STATUTORY
INSTRUMENTS
1983

PART II
(in two sections)

SECTION 2

Published by Authority

LONDON
HER MAJESTY'S STATIONERY OFFICE
1984

Printed in the UK
Dd 383005 C8 3/84 (2925)

ISBN 0 11 840228 5

Contents of the Edition

PART I

(In two sections)

PART II

(in two sections)

PART III

STATUTORY INSTRUMENTS

1983 No. 1006

CUSTOMS AND EXCISE

The Export of Goods (Control) (Amendment No. 3) Order 1983

Made - - - -	13*th July* 1983
Coming into Operation	12*th August* 1983

The Secretary of State, in exercise of powers conferred by section 1 of the Import, Export and Customs Powers (Defence) Act 1939 (**a**) and now vested in him (**b**), and of all other powers enabling him in that behalf, hereby makes the following Order:—

1. This Order may be cited as the Export of Goods (Control) (Amendment No. 3) Order 1983 and shall come into operation on 12th August 1983.

2. The Export of Goods (Control) Order 1981 (**c**) shall be further amended as follows:—

(a) in Article 1(2), there shall be inserted after the definition of "ship" the following definition—

""technological document" means any document containing information relating to the design, production, testing or use of goods or to processes and "document" includes any record or device by means of which information is recorded or stored;"

(b) at the end of Article 2 there shall be added the following paragraph—

"(ix) technological documents, other than documents generally available to the public, relating to any goods specified in Groups 1 to 3 of Part II of Schedule 1 hereto or to any goods or processes specified in Group 4 of Part II of Schedule 1 hereto are prohibited to be exported to any destination in any country specified in paragraph (v) above.";

(c) at the end of Article 3*(i)* (headed *"Ships"*) there shall be added the following sub-paragraph—

"(iii) any ship proceeding on a normal commercial sailing.";

(d) in Group 1 of Part II of Schedule 1, in the entry relating to explosives, propellants and related substances, after head (2) there shall be added the following new head—

"(2A) Spherical aluminium powder with uniform particle size and an aluminium content of 97% or more .... A";

(e) in Group 3C of Part II of Schedule 1, in the entry relating to furnaces—

(i) for the letters "C" there shall be substituted the letters "A";

(ii) at the end there shall be added the following—

"(Note exception (1) in the entry in Group 3D relating to equipment specially designed for the production of certain nickel-, cobalt- or iron-base alloys)";

(**a**) 1939 c.69.
(**b**) *See* S.I. 1970/1537.
(**c**) S.I. 1981/1641, amended by S.I. 1982/1446,1556.

(f) in Group 3D of Part II of Schedule 1—

    (i) after the entry relating to environmental chambers, there shall be added the following new entry—

"Equipment specially designed for the production of nickel-, cobalt- or iron-base alloys in crude or semi-fabricated forms having strengths superior to the AISI 300 series (as at May 1982) at temperatures over +922K (+649°C) under severe environmental conditions.. A

except—

    (1) Electric arc and induction furnaces (other than vacuum induction furnaces used in the production of powders of the aforesaid alloys), basic oxygen furnaces and re-melting equipment using other techniques for the production of carbon steels, low alloy steels and stainless steels;

    (2) Degassing equipment used for the production of carbon steels, low alloy steels and stainless steels;

    (3) Extrusion presses, hot and cold rolling mills and swaging and forging machines;

    (4) Decarburizing, annealing and pickling equipment;

    (5) Surface-finishing equipment; and

    (6) Slitting and cutting equipment;

(Note as to electric vacuum furnaces, Group 3C above and as to extrusion presses and hot and cold rolling mills, subsequent entries in this Group)";

    (ii) in the entry relating to machines and equipment specially designed for the manufacture of certain devices and assemblies relating to materials composed of certain crystals, and for the manufacture of magnetic recording media—

        (a) for the references in the heading of the entry and in heads (4) and (5) thereof to head (5) of the entry in Group 3G relating to recording or reproducing equipment, there shall be substituted references to head (4) of that entry;

        (b) for the letters "C" there shall be substituted the letters "A";

    (iii) in the entry relating to machinery, equipment and software for the manufacture or testing of electronic equipment, components or materials, at the end of sub-head (7)(b)(ii) the word "or" shall be deleted and there shall be added at the end of sub-head (iii) the word "; or" and the following new sub-head—

"(iv) measurement of rise times, fall times and edge placement times with a resolution of less than 20 nanoseconds.";

    (iv) in the entry relating to presses, at the end there shall be added the following—

"(Note exception (3) in the entry in this Group relating to equipment specially designed for the production of certain nickel-, cobalt- or iron-base alloys)";

    (v) in the entry relating to rolling mills—

        (a) for the letter "C" there shall be substituted the letter "A";

        (b) at the end there shall be added the following—

"(Note exception (3) in the entry in this Group relating to equipment specially designed for the production of certain nickel-, cobalt- or iron-base alloys)";

(g) in Group 3F of Part II of Schedule 1,

(i) in the entry relating to electronic components, assemblies, sub-assemblies, printed circuit boards and microcircuits, in exception *(b)* (v) *(b)* to head (3) (relating to certain memory microcircuits), for the letters "RAMs" there shall be substituted the letters "ROMs";

(ii) in the entry relating to semi-conductor diodes and dice and wafers therefor, in exception *(c)* to head (1), for the words "not better than" in both places where they occur there shall be substituted the words "worse than";

(h) in Group 3G of Part II of Schedule 1, in the entry relating to acoustic wave devices, in sub-head (1)*(b)* for the word "either" there shall be substituted the word "any", and sub-heads (1)*(c)* and (1)*(d)* shall be re-numbered as sub-heads (1)*(b)*(iii) and (1)*(b)*(iv) respectively;

(i) after Group 3J of Part II of Schedule 1, there shall be added the new Group 4 which appears in the Schedule hereto.

P. M. S. Corley,
An Under Secretary
Department of Trade and Industry.

13th July 1983.

SCHEDULE

Article 2(*i*)

GROUP 4

GOODS AND PROCESSES IN RESPECT OF WHICH THE EXPORT OF TECHNOLOGICAL DOCUMENTS, OTHER THAN DOCUMENTS GENER-ALLY AVAILABLE TO THE PUBLIC, IS PROHIBITED TO ANY DESTINA-TION IN ANY COUNTRY SPECIFIED IN ARTICLE 2(v)

The process of inert gas and vacuum atomising for achieving sphericity and uniform size of particles in metal powders.

EXPLANATORY NOTE

(This Note is not part of the Order.)

This Order further amends the Export of Goods (Control) Order 1981. It prohibits the export of technological documents (other than documents generally available to the public) relating to the design, production, testing or use of goods specified in Groups 1 to 3 of Part II of Schedule 1 to the 1981 Order to any destination in a country specified in Article 2(v) of that Order (Albania, Bulgaria, China, Czechoslovakia, the German Democratic Republic, Hungary, Democratic Kampuchea, the Lao People's Democratic Republic, Mongolia, North Korea, Poland, Romania, the USSR and the Socialist Republic of Vietnam). It also prohibits the exportation to such destinations of technological documents relating to goods or processes specified in the new Group 4 of Part II of Schedule 1, set out in the Schedule to this Order. The exportation of technological documents relating to inert gas and vacuum atomising for achieving sphericity and uniform size of particles in metal powders is prohibited by this provision—Article 2*(a)*, *(b)* and *(i)*.

The Order extends the categories of ships set out in Article 3 of the 1981 Order whose exportation is permitted by Article 2 to include any ships proceeding on a normal commercial sailing—Article 2*(c)*.

The Order prohibits the exportation of certain spherical aluminium powder (Article 2*(d)*) and equipment specially designed for the production of certain metal alloys—Article 2*(f)*(i). It also extends the control imposed by the 1981 Order over digitally controlled test equipment specially designed for testing microcircuits and assemblies thereof to those capable of time measurement of a specific resolution—Article 2*(f)*(iii). Restrictions on the exportation of certain electric vacuum furnaces (Article 2*(e)*), certain machines and equipment specially designed for the manufacture of certain devices and assemblies relating to materials composed of certain crystals and for the manufacture of magnetic recording media (Article 2*(f)*(ii)) and for certain rolling mills (Article 2*(f)*(v)) are extended to all destinations. The Order also makes amendments to entries in Groups 3F and 3G of Part II of Schedule 1 relating to certain memory microcircuits, Schottky diodes and acoustic wave devices—Article 2*(g)*(i) and (ii); Article 2*(h)*.

STATUTORY INSTRUMENTS

1983 No. 1008 (S. 91)

PUBLIC HEALTH, SCOTLAND

The Public Health (Infectious Diseases) (Scotland) Amendment Regulations 1983

Made - - - -	*6th July* 1983
Laid before Parliament	*25th July* 1983
Coming into Operation	*15th August* 1983

In exercise of the powers conferred on me by section 1 of the Public Health (Scotland) Act 1945(**a**), and of all other powers enabling me in that behalf, I hereby make the following regulations:—

1. These regulations may be cited as the Public Health (Infectious Diseases) (Scotland) Amendment Regulations 1983 and shall come into operation on the 15th August 1983.

2. Regulation 6 (fees for notification) of the Public Health (Infectious Diseases) (Scotland) Regulations 1975(**b**) is hereby revoked.

St Andrew's House,
EDINBURGH.
6th July 1983.

George Younger,
One of Her Majesty's Principal
Secretaries of State.

(**a**) 1945 c. 15 (9 & 10 Geo. 6); section 1 was amended by section 23 of the Food and Drugs (Scotland) Act 1956 (c. 30) and section 64(1) of Schedule 6 to the National Health Service (Scotland) Act 1972 (c. 58).
(**b**) S.I. 1975/308, to which there are amendments not relevant to these regulations.

EXPLANATORY NOTE

(This Note is not part of the Regulations.)

These Regulations revoke regulation 6 of the Public Health (Infectious Diseases) (Scotland) Regulations 1975 which specifies the fee payable to medical practitioners for providing certificates reporting cases of notifiable infectious diseases.

This revocation is consequential upon the terms of section 71A of the Health Services and Public Health Act 1968 (c. 46), as inserted by section 26(2) of the Health and Social Services and Social Security Adjudications Act 1983 (c. 41), which empowers the Secretary of State to specify such fees in a direction.

STATUTORY INSTRUMENTS

1983 No. 1009

AGRICULTURE

The Sheep Variable Premium (Protection of Payments) (Amendment) Order 1983

Approved by both Houses of Parliament

Made - - - -	*14th July* 1983
Laid before Parliament	*15th July* 1983
Coming into Operation	*1st August* 1983

The Minister of Agriculture, Fisheries and Food and the Secretaries of State for Scotland, Wales and Northern Ireland, acting jointly in exercise of the powers conferred by sections 5 and 35(3) of the Agriculture Act 1957 (**a**) and now vested in them (**b**), and of all other powers enabling them in that behalf, hereby make the following Order:—

Title, commencement and interpretation

1.—(1) This Order may be cited as the Sheep Variable Premium (Protection of Payments) (Amendment) Order 1983, and shall come into operation on 1st August 1983.

(2) In this Order "the principal order" means the Sheep Variable Premium (Protection of Payments) (No. 2) Order 1980 (**c**).

Amendment of article 2 of the principal order

2. In the definition of "certified" in article 2(1) of the principal order the word "certification" shall be substituted for the word "certificate".

Insertion of article 6A in the principal order

3. After article 6 of the principal order there shall be inserted the following article:—

"*Disposal requirement*

6A.—(1) In this article—

"disposal period", in relation to an animal, means the period of twenty-one days immediately following the date of its certification;

"disposal requirement" means the requirement contained in paragraph (2) below.

(2) Every animal shall, before the expiry of the disposal period in relation thereto, be—

   (a) slaughtered in Great Britain; or

(**a**) 1957 c.57. Section 5 is applied to Community arrangements for or related to the regulation of the market for any agricultural produce by section 6(3) of the European Communities Act 1972 (1972 c.68).

(**b**) In the case of the Secretary of State for Wales, by virtue of S.I. 1978/272.

(**c**) S.I. 1980/1811, amended by S.I. 1981/751, 1982/726.

(*b*) exported from Great Britain; or

(*c*) removed from Great Britain to Northern Ireland.

(3) For the purpose of paragraph (2) above, an animal which is kept in quarantine or isolation until it is exported or removed as aforesaid shall be deemed to have been so exported or removed on the day such quarantine or isolation commenced.

(4) A person shall be deemed to have notice of the date of certification and the disposal requirement in relation to an animal, if he or his agent or employee has received from the authorised officer who certified the animal, or from any person who has sold the animal after its certification, an invoice or similar account or other document informing him in writing of the said date and disposal requirement.

(5) Any person who has claimed a premium payment in respect of an animal after selling it, and who has notice of the date of certification and the disposal requirement in relation thereto, shall, within two days of such certification, inform the purchaser of the animal in writing of the said date and disposal requirement.

(6) No person who has notice of the date of certification and the disposal requirement in relation to an animal shall—

(*a*) sell the animal before the expiry of the disposal period in relation thereto, without informing the purchaser in writing of the said date and disposal requirement;

(*b*) sell the animal after the expiry of the disposal period in relation thereto;

(*c*) (subject to paragraph (7) below) have the animal in his possession or under his control after the expiry of the disposal period in relation thereto.

(7) Paragraph (6)(*c*) above shall not apply to a person who buys an animal after the expiry of the disposal period in relation thereto provided he slaughters it within one week after the date of purchase and he notifies the purchase in writing to an authorised officer.".

Amendment of article 8 of the principal order

4. For article 8 of the principal order there shall be substituted the following article:—

"Records of transactions

8.—(1) A person who buys or sells certified animals shall—

(*a*) keep a record showing, in respect of every purchase or sale by him of such animals, the particulars specified in Schedule 3 to this Order; and

(*b*) make a copy of every document issued by him informing a purchaser in writing of the date of certification and the disposal requirement in relation to such animals.

(2) A person who buys or sells certified animals shall retain, for at least three years after the end of the calendar year in which they were drawn up or issued—

(*a*) all records kept pursuant to paragraph (1)(*a*) above;

(b) all invoices and similar accounts in respect of his purchases and sales of such animals, and all documents informing him or his agent or employee in writing of the date of certification and the disposal requirement in relation to such animals;

(c) all copies made pursuant to paragraph (1)(b) above;

(d) all documents received by him in respect of any such animals exported from Great Britain, or removed from Great Britain to Northern Ireland.

(3) For the purpose of paragraphs (1) and (2) above "certified animal" shall include an animal in respect of which a premium payment is claimed after it has been sold.

(4) A person who is required by paragraph (2) above to retain records, invoices, accounts, copies or documents shall produce the same for inspection if so required by an authorised officer.".

Amendment to Schedule 3 to the principal order

5. For Schedule 3 to the principal order there shall be substituted the following Schedule:—

"SCHEDULE 3 Article 8

Particulars to be recorded of purchases, sales and disposals of certified animals

1. The date of the transaction.

2. Numbers and descriptions of animals.

3. In the case of a purchase or sale by auction at an auction market, the name and address of the auctioneer, and, in any other case, the name and address of the other party to the transaction.

4. The date of certification.

5. The date of slaughter, export from Great Britain or removal from Great Britain to Northern Ireland of unsold live animals.".

In Witness whereof the Official Seal of the Minister of Agriculture, Fisheries and Food is hereunto affixed on 14th July 1983.

Michael Jopling,
Minister of Agriculture, Fisheries
and Food.

George Younger,
Secretary of State for Scotland.

13th July 1983.

Nicholas Edwards,
Secretary of State for Wales.

13th July 1983.

James Prior,
Secretary of State for
Northern Ireland.

14th July 1983.

EXPLANATORY NOTE

(This Note is not part of the Order.)

This Order amends the Sheep Variable Premium (Protection of Payments) (No. 2) Order 1980 ("the principal order") by inserting a requirement that animals certified as eligible for a premium payment shall within twenty-one days after the date of their certification be slaughtered, exported from Great Britain, or removed from Great Britain to Northern Ireland.

This is in implementation of Commission Regulation (EEC) No. 1689/83 (O.J. No. L165, 24.6.83, p.23) which adds this requirement to Commission Regulation (EEC) No. 2661/80 laying down detailed rules for applying the variable slaughter premium for sheep (O.J. No. L276, 20.10.80, p.19) as paragraph 4 of Article 1 thereof.

The Order also provides for the enforcement of this requirement.

Article 3 contains the requirement itself, provides that notice thereof shall be given to anyone who purchases a certified animal, and prohibits the sale or holding of a certified animal after the expiry of the twenty-one day period.

Articles 4 and 5 extend the provisions of the principal order concerning the keeping, retention and production of records in respect of sales and purchases of certified animals and remove the record-keeping provisions applying to certified carcases.

Article 2 corrects a small defect in the principal order.

Any contravention or failure to comply with the provisions contained in this Order is an offence under section 7 of the Agriculture Act 1957.

STATUTORY INSTRUMENTS

1983 No. 1010

AGRICULTURE

The Sheep Variable Premium (Recovery Powers) Regulations 1983

Made - - - -		*14th July* 1983
Laid before Parliament		*15th July* 1983
Coming into Operation		*5th August* 1983

The Minister of Agriculture, Fisheries and Food and the Secretary of State, being Ministers designated(**a**) for the purposes of section 2(2) of the European Communities Act 1972(**b**) in relation to the common agricultural policy of the European Economic Community, acting jointly in exercise of powers conferred upon them by the said section 2(2), and of all other powers enabling them in that behalf, hereby make the following regulations:—

Title, commencement and interpretation

1.—(1) These regulations may be cited as the Sheep Variable Premium (Recovery Powers) Regulations 1983, and shall come into operation on the 5th August 1983.

(2) In these regulations—

"animal" means an animal of the ovine species;

"the Board" means the Intervention Board for Agricultural Produce;

"contravention" includes failure to comply;

"disposal period" has the same meaning as in Article 6A of the Protection Order;

"premium payment" has the same meaning as in the Protection Order;

"the Protection Order" means the Sheep Variable Premium (Protection of Payments) (No. 2) Order 1980(**c**).

(**a**) S.I. 1972/1811.   (**b**) 1972 c. 68.
(**c**) S.I. 1980/1811, amended by S.I. 1981/751, 1982/726, 1983/1009.

Recovery of premium payments

2. Where a person—

    (*a*) permits an animal in respect of which a premium payment has been made to be used for breeding, in contravention of Article 6 of the Protection Order; or

    (*b*) sells such an animal, or has such an animal in his possession or under his control, after the expiry of the disposal period in relation thereto, in contravention of Article 6A of the Protection Order;

he shall be liable to pay to the Board on demand an amount equal to the premium payment, and in the event of default in payment that amount shall be recoverable by the Board as a civil debt.

Evidence

3. For the purpose of any proceedings under these regulations, an animal which is proved to have been marked as prescribed for an animal in Schedule 1 to the Protection Order shall be deemed to be an animal in respect of which a premium payment has been made unless the contrary is proved.

Revocation

4. The Sheep Variable Premium (Recovery Powers) Regulations 1980(**a**) are hereby revoked.

In Witness whereof the Official Seal of the Minister of Agriculture, Fisheries and Food is hereunto affixed on 14th July 1983.

    (L.S.)

Michael Jopling,
Minister of Agriculture, Fisheries and Food.

George Younger,
One of Her Majesty's Principal
Secretaries of State.

13th July 1983.

(**a**) S.I. 1980/1578.

AGRICULTURE

EXPLANATORY NOTE

(This Note is not part of the Regulations.)

These regulations replace the Sheep Variable Premium (Recovery Powers) Regulations 1980 ("the 1980 Regulations"). They implement the obligation to recover an amount equal to the variable slaughter premium paid in respect of sheep which is contained in Article 5.2 of Commission Regulation (EEC) No. 2661/80 laying down detailed rules for applying the variable slaughter premium for sheep (O.J. No. L276, 20.10.80, p.19).

The regulations enable the Intervention Board for Agricultural Produce to recover this amount—

(a) if an animal is used for breeding, in contravention of Article 6 of the Sheep Variable Premium (Protection of Payments) (No. 2) Order 1980 (a provision repeated from the 1980 Regulations); or

(b) if an animal is sold or held after the expiry of its "disposal period"—the period within which it must under Article 6A of that Order be slaughtered, exported, or removed to Northern Ireland. Article 6A implements a requirement added to Commission Regulation (EEC) No. 2661/80 as paragraph 4 of Article 1 thereof by Commission Regulation (EEC) No. 1689/83 (O.J. No. L165, 24.6.83, p.23).

STATUTORY INSTRUMENTS

1983 No. 1011

OFFSHORE INSTALLATIONS

The Offshore Installations (Safety Zones) (Revocation) (No. 16) Order 1983

Made - - - -	*14th July* 1983
Coming into Operation	*16th July* 1983

The Secretary of State, in exercise of the power conferred on him by section 21(1) of the Oil and Gas (Enterprise) Act 1982(**a**), and of all other powers enabling him in that behalf, hereby makes the following Order:—

1. This Order may be cited as the Offshore Installations (Safety Zones) (Revocation) (No. 16) Order 1983 and shall come into operation on 16th July 1983.

2. The Offshore Installations (Safety Zones) (No. 19) Order 1983(**b**) is hereby revoked.

Alick Buchanan-Smith,
Minister of State,
Department of Energy.

14th July 1983.

EXPLANATORY NOTE

(This Note is not part of the Order.)

This Order revokes the Offshore Installations (Safety Zones) (No. 19) Order 1983. The installation known as Dixilyn-Field 97 which was protected by the safety zone established by that Order has been removed and accordingly that Order is no longer required.

(**a**) 1982 c. 23.   (**b**) S.I. 1983/855.

STATUTORY INSTRUMENTS

1983 No. 1012

OFFSHORE INSTALLATIONS

The Offshore Installations (Safety Zones) (No. 23) Order 1983

Made - - - - -		14*th July* 1983
Coming into Operation		16*th July* 1983

The Secretary of State, in exercise of the powers conferred on him by section 21(1), (2) and (3) of the Oil and Gas (Enterprise) Act 1982**(a)** (hereinafter referred to as "the Act"), and of all other powers enabling him in that behalf, hereby makes the following Order:—

1. This Order may be cited as the Offshore Installations (Safety Zones) (No. 23) Order 1983 and shall come into operation on 16th July 1983.

2.—(1) A safety zone is hereby established around the installation specified in Column 1 of the Schedule hereto (being an installation maintained in waters in an area designated under section 1(7) of the Continental Shelf Act 1964**(b)**) having a radius of five hundred metres from the point as respects that installation which has the co-ordinates of latitude and longitude according to European Datum (1950) specified in Columns 2 and 3 of the Schedule.

(2) The prohibition under section 21(3) of the Act on a vessel entering or remaining in a safety zone without the consent of the Secretary of State shall not apply to a vessel entering or remaining in the safety zone established under paragraph (1) above:

(*a*) in connection with the laying, inspection, testing, repair, alteration, renewal or removal of any submarine cable or pipe-line in or near that safety zone;

(*b*) to provide services for, to transport persons or goods to or from, or under the authority of a government department to inspect, any installation in that safety zone;

(*c*) if it is a vessel belonging to a general lighthouse authority performing duties relating to the safety of navigation;

(*d*) in connection with the saving or attempted saving of life or property;

(a) 1982 c. 23. **(b)** 1964 c. 29.

(*e*) owing to stress of weather; or

(*f*) when in distress.

Alick Buchanan-Smith,
Minister of State,
Department of Energy.

14th July 1983.

SCHEDULE

Article 2(1)

SAFETY ZONE

1	2	3
Name or other designation of the offshore installation	Latitude North	Longitude East
Dundee Kingsnorth	59° 27' 29·29"	01° 36' 39·71"

EXPLANATORY NOTE

(This Note is not part of the Order.)

This Order establishes, under section 21 of the Oil and Gas (Enterprise) Act 1982, a safety zone, having a radius of 500 metres from a specified point, around the installation known as Dundee Kingsnorth maintained in waters in an area designated under section 1(7) of the Continental Shelf Act 1964.

Vessels (which includes hovercraft, submersible apparatus and installations in transit) are prohibited from entering or remaining in the safety zone except with the consent of the Secretary of State or in the circumstances mentioned in Article 2(2) of the Order.

STATUTORY INSTRUMENTS

1983 No. 1013 (S. 92)

SPORTS GROUNDS AND SPORTING EVENTS

The Safety of Sports Grounds (Designation) (Scotland) Order 1983

Made - - - - -	*6th July* 1983
Laid before Parliament	*26th July* 1983
Coming into Operation	*1st January* 1984

In exercise of the powers conferred on me by section 1(1) of the Safety of Sports Grounds Act 1975**(a)**, and of all other powers enabling me in that behalf, and, as required by section 18(4) of that Act, after consultation with such persons or bodies of persons as appear to me requisite, I hereby make the following order:—

1. This order may be cited as the Safety of Sports Grounds (Designation) (Scotland) Order 1983 and shall come into operation on 1st January 1984.

2. The stadium in Scotland specified in the Schedule to this order, being a sports stadium which in the opinion of the Secretary of State has accommodation for more than 10,000 spectators, is hereby designated as a stadium requiring a safety certificate under the Safety of Sports Grounds Act 1975.

New St. Andrew's House,
Edinburgh.
6th July 1983.

George Younger,
One of Her Majesty's Principal
Secretaries of State.

Article 2　　　　　　　　　　**SCHEDULE**

STADIUM IN SCOTLAND DESIGNATED AS REQUIRING A SAFETY CERTIFICATE
UNDER THE
SAFETY OF SPORTS GROUNDS ACT 1975

Muirton Park, Perth

(a) 1975 c. 52.

EXPLANATORY NOTE

(This Note is not part of the Order.)

This Order designates Muirton Park, Perth as a stadium which requires a safety certificate under the Safety of Sports Grounds Act 1975. Other sports stadia in Scotland which require safety certificates are designated under the Safety of Sports Grounds (Designation) (Scotland) Orders 1976 (S.I. 1976/1285), 1977 (S.I. 1977/1345) (as varied by the Safety of Sports Grounds (Designation) (Scotland) Variation Order 1982 (S.I. 1982/60)), 1978 (S.I. 1978/1099), 1979 (S.I. 1979/1026), and 1980 (S.I. 1980/1034).

STATUTORY INSTRUMENTS

1983 No. 1014

HOUSING, ENGLAND AND WALES
HOUSING, SCOTLAND
RATING AND VALUATION

The Housing Benefits Amendment
Regulations 1983

Made - - - - - -	*14th July* 1983
Laid before Parliament	*18th July* 1983
Coming into Operation	*21st November* 1983

The Secretary of State for Social Services, in exercise of the powers conferred on him by section 28(1) of the Social Security and Housing Benefits Act 1982(a) and of all other powers enabling him in that behalf, with the consent of the Treasury, and, in so far as is required(b), after consultation with organisations appearing to him to be representative of authorities concerned(c) and after agreement by the Social Security Advisory Committee that proposals to make these regulations should not be referred to it(d), hereby makes the following regulations:—

Citation and commencement

1. These regulations, which may be cited as the Housing Benefits Amendment Regulations 1983, amend the Housing Benefits Regulations 1982(e) (hereinafter referred to as "the principal regulations") and shall come into operation on 21st November 1983.

(a) 1982 c. 24.
(b) These requirements apply only in the case of the amendments to paragraph 4(*a*) and (*b*) of Schedule 2 to the Housing Benefits Regulations 1982 (S.I. 1982/1124).
(c) *See* section 36(1)(*a*) of the Social Security and Housing Benefits Act 1982.
(d) *See* section 10(2)(*b*) of the Social Security Act 1980 (c. 30).
(e) S.I. 1982/1124; the relevant amending instrument is S.I. 1982/1519.

Amendment of Schedules 2 and 3 to the principal regulations

2. For each amount specified in column 3 of the Schedule to these regulations, where it appears in the provision of the principal regulations specified in relation to it in column 1 of that Schedule (the subject matter of which is indicated in column 2 of that Schedule), there is substituted the amount specified in relation to it in column 4 of that Schedule.

Signed by Authority of the Secretary of State for Social Services.

Rhodes Boyson,
Minister of State,
Department of Health and Social Security.

12th July 1983.

We consent,

Alastair Goodlad,
Ian B. Lang,
Two of the Lords Commissioners
of Her Majesty's Treasury.

14th July 1983.

HOUSING, ENGLAND AND WALES
HOUSING, SCOTLAND
RATING AND VALUATION

Regulation 2

SCHEDULE

AMOUNTS SUBSTITUTED IN THE PRINCIPAL REGULATIONS

Column 1	Column 2	Column 3	Column 4
Provision of the principal regulations	Subject matter	Old amount	New amount
Schedule 2—	disregarded income—		
paragraph 4(*a*)	earnings of an eligible person whose partner's earnings are not greater than his	£18.00	£17.45
paragraph 4(*b*)	earnings of an eligible person's partner greater than those of that person	£18.00	£17.45
paragraph 14(*b*)	lodging allowance from Manpower Services Commission	£11.30	£15.00
paragraph 16(*ab*)	payment by parents to certain students under 25	£18.60	£21.45
Schedule 3—	deductions, when computing eligible rent, for fuel, services and rent—		
paragraph 3(*a*)	heating (in certificated cases)	£5.60	£6.05
paragraph 3(*b*)	hot water (in such cases)	£0.65	£0.70
paragraph 3(*c*)	lighting (in such cases)	£0.45	£0.50
paragraph 3(*d*)	cooking (in such cases)	£0.65	£0.70
paragraph 11(*a*)(i)	rent payable to an eligible person	£2.50	£2.70
paragraph 11(*a*)(ii)		£1.25	£1.35

EXPLANATORY NOTE

(This Note is not part of the Regulations.)

These Regulations amend the Housing Benefits Regulations 1982, which contain the statutory schemes for the granting by local authorities of rate rebates, rent rebates and rent allowances, by altering certain amounts specified in those regulations. The amounts altered (set out in the Schedule to these regulations) are relevant for the purposes of calculating a person's entitlement to rebate or allowance. All the amounts altered are increased except for the amounts of earnings of an eligible person, or in certain cases of his partner, falling to be disregarded, which are decreased from £18.00 to £17.45.

STATUTORY INSTRUMENTS

1983 No. 1015

SOCIAL SECURITY

The Social Security (Attendance Allowance) Amendment Regulations 1983

Made - - - -	*15th July* 1983
Laid before Parliament	*18th July* 1983
Coming into Operation	*8th August* 1983

The Secretary of State for Social Services, in exercise of the powers conferred on him by sections 35, 81(1) and 85(1) of the Social Security Act 1975(**a**) and of all other powers enabling him in that behalf, hereby makes the following regulations which relate only to matters which, in accordance with that Act, have been referred to the Attendance Allowance Board and which accordingly, by virtue of section 10(2) of, and paragraph 12(3) of Part II of Schedule 3 to, the Social Security Act 1980(**b**) are not subject to the requirement for prior reference to the Social Security Advisory Committee.

Citation commencement and interpretation

1.—(1) These regulations may be cited as the Social Security (Attendance Allowance) Amendment Regulations 1983 and shall come into operation on 8th August 1983.

(2) In these regulations—

"the principal regulations" means the Social Security (Attendance Allowance) (No. 2) Regulations 1975(**c**), and

"the Claims and Payments Regulations" means the Social Security (Claims and Payments) Regulations 1979(**d**).

Amendment of the principal regulations

2.—(1) In regulation 5 of the principal regulations (circumstances in which attendance allowance may be paid to adults in hospital and certain other accommodation) after paragraph (2) there is inserted—

(**a**) 1975 c. 14; section 35 was amended by section 129 of, and paragraph 63 of Schedule 15 to, the National Health Service Act 1977 (c. 49), section 2 of the Social Security Act 1979 (c. 18) and sections 2 and 21 of, and paragraph 8 of Part II of Schedule 1 to, the Social Security Act 1980 (c. 30).
(**b**) 1980 c. 30.
(**c**) S.I. 1975/598; relevant amending instruments are S.I. 1977/342, 417 and 1979/1684.
(**d**) S.I. 1979/628; the relevant amending instrument is S.I. 1980/1136.

"(3) Where a child who was resident in accommodation to which regulation 7(1) refers (children in hospital and certain other accommodation) attains the age of 16, the periods to which this regulation applies shall include any periods to which regulation 7(1) and (2) formerly applied, provided that the final period to which regulation 7(1) or (2) applied and the first period to which either regulation 3 or 4 applies are not separated by more than 28 days.".

(2) In regulation 7 of the principal regulations (children in hospital and certain other accommodation) for paragraph (2) there shall be substituted—

"(2) Where any person was entitled to attendance allowance in respect of a child for the period immediately before that child entered any accommodation mentioned in sub-paragraph (1)(a) or (1)(b) or that child commenced to undergo any treatment mentioned in sub-paragraph (1)(c) as the case may be, those sub-paragraphs shall not apply to the first 4 weeks of any period during which the child is in such accommodation or is undergoing such treatment, so however for the purposes of this paragraph—

(a) 2 or more distinct periods separated by an interval not exceeding 28 days, or by 2 or more such intervals, shall be treated as a continuous period equal in duration to the total of such distinct periods and ending on the last day of the later or last such period;

(b) any period or periods to which sub-paragraph (1)(a), (1)(b) or (1)(c) refers shall be taken into account and aggregated with any other period to which the other sub-paragraphs refer.".

Amendment of the Claims and Payments Regulations

3.—(1) This regulation shall amend the Claims and Payments Regulations.

(2) In regulation 16 (time and manner of payment of certain pensions and allowances)—

(a) in paragraph (10) after the words "by the Act" shall be inserted the words "except regulation 18 below,";

(b) in paragraph (11) at the end there shall be added "except in a case to which regulation 18 below applies.".

(3) For regulation 18 (attendance allowance payable at a daily rate between periods where no allowance is payable) there shall be substituted—

"*Circumstances in which attendance allowance is to be paid at a daily rate*

18.—(1) Attendance allowance shall be paid in respect of any person for any day falling within a period to which paragraph (2) below applies at the daily rate (which shall be equal to $\frac{1}{7}$th of the weekly rate) and attendance allowance payable in pursuance of this regulation shall be paid weekly or as the Secretary of State may direct in any case.

(2) This paragraph applies to any period which—

(a) begins on the day immediately following the last day of a period during which a person was living in hospital or other accommodation specified in regulation 3, 4, or 7(1) of the Social Security (Attendance Allowance) (No. 2) Regulations 1975; and

(*b*) ends—

(i) if the first day of the period was a day of payment, at midnight on the day preceding the 13th following day of payment, or

(ii) if that day was not a day of payment, at midnight on the day preceding the 14th following day of payment, or

(iii) if earlier, on the day immediately preceding the day on which regulation 3, 4, 5, 7(1) or 7(2) next applies to his case;

if on the first day of the period it is expected that, before the expiry of the period of 13 weeks beginning with that day, he will return to hospital or other accommodation to which regulation 3, 4, 5 or 7 applies.

(3) In this regulation "day of payment" means the appropriate day of the week for the payment of attendance allowance to the person concerned determined in accordance with regulation 16(7) of these regulations.".

Signed by authority of the Secretary of State for Social Services.

Rhodes Boyson,
Minister of State,
Department of Health and Social Security.

15th July 1983.

EXPLANATORY NOTE

(*This Note is not part of the Regulations.*)

These Regulations amend the Social Security (Attendance Allowance) (No. 2) Regulations 1975 (the principal regulations) and, as respects attendance allowance only, the Social Security (Claims and Payments) Regulations 1979 (the Claims and Payments regulations).

Regulation 5 of the principal regulations, which provides that attendance allowance remains payable for the first 4 weeks during which a person over 16 is undergoing treatment in hospital or is resident in certain other accommodation where the cost is borne or may be borne out of public or local funds, is amended so that periods spent in similar accommodation before that person reaches 16 are to be taken into account for the purposes of the regulation.

Regulation 7 of the principal regulations is amended so that attendance allowance will be payable, as it is for adults, for the first 4 weeks during which a child is living in accommodation to which the enactments mentioned in the Schedule to the principal regulations refer.

A new regulation 18 is substituted in the Claims and Payments Regulations which specifies the circumstances in which attendance allowance will be paid at a daily rate instead of a weekly rate during an interval between two periods when a person is in hospital or certain other accommodation.

STATUTORY INSTRUMENTS

1983 No. 1017

EDUCATION, ENGLAND AND WALES

The Education (Grants) (Music and Ballet Schools) (Amendment) (No. 2) Regulations 1983

Made - - - - -	14*th July* 1983
Laid before Parliament	28*th July* 1983
Coming into Operation	1*st September* 1983

In exercise of the powers conferred by section 100(1)(*b*) and (3) of the Education Act 1944(**a**) and vested in the Secretary of State(**b**), the Secretary of State for Education and Science hereby makes the following Regulations:—

1. These Regulations may be cited as the Education (Grants) (Music and Ballet Schools) (Amendment) (No. 2) Regulations 1983 and shall come into operation on 1st September 1983.

2.—(1) In these Regulations a reference to the principal Regulations is a reference to the Education (Music and Ballet Schools) Regulations 1981(**c**).

(2) These Regulations shall be construed as one with the principal Regulations.

3.—(1) Regulation 4(2) of the principal Regulations (reference to a school confined in the case of the Royal Ballet School to the Lower Division thereof) is hereby revoked.

(2) A child holding an aided place in the Lower Division at the Royal Ballet School immediately before 1st September 1983 shall be treated for the purposes of the principal Regulations and the Aided Pupil Scheme specified in Schedule 1 thereto as if he had been selected to hold an aided place in the Lower and Upper Divisions at that school unless, before 1st October 1983, the school notify his parent that he will cease to be an aided pupil on leaving the Lower Division.

(**a**) 1944 c. 31.   (**b**) S.I. 1964/490, 1970/1536, 1978/274.
(**c**) S.I. 1981/786; the amending instruments are not relevant to the subject matter of these Regulations.

Article 2

SCHEDULE

EXEMPTED CLASS OF FIREPLACE

(1) Class of Fireplace	(2) Conditions
The fireplace known as the Trianco 'Coal King' Boiler and manufactured by Trianco Redfyre Limited.	1. The fireplace shall be installed, maintained and operated so as to minimise the emission of smoke at all times, and in accordance with the manufacturer's instructions dated May 1983 and which— (a) in the case of the installation instructions bear the reference '47664', and (b) in the case of the user instructions bear the reference '47665'. 2. No fuel shall be used other than selected washed coal doubles.

Patrick Jenkin,
Secretary of State for the Environment.

14th July 1983.

EXPLANATORY NOTE

(This Note is not part of the Order.)

Section 11 of the Clean Air Act 1956 empowers local authorities to declare the whole or any part of their district to be a smoke control area in which the emission of smoke is generally prohibited.

This order, which applies to England and Wales, exempts a class of fireplace known as the Trianco 'Coal King' Boiler manufactured by Trianco Redfyre Limited, from the provisions of that section, subject to certain conditions as to the method of operation and the type of fuel to be used.

STATUTORY INSTRUMENTS

1983 No. 1021

COMPANIES

The Companies (Forms) Regulations 1983

Made - - - -	*14th July* 1983
Coming into Operation	*1st January* 1984

The Secretary of State, in exercise of the powers conferred by those sections of the Companies Acts specified in Schedule 1 hereto, and now vested in him**(a)**, hereby makes the following Regulations:—

1.—(1) These Regulations may be cited as the Companies (Forms) Regulations 1983 and shall come into operation on 1st January 1984.

(2) In these Regulations "the Companies Acts" means the Companies Act 1948, the Companies Act 1976 and the Companies Act 1980.

2.—(1) The forms numbered 1, 7, 9b, 19, 47, 47a, 47c, 48, 49, 49a, 49b, F1, F8, F9, F10, F11, F12, F12a and F12b and set out in Schedule 2 hereto shall be substituted for the forms respectively bearing those numbers set out in Schedule B to the Companies (Forms) Regulations 1979**(b)** and the particulars contained therein are the particulars prescribed for the purposes of the provisions of the Companies Acts referred to therein.

(2) The prescribed manner for the certification of a copy of any document referred to in section 407(1)*(a)* of the Companies Act 1948 shall be the manner specified in note 1 to the form numbered F1 set out in Schedule 2 hereto.

(3) The prescribed manner for the certification of a translation of any document referred to in section 407(1)*(a)* of the Companies Act 1948 shall be the manner specified in note 2 to the form numbered F1 set out in Schedule 2 hereto.

3. The forms numbered 15, 16, 17 and 18 set out in Schedule 3 hereto with such variations as circumstances require are the forms prescribed for the purposes of the provisions of the Companies Acts referred to therein and the forms numbered 21 and 23 set out in Schedule B to the Companies (Forms) Regulations 1979 and those numbered 17b, 17c, 17d, 18b and 18c set out in Schedule B to the Companies (Forms) Regulations 1980**(c)** are hereby revoked.

(a) S.I. 1970/1537.
(b) S.I. 1979/1547.
(c) S.I. 1980/1826.

4. The form set out in Schedule 4 hereto with such variations as circumstances require is the form prescribed for the purpose of any return of any allotment of bonus shares required to be delivered by section 52(1)*(a)* of the Companies Act 1948.

Alexander Fletcher,
Parliamentary Under Secretary of State,
14th July 1983.   Department of Trade and Industry.

SCHEDULE 1

Sections 52(1), 95, 97, 100, 106, 125, 200, 382(1), 382(3) and (4), 384, 386, 407, 415 and 455 of the Companies Act 1948(a).

Sections 21, 23(2) and 44(2) of the Companies Act 1976 (b).

Sections 13(4) and 87(5) of the Companies Act 1980.

(a) 1948 c. 38; sections 52, 95, 100, 125, 382, 384, 386 and 407 of the Companies Act 1948 were amended by section 34 of and Schedule 1 to the Companies Act 1976 (c.69). Section 52 was also amended by section 42 of and Schedule 2 to the Companies Act 1976; section 95 was also amended by section 88 of and Schedule 3 to the Companies Act 1980 (c. 22); section 106 was amended by section 119 of and Schedule 3 to the Companies Act 1981 (c. 62); section 200 was amended by section 22 of the Companies Act 1976 and section 95 of the Companies Act 1981; sections 382 and 384 were also amended by section 88 of and Schedule 3 to the Companies Act 1980 and section 119 of and Schedule 3 to the Companies Act 1981. There are also amendments not relevant to this instrument.
(b) There are amendments to section 21 which are not relevant to this instrument.

SCHEDULE 2

Form No. 1

THE COMPANIES ACTS 1948 TO 1981

Statement of first directors and secretary and intended situation of registered office

Pursuant to sections 21 and 23(2) of the Companies Act 1976

G

Please do not
write in this
binding margin

**Please complete
legibly, preferably
in black type, or
bold block lettering**

* delete if
inappropriate

To the Registrar of Companies

For official use

Name of Company

Limited*

The intended situation of the registered office of the company
on incorporation is as stated below

If the memorandum is delivered by an agent for the subscribers of
the memorandum please mark 'X' in the box opposite and insert the
agent's name and address below

Number of continuation sheets attached (see note 1)

Presentor's name, address and
reference (if any):

For official use
General section

Post room

The name(s) and particulars of the person who is, or the persons who are, to be the first director or directors of the company(note 2) are as follows:

Name (note 3)	Business occupation
Previous name(s) (note 3)	Nationality
Address (note 4)	
	Date of birth (where applicable) (note 6)
Other directorships †	

I hereby consent to act as director of the company named on page 1

Signature   Date

Name (note 3)	Business occupation
Previous name(s) (note 3)	Nationality
Address (note 4)	
	Date of birth (where applicable) (note 6)
Other directorships †	

I hereby consent to act as director of the company named on page 1

Signature   Date

Name (note 3)	Business occupation
Previous name(s) (note 3)	Nationality
Address (note 4)	
	Date of birth (where applicable) (note 6)
Other directorships †	

I hereby consent to act as director of the company named on page 1

Signature   Date

Please do not write in this binding margin

Important
The particulars to be given are those referred to in section 21(2)(a) of the Companies Act 1976 and section 200(2) of the Companies Act 1948 as amended by section 95 of the Companies Act 1981. Please read the notes on page 4 before completing this part of the form.

† enter particulars of other directorships held or previously held (see note 5). If this space is insufficient use a continuation sheet.

COMPANIES

Please do not
write in this
binding margin

Important
The particulars
to be given are
those referred to
in section
21(2)(b) of the
Companies Act
1976 and section
200(3) of the
Companies Act
1948. Please
read the notes
on page 4 before
completing this
part of the form.

The name(s) and particulars of the person who is, or the persons who are, to be the first secretary, or joint secretaries, of the company are as follows:

Name (notes 3 & 7)

Previous name(s) (note 3)

Address (notes 4 & 7)

I hereby consent to act as secretary of the company named on page 1

Signature   Date

Name (notes 3 & 7)

Previous name(s) (note 3)

Address (notes 4 & 7)

I hereby consent to act as secretary of the company named on page 1

Signature   Date

---

* as required by
 section 21(3) of
 the Companies
 Act 1976

† delete as
 appropriate

Signed by or on behalf of the subscribers of the memorandum*

Signature   [Subscriber] [Agent]† Date

Signature   [Subscriber] [Agent]† Date

Notes

1 If the spaces on Page 2 are insufficient the names and particulars must be entered on the prescribed continuation sheet(s).

2 'Director' includes any person who occupies the position of a director by whatever name called, and any person in accordance with whose directions or instructions the directors are accustomed to act.

3 Full names must be given. In the case of an individual, his present Christian name(s) and surname must be given together with any previous Christian names or surname. 'Christian name' includes a forename and 'surname', in the case of a peer or person usually known by a title different from his surname, means that title. In the case of a corporation, its corporate name must be given. 'Previous Christian names or surname' does not include:-

  (a) in the case of a peer or a person usually known by a British title different from his surname, the name by which he was known previous to the adoption of or succession to the title; or

  (b) in the case of any person, a previous Christian name or surname where that name or surname was changed or disused before the person bearing the name attained the age of eighteen years or has been changed or disused for a period of not less than twenty years; or

  (c) in the case of a married woman, the name or surname by which she was known previous to the marriage.

4 Usual residential address must be given or, in the case of of a corporation, the registered or principal office.

5 The names of all bodies corporate incorporated in Great Britain of which the director is also a director (see note 2) or has been a director at any time during the preceding five years must be given. A current or past directorship need not be disclosed however if it has been held in a body corporate which, throughout that directorship (excluding any period of the directorship held more than five years ago), has been a dormant company, ie one for which no significant accounting transaction (within the meaning of section 12(6) of the Companies Act 1981) has occurred.

6 Dates of birth need only be given in the case of directors of a company which is subject to section 185 of the Companies Act 1948, namely a company which is a public company or, being a private company, is a subsidiary of a public company, or of a body corporate registered as a public company under the law relating to companies for the time being in force in Northern Ireland.

7 Where all the partners in a firm are joint secretaries, only the name and principal office of the firm need be stated.

Where the secretary or one of the joint secretaries is a Scottish firm the details required are the firm name and its principal office.

THE COMPANIES ACTS 1948 TO 1981

⊻ Statement of first directors and
secretary and intended situation
of registered office (continuation)

Continuation sheet No._____
to Form No. 1

For official use

**Please complete
legibly, preferably
in black type, or
bold block lettering** Name of Company

* delete if
   inappropriate

Limited*

Particulars of the first directors (continued) (note 2).

Name (note 3)	Business occupation
Previous name(s) (note 3)	Nationality
Address (note 4)	
	Date of birth (where applicable) (note 6)

† enter particulars
of other director-
ships held or
previously held
(see note 5). If
this space is
insufficient
continue over-
leaf.

Other directorships †

I hereby consent to act as director of the company named on page 1

Signature   Date

Name (note 3)	Business occupation
Previous name(s) (note 3)	Nationality
Address (note 4)	
	Date of birth (where applicable) (note 6)

Other directorships †

I hereby consent to act as director of the company named on page 1

Signature   Date

Particulars of other directorships held or previously held (note 5) specifying the director in question

Please do not
write in this
binding margin

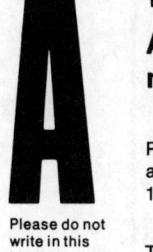

Form No. 7

THE COMPANIES ACTS 1948 TO 1981

Annual return of a company not having a share capital

Pursuant to section 125 of the Companies Act 1948
as amended by the Companies Act 1976 and to section
126 of the Companies Act 1948

Please do not
write in this
binding margin

To the Registrar of Companies

For official use

Company number

Annual return of

**Please complete
legibly, preferably
in black type, or
bold block lettering**

Limited*

*delete if
inappropriate

made up to the _____ **19**_____ (hereinafter called "the
date of this return")

Address of registered office of the company

Total amount of indebtedness of the company in respect of all mortgages and charges

which are required to be registered with the Registrar of Companies (note 1)

If the register of members or any register of
debenture holders is kept at a place other than
the registered office, insert the address of the
place where it is kept, or, if either register is
kept otherwise than in a legible form and the
place for inspection of the register is elsewhere
than at the registered office, insert the address
where inspection may be made. (see note 2)

Register of members

Register of debenture holders

†enter number
of continuation
sheets attached

We certify this return which comprises pages 1 and 2 [plus†_____continuation sheets]*

Signed_____Director, and _____ Secretary

Presentor's name, address and
reference (if any):

For official use
General section

Post room

Page 1

Particulars of the person who is the secretary of the company at the date of this return

Name   (notes 3, 4 and 5)

Previous name(s)   (note 3)

Address (notes 4, 5 and 6)

Particulars of the persons who are directors of the company at the date of this return (note 7)

Name (note 3)	Business occupation
Previous name(s) (note 3)	Nationality
Address (note 6)	
	Date of birth (where applicable) (note 8)

Other directorships †

† enter particulars
of other director-
ships held or
previously held
(see note 9). If
this space is
insufficient use
a continuation
sheet.

Name (note 3)	Business occupation
Previous name(s) (note 3)	Nationality
Address (note 6)	
	Date of birth (where applicable) (note 8)

Other directorships †

Important

The particulars
to be given are
those referred
to in section
200 of the
Companies Act
1948 as amended
by section 95 of
the Companies
Act 1981.

Name (note 3)	Business occupation
Previous name(s) (note 3)	Nationality
Address (note 6)	
	Date of birth (where applicable) (note 8)

Other directorships †

Notes for guidance on the completion of the form of annual return of a company not having a share capital

Indebtedness

1 Section 125(2) of the Companies Act 1948 requires that a statement be annexed to this return of the total amount of indebtedness of the company in respect of all mortgages and charges which are required to be registered with the Registrar of Companies under the Companies Act 1948 or which would have been required so to be registered if created after 1 July 1908. If the company is registered in Scotland the indebtedness of the company in respect of all mortgages and charges which would be required to be registered with the Registrar of Companies had the company been registered in England should be inserted, including those which would have been required so to be registered if created after 1 July 1908. The total amount of indebtedness may be entered in the appropriate box on page 1.

Register of members and debenture holders

2 If the register of members or any register of debenture holders is kept otherwise than in a legible form (eg on computer) the Companies (Registers and other Records) Regulations 1979 (SI 1979/53) made under section 3 of the Stock Exchange (Completion of Bargains) Act 1976 requires notification in the annual return of the place in Great Britain where such register may be inspected if that place of inspection is elsewhere than at the registered office.
If any register of debenture holders or any part of it is kept outside Great Britain , insert the address in Great Britain where any duplicate of such register or part is kept unless it is kept at the registered office. See Section 86 of the Companies Act 1948, which prohibits a company registered in England and Wales from keeping in Scotland a register of debenture holders or a duplicate of such register, and prohibits a company registered in Scotland from keeping any such register or duplicate in England and Wales.

3 **Particulars of secretary and director**
Full names must be given. In the case of an individual, his present Christian name(s) and surname must be given together with any previous Christian names or surname. 'Christian name' includes a forename and 'surname', in the case of a peer or person usually known by a title different from his surname, means that title. In the case of a corporation, its corporate name must be given. 'Previous Christian names or surname' does not include:-
(a) in the case of a peer or a person usually known by a British title different from his surname, the name by which he was known previous to the adoption of or succession to the title; or
(b) in the case of any person, a previous Christian name or surname where that name or surname was changed or disused before the person bearing the name attained the age of eighteen years or has been changed or disused for a period of not less than twenty years; or
(c) in the case of a married woman, the name or surname by which she was known previous to the marriage.

4 Where all the partners in a firm are joint secretaries, only the name and principal office of the firm need be stated.

5 Where the secretary or one of the joint secretaries is a Scottish firm the details required are the firm name and its principal office .

6 Usual residential address must be given or, in the case of a corporation, the registered or principal office.

7 'Director' includes any person who occupies the position of a director by whatever name called, and any person in accordance with whose directions or instructions the directors are accustomed to act.

8 Dates of birth need only be given in the case of directors of a company which is subject to section 185 of the Companies Act , 1948 namely a company which is a public company or, being a private company, is a subsidiary of a public company, or of a body corporate registered as a public company under the law relating to companies for the time being in force in Northern Ireland.

9 The names of all bodies corporate incorporated in Great Britain of which the director is also a director (see note 7) or has been a director at any time during the preceding five years must be given. A current or past directorship need not be disclosed however if it has been held in a body corporate which, throughout that directorship (excluding any period of that directorship held more than five years ago), has been:-
(a) a dormant company, ie one for which no significant accounting transaction (within the meaning of section 12(6) of the Companies Act 1981) has occurred;
(b) a body corporate of which the company making the return was a wholly owned subsidiary;
(c) a wholly owned subsidiary of the company making the present return; or
(d) a wholly owned subsidiary of a body corporate of which the company making the return was also a wholly owned subsidiary.

A body corporate is deemed to be the wholly owned subsidiary of another if it has no members except that other and that other's wholly owned subsidiaries and its or their nominees.

S.I. 1983/1021

3191

THE COMPANIES ACTS 1948 TO 1981

Form No. 7
continuation

Annual return of a company not having a share capital (continuation)

This list should be attached to and forms part of the annual return for the company made up

to the_____19_____   Continuation sheet No._____

of_____

Please do not write in this binding margin

Please complete legibly, preferably in black type, or bold block lettering

*delete if inappropriate

† enter particulars of other directorships held or previously held (see note 9). If this space is insufficient continue overleaf.

Company number

Name of company

Limited*

Particulars of other directors (continued)

Name (note 3)	Business occupation
Previous name(s) (note 3)	Nationality
Address (note 6)	
	Date of birth (where applicable) (note 8)
Other directorships †	

Name (note 3)	Business occupation
Previous name(s) (note 3)	Nationality
Address (note 6)	
	Date of birth (where applicable) (note 8)
Other directorships †	

Name (note 3)	Business occupation
Previous name(s) (note 3)	Nationality
Address (note 6)	
	Date of birth (where applicable) (note 8)
Other directorships †	

Particulars of other directorships held or previously held (note 9) specifying the director in question

G

Form No. 9b

THE COMPANIES ACTS 1948 TO 1981

Notice of change of directors or secretaries or in their particulars

Pursuant to section 200 of the Companies Act 1948
as amended by section 22 of the Companies Act 1976
and section 95 of the Companies Act 1981

9b

Please do not
write in this
binding margin.

To the Registrar of Companies

For official use

Company number

**Please complete
legibly, preferably
in black type, or
bold block lettering**

Name of Company

Limited*

* delete if
inappropriate

hereby notifies you of the following change(s):

† specify the
change and
date thereof
and if this
consists of the
appointment of
a new director
or secretary
complete the
box below.
If this space is
insufficient use
a continuation
sheet.

†

Particulars of new director or secretary (see note 1)

Name (notes 2 & 3)

Business occupation ‡

‡ Applicable to
directors only.

Previous name(s) (note 2)

Nationality ‡

Address (notes 3 & 4)

Date of birth (where applicable)
(note 5) ‡

+ Enter particulars
of other
directorships
held or previously
held (see note 6).
If this space is
insufficient use
a continuation
sheet.
§ delete as
appropriate

Other directorships ‡ +

I hereby consent to act as [director] [secretary] § of the above-named company

Signature

Date

Name (notes 2 & 3)

Business occupation ‡

Previous name(s) (note 2)

Nationality ‡

Address (notes 3 & 4)

Date of birth (where applicable)
(note 5) ‡

Other directorships ‡ +

I hereby consent to act as [director] [secretary] § of the above-named company

Signature

Date

number of continuation sheets attached (see note 7)

Signature

[Director] [Secretary] § Date

Presentor's name, address and
reference (if any):

For official use
General section

Post room

Notes

1 'Director' includes any person who occupies the position of a director by whatsoever name called, and any person in accordance with whose directions or instructions the directors are accustomed to act.

2 Full names must be given. In the case of an individual his present Christian name(s) and surname must be given together with any previous Christian names or surname. 'Christian name' includes a forename and 'surname', in the case of a peer or person usually known by a title different from his surname, means that title. In the case of a corporation, its corporate name must be given. 'Previous Christian names or surname' does not include:-

(a) in the case of a peer or a person usually known by a British title different from his surname, the name by which he was known previous to the adoption of or succession to the title; or

(b) in the case of any person, a previous Christian name or surname where that name or surname was changed or disused before the person bearing the name attained the age of eighteen years or has been changed or disused for a period of not less than twenty years; or

(c) in the case of a married woman, the name or surname by which she was known previous to the marriage.

3 Where the secretary or one of the joint secretaries is a Scottish firm the details required are the firm name and its principal office. Where all the partners in a firm are joint secretaries only the name and principal office of the firm need be stated.

4 Usual residential address must be given or, in the case of a corporation, the registered or principal office.

5 Dates of birth need only be given in the case of directors of a company which is subject to section 185 of the Companies Act 1948, namely a company which is a public company or, being a private company, is a subsidiary of a public company or of a body corporate registered as a public company under the law relating to companies for the time being in force in Northern Ireland.

6 The names of all bodies corporate incorporated in Great Britain of which the director is also a director (see note 1) or has been a director at any time during the preceding five years must be given. A current or past directorship need not be disclosed however if it has been held in a body corporate which, throughout that directorship (excluding any period of the directorship held more than five years ago), has been:-

(a) a dormant company, ie one for which no significant accounting transaction (within the meaning of section 12(6) of the Companies Act 1981) has occurred;

(b) a body corporate of which the company named on page 1 was a wholly owned subsidiary;

(c) a wholly owned subsidiary of the company named on page 1; or

(d) a wholly owned subsidiary of a body corporate of which the company named on page 1 was also a wholly owned subsidiary.

A body corporate is deemed to be the wholly owned subsidiary of another if it has no members except that other and that other's wholly owned subsidiaries and its or their nominees.

7 If the space overleaf is insufficient, the names and particulars must be entered on the prescribed continuation sheet(s).

Please do not
write in this
binding margin

Please complete
legibly, preferably
in black type, or
bold block lettering

* delete if
inappropriate

THE COMPANIES ACTS 1948 TO 1981

Notice of change of directors or secretaries or in their particulars (continuation)

Continuation sheet No _____
to Form No. 9b

Company number

Name of company

Limited*

Particulars of new directors (continued)

Name (note 2)	Business occupation
Previous name(s) (note 2)	Nationality
Address (note 4)	
	Date of birth (where applicable) (note 5)

† enter particulars
of other director-
ships held or
previously held
(see note 6). If
this space is
insufficient
continue over-
leaf.

Other directorships †

I hereby consent to act as director of the above-named company

Signature

Date

Name (note 2)	Business occupation
Previous name(s) (note 2)	Nationality
Address (note 4)	
	Date of birth (where applicable) (note 5)

Other directorships †

I hereby consent to act as director of the above-named company

Signature

Date

COMPANIES

Particulars of changes, or of other directorships held or previously held (note 6) specifying the director in question

THE COMPANIES ACTS 1948 TO 1981

Form No. 19

Registration of an existing joint stock company
List of members

Pursuant to section 384(a) of the Companies Act 1948
as amended by the Companies Act 1976

19

Please do not write in this binding margin

Please complete legibly, preferably in black type, or bold block lettering

* Not more than six clear days before the day of registration

For official use ☐☐☐☐

For official use

Name of company

List of members of the above company made up to the_____19____*

1 Full name

Address

Occupation

Number of shares or amount of stock held

Distinctive numbers (if any) of the shares

2 Full name

Address

Occupation

Number of shares or amount of stock held

Distinctive numbers (if any) of the shares

3 Full name

Address

Occupation

Number of shares or amount of stock held

Distinctive numbers (if any) of the shares

4 Full name

Address

Occupation

Number of shares or amount of stock held

Distinctive numbers (if any) of the shares

(continue overleaf if necessary)

* delete as appropriate

Signed_____ [Director] [Secretary]† Date _____

Presentor's name, address and reference (if any):

For official use

New companies section | Post room

COMPANIES

List of members (continued)

5 Full name

Occupation

Number of shares or amount of stock held

Address

Distinctive numbers (if any) of the shares

6 Full name

Occupation

Number of shares or amount of stock held

Address

Distinctive numbers (if any) of the shares

7 Full name

Occupation

Number of shares or amount of stock held

Address

Distinctive numbers (if any) of the shares

8 Full name

Occupation

Number of shares or amount of stock held

Address

Distinctive numbers (if any) of the shares

9 Full name

Occupation

Number of shares or amount of stock held

Address

Distinctive numbers (if any) of the shares

10 Full name

Occupation

Number of shares or amount of stock held

Address

Distinctive numbers (if any) of the shares

11 Full name

Occupation

Number of shares or amount of stock held

Address

Distinctive numbers (if any) of the shares

If the space above and overleaf is insufficient the information must be continued on separate sheets and must appear in the same form as above. Please tick the box below if continuation sheets have been used and state how many sheets are attached.

Number of sheets attached

THE COMPANIES ACTS 1948 TO 1981

Particulars of a mortgage or charge

Pursuant to section 95 of the Companies Act 1948

Form No. 47

47

Please do not
write in this
binding margin

**Please complete
legibly, preferably
in black type, or
bold block lettering**

*delete if
inappropriate

For official use

Company number

Name of company

Limited*

Date and description of the instrument creating or evidencing the mortgage or charge (note 2)

Amount due or owing on the mortgage or charge

Names, addresses and descriptions of the mortgagees or persons entitled to the charge

Presentor's name, address and
reference (if any):

For official use

Mortgage section

Post room

Time critical reference

Short particulars of all the property mortgaged or charged

Particulars as to commission, allowance or discount (note 3)

Signed   Date

Designation of position in relation to the company _____

Notes

1 The original instrument creating or evidencing the charge, together with this form, must be delivered to the Registrar of Companies within 21 days after the date of creation of the charge (Section 95(1)). If the property is situated and the charge was created outside the United Kingdom delivery to the Registrar must be effected within 21 days after the date on which the instrument or copy instrument could in due course of post, and if despached with due diligence, have been received in the United Kingdom (Section 95(3)). A copy of the instrument creating the charge will be accepted where the property charged and the charge so created are both outside the United Kingdom (Section 95(3))and in such cases the copy must be verified as a true copy under the seal of the Company or under the hand of some person interested therein otherwise than on behalf of the company. A copy will also be accepted where Section 95(5) applies and Form 47c is submitted.

2 A description of the instrument, eg "Trust Deed", "Debenture", "Mortgage" or "legal charge", etc, as the case may be, should be given.

3 In this section there should be inserted the amount of rate per cent. of the commission, allowance or discount (if any) paid or made either directly or indirectly by the company to any person in consideration of his subscribing or agreeing to subscribe, whether absolutely or conditionally, or procuring or agreeing to procure subscriptions, whether absolute or conditional, for any of the debentures included in this return. The rate of interest payable under the terms of the debentures should not be entered.

4 If any of the spaces in this form provide insufficient space the particulars must be entered on the prescribed continuation sheet.

Please do not
write in this
binding margin

THE COMPANIES ACTS 1948 TO 1981

Particulars of a mortgage or charge

Continuation sheet No._____
to Form No. 47

**Please complete
legibly, preferably
in black type, or
bold block lettering** Name of company

Company number

*delete if
inappropriate

Limited*

Date and description of the instrument creating or evidencing the mortgage or charge
(continued) (note 2)

Page I

COMPANIES

Amount due or owing on the mortgage or charge (continued)

Please do not write in this binding margin

Please complete legibly, preferably in black type, or bold block lettering

Names, addresses and descriptions of the mortgagees or persons entitled to the charge (continued)

lease do not
rite in this
nding margin

lease complete
egibly, preferably
a black type, or
old block lettering

Short particulars of all the property mortgaged or charged (continued)

Form No. 47a

THE COMPANIES ACTS 1948 TO 1981

Particulars of a series of debentures

Pursuant to section 95 of the Companies Act 1948
as amended by the Companies Acts 1976 and 1980

47a

ease do not
ite in this
nding margin

≫

ease complete
gibly, preferably
black type, or
ld block lettering

For official use ⌐ ⌐ ⌐ ⌐ ⌐ ⌐ ⌐

Company number

Name of company

ete if
ppropriate

Limited*

Date of the covering deed (if any) (note 2) _____

Total amount secured by the whole series _____

_____

Date and amount of the present issue (if any) of debentures of the series _____

Dates of resolutions authorising the issue of the series _____

Names of the trustees (if any) for the debenture holders

General description of the property charged

Continue overleaf as necessary

Presentor's name, address and
reference (if any):

For official use
Mortgage section

Post room

Time critical reference

e 1

COMPANIES

General description of the property charged (continued)

Particulars as to commission, allowance or discount (note 3)

Signed _____ Date _____

Designation of position in relation to the company _____

Notes

1 Particulars should be given on this form of a series of debentures containing (or giving by reference to any other instrument) any charge to the benefit of which the debenture holders of the said series are entitled pari passu. The form is to be used for registration of particulars of the entire series. When any subsequent issue of debentures in the series is made, particulars of each issue should be sent to the Registrar of Companies on Form No.48.

2 The date should be given of the covering deed (if any) by which the security is created or defined.

3 In this section there should be inserted the amount or rate per cent of the commission, allowance or discount (if any) paid or made either directly or indirectly by the company to any person in consideration of his subscribing or agreeing to subscribe, whether absolutely or conditionally, or procuring or agreeing to procure subscriptions, whether absolute or conditional, for any of the debentures included in this return. The rate of interest payable under the terms of the debentures should not be entered.

4 The deed, if any, containing the charge particulars to the Registrar within 21 days after the execution of such deed; or, if there is no such deed, one of the debentures must be so delivered within 21 days after the execution of any debenture of the series.

5 If the spaces overleaf are insufficient, the particulars may be continued on a separate sheet.

Form No. 47 c

THE COMPANIES ACTS 1948 TO 1981

Certificate of registration in Scotland or Northern Ireland of a charge comprising property situate there

Pursuant to section 95(5) of the Companies Act 1948

47c

ease do not
te in this
ding margin

ase complete
ibly, preferably
black type, or
d block lettering

ete if
ppropriate

ete as
ropriate

s certificate
uld be given
a director or
retary of the
pany or by a
son interested
e charge
rwise than
ehalf of the
pany or by
licitor
ng on behalf
e company
some
r person so
rested as
esaid. The
acity in
h the
ficate is
n must be
ed

date and
es to charge

Company number

Name of company

Limited*

[I] [We]†

of

being‡

hereby certify that the charge §

of which a true copy is annexed hereto was presented for registration on _____ 19 _____

in [Scotland] [Northern Ireland] †

Signed‡

Presentor's name, address and reference (if any):

For official use
Mortgage section   Post room

Form No. 4

THE COMPANIES ACTS 1948 TO 1981

Particulars of an issue of debentures in a series

Pursuant to section 95(8) and(9) of the Companies Act 1948
as amended by the Companies Acts 1976 and 1980

Please do not
write in this
binding margin

**Please complete
legibly, preferably
in black type, or
bold block lettering** Name of company

For official use

Company number

*delete if
inappropriate

Limited*

Note
Please refer to
notes overleaf
before
completing this
form.

Date of present issue _____

Amount of present issue _____

Particulars as to commission, allowance or discount (note 2) _____

Signed _____ Date _____

Designation of position in relation to the company _____

Presentor's name, address and
reference (if any):

For official use
Mortgage section

Post room

Time critical reference

Notes

1 This form is for use when an issue
  is made of debentures in a
  series; for registration of particulars of
  the entire series, form No. 47a should
  be used.

2 In this space there should be inserted
  the amount or rate per cent of the
  commission, allowance or discount
  (if any) paid or made either directly or
  indirectly by the company to any
  person in consideration of his
  subscribing or agreeing to subscribe,
  whether absolutely or conditionally, or
  procuring or agreeing to procure
  subscriptions, whether absolute or
  conditional for any of the debentures
  included in this return. The rate of
  interest payable under the terms of the
  debentures should not be entered.

Form No. 49

THE COMPANIES ACTS 1948 TO 1981

Memorandum of complete satisfaction of mortgage or charge

Please do not write in this binding margin

Please complete legibly, preferably in black type, or bold block lettering

*delete if inappropriate

†A description of the Instrument(s) creating or evidencing the charge, eg 'Mortgage', 'Charge', 'Debenture' etc, with the date thereof should be given.

‡Insert brief details of property

§The date of registration may be confirmed from the certificate of registration and (except in the case of a series of debentures) from the registration stamp affixed to the instrument(s) registered.

For verification see overleaf

For official use

Company number

Name of company

Limited*

Particulars to be verified

The above-named company hereby gives notice that with respect to the registered charge being [†_____ dated _____ 19____*] [a series of Debentures authorised by resolution dated _____ 19____*] secured on property‡_____

_____

of which particulars were registered with the Registrar of Companies on §_____ 19_____ the debt for which the charge was given was wholly paid or satisfied on_____ _____ 19_____

The above-named company hereby gives notice that with respect to the registered charge being [†_____ dated _____ 19____*] [a series of Debentures authorised by resolution dated _____ 19____*] secured on property ‡_____

_____

of which particulars were registered with the Registrar of Companies on §_____ 19_____ the debt for which the charge was given was wholly paid or satisfied on_____ _____ 19_____

Presentor's name, address and reference (if any):

For official use

Mortgage section

Post room

Time critical reference

page 1

The above-named company hereby gives notice that with respect to the registered charge being

[†_____ dated _____ 19____ *] [a series of Debentures

authorised by resolution dated _____ 19____ *] secured on property‡ _____

_____

of which particulars were registered with the Registrar of Companies on§_____

19_____ the debt for which the charge was given was wholly paid or satisfied on___ _ ___ __ __

_____ _____ 19_____

Declaration verifying above particulars relating to a registered mortgage or charge

Pursuant to section 100 of the Companies Act 1948 as amended by the Companies Act 1976

Name of company

Limited*

We, _____

of _____

_____

_____ a director of the above-named company

and _____

of _____

_____

the secretary thereof, do solemnly and sincerely declare that the particulars relating to
_____¶ charges entered above are true to the best of our knowledge, information
and belief. And we make this solemn declaration conscientiously believing the same to be
true and by virtue of the provisions of the Statutory Declarations Act 1835.

Declared at _____

_____

_____

the _____ day of _____ one

thousand nine hundred and _____

before me _____

A Commissioner for Oaths **

Declarants sign here

Please do not
write in this
binding margin

Please complete
legibly, preferably
in black type, or
bold block lettering

*delete if
inappropriate

†A description of
the Instrument(s)
creating or
evidencing the
charge, eg
'Mortgage',
'Charge',
'Debenture' etc,
with the date
thereof should
be given.

‡Insert brief
details of
property

§The date of
registration may
be confirmed
from the
certificate of
registration and
(except in the
case of a series
of debentures)
from the
registration
stamp affixed to
the instrument(s)
registered.

¶ insert number
of charges

**or Notary Public
or Justice of the
Peace or
Solicitor having
the powers
conferred on a
Commissioner
for Oaths

Form No. 49a

THE COMPANIES ACTS 1948 TO 1981

Memorandum of (1) partial payment or satisfaction of mortgage or charge (2) release of part of property or undertaking from mortgage or charge

49a

Please do not write in this binding margin

Please complete legibly, preferably in black type, or bold block lettering

*delete if inappropriate

†A description of the Instrument(s) creating or evidencing the charge, eg 'Mortgage', 'Charge', 'Debenture' etc, with the date thereof should be given.

‡Insert brief details of property

§The date of registration may be confirmed from the certificate of registration and (except in the case of a series of debentures) from the registration stamp affixed to the instrument(s) registered.

¶delete as appropriate

For verification see overleaf

For official use

Company number

Name of company

Limited*

Particulars to be verified

The above-named company hereby gives notice that with respect to the registered charge being
[†_____ dated _____ 19 _____ *]
[a series of Debentures authorised by resolution dated _____ 19_____ *]
secured on property ‡_____
_____ of which particulars were registered with the Registrar
of Companies on §_____ 19 _____ , [the debt for which the charge was given was
partly paid or satisfied to the extent of _____] ¶[and] ¶ [part of the property or undertaking
charged was released from the charge]¶on _____19___[Short particulars of property or
undertaking no longer charged: _____
_____]¶

The above-named company hereby gives notice that with respect to the registered charge being
[†_____ dated _____19_____*]
[a series of Debentures authorised by resolution dated _____ 19_____ *]
secured on property ‡_____
_____ of which particulars were registered with the Registrar
of Companies on §_____ 19 _____ , [the debt for which the charge was given was
partly paid or satisfied to the extent of _____]¶ [and]¶ [part of the property or undertaking
charged was released from the charge]¶on _____ 19___[Short particulars of property or
undertaking no longer charged: _____
_____]¶

Presentor's name, address and reference (if any):

For official use
Mortgage section

Post room

Time critical reference

The above-named company hereby gives notice that with respect to the registered charge being

[† _____ dated _____ 19 ____ *]

[a series of Debentures authorised by resolution dated _____ 19 ____ *]

secured on property.‡_____

_____ of which particulars were registered with the Registrar

of Companies on § _____ 19 _____ , [the debt for which the charge was given was

partly paid or satisfied to the extent of _____]¶ [and]¶ [part of the property or undertaking

charged was released from the charge]ᶜ on _____ 19 ___ [Short particulars of property or

undertaking no longer charged: _____

_____]¶

Declaration verifying above particulars relating to a registered mortgage or charge

Pursuant to section 100 of the Companies Act 1948 as amended by the Companies Act 1976

Name of company

Limited*

We, _____

of _____

_____

_____ a director of the above-named company

and _____

of _____

_____

the secretary thereof, do solemnly and sincerely declare that the particulars relating to _____ charges entered above are true to the best of our knowledge, information and belief. And we make this solemn declaration conscientiously believing the same to be true and by virtue of the provisions of the Statutory Declarations Act 1835.

Declared at _____

_____

_____

the _____ day of _____ one

thousand nine hundred and _____

before me _____

A Commissioner for Oaths **

Declarants sign here

Please do not write in this binding margin

Please complete legibly, preferably in black type, or bold block lettering

*delete if inappropriate

†A description of the Instrument(s) creating or evidencing the charge, eg 'Mortgage', 'Charge', 'Debenture' etc. with the date thereof should be given.

‡Insert brief details of property

§The date of registration may be confirmed from the certificate of registration and (except in the case of a series of debentures) from the registration stamp affixed to the instrument(s) registered.

¶delete as appropriate

insert number of charges

**or Notary Public or Justice of the Peace or Solicitor having the powers conferred on a Commissioner for Oaths

Form No. 49

THE COMPANIES ACTS 1948 TO 1981

Memorandum of fact that part of property or undertaking mortgaged or charged has ceased to form part of property or undertaking of company

49b

Please do not write in this binding margin

Please complete legibly, preferably in black type, or bold block lettering

*delete if inappropriate

†A description of the Instrument(s) creating or evidencing the charge, eg 'Mortgage', 'Charge', 'Debenture' etc, with the date thereof should be given.

For official use

Company number

Name of company

Limited*

Particulars to be verified

The above-named company hereby gives notice that on_____19_____part of

the property or undertaking subject to the registered charge being [†_____

_____ dated _____19____ *]

[a series of Debentures authorised by resolution dated_____19___ *] of

which particulars were registered with the Registrar of Companies on §_____

19_____ceased to form part of the company's property or undertaking. Short

particulars of such property:_____

_____

_____

The above-named company hereby gives notice that on_____19_____part of

the property or undertaking subject to the registered charge being [†_____

_____ dated _____19____ *

[a series of Debentures authorised by resolution dated_____19___ *] of

which particulars were registered with the Registrar of Companies on §_____

19_____ceased to form part of the company's property or undertaking. Short

particulars of such property:_____

_____

_____

§The date of registration may be confirmed from the certificate of registration and (except in the case of a series of debentures) from the registration stamp affixed to the instrument(s) registered.

For verification see overleaf

Presenter's name, address and reference (If any):

For official use

Mortgage section

Post room

Time critical reference

page 1

Please do not
write in this
binding margin

The above-named company hereby gives notice that on _____ 19 _____ part of

the property or undertaking subject to the registered charge being [† _____

_____ dated _____ 19 ___ *]

a series of Debentures authorised by resolution dated _____ 19 ___ *] of

which particulars were registered with the Registrar of Companies on § _____

9 _____ ceased to form part of the company's property or undertaking. Short particulars

of such property: _____

_____

_____

Please complete
legibly, preferably
in black type, or
bold block lettering

*delete if
inappropriate

†A description of
the Instrument(s)
creating or
evidencing the
charge, eg
'Mortgage',
'Charge',
'Debenture' etc,
with the date
thereof should
be given.

§The date of
registration may
be confirmed
from the
certificate of
registration and
(except in the
case of a series
of debentures)
from the
registration
stamp affixed to
the instrument(s)
registered.

Declaration verifying above particulars relating to a registered mortgage or charge

Pursuant to section 100 of the Companies Act 1948 as amended by the Companies Act 1976

Name of company

_____

Limited*

We, _____

of _____

_____

_____ a director of the above-named company

and _____

of _____

_____

the secretary thereof, do solemnly and sincerely declare that the particulars relating to

_____ ** charges entered above are true to the best of our knowledge, information

and belief. And we make this solemn declaration conscientiously believing the same to be

true and by virtue of the provisions of the Statutory Declarations Act 1835.

**insert number
of charges

Declared at _____

_____

_____

the _____ day of _____ one

thousand nine hundred and _____

Declarants sign here

before me _____

A Commissioner for Oaths ‡

‡or Notary Public
or Justice of the
Peace or
Solicitor having
the powers
conferred on a
Commissioner
for Oaths

page 2

Form No.

G

F

THE COMPANIES ACTS 1948 TO 1981

List of documents delivered for registration by an oversea company

Pursuant to section 407(1) of the Companies Act 1948
as amended by the Companies Act 1976

Please do not
write in this
binding margin

Please complete
legibly, preferably
in black type, or
bold block lettering

To the Registrar of Companies

For official use   For official use

F

Name of company

*Insert country
of origin.

Incorporated in*

Place of business in Great Britain established at

Note
Please read
notes overleaf
before completing
this form.

The following documents are delivered for registration:

†Insert 'Charter',
'Statutes',
'Memorandum
and Articles of
Association' or
other instrument
as the case may
be.

1 A certified copy of the† _____
constituting or defining the constitution of the above named company [and, the instrument being
written in a language other than English, a certified translation thereof] . ‡

2 A list (on form No. F2) of the directors and secretary of the company containing the particulars
required by section 407 (2) of the Companies Act 1948.

‡Delete if
inappropriate

3 A list (on form No. F3) of the names and addresses of some one or more persons resident in
Great Britain authorised to accept on behalf of the company service of process and any notices
required to be served on the company.

Signature(s) of the person(s)
authorised under section
407(1)(c) of the Companies Act
1948, or of some other person in
Great Britain duly authorised by
the company

Date

Presentor's name, address and
reference (if any):

For official use
New Companies section   Post room

Notes

1 The copy of the charter, statutes or memorandum and articles of the company or other instrument constituting or defining the constitution of the company required to be delivered by an oversea company to the registrar under section 407 of the Act shall be certified as a true copy in the place of incorporation of the company:

a by an official of the Government to whose custody the original is committed; or

b by a notary public of the place of incorporation; or

c on oath by some officer of the company before some person having authority to administer an oath as provided by section 3 of the Commissioners for Oaths Act 1889 (52 & 53 Vict. c. 10).

2 The translation of the charter, statutes or memorandum and articles of association or other instrument constituting or defining the constitution of a company shall be certified to be a correct translation

a if made in a foreign country, by any of the British officials mentioned in section 6 of the Commissioners for Oaths Act 1889, or by any person whom any such official certifies is known to him as competent to translate it into the English language;

b if made outside the United Kingdom in any of Her Majesty's dominions or in any place under Her Majesty's protection or where Her Majesty has jurisdiction, by a person having authority to administer an oath as provided by Section 3 of the Commissioners for Oaths Act 1889;

c if made in Northern Ireland, by–

i a notary public in Northern Ireland, or

ii a solicitor of the Supreme Court of Judicature of Northern Ireland;

d if made in Scotland, by–

i a notary public in Scotland, or

ii a solicitor;

e if made in England, by–

i a notary public in England, or

ii a solicitor of the Supreme Court of Judicature of England.

3 A statutory declaration stating the date on which the place of business was established in Great Britain must be made in the prescribed form (form F14) and be delivered to the registrar within one month of the establishment of the place of business. See section 407 (2A) of the Companies Act 1948 as introduced by paragraph 15 of Schedule 3 to the Companies Act 1981.

Form No.

THE COMPANIES ACTS 1948 TO 1981

Particulars of a mortgage or charge on property in England and Wales created by a company incorporated outside **Great Britain**

Pursuant to sections 95 and 106 of the Companies Act 1948 as amended by the Companies Act 1981

F8

Please do not write in this binding margin

Please complete legibly, preferably in black type, or bold block lettering

For official use

Company number

F

Name of company

*Country of origin

Incorporated in*

Place of business in **England and Wales** established at

Note
Please read notes overleaf before completing this form

Date and description of the instrument creating or evidencing the mortgage or charge

Amount due or owing under the mortgage or charge

Names, addresses and descriptions of the mortgagees or persons entitled to the mortgage or charge

Presentor's name, address and reference (if any):

For official use
Mortgage section

Post room

hort particulars of all the property mortgaged or charged

Please do not
write in this
binding margin

⩔

Please complete
legibly, preferably
in black type, or
bold block lettering

articulars as to commission, allowance or discount (if any) paid (note 2)

Signature(s) of the person(s)
authorised under section 407
1)(c) of the Companies Act
1948, or of some other person
n Great Britain duly authorised
by the company

Date

Notes

A description of the instrument, eg
'Trust Deed', 'Debenture', 'Charge
by way of legal mortgage' etc., as the
case may be should be given.

In this space there should be inserted
the amount or rate per cent of the
commission, allowance or discount
(if any) paid or made either directly or
indirectly by the company to any
person in consideration of his
subscribing or agreeing to subscribe,
whether absolutely or conditionally or
procuring or agreeing to procure
subscriptions, whether absolute or
conditional for any debentures
included in this return. The rate of
interest payable under the terms of the
debentures should not be entered.

3   The original instrument creating or
evidencing the charge together with
this form, must be delivered to the
registrar of companies within 21 days
after the date of creation of the
charge (section 95(1)).

Form No. F9

THE COMPANIES ACTS 1948 TO 1981

Particulars of a mortgage or charge subject to which property in England and Wales has been acquired by a company incorporated outside Great Britain

Pursuant to sections 97 and 106 of the Companies Act 1948 as amended by the Companies Act 1981

Please do not write in this binding margin

Please complete legibly, preferably in black type, or bold block lettering

For official use

Company number

F

Name of company

Incorporated in*

*Country of origin

Place of business in **England and Wales** established at

Note
Please read notes overleaf before completing this form

Date and description of the instrument creating or evidencing the mortgage or charge (note 1)

Date of the acquisition of the property

Amount due or owing under the mortgage or charge

Names, addresses and descriptions of the mortgagees or persons entitled to the mortgage or charge

Presentor's name, address and reference (if any):

For official use
Mortgage section

Post room

hort particulars of the property mortgaged or charged (continued)

Please do not
write in this
binding margin

Please complete
legibly, preferably
in black type, or
bold block lettering

Signature(s) of the person(s)
authorised under section 407
(1)(c) of the Companies Act
1948 or of some other person
in Great Britain duly authorised
by the company

Date

Notes

A description of the instrument, eg
'Trust Deed', 'Mortgage', 'Debenture',
etc., as the case may be, should
be given.

This return must be delivered to the
Registrar of Companies within 21 days
after the date of the acquisition of the
property which is subject to the
mortgage or charge.

3 A copy of the instrument by which a
charge is created or evidenced, to be
delivered to the Registrar under the
provisions of subsection (1) of section
97 of the Act, shall be certified to be
a true copy under the seal of the
company or under the hand of some
person interested therein otherwise
than on behalf of the company.

Form No. F10

M

THE COMPANIES ACTS 1948 TO 1981

Particulars of a series of debentures containing, or giving by reference to any other instrument, any charge on property in England and Wales, to the benefit of which the debenture holders of the said series are entitled, pari passu, created by a company incorporated outside Great Britain

Please do not write in this binding margin

Pursuant to sections 95(8), (9) and 106 of the Companies Act 1948 as amended by the Companies Acts 1976 to 1981

F10

Please complete legibly, preferably in black type, or bold block lettering

For official use   Company number

[_ _ _ _] **F**

Name of company

*Insert country of origin

Incorporated in*

Place of business in England and Wales established at

Note
Please read notes overleaf before completing this form

Particulars of a series of debentures created by the above-named company (note 1)

Total amount secured by the whole series _____

Date and amount of the present issue (if any) of debentures of the series _____

Dates of resolutions authorising the issue of the series _____

Date of the covering deed (if any) (note 2) _____
General description of the property charged

Presentor's name, address and reference (if any):

For official use
Mortgage section   Post room

Names of the trustees (if any) for the debenture holders

Particulars as to commission, allowance or discount (if any) paid (note 3)

Signature(s) of the person(s)
authorised under section
407(1)(c) of the Companies Act
1948 or of some other person
in Great Britain duly authorised
by the company

Date

Notes

This form is to be used for
registration of particulars of the
entire series. When any subsequent
issue of debentures in the series is
made, particulars of the date and
amount of each issue should be
sent to the Registrar on Form No. F11.

The date should be given of the
covering deed (if any) by which the
security is created or defined.

In this space there should be
inserted the amount, or rate per cent
of the commission, allowance or
discount (if any) paid or made either
directly or indirectly by the company
to any person in consideration of his
subscribing or agreeing to subscribe,
whether absolutely or conditionally,
or procuring or agreeing to procure
subscriptions, whether absolute or
conditional, for any of the debentures
included in this return. The rate of
interest payable under the terms
of the debentures should not be
entered.

4 The deed, if any, containing the charge
charge must be delivered with these
particualrs to the Registrar within
21 days after the execution of such
deed; or, if there is no such deed,
one of the debentures must be so
delivered within 21 days after the
execution of any debenture of the
series.

Form No. F1

M

Please do not
write in this
binding margin

THE COMPANIES ACTS 1948 TO 1981

Particulars of an issue of debentures in a series by a company incorporated outside Great Britain

Pursuant to sections 95(8), (9) and 106 of the Companies Act 1948
as amended by the Companies Acts 1976 to 1981

**Please complete
legibly, preferably
in black type, or
bold block lettering**

For official use

Company number

F

Name of company

*Country of
origin

Incorporated in*

Place of business in England and Wales established at

Note
Please read
notes overleaf
before
completing this
form

Particulars of an issue of debentures in a series (note 1)

Date of present issue

Amount of present issue

Particulars as to commission, allowance or discount (if any) paid (note 2)

Signature(s) of the person(s)
authorised under section 407
(1)(c) of the Companies Act
1948 or of some other person
in Great Britain duly authorised
by the company

Date

Presentor's name, address and
reference (if any):

For official use
Mortgage section

Post room

Notes

1 This form is for use when an issue is
made in debenture in a series; for
registration of particulars of the
entire series, Form number F10
should be used.

2 In this space there should be inserted
the amount or rate per cent of the
commission, allowance or discount
(if any) paid or made either directly or
indirectly by the company to any
person in consideration of his
subscribing or agreeing to subscribe,
whether absolutely or conditionally, or
procuring or agreeing to procure
subscriptions, whether absolute or
conditional for any of the debentures
included in this return. The rate of
interest payable under the terms of the
debentures should not be entered.

M

Form No. F12

THE COMPANIES ACTS 1948 TO 1981

Memorandum of complete satisfaction of mortgage or charge registered by a company incorporated outside Great Britain

F12

Please do not write in this binding margin.

Please complete legibly, preferably in black type, or bold block lettering

For official use

Company number

F

Name of company

Incorporated in†

†Country of origin

Place of business in England and Wales established at

Particulars to be verified

‡ A description of the instrument(s) creating or evidencing the charge, eg 'Mortgage', 'Charge', 'Debenture' etc, with the date thereof should be given.

The above-named company hereby gives notice that with respect to the registered charge being [‡_____dated_____19_____*] [a series of Debentures authorised by resolution dated_____19_____*] secured on property§_____

of which particulars were registered with the Registrar of Companies on¶_____ 19_____ the debt for which the charge was given was wholly paid or satisfied on _____ _____ 19 _____

*delete as appropriate

§Insert brief details of property

¶The date of registration may be confirmed from the certificate of registration and (except in the case of a series of debentures) from the registration stamp affixed to the instrument(s) registered.

The above-named company hereby gives notice that with respect to the registered charge being [‡_____dated_____19_____*] [a series of Debentures authorised by resolution dated_____19_____*] secured on property§_____

of which particulars were registered with the Registrar of Companies on¶ _____ 19_____ the debt for which the charge was given was wholly paid or satisfied on _____ _____19_____

For verification see overleaf

Presentor's name, address and reference (if any):

For official use

Mortgage section

Post room

Time critical reference

page 1

Please do not
write in this
binding margin

Name of company

⋙

Please complete
legibly, preferably
in black type, or
bold block lettering

The above-named company hereby gives notice that with respect to the registered charge being

[†_____ dated _____19____*] [a series of Debentures

authorised by resolution dated_____19____*] secured on property‡_____

of which particulars were registered with the Registrar of Companies on§ _____

19_____the debt for which the charge was given was wholly paid or satisfied on _____

_____ 19 _____

*delete as
appropriate

†A description of
the Instrument(s)
creating or
evidencing the
charge, eg
'Mortgage',
'Charge',
'Debenture' etc,
with the date
thereof should
be given.

‡Insert brief
details of
property

Signature(s) of the person(s) authorised

under section 407(1)(c) of the Companies

Act 1948

Date _____

§The date of
registration may
be confirmed
from the
certificate of
registration and
(except in the
case of a series
of debentures)
from the
registration
stamp affixed to
the instrument(s)
registered.

Declaration

Pursuant to section 100 of the Companies Act 1948 as amended by the Companies Act 1976 and

pursuant to section 106 of the Companies Act 1948 as amended by the Companies Act 1981

[I] [We],*_____

of _____

_____

_____

the person(s) authorised under section 407(1)(c) of the Companies Act 1948 by the above-named

company do solemnly and sincerely declare that the particulars relating to the** _____

charge(s) entered above are true to the best of [my] [our] * knowledge, information and belief. And

[I] [We] * make this solemn Declaration conscientiously believing the same to be true and by virtue

of the provisions of the Statutory Declarations Act 1835.

**insert number of
charges

Declared at _____ ⎫ Signature of declarants:

⎪ _____

the _____ day of _____ one ⎬

thousand nine hundred and _____ ⎪ _____

before me _____ ⎭

A Commissioner for Oaths ⁋

*or Notary Public
or Justice of the
Peace or
Solicitor having
the powers
conferred on a
Commissioner
for Oaths

Form No. F12a

THE COMPANIES ACTS 1948 TO 1981

Memorandum of (1) partial payment or satisfaction of mortgage or charge (2) release of part of property or undertaking from mortgage or charge registered by a company incorporated outside Great Britain

F12a

Please do not
write in this
binding margin.

**Please complete
legibly, preferably
in black type, or
bold block lettering**

†Country of origin

‡A description of
the Instrument(s)
creating or
evidencing the
charge, eg
'Mortgage',
'Charge',
'Debenture' etc,
with the date
thereof should
be given.

§Insert brief
details of
property

¶The date of
registration may
be confirmed
from the
certificate of
registration and
(except in the
case of a series
of debentures)
from the
registration
stamp affixed to
the instrument(s)
registered.

*delete as
appropriate

For verification
see overleaf

For official use

Company number

F

Name of company

Incorporated in†

Place of business in England and Wales established at

Particulars to be verified

The above-named company hereby gives notice that with respect to the registered charge being

[‡ _____ dated _____ 19_____ *]

[a series of Debentures authorised by resolution dated _____ 19_____ *]

secured on property § _____

_____ of which particulars were registered with the Registrar

of Companies on¶ _____ 19 _____ , [the debt for which the charge was given was

partly paid or satisfied to the extent of _____]* [and]* [part of the property or undertaking

charged was released from the charge]* on _____ 19___[Short particulars of property or

undertaking no longer charged: _____

_____ *]

Presentor's name, address and
reference (if any):

For official use
Mortgage section

Post room

Time critical reference

Name of company

The above-named company hereby gives notice that with respect to the registered charge being

[†_____ dated _____ 19 _____ *]

[a series of Debentures authorised by resolution dated _____ 19 _____ *]

secured on property _____

_____ of which particulars were registered with the Registrar

of Companies on _____ 19 _____ , [the debt for which the charge was given was

partly paid or satisfied to the extent of _____]* [and]* [part of the property or undertaking

charged was released from the charge]* on _____ 19 __ [Short particulars of property or

undertaking no longer charged: _____

_____ *]

†A description of the Instrument(s) creating or evidencing the charge, eg 'Mortgage', 'Charge', 'Debenture' etc. with the date thereof should be given.

Signature(s) of the person(s) authorised
under section 407 (1) (c) of the Companies
Act 1948

Date _____

§The date of registration may be confirmed from the certificate of registration and (except in the case of a series of debentures) from the registration stamp affixed to the instrument(s) registered.

*delete as appropriate

‡Insert brief details of property

Declaration

pursuant to section 100 of the Companies Act 1948 as amended by the Companies Act 1976 and
pursuant to section 106 of the Companies Act 1948 as amended by the Companies Act 1981

I [We],*_____

_____

the person(s) authorised under section 407 (1) (c) of the Companies Act 1948 by the above-named
company do solemnly and sincerely declare that the particulars relating to the **_____
charge(s) entered above are true to the best of [my] [our] * knowledge, information and belief.
and [I] [We] * make this solemn declaration conscientiously believing the same to be true and
by virtue of the provisions of the Statutory Declarations Act 1835.

**insert number of charges

Declared at_____   Signatures of declarants:

the_____ day of_____ one
thousand nine hundred and_____
before me_____
Commissioner for Oaths⸢

⸢or Notary Public or Justice of the Peace or Solicitor having the powers conferred on a Commissioner for Oaths

Form No. F12b

THE COMPANIES ACTS 1948 TO 1981

Memorandum of fact that part of property or undertaking mortgaged or charged has ceased to form part of property or undertaking of company registered by a company incorporated outside Great Britain

F12b

Please do not write in this binding margin.

Please complete legibly, preferably in black type, or bold block lettering

†Country of origin

For official use

Company number

F

Name of Company

Incorporated in†

Place of business in England and Wales established at

Particulars to be verified

*delete as appropriate

‡A description of the Instrument(s) creating or evidencing the charge, eg 'Mortgage', 'Charge', 'Debenture' etc, with the date thereof should be given.

¶The date of registration may be confirmed from the certificate of registration and (except in the case of a series of debentures) from the registration stamp affixed to the instrument(s) registered.

For verification see overleaf

The above named company hereby gives notice that on _____ 19 _____

part of the property or undertaking subject to the registered charge being [‡ _____

dated _____ 19 _____] * [a series of Debentures authorised by resolution

dated _____ 19 _____ *] of which particulars were registered with the

Registrar of Companies on ¶ _____ 19 _____ ceased to form part of the

company's property or undertaking. Short particulars of such property: _____

_____

_____

Presentor's name, address and reference (if any):

For official use

Mortgage section

Post room

Time critical reference

page 1

Please do not write in this binding margin

⌄⌄

Please complete legibly, preferably in black type, or bold block lettering

The above named company hereby gives notice that on _____ 19_____

part of the property or undertaking subject to the registered charge being [† _____

_____

dated _____ 19 _____ *] [a series of Debentures authorised by resolution

dated _____ 19 _____ *] of which particulars were registered with the

Registrar of Companies on § _____ 19 _____ ceased to form part of the company's

property or undertaking. Short particulars of such property: _____

_____

†A description of the Instrument(s) creating or evidencing the charge, eg 'Mortgage', 'Charge', 'Debenture' etc. with the date thereof should be given.

Signature(s) of the person(s) authorised _____

under section 407 (1) (c) of the Companies _____

Act 1948 _____

_____

Date _____   _____

§The date of registration may be confirmed from the certificate of registration and (except in the case of a series of debentures) from the registration stamp affixed to the instrument(s) registered.

Declaration

Pursuant to section 100 of the Companies Act 1948 as amended by the Companies Act 1976 and

pursuant to section 106 of the Companies Act 1948 as amended by the Companies Act 1981

[I] [We], * _____

_____

of _____

_____

_____

_____

*delete as appropriate

the person(s) authorised under section 407 (1) (c) of the Companies Act 1948 by the above-named

company do solemnly and sincerely declare that the particulars relating to the ** _____

charge(s) entered above are true to the best of [my] [our] * knowledge, information and belief.

And [I] [We] * make this solemn declaration conscientiously believing the same to be true and

by virtue of the provisions of the Statutory Declarations Act 1835.

**insert number of charges

Declared at _____   Signatures of declarants:

_____   _____

_____   _____

the _____ day of _____ one   _____

thousand nine hundred and _____   _____

before me _____   _____

A Commissioner for Oaths ¶

¶ or Notary Public or Justice of the Peace or Solicitor having the powers conferred on a Commissioner for Oaths

COMPANIES

SCHEDULE 3

THE COMPANIES ACTS 1948 TO 1981

Application for registration under Part VIII of the Companies Act 1948

G

Please do not
write in this
binding margin

Pursuant to section 382(1) of the Companies Act 1948 (as
amended by the Companies Acts 1976 and 1980) and where
appropriate section 13(4) of the Companies Act 1980.

15

Please complete
legibly, preferably
in black type, or
bold block
lettering

*Insert full name
of Company

To the Registrar of Companies

For official use

For official use

Name of company

*

The above named company constituted by _____

_____

†delete as
appropriate

§ delete if
inappropriate

dated _____ 19 _____ desires to be registered as [a company

limited by [shares] [guarantee] †] [an unlimited company] † under the Companies Acts 1948 to

1981 [and being a joint stock company applying to be registered as a company limited by shares,

desires to be so registered as a public company]§

Signed _____ [Director] [Secretary] † Date _____

Notes

There must also be delivered to the registrar:—
  (a) Form 16 as required by section 382(3) and (4).
  (b) Form 17 as required by section 386.
  (c) In the case of an application by a company other than a joint stock company, the documents
      required by section 385 (a) (b) and (c).
  (d) In the case of an application by a joint stock company:—
      (i)   form 18, as required by section 384(c), where the company is intended to be registered
            as a limited company;
      (ii) form 19, as required by section 384(a);
      (iii) the documents required by section 384(b);
      (iv) the documents listed in paragraphs (a) to (e) of section 13(4) of the Companies Act 1980,
            where the company is applying to be registered as a public company.
  (e) Declaration required by section 25 (4) (b) of the Companies Act 1981 if appropriate. (Form 62)

Presentor's name, address and
reference (if any):

For official use
New companies section

Post room

THE COMPANIES ACTS 1948 TO 1981

Form No. 16

Application for registration under Part VIII of the Companies Act 1948

Statement under section 382 (3) and (4) of the Companies Act 1948 as amended by the Companies Acts 1980 and 1981

Please do not write in this binding margin

Please complete legibly, preferably in black type, or bold block lettering

* Insert full name of Company

†delete as appropriate

Delete if inappropriate

To the Registrar of Companies

For official use

For official use

Name of company

*

1. The above named company, desires to be registered under the Companies Acts 1948 to 1981

2. The registered office is to be situated in [England] [Scotland] [Wales] †

3. The intended situation of the registered office after registration is

[4. The company wishes to be registered with the Welsh equivalent of ["public limited company"] ["limited"] † as the last word(s) of its name.]‡

Signed _____ [Director] [Secretary] † Date _____

Presentor's name, address and reference (if any):

For official use

General Section

Post room

Form No. 17

G

THE COMPANIES ACTS 1948 TO 1981

Registration under Part VIII of the Companies Act 1948
Declaration verifying documents delivered to the
Registrar of Companies with application for registration

Pursuant to section 386 of the Companies Act 1948
as amended by the Companies Act 1976

Please do not
write in this
binding margin

**Please complete
legibly, preferably
in black type, or
bold block lettering**

To the Registrar of Companies

For official use   For official use

Name of company

°Enter full names
and addresses
of two or more
directors or
other principal
officers of the
company

We*,

†Enter
description
of status

being† _____ of the above named company

do solemnly and sincerely declare that the particulars set forth in the several documents accompanying

§ The documents
to accompany
the declaration
are the documents
containing
particulars
relating to the
company required
to be delivered to
the registrar on
application for
registration

this Declaration,§ and marked respectively with the letters _____ are true; and

we make this solemn Declaration conscientiously believing the same to be true, and by virtue of the

provisions of the Statutory Declarations Act 1835

Declared at _____

_____

_____

the _____ day of _____

One thousand nine hundred and_____

‡or Notary Public
or Justice of the
Peace or
Solicitor having
the powers
conferred on a
Commissioner
for Oaths

before me_____

A Commissioner for Oaths‡

Signatures of Declarants

Presentor's name, address and
reference (if any):

For official use
New companies section   Post room

Form No. 18

THE COMPANIES ACTS 1948 TO 1981

Registration of an existing joint stock company as a limited company

Statement of particulars

Pursuant to section 384(c) of the Companies Act 1948
as amended by the Companies Acts 1976, 1980 and 1981

Please do not
write in this
binding margin

Please complete
legibly, preferably
in black type, or
bold block lettering

Please read notes
overleaf before
completing
this form

See notes 1
and 2.

So as to conform
to the details on
Form 19

Delete as
appropriate

To the Registrar of Companies

For official use   For official use

Name of company

*

1 Amount of nominal capital £_____

Number of shares into which it is divided_____

or amount of stock of which it consists_____

2

Number of shares taken †   Amount paid on each share

3

Resolution declaring the amount of the guarantee

Signed   [Director] [Secretary] ‡ Date

Presentor's name, address and
reference (if any):

For official use
New companies section   Post room

Notes

1. Where the company is to be registered
   as a public company the name inserted
   should be the name of the company
   with the addition as the last words of
   the name, "public limited company",
   or, if the company has delivered a
   statement under section 382 (3) (c) of
   the Companies Act 1948, "cwmni
   cyfyngedig cyhoeddus".

2. Where the company is to be registered
   as a private company, the name
   inserted should be the name of the
   company with the addition as the
   last word of the name (subject to
   section 25 of the Companies Act
   1981) "limited" or, if the company
   has delivered a statement under section
   382 (3) (c) of the Companies Act
   1948, "cyfyngedig".

3. In the case of a company having a
   share capital, please complete paragraphs
   1 and 2. In the case of a company
   intended to be registered as a company
   limited by guarantee please complete
   paragraph 3.

SCHEDULE 4

Return of allotments of shares issued by way of capitalisation of reserves (bonus issues)

Form No. PUC7 (revised)

Pursuant to section 52(1) of the Companies Act 1948 as amended by the Companies Act 1976

PUC7

ase do not
te in this
ding margin.

ase complete
bly, preferably
lack type, or
d block lettering

ete if
ppropriate

tinguish
ween
nary,
ference, etc.

uding premium
any)

For official use   Company number

Name of Company

Limited*

Description of shares †	A Number of shares allotted	B Nominal amount of each	C Amount treated as paid up	D Amount paid or due and payable on each ‡
i		£	£	£
ii		£	£	£
iii		£	£	£

ete or complete
ppropriate

Date(s) of allotment(s)

[made on the_____19____]*

[from the_____19____to the _____19____] §

The names, descriptions and addresses of the allottees should be given overleaf

Notes

If there is any non- bonus element, any amount paid on any call or calls should be stated on Form PUC 5.

No capital duty is payable in respect of capitalisation of reserves.

This form should be delivered to the Registrar of Companies within one month of the (first) date of allotment and should be accompanied by the duly stamped contract referred to in section 52(1) (b) of the Companies Act 1948 or, where the contract has not been reduced to writing by a form 52 (Particulars of contract).

Presentor's name, address and reference (if any):

For official use

Capital section   Post room

1

Names, descriptions and addresses of the allottees

Please do not write in this binding margin.

Please complete legibly, preferably in black type, or bold block lettering

Name and description	Address	Number of shares allotted		
		Preference	Ordinary	Other kinds
	Total			

Where the space given on this form is inadequate, continuation sheets should be used and the number of sheets attached should be indicated in the box opposite:

I hereby certify that the details entered on this form are correct.

‡delete as appropriate

Signed_____ [Director] [Secretary]‡   Date_____

EXPLANATORY NOTE

(This Note is not part of the Regulations.)

These Regulations:—

(a) provide that the forms set out in Schedule 2 to the Regulations are prescribed for the purposes of the provisions of the Companies Acts 1948 to 1980 referred to therein, in place of the forms bearing the same number which are set out in Schedule B to the Companies (Forms) Regulations 1979;

(b) prescribe the manner for the certification of a copy of any document referred to in s. 407(1)*(a)* of the Companies Act 1948 and of any translation of such a document;

(c) prescribe a form for the statements required by section 382(3) of the Companies Act 1948 and prescribe certain new forms for the purpose of applications for the registration of unregistered companies under Part VIII of the Companies Act 1948 in place of forms 21 and 23 in Schedule B to the Companies (Forms) Regulations 1979 and forms 17b, 17c, 17d, 18b and 18c in Schedule B to the Companies (Forms) Regulations 1980;

(d) prescribe the form of a return of allotments required by section 52(1)*(a)* of the Companies Act 1948 when the shares allotted are bonus shares. The allotment of bonus shares is not a transaction chargeable to capital duty so that regulation 4(3) of the Companies (Forms) Regulations 1979 does not in that case supply an appropriate form.

STATUTORY INSTRUMENTS

1983 No. 1022 (C. 28)

COMPANIES

The Companies Act 1980 (Commencement No. 4) Order 1983

Made - - - -	*14th July* 1983
Coming into Operation	1*st October* 1983

The Secretary of State, in exercise of his powers under section 90(3) of the Companies Act 1980(**a**), hereby makes the following Order:—

1. This Order may be cited as the Companies Act 1980 (Commencement No. 4) Order 1983.

2. All those provisions of the Companies Act 1980 not yet brought into operation shall come into operation on 1st October 1983.

Alexander Fletcher,
Parliamentary Under-Secretary of State,
Department of Trade and Industry.

14th July 1983.

EXPLANATORY NOTE

(*This Note is not part of the Order.*)

Certain provisions of the Companies Act 1980 "the Act" were brought into force by the Companies Act 1980 (Commencement) Order 1980 (S.I. 1980/745), the Companies Act 1980 (Commencement No. 2) Order 1980 (S.I. 1980/1785) and the Companies Act 1980 (Commencement No. 3) Order 1981 (S.I. 1981/1683).

This Order brings into force all the provisions of the Act not previously brought into force, ie:—

(i) section 82(*f*) of the Act (which repeals section 438 of and Schedule 15 to the Companies Act 1948 (1948 c. 38) (penalty for false statements));

(ii) section 88(2) of and Schedule 4 to the Act so far as they relate to the repeal of section 438 of and Schedule 15 to the Companies Act 1948.

(**a**) 1980 c. 22.

STATUTORY INSTRUMENTS

1983 No. 1023

COMPANIES

The Companies (Annual Return) Regulations 1983

Made - - - -	*14th July* 1983
Laid before Parliament	*27th July* 1983
Coming into Operation	*1st January* 1984

The Secretary of State, in exercise of the powers conferred by section 454(2) of the Companies Act 1948(a) and now vested in him(b), hereby makes the following Regulations:—

1. These Regulations may be cited as the Companies (Annual Return) Regulations 1983 and shall come into operation on 1st January 1984.

2. The Companies (Annual Return) Regulations 1977(c) and the Companies (Annual Return) (Amendment) Regulations 1979(d) are hereby revoked.

3. There shall be substituted for the form set out in Part II of the Sixth Schedule to the Companies Act 1948(e), the form set out in the Schedule to these Regulations.

Alexander Fletcher,
Parliamentary Under Secretary of State,
14th July 1983.   Department of Trade and Industry.

(a) 1948 c. 38; section 454(2) was amended by section 88 of and Schedule 4 to the Companies Act 1980 (c. 22) and other provisions not relevant to this instrument.
(b) S.I. 1970/1537.
(c) S.I. 1977/1368.
(d) S.I. 1979/54.
(e) The form of the annual return in Part II of the Sixth Schedule was substituted by the Companies (Annual Return) Regulations 1977 and amended by the Companies (Annual Return) (Amendment) Regulations 1979 and by section 88 of and Schedules 3 and 4 to the Companies Act 1980.

SCHEDULE

THE COMPANIES ACTS 1948 TO 1981

Annual return of a company having a share capital

Pursuant to sections 124 and 126
of the Companies Act 1948

Form No. 6

6a

Please do not write in this binding margin

To the Registrar of Companies

For official use

Company number

Please complete legibly, preferably in black type, or bold block lettering.

Annual return of

Limited*

* delete if inappropriate

made up to the ....19............ (hereinafter called 'the date of this return')

being the fourteenth day after the date of the annual general meeting for the year 19.........

Address of registered office of the company

† Scottish companies see also note 2

Total amount of indebtedness of the company in respect of all mortgages and charges which are required to be registered with the Registrar of Companies (note 1). †

If the register of members or any register of debenture holders is kept at a place other than the registered office, insert the address of the place where it is kept, or, if such a register is kept otherwise than in a legible form and the place for inspection of the register is elsewhere than at the registered office, insert the address where inspection may be made. (see note 3)

Register of members

Register of debenture holders

Particulars of the person who is the secretary at the date of this return

Name (notes 4, 5 and 6)

Previous name(s) (note 4)

Address (notes 5, 6 and 7)

We certify this return which comprises pages 1, 2 and 3 [plus ‡_____ continuation sheets]

‡ enter number of continuation sheets attached

Signed _____ Director, and _____ Secretary

Presentor's name, address and reference (if any):

For official use

General section

Post room

ummary of share capital and debentures

Nominal share capital   £

divided into:-

Number of shares	Class	Nominal value of each share
		£
		£
		£
		£

Issued share capital and debentures

	Number	Class

Number of shares of each class taken up to the date of this return (which must agree with the total shown in the list as held by existing members)

Number of shares of each class issued subject to payment wholly in cash

Number of shares of each class issued as fully paid up for a consideration other than cash

Amount   *per share

Number of shares of each class issued as partly paid up for a consideration other than cash and extent to which each such share is so paid up   £   *

Number of shares (if any) of each class issued at a discount

Amount of discount on the issue of shares which has not been written off at the date of this return

Amount called up on number of shares of each class   £   *

Total amount of calls received (note 8)   £

Total amount (if any) agreed to be considered as paid on number of shares of each class issued as fully paid up for a consideration other than cash   £

Total amount (if any) agreed to be considered as paid on number of shares of each class issued as partly paid up for a consideration other than cash   £

Total amount of calls unpaid   £

Total amount of sums (if any) paid by way of commission in respect of any shares or debentures   £

Total amount of the sums (if any) allowed by way of discount for any debentures since the date of the last return   £

Total number of shares of each class forfeited

Total amount paid (if any) on shares forfeited   £

Total amount of shares for which share warrants to bearer are outstanding   £

Total amount of share warrants to bearer issued   ISSUED   £
and surrendered respectively since the date of
the last return   SURRENDERED   £

Number of shares comprised in each share warrant to bearer, specifying in the case of warrants of different kinds, particulars of each kind

LIST OF PAST

Folio in register ledger containing particulars	Names and addresses

Please do not write in this binding margin

Please complete legibly, preferably in black type, or bold block lettering

Important
The particulars to be given are those referred to in section 200 of the Companies Act 1948 as amended by section 95 of the Companies Act 1981.

*enter particulars of other director-ships held or previously held (see note 10). If this space is insufficient use a continuation sheet.

Particulars of the director(s) of the company at the date of the return (note **9**)

Name (note 4)	Business occupation
Previous name(s) (note 4)	Nationality
Address (note 7)	
	Date of birth (note 11)
Other directorships *	

Name (note 4)	Business occupation
Previous name(s) (note 4)	Nationality
Address (note 7)	
	Date of birth (note 11)
Other directorships *	

Name (note 4)	Business occupation
Previous name(s) (note 4)	Nationality
Address (note 7)	
	Date of birth (note 11)
Other directorships *	

AND PRESENT MEMBERS (notes 12, 13 and 14)

	Account of shares			
Number of shares or amount of stock held by existing members at date of return. (notes 15 and 16)	Particulars of shares transferred since the date of the last return, or, in the case of the first return, of the incorporation of the company, by (a) persons who are still members, and (b) persons who have ceased to be members (note 17)			Remarks
	Number (note 16)	Date of registration of transfer (a)	(b)	

Notes

1   Include also any indebtedness in respect of mortgages and charges which would have been required to be so registered if created after 1st July 1908.

2   Scottish companies must state the total amount of indebtedness of the company in respect of all mortgages and charges which if the company had been registered in England would be required to be registered with the Registrar of Companies including indebtedness required by virtue of note 1.

3   If the register of members or any register of debenture holders is kept otherwise than in a legible form (eg on a computer) the Companies (Registers and other Records) Regulations 1979 (SI 1979/53) made under section 3 of the Stock Exchange (Completion of Bargains) Act 1976 requires notification in the annual return of the place in Great Britain where such register may be inspected if that place of inspection is elsewhere than at the registered office.
If any register of debenture holders or any part of it is kept outside Great Britain, insert the address in Great Britain where any duplicate of such register or part is kept unless it is kept at the registered office. See section 86 of the Companies Act 1948, which prohibits a company registered in England and Wales from keeping in Scotland a register of debenture holders or a duplicate of such register, and prohibits a company registered in Scotland from keeping any such register or duplicate in England and Wales.

4   Full names must be given. In the case of an individual his present Christian name(s) and surname must be given together with any previous Christian names or surname. 'Christian name' includes a forename and 'surname', in the case of a peer or person usually known by a title different from his surname, means that title. In the case of a corporation its corporate name must be given. 'Previous Christian names or surname' does not include:-

  (a) in the case of a peer or a person usually known by a British title different from his surname, the name by which he was known previous to the adoption of or succession to the title, or

  (b) in the case of any person, a previous Christian name or surname where that name or surname was changed or disused before the person bearing the name attained the age of eighteen years or has been changed or disused for a period of not less than twenty years, or

  (c) in the case of a married woman, the name or surname by which she was known previous to the marriage.

5   Where all the partners in a firm are joint secretaries, only the name and principal office of the firm need be stated.

6   Where the secretary or one of the joint secretaries is a Scottish firm the details required are the firm name and its principal office.

7   Usual residential address must be given or, in the case of a corporation, the registered or principal office.

8   Include payments on application and allotment and any sums received on shares forfeited.

9   If there is insufficient space use a prescribed continuation sheet. 'Director' includes any person who occupies the position of a director by whatever name called, and any person in accordance with whose directions or instructions the directors of the company are accustomed to act.

10   The names of all bodies corporate incorporated in Great Britain of which the director is also a director (see note 9) or has been a director at any time during the preceding five years must be given. A current or past directorship need not be disclosed however if it has been held in a body corporate which, throughout that directorship (excluding the the period of the directorship held more than five years ago), has been

  (a) a dormant company, ie one for which no significant accounting transaction (within the meaning of section 12(6) of the Companies Act 1981) has occurred,

  (b) a body corporate of which the company making the return was a wholly owned subsidiary,

  (c) a wholly owned subsidiary of the company making the return, or

  (d) a wholly owned subsidiary of a body corporate of which the company making the return was also a wholly owned subsidiary.

A body corporate is deemed to be the wholly owned subsidiary of another if it has no members except that other and that other's wholly owned subsidiaries and its or their nominees.

11   Dates of birth need only be given in the case of directors of a company which is subject to section 185 of the Companies Act 1948, namely a company which is a public company or, being a private company, is a subsidiary of a public company or of a body corporate registered as a public company under the law relating to companies for the time being in force in Northern Ireland.

12   Give list of persons holding shares or stock in the company on the fourteenth day after the holding of the annual general meeting. Show also those persons who have ceased to hold shares or stock in the company since the date of the last return or, if this is the company's first return, since the date of incorporation. If this space is insufficient use a prescribed continuation sheet.
Where a company keeping a dominion register receives at its registered office after the date when the annual return is completed, copies of entries made in the dominion register, the relevant particulars of those entries shall be included in a subsequent return.

13   If the names in the list are not arranged in alphabetical order, an index sufficient to enable the name of any person to be readily found must be annexed.

14   If the return for either of the two immediately preceding years has given as at the date of that return the full particulars required as to past and present members and the shares and stock held and transferred by them, the only particulars which need to be given are those relating to persons ceasing to be or becoming members since the date of the last return, the shares transferred since that date or the changes since that date in the amount of stock held by a member. In the case of a company keeping a dominion register the full particulars referred to above do not include particulars of entries in the dominion register not received at the registered office before the date when the relevant annual return was completed.

15   The aggregate number of shares held by each member must be stated and the aggregate must be added up so as to agree with the number of shares stated in the 'summary of share capital and debentures' (page 2 item 1) to have been taken up.

16   When the shares are of different classes these columns should be sub divided, so that the number of each class held, or transferred, may be shown separately. Where any shares have been converted into stock the amount of stock held by each member must be shown.

17   The date of registration of each transfer should be given as well as the number of shares transferred on each date. The particulars should be placed opposite the name of the transferor and not opposite that of the transferee, but the name of the transferee may be inserted in the 'remarks' column immediately opposite the particulars of each transfer.

THE COMPANIES ACTS 1948 TO 1981

Form No. 6a
continuation

Annual return of a company
having a share capital (continuation)

Continuation sheet No._____

of _____

This sheet should be attached to and forms part of the annual return for _____

_____ made up

to the _____ 19 ____

Company number

Particulars of the directors of the company at the date of this return   (note 9)

Name (note 4)	Business occupation
Previous name(s) (note 4)	Nationality
Address (note 7)	Date of birth (where applicable) (note 11)

Other directorships *

Name (note 4)	Business occupation
Previous name(s) (note 4)	Nationality
Address (note 7)	Date of birth (where applicable) (note 11)

Other directorships *

Name (note 4)	Business occupation
Previous name(s) (note 4)	Nationality
Address (note 7)	Date of birth (where applicable) (note 11)

Other directorships *

Name (note 4)	Business occupation
Previous name(s) (note 4)	Nationality
Address (note 7)	Date of birth (where applicable) (note 11)

Other directorships *

List of Past and Present

Folio in register ledger containing particulars.	Names and addresses	Please do not write in this binding margin. ⅩⅩ
		Please complete legibly, preferably in black type, or bold block lettering

Members (notes 12, 13 and 14)

Please do not write in this binding margin

Please complete legibly, preferably in black type, or bold block lettering

Number of shares or amount of stock held by existing members at date of return. (notes 15 and 16)	Account of shares		Remarks
	Particulars of shares transferred since the date of the last return, or, in the case of the first return, of the incorporation of the company, by (a) persons who are still members, and (b) persons who have ceased to be members (note 17)		
	Number (note 16)	Date of registration of transfer (a) (b)	

Particulars of other directorships held or previously held (note 10) **specifying** the director in question

Please do not
write in this
binding margin

Please complete
legibly, preferably
in black type, or
bold block letterir

EXPLANATORY NOTE

(This Note is not part of the Regulations.)

These Regulations alter the form of the annual return required to be made by a company having a share capital, presently set out in the Schedule to the Companies (Annual Return) Regulations 1977, as amended by the Companies (Annual Return) (Amendment) Regulations 1979 and the Companies Act 1980.

STATUTORY INSTRUMENTS

1983 No. 1024 (C. 29)

COMPANIES

The Companies Act 1981 (Commencement No. 5) Order 1983

Made - - - - -	14*th July* 1983
Coming into Operation	1*st January* 1984

The Secretary of State, in exercise of the powers conferred on him by section 119(3) of the Companies Act 1981**(a)**, hereby makes the following Order:—

1. This Order may be cited as the Companies Act 1981 (Commencement No. 5) Order 1983.

2. The following provisions of the Companies Act 1981 shall come into operation on 1st January 1984:—

(*a*) section 95;

(*b*) section 119(4) (so far as it relates to paragraph 13(*b*) of Schedule 3) and the said paragraph 13(*b*); and

(*c*) section 119(5) and Schedule 4 so far as they provide for the repeal of

   (i) section 16(3) of the Companies Act 1967**(b)**, and

   (ii) the entry in Schedule 2 to the Companies Act 1980**(c)** relating to section 200 of the Companies Act 1948**(d)**.

Alexander Fletcher,
Parliamentary Under-Secretary of State,
Department of Trade and Industry.

14th July 1983.

(**a**) 1981 c. 62.   (**b**) 1967 c. 81.   (**c**) 1980 c. 22.   (**d**) 1948 c. 38.

EXPLANATORY NOTE

(This Note is not part of the Order.)

Certain provisions of the Companies Act 1981 have been brought into force by the Companies Act 1981 (Commencement No. 1) Order 1981 (S.I. 1981/1621), the Companies Act 1981 (Commencement No. 2) Order 1981 (S.I. 1981/1684), the Companies Act 1981 (Commencement No. 3) Order 1982 (S.I. 1982/103) and the Companies Act 1981 (Commencement No. 4) Order 1982 (S.I. 1982/672).

This present Order brings into operation on 1st January 1984,

- (*a*) section 95 (register of past directorships);
- (*b*) section 119(4), so far as specified in Article 2 of the Order, and paragraph 13(*b*) of Schedule 3; and
- (*c*) section 119(5) and Schedule 4 (repeals) so far as specified in Article 2 of the Order.

NOTE AS TO EARLIER COMMENCEMENT ORDERS

(This Note is not part of the Order.)

Sections 33, 36 to 41 and 107 of the Act came into force on Royal Assent (30 October 1981).

The following provisions have been brought into force by commencement orders made before the date of this order:—

Provision	*S.I. Number*
Part I partially (except ss. 16(2), 19 and 20)	1982/672
s. 16(2) partially	1981/1684 and 1982/672
s. 19	1982/672
ss. 22 to 30	1982/103
s. 31	1981/1684
ss. 32 and 34	1981/1684 and 1982/103
s. 35	1982/103
ss. 42 to 44	1981/1621
ss. 45 to 59	1982/672
s. 60	1981/1621 and 1982/672
s. 61	1982/672
s. 62	1981/1621 and 1982/672
ss. 63 to 84	1982/672
s. 85	1981/1684 and 1982/672
ss. 86 to 92	1981/1684
ss. 93 and 94	1982/672
ss. 96 to 100	1981/1684
ss. 101 and 102	1982/672
ss. 103 to 106 and 108	1981/1684
s. 109	1982/103
ss. 110 to 112	1981/1684
ss. 113 to 115	1981/1621
s. 116	1981/1684
ss. 117 and 118	1981/1621
s. 119 partially and Schedules 3 and 4 partially	1981/1621, 1981/1684 1982/103 and 1982/672

STATUTORY INSTRUMENTS

1983 No. 1025

ROAD TRAFFIC

The Road Transport (International Passenger Services) (Amendment) Regulations 1983

Made - - - -	*18th July* 1983
Laid before Parliament	*27th July* 1983
Coming into Operation	*18th August* 1983

The Secretary of State for Transport being a Minister designated(**a**) for the purposes of section 2(2) of the European Communities Act 1972(**b**) in relation to the international carriage of passengers by road, in exercise of the powers conferred by that section and, with the consent of the Treasury, in exercise of the powers conferred by section 56(1) and (2) of the Finance Act 1973(**c**), and now vested in him(**d**), hereby makes the following Regulations:—

1. These Regulations shall come into operation on 18th August 1983 and may be cited as the Road Transport (International Passenger Services) (Amendment) Regulations 1983.

2. The Road Transport (International Passenger Services) Regulations 1980(**e**) shall be amended in accordance with the following provisions of these Regulations.

3. In Regulation 14 (Applications for, issue of, and fees payable in respect of, authorisations for international passenger services) for paragraphs (3) to (6) there shall be substituted the following paragraphs:—

'(3) An applicant for—

> (*a*) a shuttle service authorisation, or a regular, or special regular, service authorisation, or

> (*b*) an international passenger transport authorisation required by section 30 of the Public Passenger Vehicles Act 1981(**f**), as modified by Regulation 5,

shall pay, when the application is made, a fee of £110 in respect of the application.

(**a**) S.I. 1972/1811, 1979/571 and 1981/238.   (**b**) 1972 c. 68.
(**c**) 1973 c. 51.   (**d**) S.I. 1979/571, 1981/238.
(**e**) S.I. 1980/1459; there is no relevant amending instrument.
(**f**) 1981 c. 14.

(4) An applicant for a regular, or special regular, service authorisation shall pay, when the application is made, in addition to the fee required by paragraph (3) above, a fee of £25 in respect of each year of validity of the authorisation.

(5) In this Regulation "shuttle service authorisation" means such an authorisation under Council Regulation No. 516/72 and "regular service authorisation" and "special regular service authorisation" mean respectively such an authorisation under Council Regulation No. 517/72.'.

4. After Regulation 21 (Forgery and false statements, etc.) there shall be inserted the following Regulation:—

'*Amendment of Road Traffic (Foreign Vehicles) Act 1972*

21A.—(1) The Road Traffic (Foreign Vehicles) Act 1972**(a)** is amended in accordance with the following provisions of this Regulation.

(2) In section 1(1)(*a*) and (2)(*a*) after "enactment", in each place where it occurs, there shall be inserted "or instrument".

(3) In Schedule 1 (Enactments conferring functions on examiners)—

    (*a*) in the headings for "ENACTMENTS" and "*Enactment*" there shall be substituted "PROVISIONS" and "*Provisions*", and

    (*b*) there shall be added at the end—

"Regulation 16 of the Road Transport (International) Passenger Services) Regulations 1980.	To require the production of, and to inspect, copy and mark, documents required to be kept or carried on certain passenger vehicles."

(a) 1972 c. 27.

(4) In Schedule 2 (Provisions relating to vehicles and their drivers) there shall be added at the end:—

"Regulation 19 of the Road Transport (International Passenger Services) Regulations 1980	To impose penalties for contravention of Community instruments relating to international passenger services." '

Tom King,
Secretary of State for Transport.

11th July 1983.

We consent to the making of these Regulations.

Alastair Goodlad,
Ian B. Lang,
Two of the Lords Commissioners of Her
Majesty's Treasury.

18th July 1983.

EXPLANATORY NOTE

(This Note is not part of the Regulations.)

These Regulations amend Regulation 14 of the Road Transport (International Passenger Services) Regulations 1980. They introduce a fee of £110 for an application for any authorisation required for an international passenger service (a shuttle service authorisation or a regular or special regular service authorisation in the case of Community regulated services or an international passenger transport authorisation in the case of non-Community regulated services) in place of the fees of differing amounts prescribed by Regulation 14(3), (4)(*a*) and (5). The separate fee of £20 payable by an applicant for the variation of the conditions of a regular, or special regular, service authorisation under Regulation 14(4)(*b*) is abolished and the additional fee payable under Regulation 14(4)(*a*) by an applicant for a regular, or special regular, service authorisation in respect of each year of validity of the authorisation is increased to £25.

They also insert a new Regulation 21A which amends the Road Traffic (Foreign Vehicles) Act 1972 so as to apply the powers to prohibit the driving of foreign public service vehicles to such vehicles being used in contravention of Regulation 19 of the 1980 Regulations, that is otherwise than under and in accordance with an authorisation or other document referred to in that Regulation.

STATUTORY INSTRUMENTS

1983 No. 1026

HEALTH AND SAFETY
MINES AND QUARRIES

The Quarries (Metrication) Regulations 1983

Made - - - -	18*th July* 1983
Laid before Parliament	27*th July* 1983
Coming into Operation	17*th August* 1983

The Secretary of State, in exercise of the powers conferred on him by sections 49(1), (2) and (4) and 82(3)(*a*) of the Health and Safety at Work etc. Act 1974 (**a**) ("the 1974 Act") and of all other powers enabling him in that behalf and for the purpose of giving effect without modification to proposals submitted to him by the Health and Safety Commission under section 11(2)(*d*) of the 1974 Act after the carrying out by the said Commission of consultations in accordance with section 50(3) of that Act, hereby makes the following Regulations:—

Citation, commencement and interpretation

1.—(1) These Regulations may be cited as the Quarries (Metrication) Regulations 1983 and shall come into operation on 17th August 1983.

(2) In these Regulations "the principal Regulations" means the Regulations amended by these Regulations, that is to say—

The Quarries (General) Regulations 1956 (**b**);

The Quarries (Electricity) Regulations 1956 (**c**);

The Quarries (Ropeways and Vehicles) Regulations 1958 (**d**); and

The Quarries (Explosives) Regulations 1959 (**e**).

Amendments to Regulations to substitute metric measurements for imperial measurements

2. The provisions of the Regulations specified in the Schedule to these Regulations in column 1 shall be amended by substituting for the measurements set out opposite thereto in column 3 the measurements set out in the corresponding entry in column 4.

(**a**) 1974 c.37; section 49 was amended by the Employment Protection Act 1975 (c.71), Schedule 15, paragraph 15.
(**b**) S.I. 1956/1780, to which there are amendments not relevant to these Regulations.
(**c**) S.I. 1956/1781, to which there are amendments not relevant to these Regulations.
(**d**) S.I. 1958/2110, to which there are amendments not relevant to these Regulations.
(**e**) S.I. 1959/2259, to which there are amendments not relevant to these Regulations.

Application to existing premises and plant or premises and plant under construction

3. Where any premises or plant in existence or under construction immediately before the coming into operation of these Regulations complied with the requirements of the principal Regulations as then in force, then those premises or that plant shall be deemed to comply with the principal Regulations as amended by these Regulations.

Signed by order of the Secretary of State.

John Selwyn Gummer,
Joint Parliamentary Under Secretary of State,
Department of Employment.

18th July 1983.

AMENDMENTS TO REGULATIONS

Column 1 Regulations to be amended	Column 2 Subject-matter of measurement(s)	Column 3 Present measurement	Column 4 Substituted measurement
The Quarries (General) Regulations 1956			
1. Regulation 4(2)	(a) Maximum interval allowed between platforms on a ladder	(a) Thirty feet	(a) 10 metres
	(b) Length of ladder at or below which the requirement at (a) above does not apply	(b) Thirty feet	(b) 10 metres
	(c) Minimum distance a ladder must project above a platform	(c) Three feet	(c) 920 millimetres
2. Regulation 6	(a) Minimum height of skirting board on the open side of any gantry or platform forming a bridge	(a) Nine inches	(a) 230 millimetres
	(b) Minimum height of skirting board on the open side of any gantry or platform other than one forming a bridge	(b) Six inches	(a) 150 millimetres
3. Regulation 23	Minimum gauge of railway line to which certain Regulations apply	Four feet eight and one half inches	1.432 metres
4. Regulation 25 (b)	Maximum length of pointed wooden sprags required to be provided	Three feet	920 millimetres
5. Regulation 32	Minimum width of space required to be left between two vehicles stationary on one track of rails	Fifteen feet	5 metres
6. Regulation 35	Distance from railway line within which, if material is stacked, certain precautions must be taken	Three feet	920 millimetres

AMENDMENTS TO REGULATIONS

Column 1 Regulations to be amended	Column 2 Subject-matter of measurement(s)	Column 3 Present measurement	Column 4 Substituted measurement
7. Regulation 35(*b*)	(*a*) Maximum length of material which may be stacked alongside a railway line without the provision of adequate spaces or recesses	(*a*) Sixty feet	(*a*) 20 metres
	(*b*) Maximum permitted distances between spaces or recesses in stacks of material	(*b*) Sixty feet	(*b*) 20 metres
The Quarries (Electricity) Regulations 1956			
8. Regulation 3(2)	Minimum permitted cross-sectional area of earthing conductors	0.022 square inches	14 square millimetres
9. Regulation 5	Minimum permitted cross-sectional area of a conductor connecting two or more earthplates with resistances exceeding 2 ohms between them	0.022 square inches	14 square millimetres
10. Regulation 7(3)	Minimum permitted cross-sectional area of an earthing conductor	0.022 square inches	14 square millimetres
11. Regulation 9(3)(*a*)	Cross-sectional area of a copper conductor which has a conductivity equivalent to the minimum required conductivity for a metallic covering containing all the conductors in the relevant circuit	0.022 square inches	14 square millimetres

Column 1 Regulations to be amended	Column 2 Subject-matter of measurement(s)	Column 3 Present measurement	Column 4 Substituted measurement
12. Regulation 9(3)(b)	Cross-sectional area of a copper conductor which has a conductivity equivalent to the minimum required conductivity of a screen of wires containing more or less completely all the conductors forming part of the relevant circuit	0.022 square inches	14 square millimetres
13. Regulation 10(2)(a)	Rating of at least one motor in apparatus above which electricity at a voltage exceeding two hundred and fifty direct current or one hundred and ten alternating current may be supplied	Four horse power	3 kilowatts
14. Regulation 16	Minimum height of fencing to be provided around transformers or switchgear installed otherwise than in a building	Eight feet	2.4 metres
The Quarries (Ropeways and Vehicles) Regulations 1958			
15. Regulation 4(1)(a)	Minimum height of enclosure on a conveyance used for carrying persons by means of a ropeway	Four feet	1.2 metres
16. Regulation 9(1)	Minimum length of rope to be cut when that rope re-capped if used in certain haulage apparatus	Six feet	2 metres
17. Regulation 15(2)	Maximum intervals of length at which certain ropes must be cleaned and thoroughly examined for wear	One hundred and fifty feet	45 metres

Column 1 Regulations to be amended	Column 2 Subject-matter of measurement(s)	Column 3 Present measurement	Column 4 Substituted measurement
The Quarries (Explosives) Regulations 1959			
18. Regulation 2(1)	Length of safety fuse to be used in calculation of rate of burning	Three feet	900 millimetres
19. Regulation 19	(a) Nearest point to any explosive, detonator or explosives store at which a person may smoke or carry or ignite a naked light	(a) Twenty feet	(a) 6 metres
	(b) Nearest point to a naked light to which a person may take any explosive or detonator	(b) Twenty feet	(b) 6 metres
20. Regulation 39(1)	Minimum permitted difference between the diameter of a shothole and the diameter of a cartridge	One eighth of an inch	3 millimetres
21. Regulation 39(2)	Depth of a shothole beyond which a wooden tool with non-ferrous joints may be used in certain circumstances	Nine feet	3 metres
22. Regulation 41	Depth beyond which in certain circumstances a shothole shall only be charged with explosive in a cartridge or container	Nine feet	3 metres
23. Regulation 53(1)(b)	Minimum thickness of stemming between charge and charging or stemming apparatus made wholly or partly of iron or steel	One foot	300 millimetres

EXPLANATORY NOTE

(This Note is not part of the Regulations.)

These Regulations amend the Quarries (General) Regulations 1956, the Quarries (Electricity) Regulations 1956, the Quarries (Ropeways and Vehicles) Regulations 1958 and the Quarries (Explosives) Regulations 1959 by substituting measurements expressed in metric units for measurements not so expressed. The substituted measurements preserve the effect of the original provisions except to the extent necessary to obtain amounts expressed in convenient and suitable terms.

Regulation 3 provides that the amendments do not affect premises or plant in existence or under construction immediately before the coming into operation of these Regulations if those premises or that plant complied with the then existing Regulations.

STATUTORY INSTRUMENTS

1983 No. 1027 (S. 93)

NATIONAL HEALTH SERVICE, SCOTLAND

The National Health Service (Functions of Health Boards) (Scotland) Order 1983

Made - - - -	14*th July* 1983
Laid before Parliament	25*th July* 1983
Coming into Operation	15*th August* 1983

In exercise of the powers conferred on me by sections 2(1) and 105(6) and (7) of the National Health Service (Scotland) Act 1978 (**a**) and of all other powers enabling me in that behalf, I hereby make the following order:—

Citation, commencement and interpretation

1. This order may be cited as the National Health Service (Functions of Health Boards) (Scotland) Order 1983 and shall come into operation on 15th August 1983.

2. In this order, "the Act" means the National Health Service (Scotland) Act 1978.

Functions to be exercised by Health Boards

3.—(1) The functions of the Secretary of State under the Act which are to be exercised by every Health Board shall be the functions conferred or imposed upon him by the provisions of the Act which are specified in the following sub-paragraphs, subject to any exception, qualification or condition specified therein and in the other provisions of this order—

    (a) section 7(6) (Payment of allowances to members of local health councils etc) but not including the function of the Secretary of State to determine, with the approval of the Treasury (**b**), the amount of the allowances so payable;

    (b) section 16(1) (Assistance to voluntary organisations);

    (c) section 16B (**c**) (Financial assistance by Secretary of State to voluntary organisations) but not including the function of the Secretary of State to determine, with the approval of the Treasury, the terms and conditions upon which such assistance may be given;

    (d) Part III (Other Services and Facilities), but not including any function of the Secretary of State under sections 44, 45 and 46;

    (e) section 50 (**d**) (Power as to accommodation and services);

(**a**) 1978 c.29; section 2(1) was amended by the Health and Social Services and Social Security Adjudications Act 1983 (c.41), section 14(2) and Schedule 7, paragraph 1. Section 105(7) was amended by the Health Services Act 1980 (c.53), Schedule 6, paragraph 5(1)*(c)* and *(d)* and Schedule 7.

(**b**) Section 7(6) was amended by the Health Services Act 1980 (c.53), Schedule 6, paragraph 1(1). The function of the Minister for the Civil Service under section 7(6) of the Act was transferred to the Treasury by S.I. 1982/1670.

(**c**) Section 16B was inserted by the Health and Social Services and Social Security Adjudications Act 1983 (c.41), section 3.

(**d**) Section 50 was amended by the Health Services Act 1980 (c.53), section 10(2).

(f) section 55(1) (Hospital accommodation on part payment) but not including the function of the Secretary of State to determine the charges for part of the cost of the accommodation which is being made available;

(g) section 57(1) (a) and (2) (Accommodation and services for private resident patients) but not including the functions of the Secretary of State under section 57(1) to authorise accommodation and services to be made available and to determine the charges payable therefor;

(h) section 58(1) (b) and (2) (Accommodation and services for private non-resident patients) but not including the function of the Secretary of State under section 58(1)*(a)* to authorise the accommodation and services to be made available;

(i) section 64 (Permission for use of facilities in private practice);

(j) section 79(1) (Purchase of land and moveable property) but not including the function of the Secretary of State to acquire land compulsorily;

(k) section 79(1A) (c) (Disposal of land) but not including the function of the Secretary of State to authorise certain officers to execute instruments on his behalf;

(l) paragraph 4 of Schedule 1 (Payment of remuneration to Chairman of a Health Board) but not including the function of the Secretary of State, with the approval of the Treasury (d), to determine the amount of the remuneration so payable; and

(m) paragraph 13 of Schedule 1 (Payment of allowances to members of a Health Board etc) but not including the function of the Secretary of State, with the approval of the Treasury (d), to determine the amount of the allowances so payable.

(2) In exercising, by virtue of paragraph (1)*(e)* of this article, the powers conferred by section 50 of the Act, a Health Board shall exercise any function conferred upon the Secretary of State by section 54 of the Act in relation to the exercise of those powers.

(3) In exercising, by virtue of paragraph (1)*(g)* or *(h)* of this article, the powers conferred by section 57 or 58 of the Act, a Health Board shall exercise any function conferred upon the Secretary of State by section 54, as read with section 58A (e), of the Act in relation to the exercise of those powers.

(4) In exercising, by virtue of paragraph (1)*(j)* or *(k)* of this article, the functions conferred by section 79(1) or 79(1A) of the Act, a Health Board shall have power to manage any land vested in the Secretary of State under the Act.

4.—(1) Notwithstanding the foregoing provisions of this order a Health Board shall not, except with the consent of the Secretary of State—

(a) in exercising, by virtue of article 3(1)*(d)* of this order, the powers conferred by section 36 of the Act, undertake any building or civil engineering project or scheme, the estimated cost of which exceeds £1 million;

(a) Section 57(1) was amended by the Health Services Act 1980 (c.53), section 11(2).
(b) Section 58(1) was amended by the Health Services Act 1980 (c.53), section 11(2).
(c) Section 79(1A) was inserted by the Health and Social Services and Social Security Adjudications Act 1983 (c.41), Schedule 7, paragraph 3.
(d) The functions of the Minister for the Civil Service under paragraphs 4 and 13 of Schedule 1 to the Act were transferred to the Treasury by S.I. 1982/1670.
(e) Section 58A was inserted by the Health Services Act 1980 (c.53), section 11(2).

(b) in exercising, by virtue of article 3(1)*(i)* of this order, the powers conferred by section 64 of the Act, refuse any application under that section; or

(c) in exercising, by virtue of article 3(1)*(j)* or *(k)* or (4) of this order, the powers conferred by section 79(1) or 79(1A) of the Act, acquire or dispose of land in any case where the consideration paid or received for that land exceeds £100,000.

(2) In exercising, by virtue of article 3(1)*(j)* or *(k)* or (4) of this order but subject to paragraph (1)*(c)* of this article, any of the functions conferred upon the Secretary of State by section 79 or 79(1A) to acquire, manage or dispose of land, a Health Board shall ensure—

(a) that any instrument in connection with the exercise of those functions is in the name of the Secretary of State for Scotland and not that of the Health Board; and

(b) that, where any such instrument requires to be executed by the Secretary of State for Scotland and it is not executed in accordance with section 1(8) of the Reorganisation of Offices (Scotland) Act 1939 (**a**) , it is executed, on his behalf, in accordance with section 79(1A) of the Act.

(3) Nothing in this order shall prevent the Common Services Agency for the Scottish Health Service from exercising any function conferred on it by or under section 10 of the Act.

(4) Nothing in this order shall prevent the Secretary of State from exercising any function conferred or imposed upon him by the provisions of the Act.

Revocation

5. The National Health Service (Functions of Health Boards) (Scotland) Order 1974 (**b**) and the National Health Service (Functions of Health Boards) (Scotland) Order 1981 (**c**) are hereby revoked.

George Younger,
One of Her Majesty's Principal
Secretaries of State.

New St Andrew's House,
Edinburgh.
14th July 1983.

(**a**) 1939 c.20.　　　　(**b**) S.I. 1974/466.　　　　(**c**) S.I. 1981/106.

EXPLANATORY NOTE

(This Note is not part of the Order.)

This Order specifies the functions of the Secretary of State under the National Health Services (Scotland) Act 1978 ("the Act") which are to be exercised by Health Boards.

The functions specified in the order are the functions conferred or imposed upon the Secretary of State by the following provisions of the Act, but subject to the exceptions, qualifications or conditions specified in articles 3 and 4 of the order, namely section 7(6) (Payment of allowances to members of local health councils etc), section 16(1) and 16B (Assistance to voluntary organisations), Part III (Other Services and Facilities), section 50 (Power as to accommodation and services), section 55 (Hospital accommodation part payment), section 57 (Accommodation and services for private resident patients), section 58 (Accommodation and services for private non-resident patients), section 64 (Permission for use of facilities in private practice), section 79(1) (Purchase of land and moveable property), section 79(1A) (Disposal of land) and paragraphs 4 and 13 of Schedule 1 (Payment of remuneration to Chairmen and allowances to members of a Health Board).

Article 5 of this order also revokes the National Health Service (Functions of Health Boards) (Scotland) Order 1974 and the National Health Service (Functions of Health Boards) (Scotland) Order 1981.

STATUTORY INSTRUMENTS

1983 No. 1028 (S. 94)

SHERIFF COURT, SCOTLAND

The Sheriff Court Districts (Amendment) Order 1983

Made - - - -	11*th July* 1983
Coming into Operation	1*st September* 1983

In exercise of the powers conferred on me by section 3 of the Sheriff Courts (Scotland) Act 1971(**a**), and of all other powers enabling me in that behalf, I hereby make the following order:—

1. This order may be cited as the Sheriff Court Districts (Amendment) Order 1983 and shall come into operation on 1st September 1983.

2. The Sheriff Court Districts Reorganisation Order 1975(**b**) is hereby amended by substituting in column 3 of the Schedule thereto for the description of the new sheriff court district of Peterhead the following words:—

"That part of the district of Banff and Buchan comprising the parishes of Aberdour, Crimond, Cruden, Fraserburgh, Longside, Lonmay, New Deer, Old Deer, Peterhead, Pitsligo, Rathen, St. Fergus, Strichen and Tyrie".

New St Andrew's House,
Edinburgh.
11th July 1983.

George Younger,
One of Her Majesty's Principal
Secretaries of State.

EXPLANATORY NOTE

(*This Note is not part of the Order.*)

This order transfers the parishes of Aberdour, Fraserburgh, Pitsligo and Tyrie from the sheriff court district of Banff to the sheriff court district of Peterhead.

(**a**) 1971 c. 58.
(**b**) S.I. 1975/637, to which there are amendments not relevant to this order.

STATUTORY INSTRUMENTS

1983 No. 1029 (S. 95)

LOCAL GOVERNMENT, SCOTLAND
LICENCES AND LICENSING

The Local Authorities (Prohibited Conditions for Licensing of Taxis and Private Hire Cars and their Drivers) (Scotland) Regulations 1983

Made - - - -	*12th July* 1983
Laid before Parliament	*27th July* 1983
Coming into Operation	*17th August* 1983

In exercise of the powers conferred on me by section 20(1) and (3) of the Civic Government (Scotland) Act 1982(**a**) and of all other powers enabling me in that behalf, I hereby make the following regulations:—

Citation, commencement and interpretation

1.—(1) These regulations may be cited as the Local Authorities (Prohibited Conditions for Licensing of Taxis and Private Hire Cars and their Drivers) (Scotland) Regulations 1983 and shall come into operation on 17th August 1983.

(2) In these regulations "the Act" means the Civic Government (Scotland) Act 1982.

Prohibited licensing conditions

2. No licensing authority shall impose conditions under the Act on any taxi licence, private hire car licence, taxi driver's licence or private hire car driver's licence which would have the effect of—

(*a*) limiting the holder of a taxi licence or private hire car licence to a licence for only one vehicle;

(*b*) requiring the holder of a taxi licence or private hire car licence or a taxi driver's licence or a private hire car driver's licence to reside within the area of the licensing authority;

(*c*) prohibiting or restricting the use of radios or other means of external communication in private hire cars or imposing additional licensing conditions on the operation of private hire cars solely because they have radios or other means of external communication;

(**a**) 1982 c. 45.

(*d*) preventing the holder of a taxi licence or private hire car licence or a taxi driver's licence or a private hire car driver's licence from engaging in an employment or business other than that for which he is licensed.

New St Andrew's House,
Edinburgh.
12th July 1983.

George Younger,
One of Her Majesty's Principal
Secretaries of State.

EXPLANATORY NOTE

(*This Note is not part of the Regulations.*)

Section 20(1) of the Civic Government (Scotland) Act 1982 empowers the Secretary of State to make Regulations prescribing the conditions which a licensing authority must impose or shall not impose in granting licences to taxi and private hire car operators and taxi and private hire car drivers. These Regulations provide that a licensing authority cannot impose conditions which would have the effect of—

(*a*) limiting a taxi or private hire car operator to only one vehicle,

(*b*) requiring the licence holder to reside within the area of the licensing authority,

(*c*) banning radios or other means of communication in private hire cars or imposing additional conditions solely because they have radios, and

(*d*) preventing licence holders from engaging in other employment or business.

STATUTORY INSTRUMENTS

1983 No. 1030 (S. 96)

EDUCATION, SCOTLAND

The Education (Assisted Places) (Scotland) Amendment Regulations 1983

Made - - - -	*15th July* 1983
Laid before Parliament	*27th July* 1983
Coming into Operation	*17th August* 1983

In exercise of the powers conferred on me by sections 75A(9) and (10) and 75B of the Education (Scotland) Act 1980(a) and of all other powers enabling me in that behalf and after having consulted such bodies as appear to me to be appropriate and to be representative of participating schools in accordance with section 75A(11) of that Act, I hereby make the following regulations:—

Citation and commencement

1. These regulations may be cited as the Education (Assisted Places) (Scotland) Amendment Regulations 1983 and shall come into operation on 17th August 1983.

Interpretation

2. In these regulations, a reference to the principal regulations is a reference to the Education (Assisted Places) (Scotland) Regulations 1982(b).

Amendment of principal regulations

3. In regulation 2(3) of the principal regulations (interpretation) for sub-paragraph *(b)* and the words to the end of the paragraph, there shall be substituted the following provision:—

"*(b)* he is either received into the care of a local authority or is in the care of a voluntary organisation under the Social Work (Scotland) Act 1968(c),

then, for the purposes of these regulations he shall be treated as a child or assisted pupil whose parents have no income and subject thereto, any reference in these regulations to his parents shall be construed as a reference to the authority or organisation in whose care he is.".

(a) 1980 c. 44; sections 75A and 75B were inserted by section 5 of the Education (Scotland) Act 1981 (c. 58).
(b) S.I. 1982/949.
(c) 1968 c. 49.

4. In regulation 6 of the principal regulations (conditions as to age and education)—

    (a) at the commencement there shall be inserted a paragraph number "(1)" and the reference therein to "(i)" shall be deleted;

    (b) paragraph *(b)*(ii) is hereby revoked; and

    (c) at the end, there shall be added the following provision:—

        "(2) A participating school shall not admit to an assisted place a child in relation to whom they are not satisfied that he will be committed throughout the whole of his first assisted year and any subsequent assisted year to follow a course of school education comprising wholly or mainly secondary education.".

5.—(1) In regulation 10(3) of the principal regulations (references to income) for the sum of "£800" there shall be substituted the sum of "£850".

(2) At the end of that regulation there shall be added the following provision:—

"(4) In this regulation, any reference to the parents of an assisted pupil is a reference to the persons who are his parents at the time the relevant income is calculated.".

6. For regulation 13(2) of the principal regulations (calculation of remission) there shall be substituted the following provision:—

"(2) Where one of the pupil's parents has died after remission questions have been determined but before the end of the current financial year and the school are satisfied that the income of the surviving parent in that year, when aggregated with that of the deceased parent, is likely to be less than their aggregated income in the preceding financial year, the remission questions shall be redetermined by reference to the current financial year; and in such case, paragraph (1) shall have effect as if the reference therein to the preceding financial year were a reference to the current financial year and the reference to the pupil's parents in paragraph (2) of regulation 10 included a reference to the deceased parent (notwithstanding the provision of paragraph (4) of that regulation).".

7. In regulation 14(2) of the principal regulations (scale of remission) for the sum of "£5,275" there shall be substituted the sum of "£5,622".

8.—(1) In regulation 16(4)(*a*) of the principal regulations (travel grants) for the words "14(1)" there shall be substituted the words "16(2)".

(2) In regulation 16(5)(*a*) for the sum of "£5,275" there shall be substituted the sum of "£5,622".

(3) In regulation 16(5)(*b*) for the sum of "£5,100" there shall be substituted the sum of "£5,450".

9.—(1) In regulation 18(3) of the principal regulations (clothing grants) for the sum of "£5,800" there shall be substituted the sum of "£6,200"; and for sub-paragraphs *(a)* to *(d)* there shall be substituted the following sub-paragraphs—

"*(a)* £96, where the relevant income does not exceed £5,450;

(b) £72, where that income exceeds £5,450 but does not exceed £5,700;

(c) £48 where that income exceeds £5,700 but does not exceed £5,950;

(d) £24 where that income exceeds £5,950 but does not exceed £6,200.".

(2) In regulation 18(4) for the sum of "£5,350" there shall be substituted the sum of "£5,700"; and for sub-paragraphs *(a)* and *(b)*, there shall be substituted the following sub-paragraphs—

"*(a)* £48, where the relevant income does not exceed £5,450;

(b) £24, where that income exceeds £5,450 but does not exceed £5,700.".

10. In regulation 19(2) of the principal regulations (remission of charges for meals) for the sum of "£4,400" there shall be substituted the sum of "£4,700".

11. At the end of regulation 20(1) of the principal regulations (questions on grants and remission of charges) there shall be added the following provision:—

"Provided that in any case where the circumstances are such as are mentioned in either regulation 12(2)*(a)* or *(b)* and the amount or extent of a school clothing grant requires to be determined, the foregoing provision shall not apply.".

12.—(1) For paragraph 3 of Schedule 1 to the principal regulations (computation of income) there shall be substituted the following provision—

"3. In so far as in ascertaining a person's total income any deductions fall to be made—

(a) by way of personal reliefs provided for in Chapter II of Part I of the Act of 1970, otherwise than in section 18 thereof (reliefs for blind persons);

(b) in pursuance of Part IX of the Act of 1970 or of Chapter II of Part II of the Finance Act 1970(**a**), in respect of superannuation or other payments made by a person, or in respect of deductions made from his salary, for the purpose of securing the payment to or in respect of him of pensions, annuities or other future benefits;

(c) in respect of payments by way of relevant loan interest within the meaning of paragraph 2 of Schedule 7 to the Finance Act 1982(**b**);

(d) in pursuance of section 75 of the Finance Act 1972(**c**), in respect of interest payments eligible for relief under that section by virtue of Part 1 of Schedule 9 to that Act and paragraphs 4(1)*(a)* and 4A of Schedule

(**a**) 1970 c. 24.
(**b**) 1982 c. 39.
(**c**) 1972 c. 41; section 75 was amended by section 19 of the Finance Act 1974 (c. 30) and section 26 of the Finance Act 1982 (c. 39).

1 to the Finance Act 1974(**a**) (loan for purchase or improvement of land) or by virtue of paragraph 24 of the said Schedule 1 (loan to purchase life annuity);

(*e*) in respect of any sums paid under a deed of covenant otherwise than to a child of the person concerned who is wholly or mainly dependent upon him;

(*f*) in pursuance of section 31 of the Finance Act 1977(**b**), in respect of earnings from work done abroad;

(*g*) by way of the relief for persons carrying on a trade, profession or vocation partly abroad provided for in section 27 of the Finance Act 1978(**c**);

(*h*) in pursuance of section 37 of the Finance Act 1980(**d**) (relief for losses on unquoted shares in trading companies); or

(*i*) in pursuance of Chapter II of Part IV of the Finance Act 1981(**e**) (relief for investment in new corporate trades);

his income for the purposes of these regulations shall be computed as though those deductions did not fall to be made.".

(2) Paragraph 4 shall be omitted from the said Schedule.

13. For Schedule 2 to the principal regulations (scale of remission) there shall be substituted the Schedule to these regulations which shall stand as Schedule 2 to the principal regulations.

George Younger,
One of Her Majesty's Principal
Secretaries of State.

New St Andrew's House,
Edinburgh.
15 July 1983.

(**a**) 1974 c. 30; paragraph 4A of Schedule 1 was inserted by section 36 of the Finance Act 1977 (c. 36).
(**b**) 1977 c. 36.
(**c**) 1978 c. 42.
(**d**) 1980 c. 48.
(**e**) 1981 c. 35.

SCHEDULE

(to stand as Schedule 2 to the principal regulations)

Col. 1 Relevant Income	Col. 2 Parental Contribution	Col. 1 Relevant Income	Col. 2 Parental Contribution	Col. 1 Relevant Income	Col. 2 Parental Contribution
£5,622	NIL	£6,940	£171	£7,980	£405
£5,655	£18	£6,960	£174	£8,000	£411
£5,689	£21	£6,980	£177	£8,020	£417
£5,722	£24	£7,000	£180	£8,040	£423
£5,755	£27	£7,020	£183	£8,060	£429
£5,789	£30	£7,040	£186	£8,080	£435
£5,822	£33	£7,060	£189	£8,100	£441
£5,855	£36	£7,080	£192	£8,120	£447
£5,889	£39	£7,100	£195	£8,140	£453
£5,922	£42	£7,120	£198	£8,160	£459
£5,955	£45	£7,140	£201	£8,180	£465
£5,989	£48	£7,160	£204	£8,200	£471
£6,022	£51	£7,180	£207	£8,220	£477
£6,050	£54	£7,200	£210	£8,240	£483
£6,075	£57	£7,220	£213	£8,260	£489
£6,100	£60	£7,240	£216	£8,280	£495
£6,125	£63	£7,260	£219	£8,300	£501
£6,150	£66	£7,280	£222	£8,320	£507
£6,175	£69	£7,300	£225	£8,340	£513
£6,200	£72	£7,320	£228	£8,360	£519
£6,225	£75	£7,340	£231	£8,380	£525
£6,250	£78	£7,360	£234	£8,400	£531
£6,275	£81	£7,380	£237	£8,420	£537
£6,300	£84	£7,400	£240	£8,440	£543
£6,325	£87	£7,420	£243	£8,460	£549
£6,350	£90	£7,440	£246	£8,480	£555
£6,375	£93	£7,460	£249	£8,500	£561
£6,400	£96	£7,480	£255	£8,520	£567
£6,425	£99	£7,500	£261	£8,540	£573
£6,450	£102	£7,520	£267	£8,560	£579
£6,475	£105	£7,540	£273	£8,580	£585
£6,500	£108	£7,560	£279	£8,600	£591
£6,525	£111	£7,580	£285	£8,620	£597
£6,550	£114	£7,600	£291	£8,640	£603
£6,575	£117	£7,620	£297	£8,660	£609
£6,600	£120	£7,640	£303	£8,680	£615
£6,620	£123	£7,660	£309	£8,700	£621
£6,640	£126	£7,680	£315	£8,720	£627
£6,660	£129	£7,700	£321	£8,740	£633
£6,680	£132	£7,720	£327	£8,760	£639
£6,700	£135	£7,740	£333	£8,780	£645
£6,720	£138	£7,760	£339	£8,800	£651
£6,740	£141	£7,780	£345	£8,820	£657
£6,760	£144	£7,800	£351	£8,840	£663
£6,780	£147	£7,820	£357	£8,860	£669
£6,800	£150	£7,840	£363	£8,880	£675
£6,820	£153	£7,860	£369	£8,900	£681
£6,840	£156	£7,880	£375	£8,920	£687
£6,860	£159	£7,900	£381	£8,940	£693
£6,880	£162	£7,920	£387	£8,960	£699
£6,900	£165	£7,940	£393	£8,980	£705
£6,920	£168	£7,960	£399	£9,000	£711

Col. 1 Relevant Income	Col. 2 Parental Contribution	Col. 1 Relevant Income	Col. 2 Parental Contribution
£9,020	£717	£10,020	£1,017
£9,040	£723	£10,040	£1,023
£9,060	£729	£10,060	£1,029
£9,080	£735	£10,080	£1,035
£9,100	£741	£10,100	£1,041
£9,120	£747	£10,120	£1,047
£9,140	£753	£10,140	£1,053
£9,160	£759	£10,160	£1,059
£9,180	£765	£10,180	£1,065
£9,200	£771	£10,200	£1,071
£9,220	£777	£10,220	£1,077
£9,240	£783	£10,240	£1,083
£9,260	£789	£10,260	£1,089
£9,280	£795	£10,280	£1,095
£9,300	£801	£10,300	£1,101
£9,320	£807	£10,320	£1,107
£9,340	£813	£10,340	£1,113
£9,360	£819	£10,360	£1,119
£9,380	£825	£10,380	£1,125
£9,400	£831	£10,400	£1,131
£9,420	£837	£10,420	£1,137
£9,440	£843	£10,440	£1,143
£9,460	£849	£10,460	£1,149
£9,480	£855	£10,480	£1,155
£9,500	£861	£10,500	£1,161
£9,520	£867	£10,520	£1,167
£9,540	£873	£10,540	£1,173
£9,560	£879	£10,560	£1,179
£9,580	£885	£10,580	£1,185
£9,600	£891	£10,600	£1,191
£9,620	£897	£10,620	£1,197
£9,640	£903	£10,640	£1,203
£9,660	£909	£10,660	£1,209
£9,680	£915	£10,680	£1,215
£9,700	£921	£10,700	£1,221
£9,720	£927	£10,720	£1,227
£9,740	£933	£10,740	£1,233
£9,760	£939	£10,760	£1,239
£9,780	£945	£10,780	£1,245
£9,800	£951	£10,800	£1,251
£9,820	£957	£10,820	£1,257
£9,840	£963		
£9,860	£969		
£9,880	£975		
£9,900	£981		
£9,920	£987		
£9,940	£993		
£9,960	£999		
£9,980	£1,005		
£10,000	£1,011		

EXPLANATORY NOTE

(This Note is not part of the Regulations.)

These Regulations amend the Education (Assisted Places) (Scotland) Regulations 1982, (the principal regulations) to uprate the qualifying income levels for the remission of fees and charges and the making of grants under the assisted places scheme and in certain other minor respects.

Regulation 3 amends regulation 2 of the principal regulations to secure that children whether in compulsory or voluntary care may be eligible for assisted places and it further amends regulation 2 to clarify its provision with respect to parental income in relation to such children.

Regulation 4 amends regulation 6 of the principal regulations to make clear that all pupils admitted to assisted places must in their first assisted year and any subsequent assisted year follow a course of wholly or mainly secondary education.

The remaining provisions relate to determining the relevant income of parents for the purposes of the assisted places scheme, the deduction to be made in respect of a dependent relative is increased from £800 to £850 (regulation 5(1)) and the parental income to be taken into account is that of the persons who are the pupil's parents at the time the relevant income is calculated (regulation 5(2)). Consequential changes are made in the special provision relating to the determination of remission questions where one of the parents dies (regulation 6).

The income scale to determine the parental contribution to fees is uprated and the level of income at or below which fees are to be wholly remitted is set at £5,622 instead of £5,275 (regulation 7). The qualifying income levels for school travel grants, clothing grants and the remission of charges for meals are uprated (regulations 8 to 10).

Regulation 11 removes the provision in the principal regulations whereby parents were required to repay a proportion of any clothing grant they had received if a child held an assisted place for part of a school year.

In computing relevant income for the purpose of the scheme certain deductions made for tax purposes under the Finance Act 1982 are to be disregarded and account is taken of the provisions thereof whereby mobility allowances no longer constitute taxable income (regulation 12).

Regulation 13 substitutes for the Schedule of income scale contained in the principal regulations, a new Schedule of new income scales.

STATUTORY INSTRUMENTS

1983 No. 1032

MAGISTRATES' COURTS

The Licensing (Fees) Order 1983

Made - - - - -	18*th July* 1983
Laid before Parliament	19*th July* 1983
Coming into Operation	9*th August* 1983

In exercise of the powers conferred upon me by section 29 of the Licensing Act 1964(**a**) as extended by section 4 of the Licensing (Occasional Permissions) Act 1983(**b**), I hereby make the following Order:—

1. This Order may be cited as the Licensing (Fees) Order 1983 and shall come into operation on 9th August 1983.

2. The fee which may be charged on the grant of an occasional permission under section 1 of the Licensing (Occasional Permissions) Act 1983 shall be £4.00:

Provided that no more than £4.00 shall be charged in respect of more than one permission granted on one day to a single applicant.

Leon Brittan,
One of Her Majesty's Principal
Secretaries of State.

Home Office.
18th July 1983.

EXPLANATORY NOTE

(*This Note is not part of the Order.*)

This Order prescribes a fee of £4 to be charged by clerks to licensing justices on the grant of an occasional permission. Where more than one permission is granted on the same day to one applicant, the fee is still £4.

(**a**) 1964 c. 26.   (**b**) 1983 c. 24.

STATUTORY INSTRUMENTS

1983 No. 1033

BETTING, GAMING AND LOTTERIES

The Pool Competitions Act 1971 (Continuance) Order 1983

Laid before Parliament in draft

Made - - - -	*18th July* 1983
Coming into Operation	*26th July* 1983

Whereas a draft of this Order has been approved by a resolution of each House of Parliament:

Now, therefore, in pursuance of section 8(2) and (3) of the Pool Competitions Act 1971(**a**), I hereby make the following Order:—

1. This Order may be cited as the Pool Competitions Act 1971 (Continuance) Order 1983 and shall come into operation on 26th July 1983.

2. The period specified in section 8(1) of the Pool Competitions Act 1971 (which relates to the duration of that Act)(**b**) is hereby further extended so as to expire with 26th July 1984.

Leon Brittan,
One of Her Majesty's Principal
Home Office.   Secretaries of State.
18th July 1983.

EXPLANATORY NOTE

(*This Note is not part of the Order.*)

This Order continues in force the Pool Competitions Act 1971 until, and including, 26th July 1984.

(**a**) 1971 c. 57.   (**b**) The period was last extended by S.I. 1982/1010.

STATUTORY INSTRUMENTS

1983 No. 1038

CUSTOMS AND EXCISE

The Customs Duties (Quota Relief) (Paper, Paperboard and Printed Products) (Amendment) Order 1983

Made - - - - - - - - - -	18*th July* 1983
Laid before the House of Commons	27*th July* 1983
Coming into Operation	17*th August* 1983

The Secretary of State, in exercise of the powers conferred on him by section 1 of the Customs and Excise Duties (General Reliefs) Act 1979**(a)** and of all other powers enabling him in that behalf, hereby makes the following Order:—

1. This Order may be cited as the Customs Duties (Quota Relief) (Paper, Paperboard and Printed Products) (Amendment) Order 1983 and shall come into operation on 17th August 1983.

2. In the Customs Duties (Quota Relief) (Paper, Paperboard and Printed Products) Order 1982**(b)** in the entry in column 3 of Schedule 6 relating to subheading ex 48.07D of the common customs tariff of the European Economic Community, in respect of coated printing paper, weighing less than 225 g/m^2, for "23,707 tonnes" there shall be substituted "31,278 tonnes" and for "13,667 tonnes" there shall be substituted "21,238 tonnes".

Paul Channon,
Minister for Trade,
Department of Trade and Industry.

18th July 1983.

(a) 1979 c. 3.   **(b)** S.I. 1982/1760.

EXPLANATORY NOTE

(This Note is not part of the Order.)

This Order, which comes into operation on 17th August 1983, amends the Customs Duties (Quota Relief) (Paper, Paperboard and Printed Products) Order 1982 by increasing the duty-free tariff quota which the United Kingdom is entitled to open under Protocol No. 1 to the Agreement between the European Economic Community and Finland (OJ No. L328, 28.11.1973, p. 2) for coated mechanical printing paper weighing not more than 65 g/m^2 falling within subheading 48.07D of the common customs tariff of the European Economic Community and originating in Finland from 13,667 tonnes to 21,238 tonnes. The duty-free tariff quota for all coated printing paper, weighing less than 225 g/m^2 falling within subheading 48.07D is accordingly increased from 23,707 tonnes to 31,278 tonnes. This is in accordance with an agreement in the form of a recent exchange of letters approved by Council Regulation (EEC) No. 1678 (OJ No. L165, 24.6.1983, p. 1) amending the quota which the United Kingdom is entitled to open for 1983 under the terms of Protocol No. 1.

STATUTORY INSTRUMENTS

1983 No. 1039

CAPITAL TRANSFER TAX

The Capital Transfer Tax (Delivery of Accounts) (No. 3) Regulations 1983

Made - - - -	*19th July* 1983
Laid before the House of Commons	*22nd July* 1983
Coming into Operation	*1st September* 1983

The Commissioners of Inland Revenue, in exercise of the powers conferred on them by section 94(1) of the Finance Act 1980(**a**), hereby make the following Regulations:

Citation, commencement and extent

1. These Regulations may be cited as the Capital Transfer Tax (Delivery of Accounts (No. 3) Regulations 1983 and shall come into operation on 1st September 1983.

2. These Regulations do not extend to Scotland or Northern Ireland.

Interpretation

3. In these Regulations "the Principal Regulations" means The Capital Transfer Tax (Delivery of Accounts) Regulations 1981(**b**).

Amendments to Principal Regulations

4. In Regulation 3 of the Principal Regulations

(*a*) in paragraph (*b*) for "£25,000" there shall be substituted "£40,000";

(*b*) in paragraph (*c*) for "£1,000" there shall be substituted "£2,000";

(*c*) in paragraph (*d*) for "1st April 1981" there shall be substituted "1st April 1983".

J. M. Green,
A. J. G. Isaac,
Two of the Commissioners of Inland
Revenue.

19th July 1983.

(**a**) 1980 c. 48.   (**b**) S.I. 1981/880.

EXPLANATORY NOTE

(This Note is not part of the Regulations.)

The Principal regulations dispensed with the need to deliver an account for the purposes of capital transfer tax where (subject to specified exceptions) the value of the deceased's estate did not exceed £25,000 (where the deceased died on or after 1st April 1981). These regulations increase that limit to £40,000 for deaths on or after 1st April 1983, and increase from £1,000 to £2,000 the value in respect of property situated outside the United Kingdom which may be included in the £40,000 limit.

STATUTORY INSTRUMENTS

1983 No. 1040 (S. 108)

CAPITAL TRANSFER TAX

The Capital Transfer Tax (Delivery of Accounts) (Scotland) (No. 2) Regulations 1983

Made - - - -	*19th July* 1983
Laid before the House of Commons	*22nd July* 1983
Coming into Operation	*1st September* 1983

The Commissioners of Inland Revenue, in exercise of the powers conferred on them by section 94(1) of the Finance Act 1980(**a**), hereby make the following Regulations:

Citation, commencement and extent

1. These Regulations may be cited as the Capital Transfer Tax (Delivery of Accounts) (Scotland) (No. 2) Regulations 1983 and shall come into operation on 1st September 1983.

2. These Regulations extend to Scotland only.

Interpretation

3. In these Regulations "the Principal Regulations" means The Capital Transfer Tax (Delivery of Accounts) (Scotland) Regulations 1981(**b**).

Amendments to Principal Regulations

4. In Regulation 3 of the Principal Regulations

(*a*) in paragraph (*b*) for "£25,000" there shall be substituted "£40,000";

(*b*) in paragraph (*c*) for "£1,000" there shall be substituted "£2,000";

(*c*) in paragraph (*d*) for "1st April 1981" there shall be substituted "1st April 1983".

J. M. Green,
A. J. G. Isaac,
Two of the Commissioners of Inland
Revenue.

19th July 1983.

(**a**) 1980 c. 48.   (**b**) S.I. 1981/881.

EXPLANATORY NOTE

(This Note is not part of the Regulations.)

The Principal Regulations dispensed with the need to deliver an account for the purposes of capital transfer tax where (subject to specified exceptions) the value of the deceased's estate did not exceed £25,000 (where the deceased died on or after 1st April 1981). These regulations increase that limit to £40,000 for deaths on or after 1st April 1983, and increase from £1,000 to £2,000 the value in respect of property situated outside the United Kingdom which may be included in the £40,000 limit.

STATUTORY INSTRUMENTS

1983 No. 1042

AGRICULTURE

The Common Agricultural Policy (Wine) (Amendment) Regulations 1983

Made - - - - -	18*th July* 1983
Laid before Parliament	27*th July* 1983
Coming into Operation	17*th August* 1983

The Minister of Agriculture, Fisheries and Food and the Secretary of State, being Ministers designated**(a)** for the purposes of section 2(2) of the European Communities Act 1972**(b)** in relation to the common agricultural policy of the European Economic Community, acting jointly in exercise of the powers conferred upon them by the said section 2(2), and of all other powers enabling them in that behalf, hereby make the following regulations:—

Title, commencement and interpretation

1.—(1) These regulations may be cited as the Common Agricultural Policy (Wine) (Amendment) Regulations 1983 and shall come into operation on the 17th August 1983.

(2) In these regulations "the principal regulations" means the Common Agricultural Policy (Wine) Regulations 1982**(c)**.

Amendment of definition of "local authority" as respects Scotland

2. Regulation 3 of the principal regulations shall be amended by deleting paragraph (6)(a)(ii) and substituting therefor a new paragraph (6)(a)(ii) as follows:—

"(ii) as respects Scotland, an islands or district council which is the enforcement authority for the purposes of the Food and Drugs (Scotland) Act 1956;" **(d)**.

(a) S.I. 1972/1811.   **(b)** 1972 c. 68.   **(c)** S.I. 1982/578.
(d) 1956 c. 30.

Amendments to the Schedules to the principal regulations

3.—(1) Schedule 1 to the principal regulations (which lists regulations of the European Communities concerned with the production and marketing of wine and related products, for the purpose of which local authorities, the Minister, the Commissioners and the Wine Standards Board are designated competent authorities or agencies in the United Kingdom) shall be amended by adding—

(*a*) at the end of the first column of item 8 ", and by Commission Regulation (EEC) No: 131/83 (O.J. No: L17, p. 14) (1983 Vol. 26)";

(*b*) at the end of the first column of item 12 ", and by Council Regulation (EEC) No: 2144/82 (O.J. No: L227, p.1) (1982 Vol. 25), and by Council Regulation (EEC) No: 3082/82 (O.J. No: L326, p.1) (1982 Vol. 25)";

(*c*) at the end of the first column of item 13 ", and by Council Regulation (EEC) No: 2145/82 (O.J. No: L227, p.10) (1982 Vol. 25)";

(*d*) at the end of the first column of item 14 ", and by Council Regulation (EEC) No: 3267/82 (O.J. No: L347, p.1) (1982 Vol. 25)".

(*e*) at the end of the first column of item 25 ", and by Commission Regulation (EEC) No: 1224/83 (O.J. No: L134, p.1) (1983 Vol. 26)".

(2) Schedule 2 to the principal regulations (which lists regulations of the European Communities concerned as aforesaid which are to be enforced in the United Kingdom by local authorities, the Minister, the Commissioners or the Wine Standards Board) shall be amended by adding at the end of Column 2 of item 1 in Part III "and by regulation 1224/83: Article 1".

(3) Schedule 2 to the principal regulations shall be amended by adding in Part V thereof—

(*a*) at the end of Column 1 of item 7 "as amended by regulation 2144/82: Article 1(8)";

(*b*) at the end of Column 2 of item 8 "and regulation 3267/82: Article 1";

(*c*) at the end of Column 1 of item 12 "and by regulation 2144/82: Article 1(13)";

(*d*) at the end of Column 1 of item 17 "and by regulation 2144/82: Article 1(14)".

In Witness whereof the Official Seal of the Minister of Agriculture, Fisheries and Food is hereunto affixed on 14th July 1983.

Michael Jopling,
Minister of Agriculture, Fisheries and Food.

George Younger,
One of Her Majesty's
Principal Secretaries of State.

18th July 1983.

EXPLANATORY NOTE

(This Note is not part of the Regulations.)

These regulations amend the Common Agricultural Policy (Wine) Regulations 1982 ("the principal regulations") by—

(1) revising the definition of "local authority" so that, as respects Scotland, islands or district councils, rather than regional or islands councils, are the enforcement authorities. This revision is consequent upon the amendment of the definition of "local authority" in section 26 of the Food and Drugs (Scotland) Act 1956 by section 22 of the Local Government and Planning (Scotland) Act 1982 (c. 43); and

(2) adding to the Schedules details of relevant regulations of the European Communities which have been adopted since the principal regulations came into operation.

STATUTORY INSTRUMENTS

1983 No. 1047

COAL INDUSTRY

The Coal Industry (Borrowing Powers) Order 1983

Laid before the House of Commons in draft

Made - - - -	*18th July* 1983
Coming into Operation	*1st August* 1983

The Secretary of State, in exercise of the powers conferred upon him by section 1(3) of the Coal Industry Act 1965 (a) and with the approval of the Treasury, hereby makes the following Order, a draft of which has been approved by a resolution of the Commons House of Parliament in accordance with section 1(8) of the Coal Industry Act 1965:—

1. This Order may be cited as the Coal Industry (Borrowing Powers) Order 1983 and shall come into operation on 1st August 1983.

2. The aggregate amount outstanding in respect of the principal of any borrowing mentioned in the said section 1(3) shall not exceed £5,000 million.

Giles Shaw,
Parliamentary Under-Secretary of State,
Department of Energy.

14th July 1983.

We approve.

Alistair Goodlad,
D. J. F. Hunt,
Two of the Lords Commissioners
of Her Majesty's Treasury.

18th July 1983.

(a) 1965 c.82. Section 1(3) was substituted by the Coal Industry Act 1977 (c.39), section 1(1), and amended by the Coal Industry Act 1980 (c.50), section 1(1) and by the Coal Industry Act 1982 (c.15), section 1. Section 1(8) was added by the Coal Industry Act 1973 (c.8), section 13(1) and Schedule 1, paragraph 3*(b)*, the present section 1(8) being substituted by section 1(3) of the 1980 Act.

EXPLANATORY NOTE

(This Note is not part of the Order.)

Section 1 of the Coal Industry Act 1965, as amended, empowers the National Coal Board to borrow, temporarily or otherwise, subject to an overall limit of £4,500 million which may be increased up to £5,000 million. This Order increases that limit to £5,000 million.

STATUTORY INSTRUMENTS

1983 No. 1048

ECCLESIASTICAL LAW, ENGLAND

The Legal Officers' Fees Order 1983

Made (Approved by the General Synod)	12*th July* 1983
Laid before Parliament	20*th July* 1983
Coming into Operation	1*st October* 1983

We, the Fees Committee constituted in accordance with the provisions of section 1 of the Ecclesiastical Fees Measure 1962 **(a)** in the exercise of the powers conferred by the section, do hereby order as follows:—

1. The Fees appearing in the Schedule to the Order are established. Table I of the Schedule contains particulars of the fees which are to be received by the legal officers named in the Schedule for the carrying out by them after the commencement of this Order of the duties of their offices specified in the Appendix.

2. *(a)* The Fees established and set out in Table I of the Legal Officers' Fees Order 1980 **(b)** and in Table IV of the Legal Officers' Fees Order 1982 **(c)** shall no longer be payable.

(b) Appendix I of the Legal Officers' Fees Order 1974 is hereby repealed.

3. The diocesan registrar shall perform the duties and provide the professional services set forth in the Appendix to this Order in consideration of the annual fee set out in Table I for his diocese and shall not be entitled to receive any other remuneration for such duties or services save as provided by this Order and the Notes thereto.

4. *(a)* Subject to the provisions of this paragraph nothing in this Order shall preclude a diocesan board of finance from agreeing to pay an additional fee to a diocesan registrar by way of annual fee or retainer (hereinafter called a "supplementary annual fee") which is in addition to the annual fee payable under Table IV.

(b) Such supplementary annual fee may be agreed in respect of the following work:

(i) Services not falling within the scope of the services covered by the annual fee payable to the diocesan registrar and defined in the Appendix and/or

(ii) Services for which fees are prescribed by Table II of the Legal Officers' Fees Order 1982 **(c)** and for which the diocesan registrar has agreed with the diocesan board of finance that he will not receive the fees prescribed in the said Table.

(c) An agreement made under sub-paragraph *(a)* above shall be expressed to be a payment by way of supplementary annual fee.

(**a**) 1962 No. 1.   (**b**) S.I. 1980/952.   (**c**) S.I. 1982/939.

(d) Any agreement made under sub-paragraph *(a)* above shall be in writing. The period for which the agreement is to run shall be stated in the agreement. In the absence of any such statement the agreement shall remain binding until determined by not less than three months' notice on either side.

(e) The body responsible for paying a supplementary annual fee shall be the diocesan board of finance.

5. A fee specified in the Schedule to this Order may be increased by a sum for reasonable expenses of travel, subsistence and accommodation.

6. Where Value Added Tax is chargeable in respect of the provision of any service for which a fee is prescribed in this Order there shall be payable in addition to that fee the amount of the Value Added Tax.

7.—(1) This Order may be cited as the Legal Officers' Fees Order 1983 and shall come into operation on the first day of October 1983.

(2) The Interpretation Act 1978 shall apply to the interpretation of this Order as it applies to the interpretation of an Act of Parliament.

Dated this 28th day of June 1983.

J. R. Cumming-Bruce
T. A. C. Coningsby
T. G. Penny

Approved by the General Synod   *W. D. Pattinson,*
the 12th day of July 1983.   Secretary-General.

APPENDIX

The Scope of the Annual Fee

1. Subject to the restrictions contained in paragraphs 2 and 3 hereof, the professional services provided by the diocesan registrar in respect of the annual fee paid to him under this Order shall include:—

A. Giving of advice to the Diocesan Bishop, suffragan bishops, archdeacons, Chairmen of the Houses of the Diocesan Synod, Rural Deans and Lay Chairmen of Deanery Synods, Incumbents and all other clergymen, beneficed or licensed in the diocese, on any legal matter properly arising in connection with the discharge of their respective ecclesiastical or synodical offices;

B. Acting as Registrar to the Diocesan Synod and attendance at its meetings;

C. Occasional attendance at meetings of the Bishop's Council and Standing Committee and meetings of diocesan boards, councils and committees for the purpose of giving advice on specific matters;

D. Maintaining of all such records of the diocese as are customarily kept by the diocesan registrar including the making of entries therein, and the making of searches and reports on matters recorded in the Registry or in documents held in the diocesan muniment room at the request of persons or bodies referred to in sub-paragraphs A, C and E hereof;

E. Giving of advice to churchwardens and secretaries of PCCs on any legal matter properly arising in connection with their official business;

F. Giving of advice to any person concerned in or with the administration of an election under the Church Representation Rules on any question properly arising under those Rules;

G. Giving of advice to a bona fide enquirer concerning the law of marriage according to the rites and ceremonies of the Church of England;

H. Acting as Registrar to the Consistory Court of the diocese except in so far as a separate fee is prescribed by this Order or by Table II of the Legal Officers' Fees Order 1982 or except in so far as either of these Orders provides that a fee calculated in accordance with the Solicitors' Remuneration Order 1972 is payable;

I. Attendance at episcopal and archidiaconal visitations;

J. Drafting or preparing, approving, engrossing and registering of all notices, licences, consents, permissions, instruments and other documents required by law or customarily used in connection with the following matters:

Ordination

Certification of Ordination

Admission to Freehold Office

Certification of Institution or Collation

Presentation to a Benefice

Commission for Institution or Collation

Provision of Letters Dimissory or Letters of Request

Licensing of Non-residence, for legalising house of residence

Resignation

Under the Pastoral Measure 1968

admission to office of rector for term of years

licensing of vicar in a team ministry or for extending term of years of rector or vicar in a team ministry

issuing of notices relating to suspension or restriction under Part IV of the Measure

designation of a parish centre of worship under Part II of the Measure for the purposes of the Marriage Act 1949 and other purposes

Issuing of permission to officiate to and licensing of clerks in holy orders

Appointment of Rural Dean

Delegation by bishop of episcopal and archidiaconal powers under the Dioceses Measure 1978 and Church of England (Miscellaneous Provisions) Measure 1983

Episcopal and archidiaconal visitations

Appointment of sequestrators and matters relating to sequestrations

Provision of agreements to form a Conventional District

Consent to hold preferment under the Ecclesiastical Jurisdiction Measure 1963

Licensing of unconsecrated churches or places of worship (including temporary licences)

Licensing of Burial Ground until Consecration

Ordering of Licensed Chapel to come under Faculty Jurisdiction

K. Acting in relation to the following matters on the instructions of the Diocesan Bishop, suffragan bishops, archdeacons or on the instructions of a diocesan board or council whose business properly includes such matters:

Consecration of a Church and Burial Ground or a Church without a Burial Ground

Consecration of a Cemetery or Burial Ground

Preparation and Registration of documents required under the Consecration of Churchyards Act 1867 for consecration of additions to churchyards

Licensing of a Building for Marriages, including settling the area to which the licence should apply

Notification under section 2 of the Benefices (Transfer of Rights of Patronage) Measure 1930

Issuing of notices under the Benefices (Exercise of Rights of Presentation) Measure 1931 (including instances where body of advisers is consulted).

2. The provisions of paragraph 1 hereof shall be restricted as follows:

   (i) Where the Registrar receives a request for advice on any matter properly falling within paragraph 1 sub paragraphs A, D, E, F and G,

      (a) he shall not be required to correspond with a third party involved in the enquiry

      (b) before giving advice he shall first consider whether the matter on which his advice is sought is one which can conveniently be dealt with by the diocesan secretary or some other person or body in the diocese rather than by himself

      (c) if a legal dispute arises between parties who are both church officers he may decline to advise either party, but he shall be at liberty to advise both parties with a view to helping them to resolve their dispute if in his judgement it is desirable to do so;

   (ii) The Registrar shall not be required to attend meetings of the Bishop's Council, diocesan boards, councils and committees except upon an occasional basis to give legal advice on specific matters. (He may attend regularly such meetings to give general advice and assistance if requested to do so by the board, council or committee in question and in that case he shall be entitled to be separately remunerated for this work.)

3. The provisions of paragraph 2(i) hereof shall not apply to advice and assistance given as legal secretary or diocesan registrar to the Diocesan Bishop, or as diocesan registrar to suffragan bishops or archdeacons.

4. For the avoidance of doubt work in connection with the following matters shall not fall within the scope of the annual fee but a fee calculated in accordance with the Solicitors' Remuneration Order 1972 shall be payable:—

(i) Conveyancing and drafting of documents other than those referred to in paragraph 1 sub paragraphs J and K hereof;

(ii) Matters relating to individual diocesan, parochial or educational trusts or to individual pieces of diocesan glebe property;

(iii) Litigation;

(iv) Investigation of Title in case of change of patronage since the last presentation (the fee is payable by the patron);

(v) Deposition or deprivation consequent upon proceedings in secular courts, including the following:

    (a) Service of notice on priest or deacon of intention to depose him from Holy Orders under rule 49(1) of the Ecclesiastical Jurisdiction (Discipline) Rules 1963 (the fee is payable by the bishop)

    (b) Carrying out of a duty or exercising of a discretion following proceedings referred to in section 55 of the Ecclesiastical Jurisdiction Measure 1963 (the fee is payable by the bishop);

(vi) Work undertaken on behalf of a person who is not an official in the diocese or on behalf of a body which is not a diocesan board or council in connection with the following matters:

    Consecration or licensing of a public cemetery, a private burial ground or a private chapel

    Licensing the chapel of an extra-parochial place for the marriage of persons living or residing within that place

    Notification under Section 2 of the Benefices (Transfer of Rights of Patronage) Measure 1930 (the fee to be paid in such proportions as may be agreed between the transferor and the transferee, and in the absence of such agreement the fee to be paid by the transferee);

(vii) Acting as Chapter Clerk (whether or not the Diocesan Registrar holds the office of Chapter Clerk) and in particular doing the work for which a separate fee is prescribed by Table I of the Legal Officers' Fees Order 1980 before the coming into operation of this Order, namely work in connection with the following matters:—

    Installation to a Deanery

    Installation to a Canonry or Prebend (whether Residentiary or Honorary) or to an Archdeaconry

    Admission to a Minor Canonry.

    (These fees are payable out of Capitular Revenues.)

5. If any disbursements are incurred in the course of providing any of the professional services in paragraph 1 above the diocesan registrar shall be entitled to charge for them separately.

SCHEDULE
TABLE I

PART I

ANNUAL FEES PAYABLE TO BISHOPS' LEGAL SECRETARIES AND TO DIOCESAN
REGISTRARS SUBSTITUTED FOR TABLE IV OF THE LEGAL OFFICERS' FEES ORDER 1982

Diocese	Payable by Diocesan Board of Finance	Liability of the Diocesan Bishop	Total
	£	£	£
1. Bath and Wells	9,796	5,754	15,550
2. Birmingham	4,458	3,495	7,953
3. Blackburn	5,816	5,169	10,985
4. Bradford	3,430	4,523	7,953
5. Bristol	4,458	3,495	7,953
6. Canterbury	6,699	5,301	12,000
7. Carlisle	6,496	4,489	10,985
8. Chelmsford	9,814	5,736	15,550
9. Chester	6,543	4,442	10,985
10. Chichester	7,961	5,845	13,806
11. Coventry	4,502	4,466	8,968
12. Derby	6,039	4,946	10,985
13. Durham	5,864	5,121	10,985
14. Ely	6,741	5,259	12,000
15. Exeter	9,814	5,736	15,550
16. Gloucester	7,006	4,994	12,000
17. Guildford	3,883	4,070	7,953
18. Hereford	7,413	5,602	13,015
19. Leicester	6,479	4,506	10,985
20. Lichfield	9,170	5,814	14,984
21. Lincoln	11,898	4,829	16,727
22. Liverpool	4,757	4,211	8,968
23. London	9,083	5,901	14,984
24. Manchester	6,356	5,644	12,000
25. Newcastle	4,629	3,324	7,953
26. Norwich	11,840	4,887	16,727
27. Oxford	12,607	4,120	16,727
28. Peterborough	7,104	5,911	13,015
29. Portsmouth	3,239	4,714	7,953
30. Ripon	4,822	4,146	8,968
31. Rochester	4,948	4,020	8,968
32. St Albans	6,927	5,073	12,000
33. St Edmundsbury & Ipswich	9,096	5,888	14,984
34. Salisbury	9,563	5,421	14,984
35. Sheffield	4,269	3,684	7,953
36. Southwark	5,835	5,150	10,985
37. Southwell	5,949	5,036	10,985
38. Truro	5,163	3,805	8,968
39. Wakefield	4,605	4,363	8,968
40. Winchester	6,768	5,232	12,000
41. Worcester	4,757	4,211	8,968
42. York	9,268	5,716	14,984

Part II
Provincial Registrars

	Fee
1. Annual fee for Joint Registrars of the Province of Canterbury	£11,051
2. Annual fee for Registrar of the Province of York	£ 4,420
3. Fee for permission under Overseas and Other Clergy (Ministry and Ordination) Measure 1967	£ 25

Part III

Fees payable to diocesan registrars as presiding officers at general elections and casual elections to the General Synod transferred from Table I of the Legal Officers' Fees Order 1980

1. Fee for duties required to be performed as presiding officer at general elections to the Lower Houses of Convocations or to the House of Laity of the General Synod or at elections to fill vacancies if the full election procedure is used in accordance with Rule 35(1) of the Clergy Representation Rules 1975 and 1980 or Rule 39(5) of the Church Representation Rules, payable to the diocesan registrar.	£70 and a further fee of £15 for every hour spent on counting votes
2. Fee for duties required to be performed as presiding officer at elections to fill casual vacancies to the Lower Houses of the Convocations or to the House of Laity of the General Synod if the shortened procedure is used in accordance with Rule 35(4) of the Clergy Representation Rules 1975 and 1980 or Rule 39(7) of the Church Representation Rules, payable to the diocesan registrar.	£15 for every hour spent on counting votes

Notes

(a) Nothing in Table I shall prevent a diocesan board of finance and a diocesan registrar from agreeing that in addition to the annual fee prescribed in Part I there shall be paid to the diocesan registrar an additional annual sum in consideration of the exceptional cost of maintaining his particular diocesan registry and of performing the duties and providing the services referred to in paragraph 3 of this Order.

(b) "Exceptional cost" means either (i) where the expenses of the particular registry for such items as rent, rates and salaries are above the average in registries within the two provinces of Canterbury and York, or (ii) where the duties and services referred to in paragraph 3 hereof and specified in the Appendix provided by the particular diocesan registrar are more extensive than in the average registry as so defined.

(c) Such annual payment shall be called an "exceptional cost fee".

(d) Every diocesan board of finance shall give consideration to any request by a diocesan registrar for an exceptional cost fee as provided for in sub-paragraphs *(a)* and *(b)* above.

(e) Any agreement made under sub-paragraph *(a)* above shall be in writing. The period for which the agreement is to run shall be stated in the agreement. In the absence of any such statement the agreement shall remain binding until determined by not less than three months' notice on either side.

(f) The body responsible for paying an "exceptional cost fee" shall be the diocesan board of finance.

STATUTORY INSTRUMENTS

1983 No. 1049

LEGAL AID AND ADVICE, ENGLAND AND WALES

COURTS—MARTIAL (APPEALS)

The Legal Aid in Criminal Proceedings (Costs) (Amendment No. 2) Regulations 1983

Made - - - -	*14th July* 1983
Laid before Parliament	*22nd July* 1983
Coming into Operation	*1st September* 1983

The Lord Chancellor, in exercise of the powers conferred by section 39 of the Legal Aid Act 1974(**a**) and now vested in him(**b**) and all other powers enabling him in that behalf and having had regard to the principle of allowing fair remuneration according to the work actually and reasonably done, hereby makes the following Regulations:

1. These Regulations may be cited as the Legal Aid in Criminal Proceedings (Costs) (Amendment No. 2) Regulations 1983 and shall come into operation on 1st September 1983.

2. In regulation 2 of the Legal Aid in Criminal Proceedings (Costs) Regulations 1982(**c**), after the words ' "legal executive" means a fellow of the Institute of Legal Executives;' insert the following words:

' "proceedings in a magistrates' court" includes, for the purposes of these Regulations, proceedings in connection with an application for bail to the Crown Court after the issuing of a certificate under section 5 (6A) of the Bail Act 1976(**d**);'.

Hailsham of St. Marylebone, C.

Dated 14th July 1983.

(**a**) 1974 c. 4.   (**b**) S.I. 1980/705.
(**c**) S.I. 1982/1197, as amended by S.I. 1983/235.
(**d**) 1976 c. 63, as amended by section 60 of the Criminal Justice Act 1982 (c. 48).

EXPLANATORY NOTE

(This Note is not part of the Regulations.)

These Regulations amend the Legal Aid in Criminal Proceedings (Costs) Regulations 1982, defining "proceedings in a magistrates' court" as including proceedings in connection with an application for bail to the Crown Court, bail having been refused in the magistrates' court after a fully argued bail application. The costs of such applications (which are covered by any legal aid order made in respect of the magistrates' court proceedings) will therefore be determined under the 1982 Regulations as though they were proceedings in the magistrates' court and not in the Crown Court.

STATUTORY INSTRUMENTS

1983 No. 1050

TRUSTEES

The Public Trustee (Amendment) Rules 1983

Made - - - - -	15th July 1983
Laid before Parliament	22nd July 1983
Coming into Operation	15th August 1983

The Lord Chancellor, in exercise of the powers conferred on him by sections 3(4) and 14(1) of the Public Trustee Act 1906**(a)**, and with the concurrence of the Treasury, hereby makes the following Rules:—

1. These Rules may be cited as the Public Trustee (Amendment) Rules 1983 and shall come into operation on 15th August 1983.

2. The Public Trustee Rules 1912**(b)** shall be amended as follows:—

(1) In rule 15—

    (*a*) the words "in manner hereinafter provided and" shall be omitted from paragraph (1).

    (*b*) The following shall be substituted for paragraphs (2) and (3):—
    "(2) Any such question shall be submitted—

        (*a*) to such Judge of the Chancery Division as the Vice-Chancellor may specify; and
        (*b*) in such manner as that judge may direct."

(2) In rule 22, after the word "cheque" where it first appears, the words "on the Bank of England bearing a signature or a facsimile signature of an officer of the Public Trustee authorised in writing by him to act in that behalf or a cheque" shall be inserted.

Hailsham of St. Marylebone, C.

Dated 5th July 1983

Alastair Goodlad,

Dated 15th July 1983

Ian B. Lang,

Dated 15th July 1983

Two of the Lords Commissioners
of Her Majesty's Treasury.

(a) 1906 c. 55.   **(b)** S.R. & O. 1912/348.

EXPLANATORY NOTE

(This Note is not part of the Rules.)

These Rules—

(a) dispense with the formal nomination of a Judge of the Chancery Division to advise upon questions referred to him by the Public Trustee in the course of the administration of a trust; and

(b) provide for the signature or facsimile signature of an officer authorised by the Public Trustee to be placed on cheques making payments to beneficiaries.

STATUTORY INSTRUMENTS

1983 No. 1051 (S. 97)

EDUCATION, SCOTLAND

The Education Authority Bursaries (Scotland) Amendment Regulations 1983

Made - - - -	*18th July* 1983
Laid before Parliament	*27th July* 1983
Coming into Operation	*15th August* 1983

In exercise of the powers conferred upon me by section 49(3) of the Education (Scotland) Act 1980(**a**) and of all other powers enabling me in that behalf, I hereby make the following regulations:—

Citation and commencement

1. These regulations may be cited as the Education Authority Bursaries (Scotland) Amendment Regulations 1983 and shall come into operation on 15th August 1983.

Interpretation

2. In these regulations:—

the "principal regulations" means the Education Authority Bursaries (Scotland) Regulations 1978(**b**) and unless the context otherwise requires "bursary" and "payment period" shall have the meaning assigned to them in the principal regulations.

Amendment of principal regulations

3. The principal regulations shall be amended as follows:—

(*a*) in regulation 8(1)(*c*)(iii) and the proviso thereto (*assessment of full-time further education bursaries*) there shall be substituted for the sum of "£345" the sum of "£375" and there shall be substituted for the sum of "£500" the sum of "£540".

(*b*) In Schedule 1 (*assessment of higher school bursaries*)—

(i) in paragraph 1 for the Table there specified, there shall be substituted the following Table:—

(**a**) 1980 c. 44.
(**b**) S.I. 1978/998, amended by S.I. 1979/840, 1980/988, 1981/966 and 1982/936.

"Balance of income Column (1)	*Rate of sum to be paid* Column (2)
£3690 and under	£514 per payment period of 12 months
£3691 – £3740	£499 per payment period of 12 months
£3741 – £3790	£484 per payment period of 12 months
£3791 – £3840	£469 per payment period of 12 months
£3841 – £3890	£454 per payment period of 12 months
£3891 – £3940	£439 per payment period of 12 months
£3941 – £3990	£424 per payment period of 12 months
£3991 – £4040	£409 per payment period of 12 months
£4041 – £4090	£394 per payment period of 12 months
£4091 – £4140	£379 per payment period of 12 months
£4141 – £4190	£364 per payment period of 12 months
£4191 – £4240	£349 per payment period of 12 months
£4241 – £4290	£334 per payment period of 12 months
£4291 – £4340	£319 per payment period of 12 months
£4341 – £4390	£304 per payment period of 12 months
£4391 – £4440	£289 per payment period of 12 months
£4441 – £4490	£274 per payment period of 12 months
£4491 – £4540	£259 per payment period of 12 months
£4541 – £4590	£244 per payment period of 12 months
£4591 – £4640	£229 per payment period of 12 months
£4641 – £4690	£214 per payment period of 12 months
£4691 – £4740	£199 per payment period of 12 months
£4741 – £4790	£184 per payment period of 12 months
£4791 – £4840	£169 per payment period of 12 months
£4841 – £4890	£154 per payment period of 12 months
£4891 – £4940	£139 per payment period of 12 months
£4941 – £4990	£124 per payment period of 12 months
£4991 – £5040	£109 per payment period of 12 months
£5041 – £5090	£94 per payment period of 12 months
£5091 – £5140	£79 per payment period of 12 months
£5141 – £5190	£64 per payment period of 12 months
£5191 – £5240	£49 per payment period of 12 months
£5241 – £5290	£34 per payment period of 12 months
£5291 – £5340	£19 per payment period of 12 months
£5341 – £5390	£4 per payment period of 12 months
£5391 and over	NIL"

(ii) in paragraph 4(2) and paragraph (ii) of the proviso thereto for the sum of "£409" there shall be substituted the sum of "£427";

(iii) for paragraph 4(3) there shall be substituted the following paragraph:—

"(3) the amount of any expenditure upon contributions under superannuation schemes and premiums under retirement annuity contracts (provided that the amount assessed shall not exceed fifteen per cent of the said total income) and the amount of any expenditure on life insurance premiums;"

(c) in Part 1 of Schedule 2 (*assessment of estimated expenditure in relation to full-time further education bursaries*)—

    (i) in paragraph 1(5) for the sums of "£12.33" and "£29.22" there shall be substituted respectively the sums of "£12.86" and "£30.39";

   (ii) in paragraph 1(6) for the sums of "£17.73" and "£29.22" there shall be substituted respectively the sums of "£18.44" and "£30.39";

  (iii) for paragraph 1(7) there shall be substituted the following paragraph:—

       "(7) An allowance at the rate of £24.60 a week towards the cost of maintaining the holder, after he has attained the age of 18 years, during vacations other than the summer vacation;"

  (iv) in paragraph 1(8) for the sum of "£9.52" there shall be substituted the sum of "£9.90";

   (v) in paragraph 1(10) for the Table there specified, there shall be substituted the following Table:—

"Age	Amount
26	£160
27	£315
28	£485
29 and over	£640"

(d) in Part 2 of Schedule 2 (*assessment of contribution in relation to full-time further education bursaries*)—

    (i) in paragraph 4(3)(a) for the sum of "£409" there shall be substituted the sum of "£427";

   (ii) in paragraph 4(3)(b) for the sum of "£845" there shall be substituted the sum of "£915";

  (iii) for paragraph 4(4) there shall be substituted the following paragraph:—

       "(4) the amount of any expenditure upon contributions under superannuation schemes and premiums under retirement annuity contracts (provided that the amount assessed shall not exceed fifteen per cent of the said total income) and the amount of any expenditure on life insurance premiums;"

  (iv) in paragraph 6(a) for the sum of "£3536", in each place where it occurs, there shall be substituted the sum of "£3691";

   (v) for sub-paragraph (b) of paragraph 6 there shall be substituted the following sub-paragraph:—

       "(b) in the assessment of a category B bursary—

          (i) if the balance of the income of the parents or, as the case may be, the person legally liable to maintain the holder is not less than £7100 and not more than

£9000, the contribution shall be £20 with the addition of £1 for every complete £7 by which the balance of income exceeds £7100;

(ii) if the balance of that income is more than £9000 but not more than £14,300 the contribution shall be £291 with the addition of £1 for every complete £8 by which the balance of income exceeds £9000;

(iii) if the balance of that income is more than £14,300 the contribution shall be £954 with the addition of £1 for every complete £13 by which the balance of income exceeds £14,300

reduced in each case, in respect of each child of the parent (other than the student) who is wholly or mainly dependent on him, by £75 or, if such child holds a category B bursary or a grant for a degree or equivalent level course, by £210.";

(vi) for sub-paragraph (c) of paragraph 6 there shall be substituted the following sub-paragraph:—

"(c) in the assessment of a category B bursary—

(i) if the balance of the income of the spouse is not less than £5500 and not more than £9000 the contribution shall be £10 with the addition of £1 for every complete £5 by which the balance of income exceeds £5500; and

(ii) if the balance of that income is more than £9000 the contribution shall be £710 with the addition of £1 for every complete £10 by which the balance of income exceeds £9000

reduced in each case, in respect of each child of the spouse who is wholly or mainly dependent on him, by £75."

Transitional provision

4. Notwithstanding these regulations, the provisions of the principal regulations amended in regulation 3 above shall apply, as they were in force prior to being so amended, for the purposes of regulation 9 of the principal regulations, in relation to any payment period expiring prior to or current at the date of coming into operation of these regulations.

New St Andrew's House,
Edinburgh.
18th July 1983.

George Younger,
One of Her Majesty's Principal
Secretaries of State.

EXPLANATORY NOTE

(This Note is not part of the Regulations.)

These Regulations amend the bursary rates and the parental and spouse contribution scales which are prescribed by the Education Authority Bursaries (Scotland) Regulations 1978, as amended by the Education Authority Bursaries (Scotland) Amendment Regulations 1979, 1980, 1981 and 1982.

STATUTORY INSTRUMENTS

1983 No. 1052

PENSIONS

The Pensions Commutation (Amendment) Regulations 1983

Made - - -	*18th July* 1983
Coming into Operation	*1st August* 1983

The Treasury, in exercise of the powers conferred by sections 4 and 7 of the Pensions Commutation Act 1871 (**a**) and section 3 of the Pensions Commutation Act 1882 (**b**), and of all other powers enabling them in that behalf, hereby make the following Regulations:—

1. These Regulations may be cited as the Pensions Commutation (Amendment) Regulations 1983, and shall come into operation on 1st August 1983.

2. The Pensions Commutation Regulations 1968 (**c**) shall be amended by substituting, for the Tables set out in the Schedule thereto, the Tables set out in the Schedule to these Regulations.

Alastair Goodlad,
D. J. F. Hunt,
Two of the Lords Commissioners of
Her Majesty's Treasury.

18th July 1983.

(**a**) 1871 c.36.
(**b**) 1882 c.44. These powers were vested in the Minister for the Civil Service by S.I. 1968/1656 and revested in the Treasury by S.I. 1981/1670.
(**c**) S.I. 1968/1163, amended by S.I. 1974/734, 1441, 1977/108, 1978/1257.

SCHEDULE—PART I

TABLE FOR DETERMINING THE COMMUTATION RATE FOR PENSIONS WHICH WILL BECOME QUALIFIED FOR PENSIONS INCREASE ON THE PENSION-HOLDER'S ATTAINING THE AGE OF 55

Age next birthday	Rate for unimpaired lives	Rates for impaired lives according to the number of years added to the age of the pension-holder									
		1 year	2 years	3 years	4 years	5 years	6 years	7 years	8 years	9 years	10 years
20	13.51	13.38	13.24	13.10	12.96	12.81	12.66	12.51	12.36	12.20	12.04
21	13.64	13.50	13.35	13.21	13.06	12.91	12.76	12.60	12.44	12.27	12.10
22	13.76	13.62	13.47	13.32	13.16	13.00	12.85	12.69	12.52	12.35	12.17
23	13.89	13.74	13.58	13.43	13.26	13.10	12.94	12.78	12.60	12.42	12.23
24	14.03	13.86	13.70	13.54	13.37	13.20	13.03	12.86	12.68	12.49	12.30
25	14.16	13.99	13.82	13.65	13.48	13.30	13.12	12.94	12.75	12.56	12.37
26	14.29	14.11	13.94	13.76	13.58	13.40	13.22	13.03	12.83	12.64	12.43
27	14.43	14.24	14.06	13.87	13.68	13.50	13.31	13.12	12.92	12.71	12.49
28	14.56	14.37	14.18	13.98	13.79	13.60	13.40	13.20	12.99	12.77	12.56
29	14.70	14.50	14.30	14.10	13.90	13.70	13.49	13.28	13.06	12.83	12.62
30	14.83	14.63	14.43	14.22	14.01	13.80	13.58	13.36	13.13	12.90	12.67
31	14.97	14.76	14.55	14.33	14.12	13.90	13.67	13.44	13.20	12.96	12.73
32	15.10	14.89	14.67	14.44	14.22	14.00	13.76	13.52	13.27	13.02	12.79
33	15.24	15.02	14.79	14.55	14.32	14.09	13.85	13.60	13.34	13.08	12.84
34	15.37	15.14	14.90	14.66	14.42	14.18	13.93	13.67	13.41	13.14	12.88
35	15.49	15.25	15.01	14.77	14.52	14.27	14.01	13.74	13.47	13.20	12.93
36	15.62	15.36	15.11	14.86	14.61	14.35	14.08	13.80	13.52	13.25	12.97
37	15.74	15.48	15.22	14.96	14.70	14.43	14.15	13.87	13.58	13.29	13.00
38	15.85	15.59	15.32	15.05	14.78	14.50	14.22	13.93	13.63	13.33	13.03
39	15.96	15.69	15.41	15.13	14.85	14.56	14.27	13.97	13.67	13.37	13.06
40	16.06	15.78	15.49	15.20	14.91	14.62	14.32	14.01	13.70	13.39	13.07
41	16.15	15.87	15.57	15.27	14.97	14.67	14.37	14.05	13.73	13.41	13.08
42	16.23	15.94	15.63	15.33	15.02	14.71	14.40	14.08	13.75	13.42	13.08
43	16.30	16.00	15.68	15.37	15.06	14.74	14.42	14.09	13.75	13.41	13.07
44	16.35	16.04	15.72	15.40	15.08	14.75	14.42	14.08	13.74	13.39	13.04
45	16.39	16.07	15.75	15.42	15.09	14.75	14.41	14.07	13.72	13.37	13.01
46	16.41	16.08	15.75	15.41	15.07	14.73	14.38	14.04	13.68	13.33	12.96
47	16.40	16.07	15.73	15.39	15.04	14.69	14.34	13.99	13.62	13.27	12.90
48	16.38	16.04	15.69	15.34	14.99	14.63	14.28	13.92	13.55	13.19	12.82
49	16.32	15.97	15.62	15.27	14.91	14.55	14.19	13.83	13.46	13.09	12.72
50	16.23	15.87	15.51	15.15	14.79	14.43	14.07	13.70	13.33	12.96	12.59
51	16.10	15.74	15.38	15.02	14.65	14.28	13.92	13.55	13.18	12.81	12.44
52	15.93	15.57	15.21	14.84	14.47	14.10	13.73	13.36	12.99	12.62	12.25
53	15.72	15.35	14.98	14.61	14.24	13.87	13.50	13.14	12.77	12.40	12.03
54	15.44	15.07	14.70	14.33	13.96	13.59	13.22	12.86	12.49	12.12	11.75

PART II

TABLE FOR DETERMINING THE COMMUTATION RATE IN CASES OTHER THAN COVERED BY PART I

Age next birthday	Rate	Age next birthday	Rate
20	24.31	55	15.11
21	24.16	56	14.74
22	24.01	57	14.37
23	23.86	58	14.00
24	23.69	59	13.62
25	23.52	60	13.26
26	23.35	61	12.89
27	23.16	62	12.52
28	22.97	63	12.15
29	22.77	64	11.78
30	22.57	65	11.42
31	22.35	66	11.05
32	22.13	67	10.69
33	21.90	68	10.32
34	21.67	69	9.97
35	21.43	70	9.61
36	21.18	71	9.26
37	20.92	72	8.91
38	20.65	73	8.57
39	20.38	74	8.23
40	20.10	75	7.90
41	19.81	76	7.58
42	19.52	77	7.26
43	19.22	78	6.95
44	18.91	79	6.64
45	18.59	80	6.35
46	18.27	81	6.06
47	17.94	82	5.78
48	17.60	83	5.51
49	17.26	84	5.25
50	16.91	85	5.00
51	16.56	86	4.75
52	16.20	87	4.52
53	15.84	88	4.30
54	15.48	89	4.08

EXPLANATORY NOTE

(This Note is not part of the Regulations.)

These Regulations further amend the Pensions Commutation Regulations 1968 by substituting new tables which give the rates for the calculation of the capital sum obtained in commutation and which take account of the effect of increases payable either under the Pensions (Increase) Act 1971 (c.56) or under a Prerogative Instrument relating to the Armed Forces.

In the calculations of the amount payable in respect of pensions, interest has been reckoned at the rate of 11 per cent per annum and an appropriate allowance has been made for pensions increases.

STATUTORY INSTRUMENTS

1983 No. 1053

HORTICULTURE

The Grading of Horticultural Produce (Amendment) Regulations 1983

Made - - - -	*18th July* 1983
Laid before Parliament	*28th July* 1983
Coming into Operation	*18th August* 1983

The Minister of Agriculture, Fisheries and Food, the Secretary of State for Scotland and the Secretary of State for Wales, acting jointly, in exercise of the powers conferred by section 11(3) of the Agriculture and Horticulture Act 1964(a) and now vested in them(b) and of all other powers enabling them in that behalf, having consulted in accordance with section 23(1) of the said Act with such organisations as appear to any of them to be representative of interests affected by the regulations, hereby make the following regulations:—

Title and commencement

1. These regulations may be cited as the Grading of Horticultural Produce (Amendment) Regulations 1983 and shall come into operation on 18th August 1983.

Interpretation

2.—(1) In these regulations—

"the Act" means the Agriculture and Horticulture Act 1964;

"the 1973 regulations" means the Grading of Horticultural Produce (Amendment) Regulations 1973(c).

(2) Any reference in these regulations to a numbered regulation or schedule shall be construed as a reference to the regulation or schedule bearing that number in the 1973 regulations.

Amendment of the 1973 regulations

3. The 1973 regulations shall cease to have effect in so far as they apply section 20(1) of the Act(d) and regulation 8 is in consequence hereby revoked.

(a) 1964 c. 28; section 11(3) was inserted by paragraph 4(1) of Schedule 4 to the European Communities Act 1972 (c. 68).

(b) In the case of the Secretary of State for Wales, by virtue of S.I. 1978/272.

(c) S.I. 1973/22.

(d) Section 20(1) was amended, as respects England and Wales, by section 39(2) of, and Schedule 3 to, the Criminal Justice Act 1982 (c. 48) and, as respects Scotland, by sections 54 and 56(2) of, and Schedule 6 to, that Act.

Application of section 20(1) of the Act

4. In Part III of the Act (which relates to the grading of fresh horticultural produce), section 20(1) shall apply as prescribed in the 1973 regulations, and in consequence for section 20(1) of the Act as set out in Schedule 1 there is substituted the following subsection:—

> "20.—(1) A person guilty of an offence under section 15(1) of this Act shall be liable on summary conviction to a fine not exceeding level 3 on the standard scale.".

In Witness whereof the Official Seal of the Minister of Agriculture, Fisheries and Food is hereunto affixed on 13th July 1983.

(L.S.)

Michael Jopling,
Minister of Agriculture, Fisheries and Food.

George Younger,
Secretary of State for Scotland.

14th July 1983.

Nicholas Edwards,
Secretary of State for Wales.

18th July 1983.

EXPLANATORY NOTE

(This Note is not part of the Regulations.)

These regulations apply, for the purpose of the enforcement of European Community rules relating to the grading of horticultural produce, the maximum fine of level 3 on the standard scale (which is at present the sum of £200) on summary conviction for an offence of obstructing or otherwise impeding an authorised officer in the exercise of his functions provided by section 20(1) of the Agriculture and Horticulture Act 1964 as amended by the Criminal Justice Act 1982.

STATUTORY INSTRUMENTS

1983 No. 1058 (S. 98)

SCOTTISH LAND COURT

The Scottish Land Court (Fees) Amendment Rules 1983

Made -   -   -   -   *12th July* 1983
Coming into Operation   *15th August* 1983

The Scottish Land Court, in exercise of the powers conferred by section 29 of the Crofters Holdings (Scotland)Act 1886(**a**), and now vested in them(**b**), and by section 3(12) of the Small Landholders (Scotland) Act 1911(**c**) and of all other powers enabling them in that behalf, and with the approval of the Treasury, hereby make the following Rules:—

1. These Rules may be cited as the Scottish Land Court (Fees) Amendment Rules and shall come into operation on 15th August 1983.

2. For the Table of Fees contained in Appendix 1 to the Scottish Land Court Rules 1979(**d**) there shall be substituted the Table of Fees set out in the Schedule to these Rules.

3. The Scottish Land Court (Fees) Amendment Rules 1980(**e**) are hereby revoked.

Sealed with the Common Seal of the Scottish Land Court.

Scottish Land Court,
1 Grosvenor Crescent,
Edinburgh,
4th July 1983.

W. A. Elliott,
A. Gillespie,
Duncan D. McDiarmid,
A. B. Campbell.

We approve,

Alistair Goodlad,
D. J. F. Hunt,
Two of the Lords Commissioners of
Her Majesty's Treasury.

12th July 1983.

(**a**) 1886 c. 29.
(**b**) By the Small Landholders (Scotland) Act 1911 (c. 49), section 28(1).
(**c**) 1911. c. 49.   (**d**) S.I. 1979/379, amended by S.I. 1980/1319.
(**e**) S.I. 1980/1319.

Rule 2
SCHEDULE
TABLE OF FEES CHARGEABLE BY AND PAYABLE TO THE COURT

Column (1)	Column (2) £ p	Column (3)(a) £ p
(1) *Small Landholders (Scotland) Acts 1886 to 1931, Crofters (Scotland) Acts 1955 and 1961(b) and Crofting Reform (Scotland) Act 1976(c)*		
(*a*) Application for a Record of a holding or a croft		
Principal Application (each Applicant)	10.00	*(3.00)*
For each Respondent	2.00	*(0.75)*
(*b*) Recording Agreements for loan by (1) the Department of Agriculture and fisheries for Scotland and (2) The Highlands and Islands Development Board		
Each Agreement	5.00	*(3.00)*
(*c*) Other Applications		
Principal Application (each crave)	4.00	*(2.00)*
When more than one Applicant (each Applicant)	4.00	*(2.00)*
For each Respondent	1.00	*(0.75)*
(*d*) Appeals and Motions for Rehearing		
Each Apellant, or Motioner	4.00	(—)
Each Respondent	1.00	(—)
(2) *Sheep Stocks Valuation (Scotland) Act 1937(d) and Hill Farming Act 1946(e)*		
(*a*) Valuation of sheep stocks		
Awards not exceeding £100	5.00	*(3.50)*
Awards exceeding £100:		
For the first £100 thereof	5.00	*(3.50)*
For every additional £100 or fractional part thereof	2.00	*(1.00)*
Where application dismissed or withdrawn before valuation	15.00	*(10.75)*
(*b*) Determination of questions under sections 5 and 39(**b**) of the Hill Farming Act 1946		
Principal Application	15.00	*(11.00)*
For each Respondent	5.00	*(3.00)*

(**a**) The sums in italics are the fees chargeable under the Scottish Land Court (Fees) Amendment Rules 1980 which are revoked by these Rules.
(**b**) 1955 c. 21 and 1961 c. 58.   (**c**) 1976 c. 21.
(**d**) 1937 c. 34.   (**e**) 1946 c. 73.

Column (1)	Column (2) £ p	Column (3) £ p
(3) *Agriculture (Scotland) Act 1948(a),* *Agricultural Holdings (Scotland) Act 1949(b),* *Agriculture Act 1958(c), Agriculture (Miscella-* *neous Provisions) Act 1968(d) and Agriculture* *Holdings (Amendment) (Scotland) Act 1983(e)*		
(*a*) Arbitrations as to rents		
Rental as fixed by Court, not exceeding £50	10.00	(*4.25*)
Rental as fixed by Court, exceeding £50 but not exceeding £100	10.00	(*8.50*)
Rental, as fixed by Court exceeding £100:		
For the first £100 thereof	10.00	(*8.50*)
For every additional £100 or fractional part thereof	5.00	(*3.50*)
Where Application dismissed or withdrawn before compensation fixed	15.00	(*10.75*)
(*b*) Claims for compensation		
Awards not exceeding £50	10.00	(*4.25*)
Awards exceeding £50 but not exceeding £100	10.00	(*8.50*)
Awards exceeding £100:		
For the first £100 thereof	10.00	(*8.50*)
For every additional £100 or fractional part thereof	5.00	(*3.50*)
Where Application dismissed or with-drawn before compensation fixed	15.00	(*10.75*)
(*c*) Other Applications		
Principal Application (each crave)	25.00	(*11.00*)
When more than one Applicant (each Applicant)	25.00	(*11.00*)
For each Respondent	10.00	(*3.00*)
(*d*) Hearings		
For every day the Court sits beyond the first day of hearing	35.00	(—)
(4) *Miscellaneous*		
(*a*) Appeals and Motions for Rehearing		
Each Appellant, or Motioner for Rehearing	20.00	(*3.00*)
(*b*) For making a copy or copies of the Principal Application or any part of it, or any Order in it, or any original deed, writ, or document in process:		
For each sheet	0.70	(*0.50*)
For certifying such copy	3.00	(*2.00*)

(**a**) 1948 c. 45.   (**b**) 1949 c. 75.   (**c**) 1958 c. 71.
(**d**) 1968 c. 34.   (**e**) 1983 c. 46.

Column (1)	Column (2) £ p	Column (3) £ p
(c) Applications not otherwise specified		
Principal application (each crave)	15.00	(*11.00*)
When more than one Applicant (each Applicant)	15.00	(*11.00*)
For each Respondent	5.00	(*5.00*)

EXPLANATORY NOTE

(*This Note is not part of the Rules.*)

These Rules increase the fees payable in respect of applications to the Scottish Land Court and make provisions for new fees in respect of court hearings, appeals and rehearings. They also revoke the Scottish Land Court (Fees) Amendment Rules 1980.

STATUTORY INSTRUMENTS

1983 No. 1062 (C. 30)

MUSEUMS AND GALLERIES

The National Heritage Act 1983 (Commencement No. 1) Order 1983

Made - - - - - *20th July* 1983

The Lord President of the Council, in exercise of the powers conferred by section 41(1), (4) and (5) of the National Heritage Act 1983**(a)** and vested in him**(b)**, hereby makes the following Order:—

Citation

1. This Order may be cited as the National Heritage Act 1983 (Commencement No. 1) Order 1983.

Interpretation

2. In this Order "the Act" means the National Heritage Act 1983.

Coming into force of certain provisions of the Act

3. The provisions of the Act specified in column 1 of Schedules 1 and 2 to this Order (which relate to the matters specified in column 2 thereof) shall come into force on the day specified in the heading to the Schedule in question.

Transitional provision

4. The transitional provision contained in Schedule 3 to this Order shall have effect in connection with the bringing into force of paragraph 2 of Schedule 5 to the Act.

SCHEDULE 1

PROVISIONS COMING INTO FORCE ON 3RD AUGUST 1983

Provisions of the Act	Subject matter of provisions
Section 40.	Amendments and repeals.
In Schedule 5, paragraphs 1, 5 and 7.	Minor and consequential amendments.
Schedule 6, so far as it relates to the repeal of section 4(2) of the National Gallery and Tate Gallery Act 1954**(c)**.	Repeals.

(a) 1983 c. 47.   **(b)** S.I. 1983/879.   **(c)** 1954 c. 65.

SCHEDULE 2

PROVISIONS COMING INTO FORCE ON 30TH SEPTEMBER 1983

Provisions of the Act	Subject matter of provisions
Section 1.	Establishment of the Board of Trustees of the Victoria and Albert Museum.
Section 9.	Establishment of the Board of Trustees of the Science Museum.
In Schedule 1, paragraphs 1 to 8, 10 to 18 and 20.	Membership, proceedings etc. of the Boards of Trustees of the Victoria and Albert Museum and the Science Museum.
In Schedule 5, paragraph 2, paragraph 3 so far as it relates to the Science Museum and the Victoria and Albert Museum and paragraph 4 so far as it relates to the Boards of Trustees of those Museums.	Minor and consequential amendments.

SCHEDULE 3

TRANSITIONAL PROVISION

1. This Schedule shall have effect until section 17(1) of the Act comes into force.

2. Paragraph 2 of Schedule 5 to the Act shall apply as if the reference to the Armouries were omitted.

Whitelaw,
Lord President of the Council.

20th July 1983.

EXPLANATORY NOTE

(This Note is not part of the Order.)

This Order brings into force those provisions of the National Heritage Act 1983 which are specified in Schedules 1 and 2 to the Order.

The provisions specified in Schedule 1, which are brought into force on 3rd August 1983, concern the amendment and repeal of certain enactments relating to the transfer and loan of works of art.

The provisions specified in Schedule 2 are brought into force on 30th September 1983 (subject to a minor transitional provision). They are all related to the establishment of the Boards of Trustees of the Victoria and Albert Museum and the Science Museum. Initially these Boards are to be established without functions. A subsequent order will bring into force the functions and other provisions relating to the Boards.

STATUTORY INSTRUMENTS

1983 No. 1063

NATIONAL DEBT

The Savings Certificates (Amendment) (No. 2) Regulations 1983

Made - - - -	*21st July* 1983
Laid before Parliament	*22nd July* 1983
Coming into Operation	*15th August* 1983

The Treasury, in exercise of the powers conferred on them by section 11 of the National Debt Act 1972(**a**) and of all other powers enabling them in that behalf, hereby make the following Regulations:—

1. These Regulations may be cited as the Savings Certificates (Amendment) (No. 2) Regulations 1983, and shall come into operation on 15th August 1983.

2. The Savings Certificates Regulations 1972(**b**) shall be amended as follows:—

(*a*) in Regulation 5(1) by substituting for sub-paragraph (*r*) thereof the following sub-paragraphs:—

"(*r*) 200, in the case of certificates issued after 16th November 1982 but not later than 14th August 1983, the price of issue of which was £25 per unit certificate, and

(*s*) 200, in the case of certificates issued after 14th August 1983, the price of issue of which is £25 per unit certificate.";

(*b*) in Regulation 26(1)(iii) by deleting the words "not exceeding the rate of interest for the time being payable on ordinary deposits in the National Savings Bank".

3. The Savings Certificates (Amendment) (No. 3) Regulations 1982(**c**) and the Savings Certificates (Amendment) Regulations 1983(**d**) are hereby revoked.

Alastair Goodlad,
Donald Thompson,
Two of the Lords Commissioners
of Her Majesty's Treasury.

21st July 1983.

(**a**) 1972 c. 65.
(**b**) S.I. 1972/641; relevant amending instruments are S.I. 1979/1388, 1980/1614, 1981/670, 1482, 1982/488, 1013, 1574, 1983/495.
(**c**) S.I. 1982/1227.   (**d**) S.I. 1983/495.

EXPLANATORY NOTE

(This Note is not part of the Regulations.)

These Regulations, which amend the Savings Certificates Regulations 1972, provide that the maximum permitted holding of the 26th Issue of National Savings Certificates, which will be on sale from 15th August 1983 at a purchase price of £25 per certificate unit, shall be 200. Certificates of the 25th Issue will not be issued after 14th August 1983.

The Regulations also remove the maximum limit on the rate of interest which the Director of Savings may pay in the case of any certificates which have been forfeited under the 1972 Regulations because they were purchased or held in contravention of the relevant maximum permitted holding limit.

1983 No. 1071

ANIMALS

ANIMAL HEALTH

The Diseases of Animals (Approved Disinfectants) (Amendment) (No. 2) Order 1983

Made - - - -	*20th July* 1983
Coming into Operation	*29th July* 1983

The Minister of Agriculture, Fisheries and Food, the Secretary of State for Scotland and the Secretary of State for Wales, acting jointly, in exercise of the powers conferred on them by sections 1, 7(1)*(a)*, *(b)* and *(c)* and (2) and 23*(f)* and *(g)* of the Animal Health Act 1981 (a) and of all other powers enabling them in that behalf, hereby order as follows:—

Title and commencement

1. This order may be cited as the Diseases of Animals (Approved Disinfectants) (Amendment) (No. 2) Order 1983 and shall come into operation on 29th July 1983.

Amendment

2. The Diseases of Animals (Approved Disinfectants) Order 1978(b) shall be amended as follows:—

　(a) for Schedule 1 to that order (which lists disinfectants approved by the Minister) there shall be substituted the provisions of Schedule 1 to this order;

　(b) for Schedule 2 to that order (which lists disinfectants subject to transitional provisions) there shall be substituted the provisions of Schedule 2 to this order; and

　(c) in Article 6(2) of that order (which relates to disinfectants subject to transitional provisions) for the words "30th June 1983" there shall be substituted the words "31st December 1983".

Revocation

3. The orders mentioned in Schedule 3 to this order are hereby revoked.

In Witness whereof the Official Seal of the Minister of Agriculture, Fisheries and Food is hereunto affixed on 18th July 1983.

(a) 1981 c.22.
(b) S.I. 1978/32; relevant amending instruments are S.I. 1978/934, 1982/947 and 1983/32.

Michael Jopling,
Minister of Agriculture,
Fisheries and Food.

George Younger,
Secretary of State for
Scotland.

19th July 1983.

John Stradling Thomas,
Minister of State for Wales.

20th July 1983.

SCHEDULE 1

PROVISIONS TO BE SUBSTITUTED FOR SCHEDULE 1

"SCHEDULE 1

APPROVED DISINFECTANTS

Disinfectant	Orders in respect of which use is approved; and dilution rates				
	Foot-and-Mouth Disease Orders	Swine Vesicular Disease Order	Fowl Pest Orders	Tuberculosis Orders	General Orders
Abclean	30	—	—	—	—
Action Approved Disinfectant	240	200	80	25	145
Agridyne 2	250	300	125	30	180
Agrisan Master Approved Disinfectant	120	—	59	—	59
Alfa Laval Liquid Tank Cleaner	240	250	80	15	110
Alodine	240	250	80	15	110
Ani-Odophor GT	240	160	91	25	145
Antec Black Fluid	219	100	41	—	80
Antec Farm Fluid	450	300	39	24	29
Antec Hipodine	250	300	130	30	180
Antec Iodine Active Steriliser	—	—	125	30	180
Antec Long Life	—	160	60	—	60
Antec Long Life 200	—	—	200	—	—
Antec Long Life Extra	—	160	71	75	85
Antec New Formula Black Fluid	300	110	52	—	60
Antec New Formula Farm Fluid	—	—	70	30	65
Antec New Formula Farm Fluid Extra	250	150	80	60	85
Antec White Fluid	—	—	30	90	100
Applied 8–57 White Disinfectant	—	—	—	49	89
Arrow Agricultural Hydroclean Bactericidal Cleaner Disinfectant	30	—	—	—	—
Bactol Plus	40	—	20	28	50
Basol 99	—	—	50	20	20
Battles White Disinfectant Fluid	—	—	45	50	60
Battles Black Disinfectant Fluid	—	—	—	—	60

Items in bold type indicate additions to Schedule

Disinfectant	Orders in respect of which use is approved; and dilution rates				
	Foot-and-Mouth Disease Orders	Swine Vesicular Disease Order	Fowl Pest Orders	Tuberculosis Orders	General Orders
Battles Iofarm Iodophor Disinfectant and Dairy Detergent Steriliser	250	300	125	30	180
Betators 25	240	180	90	30	160
Biocid 30	250	300	125	30	180
Biokil Plus	40	—	50	—	40
Capriclense	240	200	80	25	145
Carbo White Disinfectant	—	—	—	49	89
Castrol Solvex ICD 109	50	—	—	—	—
Centaur New Approved Agricultural Disinfectant	250	300	125	30	180
Century Black Disinfectant	—	—	20	—	—
Ciba Geigy White Fluid	—	—	30	90	100
Citric Acid BP	500	—	—	—	—
Clearsol	250	300	125	45	180
Combat 2	50	—	100	30	100
Compass Agricultural Disinfectant	250	200	—	50	—
Compass Lysol BP 1968	9	—	39	39	49
Crown Special Detergent Disinfectant	240	—	80	25	145
C S Disinfectant	—	—	65	15	40
Dairyclean Bulk Tank Iodophor	240	250	80	—	110
Davrisol 76	—	—	30	90	100
Defender	—	—	30	90	100
Dellaphen General Purpose Soluble Disinfectant	—	—	60	65	70
Delsanex Iodel F.D.	215	234	130	26	147
Delsol	—	—	100	100	120
Dexadyne	240	—	91	—	—
Disteola	240	300	80	25	100

Items in bold type indicate additions to Schedule

SCHEDULE 1

APPROVED DISINFECTANTS (continued)

Disinfectant	Orders in respect of which use is approved; and dilution rates				
	Foot-and-Mouth Disease Orders	Swine Vesicular Disease Order	Fowl Pest Orders	Tuberculosis Orders	General Orders
Downland White Disinfectant	—	—	—	—	—
Durak 100	—	—	—	49	89
Eley's Economic Farm Fluid	250	20	55	—	49
Equivite All-Purpose Disinfectant	250	300	100	25	70
Evans White Disinfectant	—	—	125	30	180
FAM	240	250	—	49	89
FAM 30	250	300	80	15	110
Famclor	200	500	125	30	180
Famosan	120	200	59	12	70
Farm Disinfectant	—	—	30	—	59
Farmicide	40	—	50	90	100
Fensol	—	—	60	—	40
Ficare Blue Star	—	—	100	65	70
Ficare Gold Star	275	330	141	85	150
Formalin BP (Containing not less than 34% formaldehyde)	9	9	—	33	200
Gloquat SD Extra	400	200	50	—	—
GR 218	—	—	—	—	—
Halamid	20	90	200	—	—
Hullite Disinfectant Fluid	—	—	30	20	199
Hullite Farm Disinfectant Fluid	—	—	30	49	89
Hy-Co AFD	20	—	60	90	100
Hygasan	219	100	39	90	100
Hykil X	240	250	60	—	29
Iodet	240	250	80	24	110
Iofarm	240	180	80	15	100
Iosan Farm Disinfectant	120	200	80	15	80
Isocare Disinfectant	—	—	59	15	59
Izal Germicide	—	—	41	75	90

Items in bold type indicate additions to Schedule

SCHEDULE 1
APPROVED DISINFECTANTS (continued)

Disinfectant	Orders in respect of which use is approved; and dilution rates				
	Foot-and-Mouth Disease Orders	Swine Vesicular Disease Order	Fowl Pest Orders	Tuberculosis Orders	General Orders
Jeyes Fluid	—	—	30	—	50
Kilrobe WO Disinfectant Fluid Special Grade	—	—	—	—	99
Killgerm Black Disinfectant R W Co-efficient 18/22	—	—	—	—	80
Killgerm Iodair	250	260	41	—	—
Killgerm Lysol BP	—	—	61	39	49
Killgerm White Farm Disinfectant	—	—	50	66	100
Kirby Chlor	—	448	21	—	450
Kryptol	60	—	271	—	20
Lenfectant White Fluid	—	—	—	49	89
Leonard Smith's Approved Special Detergent Disinfectant	240	200	80	25	145
Low Odour Izal Germicide	—	—	20	40	40
Lysol BP Evansol	10	—	50	39	50
Lysovet	50	250	66	45	49
Lysovet J Forte	250	260	60	—	100
Marstan Dairy Hygiene Iodair	—	9	61	—	—
Master SVD Solution	—	100	250	—	210
Micro Chlor	160	140	100	—	110
Microdine	—	—	30	90	100
Microfec	—	—	60	65	70
Microl-Plus	—	—	70	—	—
Microsan	—	—	100	100	120
Microzol	—	—	80	22	—
Novagen FP	240	180	125	30	145
Nutosan	250	300	125	30	180
Orbicide	250	300	—	—	180
Ortho-phosphoric acid (Technical Grade)	330	—	—	—	—

Items in bold type indicate additions to Schedule

SCHEDULE 1

APPROVED DISINFECTANTS *(continued)*

Disinfectant	Orders in respect of which use is approved; and dilution rates				
	Foot-and-Mouth Disease Orders	Swine Vesicular Disease Order	Fowl Pest Orders	Tuberculosis Orders	General Orders
Parasept	—	—	100	100	120
Pennine Iodophor Detergent Steriliser	250	260	61	—	200
Peratol	75	75	100	75	90
Phiodin	220	180	80	11	85
Phorpass	240	280	90	30	180
Phorpass 75	380	300	180	100	—
Polykil + Disinfectant	—	300	—	—	—
Premiere White Disinfectant	—	—	—	—	89
Ropolik	240	250	80	49	110
Ryodac	250	300	125	15	180
Ry-odophor SP	240	160	91	30	145
Safeguard Abattoir Sanitiser	20	—	10	25	74
Safeguard Iodophor Concentrate	100	—	100	—	3
SEP 55	—	—	100	—	120
Sodium Carbonate (Decahydrate) Complying with BS 3674 of 1963	24	—	—	100	—
Sodium Hydroxide	—	100	—	—	—
Sorex White Farm Disinfectant	—	—	21	—	—
Special Ropolik	250	300	125	66	100
Sterilite Farm Disinfectant	—	—	30	30	180
Sterilite WD White Disinfectant	—	—	—	90	100
Sudol	—	—	60	49	89
Sulphamic Acid	500	—	—	65	70
Superdine	250	300	125	30	—
Superlin Black Disinfectant	—	—	—	70	180
Surgiclene	250	300	125	30	70
SWC General White	—	—	30	90	180
SWC Iodine	250	300	125	30	100

Items in bold type indicate additions to Schedule

APPROVED DISINFECTANTS *(continued)*

Disinfectant	Orders in respect of which use is approved; and dilution rates				
	Foot-and-Mouth Disease Orders	Swine Vesicular Disease Order	Fowl Pest Orders	Tuberculosis Orders	General Orders
SWC Poultry Terminal	—	—	100	100	120
Tekresol	—	—	90	80	135
Texol	—	—	—	—	95
Total Farm Disinfectant	250	300	125	30	180
Triphenol	—	—	—	—	50
Tynedale Dairy Hygiene Disinfectant plus	240	160	91	25	145
Unidol	—	100	60	65	70
Unifarm Universal Disinfectant	240	200	100	25	100
Unifect	10	—	—	—	—
Unilite	—	—	30	90	100
Unisep	—	100	100	100	120
Universal	240	—	100	25	100
Vapulin Black Disinfectant	—	100	41	—	80
Vesphene D39	10	—	50	70	55
VH6 Virucide	219	100	39	24	29
Warden Black Disinfectant	—	—	—	160	60
White Cresanol	—	—	30	90	100
Young's Approved Farm Disinfectant	—	—	—	69	69
Young's Disinfectant and Dairy Detergent Steriliser	250	300	125	30	180
Young's Farm Septol	—	—	40	89	99
Young's Iodophor Farm Disinfectant	215	234	130	26	147
Zenasan Farm Disinfectant	—	—	30	90	100

Items in bold type indicate additions to Schedule

PROVISIONS TO BE SUBSTITUTED FOR SCHEDULE 2

"SCHEDULE 2

Articles 4 and 6

APPROVED DISINFECTANTS SUBJECT TO TRANSITIONAL PROVISIONS

Disinfectant	Orders in respect of which use is approved; and dilution rates				
	Foot-and-Mouth Disease Orders	Swine Vesicular Disease Order	Fowl Pest Orders	Tuberculosis Orders	General Orders
Agridyne	250	300	110	30	180
Antec Iodine Active Steriliser	250	300	110	30	180
Battles Iofarm Iodophor Disinfectant and Dairy Detergent Steriliser	250	300	110	30	180
Biocid 30	250	300	110	30	180
Boots' Farm Disinfectant	—	—	30	90	100
Capriclense	250	300	110	30	180
Centaur New Approved Agricultural Disinfectant	250	300	110	30	180
Combat 2	250	300	110	30	180
Equivite All-Purpose Disinfectant	250	300	110	30	180
Fam 30	250	300	110	30	180
Nutosan	250	300	110	30	180
Orbicide	250	300	110	30	180
Ryodac	250	300	110	30	180
Sanol FM	140	90	—	30	180
Special Ropolik	250	300	110	30	180
Superdine	250	300	110	30	180
Surgiclene	250	300	110	30	180
Total Farm Disinfectant	250	300	110	30	180
Unifeeds Clear Soluble Disinfectant	—	—	60	65	70
Unifeeds Farm Disinfectant	9	—	30	90	100
Unifeeds Lysol Disinfectant	—	—	39	39	49
Unifeeds Special Disinfectant	—	—	100	100	120
Young's Approved Farm Disinfectant	—	—	30	90	100
Young's Disinfectant and Dairy Detergent Steriliser	250	300	110	30	180

Article 3

SCHEDULE 3

ORDERS WHICH ARE REVOKED

The Diseases of Animals (Approved Disinfectants) (Amendment) Order 1978 (S.I. 1978/934)

The Diseases of Animals (Approved Disinfectants) (Amendment) Order 1979 (S.I. 1979/37)

The Diseases of Animals (Approved Disinfectants) (Amendment) (No. 2) Order 1979 (S.I. 1979/773)

The Diseases of Animals (Approved Disinfectants) (Amendment) Order 1980 (S.I. 1980/25)

The Diseases of Animals (Approved Disinfectants) (Amendment) (No. 2) Order 1980 (S.I. 1980/955)

The Diseases of Animals (Approved Disinfectants) (Amendment) Order 1981 (S.I. 1981/7)

The Diseases of Animals (Approved Disinfectants) (Amendment) (No. 2) Order 1981 (S.I. 1981/1050)

The Diseases of Animals (Approved Disinfectants) (Amendment) Order 1982 (S.I. 1982/35)

The Diseases of Animals (Approved Disinfectants) (Amendment) (No. 2) Order 1982 (S.I. 1982/947)

The Diseases of Animals (Approved Disinfectants) (Amendment) Order 1983 (S.I. 1983/32)

EXPLANATORY NOTE

(*This Note is not part of the Order.*)

This order amends the Diseases of Animals (Approved Disinfectants) Order 1978 by substituting new schedules for Schedules 1 and 2 to that order. Schedule 1, which lists approved disinfectants, includes newly approved disinfectants, and Schedule 2 lists disinfectants which are now omitted from Schedule 1 but which may nevertheless continue to be used as approved disinfectants until 31st December 1983.

This order also revokes the orders listed in Schedule 3, which are spent.

STATUTORY INSTRUMENTS

1983 No. 1072 (S. 99)

ARMORIAL BEARINGS, ENSIGNS AND FLAGS

The Lyon Court and Office Fees (Variation) Order 1983

Made - - - - -	19*th July* 1983
Laid before Parliament	3*rd August* 1983
Coming into Operation	24*th August* 1983

In exercise of the powers conferred on me by section 5 of, as read with paragraph 3 of Schedule 3 to, the Public Expenditure and Receipts Act 1968**(a)**, and of all other powers enabling me in that behalf, I hereby make the following order:—

1. This order may be cited as the Lyon Court and Office Fees (Variation) Order 1983 and shall come into operation on 24th August 1983.

2. The fees in Schedule B to the Lyon King of Arms Act 1867**(b)** in respect of each of the matters specified in column 1 of the Schedule to this order shall be amended by substituting for the sum specified in respect of that matter in the said Schedule B (being the sum specified in column 2 of the Schedule to this order) the sum specified in respect thereof in column 3 of the Schedule to this order.

3. The Lyon Court and Office Fees (Variation) Order 1981**(c)** is hereby revoked.

New St. Andrew's House,
Edinburgh.
19th July 1983.

George Younger,
One of Her Majesty's Principal
Secretaries of State.

(a) 1968 c. 14.
(b) 1867 c. 17; Schedule B was last amended by S.I. 1981/1752.
(c) S.I. 1981/1752.

Article 2 SCHEDULE

1 Matter to which fee relates	2 Present fee	3 New fee
	£	£
On every patent of arms with supporters	390.00	430.00
On every patent of arms without supporters	234.00	258.00
On every matriculation of arms with supporters, without a new patent	124.00	137.00
On every matriculation of arms without supporters, without a new patent	94.00	104.00
On every matriculation of arms without a new patent of arms, but with a patent of supporters	254.00	270.00
On every genealogy recorded	78.00	86.00
Additional for each member of the pedigree	2.50	2.75
Certificate regarding change of surname	28.00	31.00
Search in register of arms	2.50	2.75
Search in register of genealogies	5.00	5.50
General search in heraldic MSS	28.00	31.00
General search in genealogical MSS	28.00	31.00
On every extract from a register	5.00	5.50
On entering a caveat	16.00	18.00
On admission of a messenger-at-arms to practise in the district of Edinburgh	86.00	95.00
On admission of a messenger-at-arms to practise out of the district of Edinburgh	74.00	82.00
Annual dues of a messenger-at-arms practising in the district of Edinburgh	13.00	15.00
Annual dues of a messenger-at-arms practising out of the district of Edinburgh	13.00	15.00
On renewal of a messenger's bond of caution	28.00	31.00
On recording resignation or change of residence of a messenger	2.50	2.75
On search for a messenger's cautioner	2.50	2.75
On every certified statement of name and designation of such cautioner, and date of bond	5.00	5.50
On each petition or paper lodged in a process against a messenger	5.00	5.50
On each interlocutor in a process against a messenger	5.00	5.50
On extracting each warrant, decree, or precept of suspension, first sheet	5.00	5.50
On ditto, each subsequent sheet	2.50	2.75
On affixing seal of office to warrant, decree or precept	5.00	5.50
On examining executions of service and intimations of precepts of suspension, marking them on the record and giving out certificates	5.00	5.50
On lending process and taking receipt	2.50	2.75
On return of process and scoring receipt	2.50	2.75
On re-admission of a messenger-at-arms	16.00	18.00
On the appointment of a herald	10.00	10.00
On the appointment of a pursuivant	10.00	10.00

N.B.—These fees are exclusive of stamp duties when such are exigible.

EXPLANATORY NOTE

(This Note is not part of the Order.)

This Order increases the fees in respect of most of the matters listed in Schedule B to the Lyon King of Arms Act 1867, as previously amended by the Lyon Court and Office Fees (Variation) Order 1981.

STATUTORY INSTRUMENTS

1983 No. 1073 (S. 100)

LANDLORD AND TENANT

The Agricultural Holdings (Specification of Forms) (Scotland) Order 1983

Made - - - -	*19th July* 1983
Coming into Operation	*28th July* 1983

In exercise of the powers conferred on me by paragraphs 10 and 23 of Schedule 6 to the Agricultural Holdings (Scotland) Act 1949(a), and of all other powers enabling me in that behalf, and after consultation with the Council on Tribunals as provided in section 10 of the Tribunals and Inquiries Act 1971(b), I hereby make the following order:—

1.—(1) This order may be cited as the Agricultural Holdings (Specification of Forms) (Scotland) Order 1983, and shall come into operation on the 28th July 1983.

(2) In this order "the Act" means the Agricultural Holdings (Scotland) Act 1949.

2. The form specified in Schedule 1 to this order shall, modified as circumstances may require, be the form of an award in an arbitration under the Act.

3. The forms specified in Schedule 2 to this order or forms as near thereto as circumstances may require may be used for proceedings in arbitrations under the Act as follows:—

(a) for the making of an application for appointment by the Secretary of State of an arbiter to determine claims, questions or differences (except as to determination of rent) arising between the landlord and tenant of an agricultural holding—Form A;

(b) for the making of an application for appointment by the Secretary of State of an arbiter to determine the rent of an agricultural holding—Form B;

(c) for the making of an application to the Secretary of State by an arbiter for extension of time for making his award in an arbitration—Form C.

(a) 1949 c. 75; paragraph 10 of Schedule 6 was amended by the Agricultural Holdings (Amendment) (Scotland) Act 1983 (c. 46), section 5(2)(c).
(b) 1971 c. 62.

4.—(1) The Agricultural Holdings (Specification of Forms) (Scotland) Instrument 1960(**a**) and the Agricultural Holdings (Specification of Forms) (Scotland) Amendment Instrument 1979(**b**) are hereby revoked.

(2) Anything whatsoever done under or by virtue of the instruments revoked by this order shall be deemed to have been done under or by virtue of the corresponding provision of this order and anything whatsoever begun under any article of the said instruments may be continued under this order as if begun under this order.

New St Andrew's House,
Edinburgh.
19th July 1983.

George Younger,
One of Her Majesty's Principal
Secretaries of State.

SCHEDULE 1   Article 2

FORM OF AWARD

AGRICULTURAL HOLDINGS (SCOTLAND) ACT 1949

Award in Arbitration between A. B. (name and address), the [outgoing] tenant, and C. D. (name and address), the landlord, with regard to the holding known as
                                        (insert name of holding, district and region),
[lately] in the occupation of the said tenant.

Whereas under the Agricultural Holdings (Scotland) Act 1949, the claims, questions or differences set forth in the Schedule to this Award are referred to arbitration in accordance with the provisions set out in Schedule 6 to the said Act:

And whereas by appointment dated the   day of   19   , signed by (on behalf of) the said tenant and landlord [or, as the case may be—given under the seal of the Secretary of State], I, (insert name and address), was duly appointed under the said Act to be the arbiter for the purpose of

^{1}(settling the said claims

{ settling the said questions or differences

(determining the rent to be paid in respect of the said holding as from^2

in accordance with the provisions set out in Schedule 6 to the said Act:

[And whereas the time for making my Award has been extended by

^{1}(the written agreement of the said tenant and landlord, dated the   day of
                    19   ,

) order of the Secretary of State, dated the   day of   19   ,

(to the   day of   19   .]

(**a**) S.I. 1960/1337.   (**b**) S.I. 1979/800.

And whereas I, the said (insert name)   , having accepted the appointment as arbiter, and having heard the parties (agents for the parties) and examined the documents and other productions lodged and the evidence led and having fully considered the whole matters referred to me, do hereby make my final Award as follows:—[3]

I award and determine that the said landlord shall pay to the said tenant the sum of   pounds and   pence, as compensation in respect of the claims set forth in the [first partof the] Schedule to this Award, the amount awarded in respect of each claim being as there stated.

I award and determine that the said tenant shall pay to the said landlord the sum of   pounds and   pence, in respect of the claims set forth in the [second part of the] Schedule to this Award, the amount awarded in respect of each claim being as there stated.

I determine the questions or differences set forth in the [third part of the] Schedule to this Award, as follows, namely:—

[1] I fix and determine the rent to be paid by the said tenant to the said landlord, as from[2]   to be the sum of   per anum. [My findings in fact and the reasons for my decision are set forth in the [fourth part of the] Schedule to this award.]

I award and direct that each party shall bear his own expenses and one half of the other expenses of and incidental to the arbitration and Award, including my remuneration [and that of the clerk].
(or otherwise as the arbiter may see fit to direct in light of the provisions of section 76(4) of, and paragraphs 16 to 18 of Schedule 6 to, the said Act) and that, subject to the provisions of the said Act, all sums including any expenses, payable under or by virtue of this Award shall be so paid not later than[4]

In witness whereof I have signed this Award this   day of   19   , in the presence of the following witnesses.

Signature . . . .

Designation . . . .   (*Arbiter*)

Address . . . .

Signature . . . .

Designation . . . .

Address . . . .

Schedule to the above Award

In the case of appointment by the Secretary of State or by the Scottish Land Court of an arbiter to determine claims questions or differences (except as to rent) the arbiter must, if either party so requests, state the reasons for any determination arrived at (section 12 of the Tribunals and Inquiries Act 1971).

In the case of appointment by the Secretary of State or by the Scottish Land Court of an arbiter to determine the rent of an agricultural holding under section 7 of the 1949 Act, the arbiter shall, in every case, and regardless of whether or not he is requested to do so, state in writing his findings of fact and the reasons for his decision under the headings set forth in Part IV of this Schedule (paragraph 9A of Schedule 6 to the 1949 Act).

Claims,[5] questions or differences to be determined.

Part I—
Claims made by the tenant.

Part II—
Claims made by the landlord.

Part III—
Questions or differences (including questions of rent in cases where the arbiter is not appointed by the Secretary of State or Scottish Land Court).

Part IV—
Variation of rent cases under section 7 of the 1949 Act in which the arbiter is appointed by the Secretary of State or Scottish Land Court

In such cases a statement under the following headings must be provided as a Schedule to the Award and made available to the parties to the case and the Secretary of State—

- (i) a summary of the statement of case submitted by or on behalf of the landlord;
- (ii) a summary of the statement of case submitted by or on behalf of the tenant;
- (iii) details of any evidence of the condition of the holding, including the state of the landlord's and tenant's fixed equipment, which emerged at the inspection of the holding and were taken into account;
- (iv) a summary of the relevant evidence considered at any hearing;
- (v) an appraisal of the evidence submitted under (i) to (iv);
- (vi) details of any other evidence of open market rents for comparable subjects introduced by the arbiter on which the parties had an opportunity to comment and which the arbiter took into account;
- (vii) the reasons for seeking evidence (in terms of the factors specifically listed in section 7(1A) of the 1949 Act) other than evidence of open market rents for comparable subjects in the surrounding area;
- (viii) details of the factors specified in section 7(1A) of the 1949 Act which the arbiter considers it desirable to take into account;

(ix) an indication of the weight attached by the arbiter to the various criteria taken into account;

(x) an explanation of any adjustment made by the arbiter to take account of differences in holdings used for comparative purpose;

(xi) any other explanation necessary to clarify the arbiter's decision.

---

[1] Adapt to meet the circumstances.

[2] Insert date from which revised rent is to run. (Where variation of rent under section 7 of the 1949 Act is concerned, the date will be the next ensuing day on which the tenancy could have been terminated by notice to quit given at the date of demanding the reference of the rent question to arbitration—usually a term of Whitsunday or Martinmas.)

[3] Such parts of the following four paragraphs as may be appropriate should be incorporated in the award, adaptations to meet the particular circumstances being made as necessary.

[4] The date of payment specified must not be later than one calendar month after the delivery of the Award.

[5] Where claims are made under Schedules 1, 2, 3 or 4 to the 1949 Act, the amounts awarded must, if either party so requires, be shown separately against each numbered item as set out in those Schedules. Where claims are made by either party under agreement or custom and not under statute, the amounts awarded must be separately stated.

SCHEDULE 2   Article 3

FORM A

(Application for appointment by the Secretary of State of an arbiter to determine claims, question or differences (except as to determination of rent) arising between the landlord and tenant of an agricultural holding).

AGRICULTURAL HOLDINGS (SCOTLAND) ACT 1949

To the Secretary of State,

In default of agreement between the landlord and the tenant of the holding specified in the Schedule to this application as to the person to act as arbiter and in the absence of any provision in any lease or agreement between them relating to the appointment of an arbiter, I/we hereby apply to the Secretary of State to appoint an arbiter for the purpose of settling the claims questions or differences set out in the Schedule to this application.

Signature(s) ....

1 ....

Date ....

SCHEDULE

(Applicants seeking determination of a claim for compensation associated with questions and differences should answer questions 1 to 11 inclusive)

Particulars required	Replies
SECTION A—*To be completed by all applicants* 1. Name and address of holding	Holding: District: Region:
2. Name and address of landlord.	
3. Name and address of landlord's agent.[2]	
4. Name and address of tenant.	
5. Name and address of tenant's agent.[2]	
6. If the tenancy has terminated state date of termination.	
7. Approximate area in hectares of holding.	
8. Description of holding.[3]	

SECTION B—*To be completed ONLY by applicants seeking determination of a claim for compensation*

9. If an extension of time has been granted under section 68(3) of the Agricultural Holdings (Scotland) Act 1949 for the settlement of claims, state date on which extension expires.

10. Nature of claim to be referred to arbitration.
    (*a*) State claim for compensation for improvements by the tenant, and give short particulars of any further claims by the tenant.
    (*b*) Give short particulars of any claims by the landlord.

SECTION C—*To be completed ONLY by applicants seeking determination of questions or differences*

11. State questions or differences to be referred to arbitration.

---

[1] State whether landlord or tenant. If an agent signs state on whose behalf he is signing. The appointment will be expedited if the application is made by both parties.

[2] If no agent, insert "None".

[3] Describe holding briefly, e.g. mixed, arable, dairying, market garden.

Form B

(Application for appointment by the Secretary of State of an arbiter to determine the rent of an agricultural holding).

Agricultural Holdings (Scotland) Act, 1949

To the Secretary of State,

In default of agreement between the landlord and the tenant of the holding specified in the Schedule to this application as to the person to act as arbiter and in the absence of any provision in any lease or agreement between them relating to the appointment of an arbiter, I/we hereby apply to the Secretary of State to appoint an arbiter to determine the rent to be paid for the said holding as from   19   :
(enter appropriate date in accordance with note 1 below)

Signature(s) ....

2 ....

Date ....

SCHEDULE

Particulars required	Replies
1. Name and address of holding.	Holding: District: Region:
2. Name and address of landlord.	
3. Name and address of landlord's agent.[3]	
4. Name and address of tenant.	
5. Name and address of tenant's agent.[3]	
6. Approximate area in hectares of holding.	
7. Description of holding.[4]	
8. Date of demand in writing for reference to arbitration.	
9. Date at which tenancy of holding could be terminated by notice to quit.	
10. (a) Date of commencement of tenancy. (b) Effective date of any previous increase or reduction of rent. (c) Effective date of any previous direction of an arbiter that the rent continue unchanged.	

[1] Where variation of rent under section 7 of the 1949 Act is concerned, the date will be the next ensuing day on which the tenancy could have been terminated by notice to quit given at the date of demanding the reference of the rent question to arbitration—usually a term of Whitsunday or Martinmas.

[2] State whether landlord or tenant. If an agent signs, state on whose behalf he is signing. The appointment will be expedited if the application is made by both parties.

[3] If no agent, insert "None" in second column.

[4] Describe holding briefly, e.g. mixed, arable, dairying, market garden.

FORM C

(Application to the Secretary of State by an arbiter for extension of time for making his award in an arbitration.)

AGRICULTURAL HOLDINGS (SCOTLAND) ACT 1949

To the Secretary of State,

As the time for making the Award in the arbitration detailed below will expire/expired on the   day of   19   , I hereby apply for an extension of the time for making the said Award to the   day of   19   .

(Signature of arbiter
or arbiter's clerk) ....

Date ....

Details to be supplied—

1. Name of holding and district and region in which situated.

2. Name and address of landlord (and agent, if any).

3. Name and address of tenant (and agent, if any).

4. Name and address of arbiter (and clerk, if any).

5. (*a*) Date on which arbiter appointed.

    (*b*) Whether appointed by agreement of parties or by the Secretary of State or Scottish Land Court.

EXPLANATORY NOTE

(This Note is not part of the Order.)

The forms specified in this Order take the place of the forms specified in the Agricultural Holdings (Specification of Forms) (Scotland) Instrument 1960, revised to take account of the provisions of the Agricultural Holdings (Amendment) (Scotland) Act 1983.

STATUTORY INSTRUMENTS

1983 No. 1074 (S. 101)

RATING AND VALUATION

The Local Government (Scotland) Act 1973 (Section 111) Amendment Order 1983

Made - - - -	*17th June* 1983
Laid before Parliament	*23rd June* 1983
Coming into Operation	*22nd July* 1983

In exercise of the powers conferred on me by section 5(6) of the Local Government (Scotland) Act 1966(**a**) and of all other powers enabling me in that behalf I hereby make the following order:—

1. This Order may be cited as The Local Government (Scotland) Act 1973 (Section 111) Amendment Order 1983 and shall come into operation on 22nd July 1983 .

2. In section 111(1)(*f*) of the Local Government (Scotland) Act 1973(**b**) the following words shall be inserted after the words "this Act":

"or under section 5(4)(*b*) of the Local Government (Scotland) Act 1966".

New St Andrew's House,
Edinburgh.
17th June 1983

George Younger,
One of Her Majesty's Principal
Secretaries of State.

EXPLANATORY NOTE

(*This Note is not part of the Order.*)

This Order amends section 111 of the Local Government (Scotland) Act 1973 (Regulations with respect to rates) and enables the Secretary of State to make regulations in respect of a rate determined or deemed to be determined in terms of section 5(4)(*b*) of the Local Government (Scotland) Act 1966.

(**a**) 1966 c. 51; subsection 5(6) was added by the Local Government and Planning (Scotland) Act 1982 (c. 43), section 1(*c*).
(**b**) 1973 c. 65; paragraph (*f*) was added by the Local Government (Miscellaneous Provisions) (Scotland) Act 1981 (c. 23), Schedule 3, paragraph 27.

STATUTORY INSTRUMENTS

1983 No. 1076

SHIPBUILDING INDUSTRY

The British Shipbuilders Borrowing Powers (Increase of Limit) Order 1983

Laid before the Commons House of Parliament in draft

Made - - - -	*20th July* 1983
Coming into Operation	*21st July* 1983

The Secretary of State, in exercise of his powers under section 11(7) of the Aircraft and Shipbuilding Industries Act 1977(**a**) and with the consent of the Treasury, hereby makes the following Order, a draft of which has been approved by the Commons House of Parliament in accordance with section 11(10) of that Act:—

1. This Order may be cited as the British Shipbuilders Borrowing Powers (Increase of Limit) Order 1983 and shall come into operation on the day after it is made.

2. The limit of £700 million specified in section 11(7) of the Aircraft and Shipbuilding Industries Act 1977 in respect of the aggregate of the amounts for the time being outstanding, otherwise than by way of interest, in respect of money borrowed by British Shipbuilders and each of its wholly owned subsidiaries (other than money borrowed on excluded loans as defined in section 11(9) of that Act) and the public dividend capital received by British Shipbuilders, is hereby increased to £800 million.

Norman Lamont,
Minister of State,
Department of Trade and Industry.

19th July 1983.

We consent to the making of this Order.

Alastair Goodlad,
Donald Thompson,
Two of the Lords Commissioners
of Her Majesty's Treasury.

20th July 1983.

(**a**) 1977 c. 3; section 11(7) was amended by the Shipbuilding Act 1982 (c. 4), section 1(1).

EXPLANATORY NOTE

(This Note is not part of the Order.)

Section 11(7) of the Aircraft and Shipbuilding Industries Act 1977, as amended by section 1(1) of the Shipbuilding Act 1982, limits the aggregate of the borrowings by British Shipbuilders and its wholly owned subsidiaries (other than money borrowed on excluded loans as defined by section 11(9) of the 1977 Act) and the public dividend capital received by British Shipbuilders to £700 million. Section 11(7), as so amended, also makes provision for that limit to be increased by order to a sum not exceeding £800 million. This Order increases the limit from £700 million to £800 million.

STATUTORY INSTRUMENTS

1983 No. 1077

WEIGHTS AND MEASURES

The Weights and Measures Act 1963 (Amendment of Schedule 3) Order 1983

Laid before Parliament in draft

Made - - - *21st July* 1983

Coming into Operation *1st December* 1983

Whereas the Secretary of State pursuant to section 54(2) of the Weights and Measures Act 1963(a) (hereinafter referred to as "the Act") has consulted with organisations appearing to him to be representative of interests substantially affected by this Order and considered the representations made to him by such organisations with respect to the subject matter of this Order:

And whereas a draft of this Order has been laid before Parliament and approved by resolution of each House of Parliament pursuant to section 54(3) of the Act:

Now, therefore, the Secretary of State, in exercise of powers conferred by sections 9A(3) and 54 of the Act and now vested in him (b) and of all other powers enabling him in that behalf, hereby makes the following Order:—

1. This Order may be cited as the Weights and Measures Act 1963 (Amendment of Schedule 3) Order 1983 and shall come into operation on 1st December 1983.

2.—(1) There shall be added to the list of metric capacity measures lawful for use for trade which is set out as paragraph 2 of Part IV of Schedule 3 to the Act measures of 125 millilitres, 150 millilitres and 175 millilitres.

(2) There shall be added to Part VI of Schedule 3 to the Act the following paragraph:—

"3. No person shall use a capacity measure of 125 millilitres, 150 millilitres or 175 millilitres for trade except for the purposes of transactions in intoxicating liquor.".

Alexander Fletcher,
Parliamentary Under Secretary of State,
Department of Trade and Industry.

21st July 1983.

(a) 1963 c.31; section 9A was added and section 54(2) was amended so as to refer to section 9A by section 2 of the Weights and Measures &c. Act 1976 (c.77) and a substituted Schedule 3 was set out in Schedule 4 to the Units of Measurement Regulations 1980 (S.I. 1980/1070).
(b) S.I. 1970/1537.

EXPLANATORY NOTE

(This Note is not part of the Order.)

This Order amends Schedule 3 to the Weights and Measures Act 1963. It adds to the list of measures lawful for use for trade capacity measures of 125 ml, 150 ml and 175 ml, but restricts their use to transactions in intoxicating liquor.

STATUTORY INSTRUMENTS

1983 No. 1078

WEIGHTS AND MEASURES

The Weights and Measures Act 1963 (Wine and Grape Must) Order 1983

Laid before Parliament in draft

Made - - - - -	*21st July* 1983
Coming into Operation	*1st January* 1984

Whereas the Secretary of State pursuant to section 54(2) of the Weights and Measures Act 1963**(a)** (hereinafter referred to as "the Act") has consulted with organisations appearing to him to be representative of interests substantially affected by this Order and considered the representations made to him by such organisations with respect to the subject matter of this Order:

And whereas a draft of this Order has been laid before Parliament and approved by resolution of each House of Parliament pursuant to section 54(3) of the Act:

Now, therefore, the Secretary of State, in exercise of the powers conferred by section 21(2), (3) and (5) of the Act and now vested in him**(b)** and of all other powers enabling him in that behalf, hereby makes the following Order:—

1. This Order may be cited as the Weights and Measures Act 1963 (Wine and Grape Must) Order 1983 and shall come into operation on 1st January 1984.

2.—(1) This Order applies to the wine (whether or not imported) and grape must specified in paragraph 1(*a*) and (*b*) of Annex III to Council Directive No. 75/106/EEC**(c)**, that is to say:—

(*a*) wine of fresh grapes; fresh grape must with fermentation arrested by the addition of alcohol including wine made of unfermented grape juice blended with alcohol, except for wines included in subheadings 22.05 A and B and liqueur wines (subheading ex 22.05 C);

(*b*) grape must, in fermentation or with fermentation arrested otherwise than by the addition of alcohol (heading 22.04); and

---

(a) 1963 c. 31, section 58 and Part VI of Schedule 4 were amended by Schedule 3 to the Alcoholic Liquor Duties Act 1979.

(b) S.I. 1970/1537.

(c) OJ No. L 42, 15.2.1975, p. 1, as amended by Council Directive No. 79/1005/EEC (OJ No. L 308, 4.12.1979, p. 25).

(c) "yellow" wines entitled to use the following designations of origin: "Côtes du Jura", "Arbois", "L'Étoile" and "Château-Chalon".

(2) In this Article references to a heading or subheading are references to a heading or subheading of the Common Customs Tariff of the European conomic Community(a).

3. Subject to the following provisions of this Order, wine and grape must shall be pre-packed only if they are made up in one of the following quantities by volume, that is to say:—

10 cl, 25 cl, 37.5 cl, 50 cl, 75 cl,
1 L, 1.5 L, 2 L, 3 L and 5 L.

4. Until 31st December 1985, wine and grape must may be pre-packed if they are made up in the quantity by volume of 73 cl; and until 31st December 1988, they may be pre-packed if they are made up in one of the following quantities by volume, that is to say:—

35 cl, 70 cl and 1.25 L.

5. Subject to Article 6 below, yellow wine specified in Article 2(1)(c) above shall be pre-packed only if it is made up in the quantity by volume of 62 cl.

6. There shall be exempted from the requirements of Articles 3 and 5 above:—

(a) wine and grape must made up in quantities of less than 5 ml and more than 10 L;

(b) wine to which Article 2(1)(a) of the Weights and Measures (Sale of Wine) Order 1976(b) applies; and

(c) wine and grape must made up in securely closed containers before the date of coming into operation of this Order.

Alexander Fletcher,
Parliamentary Under Secretary of State,
Department of Trade and Industry.

21st July 1983.

(a) See Annex to Council Regulation (EEC) No. 950/68 (OJ No. L 172, 22.7.1968, p. 1) as last amended by Council Regulation (EEC) No. 3000/82 (OJ No. L 318, 15.11.1982, p. 1).

(b) S.I. 1976/1120.

EXPLANATORY NOTE

(This Note is not part of the Order.)

This Order implements the requirements of Council Directive No. 75/106/EEC, as amended by Council Directive No. 79/1005/EEC, in so far as it relates to certain pre-packed wines known as table wines and grape must. "Wine" in this Order means wine of fresh grapes excluding:—

(*a*) sparkling wines;

(*b*) liqueur (fortified) wine;

(*c*) vermouths;

(*d*) British wine (eg fruit or tonic wines).

The Order provides that, where wine is made up in a quantity of at least 5 millilitres and not more than 10 litres, it is to be pre-packed only in prescribed metric quantities.

The Order does not apply to wine sold on the premises at which it is to be consumed otherwise than pre-packed in a securely closed bottle, nor does it apply to wine and grape must made up in a securely closed container before the date of coming into operation of this Order.

STATUTORY INSTRUMENTS

1983 No. 1079

LANDLORD AND TENANT

The Assured Tenancies (Approved Bodies) (No. 6) Order 1983

Made - - - - -	*21st July* 1983
Laid before Parliament	*2nd August* 1983
Coming into Operation	*24th August* 1983

The Secretary of State for the Environment, as respects England, and the Secretary of State for Wales, as respects Wales, in exercise of the powers conferred upon them by sections 56(4) and 151 of the Housing Act 1980(a), and of all other powers enabling them in that behalf, hereby make the following order:—

1. This order may be cited as the Assured Tenancies (Approved Bodies) (No. 6) Order 1983 and shall come into operation on 24th August 1983.

2. The bodies set out in the Schedule to this order are hereby specified for the purposes of Part II of the Housing Act 1980.

(a) 1980 c. 51.

SCHEDULE

BODIES SPECIFIED FOR THE PURPOSES OF PART II
OF THE HOUSING ACT 1980

1. Geneens (Properties) Limited.
2. Hawkestone Park Homes Limited.
3. MEPC p.l.c.
4. Zonnia Investments Limited.

Signed by authority of the Secretary of State

George Young,
Parliamentary Under-Secretary of State,
Department of the Environment.

20th July 1983.

Signed by authority of the Secretary of State

John Stradling Thomas,
Minister of State for Wales.

21st July 1983.

EXPLANATORY NOTE

(This Note is not part of the Order.)

Section 56 of the Housing Act 1980 deals with assured tenancies. Such tenancies are subject to Part II of the Landlord and Tenant Act 1954 (c. 56) as modified by Schedule 5 to the 1980 Act if they would otherwise have been protected tenancies under the Rent Act 1977 (c. 42). They can only be granted by bodies approved under section 56 of the 1980 Act in respect of dwelling-houses erected after the passing of that Act.

This order approves four bodies for the purposes of section 56.

STATUTORY INSTRUMENTS

1983 No. 1080

MERCHANT SHIPPING

The Merchant Shipping (Light Dues) (Amendment No. 2) Regulations 1983

Made - - - - -	21*st July* 1983
Laid before Parliament	1*st August* 1983
Coming into Operation	22*nd August* 1983

The Secretary of State, in exercise of powers conferred on him by section 5(2) of the Merchant Shipping (Mercantile Marine Fund) Act 1898**(a)** and of all other powers enabling him in that behalf, hereby makes the following Regulations:—

1. These Regulations may be cited as the Merchant Shipping (Light Dues) (Amendment No. 2) Regulations 1983 and shall come into operation on 22nd August 1983.

2. Part I of the Schedule to the Merchant Shipping (Light Dues) Regulations 1981**(b)** shall be further amended as follows:—

in the last line of paragraph 3 of the Scale of Payments, "10 tons" shall be substituted for "20 tons".

Signed by authority of the Secretary of State

David Mitchell,
Parliamentary Under Secretary of State
Department of Transport.

21st July 1983.

(a) 1898 c. 44; section 5(2) was substituted by the Merchant Shipping Act 1979 (c. 39), section 36(2).

(b) S.I. 1981/354, amended by S.I. 1983/573.

EXPLANATORY NOTE

(This Note is not part of the Regulations.)

This Order corrects an error in the Merchant Shipping (Light Dues) (Amendment) Regulations 1983 (which came into operation on 1st June 1983) by altering the rate of light dues payable by visiting cruise ships from 72p per 20 tons per voyage to 72p per 10 tons per voyage. (Under the Merchant Shipping (Light Dues) Regulations 1981 the rate was 80p per 10 tons per voyage.)

STATUTORY INSTRUMENTS

1983 No. 1081

RACE RELATIONS

The Race Relations Code of Practice Order 1983

Made - - - - -	*22nd July* 1983
Laid before Parliament	*25th July* 1983
Coming into Operation	*1st April* 1984

Whereas—

(1) in pursuance of section 47(1) of the Race Relations Act 1976(a) (hereinafter referred to as "the Act") the Commission for Racial Equality (hereinafter referred to as "the Commission") may issue Codes of Practice containing such practical guidance as the Commission think fit for either or both of the following purposes, namely, the elimination of discrimination in the field of employment and the promotion of equality of opportunity in that field between persons of different racial groups;

(2) in pursuance of section 47(2) of the Act the Commission prepared and published in draft a Code of Practice for the said purposes and considered representations made to them about the draft;

(3) in pursuance of section 47(3) of the Act the Commission consulted with such organisations or associations of organisations representative of employers or of workers and such other organisations or bodies as appeared to the Commission to be appropriate;

(4) in pursuance of section 47(4) of the Act the Commission transmitted the draft Code of Practice to the Secretary of State who then laid the draft before both Houses of Parliament;

(5) in accordance with section 47(5) of the Act the draft Code of Practice lay before each House of Parliament for a period of forty days during which period neither House resolved against the taking of further proceedings on the draft;

(6) in pursuance of section 47(7) of the Act the Commission issued the Code of Practice in the form of the draft in July 1983;

Now, therefore, the Secretary of State, in exercise of the power conferred on him by section 47(7) of the Act, hereby orders as follows:–

(a) 1976 c. 74.

Citation and commencement

1. This Order may be cited as the Race Relations Code of Practice Order 1983 and shall come into operation on 1st April 1984.

Code of Practice

2. The Code of Practice for the elimination of racial discrimination and the promotion of equality of opportunity in employment, issued by the Commission under subsections (1) and (7) of section 47 of the Act in July 1983, shall come into effect on 1st April 1984.

Signed by order of the Secretary of State.

Alan Clark,
Joint Parliamentary Under Secretary of State,
Department of Employment.

22nd July 1983.

EXPLANATORY NOTE

(This Note is not part of the Order.)

This order appoints 1st April 1984 as the date upon which the Code of Practice for the elimination of racial discrimination and the promotion of equality of opportunity in employment, issued by the Commission for Racial Equality under section 47 of the Race Relations Act 1976 in July 1983, shall be brought into effect.

STATUTORY INSTRUMENTS

1983 No. 1086

ROAD TRAFFIC

The Traffic Signs General (Amendment) Directions 1983

Made - - - - -	*20th July* 1983
Coming into Operation	*25th August* 1983

The Secretary of State for Transport, the Secretary of State for Scotland and the Secretary of State for Wales, acting jointly in exercise of the powers conferred by section 55(1) of the Road Traffic Regulation Act 1967**(a)**, and now vested in them **(b)** and of all other enabling powers, hereby give the following directions:—

1. These Directions shall come into operation on 25th August 1983 and may be cited as the Traffic Signs General (Amendment) Directions 1983.

2. The Traffic Signs General Directions 1981**(c)** shall be amended by

(*a*) the insertion at the foot of the Table in Direction 11 after paragraph (4) of "557.1" in column 1 and "557.2, 557.3 or 557.4" in column 2; and

(*b*) the insertion in Direction 12 of "557.2, 557.3, 557.4" after "556.4".

Tom King,
Secretary of State for Transport.

15th July 1983.

George Younger,
Secretary of State for Scotland.

20th July 1983.

Nicholas Edwards,
Secretary of State for Wales.

18th July 1983.

(a) 1967 c. 76, as modified by paragraph 24(*b*) of Schedule 3 to S.I. 1970/1681.
(b) S.I. 1979/571 and 1981/238 (as respects the Secretary of State for Transport).
(c) S.I. 1981/859; the relevant amending instrument is S.I. 1982/1880.

EXPLANATORY NOTE

(This Note is not part of the Directions.)

These Directions amend the Traffic Signs General Directions 1981. They provide for the use of the traffic signs for road humps introduced by the Traffic Signs (Amendment) Regulations 1983. (S.I. 1983/1087).

STATUTORY INSTRUMENTS

1983 No. 1087

HIGHWAYS, ENGLAND AND WALES

The Highways (Road Humps) Regulations 1983

Made - - - -	*18th July* 1983
Laid before Parliament	*3rd August* 1983
Coming into Operation	*25th August* 1983

The Secretary of State for Transport as respects England and the Secretary of State for Wales as respects Wales, in exercise of the powers conferred by sections 90C(1) and 90D(1) and (2) of the Highways Act 1980(a), and after consultation with representative organisations in accordance with sections 90C(6) and 90D(3) of that Act, hereby make the following Regulations:—

Citation and Commencement

1. These Regulations may be cited as the Highways (Road Humps) Regulations 1983 and shall come into operation on 25th August 1983.

Interpretation

2.— (1) In these Regulations—

"the Act" means the Highways Act 1980;

"hours of darkness" means the time between half-an-hour after sunset and half-an-hour before sunrise;

"local bus route" means the route of local service within the meaning of section 2(2) of the Public Passenger Vehicles Act 1981(b) not being an excursion or tour within the meaning of that Act;

"principal road" means a highway which is a road for the time being classified as a principal road by virtue of section 12 of the Act (whether as falling within subsection (1), or as being so classified under subsection (3), of that section);

"road" has the same meaning as in the Road Traffic Act 1972(c);

"traffic sign" has the same meaning as it has in section 54 of the Road Traffic Regulation Act 1967(d).

(a) 1980 c. 66; sections 62 and 329 were amended by, and sections 90A to 90F were inserted by section 32 of, and Part I of Schedule 10 to, the Transport Act 1981 (c. 56).

(b) 1981 c. 14.
(c) 1972 c. 20.
(d) 1967 c. 76.

(2) For the purpose of these Regulations road humps in a highway shall be deemed to form part of a series where they are spaced not less than 50 metres nor more than 150 metres apart.

(3) For the purposes of these Regulations measurements to or from any point to or from a road hump shall be taken to or from that edge of the hump, as shown in the Schedule, which is nearest to the point and for the purposes of Regulations 4 and 5 and this paragraph—

> *(a)* measurements to or from a horizontal bend shall be taken to or from that part of the bend which is nearest to the hump;

> *(b)* measurements to or from a road junction shall be taken to or from the point nearest the hump on an imaginary line drawn across the mouth of the junction; and

> *(c)* a horizontal bend begins and ends where a vehicle would start and finish the change of direction specified in those Regulations.

(4) A reference in these Regulations to a numbered Regulation is a reference to the Regulation bearing that number in these Regulations and a reference to the Schedule is a reference to the Schedule to these Regulations, except where the context otherwise requires.

(5) In these Regulations references to any enactment shall be construed as references to that enactment as amended by or under any subsequent enactment.

Consultation about road hump proposals

3. Where the Secretary of State or a local highway authority proposes to construct a road hump under section 90A or 90B of the Act, he or they shall, as well as consulting the chief officer of police as required by section 90C(1) of the Act, also consult the following persons or bodies:—

> *(a)* where the proposal relates to a highway outside Greater London, the District Council in whose district the highway is situated;

> *(b)* where the proposal relates to a highway on which there is a local bus route, the operator or operators of the service or services on that route;

> *(c)* in all cases, one or more organisations representing persons who use the highway to which the proposal relates, or representing persons who are otherwise likely to be affected by the road hump unless it appears to the authority or the Secretary of State that there are no such organisations.

Highways and circumstances in which road humps may be constructed

4. A road hump shall be constructed only—

> *(a)* in a highway which is not a special road, a trunk road or a principal road, and

> *(b)* in any part of such highway—

>> (i) where to afford illumination throughout the hours of darkness there is a system of street lighting furnished by at least three lamps

lit by electricity and placed not more than 38 metres apart or external lighting specially provided for the hump or a street lamp within 5 metres of the hump, and

(ii) where on each road affording access for vehicular traffic to the road hump or, in the case of a series of road humps, the first in the series to be met by such traffic, there is a feature of one or more of the following descriptions—

(a) a horizontal bend or a road junction at which such traffic would change its direction by not less than 70 degrees within an inner kerb radius of not more than 25 metres, or

(b) a traffic sign facing away from the road hump conveying to vehicular traffic the prohibition specified in diagram 616, 617 or 619 in Part II of Schedule 1 to the Traffic Signs Regulations 1981(a), or

(c) the end of a carriageway at the closed end of a cul-de-sac, or

(d) a traffic sign conveying to vehicular traffic the prohibition specified in diagram 1002.1 in the said part of the said Schedule to those Regulations,

any such feature being, in the case of (a), (b) or (c) within 30 metres and, in the case of (d) within 60 metres of the hump.

Nature, dimensions, location and spacing of road humps

5.— (1) A road hump constructed or maintained in a highway shall be so constructed and maintained that—

(a) it extends across the whole width of the carriageway of the highway and its cross-section conforms to the pattern and measurements shown in the Schedule, a measurement being deemed to conform if it is, in the case of a vertical measurement, no more than 10 per cent greater or no more than 15 per cent less, and, in the case of a horizontal measurement, no more than 5 per cent, greater or less, than the corresponding measurement so shown;

(b) no part of it is within 15 metres of a road junction, or a horizontal bend with an inner kerb radius of less than 50 metres at which vehicular traffic would change its direction by more than 45 degrees;

(c) it is at right angles to an imaginary line along the centre of the carriageway of the highway in which it is constructed;

(d) it is not within 500 metres of another road hump in that highway unless it forms part of a series with that other road hump; and

(e) where it is constructed or maintained in a carriageway with a gradient of more than 10 per cent, it is not within 20 metres of the top of that part of the carriageway which has that gradient and the distance between road humps on the gradient is not greater than 70 metres.

(2) A road hump shall not be constructed or maintained in a highway—

(a) within the limits of a pedestrian crossing provided under section 23 of

(a) S.I. 1981/859; there is no relevant amending instrument.

the Road Traffic Regulation Act 1967 or within 50 metres of the limits of any such crossing;

(b) on a railway level crossing or within 20 metres of the nearest rail forming part of the railway track at any such crossing;

(c) within 20 metres of any point on an imaginary line running at right angles across the carriageway from a bus stop sign, or within 10 metres of a bus stop road marking;

(d) under or within 25 metres of a structure over the carriageway of the highway any part of which is 6·5 metres or less above the surface of the carriageway;

(e) where it would form part of a series extending over more than a kilometre.

(3) In this Regulation "bus stop sign" means a traffic sign indicating a stopping place for stage or scheduled express carriages prescribed, or treated as if prescribed by the Traffic Signs Regulations 1981 and "bus stop road marking" means a traffic sign indicating to vehicular traffic the limits of such a stopping place so prescribed or treated as if prescribed.

(4) In the foregoing paragraph "scheduled express carriage" has the same meaning as in the Traffic Signs Regulations 1981.

Placing of traffic signs

6. Where a road hump or a series of road humps is constructed in a highway the highway authority for the highway shall forthwith cause or permit to be placed in accordance with the Traffic Signs Regulations and General Directions 1981(a)—

(a) the traffic sign shown in diagram 557.1, in combination with the traffic sign shown in diagram 557.2, 557.3 or 557.4 in Schedule 1 to those Regulations in such positions as the authority may consider requisite for the purpose of securing that adequate warning of the presence of a road hump or a series of road humps is given to persons using the highway; and

(b) on the road hump or, in the case of a series of road humps, on each hump in the series, the traffic sign shown in diagram 1060 in Schedule 2 to those Reguations.

Tom King,
Secretary of State for Transport.

15th July 1983.

Nicholas Edwards,
Secretary of State for Wales.

18 July 1983.

(a) S.I. 1981/859; the relevant amending instruments are S.I. 1982/1879, 1880, 1983/1086, 1088.

SCHEDULE

CROSS SECTION AND HUMP DIMENSIONS

Direction of Traffic

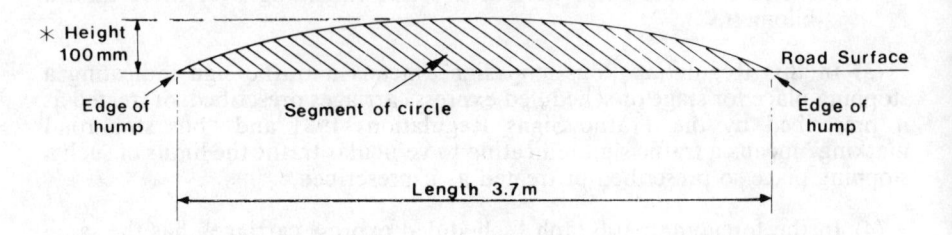

* Height 100 mm

Road Surface

Edge of hump

Segment of circle

Edge of hump

Length 3.7m

* Where the point on a highway at which the road hump is constructed
or maintained is on a local bus route at the time its construction is
completed, substitute 75mm for 100mm.

EXPLANATORY NOTE
(This Note is not part of the Regulations.)

These Regulations prescribe requirements for—

(a) consultation about proposals for the construction of road humps by
the Secretary of State or a local highway authority (Regulation 3); and

(b) the construction and maintenance of road humps including—

(i) the highways and circumstances in which they may be constructed (Regulation 4),

(ii) the nature, dimensions, location, and spacing of the humps
(Regulation 5), and

(iii) the placing of traffic signs (Regulation 6).

STATUTORY INSTRUMENTS

1983 No. 1088

ROAD TRAFFIC

The Traffic Signs (Amendment) Regulations 1983

Made - - - -	*20th July* 1983
Laid before Parliament	*3rd August* 1983
Coming into Operation	*25th August* 1983

The Secretary of State for Transport, the Secretary of State for Scotland and the Secretary of State for Wales, acting jointly in exercise of their powers under section 54(1) and (2) of the Road Traffic Regulation Act 1967(a), and now vested in them (b) and of all other enabling powers, and after consultation with representative organisations in accordance with the provisions of section 107(2) of that Act, hereby make the following Regulations:—

1. These Regulations shall come into operation on 25th August 1983 and may be cited as the Traffic Signs (Amendment) Regulations 1983.

2. The Traffic Signs Regulations 1981(c) shall be amended in accordance with the following provisions of these Regulations.

3. In Regulation 12 (Permitted variants)—

(a) in paragraph (1)(e) after "556.4," there shall be inserted "557.2, 557.3"; and

(b) in paragraph (1)(h) after "556.4" and after "553" in the second place where it appears, there shall be inserted "557.3, 557.4".

4. In Regulation 15 (Illumination of signs by steady lighting), in paragraph (5) after the word "diagrams" there shall be inserted "557.1".

5. In Regulation 25 (Use on road markings of reflecting material and studs with reflectors) after paragraph (2) there shall be inserted the following paragraph:—

"(2A) The road markings shown in diagram 1060 including the permitted variants shall be illuminated with reflecting material.".

(a) 1967 c.76, as modified by paragraph 24(b) of Schedule 3 to S.I. 1970/1681.
(b) S.I. 1979/571 and 1981/238 (as respects the Secretary of State for Transport).
(c) S.I. 1981/859; the relevant amending instrument is S.I. 1982/1879.

6. In Part I (Warning signs) of Schedule 1 there shall be inserted after diagram 557 the following diagrams:—

(Red triangle; black symbol on a white background)
Road Hump Ahead
(See Direction 11)
557.1

(Black on White)
Plate for use with sign in
diagram 557.1
(See Direction 12)
557.2

(Black on White)
Plate for use with sign in
diagram 557.1
(See Direction 12)
557.3

(Black on White)
Plate for use with sign in
diagram 557.1
Permitted variant: The
numerals shall be varied
to accord with the circumstances, distances being
expressed in yards to the nearest 5 yards.
(See Direction 12)
557.4

7. In Schedule 2 (Markings on the road) there shall be added after diagram 1059 the following diagram:—

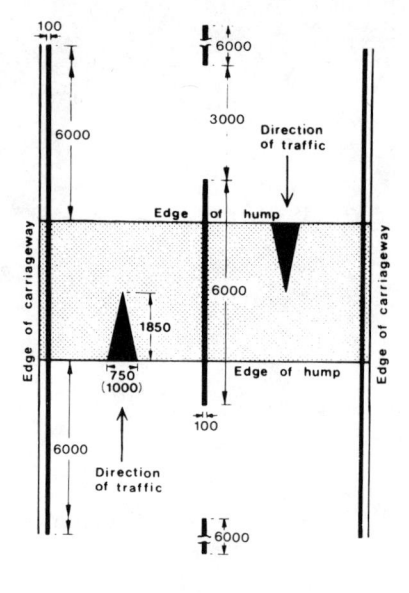

(White)

To indicate to vehicular traffic
the presence of a road hump.

Permitted variants: the longitudinal line adjacent to the edge of
the carriageway may be omitted when a longitudinal line to
Diagram 1017 or 1018 is placed in the position of that line.
Where more than one lane is open to traffic in the same
direction, the longitudinal broken line shall be placed between
each lane, and the triangular marking shall be placed on each
lane. Where, on any carriageway, traffic is permitted to travel in
one direction only, the triangular marking or markings shall be
placed only on that part of the road hump which faces the
oncoming traffic.

1060

15th July 1983.

Tom King,
Secretary of State for Transport.

20th July 1983.

George Younger,
Secretary of State for Scotland.

18th July 1983.

Nicholas Edwards,
Secretary of State for Wales.

EXPLANATORY NOTE

(This Note is not part of the Regulations.)

These Regulations amend the Traffic Signs Regulations 1981. They introduce for road humps constructed in highways new signs to be placed as required by Regulation 6 of the Highways (Road Humps) Regulations 1983 (S.I. 1983/1087).

STATUTORY INSTRUMENTS

1983 No. 1089 (C. 31)

HIGHWAYS, ENGLAND AND WALES

The Transport Act 1981 (Commencement No. 11) Order 1983

Made -   -   -   -   15*th July* 1983

The Secretary of State for Transport, in exercise of the powers conferred by sections 32(2) and 40(4) of the Transport Act 1981(**a**), and of all other enabling powers, hereby makes the following Order:—

1. This Order may be cited as the Transport Act 1981 (Commencement No. 11) Order 1983.

2. 25th August 1983 is appointed for the purpose of the coming into force of section 32 of, and Schedule 10 to, the Transport Act 1981 and the repeal of section 17 of the Road Traffic Act 1974(**b**) in Part III of Schedule 12 to the said Act of 1981, in so far as those provisions apply to England and Wales.

Tom King,
Secretary of State for Transport.

15th July 1983.

(**a**) 1981 c. 56.   (**b**) 1974 c. 50.

EXPLANATORY NOTE

(This Note is not part of the Order.)

This Order appoints 25th August 1983 for the purpose of the coming into force of section 32 of, and Schedule 10 to, the Transport Act 1981 (which provide for the construction, maintenance and removal of road humps in highways) and the repeal of section 17 of the Road Traffic Act 1974 (which provides for the experimental introduction of road humps for controlling vehicle speeds), in so far as applicable to England and Wales.

NOTE OF EARLIER COMMENCEMENT ORDERS

(This Note is not part of the Order.)

The following provisions of the Transport Act 1981 have been brought into force by commencement orders made before the date of this Order:—

Provision	Date of Commencement	S.I. No.
S. 35 (partially) and sch. 12 (partially)	12.10.81	1981/1331
Ss. 21, 22, 26 and 27, and s. 30 (partially) and sch. 9 (partially)	1.12.81	1981/1617
S. 23 (partially) and s. 30(1) (partially)	29.3.82	1982/300
S. 35 (remainder) and Part III of sch. 12 (partially)	1.4.82	1982/310
S. 23 (partially) and s. 30(1) (partially)	1.10.82	1982/866
Ss. 19, 20, sch. 7, sch. 9, paragraphs 2, 4, 5, 6, 7, 8, 9, 10, 11, 13 and 15, sch. 12, Part III, the items relating to ss. 93(3) and (5) and 177(2) of the Road Traffic Act 1972 and s. 30(1) and (2) so far as it relates to the above provisions	1.11.82	1982/1451
Sch. 12, paragraph 12 (partially)	20.12.82	1982/1803
S. 28 and 30(1) (partially)	31.1.83	1982/1341
S. 23 (remainder) and s. 30(1) (partially)	1.2.83	1982/866
Ss. 24, 25 and 30(1) (partially), sch. 9, paragraphs 1, 3, 12 (remainder), 17, 18 (remainder), 19, 20, 21, 23, 24 and 25 and sch. 12, the repeals relating to sections 89, 90 and 189 of, and paragraph 1 of Part V of sch. 4 to, the Road Traffic Act 1972	6.5.83	1983/576
Sch. 6, paragraph 10	2.8.83	1983/930

STATUTORY INSTRUMENTS

1983 No. 1090

NATIONAL HEALTH SERVICE, ENGLAND AND WALES

The National Health Service (Constitution of District Health Authorities) Amendment (No. 2) Order 1983

Made - - - - -	*22nd July* 1983
Laid before Parliament	*25th July* 1983
Coming into Operation	*15th August* 1983

The Secretary of State for Social Services, as respects England, and the Secretary of State for Wales, as respects Wales, in exercise of powers conferred upon them by section 8(1) and (1A) of the National Health Service Act 1977(a) and of all other powers enabling them in that behalf hereby make the following Order:—

Citation and commencement

1. This Order may be cited as the National Health Service (Constitution of District Health Authorities) Amendment (No. 2) Order 1983 and shall come into operation on 15th August 1983.

Amendment of the National Health Service (Constitution of District Health Authorities) Order 1981

2.—(1) The National Health Service (Constitution of District Health Authorities) Order 1981(b) shall be amended in accordance with the following provisions of this Article.

(2) In Article 5 (membership of authorities), paragraph (5) shall be omitted.

(3) In Schedule 2 (District Health Authorities in England)—

(*a*) in Part 1 (authorities in Northern Region), in column (2) (name of District Health Authority), for the name "Newcastle Health Authority (Teaching)" there shall be substituted the name "Newcastle Health Authority";

(a) 1977 c. 49; section 8(1) was amended by the Health Service Act 1980 (c. 53), Schedule 1, Part I, paragraph 28; section 8(1A) was amended by the Health and Social Services and Social Security Adjudications Act 1983 (c. 41), Schedule 10, Part I.

(b) S.I. 1981/1838, to which there are no amendments relevant to this Order.

(b) in Part 3 (authorities in Trent Region), in column (2)—

(i) for the name "Leicestershire Health Authority (Teaching)" there shall be substituted the words "Leicestershire Health Authority",

(ii) for the name "Sheffield Health Authority (Teaching)" there shall be substituted the name "Sheffield Health Authority";

(c) in Part 13 (authorities in Mersey Region), in column (2), for the name "Liverpool Health Authority (Teaching)" there shall be substituted the name "Liverpool Health Authority";

(d) in Part 14 (authorities in North Western Region), in column (2), for the name "Salford Health Authority (Teaching)" there shall be substituted the name "Salford Health Authority";

(e) in Parts 1, 3, 13 and 14, in the entries appropriate to the authorities named in sub-paragraphs (a) to (d) above, in column (7) (number of other members appointed by the Regional Health Authority), for the figure "9" there shall be substituted the figure "11";

(f) column (10) (additional members of authorities the names of which include the word "Teaching") shall be omitted.

(4) In Schedule 3 (District Health Authorities in Wales)—

(a) in column (2) (name of District Health Authority), for the name "South Glamorgan Health Authority (Teaching)" there shall be substituted the name "South Glamorgan Health Authority";

(b) in the entry appropriate to that authority, in column (7) (number of other members appointed by the Secretary of State), for the figure "9" there shall be substituted the figure "11";

(c) column (10) (additional members of authorities the names of which include the word "Teaching") shall be omitted.

Transitional provisions

3. A change of name under this Order shall not—

(*a*) affect any right or obligation of any Authority or person;

(*b*) be taken as invalidating any instrument (whether made before or after the day on which this Order comes into operation) which refers to the relevant Authority by the previous name,

but the new name shall be substituted for the previous name in all documents relating to the relevant Authority and in all instruments which refer to the previous name.

Signed by authority of the Secretary of State for Social Services

K. Clarke,
Minister of State,
Department of Health and Social Security.

22nd July 1983.

Signed by authority of the Secretary of State for Wales

John Stradling Thomas,
Minister of State for Wales.

22nd July 1983.

EXPLANATORY NOTE

(This Note is not part of the Order.)

This Order amends the National Health Service (Constitution of District Health Authorities) Order 1981. The changes made by the Order are in consequence of the repeal by Health and Social Services and Social Security Adjudications Act 1983 of provisions in the National Health Service Act 1977 concerning designation and membership of teaching authorities. Accordingly, any District Health Authority the name of which includes the designation "Teaching" is re-named so as to omit that designation. In consequence of the repeal, provision for the number of additional members to be appointed to Teaching authorities is amended in such a way as to provide that the overall number of members of the newly-named authorities remains the same.

STATUTORY INSTRUMENTS

1983 No. 1091

NATIONAL HEALTH SERVICE, ENGLAND AND WALES

The National Health Service (Constitution of District Health Authorities) (Transitory Provision) Regulations 1983

Made - - - -	*22nd July* 1983
Laid before Parliament	*25th July* 1983
Coming into Operation	*15th August* 1983

The Secretary of State for Social Services, as respects England, and the Secretary of State for Wales, as respects Wales, in exercise of the powers conferred upon them by paragraph 12 of Schedule 5 to the National Health Service Act 1977(**a**) and of all other powers enabling them in that behalf, hereby make the following regulations:—

Citation and commencement

1. These regulations may be cited as the National Health Service (Constitution of District Health Authorities) (Transitory Provision) Regulations 1983 and shall come into operation on 15th August 1983.

Transitory provision

2. An appointment of a member of an Authority, pursuant to the amendment effected by Article 2(3)(*e*) or, as the case may be, (4)(*b*) of the National Health Service (Constitution of District Health Authorities) Amendment (No. 2) Order 1983(**b**) (amendments made to principal Order in consequence of the repeal by the Health and Social Services and Social Security Adjudications Act 1983(**c**) of provisions relating to the designation of teaching authorities), shall not be made until a member of that Authority appointed, before the coming into operation of that Order, pursuant to Article 5(5) of the National Health Service (Constitution of District Health Authorities) Order 1981(**d**), ceases to be a member of that Authority.

Signed by authority of the Secretary of State for Social Services.

K. Clarke,
Minister of State,
Department of Health and Social Security.

22nd July 1983.

(**a**) 1977 c. 49.   (**b**) S.I. 1983/1090.   (**c**) 1983 c. 41.
(**d**) S.I. 1981/1838, to which there are no amendments relevant to these regulations.

Signed by authority of the Secretary of State for Wales.

John Stradling Thomas,
Minister of State for Wales.

22nd July 1983.

EXPLANATORY NOTE

(This Note is not part of the Regulations.)

These regulations are made in consequence of amendments made by the National Health Service (Constitution of District Health Authorities) Amendment (No. 2) Order 1983 to the National Health Service (Constitution of District Health Authorities) Order 1981 whereby the number of members of district health authorities, the name of which formerly included the designation "teaching", appointed by Regional Health Authorities is increased by the same number as that of the additional members appointed to such Authorities. The regulations make transitory provision so that an appointment is not to be so made by a Regional Health Authority unless a vacancy arises amongst those additional members.

STATUTORY INSTRUMENTS

1983 No. 1094

SOCIAL SECURITY

The Social Security (Industrial Injuries) (Prescribed Diseases) Amendment (No. 2) Regulations 1983

Made - - - -	21st July 1983
Laid before Parliament	27th July 1983
Coming into Operation	3rd October 1983

The Secretary of State for Social Services, in exercise of the powers conferred upon him by sections 76, 77 and 113 of the Social Security Act 1975 (a) and of all other powers enabling him in that behalf, after reference to the Industrial Injuries Advisory Council, hereby makes the following regulations:—

Citation, commencement and interpretation

1. These regulations, which may be cited as the Social Security (Industrial Injuries) (Prescribed Diseases) Amendment (No. 2) Regulations 1983, shall be read as one with the Social Security (Industrial Injuries) (Prescribed Diseases) Regulations 1980 (b) (hereinafter referred to as "the principal regulations"), and shall come into operation on 3rd October 1983.

Amendment of regulation 1 of the principal regulations

2. In regulation 1(2) of the principal regulations (interpretation)—

(a) in the definition of "diffuse mesothelioma" for the words "numbered 44" there shall be substituted the words "numbered D3";

(b) the definition of "farmer's lung" shall be omitted;

(c) in the definition of "occupational asthma" for the words "numbered 53" there shall be substituted the words "numbered D7";

(d) in the definition of "occupational deafness" for the words "numbered 48" there shall be substituted the words "numbered A10";

(e) the definition of "pneumoconiosis" shall be omitted;

(f) in the definition of "tuberculosis" for the words "numbered 38" there shall be substituted the words "numbered B5".

Amendment of regulation 2 of the principal regulations

3.—(1) In regulation 2 of the principal regulations (prescription of diseases and injuries and occupations for which they are prescribed)—

(a) in paragraph (a) for the words "paragraph (d)" there shall be substituted the words "paragraphs (b) and (d)" and for the words "regulation 56(2) and (4)" there shall be substituted the words "regulation 56(2), (3) and (4)";

(b) paragraph (c) shall be omitted;

(a) 1975 c.14.
(b) S.I. 1980/377; the relevant amending instruments are S.I. 1980/1493, 1982/249, 1983/185.

(c) for paragraph *(d)* there shall be substituted—

"*(d)* occupational deafness is prescribed in relation to all persons who have been employed in employed earner's employment—

(i) at any time on or after 5th July 1948; and

(ii) for a period or periods (whether before or after 5th July 1948) amounting in the aggregate to not less than 10 years

in one or more of the occupations set out in the second column of paragraph A10 of Part I of Schedule 1 to these regulations and in the case of a person who during such period as is specified above has been concurrently employed in two or more of the occupations described in sub-paragraphs *(a)*, *(b)*, *(d)*, *(e)*, *(f)*, *(g)* and *(h)* of the said paragraph A10 those occupations shall be treated as a single occupation for the purposes of determining whether that person has been employed wholly or mainly in work described in those sub-paragraphs."

(2) For Part I of Schedule 1 to the principal regulations there shall be substituted the Part set out in Schedule 1 to these regulations.

Amendment of regulation 4 of the principal regulations

4. Regulation 4 of the principal regulations (presumption that a disease is due to the nature of employment) shall be amended as follows—

(a) in paragraph (1) for the words "numbered 38, 41, 42 and 48" there shall be substituted the words "numbered A10, B5, D1, D2, D4 and D5";

(b) in paragraph (2) for the words "paragraph 38" there shall be substituted the words "paragraph B5";

(c) in paragraph (4) for the words "regulation 2*(c)*" there shall be substituted the words "paragraph D2 of Part I of Schedule 1 hereto".

Amendment of regulations 22 and 25 of the principal regulations

5. In regulation 22 and regulation 25(2) of the principal regulations for the words "numbered 17, 36, 37*(b)*, 40, 43, 44 and 53" there shall be substituted the words "numbered B6, C15, C17, C18, C22*(b)*, D3 and D7".

Amendment of regulation 26 of the principal regulations

6. In regulation 26 of the principal regulations (power to dispense with reference for medical report) for the words "numbered 17, 36, 37*(b)*, 40 and 43" there shall be substituted the words "numbered B6, C15, C17, C18 and C22*(b)*".

Amendment of regulation 33 of the principal regulations

7. In regulation 33 of the principal regulations (constitution and procedure of a medical board and medical appeal tribunal) for the words "numbered 17, 36, 37*(b)*, 40, 43, 44 and 53" there shall be substituted the words "numbered B6, C15, C17, C18, C22*(b)*, D3 and D7".

Amendment of regulation 40 of the principal regulations

8. Regulation 40 of the principal regulations (time for claiming benefit in respect of occupational deafness) shall be amended as follows—

(a) in paragraph (1) after the words "occupational deafness" there shall be inserted the words "except in relation to a claim for sickness benefit payable by virtue of section 50A";

(b) for paragraphs (2) to (7) there shall be substituted the following paragraph—

"(2) Subject to regulation 41(1)(c), disablement benefit, or sickness benefit payable by virtue of section 50A of the Act, shall not be paid in pursuance of a claim in respect of occupational deafness which is made later than 5 years after the latest date, before the date of the claim, on which the claimant worked in an occupation prescribed in relation to occupational deafness unless—

(a) the claimant has been employed in one or more of the occupations so prescribed for a period or periods amounting in aggregate to not less than 10 years, and

(b) that period or the last of those periods ended on or after 8th October 1977, and

(c) the claim is made within the period of one year beginning on 3rd October 1983, and

(d) either—

(i) the claimant, not being a person to whom regulation 41(1)(c) applies, has not within the period of 3 years before the claim was made previously made a claim which was disallowed because he was not suffering from occupational deafness, or

(ii) where a previous claim was made by him, a medical board or a medical appeal tribunal have not within the period of 3 years before the claim was made reassessed the extent of his disablement at less than 20 per cent."

Amendment of regulation 41 of the principal regulations

9. Regulation 41 of the principal regulations (further claims in respect of occupational deafness) shall be amended as follows—

(a) in paragraph (1) for the words "paragraph 48" there shall be substituted the words "paragraph A10" and in sub-paragraph (a) for the words "the disallowed claim" there shall be substituted the words "a claim which was disallowed because the claimant was not suffering from occupational deafness";

(b) for sub-paragraphs (b) and (c) of paragraph (1) there shall be substituted—

"(b) it is a claim made after the expiration of 3 years from the date of a reassessment by a medical board or medical appeal tribunal of the extent of the claimant's disablement at less than 20 per cent; or

(c) if the claimant would otherwise be precluded by regulation 40(2) from making a further claim after the expiration of 3 years from the date of the disallowed claim or from the date of a reassessment by a medical board or a medical appeal tribunal of the extent of his disablement at less than 20 per cent, as the case may be, it is the first claim made since that date and within 5 years from the latest date, before the date of the claim, on which he worked in any occupation specified in column 2 of paragraph A10 of Part I of Schedule 1 hereto.";

(c) in paragraph (2) for the words from "was not" to the end there shall be substituted the words "is not suffering from occupational deafness".

Revocation of regulation 42 of the principal regulations

10. Regulation 42 of the principal regulations (effect of presbyacusis on assessment) is hereby revoked.

Substitution of regulation 43 of the principal regulations

11. For regulation 43 of the principal regulations (Period to be covered by assessment of disablement in respect of occupational deafness) there shall be substituted the following regulation—

"43. Subject to the proviso to section 57(6) (cessation of pension on death of beneficiary)—

(a) every initial assessment of the extent of a claimant's disablement in respect of occupational deafness shall be a provisional assessment and the period to be taken into account by such an assessment shall be a period of 5 years;

(b) the period to be taken into account by any subsequent reassessment of the extent of the claimant's disablement in respect of occupational deafness, if not limited by reference to the claimant's life, shall not be less than 5 years."

Amendment of regulation 44 of the principal regulations

12. Regulation 44 of the principal regulations (Review of assessment for unforeseen aggravation in respect of occupational deafness) shall be renumbered as paragraph (1) of that regulation and after that provision as so renumbered there shall be inserted the following paragraph—

"(2) The provisions of section 110(2) (review of assessment in a case of unforeseen aggravation) shall not apply to an assessment of the extent of disablement in respect of occupational deafness which is less than 20 per cent."

Reassessment of disablement

13. After regulation 46 there shall be inserted the following regulation—

"Cases in which reassessment of disablement in respect of occupational deafness is final

46A. Where in any case the extent of disablement in respect of occupational deafness has been provisionally assessed at 20 per cent or more and on any reassessment the extent of disablement in respect of occupational deafness is assessed at less than 20 per cent that assessment shall be final."

Substitution of regulation 47 of the principal regulations

14. For regulation 47 of the principal regulations (Lower and upper limits of assessment in respect of occupational deafness) there shall be substituted the following regulation—

"Assessment of extent of disablement and rate of disablement benefit payable in respect of occupational deafness

47.—(1) Subject to the provisions of Schedule 8 and regulations made thereunder and the following provisions of this regulation, the first assessment of the extent of disablement in respect of occupational deafness made in pursuance of a claim made before 3rd September 1979 by a person to whom disablement benefit in respect of occupational deafness is payable for a period before 3rd September 1979 shall be the percentage calculated by applying the formula set out in Part III of Schedule 2A hereto to the percentages specified in column 2 of Part I of that Schedule opposite the appropriate amount of hearing loss in the better ear and the worse ear respectively specified in column 1 of that Schedule, being the total hearing loss due to all causes, measured in each case by pure tone audiometry over the 1, 2 and 3 kHz frequencies.

(2) Except in any case to which paragraph (1) applies and subject to the provisions of Schedule 8 and regulations made thereunder and the following provisions of this regulation, the extent of disablement in respect of occupational deafness shall be assessed at the percentage calculated by applying the formula set out in Part III of Schedule 2A hereto to the percentages specified in column 2 of Part II of that Schedule opposite the appropriate amount of hearing loss in the better ear and the worse ear respectively specified in column 1 of that Schedule, being the total hearing loss due to all causes, measured in each case by pure tone audiometry over the 1, 2 and 3 kHz frequencies.

(3) In this regulation and in Schedule 2A hereto "better ear" means that ear in which the claimant's hearing loss due to all causes is the less and "worse ear" means that ear in which the claimant's hearing loss due to all causes is the more.

(4) The extent of disablement in respect of occupational deafness may be subject to such increase or reduction of the degree of disablement as may be reasonable in the circumstances of the case where, having regard to the provisions of Schedule 8 and to regulations made thereunder, that degree of disablement does not provide a reasonable assessment of the extent of disability resulting from the relevant loss of faculty.

(5) Where on reassessment of the extent of disability in respect of occupational deafness the sensorineural hearing loss is less than 50dB in each ear, being due in the case of at least one ear to occupational noise, the extent of disablement shall be assessed at less than 20 per cent.

(6) Where the extent of disablement is reassessed at less than 20 per cent disablement benefit shall not be payable.

(7) In the case of a person to whom disablement benefit by reason of occupational deafness was payable in respect of a period before 3rd September 1979—

(a) if no assessment of the extent of his disability has been made, reviewed or varied on or after that date, the rate of any disablement benefit payable to him shall be the rate payable for the degree of disablement assessed in accordance with paragraph (1), but

(b) if such an assessment has been made, reviewed or varied in respect of a period commencing on or after that date and before 3rd October 1983, the rate of any disablement benefit payable to him shall be either—

(i) the rate which would be payable if an assessment were made in accordance with paragraph (2), or

(ii) the rate which was payable immediately before the first occasion on which such review or variation took place,

whichever is the more favourable to him.

(8) Where in the case of a person to whom disablement benefit by reason of occupational deafness was payable in respect of a period before 3rd September 1979 the extent of his disability is reassessed and the period taken into account on reassessment begins on or after 3rd October 1983 and—

  (a) immediately before that date, by virtue of paragraph (7) the rate at which disablement benefit was payable to him was higher than the rate which would otherwise have been payable, or

  (b) the reassessment is the first reassessment for a period commencing after 3rd September 1979,

the rate of disablement benefit payable to him shall be whichever of the rates specified in paragraph (9) is applicable.

(9) The rate of disablement benefit payable in the case of a person to whom paragraph (8) applies shall be—

  (a) if the current rate appropriate to the extent of his disability as reassessed is the same as or more than the rate at which disablement benefit was payable immediately before the beginning of the period taken into account on reassessment, the current rate, or

  (b) if the current rate is less than the rate at which disablement benefit was payable immediately before the beginning of the period taken into account on reassessment, the lower of the following rates—

    (i) the rate at which benefit would have been payable if the reassessment of the extent of his disability had been made in accordance with paragraph (1), or

    (ii) the rate at which benefit was payable immediately before the beginning of the period taken into account on reassessment."

Amendment of regulation 48A of the principal regulations

15. Regulation 48A of the principal regulations (Time for claiming benefit in respect of occupational asthma) shall be amended as follows—

  (a) in paragraph (1), after the words "disablement benefit" there shall be inserted the words "and sickness benefit payable by virtue of section 50A" and after the word "after" there shall be inserted the words "the latest date, before the date of the claim, on which" and for the words "ceased to be employed" there shall be substituted the word "worked";

  (b) in paragraph (4) for the words "he ceased to be employed" there shall be substituted the words "the latest date on which he worked";

  (c) in paragraph (5) the word "ceased" shall be omitted and for the words "to be employed" there shall be substituted the words "had not worked".

Amendment of regulation 49 of the principal regulations

16. In regulation 49(2) of the principal regulations (Constitution of pneumoconiosis medical panels and boards) for the words "numbered 17, 36, 37(b), 40, 43, 44 and 53" there shall be substituted the words "B6, C15, C17, C18, C22(b), D3 and D7".

Amendment of regulation 56 of the principal regulations

17.—(1) In regulation 56 of the principal regulations (transitional provisions)—

  (a) in paragraph (1), at the beginning, there shall be inserted the words

"Subject to paragraph (2)" and the words from "in relation to byssinosis" onwards shall be omitted;

(b) after paragraph (1) there shall be inserted the following paragraph—

"(1A) Where a disease set out in the first column of Schedule 3 hereto was prescribed in relation to any person by regulations which came into operation on a date earlier than the date set against that disease in the second column of that Schedule, the "relevant date" in relation to such disease is such earlier date on which the disease was prescribed in relation to the person in question.";

(c) after paragraph (2) there shall be inserted the following paragraph—

"(2A) The "relevant date" in relation to byssinosis—

(a) in the case of a person employed in an occupation involving work in any room in which the weaving of cotton or flax or any other process which takes place between, or at the same time as, the winding or beaming and weaving of cotton or flax is carried on in a factory in which any or all of those processes are carried on is 3rd October 1983;

(b) in any other case, is 6th April 1979 except that where the disease was prescribed in relation to any person by regulations which came into operation on a date earlier than 6th April 1979 the relevant date is that earlier date.";

(d) in paragraph 3(b) after the words "regulation 2(c)" there shall be inserted the words "of these regulations in force immediately before 3rd October 1983.";

(e) for paragraph (4) there shall be substituted the following paragraph—

"(4) Notwithstanding that a person does not satisfy paragraph (2) infection by leptospira is prescribed in relation to any person if he is or has been either incapable of work or suffering from a loss of faculty as a result of infection by *Leptospira icterohaemorrhagiae* in the case of a person employed in employed earner's employment before 7th January 1980 in any occupation involving work in places which are, or are liable to be, infested by rats or infection by *Leptospira canicola* in the case of a person so employed in any occupation involving work at dog kennels or the care or handling of dogs.".

(2) For Schedule 3 to the principal regulations there shall be substituted the Schedule set out in Schedule 3 to these regulations.

(3) A person in relation to whom a disease or injury was prescribed by virtue of the principal regulations immediately before the date of coming into operation of these regulations shall be treated as if these regulations had not come into operation if it would be more favourable to him.

Signed by authority of the Secretary of State for Social Services.

Tony Newton,
Parliamentary Under-Secretary of State,
Department of Health and Social Security.

21st July 1983.

SCHEDULE 1

Regulation 3(2)

PART I OF SCHEDULE INSERTED IN PRINCIPAL REGULATIONS IN SUBSTITUTION FOR
PART I OF SCHEDULE 1

PART I

LIST OF PRESCRIBED DISEASES AND THE OCCUPATIONS FOR WHICH THEY ARE
PRESCRIBED

Prescribed disease or injury	Occupation
A. *Conditions due to physical agents*	Any occupation involving:
1. Inflammation, ulceration or malignant disease of the skin or subcutaneous tissues or of the bones, or blood dyscrasia, or cataract, due to electro-magnetic radiations (other than radiant heat), or to ionising particles.	Exposure to electro-magnetic radiations (other than radiant heat) or to ionising particles.
2. Heat cataract.	Frequent or prolonged exposure to rays from molten or red-hot material.
3. Dysbarism, including decompression sickness, barotrauma and osteonecrosis.	Subjection to compressed or rarified air or other respirable gases or gaseous mixtures.
4. Cramp of the hand or forearm due to repetitive movements.	Prolonged periods of handwriting, typing or other repetitive movements of the fingers, hand or arm.
5. Subcutaneous cellulitis of the hand (Beat hand).	Manual labour causing severe or prolonged friction or pressure on the hand.
6. Bursitis or subcutaneous cellulitis arising at or about the knee due to severe or prolonged external friction or pressure at or about the knee (Beat knee).	Manual labour causing severe or prolonged external friction or pressure at or about the knee.
7. Bursitis or subcutaneous cellulitis arising at or about the elbow due to severe or prolonged external friction or pressure at or about the elbow (Beat elbow).	Manual labour causing severe or prolonged external friction or pressure at or about the elbow.
8. Traumatic inflammation of the tendons of the hand or forearm, or of the associated tendon sheaths.	Manual labour, or frequent or repeated movements of the hand or wrist.
9. Miner's nystagmus.	Work in or about a mine.
10. Substantial sensorineural hearing loss amounting to at least 50dB in each ear, being due in the case of at least one ear to occupational noise, and being the average of pure tone losses measured by audiometry over the 1, 2 and 3 kHz frequencies (occupational deafness).	*(a)* The use of, or work wholly or mainly in the immediate vicinity of, pneumatic percussive tools or high-speed grinding tools, in the cleaning, dressing or finishing of cast metal or of ingots, billets or blooms; or *(b)* the use of, or work wholly or mainly in the immediate vicinity of, pneumatic percussive tools on metal in the shipbuilding or ship repairing industries; or

Prescribed disease or injury	Occupation
	Any occupation involving:
	(c) the use of, or work in the immediate vicinity of, pneumatic percussive tools on metal, or for drilling rock in quarries or underground, or in mining coal, for at least an average of one hour per working day; or
	(d) work wholly or mainly in the immediate vicinity of drop-forging plant (including plant for drop-stamping or drop-hammering) or forging press plant engaged in the shaping of metal; or
	(e) work wholly or mainly in rooms or sheds where there are machines engaged in weaving man-made or natural (including mineral) fibres or in the bulking up of fibres in textile manufacturing; or
	(f) the use of, or work wholly or mainly in the immediate vicinity of, machines engaged in cutting, shaping or cleaning metal nails; or
	(g) the use of, or work wholly or mainly in the immediate vicinity of, plasma spray guns engaged in the deposition of metal; or
	(h) the use of, or work wholly or mainly in the immediate vicinity of, any of the following machines engaged in the working of wood or material composed partly of wood, that is to say: multi-cutter moulding machines, planing machines, automatic or semi-automatic lathes, multiple cross-cut machines, automatic shaping machines, double-end tenoning machines, vertical spindle moulding machines (including high-speed routing machines), edge banding machines, bandsawing machines with a blade width of not less than 75 millimetres and circular sawing machines in the operation of which the blade is moved towards the material being cut; or
	(i) the use of chain saws in forestry.
B. *Conditions due to biological agents*	
1. Anthrax.	Contact with animals infected with anthrax or the handling (including the loading or unloading or transport) of animal products or residues.
2. Glanders.	Contact with equine animals or their carcases.

Prescribed disease or injury	Occupation
	Any occupation involving:
3. Infection by leptospira.	(a) Work in places which are, or are liable to be, infested by rats, field mice or voles, or other small mammals; or
	(b) work at dog kennels or the care or handling of dogs; or
	(c) contact with bovine animals or their meat products or pigs or their meat products.
4. Ankylostomiasis.	Work in or about a mine.
5. Tuberculosis.	Contact with a source of tuberculous infection.
6. Extrinsic allergic alveolitis (including farmer's lung).	Exposure to moulds or fungal spores or heterologous proteins by reason of employment in:—
	(a) agriculture, horticulture, forestry, cultivation of edible fungi or malt-working; or
	(b) loading or unloading or handling in storage mouldy vegetable matter or edible fungi; or
	(c) caring for or handling birds; or
	(d) handling bagasse.
7. Infection by organisms of the genus brucella.	Contact with—
	(a) animals infected by brucella, or their carcases or parts thereof, or their untreated products; or
	(b) laboratory specimens or vaccines of, or containing, brucella.
8. Viral hepatitis.	Close and frequent contact with—
	(a) human blood or human blood products; or
	(b) a source of viral hepatitis infection by reason of employment in the medical treatment or nursing of a person or persons suffering from viral hepatitis, or in a service ancillary to such treatment or nursing.
9. Infection by *Streptococcus suis*	Contact with pigs infected by *Streptococcus suis,* or with the carcases, products or residues of pigs so infected.
C. *Conditions due to chemical agents*	
1. Poisoning by lead or a compound of lead.	The use or handling of, or exposure to the fumes, dust or vapour of, lead or a compound of lead, or a substance containing lead.

Prescribed disease or injury	Occupation
	Any occupation involving:
2. Poisoning by manganese or a compound of manganese.	The use or handling of, or exposure to the fumes, dust or vapour of, manganese or a compound of manganese, or a substance containing manganese.
3. Poisoning by phosphorus or an inorganic compound of phosphorus or poisoning due to the anti-cholinesterase or pseudo anti-cholinesterase action of organic phosphorus compounds.	The use or handling of, or exposure to the fumes, dust or vapour of, phosphorus or a compound of phosphorus, or a substance containing phosphorus.
4. Poisoning by arsenic or a compound of arsenic.	The use or handling of, or exposure to the fumes, dust or vapour of, arsenic or a compound of arsenic, or a substance containing arsenic.
5. Poisoning by mercury or a compound of mercury.	The use or handling of, or exposure to the fumes, dust or vapour of, mercury or a compound of mercury, or a substance containing mercury.
6. Poisoning by carbon bisulphide.	The use or handling of, or exposure to the fumes or vapour of, carbon bisulphide or a compound of carbon bisulphide, or a substance containing carbon bisulphide.
7. Poisoning by benzene or a homologue of benzene.	The use or handling of, or exposure to the fumes of, or vapour containing benzene or any of its homologues.
8. Poisoning by a nitro- or amino- or chloro- derivative of benzene or of a homologue of benzene, or poisoning by nitrochlorbenzene.	The use or handling of, or exposure to the fumes of, or vapour containing, a nitro- or amino- or chloro- derivative of benzene, or of a homologue of benzene, or nitrochlorbenzene.
9. Poisoning by dinitrophenol or a homologue of dinitrophenol or by substituted dinitrophenols or by the salts of such substances.	The use or handling of, or exposure to the fumes of, or vapour containing, dinitrophenol or a homologue or substituted dinitrophenols or the salts of such substances.
10. Poisoning by tetrachloroethane.	The use or handling of, or exposure to the fumes of, or vapour containing, tetrachloroethane.
11. Poisoning by diethylene dioxide (dioxan).	The use or handling of, or exposure to the fumes of, or vapour containing, diethylene dioxide (dioxan).
12. Poisoning by methyl bromide.	The use or handling of, or exposure to the fumes of, or vapour containing, methyl bromide.
13. Poisoning by chlorinated naphthalene.	The use or handling of, or exposure to the fumes of, or dust or vapour containing, chlorinated naphthalene.

Prescribed disease or injury	Occupation
	Any occupation involving:
14. Poisoning by nickel carbonyl.	Exposure to nickel carbonyl gas.
15. Poisoning by oxides of nitrogen.	Exposure to oxides of nitrogen.
16. Poisoning by gonioma kamassi (African boxwood).	The manipulation of gonioma kamassi or any process in or incidental to the manufacture of articles therefrom.
17. Poisoning by beryllium or a compound of beryllium.	The use or handling of, or exposure to the fumes, dust or vapour of, beryllium or a compound of beryllium, or a substance containing beryllium.
18. Poisoning by cadmium.	Exposure to cadmium dust or fumes.
19. Poisoning by acrylamide monomer.	The use or handling of, or exposure to, acrylamide monomer.
20. Dystrophy of the cornea (including ulceration of the corneal surface) of the eye.	(a) The use or handling of, or exposure to, arsenic, tar, pitch, bitumen, mineral oil (including paraffin), soot or any compound, product or residue of any of these substances, except quinone or hydroquinone; or (b) exposure to quinone or hydroquinone during their manufacture.
21. (a) Localised new growth of the skin, papillomatous or keratotic; (b) squamous-celled carcinoma of the skin.	The use or handling of, or exposure to, arsenic, tar, pitch, bitumen, mineral oil (including paraffin), soot or any compound, product or residue of any of these substances, except quinone or hydroquinone.
22. (a) Carcinoma of the mucous membrane of the nose or associated air sinuses; (b) primary carcinoma of a bronchus or of a lung.	Work in a factory where nickel is produced by decomposition of a gaseous nickel compound which necessitates working in or about a building or buildings where that process or any other industrial process ancillary or incidental thereto is carried on.
23. Primary neoplasm (including papilloma, carcinoma-in-situ and invasive carcinoma) of the epithelial lining of the urinary tract (renal pelvis, ureter, bladder and urethra).	(a) Work in a building in which any of the following substances is produced for commercial purposes:— (i) alpha-naphthylamine, beta-naphthylamine or methylene-bis–orthochloroaniline; (ii) diphenyl substituted by at least one nitro or primary amino group or by at least one nitro and primary amino group (including benzidine); (iii) any of the substances mentioned in sub-paragraph (ii) above if further ring substituted by halogeno, methyl or methoxy groups, but not by other groups;

Prescribed disease or injury	Occupation
	(iv) the salts of any of the substances mentioned in sub-paragraphs (i) to (iii) above;
	(v) auramine or magenta; or
	Any occupation involving:
	(b) the use or handling of any of the substances mentioned in sub-paragraph (a) (i) to (iv), or work in a process in which any such substance is used, handled or liberated; or
	(c) the maintenance or cleaning of any plant or machinery used in any such process as is mentioned in sub-paragraph (b), or the cleaning of clothing used in any such building as is mentioned in sub-paragraph (a) if such clothing is cleaned within the works of which the building forms a part or in a laundry maintained and used solely in connection with such works.
24. (a) Angiosarcoma of the liver; (b) osteolysis of the terminal phalanges of the fingers; (c) non-cirrhotic portal fibrosis.	(a) Work in or about machinery or apparatus used for the polymerization of vinyl chloride monomer, a process which, for the purposes of this provision, comprises all operations up to and including the drying of the slurry produced by the polymerization and the packaging of the dried product; or (b) work in a building or structure in which any part of that process takes place.
25. Occupational vitiligo.	The use or handling of, or exposure to, para–tertiary–butylphenol, para–tertiary–butylcatechol, para–amyl–phenol, hydroquinone or the monobenzyl or monobutyl ether of hydroquinone.
D. *Miscellaneous Conditions*	
1. Pneumoconiosis.	Any occupation— (a) set out in Part II of this Schedule; (b) specified in regulation 2(b)(ii). Any occupation involving:
2. Byssinosis.	Work in any room where any process up to and including the weaving process is performed in a factory in which the spinning or manipulation of raw or waste cotton or of flax, or the weaving of cotton or flax, is carried on.

Prescribed disease or injury	Occupation
	Any occupation involving:
3. Diffuse mesothelioma (primary neoplasm of the mesothelium of the pleura or of the pericardium or of the peritoneum).	*(a)* The working or handling of asbestos or any admixture of asbestos; or *(b)* the manufacture or repair of asbestos textiles or other articles containing or composed of asbestos; or *(c)* the cleaning of any machinery or plant used in any of the foregoing operations and of any chambers, fixtures and appliances for the collection of asbestos dust; or *(d)* substantial exposure to the dust arising from any of the foregoing operations.
4. Inflammation or ulceration of the mucous membrane of the upper respiratory passages or mouth produced by dust, liquid or vapour.	Exposure to dust, liquid or vapour.
5. Non-infective dermatitis of external origin (including chrome ulceration of the skin but excluding dermatitis due to ionising particles or electro-magnetic radiations other than radiant heat).	Exposure to dust, liquid or vapour or any other external agent capable of irritating the skin (including friction or heat but excluding ionising particles or electro-magnetic radiations other than radiant heat).
6. Carcinoma of the nasal cavity or associated air sinuses (nasal carcinoma).	*(a)* Attendance for work in or about a building where wooden goods are manufactured or repaired; or *(b)* attendance for work in a building used for the manufacture of footwear or components of footwear made wholly or partly of leather or fibre board; or *(c)* attendance for work at a place used wholly or mainly for the repair of footwear made wholly or partly of leather or fibre board.
7. Asthma which is due to exposure to any of the following agents:— *(a)* isocyanates; *(b)* platinum salts; *(c)* fumes or dusts arising from the manufacture, transport or use of hardening agents (including epoxy resin curing agents) based on phthalic anhydride, tetrachlorophthalic anhydride, trimellitic anhydride or triethylenetetramine; *(d)* fumes arising from the use of rosin as a soldering flux; *(e)* proteolytic enzymes;	Exposure to any of the agents set out in column 1 of this paragraph.

Prescribed disease or injury	Occupation
(f) animals or insects used for the purposes of research or education or in laboratories; *(g)* dusts arising from the sowing, cultivation, harvesting, drying, handling, milling, transport or storage of barley, oats, rye, wheat or maize, or the handling, milling, transport or storage of meal or flour made therefrom (occupational asthma).	

Regulation 14　　　　　　SCHEDULE 2

SCHEDULE INSERTED IN PRINCIPAL REGULATIONS

SCHEDULE 2A

ASSESSMENT OF THE EXTENT OF OCCUPATIONAL DEAFNESS

PART I

CLAIMS TO WHICH REGULATION 47(1) APPLIES

Average hearing loss (dB) over 1, 2 and 3 kHz	Degree of disablement per cent
50–52 dB	20
53–57 dB	30
58–62 dB	40
63–67 dB	50
68–72 dB	60
73–77 dB	70
78–82 dB	80
83–87 dB	90
88 dB or more	100

PART II

CLAIMS TO WHICH REGULATION 47(2) APPLIES

Average hearing loss (dB) over 1, 2 and 3 kHz	Degree of disablement per cent
50–53 dB	20
54–60 dB	30
61–66 dB	40
67–72 dB	50
73–79 dB	60
80–86 dB	70
87–95 dB	80
96–105 dB	90
106 dB or more	100

PART III

FORMULA FOR CALCULATING BINAURAL DISABLEMENT

$$\frac{(\text{Degree of disablement of better ear} \times 4) + \text{Degree of disablement of worse ear}}{5}$$

SCHEDULE 3   Regulation 17(2)

SCHEDULE INSERTED IN PRINCIPAL REGULATIONS IN SUBSTITUTION FOR SCHEDULE 3

PRESCRIBED DISEASES AND RELEVANT DATES FOR THE PURPOSES OF REGULATION 56

Description of disease or injury	Relevant date
A3 Dysbarism, including decompression sickness, barotrauma and osteonecrosis.	Except in the case of a person suffering from decompression sickness employed in any occupation involving subjection to compressed or rarefied air, 3rd October 1983.
B1 Anthrax.	In the case of a person employed in an occupation involving the loading and unloading or transport of animal products or residues, 3rd October 1983.
B3 Infection by leptospira.	(a) In the case of a person employed in an occupation in places which are or are liable to be infested by small mammals other than rats, field mice or voles, 3rd October 1983; (b) in the case of a person employed in an occupation in any other place mentioned in the second column of paragraph B3 of Part I of Schedule 1 above, 7th January 1980.
B5 Tuberculosis.	In the case of a person employed in an occupation involving contact with a source of tuberculous infection, not being an employment set out in the second column of paragraph 38 of Part I of Schedule 1 to the principal regulations in force immediately before 3rd October 1983, that date.
B6 Extrinsic allergic alveolitis (including farmer's lung).	In the case of a person suffering from extrinsic allergic alveolitis, not being farmer's lung, employed in any occupation set out in the second column of paragraph B6 of Part I of Schedule 1 above, or in the case of a person suffering from farmer's lung, employed in any occupation involving exposure to moulds or fungal spores or heterologous proteins by reason of employment in cultivation of edible fungi or maltworking, or loading or unloading or handling in storage edible fungi or caring for or handling birds, 3rd October 1983.

Description of disease or injury	Relevant date
B7 Infection by organisms of the genus brucella.	In the case of a person suffering from infection by organisms of the genus brucella, not being infection by *Brucella abortus*, or employed in an occupation set out in the second column of paragraph B7 of Part I of Schedule 1 above, not being an occupation set out in the second column of paragraph 46 of Part I of Schedule 1 to the principal regulations in force immediately before 3rd October 1983, that date.
B8 Viral hepatitis.	2nd February 1976.
B9 Infection by *Streptococcus suis*.	3rd October 1983.
C3 Poisoning by phosphorus or an inorganic compound of phosphorus or poisoning due to the anti-cholinesterase or pseudo anti-cholinesterase action of organic phosphorus compounds.	In the case of a person suffering from poisoning by an inorganic compound of phosphorus or poisoning due to the pseudo anti-cholinesterase action of organic phosphorus compounds, 3rd October 1983.
C18 Poisoning by cadmium.	In the case of a person employed in an occupation involving exposure to cadmium dust, 3rd October 1983.
C23 Primary neoplasm (including papilloma, carcinoma-in-situ and invasive carcinoma) of the epithelial lining of the urinary tract (renal pelvis, ureter, bladder and urethra).	In the case of a person employed in an occupation involving work in a building in which methylene–bis–orthochloroaniline is produced for commercial purposes, 3rd October 1983.
C24 *(a)* Angiosarcoma of the liver; *(b)* osteolysis of the terminal phalanges of the fingers; *(c)* non-cirrhotic portal fibrosis.	*(a)* In the case of a person suffering from angiosarcoma of the liver or osteolysis of the terminal phalanges of the fingers, 21st March 1977; *(b)* in the case of a person suffering from non-cirrhotic portal fibrosis, 3rd October 1983.
C25 Occupational vitiligo.	15th December 1980.
D3 Diffuse mesothelioma.	In the case of a person suffering from primary neoplasm of the pericardium, 3rd October 1983.
D6 Carcinoma of the nasal cavity or associated air sinuses (nasal carcinoma).	In the case of a person employed in an occupation involving attendance for work in or about a building where wooden goods (other than wooden furniture) are manufactured or where wooden goods are repaired, 3rd October 1983.
D7 Occupational asthma.	29th March 1982.

EXPLANATORY NOTE

(This Note is not part of the Regulations.)

These regulations further amend the Social Security (Industrial Injuries) (Prescribed Diseases) Regulations 1980.

The main changes made by the regulations are:—

(a) The regulations amend the definition of occupational deafness in the principal regulations so that it is no longer a requirement that hearing loss must be permanent and extend cover under the industrial injuries provisions of the Social Security Act 1975 in respect of occupational deafness to persons employed in employed earner's employment in occupations involving the use of, or work wholly or mainly in the immediate vicinity of, certain kinds of high-speed pneumatic percussive tools and high-speed grinding tools in certain processes and work in the immediate vicinity of machines engaged in cutting, shaping or cleaning metal nails, plasma spray guns engaged in the deposition of metal, certain woodworking machines and the use of chain saws in forestry.

(b) The period for which a person is required to have been employed in an occupation for which occupational deafness is prescribed before he can claim is reduced from 20 years to 10 years (regulation 3(1)).

(c) The time for claiming benefit in respect of occupational deafness is increased from 1 year to 5 years of the date of leaving his employment and provision is made to enable claims to be made within 1 year of the coming into operation of the regulations (regulation 8).

(d) The periods for making further claims in respect of occupational deafness after an earlier claim has been disallowed are increased in certain circumstances (regulation 9).

(e) The requirement that age-related hearing loss must be offset in assessing hearing loss is abolished (regulation 10).

(f) Initial assessments of disablement in respect of occupational deafness by medical boards and medical appeal tribunals are required to be provisional assessments for a period of 5 years and subsequent reassessments are required to be for not less than 5 years (regulation 11).

(g) The provisions of the Social Security Act 1975 relating to a review of assessment in a case of unforeseen aggravation will not apply where disability in respect of occupational deafness is assessed at less than 20 per cent (regulation 12).

(h) Any reassessment of disablement in respect of occupational deafness at less than 20 per cent will be a final assessment (regulation 13).

(i) The formula and tables for calculating assessment of the extent of disablement in respect of occupational deafness are set out in a new Schedule. In cases where the extent of disablement is reassessed at less than 20 per cent disablement benefit is not payable (regulation 14 and Schedule 2).

(j) The list of prescribed diseases and the occupations for which diseases are prescribed set out in Part I of Schedule 1 to the regulations have been rearranged under 4 categories and a number of amendments have been made to the description of the diseases and the occupations for which they are prescribed (regulation 3 and Schedule 1).

(k) The regulations contain transitional provisions relating to claims as a consequence of the changes in the descriptions of certain of the prescribed diseases and the occupations for which they are prescribed (regulation 17 and Schedule 3).

The regulations also contain consequential and other amendments of the principal regulations.

STATUTORY INSTRUMENTS

1983 No. 1095 (S. 102)

RATING AND VALUATION

The Rating (Repayment Procedures etc.) (Scotland) Amendment Regulations 1983

Made - - - -	*22nd July* 1983
Laid before Parliament	*27th July* 1983
Coming into Operation	*28th July* 1983

In exercise of the powers conferred on me by section 111(1) of the Local Government (Scotland) Act 1973(**a**), and of all other powers enabling me in that behalf, and after consultation with such associations of local authorities as appear to me to be concerned, I hereby make the following regulations:—

1. These regulations may be cited as the Rating (Repayment Procedures etc.) (Scotland) Amendment Regulations 1983 and shall come into operation on 28th July 1983.

2. In the Rating (Repayment Procedures etc.) (Scotland) Regulations 1981(**b**)—

(*a*) after the words "Local Government (Scotland) Act 1973" where they appear in regulations 2 and 4 respectively, there shall be inserted the words "or determine or are deemed to have determined a lower rate under section 5(4)(*b*) of the Local Government (Scotland) Act 1966(**c**)";

(*b*) after the word "Act" in the fifth line of regulation 2, there shall be inserted the words "of 1973";

(*c*) after the word "determination" in regulation 4, there shall be inserted the words "or deemed determination".

George Younger,
One of Her Majesty's Principal
Secretaries of State.

New St Andrew's House,
Edinburgh.
22nd July 1983.

(**a**) 1973 c. 65; section 111(1) was amended by the Local Government (Miscellaneous Provisions) (Scotland) Act 1981 (c. 23), Schedule 3, paragraph 27, by the Local Government and Planning (Scotland) Act 1982 (c. 43), Schedule 3, paragraph 20 and by the Local Government (Scotland) Act 1973 (Section 111) Amendment Order 1983 (S.I. 1983/1074).
(**b**) S.I. 1981/1045.
(**c**) 1966 c. 51; section 5(4) was inserted by section 1(*c*) of the Local Government and Planning (Scotland) Act 1982 (c. 43).

EXPLANATORY NOTE

(This Note is not part of the Regulations.)

These Regulations amend the Rating (Repayment Procedures etc.) (Scotland) Regulations 1981 and prescribe that the provisions for repayment or credit of any sums as the result of the determination of a lower rate by a local authority, and for the extra cost of levying that lower rate to be borne by that local authority, shall apply when a new rate is determined or deemed to be determined under section 5(4)(*b*) of the Local Government (Scotland) Act 1966.

STATUTORY INSTRUMENTS

1983 No. 1096

GAS

The British Gas Corporation (Further Disposal of Offshore Interests) Directions 1983

Made - - - - -	*26th July* 1983
Laid before Parliament	*26th July* 1983
Coming into Operation	*12th September* 1983

The Secretary of State, in exercise of the powers conferred on him by section 11(1) of the Oil and Gas (Enterprise) Act 1982**(a)** (hereinafter referred to as "the Act") and of all other powers enabling him in that behalf and after consultation with the British Gas Corporation (hereinafter referred to as "the Corporation") and with the approval of the Treasury, hereby gives the following directions to the Corporation:—

Citation, commencement and interpretation

1.—(1) These directions may be cited as the British Gas Corporation (Further Disposal of Offshore Interests) Directions 1983 and shall come into operation on 12th September 1983.

(2) In these directions "petroleum" has the same meaning as in Part I of the Petroleum and Submarine Pipe-lines Act 1975**(b)**.

Establishment of Subsidiary I

2. For the purpose of facilitating the eventual disposal under section 9(1)(*a*) of the Act of the property, rights and liabilities of the Corporation and of Gas Council (Exploration) Limited, a wholly owned subsidiary of the Corporation, relating to, or comprised in so much of their undertakings as relate to, the seaward areas specified in the Schedule to these directions, including in particular, but without prejudice to the generality of the foregoing—

(*a*) all rights and liabilities of the Corporation in respect of the purchase from Gas Council (Exploration) Limited of any kind of petroleum which may be won and saved from those seaward areas under any agreement which does not also confer on the Corporation rights to purchase from other persons, not being members of the group, petroleum of that kind so won and saved; and

(*b*) all rights and liabilities of the Corporation and Gas Council (Exploration) Limited under any agreement for the preparation, pursuant to Clause 6(*a*) below, of the report mentioned in that paragraph,

---

(a) 1982 c. 23.   **(b)** 1975 c. 74.

the Corporation shall exercise its powers extended by section 10(1) of the Act by establishing, before the expiry of the period of 2 months beginning on the date of the coming into operation of these directions, a wholly owned subsidiary of the Corporation (hereinafter referred to as "Subsidiary I") as a private company within the meaning of the Companies Act 1980**(a)** having as its principal object searching and boring for and getting petroleum.

Scheme relating to Subsidiary I
3.—(1) For the purpose mentioned in Clause 2 above, the Corporation shall exercise its powers under section 10(2) of the Act by making, and submitting to the Secretary of State for approval before the expiry of the period specified in Clause 2 above, a scheme for the transfer of the property, rights and liabilities mentioned in Clause 2 above to Subsidiary I.

(2) Such scheme shall, pursuant to section 10(3)(*b*) of the Act, for the purpose of facilitating the conclusion of arrangements with a view to securing participation by the British National Oil Corporation or any other body on behalf of the Government in activities connected with petroleum, confer on the Corporation, subject to any rights of other persons existing at the transfer date, rights enforceable against Subsidiary I in respect of the acquisition, at the election of the Corporation, of up to 51% of the petroleum not consisting of methane to which Subsidiary I may become entitled by virtue of its interests in each of the seaward areas specified in the Schedule to these directions.

(3) Such scheme shall also provide that in consideration of the transfer referred to in paragraph (1) above there shall be issued—

(*a*) to the Corporation a debenture of Subsidiary I which shall be credited as fully paid up for securing payment of the sum of £1; and

(*b*) to Gas Council (Exploration) Limited a debenture of Subsidiary I which shall be credited as fully paid up for securing payment of the sum of £9,998 and be subject to the right of Gas Council (Exploration) Limited to require Subsidiary I at any time before repayment of the debenture to allot and issue 9,998 ordinary shares of £1 each in Subsidiary I which shall be credited as fully paid up in exchange for and in satisfaction of the debenture.

Establishment of Subsidiary II
4. For the purpose of facilitating the eventual disposal under section 9(1)(*a*) of the Act of the rights to be conferred pursuant to Clause 3(2) above, the Corporation shall exercise its powers under section 10(1) of the Act by establishing, before the expiry of the period specified in Clause 2 above, a wholly owned subsidiary of the Corporation (hereinafter referred to as "Subsidiary II") as a private company within the meaning of the Companies Act 1980 having as its principal object the acquisition and disposal of petroleum.

(**a**) 1980 c. 22.

Scheme relating to Subsidiary II

5.—(1) For the purpose mentioned in Clause 4 above, the Corporation shall exercise its powers under section 10(2) of the Act by making, and submitting to the Secretary of State for approval before the expiry of the period specified in Clause 2 above, a scheme for the transfer between the Corporation and Subsidiary II of the rights to be conferred pursuant to Clause 3(2) above and any other rights and liabilities connected with those rights conferred or imposed by the scheme to be made under Clause 3(1) above.

(2) Such scheme shall also provide that in consideration of the transfer referred to in paragraph (1) above, there shall be issued to the Corporation a debenture of Subsidiary II which shall be credited as fully paid up for securing payment of the sum of £1.

Provisions relating to disposal

6. The Corporation shall exercise its powers under section 9(1)(*a*) of the Act to provide for the eventual disposal thereunder of property, rights and liabilities to be transferred by the scheme to be made under Clause 3(1) above in the following manner:—

    (*a*) by engaging an independent petroleum consultant to prepare, before the expiry of the period of 3 months beginning on the date of the coming into operation of these directions, a report on the proven, probable and possible reserves of petroleum in the seabed and subsoil of the seaward areas specified in the Schedule to these directions;

    (*b*) by compiling, or causing to be compiled, such information about the activities of any member of the group as may facilitate any such disposal.

Peter Walker,
Secretary of State for Energy.

21st July 1983.

We approve these directions.

Ian B. Lang,
Donald Thompson,
Two of the Lords Commissioners
of Her Majesty's Treasury.

26th July 1983.

SCHEDULE

SEAWARD AREAS

1. Blocks 29/11a, 29/12 and 29/18a now comprised in production licence P.065.

2. Block 30/22a now comprised in production licence P.143.

3. Blocks 205/23a, 206/9 and 206/10a now comprised in production licence P.170.

4. Blocks 3/11a, 9/27a, 210/24a and 211/27 now comprised in production licence P.184.

5. Blocks 13/16a, 13/21a, 15/22, 21/20a, 30/11b and 30/12b now comprised in production licence P.185.

6. Blocks 22/22a and 22/23a and the part of block 22/17 now comprised in production licence P.291 and the part of block 22/18 now comprised in production licence P.292.

7. Block 9/13b now comprised in production licence P.337.

Note. In this Schedule "block" means an area delineated on reference maps deposited at the principal office of the Department of Energy for the purposes of regulations made under section 6 of the Petroleum (Production) Act 1934**(a)**.

(a) 1934 c. 36.

EXPLANATORY NOTE

(This Note is not part of the Directions.)

These directions require the British Gas Corporation—

(*a*) to establish a wholly owned subsidiary of the Corporation, referred to as Subsidiary I, as a private company having as its principal object searching and boring for and getting petroleum and to make a scheme for the transfer to Subsidiary I of the property, rights and liabilities of the Corporation and Gas Council (Exploration) Limited, a wholly owned subsidiary of the Corporation, relating to the seaward areas comprised in production licences specified in the Schedule to the directions; such scheme—

  (i) to confer on the Corporation rights in respect of the acquisition, at the election of the Corporation, of up to 51% of the petroleum not consisting of methane to which Subsidiary I may become entitled by virtue of its interests in those seaward areas, and

  (ii) to provide, in consideration of the transfer referred to above, for the issue to the Corporation and Gas Council (Exploration) Limited respectively of a debenture for £1 and a convertible debenture for £9,998;

(*b*) to establish a wholly owned subsidiary of the Corporation, referred to as Subsidiary II, as a private company having as its principal object the acquisition and disposal of petroleum and to make a scheme for the transfer to Subsidiary II of the rights referred to in paragraph (*a*)(i) above and other rights and liabilities connected therewith; such scheme to provide, in consideration of this transfer, for the issue to the Corporation of a debenture for £1;

(*c*) to provide for the eventual disposal of property, rights and liabilities transferred by the scheme referred to in paragraph (*a*) above by engaging an independent consultant to prepare a report on the petroleum reserves in the seaward areas and compiling such information about the activities of the Corporation and its wholly owned subsidiaries as may facilitate such disposal.

STATUTORY INSTRUMENTS

1983 No. 1097

OFFSHORE INSTALLATIONS

The Offshore Installations (Safety Zones) (No. 24) Order 1983

Made - - - -	*25th July* 1983
Coming into Operation	*27th July* 1983

The Secretary of State, in exercise of the powers conferred on him by section 21(1), (2) and (3) of the Oil and Gas (Enterprise) Act 1982(**a**) (hereinafter referred to as "the Act"), and of all other powers enabling him in that behalf, hereby makes the following Order:—

1. This Order may be cited as the Offshore Installations (Safety Zones) (No. 24) Order 1983 and shall come into operation on 27th July 1983.

2.—(1) A safety zone is hereby established around the installation specified in Column 1 of the Schedule hereto (being an installation maintained in waters in an area designated under section 1(7) of the Continental Shelf Act 1964(**b**)) having a radius of five hundred metres from the point as respects that installation which has the co-ordinates of latitude and longitude according to European Datum (1950) specified in Columns 2 and 3 of the Schedule.

(2) The prohibition under section 21(3) of the Act on a vessel entering or remaining in a safety zone without the consent of the Secretary of State shall not apply to a vessel entering or remaining in the safety zone established under paragraph (1) above:

(*a*) in connection with the laying, inspection, testing, repair, alteration, renewal or removal of any submarine cable or pipe-line in or near that safety zone;

(*b*) to provide services for, to transport persons or goods to or from, or under the authority of a government department to inspect, any installation in that safety zone;

(*c*) if it is a vessel belonging to a general lighthouse authority performing duties relating to the safety of navigation;

(**a**) 1982 c. 23.   (**b**) 1964 c. 29.

(*d*) in connection with the saving or attempted saving of life or property;

(*e*) owing to stress of weather; or

(*f*) when in distress.

Alick Buchanan-Smith,
Minister of State,
Department of Energy.

25th July 1983.

SCHEDULE   Article 2(1)

SAFETY ZONE

1	2	3
Name or other designation of the offshore installation	Latitude North	Longitude East
Dixilyn-Field 97	56°43′42·10″	01°32′24.90″

EXPLANATORY NOTE

(*This Note is not part of the Order.*)

This Order establishes, under section 21 of the Oil and Gas (Enterprise) Act 1982, a safety zone, having a radius of 500 metres from a specified point, around the installation known as Dixilyn-Field 97 maintained in waters in an area designated under section 1(7) of the Continental Shelf Act 1964.

Vessels (which includes hovercraft, submersible apparatus and installations in transit) are prohibited from entering or remaining in the safety zone except with the consent of the Secretary of State or in the circumstances mentioned in Article 2(2) of the Order.

STATUTORY INSTRUMENTS

1983 No. 1098

AGRICULTURE

The Butter Subsidy (Protection of Community Arrangements) (Amendment) Regulations 1983

Made - - - -	*25th July* 1983
Laid before Parliament	*2nd August* 1983
Coming into Operation	*23rd August* 1983

The Minister of Agriculture, Fisheries and Food and the Secretary of State, being Ministers designated (**a**) for the purposes of section 2(2) of the European Communities Act 1972 (**b**) in relation to the common agricultural policy of the European Economic Community, acting jointly in exercise of the powers conferred on them by the said section 2(2) and of all other powers enabling them in that behalf, hereby make the following regulations:—

Title and commencement

1. These regulations may be cited as the Butter Subsidy (Protection of Community Arrangements) (Amendment) Regulations 1983 and shall come into operation on 23rd August 1983.

Amendment of the Butter Subsidy (Protection of Community Arrangements) Regulations 1980

2. The Butter Subsidy (Protection of Community Arrangements) Regulations 1980 (**c**) shall be further amended by substituting in regulation 1(2) thereof for the definition of "subsidy payment" the following definition:—

" 'subsidy payment' means a sum paid in pursuance of any of the following provisions:

Council Regulation (EEC) No. 2574/78 (**d**) on the granting of aid for consumption of butter in the United Kingdom;

Council Regulation (EEC) No. 1269/79 (**e**) on the marketing of reduced-price butter for direct consumption as amended by Council Regulation (EEC) No. 1362/80 (**f**) , Council Regulation (EEC) No. 854/81 (**g**) and Council Regulation (EEC) No. 1186/82 (**h**);

Commission Regulation (EEC) No. 2991/82 (**i**) on the temporary marketing during the 1982/83 milk year of reduced-price butter for direct consumption;

Council Regulation (EEC) No. 1208/83 (**j**) further amending Council Regulation (EEC) No. 1269/79 on the marketing of reduced-price butter for direct consumption."

(**a**) S.I. 1972/1811.   (**b**) 1972 c.68.
(**c**) S.I. 1980/1990, to which there are amendments not relevant to these Regulations.
(**d**) O.J. No. L309, 1.11.78, p.4.   (**e**) O.J. No. L161, 29.6.79, p.8.
(**f**) O.J. No. L140, 5.6.80, p.14.   (**g**) O.J. No. L90, 4.4.81, p.14.
(**h**) O.J. No. L140, 20.5.82, p.5.   (**i**) O.J. No. L314, 10.11.82, p.27.
(**j**) O.J. No. L132, 21.5.83, p.5.

In Witness whereof the Official Seal of the Minister of Agriculture, Fisheries and Food is hereunto affixed on 21st July 1983.

Michael Jopling,
Minister of Agriculture, Fisheries
and Food.

George Younger,
One of Her Majesty's Principal
Secretaries of State.

25th July 1983.

EXPLANATORY NOTE

(This Note is not part of the Regulations.)

These Regulations further amend the Butter Subsidy (Protection of Community Arrangements) Regulations 1980 by substituting a new definition of "subsidy payment" in regulation 1(2) thereof. The purpose of the amendment is to incorporate a reference to the current Community instrument: Council Regulation (EEC) No. 1208/83 of 17 May 1983 amending Regulation (EEC) No. 1269/79 as regards the conditions for the marketing of reduced-price butter for direct consumption during the 1983/84 milk year.

The main effect of the amendment is to apply the provisions of the principal regulations to payments made in pursuance of Council Regulation (EEC) No. 1269/79 as extended to the milk year 1983/84 by Council Regulation (EEC) No. 1208/83.

STATUTORY INSTRUMENTS

1983 No. 1099

VALUE ADDED TAX

The Value Added Tax (Horses and Ponies) Order 1983

Made - - - -	*26th July* 1983
Laid before the House of Commons	*27th July* 1983
Coming into Operation	*1st October* 1983

The Treasury, in exercise of the powers conferred on them by sections 3(9) and 14 of the Finance Act 1972(**a**) and all other powers enabling them in that behalf, hereby make the following Order:

1. This Order may be cited as the Value Added Tax (Horses and Ponies) Order 1983 and shall come into operation on 1st October 1983.

2. Except as provided in article 3, article 4 shall apply to the supply of a horse or pony by a taxable person where he acquired the horse or pony in either of the following circumstances—

(a) a supply on which no tax was chargeable;

(b) a supply on which tax was chargeable in accordance with article 4.

3. Article 4 does not apply to:

(a) a supply which is a letting on hire;

(b) a supply if an invoice or similar document showing an amount as being tax or as being attributable to tax is issued in respect of the supply;

(c) any supply by a taxable person unless he keeps such records and accounts as the Commissioners may specify in a notice published by them for the purposes of this Order.

4. Where this article applies, tax shall be charged as if the supply of the horse or pony were for a consideration equal to the excess of—

(a) the consideration for which the horse or pony is supplied, over

(b) the consideration for which the horse or pony was acquired,

and accordingly shall not be charged unless there is such an excess.

5. Where article 4 applies tax charged on the supply shall be excluded from any credit under sections 3 and 4 of the Finance Act 1972.

(a) 1972 c. 41, as amended by Schedule 6 to the Finance Act 1977 (c.36).

Ian B. Lang,
Donald Thompson,
Two of the Lords Commissioners
of Her Majesty's Treasury.

26th July 1983.

EXPLANATORY NOTE

(*This Note is not part of the Order.*)

This Order provides, subject to specified conditions, for the tax chargeable on the supply (otherwise than by hiring) of horses and ponies by a taxable person to be charged only on the excess, if any, of the price which that person obtained for a horse or pony over the price he gave for it.

STATUTORY INSTRUMENTS

1983 No. 1100

BANKS AND BANKING

The Deposit Protection Fund (Excluded Institutions) Order 1983

Made - - - -	*26th July* 1983
Laid before Parliament	*27th July* 1983
Coming into Operation	*1st September* 1983

Whereas the Treasury are satisfied, after consultation with the Deposit Protection Board, that sterling deposits with the United Kingdom offices of the State Bank of New South Wales (which is a body corporate formed under the law of the State of New South Wales in the Commonwealth of Australia) are as well protected under such law as they would be under Part II of the Banking Act 1979(**a**):—

Now therefore, the Treasury in exercise of the powers conferred on them by section 23(2) of the Banking Act 1979 and of all other powers enabling them in that behalf, hereby make the following Order:—

1. This Order may be cited as the Deposit Protection Fund (Excluded Institutions) Order 1983 and shall come into operation on 1st September 1983.

2. The State Bank of New South Wales is hereby excluded from section 23(1) of the Banking Act 1979.

Ian B. Lang,
Donald Thompson,
Two of the Lord's Commissioners of
Her Majesty's Treasury.

26th July 1983.

(**a**) 1979 c. 37.

EXPLANATORY NOTE

(This Note is not part of the Order.)

This Order excludes the State Bank of New South Wales from section 23(1) of the Banking Act 1979, thus exempting it from the requirement to contribute to the Deposit Protection Fund established by section 21 of the Act, and removing deposits with it from the protection afforded by section 28 in the event of insolvency.

STATUTORY INSTRUMENTS

1983 No. 1101

INCOME TAX

The Income Tax (Cash Equivalents of Car Fuel Benefits) Order 1983

Made - - - - - - - - - -	*26th July* 1983
Laid before the House of Commons	*27th July* 1983
Coming into Operation	*6th April* 1984

The Treasury, in exercise of the powers conferred on them by section 64A(4) of the Finance Act 1976**(a)**, hereby make the following Order—

1. This Order may be cited as the Income Tax (Cash Equivalents of Car Fuel Benefits) Order 1983 and shall come into force on 6th April 1984.

2. In section 64A(2) of the Finance Act 1976 (Tables of flat rate cash equivalents) for Tables A and B there shall be substituted the following Tables:—

TABLE A

Cylinder capacity of car in cubic centimetres	Cash equivalent
1,300 or less	£375
More than 1,300, but not more than 1,800 ..	£480
More than 1,800	£750

(a) 1976 c. 40; section 64A was inserted by section 69 of the Finance Act 1981 (c. 35) and was amended by section 46(4), (5) and (6) of the Finance Act 1982 (c. 39).

TABLE B

Original market value of car	Cash equivalent
Less than £4,950	£375
£4,950 or more, but less than £7,000	£480
£7,000 or more	£750

Ian B. Lang,
Donald Thompson,
Two of the Lords Commissioners
of Her Majesty's Treasury.

26th July 1983.

EXPLANATORY NOTE

(This Note is not part of the Order.)

This Order prescribes with effect from 6th April 1984 new amounts of cash equivalents on which directors and higher-paid employees are chargeable to income tax under the Finance Act 1976 in respect of the benefit of car fuel made available for private use by reason of their employment. For this purpose higher-paid employees are those earning at the rate of £8,500 or more a year.

STATUTORY INSTRUMENTS

1983 No. 1102

INCOME TAX

The Income Tax (Cash Equivalents of Car Benefits) Order 1983

Made - - - -	*26th July* 1983
Laid before the House of Commons	*27th July* 1983
Coming into Operation	*6th April* 1984

The Treasury, in exercise of the powers conferred on them by section 64(4) of the Finance Act 1976(**a**), hereby make the following Order—

1. This Order may be cited as the Income Tax (Cash Equivalents of Car Benefits) Order 1983 and shall come into force on 6th April 1984.

2. The money sum specified in subsection (2)(*a*) of section 64 of the Finance Act 1976 (which imposes a charge to income tax on the benefit of a car made available for private use by reason of an employment) shall be further increased to £16,000.

3. In Part 1 of Schedule 7 to the Finance Act 1976 (Tables of flat rate cash equivalents) for Tables A, B and C there shall be substituted the following Tables:—

TABLE A

CARS WITH ORIGINAL MARKET VALUE UP TO £16,000 AND HAVING A CYLINDER CAPACITY

Cylinder capacity of car in cubic centimetres	Age of car at end of relevant year of assessment	
	Under 4 years	4 years or more
1,300 or less	£375	£250
More than 1,300, but not more than 1,800	£480	£320
More than 1,800	£750	£500

(**a**) 1976 c. 40; section 64(4) was amended by section 51(2) of the Finance Act 1980 (c. 48).

TABLE B

CARS WITH ORIGINAL MARKET VALUE UP TO £16,000 AND NOT HAVING A CYLINDER CAPACITY

Original market value of car	Age of car at end of relevant year of assessment	
	Under 4 years	4 years or more
Less than £4,950	£375	£250
£4,950 or more, but less than £7,000	£480	£320
£7,000 or more, but not more than £16,000	£750	£500

TABLE C

CARS WITH ORIGINAL MARKET VALUE MORE THAN £16,000

Original market value of car	Age of car at end of relevant year of assessment	
	Under 4 years	4 years or more
More than £16,000 but not more than £24,000	£1,100	£740
More than £24,000	£1,725	£1,150

4. The money sum specified in paragraph 1(1) of Part II of Schedule 7 to the Finance Act 1976 shall be increased to £16,000.

Ian B. Lang,
Donald Thompson,
Two of the Lords Commissioners
of Her Majesty's Treasury.

26th July 1983.

EXPLANATORY NOTE

(This Note is not part of the Order.)

This Order prescribes with effect from 6th April 1984 new amounts of cash equivalents on which directors and higher-paid employees are chargeable to income tax under the Finance Act 1976 in respect of the benefit of a car made available for private use by reason of their employment. For this purpose higher-paid employees are those earning at the rate of £8,500 or more a year.

The Order replaces S.I. 1982/1159.

STATUTORY INSTRUMENTS

1983 No. 1103

NATIONAL DEBT

The National Savings Stock Register (Amendment) Regulations 1983

Made - - - - -	*26th July* 1983
Laid before Parliament	*4th August* 1983
Coming into Operation	*1st September* 1983

The Treasury, in exercise of the powers conferred on them by section 3 of the National Debt Act 1972(**a**) and of all other powers enabling them in that behalf, in conjunction, so far as the Regulations relate to the National Debt Commissioners, with those Commissioners, hereby make the following Regulations:—

1. These Regulations may be cited as the National Savings Stock Register (Amendment) Regulations 1983, and shall come into operation on 1st September 1983.

2. The National Savings Stock Register Regulations 1976(**b**) shall be amended in Regulation 7(1) by substituting for the words "£5,000" the words "£10,000".

T. Garel-Jones,
Donald Thompson,
Two of the Lords Commissioners of
Her Majesty's Treasury

21st July 1983.

P. A. Goodwin,
On behalf of the National Debt Commissioners.

26th July 1983.

(**a**) 1972 c. 65.
(**b**) S.I. 1976/2012; the relevant amending instrument is S.I. 1979/1677.

EXPLANATORY NOTE

(This Note is not part of the Regulations.)

These Regulations, which amend the National Savings Stock Register Regulations 1976, increase the limit on the amount of stock of any one description which may be purchased by any one person on any one day from £5,000 to £10,000.

1983 No. 1104

DEFENCE

The Army, Air Force and Naval Discipline Acts (Continuation) Order 1983

Laid before Parliament in Draft

Made - - - -   27*th July* 1983

At the Court at Buckingham Palace, the 27th day of July 1983

Present,

The Queen's Most Excellent Majesty in Council

Whereas a draft of the following Order in Council has been laid before Parliament and approved by a resolution of each House of Parliament:

Now, therefore, Her Majesty, in pursuance of section 1(2) of the Armed Forces Act 1981(**a**), is pleased, by and with the advice of Her Privy Council, to order, and it is hereby ordered, as follows:

1. The Army Act 1955(**b**), the Air Force Act 1955(**c**) and the Naval Discipline Act 1957(**d**) shall continue in force for a period of twelve months beyond 31st August 1983, that date being the date on which they would otherwise expire.

2. This Order may be cited as the Army, Air Force and Naval Discipline Acts (Continuation) Order 1983.

N. E. Leigh,
Clerk of the Privy Council.

(**a**) 1981 c. 55.
(**b**) 1955 c. 18.
(**c**) 1955 c. 19.
(**d**) 1957 c. 53.

STATUTORY INSTRUMENTS

1983 No. 1106

MERCHANT SHIPPING

OIL POLLUTION

The Merchant Shipping (Prevention of Oil Pollution) Order 1983

Made - - - -	*27th July* 1983
Laid before Parliament	*4th August* 1983
Coming into Operation	*2nd October* 1983

At the Court at Buckingham Palace the 27th day of July 1983

Present,

The Queen's Most Excellent Majesty in Council

Whereas by virtue of section 20(1)(a) and (c) of the Merchant Shipping Act 1979 (**a**) ("the Act of 1979") Her Majesty may by Order in Council make such provision as She considers appropriate for the purpose of giving effect to—

    (a) the International Convention for the Prevention of Pollution from Ships (including its protocols, annexes and appendices) which constitutes attachment 1 to the final act of the International Conference on Marine Pollution signed in London on 2nd November 1973 ("the Convention") (**b**), and

    (b) the Protocol relating to the said Convention which constitutes attachment 2 to the final act of the International Conference on Tanker Safety and Pollution Prevention signed in London on 17th February 1978 ("the Protocol") (**c**) :

And whereas by virtue of section 20(3)*(a)* of the Act of 1979 such an Order may apply, for the purpose of giving effect to such Convention and Protocol, any enactment relating to the pollution of the sea or other waters:

And whereas by virtue of section 20(3)*(c)* of the Act of 1979 such an Order may repeal the provisions of any enactment so far as it appears to Her Majesty that those provisions are not required having regard to provisions made by this Order:

And whereas this Order is made only for the purpose of giving effect to the Convention and the Protocol:

Now, therefore, Her Majesty, in exercise of the powers conferred by section 20(1)*(a)* and *(c)*, (3) and (4) of the Act of 1979 (**d**) and of all other powers enabling Her in that behalf, is pleased, by and with the advice of Her Privy Council, to order, and it is hereby ordered, as follows:

1. This Order may be cited as the Merchant Shipping (Prevention of Oil Pollution) Order 1983 and shall come into operation on 2nd October 1983.

(**a**) 1979 c.39.
(**b**) Cmnd. 5748.
(**c**) Cmnd. 7347.
(**d**) Section 20(3) was amended and paragraphs *(f)* and *(fa)* were substituted by section 49(2) of the Criminal Justice Act 1982 (c.48).

2. The provisions of the Prevention of Oil Pollution Act 1971 (**a**) ("the Act of 1971"), the Merchant Shipping Act 1974 (**b**) and the instruments set out in the Schedule hereto are hereby repealed and revoked subject to the limitations (if any) specified in that Schedule.

3.—(1) The Secretary of State may make regulations for the prevention of oil pollution (hereinafter referred to as "the Regulations") for the purpose of giving effect to the said Convention and Protocol and the Regulations may in particular include provisions—

(a) with respect to the carrying out of surveys and inspections for that purpose, and for the issue, duration and recognition of certificates for that purpose and the payment in connection with such a survey, inspection or certificate of fees of amounts determined with the approval of the Treasury;

(b) with respect to the application of the Regulations to the Crown and the extra-territorial operation of the Regulations;

(c) for the extension of any provision of this Order or of the Regulations, with or without modification, to any of the Channel Islands, the Isle of Man, any colony and any country or place outside Her Majesty's dominions in which Her Majesty has jurisdiction in right of the government of the United Kingdom;

(d) that specified contraventions of the Regulations shall be offences punishable on summary conviction by a fine not exceeding the statutory maximum and on conviction on indictment by imprisonment for a term not exceeding two years and a fine;

(e) that any such contraventions shall be offences punishable only on summary conviction by a maximum fine not exceeding level 5 on the standard scale or such less amount as is prescribed by the Regulations;

(f) for detaining any ship in respect of which such a contravention is suspected to have occurred and, in relation to such a ship, for applying section 692 of the Merchant Shipping Act 1894 (**c**) (which relates to the detention of a ship) with such modifications, if any, as are prescribed by the Regulations;

and the Regulations may—

(i) make different provisions for different circumstances;

(ii) provide for exemptions from any provisions of the Regulations;

(iii) provide for the delegation of functions exercisable by virtue of the Regulations; and

(iv) include such incidental, supplemental and transitional provisions as appear to the Secretary of State to be expedient for the purposes of the Regulations.

(2) The Statutory Instruments Act 1946 (**d**) shall apply to Regulations made under this Order, and shall so apply as if such Regulations were a statutory instrument.

4. Section 2(4) of the Act of 1971 (which provides that a person guilty of an offence under that section shall be liable on summary conviction to a fine not exceeding £50,000 or on conviction on indictment to a fine) shall apply in respect of any contravention of the Regulations made under this Order as may be prescribed by those Regulations as it applies to an offence under section 2 of that Act.

(**a**) 1971 c.60.   (**b**) 1974 c.43.   (**c**) 1894 c.60.
(**d**) 1946 c.36.

5. Sections 55 to 58 of the Merchant Shipping Act 1970(a) (which relate to investigations of shipping casualties) shall apply in respect of any discharge from a ship which may have been made in contravention of any Regulations made under this Order as they apply in relation to any damage caused by a ship.

6. Any discharge of oil or oily mixture from a ship to which any Regulations made under this Order apply which is not prohibited by any such Regulations is authorised by this Order.

N. E. Leigh,
Clerk of the Privy Council.

Article 2   SCHEDULE

ENACTMENTS REPEALED

(1)   The Prevention of Oil Pollution Act 1971:—

in section 1, subsections (1), (3) and (4) (discharge of certain oils into sea outside territorial waters);

in section 2, paragraphs *(a)* and *(b)* of subsection (1) (discharge of oil from a vessel into United Kingdom waters);

section 4 (equipment in ships to prevent oil pollution);

section 8(1) (discharge of certain ballast water into harbours).

(2)   The Merchant Shipping Act 1974, Part II:—

section 10 (interpretation of Part II);

section 11 (design and construction of oil tankers);

section 12 (restrictions on tankers sailing from United Kingdom ports);

section 13 (restrictions on uncertificated tankers);

Schedule 2 (oil tankers);

Schedule 3 (certificated oil tankers).

STATUTORY INSTRUMENTS REVOKED

Column 1 Instruments revoked	Column 2 References
The Oil in Navigable Waters (Ships' Equipment) (No. 1) Regulations 1956	1956/1423
The Oil in Navigable Waters (Ships' Equipment) Regulations 1957	1957/1424
The Oil in Navigable Waters (Enforcement of Convention) Order 1958	1958/1526
The Oil in Navigable Waters (Exceptions) Regulations 1972	1972/1928

(a)   1970 c.36, amended by ss.28 and 32 of the Merchant Shipping Act 1979 (c.39) and by para. 90 of Schedule 7 to the Magistrates' Courts Act 1980 (c.43).

The Oil in Navigable Waters (Records) Regulations 1972   1972/1929
except to the extent that the Regulations apply to oil tankers of less
than 150 gross registered tonnage and other ships of less than 400
gross registered tonnage (and the gross registered tonnage of a ship
having alternative such tonnages shall be taken to be the larger of
those tonnages).

EXPLANATORY NOTE

(This Note is not part of the Order.)

This Order enables effect to be given to the International Convention for
the Prevention of Pollution from Ships 1973 (Cmnd. 5748) and the Protocol of
1978 (Cmnd. 7347) relating to the Convention. The Order empowers the
Secretary of State to make Regulations for the purpose of giving effect to the
Convention and Protocol, and in particular with respect to the carrying out of
surveys, the issue of certificates, the application of the Regulations to the
Crown, the extension of the Order or Regulations to dependent territories,
the imposition of penalties and the detention of ships for that purpose.

Specified provisions of the Prevention of Oil Pollution Act 1971, and the
Merchant Shipping Act 1974 together with the statutory instruments set out in
Schedule 1, will no longer be required once those Regulations are in force and
they are accordingly repealed or revoked.

Sections 55 to 58 of the Merchant Shipping Act 1970 (investigations of
casualties) are applied in relation to a discharge of oil or oily mixture from
certain ships as they apply to damage caused by the ship. Any such discharge
from a ship to which Regulations made under this Order apply and which is
not prohibited thereby is authorised by this Order. By virtue of section
31(2)(b)(ii) of the Control of Pollution Act 1974 (c.40) any discharge so
authorised does not constitute an offence under section 31(1) of that Act.

STATUTORY INSTRUMENTS

1983 No. 1107

CARIBBEAN AND NORTH ATLANTIC TERRITORIES

The Anguilla Consequential Provisions Order 1983

Made - - - -	*27th July* 1983
Laid before Parliament	*4th August* 1983
Coming into Operation	*1st September* 1983

At the Court at Buckingham Palace, the 27th day of July 1983

Present,

The Queen's Most Excellent Majesty in Council

Whereas Anguilla ceased to form part of the territory of the associated state of St. Christopher, Nevis and Anguilla on 19th December 1980, when section 1(1) of the Anguilla Act 1980(**a**) came into force:

Now, therefore, Her Majesty, by virtue of the powers conferred upon Her by sections 13(2) and 15 of the West Indies Act 1967(**b**) and section 1(1) of the Anguilla Act 1980, is pleased, by and with the advice of Her Privy Council, to order, and it is hereby ordered, as follows:

Citation and commencement.
1. This Order may be cited as the Anguilla Consequential Provisions Order 1983 and shall come into operation on 1st September 1983.

Supreme Court.
2.—(1) Section 6(2) of the West Indies Act 1967 shall have effect as if the word 'Anguilla,' were inserted before the word 'Montserrat'.

(2) The West Indies Associated States Supreme Court Order 1967(**c**) shall, so far as it has effect as part of the law of Anguilla, have effect as if it had been made under section 6(2) of the West Indies Act 1967, as amended by the preceding paragraph.

N. E. Leigh,
Clerk of the Privy Council.

(**a**) 1980 c. 67.   (**b**) 1967 c. 4.   (**c**) S.I. 1967/223.

EXPLANATORY NOTE

(This Note is not part of the Order.)

This Order modifies section 6(2) of the West Indies Act 1967 (which relates to the Supreme Court originally established as a common court for the West Indies Associated States and retained by five States upon their independence as the Eastern Caribbean Supreme Court) in relation to Anguilla consequent upon its separation from St. Christopher and Nevis.

STATUTORY INSTRUMENTS

1983 No. 1108

CARIBBEAN AND NORTH ATLANTIC TERRITORIES

The Anguilla, Montserrat and Virgin Islands (Supreme Court) Order 1983

Made - - - -	*27th July* 1983
Coming into Operation	1*st September* 1983

At the Court at Buckingham Palace, the 27th day of July 1983

Present,
The Queens Most Excellent Majesty in Council

Her Majesty, by virtue and in exercise of Her powers under section 6(2) and 17(4) of the West Indies Act 1967(a), section 1(2) of the Anguilla Act 1980(b) and section 1 of the Judicial Committee Act 1844(c), is pleased, by and with the advice of Her Privy Council, to order, and it is hereby ordered, as follows:

Citation and commencement.

1. This Order may be cited as the Anguilla, Montserrat and Virgin Islands (Supreme Court) Order 1983 and shall come into operation on 1st September 1983.

Amendment of Supreme Court Order.

2.—(1) The following provisions shall have effect in relation to the West Indies Associated States Supreme Court Order 1967(d) (referred to below as the Order) so far as the Order has effect as part of the law of Anguilla, the law of Montserrat or, as the case may be, the law of the Virgin Islands.

(2) The Order may be cited as the Supreme Court Order and shall have effect as if section 1(1) thereof were deleted.

(3) The Court established by this Order shall be styled the Eastern Caribbean Supreme Court and accordingly section 4(1) of the Order shall have effect as if the words "Eastern Caribbean" were substituted for the words "West Indies Associated States".

(a) 1967 c. 4.　　(b) 1980 c. 67.　　(c) 1844 c. 69.　　(d) S.I. 1967/223.

(4) References in the Order to the Premier of any State shall be construed as references to the Prime Minister of that State.

(5) The Order shall have effect as if—

  (a) in sections 2(1) and 18(2) references to Antigua were references to Antigua and Barbuda, references to Grenada were deleted, references to Saint Christopher, Nevis and Anguilla were references to Saint Christopher and Nevis and references to Saint Vincent were references to Saint Vincent and the Grenadines; and

  (b) in sections 10 and 15 the word "Anguilla," were inserted before the word "Montserrat" wherever it occurs.

(6) For the purposes of the Order, Anguilla shall not be regarded as a State.

(7) References to the Order in any law in force in Anguilla, in Montserrat or, as the case may be, in the Virgin Islands shall, unless the context otherwise requires, be construed as including any law amending the Order.

3. The Montserrat (Appeals to Privy Council) Order 1967(**a**) and the Virgin Islands (Appeals to Privy Council) Order 1967(**b**) shall have effect as if—   Amendment of Appeals to Privy Council Orders.

  (a) the definition of "Courts Order" in section 2(1) were deleted; and

  (b) the words "the Supreme Court Order" were substituted for the words "the Courts Order" wherever they appear in section 2(1).

4. Subsections (1) and (2) of section 3 of the Anguilla Constitution Order 1982(**c**) are revoked.   Revocation.

N. E. Leigh,
Clerk of the Privy Council.

(**a**) S.I. 1967/233.   (**b**) S.I. 1967/234.   (**c**) S.I. 1982/334.

EXPLANATORY NOTE

(This Note is not part of the Order.)

For purposes of consistency, this Order makes alterations to the West Indies Associated States Supreme Court Order 1967 so far as it has effect as part of the law of Anguilla, of Montserrat and of the Virgin Islands. These are similar to those already made to the Order as it has effect as part of the law of the five States that have retained the Supreme Court that Order established, originally as a common court for the West Indies Associated States. On the independence of each State, the Court under its law is styled the Eastern Caribbean Supreme Court and the Order is cited as the Supreme Court Order.

STATUTORY INSTRUMENTS

1983 No. 1109

JUDICIAL COMMITTEE

The Anguilla (Appeals to Privy Council) Order 1983

Made - - - -	*27th July* 1983
Coming into Operation	*1st September* 1983

At the Court at Buckingham Palace, the 27th day of July 1983

Present,

The Queen's Most Excellent Majesty in Council

Her Majesty, by virtue and in the exercise of the powers in that behalf by section 1 of the Judicial Committee Act 1844 (a) or otherwise in Her Majesty vested, is pleased, by and with the advice of Her Privy Council, to order, and it is hereby ordered, as follows:—

1. This Order may be cited as the Anguilla (Appeals to Privy Council) Order 1983 and shall come into operation on 1st September 1983.

Citation and commencement.

2. In this Order, unless the context otherwise requires—

Interpretation.

"appeal" means appeal from a decision of the Court to Her Majesty in Council;

"Court" means the Court of Appeal established by the Supreme Court Order (b);

"decision" means a decision in any proceedings originating in Anguilla;

"Judicial Committee" means the Judicial Committee of the Privy Council;

"record" means the aggregate of papers relating to an appeal (including pleadings, proceedings, evidence and decisions) proper to be laid before Her Majesty in Council on the hearing of an appeal;

"Registrar" means the Registrar of the Court or other proper officer having custody of the records of the Court.

3.—(1) Subject to the provisions of this Order, an appeal shall lie as of right from decisions of the Court to Her Majesty in Council in the following cases—

Appeals to Her Majesty in Council.

(*a*) final decisions in any civil proceedings, where the matter in dispute on the appeal to Her Majesty in Council is of the value of £300 sterling or upwards or where the appeal involves directly or indirectly a claim to or question respecting property or a right of the value of £300 sterling or upwards;

(a) 1844 c.69.   (b) S.I. 1967/223.

(b) final decisions in proceedings for dissolution or nullity of marriage; and

(c) such other cases as may be prescribed by any law for the time being in force in Anguilla.

(2) Subject to the provisions of this Order, an appeal shall lie from decisions of the Court to Her Majesty in Council with the leave of the Court in the following cases—

(a) decisions in any civil proceedings, where in the opinion of the Court the question involved in the appeal is one that, by reason of its great general or public importance or otherwise, ought to be submitted to Her Majesty in Council; and

(b) such other cases as may be prescribed by any law for the time being in force in Anguilla.

(3) An appeal shall lie to Her Majesty in Council with the special leave of Her Majesty from any decision of the Court in any civil or criminal matter.

Applications for leave to appeal.

4. Applications to the Court for leave to appeal shall be made by motion or petition within twenty-one days of the date of the decision to be appealed from, and the applicant shall give all other parties concerned notice of his intended application.

Conditional leave to appeal.

5. Leave to appeal to Her Majesty in Council in pursuance of the provisions of this Order shall, in the first instance, be granted by the Court only—

(a) upon condition of the appellant, within a period to be fixed by the Court but not exceeding ninety days from the date of the hearing of the application for leave to appeal, entering into good and sufficient security to the satisfaction of the Court in a sum not exceeding £500 sterling for the due prosecution of the appeal and the payment of all such costs as may become payable by the applicant in the event of his not obtaining an order granting him final leave to appeal, or of the appeal being dismissed for non-prosecution, or of the Judicial Committee ordering the appellant to pay the costs of the appeal (as the case may be); and

(b) upon such other conditions (if any) as to the time or times within which the appellant shall take the necessary steps for the purposes of procuring the preparation of the record and the despatch thereof to England as the Court, having regard to all the circumstances of the case, may think it reasonable to impose.

Powers of a single judge.

6. A single judge of the Court shall have power and jurisdiction—

(a) to hear and determine any application to the Court for leave to appeal in any case where under any provision of law an appeal lies as of right from a decision of the Court;

(b) generally in respect of any appeal pending before Her Majesty in Council, to make such order and to give such other directions as he shall consider the interests of justice or circumstances of the case require:

Provided that any order, directions or decision made or given in pursuance of this section may be varied, discharged or reversed by the Court when consisting of three judges which may include the judge who made or gave the order, directions or decision.

7. Where the decision appealed from requires the appellant to pay money or do any act, the Court shall have power, when granting leave to appeal, either to direct that the said decision shall be carried into execution or that the execution thereof shall be suspended pending the appeal, as to the Court shall seem just, and in case the Court shall direct the said decision to be carried into execution, the person in whose favour it was given shall, before the execution thereof, enter into good and sufficient security to the satisfaction of the Court, for the due performance of such Order as Her Majesty in Council shall think fit to make thereon.

Stay of execution.

8. For the purposes of articles 5 and 7, a person may provide security in any manner that the Court may approve in his case, and for the avoidance of doubt it is declared that such security may with the approval of the Court consist in whole or in part of a deposit of money.

Manner of providing security.

9.—(1) The preparation of the record shall be subject to the supervision of the Court, and the parties may submit any disputed question arising in connection therewith to the decision of the Court, and the Court shall give such directions thereon as the justice of the case may require.

Preparation of record.

(2) The Registrar, as well as the parties, shall endeavour to exclude from the record all documents which are merely formal and are not relevant to the subject-matter of the appeal and, generally, to reduce the bulk of the record as far as practicable, taking special care to avoid the repetition of documents and headings and other merely formal parts of documents.

(3) Documents excluded from the record shall be enumerated in a list to be transmitted with the record.

(4) Where in the course of the preparation of a record one party objects to the inclusion of a document on the ground that it is unnecessary or irrelevant and the other party nevertheless insists upon its being included, the record, as finally reproduced (whether in Anguilla or in England) shall, with a view to the subsequent adjustment of the costs of and incidental to such document, indicate in the index or elsewhere the fact that, and the party by whom, the inclusion of the documents was objected to.

(5) The reasons given by judges of the Court for or against any decision pronounced in the course of the proceedings out of which the appeal arises shall be communicated by them in writing to the Registrar, and shall be included in the record.

10.—(1) The record may be reproduced either in Anguilla or in England.

Printing of the record.

(2) The reproduction shall comply with the provisions contained in the Schedule hereto.

(3) Where the record is reproduced in Anguilla the Registrar shall, at the expense of the appellant, transmit to the Registrar of the Privy Council 30 copies, one of which he shall certify to be correct by signing his name on, or initialling, every eighth page thereof and by affixing thereto the seal of the Court.

(4) Where the record is to be reproduced in England the Registrar shall, at the expense of the appellant, transmit to the Registrar of the Privy Council one certified copy, together with an index of all the papers and exhibits in the case.

(5) No other certified copies of the record shall be transmitted to the agents in England by or on behalf of the parties to the appeal.

Consolidation of appeals.

11. Where there are two or more applications for leave to appeal arising out of the same matter, and the Court is of opinion that it would be for the convenience of the Lords of the Judicial Committee and all parties concerned that the appeals should be consolidated, the Court may direct the appeals to be consolidated and grant leave to appeal by a single order.

Failure to prosecute appeal.

12. Where an appellant, having obtained an order granting him conditional leave to appeal, and having complied with the conditions imposed on him by such order, fails thereafter to apply with due diligence to the Court for an order granting him final leave to appeal, the Court may, on an application in that behalf made by the respondent, rescind the order granting conditional leave to appeal notwithstanding the appellant's compliance with the conditions imposed by such an order, and may give such directions as to the costs of the appeal and security entered into by the appellant as the Court shall think fit, or make such further or other order in the premises as, in the opinion of the Court, the justice of the case requires.

Notice to other parties.

13.—(1) On an application for final leave to appeal, the Court may enquire whether notice or sufficient notice of the application has been given by the appellant to parties concerned and, if not satisfied as to the notices given, may defer the granting of the final leave to appeal, or may give such other directions in the matter as, in the opinion of the Court, the justice of the case requires.

(2) The Registrar shall, with all convenient speed, transmit to the Registrar of the Privy Council a certificate to the effect that the respondent has received notice, or is otherwise aware, of the order of the Court granting final leave to appeal and of the transmission of the record to England.

Prosecution of appeal.

14. An appellant who has obtained final leave to appeal shall prosecute his appeal in accordance with the Rules for the time being regulating the general practice and procedure in appeals to Her Majesty in Council.

Withdrawal of appeal.

15.—(1) An appellant who has obtained an order granting him conditional leave to appeal may at any time prior to the making of an order granting him final leave to appeal withdraw his appeal on such terms as to costs and otherwise as the Court may direct.

(2) Where an appellant, having obtained final leave to appeal, desires, prior to the despatch of the record to England, to withdraw his appeal, the Court may, upon an application in that behalf made by the appellant, grant him a certificate to the effect that the appeal has been withdrawn, and the appeal shall thereupon be deemed, as from the date of such certificate, to stand dismissed without express Order of Her Majesty in Council, and the costs of the appeal and the security entered into by the appellant shall be dealt with in such manner as the Court may think fit to direct.

16. Where an appellant, having obtained final leave to appeal, fails to show due diligence in taking all necessary steps for the purpose of procuring the despatch of the record to England, any respondent may, after giving the appellant due notice of his intended application, apply to the Court for a certificate that the appeal has not been effectually prosecuted by the appellant, and if the Court sees fit to grant such a certificate the appeal shall be deemed, as from the date of such certificate, to stand dismissed for non-prosecution without express Order of Her Majesty in Council, and the costs of the appeal and the security entered into by the appellant shall be dealt with in such manner as the Court may think fit to direct.

Dismissal for non-prosecution.

17.—(1) Where at any time between the order granting final leave to appeal and the despatch of the record to England, the record becomes defective by reason of the death or change of status of a party to the appeal, the Court may, notwithstanding the order granting final leave to appeal, on an application in that behalf made by any person interested, grant a certificate showing who, in the opinion of the Court, is the proper person to be substituted or entered on the record in place of or in addition to the party who has died or undergone a change of status, and the name of such person shall thereupon be deemed to be so substituted or entered on the record as aforesaid without express Order of Her Majesty in Council.

Substituting parties.

(2) Where the record subsequently to its despatch to England becomes defective by reason of the death or change of status of a party to the appeal, the Court shall, upon an application in that behalf made by any person interested, cause a certificate to be transmitted to the Registrar of the Privy Council showing who, in the opinion of the Court, is the proper person to be substituted, or entered on the record, in place of, or in addition to, the party who has died or undergone a change of status.

18. The case of each party to the appeal which may be reproduced in Anguilla or in England, shall comply with the provisions contained in the Schedule to this Order and shall be signed by at least one of the counsel who attends at the hearing of the appeal, or by the party himself if he conducts his appeal in person.

Printing of case.

19.—(1) The form of the case shall comply with the following requirements of this rule—

Form of case.

    (a) it shall consist of paragraphs numbered consecutively;

    (b) it shall state, as concisely as possible, the circumstances out of which the appeal arises, the contentions to be urged by the party lodging it, and the reasons of appeal;

    (c) references by page and line to the relevant portions of the record as reproduced shall, as far as practicable, be reproduced in the margin;

    (d) care shall be taken to avoid, as far as possible, the recital of long extracts from the record.

(2) The taxing officer, in taxing the costs of the appeal, may, either of his own motion or at the instance of the opposite party, inquire into any unnecessary prolixity in the case and disallow the costs occasioned thereby.

Costs in
Anguilla.

20. Where the Judicial Committee directs a party to bear the costs of an appeal incurred in Anguilla, such costs shall be taxed by the proper officer of the Court in accordance with the rules for the time being regulating taxation in the Court.

Enforcing
Order.

21. Any Order which Her Majesty in Council may think fit to make on an appeal from a decision of the Court may be enforced in like manner as any decision of the Court should or might have been executed.

Revocation
of Order
of 1967.

22. The West Indies Associated States (Appeals to Privy Council) Order 1967 (a) is revoked in so far as it relates to Anguilla.

N. E. Leigh,
Clerk of the Privy Council.

THE SCHEDULE

Sections 10(2)
and 18.

RULES AS TO REPRODUCTION OF DOCUMENTS

1.—(1) All records, cases and other proceedings in appeals or other matters pending before Her Majesty in Council or the Judicial Committee which are required by the above Rules to be reproduced shall be reproduced on A4 ISO paper.

(2) Each page shall be numbered.

(3) The number of lines on each page of type shall be 47 or thereabouts, and every tenth line shall be numbered in the margin.

2. The record shall, where practicable, be arranged in two parts in the same volume, viz:—

Part I. The pleadings and proceedings, the transcript of the evidence of the witnesses, the judgments, orders etc., of the courts below down to the order admitting the appeal.

Part II. The exhibits and documents.

3.—(1) The index to both parts of the record shall be placed at the beginning of Part I.

(2) Where a record is in more than one volume, each volume shall contain an index of its contents.

(3) The index to Part I shall be in chronological order; the index to Part II shall follow the order of the exhibit mark.

(4) A list of any documents transmitted to the Privy Council but not reproduced shall be inserted in the record after the index to Part II.

4.—(1) The documents in Part I of the record shall be arranged in chronological order.

(a) S.I. 1967/224.

(2) *(a)* Part II shall be arranged in the most convenient way for the use of the Judicial Committee, as the circumstances of the case require.

(b) The documents shall be as far as suitable in chronological order, mixing plaintiff's and defendant's documents together when necessary.

(c) Each documents shall show its exhibit mark and whether it is a plaintiff's or defendant's document (unless this is clear from the exhibit mark).

(d) Documents relating to the same matter, such as—

  (i) a series of correspondence, or

  (ii) proceedings in a suit other than the one under appeal,

  shall be kept together.

(e) The page number of each document shall be inserted in the index.

5.—(1) The documents in Part I shall be numbered consecutively.

(2) The documents in Part II shall not be numbered, apart from the exhibit mark.

6. Each document shall have a heading which shall consist of the number or exhibit mark and the description of the document in the index, without the date.

7. Each document shall have a marginal note which shall be repeated on each page over which the document extends, viz:—

PART I

(a) Where the case has been before more than one Court, the short name of the Court shall first appear. Where the case has been before only one Court, the name of the Court need not appear.

(b) The marginal note of the document shall then appear consisting of the number and the description of the document in the index, with the date, except in the case of oral evidence.

(c) In the case of oral evidence, "plaintiff's evidence" or "defendant's evidence" shall appear beneath the name of the Court, and then the marginal note consisting of the number in the index and the witness's name, with "examination", "cross-examination" or "re-examination", as the case may be.

PART II

The word "Exhibits" shall first appear.

The marginal note of the exhibit shall then appear consisting of the exhibit mark and the description of the document in the index, with the date.

8.—(1) The parties shall agree to the omission of formal and irrelevant documents, but the description of the document may appear (both in the index and in the record), if desired, with the words "not reproduced" against it.

(2) A long series of documents, such as accounts, rent rolls, inventories, etc., shall not be reproduced in full unless Counsel so advise, but the parties shall agree to short extracts being reproduced as specimens.

EXPLANATORY NOTE

(This Note is not part of the Order.)

This Order makes provision in relation to appeals to Her Majesty in Council from the Court of Appeal established by the Supreme Court Order (formerly cited as the West Indies Associated States Supreme Court Order 1967) given in exercise of its jurisdiction under the law of Anguilla.

STATUTORY INSTRUMENTS

1983 No. 1110

SOUTH ATLANTIC TERRITORIES

The Falkland Islands and Dependencies (Interim Administration) (Amendment) Order 1983

Made - - - -	*27th July* 1983
Laid before Parliament	*4th August* 1983
Coming into Operation	*In accordance with section* 1(2)

At the Court at Buckingham Palace, the 27th day of July 1983

Present,

The Queen's Most Excellent Majesty in Council

Her Majesty, by virtue and in exercise of the powers vested in Her by the British Settlements Acts 1887 and 1945(**a**), and of all other powers enabling Her in that behalf, is pleased, by and with the advice of Her Privy Council, to order, and it is hereby ordered, as follows:—

Citation, construction and commencement

1.—(1) This Order may be cited as the Falkland Islands and Dependencies (Interim Administration) (Amendment) Order 1983, and shall be construed as one with the Falkland Islands and Dependencies (Interim Administration) Order 1982(**b**), which Order is hereinafter referred to as "the principal Order".

(2) This Order shall come into operation on a date to be notified by the Civil Commissioner by Proclamation in the Falkland Islands Government Gazette, which shall be a date not earlier than the day after the day on which this Order shall have been laid before both Houses of Parliament.

Amendment of section 2 of the principal Order

2. Section 2 of the principal Order is amended by adding the following new subsection and numbering the existing subsection "(1)":

"(2) For the purposes of this Order, unless the context otherwise requires, a reference to the holder of an office by the term designating his office shall be construed as including, to the extent of his authority, a reference to any person for the time being authorised to exercise the functions of that office.".

(**a**) 1887 c. 54 and 1945 c. 7.   (**b**) S.I. 1982/824.

Modification of existing law

3. In any law (including the Royal Instructions) in force in the Colony or the Dependencies immediately before the commencement of this Order any reference to "the Chief Secretary" shall be construed as a reference to "the Chief Executive".

N. E. Leigh,
Clerk of the Privy Council.

EXPLANATORY NOTE

(*This Note is not part of the Order.*)

This Order amends section 2 of the Falkland Islands and Dependencies (Interim Administration) Order 1982 to provide for acting appointments and makes changes to constitutional instruments and other laws of the Falkland Islands and the Falkland Islands Dependencies consequent upon the change in title of the office of Chief Secretary to that of Chief Executive.

STATUTORY INSTRUMENTS

1983 No. 1111

INTERNATIONAL IMMUNITIES AND PRIVILEGES

The International Jute Organization (Immunities and Privileges) Order 1983

Laid before Parliament in draft

Made - - - -	*27th July* 1983
Coming into Operation	*On a date to be notified in the London, Edinburgh and Belfast Gazettes*

At the Court at Buckingham Palace, the 27th day of July 1983

Present,

The Queen's Most Excellent Majesty in Council

Whereas a draft of this Order has been laid before Parliament in accordance with section 10(1) of the International Organisations Act 1968(**a**) (hereinafter referred to as the Act) and has been approved by resolution of each House of Parliament:

Now, therefore, Her Majesty, by virtue and in exercise of the powers conferred on Her by section 1 of the Act(**b**) or otherwise in Her Majesty vested, is pleased, by and with the advice of Her Privy Council, to order, and it is hereby ordered, as follows:—

1. This Order may be cited as the International Jute Organization (Immunities and Privileges) Order 1983. It shall come into operation on the date on which the International Agreement on Jute and Jute Products(**c**), open for signature at New York from 3rd January to 30th June 1983, enters into force in respect of the United Kingdom. That date shall be notified in the London, Edinburgh and Belfast Gazettes.

2. The International Jute Organization (hereinafter referred to as the Organisation) is an organisation of which Her Majesty's Government in the United Kingdom and the Governments of other sovereign Powers are members.

(**a**) 1968 c. 48.
(**b**) As amended by section 1 of the International Organisations Act 1981 (c. 9).
(**c**) Cmnd. 8825.

3. The Organisation shall have the legal capacities of a body corporate.

N. E. Leigh,
Clerk of the Privy Council.

EXPLANATORY NOTE

(*This Note is not part of the Order.*)

This Order confers the legal capacities of a body corporate on the International Jute Organization. It will enable the United Kingdom to give effect to Article 17(1) of the International Agreement on Jute and Jute Products (Cmnd. 8825), which was signed by the Government of the United Kingdom on 6th June 1983.

STATUTORY INSTRUMENTS

1983 No. 1112

CARIBBEAN AND NORTH ATLANTIC TERRITORIES

The Montserrat and Virgin Islands (Supreme Court) Modifications Order 1983

Made - - - -	*27th July* 1983
Laid before Parliament	*4th August* 1983
Coming into Operation	*1st September* 1983

At the Court at Buckingham Palace, the 27th day of July 1983

Present,
The Queen's Most Excellent Majesty in Council

Her Majesty, by virtue and in exercise of Her powers under sections 4, 5 and 7 of the West Indies Act 1962(**a**), is pleased, by and with the advice of Her Privy Council, to order, and it is hereby ordered, as follows:

Citation and commencement

1. This Order may be cited as the Montserrat and Virgin Islands (Supreme Court) Modifications Order 1983 and shall come into operation on 1st September 1983.

Modifications relating to Supreme Court

2.—(1) The Montserrat Order 1967(**b**) and the Virgin Islands (Courts) Order 1967(**c**) shall have effect as if—

(*a*) the definition of 'the Courts Order' in section 2(1) were deleted; and

(*b*) the words 'the Supreme Court Order' were substituted for the words 'the Courts Order' wherever they appear elsewhere in section 2(1) and in section 6(3).

(**a**) 1962 c. 19.   (**b**) S.I. 1967/230.   (**c**) S.I. 1967/231.

(2) Article 8 of the Montserrat Letters Patent 1959(a) (as amended by section 4(2) of the Montserrat Order 1967) shall have effect as if the words 'the Supreme Court Order' were substituted for the words 'the West Indies Associated States Supreme Court Order 1967' in the proviso.

N. E. Leigh,
Clerk of the Privy Council.

EXPLANATORY NOTE

(This Note is not part of the Order.)

This Order amends the Montserrat Order 1967, the Montserrat Letters Patent 1959 and the Virgin Islands (Courts) Order 1967 so as to bring them into conformity with the Anguilla, Montserrat and Virgin Islands (Supreme Court) Order 1983(b).

(a) 1959 II, p.3386.   (b) S.I. 1983/1108.

STATUTORY INSTRUMENTS

1983 No. 1113

SOUTH ATLANTIC TERRITORIES

The St. Helena Supreme Court (Amendment) Order 1983

Made - - - -	*27th July* 1983
Laid before Parliament	*4th August* 1983
Coming into Operation	*1st September* 1983

At the Court at Buckingham Palace, the 27th day of July 1983

Present,
The Queen's Most Excellent Majesty in Council

Her Majesty, by virtue and in exercise of the powers in that behalf conferred by section 112 of the Government of India Act 1833(**a**), the British Settlements Acts 1887 and 1945(**b**) or otherwise in Her Majesty vested, is pleased, by and with the advice of Her Privy Council, to order, and it is hereby ordered, as follows:

1.—(1) This Order may be cited as the St Helena Supreme Court Citation a (Amendment) Order 1983 and shall be construed as one with the St commence Helena Supreme Court Order 1969, as amended, (**c**) (hereinafter called 'the Principal Order').

(2) The Principal Order, the St Helena Supreme Court (Amendment) Order 1975, (**d**), and this Order may be cited together as the St Helena Supreme Court Orders 1969 to 1983.

(3) This Order shall come into operation on 1st September 1983.

(**a**) 1833 c. 85. (**b**) 1887 c. 54 and 1945 c. 7.
(**c**) S.I. 1969/857. (**d**) S.I. 1975/1211.

mendment of
rder of 1969.

2. Section 4 of the Principal Order is amended as follows:

(*a*) in subsection (4) by deleting the proviso and substituting therefor the following:

"Provided that the Court shall sit in the United Kingdom for the purpose only of hearing an application or an appeal and then only if all parties to be heard on the application or all parties to the appeal, as the case may be, have agreed to the application or appeal being heard in the United Kingdom."; and

(*b*) in subsection (5) by inserting after the word "appeals" the words "and applications".

N. E. Leigh,
Clerk of the Privy Council.

EXPLANATORY NOTE

(*This Note is not part of the Order.*)

This Order amends the St. Helena Supreme Court Order 1969 by permitting the Court with the consent of the parties to hear applications to the Court in the United Kingdom.

STATUTORY INSTRUMENTS

1983 No. 1114

NATIONAL HEALTH SERVICE, ENGLAND AND WALES

The Health Service Commissioner for England (Mental Health Act Commission) Order 1983

Made - - - - -	*27th July* 1983
Laid before Parliament	*4th August* 1983
Coming into Operation	*1st September* 1983

At the Court at Buckingham Palace, the 27th day of July 1983

Present,

The Queen's Most Excellent Majesty in Council.

Her Majesty, in pursuance of section 109(*d*) of the National Health Service Act 1977**(a)**, is pleased, by and with the advice of Her Privy Council, to order, and it is hereby ordered, as follows:—

Citation and commencement

1. This Order may be cited as the Health Service Commissioner for England (Mental Health Act Commission) Order 1983 and shall come into operation on 1st September 1983.

Designation as body subject to investigation

2. The Mental Health Act Commission is hereby designated as an authority to which section 109 of the National Health Service Act 1977 (bodies subject to investigation by Health Service Commissioner) applies.

N. E. Leigh,
Clerk of the Privy Council.

(a) 1977 c. 49; in section 109, paragraph (*bb*) was inserted by paragraph 72 of Schedule 1, and paragraph (*g*) was repealed by paragraph 7 of Schedule 2 and by Schedule 7, to the Health Services Act 1980 (c.53).

EXPLANATORY NOTE

(This Note is not part of the Order.)

This Order provides that the Mental Health Act Commission is to be a "relevant body" within the meaning of section 109 of the National Health Service Act 1977 so that the Health Service Commissioner for England may investigate complaints which relate to the Commission or its officers.

STATUTORY INSTRUMENTS

1983 No. 1115

NATIONAL HEALTH SERVICE, ENGLAND AND WALES

The Health Service Commissioner for England (Rural Dispensing Committee) Order 1983

Made - - - - -	*27th July* 1983
Laid before Parliament	*4th August* 1983
Coming into Operation	*25th August* 1983

At the Court at Buckingham Palace, the 27th day of July 1983

Present,

The Queen's Most Excellent Majesty in Council

Her Majesty, in pursuance of section 109(*d*) of the National Health Service Act 1977**(a)**, is pleased, by and with the advice of Her Privy Council, to order, and it is hereby ordered, as follows:—

1. This Order may be cited as the Health Service Commissioner for England (Rural Dispensing Committee) Order 1983 and shall come into operation on 25th August 1983.

2. The special health authority established by the Rural Dispensing Committee (Establishment and Constitution) Order 1983**(b)** and known as the Rural Dispensing Committee is hereby designated as an authority to which section 109 of the National Health Service Act 1977 (bodies subject to investigation by Health Service Commissioner) applies.

N. E. Leigh,
Clerk of the Privy Council.

(a) 1977 c. 49; in section 109, paragraph (*bb*) was inserted by paragraph 72 of Schedule 1, and paragraph (*g*) was repealed by paragraph 7 of Schedule 2 and by Schedule 7, to the Health Services Act 1980 (c. 53).
(b) S.I. 1983/312.

EXPLANATORY NOTE

(This Note is not part of the Order.)

This Order designates the Rural Dispensing Committee as an authority to which section 109 of the National Health Service Act 1977 applies so that the Health Service Commissioner for England may investigate complaints which relate to that Committee or its officers.

STATUTORY INSTRUMENTS

1983 No. 1116

PENSIONS

The Naval, Military and Air Forces etc. (Disablement and Death) Service Pensions Amendment Order 1983

Made - - - -	*27th July* 1983
Laid before Parliament	*4th August* 1983
Coming into Operation	*21st November* 1983

At the Court at Buckingham Palace, the 27th day of July 1983

Present

The Queen's Most Excellent Majesty in Council

WHEREAS Her Majesty deems it expedient to amend the Naval, Military and Air Forces etc. (Disablement and Death) Service Pensions Order 1983(a) and to do so by Order in Council in pursuance of section 12(1) of the Social Security (Miscellaneous Provisions) Act 1977(b):

NOW, THEREFORE, Her Majesty, in exercise of the powers conferred by the said section 12(1) and of all other powers enabling Her in that behalf, is pleased, by and with the advice of Her Privy Council, to order, and it is hereby ordered, as follows:—

Citation, commencement and interpretation

1.—(1) This Order, which may be cited as the Naval, Military and Air Forces etc. (Disablement and Death) Service Pensions Amendment Order 1983, shall come into operation on 21st November 1983.

(2) In this Order the expression "the principal Order" means the Naval, Military and Air Forces etc. (Disablement and Death) Service Pensions Order 1983.

(3) In relation to any award under the principal Order which is payable weekly and to which any provision of this Order relates, the foregoing reference to 21st November 1983 shall, where that date is not the normal weekly pay day for that award, be construed as a reference to the date of the first weekly pay day for that award immediately following 21st November 1983.

(a) S.I. 1983/883.
(b) 1977 c. 5.

Amendment of article 2 of the principal Order

2. In article 2 of the principal Order (scheduled rates and amounts of pensions, grants and allowances etc. and construction of Schedules relevant thereto)—

(*a*) after the word "allowances" there shall be inserted the word ", supplement"; and

(*b*) for the words "and 25(1)" there shall be substituted the words "25(1) and 26A(1)".

Amendment of article 18 of the principal Order

3. For the amount "£1040" in paragraph (2) of article 18 of the principal Order (earnings allowed in relation to unemployability allowances) there shall be substituted the amount "£1170".

Insertion of new article in the principal Order

4. In Part III of the principal Order (awards in respect of disablement) after article 26 there shall be inserted the following new article:—

"*Mobility supplement*

26A.—(1) Subject to the provisions of this article a mobility supplement may be awarded at the rate specified in paragraph 13 of Part IV of Schedule 1 to a member of the armed forces who is in receipt of retired pay or a pension in respect of—

(*a*) disablement as a result of the amputation of both legs, at least one of which has been amputated either through or at a point above the knee; or

(*b*) disablement due to any other injury which is, and is likely to remain for at least 12 months from the date on which the question of eligibility for a supplement under this article is considered by the Secretary of State (either at first instance or on review), wholly or mainly responsible for—

(i) rendering him unable to walk, or

(ii) restricting his leg movements to such an extent that his ability to walk without severe discomfort is of little or no practical use to him, or

(iii) rendering the exertion required to walk a danger to his life or a likely cause of serious deterioration in his health; or

(*c*) disablement by reason of which, immediately prior to the date on which the question of his eligibility for a supplement under this article is first considered by the Secretary of State, he—

(i) has had the use of an invalid carriage or other vehicle provided by the Secretary of State under section 5(2) of, and Schedule 2 to, the

National Health Service Act 1977(**a**) or section 46 of the National Health Service (Scotland) Act 1978(**b**), or by the Department of Health and Social Services for Northern Ireland under article 30 of the Health and Personal Social Services (Northern Ireland) Order 1972(**c**), which is a vehicle propelled by petrol engine or by electric power for use on the road and to be controlled by the occupant, or

(ii) has received any payment by way of grant under the said section 5(2) and Schedule 2 or the said section 46 or the said article 30 towards the cost of running a private car, or any payment out of public funds which the Secretary of State is satisfied is analogous thereto, or

(iii) has been in receipt of a mobility allowance under section 37A of the Social Security Act 1975(**d**) or section 37A of the Social Security (Northern Ireland) Act 1975(**e**) having been deemed, by virtue of section 13 of the Social Security (Miscellaneous Provisions) Act 1977 or, as the case may be, article 10 of the Social Security (Miscellaneous Provisions) (Northern Ireland) Order 1977(**f**), to be suffering from such disablement as is mentioned in subsection (1) of that section 37A and to satisfy the requirements of subsection (2)(*a*) of that section.

(2) In determining for the purposes of paragraph (1)(*b*)(i) and (ii) the extent of a person's walking ability regard shall be had to his ability to walk with a suitable prosthesis or artificial aid which he habitually wears or uses, or which he might reasonably be expected to wear or use.

(3) A mobility supplement under this article shall not be payable to a member for any period in respect of which he—

(*a*) has the use of an invalid carriage or other vehicle provided under any of the statutory provisions referred to in paragraph (1)(*c*); or

(*b*) is in receipt of a mobility allowance under section 37A of the Social Security Act 1975 or section 37A of the Social Security (Northern Ireland) Act 1975.".

Amendment of Schedules to the principal Order

5.—(1) In Schedule 1 to the principal Order (rates of pension and other grants payable in respect of disablement)—

(*a*) for Tables 1 and 3 of Part II there shall respectively be substituted the Tables set out in Schedules 1 and 2 hereto;

(*b*) for Tables 1 and 2 of Part III there shall respectively be substituted the Tables set out in Schedules 3 and 4 hereto;

(**a**) 1977 c. 49.
(**b**) 1978 c. 29.
(**c**) S.I. 1972/1265 (N.I. 14), as amended by section 40 of, and paragraph 8 of Schedule 5 to, the Northern Ireland Constitution Act 1973 (c. 36).
(**d**) 1975 c. 14; section 37A was inserted by section 22(1) of the Social Security Pensions Act 1975 (c. 60), and amended by section 3 of the Social Security Act 1979 (c. 18).
(**e**) 1975 c. 15 (N.I.); section 37A was inserted by article 24 of the Social Security Pensions (Northern Ireland) Order 1975 (S.I. 1975/1503 (N.I. 15)).
(**f**) S.I. 1977/610 (N.I. 11).

(*c*) for Part IV there shall be substituted the Part set out in Schedule 5 hereto.

(2) In Schedule 2 to the principal Order (rates of pension and other grants payable in respect of death)—

(*a*) for Table 1A of Part II there shall be substituted the Table set out in Schedule 6 hereto;

(*b*) for the amount "£2226" in the second column of Table 1B of Part II there shall be substituted the amount "£2307";

(*c*) for the amounts "£42.70" and "£9.86" in the second and third columns of Table 3 of Part II there shall respectively be substituted the amounts "£44.25" and "£10.22";

(*d*) for Table 5 of Part II there shall be substituted the Table set out in Schedule 7 hereto;

(*e*) for Part III there shall be substituted the Part set out in Schedule 8 hereto.

N. E. Leigh,
Clerk of the Privy Council.

SCHEDULE 1 Article 5(1)(*a*)

Table to be substituted for Table 1 of Part II of Schedule 1 to the principal Order.

TABLE 1

YEARLY RATES OF—

A. RETIRED PAY AND PENSIONS FOR DISABLED OFFICERS AND NURSES FOR ALL RANKS IN GROUPS 1–9 OF PART I OF THIS SCHEDULE

B. DISABLEMENT ADDITION ON A PENSION BASIS (ARTICLE 43(3)(*a*)) FOR ALL RANKS IN GROUPS 1–9 OF PART I OF THIS SCHEDULE AND GROUPS 2 AND 3 OF PART I OF SCHEDULE 2

Degree of Disability	Yearly Rate
Per cent.	£
100	2934
90	2641
80	2347
70	2054
60	1760
50	1467
40	1174
30	880
20	587

SCHEDULE 2 Article 5(1)(*a*)

Table to be substituted for Table 3 of Part II of Schedule 1 to the principal Order

TABLE 3

WEEKLY RATES OF PENSION FOR DISABLED OTHER RANKS
GROUPS 10–15

Degree of Disability	Weekly Rate
Per cent.	£
100	55.60
90	50.04
80	44.48
70	38.92
60	33.36
50	27.80
40	22.24
30	16.68
20	11.12

Article 5(1)(*b*) **SCHEDULE 3**

Table to be substituted for Table 1 of Part III of Schedule 1 to the principal Order

TABLE 1

GRATUITIES PAYABLE FOR SPECIFIED MINOR INJURIES

Description of Injury	Assessments Per cent.	Groups 1–9	Groups 10–15
For the loss of:—		£	£
A. FINGERS:—			
Index finger—			
Whole	14	2828	2798
2 phalanges	11	2264	2239
1 phalanx	9	1885	1865
Guillotine amputation of tip without loss of bone	5	1127	1117
Middle finger—			
Whole	12	2449	2424
2 phalanges	9	1885	1865
1 phalanx	7	1506	1491
Guillotine amputation of tip without loss of bone	4	943	933
Ring or little finger—			
Whole	7	1506	1491
2 phalanges	6	1322	1307
1 phalanx	5	1127	1117
Guillotine amputation of tip without loss of bone	2	564	559
B. TOES:—			
Great toe—			
through metatarso-phalangeal joint	14	2828	2798
part, with some loss of bone...	3	748	743
1 other toe—			
through metatarso-phalangeal joint	3	748	743
part, with some loss of bone...	1	379	374
2 toes, excluding great toe—			
through metatarso-phalangeal joint	5	1127	1117
part, with some loss of bone...	2	564	559
3 toes, excluding great toe—			
through metatarso-phalangeal joint	6	1322	1307
part, with some loss of bone...	3	748	743
4 toes, excluding great toe—			
through metatarso-phalangeal joint	9	1885	1865
part, with some loss of bone...	3	748	743

SCHEDULE 4   Article 5(1)(*b*)

Table to be substituted for Table 2 of Part III of Schedule 1 to the principal Order

TABLE 2

GRATUITIES PAYABLE TO MEMBERS OF THE ARMED FORCES FOR DISABLEMENT ASSESSED AT LESS THAN 20 PER CENT. NOT BEING A MINOR INJURY SPECIFIED IN TABLE 1

Group	Estimated duration of the disablement within the degree referred to								
	Temporary less than a year			Temporary more than a year			Indeterminate		
	Per cent.			Per cent.			Per cent.		
	1–5	6–14	15–19	1–5	6–14	15–19	1–5	6–14	15–19
	£	£	£	£	£	£	£	£	£
1	166	370	646	331	737	1290	995	2213	3872
3	164	365	639	327	728	1274	983	2186	3825
4	162	361	631	323	719	1258	971	2159	3778
5	160	358	625	321	713	1248	963	2141	3746
6	159	355	620	318	707	1237	955	2123	3715
7, 8	157	350	612	314	698	1221	943	2096	3668
9	155	346	604	310	689	1206	931	2069	3620
10	156	347	606	312	692	1210	930	2067	3612
11	156	346	605	311	691	1207	928	2062	3603
12	155	346	603	310	689	1204	926	2057	3594
13	155	345	602	310	687	1201	924	2052	3586
14	154	344	600	309	686	1198	921	2047	3577
15	154	343	599	308	684	1195	919	2042	3568

Article 5(1)(*c*) **SCHEDULE 5**

Part to be substituted for Part IV of Schedule 1 to the principal Order

PART IV

RATES OF ALLOWANCES PAYABLE IN RESPECT OF DISABLEMENT

Description of Allowance	Rate	
	Groups 1–9	*Groups 10–15*
1. Education allowance under article 13	£120 per annum (maximum)	£120 per annum (maximum)
2. Constant attendance allowance—		
(*a*) under article 14(1)(*b*) ...	£2325 per annum (maximum)	£44.60 per week (maximum)
(*b*) under article 14(1)(*a*) ...	£1163 per annum (maximum)	£22.30 per week (maximum)
3. Exceptionally severe disablement allowance under article 15	£1163 per annum	£22.30 per week
4. Severe disablement occupational allowance under article 16	£581 per annum	£11.15 per week
5. Allowance for wear and tear of clothing—		
(*a*) under article 17(1)(*a*) ...	£48 per annum	£48 per annum
(*b*) under article 17(1)(*b*) and 17(2)	£75 per annum	£75 per annum
6. Unemployability allowances—		
(*a*) personal allowance under article 18(1)(*a*)	£1885 per annum	£36.15 per week
(*b*) additional allowances for dependants by way of—		
(i) increase of allowance in respect of a wife, husband or unmarried dependant living as a wife, under article 18(5)(*b*)	£1066 per annum (maximum)	£20.45 per week (maximum)
(ii) allowance in respect of an adult dependant under article 18(5)(*c*)	£1066 per annum (maximum)	£20.45 per week (maximum)
(iii) increase of allowance in respect of each child under article 18(5)(*d*) ...	£396 per annum	£7.60 per week

SCHEDULE 5 *(Contd.)*

Description of Allowance	Rate	
	Groups 1–9	Groups 10–15
7. Invalidity allowance under article 19—		
(a) if— (i) the relevant date fell before 5th July 1948; or (ii) on the relevant date the member was under the age of 35; or (iii) on the relevant date the member was under the age of 40 and had not attained the age of 65, in the case of the member being a man, or 60, in the case of the member being a woman, before 6th April 1979 and the period in respect of which payment of the allowance is to relate begins on or after 6th April 1979	£373 per annum	£7.15 per week
(b) if— (i) on the relevant date the member was under the age of 45; or (ii) on the relevant date the member was under the age of 50 and had not attained the age of 65, in the case of the member being a man, or 60, in the case of the member being a woman, before 6th April 1979 and the period in respect of which payment of the allowance is to relate begins on or after 6th April 1979	£240 per annum	£4.60 per week
(c) if heads (a) and (b) do not apply, and on the relevant date the member was a man under the age of 60 or a woman under the age of 55 ...	£120 per annum	£2.30 per week
8. Comforts allowance— (a) under article 20(1)(a) ... (b) under article 20(1)(b) ...	£501 per annum £250 per annum	£9.60 per week £4.80 per week
9. Allowance for lowered standard of occupation under article 21	£1160 per annum (maximum)	£22.24 per week (maximum)

SCHEDULE 5 *(Contd.)*

Description of Allowance	Rate	
	Groups 1–9	Groups 10–15
10. Age allowance under article 22 where the degree of pensioned disablement is—		
(a) 40 to 50 per cent.	£201 per annum	£3.85 per week
(b) over 50 per cent., but not exceeding 70 per cent.	£315 per annum	£6.05 per week
(c) over 70 per cent., but not exceeding 90 per cent.	£451 per annum	£8.65 per week
(d) over 90 per cent.	£631 per annum	£12.10 per week
11. Treatment allowances— increase of personal allowance under article 23(3)...	£631 per annum (maximum)	£12.10 per week (maximum)
12. Part-time treatment allowance under article 25	£21 per day (maximum)	£21 per day (maximum)
13. Mobility supplement under article 26A	£21.15 per week	£21.15 per week

Article 5(2)(a)   **SCHEDULE 6**

Table to be substituted for Table 1A of Part II of Schedule 2 to the principal Order

TABLE 1

YEARLY RATES OF PENSIONS FOR WIDOWS OF OFFICERS

A.—Pensions other than pensions awarded under article 11(1) or (2) of the 1921 (Officers) Order or article 11(1) of the 1921 (Warrant Officers) Order, of the 1920 Warrant or of the 1921 Order

Group (1)	Rate (2)	Rate (3)
	£	£
1		
2		
3		
4		2307
5		
6	2307	
7		
8		817
9		729
10		641
11		567

SCHEDULE 7   Article 5(2)(*d*)

Table to be substituted for Table 5 of Part II of Schedule 2 to the principal Order

TABLE 5

MAXIMUM YEARLY RATES OF PENSION FOR RELATIVES OF 1914 WORLD WAR OFFICERS

Group (1)	Rate (2)
	£
1	
2	
3	
4	2307
5	
6	
7	
8	817
9	729
10	641
11	567

Article 5(2)(e)   **SCHEDULE 8**

Part to be substituted for Part III of Schedule 2 to the principal Order

PART III

RATES OF PENSIONS, OTHER THAN WIDOWS' PENSIONS AND
ALLOWANCES, PAYABLE IN RESPECT OF DEATH

Description of Pension or Allowance	Rate	
	Groups 1–11	Groups 12–17
1. Pension under article 30 to unmarried dependant who lived as wife	£2200 per annum (maximum)	£42.20 per week (maximum)
2. Rent allowance under article 31	£16.85 per week (maximum)	£16.85 per week (maximum)
3. Allowance under article 32 to elderly widow or unmarried dependant who lived as wife— (a) if age 65 but under 70... (b) if age 70 or over	£224 per annum £448 per annum	£4.30 per week £8.60 per week
4. Pension to widower under article 34	£2307 per annum (maximum)	£44.25 per week (maximum)
5. Allowances in respect of children— (a) under article 35(1) in respect of each child ... ... (b) under article 35(3)... ...	£571 per annum £620 per annum	£10.95 per week £11.90 per week
6. Pension under article 36 to a motherless or fatherless child of a member	£620 per annum	£11.90 per week
7. Pension or allowance under article 37(3) to or in respect of a child over the age limit	£1775 per annum (maximum)	£34.05 per week (maximum)
8. Education allowance under article 38	£120 per annum (maximum)	£120 per annum (maximum)

SCHEDULE 8 *(Contd.)*

Description of Pension or Allowance	Rate	
	Groups 1–11	*Groups* 12–17
9. Pensions to parents— (a) minimum rate under article 40(3)	£15 per annum	£0.25 per week
(b) under paragraphs (a) and (b) of article 40(3)— (i) where there is only one eligible parent	(i) Groups 1–10— £75 per annum (maximum) (ii) Group 11— £60 per annum (maximum)	£1.00 per week (maximum)
(ii) where there is more than one eligible parent... ...	(i) Groups 1–10— £100 per annum (maximum) (ii) Group 11— £85 per annum (maximum)	£1.38 per week (maximum)
(c) increase under article 40(3)(c)	£20 per annum (maximum)	(i) where there is only one eligible parent —£0.38 per week (maximum) (ii) where there is more than one eligible parent — £0.62 per week (maximum)
(d) under paragraph (d) of article 40(4)	—	£1.00 per week (maximum)
10. Pensions to other dependants— (a) under article 41(2)... ...	£54 per annum (maximum)	£1.00 per week (maximum)
(b) for each juvenile dependant under article 41(3) ...	(i) Groups 1–10— £26 per annum (maximum) (ii) Group 11— £20 per annum (maximum)	£0.30 per week (maximum)
(c) aggregate rate under article 41(3)	(i) Groups 1–10— £75 per annum (maximum) (ii) Group 11— £65 per annum (maximum)	£1.00 per week (maximum)

EXPLANATORY NOTE
(This Note is not part of the Order.)

This Order amends the Naval, Military and Air Forces etc. (Disablement and Death) Service Pensions Order 1983 ("the principal Order").

The Order inserts in the principal Order a new article 26A to make provision for a mobility supplement to be payable to certain members of the armed forces who are in receipt of retired pay or a pension in respect of disablement. Consequential amendments are also made to article 2 of the principal Order.

The Order raises the maximum amount of annual earnings which may be received by a member of the armed forces in receipt of retired pay or a pension while that person is deemed to be unemployable for the purposes of an award of unemployability allowances under article 18 of the principal Order.

The Order also varies the rates of retired pay, pensions, gratuities and allowances in respect of disablement and death due to service in the Naval, Military and Air Forces of the Crown during the 1914 World War and after 2nd September 1939. In the Part to be substituted for Part IV of Schedule 1 to the principal Order, which sets out the rates of allowances payable in respect of disablement, the rate for mobility supplement is inserted.

STATUTORY INSTRUMENTS

1983 No. 1122

NORTHERN IRELAND

The Housing (Northern Ireland Consequential Amendments) Order 1983

Laid before Parliament in draft

Made - - - -	*27th July* 1983
Coming into Operation	*28th September* 1983

At the Court at Buckingham Palace, the 27th day of July 1983

Present,

The Queen's Most Excellent Majesty in Council

Whereas a draft of this Order has been approved by a resolution of each House of Parliament:

Now, therefore, Her Majesty, in exercise of the powers conferred by section 38(2) of the Northern Ireland Constitution Act 1973(**a**) as extended by paragraph 1(7) of Schedule 1 to the Northern Ireland Act 1974(**b**), and of all other powers enabling Her in that behalf, is pleased, by and with the advice of Her Privy Council, to order, and it is hereby ordered, as follows:—

Title, commencement and extent

1. This Order—

(*a*) may be cited as the Housing (Northern Ireland Consequential Amendments) Order 1983;

(*b*) shall come into operation on the same day as the Housing (Northern Ireland) Order 1983(**c**); and

(*c*) extends to the whole of the United Kingdom.

(**a**) 1973 c. 36; section 38 was amended by paragraph 6 of Schedule 2 to the Northern Ireland Act 1982 (c. 38).
(**b**) 1974 c. 28.
(**c**) S.I. 1983/1118 (N.I. 15).

Amendment of Housing Act 1980

2.—(1) The Housing Act 1980(**a**) shall be amended in accordance with the following provisions of this Article.

(2) In section 111(8) (exclusion of certain recommendations made to building societies from the scope of section 16(3) and (5) of the Restrictive Trade Practices Act 1976(**b**)):—

(*a*) after the words "this section" there shall be inserted the words "or under Article 156 of the Housing (Northern Ireland) Order 1981" and

(*b*) after the words "Secretary of State" there shall be inserted the words "or of the Department of the Environment for Northern Ireland, as the case may be,".

(3) In section 155(3) (provisions extending to Northern Ireland), after the word "Sections" there shall be inserted "111(8),".

N. E. Leigh,
Clerk of the Privy Council.

EXPLANATORY NOTE

(This Note is not part of the Order.)

This Order makes amendments to the Housing Act 1980 which are expedient in consequence of Article 87 of the Housing (Northern Ireland) Order 1983. That Article amends the Housing (Northern Ireland) Order 1981 (S.I. 1981/156 (N.I. 3)) by substituting for Article 156 of that Order a new Article.

The effect of Article 2(2) and (3) is to exclude from the scope of section 16(3) and (5) of the Restrictive Trade Practices Act 1976 certain recommendations which may be made to building societies about entering into indemnity agreements with the Northern Ireland Housing Executive.

(**a**) 1980 c. 51.   (**b**) 1976 c. 34.

STATUTORY INSTRUMENTS

1983 No. 1123

ROAD TRAFFIC

The International Carriage of Perishable Foodstuffs Act 1976 (Amendment) Order 1983

Laid before Parliament in draft

Made - - - -	*27th July* 1983

Coming into operation in accordance with Article 1

At the Court at Buckingham Palace, the 27th day of July 1983

Present,

The Queen's Most Excellent Majesty in Council

Whereas it appears to Her Majesty in Council that Her Majesty's Government in the United Kingdom have agreed to certain alterations of the Agreement on the International Carriage of Perishable Foodstuffs and on the Special Equipment to be Used for such Carriage (ATP)(a):

And whereas a draft of this Order has been laid before Parliament and approved by resolution of each House of Parliament:

Now, therefore, Her Majesty, in exercise of the powers conferred on Her by section 16(1) of the International Carriage of Perishable Foodstuffs Act 1976(b), is pleased, by and with the advice of Her Privy Council, to order, and it is hereby ordered, as follows:—

Citation and Commencement

1. This Order may be cited as the International Carriage of Perishable Foodstuffs Act 1976 (Amendment) Order 1983 and shall come into operation on the day after the day on which it is made.

(a) Cmnd. 8272.
(b) 1976 c. 58; sections 6(3) and (4), 7(2), 8(1) and (2), 9(1), 10(3) and 11(5) are modified by Parts III and IV of the Criminal Justice Act 1982 (c. 48); section 9 is modified by section 289B(2) of the Criminal Procedure (Scotland) Act 1975 (c. 21) (inserted by section 63 of, and paragraph 5 of Schedule 11 to, the Criminal Law Act 1977 (c. 45)) and by section 32(2) of the Magistrates' Courts Act 1980 (c. 43), and repealed in part by section 30 of, Part I of the Schedule to, the Forgery and Counterfeiting Act 1981 (c. 45); section 16 is amended by section 9 of, and paragraph 4 of Schedule 2 to, the International Transport Conventions Act 1983 (c. 14).

Interpretation

2. In this Order the "1976 Act" means the International Carriage of Perishable Foodstuffs Act 1976.

Amendment of the 1976 Act

3. The 1976 Act shall be amended in accordance with the Schedule to this Order.

N. E. Leigh,
Clerk of the Privy Council.

Article 3   SCHEDULE

AMENDMENTS OF THE 1976 ACT.

1. In section 2 (provisions as to examination and testing), in subsection (1)—

(*a*) in paragraph (*a*) there shall be added at the end "or of a certification plate"; and

(*b*) in paragraph (*b*) after "certificate" there shall be inserted "or plate".

2. In section 3 (provisions supplementary to section 2)—

(*a*) in subsection (1)—

   (i) in paragraph (*f*) after "certificates" there shall be inserted "and plates";

   (ii) in paragraph (*g*) after "certificates" there shall be inserted "or duplicates of plates";

   (iii) after paragraph (*g*) there shall be inserted—

      "(gg) the position and the manner in which certification plates are to be affixed;"; and

   (iv) in paragraphs (*i*), (*k*), (*l*) and (*m*) after "certificate" there shall be inserted "or plate"; and

(*b*) in subsection (3) after "documents" there shall be inserted "or plates".

3. In section 6 (powers of entry and inspection)—

(*a*) in subsection (2)(*b*) after "certificate of compliance" there shall be inserted "or certification plate"; and

(*b*) after subsection (2) there shall be inserted—

      "(2A) Subsection (2)(*c*) above shall not apply in relation to any vehicle or container to which a valid certification plate is affixed in accordance with regulations under this Act; but an examiner may, at any time and on production if so required of his authority, detain any such vehicle or container for the purpose of inspecting the plate and copying the particulars contained in it.".

4. In section 7 (offences as to use of transport equipment) for subsection (1)(*a*) there shall be substituted—

"(*a*) without there being either a certificate of compliance in force for that equipment or a valid certification plate affixed to it in accordance with regulations under this Act,".

5. In section 9 (forgery of certificates of compliance) after subsection (1) there shall be inserted the following subsections—

"(2) Any person who, with intent to deceive—

(*a*) forges, or alters, or uses or lends to, or allows to be used by, any other person, a certification plate, or

(*b*) makes or has in his possession a plate so closely resembling a certification plate as to be calculated to deceive,

shall be guilty of an offence and shall be liable as mentioned in paragraphs (i) and (ii) of subsection (1) above.

(3) In the application of subsection (2) above to England, Wales and Northern Ireland "forges" means makes a false plate in order that it may be used as genuine.".

6. In section 10 (false statements and withholding material information in subsection (1) after "certificate of compliance" there shall be inserted "or a certification plate".

7. In section 11 (power to prohibit driving of foreign goods vehicles) for subsection (1)(*a*) there shall be substituted—

(*a*) the vehicle is required to comply with regulations under this Act and—

(i) there is not produced to him in respect of the vehicle a certificate of compliance, and

(ii) no valid certification plate is affixed to it in accordance with regulations under this Act; or".

8. In section 19 (Interpretation) in subsection (1) after the definition of "certificate of compliance" there shall be inserted—

"certification plate" means a plate issued under section 2 of this Act, and includes a duplicate plate issued under section 3 of this Act and a plate recognised under that section;".

EXPLANATORY NOTE

(This Note is not part of the Order.)

This Order amends the International Carriage of Perishable Foodstuffs Act 1976 in consequence of alterations of the Agreement on the International Carriage of Perishable Foodstuffs and on the Special Equipment to be Used for such Carriage (ATP) concluded in Geneva on 1st September 1970.

The alterations are made to Annex I to the Agreement and are published in Cmnd. 8842.

The alterations provide for the introduction of a certification plate as an alternative to a certificate of compliance as evidence of the compliance of transport equipment with ATP standards for the international carriage of perishable foodstuffs.

STATUTORY INSTRUMENTS

1983 No. 1124

MAINTENANCE OF DEPENDANTS

The Maintenance Orders (Facilities for Enforcement) (Revocation) Order 1983

Made - - - -	*27th July* 1983
Coming into Operation	1*st September* 1983

At the Court at Buckingham Palace, the 27th day of July 1983

Present,

The Queen's Most Excellent Majesty in Council

Her Majesty, in exercise of the powers conferred by section 19 of the Maintenance Orders Act 1958(**a**), is pleased, by and with the advice of Her Privy Council, to order, and it is hereby ordered, as follows:—

1. This Order may be cited as the Maintenance Orders (Facilities for Enforcement) (Revocation) Order 1983 and shall come into operation on 1st September 1983.

2. In this Order—

 (*a*) "the Order of 1959" means the Maintenance Orders (Facilities for Enforcement) Order 1959(**b**);

 (*b*) "the Act of 1920" means the Maintenance Orders (Facilities for Enforcement) Act 1920(**c**).

3.—(1) Insofar as the Order of 1959 provides that the Act of 1920 shall extend to the countries and territories specified in paragraph (2) below, that Order is hereby revoked, and accordingly the names of those countries and territories shall be omitted from the First Schedule to that Order.

(2) The countries and territories referred to in paragraph (1) above are—

Anguilla
Falkland Islands and Dependencies
Isle of Man
Papua
St. Helena.

(**a**) 1958 c. 39.   (**b**) S.I. 1959/377.   (**c**) 1920 c. 33.

4. Insofar as the Order of 1959, as it has effect by virtue of paragraph 3 of Schedule 2 to the Zimbabwe Act 1979(**a**), provides that the Act of 1920 shall extend to Zimbabwe, that Order is hereby revoked and, accordingly, the name of Southern Rhodesia shall be omitted from the First Schedule to that Order.

N. E. Leigh,
Clerk of the Privy Council.

EXPLANATORY NOTE

(*This Note is not part of the Order.*)

This Order revokes the Maintenance Orders (Facilities for Enforcement) Order 1959 insofar as it extends the Maintenance Orders (Facilities for Enforcement) Act 1920 to Anguilla, the Falkland Islands and Dependencies, the Isle of Man, Papua, St. Helena and Zimbabwe. These countries and territories are designated as reciprocating countries for the purposes of Part I of the Maintenance Orders (Reciprocal Enforcement) Act 1972 (c. 18) by the Reciprocal Enforcement of Maintenance Orders (Designation of Reciprocating Countries) Order 1983 (S.I. 1983/1125) which comes into operation on the same date as this Order.

(**a**) 1979 c. 60.

STATUTORY INSTRUMENTS

1983 No. 1125

MAINTENANCE OF DEPENDANTS

The Reciprocal Enforcement of Maintenance Orders (Designation of Reciprocating Countries) Order 1983

Made - - - -	*27th July* 1983
Laid before Parliament	*4th August* 1983
Coming into Operation	*1st September* 1983

At the Court at Buckingham Palace, the 27th day of July 1983

Present,

The Queen's Most Excellent Majesty in Council

Whereas Her Majesty is satisfied that, in the event of the benefits conferred by Part I of the Maintenance Orders (Reciprocal Enforcement) Act 1972(**a**) being applied to, or to particular classes of, maintenance orders made by the courts of each of the countries and territories specified in column (1) of the Schedule to this Order, similar benefits will in that country or territory be applied to, or to those classes of, maintenance orders made by the courts of the United Kingdom:

And whereas Her Majesty considers the provisions contained in Article 5 of this Order expedient for the purpose of securing the matters set out in section 24 of the said Act of 1972:

Now, therefore, Her Majesty, in exercise of the powers conferred by sections 1, 24 and 45(1) of the Maintenance Orders (Reciprocal Enforcement) Act 1972, is pleased, by and with the advice of Her Privy Council, to order, and it is hereby ordered, as follows:—

1. This Order may be cited as the Reciprocal Enforcement of Maintenance Orders (Designation of Reciprocating Countries) Order 1983 and shall come into operation on 1st September 1983.

2. In this Order—

"the Act of 1972" means the Maintenance Orders (Reciprocal Enforcement) Act 1972;

"the Act of 1920" means the Maintenance Orders (Facilities for Enforcement) Act 1920(**b**);

(**a**) 1972 c. 18.   (**b**) 1920 c. 33.

"the Order of 1974" means the Reciprocal Enforcement of Maintenance Orders (Designation of Reciprocating Countries) Order 1974(a);

"column (1)" and "column (2)" in Articles 3 and 5 below mean respectively columns (1) and (2) of the Schedule to this Order.

3. Each of the countries and territories specified in column (1) is hereby designated as a reciprocating country for the purposes of Part I of the Act of 1972 as regards maintenance orders of the description specified in respect of that country or territory in column (2).

4. Column (2) of the Schedule to the 1974 Order shall be varied as follows:—

  (a) in the entry in respect of Manitoba for the words "other than provisional affiliation orders" there shall be substituted the words "generally";

  (b) for the entry in respect of New Zealand there shall be substituted the following entry:—

    "Maintenance orders generally"; and

  (c) in the entry relating to Nova Scotia for the words "the said paragraph (b), and" in paragraph (a) there shall be substituted the words "paragraph (b) of the definition of "maintenance order" in section 21(1) of the Act of 1972 (orders for the payment of birth and funeral expenses of child), and".

5.—(1) Sections 5, 12 to 15, 17, 18 and 21 of the Act of 1972 shall apply in relation to a maintenance order transmitted under section 2 or 3 of the Act of 1920 to one of the countries and territories specified in column (1), being an order of the description specified in respect of that country or territory in column (2) to which immediately before the coming into operation of this Order the Act of 1920 applied, as they apply in relation to a maintenance order sent to that country or territory in pursuance of section 2 of the Act of 1972 or made by virtue of section 3 or 4 of the Act of 1972 and confirmed by a competent court in that country or territory.

(2) Sections 8 to 21 of the Act of 1972 shall apply in relation to a maintenance order made in one of the countries and territories specified in column (1), being an order of the description specified in respect of that country or territory in column (2) to which immediately before the coming into operation of this Order the Act of 1920 applied and not being an order which immediately before that date is registered in the High Court or the High Court of Justice in Northern Ireland under section 1 of the Act of 1920, as they apply in relation to a registered order.

(3) A maintenance order made by a court in one of the countries and territories specified in column (1) being an order of the description specified in respect of that country or territory in column (2) which has been confirmed by a court in England, Wales or Northern Ireland under section 4 of the Act of

---

(a) S.I. 1974/556, to which there are amendments not relevant to this Order.

1920 and is in force immediately before the coming into operation of this Order, shall be registered under section 7(5) of the Act of 1972 in like manner as if it had been confirmed by that court in England, Wales or Northern Ireland under subsection (2) of that section.

(4) Any proceedings brought under or by virtue of any provision of the Act of 1920 in a court in England, Wales or Northern Ireland which are pending immediately before the coming into operation of this Order, being proceedings affecting a person resident in one of the countries or territories specified in column (1), shall be continued as if they had been brought under or by virtue of the corresponding provision of the Act of 1972.

N. E. Leigh,
Clerk of the Privy Council.

SCHEDULE   *Article 3*

COUNTRIES AND TERRITORIES DESIGNATED AS RECIPROCATING COUNTRIES

(1) Country or territory	(2) Description of maintenance orders to which designation extends
Anguilla	Maintenance orders generally
Falkland Islands and Dependencies	Maintenance orders generally
Isle of Man	Maintenance orders generally
Nauru	Maintenance orders generally
Papua New Guinea	Maintenance orders other than provisional affiliation orders
St. Helena	Maintenance orders generally
Zimbabwe	Maintenance orders other than— (*a*) affiliation orders; and (*b*) maintenance orders of the description contained in paragraph (*b*) of the definition of "maintenance order" in section 21(1) of the Act of 1972 (orders for the payment of birth and funeral expenses of child).

EXPLANATORY NOTE

(This Note is not part of the Order.)

Article 3 of this Order designates as reciprocating countries for the purposes of Part I of the Maintenance Orders (Reciprocal Enforcement) Act 1972 the following countries and territories: Anguilla, Falkland Islands and Dependencies, Isle of Man, Nauru, Papua New Guinea, St. Helena and Zimbabwe.

The Reciprocal Enforcement of Maintenance Orders (Designation of Reciprocating Countries) Order 1974 designated, for the purposes of Part I of the Act of 1972, Manitoba subject to the exclusion of provisional affiliation orders and New Zealand subject to the exclusion of provisional affiliation orders and orders for the payment of a child's birth and funeral expenses. Article 4 of this Order varies the Order of 1974 so as to extend the designation in respect of Manitoba and New Zealand to maintenance orders generally.

Article 5 of this Order contains transitional provisions in respect of maintenance orders and proceedings to which the Maintenance Orders (Facilities for Enforcement) Act 1920 applied before the coming into operation of this Order.

STATUTORY INSTRUMENTS

1983 No. 1126

SAVINGS BANKS

The Trustee Savings Banks Act 1981 (Channel Islands) Order 1983

Made - - - -	*27th July* 1983
Coming into Operation	*27th August* 1983

At the Court at Buckingham Palace, the 27th day of July 1983

Present,

The Queen's Most Excellent Majesty in Council

Her Majesty, in pursuance of section 56 of the Trustee Savings Banks Act 1981 (**a**), is pleased, by and with the advice of Her Privy Council, to order, and it is hereby ordered, as follows:—

1. This Order may be cited as the Trustee Savings Banks Act 1981 (Channel Islands) Order 1983 and shall come into operation on 27th August 1983.

2. The Trustee Savings Banks Act 1981 in its extension to the Bailiwick of Guernsey shall have effect subject to the adaptations and modifications specified in Schedule 1 to this Order and in its extension to the Bailiwick of Jersey shall have effect subject to the adaptations and modifications specified in Schedule 2 to this Order.

3. The Trustee Savings Banks (Channel Islands) Order 1970 (**b**) and the Trustee Savings Banks Act 1976 (Channel Islands) Order 1976 (**c**) are hereby revoked.

N. E. Leigh,
Clerk of the Privy Council.

(**a**) 1981 c.65.   (**b**) S.I. 1970/1440.   (**c**) S.I. 1976/2149.

Article 2   SCHEDULE 1

ADAPTATIONS AND MODIFICATIONS TO THE TRUSTEE SAVINGS BANKS ACT 1981 AS
EXTENDING TO THE BAILIWICK OF GUERNSEY

1.   In this Schedule, "the Bailiwick" means the Bailiwick of Guernsey and the
territorial waters adjacent thereto.

2.   Subject as hereinafter provided and save where the context otherwise requires,
any reference to the Trustee Savings Banks Act 1981 or to any other enactment shall
be construed as a reference to that enactment as it has effect in the Bailiwick.

3.   Section 7(6) shall be omitted.

4.   Section 11(5) shall be omitted.

5.   In section 24(2), all the words after paragraph (d) shall be omitted.

6.   In section 31, for paragraph (b) there shall be substituted the following
paragraph:—

"(b) the bank is wound up by order of the Royal Court sitting as an Ordinary Court
    under the provisions of the Law entitled "Loi Relative aux Sociétés Anonymes
    ou à Responsibilité Limitée" registered on the 21st March, 1908, or by order
    of the Court of Alderney under the provisions of the Companies (Amend-
    ment) (Alderney) Law, 1962 and the provisions with respect to compulsory
    winding up under either of those Laws shall apply in relation to the bank
    subject to such modifications as may be provided by rules made by the Royal
    Court sitting as a Full Court.".

7.   In section 35(2), for the words from "any judge of the High Court" to "standing
in Scotland," there shall be substituted the words "the Bailiff of Guernsey who, if
satisfied that an examination into the affairs of the bank is desirable, may thereupon
appoint an Advocate of the Royal Court of Guernsey of not less than seven years'
standing,".

8.   In section 35(4), for paragraphs (a) and (b) there shall be substituted the words
"in the Bailiwick, to a fine not exceeding £25.".

9.   In section 35(5), for the words from "a master or taxing officer" to "Scotland"
there shall be substituted the words "Her Majesty's Procureur".

10.   In section 36(4), for all the words after the word "conviction," there shall be
substituted the words "has the same meaning as it has for the time being in those
sections as they have effect in England and Wales (that is to say, the prescribed sum
within the meaning of section 32 of the Magistrates' Courts Act 1980).".

11.   In section 40, for subsection (1) and the marginal note to the section there shall
be substituted the following:—

"Time limit   40 (1) Proceedings in the Bailiwick for any offence under section 36 or
for   38 may, subject to subsection (2) of this section, be commenced at any
commence-   time—
ment of
proceeding   (a) within the period of one year beginning with the date on which
under s.36   evidence, sufficient in the opinion of Her Majesty's Procureur to
or 38.   justify proceedings, comes to his knowledge, or

                    (b) where such evidence was reported to him by the Chief Registrar
                        of Friendly Societies within one year after the date on which it
                        came to the knowledge of the Chief Registrar.".

12.   In section 40(3), for the words from "the Lord Advocate" to "for Scotland"
there shall be substituted the words "Her Majesty's Procureur or the Chief Registrar
of Friendly Societies".

13.   In section 41(1), for the words "the United Kingdom" there shall be
substituted the words "the Bailiwick".

14.   In section 41(2), for the words from "by a court" to "Northern Ireland" there shall be substituted the words "by the Royal Court sitting as a Full Court".

15.   In section 45(2), for the word "Scotland" there shall be substituted the words "the Bailiwick".

16.   In section 50, after the words "stamp duty" there shall be inserted the words "or, in Guernsey, document duty".

17.   In section 52(1), for the words "the United Kingdom" there shall be substituted the words "the Bailiwick".

18.   In section 52(2), for the words from "by a court" to "Northern Ireland" there shall be substituted the words "by the Royal Court sitting as a Full Court".

19.   In section 54(1)—

(a) for the definition of "enactment" there shall be substituted the following definitions:—

" "document duty" has the meaning assigned to it by section 1(1) of the Document Duty (Guernsey) Law 1973;

"enactment" means any enactment in force in the Bailiwick or any part thereof;";

(b) after the definition of "financial year" there shall be inserted the following definition:—

" "Her Majesty's Procureur" includes Her Majesty's Comptroller;"; and

(c) for the definition of "subsidiary" there shall be substituted the following definition:—

" "subsidiary" has the meaning assigned to it by section 20 of the Protection of Depositors (Bailiwick of Guernsey) Ordinance 1971;".

20.   Section 54(2) shall be omitted.

21.   In section 56 there shall be added at the end the following subsection:—

"(2) Any order, regulations or warrant made under any of the preceding provisions of this Act, other than this section, shall not have effect in the Bailiwick until registered by the Royal Court.".

22.   In paragraph 14(2) of Schedule 2, for the words "the United Kingdom" there shall be substituted the words "the Bailiwick".

23.   In Part II of Schedule 4 there shall be added at the end the following paragraph:—

"23. Any security issued by the States of Guernsey or Jersey of which principal and interest are charged on the annual income of the States issuing that security.".

SCHEDULE 2   Article 2

ADAPTATIONS AND MODIFICATIONS TO THE TRUSTEE SAVINGS BANKS ACT 1981 AS EXTENDING TO THE BAILIWICK OF JERSEY

1.   In this Schedule, "the Bailiwick" means the Bailiwick of Jersey and the territorial waters adjacent thereto.

2.   Subject as hereinafter provided and save where the context otherwise requires, any reference to the Trustee Savings Banks Act 1981 or to any other enactment shall be construed as a reference to that enactment as it has effect in the Bailiwick.

3.   Section 7(6) shall be omitted.

4.   Section 11(5) shall be omitted.

5.   In section 24(2), all the words after paragraph (d) shall be omitted.

6.   In section 31, paragraph (b) shall be omitted.

7.   In section 35(2), for the words from "any judge of the High Court" to "standing in Scotland," there shall be substituted the words "the Bailiff of Jersey who, if satisfied that an examination into the affairs of the bank is desirable, may thereupon appoint an Advocate of the Royal Court of not less than 7 years' standing".

8.   In section 35, for the words from "on summary conviction" where they appear in subsection (4) to the end of that subsection there shall be substituted the words "on conviction, for each offence be liable to a fine not exceeding £25.".

9.   In section 35(5), for the words from "a master or taxing officer" to "Scotland" there shall be substituted the words "the Judicial Greffe".

10.   In section 36, for subsection (3) there shall be substituted the following subsection:—

"(3) If a trustee savings bank contravenes a direction under this section, it shall be liable to a fine, and every trustee who knowingly authorises or permits such a contravention shall be liable to a fine or to imprisonment for a term not exceeding two years, or to both.".

11.   Section 36(4) shall be omitted.

12.   In section 38, for subsection (4) there shall be substituted the following subsection:—

"(4) If a trustee savings bank contravenes any provision contained in regulations under this section, it shall be liable to a fine, and every trustee who knowingly contravenes or authorises or permits a contravention of any provision contained in regulations under this section shall be liable to a fine or to imprisonment for a term not exceeding two years, or to both.".

13.   In section 38, for subsection (5) there shall be substituted the following subsection:—

"(5) If an employee of a trustee savings bank knowingly contravenes any provision contained in regulations under this section he shall be liable to a fine or to imprisonment for a term not exceeding two years, or to both.".

14.   Section 38(6) shall be omitted.

15.   In section 40, for subsection (1) and the marginal note to the section there shall be substituted the following:—

"Time limit for commencement of proceedings under s.36 or 38.

40 (1) Proceedings in the Bailiwick for any offence under section 36 or 38 may, subject to subsection (2) of this section, be commenced at any time—

(a) within the period of one year beginning with the date on which evidence, sufficient in the opinion of the Attorney General to justify proceedings, comes to his knowledge, or

(b) where such evidence was reported to him by the Chief Registrar of Friendly Societies within one year after the date on which it came to the knowledge of the Chief Registrar.".

16.   In section 40(3), for the words from "the Lord Advocate" to "for Scotland" there shall be substituted the words "Attorney General or the Chief Registrar of Friendly Societies".

17.   In section 41(1), for the words "the United Kingdom" there shall be substituted the words "the Bailiwick".

18.   In section 41(2), the words "on indictment" and "by a court in England, Wales or Northern Ireland" shall be omitted.

19.   In section 45(2), for the word "Scotland" there shall be substituted the words "the Bailiwick".

20.   In section 52(1), for the words "the United Kingdom" there shall be substituted the words "the Bailiwick".

21. In section 52(2), the words "on indictment" and "by a court in England, Wales or Northern Ireland" shall be omitted.

22. In section 54(1)—

(a) for the definition of "enactment" there shall be substituted the following definition:—

""enactment" means any enactment in force in the Bailiwick"; and

(b) in the definition of "subsidiary" the words from "or section 148" to the end shall be omitted.

23. Section 54(2) shall be omitted.

24. In section 56, there shall be added at the end the following subsection:—

"(2) Any order, regulations or warrant made under any of the preceding provisions of this Act, other than this section, shall not have effect in the Bailiwick until registered by the Royal Court.".

25. In paragraph 14(2) of Schedule 2, for the words "the United Kingdom" there shall be substituted the words "the Bailiwick".

26. In Part II of Schedule 4, there shall be added at the end the following paragraph:—

"23. Any security issued by the States of Jersey or Guernsey of which principal and interest are charged on the annual income of the States issuing that security.".

EXPLANATORY NOTE

(This Note is not part of the Order.)

The Trustee Savings Banks Act 1981 extends to the Channel Islands, subject to such adaptations and modifications as may be specified by Order in Council. This Order provides for those adaptations and modifications.

STATUTORY INSTRUMENTS

1983 No. 1127

MINISTERS OF THE CROWN

The Transfer of Functions (Trade and Industry) Order 1983

Made - - - - -	*27th July* 1983
Laid before Parliament	*4th August* 1983
Coming into Operation	*11th August* 1983

At the Court at Buckingham Palace, the 27th day of July 1983

Present,

The Queen's Most Excellent Majesty in Council

Her Majesty, in pursuance of sections 1 and 2 of the Ministers of the Crown Act 1975**(a)**, is pleased, by and with the advice of Her Privy Council, to order, and it is hereby ordered, as follows:

Citation, interpretation and commencement

1.—(1) This Order may be cited as the Transfer of Functions (Trade and Industry) Order 1983.

(2) In this Order—

(*a*) "civil aviation and shipping functions" means functions relating to civil aviation, merchant shipping or hovercraft, including any functions relating to harbours, docks, tidal waters, lighthouses or the coastguard service but does not include any wireless telegraphy functions, and except in Article 2 below any reference to civil aviation and shipping functions includes a reference to any such functions which before the making of this Order have been entrusted to the Secretary of State for Transport; and

(*b*) "wireless telegraphy functions" means functions relating to wireless telegraphy which before the making of this Order have been entrusted to the Secretary of State for Trade and Industry.

(3) This Order shall come into operation on 11th August 1983.

Transfer of functions and property

2.—(1) The functions of the Secretary of State for Industry and of the Secretary of State for Trade, other than any civil aviation and shipping functions, are hereby transferred to the Secretary of State for Trade and Industry.

(a) 1975 c. 26.

(2) The functions of the Secretary of State and the Board of Trade under section 111 of the Companies Act 1967**(a)** (disclosure of information, except for specified purposes, only to a competent authority), which by virtue of Article 2(1) of the Secretary of State for Trade and Industry Order 1970**(b)** are exercisable concurrently, are hereby transferred to the Secretary of State for Trade and Industry.

(3) The civil aviation and shippiung functions of the Secretary of State for Trade are hereby transferred to the Secretary of State for Transport.

(4) It is hereby directed that the civil aviation and shipping functions of the Board of Trade which at the coming into operation of this Order are exercisable concurrently with any other Minister of the Crown shall cease to be exercisable by the Board of Trade.

3.—(1) Subject to paragraph (3) below, there are hereby transferred to the Secretary of State for Trade and Industry all property, rights and liabilities to which the Secretary of State for Industry or the Secretary of State for Trade was, immediately before the coming into operation of this Order, entitled or subject.

(2) There are hereby transferred to the Secretary of State for Trade and Industry all property, rights and liabilities to which the Secretary of State for the Home Department was immediately before the coming into operation of this Order entitled or subject in connection with any wireless telegraphy functions.

(3) There are hereby transferred to the Secretary of State for Transport all property, rights and liabilities to which the Secretary of State for Trade was immediately before the coming into operation of this Order entitled or subject in connection with any civil aviation and shipping functions.

Supplemental
4.—(1) This Order shall not affect the validity of anything done before the coming into operation of this Order by or in relation to a Secretary of State and anything (including legal proceedings) which is then in the process of being done by or in relation to the Secretary of State for the Home Department in connection with any wireless telegraphy functions or the Secretary of State for Industry or the Secretary of State for Trade may be continued—

    (*a*) by or in relation to the Secretary of State for Transport in the case of anything in the process of being done in connection with any civil aviation and shipping functions;

    (*b*) by or in relation to the Secretary of State for Trade and Industry in any other case.

(2) Any authorisation given (by way of approval or otherwise), requirement imposed or appointment made by—

    (*a*) the Secretary of State for the Home Department in connection with any wireless telegraphy functions, or

    (*b*) the Secretary of State for Industry, or

    (*c*) the Secretary of State for Trade,

(a) 1967 c. 81.   **(b)** S.I. 1970/1537.

or having effect as if so given, imposed or made shall, if in force on the coming into operation of this Order and so far as may be necessary for it to continue in force thereafter, have effect as if given, imposed or made by the Secretary of State for Transport, if it was given, imposed or made in exercise of any civil aviation and shipping functions, or, in any other case, by the Secretary of State for Trade and Industry.

(3) Any enactment, instrument, contract or other document passed, made or printed before the coming into operation of this Order shall have effect so far as may be necessary for the purposes of or in consequence of any of the preceding provisions of this Order or of any functions of the Secretary of State which had been entrusted to the Secretary of State for the Home Department or the Secretary of State for Industry or the Secretary of State for Trade having been entrusted to the Secretary of State for Trade and Industry or the Secretary of State for Transport—

(a) if it is connected with any civil aviation and shipping functions, as if any reference to the Secretary of State for Trade, the Department of Trade or an officer of that Minister or to the President of the Board of Trade, to the Board of Trade or an officer of the Board were or included a reference to the Secretary of State for Transport, the Department of Transport or an officer of that Minister;

(b) if it is connected with any wireless telegraphy functions, as if any reference to the Secretary of State for the Home Department, an officer of his or the Home office were or included a reference to the Secretary of State for Trade and Industry, an officer of his or the Department of Trade and Industry; and

(c) in any other case, as if any reference to the Secretary of State for Industry or the Secretary of State for Trade, an officer of either or the Department of Industry or the Department of Trade were or included a reference to the Secretary of State for Trade and Industry, an officer of his or the Department of Trade and Industry.

5.—(1) In Schedule 2 to the Parliamentary Commissioner Act 1967**(a)** (departments subject to investigation)—

(a) the words "Department of Industry" shall cease to have effect, and

(b) for the words "Department of Trade" here shall be substituted "Department of Trade and Industry".

(2) In section 1(5) of the Air Travel Reserve Fund Act 1975**(b)** (restrictions on eligibility for appointment as chairman of the Air Travel Reserve Fund Agency) for the words "the Department of Trade" there shall be substituted the words "the Department of Transport".

(a) 1967 c. 13, amended by S.I. 1974/692, Article 4(1).
(b) 1975 c. 36.

(3) In paragraph 1 of Schedule 9 to the Finance Act 1981**(a)** for the words "the Department of Industry" there shall be substituted the words "the Department of Trade and Industry".

N. E. Leigh,
Clerk of the Privy Council.

EXPLANATORY NOTE

(*This Note is not part of the Order.*)

This Order transfers certain functions to the Secretary of State for Trade and Industry and others to the Secretary of State for Transport and makes provision in consequence of various functions having been entrusted to the Secretary of State for Trade and Industry or the Secretary of State for Transport.

It transfers all the functions of the Secretary of State for Industry and of the Secretary of State for Trade to the Secretary of State for Trade and Industry except civil aviation and shipping functions of the Secretary of State for Trade, which are transferred to the Secretary of State for Transport. It also has the effect that civil aviation and shipping functions shall cease to be exercisable concurrently by the Board of Trade.

The functions under section 111 of the Companies Act 1967 which are exercisable concurrently by the Secretary of State and the Board of Trade are transferred to the Secretary of State for Trade and Industry.

The Order transfers to the Secretary of State for Trade and Industry all property, rights and liabilities of the Secretary of State for Industry and the Secretary of State for Trade except those connected with civil aviation and shipping functions, which are transferred to the Secretary of State for Transport. It also transfers to the Secretary of State for Trade and Industry property, rights and liabilities connected with the wireless telegraphy functions which have been entrusted to him and were previously entrusted to the Secretary of State for the Home Department.

The Order also contains supplemental provisions set out in Article 4.

(a) 1981 c. 35.

STATUTORY INSTRUMENTS

1983 No. 1128

PARLIAMENT

The Ministerial and other Salaries Order 1983

Laid before Parliament in draft

Made - - - -	*27th July* 1983
Coming into Operation	*27th July* 1983

At the Court at Buckingham Palace, the 27th day of July 1983

Present,

The Queen's Most Excellent Majesty in Council

Whereas a draft of this Order has been approved by resolution of each House of Parliament:

Now, therefore, Her Majesty, in pursuance of section 1(4) of the Ministerial and other Salaries Act 1975(**a**) is pleased, by and with the advice of Her Privy Council, to order, and it is hereby ordered, as follows:—

Citation, commencement and revocation

1.—(1) This Order may be cited as the Ministerial and other Salaries Order 1983.

(2) This Order shall come into operation on 27th July 1983.

(3) The Ministerial and other Salaries Order 1982(**b**) is hereby revoked.

Increase of Ministerial salaries

2.—(1) For the amount specified in section 1(2) of the Ministerial and other Salaries Act 1975 ("the 1975 Act") as the aggregate annual amount of the salary payable to the Lord Chancellor under that subsection and the salary payable to him as Speaker of the House of Lords there shall be substituted—

     (a) for the period beginning with 27th July 1983 and ending with 31st December 1983, £58,500,

     (b) for 1984 and any subsequent period, £62,000.

(2) For the annual amount, or the maximum or minimum annual amount, of salary specified in Parts I, II, III and IV of Schedule 1 to the 1975 Act in relation to each of the offices specified in the first column of Schedule 1 to this Order there shall be substituted—

(**a**) 1975 c. 27.   (**b**) S.I. 1982/848.

(a) for the period beginning with 27th July 1983 and ending with 31st December 1983, the amount, or the maximum or minimum amount, of salary specified in relation to that office in the second column of that Schedule;

(b) for 1984, the amount, or the maximum or minimum amount, of salary specified in relation to that office in the third column of that Schedule;

(c) for 1985, the amount, or the maximum or minimum amount, of salary specified in relation to that office in the fourth column of that Schedule;

(d) for 1986, the amount, or the maximum or minimum amount, of salary specifed in relation to that office in the fifth column of that Schedule; and

(e) for 1987 and any subsequent period, the amount, or the maximum or minimum amount, of salary specified in relation to that office in the sixth column of that Schedule.

Increase of salaries of Opposition Leaders and Whips

3. For the annual amount of salary specified in Part I of Schedule 2 to the 1975 Act in relation to each of the positions specified in the first column of Schedule 2 to this Order there shall be substituted—

(a) for the period beginning with 27th July 1983 and ending with 31st December 1983, the amount specified in relation to that position in the second column of that Schedule;

(b) for 1984, the amount specified in relation to that position in the third column of that Schedule;

(c) for 1985, the amount specified in relation to that position in the fourth column of that Schedule;

(d) for 1986, the amount specified in relation to that position in the fifth column of that Schedule; and

(e) for 1987 and any subsequent period, the amount specified in relation to that position in the sixth column of that Schedule.

Increase of the Speaker's salary

4. For the annual amount specified in section 1(3) of the 1975 Act as the salary of the Speaker of the House of Commons there shall be substituted—

(a) for the period beginning with 27th July 1983 and ending with 31st December 1983, £30,797;

(b) for 1984, £31,814;

(c) for 1985, £32,851;

(d) for 1986, £33,858; and

(e) for 1987 and any subsequent period, £34,875.

N. E. Leigh,
Clerk of the Privy Council.

Article 2(2)

SCHEDULE 1

MINISTERIAL SALARIES

PART I

Office	Salary until end of 1983 £	Salary in 1984 £	Salary in 1985 £	Salary in 1986 £	Salary in and after 1987 £
Prime Minister and First Lord of the Treasury ...	38,987	40,424	41,891	43,328	44,775
Chancellor of the Exchequer ... ... Secretary of State ... ... Minister of Agriculture, Fisheries and Food	30,110	31,680	33,260	34,820	36,390

Any of the following offices for so long as the holder is a member of the Cabinet:—

   (a) Lord President of the Council;
   (b) Lord Privy Seal;
   (c) Chancellor of the Duchy of Lancaster;
   (d) Paymaster General;
   (e) Chief Secretary to the Treasury;
   (f) Parliamentary Secretary to the Treasury;
   (g) Minister of State.

PART II

Office	Salary until end of 1983 £	Salary in 1984 £	Salary in 1985 £	Salary in 1986 £	Salary in and after 1987 £
1. Any of the offices listed at (a) to (g) in Part I above for so long as the holder is not a member of the Cabinet ...					
2. Minister in charge of a public department of Her Majesty's Government in the United Kingdom who is not a member of the Cabinet, and whose office is not specified elsewhere in this Schedule	20,867– 25,350	21,364– 26,670	21,881– 28,000	22,378– 29,320	22,875– 30,640
3. Financial Secretary to the Treasury					

PART III

Office	Salary until end of 1983 £	Salary in 1984 £	Salary in 1985 £	Salary in 1986 £	Salary in and after 1987 £
Attorney General	31,187	32,224	33,281	34,308	35,345
Lord Advocate	30,160	31,730	33,320	34,890	36,460
Solicitor General	25,617	26,364	27,131	27,878	28,625
Solicitor General for Scotland	21,877	22,424	22,991	23,538	24,085

PART IV

Office	Salary until end of 1983 £	Salary in 1984 £	Salary in 1985 £	Salary in 1986 £	Salary in and after 1987 £
Captain of the Honourable Corps of Gentleman-at-Arms Treasurer of Her Majesty's Household ...	25,350	26,670	28,000	29,320	30,640
Parlimentary Secretary other than Parlimentary Secretary to the Treasury ...	20,867	21,364	21,881	22,378	22,875
Captain of the Queen's Bodyguard of the Yeomen of the Guard ...	20,390	21,450	22,520	23,580	24,640
Lord in Waiting	20,390	21,450	22,520	23,580	24,640
Comptroller for Her Majesty's Household ...	17,840	18,770	19,710	20,640	21,570
Vice-Chamberlain of Her Majesty's Household Junior Lord of the Treasury Assistant Whip, House of Commons ...	13,367	13,474	13,601	13,708	13,815

Article 3

SCHEDULE 2

OPPOSITION LEADERS AND WHIPS

Position	Salary until end of 1983 £	Salary in 1984 £	Salary in 1985 £	Salary in 1986 £	Salary in and after 1987 £
In the House of Commons—					
Leader of the Opposition	26,947	27,764	28,601	29,408	30,225
Chief Opposition Whip	20,867	21,364	21,881	22,378	22,875
Assistant Opposition Whip	13,367	13,474	13,601	13,708	13,815
In the House of Lords—					
Leader of the Opposition	20,390	21,450	22,520	23,580	24,640
Chief Opposition Whip	17,840	18,770	19,710	20,640	21,570

EXPLANATORY NOTE

(This Note is not part of the Order.)

This Order increases salaries payable under the Ministerial and other Salaries Act 1975 to Ministers, to salaried Members of the Opposition and to the Speaker of the House of Commons. The salaries specified in the Schedules to the Order which are payable from 27th July 1983 represent an average increase of 2·1 per cent. Those so specified which are payable for 1984, 1985, 1986 and 1987 represent average increases of 3 per cent., 3 per cent., 2·8 per cent. and 2·7 per cent. respectively. The amounts specified in this Order are the maximum salaries payable. The actual salaries in payment may therefore be below these levels.

STATUTORY INSTRUMENTS

1983 No. 1129

ELECTRICITY

The Electricity (Consumers' Council) Regulations 1983

Made - - - -	*26th July* 1983
Laid before Parliament	*28th July* 1983
Coming into Operation	*1st September* 1983

The Secretary of State, in exercise of the powers conferred on him by paragraph 8(1) of Schedule 2 to the Energy Act 1983(a) and of all other powers enabling him in that behalf, hereby makes the following Regulations:—

Citation and commencement

1. These Regulations may be cited as the Electricity (Consumers' Council) Regulations 1983 and shall come into operation on 1st September 1983.

Appointment and tenure of office

2.—(1) The appointment of a member of the Electricity Consumers' Council (hereinafter referred to as "the Council") shall be for such term not exceeding three years as may before that member's appointment be determined by the Secretary of State and shall be subject to Regulation 3 and to any conditions notified to him in writing by the Secretary of State.

(2) Any member of the Council may, on the expiry of his term of office, be reappointed.

(3) Such member of the Council as the Secretary of State may appoint shall act as deputy chairman of the Council.

(4) Any member of the Council may resign his office by giving to the Secretary of State either one month's notice in writing or such shorter notice as he may approve.

Vacation of office

3. If the Secretary of State is satisfied that a member of the Council—

    (*a*) has become bankrupt or made an arrangement with his creditors;

    (*b*) is incapacitated by physical or mental illness;

    (*c*) has been absent from meetings of the Council for a period longer than six consecutive months without the permission of the Secretary of State; or

    (*d*) is otherwise unable or unfit to discharge the functions of a member,

---

(a) 1983 c. 25.

the Secretary of State may declare his office as a member to be vacant; and thereupon the office shall become vacant.

Frequency and constitution of meetings

4.—(1) The Council shall meet as often as may be necessary for the proper discharge of their duties; and the period between any two consecutive meetings shall not be longer than six months.

(2) Where one third or more of all existing members of the Council deliver to the Secretary of the Council a written requisition for a meeting, the chairman or, if the chairman is not available, the deputy chairman shall ensure that a meeting is held before the expiry of fourteen days from the delivery of that requisition.

(3) No meetings of the Council shall be held unless either the chairman or deputy chairman is present, but if by reason of vacancy in their offices or their serious illness or absence from England and Wales neither of them is available, or a meeting is not held before the expiry of fourteen days from the delivery of the said requisition, the Council may meet and pass provisional resolutions which shall have effect until the next duly constituted meeting after they were passed and which may be ratified at that meeting.

(4) The Council may determine its own quorum.

Voting

5. Every resolution of the Council shall be passed by a majority of the votes of the members of the Council present and voting, and in the event of an equality of votes the proposal in question shall be deemed to have been rejected.

Minutes and evidence of proceedings

6. The Council shall keep, or cause to be kept, minutes of their proceedings, and a record in any such minutes specifying the terms of a resolution passed at any meeting, and, in the case of a resolution that a representation be made to the Electricity Council or the Secretary of State, the number of votes cast for and against it shall, if signed by the person purporting to be acting as chairman of the meeting to which the minutes relate, or of a meeting at which they were read, be evidence of those proceedings.

Execution of documents

7. Any document requiring to be executed by or on behalf of the Council shall be signed by the chairman and secretary of the Council or by such one or more of the members and officers of the Council as the Council may in any particular case determine.

Alexander Fletcher,
Parliamentary Under Secretary of State,
Department of Trade and Industry.

26th July 1983.

EXPLANATORY NOTE

(This Note is not part of the Regulations.)

These Regulations make provision for the appointment and tenure of office of members of the Electricity Consumers' Council established by the Energy Act 1983 for England and Wales, including the power of the Secretary of State to terminate such an appointment and to appoint a deputy chairman of the Council, the proceedings and meetings of the Council, and the execution of documents by or on behalf of the Council.

STATUTORY INSTRUMENTS

1983 No. 1130

HEALTH AND SAFETY

MINES AND QUARRIES

The Mines (Miscellaneous Amendments) Regulations 1983

Made - - - - -	*25th July* 1983
Laid before Parliament	*27th July* 1983
Coming into Operation	*18th August* 1983

The Secretary of State, in exercise of the powers conferred on him by section 15(1), (2) and (3)(*a*) of, and paragraphs 1(1)(*a*), (2) and (3), 12 and 18(*a*) of Schedule 3 to, the Health and Safety at Work etc. Act 1974**(a)** ("the 1974 Act") and of all other powers enabling him in that behalf, and for the purpose of giving effect without modifications to proposals submitted to him by the Health and Safety Commission under section 11(2)(*d*) of the 1974 Act after the carrying out by the said Commission of consultations in accordance with section 50(3) of that Act, hereby makes the following Regulations:—

Citation and commencement

1. These Regulations may be cited as the Mines (Miscellaneous Amendments) Regulations 1983 and shall come into operation on 18th August 1983.

Amendment to Regulations

2.—(1) In Regulation 5 of the Miscellaneous Mines (Electricity) Regulations 1956**(b)** after "conditions" there shall be inserted "or electrical equipment which has received a certificate of conformity or a certificate of inspection in accordance with Article 4(1) of the Council Directive No. 82/130/EEC**(c)** 'on the approximation of the laws of the Member States concerning electrical equipment for use in potentially explosive atmospheres in mines susceptible to fire-damp' and which bears the distinctive Community mark provided for in Article 11 of that Directive".

(a) 1974 c. 37; section 15 was amended by the Employment Protection Act 1975 (c. 71), Schedule 15, paragraph 6.

(b) S.I. 1956/1779; the relevant amending instrument is S.I. 1974/2013.

(c) OJ No. L59, 2.3.82, p. 10.

(2) In Regulation 12(1)(*b*) of the Coal Mines (Firedamp Drainage) Regulations 1960**(a)** after "flameproof" there shall be added "or is electrical equipment which has received a certificate of conformity or a certificate of inspection in accordance with Article 4(1) of Council Directive No. 82/130/EEC 'on the approximation of the laws of the Member States concerning electrical equipment for use in potentially explosive atmospheres in mines susceptible to fire-damp' and which bears the distinctive Community mark provided for in Article 11 of that Directive".

Giles Shaw,
Parliamentary Under Secretary of State,
Department of Energy.

25th July 1983.

John Selwyn Gummer,
Parliamentary Under Secretary of State,
Department of Employment.

25th July 1983.

EXPLANATORY NOTE

(*This Note is not part of the Regulations.*)

These Regulations amend the Miscellaneous Mines (Electricity) Regulations 1956 and the Coal Mines (Firedamp Drainage) Regulations 1960. They implement the provisions of Council Directive No. 82/130/EEC (which relates to the approximation of the laws of the Member States concerning electrical equipment for use in potentially explosive atmospheres in mines susceptible to firedamp) by allowing the use of electrical equipment which has been certified and marked in accordance with the Directive in areas specified in those Regulations.

(a) S.I. 1960/1015; the relevant amending instrument is S.I. 1974/2013.

STATUTORY INSTRUMENTS

1983 No. 1132

INDUSTRIAL TRAINING

The Industrial Training Levy (Clothing and Allied Products) Order 1983

Made - - - -	*26th July* 1983
Laid before Parliament	*4th August* 1983
Coming into Operation	*26th August* 1983

Whereas proposals made by the Clothing and Allied Products Industry Training Board for the raising and collection of a levy have been submitted to, and approved by, the Manpower Services Commission under section 11(1) of the Industrial Training Act 1982 (a) ("the 1982 Act") and have thereafter been submitted by the said Commission to the Secretary of State under that subsection;

And whereas in pursuance of section 11(3) of the 1982 Act the said proposals include provision for the exemption from the levy of employers who, in view of the small number of their employees, ought in the opinion of the Secretary of State to be exempted from it;

And whereas the Secretary of State estimates that the amount which, disregarding any exemptions, will be payable by virtue of this Order by any employer in the clothing and allied products industry, does not exceed an amount which the Secretary of State estimates is equal to one per cent. of the relevant emoluments, being the aggregate of the emoluments and payments intended to be disbursed as emoluments which have been paid or are payable by any such employer to or in respect of persons employed in the industry, in respect of the period specified in the said proposals as relevant, that is to say the period hereafter referred to in this Order as "the fourteenth base period";

Now, therefore, the Secretary of State in exercise of the powers conferred on him by sections 11(2), 12(3) and 12(4) of the 1982 Act and of all other powers enabling him in that behalf hereby makes the following Order:—

Citation and commencement

1. This Order may be cited as the Industrial Training Levy (Clothing and Allied Products) Order 1983 and shall come into operation on 26th August 1983.

Interpretation

2.—(1) In this Order unless the context otherwise requires:—

    (*a*) "agriculture" has the same meaning as in section 109(3) of the Agriculture Act 1947 (b) or, in relation to Scotland, as in section 86(3) of the Agriculture (Scotland) Act 1948 (c) ;

    (*b*) "assessment" means an assessment of an employer to the levy;

(a) 1982 c.10.   (**b**) 1947 c.48.   (c) 1948 c.45.

(c) "the Board" means the Clothing and Allied Products Industry Training Board;

(d) "business" means any activities of industry or commerce;

(e) "charity" has the same meaning as in section 360 of the Income and Corporation Taxes Act 1970(a) ;

(f) "clothing and allied products establishment" means an establishment in Great Britain engaged in the fourteenth base period wholly or mainly in the clothing and allied products industry for a total of twenty-seven or more weeks or, being an establishment that commenced to carry on business in the fourteenth base period, for a total number of weeks exceeding one half of the number of weeks in the part of the said period commencing with the day on which business was commenced and ending on the last day thereof;

(g) "the clothing and allied products industry" does not include any activities which have been transferred from the industry of the Board to the industry of another industrial training board by one of the transfer orders but save as aforesaid means any one or more of the activities which, subject to the provisions of paragraph 2 of Schedule 1 to the industrial training order, are specified in paragraph 1 of that Schedule as the activities of the clothing and allied products industry or, in relation to an establishment whose activities have been transferred to the industry of the Board by one of the transfer orders, any activities so transferred;

(h) "emoluments" means all emoluments assessable to income tax under Schedule E (other than pensions), being emoluments from which tax under that Schedule is deductible, whether or not tax in fact falls to be deducted from any particular payment thereof;

(i) "employer" means a person who is an employer in the clothing and allied products industry at any time in the fourteenth levy period;

(j) "the industrial training order" means the Industrial Training (Clothing and Allied Products Board) Order 1969(b) ;

(k) "the levy" means the levy imposed by the Board in respect of the fourteenth levy period;

(l) "notice" means a notice in writing;

(m) "the transfer orders" means

(i) the Industrial Training (Transfer of the Activities of Establishments) (No. 3) Order 1976(c) , and

(ii) the Industrial Training (Transfer of the Activities of Establishments) Order 1977(d) ;

(n) "the fourteenth base period" means the period of twelve months that commenced on 6th April 1982;

(o) "the fourteenth levy period" means the period commencing with the day upon which this Order comes into operation and ending on 31st March 1984.

(2) Any reference in this Order to persons employed at or from a clothing and allied products establishment shall in any case where the employer is a company be construed as including a reference to any director of the company (or any person occupying the position of director by whatever name he was called) who was, at the material time, in receipt of a salary from the company.

(a) 1970 c.10.   (b) S.I. 1969/1375, amended by S.I. 1982/920.
(c) S.I. 1976/2110.   (d) S.I. 1977/1951.

(3) Any reference in this Order to an establishment that commences to carry on business or that ceases to carry on business shall not be taken to apply where the location of the establishment is changed but its business is continued wholly or mainly at or from the new location, or where the suspension of activities is of a temporary or seasonal nature.

Imposition of the levy

3.—(1) The levy to be imposed by the Board on employers in respect of the fourteenth levy period shall be assessed in accordance with the provisions of this Article.

(2) Subject to the provisions of this Article, the levy shall be assessed by the Board in respect of each employer and the amount thereof shall be equal to 0·11 per cent. of the sum of the emoluments of all the persons employed by the employer at or from the relevant establishment or establishments (that is to say the clothing and allied products establishment or establishments of the employer other than one which is an establishment of an employer who is exempted by virtue of paragraph (3) of this Article) in the fourteenth base period.

(3) There shall be exempt from the levy:—

    (a) an employer in respect of whom the sum of the emoluments of the persons mentioned in the last foregoing paragraphs is less than £68,250;

    (b) a charity.

(4) Where any persons whose emoluments are taken into account for the purposes of this Article were employed at or from an establishment that ceases to carry on business in the fourteenth levy period, the sum of the emoluments of those persons shall be reduced for such purposes in the same proportion as the number of days between the commencement of the said levy period and the date of cessation of business (both dates inclusive) bears to the number of days in the said levy period.

(5) For the purposes of this Article, no regard shall be had to the emoluments of any person wholly engaged:—

    (a) in agriculture; or

    (b) in the supply of food or drink for immediate consumption.

Assessment notices

4.—(1) The Board shall serve an assessment notice on every employer assessed to the levy.

(2) The amount of an assessment shall be rounded down to the nearest £1.

(3) An assessment notice shall state the Board's address for the service of a notice of appeal or of an application for an extension of time for appealing.

(4) An assessment notice may be served on the person assessed to the levy either by delivering it to him personally or by leaving it, or sending it to him by post, at his last known address or place of business in the United Kingdom or, if that person is a corporation, by leaving it, or sending it by post to the corporation, at such address or place of business or at its registered or principal office.

Payment of the levy

5.—(1) Subject to the provisions of this Article and of Articles 6 and 7, the amount of the assessment payable under an assessment notice served by the Board shall be due and payable to the Board one month after the date of the notice.

(2) The amount of an assessment shall not be recoverable by the Board until there has expired the time allowed for appealing against the assessment by Article 7(1) of this Order and any further period or periods of time that the Board or an industrial tribunal may have allowed for appealing under paragraph (2) or (3) of that Article or, where an appeal is brought, until the appeal is decided or withdrawn.

Withdrawal of assessment

6.—(1) The Board may, by a notice served on the person assessed to the levy in the same manner as an assessment notice, withdraw an assessment if that person has appealed against that assessment under the provisions of Article 7 of this Order and the appeal has not been entered in the Register of Appeals kept under the appropriate Regulations specified in paragraph (5) of that Article.

(2) The withdrawal of an assessment shall be without prejudice to the power of the Board to serve a further assessment notice on the employer.

Appeals

7.—(1) A person assessed to the levy may appeal to an industrial tribunal against the assessment within one month from the date of the service of the assessment notice or within any further period or periods of time that may be allowed by the Board or an industrial tribunal under the following provisions of this Article.

(2) The Board by notice may for good cause allow a person assessed to the levy to appeal to an industrial tribunal against the assessment at any time within the period of four months from the date of the service of the assessment notice or within such further period or periods as the Board may allow before such time as may then be limited for appealing has expired.

(3) If the Board shall not allow an application for extension of time for appealing, an industrial tribunal shall upon application made to the tribunal by the person assessed to the levy have the like powers as the Board under the last foregoing paragraph.

(4) In the case of an assessment that has reference to an establishment that ceases to carry on business in the fourteenth levy period on any day after the date of the service of the assessment notice, the foregoing provisions of this Article shall have effect as if for the period of four months from the date of the service of the assessment notice mentioned in paragraph (2) of this Article there were substituted the period of six months from the date of the cessation of business.

(5) An appeal or an application to an industrial tribunal under this Article shall be made in accordance with the Industrial Tribunals (England and Wales) Regulations 1965 (a) except where the assessment has reference to persons employed at or from one or more establishments that are wholly in Scotland and to no other persons, in which case the appeal or application shall be made in accordance with the Industrial Tribunals (Scotland) Regulations 1965(b).

(6) The powers of an industrial tribunal under paragraph (3) of this Article may be exercised by the President of the Industrial Tribunals (England and Wales) or by the President of the Industrial Tribunals (Scotland) as the case may be.

Evidence

8.—(1) Upon the discharge by a person assessed to the levy of his liability under an assessment the Board shall if so requested issue to him a certificate to that effect.

(2) The production in any proceedings of a document purporting to be certified by the Secretary of the Board to be a true copy of an assessment or other notice issued by the Board or purporting to be a certificate such as is mentioned in the foregoing paragraph of this Article shall, unless the contrary is proved, be sufficient evidence of the document and of the facts stated therein.

Signed by order of the Secretary of State.

Peter Morrison,
Minister of State,
Department of Employment.

26th July 1983.

(a) S.I. 1965/1101, amended by S.I. 1967/301, 1977/1473.
(b) S.I. 1965/1157, amended by S.I. 1967/302, 1977/1474.

EXPLANATORY NOTE

(This Note is not part of the Order.)

This Order, which comes into operation on 26th August 1983 gives effect to proposals of the Clothing and Allied Products Industry Training Board which were submitted to and approved by the Manpower Services Commission, and thereafter submitted by the Manpower Services Commission to the Secretary of State. The proposals are for the imposition of a levy on employers in the Clothing and Allied Products industry for the purpose of raising money towards meeting the expenses of the Board.

The levy is to be imposed in respect of the fourteenth levy period commencing with the day upon which this Order comes into operation and ending on 31st March 1984. The levy will be assessed by the Board and there will be a right of appeal against an assessment to an industrial tribunal.

STATUTORY INSTRUMENTS

1983 No. 1133

INDUSTRIAL TRAINING

The Industrial Training Levy (Hotel and Catering) Order 1983

Made - - - -	*26th July* 1983
Laid before Parliament	*4th August* 1983
Coming into Operation	*26th August* 1983

Whereas proposals made by the Hotel and Catering Industry Training Board for the raising and collection of a levy have been submitted to, and approved by, the Manpower Services Commission under section 11(1) of the Industrial Training Act 1982 (a) ("the 1982 Act") and have thereafter been submitted by the said Commission to the Secretary of State under that subsection;

And whereas in pursuance of section 11(3) of the 1982 Act the said proposals include provision for the exemption from the levy of employers who, in view of the small number of their employees, ought in the opinion of the Secretary of State to be exempted from it;

And whereas the Secretary of State estimates that the amount which, disregarding any exemptions, will be payable by virtue of this Order by any employer in the hotel and catering industry, does not exceed an amount which the Secretary of State estimates is equal to one per cent. of the relevant emoluments being the aggregate of the emoluments and payments intended to be disbursed as emoluments which have been paid or are payable by any such employer to or in respect of persons employed in the industry, in respect of the period specified in the said proposals as relevant, that is to say the period hereafter referred to in this Order as "the seventeenth base period";

And whereas the Secretary of State is satisfied that proposals published by the said Board in pursuance of section 13 of the 1982 Act provide for exemption certificates relating to the levy in such cases as he considers appropriate;

Now, therefore, the Secretary of State in exercise of the powers conferred on him by sections 11(2), 12(3) and 12(4) of the 1982 Act and of all other powers enabling him in that behalf hereby makes the following Order:—

Citation and commencement

1. This Order may be cited as the Industrial Training Levy (Hotel and Catering) Order 1983 and shall come into operation on 26th August 1983.

Interpretation

2.—(1) In this Order unless the context otherwise requires:—

(a) "agriculture" has the same meaning as in section 109(3) of the Agriculture Act 1947 (b) or, in relation to Scotland, as in section 86(3) of the Agriculture (Scotland) Act 1948 (c) ;

(b) "assessment" means an assessment of an employer to the levy;

(a) 1982 c.10.   (b) 1947 c.48.   (c) 1948 c.45.

(c) "the Board" means the Hotel and Catering Industry Training Board;

(d) "British Airways Group" means the British Airways Board, and all subsidiaries and joint subsidiaries, and "member of the British Airways Group" shall be construed accordingly;

(e) "charity" has the same meaning as in section 360 of the Income and Corporation Taxes Act 1970 (a) ;

(f) "emoluments" means all emoluments assessable to income tax under Schedule E (other than pensions), being emoluments from which tax under that Schedule is deductible, whether or not tax in fact falls to be deducted from any particular payment thereof;

(g) "employer" means a person who is an employer in the hotel and catering industry at any time in the seventeenth levy period;

(h) "establishment" (except in sub-paragraphs (i) and (k) of this paragraph) means an establishment comprising catering activities or a hotel and catering establishment;

(i) "establishment comprising catering activities" means an establishment in Great Britain at or from which persons were employed in the seventeenth base period in the supply of food or drink to persons for immediate consumption, but does not include:—

    (i) a hotel and catering establishment; or

    (ii) an establishment in which the employer supplied for immediate consumption light refreshments to persons employed at or from the same where the employer was not otherwise engaged at or from the establishment in any activities to which paragraph 1 of the Schedule to the industrial training order applies or in the manufacture of any chocolate or flour confectionery so supplied as light refreshments;

(j) "exemption certificate" means a certificate issued by the Board under section 14 of the 1982 Act;

(k) "hotel and catering establishment" means an establishment in Great Britain that was engaged in the seventeenth base period wholly or mainly in the hotel and catering industry;

(l) "hotel and catering industry" does not include any activities of an establishment which has been transferred from the industry of the Board to the industry of another industrial training board by one of the transfer orders but save as aforesaid means any one or more of the activities which, subject to the provisions of paragraph 2 of the Schedule to the industrial training order, are specified in paragraph 1 of that Schedule as the activities of the hotel and catering industry or, in relation to an establishment whose activities have been transferred to the industry of the Board by one of the transfer orders, any activities so transferred;

(m) "the industrial training order" means the Industrial Training (Hotel and Catering Board) Order 1966 (b);

(n) "the levy" means the levy imposed by the Board in respect of the seventeenth levy period;

(o) "notice" means a notice in writing;

(p) "the seventeenth base period" means the period of twelve months that commenced on 6th April 1982;

(a) 1970 c.10.
(b) S.I. 1966/1347, amended by S.I. 1969/1405.

(q) "the seventeenth levy period" means the period commencing with the day upon which this Order comes into operation and ending on 31st March 1984;

(r) "subsidiary" and "joint subsidiary" have the same meanings as in section 60(1) of the Civil Aviation Act 1971 (a);

(s) "the supply of food or drink to persons for immediate consumption" means such a supply either by way of business or by a person carrying on a business to persons employed in the business;

(t) "the transfer orders" means:—

(i) the Industrial Training (Transfer of the Activities of Establishments) Order 1980 (b);

(ii) the Industrial Training (Transfer of the Activities of Establishments) (No. 2) Order 1980 (c);

(u) other expressions have the same meanings as in the industrial training order.

(2) Any reference in this Order to an establishment that ceases to carry on business shall not be taken to apply where the location of the establishment is changed but its business is continued wholly or mainly at or from the new location, or where the suspension of activities is of a temporary or seasonal nature.

Imposition of the levy

3.—(1) The levy to be imposed by the Board on employers in respect of the seventeenth levy period shall be assessed in accordance with the provisions of this Article.

(2) Subject to the provisions of this Article the levy on each employer shall be assessed by the Board in respect of the emoluments paid by him to all persons to whom paragraph (3) below applies employed by the employer in the seventeenth base period at relevant establishments of his (that is to say, any hotel and catering establishment or establishments, or any establishment or establishments comprising catering activities other than an establishment of an employer who is exempt from the levy by virtue of paragraph (4) of this Article) and the amount thereof shall be:—

(a) equal to 1 per cent. of the sum of the emoluments where such emoluments are £100,000 or more;

(b) £60 where the emoluments are less than £100,000.

(3) This paragraph applies to:—

(a) in the case of a hotel and catering establishment, all persons employed;

(b) in the case of an establishment comprising catering activities, all persons employed wholly or mainly in the supply of food or drink to persons for immediate consumption.

(4) There shall be exempt from the levy:—

(a) an employer in whose case the sum of the emoluments of all the persons employed by him in the seventeenth base period in the hotel and catering industry at or from the establishment or establishments of the employer was less than £70,000;

(b) a charity.

(a) 1971 c.75. (b) S.I. 1980/586. (c) S.I. 1980/1753.

(5)

(a) Levy shall not be imposed in respect of an establishment that ceases to carry on business prior to the commencement of the seventeenth levy period;

(b) the amount of the levy imposed in respect of an establishment that ceases to carry on business in the seventeenth levy period shall be in the same proportion to the amount that would otherwise be due under the foregoing provisions of this Article as the number of days between the commencement of the said levy period and the date of cessation of business (both dates inclusive) bears to the number of days in the said levy period.

(6) For the purposes of this Article, no regard shall be had to the emoluments of any person employed as follows:—

(a) wholly in the supply (except at or in connection with an hotel, restaurant, café, snack bar, canteen, mess room or similar place of refreshment) of:—

   (i) ice-cream, chocolate confectionery, sugar confectionery or soft drink;

   (ii) shellfish or eels; or

   (iii) food or drink by means of an automatic vending machine;

(b) wholly in agriculture;

(c) otherwise than wholly in the supply of food or drink to persons for immediate consumption, where the employment is at or from an establishment engaged mainly in any activities of an industry specified in column 1 of the Schedule to this Order by virtue of the relevant industrial training order specified in column 2 of that Schedule or in any activities of two or more such industries;

(d) as a member of the crew of an aircraft, or as the master or a member of the crew of a ship or, in the case of a person ordinarily employed as a seaman, in or about a ship in port by the owner or charterer thereof on work of a kind ordinarily done by a seaman on a ship while it is in port;

(e) by a local authority in any activities mentioned in sub-paragraph (d) or (e) of paragraph 1 of the Schedule to the industrial training order, not being activities mentioned in head (ii) or head (iv) of paragraph 3(l) of that Schedule; or

(f) in any activities mentioned in sub-paragraph (b), (c) (ii), (d) or (e) of paragraph 1 of the Schedule to the industrial training order when carried out by:—

   (i) a harbour authority while acting in that capacity;

   (ii) the Electricity Council, the Central Electricity Generating Board or an Area Electricity Board;

   (iii) the North of Scotland Hydro-Electric Board or the South of Scotland Electricity Board;

   (iv) the British Gas Corporation;

   (v) statutory water undertakers within the meaning of the Water Act 1973 (a) or water authorities within the meaning of the Local Government (Scotland) Act 1973 (b) or water development boards within the meaning of the Water (Scotland) Act 1967 (c) , being the activities of such undertakers, authorities or boards in

---

(a) 1973 c.37.   (b) 1973 c.65.   (c) 1967 c.78.

the exercise of their powers or duties as such;

(vi) the British Airports Authority or a member of the British Airways Group;

(vii) a marketing board; or

(viii) the United Kingdom Atomic Energy Authority.

Exemption Certificates

4. Exemption Certificates issued by the Board shall not exempt any employer in the industry from that portion of the levy which equals 0.06 per cent. of the sum of the emoluments upon which the levy is to be assessed under article 3(2)(a) above.

Assessment notices

5.—(1) The Board shall serve an assessment notice on every employer assessed to the levy, but one notice may comprise two or more assessments.

(2) An assessment notice shall state the Board's address for the service of a notice of appeal or of an application for an extension of time for appealing.

(3) An assessment notice may be served on the person assessed to the levy either by delivering it to him personally or by leaving it, or sending it to him by post, at his last known address or place of business in the United Kingdom or, if that person is a corporation, by leaving it, or sending it by post to the corporation, at such address or place of business or at its registered or principal office.

Payment of the levy

6.—(1) Subject to the provisions of this article and of articles 7 and 8, the amount of the levy payable under an assessment notice served by the Board shall be due and payable to the Board as follows:—

(a) where the amount of the levy is calculated under Article 3(2)(a) above it shall be due and payable in two instalments:—

(i) the first instalment, being 0.06 per cent. of the levy, on 31st August 1983, and

(ii) the second instalment, being the remainder of the levy, on 1st August 1984;

(b) where the amount of the levy is calculated under Article 3(2)(b) above it shall be due and payable on 31st August 1983.

(2) The amount of an assessment shall not be recoverable by the Board until there has expired the time allowed for appealing against the assessment by Article 8(1) of this Order and any further period or periods of time that the Board or an industrial tribunal may have allowed for appealing under paragraph (2) or (3) of that Article or, where an appeal is brought, until the appeal is decided or withdrawn.

Withdrawal of assessment

7.—(1) The Board may, by a notice served on the person assessed to the levy in the same manner as an assessment notice, withdraw an assessment if that person has appealed against that assessment under the provisions of Article 8 of this Order and the appeal has not been entered in the Register of Appeals kept under the appropriate Regulations specified in paragraph (5) of that Article, and such withdrawal may be extended by the Board to any other assessment appearing in the assessment notice.

(2) The withdrawal of an assessment shall be without prejudice:—

(a) to the power of the Board to serve a further assessment notice in respect of any establishment to which that assessment related and, where the withdrawal is made by reason of the fact that an establishment has ceased to carry on business in the seventeenth levy period, the said notice may provide that the whole amount payable thereunder in respect of the establishment shall be due one month after the date of the notice; or

(b) to any other assessment included in the original assessment notice and not withdrawn by the Board, and such notice shall thereupon have effect as if any assessment withdrawn by the Board had not been included therein.

Appeals

8.—(1) A person assessed to the levy may appeal to an industrial tribunal against the assessment within one month from the date of the service of the assessment notice or within any further period or periods of time that may be allowed by the Board or an industrial tribunal under the following provisions of this Article.

(2) The Board by notice may for good cause allow a person assessed to the levy to appeal to an industrial tribunal against the assessment at any time within the period of four months from the date of the service of the assessment notice or within such further period or periods as the Board may allow before such time as may then be limited for appealing has expired.

(3) If the Board shall not allow an application for extension of time for appealing, an industrial tribunal shall upon application made to the tribunal by the person assessed to the levy have the like powers as the Board under the last foregoing paragraph.

(4) In the case of an establishment that ceases to carry on business in the seventeenth levy period on any day after the date of the service of the relevant assessment notice, the foregoing provisions of this Article shall have effect as if for the period of four months from the date of the service of the assessment notice mentioned in paragraph (2) of this Article there were substituted the period of six months from the date of the cessation of business.

(5) An appeal or an application to an industrial tribunal under this Article shall be made in accordance with the Industrial Tribunals (England and Wales) Regulations 1965 (a) except where the establishment to which the relevant assessment relates is wholly in Scotland in which case the appeal or application shall be made in accordance with the Industrial Tribunals (Scotland) Regulations 1965 (b) .

(6) The powers of an industrial tribunal under paragraph (3) of this Article may be exercised by the President of the Industrial Tribunals (England and Wales) or by the President of the Industrial Tribunals (Scotland) as the case may be.

Evidence

9.—(1) Upon the discharge by a person assessed to the levy of his liability under an assessment the Board shall if so requested issue to him a certificate to that effect.

(a) S.I. 1965/1101; relevant amending instruments are S.I. 1967/301, 1977/1473.
(b) S.I. 1965/1157; relevant amending instruments are S.I. 1967/302, 1977/1474.

(2) The production in any proceedings of a document purporting to be certified by the Secretary of the Board to be a true copy of an assessment or other notice issued by the Board or purporting to be a certificate such as is mentioned in the foregoing paragraph of this Article shall, unless the contrary is proved, be sufficient evidence of the document and of the facts stated therein.

Signed by order of the Secretary of State.

Peter Morrison,
Minister of State,
Department of Employment.

26th July 1983.

SCHEDULE
Article 3

THE INDUSTRIES REFERRED TO IN ARTICLE 3(6)(*c*) OF THIS ORDER

Column 1	Column 2
The construction industry	The Industrial Training (Construction Board) Order 1964 (a)
The engineering industry	The Industrial Training (Engineering Board) Order 1964 (b)
The agricultural, horticultural and forestry industry	The Industrial Training (Agricultural, Horticultural and Forestry Board) Order 1966 (c)
The road transport industry	The Industrial Training (Road Transport Board) Order 1966 (d)
The offshore petroleum industry	The Industrial Training (Petroleum Board) Order 1967 (e)
The clothing and allied products industry	The Industrial Training (Clothing and Allied Products Board) Order 1969 (f)
The plastics processing industry	The Industrial Training (Rubber and Plastics Processing Board) Order 1967 (g)

(a) S.I. 1964/1079, amended by S.I. 1980/1274, 1982/922.
(b) S.I. 1964/1086, amended by S.I. 1980/1273.
(c) S.I. 1966/969, amended by S.I. 1970/1886.
(d) S.I. 1966/1112, amended by S.I. 1982/664.
(e) S.I. 1967/648, amended by S.I. 1982/921.
(f) S.I. 1969/1375, amended by S.I. 1982/920.
(g) S.I. 1967/1062, amended by S.I. 1982/923.

EXPLANATORY NOTE

(This Note is not part of the Order.)

This Order, which comes into operation on 26th August 1983, gives effect to proposals of the Hotel and Catering Industry Training Board which were submitted to and approved by the Manpower Services Commission, and thereafter submitted by the Manpower Services Commission to the Secretary of State. The proposals are for the imposition of a levy on employers in the hotel and catering industry for the purpose of raising money towards meeting the expenses of the Board.

The levy is to be imposed in respect of the seventeenth levy period commencing with the day upon which this Order comes into operation and ending on 31st March 1984. The levy will be assessed by the Board and there will be a right of appeal against an assessment to an industrial tribunal.

STATUTORY INSTRUMENTS

1983 No. 1134

OFFSHORE INSTALLATIONS

The Offshore Installations (Safety Zones) (Revocation) (No. 17) Order 1983

Made - - - -	*27th July* 1983
Coming into Operation	*28th July* 1983

The Secretary of State, in exercise of the power conferred on him by section 21(1) of the Oil and Gas (Enterprise) Act 1982(a) , and of all other powers enabling him in that behalf, hereby makes the following Order:—

1. This Order may be cited as the Offshore Installations (Safety Zones) (Revocation) (No. 17) Order 1983 and shall come into operation on 28th July 1983.

2. The Offshore Installations (Safety Zones) (No. 7) Order 1983 (b) is hereby revoked.

Alick Buchanan-Smith,
Minister of State,
Department of Energy.

27th July 1983.

EXPLANATORY NOTE

(This Note is not part of the Order.)

This Order revokes the Offshore Installations (Safety Zones) (No. 7) Order 1983. The installation known as Gilbert Rowe which was protected by the safety zone established by that Order has been removed and accordingly that Order is no longer required.

(a) 1982 c.23.   (b) S.I. 1983/330.

STATUTORY INSTRUMENTS

1983 No. 1135

EDUCATION, ENGLAND AND WALES

The Education (Mandatory Awards) Regulations 1983

Made - - - -	*25th July* 1983
Laid before Parliament	*9th August* 1983
Coming into Operation	*1st September* 1983

ARRANGEMENT OF REGULATIONS

SCHEDULES AND APPENDIX

The Secretary of State for Education and Science, in exercise of the powers conferred by sections 1 and 4(2) of, and paragraphs 3 and 4 of Schedule 1 to, the Education Act 1962(**a**), hereby makes the following Regulations:—

PART I

GENERAL

Citation and commencement

1. These Regulations may be cited as the Education (Mandatory Awards) Regulations 1983 and shall come into operation on 1st September 1983.

Definitions

2. In these Regulations, unless the context otherwise requires—

"academic authority" means, in relation to an establishment, the governing body, or other body having the functions of a governing body and includes a person acting with the authority of that body;

"authority" means a local education authority;

"award" includes an award bestowed under previous Awards Regulations;

"British Islands" means the United Kingdom, the Channel Islands and the Isle of Man;

"Certificate in Education" includes a Teacher's Certificate;

"course", "designated course", "sandwich course" and other qualified references to courses have the meanings respectively assigned to them by Regulation 4;

"dependent" means wholly or mainly financially dependent;

(**a**) 1962 c. 12; the relevant provisions, as amended, are set out in Schedule 5 to the Education Act 1980 (c. 20).

"employment" **means full-time employment or part-time employment which, in a normal week, involves a significant number of hours of work and "employed" shall be construed accordingly,** and for the purposes hereof the references to employment include references to the holding of any office and to any occupation for gain;

"establishment" means a university or establishment of further education in the United Kingdom, and "establishment of further education" excludes a university;

"European Community" means the area comprised by the member states of the European Economic Community (including the United Kingdom) as constituted from time to time;

"high-cost country" means Austria, Belgium, Denmark, Federal Republic of Germany, Finland, France, Japan, Netherlands, Norway, Sweden, Switzerland or the United States of America;

"independent student" has the meaning assigned to it by Regulation 3;

"maintenance grant", "full maintenance grant" and "minimum maintenance payment" have the meanings respectively assigned to them by Regulation 17;

"national of a member state of the European Community" means a person who is a national for the purposes of the Community Treaties of any member state of the European Economic Community (including the United Kingdom) as constituted from time to time;

"period of experience", "prescribed proportion" and "sandwich year", in relation to a sandwich course, have the meanings respectively assigned to them by paragraph 1 of Schedule 5;

"previous Awards Regulations" means the Regulations revoked by Regulation 6 and any Regulations made but revoked under section 1 of the Education Act 1962 before the coming into operation of these Regulations;

"refugee" means a person who is recognised by Her Majesty's government as a refugee within the meaning of the United Nations Convention relating to the Status of Refugees done at Geneva on 28th July 1951 as extended by the Protocol thereto which entered into force on 4th October 1967 or a person who enjoys asylum in the United Kingdom in pursuance of a decision of Her Majesty's government though not so recognised, **and any reference to the child of a refugee includes a reference to a person adopted in pursuance of adoption proceedings, a step-child and an illegitimate child of whom the refugee is the mother or in whose case the refugee has admitted paternity or been adjudged the putative father;**

"statutory award" means any award bestowed or grant paid by virtue of the Education Act 1962 or any comparable award or grant which is paid out of moneys provided by Parliament;

"student" means a person upon whom an award has been bestowed under these Regulations or previous Awards Regulations;

"university" means a university in the United Kingdom and includes a university college and a constituent college, school or hall of a university;

"year", in relation to a course, means the period of twelve months beginning on 1st January, 1st April or 1st September according as the academic year of the course in question begins in the spring, the summer or the autumn respectively; and references to the first year of a designated course shall be construed accordingly.

References to independent students

3.—(1) In these Regulations "independent student" means a student who either—

(a) has attained the age of 25 years before the beginning of the year for which payments in pursuance of his award fall to be made, or

(b) has supported himself out of his earnings for periods before the first year of his course aggregating not less than three years.

(2) For the purposes of paragraph (1) a student shall be treated as having supported himself out of his earnings for any period or periods, not exceeding twelve months in the aggregate, for which—

(a) the student was in receipt of training in pursuance of the Manpower Services Commission's Training Opportunities Programme or Youth Opportunities Programme; or

(b) the student was in receipt of unemployment benefit under section 14(1)(a) of the Social Security Act 1975(a); or

(c) before 24th November 1980 (when Schedule 2 to the Social Security Act 1980(b) came into force), the student was registered for employment; or

(d) on and after that date but before 18th October 1982, the student was registered and available for employment; or

(e) on and after 18th October 1982, the student was available for employment and, if under the age of 18 years, registered for employment.

(3) For the purposes aforesaid a student shall also be treated as having supported himself out of his earnings for any period—

(a) for which the student held a State Studentship or comparable award; or

(b) for which the student received sickness benefit, invalidity pension or maternity allowance under section 14(1)(b), 15(1)(b), 22(1) or 36(1) of the Social Security Act 1975; or

(c) for which the student could not reasonably have been expected to support himself out of his earnings because he had the care of a person under the age of 18 years who was dependent upon him.

(4) In this Regulation—

(a) any reference to a person registered or available for employment is a reference to his being so registered or available for the purposes of section 5 of the Supplementary Benefits Act 1976(c);

(b) any reference to an enactment contained in the Supplementary Benefits Act 1976 or the Social Security Act 1975 is a reference to that enactment as from time to time in force and includes, in relation to a period before the coming into force of the enactment in question, a reference to the corresponding enactment then in force.

(a) 1975 c. 14.
(b) 1980 c. 30.
(c) 1976 c. 71, amended by Schedule 2 to the Social Security Act 1980.

References to courses

4.—(1) In these Regulations any reference to a designated course shall be construed as a reference to a course prescribed as such by or under Regulation 10 and, in relation to any person, any reference to such a course (otherwise unqualified) shall, as the context requires, be construed as a reference to a designated course which the person in question attends or has applied to attend; and, in relation to any designated course except one prescribed under Regulation 10(1)*(d)*(ii) or (iii), any reference to a course shall be construed as a reference to either a course of full-time study or a sandwich course.

(2) In these Regulations any reference to a first degree course, a Dip HE course, a course for the Higher Diploma, a course of initial training for teachers, a course comparable to a first degree course or an international course shall be construed in accordance with Regulation 10.

(3) In these Regulations any reference to a sandwich course shall be construed as a reference to such a course within the meaning of paragraph 1 of Schedule 5.

(4) In these Regulations any reference to a course of advanced further education is a reference to a course such as is mentioned in Schedule 2 to the Education (Schools and Further Education) Regulations 1981(a).

General construction and interpretation

5.—(1) In these Regulations references to payments made to a student include references to payments made to the academic authority in respect of the student by virtue of Regulation 25(2).

(2) In calculating a person's income for any year any reduction for income tax is to be made by calculating the tax payable on the income received in that year as if the year were a year of assessment within the meaning of the Income Tax Acts (the necessary apportionment being made in any case where the relevant provisions of those Acts change during the year).

(3) For the purposes of these Regulations a person's marriage is to be treated as having been terminated, not only by the death of the other spouse or the annulment or dissolution of the marriage by an order of a court of competent jurisdiction, but also by virtue of the parties to the marriage ceasing ordinarily to live together, whether or not an order for their separation has been made by any court.

(4) A person shall be treated, for the purposes of Regulation 9(2)(*a*) or 13, as ordinarily resident in England and Wales, in the British Islands or in the European Community, if the authority are satisfied that he is not, or has not been, so resident at the relevant time only because he, his spouse or his parent is, or was temporarily employed outside England and Wales, outside the British Islands or, as the case may be, outside the European Community, **and paragraph (1)(*b*) of Regulation 13 shall not apply in the case of such a person.**

(5) Except where the context otherwise requires, in these Regulations any reference to a Regulation or a Schedule is a reference to a Regulation

contained therein or a Schedule thereto; and a reference in a Regulation or a Schedule to a paragraph is a reference to a paragraph of that Regulation or Schedule, and a reference in a paragraph to a sub-paragraph is a reference to a sub-paragraph thereof.

Revocations and transitional provisions

6.—(1) **The Education (Mandatory Awards) Regulations 1982(a) and the Regulations amending those Regulations (specified in the Appendix hereto) are hereby revoked.**

(2) Without prejudice to section 17(2)*(b)* of the Interpretation Act 1978(b) and the definition of "award" in Regulation 2, an award bestowed in pursuance of the said Regulations before the coming into operation of these Regulations, in so far as it could have been bestowed in pursuance of these Regulations, shall, for the purposes thereof, be treated as having been so bestowed.

(3) Where the current academic year of a student's course began in the spring or summer of 1983 then, notwithstanding anything in these Regulations, payments in pursuance of his award in respect of the year beginning on 1st January or, as the case may be, 1st April 1983 shall be the aggregate of—

(a) two-thirds or, as the case may be, one-third of the payments which would have fallen to be made in respect of that year under the Regulations referred to in paragraph (1) had they not been revoked, and

(b) one-third or, as the case may be, two-thirds of the payments which would have fallen to be made in respect of the year beginning on 1st September 1983 under these Regulations had the academic year of his course begun in the autumn of 1983.

(4) Where an award was bestowed on a student under section 2 of the Education Act 1962 ("the discretionary award") in respect of a course to which section 1 of that Act did not then apply but the course becomes or has become a designated course and an award within the meaning of these Regulations is or has been bestowed on the student in respect of that course ("the mandatory award") then, if the discretionary award continues to be payable, it shall be disregarded in calculating the student's income for the purposes of Regulation 18(1)*(b)* and for the purposes of Regulation 23; but payments on account of the mandatory award in respect of fees and in respect of maintenance for any period shall be respectively reduced or extinguished by those on account of the corresponding element of the discretionary award.

PART II

AWARDS

Duty to bestow an award

7. In pursuance of section 1(1) of the Education Act 1962 it shall be the duty of an authority, subject to the conditions and exceptions hereinafter provided,

(a) S.I. 1982/954.
(b) 1978 c. 30.

to bestow an award in respect of a person's attendance at a designated course within the meaning of these Regulations during an academic year beginning after 31st August 1983 if the person concerned is ordinarily resident in the authority's area within the meaning of section 1 of the said Act of 1962 and Schedule 1 thereto, read with these Regulations.

Modification of provisions for determining ordinary residence

8.—(1) This Regulation shall have effect for modifying paragraph 2 of Schedule 1 to the Education Act 1962 in the case of a person who, apart from this Regulation, would be treated by virtue of that paragraph as having been ordinarily resident in the area of more than one authority within the period of twelve months ending with the date of the beginning of the course.

(2) Any such person as is described in paragraph (1) shall be treated as being ordinarily resident in the area of the authority in which he was so resident on the last day of the month of October, February, or June (according as the academic year of the course begins in the spring, the summer or the autumn respectively) preceding the beginning of the course.

No area students

9.—(1) This Regulation shall apply in the case of such a person as is mentioned in paragraph (2) who, apart from this Regulation, would by virtue of paragraph 2 of Schedule 1 to the Education Act 1962 fall to be treated for the purposes of section 1 of that Act as not being ordinarily resident in the area of any authority.

(2) The person referred to in paragraph (1) is a person who—

    (a) is ordinarily resident in England and Wales on the relevant day,

    (b) **is resident in England and Wales on the relevant day and is a national of a member state of the European Community who—**

        (i) **entered the United Kingdom wholly or mainly for the purpose of taking up, or of seeking, employment;**

        (ii) **during the year preceding the relevant day has been in employment in England and Wales for an aggregate period of not less than nine months; and**

        (iii) **has applied for an award in respect of a course provided by a vocational training establishment, being a course leading to a qualification which is needed for, or is designed to fit a person for, engagement in a specific profession or trade;** or

    (c) is resident in England and Wales on the relevant day and is the child of a national of a member state of the European Community who—

        (i) where he is employed on the relevant day, is then in employment in England and Wales, or

        (ii) where he is not employed on that day (by reason of retirement or otherwise), was last employed in such employment, or

        (iii) whether or not he is employed on that day, has, during the period of three years ending therewith, been in such employment for an aggregate period of not less than a year.

(3) A person to whom this Regulation applies shall be treated for the purposes of section 1 of the Education Act 1962 as ordinarily resident—

  (a) if at any time during the period of two years preceding the relevant day he would have fallen to be treated as belonging to the area of an authority for the purposes of section 31(3) of the Education Act 1980(**a**) or of section 7 of the Education (Miscellaneous Provisions) Act 1953(**b**), in the last such area;

  (b) if sub-paragraph (a) does not apply but at any time during the said period he was resident in the area of an authority, in the last such area;

  (c) if neither sub-paragraph (a) nor (b) applies, in the area of the authority in which the establishment providing his course is situate.

(4) In paragraphs (2) and (3)—

"child" includes a person adopted in pursuance of adoption proceedings and a step-child;

"qualification" includes authorisation, recognition, registration, enrolment, approval and certification;

"relevant day" means, except in the case specified in paragraph (5), the last day of the month of October, February or June (according as the academic year of the course begins in the spring, the summer or the autumn respectively) preceding the beginning of the course;

"vocational training establishment" means a further education establishment being a vocational school within the meaning of Article 7 of Council Regulation (EEC) No. 1612/68 on freedom of movement for workers within the Community(c).

(5) In the case of a refugee, **or the spouse or child of a refugee,** who entered the United Kingdom on or after the relevant day as defined in paragraph (4), "relevant day" in paragraphs (2) and (3) means—

  (a) where he had entered the United Kingdom before the day one month earlier than that of the beginning of the term in which he commences his course, the said day or the day on which he applies for an award, whichever is the earlier;

  (b) where he had not so entered the United Kingdom, the day of the beginning of that term or the day on which he applies for an award, whichever is the earlier.

Designated courses

10.—(1) The following are prescribed as designated courses—

  (a) a first degree course, that is to say—

    (i) a course provided by an establishment for a first degree of a university or for the degree of Bachelor of Medicine or an equivalent degree;

(**a**) 1980 c. 20.
(**b**) 1953 c. 33.
(**c**) OJ No. L257, 19.10.68, p. 2 (OJ/SE 1968(II), p. 475).

    (ii) a course provided by an establishment of further education for a first degree of the Council for National Academic Awards;

    (iii) a course provided by the Cranfield Institute of Technology for a first degree of that Institute;

(b) a Dip HE course, that is to say—

    (i) a course provided by an establishment for the Diploma of Higher Education;

    (ii) a course provided by an establishment for the Diploma of Higher Education or a first degree as the student may elect after the commencement of the course;

(c) a course for the Higher Diploma, that is to say, a course provided by an establishment of further education for the Higher National Diploma, the Higher Diploma of the Technician Education Council ("TEC") or the Higher National Diploma of the Business Education Council ("BEC");

(d) a course of initial training for teachers, that is to say—

    (i) a course for the initial training of teachers (other than a course for the degree of Bachelor of Education) provided by an establishment;

    (ii) a part-time day course of teacher training, involving not less than 3 days' attendance a week during the course, for the time being prescribed for the purposes of this provision by the Secretary of State;

    (iii) any other course of teacher training, whether part-time or partly full-time and partly part-time, for the time being so prescribed;

(e) a course comparable to a first degree course, that is to say—

    (i) a course of at least 3 academic years' duration provided by a university for a certificate, diploma or other academic award;

    (ii) a course for the time being prescribed for the purposes of this provision by the Secretary of State;

(f) an international course, that is to say, a course provided by an establishment in the United Kingdom in conjunction with a university, college or other institution in another country for a first degree of a university or a course so provided comparable to a first degree course being, in either case, a course prescribed for the purposes of this provision by the Secretary of State.

(2) In this Regulation references to an establishment and an establishment of further education do not include references to establishments of further education which are neither maintained, nor assisted by recurrent grants, out of public funds.

Conditions

11.—(1) Subject to paragraph (2), the duty of an authority to bestow an award shall be subject to the conditions that—

(a) an application in writing reaches the authority before the end of the term in which the student commences his course; and

(b) the applicant gives the authority a written undertaking that, where any provisional or other payments made in pursuance of the award in respect of a year exceed (for whatever reason) the grant payable in respect of that year, he will, if called upon to do so, repay the excess amount.

(2) For the purposes of paragraph (1)(a), an application shall be treated as having reached the authority as there mentioned—

(a) where, to the knowledge of the authority, an application has so reached some other authority;

(b) where before the end of the term in which the student commenced his course it had not become a designated course and the application reaches the authority before the end of the first term after it becomes a designated course;

(c) in the case of a refugee, **or the spouse or child of a refugee,** where the application reaches the authority before the end of the term of his course first beginning after the date on which the refugee was recognised as a refugee or was accorded asylum, or

(d) where, having regard to the circumstances of the particular case, the authority consider that it should be so treated.

(3) If the applicant is a minor, paragraph (1)(b) shall have effect, with the necessary modifications, as if the references to the applicant were references to the applicant or his parent.

Exceptions relating to attendance at previous courses

12.—(1) An authority shall not bestow an award on a person in respect of his attendance at a course if it is their duty under Regulation 14 to transfer an award already bestowed on him so that it is held in respect of his attendance at that course.

(2) An authority shall not be under a duty to bestow an award on any person in respect of his attendance at any course prescribed by Regulation 10(1)(b) or (c) if he has previously—

(a) successfully completed a course of teacher training prescribed under sub-paragraph (d)(ii) or (iii) of Regulation 10(1), or

(b) attended any other course prescribed by or under Regulation 10(1).

(3) An authority shall not be under a duty to bestow an award on any person in respect of his attendance at any course of two academic years' duration prescribed under sub-paragraph (e)(ii) of Regulation 10(1) if he has previously attended such a course.

(4) Subject to paragraphs (5) to (8), an authority shall not be under a duty to bestow an award on any person where he has previously attended one or more full-time, or satisfactorily completed one or more part-time, courses of advanced further education and the aggregate duration of—

(a) such full-time courses which he has attended, and

(b) the full-time courses equivalent to such part time courses which he has successfully completed,

(ignoring, in the case of a sandwich course, periods of experience) exceeds two academic years; and, for the purposes hereof, a full-time or part-time course outside England and Wales which is comparable to full-time or, as the case may be, part-time course of advanced further education shall be treated as if it were such a course.

(5) A previous course shall be disregarded for the purposes of paragraph (4) if it was provided by a college providing long term residential courses of full-time education for adults which is specified in Regulation 7 of the State Awards Regulations 1978(a).

(6) A previous course shall be disregarded for the purposes of paragraph (4) if—

(a) the student is such a person as is mentioned in Regulation 9(2)(c);

(b) the previous course was provided by an institution outside the British Islands but within the European Community, and

(c) the authority are satisfied—

(i) by the student, that he has ceased to attend the previous course without completing it during the year immediately preceding the first year of the course to which his application for an award relates, and

(ii) by the academic authority of the establishment providing that course, that it is comparable, in terms of content, to the uncompleted part of the previous course.

(7) Nothing in paragraph (4) shall affect the duty of an authority to bestow an award on a person—

(a) in respect of his attendance at a course for the post-graduate Certificate in Education, the Art Teacher's Certificate or the Art Teacher's Diploma (or for a qualification comparable with any such certificate or diploma) unless he has previously attended such a course or successfully completed a course which—

(i) was for the degree of Bachelor of Education or a comparable academic award of either a university in the United Kingdom or of the Council for National Academic Awards, and

(ii) was approved as a course for the initial training of teachers for the purposes of Regulation 16(2)(a) of the Schools Regulations 1959(b) or of any corresponding provision of regulations from time to time in force under section 27 of the Education Act 1980(c).

(b) in respect of his attendance at any full-time course of initial training as a teacher of one academic year's duration, or a comparable part-time course, not within sub-paragraph (a) above, unless he has for more than three years held a statutory award in respect of his attendance at

(a S.I. 1978/1096, to which there are amendments not relevant to these Regulations.
(b) S.I. 1959/364, revoked by S.I. 1982/106.
(c) 1980 c. 20; the relevant regulations currently in force are the Education (Teachers) Regulations 1982 (S.I. 1982/106).

a full-time course of advanced further education or a comparable course outside England and Wales.

(8) Nothing in paragraph (4) shall affect the duty of an authority to bestow an award on a person if—

(a) he is a refugee, **or the spouse or child of a refugee;**

(b) the previous course was a full-time course provided by an institution outside the British Islands, and

(c) he satisfies the authority that he ceased to attend the previous course, without completing it, during the four years immediately preceding his entering the United Kingdom.

(9) For the purposes of this Regulation a person shall not be treated as having previously attended a course by reason only of his having attended from its beginning the course to which his application for an award relates.

(10) For the purposes of this Regulation a person shall only be treated as having attended a course if he has attended either more than one course or one course for a period of more than one term; and it is hereby declared that any reference to a person having attended or completed a course shall be construed as a reference to his having done so before or after the coming into operation of these Regulations.

Other exceptions

13.—(1) An authority shall not be under a duty to bestow an award in respect of a person's attendance at a course—

(a) upon a person who has not been ordinarily resident, throughout the three years preceding the first year of the course in question, in the British Islands or, in the case of such a person as is mentioned in Regulation 9(2)(b) or (c), has not been so resident in the European Community;

(b) upon a person whose residence in the British Islands or, in the case of such a person as is mentioned in Regulation 9(2)(b) or (c), in the European Community, has during any part of the period referred to in sub-paragraph (a) been wholly or mainly for the purposes of receiving full-time education; or

(c) upon a person who has, in the opinion of the authority, shown himself by his conduct to be unfitted to receive an award.

(2) Paragraph (1)(a) shall not apply in the case of a refugee, ordinarily resident in the British Islands who has not ceased to be so ordinarily resident since he was recognised as a refugee or was granted asylum, **or in the case of the spouse or child of such a refugee.**

Transfer of awards

14.—(1) An award shall be transferred by the authority so as to be held in respect of attendance at a course other than that in respect of which it is held in any case where either—

(a) subject to paragraph (2), on the recommendation of the academic authority the student commences to attend another course ("the new course") at the establishment;

(b) subject to paragraph (2), with the written consent of the academic authorities of both establishments concerned, given on educational grounds, the student commences to attend a course ("the new course") at another establishment;

(c) subject to paragraph (4), after commencing a course for the Certificate in Education, the student is, on or before the completion of that course, admitted to a course for the degree of Bachelor of Education;

(d) on the completion of a course for the Certificate in Education or the degree of Bachelor of Education, the student is admitted to a course of initial training for teachers of the deaf, or

(e) subject to paragraph (4), after commencing a course for the degree (other than an honours degree) of Bachelor of Education, the student is, on or before the completion of that course, admitted to a course for the honours degree of Bachelor of Education.

(2) An award shall not be transferred in pursuance of paragraph (1)*(a)* or *(b)* unless either—

(a) the requisite recommendation or consent is given before the expiry of two months after the end of the first year of the course in respect of which the award was originally bestowed, or

(b) the authority, after consulting the academic authority or authorities concerned, are satisfied that the period which the student in question will ordinarily require for the completion of the new course will expire not later than the period which he would now so require for the completion of the course in respect of which the award is held, ignoring—

    (i) in each case, periods of experience which are part of a sandwich course; and

    (ii) **in the case of the course in respect of which the award is held, any period during which the student would now be required by the academic authority concerned to repeat part of the course, if the authority would not make any payment for maintenance in respect of that period under Regulation 26(1).**

(3) An authority may, after consulting the academic authority concerned, refuse the transfer of an award in pursuance of paragraph (1)(a) or (b) if they are satisfied that when the student applied for it he did not intend to complete the course to which his application related.

(4) An award shall not be transferred in pursuance of paragraph (1)*(c)* or *(e)* so as to be held in respect of his attendance at a course for the degree of Bachelor of Education if the period which the student in question would ordinarily require for the completion of that course, when aggregated with the period for which the student has already pursued a course in respect of which the award was held, exceeds—

(a) five years where the award would be held in respect of a course for the honours degree of Bachelor of Education, or

(b) four years where the award would be held in respect of a course for that degree not being an honours degree;

so, however, that where the student has pursued a part-time course, for the purposes hereof account shall only be taken of that proportion of the period for which he pursued that course which the period ordinarily required to complete the full-time course equivalent to the part-time course bears to the period so required to complete the part-time course.

(5) For the purposes of the duty of an authority to transfer an award in pursuance of paragraph (1)*(c)*, *(d)* or *(e)* it shall be immaterial whether or not the two courses are provided by the same establishment.

Termination of awards

15.—(1) An award shall terminate on the expiry of the period ordinarily required for the completion of the course;

Provided that—

(a) if the academic authority refuse to allow the student to complete the course, the authority shall terminate the award forthwith;

(b) if the student does not complete the course within the period ordinarily required, the authority—

(i) may extend the award until the student has completed the course; and

(ii) shall extend it for a period equivalent to any period in respect of which they have made any payment under Regulation 26(1).

(2) The authority may, after consultation with the academic authority, terminate the award if they are satisfied that the student has either—

(a) abandoned the course in respect of which it is held and the award does not fall to be transferred in pursuance of Regulation 14, or

(b) shown himself by his conduct to be unfitted to hold the award.

Supplementary provisions

16. The authority may require the student to provide from time to time such information as they consider necessary for the exercise of their functions under this Part, and if in the case of any student the authority are satisfied that he has wilfully failed to comply with any such requirement or has provided information which he knows to be false in a material particular or has recklessly provided information which is false in a material particular, they may terminate the award or withhold any payments due under it as they see fit.

PART III

PAYMENTS

Payments

17. Subject to Regulations 16, 23, 26 and 27, the authority shall in respect of each year pay in pursuance of the award—

(a) in respect of fees, a sum equal to the aggregate of any such fees payable in respect of the student as are described in Schedule 1;

(b) in respect of maintenance—

(i) except in a case in which Regulations 20, 21, 22 or 24 applies, either the sum of £410 (in these Regulations called "the minimum maintenance payment") or a grant calculated in accordance with Regulation 18 (in these Regulations called "the maintenance grant" or "the full maintenance grant"), whichever is the greater;

(ii) in a case in which one of those Regulations applies (subject to Regulation 20(2)) a sum or grant determined in accordance with the Regulation in question;

and so much of the sum or grant referred to in sub-paragraph *(b)* as appears to the authority to be appropriate shall be treated as being in respect of the Easter and Christmas vacations.

Calculation of maintenance grant

18.—(1) The maintenance grant in respect of any year shall be the amount by which the student's resources fall short of his requirements and for the purpose of ascertaining that amount—

(a) the requirements of the student shall be taken to be the aggregate of such of the amounts specified in Schedule 2 as are applicable in his case;

(b) the resources of the student shall be taken to be the aggregate of his income for the year calculated in accordance with Part 1 of Schedule 3 and any contribution applicable in his case by virtue of Part 2 or 3 of that Schedule.

(2) This Regulation and Schedules 2 and 3 shall have effect—

(a) in the case of such a student as is mentioned in Schedule 4, subject to the provisions thereof;

(b) where Regulation 20 applies, subject as therein provided.

Assessment of requirements and resources

19. The requirements and resources of a student shall be assessed by the authority and, for the purpose of the exercise of their functions under this Regulation, the authority shall require the student to provide from time to time such information as they consider necessary as to the resources of any person whose means are relevant to the assessment of his requirements and resources.

Sandwich courses

20.—(1) This Regulation shall apply where the course is a sandwich course unless the student is a member of a religious order and Regulation 21 applies.

(2) For the purpose of calculating payments in respect of maintenance under Regulation 17*(b)* in respect of a sandwich year, that Regulation and Schedules 2 and 3 shall have effect subject to the provisions of Schedule 5; but no such

payments shall be made in respect of a year in which there are no periods of full-time study.

Members of religious orders

21.—(1) This Regulation shall apply where the student is a member of a religious order ("the Order") unless the course is a course of teacher training prescribed under Regulation 10(1)*(d)*(iii) and Regulation 22 applies.

(2) Subject to paragraph (5), the payment in respect of maintenance under Regulation 17*(b)* shall be the sum specified as appropriate in the case of the student in paragraph (3) or (4):

Provided that—

(a) where the course is a sandwich course, the payment in respect of a sandwich year shall be the prescribed proportion of the sum so specified and no payment shall be made in respect of a year which includes no periods of full-time study;

(b) where the course is a part-time course of teacher training prescribed under Regulation 10(1)*(d)*(ii), the payment shall be three-quarters of the sum so specified.

(3) In the case of a student who resides at his parents' home or in a house of the Order, the appropriate sum shall be **£700**.

(4) In the case of any other student, the appropriate sum shall be **£915** except that, where he is attending a course—

(a) at the University of London,

(b) at an establishment within the area comprising the City of London and the metropolitan police district, or

(c) at an institution in a country outside the United Kingdom which is not a high-cost country,

it shall be **£1,085 and, where he is attending a course at an institution in a high-cost country, it shall be £1,230.**

(5) The payment in respect of maintenance, determined as aforesaid, shall, in the case of any student who is attending such a course as is mentioned in paragraph 13(1) of Part 2 of Schedule 2 and for the purposes thereof necessarily incurs expenditure in the purchase of special equipment, be increased by so much of that expenditure as does not during the course exceed **£80**.

Courses of teacher training

22.—(1) This Regulation shall apply—

(a) where the course is a part-time course of teacher training prescribed under sub-paragraph *(d)*(ii) or *(d)*(iii) of Regulation 10(1), or

(b) where it is a partly full-time and partly part-time one prescribed under the said sub-paragraph *(d)*(iii),

unless the student is a member of a religious order, the course is a part-time course of teacher training prescribed under the said sub-paragraph *(d)*(ii) and Regulation 21 applies.

(2) Where the course is prescribed under the said sub-paragraph *(d)*(ii), the payment in respect of maintenance under Regulation 17*(b)* shall be the minimum maintenance payment or a grant equal to three-quarters of the full maintenance grant, whichever is the greater.

(3) Subject to the following paragraphs, where the course is prescribed under the said sub-paragraph *(d)*(iii), the said payment under Regulation 17*(b)* shall be:—

  (a) in a year in which the student's periods of study are all periods of full-time study or in which his aggregate period of full-time study is 30 weeks or more, the minimum maintenance payment or the full maintenance grant, whichever is the greater;

  (b) in a year in which the student's periods of study are all periods of part-time study, a sum equal to the aggregate of—

    (i) his requirement in respect of such expenditure as is mentioned in paragraph 10 of Part 2 of Schedule 2, determined as therein provided ("travelling requirement"), and

    (ii) the sum of £230;

  (c) in any other year, a sum equal to the aggregate of—

    (i) his travelling requirement;

    (ii) the appropriate proportion of the difference between his travelling requirement and either the minimum maintenance payment or the full maintenance grant, whichever is the greater, namely, the proportion which the student's aggregate period of full-time study in the year, expressed in weeks, bears to 30, and

    (iii) the appropriate proportion of £230, namely, the proportion which the difference between the said aggregate period and thirty weeks bears to 30.

(4) Where the first year of a student's course began before 1st September 1978, sub-paragraphs *(b)*(ii) and *(c)*(iii) of paragraph (3) shall have effect as if the references therein to the sum of £230 were references to the sum of £245.

(5) In relation to a student employed full-time as a teacher, paragraph (3) shall have effect, except in such a year as is mentioned in sub-paragraph *(a)* thereof, as if it provided that the said payment under Regulation 17*(b)* should equal the aggregate of such expenditure which he is obliged to incur as mentioned in paragraph 10 of Part 2 of Schedule 2 subject, however, to the proviso to sub-paragraph (2) of that paragraph.

(6) In relation to a student attending a course provided by the University of Oxford or Cambridge, sub-paragraphs *(a)* and *(c)*(ii) and (iii) of paragraph (3) shall have effect as if any reference therein to—

  (a) a period of 30 weeks were a reference to a period of 25 weeks, and

  (b) the proportion which a period expressed in weeks bears to 30 were a reference to the proportion which that period bears to 25.

(7) For the purposes of this Regulation a day shall be reckoned as a seventh of a week.

Assisted students

23.—(1) Notwithstanding anything in the preceding provisions of these Regulations, no payment under Regulation 17*(a)* or *(b)* shall be made to a student in respect of any year in respect whereof he receives such payments as are mentioned in paragraph (2) amounting to not less than the aggregate of—

   (a) such fees payable in respect of him as are described in Schedule 1; and

   (b) his requirements for maintenance ascertained in accordance with—

      (i) Part 1 of Schedule 2,

      (ii) paragraphs 6 and 7 of Part 2 of that Schedule, and

      (iii) Parts 3 and 4 of that Schedule.

(2) The payments referred to in paragraph (1) are the aggregate payments received by the student—

   (a) in pursuance of any scholarship, studentship, exhibition or award of similar description bestowed on him in respect of the course (otherwise than in pursuance of section 1 of the Education Act 1962), and

   (b) if he is in gainful employment, by way of remuneration (reduced by income tax and social security contributions) paid in respect of any period for which he has leave of absence or is relieved of his normal duties for the purpose of attending the course;

except that, if the student's course is a part-time course of teacher training prescribed under Regulation 10(1)*(d)*(iii), or the part-time part of a course so prescribed which is partly full-time and partly part-time , any payments by way of remuneration shall be disregarded.

Students provided with free board and lodging

24.—(1) This Regulation shall apply where the student is provided with free board and lodging by the academic authority in accordance with arrangements whereunder charges for board and lodging are made only in the case of students whose resources exceed their requirements (ascertained as provided in Regulation 18), unless the student is a member of a religious order and Regulation 21 applies.

(2) The payment in respect of maintenance under Regulation 17*(b)* shall be a maintenance grant calculated in accordance with Regulation 18.

Method of payment

25.—(1) The authority shall make any payment due under these Regulations in such instalments (if any) and at such times as they consider appropriate; and in the exercise of their functions under this paragraph the authority may in particular make provisional payments pending the final calculation of the award.

(2) Any payment in respect of such fees as are described in Schedule 1 may be made to the academic authority but subject thereto all payments shall be made to the student.

(3) Where, in pursuance of this Regulation, a payment in respect of any

period is made in advance or is provisional then, without prejudice to Regulation 27 or the recovery of an over-payment by way of a deduction from a subsequent payment, any over-payment or under-payment shall be adjusted by payment between the student or, as the case may be, the academic authority and the authority.

Discretionary payments

26.—(1) In respect of any period during which the student repeats any part of his course, the authority shall not be required to make any payments under Regulation 17*(a)* or *(b)* but may pay in pursuance of the award such sums (if any) as they consider appropriate, being sums not exceeding the amount of any payments that would, apart from this Regulation, be payable to that student in respect of that period.

(2) Subject to paragraph (3), paragraph (4) shall apply in the case of a student who—

> *(a)* has previously attended a course of advanced further education being—
>
> > (i) a course of up to two academic years' duration, in the case of one designated by or under Regulation 10(1), or
> >
> > (ii) a course of two academic years' duration, in the case of one not so designated,
>
> (ignoring, in the case of a sandwich course, periods of experience) or has previously successfully completed a part-time course corresponding to such a course as is mentioned above ("the previous course"), and
>
> *(b)* holds an award, bestowed so as to be held, in respect of a course prescribed by or under Regulation 10(1)*(a)*, *(d)*, *(e)* or *(f)* being a course ordinarily of more than one year's duration ("the current course").

(3) Paragraph (4) shall not apply if the current course is for the degree of Bachelor of Education and a subject thereof is—

> *(a)* physics, chemistry or mathematics (or a combination of those subjects), or
>
> *(b)* craft, design and technology, or
>
> *(c)* business studies, or
>
> *(d)* some other subject the study of which the authority are satisfied fits a person to teach in schools any of the above mentioned subjects.

(4) Where this paragraph applies, the authority shall only be required to make payments under Regulation 17*(a)* or *(b)* in pursuance of the award in respect of the current course—

> *(a)* where that course is ordinarily of not more than two years' duration, in respect of the final year of the student's course which, in the case of a sandwich course, includes periods of full-time study;
>
> *(b)* where that course is ordinarily of a greater number of years' duration in respect of that number less two of the final years of the student's

course which, in the case of a sandwich course, include periods of full-time study;

but, in respect of any other year of the student's current course, they may make such payments as they consider appropriate not exceeding those which would, apart from this Regulation, have been payable under Regulation 17*(a)* or *(b)* as aforesaid.

(5) In this Regulation any reference—

(a) to the ordinary duration of a course is a reference to the period ordinarily required for its completion by a student who is not excused part of the course on account of his having attended a previous course (ignoring, in the case of a sandwich course, periods of experience);

(b) to the final year or years of a student's course is, in the case of a student so excused part of the course, a reference thereto after taking account of the consequential reduction in the duration of his course, and

(c) to a person having attended a course shall be construed as provided in Regulation 12(10).

Withholding and reduction of payments

27.—(1) Without prejudice to Regulation 16, in the case of any student who is for the time being in default of any requirement to provide such information as is described in Regulation 19, the authority may withhold, in part, any payment due to him in respect of maintenance and calculated or determined in accordance with Regulation 18, 20 or 22 or, in whole or in part, any such payment determined in accordance with Regulation 24:

Provided that a partial payment made to the student in respect of any year in which he remains in default shall not (unless Regulation 24 applies to him) be less than the minimum maintenance payment.

(2) In respect of any period—

(a) after the termination of an award,

(b) during which a student is excluded from attendance at the course by the academic authority, or

(c) during which a student is absent from his course without leave,

any payment otherwise due in pursuance of the award shall be reduced by the aggregate sum mentioned in paragraph (4).

(3) In respect of any other period being—

(a) a period during which a student is absent from his course (other than a period of not more than 28 days due to illness),

(b) where an award held in respect of one course is transferred in pursuance of Regulation 14 so as to be held in respect of another course, a period during which the student is not required to attend either course (other than the period of a single vacation), or

(c) **a period during which the student is detained in pursuance of an order made by any court,**

the authority may reduce any payment otherwise due in pursuance of the award by such amount, not exceeding the aggregate sum mentioned in paragraph (4), as having regard to all relevant circumstances they consider appropriate.

(4) The sum referred to in paragraph (2) and (3) is the aggregate of—

(a) fees otherwise due that are not payable by reason of the student's non-attendance, and

(b) the appropriate proportion of the balance of any payments in respect of maintenance payable in pursuance of Regulation 17*(b)*.

SCHEDULE 1   Regulations 17, 23(1)
and 25(2)

FEES

The fees referred to in Regulation 17*(a)* are—

(*a*) the aggregate of any fees for admission, registration or matriculation (including matriculation exemption), any sessional or tuition fees, any composition fee and any graduation fee (in each case excluding any element thereof representing or attributable to any such fee as is mentioned in the following sub-paragraphs, or to maintenance) subject to a maximum of £480:

Provided that the said maximum—

(i) shall be **£1,355** in the case of a course at the University of Buckingham;

(ii) shall be £240 in the case of a course prescribed under Regulation 10(1)*(d)*(iii) unless the course is partly full-time and involves more than 10 weeks full-time attendance in the relevant year, and

(iii) shall not apply in the case of a course at the Guildhall School of Music, the Heythrop College, the London College of Music, the Royal Academy of Music, the Royal Academy Schools, the Royal College of Music or the Trinity College of Music;

(*b*) college fees or dues at the universities of Cambridge, Durham, Kent, Lancaster, Oxford and York (excluding any element thereof representing or attributable to any such fee as is mentioned in the following sub-paragraph or to maintenance);

(*c*) any fees charged by an external body in respect of examinations or the validation of the course or otherwise charged by such a body whose requirements must (for the purposes of the course) be satisfied, or any fees attributable to fees so charged.

SCHEDULE 2   Regulations 18, 20(2), 21(5),
22(3) and 23(1)

REQUIREMENTS

PART 1

ORDINARY MAINTENANCE

1.—(1) The requirements of the student referred to in Regulation 18(1)*(a)* shall include his requirement for ordinary maintenance during—

(*a*) any period while he is attending the course, and

(*b*) the Christmas and Easter vacations;

and the amount of such requirement ("ordinary maintenance requirement") shall be determined in accordance with this Part of this Schedule.

(2) Where a student's ordinary maintenance requirements are different in respect of different parts of a year, his ordinary maintenance requirement for

that year shall be the aggregate of the proportionate parts of those differing requirements.

2.—(1) Subject to paragraph 4 below, this paragraph shall apply in the case of—

(a) any student who, on the recommendation of the academic authority, resides in the establishment or in a hostel or other accommodation administered by the academic authority;

(b) any independent or married student who does not reside at his parents' home;

(c) any other student who does not reside at his parents' home, except where he can in the opinion of the authority conveniently attend the course from his parents' home and the authority, after consultation with the academic authority, consider that in all the circumstances the ordinary maintenance requirement specified in paragraph 3(2) would be appropriate; and

(d) any student residing at his parents' home whose parents by reason of age, incapacity or otherwise cannot reasonably be expected to support him and in respect of whom the authority are satisfied that in all the circumstances the ordinary maintenance requirement specified herein would be appropriate.

(2) In the case of such a student the ordinary maintenance requirement shall be **£1,660** except that—

(a) where he is attending a course at the University of London or at an establishment within the area comprising the City of London and the metropolitan police district, it shall be **£1,975**;

(b) where he is attending, for at least one term and as a necessary part of his course, at an institution in a country outside the United Kingdom,

it shall be **£1,975 or, if that country is a high-cost country, £2,240 (notwithstanding anything in sub-paragraph (a)).**

3.—(1) Subject to paragraph 4, this paragraph shall apply in the case of any other student, that is to say, in the case of—

(a) a student residing at his parents' home, except where the conditions specified in paragraph 2(1)(d) are satisfied;

(b) a student whose case falls within the exception to paragraph 2(1)(c).

(2) In the case of such a student the ordinary maintenance requirement shall be **£1,275**.

4.—(1) This paragraph shall apply, to the exclusion of paragraph 2 or 3, in the case of a student who is provided with board and lodging by the academic authority in accordance with arrangements under which charges for board and lodging are made only in the case of those students whose resources exceed their requirements (ascertained as provided in Regulation 18).

(2) In the case of such a student the ordinary maintenance requirement shall be **£680**.

PART 2

SUPPLEMENTARY MAINTENANCE ETC

5. The requirements referred to in Regulation 18(1)*(a)* shall include the student's requirements—

(a) for supplementary maintenance in the cases and for the periods mentioned in paragraphs 6, 7, 8 and 14, and

(b) in respect of such expenditure as is mentioned in paragraphs 9 to 13 and 15;

and the amount of any such requirement ("supplementary requirement") shall be determined in accordance with this Part of this Schedule.

6.—(1) This paragraph shall apply in the case of a student who having, in any academic year, attended his course—

(a) in the case of a course provided by the University of Oxford or Cambridge, for a period of 25 weeks 3 days, or

(b) in the case of any other course, for a period of 30 weeks 3 days,

in that year attends his course, howsoever provided, for a further period ("the excess period") unless, as respects that period, he is provided with board and lodging as mentioned in paragraph 4.

(2) In respect of each week and any part of a week comprised in the excess period the supplementary requirement shall be—

(a) in the case of a student residing at his parents' home, **£17.65**;

(b) in the case of a student not so residing, **£30.45** except that—

(i) where he is attending a course at the University of London or at an establishment within the area comprising the City of London and the metropolitan police district, it shall be **£40.85**;

(ii) where he is attending, for at least one term and as a necessary part of his course, at an institution in a country outside the United Kingdom, it shall be **£40.85 or, if that country is a high-cost country, £46.40 (notwithstanding anything in sub-paragraph (i)).**

7.—(1) This paragraph shall apply in the case of a student who attends at his course for a period of not less than 45 weeks in any continuous period of 52 weeks.

(2) In respect of each aggregate period of a complete week for which he does not attend at his course in the period of 52 weeks in question, the student's supplementary requirement shall be determined in accordance with paragraph 6(2).

8.—(1) This paragraph shall apply, unless paragraph 7 applies, in the case of a student at an establishment of further education which is not wholly maintained out of public funds, or at a service establishment mentioned in sub-paragraph (3), who undertakes a period of vacation study on the recommendation of the academic authority—

    (a) under the guidance of that authority, or

    (b) where he is studying modern languages, with a family (approved for the purposes hereof by that authority) in a country whose language is a main language of the course.

(2) In respect of each day of such vacation study the supplementary requirement shall be such amount, if any, as the authority consider appropriate not exceeding the maximum amount hereinafter specified, that is to say—

    (a) in the case of a student residing at his parents' home, the maximum amount of **£3.65**,

    (b) in the case of a student not so residing, the maximum amount of **£5.50** except that—

        (i) where he is studying at an establishment within the area comprising the City of London and the metropolitan police district, it shall be **£7.00**;

        (ii) where he is studying (either at an institution or as mentioned in sub-paragraph (1)*(b)*) in a country outside the United Kingdom,

    it shall be **£7.00 or, if that country is a high-cost country, £8.25.**

(3) The service establishments referred to in paragraph (1) are the Royal Military College of Science, Shrivenham, and the Royal Naval Engineering College, Manadon.

9.—(1) This paragraph shall apply in the case of a student at an establishment of further education which is not wholly maintained out of public funds, or at a service establishment mentioned in paragraph 8(3), who incurs additional expenditure on his maintenance for the purpose of attending, as part of his course, a period of term-time residential study away from the establishment, being study within the United Kingdom unless (apart from the said period) he is attending, as part of his course, at an institution in a country outside the United Kingdom and the study is away from that institution.

(2) In respect of each day for which the student incurs such additional expenditure his supplementary requirement shall be **£4.65** or the daily additional expenditure, whichever is the less:

Provided that where the expenditure was incurred for the purposes of a period of study which was not a necessary part of his course, his requirement in respect thereof shall be such amount as the authority consider appropriate, not exceeding the amount determined as aforesaid.

10.—(1) This paragraph shall apply in the case of a student who is obliged to incur expenditure—

    (a) within the United Kingdom for the purpose of attending the establishment;

    (b) within or outside the United Kingdom, for the purpose of attending, as part of his course, any period of study at an institution in a country outside the United Kingdom;

(c) in the case of a student at an establishment of further education which is not wholly maintained out of public funds, or at a service establishment mentioned in paragraph 8(3)—

  (i) within or outside the United Kingdom, for the purpose of attending a period of vacation study or of term-time residential study in respect of which he has a supplementary requirement under paragraph 8 or 9 above, and

  (ii) without prejudice to the preceding provisions of this pararaph, on any other term-time travel within the United Kingdom in connection with his course.

(2) The student's supplementary requirement in respect of such expenditure shall be the amount by which, in the aggregate, it exceeds £50:

Provided that, where a period of study outside the United Kingdom (whether or not at an institution) is not a necessary part of the student's course, in arriving at the said aggregate the authority, save in so far and to the extent that they otherwise consider appropriate, shall take no account of so much of his expenditure for the purpose of attending that period of study as—

(a) was incurred outside the United Kingdom, or

(b) was incurred within the United Kingdom but is in respect of a journey between a port or airport within, and a place outside, the United Kingdom or is in respect of a benefit to be enjoyed outside the United Kingdom.

(3) The reference in sub-paragraph (1)(a) to the student attending the establishment shall be construed—

(a) in the case of any establishment which is a constituent college, hall or school (including medical school) of a university or is a university with such constituent establishments, as including a reference to his attending, in connection with his course, any constituent establishment of the university, and

(b) in the case of a student attending a course in medicine, dentistry, or nursing a necessary part of which is a period of study by way of clinical training, as including a reference to his attending, in connection with his course but otherwise than for the purposes of residential study away from the establishment, any hospital not comprised therein at which facilities for clinical training are provided.

(4) For the purposes of this paragraph any reference to expenditure incurred for the purpose of attending an establishment or period of study includes expenditure both before and after so attending.

11.—(1) This paragraph shall apply in the case of a student whose home is for the time being outside the United Kingdom and who incurs expenditure travelling between his home and the establishment at the beginning and end of term.

(2) The student's supplementary requirement in respect of such expenditure shall be such amount, not exceeding the expenditure the student was obliged to incur, as the authority consider appropriate having regard to his supplementary requirement under paragraph 10.

12.—(1) This paragraph shall apply in the case of a student who reasonably incurs any expenditure in insuring against liability for the cost of medical treatment provided outside the United Kingdom for any illness or bodily injury contracted or suffered during a period of study outside the United Kingdom.

(2) The student's supplementary requirement in respect of such expenditure shall be the amount reasonably incurred:

Provided that where the expenditure was incurred in connection with a period of study which was not a necessary part of his course, his requirement in respect thereof shall be such amount as the authority consider appropriate, not exceeding the said amount.

13.—(1) This paragraph shall apply in the case of a student who—

    (a) is attending a course in architecture, art and design, home economics, landscape architecture, medicine, music, ophthalmic optics, physical education, town and country planning or veterinary science (or medicine) or a course comprising any of those subjects as a principal subject, and

    (b) for the purposes thereof necessarily incurs expenditure in the purchase of special equipment.

(2) The student's supplementary requirement in respect of such expenditure shall be so much of the expenditure as does not during the course exceed **£80**.

14.—(1) This paragraph shall apply in the case of a student who, in any week during a vacation (not being a week in respect of which a supplementary requirement falls to be determined under paragraph 7 or 8) would, in the opinion of the authority, suffer undue hardship but for this paragraph.

(2) The student's supplementary requirement in respect of each such week shall be such amount as the authority consider appropriate having regard to his means, not exceeding **£39.65**.

15.—(1) This paragraph shall apply in the case of a disabled student where the authority are satisfied that, by reason of his disability, he is obliged to incur additional expenditure in respect of his attendance at the course.

(2) The student's supplementary requirement in respect of such expenditure shall be such amount as the authority consider appropriate not exceeding **£520**.

PART 3

MAINTENANCE OF DEPENDANTS

16.—(1) The requirements referred to in Regulation 18(1)*(a)* shall include the student's requirements for the maintenance of dependants during the year and the amount of any such requirement ("dependants requirement") shall be determined in accordance with this Part of this Schedule.

(2) Where a student's requirements for the maintenance of dependants are

different in respect of different parts of a year, his dependants requirement for that year shall be the aggregate of the proportionate parts of those differing requirements.

17.—(1) In this Part of this Schedule—

"adult dependant" means, in relation to a student, an adult person dependent on the student not being his child, his spouse or a person living with him as his spouse or his former spouse, subject however to sub-paragraphs (2), (3) and (4);

"child", in relation to a student, includes a person adopted in pursuance of adoption proceedings and a step-child but does not include a child born during the student's course unless born of a marriage contracted before the first year of that course or adopted jointly by the student and his spouse by such a marriage, subject however to sub-paragraph (4);

"dependant" means, in relation to a student, his dependent child, his spouse or an adult dependant, subject however to sub-paragraphs (2) and (3);

"income" means income for the year from all sources less income tax, social security contributions and child benefit and, in the case of the student's spouse, less—

(a) where she holds an award in respect of a course of teacher training prescribed under Regulation 10(1)(d)(iii), being a part-time course or a course which is partly full-time and partly part-time, the payments in respect of maintenance made to her in pursuance of Regulation 17(b) or so much of those payments as relates to the part-time part of the course,

(b) where she or the student make any payment which was previously made by him in pursuance of an obligation incurred before the first year of his course—

(i) if, in the opinion of the authority the obligation had been reasonably so incurred, an amount equal to the payment in question,

(ii) if, in their opinion only a lesser obligation could have been reasonably so incurred, such correspondingly lesser amount (if any) as appears to them appropriate,

(c) any allowance payable to her by an adoption agency in pursuance of a scheme approved by the Secretary of State under section 50 of the Adoption Act 1958(a),

(d) **any guardian's allowance to which she is entitled under section 38 of the Social Security Act 1975(b), and**

(e) where a child in the care of a local authority is boarded out with her, any payment made to her in pursuance of section 21(1) of the Child Care Act 1980(c),

---

(a) 1958 c. 5, amended by section 32 of the Children Act 1975 (c. 72).
(b) 1975 c. 14; section 38 was amended by paragraph 12 of Schedule 4 and by Schedule 5 to the Child Benefit Act 1975 (c. 61).
(c) 1980 c. 5.

except that "income" does not include any attendance or mobility allowance under section 35 or 37A of the Social Security Act 1975(a);

"relevant award" means a statutory award in respect of a person's attendance at—

 (a) a full-time course of advanced further education or a comparable course outside England and Wales,

 (b) a course prescribed under sub-paragraph *(d)*(ii) of Regulation 10(1), or

 (c) the full-time part of a course prescribed under sub-paragraph *(d)*(iii) of Regulation 10(1) which is partly full-time and partly part-time;

"spouse", except in the definition above of adult dependant, means in relation to a student his spouse by a marriage contracted before the first year of his course, so however that a person shall be treated as though not the student's spouse if they have ceased ordinarily to live together whether or not an order for their separation has been made by any court, subject however to sub-paragraph (4).

(2) A person, including the student's spouse, shall not be treated as a dependant of the student during any period for which that person—

 (a) holds a relevant award, or

 (b) (save for the purposes of paragraph 20) is ordinarily living outside the United Kingdom.

(3) A person shall not be treated as a student's adult dependant or as his dependent child—

 (a) in the case of a person other than a child of the student, if his income exceeds by £375 or more the sum specified in paragraph 18(4)*(a)*;

 (b) in the case of a child of a student who either has a spouse who is, or but for sub-paragraph (2) would be, his dependant or has an adult dependant, if the child's income so exceeds the sum specified in paragraph 18(4)*(b)* and applicable to his age;

 (c) in the case of a child of a student not falling within sub-paragraph *(b)*, unless either—

  (i) the child is the only or eldest child dependent on the student whose income does not so exceed the sum specified in paragraph 18(4)*(a)*, or

  (ii) the child's income does not so exceed the sum specified in paragraph 18(4)*(b)* and applicable to his age,

subject, however to sub-paragraph (4).

(4) In the case of a student—

 (a) who began his course before 1st September 1981;

 (b) whose dependants requirement under paragraph 18 of Part 3 of Schedule 2 to the Education (Mandatory Awards) Regulations 1980(b), before the revocation of those Regulations, took account of an

---

(a) Section 37A was inserted by section 22 of the Social Security Pensions Act 1975 (c. 60).
(b) S.I. 1980/974.

adult dependant, spouse or child who falls outside the definitions in sub-paragraph (1) above, and

(c) whose dependants requirement thereunder would have continued to take account of the person in question if those Regulations had not been revoked and no subsequent regulations had been made under section 1 of the Education Act 1962,

the person in question shall be treated as the student's adult dependant, spouse, or as the case may be, child for the purposes of paragraph 18 below and, in relation to that person, sub-paragraph (3) above shall not apply.

18.—(1) This paragraph shall apply in the case of a student who married before the first year of his course where he is an independent student with dependants except that for the purpose of determining a student's dependants requirement for an adult dependant it shall be immaterial whether or not he married as aforesaid.

(2) The dependants requirement of the student shall, subject to paragraphs 19 and 20, be—

(a) if the student's spouse holds a statutory award and in calculating payments under it account is taken of the spouse's dependants requirement, one half of the amount determined in accordance with sub-paragraphs (3) and (4);

(b) in any other case, the whole of the amount so determined.

(3) The amount referred to in sub-paragraph (2) shall be the amount which is $X-(Y-Z)$ where—

(a) X is the aggregate of the relevant sums specified in sub-paragraph (4);

(b) Y is the aggregate of the income of the student's dependants;

(c) Z is so much of the sum ascertained by multiplying £375 by the number of his dependants as does not exceed Y.

(4) The relevant sums referred to in sub-paragraph (3) are—

(a) except where the student has a spouse who is the holder of a relevant award, **£1,115,** and

(b) in respect of each dependent child—

(i) under the age of 11 immediately before the beginning of the academic year, or born during that year, **£215,**

(ii) then aged 11 or over, but under 16, **£450,**

(iii) then aged 16 or over, but under 18, **£595,**

(iv) then aged 18 or over, **£850,**

except that the only or eldest dependent child shall be disregarded for the purposes hereof if the student has neither an adult dependant nor a spouse who is, or but for paragraph 17(2) would be, a dependant.

19.—(1) This paragraph shall apply in the case of an independent student with dependants who maintains a home for himself and a dependant at a place other than that at which he resides while attending the course.

(2) The dependants requirement of the student (determined in accordance with paragraph 18(2)*(a)* or *(b)*) shall be increased by **£385**.

20.—(1) This paragraph shall apply in the case of a student, in whose case paragraph 18 applies, who maintains any dependant outside the United Kingdom.

(2) Notwithstanding anything in the foregoing paragraphs of this Part of this Schedule, the dependants requirement of the student shall be of such amount, if any, as the authority consider reasonable in all the circumstances, not exceeding the amount determined in accordance with those paragraphs.

PART 4

OLDER STUDENTS

21. This Part of this Schedule shall apply in the case of a student who attained the age of 26 before the first year of the course in respect of which his award was originally bestowed and either—

(a) was in full-time employment for a total of three of the six years immediately preceding that year; or

(b) held an award (or was in receipt of a grant under arrangements made under section 2(3) of the Education Act 1962) in respect of his attendance at a previous course and either was in full-time employ-ment as aforesaid immediately preceding the first year of that course or was a person to whom paragraph 14 of Schedule 1 to the 1971 Regulations applied (or any provision to the like effect in such arrangements as aforesaid).

22. The requirements referred to in Regulation 18(1)*(a)* shall, in the case of such a student, include—

(a) where at the beginning of the first year of his course he was aged 26 years, the sum of **£160**;

(b) where he was so aged 27 years, the sum of **£315**;

(c) where he was so aged 28 years, the sum of **£485**;

(d) where he was so aged 29 or more years, the sum of **£640**.

PART 5

CONSTRUCTION OF PARTS 1 TO 4

23.   In this Schedule, any reference to the home of the student's parents shall be construed, in the case of a student whose spouse attends a full-time course at any establishment, as including a reference to the home of the parents of the student's spouse.

24. In this Schedule, except where the context otherwise requires, any reference to a requirement, expenditure or attendance in respect of which no period of time is specified shall be construed as a reference to a requirement, expenditure or attendance for the year.

25. For the purposes of this Schedule, attendance at an institution, or a period of study, is a necessary part of a student's course only where the authority are satisfied that if the student did not attend the institution, or undertake the period of study, he would not be eligible to complete his course; and, for the purpose of being so satisfied, the authority may require the matter to be evidenced by a certificate given by the academic authority.

SCHEDULE 3 Regulation 18

RESOURCES

PART 1

STUDENT'S INCOME

Calculation of student's income

1.—(1) In calculating the student's income for the purposes of Regulation 18(1)*(b)* there shall be taken into account his income (reduced by income tax and social security contributions) from all sources, but there shall be disregarded the following resources—

(a) the first **£375** of the aggregate of—

(i) any income other than income of a kind mentioned in sub-paragraphs (b) to (o) **and other than any sum treated as income under sub-paragraph (3),** and

(ii) so much of any income mentioned in sub-paragraph *(b)* as is not disregarded under that sub-paragraph;

(b) the first **£540** of any income by way of—

(i) scholarship, studentship, exhibition or award of a similar description bestowed on the student in respect of the course (in pursuance of a sponsorship scheme or otherwise) not being an award bestowed in pursuance of section 1 of the Education Act 1962(a), and

(ii) in the case of a student released by his employer to attend the course, any payments made by that employer,

so, however, that in the case of a student who holds an Industrial Scholarship this sub-paragraph shall have effect as if for the sum "£540" there were substituted the sum "£795";

(c) in the case of a student, other than one mentioned in paragraph 3*(a)*, for whose benefit any income is applied, or payments are required to be applied, as mentioned in paragraph 5(5)—

(i) the whole of that income or those payments, unless he is such a student as is mentioned in paragraph 3*(b)* or *(c)* or

(ii) so much of that income or those payments as, when aggregated

(a) 1962 c. 12.

with any amount disregarded under sub-paragraph *(a)*, does not exceed **£740**, if he is such a student as is so mentioned;

(d) any disability pension not subject to income tax;

(e) any bounty received as a reservist with the armed forces;

(f) remuneration for work done in vacations;

(g) in the case of a student in respect of whom a parental contribution is by virtue of Part 2 of this Schedule treated as forming part of his resources, any payment made under covenant by a parent by reference to whose income that contribution falls to be ascertained;

(h) any payment made for a specific educational purpose otherwise than to meet such fees and such requirements for maintenance as are specified in Schedules 1 and 2;

(i) child benefit;

(j) any benefit under the Supplementary Benefits Act 1976(**a**);

(k) any attendance or mobility allowance under section 35 or 37A of the Social Security Act 1975;

(l) any allowance granted to him in pursuance of a scheme under section 19 of the Housing Finance Act 1972(**b**);

(m) any allowance payable to him by an adoption agency in pursuance of a scheme approved by the Secretary of State under section 50 of the Adoption Act 1958(**c**);

(n) **any guardian's allowance to which he is entitled under section 38 of the Social Security Act 1975;**

(o) in the case of a student with whom a child in the care of a local authority is boarded out, any payment made to him in pursuance of section 21(1) of the Child Care Act 1980(**d**).

(2) In the case of such a student as is described in paragraph 3*(a)* who makes any payment in pursuance of an obligation incurred before the first year of his course, in calculating his income for the purposes aforesaid there shall be deducted therefrom—

(a) if, in the opinion of the authority, the obligation had been reasonably so incurred, an amount equal to the payment in question;

(b) if, in their opinion, only a lesser obligation could have been reasonably so incurred, such correspondingly lesser amount (if any) as appears to them appropriate;

except that no deduction shall be made from the student's income under this sub-paragraph if he is married, his spouse is a dependant for the purposes of Part 3 of Schedule 2 and, in pursuance of paragraph 17(1) thereof, the payment is taken into account in determining her income.

(3) **In a case where the student is the parent or step-parent of an award holder in respect of whom a contribution is ascertained under Part 2 of this**

(**a**) 1976 c. 71.
(**b**) 1972 c. 47.
(**c**) 1958 c 5, amended by section 32 of the Children Act 1975 (c.72).
(**d**) 1980 c. 5.

Schedule, so much of the amount (if any) by which the contribution is reduced under paragraph 4(2) as the authority consider just shall be treated as part of the student's income for the purposes of Regulation 18(1) *(b)*.

(4) For the purposes of sub-paragraph (1)*(b)*, the reference therein to an Industrial Scholarship is a reference to a Scholarship awarded by the Industrial Scholarships Trust.

PART 2

PARENTAL CONTRIBUTION

Definitions and construction of Part 2

2.—(1) In this Part of this Schedule—

"child" includes a person adopted in pursuance of adoption proceedings and a step-child but, except in paragraph 4, does not include a child who holds a statutory award; and, except as otherwise provided by paragraph 5, "parent" shall be construed accordingly;

"gross income" has the meaning assigned to it by paragraph 5;

"income of the student's parent" means the total income of the parent from all sources computed as for income tax purposes, except as otherwise provided by paragraph 5 or 6;

"residual income" means, subject to sub-paragraph (2), the balance of gross income remaining in any year after the deductions specified in paragraph 6 have been made;

"total income" has the same meaning as in section 32 of the Finance Act 1971(**a**).

(2) Where, in a case not falling within paragraph 5(3) or (4), the authority are satisfied that the income of the parent in any financial year is as a result of some event beyond his control likely to be, and to continue after that year to be, not more than 85% of his income in the financial year preceding that year, they may, for the purpose of enabling the student to attend the course without hardship, ascertain the parental contribution for the year of his course in which that event occurred by taking as the residual income the average of the residual income for each of the financial years in which that year falls.

(3) Where the student's parent satisfies the authority that his income is wholly or mainly derived from the profits of a business or profession carried on by him, then, if the authority and the parent so agree, any reference in this Part of this Schedule to a financial year shall be construed as a reference to a year ending with such date as appears to the authority expedient having regard to the accounts kept in respect of that business or profession and the periods covered thereby.

Application of Part 2

3. A parental contribution ascertained in accordance with this Part shall be applicable in the case of every student except—

(a) 1971 c. 68.

(a) an independent student;

(b) a student who has no parent living or in respect of whom the authority are satisfied either—

　(i) that his parents cannot be found, or

　(ii) that it is not reasonably practicable to get in touch with them;

(c) a student who has been in the care of a local authority or in care of a voluntary organisation within the meaning of section 88 of the Children Act 1975(a) throughout the three years immediately preceding—

　(i) the first year of his course, or

　(ii) without prejudice to sub-paragraph (i), his attaining the age of 18 years where he had attained that age before the first year of his course,

and has not, at any time in the said period, been allowed by the local authority to be under the charge and control of his parents or, in the case of a student who has been in the care of a voluntary organisation, has not, at any such time, in fact been under such charge and control.

Parental contribution

4.—(1) Subject to sub-paragraph (2), the parental contribution shall be—

(a) in any case in which the residual income is **£7,100** or more but less than **£9,000**, £20 with the addition of £1 for every complete £7 by which it exceeds **£7,100**;

(b) in any case in which the residual income is **£9,000** or more but less than **£14,300**, **£291** with the addition of £1 for every complete £8 by which it exceeds **£9,000**; and

(c) in any case in which the residual income is **£14,300** or more, **£953** with the addition of £1 for every complete £13 by which it exceeds **£14,300**,

reduced in each case, in respect of each child of the parent (other than the student) who is wholly or mainly dependent on him on the first day of the year for which the contribution falls to be ascertained, by **£75** or, if the child holds a statutory award, by **£210** and in any case in which the residual income is less than **£7,100** the parental contribution shall be nil.

(2) For any year in which a statutory award is held by—

(a) more than one child of the parent;

(b) the parent; or

(c) the student's step-parent—

the parental contribution for the student shall be such proportion of any contribution ascertained in accordance with this Part as the authority (after consultation with any other authority concerned) consider just:

Provided that where a contribution is ascertained in respect of more than one child of the parent, the aggregate amount of the contributions in respect of each shall not exceed the amount of the contribution that would be applicable if only one child held an award.

(a) 1975 c. 72.

Gross income

5.—(1) For the purposes of this paragraph "preceding financial year" means the financial year preceding the year in respect of which the resources of the student fall to be assessed and "current financial year" means the financial year which includes the first day of that year:

Provided that where references to a financial year fall to be construed in accordance with paragraph 2(3) as references to a year ending less than five months before the beginning of a year of the student's course, "preceding financial year" shall mean the year last ending five or more months before the year in respect of which the resources of the student fall to be assessed and "current financial year" shall mean the year ending within those five months.

(2) Subject to the provisions of this paragraph, "gross income" means the income of the student's parent in the preceding financial year or, for the purpose of calculating residual income under paragraph 2(2), in a financial year there mentioned.

(3) Where the authority are satisfied that the income of the parent in the current financial year is likely to be not more than 85% of his income for the preceding financial year, they may for the purpose of calculating the parental contribution ascertain the gross income by reference to the current financial year; and, in such case sub-paragraph (2) shall have effect, in relation to the year in respect of which the student's resources fall to be assessed and, if the authority so determine, any subsequent year, as if the reference therein to the preceding financial year were a reference to the current financial year.

(4) Where one of the student's parents has died in either the preceding or the current financial year and the authority are satisfied that the income of the surviving parent in the current financial year, when aggregated with that of the deceased parent where he died in that year, is likely to be less than their aggregated income in the preceding financial year, they may for the purpose of calculating the parental contribution ascertain the gross income by reference to the current financial year; and, in such case, sub-paragraph (2) shall have effect, in relation to the year in which the student's resources fall to be assessed as if the reference therein to the preceding financial year were a reference to the current financial year and, if the deceased parent died in that year, the reference to the student's parent included a reference to his deceased parent.

(5) Without prejudice to sub-paragraph (7), where, in pursuance of any trust deed or other instrument or by virtue of section 31(1) of the Trustee Act 1925(**a**) or any other enactment, any income is applied by any person for or towards the maintenance, education or other benefit of the student or of any person dependent on the student's parent, or payments made to his parent are required to be so applied, that income, or those payments, shall be treated as part of the gross income of the parent.

(6) Any dividends or interest paid or credited to the parent by a building society which has entered into arrangements with the Commissioners of Inland Revenue under section 343(1) of the Income and Corporation Taxes Act 1970(**b**) shall be deemed to have been received by him after deduction of

---

(**a**) 1925 c. 19.
(**b**) 1970 c. 10; all the provisions of this Act referred to in paragraphs 5 and 6 have been amended extensively by subsequent Finance Acts.

income tax at the reduced rate determined under those arrangements for the year of assessment in which the dividends or interest are paid or credited; and the amount deemed to have been so deducted shall be treated as part of his gross income.

(7) Where any such benefit as is mentioned in paragraph 1(1)*(b)*(i) of Part 1 of this Schedule is provided, by reason of the parent's employment, for any member of his family or household who holds a statutory award (whether the student or some other such member) then, notwithstanding the provisions of section 61 of the Finance Act 1976(a), that benefit shall not be treated as part of the gross income of the parent.

(8) There shall be treated as part of the gross income all income arising from an office or employment which by virtue of any enactment is, as such, exempt from tax.

(9) Where the parents do not ordinarily live together throughout the year in respect of which the resources of the student fall to be ascertained ("the relevant year"), the parental contribution shall be determined by reference to the income of whichever parent the authority consider the more appropriate in the circumstances.

(10) Where the parents do not ordinarily live together for part only of the relevant year, the parental contribution shall be the aggregate of—

   (a) the appropriate proportion of the contribution determined as provided in sub-paragraph (9), that is to say, such proportion thereof as the part of the relevant year for which the parents do not so live together bears to the full year, and

   (b) the appropriate proportion of the contribution determined without regard to this sub-paragraph, that is to say, such proportion thereof as the part of the relevant year for which the parents so live together bears to the full year.

(11) Where one of the student's parents is his step-parent, the parental contribution shall be ascertained by reference only to the income of the other parent.

Deductions

6.—(1) For the purpose of determining the income of a student's parent (and, accordingly, the parent's gross income), in so far as in computing his total income for income tax purposes any deductions fall to be made—

   (a) by way of personal reliefs provided for in Chapter II of Part I of the Income and Corporation Taxes Act 1970;

   (b) **in pursuance of any Act passed after the passing of the Finance Act 1982(b) on 30th July 1982,** or

   (c) without prejudice as aforesaid, of a kind mentioned in sub-paragraph (2),

the parent's income shall be determined as though those deductions did not fall to be made.

(a) 1976 c. 40.
(b) 1982 c. 39.

(2) For the purpose of determining a parent's residual income there shall be deducted from his gross income—

(a) in respect of any person, other than a spouse, child or holder of a statutory award, dependent on the parent during the year for which the contribution falls to be ascertained, the amount by which **£915** exceeds the income of that person in that year;

(b) the gross amount of any sums paid as interest (including interest on a mortgage) in respect of which relief is given under the Income Tax Acts, or as interest under the option mortgage scheme, in respect of a loan to the parent;

(c) the gross amount of any premium or other sum in respect of which relief is given to the parent **in the relevant year** under sections 19, 20 or **227** of the Income and Corporation Taxes Act 1970 (life insurance and retirement annuity premiums and certain other payments);

(d) where the parents ordinarily live together and one of them is incapacitated, so much of the cost in wages of domestic assistance as does not exceed **£730**;

(e) where a parent whose marriage has terminated either is gainfully employed or is incapacitated, so much of the cost in wages of domestic assistance as does not exceed **£730**;

(f) in respect of additional expenditure incurred by reason of the fact that the parent lives in a place where the cost of living is higher than that cost in the United Kingdom, such sum (if any) as the authority consider reasonable in all the circumstances;

(g) in the case of a parent who holds a statutory award, the amount by which the aggregate of his requirements for his ordinary maintenance (ascertained in accordance with Part 1 of Schedule 2) and **£375** exceeds the sum payable in respect of maintenance in pursuance of that award.

PART 3

SPOUSE'S CONTRIBUTION

Application of Part 3

7. A spouse's contribution ascertained in accordance with this Part shall be applicable in the case of every man student ordinarily living with his wife and every woman student so living with her husband except—

(a) a student in whose case a parental contribution is applicable in accordance with Part 2, and

(b) **a student whose child holds an award in respect of which a parental contribution is applicable.**

Spouse's contribution

8.—(1) Subject to sub-paragraphs (3) and (4), Part 2 above, except paragraphs 3, 4(1) and (2)(a), 5(4), (9) and (10) and 6(2)(d) shall apply with the necessary modifications for the ascertainment of the spouse's contribution as it applies for the ascertainment of the parental contribution, references to the parent being construed except where the context otherwise requires as references to the student's spouse and, unless the context otherwise requires, this Part shall be construed as one with the said Part 2.

(2) The spouse's contribution shall be—

    (a) in any case in which the residual income is **£5,500** or more but less than **£9,000,** £10 with the addition of £1 for every complete £5 by which it exceeds **£5,500;** and

    (b) in any case in which the residual income is **£9,000** or more, **£710** with the addition of £1 for every complete £10 by which it exceeds **£9,000;**

reduced in either case, by **£75** in respect of each child of the student who is dependent on him or his spouse on the first day of the year for which the contribution falls to be ascertained; and in any case in which the residual income is less than **£5,500** the spouse's contribution shall be nil.

(3) If the student marries during any year for which the contribution falls to be ascertained the contribution for that year shall be the fraction of the sum ascertained in accordance with the provisions of sub-paragraphs (1) and (2) of which the denominator is 52 and the numerator is the number of complete weeks between the date of the marriage and whichever is the earlier of the end of that year and the end of the course.

(4) If the student's marriage terminates during any year for which the contribution falls to be ascertained the contribution for that year shall be the fraction of the sum ascertained in accordance with the provisions of sub-paragraphs (1) and (2) of which the denominator is 52 and the numerator is the number of complete weeks between the beginning of that year and the termination of the marriage.

Regulation 18(2)   SCHEDULE 4

WIDOWS, WIDOWERS, DIVORCED AND SEPARATED PERSONS

1. This Schedule shall apply in the case of a student whose marriage has terminated (either before or during his course) unless and until—

    (a) he remarries, or

    (b) where the marriage terminated by reason of the parties ceasing ordinarily to live together, they again so live together.

2.—(1) This paragraph shall apply where the student has dependants within the meaning of Part 3 of Schedule 2 and paragraph 18 thereof applies to him.

(2) In the case of such a student—

    (a) the sum to be disregarded under paragraph 1(1)*(a)* of Schedule 3 shall be **£940** instead of **£375,** or

    (b) his requirements under paragraph 18 of Part 3 of Schedule 2 shall be treated as increased by the sum of **£565,** or

    (c) in the case of a student to whom Part 4 of Schedule 2 applies, his requirements shall be treated as including the sum specified in paragraph 22 thereof,

whichever is the most favourable to him (disregarding sub-paragraph *(b)* where, in pursuance of the following paragraph, he elects as there mentioned).

3.—(1) This paragraph shall apply in the case of a student with one or more children (including persons adopted in pursuance of adoption proceedings and step-children) who are both under the age of nineteen years and dependent on him.

(2) Such a student may elect that the sum specified as his requirements in Part 3 of Schedule 2 shall be disregarded and that instead there shall in calculating his income be disregarded **£1,225** in respect of his only or eldest such child and **£395** in respect of every other such child.

SCHEDULE 5   Regulations 2, 4(3) and 20

SANDWICH COURSES

1.—(1) In this Schedule—

"sandwich course" means a course consisting of alternate periods of full-time study in an establishment and periods of experience so organised that, taking the course as a whole, the student attends the periods of full-time study for an average of not less than 19 weeks in each year; and for the purpose of calculating his attendance the course shall be treated as beginning with the first period of full-time study and ending with the last such period;

"periods of experience" means, subject to sub-paragraph (2), periods of industrial, professional or commercial experience associated with full-time study at the establishment but at a place outside the establishment, other than periods of—

(a) unpaid service in a hospital or in a public health service laboratory,

(b) unpaid service with a local authority acting in the exercise of their functions relating to health, welfare or the care of children and young persons or with a voluntary organisation providing facilities or carrying out activities of a like nature,

(c) unpaid service in the probation and aftercare service,

(d) teaching practice,

(e) unpaid research in an establishment, or

(f) such experience as aforesaid falling wholly within the terms at the establishment in any year which do not comprise paid service or employment and either—

  (i) do not aggregate more than 6 weeks during that year, or

  (ii) do not aggregate more than 12 weeks during that and some other year taken together, where that other year has not already been taken into account for the purposes hereof;

"sandwich year" means, as respects any student, any year of a sandwich course which includes both periods of full-time study in the establishment and periods of experience;

"prescribed proportion" means the proportion which the number of weeks in the year for which the student in question attends the establishment bears to 30, except that where that proportion is greater than the whole it means the whole;

"modified proportion" means the proportion which the number of weeks in the year in which there are no periods of experience for the student in question bears to 52.

(2) In the case of a student studying modern languages whose course includes periods of residence in a country whose language is a main language of that course, "periods of experience" means such periods of residence for which he is in gainful employment.

(3) For the purposes of determining the prescribed proportion or the modified proportion where the number of weeks in question is not a whole number, a day shall be reckoned as a seventh of a week.

(4) In the application of this Schedule to a student whose marriage has terminated, references to Schedules 2 and 3 are to be construed as references to those Schedules as modified in accordance with Schedule 4.

(5) In the application of this Schedule to a student attending a course provided by the University of Oxford or of Cambridge the provisions thereof shall have effect as if—

> (a) in the definitions of "prescribed proportion" in sub-paragraph (1) for the number "30" there were substituted the number "25", and

> (b) in paragraph 3 for the words "30 weeks 3 days", in both places where they occur, there were substituted the words "25 weeks 3 days".

2. The provisions of Regulation 17(b) shall, as respects any sandwich year where the period of full-time study does not exceed 30 weeks 3 days, have effect as if the minimum maintenance payment there mentioned were the prescribed proportion of the sum of £410 so mentioned.

3. The provisions of Schedule 2 shall, as respects any sandwich year, have effect subject to the following modifications—

> (a) where the period of full-time study does not exceed 30 weeks 3 days, the student's requirements for his ordinary maintenance shall be the prescribed proportion of the appropriate amount specified in Part 1;

> (b) where the period of full-time study exceeds 30 weeks 3 days, the student's requirements for his ordinary and supplementary maintenance shall be the aggregate of the appropriate amount specified in Part 1 and the appropriate amount specified in paragraph 6 of Part 2;

> (c) the student's requirements in respect of such expenditure as is referred to in paragraph 5(b) of Part 2 shall be determined in accordance with that Part except that his requirements in respect of such expenditure as is mentioned in paragraph 10 shall be the amount by which the expenditure exceeds the prescribed proportion of £50;

> (d) the student's requirement for the maintenance of a dependant shall be the modified proportion of the sum specified in Part 3 except that

where such a requirement falls to be increased under paragraph 19 it shall be increased by the prescribed proportion of the sum there specified; and

(e) if the student is a person to whom Part 4 applies, his requirements under that Part shall be the prescribed proportion of the amount there specified.

4. The provisions of Schedule 3 shall, as respects any sandwich year, have effect subject to the following modifications—

(a) the sum to be disregarded under paragraph 1(1)*(a)* of Part 1 shall be the prescribed proportion of **£375** and the reference in paragraph 1(1)*(c)* to **£740** shall be construed as a reference to the aggregate of **£365** and the prescribed proportion of **£375**.

(b) in calculating the student's income there shall be disregarded any payment made to him by his employer in respect of any period of experience;

(c) the amount of the parental contribution applicable to his case shall be the prescribed proportion of the contribution ascertained in accordance with Part 2; and

(d) the amount of the spouse's contribution applicable to his case shall be the prescribed proportion of the contribution ascertained in accordance with Part 3.

Keith Joseph,
Secretary of State for
Education and Science.

25th July 1983.

Regulation 6(1)   **APPENDIX**

REGULATIONS AMENDING THE EDUCATION (MANDATORY AWARDS)
REGULATIONS 1982 REVOKED BY REGULATION 6(1)

Title	Reference
The Education (Mandatory Awards) (Amendment) Regulations 1982	SI 1982/1295
The Education (Mandatory Awards) (Amendment) Regulations 1983	SI 1983/114
The Education (Mandatory Awards) (Amendment) (No. 2) Regulations 1983	SI 1983/477

EXPLANATORY NOTE
(This Note is not part of the Regulations.)

These Regulations, which come into operation on 1st September 1983, consolidate, with amendments, the Education (Mandatory Awards) Regulations 1982 and the Regulations amending those Regulations. Changes other than minor drafting and consequential changes are indicated by the use of heavy type; the changes of substance are described below.

New provisions for the payment of awards to EEC migrant workers undertaking vocational training courses are included in Regulations 9 and 13. Provisions in Regulations 9 and 11–13 concerning the payment of awards to refugees are extended to relate to the spouse and child of a refugee.

The obligation of local education authorities under Regulation 14 to transfer an award where a student changes courses is modified in cases where the student would have had to undertake a period of repeat study in order to complete his original course.

In Regulation 27, authorities are given a discretion to reduce the payments under an award to a student who is detained under a court order.

The Regulations increase the amounts payable in respect of both fees and maintenance requirements; new figures are specified in Regulations 21 and 22 and in Schedules 1–5. Part 3 of Schedule 2 and Part 1 of Schedule 3 are amended to provide that any guardian's allowance shall be disregarded in calculating the income of a student or his spouse in order to determine the amount of a maintenance grant. The requirements in Schedule 3 to ascertain parental and spouses' contributions to a student's resources are modified in cases where there is more than one award-holder in the student's family. The provisions in Part 2 of Schedule 3 for life insurance premiums and certain similar payments to be disregarded in calculating the income of a student's parent are amended so as to reflect more closely the treatment given to such premiums for tax purposes.

STATUTORY INSTRUMENTS

1983 No. 1136

LICENSING (LIQUOR)

The Occasional Permissions (Isles of Scilly) Order 1983

Made - - - -	*26th July* 1983
Coming into Operation	*9th August* 1983

In exercise of the powers conferred upon me by section 198(2) of the Licensing Act 1964(**a**) and section 202 of that Act, as amended by section 4(4) of the Licensing (Occasional Permissions) Act 1983(**b**), I hereby make the following Order:—

1. This Order may be cited as the Occasional Permissions (Isles of Scilly) Order 1983 and shall come into operation on 9th August 1983.

2. In relation to the Isles of Scilly the functions of licensing justices under the Licensing (Occasional Permissions) Act 1983 shall be exercised by the Joint Police Committee for the Isles of Scilly and, accordingly, that Act shall have effect in the Isles of Scilly as if–

(*a*) each reference to the licensing justices were a reference to the Joint Police Committee;

(*b*) each reference to a licensing district were a reference to the Isles of Scilly;

(*c*) each reference to licensing sessions were a reference to a meeting of the Joint Police Committee held for the purposes of the Isles of Scilly (Sale of Intoxicating Liquor) Order 1973(**c**); and

(*d*) the reference in section 2(3) to the chief officer of police were a reference to the Chief Constable of the Devon and Cornwall Police Area.

(**a**) 1964 c. 26.   (**b**) 1983 c. 24.   (**c**) S.I. 1973/1958.

3.—(1) In Article 9 of the Isles of Scilly (Sale of Intoxicating Liquor) Order 1973, after the words "a permit," there shall be inserted the words "or an occasional permission,".

(2) In Article 14 of that Order, after the words "annual permits" and "justices' licences" in the first places where they occur, there shall be inserted the words "or the issue of occasional permissions".

(3) In Article 15 of that Order, after the words "a permit", there shall be inserted the words ", an occasional permission," and after the words "the Licensing Act 1964," there shall be inserted the words "or the Licensing (Occasional Permissions) Act 1983,".

Leon Brittan,
One of Her Majesty's Principal
Secretaries of State.

Home Office.
26th July 1983.

EXPLANATORY NOTE

(*This Note is not part of the Order.*)

This Order provides that the functions of licensing justices under the Licensing (Occasional Permissions) Act 1983 shall, in the Isles of Scilly, be exercised by the Joint Police Committee for the Isles of Scilly, which is responsible for liquor licensing in the Isles of Scilly.

STATUTORY INSTRUMENTS

1983 No. 1137

SOCIAL SECURITY

The Social Security (Attendance Allowance) Amendment (No. 2) Regulations 1983

Made - - - - -	*27th July* 1983
Laid before Parliament	*29th July* 1983
Coming into Operation	*8th August* 1983

The Secretary of State for Social Services, in exercise of the powers conferred on him by sections 35 and 85(1) of the Social Security Act 1975(a) and of all other powers enabling him in that behalf, hereby makes the following regulations which relate only to matters which, in accordance with that Act, have been referred to the Attendance Allowance Board and which accordingly, by virtue of section 10(2) of, and paragraph 12(3) of Part II of Schedule 3 to, the Social Security Act 1980(b) are not subject to the requirement for prior reference to the Social Security Advisory Committee.

Citation and commencement

1. These regulations may be cited as the Social Security (Attendance Allowance) Amendment (No. 2) Regulations 1983 and shall come into operation on 8th August 1983.

Amendment of the Social Security (Attendance Allowance) (No. 2) Regulations 1975

2.—(1) The Social Security (Attendance Allowance) (No. 2) Regulations 1975(c) shall be amended in the following manner.

(2) In paragraph (2) of regulation 7 (children in hospital and certain other accommodation) at the beginning there shall be inserted—

"Subject to paragraph (2A)".

(a) 1975 c. 14; section 35 was amended by section 129 of, and paragraph 63 of Schedule 15 to, the National Health Service Act 1977 (c. 49), section 2 of the Social Security Act 1979 (c. 18) and sections 2 and 21 of, and paragraph 8 of Part II of Schedule 1 to, the Social Security Act 1980 (c. 30).

(b) 1980 c. 30.

(c) S.I. 1975/598; relevant amending instruments are S.I. 1977/342, 417, 1979/1684 and 1983/1015.

(3) After paragraph (2) of regulation 7 a new paragraph (2A) shall be inserted—

"(2A) Where—

(*a*) on a day or days falling within the period of 4 weeks ending immediately before 8th August 1983 a child has been living in accommodation in circumstances in which paragraph (1)(b) applies in his case; and

(*b*) since that day or the last of those days there has not been an interval of at least 29 consecutive days when that paragraph did not apply in the case of that child,

paragraph (2) shall not operate to make attendance allowance payable in respect of that child for any day throughout which he is living in such accommodation."

Signed by authority of the Secretary of State for Social Services.

Rhodes Boyson,
Minister of State,
Department of Health and Social Security.

27th July 1983.

EXPLANATORY NOTE

(This Note is not part of the Regulations.)

These regulations further amend regulation 7 of the Social Security (Attendance Allowance) (No. 2) Regulations 1975 relating to children in hospital and other accommodation, so that the provision whereby attendance allowance may be paid in respect of a child for the first 4 weeks that a child is residing in accommodation where the cost is borne or may be borne out of public or local funds shall not apply in respect of a child who was living in such accommodation on any day in the 4 weeks before 8th August 1983 until an interval of at least 29 days elapses during which he does not live in such accommodation.

1983 No. 1139

SEA FISHERIES

CONSERVATION OF SEA FISH

The Receiving of Trans-shipped Sea Fish (Licensing) (Variation) Order 1983

Made - - - - -	*27th July* 1983
Laid before Parliament	*28th July* 1983
Coming into Operation	*10th August* 1983

The Minister of Agriculture, Fisheries and Food and the Secretaries of State respectively concerned with the sea fish industry in Scotland, Wales and Northern Ireland, acting jointly, in exercise of the powers conferred on them by sections 4A(1) and (2) and 20(1) of the Sea Fish (Conservation) Act 1967(a), and of all other powers enabling them in that behalf, hereby make the following order:—

Title and commencement

1. This order may be cited as the Receiving of Trans-shipped Sea Fish (Licensing) (Variation) Order 1983 and shall come into operation on 10th August 1983.

Variation of the Receiving of Trans-shipped Sea Fish (Licensing) Order 1982

2. The Receiving of Trans-shipped Sea Fish (Licensing) Order 1982(b) shall be varied by substituting for article 3 thereof the following articles:—

"*Prohibition of receiving trans-shipped sea fish without a licence*

3. Within British fishery limits the receiving by any vessel (whether British or foreign) of any pelagic sea fish trans-shipped from any other vessel is prohibited unless authorised by a licence granted by one of the Ministers.

Defence

3A. In any proceedings under article 3 of this order in respect of the receiving of pelagic sea fish caught by a foreign fishing boat, it shall be a defence, unless the receiving of the fish took place within the territorial sea adjacent to the United Kingdom, the Channel Islands and the Isle of Man, for the person charged to prove that the fish to which the charge relates were caught outside British fishery limits.".

(a) 1967 c. 84; section 4A was inserted by section 21 of the Fisheries Act 1981 (c. 29); section 22(2)(*a*), which contains a definition of "the Ministers" for the purposes of section 4A(1), was amended by the Fisheries Act 1981, sections 19(2)(*d*) and 45(*b*).
(b) S.I. 1982/80.

In Witness whereof the Official Seal of the Minister of Agriculture, Fisheries and Food is hereunto affixed on 25th July 1983.

(L.S.)

Michael Jopling,
Minister of Agriculture, Fisheries and Food.

26th July 1983.

George Younger,
Secretary of State for Scotland.

27th July 1983.

Nicholas Edwards,
Secretary of State for Wales.

26th July 1983.

James Prior,
Secretary of State for Northern Ireland.

EXPLANATORY NOTE

(This Note is not part of the Order.)

This order varies the Receiving of Trans-shipped Sea Fish (Licensing) Order 1982, which prohibits the receiving within British fishery limits by any vessel (whether British or foreign) of any pelagic sea fish which—

(*a*) have been caught by any British fishing boat registered in the United Kingdom, and

(*b*) are trans-shipped from a boat so registered to the receiving vessel,

unless authorised by a licence granted by one of the Ministers.

The variation made by this order extends this prohibition on receiving fish without a licence so that it applies in respect of any pelagic sea fish trans-shipped within British fishery limits from any vessel, whether caught by a British fishing boat or by a foreign fishing boat. However, the variation also provides that where the fish were caught by a foreign fishing boat, it shall be a defence, unless the receiving took place in British territorial waters, to show that the fish were caught outside British fishery limits.

STATUTORY INSTRUMENTS

1983 No. 1140

HEALTH AND SAFETY

The Classification and Labelling of Explosives Regulations 1983

Made - - - -	*21st July* 1983
Laid before Parliament	*9th August* 1983
Coming into Operation	*1st November* 1983

The Secretary of State, in exercise of the powers conferred upon him by sections 15(1), (2), (3)*(a)* and *(c)*, (4)*(a)* and *(b)*, (5)*(a)* and *(b)*, and (6)*(b)*, 43(2) and (4), 47(3), and 82(3)*(a)* of, and paragraphs 1(1)*(b)* and *(c)* and (4), 2(1), and 3(1) and (2) of Schedule 3 to, the Health and Safety at Work etc. Act 1974(a) ("the 1974 Act") and of all other powers enabling him in that behalf and for the purpose of giving effect without modifications to proposals submitted to him by the Health and Safety Commission under section 11(2)*(d)* of the 1974 Act after the carrying out by the said Commission of consultations in accordance with section 50(3) of that Act, hereby makes the following Regulations:—

ARRANGEMENT OF REGULATIONS

1. Citation and commencement.
2. Interpretation.
3. Classification and labelling of explosive articles and explosive substances and of combinations and unit loads thereof.
4. Cases to which these Regulations do not apply.
5. Fees for testing.
6. Labelling of an article, substance or combination in Class 1.
7. Labelling of an article, substance or combination not in Class 1.
8. Labelling of outer and inner packagings.
9. Labelling or arrangement of a unit load.
10. Labelling generally.
11. Classification and labelling under these Regulations shall satisfy classification and labelling provisions of the Explosives Act 1875(b).
12. Defence in proceedings for contravening these Regulations.
13. Enforcement.
14. Power to grant exemptions.
15. Revocations.

Schedule 1. The Divisions.
Schedule 2. The Compatibility Groups.
Schedule 3. Labels.

(a) 1974 c. 37; section 15 was amended by the Employment Protection Act 1975 (c. 71), Schedule 15, paragraph 6.
(b) 1875 c. 17.

Schedule 4. Explosive articles in respect of which outer packaging is to be labelled.

Schedule 5. Explosive substances in respect of which inner and outer packagings are to be labelled.

Citation and commencement

1. These Regulations may be cited as the Classification and Labelling of Explosives Regulations 1983 and shall come into operation on 1st November 1983.

Interpretation

2.—(1) In these Regulations, unless the context otherwise requires—

"Class 1" means Class 1 in respect of explosives or the classification of dangerous goods as set out in the Second Revised Edition of the Recommendations prepared by the United Nations Committee of Experts on the Transport of Dangerous Goods published in Chicago in 1982 on behalf of the United Nations by the International Regulations Publishing and Distributing Organization(**a**);

"classified" in relation to an article, substance, combination or unit load means assessed by the Health and Safety Executive or, in the case of a military explosive, by the Secretary of State and—

    (a) (i) assigned to Class 1,

        (ii) assigned to a Division and Compatibility Group,

        (iii) designated as an article, substance, combination or unit load, and

        (iv) in the case of an article or substance, allocated a United Nations Serial Number, or

    (b) excluded from Class 1 and designated as or as not presenting a significant hazard from explosion;

"combination" means a combination in the same packaging of articles or substances or of one or more of each of them;

"Compatibility Group" means one of the compatibility groups in Class 1 set out in column 1 of Schedule 2 and "Compatibility Group letter" means the letter assigned to a Compatibility Group by column 2 of that Schedule;

"Division" means one of the divisions, into which Class 1 is divided, set out in column 1 of Schedule 1 and "Division number" means the number assigned to a Division by column 2 of that Schedule;

"explosive article" means an article containing one or more explosive substances;

"explosive substance" means—

    (a) a solid or liquid substance, or

    (b) a mixture of solid or liquid substances or both,

which is capable by chemical reaction in itself of producing gas at such a

---

(**a**) ISBN–0–940394–04–9.

temperature and pressure and at such a speed as could cause damage to surroundings or which is designed to produce an effect by heat, light, sound, gas or smoke or a combination of these as a result of non-detonative self-sustaining exothermic chemical reactions;

"hazard classification code" means the Division number followed by the Compatibility Group letter of an article, substance, combination or unit load as assigned on classification;

"inner packaging" means the packaging immediately surrounding an article, substance or combination, except when it is the only packaging, but it does not include any envelope, case or contrivance forming part of an article;

"label" includes "mark" and related expressions shall be construed accordingly;

"military explosive" means any article, substance, combination or unit load to which these Regulations apply—

    (a) under the control of the Secretary of State, or otherwise held for the service of the Crown, for the purposes of the Ministry of Defence,

    (b) under the control of a headquarters or organisation designated for the purposes of the International Headquarters and Defence Organisations Act 1964(**a**) or of the service authorities of a visiting force within the meaning of any of the provisions of Part 1 of the Visiting Forces Act 1952(**b**), or otherwise held for the service of such a headquarters, organisation or visiting force, or

    (c) the conveyance of which is certified by the Secretary of State to be in connection with the execution of a contract with the Secretary of State or with a headquarters or organisation designated for the purposes of the International Headquarters and Defence Organisations Act 1964 or with the service authorities of a visiting force within the meaning of any of the provisions of Part 1 of the Visiting Forces Act 1952;

"name" means in relation to an explosive article or explosive substance its name—

    (a) as shown in "List of Authorised Explosives" or "List of Classifications of Explosives" both being lists issued by the Health and Safety Executive or in any of the various lists of classifications for military explosives issued by the Ministry of Defence, all the foregoing as revised or re-issued from time to time;

    (b) as shown in a licence issued in respect of its manufacture or importation by the Health and Safety Executive or the Secretary of State, or

    (c) as otherwise approved in writing by the Secretary of State;

"outer packaging" means the packaging immediately surrounding an article, substance or combination where it is the only packaging and in any other case the outermost packaging but does not include—

    (a) any envelope, case or contrivance forming part of an article, or

(**a**) 1964 c. 5.
(**b**) 1952 c. 67.

(b) any type of freight container, aircraft container, container with integral pallet, aircraft pallet or vehicle;

"supply" means (whether as principal or agent for another) supply in the course of, or for use at, work by way of—

(a) sale, offer for sale, lease, hire or hire purchase,

(b) commercial sample,

(c) transfer from a factory, warehouse or other place of work and its curtilage to another place of work, whether or not in the same ownership, or

(d) importation into the United Kingdom,

and related expressions shall be construed accordingly;

"unit load" means the unit formed when packages or unpackaged articles are assembled on or in a device which enables them to be mechanically handled as one unit, but which is not any type of freight container, aircraft container, container with integral pallet, aircraft pallet, or vehicle;

"United Nations Serial Number" means one of the four-digit numbers devised by the United Nations and allocated by the Health and Safety Executive or the Secretary of State to an explosive article or explosive substance as a means of identification.

(2) Unless the context otherwise requires, any reference in these Regulations to—

(a) a numbered Regulation or Schedule is a reference to the Regulation of, or Schedule to, these Regulations bearing that number;

(b) a numbered paragraph is a reference to the paragraph bearing that number in the Regulation or Schedule in which the reference appears.

Classification and labelling of explosive articles and explosive substances and of combinations and unit loads thereof

3.—(1) Subject to Regulation 4, these Regulations shall apply to—

(a) explosive articles or explosive substances, whether in packaging or not;

(b) combinations in the same packaging of explosive articles or explosive substances or of one or more of each of such articles and substances;

(c) unit loads of any of the following—

(i) explosive articles, whether in packaging or not,

(ii) packaged explosive substances,

(iii) combinations in the same packaging of explosive articles or explosive substances or of one or more of each of such articles and substances;

except that in relation to supply only, these Regulations shall apply to the items specified in this paragraph only in so far as they are supplied with a view to producing a practical effect by explosion or a pyrotechnic effect.

(2) An article, substance, combination or unit load to which these Regulations apply may not be conveyed, kept or supplied unless—

(a) it has been classified for the time being according to composition and in the form and packaging, if any, in which it is to be conveyed, kept or supplied; and

(b) it and any packaging comply with the labelling requirements, if any, imposed in respect of them by these Regulations.

(3) Subject to Regulation 11, nothing in paragraph (2) shall be construed as affecting any other requirement of law relating to the conveyance, keeping or supply of any article, substance, combination or unit load to which these Regulations apply.

Cases to which these Regulations do not apply

4.—(1) These Regulations shall not apply to an article, substance, combination or unit load—

(a) which complies with the classification and labelling requirements imposed in respect of it by or under the Explosives Act 1875, but this exception shall not apply after 1st November 1988, other than to the keeping of articles and substances manufactured, and combinations and unit loads formed, before 1st November 1983; or

(b) which is conveyed, kept or supplied solely in connection with an application for its classification; or

(c) which has not been classified and—

  (i) is the subject of, or is used in, a research project, and

  (ii) is not kept at, or conveyed through, any place to which persons not employed in, or otherwise concerned with, the project have access; or

(d) which is in transit on any aircraft, vessel or hovercraft, if—

  (i) it is not to be unloaded in the United Kingdom, and

  (ii) notification of its nature is given, before it enters the United Kingdom, to the airport manager, harbour master or person in charge of the hoverport, at the place at which it is to land or berth, except that such notification need not be given in the case of articles lawfully carried on board for the purpose of safety or in relation to anything carried on board a warship; or

(e) which is being transhipped from one aircraft, vessel or hovercraft to another for the purpose of being conveyed to a place outside the United Kingdom provided that there is compliance with the appropriate classification and labelling provisions of the International Maritime Dangerous Goods Code or the Technical Instructions for the Safe Transport of Dangerous Goods by Air, both as revised or re-issued from time to time and published respectively by the International Maritime Organisation and the Council of the International Civil Aviation Organisation; or

(f) which is being lawfully carried on the person, or in the baggage, of a passenger or member of the crew on an aircraft, vessel or hovercraft or in transit between one aircraft, vessel or hovercraft and another; or

(g) which is undergoing explosive ordnance disposal, other than dumping at sea, under the directions of a member of Her Majesty's forces or a constable.

(2) These Regulations shall not apply to an article or substance—

(a) which is in the process of manufacture, including any examination or testing carried out at the place of manufacture; or

(b) which has been removed from its packaging for the purpose of immediate use.

(3) These Regulations shall not apply to fireworks, small arms ammunition or combinations in the same packaging of fireworks or small arms ammunition that—

(a) are kept or supplied by the retailer thereof; or

(b) have been obtained from such a person.

(4) These Regulations shall not apply to any explosive nuclear device or any component thereof.

Fees for testing

5. If any testing is carried out by or on behalf of the Health and Safety Executive with the agreement of the applicant in connection with his application for the classification of an article, substance, combination or unit load, the applicant shall pay, prior to the issue of the decision, a fee of £25 for each man-hour of work certified as having been done in respect of that testing, excluding any typing, messenger or other ancillary work (for which no fee shall be payable).

Labelling of an article, substance or combination in Class 1

6.—(1) A packaged article or substance or a combination to which these Regulations apply, assigned on classification to Class 1, Division 1.1, 1.2 or 1.3, shall bear two labels on its outer packaging, one in accordance with paragraphs 1, 2, 10 and 11, the other in accordance with paragraph 12, of Schedule 3.

(2) An unpackaged article to which these Regulations apply, assigned on classification to Class 1, Division 1.1, 1.2 or 1.3, shall bear two labels, one in accordance with paragraphs 3, 10 and 11, the other in accordance with paragraph 13, of Schedule 3.

(3) A packaged article or substance or a combination to which these Regulations apply, assigned on classification to Class 1, Division 1.4 or 1.5, shall bear two labels on its outer packaging, one in accordance with paragraphs 4 to 7 and 10 and 11, the other in accordance with paragraph 12, of Schedule 3.

(4) An unpackaged article, other than a firework, to which these Regulations apply, assigned on classification to Class 1, Division 1.4, shall bear two labels, one in accordance with paragraphs 8, 10 and 11, the other in accordance with paragraph 13, of Schedule 3.

Labelling of an article, substance or combination not in Class 1

7. An article, whether in packaging or not, a packaged substance or a combination to which these Regulations apply, which on classification is both excluded from Class 1 and designated as presenting a significant hazard from explosion, shall be labelled in accordance with paragraphs 9 to 11 of Schedule 3 when it is conveyed or kept.

Labelling of outer and inner packagings

8.—(1) In addition to any labelling required by Regulation 6, where an outer packaging contains an explosive article listed in Schedule 4 or an explosive substance listed in Schedule 5, it shall be labelled in accordance with paragraph 14 of Schedule 3.

(2) Where an inner packaging contains an explosive substance listed in Schedule 5, it shall be labelled in accordance with paragraph 15 of Schedule 3.

Labelling or arrangement of a unit load

9.—(1) A unit load to which these Regulations apply shall be labelled or arranged as follows—

(a) if the same hazard classification code applies to all articles, substances or combinations to which these Regulations apply in the unit load, they shall be arranged so that the label on at least one such article or outer packaging is visible on each vertical face of the load, except that, in the case of a unit load assembled on or in a device with a base or straps, it shall be sufficient if such labels are placed on the base or the straps so that they are as visible as if they were on the load itself;

(b) in any other case, the labels specified in paragraph (2) shall be placed on the base or straps of the device on or in which the unit load is assembled so that they are as visible as if they were on each vertical face of the load, or, if there is no base or straps or it is impracticable to fix the labels there, they may be placed on each vertical face of the load.

(2) The labels referred to in paragraph (1)(b) shall be those appropriate under Regulations 6(1) or (3) or 7, as the case may be, for a combination which has the same hazard classification code as the unit load as a whole except that the label described in paragraph 12 of Schedule 3 need not be shown.

Labelling generally

10.—(1) The requirements of Regulations 6, 7, 8 and 9 and Schedule 3 shall be implemented by the use of durable labelling either—

(a) directly onto the outside of the packaging, article, base or strap, as the case may be, or

(b) on a piece of paper or other suitable material securely fixed to the outside of the packaging, article, base or strap, as the case may be, with one entire side of the label in contact with the relevant surface.

(2) Where, in order to comply with paragraph (1), the size of the packaging, article, base or strap, as the case may be, would necessitate a reduction in the

size of the label, as an alternative, a full sized label may be affixed in some other safe and suitable manner.

Classification and labelling under these Regulations shall satisfy classification and labelling provisions of the Explosives Act 1875

11. Where an article, substance, combination or unit load, assigned on classification to Class 1, complies with the labelling requirements, if any, imposed in respect of it by these Regulations, that classification and labelling shall be deemed to satisfy any corresponding provisions of the Explosives Act 1875 and of any instrument made under it; and that Act and any such instrument shall be modified accordingly.

Defence in proceedings for contravening these Regulations

12. In any proceedings for an alleged contravention of, or breach of duty imposed by, these Regulations it shall be a defence for any person to prove that he took all reasonable precautions and exercised all due diligence to avoid the commission of such an offence or breach.

Enforcement

13. Notwithstanding the provisions of the Health and Safety (Enforcing Authority) Regulations 1977(**a**), the enforcing authority for the purposes of these Regulations shall in all cases be the Health and Safety Executive.

Power to grant exemptions

14.—(1) Subject to paragraph (2), the Health and Safety Executive may, by a certificate in writing, exempt from all or any requirements or prohibitions imposed by these Regulations any particular, or class of, article, substance, combination or unit load and any such exemption may be granted subject to conditions and to a limit of time and may be revoked by a certificate in writing at any time.

(2) The Executive shall not grant any such exemption unless, having regard to the circumstances of the case, and in particular to—

    (a) the conditions, if any, which it proposes to attach to the exemption, and

    (b) any other requirements imposed by or under any enactment which apply to the case,

it is satisfied that neither the health and safety of persons who are likely to be affected by the exemption nor the security of the explosives will be prejudiced.

(3) The Secretary of State may, by a certificate in writing, exempt from all or any requirements or prohibitions imposed by these Regulations any particular or class of military explosive and any such exemption may be granted subject to conditions and to a limit of time and may be revoked by a certificate in writing at any time.

(**a**) S.I. 1977/746, amended by S.I. 1980/1744.

Revocations

15. The following Regulations are hereby revoked—

(a) Regulation 6(1)*(a)* and *(c)*, (2) and (4) of the Conveyance by Road of Military Explosives Regulations 1977(**a**);

(b) Regulation 6(1)*(a)* and *(c)*, (2) and (4) of the Conveyance by Rail of Military Explosives Regulations 1977(**b**);

(c) Regulation 7(1)*(a)* and *(c)*, (2) and (3) of the Conveyance in Harbours of Military Explosives Regulations 1977(**c**).

Signed by order of the Secretary of State.

John Selwyn Gummer,
Joint Parliamentary Under Secretary of State,
Department of Employment.

21st July 1983.

(**a**) S.I. 1977/888.
(**b**) S.I. 1977/889.
(**c**) S.I. 1977/890.

Regulation 2(1) SCHEDULE 1

THE DIVISIONS

1 Division	2 Division number
Substances and articles which have a mass explosion hazard.	1.1
Substances and articles which have a projection hazard but not a mass explosion hazard.	1.2
Substances and articles which have a fire hazard and either a minor blast hazard or a minor projection hazard or both, but not a mass explosion hazard.	1.3
Substances and articles which present no significant hazard.	1.4
Very insensitive substances which have a mass explosion hazard.	1.5

SCHEDULE 2   Regulation 2(1)

THE COMPATIBILITY GROUPS

1 Compatibility Group	2 Compatibility Group letter
Primary explosive substance.	A
Article containing a primary explosive substance and not containing two or more independent safety features.	B
Propellant explosive substance or other deflagrating explosive substance or article containing such explosive substance.	C
Secondary detonating explosive substance or black powder or article containing a secondary detonating explosive substance, in each case without means of initiation and without a propelling charge, or article containing a primary explosive substance and containing two or more independent safety features.	D
Article containing a secondary detonating explosive substance, without means of initiation and with a propelling charge (other than a charge containing a flammable or hypergolic liquid).	E
Article containing a secondary detonating explosive substance, with means of initiation, and either with a propelling charge (other than a charge containing a flammable or hypergolic liquid) or without a propelling charge.	F
A substance which is an explosive substance because it is designed to produce an effect by heat, light, sound, gas or smoke or a combination of these as a result of non-detonative self-sustaining exothermic chemical reactions or an article containing such a substance or an article containing both a substance which is explosive because it is capable by chemical reaction in itself of producing gas at such a temperature and pressure and at such a speed as could cause damage to surroundings and an illuminating, incendiary, lachrymatory or smoke-producing substance (other than a water-activated article or one containing white phosphorus, phosphide or a flammable liquid or gel).	G
Article containing both an explosive substance and white phosphorus.	H
Article containing both an explosive substance and a flammable liquid or gel.	J
Article containing both an explosive substance and a toxic chemical agent.	K
Explosive substance or explosive article presenting a special risk needing isolation of each type.	L
Substance or article so packed or designed that any hazardous effects arising from accidental functioning are confined within the package unless the package has been degraded by fire, in which case all blast or projection effects are limited to the extent that they do not significantly hinder or prohibit fire fighting or other emergency response efforts in the immediate vicinity of the package.	S

Regulations 6, 7, 8 and 10　　SCHEDULE 3

LABELS

A packaged article or substance or a combination in Class 1, Division 1.1, 1.2 or 1.3

1. One of the labels required by Regulation 6(1) shall—

    (a) be a square set with its sides at an angle of 45° to the vertical;

    (b) be in the form of the following diagram (the hazard classification code "1.2 E" is only an example); and

    (c) comply with the measurements in the diagram except that—

    (i) larger measurements may be used in which case the measurements shall be increased proportionally, or

    (ii) where, in order to comply with Regulation 10(1), a smaller label is necessary, the dimensions may be decreased proportionally whilst remaining as large as is reasonably practicable for the purpose of such compliance.

2.—(1) The above label shall have a pictograph of a bomb blast filling most of its upper half.

(2) In the lower half of the label, the word "EXPLOSIVE" shall be written in capital letters which shall each be smaller than the Compatibility Group letter in the hazard classification code required by sub-paragraph (3) below.

(3) Below the word "EXPLOSIVE", the hazard classification code appropriate for the contents when in the packaging on which the label is put shall be written.

(4) Below the hazard classification code, the Class number "1" shall be written in the bottom corner of the label.

(5) The label shall have a line at least 1mm wide approximately 5mm inside the edge and running parallel to it.

An unpackaged article in Class 1, Division 1.1, 1.2 or 1.3

3. One of the labels required by Regulation 6(2) shall be as described in paragraphs 1 and 2 except that the hazard classification code shall be that appropriate for the article when not packaged.

A packaged article or substance or a combination in Class 1, Division 1.4 or 1.5

4. Subject to the alternatives in paragraphs 6 and 7 which may be used instead where appropriate, one of the labels required by Regulation 6(3) shall—

    (a) be a square set with its sides at an angle of 45° to the vertical;

    (b) be in the form of the following diagram (the Division number "1.4" and the Compatibility Group letter "G" are only examples); and

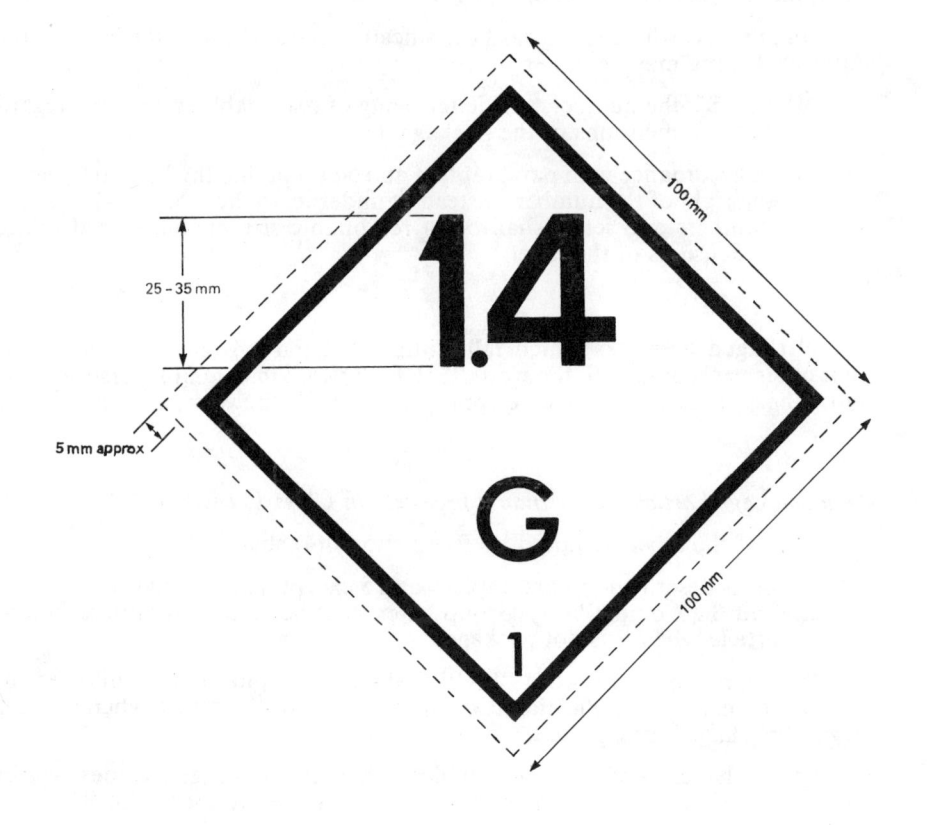

(c) comply with the measurements in the diagram except that—

    (i) larger measurements may be used in which case the measurements shall be increased proportionally, or

    (ii) where, in order to comply with Regulation 10(1), a smaller label is necessary, the dimensions may be decreased proportionally whilst remaining as large as is reasonably practicable for the purpose of such compliance.

5.—(1) The Division number appropriate for the contents when in the packaging on which the label is put shall be written in the upper half of the label.

(2) The Compatibility Group letter appropriate for the contents when in the packaging on which the label is put shall be written in the lower half of the label.

(3) Below the Compatibility Group letter, the Class number "1" shall be written in the bottom corner of the label.

(4) The label shall have a line at least 1mm wide approximately 5mm inside the edge and running parallel to it.

Alternatives to the provisions of paragraphs 4 and 5

6. In any case where the hazard classification code is "1.4 S" the label on the outer packaging may be either—

    (a) "1.4 S", the numbers and letter being of reasonable size having regard to the dimensions of the package; or

    (b) in accordance with paragraphs 4 and 5 except that the letter may be on the right of the numbers instead of underneath them, in which case the numbers and letter shall be of reasonable size having regard to the dimensions of the label.

7. Packaged fireworks which fall within Division 1.4 may be labelled on their outer packaging with the word "FIREWORK" in capital letters followed by the hazard classification code appropriate for the fireworks as so packaged.

An unpackaged article, other than a firework, in Class 1, Division 1.4

8. One of the labels required by Regulation 6(4) shall—

    (a) be as described in paragraphs 4 and 5 except that the Division number and the Compatibility Group letter shall be those appropriate for the article when it is not packaged; or

    (b) clearly show the word "EXPLOSIVE" in capital letters followed by the hazard classification code appropriate for the article when it is not packaged; or

    (c) in the case of an article which when not packaged comes within Division 1.4 and Compatibility Group S, clearly show "1.4 S".

An article, substance or combination not in Class 1

9. The label required by Regulation 7 shall—

   (a) be a square set with its sides at an angle of 45° to the vertical;

   (b) be in the form of the following diagram; and

   (c) comply with the measurements in the diagram except that—

      (i) larger measurements may be used in which case the measurements shall be increased proportionally, or

      (ii) where, in order to comply with Regulation 10(1), a smaller label is necessary, the dimensions may be decreased proportionally whilst remaining as large as is reasonably practicable for the purpose of such compliance.

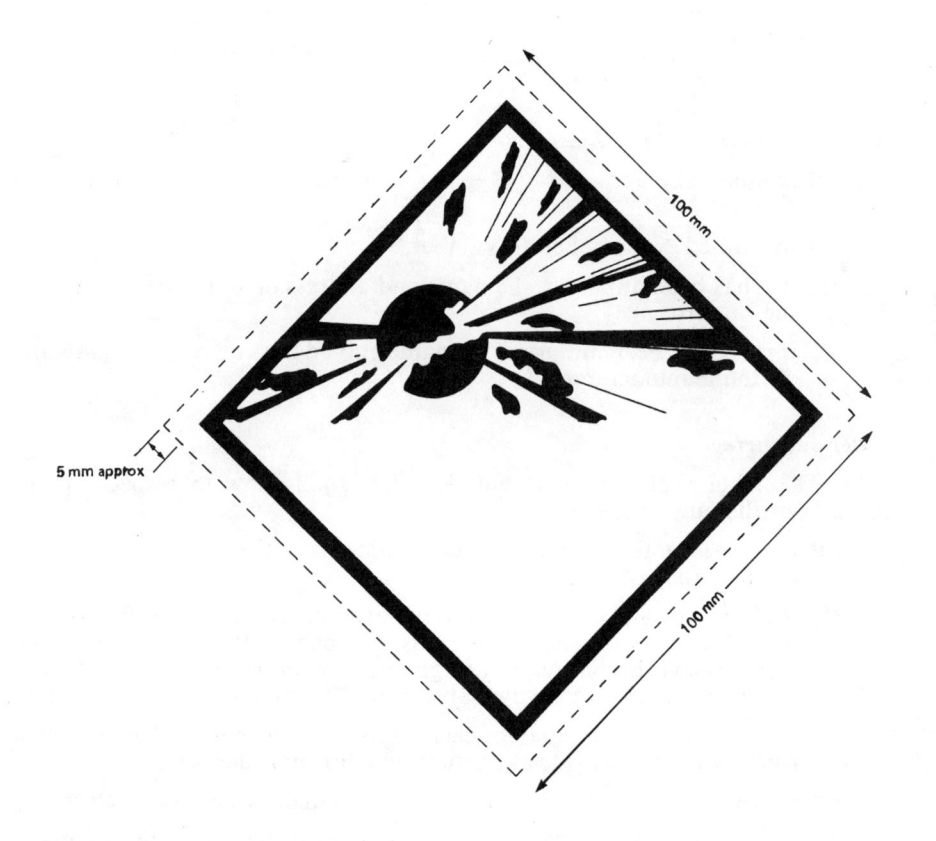

Colour of labels described in paragraphs 1 to 9

10. The background colour of the labels shall be orange.

11. Pictographs, numbers, letters and lines shall be in black.

A packaged article or substance or a combination in Class 1

12. The other label required by Regulation 6(1) and (3) shall show in respect of each explosive article or explosive substance, whether or not in a combination—

  (a) its United Nations Serial Number;

  (b) its name;

  (c) if it has been imported, the name and address of, or the monogram of, the importer;

  (d) if it has not been imported, the name and address of, or the monogram of, the manufacturer.

An unpackaged article in Class 1

13. The other label required by Regulation 6(2) and (4) shall show in respect of the article—

  (a) its United Nations Serial Number;

  (b) if it has been imported, the name and address of, or the monogram of, the importer;

  (c) if it has not been imported, the name and address of, or the monogram of, the manufacturer.

Outer packaging

14. The label required by Regulation 8(1) shall show in respect of the contents of the outer packaging—

  (a) the total number of any explosive articles and the total nominal mass of any explosive substances;

  (b) the month and year of manufacture or leaving the factory of manufacture, with an indication as to which of the two dates is being given, such information may be given in a manufacturer's code, details of which shall be made available to the Health and Safety Executive;

  (c) a description which enables each explosive article to be distinguished from every other explosive article which is not identical;

  (d) in the case of articles in cord form, the length of cord on each spool;

  (e) in the case of explosive substances in cartridge form, the number, nominal diameter and either the nominal mass or nominal length of each kind of cartridge.

Inner packaging

15. The label required by Regulation 8(2) shall show in respect of the contents of the inner packaging—

    (a) the name of each explosive substance;

    (b) the total nominal mass of explosive substances or, as an alternative, in the case of explosive substances in cartridge form, their nominal length;

    (c) in the case of explosive substances in cartridge form, their nominal diameter;

    (d) the month and year of manufacture or leaving the factory of manufacture, with an indication as to which of the two dates is being given, such information may be given in a manufacturer's code, details of which shall be made available to the Health and Safety Executive.

Regulation 8(1) SCHEDULE 4

EXPLOSIVE ARTICLES IN RESPECT OF WHICH OUTER PACKAGING IS TO BE LABELLED

In this Schedule "N.O.S." means "not otherwise specified"

1 United Nations Serial Number	2 Article	3 Hazard Classification Code
0354	ARTICLES, EXPLOSIVE, N.O.S.	1.1 L
0355	ARTICLES, EXPLOSIVE, N.O.S.	1.2 L
0356	ARTICLES, EXPLOSIVE, N.O.S.	1.3 L
0350	ARTICLES, EXPLOSIVE, N.O.S.	1.4 B
0351	ARTICLES, EXPLOSIVE, N.O.S.	1.4 C
0352	ARTICLES, EXPLOSIVE, N.O.S.	1.4 D
0353	ARTICLES, EXPLOSIVE, N.O.S.	1.4 G
0349	ARTICLES, EXPLOSIVE, N.O.S.	1.4 S
0225	BOOSTERS WITH DETONATOR	1.1 B
0268	BOOSTERS WITH DETONATOR	1.2 B
0042	BOOSTERS without detonator	1.1 D
0283	BOOSTERS without detonator	1.2 D
0048	CHARGES, DEMOLITION	1.1 D
0442	CHARGES, EXPLOSIVE, COMMERCIAL without detonator	1.1 D
0443	CHARGES, EXPLOSIVE, COMMERCIAL without detonator	1.2 D
0444	CHARGES, EXPLOSIVE, COMMERCIAL without detonator	1.4 D
0445	CHARGES, EXPLOSIVE, COMMERCIAL without detonator	1.4 S
0059	CHARGES, SHAPED, COMMERCIAL without detonator	1.1 D
0439	CHARGES, SHAPED, COMMERCIAL without detonator	1.2 D
0440	CHARGES, SHAPED, COMMERCIAL without detonator	1.4 D
0441	CHARGES, SHAPED, COMMERCIAL without detonator	1.4 S

1 United Nations Serial Number	2 Article	3 Hazard Classification Code
0288	CHARGES, SHAPED, FLEXIBLE, LINEAR metal clad	1.1 D
0237	CHARGES, SHAPED, FLEXIBLE, LINEAR metal clad	1.4 D
0060	CHARGES, SUPPLEMENTARY, EXPLOSIVE	1.1 D
0382	COMPONENTS, EXPLOSIVE TRAIN, N.O.S.	1.2 B
0383	COMPONENTS, EXPLOSIVE TRAIN, N.O.S.	1.4 B
0384	COMPONENTS, EXPLOSIVE TRAIN, N.O.S.	1.4 S
0248	CONTRIVANCES, WATER-ACTIVATED with burster, expelling charge or propelling charge	1.2 L
0249	CONTRIVANCES, WATER-ACTIVATED with burster, expelling charge or propelling charge	1.3 L
0065	CORD, DETONATING, flexible	1.1 D
0289	CORD, DETONATING, flexible	1.4 D
0290	CORD (FUSE), DETONATING, metal clad	1.1 D
0102	CORD (FUSE), DETONATING, metal clad	1.2 D
0104	CORD (FUSE), DETONATING, MILD EFFECT, metal clad	1.4 D
0066	CORD, IGNITER	1.4 G
0030	DETONATORS, ELECTRIC for blasting	1.1 B
0255	DETONATORS, ELECTRIC for blasting	1.4 B
0029	DETONATORS, NON-ELECTRIC for blasting	1.1 B
0267	DETONATORS, NON-ELECTRIC for blasting	1.4 B
0360	DETONATOR ASSEMBLIES, NON-ELECTRIC for blasting	1.1 B

1 United Nations Serial Number	2 Article	3 Hazard Classification Code
0361	DETONATOR ASSEMBLIES, NON-ELECTRIC for blasting	1.4 B
0099	FRACTURING DEVICES, EXPLOSIVE, for oil wells, without detonator	1.1 D
0103	FUSE, IGNITER, tubular, metal clad	1.4 G
0101	FUSE, INSTANTANEOUS, NON-DETONATING	1.3 G
0105	FUSE, SAFETY	1.4 S
0106	FUZES, DETONATING	1.1 B
0107	FUZES, DETONATING	1.2 B
0257	FUZES, DETONATING	1.4 B
0367	FUZES, DETONATING	1.4 S
0408	FUZES, DETONATING with protective features	1.1 D
0409	FUZES, DETONATING with protective features	1.2 D
0410	FUZES, DETONATING with protective features	1.4 D
0121	IGNITERS	1.1 G
0314	IGNITERS	1.2 G
0315	IGNITERS	1.3 G
0325	IGNITERS	1.4 G
0124	JET PERFORATING GUNS, CHARGED, oil well, without detonator	1.1 D
0173	RELEASE DEVICES, EXPLOSIVE	1.4 S
0374	SOUNDING DEVICES, EXPLOSIVE	1.1 E
0296	SOUNDING DEVICES, EXPLOSIVE	1.1 F
0375	SOUNDING DEVICES, EXPLOSIVE	1.2 E
0204	SOUNDING DEVICES, EXPLOSIVE	1.2 F

SCHEDULE 5   Regulation 8(1) and (2)

EXPLOSIVE SUBSTANCES IN RESPECT OF WHICH INNER AND OUTER PACKAGINGS
ARE TO BE LABELLED

In this Schedule "N.O.S." means "not otherwise specified"

1 United Nations Serial Number	2 Substance	3 Hazard Classification Code
0224	BARIUM AZIDE, dry or wetted with less than 50 per cent water, by weight	1.1 A
0027	BLACK POWDER (GUNPOWDER) granular or as a meal	1.1 D
0028	BLACK POWDER (GUNPOWDER) COMPRESSED, or BLACK POWDER (GUNPOWDER) IN PELLETS	1.1 D
0226	CYCLOTETRAMETHYLENETETRANI-TRAMINE (HMX; OCTOGEN), WETTED with not less than 15 per cent water, by weight, or CYCLOTETRAMETHYLENE-TETRANITRAMINE (HMX; OCTOGEN), DESENSITIZED with not less than 10 per cent phlegmatiser, by weight	1.1 D
0391	CYCLOTRIMETHYLENETRINITRA-MINE(CYCLONITE; HEXOGEN; RDX) AND CYCLOTETRAMETHYLENETETRA-NITRAMINE (HMX; OCTOGEN) MIXTURES, WETTED with not less than 15 per cent water by weight, or CYCLOTRI-METHYLENETRINITRAMINE (CYCLO-NITE; HEXOGEN; RDX) AND CYCLO-TETRAMETHYLENETETRANITRA-MINE (HMX; OCTOGEN) MIXTURES, DESENSITIZED with not less than 10 per cent phlegmatiser, by weight	1.1 D
0072	CYCLOTRIMETHYLENETRINITRA-MINE (CYCLONITE; HEXOGEN; RDX), WETTED with not less than 15 per cent water, by weight, or CYCLOTRI-METHYLENETRINITRAMINE (CYCLO-NITE; HEXOGEN; RDX), DESENSITIZED with not less than 10 per cent phlegmatiser, by weight	1.1 D
0074	DIAZODINITROPHENOL, WETTED with not less than 40 per cent water, by weight (or mixture of alcohol and water) ..	1.1 A
0081	EXPLOSIVE, BLASTING, TYPE A	1.1 D
0082	EXPLOSIVE, BLASTING, TYPE B	1.1 D
0331	EXPLOSIVE, BLASTING, TYPE B	1.5 D

1 United Nations Serial Number	2 Substance	3 Hazard Classification Code
0083	EXPLOSIVE, BLASTING, TYPE C	1.1 D
0084	EXPLOSIVE, BLASTING, TYPE D	1.1 D
0241	EXPLOSIVE, BLASTING, TYPE E	1.1 D
0332	EXPLOSIVE, BLASTING, TYPE E	1.5 D
0113	GUANYL NITROSAMINOGUANYLI- DENE HYDRAZINE, WETTED with not less than 30 per cent water, by weight	1.1 A
0114	GUANYL NITROSAMINOGUANYL- TETRAZENE (TETRAZENE), WETTED with not less than 30 per cent water, by weight (or mixture of alcohol and water)	1.1 A
0079	HEXANITRODIPHENYLAMINE (DIPICRYLAMINE; HEXYL)	1.1 D
0392	HEXANITROSTILBENE	1.1 D
0393	HEXATONAL, CAST	1.1 D
0118	HEXOLITE, dry or wetted with less than 15 per cent water, by weight	1.1 D
0129	LEAD AZIDE, WETTED with not less than 20 per cent water, by weight (or mixture of alcohol and water)	1.1 A
0130	LEAD STYPHNATE (LEAD TRI- NITRORESORCINATE), WETTED with not less than 20 per cent water, by weight (or mixture of alcohol and water)	1.1 A
0133	MANNITOL HEXANITRATE (NITROMANNITE), WETTED with not less than 40 per cent water, by weight (or mixture of alcohol and water)	1.1 D
0135	MERCURY FULMINATE, WETTED with not less than 20 per cent water, by weight (or mixture of alcohol and water)	1.1 A
0340	NITROCELLULOSE, dry or wetted with less than 25 per cent water (or alcohol), by weight	1.1 D

1 United Nations Serial Number	2 Substance	3 Hazard Classification Code
0341	NITROCELLULOSE, unmodified or plasticized with less than 18 per cent plasticizing substance, by weight	1.1 D
0343	NITROCELLULOSE, PLASTICIZED with not less than 18 per cent plasticizing substance, by weight	1.3 C
0342	NITROCELLULOSE, WETTED with not less than 25 per cent alcohol, by weight	1.3 C
0143	NITROGLYCERIN, DESENSITIZED with not less than 40 per cent non-volatile water-insoluble phlegmatiser, by weight	1.1 D
0144	NITROGLYCERIN, SPIRIT OF, with more than 1 per cent but not more than 10 per cent nitroglycerin in solution in alcohol	1.1 D
0282	NITROGUANIDINE, (PICRITE), dry or wetted with less than 20 per cent water, by weight	1.1 D
0146	NITROSTARCH, dry or wetted with less than 20 per cent water, by weight	1.1 D
0147	NITRO UREA	1.1 D
0266	OCTOLITE, (OCTOL), dry or wetted with less than 15 per cent water, by weight	1.1 D
0411	PENTAERYTHRITE TETRANITRATE (PETN) with not less than 7 per cent wax, by weight	1.1 D
0150	PENTAERYTHRITE TETRANITRATE (PENTAERYTHRITOL TETRA-NITRATE; PETN), WETTED with not less than 25 per cent water, by weight, or PENTAERYTHRITE TETRANITRATE (PENTAERY-THRITOL TETRANITRATE; PETN), DESENSITIZED with not less than 15 per cent phlegmatiser, by weight	1.1 D
0151	PENTOLITE, dry or wetted with less than 15 per cent water, by weight	1.1 D

1 United Nations Serial Number	2. Substance	3 Hazard Classification Code
0433	POWDER CAKE, WETTED with not less than 17 per cent alcohol, by weight	1.1 C
0159	POWDER CAKE (POWDER PASTE), WETTED with not less than 35 per cent water, by weight	1.3 C
0160	POWDER, SMOKELESS	1.1 C
0161	POWDER, SMOKELESS	1.3 C
0190	SAMPLES, EXPLOSIVE, other than initiating explosive	As appropriate
0357	SUBSTANCES, EXPLOSIVE, N.O.S.	1.1 L
0358	SUBSTANCES, EXPLOSIVE, N.O.S.	1.2 L
0359	SUBSTANCES, EXPLOSIVE, N.O.S.	1.3 L
0208	TRINITROPHENYLMETHYLNITRA-MINE (TETRYL)	1.1 D
0209	TRINITROTOLUENE (TNT), dry or wetted with less than 30 per cent water, by weight	1.1 D
0388	TRINITROTOLUENE (TNT) AND TRINITROBENZENE MIXTURES or TRINITROTOLUENE (TNT) AND HEXANITROSTILBENE MIXTURES	1.1 D
0389	TRINITROTOLUENE (TNT) MIXTURES CONTAINING TRINITROBENZENE AND HEXANITROSTILBENE	1.1 D
0390	TRITONAL	1.1 D
0220	UREA NITRATE, dry or wetted with less than 20 per cent water, by weight	1.1 D

EXPLANATORY NOTE
(This Note is not part of the Regulations.)

These Regulations provide for the classification of explosive articles, explosive substances and combinations and unit loads thereof by the Health and Safety Executive or, in the case of military explosives, by the Secretary of State for Defence, according to the type of explosive hazard which they present and their compatibility with other explosives.

Explosives which are assigned to Class 1 or designated as presenting a significant hazard from explosion must comply, whenever they are conveyed or kept and in certain circumstances supplied, with the requirements as to labelling set out in the Regulations.

Copies of the Second Revised Edition of the Recommendations prepared by the United Nations Committee of Experts on the Transport of Dangerous Goods (mentioned in the definition of "Class 1" in Regulation 2(1)) and the Technical Instructions for the Safe Transport of Dangerous Goods by Air (mentioned in Regulation 4(1)*(e)*) can be obtained from IAL Merchandising Service, Aeradio House, Hayes Road, Southall, Middlesex UB2 5NJ.

The lists mentioned in the definition of "name" in Regulation 2(1) can be obtained as follows:–

(a) "List of Authorised Explosives" is published by and obtainable from Her Majesty's Stationery Office;

(b) copies of "List of Classifications of Explosives" can be obtained from Her Majesty's Explosives Inspectorate, Health and Safety Executive, Magdalen House, Stanley Precinct, Bootle, Merseyside, L20 3LZ;

(c) copies of the Ministry of Defence lists of classifications for military explosives can be obtained from the Ministry of Defence Explosives Storage and Transport Committee, Empress State Building, Lillie Road, London SW6 1TR.

Copies of The International Maritime Dangerous Goods Code mentioned in Regulation 4(1)(e) can be obtained from the International Maritime Organisation, Publications Section, 4 Albert Embankment, London SE1 7SR.

Classifications given by the Health and Safety Executive are shown in "List of Authorised Explosives" and "List of Classifications of Explosives." Classifications given by the Secretary of State for Defence are shown in the Ministry of Defence lists of classifications for military explosives. If there is doubt whether an article, substance, combination or unit load has been classified since the date of the most recent lists, enquiries can be made of Her Majesty's Explosives Inspectorate and the Ministry of Defence Explosives Storage and Transport Committee, as appropriate, at the addresses given above.

STATUTORY INSTRUMENTS

1983 No. 1142

LEGAL AID AND ADVICE, ENGLAND AND WALES

The Legal Advice and Assistance (Amendment) (No. 3) Regulations 1983

Made - - - - -	*27th July* 1983
Laid before Parliament	*29th July* 1983
Coming into Operation	*30th September* 1983

The Lord Chancellor, in exercise of the powers conferred on him by sections 2A and 20 of the Legal Aid Act 1974(a), hereby makes the following Regulations:

1. These Regulations may be cited as the Legal Advice and Assistance (Amendment) (No. 3) Regulations 1983 and shall come into operation on 30th September 1983.

2. In these Regulations a regulation referred to by number means a regulation so numbered in the Legal Advice and Assistance Regulations (No. 2) 1980(b).

3. For paragraph (3) of regulation 17 there shall be substituted the following paragraph—

"(3) An application for approval shall not be granted unless—

(*a*) it is made in respect of proceedings specified in Schedule 4 and it is shown that there are reasonable grounds for taking, defending or being a party to the proceedings to which the application relates, or

(*b*) it is made in respect of proceedings before a Mental Health Review Tribunal under the Mental Health Act 1983(c) by a solicitor acting on behalf of the person whose application to the Tribunal or whose case is or is to be the subject of those proceedings, or

---

(a) 1974 c. 4, as amended by the Legal Aid Act 1979 (c. 26).
(b) S.I. 1980/1898, as amended by S.I. 1982/1592 and 1983/470.
(c) 1983 c. 20.

(c) it is made in respect of proceedings in respect of a child under section 1, 2(12), 15(1), 16(8), 21(2) or 21(4) of the Children and Young Persons Act 1969(a) by a solicitor acting on behalf of the parent or guardian of the child who is the subject of the proceedings and it appears to the general committee both that there is or may be a conflict on any matter relevant to the proceedings between the interests of the child and those of his parent or guardian, and that it is desirable to grant it in the interests of justice,

provided that an application made in respect of proceedings under paragraph (a) or (b) above may be refused if it appears unreasonable that approval should be granted in the particular circumstances of the case.".

4. In regulation 20, for the words "paragraph (3A)" there shall be substituted the words "paragraph (3)(c)".

Hailsham of St. Marylebone, C.

Dated 27th July 1983

EXPLANATORY NOTE

(This Note is not part of the Regulations.)

These Regulations consolidate, with minor drafting amendments, earlier amendments to regulation 17(3) of the Legal Advice and Assistance Regulations (No. 2) 1980 which extended assistance by way of representation under section 2A of the Legal Aid Act 1974 to applicants before Mental Health Review Tribunals and to the parents or guardians of children who are the subject of care proceedings under the Children and Young Persons Act 1969. Assistance by way of representation is also now extended to all persons whose cases are the subject of proceedings before Mental Health Review Tribunals.

(a) 1969 c. 54.

STATUTORY INSTRUMENTS

1983 No. 1147

ROAD TRAFFIC

The Motor Vehicles (Tests) (Amendment) Regulations 1983

Made - - - -		*25th July* 1983
Laid before Parliament		10*th* August 1983
Coming into Operation		1*st September* 1983

The Secretary of State for Transport, in exercise of the powers conferred by section 43(2) and (6) of the Road Traffic Act 1972(**a**) and now vested in him(**b**), and of all other enabling powers, and after consultation with representative organisations in accordance with the provisions of section 199(2) of that Act, hereby makes the following Regulations:—

1. These Regulations shall come into operation on 1st September 1983, and may be cited as the Motor Vehicles (Tests) (Amendment) Regulations 1983.

2. The Motor Vehicles (Tests) Regulations 1981(**c**) are hereby amended so that in the Regulations specified in column 1 of the Table below for the words specified in column 2 of that Table there are substituted the words specified in column 3 of that Table.

TABLE

1	2	3
Regulation	Existing words	Substituted words
20(1)(*a*)	£4.50	£5.40
20(1)(*c*)	£7.50	£9
25(2)	£18	£20

Tom King,
Secretary of State for Transport.

25th July 1983.

(**a**) 1972 c. 20.   (**b**) S.I. 1979/571 and 1981/238.
(**c**) S.I. 1981/1694; the relevant amending Instrument is S.I. 1982/783.

EXPLANATORY NOTE

(This Note is not part of the Regulations.)

These Regulations amend the Motor Vehicles (Tests) Regulations 1981 so that:—

   (i) the fee for the examination of a motor bicycle (without a sidecar) is increased from £4.50 to £5.40;

  (ii) the fee for examination of any other vehicle (not being a vehicle in Class VI) is increased from £7.50 to £9.00; and

 (iii) the fee for the supply of 100 forms of test certificate is increased from £18 to £20.

STATUTORY INSTRUMENTS

1983 No. 1148 (L. 19)

MAGISTRATES' COURTS

PROCEDURE

The Magistrates' Courts (Reciprocal Enforcement of Maintenance Orders) (Amendment) Rules 1983

Made - - - - -	28*th July* 1983
Laid before Parliament	1*st August* 1983
Coming into Operation	1*st September* 1983

The Lord Chancellor, in exercise of the powers conferred on him by section 144 of the Magistrates' Courts Act 1980**(a)**, as extended by section 18(1) of the Maintenance Orders (Reciprocal Enforcement) Act 1972**(b)**, and after consultation with the Rule Committee appointed under the said section 144, hereby makes the following Rules:—

1. These Rules may be cited as the Magistrates' Courts (Reciprocal Enforcement of Maintenance Orders) (Amendment) Rules 1983 and shall come into operation on 1st September 1983.

2. In these Rules "the principal Rules" means the Magistrates' Courts (Reciprocal Enforcement of Maintenance Orders) Rules 1974**(c)**.

3. Schedule 1 to the principal Rules shall be amended by inserting after the words "United Republic of Tanzania (except Zanzibar)" the following words:—

"Papua New Guinea
Zimbabwe".

(a) 1980 c. 43. **(b)** 1972 c. 18.
(c) S.I. 1974/668, amended by S.I. 1975/2236, 1979/170.

4. Schedule 2 to the principal Rules shall be amended by inserting after the words "United Republic of Tanzania (except Zanzibar)" the following words:—

"Anguilla
Falkland Islands and Dependencies
St. Helena".

Hailsham of St. Marylebone, C.

Dated 28th July 1983.

EXPLANATORY NOTE

(This Note is not part of the Rules.)

These Rules amend the Magistrates' Courts (Reciprocal Enforcement of Maintenance Orders) Rules 1974. Rules 3 and 4 add to Schedule 1 (reciprocating countries to which documents are transmitted via the Secretary of State) and Schedule 2 (countries and territories in which sums are payable through Crown Agents for Overseas Governments and Administrations) certain of the countries and territories which are designated as reciprocating countries for the purposes of Part I of the Maintenance Orders (Reciprocal Enforcement) Act 1972 by the Reciprocal Enforcement of Maintenance Orders (Designation of Reciprocating Countries) Order 1983 (S.I. 1983/1125) which comes into operation on the same date as these Rules.

STATUTORY INSTRUMENTS

1983 No. 1149

INDUSTRIAL ORGANISATION AND DEVELOPMENT

The Iron Casting Industry (Scientific Research Levy) (Amendment) Order 1983

Laid before Parliament in draft

Made - - - *28th July* 1983

Coming into Operation *2nd October* 1983

Whereas it appears to the Secretary of State that it is expedient that funds should be made available for the purpose of scientific research in connection with the iron casting industry for which there is not a Development Council:

And whereas it appears to the Secretary of State that there is an incorporated body limited by guarantee called BCIRA (formerly called the British Cast Iron Research Association) which is capable of carrying out such scientific research satisfactorily:

And whereas the Secretary of State has consulted the organisations appearing to him to be representative of substantial numbers of persons carrying on business in the iron casting industry and the organisations representative of persons employed in that industry appearing to him to be appropriate:

And whereas the Secretary of State is satisfied that the incidence of the charges imposed by the following order as between different classes of undertakings in the iron casting industry will be in accordance with a fair principle:

And whereas a draft of this Order has been approved by a resolution of each House of Parliament:

Now, therefore, the Secretary of State, in exercise of the powers conferred on him by section 9 of the Industrial Organisation and Development Act 1947**(a)**, hereby orders as follows:—

1. This Order may be cited as the Iron Casting Industry (Scientific Research Levy) (Amendment) Order 1983 and shall come into operation on 2nd October 1983.

(a) 1947 c.40.

2. The Iron Casting Industry (Scientific Research Levy) Order 1971(a) shall, in relation to charges imposed in respect of the levy period beginning on 2nd October 1983 and each subsequent levy period, have effect subject to the following amendments:—

(*a*) for Article 7 there shall be substituted the following Article:—

"**7.**—(1) The charge to be paid by a person by virtue of the provisions of Article 6 hereof in respect of any levy period shall be the aggregate of—

(*a*) an amount equal to 0.15 per cent. of the chargeable amount of the emoluments paid or payable by him in respect of the relevant production quarter; and

(*b*) an amount calculated at the appropriate number of pence (hereinafter called the "appropriate number") for every metric tonne of leviable iron castings produced by him in the relevant production quarter.

(2) The chargeable amount of the emoluments paid or payable by a person in respect of the relevant production quarter shall be calculated by aggregating—

(*a*) the total amount of the emoluments of persons employed by him during that quarter, under a contract of service, wholly or mainly in the actual performance of any process comprised in the activity of casting iron (other than pig iron) or the purposes ancillary to such performance including persons employed as pattern makers or in the maintenance or security of premises, plant or machinery but excluding persons engaged in the supply of food or drink; and

(*b*) the total amount of the emoluments of persons employed by him during that quarter, under a contract of service, including directors, managers and administrative, scientific, technical, laboratory and clerical staff, wholly or mainly in respect of—

(i) the payment of persons specified in head (a);

(ii) the direction, management, control, supervision, administration or costing of the industry; or

(iii) activities carried on for the purposes of scientific research and development in connection with the industry.

(3) Subject to paragraphs (4) and (5) below, the appropriate number shall be 23.5.

(4) If the number of the index for the December of any year after 1982 ("the relevant December") differs from 231.7 (being the number of the index for December 1982) the appropriate number in relation to the relevant levy period shall be 23.5 divided by 231.7 multiplied by the number of the index for the relevant December the result having been rounded up or down to the nearest halfpenny.

(a) S.I. 1971/253, as amended by S.I. 1976/1016 and 1979/748.

(5) If the base year of the index is changed at any time or times after the coming into operation of this Order—

(a) paragraph (3) above shall have effect as if for 23.5 or for such number as for the time being has effect in place of that number in accordance with this paragraph there were substituted the appropriate number which was operative at the commencement of the new base year; and

(b) paragraph (4) above shall have effect as if—

(i) for 23.5 or for such number as for the time being has effect in place of that number in accordance with this paragraph there were substituted the appropriate number so operative;

(ii) for 231.7 or for such number as for the time being has effect in place of that number in accordance with this paragraph there were substituted the number by which the number of the index at the date when such change of base year is made has been replaced for the purposes of the new base year; and

(iii) for "1982" in both places that it occurs or for such year as for the time being has effect in place of that year in accordance with this paragraph, there shall be substituted the year in which the base year is so changed.

(6) In this Article—

"the index" means—

(a) before 8th August 1983, the index of wholesale selling prices of iron castings produced in the United Kingdom (as compiled by the Department of Industry and published in "British Business");

(b) on and after 8th August 1983, the index of producer prices of iron castings in the rough or machined produced in the United Kingdom (as compiled by the Department of Trade and Industry and published in "British business"); and

"the relevant levy period" means any levy period commencing in the twelve months after 24th June next following the relevant December.";

(b) for Article 8, there shall be substituted the following Article:—

"8.   No person shall be liable to pay any charge—

(a) in respect of the levy period in which he began to carry on business in the industry; or

(b) in respect of a levy period if the amount of charge calculated as aforesaid in respect of that levy period is less than £100."; and

(c) in Article 9(3)—

(i) for "the British Cast Iron Research Association" there shall be substituted "BCIRA"; and

(ii) for "the Association" there shall be substituted "that body".

3. The Iron Casting Industry (Scientific Research Levy) (Amendment) Order 1976(a) and the Iron Casting Industry (Scientific Research Levy) (Amendment) Order 1979(b) are hereby revoked.

John Butcher,
Department of Trade and Industry.

28th July 1983.

EXPLANATORY NOTE

(This Note is not part of the Order.)

This Order further amends the Iron Casting Industry (Scientific Research Levy) Order 1971 and revokes the Iron Casting Industry (Scientific Research Levy) (Amendment) Order 1976 and the Iron Casting Industry (Scientific Research Levy) (Amendment) Order 1979.

It consolidates the provisions previously made for the computation of levies and makes minor amendments. In particular it amends the basis of computation so as to reflect the current wholesale selling prices of iron castings produced in the United Kingdom and it provides for the basis of computation to be up-dated from time to time in order to accord with current price levels.

The basis is up-dated by reference to an index (which is published in "British business", a publication obtainable from Her Majesty's Stationery Office, PO Box 276, London SW8 5DT).

(a) S.I. 1976/1016.   (b) S.I. 1979/748.

STATUTORY INSTRUMENTS

1983 No. 1151

REPRESENTATION OF THE PEOPLE

The Parish and Community Meetings (Polls) (Amendment) Rules 1983

Made - - - - -	*27th July* 1983
Laid before Parliament	*5th August* 1983
Coming into Operation	*1st September* 1983

In exercise of the powers conferred upon me by paragraph 18(5) of Part III of, and paragraph 34(5) of Part V of, Schedule 12 to the Local Government Act 1972**(a)**, I hereby make the following Rules:—

1.—(1) These Rules may be cited as the Parish and Community Meetings (Polls) (Amendment) Rules 1983.

(2) These Rules shall come into operation on 1st September 1983, except that paragraphs (2), (3), (5) and (6) of Rule 4 shall not apply to any poll notice which is published before the coming into operation of these Rules.

2. Rule 4 of the Parish and Community Meetings (Polls) Rules 1973**(b)** shall be amended as follows:—

(*a*) for "Representation of the People Act 1949" there shall be substituted "Representation of the People Act 1983";

(*b*) for "section 165(1)" there shall be substituted "section 187(1)";

(*c*) for "section 53" there shall be substituted "section 66";

(*d*) for the sections cited in paragraph (*a*) there shall be substituted "sections 60, 113, 114, 115, 168, 173 (except paragraph (*b*) thereof), 176, 179, 180, 181 and 186";

(*e*) in paragraph (*c*) for "section 115(7)" there shall be substituted "section 130(6)";

(*f*) in paragraph (*d*) for "sections 47(2), 86(1) and 87(1)" there shall be substituted "sections 60(2), 99(1) and 100(1)"; and

(*g*) in paragraph (*e*) for "section 119(2)(*b*)" there shall be substituted "section 136(2)(*b*)".

(a) 1972 c. 70; those paragraphs were amended by paragraph 14 of Schedule 8 to the Representation of the People Act 1983 (c. 2).
(b) S.I. 1973/1911, to which there are amendments not relevant to these Rules.

3. In Rule 5 of the Parish and Community Meetings (Polls) Rules 1973 for "section 53 of the Representation of the People Act 1949" there shall be substituted "section 66 of the Representation of the People Act 1983".

4.—(1) The rules in the Schedule to the Parish and Community Meetings (Polls) Rules 1973 shall be amended as follows.

(2) In rule 2(1) after the words "The Timetable a" there shall be inserted "Saturday,".

(3) At the end of rule 2 there shall be added the following paragraph:—

"(3) In this rule "weekday" does not include a Saturday.".

(4) At the end of rule 15(1) there shall be added the words "but the constables on duty at polling stations or at the counting of the votes shall not be required to make the declaration of secrecy.".

(5) Rule 22(1)(*b*) shall be omitted.

(6) In rule 27(1)(*f*) the word "Jews" shall be omitted.

Leon Brittan,
One of Her Majesty's Principal
Secretaries of State.

Home Office.
27th July 1983.

EXPLANATORY NOTE

(*This Note is not part of the Rules.*)

These Rules amend the Parish and Community Meetings (Polls) Rules 1973. The principal change is to exclude Saturdays from the computation of time for the purposes of the election timetable (rule 4(2), (3), (5) and (6)).

These Rules also make amendments consequential on the consolidation of the Representation of the People Acts by the Representation of the People Act 1983 (rules 2 and 3). Rule 4(4) inserts a provision which expressly states that constables on duty at polling stations or at the counting of the votes are not required to make the declaration of secrecy.

STATUTORY INSTRUMENTS

1983 No. 1152

REPRESENTATION OF THE PEOPLE

The European Assembly Elections (Day of Election) Order 1983

Made - - - -	*27th July* 1983
Laid before Parliament	*5th August* 1983
Coming into Operation	*1st January* 1984

In exercise of the powers conferred upon me by paragraph 3(1) of Schedule 1 to the European Assembly Elections Act 1978(a), I hereby make the following Order:—

1. This Order may be cited as the European Assembly Elections (Day of Election) Order 1983 and shall come into operation on 1st January 1984.

2. A general election of United Kingdom representatives to the Assembly of the European Communities shall be held on 14th June 1984.

Leon Brittan,
One of Her Majesty's Principal
Secretaries of State.

Home Office.
27th July 1983.

EXPLANATORY NOTE
(This Note is not part of the Order.)

This Order appoints 14th June 1984 as the day on which the next general election of representatives to the European Assembly shall be held.

(a) 1978 c.10.

STATUTORY INSTRUMENTS

1983 No. 1153

REPRESENTATION OF THE PEOPLE

The Local Elections (Parishes and Communities) (Amendment) Rules 1983

Made - - - -	*27th July* 1983
Laid before Parliament	*5th August* 1983
Coming into Operation	*1st September* 1983

In exercise of the powers conferred upon me by section 36 of the Representation of the People Act 1983 (a), I hereby make the following Rules:—

1.—(1) These Rules may be cited as the Local Elections (Parishes and Communities) (Amendment) Rules 1983.

(2) These Rules shall come into operation on 1st September 1983, except that paragraphs (2), (3), (8) and (9) of Rule 4 shall not apply to any election notice of which is published before the coming into operation of these Rules.

2. Rule 3 of the Local Elections (Parishes and Communities) Rules 1973(b) shall have effect as though, for the reference in that rule to Schedule 2 to the Representation of the People Act 1949, there were substituted a reference to Schedule 1 to the Representation of the People Act 1983.

3. Rule 4 of the Local Elections (Parishes and Communities) Rules 1973 shall be amended as follows:—

(a) for "Representation of the People Act 1949" there shall be substituted "Representation of the People Act 1983";

(b) for "section 165(1)" there shall be substituted "section 187(1)", and

(c) for "section 119(2)*(b)*" there shall be substituted "section 136(2)*(b)*".

4.—(1) The rules in Schedule 1 to the Local Elections (Parishes and Communities) Rules 1973 shall be amended as follows.

(2) In rule 2(1) after the words "of the timetable in rule 1 a" there shall be inserted "Saturday,".

(3) At the end of rule 2 there shall be added the following paragraph:—

"(3) In this rule "weekday" does not include a Saturday.".

(4) At the beginning of rule 7(1) there shall be inserted the words "Subject to section 38(1)*(b)* of the Representation of the People Act 1983,".

(5) At the end of rule 25(1) there shall be added the words "but the constables on duty at polling stations or at the counting of the votes shall not be required to make the declaration of secrecy".

(a) 1983 c.2; the powers are extended by section 187(1) of the 1983 Act and section 89(6) of the Local Government Act 1972 (c.70), as amended by paragraph 13 of Schedule 8 to the 1983 Act.

(b) S.I. 1973/1910, to which there are amendments not relevant to these Rules.

(6) In rule 25(3) and (4) for "section 53 of the Representation of the People Act 1949", in each place where the words occur, there shall be substituted "section 66 of the Representation of the People Act 1983".

(7) In rule 26(3) for "Representation of the People Act 1949" there shall be substituted "Representation of the People Act 1983".

(8) Rule 32(1)*(b)* shall be omitted.

(9) In rule 37(1)*(f)* the word "Jews" shall be omitted.

(10) Rule 51(1) shall be omitted.

(11) In rule 52(1) for "two electors" there shall be substituted "ten electors".

(12) In rule 52(2) and (4) for "filled by election", in each place where the words occur, there shall be substituted "required to be filled by election".

Leon Brittan,
One of Her Majesty's Principal
Secretaries of State.

Home Office.
27th July 1983.

EXPLANATORY NOTE

(*This Note is not part of the Rules.*)

These Rules amend the Local Elections (Parishes and Communities) Rules 1973 ("the 1973 Rules").

There are two principal changes. One is to exclude Saturdays from the computation of time for the purposes of the election timetable (rule 4(2), (3), (8) and (9)). The other is to increase from two to ten the number of electors who may require that an election be held to fill a casual vacancy in the office of a parish or community councillor (rule 4(11)).

These Rules also make amendments consequential on the consolidation of the Representation of the People Acts by the Representation of the People Act 1983 (rules 2, 3 and 4(4), (6) and (7)). Rule 4(5) inserts a provision which expressly states that constables on duty at polling stations or at the counting of the votes are not required to make the declaration of secrecy. Rule 4(10) omits a provision from the 1973 Rules because the substance of that provision is to be found in primary legislation, namely, section 38(2) of the Representation of the People Act 1983. Rule 4(12) is intended to clarify a provision in the 1973 Rules.

STATUTORY INSTRUMENTS

1983 No. 1154

REPRESENTATION OF THE PEOPLE

The Local Elections (Principal Areas) (Amendment) Rules 1983

Made - - - -	*27th July* 1983
Laid before Parliament	*5th August* 1983
Coming into Operation	*1st September* 1983

In exercise of the powers conferred upon me by section 36 of the Representation of the People Act 1983(**a**), I hereby make the following Rules:—

1.—(1) These Rules may be cited as the Local Elections (Principal Areas) (Amendment) Rules 1983.

(2) These Rules shall come into operation on 1st September 1983, except that paragraphs (2), (3) and (10)(*a*) and (*b*) of Rule 3 shall not apply to any election notice of which is published before the coming into operation of these Rules.

2. Rule 3(1) of the Local Elections (Principal Areas) Rules 1973(**b**) shall have effect as though, for the reference in that rule to Schedule 2 to the Representation of the People Act 1949, there were substituted a reference to Schedule 1 to the Representation of the People Act 1983.

3.—(1) The rules in Schedule 2 to the Local Elections (Principal Areas) Rules 1973 shall be amended as follows.

(2) In rule 2(1) after the words "of the timetable in rule 1 a" there shall be inserted "Saturday,"; and in the proviso to that rule the words "or on the Saturday in the Easter break" shall be omitted.

(3) At the end of rule 2, there shall be added the following paragraph:—

"(3) In this rule "weekday" does not include a Saturday.".

(4) At the beginning of rule 7 there shall be inserted the words "Subject to section 38(1)(*b*) of the Representation of the People Act 1983,".

(5) In rule 20 for "Representation of the People Regulations 1969" there shall be substituted "Representation of the People Regulations 1983".

(**a**) 1983 c. 2.
(**b**) S.I. 1973/79, to which there are amendments not relevant to these Rules.

(6) In rule 26(5) for "section 60(1) of the Representation of the People Act 1949" there shall be substituted "section 72(1) of the Representation of the People Act 1983".

(7) At the end of rule 27(1) there shall be added the words "but the constables on duty at polling stations or at the counting of the votes shall not be required to make the declaration of secrecy".

(8) In rule 27(3) and (4) for "section 53 of the Representation of the People Act 1949", in each place where the words occur, there shall be substituted "section 66 of the Representation of the People Act 1983".

(9) In rule 28(3) for "Representation of the People Act 1949" there shall be substituted "Representation of the People Act 1983".

(10) The following provisions shall be omitted:—

(*a*) rule 34(1)(*b*);

(*b*) in rule 39(1)(*f*), the word "Jews", and

(*c*) rule 53(1).

Leon Brittan,
One of Her Majesty's Principal
Secretaries of State.

Home Office.
27th July 1983.

EXPLANATORY NOTE

(*This Note is not part of the Rules.*)

These Rules amend the Local Elections (Principal Areas) Rules 1973 ("the 1973 Rules"). The principal change is to exclude Saturdays from the computation of time for the purposes of the election timetable (rule 3(2), (3) and (10)(*a*) and (*b*)).

These Rules also make amendments consequential on the consolidation of the Representation of the People Acts by the Representation of the People Act 1983 and the making of the Representation of the People Regulations 1983 (S.I. 1983/435) (rules 2 and 3(4), (5), (6), (8) and (9)). Rule 3(7) inserts a provision which expressly states that constables on duty at polling stations or at the counting of the votes are not required to make the declaration of secrecy. Rule 3(10)(*c*) omits a provision from the 1973 Rules because the substance of that provision is to be found in primary legislation, namely, section 38(2) of the Representation of the People Act 1983.

STATUTORY INSTRUMENTS

1983 No. 1156

MEDICINES

The Medicines (Exemptions from Restrictions on the Retail Sale or Supply of Veterinary Drugs) (Amendment) (No. 2) Order 1983

Made - - - -	*28th July* 1983
Laid before Parliament	*10th August* 1983
Coming into Operation	*1st September* 1983

The Secretary of State concerned with health in England, the Secretaries of State respectively concerned with health and with agriculture in Scotland and in Wales, the Minister of Agriculture, Fisheries and Food, the Department of Health and Social Services for Northern Ireland, and the Department of Agriculture for Northern Ireland, acting jointly, in exercise of the powers conferred by sections 57(1), (2) and 129(4) of the Medicines Act 1968(a) and now vested in them(b), and of all other powers enabling them in that behalf, after consulting such organisations as appear to them to be representative of interests likely to be substantially affected by the following order in accordance with section 129(6) of the said Act, hereby make the following order:—

Title and commencement

1. This order may be cited as the Medicines (Exemptions from Restrictions on the Retail Sale or Supply of Veterinary Drugs) (Amendment) (No. 2) Order 1983 and shall come into operation on 1st September 1983.

Amendment of principal order

2. For the Schedules to the Medicines (Exemptions from Restrictions on the Retail Sale or Supply of Veterinary Drugs) Order 1979(c) there shall be substituted the Schedules to this Order.

(a) 1968 c. 67.
(b) In the case of the Secretaries of State concerned with health in England and Wales by virtue of S.I. 1969/388, in the case of the Secretary of State concerned with agriculture in Wales by virtue of S.I. 1978/272 and in the case of the Northern Ireland Departments by virtue of section 40 of, and Schedule 5 to, the Northern Ireland Constitution Act 1973 (c. 36) and section 1(3) of, and paragraph 2(1)(*b*) of Schedule 1 to, the Northern Ireland Act 1974 (c. 28).
(c) S.I. 1979/45; relevant amending instrument is S.I. 1983/274.

14th July 1983.

Norman Fowler,
Secretary of State for Social Services.

18th July 1983.

George Younger,
Secretary of State for Scotland.

20th July 1983.

John Stradling Thomas,
Minister of State for Wales.

In Witness where of the Official Seal of the Minister of Agriculture, Fisheries and Food is hereunto affixed on 7th July 1983.
    (L.S.)

Michael Jopling,
Minister of Agriculture, Fisheries and Food.

Sealed with the Offical Seal of the Department of Health and Social Services for Northern Ireland this 25th day of July 1983.
    (L.S.)

N. Dugdale,
Permanent Secretary.

Sealed with the Official Seal of the Department of Agriculture for Northern Ireland this 28th day of July 1983.
    (L.S.)

J. A. Young,
Permanent Secretary.

SCHEDULE 1

PART A

LICENCE OF RIGHT VETERINARY DRUGS

Article 3

Group/Class	Substance	Maximum strength or concentration	Pharmaceutical form or route of administration	Maximum daily dose	Other restrictions
1. GROWTH PROMOTERS	Bacitracin Zinc	6,300,000 i.u./kg	Incorporation in feed		
	Bambermycin	30 g/kg	Incorporation in feed		
	Nitrovin		Incorporation in feed		
	Tylosin Phosphate		Incorporation in feed		
	Virginiamycin	20 g/kg	Incorporation in feed		
	Zeranol				For pigs
2. IMPLANTS	Amprolium hydrochloride				
3. COCCIDIOSTATS	Clopidol	33%			
	Decoquinate	80 g/kg	Incorporation in feed		
	Diaveridine				
	Dinitolmide	33%			

Group/Class	Substance	Maximum strength or concentration	Pharmaceutical form or route of administration	Maximum daily dose	Other restrictions
	Ethopabate Methyl benzoquate	1·75%	Incorporation in feed		When combined with not more than 20·6 per cent of Clopidol
	Pyrimethamine		Incorporation in feed		For broiler chickens at levels not exceeding 5 ppm
	Robenidine				
	Sulphaquinoxaline	12%	Incorporation in feed		When combined with not more than 20 per cent of Amprolium hydrochloride and 1 per cent of Ethopabate with or without 1 per cent of Pyrimethamine
4. ANTI-BLACKHEAD PREPARATIONS	Acinitrazole Aminonitrothiazole Nifursol				

5. SHEEP DIPS AND ECTO-PARASITICIDES

Allethrin		
Amitraz		
Benzyl Benzoate		
Bromophos		
Bucarpolate		
Butacarb		
Carbaryl		
Carbophenothion		
Chlorfenvinphos		
Chlorpyrifos		
Coal Tar Phenols		External use only
Coumaphos		
Crotoxyphos		
Cresol	4%	
Cresylic Acid		External use only
Derris Resins		
Diazinon		
Dichlofenthion		

SCHEDULE 1: *Continued*

Group/Class	Substance	Maximum strength or concentration	Pharmaceutical form or route of administration	Maximum daily dose	Other restrictions
	Dicophane				
	Dioxathion				
	Dursban				
	Fenchlorphos				
	Fenitrothion				
	Gamma BHC				
	Iodofenphos				
	Lethane				
	Malathion				
	Phosalone				
	Pyractone				
	Pyrimithate				
	Rotenone				

6. ANTHELMINTICS	Bephenium and its salts			
	4-brom-2, 6 dihydroxy-benzanilide			
	Bunamidine and its salts			
	Cyacetazide			
	Dichlorvos			
	Diethyl-carbamazine and its salts			
	Extract Filicis BP			
	Haloxon			
	Levamisole and its salts			
	Mebendazole			
	Metriphonate			
	Morantel and its salts			
	Naphthalophos			

SCHEDULE 1: *Continued*

Group/Class	Substance	Maximum strength or concentration	Pharmaceutical form or route of administration	Maximum daily dose	Other restrictions
	Niclosamide				
	Parbendazole				
	Phenothiazine				
	Piperazine Carbon Disulphide Complex				
	Pyrantel and its salts				
	Sodium glycarsamate				
	Tetramisole and its salts				
	Thenium and its salts				
	Thiabendazole				
	Thiophanate				

7. MILK FEVER PREPARATIONS	Calcium borogluconate Injection whether or not containing all or any of the following substances:
	Dextrose, Magnesium and Phosphorus
8. WARBLE FLY DRESSINGS	Crufomate
	Famphur
	Fenchlorphos
	Fenthion
	Metriphonate
	Prolate
	Brotianide
	Carbon Tetrachloride
9. LIVER FLUKE REMEDIES	Diamphenethide
	Hexachloroethane
	Hexachlorophane

SCHEDULE 1: *Continued*

Group/Class	Substance	Maximum strength or concentration	Pharmaceutical form or route of administration	Maximum daily dose	Other restrictions
	Nitroxynil and its salts				
	Oxyclozanide				
	Rafoxanide				
	Tribromsalan				
	Black Disease Antisera				
	Black Disease Vaccines				
	Blackleg (Black-quarter) Vaccine and Antiserum				
	Braxy Vaccines and Antisera				
	Enterotoxaemia Vaccines and Antisera				
	Lamb Dysentry Antisera				
10. SHEEP AND CATTLE CLOSTRIDIAL VACCINES AND ANTISERA					

11. POULTRY VACCINES

Lamb Dysentry Vaccines	
Pulpy Kidney Vaccines and Antisera	
Struck Vaccine and Antiserum	
Tetanus Antitoxins	
Tetanus Toxoids	
Combinations of two or more of Braxy, Blackleg (Black-quarter), Lamb Dysentry, Pulpy Kidney, Entero-toxaemia, Struck, Tetanus, Black Disease and Pasteurella Vaccines	
Avian Encephalo-myelitis Vaccine (Living and Inactivated)	
Duck Hepatitis Vaccine (Living)	

SCHEDULE 1: *Continued*

Group/Class	Substance	Maximum strength or concentration	Pharmaceutical form or route of administration	Maximum daily dose	Other restrictions
	Fowl Pox Vaccine				
	Fowl Typhoid Vaccines (Salmonella gallinarum)				
	Infectious Bronchitis Vaccines (Living)				
	Infectious Bronchitis Vaccines (Inactivated)				
	Infectious Bursal Disease Vaccines				
	Infectious Laryngotracheitis Vaccines (Living)				
	Marek's Disease Vaccine				

	Newcastle Disease Vaccine (Living)
	Newcastle Disease Vaccine (Inactivated)
	Combinations of Newcastle Disease Vaccines and Avian Encephalomyelitis Vaccines
	Combinations of Newcastle Disease Vaccines with Infectious Bronchitis Vaccines
12. ERYSIPELAS VACCINES	Avian Erysipelas Vaccines
	Swine Erysipelas Vaccines
13. SALMONELLA AND E. COLI VACCINES	E. Coli Vaccines (Killed)
	Salmonella Vaccines (Killed)

Group/Class	Substance	Maximum strength or concentration	Pharmaceutical form or route of administration	Maximum daily dose	Other restrictions
14. OTHER SHEEP AND CATTLE VACCINES	E. Coli and Salmonella Sero Vaccines				
	Foot Rot Vaccine				
	Louping Ill Vaccines (Killed)				
	Orf Vaccine (Live)				
	Ovine Enzootic Abortion Vaccines				
	Pasteurella Vaccines (Killed)				
	Pneumonia Combined Vaccine (Pasteurella)				
15. MISCELLANEOUS VACCINES	Botulism Vaccine (Mink)				
	Epidemic Tremors Vaccine				

	Combinations of E. Coli, Salmonella and Pasteurella Vaccines (Killed)
16. SULPHANILAMIDE SURFACE WOUND DRESSINGS	Pigeon Pox Vaccine (Living)
	This group comprises powdered surface wound dressings containing not more than 5 per cent of sulphanilamide for application to farm animals
17. LOCAL ANAESTHETICS	This group comprises injections containing not more than 2 per cent of procaine hydrochloride, lignocaine, or lignocaine hydrochloride with or without not more than 0·002 per cent of adrenaline,

SCHEDULE 1: *Continued*

Group/Class	Substance	Maximum strength or concentration	Pharmaceutical form or route of administration	Maximum daily dose	Other restrictions
	adrenaline acid tartrate or noradrenaline				
	Ammonia Solution Conc.	4%			
	Azaperone				For pigs
	Broxyquinoline				
	Butafosfan				
	Butyl amino benzoate		Non-parenteral use only		
	Butynorate		External use only		
	Chlorprothixene				For pigs
18. OTHERS	Clioquinol	5%			
	Cobalt Carbonate				For use only in combination with anthelmintics

Cobalt Oxide		Non-parenteral use only		For use only in combination with anthelmintics and in ruminal pellets
Copper its salts and organic preparations except Copper Sulphate				
Copper Sulphate	21%	External use only		
Creosote		Internal use		
Dextrose Injection				
Dill, oil of				
Dimethyl Sulphoxide				
Etisazole		External use only		
Halquinol	5%			
Iron Dextran Complex				
Iron Dextrin				
Iron Galactan				
Iron Organic Complexes				

SCHEDULE 1: *Continued*

Group/Class	Substance	Maximum strength or concentration	Pharmaceutical form or route of administration	Maximum daily dose	Other restrictions
	Magnesium salts				
	Menaphthone Sodium Bisulphite				
	Menaphthone Dimethyl Pyrimidinol Bisulphite				
	Methimazole				
	Phenol				
	Poloxalene				
	Turpentine	40%	Internal use		
	Vitamin A				
	Vitamin D$_2$				
	Vitamin D$_3$				
	Vitamin E Injection				

SCHEDULE 1   Article 3

PART B

VETERINARY DRUGS

Product Licence No.   Name of Product*

1. Growth Promoters

PL 4131/4000 Advantage with Romensin[R]
PL 0095/4026 { Avotan 50 Avoparcin / *Avotan 50*
PL 0095/4028 Avotan 50c Avoparcin
PL 3832/4031 Eskalin 100
PL 0002/4055 Eskalin S400
PL 0002/4045 Eskalin 500
PL 0029/4102 Fedan 10% Premix
PL 0086/4124 { Flavomycin 40 / Flavomycin 40 g/kg
PL 4869/4000 Panazone 250– Nitrovin
PL 0095/4007 Payzone 50 MA Nitrovin Milk Replacer Additive
PL 4188/4008 Pentazone 250
PL 2969/4006 Rumevite with Romensin
PL 0006/4052 Romesin (Monensin Sodium) Premix
PL 0006/4055 Tylamix Premix 100 g/kg
PL 0006/4062 Tylamix Premix 250 g/kg
PL 3405/4007 Tylosin 100 Premix
PL 3405/4002 ZB 100
PL 3405/4005 ZB 150
PL 3734/4000 Zinc Bacitracin Dumex Feed Grade
PL 3734/4001 Zinc Bacitracin "Dumex" 150 Premix
PL 0109/4001 Zinc Bacitracin Premix

2. Implants

PL 0829/4119 Ralgro

3. Coccidiostats

PL 0025/4035 Arpocox
PL 0031/4011 Avatec Premix
PL 0109/4000 Dinormix SR 25
PL 4188/4004 { Dinitolmide (DOT) 3·5— / Dinitro-ortho-toluamide / Unicox Pure
PL 0109/4002 DOT (dinitolmide)
PL 1598/4032 DOT Premix 12·5%
PL 1598/4033 DOT Premix 25%
PL 0006/4047 { Elancoban / *Elancoban Premix*
PL 3405/4006 Elancoban Premix
PL 0621/4015 Lerbek
PL 0006/4061 Monteban 100 Premix

*Alternative product names used by specially authorised persons are not shown.

PL 0025/4019 Nicrazin (Premix)
PL 0086/4135 Sacox 60 Premix
PL 0086/4117 Stenorol
PL 0025/4003 Supacox

4. Anti-Blackhead Preparations

5. Sheep Dips and Ectoparasiticides

PL 0010/4041 Asuntol Scab Dip
PL 1300/4010 Barricade
PL 0676/4089 Battles Improved Organo-Phosphorus Single-Dipping Fluid Dip
PL 0676/4088 Battles Improved Special Single-Dipping Fluid Dip
PL 0676/4087 Battles Organo-Phosphorus Single-Dipping Fluid Dip
PL 0676/4086 Battles Liquid Summer Fly Dip (Scab Approved)
PL 0010/4047 Bayverm Suspension 2·5%
PL 0010/4048 Bayverm Suspension 10%
PL 0014/4064 Boots Fly Dip
PL 2613/4003 Cheviot Sheep Head Ointment
PL 1300/4004 Ciodrin Insecticide
PL 0805/4015 Cooper MD Powder Dip (BHC)
PL 0003/4124 Cooper-Summer Dip 400
PL 0003/4116 Cooper Winter Dip 200
PL 1300/4011 C Tag 97 Fly Tag/Flectron Fly Tag
PL 4149/4001 Deodorised Malathion Premium Grade
PL 1476/4018 Deosan Dysect
PL 1476/4026 Deosan Flectron
PL 1476/4021 Deosan Summer Dip
PL 1476/4020 Deosan Winter Dip
PL 0829/4127 Dermol
PL 1978/4000 Ectoral Emulsifiable Concentrate
PL 1978/4001 Ectoral Tablets No. 1, 2 and 3
PL 0038/4061 Flockcare Fly and Scab Dip
PL 0038/4063 Flockcare Winter Dip
PL 2759/4006 Killgerm and Marstan Sheep Dip
PL 2759/4009 Killgerm Scab and Fly Sheep Dip
PL 2759/4007 { Killgerm Single Dipping Type Liquid—Sheep Dip
Marstan Single Dipping Type Liquid—Sheep Dip
PL 4055/4012 Lice and Mange Remedy
PL 1826/4004 Lice Tick and Mange Dressing (LTM)
PL 0430/4001 Lorexane Medicated Shampoo
PL 3317/4070 Milocide 50%
PL 0015/4003 Nexion (Bromophos) 2% Dusting Powder
PL 1826/4001 Northern Fly Dip
PL 4055/4003 Northern Fly Dip
PL 1728/4055 Nuvanol Vet
PL 1826/4023 Osmond's Wintol Sheep Dip (1–200)
PL 0038/4068 Porect
PL 1447/4083 { Rycopel
Young's SP Fly Spray
PL 0003/4113 Stomoxin
PL 4055/4001 Supona Fly and Tick Dip
PL 1300/4005 Supona Sheep Dip
PL 0014/4065 Taktic
PL 1345/4040 Taskill

PL 1728/4050 { Topclip Dri-Dress / Neocidal Veterinary Powder
PL 1826/4025 { Viper Winter Dip / Viper Dip
PL 4055/4000 Viper Winter Dip
PL 4055/4002 Vipex 200 Liquid Dip
PL 0014/4066 Winter Dip
PL 1447/4096 Young's Cypor
PL 1447/4086 Young's Dursban 400 Winter Dip
PL 1447/4080 { Young's Ectomort Sheep Dip / *Young's Scab Approved Summer Dip*
PL 1447/4087 Young's 400 Fly Dip
PL 1447/4085 Young's Scab Approved Diazinon Winter Dip
PL 1447/4041 Young's Scab Approved Liquid Fly Dip
PL 1447/4052 Young's 200 Liquid Tick Dip
PL 1447/4055 Young's Scab Approved Killtick Liquid Tick Dip
PL 1447/4058 Young's Scab Approved 200 Liquid Tick Dip
PL 1447/4060 Young's Sheep Blowfly Spray
PL 1447/4063 Young's Scab Approved 400 Fly Dip
PL 1447/4050 Young's Scab Approved 200 Winter Dip
PL 1447/4071 Young's Scab Approved Dursban 400 Winter Dip
PL 1447/4070 Young's Scab Approved Dursban Winter Dip
PL 1447/4068 Young's Scab Approved Bromophos Winter Dip
PL 1447/4073 Young's Scab Approved Iodofenphos Winter Dip
PL 1447/4015 { Young's Powder Fly Dip / Young's Summer Mycotic Dip
PL 1447/4056 { Young's Scab Approved Powder Fly Dip / Young's Scab Approved Summer Mycotic Dip

6. Anthelminitics

PL 0829/4135 Action Paranil Pellets
PL 0029/4105 'Amatron' Sheep Drench
PL 1447/4092 Anthelpor
PL 3413/4014 Ascapilla
PL 0010/4054 Bayverm L.V. Paste
PL 0010/4049 Bayverm Premix 0·6%
PL 0010/4050 Bayverm Premix 2·4%
PL 1861/4055 Day's Worm Drench
PL 0010/4046 Droncit
PL 0025/4023 Equiben
PL 0002/4074 Equitac
PL 0025/4027 Equizole Pony Paste
PL 0829/4044 Equivurm Plus
PL 0829/4058 Equivurm Plus Paste
PL 0829/4120 Flubenol
PL 0829/4131 Flubenol Pellets
PL 0010/4055 Flukombin
PL 3763/4000 Gapex
PL 0002/4004 Helmatac In-Feed Wormer
PL 0025/4041 Ivomec Drench
PL 1447/4091 Levanthel
PL 0829/4126 Mebatreat
PL 0829/4113 Mebenvet (1·2%)
PL 0829/4123 Mebenvet (5%)
PL 0010/4026 Neguvon
PL 0012/4003 Nemafax Drench

PL 0012/4150 Nemafax P Wormer Pellets
PL 0012/4149 { Nemafax 14
{ Nemafax 5
PL 0012/4151 { Nemafax Sow
{ Nemafax Cattle, Sheep and Goat Wormer Pellets
PL 0012/4153 Nemafax Wettable Powder
PL 0029/4101 Nemicide Cattle Drench
PL 0029/4101 Nilverm Cattle Special
PL 0029/4100 Nilverm C. Small Dose Cattle Drench
PL 0029/4098 Nilzan C
PL 0829/4114 { Ovitelmin
{ Telmin Liquid
PL 0086/4119 Panacur Paste
PL 0086/4110 Panacur 4% Powder
PL 0086/4130 { Panacur SC
{ *Panacur SC Sheep Wormer*
PL 0086/4136 Panacur SC Cattle Wormer
PL 0086/4106 Panacur 10% Suspension
PL 0086/4105 { Panacur 2·5% Suspension
{ Panacur 2·5% Sheep Wormer
PL 0086/4121 Panacur 1·5% Pellets
PL 0086/4107 Panacur 22% Granules
PL 0057/4075 Paratect Sustained Release Bolus
PL 0025/4031 Porcam
PL 0025/4038 Ranizole Paste
PL 0829/4150 Ripercol
PL 0829/4151 Ripercol 7·5% Injectable
PL 0829/4140 Ripercol 5% Injectable Solution
PL 0829/4132 Ripercol 15% Injectable Solution
PL 0829/4133 Ripercol 3·2% Oral Solution
PL 0086/4115 Rumevite Wormablok with Panacur for Cattle
PL 0086/4114 Rumevite Wormablok with Panacur for Sheep
PL 1447/4094 Rycovet Horse and Pony Wormer
PL 0029/4099 Spectril
PL 0057/4060 Strongid-P (Granules)
PL 0057/4062 Strongid-P Paste
PL 0057/4063 Suiminth (Morantel Tartrate)
PL 0286/4039 Synanthic Horse Paste
PL 0286/4035 Synanthic Horse Pellets
PL 0286/4032 Synanthic
PL 0286/4034 Synanthic DC
PL 0003/4127 Systamex Paste 18·5% and Horse Wormer
PL 0003/4112 Systamex Worm Drench for Cattle and Sheep
PL 0003/4121 Systamex 906 Concentrated Cattle Wormer
PL 1300/4002 Task
PL 0829/4112 Telmin KH
PL 4462/4002 Tetramisole Hydrochloride BP (Vet)
PL 0025/4024 { Thibenzole 50% Paste
{ *Thibenzole Paste*
PL 1728/4060 Topclip Wormer
PL 1728/4061 Topclip Wormer Pellets
PL 0829/4136 Triban Drench
PL 3832/4016 Valbazen Cattle Wormer Pellets
PL 3832/4025 Valbazen C10% Total Spectrum Wormer
PL 0002/4062 { Valbazen 10% Drench
{ Valbazen 10% Total Spectrum Wormer

PL 3832/4026 *Valbazen SC 2·5% Total Spectrum Wormer*
PL 0002/4061 { Valbazen 2·5% Suspension
Valbazen 2·5% Total Spectrum Wormer
PL 0012/4172 Vermadax
PL 1447/4091 Young's Anthelpor 20
PL 1447/4075 { Young's Anthelworm
Young's Anthelworm (New Formula)
PL 1447/4090 Young's Anthelworm Feed Pellets
PL 1447/4076 { Young's Anthelworm L
Young's Anthelworm L (New Formula)
PL 1447/4066 Young's Nemtrem Cattle
PL 1447/4067 Young's Nemtrem Sheep
PL 1447/4079 { Young's Nemtrem
Young's New Formula Nemtrem

7. Milk Fever Preparations

PL 4134/4003 { Astracalc (Calcium Borogluconate 20%) No. 1
Flexopax (Calcium Borogluconate 20%) No. 1
PL 4134/4004 { Astacalc (Calcium Borogluconate 40%) No. 2
Flexopax (Calcium Borogluconate 40%) No. 2
PL 4134/4005 { Astracalc (Calcium Borogluconate PM) No. 3
Flexopax (Calcium Borogluconate PM) No. 3
PL 4134/4006 Astracalc (Calcium Borogluconate PM 29) No. 4
PL 4134/4007 Astracalc (Calcium Borogluconate PM 40) No. 5
PL 4134/4008 { Astracalc (Calcium Borogluconate PMD) No. 6
Flexopax (Calcium Borogluconate PMD) No. 6
PL 4134/4009 Astracalc (Calcium Borogluconate M) No. 7
PL 0123/4034 Calcibor C.B.G. 20% w/v
PL 0123/4035 Calcibor C.B.G. 40% w/v
PL 0123/4036 Calcibor C.M.P. 20
PL 0123/4037 Calcibor C.M.P. 30
PL 0123/4038 Calcibor C.M.P. 40
PL 0123/4039 Calcibor C.M.P. and D
PL 2324/4077 Calcium Borogluconate 30% and Magnesium
Hypophosphite 2·2% Solution CMP 30
PL 0829/4118 Calcium Borogluconate 40% with Magnesium and
Phosphorus
PL 2848/4018 Calcium Borogluconate Injection B Vet C 20%
PL 2848/4019 Calcium Borogluconate Injection B Vet C 30%
PL 2848/4020 Calcium Borogluconate Injection B Vet C 40%
PL 2324/4076 Calcium Borogluconate Solution CBG 20
PL 2324/4079 Glucose Saline Injection
PL 2324/4078 Injection of Calcium Borogluconate 40% and Magnesium
Hypophosphite 2·2% Solution CMP 40
PL 4134/4012 Novocalc
PL 1345/4007 TVL Calcium Borogluconate "Borocal"

8. Warble Fly Dressings

PL 0003/4115 Cooper Warble Fly Liquid
PL 0829/4127 Dermol
PL 0010/4045 Neguvon Spot-on

PL 0038/4062 { Orbisect Warble Fly Liquid
and Louse Liquid for Cattle
Orbisect Warble Fly Liquid

PL 0621/4017 Ruelene Ready to Use (New Formulation)
PL 0621/4013 Trolene FM
PL 0095/4024 Warbex 16·7% Famphur Pour-on
PL 4436/4000 Warbexol—Ready To Use Systemic Warble Fly Dressing
PL 1447/4059 Young's Concentrated Poron
PL 1447/4074 Young's New Poron
PL 1447/4077 Young's Poron 20

9. Liver Fluke Remedies

PL 1937/4012 Carbon Tetrachloride Capsules BPC
PL 0010/4031 Dirian
PL 0025/4036 { Flukanide Injection
             { Flukanide
PL 1826/4000 Hexol
PL 1826/4002 Osmond's Fluke Drench
PL 0002/4062 Valbazen 10% Drench
PL 3832/4025 Valbazen C10% Total Spectrum Wormer
PL 0002/4061 Valbazen 2·5% Suspension
PL 3832/4026 Valbazen SC 2·5% Total Spectrum Wormer
PL 1447/4066 Young's Nemtrem Cattle
PL 1447/4067 Young's Nemtrem Sheep
PL 1447/4065 Young's Flukol

10. Sheep and Cattle Clostridial Vaccines and Antisera

PL 1345/4062 Tasvax 8
PL 1345/4063 Nilvax

11. Poultry Vaccines

PL 1531/4001 Addervax ND Vaccine (Living) HB 1
PL 3359/4024 Avian Encephalomyelitis Vaccine Delvax AE
PL 1598/4001 Avian Encephalomyelitis Vaccine (Living) Calnek Strain
PL 1708/4133 Avian Encephalomyelitis Vaccine (Living) Nobilis
PL 3317/4086 Avivac-Avian Encephalomyelitis Vaccine (Live)
PL 1531/4009 Avivac-Infectious Bronchitis Vaccine H52 (Live)
              Massachusetts Strain (IB two)
PL 1531/4010 Avivac-Infectious Bronchitis Vaccine H120 (Live)
              Massachusetts Strain (IB one)
PL 1531/4008 Avivac-Newcastle Disease Vaccine (Live) Hitchner B1
              strain
PL 0002/4053 Bronchimune IB Vaccine
PL 0002/4034 Combimune
PL 1598/4029 Combined ND (HB1) and IB (Massachusetts MM)
              Vaccine (Living)
PL 1598/4028 Combined ND La Sota and IB Vaccine (Living)
PL 3359/4004 Delvax IB H52
PL 3359/4003 Delvax IB H120
PL 3350/4001 Delvax Marek THV Freeze-dried
PL 3359/4035 Delvax ND Hitchner
PL 3359/4006 Delvax ND La Sota
PL 3359/4005 Delvax ND HB1
PL 2592/4055 Eavax
PL 3317/4083 Fowl Laryngotracheitis Vaccine (Modified Live Virus)
PL 1598/4055 Fowl Pox Vaccine Poxine
PL 1598/4053 Fowl Pox Vaccine Poxinet
PL 1708/4139 Gumboro Disease Vaccine (Living) Nobilis

PL 4978/4004 Iblin Emulsion
PL 2592/4037 Ibvax
PL 0002/4003 IB Vaccine (Living) Massachusetts H120 Strain
PL 0002/4002 IB Vaccine (Living) Massachusetts H52 Strain
PL 1708/4135 Inactivated ND Vaccine (oil emulsion) Newcavac
                Nobilis
PL 1598/4056 Infectious Laryngotracheitis Vaccine (LT-VAC)
PL 2592/4074 Ivamarek Marek's Disease Vaccine
PL 2592/4044 Lentogen HB1
PL 2592/4043 Lentogen La Sota
PL 0086/4004 Marek's Disease Vaccine, Behringwerke
PL 0002/4001 Marek's Disease Vaccine (Living) THV (Marimune)
PL 3317/4085 Marek's Disease Vaccine (Live) THV
PL 1598/4026 Marek's Disease Vaccine MD-VAC (Living) THV
                (Witter Strain) Frozen (Wet)
PL 1598/4027 Marek's Disease Vaccine (Lyophilised) MD-VAC
PL 1708/4141 Marexine MD
PL 1708/4169 Marexine THV/CA
PL 4978/4005 Maternalin Emulsion
PL 4978/4003 Myxilin Emulsion
PL 2592/4033 Newcastle Disease Vaccine (Inactivated) Oil Emulsion
                (Layer Plus)
PL 0039/4040 ⎫
PL 4978/4002 ⎬ Newcadin Day Old
PL 3317/4087 Newcastle Disease Vaccine K2C (Inactivated)
PL 1708/4142 Newcastle Disease Vaccine (Living) Nobilis Clone 30
PL 3317/4086 Newcastle Disease Vaccine (Live) La Sota Strain
PL 1708/4150 Newcavac + EDS '76 Vaccine
PL 1598/4000 NDV (Living) La Sota
PL 0020/4000 ND Vaccine (Living) La Sota
PL 0039/4000 ⎫
PL 4978/4000 ⎬ ND Vaccine (Living) HB 1 Strain (Newcadin L)
PL 0039/4029 ⎫ ND Oil Adjuvant Vaccine (Inactivated) (Newcadin
PL 4978/4001 ⎭   Emulsion)
PL 3318/4000 ND Vaccine (Inactivated) Oil Emulsion
PL 1708/4143 Nobi-Vac Egg Drop Syndrome 76 Vaccine BC14
                (Inactivated)
PL 1708/4155 Nobi-Vac Gumboro Inactivated
PL 1596/4034 Poulvac AE
PL 1596/4040 Poulvac EDS
PL 1596/4029 Poulvac IB Vaccine H52 (Living)
PL 1596/4030 Poulvac IB Vaccine H120 (Living)
PL 1596/4025 Poulvac Marek THV
PL 1596/4026 Poulvac ND Vaccine (Living) HB 1
PL 1596/4027 Poulvac ND Vaccine (Living) La Sota
PL 0002/4005 Tremimune

12. Erysipelas Vaccines

PL 1345/4004 Swine Erysipelas Vaccine, Inactivated (Oil Adjuvant)
                Erysivax

13. Salmonella and E. coli Vaccines

PL 0003/4110 ⎧ Gletvac-Porcine E. coli Vaccine (Polyvalent)
             ⎨ Gletvac-Porcine E. coli Vaccine (Polyvalent) + K88
             ⎩ Gletvax K88-Porcine E. coli Vaccine (Polyvalent)

PL 0086/4113 Porcovac AT

14. Other Sheep and Cattle Vaccines

PL 0086/4132 Heptavac P
PL 0003/4135 Ovine Enzootic Abortion (Improved) Vaccine
PL 0086/4133 Ovipast
PL 0086/4129 Ovivac P
PL 1345/4003 TVL Scabivax

15. Miscellaneous Vaccines

PL 1708/4152 Nobi-Vac L.T. K88
PL 3317/4088 Pigeon Pox Vaccine (Live Virus-Chicken Embryo
              Origin)

16. Sulphanilamide Surface Wound Dressings

PL 2428/4002 Sulphonamide Wound and Navel Dressing Powder

17. Local Anaesthetics

PL 3317/4049 Lignavet Plus Injection
PL 2324/4074 Lignocaine Anaesthetic Injection
PL 2000/4029 Lignocaine and Adrenalin Injection
PL 1393/4107 Lignocaine Hydrochloride Injection BP 1973
PL 2428/4021 Lignocaine Injection
PL 1599/4005 Ruby Freezaject

18. Others

PL 4318/4002 Ashfer 100
PL 4134/4010 Astracalc (Glucose (Dextrose) 40%) No. 8
PL 4134/4011 Astracalc (Magnesium Sulphate 25%) No. 9
PL 2428/4026 Bactasorb Tablets
PL 0002/4043 Bloat Guard
PL 0002/4054 Bloat Guard Drench
PL 0002/4051 Bloat Guard Liquid
PL 4261/4000 Bovinyl
PL 2613/4000 Cheviot Veterinary Oil
PL 2545/4009 Codifer 10
PL 0676/4091 Colostrene-Watery Mouth Drench for Young Lambs
PL 3317/4010 Copavet
PL 2987/4003 Copper (Cupric) Carbonate
PL 1345/4012 Cujec
PL 2987/4002 Cupric Oxide
PL 2987/4001 Cuprous Chloride
PL 3656/4012 Dio-Iron
PL 1596/4031 Ducrofer
PL 1532/4026 Ferriphor
PL 3317/4041 Ferrofax 10
PL 0113/4006 Fisons Vitamin A, D & E Injection
PL 3026/4009 "Flex Flac" Pack for infusion 25% Dextrose Injection BP
PL 0113/4007 Gleptosil
PL 2323/4079 Glucose Saline Injection
PL 1708/4121 Haemalift
PL 0829/4117 { Iron Dextran 10% (Pharmacosmos)
               Tendex

PL 0025/4040 Ivomec Injection
PL 3058/4002 Iron Dextran Injection 100 mg/ml BVC (Ronidex)
PL 0043/4000 Leodex
PL 0043/4042 Leodex 20%
PL 0043/4036 Leodex Plus
PL 2000/4043 Magnesium Sulphate Injection 25% w/v
PL 4127/4000 Micro Anti-Bloat Premix
PL 2592/4059 Microdex
PL 0010/4006 Netrosylla
PL 0676/4090 Orfoids-Capsules for Orf
PL 0032/4060 Pegasus DE Mineral Mixture
PL 0032/4041 Pegasus Minerals JGW 343
PL 0032/4087 Pegasus OCU Mineral Mixture
PL 1345/4051 Permasel-C
PL 1345/4052 Permasel-S
PL 1345/4042 Permaco C
PL 1345/4041 Permaco S
PL 0295/4000 Poudre Armoricaine
PL 4134/4000 Proviton
PL 4262/4000 Quay-Iron
PL 0829/4140 Ripercol 5% Injectable Solution
PL 0829/4132 Ripercol 15% Injectable
PL 0829/4133 Ripercol 3·2% Oral
PL 1011/4001 Roscofer 10% Vet
PL 1011/4000 Roscoral Vet
PL 3317/4077 Sildex
PL 3317/4022 Super Suntax
PL 1599/4004 Swipoul
PL 0032/4039 Telmin Pellet JGW 343
PL 2868/4000 Vache Ointment
PL 2428/4000 Vetrion 200
PL 3317/4047 Vetrivite Plus
PL 0829/4121 Vital Multivitamin Solution
PL 0038/4060 Vitament Vitamin A, D_3 & E Injection
PL 1532/4020 Vitamin AD_3 E Oral
PL 3317/4069 Vitapol
PL 2969/4001 Vituramag
PL 2969/4005 Vituramol 60 with Romensin
PL 0038/4057 Whitmoyer V—Mix
PL 1447/4036 Young's Swaycop

Article 4   SCHEDULE 2
                                     PART A
                    LICENCE OF RIGHT VETERINARY DRUGS

Group/Class   Substance
1. GROWTH   Bacitracin Zinc
     PROMOTERS   Bambermycin
                              Nitrovin
                              Tylosin Phosphate
                              Virginiamycin

2. COCCIDIOSTATS   Amprolium hydrochloride
                              Clopidol
                              Decoquinate
                              Diaveridine
                              Dinitolmide
                              Ethopabate
                              Pyrimethamine
                              Robenidine

3. ANTI-BLACKHEAD   Acinitrazole
     PREPARATIONS   Aminonitrothiazole
                              Nifursol

4. ANTHELMINTICS   Haloxon
                              Mebendazole
                              Parbendazole
                              Phenothiazine
                              Piperazine Carbon Disulphide Complex
                              Tetramisole
                              Thiabendazole

5. OTHERS   Menaphthone Dimethyl Pyrimidinol Bisulphite
                              Menaphthone Sodium Bisulphite

Article 4   SCHEDULE 2
                                     PART B
                              VETERINARY DRUGS
Product Licence No.   Name of Product*
1. Growth Promoters
    PL 0095/4026 { Avotan 50 Avoparcin
                 { *Avotan 50*
    PL 0095/4028 Avotan 50c Avoparcin
    PL 3832/4031 Eskalin 100
    PL 0002/4045 Eskalin 500
    PL 0002/4055 Eskalin S400
    PL 0029/4102 Fedan 10% Premix
    PL 0086/4124 { Flavomycin 40
                 { Flavomycin 40 g/kg
    PL 4869/4000 Panazone 250 Nitrovin
    PL 0095/4007 Payzone 50 MA Nitrovin Milk Replacer Additive
    PL 4188/4008 Pentazone 250
    PL 2969/4006 Rumevite with Romensin
    PL 0006/4052 Romensin (Monensin Sodium) Premix
    PL 0006/4055 Tylamix Premix 100 g/kg

---

*Alternative product names used by specially authorised persons are not shown.

PL 0006/4062 Tylamix Premix 250 g/kg
PL 3405/4007 Tylosin 100 Premix
PL 3734/4000 Zinc Bacitracin Dumex Feed Grade
PL 3734/4001 Zinc Bacitracin "Dumex" 150 Premix
PL 0109/4001 Zinc Bacitracin Premix
PL 3405/4002 ZB100
PL 3405/4005 ZB150

2. Coccidiostats

PL 0025/4035 Arpocox
PL 0031/4011 Avatec Premix
PL 0012/4056 "Deccox" Pure
PL 0109/4000 Dinormix SR 25
PL 4188/4004 { Dinitolmide (DOT) 3·5-Dinitro-ortho-toluamide
　　　　　　　Unicox Pure
PL 0109/4002 DOT (dinitolmide)
PL 1598/4032 DOT Premix 12·5%
PL 1598/4033 DOT Premix 25%
PL 0006/4047 { Elancoban
　　　　　　　Elancoban Premix
PL 3405/4006 Elancoban Premix
PL 0621/4015 Lerbek
PL 0006/4061 Monteban 100 Premix
PL 0025/4019 Nicrazin (Premix)
PL 0025/4010 Pancoxin
PL 0086/4135 Sacox 60 Premix
PL 1598/4036 Salcostat
PL 0086/4117 Stenorol
PL 0025/4003 Supacox

3. Anti-Blackhead Preparations

4. Anthelmintics

PL 0010/4049 Bayverm Premix 0·6%
PL 0010/4050 Bayverm Premix 2·4%
PL 0829/4131 Flubenol Pellets
PL 0002/4004 Helmatac In-Feed Wormer
PL 0829/4113 Mebenvet (1·2%)
PL 0829/4123 Mebenvet (5%)
PL 0012/4149 { Nemafax 14
　　　　　　　Nemafax 5
　　　　　　　Nemafax Premix
PL 0012/4153 Nemafax Wettable Powder

5. Others

PL 0002/4043 Bloat Guard
PL 4127/4000 Micro Anti-Bloat Premix
PL 0032/4041 Pegasus Minerals JGW 343
PL 0032/4039 Telmin Pellet JGW 343
PL 2969/4005 Vituramol 60 with Romensin
PL 0038/4057 Whitmoyer V—Mix

Article 4   SCHEDULE 3

PART A

LICENCE OF RIGHT VETERINARY DRUGS

Aklomide
Ampicillin Trihydrate
Arsanilic Acid
Benzylpenicillin
Chlortetracycline
E. coli oral vaccine (Inactivated)
Erythromycin
Framycetin Sulphate
Furazolidone
4 hydroxy-3 nitrophenyl arsonic acid
Lincomycin Hydrochloride
Methyl Benzoquate
Nitrofurazone
Oxytetracycline
Procaine Penicillin
Sulphadimidine
Sulphanitran
Sulphaquinoxaline
Tylosin phosphate

Article 4   SCHEDULE 3

PART B

VETERINARY DRUGS

Product Licence No.   Name of Product*

PL 0006/4053 Apralan Soluble Powder
PL 0006/4057 Apralan 20 Premix
PL 0006/4058 Apralan 100 Premix
PL 4188/4002 { Chlortetracycline Feedgrade
               Auromix 100
PL 0095/4029 Cycostat 66R Robenidine Feed Additive
PL 0034/4031 Dynamutilin 2% Premix
PL 0006/4063 Elancoban for Turkeys and Replacement Chickens
PL 0012/4158 Emtrymore
PL 1596/4018 Engemycin 5% Soluble Powder
PL 0002/4071 'Eskalin' 500 POM for laying and breeding hens
PL 0057/4068 Fortigro S Premix
PL 1654/4012 Fortracin BMDᴿ
PL 3317/4031 Framomycin Soluble Powder 25%
PL 3317/4023 Framomycin Feed Additive
PL 3405/4012 Furazolidone BP
PL 0131/4002 Furazolidone BPC 68
PL 4188/4003 { Furazolidone BPC 68 or USNF 13
               Unidone
PL 3058/4000 Furazolidone NF BVC
PL 2592/4036 Furazolidone Premix

---

*Alternative product names used by specially authorised persons are not shown.

PL 0006/4050 Granulated Tylosin Concentrate
PL 1754/4000 Intagen
PL 0032/4084 Lincocin Premix
PL 2592/4065 Micro-Bio Sulphadimidine Premix
PL 0364/4003 Neftin Premix
PL 0364/4004 Neftin Supplement
PL 1598/4037 {
    Nifulidone Premix 11·6%
    Nifulidone Premix 22·4%
    Nifulidone Premix 44·8%
PL 4188/4001 Oxytetracycline HCI Feedgrade
PL 0034/4001 Quixalud Feed Additive
PL 0034/4026 Quixalud Premix 12%
PL 0025/4028 Ridzol 12% Premix
PL 1728/4041 Sermix
PL 1754/4002 Sow Intagen O/I
PL 0086/4120 Stenorol for Turkeys
PL 4219/4000 Sulphadimidine
PL 0057/4061 Terramycine Concentrate 20%
PL 0057/4031 Terramycine 5% Feed Supplement
PL 0057/4065 Terramycine 20% Feed Supplement
PL 0003/4105 Tribrissen Powder
PL 0006/4045 Tylan Premix 20 g/kg
PL 0006/4001 {
    Tylasul Premix Veterinary
    Tylasul Premix
PL 0006/4064 Tylasul Premix 100
PL 4188/4000 Unidim
PL 0131/4008 Unidim
PL 4188/4007 Unidim 100
PL 3317/4076 Vi-Mycin Soluble Powder
PL 0038/4037 Whitsyn 10

EXPLANATORY NOTE

(This Note is not part of the Order.)

This Order further amends the Medicines (Exemptions from Restrictions on the Retail Sale or Supply of Veterinary Drugs) Order 1979 by replacing all the Schedules to that Order with updated New Schedules. Certain items, which are shown in italics in the schedules to this Order, have been added to the Schedules to the 1979 Order, and certain other items contained in those Schedules have been deleted from the new Schedules.

STATUTORY INSTRUMENTS

1983 No. 1157

AGRICULTURE

AGRICULTURAL GRANTS, GOODS AND SERVICES

The Agricultural and Horticultural Co-operation (Variation) Scheme 1983

Laid before Parliament in draft

Made - - - - -	*28th July* 1983
Coming into Operation	*29th July* 1983

The Minister of Agriculture, Fisheries and Food, the Secretary of State for Scotland and the Secretary of State for Wales, acting jointly, in exercise of the powers conferred by sections 61 and 62 of the Agriculture Act 1967(a) and now vested in them(b) and of all other powers enabling them in that behalf, with the approval of the Treasury, hereby make the following scheme, a draft whereof has been laid before Parliament and approved by a resolution of each House of Parliament:—

Title, application and commencement

1. This scheme, which applies throughout the United Kingdom, may be cited as the Agricultural and Horticultural Co-operation (Variation) Scheme 1983, and shall come into operation on the day after the day on which it is made.

Variation of the Agricultural and Horticultural Co-operation Scheme 1971

2. The Agricultural and Horticultural Co-operation Scheme 1971(c) shall be further varied as follows:—

(1) In column 1 of the Schedule—

(*a*) the heading "BUILDINGS" immediately above item 1 shall be amended to read—

"BUILDINGS FOR PURPOSES OTHER THAN THE STORAGE OR DRYING OF GRAIN";

(*b*) the heading "FACILITIES" immediately above item 4 shall be amended to read—

"FACILITIES FOR PURPOSES OTHER THAN THE STORAGE OR DRYING OF GRAIN";

(a) 1967 c. 22.
(b) In the case of the Secretary of State for Wales, by virtue of S.I. 1978/272.
(c) S.I. 1971/415, previously varied by S.I. 1977/846 and 1980/1382.

(*c*) the heading "LAND IMPROVEMENT" immediately above item 7 shall be amended to read—

"LAND IMPROVEMENT FOR PURPOSES OTHER THAN THE STORAGE OR DRYING OF GRAIN";

(*d*) Item 13(iii) shall be deleted; and

(*e*) in item 17, for "paragraphs 1–16" there shall be substituted "items 1 to 16 inclusive, 23 and 24".

(2) Immediately after item 22 of the Schedule the following heading and items shall be inserted:

STORAGE OR DRYING OF GRAIN			
23. Any proposal of a kind described in item 1 or items 4 to 9 inclusive of this Schedule for the purposes of or in connection with the storage or drying of grain	$22\frac{1}{2}$	—	—
24. Supply and installation of new plant and equipment for grain storage	15	5	—

In Witness whereof the Official Seal of the Minister of Agriculture, Fisheries and Food is hereunto affixed on 27th July 1983.

Michael Jopling,
Minister of Agriculture,
Fisheries and Food.

George Younger,
Secretary of State for Scotland.

27th July 1983.

John Stradling Thomas,
Minister of State for Wales.

28th July 1983.

We approve,

T. Garel-Jones,
Ian B. Lang,
Two of the Lords Commissioners
of Her Majesty's Treasury.

28th July 1983.

EXPLANATORY NOTE

(This Note is not part of the Scheme.)

This scheme, which applies throughout the United Kingdom, varies for the third time the Agricultural and Horticultural Co-operation Scheme 1971, under which grants are paid towards the cost of carrying out approved proposals designed to promote co-operative activities in agriculture or horticulture.

The scheme affects the payment of grant towards expenditure incurred in connection with the provision, replacement or improvement of buildings, facilities or plant and equipment, or work done by way of land improvement, for the purposes of the storage or drying of grain. Upon the scheme's coming into operation the rate of grant is reduced from $32\frac{1}{2}$ per cent to $22\frac{1}{2}$ per cent in the case of buildings, facilities or land improvement, from 25 per cent to 15 per cent in the case of new plant and equipment installed on land not used for agriculture, and from 15 per cent to 5 per cent in the case of new plant and equipment installed on land used for agriculture.

1983 No. 1158

AGRICULTURE

The Sheep and Goats (Removal to Northern Ireland) Regulations 1983

Laid before Parliament in draft

Made - - - -	*28th July* 1983
Coming into Operation	*29th July* 1983

The Minister of Agriculture, Fisheries and Food and the Secretary of State, being Ministers designated(a) for the purposes of section 2(2) of the European Communities Act 1972(b) in relation to the common agricultural policy of the European Economic Community, acting jointly in exercise of the powers conferred upon them by the said section 2(2) and of all other powers enabling them in that behalf, hereby make the following regulations, of which a draft has been approved by resolution of each House of Parliament:—

Title and commencement

1. These regulations may be cited as the Sheep and Goats (Removal to Northern Ireland) Regulations 1983, and shall come into operation on the day after the day on which they are made.

Interpretation

2.—(1) In these regulations, unless the context otherwise requires—

"animal" means an animal of the ovine or caprine species;

"authorised officer" means, for any purpose referred to in these regulations, a person authorised to act for that purpose by the Board, or, in relation to Great Britain, by the Meat and Livestock Commission when acting for the Board, or, in relation to Northern Ireland, by the Department of Agriculture for Northern Ireland when so acting;

"the Board" means the Intervention Board for Agricultural Produce established under section 6 of the European Communities Act 1972;

"carcase" means the carcase of an animal (whether in whole or in part), fresh, chilled, frozen, salted in brine, dried or smoked;

(a) S.I. 1972/1811.
(b) 1972 c. 68.

"the Commission Regulation" means Commission Regulation (EEC) No. 2661/80(a) laying down detailed rules for applying the variable slaughter premium for sheep;

"the departure charge" means the amount to be charged on departure as referred to in Article 4.1 of the Commission Regulation;

"removal" means removal from a port in Great Britain to a port in Northern Ireland, and "remove" shall be construed accordingly;

"removal declaration" means a written declaration of intention to remove an animal or carcase, containing the particulars specified in Schedule 1;

"the security" means the security referred to in Article 4.2 of the Commission Regulation.

(2) In these regulations, unless the context otherwise requires, "qualified person" means—

(a) in relation to any part of the United Kingdom, an officer of the Board specially authorised for the purposes of these regulations by the Board;

(b) in relation to England, an officer of the Ministry of Agriculture, Fisheries and Food so authorised by the Minister of Agriculture, Fisheries and Food;

(c) in relation to Scotland, an officer of the Department of Agriculture and Fisheries for Scotland so authorised by the Secretary of State;

(d) in relation to Wales, an officer of the Secretary of State so authorised by the Secretary of State;

(e) in relation to Northern Ireland, an officer of the Department of Agriculture for Northern Ireland so authorised by that Department.

(3) In these regulations, unless the context otherwise requires, any reference to a numbered regulation or schedule is a reference to the regulation or schedule bearing that number in these regulations.

Removal of animals and carcases

3.—(1) No person shall remove, or attempt to remove, or cause or permit to be removed, any animal (other than a pure-bred breeding animal) or carcase unless, not less than three working days previously, he has delivered to the Board, or (in the case of the item referred to in sub-paragraph (a) of this paragraph) to an authorised officer, in respect of that animal or carcase—

(a) a removal declaration; and

(b) the security.

(2) No person shall remove, or attempt to remove, or cause or permit to be removed, any pure-bred breeding animal unless, not less than three working days previously, he has delivered to the Board or to an authorised officer in respect of that animal—

(a) a removal declaration; and

(a) O.J. No. L 276, 20.10.80, p.19, as amended by Commission Regulation (EEC) No. 1238/82, O.J. No. L 143, 20.5.82, p.10.

(b) a certificate or equivalent document issued by the appropriate breed society identifying that animal as a pure-bred specimen of its breed.

(3) The certificate or equivalent document referred to in sub-paragraph (2)(b) of this regulation shall not be required if the Board are otherwise satisfied that the animal is a pure-bred breeding animal.

(4) In this regulation "working day" means any day other than a Saturday or Sunday, Christmas Day, Good Friday or any other day which, in the part of Great Britain from which the animal or carcase is to be removed, is a bank holiday under section 1 of the Banking and Financial Dealings Act 1971(a).

Inspection of animals and carcases

4.—(1) Any person having possession, charge or control of any animal or carcase in respect of which a removal declaration has been delivered shall permit an authorised officer to inspect that animal or carcase and (except in the case of a pure-bred breeding animal) weigh the same at any reasonable time before removal.

(2) Any person having possession, charge or control of any such animal shall present it for the purposes of paragraph (1) of this regulation at such premises as the Board may direct.

Prohibition against removals other than from specified ports

5. No person shall remove, or attempt to remove, or cause or permit to be removed, any animal or carcase except from a port specified in Schedule 2.

Production of books, accounts and records

6. A qualified person who reasonably suspects that there has been a removal or attempted removal of an animal (other than a pure-bred breeding animal) or carcase in respect of which the security has not been delivered to the Board, may require any person (whether a principal, agent or employee) who has, or whom he reasonably believes has, bought, sold, transported or removed that animal or carcase to produce for inspection any books, accounts or records in his possession or control relating to transactions in or movements of animals or carcases; and that person shall comply with every such requirement made of him.

Power to prevent removal or detain

7. A qualified person who reasonably suspects that there has been a contravention of, or failure to comply with, regulation 3(1), 3(2), 4 or 5 may prevent the removal of, or detain, any animal or carcase until he is reasonably satisfied that—

(a) a removal declaration in respect thereof has been delivered to the Board or to an authorised officer and (except in the case of a pure-bred

---

(a) 1971 c. 80.

breeding animal) the security in respect thereof has been delivered to the Board; and

(b) the animal or carcase has been inspected and (except in the case of a pure-bred breeding animal) weighed by an authorised officer.

Powers of entry and to obtain evidence

8. A qualified person who reasonably suspects that there has been an offence under these regulations may, for the purpose of investigating such an offence—

(a) enter upon land on which animals or carcases are being held for the time being and inspect any animal or carcase found thereon;

(b) enter and examine the contents of any vehicle, vessel or aircraft which he reasonably suspects of being or having been used in connection with any such offence, or open and examine the contents of any container which he reasonably suspects of being or having been so used;

(c) take possession of, or take a copy of, or extract from, any book, account or record appearing to him to be material which is produced pursuant to regulation 6, or which is in the possession or control of a person whom he reasonably suspects is guilty of such an offence.

Warrants of qualified persons

9. A qualified person acting in exercise of the powers conferred by regulation 6, 7 or 8 shall carry a warrant of his authority so to act, and shall produce the same on demand.

Offences and penalties

10.—(1) If any person contravenes, or fails to comply with, any provision of regulation 3(1), he shall be guilty of an offence and liable on summary conviction to a fine not exceeding four hundred pounds.

(2) If any person contravenes, or fails to comply with, any provision of regulation 3(2), 4 or 5, he shall be guilty of an offence and liable on summary conviction to a fine not exceeding two hundred pounds.

(3) If any person—

(a) fails without reasonable cause to comply with a requirement made of him under regulation 6; or

(b) intentionally obstructs a qualified person in the exercise of any of the powers conferred upon him by regulation 6, 7 or 8;

he shall be guilty of an offence and liable on summary conviction to a fine not exceeding two hundred pounds.

(4) If any person knowingly or recklessly, for the purpose of avoiding in respect of any animal or carcase payment of the departure charge—

(a) signs or delivers, or causes to be signed or delivered, a removal declaration; or

(b) makes any statement;

which is untrue in any material respect, he shall be guilty of an offence and liable on summary conviction to a fine not exceeding one thousand pounds or to imprisonment for a term not exceeding three months or both, or on conviction on indictment to a fine or to imprisonment for a term not exceeding two years or both.

Offences by officers of bodies corporate

11.—(1) Where an offence under these regulations which has been committed by a body corporate is proved to have been committed with the consent or connivance of, or to be attributable to any neglect on the part of, any director, manager, secretary or other similar officer of the body corporate, or any person who was purporting to act in any such capacity, he as well as the body corporate shall be deemed to be guilty of that offence and shall be liable to be proceeded against and punished accordingly.

(2) Where the affairs of a body corporate are managed by its members, the provisions of paragraph (1) of this regulation shall apply in relation to the acts and defaults of a member in connection with his functions of management as if he were a director of the body corporate.

Defence

12. In any proceedings for an offence under regulation 10(1) or (2), it shall be a defence for the person charged to prove that he took all reasonable precautions and exercised all due diligence to avoid the commission of such an offence.

Recovery of departure charge

13. Any person who removes, or causes or permits or be removed, any animal (other than a pure-bred breeding animal) or carcase shall be liable to pay the departure charge to the Board on demand, and in the event of default in payment the departure charge shall be recoverable by the Board as a civil debt.

In Witness whereof the Official Seal of the Minister of Agriculture, Fisheries and Food is hereunto affixed on 27th July 1983.

Michael Jopling,
Minister of Agriculture, Fisheries and Food.

George Younger,
One of Her Majesty's Principal
Secretaries of State.

28th July 1983.

AGRICULTURE

Regulation 2(1) SCHEDULE 1

Particulars to be contained in removal declarations

1. The name, address and signature of the consignor of the animals or carcases to be removed.

2. The numbers, weights and descriptions, including full Common Customs Tariff headings, of the animals or carcases to be removed.

3. For animals, the address of the farm premises, and for carcases, the address of the slaughterhouse, from which they originate, if different from that of the consignor.

4. The names of the ports from and to which the animals or carcases are to be removed.

5. The expected date of the removal.

6. The name and address of the consignee of the animals or carcases.

7. The name and address of the haulage contractor by whom removal is to be effected.

Regulation 5 SCHEDULE 2

Ports through which removals of animals and carcases may take place.

Bristol.

Cairnryan.

Cardiff.

Fishguard.

Heysham.

Holyhead.

Liverpool.

Milford Haven.

Pembroke.

Silloth.

Stranraer.

EXPLANATORY NOTE

(This Note is not part of the Regulations.)

These regulations make provision for the protection of arrangements of the European Economic Community for the regulation of the market in sheepmeat and goatmeat. Under Article 9 of Council Regulation (EEC) No. 1837/80 on the common organisation of the market in sheepmeat and goatmeat (O.J. No. L 183, 16.7.1980, p.l), as amended by Council Regulation (EEC) No. 1195/82 (O.J. No. L 140, 20.5.1982, p.22), and implemented by Commission Regulation (EEC) No. 2661/80 laying down detailed rules for applying the variable slaughter premium for sheep (O.J. No. L 276, 20.10.80, p.19), as amended by Commission Regulation (EEC) No. 1238/82 (O.J. No. L 143, 20. 5.1982, p.10), an amount equivalent to the variable slaughter premium paid in Great Britain is to be charged on departure of live sheep and goats (other than pure–bred breeding animals), sheepmeat and goatmeat to Northern Ireland. Article 4.2 of Commission Regulation (EEC) No. 2661/80 (as amended by Article 1.5 of Commission Regulation (EEC) No. 1238/82) provides that on departure a security shall be lodged to cover the amount to be charged.

Under Article 5.3 of Commission Regulation (EEC) No. 2661/80 (as amended by Article 1.6 of Commission Regulation (EEC) No. 1238/80), the competent authorities in the United Kingdom must take all the necessary steps to prevent irregular movements of the products referred to in the first paragraph of this note.

In implementation of these provisions, regulation 3 of these regulations prohibits the removal or attempted removal of live sheep or goats, sheepmeat or goatmeat from Great Britain to Northern Ireland unless there have been lodged with the Intervention Board for Agricultural Produce a written declaration of intention to remove (containing the particulars specified in Schedule 1) and either, in the case of animals (other than pure-bred breeding animals) and meat, the security referred to in the first paragraph of this note, or, in the case of pure-bred breeding animals, evidence of pure-bred status.

Regulation 4 provides for inspection and weighing of animals and meat on behalf of the Intervention Board for Agricultural Produce. Regulation 5 prohibits removals other than from the ports specified in Schedule 2.

Regulations 6, 7 and 8 confer on "qualified persons" (who are defined in regulation 2(2) and must carry and produce warrants of their authority pursuant to regulation 9) power to require the production of documents, power to prevent the removal of, or detain, animals and meat, powers of entry and power to obtain evidence, when an offence under these regulations is reasonably suspected.

Regulations 10, 11 and 12 deal with offences and regulation 13 with recovery of the amount to be charged on departure, if payment of this is evaded.

STATUTORY INSTRUMENTS

1983 No. 1159

INDUSTRIAL TRAINING

The Industrial Training Levy (Road Transport) Order 1983

Made - - - - -	*29th July* 1983
Laid before Parliament	*2nd August* 1983
Coming into Operation	*23rd August* 1983

Whereas proposals made by the Road Transport Industry Training Board for the raising and collection of a levy have been submitted to, and approved by, the Manpower Services Commission under section 11(1) of the Industrial Training Act 1982(a) ("the 1982 Act") and have thereafter been submitted by the said Commission to the Secretary of State under that subsection;

And whereas in pursuance of section 11(3) of the 1982 Act the said proposals include provision for the exemption from the levy of employers who, in view of the small number of their employees, ought in the opinion of the Secretary of State to be exempted from it;

And whereas the Secretary of State is satisfied that proposals made in pursuance of section 11(4)(*b*) of the 1982 Act and falling within section 11(5)(*b*) of the said Act are necessary as mentioned in the said section 11(5) and the condition mentioned in section 11(6)(*a*) of the 1982 Act is satisfied;

Now, therefore, the Secretary of State in exercise of the powers conferred on him by sections 11(2), 12(3) and 12(4) of the 1982 Act and of all other powers enabling him in that behalf hereby makes the following Order:—

Citation and commencement
1. This Order may be cited as the Industrial Training Levy (Road Transport) Order 1983 and shall come into operation on 23rd August 1983.

(a) 1982 c. 10.

Interpretation

2.—(1) In this Order unless the context otherwise requires:—

(*a*) "assessment" means an assessment of an employer to the levy;

(*b*) "the Board" means the Road Transport Industry Training Board;

(*c*) "business" means any activities of industry or commerce;

(*d*) "employer" means a person who is an employer in the road transport industry at any time in the seventeenth levy period;

(*e*) "the industrial training order" means the Industrial Training (Road Transport Board) Order 1966**(a)**;

(*f*) "the levy" means the levy imposed by the Board in respect of the seventeenth levy period;

(*g*) "notice" means a notice in writing;

(*h*) "road transport establishment" means an establishment in Great Britain engaged in the seventeenth base period wholly or mainly in the road transport industry for a total of twenty-seven or more weeks or, being an establishment that commenced to carry on business in the seventeenth base period, for a total number of weeks exceeding one-half of the number of weeks in the part of the said period commencing with the day on which business was commenced and ending on the last day thereof;

(*i*) "the road transport industry" does not include any activities which have been transferred from the industry of the Board to the industry of another industrial training board by one of the transfer orders but save as aforesaid means any one or more of the activities which, subject to the provisions of paragraph 2 of Schedule 1 to the industrial training order, are specified in paragraph 1 of that Schedule as the activities of the road transport industry or, in relation to an establishment whose activities have been transferred to the industry of the Board by one of the transfer orders, any activities so transferred;

(*j*) "the seventeenth base period" means the period of twelve months that commenced on 6th April 1982;

(*k*) "the seventeenth levy period" means the period commencing with the day upon which this Order comes into operation and ending on 31st July 1984;

(*l*) "the transfer orders" means:—

　　(i) the Industrial Training (Transfer of the Activities of Establishments) (No. 2) Order 1974**(b)**,

　　(ii) the Industrial Training (Transfer of the Activities of Establishments) (No. 2) Order 1975**(c)**,

　　(iii) the Industrial Training (Transfer of the Activities of Establishments) Order 1976**(d)**.

(a) S.I. 1966/1112, amended by S.I. 1982/664.　　　　**(b)** S.I. 1974/1495.
(c) S.I. 1975/1157.　　　　**(d)** S.I. 1976/396.

    (iv) the Industrial Training (Transfer of the Activities of Establish-ments) (No. 3) Order 1976**(a)**,

    (v) the Industrial Training (Transfer of the Activities of Establish-ments) Order 1977**(b)**,

    (vi) the Industrial Training (Transfer of the Activities of Establish-ments) Order 1978**(c)**,

    (vii) the Industrial Training (Transfer of the Activities of Establish-ments) (No. 2) Order 1978**(d)**,

    (viii) the Industrial Training (Transfer of the Activities of Establish-ments) Order 1979**(e)**,

    (ix) the Industrial Training (Transfer of the Activities of Establish-ments) Order 1980**(f)**,

    (x) the Industrial Training (Transfer of the Activities of Establish-ments) (No. 2) Order 1980**(g)**, and

    (xi) the Industrial Training (Transfer of the Activities of Establish-ments) Order 1981**(h)**.

(2) Any reference in this Order to persons employed at or from a road transport establishment shall in any case where the employer is a company be construed as including a reference to any director of the company (or any person occupying the position of director by whatever name he is called) who devotes substantially the whole of his time to the service of the company.

(3) Any reference in this Order to an establishment that commences to carry on business or that ceases to carry on business shall not be taken to apply where the location of the establishment is changed but its business is continued wholly or mainly at or from the new location, or where the suspension of activities is of a temporary or seasonal nature.

Imposition of the levy
3. The levy to be imposed by the Board on employers in respect of the seventeenth levy period shall be assessed in accordance with the provisions of the Schedule to this Order.

Assessment notices
4.—(1) The Board shall serve an assessment notice on every employer assessed to the levy.

(2) The amount payable under an assessment notice shall be rounded down to the nearest £1.

(3) An assessment notice shall state the Board's address for the service of a notice of appeal or of an application for an extension of time for appealing.

(4) An assessment notice may be served on the person assessed to the levy either by delivering it to him personally or by leaving it, or sending it to him by post, at his last known address or place of business in the United Kingdom or, if that person is a corporation, by leaving it, or sending it by post to the corporation at such address or place of business or at its registered or principal office.

(a) S.I. 1976/2110.   **(b)** S.I. 1977/1951.   **(c)** S.I. 1978/448.
(d) S.I. 1978/1225.   **(e)** S.I. 1979/793.   **(f)** S.I. 1980/586.
(g) S.I. 1980/1753.   **(h)** S.I. 1981/1041.

Payment of levy

5.—(1) Subject to the provisions of this Article and of Articles 6 and 7, the amount of the levy payable under an assessment notice served by the Board shall be due and payable to the Board in two instalments, as follows:—

(*a*) the first instalment, being one quarter of the levy, shall be due and payable on 1st September 1983 or one month after the date of the assessment notice, whichever is the later;

(*b*) the second instalment, being the remainder of the levy, shall be due and payable on 1st December 1983 or one month after the date of the assessment notice, whichever is the later.

(2) The amount of an assessment shall not be recoverable by the Board until there has expired the time allowed for appealing against the assessment by Article 7(1) of this Order and any further period or periods of time that the Board or an industrial tribunal may have allowed for appealing under paragraph (2) or (3) of that Article or, where an appeal is brought, until the appeal is decided or withdrawn.

Withdrawal of assessment

6.—(1) The Board may, by a notice served on the person assessed to the levy in the same manner as an assessment notice, withdraw an assessment if that person has appealed against that assessment under the provisions of Article 7 of this Order and the appeal has not been entered in the Register of Appeals kept under the appropriate Regulations specified in paragraph (5) of that Article.

(2) The withdrawal of an assessment shall be without prejudice to the power of the Board to serve a further assessment notice on the employer.

Appeals

7.—(1) A person assessed to the levy may appeal to an industrial tribunal against the assessment within one month from the date of the service of the assessment notice or within any further periods or periods of time that may be allowed by the Board or an industrial tribunal under the following provisions of this Article.

(2) The Board by notice may for good cause allow a person assessed to the levy to appeal to an industrial tribunal against the assessment at any time within the period of four months from the date of the service of the assessment notice or within such further period or periods as the Board may allow before such time as may then be limited for appealing has expired.

(3) If the Board shall not allow an application for extension of time for appealing, an industrial tribunal shall upon application made to the tribunal by the person assessed to the levy have the like powers as the Board under the last foregoing paragraph.

(4) In the case of an assessment that has reference to an establishment that ceases to carry on business in the seventeenth levy period on any day after the date of the service of the assessment notice, the foregoing provisions of this Article shall have effect as if for the period of four months from the date of the service of the assessment notice mentioned in paragraph (2) of this Article there were substituted the period of six months from the date of the cessation of business.

(5) An appeal or an application to an industrial tribunal under this Article shall be made in accordance with the Industrial Tribunals (England and Wales) Regulations 1965(a) except where the assessment relates to persons employed at or from one or more establishments which are wholly in Scotland and to no other persons in which case the appeal or application shall be made in accordance with the Industrial Tribunals (Scotland) Regulations 1965(b).

(6) The powers of an industrial tribunal under paragraph (3) of this Article may be exercised by the President of the Industrial Tribunals (England and Wales) or by the President of the Industrial Tribunals (Scotland) as the case may be.

Evidence

8.—(1) Upon the discharge by a person assessed to the levy of his liability under an assessment the Board shall if so requested issue to him a certificate to that effect.

(2) The production in any proceedings of a document purporting to be certified by the Secretary of the Board to be a true copy of an assessment or other notice issued by the Board or purporting to be a certificate such as is mentioned in the foregoing paragraph of this Article shall, unless the contrary is proved, be sufficient evidence of the document and of the facts stated therein.

Signed by order of the Secretary of State.

Peter Morrison,
Minister of State,
Department of Employment.

29th July 1983.

(a) S.I. 1965/1101; relevant amending instruments are S.I. 1967/301, 1977/1473.
(b) S.I. 1965/1157; relevant amending instruments are S.I. 1967/302, 1977/1474.

SCHEDULE   Article 3

1.—(1) In this Schedule unless the context otherwise requires—

(a) "emoluments" means all emoluments assessable to income tax under Schedule E (other than pensions), being emoluments from which tax under that Schedule is deductible, whether or not tax in fact falls to be deducted from any particular payment thereof;

(b) "the relevant date" means the 5th April 1983;

(c) "the relevant establishment" means the road transport establishment of an employer other than one which is an establishment of an employer who is exempted by virtue of paragraph 3 of this Schedule;

(d) other expressions have the meanings assigned to them respectively by paragraph 3 or 4 of the Schedule to the industrial training order or by Article 2 of this Order.

(2) For the purposes of this Schedule no regard shall be had to the emoluments of any person employed as follows:—

(a) wholly in agriculture;

(b) **wholly as a registered dock worker on dock work; or**

(c) wholly in the supply of food or drink for immediate consumption.

2. Subject to the provisions of this Schedule, the levy shall be assessed by the Board in respect of each employer and the amount thereof shall be equal to 0·8 per cent. of the sum of the emoluments of all the persons employed by the employer in the seventeenth base period at or from the relevant establishment or establishments.

3. There shall be exempt from the levy an employer—

(a) in whose case the sum of the emoluments of all the persons employed by him in the seventeenth base period at or from his road transport establishment or establishments (whether or not any such establishment is a relevant establishment) is £21,000 or less (£24,500 or less in the case of an employer wholly or mainly engaged on the relevant date in any of the activities comprised in Group 1 of the Appendix to this Schedule, or £36,000 or less in the case of an employer wholly or mainly engaged on the relevant date in any of the activities comprised in Group 2 of the said Appendix);

(b) who was wholly or mainly engaged on the relevant date in giving instruction by way of business in the driving of heavy goods vehicles.

4. Where any persons whose emoluments are taken into account for the purpose of the preceding paragraphs of this Schedule were employed at or from an establishment that ceases to carry on business in the seventeenth levy period, the sum of the emoluments of those persons shall, for the purposes only of paragraph 2 above, be reduced in the same proportion as the number of days between the commencement of the said levy period and the date of cessation of business (both dates inclusive) bears to the number of days in the said levy period.

APPENDIX

Column 1	Column 2
Group No.	*Description of Activities*
1.	Dealing (not being selling by retail) in components, replacements, spare parts or accessories (not being tyres) for motor vehicles or goods vehicles; and the removal of furniture by way of business.
2.	The letting out on hire (without the services of the drivers) of motor vehicles for the conveyance of eight passengers or less.

EXPLANATORY NOTE

(This Note is not part of the Order.)

This Order, which comes into operation on 23rd August 1983 gives effect to proposals of the Road Transport Industry Training Board which were submitted to and approved by the Manpower Services Commission, and thereafter submitted by the Manpower Services Commission to the Secretary of State. The proposals are for the imposition of a levy on employers in the road transport industry for the purpose of raising money towards meeting the expenses of the Board.

The levy is to be imposed in respect of the seventeenth levy period commencing with the day upon which this Order comes into operation and ending on 31st July 1984. The levy will be assessed by the Board and there will be a right of appeal against an assessment to an industrial tribunal.

STATUTORY INSTRUMENTS

1983 No. 1160

TERMS AND CONDITIONS OF EMPLOYMENT

The Redundancy Payments (Local Government) (Modification) Order 1983

Laid before Parliament in draft

Made - - - - - - *28th July* 1983

Coming into Operation on the fourteenth day after the day on which it is made

Whereas a draft of the following Order was laid before Parliament in accordance with section 149(4) of the Employment Protection (Consolidation) Act 1978(**a**) and approved by resolution of each House of Parliament:

Now, therefore, the Secretary of State in exercise of the powers conferred on him by sections 149(1)(b) and 154(3) of the 1978 Act and of all other powers enabling him in that behalf hereby makes the following Order:

Citation, commencement and interpretation

1.—(1) This Order may be cited as the Redundancy Payments (Local Government) (Modification) Order 1983 and shall come into operation on the fourteenth day after the day on which it is made.

(2) In this Order, unless the context otherwise requires—

(a) "relevant event" means any event occurring on or after the coming into operation of this Order on the happening of which an employee may become entitled to a redundancy payment in accordance with the provisions of the 1978 Act;

(b) "the 1978 Act" means the Employment Protection (Consolidation) Act 1978.

Application of order

2. This Order applies to any person who immediately before the occurrence of the relevant event is employed by an employer described in Schedule 1 to this Order, for the purposes of determining that person's entitlement to a redundancy payment under the 1978 Act and the amount of such payment.

(**a**) 1978 c. 44.

Application of certain redundancy payments provisions with modifications

3. In relation to any person to whom this Order applies the provisions of the 1978 Act mentioned in Schedule 2 to this Order shall have effect subject to the modifications specified in that Schedule.

Transitional, supplementary and incidental provisions

4.—(1) Any reference to the 1978 Act in any enactment shall have effect as a reference to that Act as modified by this Order in relation to persons to whom this Order applies.

(2) Any document which refers, whether specifically or by means of a general description, to an enactment which is modified by any provision of this Order shall, except so far as the context otherwise requires, be construed as referring or as including a reference, to that provision.

(3) Where a period of employment of a person to whom this Order applies falls to be computed in accordance with the provisions of the 1978 Act as modified by this Order, the provisions of this Order shall have effect in relation to any period whether falling wholly or partly before or after the coming into operation of this Order.

28th July 1983.

N. B. Tebbit,
Secretary of State for Employment.

Article 2   SCHEDULE 1

EMPLOYMENT TO WHICH THIS ORDER APPLIES: EMPLOYERS IMMEDIATELY BEFORE
THE RELEVANT EVENT.

1. A county council, the Greater London Council, a district council, a London borough council, the Common Council of the City of London, the Council of the Isles of Scilly.

2. A regional council, islands council or district council established by or under the Local Government (Scotland) Act 1973(**a**).

3. A joint board or joint body constituted by or under any enactment for the purpose of exercising the functions of two or more bodies described in paragraph 1 or 2 above, and any special planning board within the meaning of paragraph 3 of Schedule 17 to the Local Government Act 1972(**b**).

4. Any other authority or body, not specified in paragraph 1, 2 or 3 above, established by or under any enactment for the purpose of exercising the functions of, or advising, one or more of the bodies specified in paragraph 1, 2 or 3 above.

5. Any committee (including a joint committee) established by or under any enactment for the purpose of exercising the functions of, or advising, one or more of the bodies specified in paragraph 1, 2, 3 or 4 above.

6. Any two or more bodies described in paragraph 1, 2, 3, 4 or 5 above acting jointly or as a combined authority.

7. Any association which is representative of any two or more authorities described in paragraph 1 or 2 above.

8. Any committee established by one or more of the associations described in paragraph 7 above for the purpose of exercising the functions of, or advising, one or more of such associations.

9. An association which is representative of one or more of the associations described in paragraph 7 above and of another body or other bodies, and included in whose objects is the assembling and dissemination of information and advising with regard to conditions of service generally and in local government service.

10. An organisation which is representative of an association or associations described in paragraph 7 above and employees' organisations and among

---

(**a**) 1973 c. 65.   (**b**) 1972 c. 70.

whose objects is the negotiation of pay and conditions of service in local government service.

11. The Local Government Training Board.

12. A probation committee within the meaning of the Criminal Justice Act 1982(**a**).

13. A magistrates' courts committee or the Committee of Magistrates for the Inner London Area, within the meaning of the Justices of the Peace Act 1979(**b**).

14. The Commission for the New Towns.

15. The Housing Corporation.

16. A development corporation within the meaning of the New Towns Act 1981(**c**).

17. A development corporation established under section 2 of the New Towns (Scotland) Act 1968(**d**).

18. A Passenger Transport Executive established under section 9(1) of the Transport Act 1968(**e**).

19. An Urban Development Corporation established under section 135 of the Local Government Planning and Land Act 1980(**f**).

20. The English Industrial Estates Corporation established by section 8 of the Local Employment Act 1960(**g**).

21. The Welsh Development Agency.

22. The Development Board for Rural Wales.

(**a**) 1982 c. 48.   (**b**) 1979 c. 55.   (**c**) 1981 c. 64.
(**d**) 1968 c. 16.   (**e**) 1968 c. 73.   (**f**) 1980 c. 65.
(**g**) 1960 c. 18.

23. The Scottish Development Agency.

24. The Scottish Special Housing Association.

25. A fire authority constituted by a combination scheme, or in Scotland an administration scheme, made under the Fire Services Act 1947(**a**).

26. A police authority, other than the Secretary of State, or a combined police authority within the meaning of the Police Act 1964(**b**) or the Police (Scotland) Act 1967(**c**), as amended by section 146 of the Local Government (Scotland) Act 1973(**d**).

27. The Central Scotland Water Development Board.

28. A river purification board established under section 135 of the Local Government (Scotland) Act 1973.

29. The governing body of a further education establishment for the time being mainly dependent for its maintenance on assistance from local education authorities, on grants under section 100(1)(b) of the Education Act 1944(**e**) or on such assistance and grants taken together.

30. The governing body of a voluntary school (within the meaning of section 9(2) of the Education Act 1944).

31. The proprietors (within the meaning of section 114(1) of the Education Act 1944) of a school for the time being recognised as a grammer school for the purposes of Regulation 4(1) of the Direct Grant Schools Regulations 1959(**f**), being a school—

    (a) in relation to which, before 1st January 1976, the Secretary of State was satisfied as mentioned in Regulation 3(1) of the Direct Grant Grammar Schools (Cessation of Grant) Regulations 1975(**g**), and

    (b) In the case of which grants are paid under the said Regulations of 1959 for the educational year (within the meaning of those Regulations) within which the relevant event falls either—

        (i) in respect of pupils admitted in that year, or

        (ii) if, on or after the coming into operation of this Order, Regulation

---

(**a**) 1947 c. 41.   (**b**) 1964 c. 48.   (**c**) 1967 c. 77.
(**d**) 1973 c. 65.   (**e**) 1944 c. 31.
(**f**) S.I. 1959/1832; relevant modifications are made by S.I. 1975/1198.
(**g**) S.I. 1975/1198; the relevant amending instrument is S.I. 1981/1788.

5 of the said Regulations of 1975 applies to the school by virtue of paragraph (3) thereof, in respect of any pupils.

32. The managers of a grant-aided school as defined in section 135(1) of the Education (Scotland) Act 1980(**a**).

33. The governing body of a central institution as defined in section 135(1) of the Education (Scotland) Act 1980 other than a college of agriculture.

34. The governing body of a College of Education as defined in section 135(1) of the Education (Scotland) Act 1980.

35. The managers of a school which immediately before the commencement of Part III of the Social Work (Scotland) Act 1968(**b**) was approved under section 83 of the Children and Young Persons (Scotland) Act 1937(**c**) if that approval remains in force at the date of termination of employment.

36. A local valuation panel established under the General Rate Act 1967(**d**).

37. The Sports Council.

38. The Sports Council for Wales.

39. The Scottish Sports Council.

40. The Forth Road Bridge Joint Board.

41. The Tay Road Bridge Joint Board.

42. The Commission for Local Administration in England.

43. The Commission for Local Administration in Wales.

44. The Commissioner for Local Administration in Scotland.

45. The Commission for Local Authority Accounts in Scotland.

46. The Land Authority for Wales.

(**a**) 1980 c. 44.   (**b**) 1968 c. 49.   (**c**) 1937 c. 37.
(**d**) 1967 c. 9.

Article 3 SCHEDULE 2

MODIFICATIONS TO CERTAIN REDUNDANCY PAYMENTS PROVISIONS OF THE 1978 ACT

1. Section 81 of the 1978 Act shall have effect as if:—

(a) in subsection (1) for the words "has been continuously employed for the requisite period" there were substituted the words "has been employed in relevant local government service for the requisite period" and for the words "Schedules 4, 13 and 14" there were substituted the words "Schedule 4, as modified by the Redundancy Payments (Local Government) (Modification) Order 1983, and Schedules 13 and 14";

(b) after subsection (4) there were inserted the following subsection:—

"(5) In this section and Schedule 4—

(a) "relevant local government service" means—

(i) continuous employment by an employer referred to in the Appendix to Schedule 2 to the Redundancy Payments (Local Government) (Modification) Order 1983, or

(ii) where immediately before the relevant event a person has been successively employed by two or more employers referred to in the Appendix to Schedule 2 to the said Order, such aggregate period of service with such employers as would be continuous employment if they were a single employer;

(b) "relevant event" means any event occurring on or after the coming into operation of the Redundancy Payments (Local Government) (Modification) Order 1983 on the happening of which an employee may become entitled to a redundancy payment in accordance with this Act."

2. Section 82 of the 1978 Act shall have effect as if immediately after subsection (7) there were inserted:—

"(7A) Any reference in this section to re-engagement by the employer shall be construed as including a reference to re-engagement by any employer referred to in the Appendix to Schedule 2 to the Redundancy Payments (Local Government) (Modification) Order 1983 and any reference in this section to an offer by the employer shall be construed as including a reference to an offer made by any such employer."

3. Section 84 of the 1978 Act shall have effect as if immediately after subsection (7) thereof there were inserted the following subsection:—

"(7A) Any reference in this section to re-engagement by the employer shall be construed as including a reference to re-engagement by any employer referred to in the Appendix to Schedule 2 to the Redundancy Payments (Local Government) (Modification) Order 1983 and any reference in this section to an offer made by the employer shall be construed as including a reference to an offer made by any such employer."

4. Section 94(6) of the 1978 Act shall have effect as if for the words "Section 82(7) and 84(7)" there were substituted the words "Sections 82(7), 82(7A), 84(7) and 84(7A)."

5. Schedule 4 to the 1978 Act shall have effect as if for paragraph 1 there were substituted the following paragraph:—

"1. The amount of a redundancy payment to which an employee is entitled in any case to which the Redundancy Payments (Local Government) (Modification) Order 1983 applies shall, subject to the following provisions of this Schedule, be calculated by reference to the period ending with the relevant date during which he has been employed in relevant local government service."

6. Schedule 6 to the 1978 Act shall have effect as if in paragraph 1 for the words "Schedule 4" there were substituted the words "Schedule 4 as modified by the Redundancy Payments (Local Government) (Modification) Order 1983".

APPENDIX

Employers with which Employment may constitute Relevant Local Government Service

1. Any employer described in Schedule 1 whether or not in existence at the time of the relevant event.

2. The council of an administrative county, county borough, metropolitan borough or county district.

3. The council of a county, county of a city, large burgh, small burgh or district ceasing to exist after 15 May 1975.

4. Any joint board or joint body constituted by or under any enactment for the purpose of exercising the functions of two or more of the bodies described in paragraph 2 or 3 above.

5. Any other body, not specified in paragraph 2, 3 or 4 above, established by or under any enactment for the purpose of exercising the functions of, or advising, one or more of the bodies specified in paragraph 2, 3 or 4 above.

6. Any committee (including a joint committee) established by or under any enactment for the purpose of exercising the functions of, or advising, one or more of the bodies described in paragraph 2, 3, 4 or 5 above.

7. Any two or more bodies described in paragraph 2, 3, 4, 5 or 6 above acting jointly or as a combined authority.

8. Any association which was representative of any two or more bodies described in paragraph 2 or 3 above.

9. Any committee established by one or more of the associations described in paragraph 8 above for the purpose of exercising the functions of, or advising, one or more of such associations.

10. An organisation which was representative of an association or association described in paragraph 8 above and employees' organisations and among whose objects was to negotiate pay and conditions of service in local government service.

11. A local valuation panel constituted under the Local Government Act 1948(**a**).

12. A previous police authority for which Schedule 11 to the Police Act 1964 had effect or which was the police authority for an area or district which was before 1st April 1947 or after 31 March 1946 a separate police area or, in Scotland, a previous police authority for an area which was before 16 May 1975 a separate or combined police area.

13. The proprietors (within the meaning of section 114(1) of the Education Act 1944) of a school not falling within paragraph 31 of Schedule I which throughout the period of employment was recognised as a grammar school or, as the case may be, as a direct grant grammar school for the purposes of Regulation 4(1) of the Direct Grant Schools Regulations 1959, of Part IV of the Schools Grant Regulations 1951(**b**) or of Part IV of the Primary and Secondary Schools (Grant Conditions) Regulations 1945(**c**).

14. The managers of a school which during the period of employment was approved under section 83 of the Children and Young Persons (Scotland) Act 1937.

15. The managers of a school which during the period of employment was a grant-aided school within the meaning of section 143(1) of the Education (Scotland) Act 1946(**d**), section 145(22) of the Education (Scotland) Act 1962(**e**) or section 135(1) of the Education (Scotland) Act 1980.

(**a**) 1948 c. 26.   (**b**) S.I. 1951/1743.   (**c**) S.R.&O. 1945/636.
(**d**) 1946 c. 72.   (**e**) 1962 c. 47.

16. The Secretary of State for Defence in relation only to employees in schools administered by the Service Children's Education Authority.

17. A regional water board established under section 5 of the Water (Scotland) Act 1967(**a**).

18. A river purification board established under section 2 of the Rivers (Prevention of Pollution) (Scotland) Act 1951(**b**).

19. The Scottish Industrial Estates Corporation (formerly the Industrial Estates Management Corporation for Scotland) established by section 8 of the Local Employment Act 1960.

20. The Welsh Industrial Estates Corporation (formerly the Industrial Estates Management Corporation for Wales) established by section 8 of the Local Employment Act 1960.

21. The Small Industries Council for Rural Areas of Scotland, being a company which was registered under the Companies Act and dissolved by section 15(5) of the Scottish Development Agency Act 1975(**c**).

22. A person or body of persons responsible for the management of an assisted community home within the meaning of section 36 of the Children and Young Persons Act 1969(**d**) or of an approved institution within the meaning of section 46 of that Act.

23. A development Corporation within the meaning of the New Towns Act 1946(**e**) or the New Towns Act 1965(**f**).

(**a**) 1967 c. 78.   (**b**) 1951 c. 66.   (**c**) 1975 c. 69.
(**d**) 1969 c. 54.   (**e**) 1946 c. 68.   (**f**) 1965 c. 59.

EXPLANATORY NOTE
(This Note is not part of the Order.)

This Order, which comes into operation on the fourteenth day after the day on which it is made, modifies certain redundancy payments provisions of the Employment Protection (Consolidation) Act 1978 in their application to persons employed in relevant local government service (service with the employers referred to in the Appendix to Schedule 2 to the Order) so that their employment in the service is to be treated as if it was continuous for the purposes of those provisions.

STATUTORY INSTRUMENTS

1983 No. 1164

PENSIONS

The Personal Injuries (Civilians) Amendment Scheme 1983

Made - - - -	*27th July* 1983
Laid before Parliament	*4th August* 1983
Coming into Operation	*21st November* 1983

The Secretary of State for Social Services, with the consent of the Treasury, in exercise of the powers conferred by section 2 of the Personal Injuries (Emergency Provisions) Act 1939 (a) and now vested in him (b), and of all other powers enabling him in that behalf, hereby makes the following Scheme:—

Citation, commencement and interpretation

1.—(1) This Scheme may be cited as the Personal Injuries (Civilians) Amendment Scheme 1983 and shall come into operation on 21st November 1983.

(2) In this Scheme the expression "the principal Scheme" means the Personal Injuries (Civilians) Scheme 1983 (c).

(3) In relation to any award under the principal Scheme which is payable weekly and to which any provision of this Scheme relates, the foregoing reference to 21st November 1983 shall, where that date is not the normal weekly pay day for that award, be construed as a reference to the date of the first weekly pay day for that award immediately following 21st November 1983.

Amendment of Article 18 of the principal Scheme

2. For the amount "£1040" in paragraph (2) of Article 18 of the principal Scheme (earnings allowed in relation to unemployability allowances) there shall be substituted the amount "£1170".

Insertion of new Article in the principal Scheme

3. In Part III of the principal Scheme (awards in respect of disablement of gainfully occupied persons and civil defence volunteers) after Article 25 there shall be inserted the following new Article:—

"Mobility supplement

25A.—(1) Subject to the provisions of this Article a mobility supplement may be awarded at the rate specified in paragraph 14 of Schedule 3 to a

(a) 1939 c.82.
(b) *See* Transfer of Functions (Ministry of Pensions) Order 1953 (S.I. 1953/1198), Article 2; Ministry of Social Security Act 1966 (c.20), section 2; Secretary of State for Social Services Order 1968 (S.I. 1968/1699), Article 2.
(c) S.I. 1983/686.

person in receipt of a pension under Article 11 in respect of—

(a) disablement as a result of the amputation of both legs, at least one of which has been amputated either through or at a point above the knee; or

(b) disablement due to any other injury which is, and is likely to remain for at least 12 months from the date on which the question of eligibility for a supplement under this Article is considered by the Secretary of State (either at first instance or on review), wholly or mainly responsible for—

    (i) rendering him unable to walk, or

    (ii) restricting his leg movements to such an extent that his ability to walk without severe discomfort is of little or no practical use to him, or

    (iii) rendering the exertion required to walk a danger to his life or a likely cause of serious deterioration in his health; or

(c) disablement by reason of which, immediately prior to the date on which the question of his eligibility for a supplement under this Article is first considered by the Secretary of State, he—

    (i) has had the use of an invalid carriage or other vehicle provided by the Secretary of State under section 5(2) of, and Schedule 2 to, the National Health Service Act 1977 (**a**) or section 46 of the National Health Service (Scotland) Act 1978 (**b**), or by the Department of Health and Social Services for Northern Ireland under Article 30 of the Health and Personal Social Services (Northern Ireland) Order 1972 (**c**), which is a vehicle propelled by petrol engine or by electric power for use on the road and to be controlled by the occupant, or

    (ii) has received any payment by way of grant under the said section 5(2) and Schedule 2 or the said section 46 or the said Article 30 towards the cost of running a private car, or any payment out of public funds which the Secretary of State is satisfied is analogous thereto, or

    (iii) has been in receipt of a mobility allowance under section 37A of the Social Security Act 1975 (**d**) or section 37A of the Social Security (Northern Ireland) Act 1975 (**e**) having been deemed, by virtue of section 13 of the Social Security (Miscellaneous Provisions) Act 1977 (**f**) or, as the case may be, Article 10 of the Social Security (Miscellaneous Provisions) (Northern Ireland) Order 1977 (**g**), to be suffering from such disablement as is mentioned in subsection (1) of that section 37A and to satisfy the requirements of subsection (2)*(a)* of that section.

(2) In determining for the purposes of paragraph (1)*(b)* (i) and (ii) the extent of a person's walking ability regard shall be had to his ability to walk with a suitable prosthesis or artificial aid which he habitually wears or uses, or which he might reasonably be expected to wear or use.

(**a**) 1977 c.49.
(**b**) 1978 c.29.
(**c**) S.I. 1972/1265 (N.I. 14), as amended by section 40 of, and paragraph 8 of Schedule 5 to, the Northern Ireland Constitution Act 1973 (c.36).
(**d**) 1975 c.14; section 37A was inserted by section 22(1) of the Social Security Pensions Act 1975 (c.60), and amended by section 3 of the Social Security Act 1979 (c.18).
(**e**) 1975 c.15 (N.I.); section 37A was inserted by Article 24 of the Social Security Pensions (Northern Ireland) Order 1975 (S.I. 1975/1503 (N.I. 15)).
(**f**) 1977 c.5.
(**g**) S.I. 1977/610 (N.I. 11).

(3) A mobility supplement under this Article shall not be payable to a person for any period in respect of which he—

(a) has the use of an invalid carriage or other vehicle provided under any of the statutory provisions referred to in paragraph (1)*(c)*; or

(b) is in receipt of a mobility allowance under section 37A of the Social Security Act 1975 or section 37A of the Social Security (Northern Ireland) Act 1975."

Substitution of Schedules 3 and 4 to the principal Scheme

4. For Schedules 3 and 4 to the principal Scheme (rates of pensions and allowances payable in respect of disablement and death) there shall respectively be substituted the Schedules set out in the Schedule hereto and numbered 3 and 4.

Signed by authority of the Secretary of State for Social Services.

Glenarthur,
Parliamentary Under-Secretary of State,
Department of Health and Social Security.

26th July 1983.

We consent,

T. Garel-Jones,
Ian B. Lang,
Two of the Lords Commissioners of
Her Majesty's Treasury.

27th July 1983.

Article 4

SCHEDULE

Schedules to be substituted in the principal Scheme

"SCHEDULE 3

RATES OF PENSIONS AND ALLOWANCES PAYABLE
IN RESPECT OF DISABLEMENT

Description of Pension or Allowance	*Rate*
1. Pension for 100 per cent. disablement under Article 11 ..	£55.60 per week
2. Education allowance under Article 13	£120 per annum*
3. Constant attendance allowance—	
(a) under the proviso to Article 14	£44.60 per week*
(b) in any other case under that Article	£22.30 per week*
4. Exceptionally severe disablement allowance under Article 15	£22.30 per week
5. Severe disablement occupational allowance under Article 16	£11.15 per week
6. Allowance for wear and tear of clothing—	
(a) under Article 17(1)(a)	£48 per annum
(b) under Article 17(1)(b) and 17(2)	£75 per annum
7. Unemployability allowances—	
(a) personal allowance under Article 18(1)(i)	£36.15 per week
(b) additional allowances for dependants by way of—	
(i) increase of allowance in respect of a wife or a dependent husband under Article 18(5)(b) ..	£20.45 per week*
(ii) allowance in respect of an adult dependant under Article 18(5)(c)	£20.45 per week*
(iii) increase of allowance in respect of each child under Article 18(5)(d)	£7.60 per week
8. Invalidity allowance payable under Article 19	
(a) if—	
(i) the relevant date fell before 5th July 1948; or	
(ii) on the relevant date the disabled person was under the age of 35; or	£7.15 per week
(iii) on the relevant date the disabled person was under the age of 40 and had not attained the age of 65, in the case of the disabled person being a man, or 60, in the case of that person being a woman, before 6th April 1979 and the period in respect of which payment of the allowance is to relate begins on or after 6th April 1979	

Description of Pension or Allowance	Rate
(b) if—	
(i) on the relevant date the disabled person was under the age of 45; or	
(ii) on the relevant date the disabled person was under the age of 50 and had not attained the age of 65, in the case of the disabled person being a man, or 60, in the case of that person being a woman, before 6th April 1979 and the period in respect of which payment of the allowance is to relate begins on or after 6th April 1979	£4.60 per week
(c) if heads (a) and (b) do not apply and on the relevant date the disabled person was a man under the age of 60 or a woman under the age of 55	£2.30 per week
9. Comforts allowance—	
(a) under Article 20(1)(a)	£9.60 per week
(b) under Article 20(1)(b) or 45(1)	£4.80 per week
10. Allowance for lowered standard of occupation under Article 21	£22.24 per week*
11. Age allowance under Article 22 where the degree of pensioned disablement is—	
(a) 40 or 50 per cent.	£3.85 per week
(b) 60 or 70 per cent.	£6.05 per week
(c) 80 or 90 per cent.	£8.65 per week
(d) 100 per cent.	£12.10 per week
12. Treatment allowances—	
increase of personal allowance under Article 23(2) ..	£12.10 per week*
13. Part-time treatment allowance under Article 25 ..	£21 per day*
14. Mobility supplement under Article 25A	£21.15 per week

*Maximum

SCHEDULE 4

RATES OF PENSIONS AND ALLOWANCES PAYABLE
IN RESPECT OF DEATH

Description of Pension or Allowance	Rate
1. Pension to widow—	
(a) under Article 27(1)	£44.25 per week
(b) under Article 27(2)	£10.22 per week
2. Rent allowance under Article 28	£16.85 per week*
3. Allowance under Article 29 or 50 to an elderly widow—	
(a) if age 65 but under age 70	£4.30 per week
(b) if age 70 or over..	£8.60 per week
4. Pension under Article 30 to unmarried dependant who lived as wife..	£1.00 per week*
5. Pension to dependent widower under Article 32	£44.25 per week*
6. Allowances under Article 33 in respect of each child under the age of 15	£10.95 per week
7. Pensions under Article 34(1) to motherless or fatherless children under the age of 15	£11.90 per week
8. Pension or allowance under Article 35(3) to or in respect of a child over the age of 15—	
(a) where the child has attained the age of 18 and is incapable of self-support by reason of an infirmity which arose before he attained the age of 15	£34.05 per week*
(b) any other case	£11.90 per week*
9. Education allowance under Article 36	£120 per annum*
10. Pensions to parents—	
(a) minimum rate under Article 38(4)	£0.25 per week
(b) maximum rate under Article 38(4)—	
(i) where there is only one eligible parent	£1.00 per week
(ii) where there is more than one eligible parent	£1.38 per week
(c) increase under the proviso to Article 38(4)—	
(i) where there is only one eligible parent	£0.38 per week*
(ii) where there is more than one eligible parent	£0.62 per week*
11. Pensions to other dependants—	
(a) for each juvenile dependant under Article 39(4)	£0.30 per week*
(b) aggregate rate under Article 39(4)..	£1.00 per week*
(c) under Article 39(5)	£1.00 per week*
12. Funeral Grant under Article 40(1) ..	£30.00*"

*Maximum.

EXPLANATORY NOTE

(This Note is not part of the Scheme.)

This Scheme amends the Personal Injuries (Civilians) Scheme 1983 ("the principal Scheme").

The Scheme inserts in the principal Scheme a new Article 25A to make provision for a mobility supplement to be payable to certain persons who are in receipt of a pension in respect of disablement under Article 11 of the principal Scheme.

The Scheme also raises the maximum amount of annual earnings which may be received by a disabled person while he is deemed to be unemployable for the purposes of unemployability allowances under Article 18 of the principal Scheme and varies the rates of pensions and allowances in respect of disablement and death in the 1939/45 War. In the Schedule to be substituted for Schedule 3 to the principal Scheme, which sets out the rates of pensions and allowances payable in respect of disablement, the rate for mobility supplement is inserted.

STATUTORY INSTRUMENTS

1983 No. 1165

NATIONAL HEALTH SERVICE, ENGLAND AND WALES

The National Health Service (Charges for Drugs and Appliances) Amendment (No. 2) Regulations 1983

Made - - - - -	*28th July* 1983
Laid before Parliament	*8th August* 1983
Coming into Operation	*1st September* 1983

The Secretary of State for Social Services, in exercise of powers conferred by section 77(1) of and paragraph 1(2) of Schedule 12 to the National Health Service Act 1977(a) and of all other powers enabling him in that behalf, hereby makes the following regulations:—

Citation and commencement

1. These regulations may be cited as the National Health Service (Charges for Drugs and Appliances) Amendment (No. 2) Regulations 1983 and shall come into operation on 1st September 1983.

Amendment of regulation 4(1) of the National Health Service (Charges for Drugs and Appliances) Regulations 1980

2. In regulation 4(1) of the National Health Service (Charges for Drugs and Appliances) Regulations 1980(b) (supply of drugs and appliances by doctors), for the words "not being a supply needed for immediate treatment of that patient before a supply can be obtained otherwise" there are substituted the words "being neither a supply needed for immediate treatment of that patient before a supply can be obtained otherwise nor a drug or appliance which that doctor personally administers or, as the case may require, applies to that patient".

Signed by authority of the Secretary of State for Social Services.

K. Clarke,
Minister of State,
Department of Health and Social Security.

28th July 1983.

(a) 1977 c. 49.
(b) S.I. 1980/1503; relevant amending instruments are S.I. 1982/289, 1983/306.

EXPLANATORY NOTE

(This Note is not part of the Regulations.)

These regulations amend regulation 4 of the National Health Service (Charges for Drugs and Appliances) Regulations 1980 by adding to the cases where the provision for a doctor to make and recover from a patient a charge for supplying drugs or appliances does not apply, the case where the doctor personally administers or applies to the patient the drug or appliance supplied.

STATUTORY INSTRUMENTS

1983 No. 1166

HOVERCRAFT

The Hovercraft (Fees) Regulations 1983

Made - - - -	*28th July* 1983
Coming into Operation	*2nd September* 1983

The Secretary of State, in exercise of powers conferred on him by article 35 of the Hovercraft (General) Order 1972(**a**) and of all other powers enabling him in that behalf, and with the approval of the Treasury, hereby makes the following Regulations:

Citation and Commencement

1. The Regulations may be cited as the Hovercraft (Fees) Regulations 1983 and shall come into operation on 2nd September 1983.

Interpretation and Revocation

2.—(1) In these Regulations, unless the context otherwise requires—

"costs of making any investigation" means any costs incurred by the CAA in making an investigation;

"hoverplatform" means a hovercraft with no installed means of propulsion or directional control and where any external agency providing propulsion or directional control is not itself a hovercraft;

"item" means an engine, propeller, fan, instrument, component, radio apparatus or equipment;

"maximum weight of the hovercraft" means the maximum total weight specified in the relevant application;

"the Order" means the Hovercraft (General) Order 1972;

"the weight of the type of hovercraft" means the maximum permissible weight specified in the Type Certificate.

(2) The Hovercraft (Fees) Regulations 1981(**b**) and the Hovercraft (Fees) (Amendment) Regulations 1982(**c**) are hereby revoked.

3. The provisions of the Schedule to these Regulations shall have effect with

---

(**a**) S.I. 1972/674.
(**b**) S.I. 1981/396.
(**c**) S.I. 1982/361.

respect to the fees to be paid in connection with the Certificates and other documents and with tests, inspections, investigations, permissions and approvals, required by or for the purposes of the Order.

4. For the purposes of these Regulations a variation of a document incorporated by reference in a Certificate shall be treated as variation of the Certificate itself.

David Mitchell,
Parliamentary Under-Secretary of State,
25th July 1983. Department of Transport.

We approve the making of these Regulations.

T. Garel Jones,
Donald Thompson,
Two of the Lords Commissioners of
28th July 1983. Her Majesty's Treasury.

THE SCHEDULE

Certificate of registration

1. The fee to be paid for the issue of a certificate of registration pursuant to Article 5(7) of the Order shall be £13.

Experimental Certificate

2. Where an application is made for the issue, variation, or renewal of an Experimental Certificate in respect of a hovercraft there shall be paid for any investigations required by the CAA in pursuance of Article 9 of the Order, a fee of an amount equal to the cost of making the investigations:

Provided that the fee shall not exceed, for the first period of 6 months or part thereof required for carrying out the investigations, £13,500 or 27p per kg. of the maximum weight of the hovercraft, whichever is the greater amount, and thereafter pro rata for every month or part thereof.

Type Certificates for types of hovercraft

3. Where an application is made for the issue or variation of a Type Certificate in respect of a type of hovercraft, there shall be paid, for any investigations required by the CAA in pursuance of Article 10 of the Order, a fee of an amount equal to the cost of making the investigations:

Provided that

(a) the fee shall not exceed, for the first period of 12 months or part thereof required for carrying out the investigations £32,500 or 65p per kg. of the maximum weight of the hovercraft, whichever is the greater amount, and thereafter pro rata for every month or part thereof;

(b) the cost of the investigations shall not include the cost of investigating any items for which the CAA requires separate type approval;

(c) the cost of the investigations shall not include the cost of any inspection of a craft which also serves as evidence leading to the first issue of a Safety Certificate for that craft.

Type Certificates for items

4. Where an application is made for the issue or variation of a Type Certificate in respect of a type of item, there shall be paid for any investigations required by the CAA in pursuance of Article 10 of the Order, a fee of an amount equal to the cost of making the investigations:

Provided that the fee shall not exceed, for the first period of 12 months or part thereof required for carrying out the investigations, £16,000 and thereafter pro rata for every month or part thereof.

Safety Certificates (Issue)

5.—(1) Where an application is made for the issue of a Safety Certificate, in pursuance of Article 11 of the Order, in respect of a hovercraft which has been used solely in accordance with the conditions of an Experimental Certificate issued by the CAA, the fee to be paid in respect thereof (including any investigations undertaken by the CAA in connection with the application) shall be, for each month or part thereof for which the Safety Certificate is to be in force, on the following scale:—

Maximum weight of the Hovercraft	Fee per tonne or part thereof
For the first 10 tonnes	£5.50
For the next 10 tonnes	£4.10
For the next 10 tonnes	£2.70
For the next 10 tonnes	£1.35
For any excess over 40 tonnes	90p

plus in each case an amount equal to the fee for an additional 3 months.

(2) Where an application is made for the issue of a Safety Certificate, in pursuance of Article 11 of the Order, in respect of a hovercraft which has not been used solely in accordance with the conditions of an Experimental Certificate issued by the CAA, the fee to be paid in respect thereof shall be in accordance with the scale of sub-paragraph (1) of this paragraph together with a fee equal to the cost of any additional investigations deemed necessary in the circumstances by the CAA:

Provided that the total fee shall not exceed £16,000 or 32p per kg. of the maximum weight of the hovercraft, whichever is the greater amount, for the first period of 12 months or part thereof.

Safety Certificates (Renewal)

6.—(1) Where an application is made for the renewal of a Safety Certificate in pursuance of Article 12 of the Order in respect of a hovercraft, within a period of 7 days from the date of expiry of the previous Certificate and where there has been no change in the conditions affecting maintenance during that period, the fee to be paid in respect thereof (including any investigations undertaken by the CAA in connection with the application) shall be, for each month, or part thereof, for which the Certificate is to be renewed, on the following scale:—

Maximum weight of the Hovercraft	Fee per tonne or part thereof
For the first 10 tonnes	£5.50
For the next 10 tonnes	£4.10
For the next 10 tonnes	£2.70
For the next 10 tonnes	£1.35
For any excess over 40 tonnes	90p

(2) Where an application for the renewal of a Safety Certificate is not in accordance with the conditions of sub-paragraph (1) of this paragraph or where the storage of the hovercraft has not been in accordance with arrangements having prior CAA approval, the fee to be paid shall be that specified in the

scale of sub-paragraph (1) together with the cost of any additional investigations deemed necessary by the CAA:

Provided that the total fee shall not exceed for the first period of 12 months or part thereof £16,000 or 32p per kg. of the maximum weight of the hovercraft, whichever is the greater amount.

Variation of Safety Certificates

7. Where an application is made for the variation of a Safety Certificate there shall be paid for the investigations required by the CAA a fee equal to the cost of making the investigations:

Provided that the fee shall not exceed for any period of 12 months, or part thereof, required for carrying out the investigations £32,500 or 65p per kg. of the maximum weight of the hovercraft, whichever is the greater amount, and thereafter pro rata for every month or part of a month.

Approval of Persons

8.—(1) Subject to sub-paragraph (2) of this paragraph, the fee to be paid per annum by a person for the inspection of his organisation for the purposes of Article 14 of the Order shall, for each branch of the organisation which is separately inspected, be in accordance with the following tables—

A: HOVERCRAFT (EXCLUDING HOVERPLATFORMS)

TABLE 1: Design and construction

Purpose of approval	Fee per tonne of maximum weight of hovercraft for which approval is applied for and granted	Minimum Fee
Either or both of the following: Design and construction of hovercraft	£2.80	£84

TABLE 2: Maintenance, overhaul and repair

Purpose of approval	Fee per tonne of the weight of the type of hovercraft having the greatest weight of any types of hovercraft for which approval is applied for and granted	Minimum Fee
Any or all of the following: *Maintenance, overhaul and repair of hovercraft	£1.40	£42

*1. No fee is payable under Table 2 by an organisation or branch approved for the purposes of construction in respect of approval for the purpose of maintenance, overhaul or repair of hovercraft constructed by that organisation as the case may be.

2. For approval for the purposes of maintenance, overhaul or repair of hovercraft of which the applicant is the sole operator a fixed fee of £42 will be charged in place of any fees which might otherwise be payable in accordance with Tables 2, 4 or 5.

B: ENGINES, PROPELLERS AND FANS

TABLE 3: Design and manufacture

Purpose of approval	Fee per maximum shaft h.p. of engine, propeller or fan for which approval is applied for and granted	Minimum Fee
Any or all of the following: Design and manufacture of engines, propellers or fans	14p	£84

TABLE 4: Maintenance, overhaul and repair

Purpose of approval	Fee per shaft h.p. of the type of engine, propeller or fan having the greatest shaft h.p. of a type of engine propeller or fan for which approval is applied for and granted	Minimum Fee
Any or all of the following: †Maintenance, overhaul and repair of engines propellers or fans	7p	£42

C: OTHER ITEMS

TABLE 5

Purpose of approval	Fee
Any or all of the following: Manufacture and design of items not referred to in Table 3 ... ... Maintenance, overhaul and repair of such items	£84 £42

TABLE 6

Purpose of approval	Fee
Design and construction of hover-platforms	An amount equal to the cost of inspection of his organisation: Provided that the fee shall not exceed £2,750

(2) In the application of sub-paragraph (1) of this paragraph:

    (a) Where a fee would otherwise be payable in respect of an organisation or branch under Table 1, and also under Tables 3 or 5 or both, a fee shall only be payable in accordance with Table 1.

---

† No fee is payable under Table 4 by an organisation or branch approved for the purpose of manufacture in respect of approval for the purpose of maintenance, overhaul or repair of engines, propellers or fans manufactured by that organisation or branch as the case may be.

　　　(b) Where a fee would otherwise be payable in respect of an organisation or branch under Table 2, and also under Tables 4 or 5 or both, a fee shall only be payable in accordance with Table 2.

　　　(c) Where a fee would be payable in respect of a branch or organisation under Table 3, and also under Table 5, a fee shall only be payable in accordance with Table 3.

　　　(d) Where a fee would be payable in respect of a branch or organisation under Table 4, and also under Table 5, a fee shall only be payable in accordance with Table 4.

Maintenance

　　9.—(1)*(a)* Where an operator's organisation is not approved for maintenance, there shall be paid for any visits of inspection pursuant to Article 13 of the Order in excess of one per month made by the CAA to the said operator, a fee equal to the cost of making such visits:

Provided that such fee in no case exceed £275 per visit.

　　　(b) Where the said unapproved operator obtains for the purpose of maintenance either goods or services or both from an organisation which is not approved by the CAA for such purpose, there shall be paid by the operator for any visits of inspection made to the suppliers of such goods or services or both, a fee equal to the cost of making such visits:

Provided that

　　　　　　(i) a total of one visit per month to the said operator or such suppliers shall not be subject to charges;

　　　　　　(ii) such fee shall in no case exceed £275 per visit.

　　(2) In this paragraph the term "maintenance" shall be deemed to include the installation of a modification covered by a variation of a document incorporated by reference in a Type Certificate.

　　(3) In sub-paragraph (1) above "visits of inspection" means visits made to an organisation for the purpose of investigating and approving maintenance arrangements. A visit shall be any visit of twenty-four hours or less.

Operating Permits

　　10.—(1) The fees to be paid for the issue of an Operating Permit pursuant to Article 18(2) of the Order shall be determined by the amount of work involved (including any investigations carried out preparatory to the issue of the Permit) charged at an hourly rate of £36.95 for each type of hovercraft.

　　(2) The fee to be paid for amending, at the request of the operator:

　　　(a) the area of operation of a type of hovercraft specified in an existing Operating Permit,

　　　(b) a condition under which an existing Operating Permit has been issued other than that referred to in *(a)* above,

shall also be determined by the amount of work involved (including any investigations carried out preparatory to the amendment of the Permit) charged at an hourly rate of £36.95.

(3) Notwithstanding sub-paragraph (1) of this paragraph, no fee shall be payable for the issue of an Operating Permit in respect of hovercraft of a type and operating in an area specified in a permit to fly issued to the applicant pursuant to Article 7 of the Air Navigation Order 1980(a) or having effect as if made thereunder.

Payment of Fees

11.—(1) The fees specified in paragraphs 1 and 10 of this Schedule shall be payable to the Secretary of State; and the fees specified in paragraphs 2 to 9 shall be payable to the CAA.

(2) The fees specified in these Regulations shall be payable upon application being made for the certificate, other document or approval, as the case may be:

Provided that where the amount of the fee depends on the actual costs incurred by the CAA—

(i) they may require that the application shall be accompanied by payment of an amount up to 5 per cent. of the maximum of such fee;

(ii) the fee in respect of the investigations made during any month shall be payable at the end of that month, and any amount paid on application shall be deducted from the fee payable at the end of the final month of investigations.

EXPLANATORY NOTE
(This Note is not part of the Regulations.)

These Regulations revoke the Hovercraft (Fees) Regulations 1981 as amended.

These regulations prescribe an increase of 10.8% in the fees to be paid to the Secretary of State for the issue or amendment of operating permits for hovercraft and an average increase of 9.8% in the fees to be paid to the Civil Aviation Authority for the issue of Type and Safety Certificates, and other matters under Part II (Certification and Maintenance) of the Hovercraft (General) Order 1972.

(a) S.I. 1980/1965, amended by S.I. 1982/161.

STATUTORY INSTRUMENTS

1983 No. 1167

MERCHANT SHIPPING

The Merchant Shipping (Fees) Regulations 1983

Made - - - -	*28th July* 1983
Laid before Parliament	*12th August* 1983
Coming into Operation	*2nd September* 1983

ARRANGEMENT OF REGULATIONS

SCHEDULE

The Secretary of State, in exercise of powers conferred by section 5(3) of the Merchant Shipping Act 1948(a), section 33 of the Merchant Shipping (Safety Convention) Act 1949(b) as extended by section 2(4) of the Merchant Shipping Act 1964(c), section 26 of the Merchant Shipping (Load Lines) Act 1967(d), section 6 of the Fishing Vessels (Safety Provisions) Act 1970(e), section 84 of the Merchant Shipping Act 1970(f), section 17 of and Schedule 5 to the Merchant Shipping Act 1974(g) and section 21(1) and (3)*(r)* of the Merchant Shipping Act 1979(h) and now vested in him(i), and of all other powers enabling him in that behalf, and with the consent and approval of the Treasury (except in respect of the powers conferred by the Acts of 1948 and 1974) hereby makes the following Regulations:—

Citation and commencement

1. These Regulations may be cited as the Merchant Shipping (Fees) Regulations 1983 and shall come into operation on 2nd September 1983.

Interpretation

2.—(1) In these Regulations:—

"the Act of 1948" means the Merchant Shipping Act 1948;

"the Act of 1949" means the Merchant Shipping (Safety Convention) Act 1949;

"the Act of 1967" means the Merchant Shipping (Load Lines) Act 1967;

"the Act of 1970" means the Merchant Shipping Act 1970;

"the Act of 1974" means the Merchant Shipping Act 1974;

"the Act of 1979" means the Merchant Shipping Act 1979;

"the principal Act" means the Merchant Shipping Act 1894(j);

"tons" means gross tons and the gross tonnage of a ship having alternative gross tonnages shall be taken to be the larger of those tonnages.

(2) Nothing in these Regulations shall apply to any service started before the date on which these Regulations come into operation, and as respects any such service the fee payable shall be that applicable at the time of starting the service.

(3) The fees set out in the Schedule to these Regulations shall apply in respect of any service started on or after the date on which these Regulations come into operation if it is completed within 12 months of starting the service.

(a) 1948 c. 44.
(b) 1949 c. 43.
(c) 1964 c. 47, amended by S.I. 1980/539.
(d) 1967 c. 27.
(e) 1970 c. 27.
(f) 1970 c. 36.
(g) 1974 c. 43.
(h) 1979 c. 39.
(i) *See* S.I. 1970/1537.
(j) 1894 c. 60.

(4) In respect of any service referred to in (3) above not completed within that 12 months' period, the fees set out in the Schedule to these Regulations shall be increased by $1\frac{1}{2}$ per cent. for each month or part of a month by which the completion date falls outside the 12 months' period.

Revocation

3. The following Regulations are hereby revoked:—

The Merchant Shipping (Fees) Regulations 1982(**a**);

The Merchant Shipping (Fees) (Amendment) Regulations 1982(**b**).

Payment of fees

4.—(1) The fees, or maximum fees as the case may be, payable for the services specified in the Schedule to these Regulations shall be the fees, or maximum fees, specified in relation thereto in that Schedule and are payable under the enactments so specified.

(2) The fee in the case of a survey or periodical inspection for the issue, renewal or endorsement of a certificate shall cover the issue or endorsement of that certificate.

Tom King,
Secretary of State for Transport.

26th July 1983.

We consent to and approve the making of these Regulations.

T. Garel Jones,
Donald Thompson,
Two of the Lords Commissioners
of Her Majesty's Treasury.

28th July 1983.

(**a**) S.I. 1982/355.
(**b**) S.I. 1982/864.

SCHEDULE

In Parts I to V of this Schedule:—

"Class" in relation to a ship means the Class of that ship as determined by the construction rules for the time being in force made under section 1 of the Act of 1949 or the construction regulations for the time being in force made under section 21 of the Act of 1979;

"overall length" in relation to a ship means the distance between the foreside of the foremost fixed permanent structure and the aftside of the aftermost fixed permanent structure;

"passenger certificate" means a passenger steamer's certificate issued under section 274 of the principal Act;

"safety certificate" means a safety certificate for the purposes of the Act of 1949 and includes a qualified safety certificate together with a corresponding exemption certificate;

"safety equipment certificate" includes a qualified safety equipment certificate together with a corresponding exemption certificate.

PART I: PASSENGER SHIPS

FEES FOR PASSENGER CERTIFICATES AND SAFETY CERTIFICATES

1. The fees prescribed in this Part are payable under the following enactments:—

for passenger certificates—section 277 of the principal Act(a);

for safety certificates—section 33(1) of the Act of 1949.

2. All such fees shall be determined by the amount of work involved, charged at an hourly rate of £36.95 subject to the following maxima:

(1) The survey of a ship (not being a ship to which sub-paragraph (2) refers) for the issue of a passenger certificate, a safety certificate or a passenger certificate combined with a safety certificate

---

(a) As amended by section 33(2) of the Act of 1949.

(1) Gross tonnage of ship where the ship		(2)	(3)
exceeds (tons):	**does not exceed (tons):**	**Initial Survey (Maximum fee)**	**Renewal Survey (Maximum fee)**
	25 tons or, if unregistered, 15 metres (49.2 feet) in overall length	£ 2,382	£280
25	50		
50	50 tons or, if unregistered, 15 metres (49.2 feet) in overall length	£ 5,983	£500
50	100		
100	200	£11,634	
	30,000		£500 plus an additional £221.60 for each 500 tons or part thereof by which the ship exceeds 100 tons
200	10,000	£11,634 plus an additional £1,662 for each 100 tons or part thereof by which the ship exceeds 200 tons no maximum	
10,000			
30,000			£13,800 plus an additional £130 for each 1,000 tons or part thereof by which the ship exceeds 30,000 tons

Service	*Maximum fee*
(2)—(a) The initial survey of a ship of Class I, II or IIA carrying not more than 36 passengers, for the issue of a certificate specified in sub-paragraph (1)	60% of the appropriate maximum fee in sub-paragraph (1)
(b) The survey of a ship of Class I, II or IIA carrying not more than 36 passengers, for the renewal of a certificate specified in sub-paragraph (1)	80% of the appropriate maximum fee in sub-paragraph (1)
(3) The survey of a ship for the issue of a passenger certificate, safety certificate, or a passenger certificate combined with a safety certificate, being in each case a certificate granted exceptionally to cover a period of not more than 3 months commencing with the expiration date of an existing certificate	25% of the appropriate maximum fee in sub-paragraph (1)

Service	*Maximum Fee*

(4) The issue of a passenger certificate, a safety certificate, or a passenger certificate combined with a safety certificate and including a survey where necessary, being in each case a certificate issued in substitution for an existing certificate of the same kind, for the purpose of effecting any one of the following changes:—

changing the plying limits;

giving additional plying limits;

decreasing the number of passengers the ship may carry;

increasing the number of passengers the ship may carry;

any other change (not being a change in ownership or a change of the ship's name) 　　　　　£163 for each category of change effected.

(5) The survey for a passenger certificate issued in respect of a passenger ship not registered in the United Kingdom stating only the number of passengers the ship may carry:—

for the first 200, or fraction of 200, passengers	£382
for every additional 200, or fraction of 200, passengers	£294

PART II: CARGO SHIPS

FEES FOR CARGO SHIPS SAFETY CONSTRUCTION SURVEYS AND CERTIFICATION

1. The fees prescribed in this Part are payable under section 33 of the Act of 1949, as extended by section 2(4) of the Merchant Shipping Act 1964(a), and under section 21(3)*(r)* of the Act of 1979.

2. The standard fee payable in respect of a service described in paragraph 8 below shall, subject to paragraph 3 below, be the fee therein specified which is appropriate to the tonnage of the ship in relation to which the service is carried out.

3. The standard fee described in paragraph 2 shall be adjusted in accordance with the provisions of paragraphs 5 to 7 of this Part.

4. In this Part "Certifying Authority" means a body which is a Certifying Authority for the purposes of the construction rules for the time being in force made under section 2 of the Act of 1964 or, as the case may be, for the purposes of the Merchant Shipping (Cargo Ship Construction and Survey) Regulations 1981(b).

Service

5. Where a surveyor appointed by a Certifying Authority other than the Department of Transport carries out concurrently with a survey for classification purposes a survey for the issue or renewal of a Cargo Ship Safety Construction Certificate or an intermediate survey, £166 shall be payable under this Part.

(a) As amended by S.I. 1980/539.
(b) S.I. 1981/572.

6. Where a Department of Transport surveyor carries out a survey of a ship for the issue of a Cargo Ship Safety Construction Certificate which is to remain in force for a period not exceeding three months, and the ship is one in respect of which there is or has within the period of 12 months preceding the survey been in force a passenger certificate, a safety certificate, or a passenger certificate combined with a safety certificate, the fee payable for such survey shall be as follows:—

(1) if the survey is carried out before or within one
month after the expiry of the certificate   £355

(2) if the survey is carried out more than one month
but within 12 months after the expiry of the
certificate   £710

7. Where a Department of Transport surveyor carries out a survey of a ship to which the Merchant Shipping (Cargo Ship Construction and Survey) Regulations 1981 apply before a survey for the issue or renewal of a Cargo Ship Safety Construction Certificate or an intermediate survey, there shall be paid, in addition to the fee payable under paragraph 8(1), (2) or (3), as the case may be, an additional fee which will be determined by the amount of work involved, charged at an hourly rate of £36.95.

8. The fees for the following services shall be determined by the amount of work involved, charged at an hourly rate of £36.95 subject to the following maxima.

Service	*Maximum Fee*
(1) The survey of a ship for the issue of an initial Cargo Ship Safety Construction Certificate, where the ship:	
(a) is 500 tons or over but does not exceed 600 tons	£7,202
(b) exceeds 600 tons but does not exceed 30,000 tons	£7,202 plus an additional £1,994.40 for each 500 tons or part thereof by which the ship exceeds 600 tons
(c) exceeds 30,000 tons	£124,875 plus an additional £1,785 for each 1,000 tons or part thereof by which the ship exceeds 30,000 tons
(2) The survey of a ship for the renewal of a Cargo Ship Safety Construction Certificate, where the ship:	
(a) is 500 tons or over but does not exceed 1,000 tons	£1,440
(b) exceeds 1,000 tons but does not exceed 30,000 tons	£1,440 plus an additional £122 for each 500 tons or part thereof by which the ship exceeds 1,000 tons
(c) exceeds 30,000 tons	£8,516 plus an additional £111 for each 1,000 tons or part thereof by which the ship exceeds 30,000 tons
(3) The intermediate survey of a ship during the period of validity of a Cargo Ship Safety Construction Certificate, where the ship:	

Service	*Maximum Fee*
(a) is 500 tons or over but does not exceed 1,000 tons	£388
(b) exceeds 1,000 tons but does not exceed 30,000 tons	£388 plus an additional £33.24 for each 500 tons or part thereof by which the ship exceeds 1,000 tons
(c) exceeds 30,000 tons	£2,316 plus an additional £27.70 for each 1,000 tons or part thereof by which the ship exceeds 30,000 tons

(4) The annual survey of a ship during the period of validity of a Cargo Ship Safety Construction Certificate, where the ship:

(a) is 500 tons or over but does not exceed 1,000 tons	£240
(b) exceeds 1,000 tons but does not exceed 30,000 tons	£240 plus an additional £27.70 for each 500 tons or part thereof by which the ship exceeds 1,000 tons
(c) exceeds 30,000 tons	£1,847 plus an additional £27.70 for each 1,000 tons or part thereof by which the ship exceeds 30,000 tons.

PART III: RADIO

FEES FOR RADIO CERTIFICATES AND RADIO EXEMPTION CERTIFICATES AND FOR THE INSPECTION OF RADIO INSTALLATIONS ON BOARD SHIPS AND FISHING VESSELS

1. The fees prescribed in this Part are payable under section 33(1) of the Act of 1949, section 84 of the Act of 1970, and section 21(3)*(r)* of the Act of 1979.

2. In this Part:—

"Class" in relation to a fishing vessel means the class of that vessel as determined by Rule 2 of the fishing vessels Radio Rules;

"the Radio Rules" means the Merchant Shipping (Radio Installations) Regulations 1980(**a**);

"the fishing vessels Radio Rules" means the Merchant Shipping (Radio) (Fishing Vessels) Rules 1974(**b**).

Service	*Fee*
3.—(1) Survey of a ship for the issue of a radio certificate, or a qualified radio certificate together with an exemption certificate, in the case of a ship:—	
not exceeding 1,600 tons	£143
exceeding 1,600 tons	£223

(**a**) S.I. 1980/529.
(**b**) S.I. 1974/1919.

Service	Fee
(2) The issue of an exemption certificate only, relating to radio	£24
(3) Inspection of a ship under section 76(1) of the Act of 1970 (not being an inspection made with a view to the issue of a passenger certificate or any of the certificates referred to in sections 7 and 9 of the Act of 1949):—	
(a) on the application of the owner for the purpose of seeing that she is properly provided with a radio installation and radio officers or radio-telephone operators in conformity with the Radio Rules or	
(b) otherwise than on the application of the owner, as a result of changes or modification in her radio equipment or as a result of an accident to the ship or a defect which affects the efficiency or completeness of a radio installation, being:—	
(i) a complete inspection, in the case of a ship:—	
not exceeding 1,600 tons	£143
exceeding 1,600 tons	£223
(ii) a partial inspection—for each visit to the ship	£64 subject to a maximum of the appropriate fee for a complete inspection.
(4) Inspection of a ship, otherwise than on the application of the owner, under section 76(1) of the Act of 1970 where the ship is found not to be properly provided with a radio installation or radio officers or radio-telephone operators:—	
for each visit made to the ship	£64 subject to a maximum of the appropriate fee for a complete inspection.
(5) Inspection of a ship, on the application of the owner, under section 76(1) of the Act of 1970, for the purpose of seeing that she is properly provided with radio equipment not required by the Radio Rules but which has been fitted as a condition of exemption from specific requirements of the Radio Rules	£64

Fishing Vessels

4.—(1) Inspection of a fishing vessel, on the application of the owner, under section 76(1) of the Act of 1970 for the purpose of seeing that the vessel is properly provided with a radio installation and radio operators in compliance with the fishing vessels Radio Rules, for the issue or renewal of a United Kingdom fishing vessel certificate issued under Rule 126 of the Fishing Vessels

Service	*Fee*
(Safety Provisions) Rules 1975(a), in the case of a vessel of:—	

Class I

exceeding 1,600 tons	£223
not exceeding 1,600 tons	£119

Class II or III £119

(2) Periodical inspection of a fishing vessel, on the application of the owner, under section 76(1) of the Act of 1970 pursuant to Rule 130 of the Fishing Vessels (Safety Provisions) Rules 1975 for the purpose of seeing that the radio equipment and installations are in compliance with the fishing vessels Radio Rules, in the case of a vessel of:—

Class I

exceeding 1,600 tons	£223
not exceeding 1,600 tons	£119

Class II or III £119

(3) Inspection of a fishing vessel under section 76(1) of the Act of 1970:—

(a) on the application of the owner (not being a case to which sub-paragraphs (1) and (2) above apply) for the purpose of seeing that the vessel is properly provided with a radio installation and radio operators in compliance with the fishing vessels Radio Rules, or

(b) otherwise than on the application of the owner, as a result of changes or modification in the radio equipment after compliance with the fishing vessels Radio Rules:—

(i) a complete inspection, in the case of a vessel of:—

Class I

exceeding 1,600 tons	£223
not exceeding 1,600 tons	£119

Class II or III £119

(ii) a partial inspection—for each visit made to the vessel £60

subject to a maximum of the appropriate fee for a complete inspection.

(4) Inspection of a fishing vessel, otherwise than on the application of the owner, under section 76(1) of the Act of 1970 where the vessel is found not to be properly provided with a radio installation or radio operators required by the fishing vessels Radio Rules or any condition subject to which the vessel has been exempted from a requirement of the fishing vessels Radio Rules:—

(a) S.I. 1975/330, to which there are amendments not expressly relevant to these Regulations.

Service	*Fee*
for each visit made to the vessel	£60 subject to a maximum of the appropriate fee for a complete inspection.

(5) Inspection of a fishing vessel, on the application of the owner, under section 76(1) of the Act of 1970 for the purpose of exempting the vessel from a requirement of the fishing vessels Radio Rules   £60

(6) The issue of an exemption certificate only, relating to radio   £18

PART IV: RADAR

FEES FOR THE INSPECTION OF RADAR INSTALLATIONS ON BOARD SHIPS

1. The fees prescribed in this Part are payable under section 84 of the Act of 1970 and section 21(3)*(r)* of the Act of 1979.

2. In this Part, "the Rules" means the Merchant Shipping (Navigational Equipment) Regulations 1980(**a**);

Service	*Fee*
3. Inspection of the radar installation on a ship under section 76(1) of the Act of 1970:—	
(a) on the application of the owner for the purpose of seeing that the radar installation provided is in accordance with the Rules or	
(b) otherwise than on the application of the owner, where the ship is found not to be complying with the provisions of the Rules or any condition subject to which the ship has been exempted from a requirement of the Rules or as a result of an accident to the ship or a defect which affects the efficiency or completeness of the radar installation	the fee will be determined by the amount of work involved, charged at an hourly rate of £36.95.

PART V: SAFETY EQUIPMENT

FEES FOR SAFETY EQUIPMENT CERTIFICATES AND FOR THE INSPECTION OF LIFE-SAVING APPLIANCES (INCLUDING EQUIPMENT NECESSARY FOR A SAFETY EQUIPMENT CERTIFICATE), LIGHTS AND FOG SIGNALS

1. The fees prescribed in this Part are payable under the following enactments:—

(**a**) S.I. 1980/530, amended by S.I. 1981/579.

Safety Equipment Certificates (paragraph 2(1)).   Section 21(3)*(r)* of the Act of 1979.

Inspection of life-saving appliances including equipment certificate (paragraph 2(2) and 2(3)).   Section 2(3) of the Fees (Increase) Act 1923**(a)** and section 21(3)*(r)* of the Act of 1979.

Inspection of lights and fog signals (paragraph 2(4)).   Section 420(8)**(b)** of the Principal Act.

and shall be determined by the amount of work involved, charged at an hourly rate of £36.95, subject to the following maxima:

Service	*Maximum Fee*
2.—(1) The survey of a ship for the initial issue of a safety equipment certificate where the ship:—	
(a) is 500 tons or over but under 1,600 tons	£4,432
(b) is 1,600 tons or over but under 15,000 tons	£4,432 plus an additional £609.40 for each 1,000 tons or part thereof by which the ship exceeds 1,600 tons
(c) is 15,000 tons or over	£13,296
(2) The survey of a ship for the renewal of a safety equipment certificate where the ship:—	
(a) is 500 tons or over but under 1,600 tons	£554
(b) is 1,600 tons or over but under 3,000 tons	£886
(c) is 3,000 tons or over	£1,220
(3) The survey of a ship for a safety equipment certificate under regulation 4 of the Merchant Shipping (Cargo Ship Safety Equipment Survey) Regulations 1981**(c)** where the ship:—	
(a) is 500 tons or over but under 1,600 tons	£333
(b) is 1,600 tons or over but under 3,000 tons	£665
(c) is 3,000 tons or over	£776
3.—(1) The initial inspection of the life-saving appliances (including equipment necessary for a safety equipment certificate) of a ship (other than a passenger steamer) on the application of the owner under section 431 of the principal Act**(d)** in the case of a ship of:—	
(a) under 50 tons	£886
(b) 50 tons or over but under 3,000 tons	£886 plus an additional £277 for each 100 tons or part thereof by which the ship exceeds 50 tons
(c) 3,000 tons or over	£9,418
(2) A subsequent inspection as described in sub-paragraph (1) above in the case of a ship of:—	
(a) under 500 tons	£388

(**a**) 1923 c. 4, as amended by section 33(2) of the Act of 1949.
(**b**) As amended by section 33(2) of the Act of 1949.
(**c**) S.I. 1981/573.
(**d**) As substituted by section 5(3) of the Merchant Shipping (Safety and Load Line Conventions) Act 1932 (c. 9).

Service	Maximum fee
(b) 500 tons or over but under 3,000 tons	£388 plus an additional £111 for each 500 tons or part thereof by which the ship exceeds 500 tons
(c) 3,000 tons or over	£1,000

(3) A partial inspection of the equipment described in sub-paragraph (1) above of a ship under section 431 of the principal Act, being an inspection:—

(i) made on application of the owner or

(ii) made otherwise than on the application of the owner, where equipment is found defective or

(iii) made otherwise than on the application of the owner and in consequence of changes or modification in the equipment — No maximum

(4) Where the survey or inspection of the safety equipment of a ship is to be carried out at a port outside the United Kingdom by a ship surveyor not employed by the Department of Transport but specially appointed for the purpose under the Merchant Shipping Acts — The fee payable to the Department of Transport for arranging that appointment shall be determined by the amount of work involved. (The fee is in addition to the fee payable for the service of the specially appointed surveyor or his employer.)

(5) The inspection of lights and fog signals on a ship under section 420 of the principal Act, either on the application of the owner or where equipment is found defective — No maximum

PART VI: LOAD LINE SURVEYS AND INSPECTIONS

1. The fees prescribed in this Part are payable under section 26 of the Act of 1967 and shall be determined by the amount of work involved, charged at an hourly rate of £36.95 subject to the maxima prescribed in Sections A, B and C below.

2. In this Part:—

"Assigning Authority" means a body which is an Assigning Authority for the purposes of the Rules;

"a classed ship" means a ship which has been surveyed by or on behalf of an Assigning Authority other than the Department of Transport and has, following such survey, been classified by that authority in accordance with standards set for ships by it and remains so classified at the date of the survey or inspection for which the relevant fee is payable; and "unclassed ship" means a ship which is not a classed ship;

"extended international voyage" means an outward voyage from a port or place in the United Kingdom, to a port or place outside the United Kingdom not being a short international voyage as defined in section 36 of the Act of 1949;

"periodical survey" means a survey (other than a survey specified in Section C of this Part) of a ship in respect of which there is in force at the time of the survey, or was in force immediately before that time, a load line certificate or a load line exemption certificate issued under the Act of 1967;

"the Rules" means the Merchant Shipping (Load Line) Rules 1968(a).

3. The standard fee prescribed in paragraph 1 above (read with Section A) shall be adjusted in accordance with the provisions of Section B and for special cases in accordance with Section C.

4. References in Section B or Section C of this Part to a standard fee are references to the standard fee appropriate to the tonnage of the ship prescribed by paragraph 1 above (read with Section A) and references to a maximum standard fee shall be construed accordingly.

SECTION A

TABLE OF MAXIMUM STANDARD FEES

Gross Tonnage of ship		Initial Survey	Periodical Survey	Periodical Inspection
Exceeds (tons)	Does not exceed (tons)			
	50	£526	£500	£277
50	100	£942	£886	£554
100	500		£1,995	
100	3,000			£554 plus an additional £27.70 for each 100 tons or part thereof by which the ship exceeds 100 tons
100	8,000	£8,864		
500			£3,324	
3,000				£1,385
8,000		£9,141		

SECTION B

ADJUSTMENTS OF STANDARD FEES

Service	*Maximum Fee*
1. Survey or inspection of a classed ship carried out by a surveyor on behalf of an Assigning Authority other than the Department of Transport at the same time as a classification survey for which a fee is charged by that Authority:—	
an initial survey	25% of the maximum standard fee for an initial survey.
a periodical survey	The standard periodical inspection fee.

(a) S.I. 1968/1053, as amended by S.I. 1970/1003, 1975/595.

Service	Maximum Fee
a periodical inspection	50% of the maximum standard periodical inspection fee.

2. Survey of a classed ship carried out by a surveyor appointed by the Department of Transport:

an initial survey	30% of the maximum standard fee for an initial survey.
a periodical survey	125% of the maximum standard periodical inspection fee.

3. Survey or inspection of a ship carried out concurrently with a survey for a passenger certificate, a safety certificate, a passenger certificate combined with a safety certificate or a United Kingdom fishing vessel certificate by a surveyor appointed by the Department of Transport:—

an initial survey	$12\frac{1}{2}$% of the maximum standard fee for an initial survey.
a periodical survey	50% of the maximum standard periodical inspection fee.
a periodical inspection	No fee.

4. Survey of a ship in respect of which a load line certificate or load line exemption certificate is in force, where alterations have been made to the ship which involve the assignment of new freeboards but are not such as to necessitate a complete survey of the ship for that purpose — The standard periodical inspection fee.

5. Survey of a ship where the survey involves the attendance of a surveyor appointed by the Department of Transport at the loading trial of the ship in respect of which the owners apply for exemption from the necessity to fit hatch covers — The standard fee appropriate to the survey, plus an additional fixed fee of £715 for the surveyor's attendance at the first loading trial and of £344 for his attendance at any subsequent loading trial.

6. Survey or inspection of a ship not exceeding 25 tons or, if unregistered, not exceeding 15 metres (49.2 feet) in overall length, which on voyages to sea carries neither cargo nor more than 12 passengers — 50% of the maximum appropriate standard fee for survey or inspection as the case may be.

Service	*Maximum Fee*

Stability requirements

7. Survey of a ship (other than a ship to which paragraph 8 applies) where it is necessary to determine compliance in respect of the ship with the stability requirements in Schedules 4 and 7 of the Rules

The standard fee appropriate to the survey plus an additional fee of:—

Where the ship:—

does not exceed 2,000 tons

£665

exceeds 2,000 tons

£665 plus an additional £277 for each 1,000 tons or part thereof by which the ship exceeds 2,000 tons.

8. Survey as described in paragraph 7 in the case of a sister ship in respect of which an inclining test has been dispensed with, a "sister ship" for this purpose being a ship:—

(1) which corresponds in the following respects with a ship (referred to below as the "principal ship") which has been surveyed as described in paragraph 7, or which will have been so surveyed prior to the survey of the sister ship:—

   (a) the hydrostatic particulars and cross curves of stability are identical to those of the principal ship;

   (b) the amounts and dispositions of the items included in the lightweight of the ship are substantially the same as those of the principal ship;

(2) as to which, prior to the commencement of the survey, application is made in writing by or on behalf of the owner of the ship to be treated as a sister ship, accompanied by a declaration that it complies with the foregoing requirements

The standard fee appropriate to the survey plus an additional fee to be determined by the amount of work involved subject to a maximum of 50% of the appropriate maximum additional fee under paragraph 7.

9. Survey of a ship (other than a ship to which paragraph 10 applies) where the survey involves calculations in accordance with the Rules as to the ability of the ship to withstand the flooding of compartments

The standard fee appropriate to the survey plus an additional fixed fee of £1,091.

Service	*Maximum Fee*
10. Survey as described in paragraph 9 in the case of a sister ship as defined in paragraph 8	The standard fee appropriate to the survey plus an additional fixed fee of £543.

SECTION C

FEES FOR SURVEY AND INSPECTION:

SPECIAL CASES

Service	*Maximum Fee*

Exemptions for deeper loading

1. Survey or inspection (except in a case to which paragraph 2 applies) carried out on a ship in respect of which a load line certificate is in force, for the purpose of an exemption for deeper loading:—

a first survey for the exemption	25% of the maximum standard fee for an initial survey plus 50% of the maximum standard periodical inspection fee.
a subsequent survey or inspection for the continuing of the exemption in force:—	
(a) made concurrently with a periodical inspection respectively carried out by the Department of Transport	No fee.
(b) not so made	The standard periodical inspection fee.

2. Survey or inspection as described in paragraph 1 where the ship is a classed ship and the load line Assigning Authority certify in writing that the scantlings of the ship are sufficient for the deeper loading:—

a first survey for the exemption	25% of the maximum standard fee for an initial survey plus the standard periodical inspection fee.
a subsequent survey or inspection for the continuing of the exemption in force:—	
(a) made concurrently with a periodical survey or periodical inspection respectively carried out by the Department of Transport	No fee.
(b) not so made	The standard periodical inspection fee.

Exemptions for single voyages

3. Survey carried out on a ship in respect of which a load line certificate or load line exemption certificate is in force and the owners of which require it to make a single voyage outside the limits specified in that certificate not being an extended international voyage	The standard periodical inspection fee.

Service	Maximum Fee
4. Survey carried out on a ship in respect of which a load line certificate or load line exemption certificate is not in force and the owners of which require it to make either a single short international voyage or a single coastal voyage	25% of the maximum standard initial survey fee.
5. Survey carried out on a ship in respect of which a load line certificate or load line exemption certificate is in force for prescribed coastal limits and the owners of which require it to make a single extended international voyage	25% of the maximum standard initial survey fee.
6. Survey carried out on a ship in respect of which a load line certificate or load line exemption certificate is not in force and the owners of which require it to make a single extended international voyage	50% of the maximum standard initial survey fee.
7. Survey carried out on a ship the owners of which require it to make a single voyage under tow	No maximum.

Stability requirements

8. Survey of a ship (other than a ship to which paragraph 9 applies) to determine compliance in respect of the ship with the stability information requirements in Schedule 7 of the Rules in the case of a ship which was an existing ship on 21st July 1968:—

(a) on which stability information was carried for the guidance of the master pursuant to the Act of 1949:—

Where the ship:—

does not exceed 2,000 tons	£333
is 2,000 tons or over	£333 plus an additional £55.40 for each 400 tons or part thereof by which the ship exceeds 2,000 tons.

(b) on which stability information was not carried for the guidance of the master pursuant to the Act of 1949:—

The fee shall be that prescribed as an additional fee in paragraph 7 of Section B of this part.

9. Survey as described in paragraph 8 in the case of a sister ship as defined in paragraph 8 of Section B	50% of the maximum appropriate fee in paragraph 8.

General

10. The issue, in substitution for an existing load line

	Service	*Maximum Fee*

certificate, or load line exemption certificate, of a corresponding certificate showing amended or extended plying limits (including such survey or inspection as may be necessary) — A fixed fee of £104.

11. The endorsement of a load line exemption certificate — A fixed fee of £52.

PART VII: CREW ACCOMMODATION—MERCHANT SHIPS

FEES FOR THE INSPECTION OF CREW ACCOMMODATION IN MERCHANT SHIPS

1. The fees prescribed in this Part are payable under section 84 of the Act of 1970 and shall be determined by the amount of work involved, charged at an hourly rate of £36.95, subject to the following maxima.

2. In this Part:—

"the Regulations" means the Merchant Shipping (Crew Accommodation) Regulations 1978(**a**) and references to specific regulations shall be construed accordingly.

Service	*Maximum Fee*

3.—(1) Inspection of crew accommodation in a ship, on the application of the owner, under section 76(1) of the Act of 1970 on first registry or re-registry in the United Kingdom:—

Where the ship:—

does not exceed 2,000 tons — £665 plus an additional £111 for each 50 tons or part thereof by which the ship exceeds 50 tons.

is 2,000 or over but does not exceed 3,000 tons — £4,995 plus an additional £310 for each 1,000 tons or part thereof by which the ship exceeds 2,000 tons.

is 30,000 tons or over — £13,850

(2) Inspection of crew accommodation in a ship, on the application of the owner under section 76(1) of the Act of 1970:—

(a) consequent upon alterations or repairs to any part of the crew accommodation, other than as described in (b) below

(b) concurrent with tonnage measurement in relation to registry under Part 1 of the principal Act carried out consequent upon alterations or repairs to any part of the crew accommodation — 50% of the appropriate maximum fee under sub-paragraph (1) above.

(3) Inspection of crew accommodation in a ship under Section 76(1) of the Act of 1970:—

(**a**) S.I. 1978/795, to which there are amendments not relevant to these Regulations.

Service	Maximum Fee

(a) on the application of the owner (not being a case to which sub-paragraph (1) above applies) or on the application of any organisation which appears to the Department of Transport to be representative of the owners of British ships or the seamen concerned (other than upon a complaint by the crew), or

(b) on the application of the owner consequent upon an increase in the number of persons accommodated in any sleeping room above that marked in accordance with regulation 20(1) of the Regulations, or

(c) otherwise than on the application of the owner, where the ship is found not to be complying with the provisions of the Regulations or any condition subject to which the ship has been exempted from a requirement of the Regulations:—

The appropriate maximum fee under sub-paragraph (1) above.

(4) Where a service described in sub-paragraphs (1) to (3) above is to be carried out at a port outside the United Kingdom by a ship surveyor not employed by the Department of Transport but specially appointed for the purpose under the Merchant Shipping Acts

The fee payable to the Department of Transport for arranging the appointment will be $66\frac{2}{3}\%$ of the appropriate maximum fee under sub-paragraphs (1) to (3) above. (The fee in each case is in addition to the fee payable for the service to the specially appointed surveyor or his employer.)

PART VIII: CREW ACCOMMODATION—FISHING VESSELS

FEES FOR THE INSPECTION OF CREW ACCOMMODATION IN FISHING VESSELS

1. The fees prescribed in this Part are payable under section 84 of the Act of 1970 and shall be determined by the amount of work involved, charged at an hourly rate of £24.15, subject to the following maxima.

2. In this Part:—

"length" means the length measured from the fore part of the stem on the line of the forecastle deck to the after side of the head of the stern post, or, if there is no stern post, to the foreside of the rudder stock at the point where the rudder stock passes out of the hull;

"the Regulations" means the Merchant Shipping (Crew Accommodation) (Fishing Vessels) Regulations 1975(**a**) and references to specific regulations shall be construed accordingly.

_____

(**a**) S.I. 1975/2220.

Service	*Maximum Fee*

3.—(1) Inspection of crew accommodation in a fishing vessel on the application of the owner under section 76(1) of the Act of 1970 on first registry or re-registry in the United Kingdom:—

Where the length of the fishing vessel is 24.4 metres or more — £402.50 plus an additional £39.10 for each metre or part thereof by which the fishing vessel exceeds 25 metres.

(2) Inspection of the crew accommodation in a fishing vessel, on the application of the owner, under section 76(1) of the Act of 1970:—

(a) consequent upon alterations or repairs to any part of the crew accommodation; or

(b) concurrent with tonnage measurement in relation to registry under Part 1 of the principal Act carried out consequent upon alterations or repairs to any part of the crew accommodation — 50% of the appropriate maximum fee under sub-paragraph (1) above.

(3) Inspection of crew accommodation in a fishing vessel under section 76(1) of the Act of 1970:—

(a) on the application of the owner (not being a case to which sub-paragraph (1) above applies) or on the application of any organisation which appears to the Department of Transport to be representative of the owners of British fishing vessels or the fishermen concerned (other than upon a complaint by the crew), or

(b) on an application of the owner consequent upon an increase in the number of persons accommodated in any sleeping room above that marked in accordance with regulation 19(1) of the Regulations, or

(c) otherwise than on the application of the owner, where the vessel is found not to be complying with the provisions of the Regulations or any condition subject to which the vessel has been exempted from a requirement of the Regulations — The appropriate maximum fee under sub-paragraph (1) above.

Service	Maximum Fee
(4) Where a service described in sub-paragraph (1) to (3) above is to be carried out at a port outside the United Kingdom by a ship surveyor not employed by the Department of Transport but specially appointed for the purpose under the Merchant Shipping Acts	The fee payable to the Department of Transport for arranging the appointment will be $66\frac{2}{3}\%$ of the appropriate maximum fee under sub-paragraphs (1) to (3) above. (The fee in each case is in addition to the fee payable to the specially appointed surveyor or his employer.)

PART IX: TONNAGE MEASUREMENT

FEES FOR MEASUREMENT OF SHIP'S TONNAGE

1. The fees prescribed in this Part are payable under section 83 of the principal Act(**a**) and where they relate to the tonnage measurement of a ship they include the survey and certification under section 6 and the inspection of markings under section 7(1) of the principal Act.

2. In this Part:—

"the Regulations" means the Merchant Shipping (Tonnage) Regulations 1982(**b**) and references to specific Regulations shall be construed accordingly;

"sister ship" means a ship which corresponds in all major respects relevant to the measurement for tonnage with a ship the tonnage of which has been previously ascertained under the Regulations, and for which the calculation for tonnage is available to the Certifying Authority to which, prior to the commencement of its measurement for tonnage, application has been made in writing by or on behalf of the owner of the ship requesting it to be treated as a sister ship.

(**a**) 1894 c. 60, as amended by section 33(2) of the Act of 1949.
(**b**) S.I. 1982/841.

3. *Tonnage Measurement of Ships*

TABLE A

A ship which:—   Fee

exceeds (tons):	does not exceed (tons):	£
	90	273
90	180	410
180	270	545
270	450	683
450	900	907
900	1,450	1,131
1,450	1,800	1,249
1,800	2,700	1,366
2,700	3,600	1,589
3,600	4,500	1,815
4,500	6,000	2,040
6,000	7,000	2,274
7,000	8,000	2,497
8,000	9,000	2,723
9,000	10,000	2,946
10,000	11,000	3,123
11,000	12,000	3,288
12,000	13,000	3,464
13,000	14,000	3,629
14,000	15,000	3,806
15,000	16,000	3,972
16,000	17,000	4,089
17,000	18,000	4,196
18,000	19,000	4,257
19,000	20,000	4,420
20,000	21,000	4,537
21,000	22,000	4,654
22,000	23,000	4,762
23,000	24,000	4,879
24,000	25,000	4,996
25,000	27,500	5,221
27,500	30,000	5,445
30,000	32,500	5,680
32,500	35,000	5,901
35,000	40,000	6,352
40,000	45,000	6,812
45,000	50,000	7,378
50,000	55,000	7,943
55,000	60,000	8,509
60,000		9,076

(1)*(a)* The fees to be charged for the tonnage measurement of a ship in accordance with Part II of the Regulations (that is to say, the International Tonnage Convention, 1969) shall be 70% of the fees set out in Table A.

   (b) The fees for a sister ship, or a foreign ship with an International Tonnage Certificate (1969) transferring to the United Kingdom register, shall be determined by the amount of work involved, charged at an hourly rate of £36.95 subject to the maximum fee chargeable under paragraph (1)*(a)* above.

(2)*(a)* The fees to be charged for the tonnage measurement of a ship in accordance with either Schedule 5 Part I paragraph 2(2) (single tonnage) or Schedule 5

Part III paragraph 12 (modified tonnage) of the Regulations shall be 100% of the fees set out in Table A.

(b) The fees for a sister ship shall be determined by the amount of work involved, charged at an hourly rate of £36.95 subject to the maximum fee chargeable under sub-paragraph (2)*(a)* above.

(3)*(a)* The fees to be charged for the tonnage measurement of a ship in accordance with Schedule 5 Part III paragraph 13 (alternative tonnages) shall be 150% of the fees set out in Table A.

(b) The fees for a sister ship shall be determined by the amount of work involved charged at an hourly rate of £36.95 subject to the maximum fee chargeable under sub-paragraph (3)*(a)* above.

(4)*(a)* The fees to be charged for the tonnage measurement of a ship in accordance with Part VI of the Regulations (gross tonnage for Interim Scheme for tonnage measurement for certain ships) shall be 80% of the fees set out in Table A.

(b) The fees for a sister ship shall be determined by the amount of work involved charged at an hourly rate of £36.95 subject to the maximum fee chargeable under sub-paragraph (4)*(a)* above.

(5) The fees to be charged for the tonnage measurement or measurement of a pleasure yacht under 13.7m (45 feet) in overall length in accordance with Schedule 5, Part IV and Appendix 5 shall:

(i) when undertaken in the United Kingdom, not exceed £95.55 and

(ii) when undertaken outside the United Kingdom, not exceed £191,10.

(6) The fees to be charged for the tonnage measurement of a ship to which Schedule 5 Part I paragraph 2(3) of the Regulations (girthing of a loaded ship) applies, shall be 50% of the fees set out in Table A.

(7) The fee to be charged for the remeasurement of a ship for tonnage purposes, verification of changes in any of the registered particulars or any other services associated with the tonnage measurement shall be determined by the amount of work involved charged at an hourly rate of £36.95 subject to the maximum fee shown for a ship of that tonnage in Table A.

PART X: FISHING VESSELS

FEES FOR FISHING VESSEL SURVEYS AND PERIODICAL INSPECTIONS AND CERTIFICATION

1. The fees prescribed in this Part are payable under section 6 of the Fishing Vessels (Safety Provisions) Act 1970.

2. In this Part:—

"the Rules" means the Fishing Vessels (Safety Provisions) Rules 1975(a);

"survey" means the survey of a fishing vessel carried out pursuant to rule 124 of the Rules with a view to the issue of a certificate for the vessel;

"certificate" means a United Kingdom fishing vessel certificate issued under rule 126 of the Rules;

"periodical inspection" means the inspection of a fishing vessel for which a certificate is in force, being an inspection carried out pursuant to rule 130 of the Rules;

(a) S.I. 1975/330; relevant amending instruments are S.I. 1976/432, 1977/313, 1978/1598.

"Category A vessel" means a fishing vessel which is not a Category B vessel;

"Category B vessel" means a fishing vessel which, at a time when a survey or periodical inspection of the vessel is carried out by a surveyor appointed by the Secretary of State, is surveyed or inspected in order to ascertain whether the vessel complies with such requirements of rules 2 to 14 inclusive and 17 to 54 inclusive of the Rules as apply to it:—

(i) by a person appointed by Lloyd's Register of Shipping; or

(ii) *(a)* by an officer authorised by the White Fish Authority under section 13(1) of the Sea Fish Industry Act 1970(**a**); or

 (b) by a person authorised by the White Fish Authority or the Herring Industry Board under a scheme made under that Act, or

 (c) by a person authorised by the Department of Agriculture for Northern Ireland under a scheme made under section 1 of the Fishing Vessels (Grants) Act (Northern Ireland) 1967(**b**), or under section 5 of the Development Loans (Agriculture and Fisheries) Act (Northern Ireland) 1968(**c**);

"new vessel" means a fishing vessel the keel of which was laid on or after 1st May 1975 pursuant to an agreement for the construction of the vessel entered into on or after that date;

"existing vessel" means a fishing vessel which is not a new vessel.

3. The fees prescribed by this Part shall be payable in respect of a survey or a periodical inspection only in so far as it is a survey or inspection carried out by a surveyor appointed by the Secretary of State.

4.—(1) Subject to paragraph 3 above and to sub-paragraphs (3) and (4) below, the provisions contained in the Table set out below shall apply for determining, in relation to a vessel of a description and registered length specified in that Table, the fee payable in respect of:—

 (a) a survey of that vessel and

 (b) a periodical inspection of the vessel.

(2) The fee payable in respect of a survey of a vessel shall cover the issue of a certificate for the vessel following that survey, and the fee payable in respect of a periodical inspection of that vessel shall cover the endorsement of the certificate for the vessel (pursuant to rule 130(5) of the Rules) following that inspection.

(3) Where alterations have been made to a fishing vessel which affect its stability and are such as, in the opinion of a surveyor carrying out a survey or periodical inspection of the vessel, to make it necessary for the vessel to be examined to ensure that it complies with rule 16 of the Rules (which relates to stability), the fee payable in respect of the survey or inspection by virtue of sub-paragraph (1) above shall be increased by the sum of £207 together with a further £3.65 for every metre, if any, by which the length of the vessel exceeds 24.4 metres, subject to a maximum increase in any such case of £381.

(4) Where a survey is carried out on a vessel with a view to the issue of a certificate for the vessel which (in accordance with rule 127 of the Rules) is to be in force for a period not exceeding 12 months, the fee payable in respect of that survey shall be:—

(a) 1970 c. 11.
(**b**) 1967 c. 8. (N.I.)
(**c**) 1968 c. 21. (N.I.)

(a) in respect of a survey for the issue of a certificate which is to be in force for 12 months, half of the fee which would otherwise be payable in respect thereof by virtue of paragraph (1) above; or

(b) in respect of a survey for the issue of a certificate which is to be in force for less than 12 months, a fee which bears the same proportion to the fee which would otherwise be payable in respect thereof by virtue of sub-paragraph (a) above, as the period of months for which the certificate is to be in force (part of a month being reckoned as a full month) bears to a period of 12 months, subject to a minimum fee being payable appropriate to a survey for the issue of a certificate which is to be in force for three months.

TABLE

(This Table has effect subject to paragraph 4(3) and (4) above)

Registered length of vessel	FEES						
	In respect of a survey before the first issue of a certificate				In respect of a survey before the renewal of a certificate		In respect of a periodical inspection
	Category A vessels		Category B vessels		Category A vessels	Category B vessels	All vessels
	New vessels	Existing vessels	New vessels	Existing vessels			
	£	£	£	£	£	£	£
12m and under 15m	2,075	1,065	855	855	645	435	275
15m and under 18m	2,525	1,205	910	910	750	475	310
18m and under 21m	2,985	1,405	1.020	1,020	880	540	335
21m and under 24.4m	3,640	1,665	1,125	1,125	1,100	580	350
24.4m and under 30m	4,285	1,940	1,225	1,225	1,330	645	410
30m and under 75m	5,890	2,435	1,395	1,395	1,735	705	450
Plus amount shown for each 1m or part increase in length over 30.99m	263	95	32	32	83	17	14
75m and over	17,725	6,705	2,835	2,835	5,470	1,470	1,080

PART XI: FEES FOR EXAMINATIONS FOR CERTIFICATES OF COMPETENCY

SECTION A

FEES FOR EXAMINATION FOR CERTIFICATES OF COMPETENCY AS MASTERS, DECK OFFICERS AND MARINE ENGINEER OFFICERS AND OTHER SERVICES

1. The fees prescribed in paragraph 2 of this Part are payable under section 84 of the Act of 1970, and section 21(3)(r) of the Act 1979.

Service	*Fee*

2.—(1) For examination for a certificate of competency on each occasion on which a candidate presents himself for the whole examination as:—

(a)	deck officer class 1 (master mariner)	£390
(b)	deck officer class 2	£226
(c)	deck officer class 3	£198
(d)	deck officer class 4	£177
(e)	deck officer class 5	£148.50
(f)	marine engineer officer class 1	£390
(g)	marine engineer officer class 2	£226
(h)	marine engineer officer class 3	£198
(i)	marine engineer officer class 4	£108

Provided that where in cases *(b)*, *(c)*, *(d)* or *(e)* the examination in signalling is taken separately from the remainder of the examination, there shall be paid an additional fee of £99

(2) Where a candidate for a class 1, class 2 or class 3 marine engineer officer's certificate is examined only in Part A or Part B, or for a portion of either:—

For a marine engineer officer class 1	£195
For a marine engineer officer class 2	£113
For a marine engineer officer class 3	£99

(3) Where in case (2) above a class 1 or class 2 candidate is examined in both steam and motor engineering knowledge in a Part B examination in the same week:—

For a marine engineer officer class 1	£361
For a marine engineer officer class 2	£220

(4) Where a candidate in class (1) *(a)*, *(b)*, *(c)*, *(d)* or *(e)* is examined in any part of the written but not in the practical oral part of the examination, or vice versa — 50% of the appropriate fee in (1) subject to a minimum of £99.

(5) For examination of a class 1, class 2, or class 4 marine engineer officer for the endorsement of his ordinary (steam) certificate to the effect that he is qualified to act in the capacity stated in his certificate on board a motor vessel, or vice versa:—

marine engineer officer class 1	£166
marine engineer officer class 2	£107
marine engineer officer class 4	£70

(6) For examination for a command endorsement as:—

(a)	master (middle trade)	£296

Service	Fee
(b) master (near continental)	£238
(c) tugmaster	£296
(d) tugmaster (near continental)	£238

(7) Where a candidate in case (6) *(a), (b), (c)* or *(d)* is examined in any part of the written but not in the practical oral part of the examination, or vice versa — 50% of the appropriate fee in (6).

(8) For examination for a service endorsement to a certificate of competency as marine engineer officer — £70

(9) Where the holder of a deck officer class 4 certificate of competency is granted a class 3 certificate without further examination — £19.30

(10) Removal of a For Tug Service Only endorsement from a certificate of competency — £19.30

(11) For a dangerous cargo endorsement to a certificate of competency or service — £19.30

(12) For eexamination for and the grant of a radar maintenance certificate — £107

(13) Where in case (12) a candidate is examined in the written part (Part A) of the examination only and for the grant of such a certificate — £53

(14) Where in case (12) a candidate is examined in the practical part (Part BII) of the examination only and for the grant of such a certificate — £79

(15) For examination for and for the grant of a radar observer certificate — £19.30

(16) For examination for and for the grant of an electronic navigational aids (operation) certificate — £19.30

(17) For examination for and for the grant of an electronic navigation systems certificate — £19.30

(18) For an electronic navigational equipment maintenance examination and for the grant of an electronic navigational equipment maintenance or radar maintenance certificate — £107 or £55 in the case of the holder of a valid radar maintenance certificate.

(19) Where in case (18) a candidate is examined in part of the written part (Part C) of the examination only, for each written paper or section thereof and for the grant of a certificate — £27.50

(20) Where in case (18) a candidate is examined in the practical part (Part B4) of the examination only and for the grant of a certificate — £33

(21) For examination for a certificate of efficiency as lifeboatman, except where the examination is sat at a

Service	Fee
centre specially approved by the Secretary of State, and for the grant of a certificate to a person passing the examination	£9.90
(22) For the grant of a certificate of efficiency as lifeboatman where the examination was sat at a centre specially approved by the Secretary of State	£5.30
(23) For examination for a certificate of qualification as efficient deck hand except where the examination is sat at a centre specially approved by the Secretary of State, and for the grant of a certificate to a person passing the examination	£9.90
(24) For the grant of a certificate of qualification as efficient deck hand where the examination was sat at a centre specially approved by the Secretary of State	£5.30

SECTION B

FEES FOR THE EXAMINATION FOR CERTIFICATES OF COMPETENCY AS A.B

1. The fees prescribed in paragraph 2 of this Part are payable under section 5(3) of the Act of 1948.

2. For Schedule 3 to the Merchant Shipping (Certificates of Competency as A.B.) Regulations 1970(**a**), there shall be substituted the following:—

"SCHEDULE 3

FEES

Service	Fee
1. For sitting the examination specified in regulation 4(1)*(c),* except in cases to which paragraph 3 of this Schedule applies or where the examination is sat at a centre specially approved by the Secretary of State	£9.90
2. For the grant of a certificate of competency, except in cases to which paragraph 3 of this Schedule applies	£5.30
3. For sitting the said examination and for the grant of a certificate of competency in the case of a person making application therefor under regulation 5(6) and passing the examination	£9.90
4. For a copy of a certificate of competency issued pursuant to regulation 10, except where the loss or destruction of the original certificate was occasioned by the wreck or loss of a ship or by a fire on board ship, in which case no fee shall be payable	£5.80

(**a**) S.I. 1970/294; the relevant amending instrument is S.I. 1982/355.

PART XII: REGISTRATION, ETC. OF SHIPS

FEES FOR REGISTRATION, TRANSFER AND MORTGAGE OR SHIPS (EXCLUDING VESSELS NOT EXCEEDING 10 TONS EMPLOYED SOLELY IN FISHING) AND INSPECTION OF THE REGISTER BOOK

1. The fees prescribed in this Part are payable under the following enactments:—

For registration, transfer and mortgage of ships	Section 3 of the Merchant Shipping (Mercantile Marine Fund) Act 1898(**a**).
For inspection of the Register Book	Section 64(1) of the principal Act(**b**).

2. In this Part "ship" does not include vessels not exceeding 10 tons employed solely in fishing.

Service	Fee
3.—(1) First registry, registry anew or re-registry of a ship, or the transfer of registry of a ship from one port to another, where the ship:	
does not exceed 1,500 tons	£110
exceeds 1,500 tons	£160
(2) Registry of the transfer of ownership of a ship by bill of sale or by transmission, or of the mortgage of a ship or the transfer or the discharge of such a mortgage, where the ship:	
does not exceed 1,500 tons	£35
exceeds 1,500 tons	£60
(3) Each inspection of the register book	£3.50

PART XIII: COPIES OF DOCUMENTS

FEES FOR COPIES OF, OR EXTRACTS FROM, DOCUMENTS ADMISSIBLE IN EVIDENCE

1. The fees prescribed in this Part are payable under section 695(2) of the principal Act(**c**).

Service	Fee
2.—(1) Supplying a certified copy of the particulars entered by the registrar in the register book on the registry of a ship, together with a certified statement showing the ownership of the ship at the time being	£11
(2) Supplying a certified copy of any declaration or document, a copy of which is made evidence by the Merchant Shipping Acts or for a certified copy of or	

(**a**) 1898 c. 44, as amended by section 33(2) of the Act of 1949.
(**b**) As amended by section 33(2) of the Act of 1949.
(**c**) As amended by section 33(2) of the Act of 1949.

extracts from a document declared by the Merchant Shipping Acts to be admissible as evidence:—

    (a) if the declaration or document relates to the registry of a ship, for each folio of 90 words or part thereof   £3.50

    (b) in any other case, for each page or portion thereof   £3.00

PART XIV: WRECK

FEES OF RECEIVERS OF WRECK

1. The fees prescribed in this Part are payable under section 567(1) of the principal Act(**a**).

Service	*Fee*
2. Wreck taken by the Receiver into his custody	7½% of the value thereof.
Services rendered by a Receiver in respect of any vessel in distress, not being a wreck, or in respect of the cargo or other articles belonging thereto	£40 for each day during which the Receiver is employed on that service.

PART XV: INSPECTION OF SHIPS' PROVISIONS

FEES FOR THE INSPECTION OF PROVISIONS AND WATER IN SHIPS AND FISHING VESSELS AND ON PREMISES

1. The fees prescribed in this Part are payable under section 84 of the Act of 1970.

2. In this Part, "the Regulations" means the Merchant Shipping (Provisions and Water) Regulations 1972(**b**), and the Merchant Shipping (Provisions and Water) (Fishing Vessels) Regulations 1972(**c**).

3.—(1) Inspection of provisions or water in a ship or fishing vessel under section 76(1) of the Act of 1970:—

    (a) on the application of the owner for the purpose of seeing that the provisions or water provided are in accordance with the Regulations or

    (b) otherwise than on the application of the owner, where the provisions or water provided are found not to be in accordance with the Regulations or

    (c) where a complaint has been made by the crew under section 22 of the Act of 1970 to a superintendent or proper officer   the fee will be determined by the amount of work involved, charged at an hourly rate of £24.09.

(**a**) As amended by section 33(2) of the Act of 1949.
(**b**) S.I. 1972/1871, amended by S.I. 1975/733, 1978/36.
(**c**) S.I. 1972/1872, amended by S.I. 1975/733.

Provided that no fee shall be payable under *(c)* above if, upon inspection, the provisions or water provided are found to comply with the Regulations.

(2) Inspection on premises under section 76(3) of the Act of 1970 of provisions or water intended for supply to a ship or fishing vessel, where the provisions or water are found not to be in accordance with the Regulations — the fee will be determined by the amount of work involved, charged at an hourly rate of £24.09.

PART XVI: SUBMERSIBLE CRAFT

FEES FOR THE REGISTRATION OF SUBMERSIBLE CRAFT AND THE SURVEY OF SUBMERSIBLE CRAFT AND THEIR SUPPORTING EQUIPMENT

1. The fees prescribed in this Part are payable under section 17 of and paragraph 5*(g)* of Schedule 5 to the Act of 1974.

2. In this Part:—

"autonomous submersible craft" means a submersible craft which does not rely on a parent craft for launch and recovery and recharging its power source or for surface support;

"existing submersible craft" means a submersible craft which is not a new submersible craft;

"new submersible craft" means a submersible craft:

    (a) the construction of which is begun pursuant to an agreement for the construction of the craft entered into on or after 1st October 1981; or

    (b) which is used or operated for the first time on or after 1st October 1981;

"the Regulations" means the Merchant Shipping (Submersible Craft Construction and Survey) Regulations 1981(a);

"submersible craft" means any description of manned mobile submersible craft which is designed to maintain some or all of its occupants at or near atmospheric pressure, and includes free, self-propelled, tethered, towed or bottom contact propelled apparatus, one man submersible craft and atmospheric diving suits;

"supporting equipment" means the launching and recovery gear used in connection with a submersible craft;

"survey" and "inspection" means a survey or inspection required under regulation 3 or 5 of the Regulations.

3. On application to register a submersible craft, the fee payable is £27.

4. Subject to paragraphs 5 and 6 below, fees for surveys and inspections of new and existing submersible craft will be determined by the amount of work involved, charged at an hourly rate of £36.95.

(a) S.I. 1981/1098.

5. The maximum fees for existing submersible craft when surveyed by a marine surveyor appointed by the Secretary of State other than a marine surveyor of the Department of Transport shall be as follows:—

TABLE

Type of Craft	In respect of initial survey before the issue of a safety certificate	In respect of survey before the renewal of a safety certificate	In respect of annual inspection
	£	£	£
(1) Diver lock-out:			
(a) craft	1,468	831	355
(b) supporting equipment	715	393	238
(2) One-man submersible craft including atmospheric diving suits			
(a) craft	947	637	277
(b) supporting equipment	554	355	238
(3) Craft not included in (1) or (2):			
(a) craft	1,313	753	321
(b) supporting equipment	715	393	238

6. The maximum fees shown in the table in paragraph 5 for surveys for the renewal of a safety certificate and for annual inspections shall also apply to new submersible craft (excluding autonomous submersible craft) where surveyed by a marine surveyor appointed by the Secretary of State other than a marine surveyor of the Department of Transport.

PART XVII: SEAMEN'S DOCUMENTS

FEES FOR THE ISSUE OF BRITISH SEAMEN'S CARDS AND DISCHARGE BOOKS

1. The fees prescribed in this Part are payable under section 84 of the Act of 1970.

2. In this Part "the Regulations" means the Merchant Shipping (Seamen's Documents) Regulations 1972(a); and the person to whom a British Seaman's Card or a discharge book has been issued is referred to as the holder of it.

(a) S.I. 1972/1295, to which there are amendments not relevant to these Regulations.

Service	*Fee*

3.—(1) For the issue of a British Seamen's Card:—

   (a) to a British Seaman under regulation 5 of the Regulations   £6.80

   (b) to a person:—

      (i) who would, but for the provisions of regulation 9 of the Regulations, be regarded as the holder of a British Seamen's Card; and

      (ii) who has ceased to be regarded as the holder of a British Seamen's Card because it has been lost, destroyed or defaced other than through circumstances beyond his control   £6.80

(2) For the issue of a discharge book under paragraph (1) or paragraph (2) of regulation 19 of the Regulations to a seaman other than:—

   (a) one who, in accordance with regulation 18(1)*(b)* of the Regulations, produces a Seamen's Record Book (as defined in regulation 1(2)*(h)* of the Regulations), which has been issued to him, or a discharge book of which he would, but for the provisions of regulation 25*(b)* of the Regulations, be regarded as the holder; or

   (b) one to whom Seaman's Record Book (as so defined) has been issued or who was the holder of a discharge book, which in either case has been lost, destroyed or defaced through circumstances beyond his control   £6.80

PART XVIII: ENGAGEMENT AND DISCHARGE OF SEAMEN

FEES FOR THE ENGAGEMENT AND DISCHARGE OF SEAMEN

1. The fees prescribed in this Part are payable under section 2(2) of the Fees (Increase) Act 1923(**a**) and section 84 of the Act of 1970.

2. In this Part "the Crew Agreements Regulations" means the Merchant Shipping (Crew Agreements, Lists of Crew and Discharge of Seamen) Regulations 1972(**b**) and the Merchant Shipping (Crew Agreements, Lists of Crew and Discharge of Seamen) (Fishing Vessels) Regulations 1972(**c**).

Service	*Fee*

3. For the engagement and discharge of seamen before a Superintendent pursuant to the Crew Agreements Regulations, or for any service rendered in connection with a crew agreement at the request of the owner, agent or master:—

(a) As amended by section 33(2) of the Act of 1949.
(b) S.I. 1972/918, to which there are amendments not relevant to these Regulations.
(c) S.I. 1972/919, to which there are amendments not relevant to these Regulations.

Service	*Fee*
(a) Where the service is performed elsewhere than in a Marine Office:—	
(1) On Monday to Friday (excluding Public Holidays) between 9.00 am and 5.00 pm	The fee will be determined by the amount of work involved, including travelling time, charged at an hourly rate of £17, subject to a minimum fee of £17.
(2) At all other times	200% of the appropriate fee under (1) above.
These fees are exclusive of travel and subsistence expenses which will be charged additionally	
(b) Where the service is performed in a Marine Office:—	
(1) On Monday to Friday (excluding Public Holidays) between 9.00 am and 5.00 pm	The fee will be determined by the amount of work involved charged at an hourly rate of £17, subject to a minimum fee of £4.25
(2) At all other times	200% of the appropriate fee under (1) above.

EXPLANATORY NOTE

(*This Note is not part of the Regulations.*)

These Regulations revoke the Merchant Shipping (Fees) Regulations 1982, as amended.

The Regulations prescribe a 10.8% increase in fees for marine surveys and inspections (Parts I, II, IV–VII, IX, XV and XVI), a 15% increase in fees for the survey of fishing vessels (Parts VIII and X), a 10.4% increase in the fees for the survey and inspection of ships' radio equipment (Part III) and a 10% increase in fees for examinations for certificates of competency (Part XI).

Fees for other services have been increased by amounts varying from 5% to 19%.

STATUTORY INSTRUMENTS

1983 No. 1168

ROAD TRAFFIC

The Electrically Assisted Pedal Cycles Regulations 1983

Approved by both Houses of Parliament

Made - - - -	*1st July* 1983
Laid before Parliament	*8th July* 1983
Coming into Operation	*12th August* 1983

The Secretary of State for Transport, in exercise of the powers conferred by section 103(1) of the Road Traffic Regulation Act 1967(**a**) and section 193(1) of the Road Traffic Act 1972(**b**), now vested in him(**c**), and of all other enabling powers, and after consultation with representative organisations in accordance with section 107(2) of the said Act of 1967 and with section 199(2) of the said Act of 1972, hereby makes the following Regulations:—

1.—(1) These Regulations shall come into operation 14 days after the date on which they are approved by resolution of each House of Parliament.

(2) These Regulations may be cited as the Electrically Assisted Pedal Cycles Regulations 1983.

2. In these Regulations—
"continuous rated output" has the same meaning as in the 1971 British Standard;

"kerbside weight", in relation to an electrically assisted pedal cycle, means the weight of the cycle without any person on it and with no load other than the loose tools and equipment with which it is normally equipped;

"nominal voltage" means the nominal voltage of the battery as defined in the 1971 British Standard;

"the 1971 British Standard" means the specification for motors for battery operated vehicles published by the British Standards Institution under the reference 1727: 1971 as amended by Amendment Slip No. 1 published on 31st January 1973, Amendment Slip No. 2 published on 31st July 1974 and Amendment Slip No. 3 published on 31st March 1978; and

"tandem bicycle" means a bicycle which is designed to carry two or more persons at least two of whom can propel the vehicle at the same time.

3. The class of electrically assisted pedal cycles prescribed for the purposes of section 103 of the Road Traffic Regulation Act 1967 and section 193 of the Road Traffic Act 1972 consists of bicycles or tricycles which comply with the requirements specified in Regulation 4 below.

(**a**) 1967 c. 76; section 103(1) of which Act has been amended by section 24 of the Transport Act 1981 (c. 56).
(**b**) 1972 c. 20; section 193(1) of which Act has been amended by section 24 of the Transport Act 1981.
(**c**) As regards 1967 c. 76 by S.I. 1970/1681, 1979/571 and 1981/238 and as regards 1972 c. 20 by S.I. 1979/571 and 1981/238.

4. The requirements referred to in Regulation 3 above are that the vehicle shall:—

(a) have a kerbside weight not exceeding—

(i) in the case of a bicycle, other than a tandem bicycle, 40 kilograms, and

(ii) in the case of a tandem bicycle and a tricycle, 60 kilograms;

(b) be fitted with pedals by means of which it is capable of being propelled; and

(c) be fitted with no motor other than an electric motor which—

(i) has a continuous rated output which, when installed in the vehicle with the nominal voltage supplied, does not exceed—

(A) in the case of a bicycle, other than a tandem bicycle, 0.2 kilowatts,

(B) in the case of a tandem bicycle and a tricycle, 0.25 kilowatts; and

(ii) cannot propel the vehicle when it is travelling at more than 15 miles per hour.

Tom King,
Secretary of State for Transport.

1st July 1983.

EXPLANATORY NOTE

(This Note is not part of the Regulations.)

1. These Regulations are made pursuant to section 24 of the Transport Act 1981 (which has been brought into force by the Transport Act 1981 (Commencement No. 9) Order 1983 (S.I. 1983/576 (c.16))). That section provided for the addition to section 103 of the Road Traffic Regulation Act 1967 (by virtue of which certain vehicles are not treated as motor vehicles for the purposes of that Act) and section 193 of the Road Traffic Act 1972 (by virtue of which certain vehicles are not treated as motor vehicles for the purposes of that Act) of an electrically assisted pedal cycle of such class as may be prescribed by regulations.

2. By Regulation 3 of these Regulations the class of electrically assisted pedal cycles prescribed for the purposes of section 103 of the 1967 Act and section 193 of the 1972 Act are vehicles which comply with the requirements specified in Regulation 4. Certain terms used in these Regulations are defined in Regulation 2.

3. Copies of the British Standard, referred to in Regulation 2, are available from the British Standards Institution at 101 Pentonville Road, London N1 9ND.

STATUTORY INSTRUMENTS

1983 No. 1172 (S. 104)

NATIONAL HEALTH SERVICE, SCOTLAND

The National Health Service (Charges for Drugs and Appliances) (Scotland) Amendment (No. 2) Regulations 1983

Made - - - - -	26*th July* 1983
Laid before Parliament	10*th August* 1983
Coming into Operation	1*st September* 1983

In exercise of the powers conferred on me by sections 69(1) and (3) and 108(1) of and paragraph 1(2) of Schedule 11 to the National Health Service (Scotland) Act 1978**(a)** and of all other powers enabling me in that behalf, I hereby make the following regulations:—

Citation, commencement and interpretation

1.—(1) These regulations may be cited as the National Health Service (Charges for Drugs and Appliances) (Scotland) Amendment (No. 2) Regulations 1983 and shall come into operation on 1st September 1983.

(2) In these regulations, "the principal regulations" means the National Health Service (Charges for Drugs and Appliances) (Scotland) Regulations 1980**(b)**.

Amendment of the principal regulations

2. In regulation 4(1) of the principal regulations (supply of drugs and appliances by doctors),

(*a*) for the words "the Medical Services Regulations or of his terms of service,", there shall be substituted the words "regulation 30 of the Medical Services Regulations (and otherwise than under paragraph 15(1) of Schedule 1 to those regulations),"; and

(*b*) sub-paragraph (ii) and the word "or" preceding it shall be revoked.

George Younger,
New St. Andrew's House, One of Her Majesty's Principal
Edinburgh. Secretaries of State.
26th July 1983.

(**a**) 1978 c. 29.
(**b**) S.I. 1980/1674; the relevant amending instruments are S.I. 1982/332 and 1983/334.

EXPLANATORY NOTE

(This Note is not part of the Regulations.)

These Regulations amend regulation 4(1) of the National Health Service (Charges for Drugs and Appliances) (Scotland) Regulations 1980 ("the principal regulations"), which make provision for the charges for the supply of drugs and appliances which a doctor, who provides pharmaceutical services, is required to make and recover from a patient.

The amendments made by these regulations restrict the scope of regulation 4(1) of the principal regulations by confining it to where a doctor provides pharmaceutical services under regulation 30 of the National Health Service (General Medical and Pharmaceutical Services) (Scotland) Regulations 1974 (S.I. 1974/506) (arrangements for supply by doctors of drugs and appliances). It also makes it clear that it does not include any case where a doctor supplies any drug or appliance under paragraph 15(1) of Schedule 1 to those regulations (which makes provision for a doctor supplying any drug or appliance for the immediate treatment of a patient or for personal administration).

As a consequence, it is no longer necessary to make an express exemption in regulation 4(1) of the principal regulations for the case where the drug or appliance is supplied for immediate treatment and sub-paragraph (ii) of that regulation is accordingly revoked.

STATUTORY INSTRUMENTS

1983 No. 1173 (C. 32)

WATER, ENGLAND AND WALES

The Water Act 1983 (Commencement No. 1) Order 1983

Made -   -   -   -   29*th July* 1983

The Secretary of State for the Environment, as respects England, and the Secretary of State for Wales, as respects Wales, in exercise of their powers under section 11(5) of the Water Act 1983(**a**) and of all other powers enabling them in that behalf, hereby order as follows:—

1. This order may be cited as the Water Act 1983 (Commencement No. 1) Order 1983.

2. The provisions of the Water Act 1983 which are specified in column 1 of the Schedule to this order and which relate to the subject matter specified in column 2 thereof shall come into force on 10th August 1983.

(**a**) 1983 c. 23.

SCHEDULE

Column 1 Provisions of the Act	Column 2 Subject matter of provisions
Section 7	Arrangements by water authorities for representation of consumers' interests
Section 8	Repeal of Water Charges Equalisation Act 1977(**a**)
Section 11(3) so far as it applies to the provisions of Schedule 5 which are specified below	Repeal or revocation of enactments and instruments
In Schedule 5, Part 1	
the entry relative to the Development of Rural Wales Act 1976(**b**)	
the entry relative to the Water Charges Equalisation Act 1977	
Local Government, Planning and Land Act 1980(**c**)	
In section 158, subsections (1) and (2)	
the entry relative to the New Towns Act 1981(**d**)	

Patrick Jenkin,
Secretary of State for the Environment.

27th July 1983.

Signed by authority of the Secretary of State.

John Stradling Thomas,
Minister of State for Wales.

29th July 1983.

(**a**) 1977 c. 41.   (**b**) 1976 c. 75.
(**c**) 1980 c. 65.   (**d**) 1981 c. 64.

STATUTORY INSTRUMENTS

1983 No. 1174

WATER, ENGLAND AND WALES

The Water Act 1983 (Water Space Amenity Commission Appointed Day) Order 1983

Made -   -   -   -   *29th July* 1983

The Secretary of State for the Environment as respects England and the Secretary of State for Wales as respects Wales, in exercise of their powers under sections 3(2) and 9(2) of the Water Act 1983(**a**) and of all other powers enabling them in that behalf, hereby make the following order:—

1. This order may be cited as the Water Act 1983 (Water Space Amenity Commission Appointed Day) Order 1983.

2. The day appointed for the purposes of section 3(2) of the Water Act 1983 (which provides for the determination of the functions of the Water Space Amenity Commission) shall be 1st October 1983.

3. The provisions of the Water Act 1983 which are specified in column 1 of the Schedule to this order and which relate to the subject matter specified in column 2 thereof shall come into force on 1st October 1983.

(**a**) 1983 c. 23.

SCHEDULE

Column 1 Provisions of the Act	Column 2 Subject matter of provisions

Section 11(3)
    so far as it applies to the provisions of
    Schedule 5 which are specified below
	Repeal or revocation of enactments and
	instruments

In Schedule 5, Part I	
Water Act 1973(a)	
Section 23	
In section 24(12)(a), the words "and to the Water Space Amenity Commission"	
Section 25(5)(a)	

In Schedule 3, in paragraph 40,
    sub-paragraph (1)(b) and the word
    "and" immediately preceding it; and
    sub-paragraph (5)	

Patrick Jenkin,
Secretary of State for the Environment.

27th July 1983.

Signed by authority of the Secretary of State.

John Stradling Thomas,
Minister of State for Wales.

29th July 1983.

EXPLANATORY NOTE

(This Note is not part of the Order.)

This Order appoints 1st October 1983 as the day on which the functions of the Water Space Amenity Commission shall determine, and as the day on which certain enactments relating to those functions shall be repealed.

(a) 1973 c. 37.

STATUTORY INSTRUMENTS

1983 No. 1175 (C. 33)

PUBLIC HEALTH, ENGLAND AND WALES
PUBLIC HEALTH, SCOTLAND

The Control of Pollution Act 1974 (Commencement No. 15)*
Order 1983

Made -   -   -   -   *28th July* 1983

The Secretary of State, in exercise of his powers under section 109(2) of the Control of Pollution Act 1974(**a**) and of all other powers enabling him in that behalf, hereby makes the following order:—

1. This order may be cited as the Control of Pollution Act 1974 (Commencement No. 15) Order 1983.

2. Section 32(3) of the Control of Pollution Act 1974 shall come into operation on 10th August 1983.

Patrick Jenkin,
One of Her Majesty's Principal
Secretaries of State.

28th July 1983.

(**a**) 1974 c. 40.
*A correction slip which inadvertently renumbered the Commencement No. of this Order as "16" was issued in August 1983.

EXPLANATORY NOTE

(This Note is not part of the Order.)

This Order, which applies to Great Britain, brings into force the provision of the Control of Pollution Act 1974 which empowers the Secretary of State to provide by order that certain discharges shall be exempt, while the Order is in force, from control under the Act.

NOTE AS TO EARLIER COMMENCEMENT ORDERS

(This Note is not part of the Order.)

Provision	Date of Commencement	S.I. No.
s. 109 (England, Wales, Scotland, Northern Ireland)		
ss. 104, 105 (England, Wales, Scotland)		
ss. 43, 44, 95, 107 and 108(1) (partially) (England, Wales)	12th December 1974	1974/2039
s. 108(1) and (2) (both partially) (England, Wales, Scotland)	1st January 1975	1974/2169
s. 108(2) (partially) (Scotland)	3rd March 1975	1975/230
ss. 75, 77, 100, 101 (England, Wales, Scotland, Northern Ireland)		
s. 12(5) (partially), ss.25, 29, 30, 78, 99, 102, 103, 108(2) (partially), Sch. 2 (England, Wales, Scotland)		
s. 12(6) and (7) (partially), ss.17, 19–21, 26, 27(1)(*a*) and (2), 28 (partially), 49, 50, 56–74, Sch. 1, 76, 79–87, 89–94, 96–8, 108(1) and (2) (both partially), 108(3), Sch. 3 (partially), Sch. 4 (partially) (England, Wales)		
s. 106 (Scotland)	1st January 1976	1975/2118
ss. 3–11, 16, 18(1) and (2), 22, 23, 88, Sch. 3 (partially) Sch. 4 (partially) (England, Wales)	14th June 1976	1976/731
ss. 108(1) and (2) (both partially) (England, Wales)	20th July 1976	1976/956

Provision	Date of Commencement	S.I. No.
s. 17 (partially), s.27(1)(*a*) and (2), ss.57(*a*), 58 (partially), 59, 62, 68, 69 (partially), 70, 71(1) and (3), 72, 73 (partially), 74, 76, 84, 85, 87, 89–93, 94 (partially), 96, 98, 108(1) and (2) (both partially), 108(3), Sch. 3 (partially), Sch. 4 (partially) (Scotland)	18th July 1976	1976/1080
ss. 12(5), 14(9), (10), (11), 108(2) (partially), Sch. 4 (partially) (England)	1st April 1977	1977/336
ss. 24(4) (England, Wales, Scotland), s.108(2) (partially), Sch. 4 (partially) (England, Wales)	1st April 1977	1977/476
ss. 3–11, 16, 17(3)(*a*), 18(1) and (2), 20, 88 (Scotland)	1st January 1978	1977/1587
s. 2 (England, Wales)	1st July 1978	1977/2164
s. 2 (Scotland)	1st September 1978	1978/816
s. 13 (partially) (England, Wales)	1st August 1978	1978/954
s. 108(2) (partially) (England, Wales, Scotland)	16th March 1981	1981/196
ss. 57(*b*), 58(6), 58(8) (partially), 60, 61, 63 – 67, 69 (partially), 71(2), 73 (partially), 79 – 83 (Scotland)	1st August 1982	1982/624

STATUTORY INSTRUMENTS

1983 No. 1176

ROAD TRAFFIC

The Pedal Cycles (Construction and Use) Regulations 1983

Made - - - - -	*1st August* 1983
Laid before Parliament	*10th August* 1983
Coming into Operation	*1st September* 1983

ARRANGEMENT OF REGULATIONS

The Secretary of State for Transport, in exercise of the powers conferred by section 66(1), (3) and (4) of the Road Traffic Act 1972**(a)**, and now vested in him**(b)**, and of all other enabling powers, and after consultation with representative organisations in accordance with the provisions of section 199(2) of that Act, hereby makes the following Regulations:—

Commencement and citation
1. These Regulations shall come into operation on 1st September 1983, and may be cited as the Pedal Cycles (Construction and Use) Regulations 1983.

Revocation
2. The Brakes on Pedal Cycles Regulations 1954**(c)** are hereby revoked.

Interpretation
3.—(1) In these Regulations:—

(*a*) a reference to the manufacturer of a vehicle means, in the case of a vehicle which has been altered so as to become an electrically assisted pedal cycle, the person who made that alteration;

(**a**) 1972 c. 20.   (**b**) S.I. 1979/571 and 1981/238.   (**c**) S.I. 1954/966.

(b) "pedal cycle" means a pedal cycle which is either—

    (i) not propelled by mechanical power, or

    (ii) an electrically assisted pedal cycle prescribed for the purposes of section 103 of the Road Traffic Regulation Act 1967(a) and section 193 of the Road Traffic Act 1972 by virtue of the Electrically Assisted Pedal Cycles Regulations 1983(b);

(c) "the 1971 British Standard" has the same meaning as in the Electrically Assisted Pedal Cycles Regulations 1983; and

(d) "the 1981 British Standard" means the Specification for safety requirements for bicycles published by the British Standard Institution under the reference BS 6102: Part I: 1981.

(2) In these Regulations, unless the context otherwise requires, a reference to a numbered Regulation is to the Regulation bearing that number in these Regulations, and a reference to a numbered paragraph is to the paragraph bearing that number in the Regulation in which the reference occurs.

Requirements as to a pedal cycle to which the Electrically Assisted Pedal Cycles Regulations 1983 apply

4. No person shall ride, or cause or permit to be ridden, on a road a pedal cycle to which the Electrically Assisted Pedal Cycles Regulations 1983 apply unless it is fitted with—

(a) a plate securely fixed in a conspicuous and readily accessible position showing—

    (i) the name of the manufacturer of the vehicle,

    (ii) the nominal voltage of the battery (as defined in the 1971 British Standard) of the vehicle, and

    (iii) the continuous rated output (as defined in the 1971 British Standard) of the motor of the vehicle;

(b) braking systems which are so designed and constructed that—

    (i) in the case of a bicycle they comply with the standards specified in clause 6 of the 1981 British Standard, and

    (ii) in the case of a tricycle they comply with standards no less than the standards of braking systems fitted to a bicycle which comply with clause 6 of the 1981 British Standard;

(c) a battery which does not leak so as to be a source of danger; and

(d) a device biased to the off position which allows power to come from the motor only when the device is operated so as to achieve that result.

5. No person shall ride, or cause or permit to be ridden, on a road a pedal cycle to which the Electrically Assisted Pedal Cycles Regulations 1983 apply unless the parts of the vehicle mentioned in—

(a) Regulation 4(b) and (c) of those Regulations, and

(a) 1967 c. 76.   (b) S.I. 1983/1168.

(*b*) Regulation 4(*b*), (*c*) and (*d*) of these Regulations,

are in efficient working order.

Requirements as to a pedal cycle to which the Electrically Assisted Pedal Cycles Regulations 1983 do not apply

6. No person shall ride, or cause or permit to be ridden, on a road a pedal cycle to which the Electrically Assisted Pedal Cycles Regulations 1983 do not apply unless it complies with such of the requirements specified in Regulation 7 or 8 as apply to it.

7.—(1) Save as provided in Regulations 8 and 9—

(*a*) every pedal cycle shall be equipped with at least one braking system;

(*b*) every bicycle or tricycle the height of the saddle of which is 635 millimetres or more and every cycle with four or more wheels shall—

   (i) if it is so constructed that one or more of the wheels is incapable of rotating independently of the pedals, be equipped with a braking system operating on the front wheel or, if it has more than one front wheel, on at least two front wheels;

   (ii) if it is not so constructed that one or more of the wheels is incapable of rotating independently of the pedals, be equipped with two independent braking systems one of which operates on the front wheel, or if it has more than one front wheel, on at least two front wheels, and the other of which operates on the rear wheel, or if it has more than one rear wheel, on at least two rear wheels.

(2) The reference in paragraph (1)(*b*) to the height of the saddle is a reference to the height above the ground of the part of the seating area of the saddle which is furthest from the ground when the cycle to which the saddle is attached is vertical and the saddle is raised to the fullest extent compatible with safety and the tyres on the wheels of the cycle are fully inflated.

8.—(1) The requirements of Regulation 7 do not apply to a pedal cycle manufactured before 1st August 1984 if, save as provided in Regulation 9 in the case where the cycle has any wheel of which the outside diameter (including any tyre when fully inflated) exceeds 460 millimetres—

   (i) the cycle is so constructed that one or more of the wheels is incapable of rotating independently of the pedals, it is equipped with a braking system operating on the front wheel or both the front wheels if it has two front wheels;

   (ii) the cycle is not so constructed, it is equipped with two independent braking systems one of which operates on the front wheel or both the front wheels if it has two front wheels, and the other of which operates on the rear wheel or one of the rear wheels if it has two rear wheels.

9.—(1) Nothing in Regulation 7 or 8 applies to—

(*a*) any pedal cycle so constructed that the pedals act on any wheel or on the axle of any wheel without the interposition of any gearing or chain; or

(*b*) any pedal cycle brought temporarily into Great Britain by a person resident abroad and intending to make only a temporary stay in Great Britain, while the cycle is being ridden by that person, provided that its brakes comply with the requirements of Article 26 of the International Convention on Road Traffic signed at Geneva on 19th September 1949**(a)** as amended**(b)**.

(2) In the case of a tricycle not constructed or adapted for the carriage of goods it shall be a sufficient compliance with the requirements specified in Regulation 7(1)(*b*)(ii) and 8(1)(*a*)(ii) if the tricycle is equipped with two independent braking systems operating on the front wheel if it has two rear wheels, or on the rear wheel if it has two front wheels.

10.—(1) No person shall ride, or cause or permit to be ridden, on a road a pedal cycle to which Regulation 6 applies unless the braking system or systems with which it is required to be fitted in accordance with Regulation 7 or, as the case may be, Regulation 8 are in efficient working order.

(2) For the purpose of this Regulation, except in the case of a cycle having four or more wheels, none of which has a diameter exceeding 250 millimetres (including any tyre when fully inflated), a braking system shall be deemed not to be in efficient working order if any brake operates directly on a pneumatic tyre on any wheel.

Testing and inspection

11. Any constable in uniform is hereby empowered to test and inspect a pedal cycle for the purpose of ascertaining whether any of the requirements specified in Regulation 4(*b*), or Regulation 7 or, as the case may be, Regulation 8, are satisfied provided he does so either—

(*a*) on any premises where the cycle is if the cycle has been involved in an accident, and the test and inspection are carried out within 48 hours of the accident and the owner of the premises consents; or

(*b*) on a road.

Requirements as to sale or supply etc of pedal cycles

12. No person shall sell or supply, or offer to sell or supply for delivery—

(*a*) a pedal cycle to which the Electrically Assisted Pedal Cycles Regulations 1983 apply unless it is equipped with braking systems as specified in Regulation 4(*b*); or

(*b*) on and after 1st August 1984, a pedal cycle to which those Regulations do not apply unless it is

(i) equipped with braking systems as specified in Regulation 7 or, as the case may be, Regulation 8; or

(a) Cmnd. 7997. **(b)** Cmnd. 3152.

(ii) a pedal cycle which has no braking system and is specifically designed for off-road racing on enclosed tracks.

Tom King,
Secretary of State for Transport.
1st August 1983.

EXPLANATORY NOTE

(This Note is not part of the Regulations.)

1. These Regulations exercise powers under section 66 of the Road Traffic Act 1972 relating to the construction and use of pedal cycles.

2. The previous Regulations made under these powers—the Brakes on Pedal Cycles Regulations 1954—are revoked (see Regulation 2).

3. Regulation 4 provides that no person shall ride, or cause or permit to be ridden, on a road a pedal cycle to which the Electrically Assisted Pedal Cycles Regulations 1983 apply unless it is fitted with a plate showing certain particulars, brakes which comply with certain standards, a battery which does not leak, and a device to control the operation of its motor. Regulation 5 provides that no person shall ride, or cause or permit to be ridden, on a road a vehicle to which those Regulations apply unless the parts of the vehicle mentioned in Regulation 4 of those Regulations (pedals and motor) and the parts mentioned in Regulation 4(*b*), (*c*) and (*d*) of these Regulations are in efficient working order.

4. Regulation 6 provides that no person shall ride, or cause or permit to be ridden, on a road a cycle to which the Electrically Assisted Pedal Cycles Regulations 1983 do not apply unless it complies with the relevant requirements specified in Regulation 7 or 8. Regulations 7 and 8 contain provisions about brakes on such cycles. Regulation 9 gives exemptions from Regulation 7 or, as the case may be, Regulation 8. Regulation 10 requires brakes on such cycles to be in efficient working order.

5. By Regulation 11 the power contained in section 66(1)(*c*) of the 1972 Act as to the testing and inspection of pedal cycles is exercised so that a constable in uniform may test a cycle to see whether braking requirements are satisfied.

6. By Regulation 12 the power contained in section 66(4) of the 1972 Act to prohibit the sale of pedal cycles is exercised so that no person shall sell or supply, or offer to sell or supply for delivery a pedal cycle to which the Electrically Assisted Pedal Cycles Regulations 1983 applies unless it is equipped with brakes as specified in Regulation 4(*b*) or, on and after 1st August 1984, a pedal cycle to which those Regulations do not apply unless it is equipped with brakes as specified in Regulation 7 or 8 or is designed for off-road racing on enclosed tracks.

7. Provisions relating to lights and reflectors on pedal cycles are not made in these Regulations; provisions in that respect remain in Part II of the 1972 Act and in the Road Vehicles Lighting Regulations 1971 (S.I. 1971/694).

8. Copies of the British Standards mentioned in these Regulations may be obtained from the British Standards Institution at 195 Pentonville Road, London N1 9ND or Linford Wood, Milton Keynes, MK14 6CE.

STATUTORY INSTRUMENTS

1983 No. 1180 (L. 20)

SUPREME COURT OF ENGLAND AND WALES

FEES

The Non-Contentious Probate Fees (Amendment) Order 1983

Made - - - -	*26th July* 1983
Laid before Parliament	*4th August* 1983
Coming into Operation	*1st September* 1983

The Lord Chancellor, in exercise of the power conferred on him by section 130 of the Supreme Court Act 1981(**a**), and with the concurrence of the Lord Chief Justice, the Master of the Rolls, the President of the Family Division, The Vice-Chancellor and the Treasury, hereby makes the following Order:—

  1. This Order may be cited as the Non-Contentious Probate Fees (Amendment) Order 1983 and shall come into operation on 1st September 1983.

  2. For paragraph 1(*a*) of the schedule to the Non-Contentious Probate Fees Order 1981(*b*) there shall be substituted the following sub-paragraph:—

"(a) if the assessed value

does not exceed £10,000	No fee
exceeds £10,000 but does not exceed £25,000 ..	40.00
exceeds £25,000 but does not exceed £40,000 ..	80.00
exceeds £40,000 but does not exceed £100,000 ..	2.50 per £1,000 or part thereof"

Hailsham of St. Marylebone, C.

Dated 25th July 1983.

(**a**) 1981 c. 54.   (**b**) S.I. 1981/861.

Lane, C.J.,
John F. Donaldson, M.R.,
John Arnold, P.,
R. E. Megarry, V-C.

Dated 26th July 1983

T. Garel-Jones,
Ian B. Lang,
Two of the Lords Commissioners of
Her Majesty's Treasury.

Dated 26th July 1983.

EXPLANATORY NOTE

(*This Note is not part of the Order.*)

This Order substitutes a fixed fee of £80 for the ad Valorem charge of £2.50 per £1,000 or part thereof in respect of estates with an assessed value exceeding £25,000 and not exceeding £40,000.

STATUTORY INSTRUMENTS

1983 No. 1181 (L. 21)

SUPREME COURT OF ENGLAND AND WALES

The Rules of the Supreme Court (Amendment No. 2) 1983

Made - - - -	*25th July* 1983
Laid before Parliament	*4th August* 1983
Coming into Operation as to Rules 1 and 2, Rule 12 and Rules 22 to 36	*1st October* 1983
as to Rules 3 to 11, Rules 13 to 21 and Rule 37	*in accordance with Rule 1*

We, the Supreme Court Rule Committee, having power under section 84 of the Supreme Court Act 1981(**a**) to make rules of court for the purpose of regulating and prescribing the practice and procedure to be followed in the Supreme Court, hereby exercise those powers as follows:—

Citation and commencement

1. These Rules may be cited as the Rules of the Supreme Court (Amendment No. 2) 1983 and shall come into operation on 1st October 1983, except for Rules 3 to 11, 13 to 21 and 37, which shall come into operation when section 2 of the Civil Jurisdiction and Judgments Act 1982(**b**) comes into force.

2. In these Rules an Order referred to by number means the Order so numbered in the Rules of the Supreme Court 1965(**c**) and, unless the context otherwise requires, a form referred to by number means the form so numbered in Appendix A to those Rules.

Issue of Writ

3. Order 6, rule 7 shall be amended by substituting for paragraph (1), the following new paragraph:—

"(1) No writ which is to be served out of the jurisdiction shall be issued

---

(**a**) 1981 c. 54.
(**b**) 1982 c. 27.
(**c**) S.I. 1965/1776; the relevant amending instruments are S.I. 1967/829, 1809, 1969/1105, 1971/1269, 1955, 1972/1898, 1976/337, 1196, 2097, 1978/1066, 1979/522, 1980/629, 1010, 1981/1734.

without the leave of the court unless it complies with the following conditions, that is to say—

(a) each claim made by the writ is either—

(i) one which by virtue of the Civil Jurisdiction and Judgments Act 1982 the Court has power to hear and determine, or

(ii) one which by virtue of any other enactment the Court has power to hear and determine notwithstanding that the person against whom the claim is made is not within the jurisdiction of the Court or that the wrongful act, neglect or default giving rise to the claim did not take place within its jurisdiction;

and

(b) where a claim made by the writ in one which the Court has power to hear and determine by virtue of the Civil Jurisdiction and Judgments Act 1982, the writ is indorsed before it is issued with a statement that the Court has power under that Act to hear and determine the claim, and that no proceedings involving the same cause of action are pending between the parties in Scotland, Northern Ireland or another Convention territory.".

4. Order 6, rule 7 shall be further amended by adding, at the end, the following new paragraph:—

"(6) For the purposes of this rule, 'Convention territory' means the territory or territories of any Contracting State, as defined by section 1(3) of that Act, to which the Conventions as defined in section 1(1) of that Act apply.".

Service of writ in pursuance of contract

5. Order 10, rule 3 shall be amended by substituting in paragraph (2), for the words from "has been granted" to the end, the words:—

"has been granted under Order 11, rule 1(1) or service of the writ is permitted without leave under Order 11, rule 1(2).".

6. Order 10, rule 3 shall be further amended by adding at the end the following new paragraph:—

"(3) Where a contract contains an agreement conferring jurisdiction to which Article 17 of Schedule 1 or of Schedule 4 to the Civil Jurisdiction and Judgments Act 1982 applies and the writ is served under Order 11, rule 1(2) the writ shall be deemed to have been duly served on the defendant.".

Service of process out of the jurisdiction

7. Order 11, rule 1 shall be amended by substituting for that rule the following new rule:—

"Principal cases in which service of writ out of jurisdiction is permissible

1.—(1) Provided that the writ does not contain any claim mentioned in Order 75, rule 2(1) and is not a writ to which paragraph (2) of this rule applies, service of a writ out of the jurisdiction is permissible with the leave of the Court if in the action begun by the writ—

(a) relief is sought against a person domiciled within the jurisdiction;

(b) an injunction is sought ordering the defendant to do or refrain from doing anything within the jurisdiction (whether or not damages are also claimed in respect of a failure to do or the doing of that thing);

(c) the claim is brought against a person duly served within or out of the jurisdiction and a person out of the jurisdiction is a necessary or proper party thereto;

(d) the claim is brought to enforce, rescind, dissolve, annul or otherwise affect a contract, or to recover damages or obtain other relief in respect of the breach of a contract, being (in either case) a contract which—

　(i) was made within the jurisdiction, or

　(ii) was made by or through an agent trading or residing within the jurisdiction on behalf of a principal trading or residing out of the jurisdiction, or

　(iii) is by its terms, or by implication, governed by English law, or

　(iv) contains a term to the effect that the High Court shall have jurisdiction to hear and determine any action in respect of the contract;

(e) the claim is brought in respect of a breach committed within the jurisdiction of a contract made within or out of the jurisdiction, and irrespective of the fact, if such be the case, that the breach was preceded or accompanied by a breach committed out of the jurisdiction that rendered impossible the performance of so much of the contract as ought to have been performed within the jurisdiction;

(f) the claim is founded on a tort and the damage was sustained, or resulted from an act committed, within the jurisdiction;

(g) the whole subject-matter of the action is land situate within the jurisdiction (with or without rents or profits) or the perpetuation of testimony relating to land so situate;

(h) the claim is brought to construe, rectify, set aside or enforce an act, deed, will, contract, obligation or liability affecting land situate within the jurisdiction;

(i) the claim is made for a debt secured on immovable property or is made to assert, declare or determine proprietary or possessory rights, or rights of security, in or over movable property, or to obtain authority to dispose of movable property, situate within the jurisdiction;

(j) the claim is brought to execute the trusts of a written instrument being trusts that ought to be executed according to English law and of which the person to be served with the writ is a trustee, or for any relief or remedy which might be obtained in any such action;

(k) the claim is made for the administration of the estate of a person who died domiciled within the jurisdiction or for any relief or remedy which might be obtained in any such action;

(l) the claim is brought in a probate action within the meaning of Order 76;

(*m*) the claim is brought to enforce any judgment or arbitral award;

(*n*) the claim is brought against a defendant not domiciled in Scotland or Northern Ireland in respect of a claim by the Commissioners of Inland Revenue for or in relation to any of the duties or taxes which have been, or are for the time being, placed under their care and management;

(*o*) the claim is brought under the Nuclear Installations Act 1965(**a**) or in respect of contributions under the Social Security Act 1975(**b**);

(*p*) the claim is made for a sum to which the Directive of the Council of the European Communities dated 15th March 1976 No. 76/308/EEC applies, and service is to be effected in a country which is a member State of the European Economic Community.

(2) Service of a writ out of the jurisdiction is permissible without the leave of the Court provided that each claim made by the writ is either:—

(*a*) a claim which by virtue of the Civil Jurisdiction and Judgments Act 1982 the Court has power to hear and determine, made in proceedings to which the following conditions apply—

(i) no proceedings between the parties concerning the same cause of action are pending in the courts of any other part of the United Kingdom or of any other Convention territory, and

(ii) either—

the defendant is domiciled in any part of the United Kingdom or in any other Convention territory, or

the proceedings begun by the writ are proceedings to which Article 16 of Schedule 1 or of Schedule 4 refers, or

the defendant is a party to an agreement conferring jurisdiction to which Article 17 of Schedule 1 or of Schedule 4 to that Act applies,

or

(*b*) a claim which by virtue of any other enactment the High Court has power to hear and determine notwithstanding that the person against whom the claim is made is not within the jurisdiction of the Court or that the wrongful act, neglect or default giving rise to the claim did not take place within its jurisdiction.

(3) Where a writ is to be served out of the jurisdiction under paragraph (2), the time to be inserted in the writ within which the defendant served therewith must acknowledge service shall be—

(*a*) 21 days where the writ is to be served out of the jurisdiction under paragraph (2)(*a*) in Scotland, Northern Ireland or in the European territory of another Contracting State, or

(*b*) 31 days where the writ is to be served under paragraph (2)(*a*) in any other territory of a Contracting State, or

(*c*) limited in accordance with the practice adopted under rule 4(4)

(**a**) 1965 c. 57.
(**b**) 1975 c. 14.

where the writ is to be served under paragraph (2)(*a*) in a country not referred to in sub-paragraphs (*a*) or (*b*) or under paragraph (2)(*b*).

(4) For the purposes of this rule, and of rule 9 of this Order, domicile is to be determined in accordance with the provisions of sections 41 to 46 of the Civil Jurisdiction and Judgments Act 1982 and "Convention territory" means the territory or territories of any Contracting State, as defined by section 1(3) of that Act, to which the Conventions as defined in section 1(1) of that Act apply.".

8. Order 11, rule 2 shall be revoked.

Application for, and grant of, leave to serve writ out of jurisdiction

9. Order 11, rule 4 shall be amended as follows:—

(1) The following paragraph shall be substituted for paragraph (1):—

"(1) An application for the grant of leave under rule 1(1) must be supported by an affidavit stating—

(*a*) the grounds on which the application is made,

(*b*) that in the deponent's belief the plaintiff has a good cause of action,

(*c*) in what place or country the defendant is, or probably may be found, and

(*d*) where the application is made under rule 1(1)*(c)*, the grounds for the deponent's belief that there is between the plaintiff and the person on whom a writ has been served a real issue which the plaintiff may reasonably ask the Court to try."

(2) In paragraph (4) the words "or 2" shall be omitted.

Service of originating summons, petition, notice of motion, etc.

10. Order 11, rule 9 shall be amended by substituting for paragraph (1) the following new paragraph:—

"(1) Subject to Order 73, rule 7, rule 1 of this Order shall aply to the service out of the jurisdiction of an originating summons, notice of motion or petition as it applies to service of a writ."

11. Order 11, rule 9 shall be further amended as follows:—

(1) Paragraphs (2) and (3) shall be revoked.

(2) There shall be inserted in paragraph (4), after the words "permissible with the leave of the Court", the words ", but leave shall not be required for such service in any proceedings in which the writ, originating summons, motion or petition may by these rules or under any Act be served out of the jurisdiction without leave".

(3) In paragraph (5) the words "or 2" shall be omitted.

Dispute as to jurisdiction

12. Order 12, rule 8 shall be amended by substituting in paragraph (1), for the words, "within 14 days thereafter", the words "within the time limited for service of a defence" and by revoking paragraph (2).

Proof of service of writ and of jurisdiction

13. Order 13 shall be amended by inserting after rule 7A the following new rule:—

"Judgments under the Civil Jurisdiction and Judgments Act 1982

7B.—(1) Where a writ has been served out of the jurisdiction under Order 11, rule 1(2)(*a*) or has been served within the jurisdiction on a defendant domiciled in Scotland or Northern Ireland or in any other Convention territory the plaintiff shall not be entitled to enter judgment under this Order except with the leave of the Court.

(2) An application for leave to enter judgment may be made ex parte and shall be supported by an affidavit stating that in the deponent's belief—

(*a*) each claim made by the writ is one which by virtue of the Civil Jurisdiction and Judgments Act 1982 the Court has power to hear and determine,

(*b*) no other court has exclusive jurisdiction within the meaning of Schedule 1 or under Schedule 4 to that Act to hear and determine such claim, and

(*c*) where the writ is served out of the jurisdiction under Order 11, rule 1(2)(*a*), such service satisfied the requirements of Schedule 1 or, as the case may require, of Article 20 of Schedule 4 to that Act,

and giving in each case the sources and grounds of such belief.

(3) For the purposes of this rule, domicile is to be determined in accordance with the provisions of sections 41 to 46 of the Civil Jurisdiction and Judgments Act 1982 and "Convention territory" means the territory or territories of any Contracting State, as defined by section 1(3) of that Act, to which the Conventions as defined in section 1(1) of that Act apply.".

Issue, service, and acknowledgement of service of third party notice

14. Order 16, rule 3 shall be amended by substituting for the full stop at the end of paragraph (4) a colon, and by adding at the end the words:—

"Provided that in the application of Order 11, r. 1(1)(*c*) leave may be granted to serve a third party notice outside the jurisdiction on any necessary or proper party to the proceedings brought against the defendant.".

Service out of the jurisdiction of an originating summons for leave to enforce an arbitral award

15. Order 73, rule 7 shall be amended by omitting in paragraph (1)(*a*) the words "or for leave to enforce an award" and shall be further amended by inserting after rule 7(1) the following new paragraph:—

"(1A) Service out of the jurisdiction of an originating summons for leave to enforce an award is permissible with the leave of the Court whether or not the arbitration is governed by English law.".

Admiralty proceedings: Merchant Shipping (Oil Pollution) Act 1971(a) and Merchant Shipping Act 1974(b)

16. Order 75, rule 4 shall be amended as follows:—

(1) paragraph (1) shall be amended by substituting for the words "in rule 2(1)" the words "in rule 2(1)(*a*) or (*b*)";

(2) there shall be inserted after paragraph (1) the following new paragraph:—

"(1A) Service out of the jurisdiction of a writ in an action containing any such claim as is mentioned in rule 2(1)(*c*) is permissible with the leave of the Court.";

(3) paragraph (3) shall be amended by substituting for the words "Paragraph (1)" the words "Paragraphs (1) and (1A)".

17. Order 75, rule 5(8) shall be amended by substituting a semi-colon for the full stop at the end of item "(*d*)", by inserting thereafter the word "and", and by inserting after item (*d*) the following new item:—

"(*e*) in the case of a claim in respect of a liability incurred under section 1 of the Merchant Shipping (Oil Pollution) Act 1971, the facts relied on as establishing that the Court is not prevented from entertaining the action by reason of section 13(2) of that Act.".

Partners—application of Order 81 to individual traders

18. Order 81, rule 9 shall be amended by inserting, after the word "may", the words "whether or not he is within the jurisdiction,".

Reciprocal enforcement of judgments

19. Order 71 shall be amended by substituting in the title, for the words "I. RECIPROCAL ENFORCEMENT", the words "I. RECIPROCAL EN-FORCEMENT: THE ADMINISTRATION OF JUSTICE ACT 1920 AND THE FOREIGN JUDGMENTS (RECIPROCAL ENFORCEMENT) ACT 1933", and by substituting in the title of Part II, for the words "EUROPEAN COMMUNITY JUDGMENTS" the words "ENFORCEMENT OF EURO-PEAN COMMUNITY JUDGMENTS".

20. Order 71 shall be further amended by revoking rule 14 and by adding at the end the following new rules:—

"III. RECIPROCAL ENFORCEMENT: THE CIVIL JURISDICTION AND JUDGMENTS ACT 1982

Interpretation

25.—(1) In this Part of this Order—

"the Act of 1982" means the Civil Jurisdiction and Judgments Act 1982;

(a) 1971 c. 59.
(b) 1974 c. 43.

"Convention territory" means the territory or territories of any Contracting State, as defined by section 1(3) of the Act of 1982, to which the Conventions as defined in section 1(1) of the Act of 1982 apply;

"judgment" is to be construed in accordance with the definition of "judgment" in section 50 of the Act of 1982;

"money provision" means a provision for the payment of one or more sums of money;

"non-money provision" means a provision for any relief or remedy not requiring payment of a sum of money;

"protective measures" means the protective measures referred to in Article 39 of Schedule 1 to the Act of 1982.

(2) For the purposes of this Part of this Order domicile is to be determined in accordance with the provisions of sections 41 to 46 of the Act of 1982.

Assignment of business and exercise of powers

26. Any application to the High Court under the Act of 1982 shall be assigned to the Queen's Bench Division and the powers conferred on the Court by that Act shall be exercised in accordance with the provisions of Order 32, rule 11.

Application for registration

27. An application for registration of a judgment under section 4 of the Act of 1982 shall be made ex parte.

Evidence in support of application

28.—(1) An application for registration under section 4 of the Act of 1982 must be supported by an affidavit—

(*a*) exhibiting—

    (i) the judgment or a verified or certified or otherwise duly authenticated copy thereof together with such other document or documents as may be requisite to show that, according to the law of the State in which it has been given, the judgment is enforceable and has been served;

    (ii) in the case of a judgment given in default, the original or a certified true copy of the document which establishes that the party in default was served with the document instituting the proceedings or with an equivalent document;

    (iii) where it is the case, a document showing that the party making the application is in receipt of legal aid in the State in which the judgment was given;

    (iv) where the judgment or document is not in the English language, a translation thereof into English certified by a notary public or a person qualified for the purpose in one of the Contracting States or authenticated by affidavit;

(*b*) stating—

    (i) whether the judgment provides for the payment of a sum or sums of money;

(ii) whether interest is recoverable on the judgment or part thereof in accordance with the law of the State in which the judgment was given, and if such be the case, the rate of interest, the date from which interest is recoverable, and the date on which interest ceases to accrue;

(c) giving an address within the jurisdiction of the Court for service of process on the party making the application and stating, so far as is known to the deponent, the name and the usual or last known address or place of business of the person against whom judgment was given;

(d) stating to the best of the information or belief of the deponent—

(i) the grounds on which the right to enforce the judgment is vested in the party making the application;

(ii) as the case may require, either that at the date of the application the judgment has not been satisfied, or the part or amount in respect of which it remains unsatisfied.

(2) Where the party making the application does not produce the documents referred to in paragraphs (1)(a)(ii) and (iii) of this rule, the Court may—

(a) fix a time within which the documents are to be produced; or

(b) accept equivalent documents; or

(c) dispense with production of the documents.

Security for costs

29. Notwithstanding the provisions of Order 23 a party making an application for registration under section 4 of the Act of 1982 shall not be required solely on the ground that he is not domiciled or resident within the jurisdiction, to give security for costs of the application.

Order for registration

30.—(1) An order giving leave to register a judgment under section 4 of the Act of 1982 must be drawn up by or on behalf of the party making the application for registration.

(2) Every such order shall state the period within which an appeal may be made against the order for registration and shall contain a notification that execution on the judgment will not issue until after the expiration of that period.

(3) The notification referred to in paragraph (2) shall not prevent any application for protective measures pending final determination of any issue relating to enforcement of the judgment.

Register of judgments registered under s. 4 of the Act of 1982

31. There shall be kept in the Central Office under the direction of the senior master a register of the judgments ordered to be registered under section 4 of the Act of 1982.

Notice of registration

32.—(1) Notice of the registration of a judgment must be served on the person against whom judgment was given by delivering it to him personally or by sending it to him at his usual or last known address or place of business or in such other manner as the Court may direct.

(2) Service of such a notice out of the jurisdiction is permissible without leave, and Order 11, rules 5, 6 and 8, shall apply in relation to such a notice as they apply in relation to a writ.

(3) The notice of registration must state—

(*a*) full particulars of the judgment registered and the order for registration,

(*b*) the name of the party making the application and his address for service within the jurisdiction,

(*c*) the right of the person against whom judgment was given to appeal against the order for registration, and

(*d*) the period within which an appeal against the order for registration may be made.

Appeals

33.—(1) An appeal under Article 37 or Article 40 of Schedule 1 to the Act of 1982 must be made by summons to a judge.

(2) A summons in an appeal to which this rule applies must be served—

(*a*) in the case of an appeal under the said Article 37 of Schedule 1, within one month of service of notice of registration of the judgment, or two months of service of such notice where that notice was served on a party not domiciled within the jurisdiction;

(*b*) in the case of an appeal under the said Article 40 of Schedule 1, within one month of the determination of the application under rule 27.

(3) If the party against whom judgment was given is not domiciled in a Convention territory and an application is made within two months of service of notice of registration, the Court may extend the period within which an appeal may be made against the order for registration.

Issue of execution

34.—(1) Execution shall not issue on a judgment registered under section 4 of the Act of 1982 until after the expiration of the period specified in accordance with rule 30(2) or, if that period has been extended by the Court, until after the expiration of the period so extended.

(2) If an appeal is made under rule 33(1), execution on the judgment shall not issue until after such appeal is determined.

(3) Any party wishing to issue execution on a judgment registered under section 4 of the Act of 1982 must produce to the proper officer an affidavit of service of the notice of registration of the judgment and of any order made by the Court in relation to the judgment.

(4) Nothing in this rule shall prevent the Court from granting protective measures pending final determination of any issue relating to enforcement of the judgment.

Application for recognition

35.—(1) Registration of the judgment under these rules shall serve for the purposes of the second paragraph of Article 26 of Schedule 1 to the Act of 1982 as a decision that the judgment is recognised.

(2) Where it is sought to apply for recognition of a judgment, the foregoing rules of this Order shall apply to such application as they apply to an application for registration under section 4 of the Act, with the exception that the applicant shall not be required to produce a document or documents which establish that according to the law of the State in which it has been given the judgment is enforceable and has been served, or the document referred to in rule 28(1)(*a*)(iii).

Enforcement of High Court judgments in other Contracting States

36.—(1) An application under section 12 of the Act of 1982 for a certified copy of a judgment entered in the High Court must be made ex parte on affidavit to the Court.

(2) An affidavit by which an application under section 12 of the Act of 1982 is made must—

(*a*) give particulars of the proceedings in which the judgment was obtained;

(*b*) have annexed to it a copy of the writ, originating summons or other process by which the proceedings were begun, the evidence of service thereof on the defendant, copies of the pleadings, if any, and a statement of the grounds on which the judgment was based together, where appropriate, with any document under which the applicant is entitled to legal aid or assistance by way of representation for the purposes of the proceedings;

(*c*) state whether the defendant did or did not object to the jurisdiction, and, if so, on what grounds;

(*d*) show that the judgment has been served in accordance with Order 65, rule 5 and is not subject to any stay of execution;

(*e*) state that the time for appealing has expired, or, as the case may be, the date on which it will expire and in either case whether notice of appeal against the judgment has been given; and

(*f*) state—

   (i) whether the judgment provides for the payment of a sum or sums of money;

   (ii) whether interest is recoverable on the judgment or part thereof and if such be the case, the rate of interest, the date from which interest is recoverable, and the date on which interest ceases to accrue.

(3) The certified copy of the judgment shall be an office copy sealed with the seal of the Supreme Court and there shall be issued with the copy of the

judgment a certificate in Form 110, signed by one of the persons referred to in Order 1, rule 4(2) and sealed with the seal of the Supreme Court, having annexed to it a copy of the writ, originating summons or other process by which the proceedings were begun.

Enforcement of United Kingdom judgments in other parts of the United Kingdom: money provisions

37.—(1) An application for registration in the High Court of a certificate in respect of any money provisions contained in a judgment given in another part of the United Kingdom to which section 18 of the Act of 1982 applies may be made by producing at the Central Office, within six months from the date of its issue, a certificate in the appropriate form prescribed under that Act together with a copy thereof certified by the applicant's solicitor to be a true copy.

(2) A certificate under paragraph (1) must be filed in the Central Office and the certified copy thereof, sealed by an officer of the office in which the certificate is filed, shall be returned to the applicant's solicitor.

(3) A certificate in respect of any money provisions contained in a judgment of the High Court to which section 18 of the Act of 1982 applies may be obtained by producing the form of certificate prescribed in Form 111 at the office in which the judgment is entered, together with an affidavit made by the party entitled to enforce the judgment—

(a) giving particulars of the judgment, stating the sum or aggregate of the sums (including any costs or expenses) payable and unsatisfied under the money provisions contained in the judgment, the rate of interest, if any, payable thereon and the date or time from which any such interest began to accrue;

(b) verifying that the time for appealing against the judgment has expired, or that any appeal brought has been finally disposed of and that enforcement of the judgment is not stayed or suspended; and

(c) stating to the best of the information or belief of the deponent the usual or last known address of the party entitled to enforce the judgment and of the party liable to execution on it.

Enforcement of United Kingdom judgments in other parts of the United Kingdom: non-money provisions

38.—(1) An application for registration in the High Court of a judgment which contains non-money provisions, being a judgment given in another part of the United Kingdom to which section 18 of the Act of 1982 applies, may be made ex parte, but the Court hearing the application may direct the issue of a summons to which paragraphs (2) and (3) of rule 2 shall apply.

(2) An application under paragraph (1) must be accompanied by a certified copy of the judgment issued under Schedule 7 to the Act of 1982 and a certificate in Form 112 issued not more than six months before the date of application.

(3) Rules 30 and 32 of this Order shall apply to judgments registered under Schedule 7 to the Act of 1982 as they apply to judgments registered under section 4 of that Act.

(4) Paragraphs (1) and (2) of rule 9 shall apply to applications to set aside registration of a judgment under Schedule 7 to the Act of 1982 as they apply to judgments registered under the Administration of Justice Act 1920 and the Foreign Judgments (Reciprocal Enforcements) Act 1933.

(5) A certified copy of a judgment of the High Court to which section 18 of the Act of 1982 applies and which contains any non-money provision may be obtained by an ex parte application on affidavit to the Court.

(6) The requirements in paragraph (3) of rule 37 shall apply with the necessary modifications to an affidavit made in an application under paragraph (5) of this rule.

(7) A certified copy of a judgment shall be an office copy sealed with the seal of the Supreme Court and indorsed with a certificate signed by a master or, where appropriate, a registrar certifying—

(a) that the copy is a true copy of a judgment obtained in the High Court;

(b) that it is issued in accordance with section 18 of the Act of 1982; and

(c) that the conditions specified in paragraphs 3(a) and (b) of Schedule 7 to that Act are satisfied in relation to the judgment.

Register of United Kingdom judgments

39. There shall be kept in the Central Office under the direction of the senior master a register of the certificates in respect of judgments and of the judgments ordered to be registered in the Central Office under Schedule 6, or, as the case may be, Schedule 7 to the Act.".

Reference to the European Court

21. Order 114, rule 1 shall be amended by inserting, after the words "Coal and Steel Community", the words ", or for a ruling on the interpretation of the Conventions referred to in section 1(1) of the Civil Jurisdiction and Judgments Act 1982".

Interpleader proceedings

22. Order 17, rule 2 shall be amended by substituting, for the words "4 days" in paragraph (2), the words "7 days".

23. Order 17, rule 3 shall be amended by adding at the end the following new paragraphs:—

"(6) Any person who makes a claim under rule 2 and who is served with a summons under this rule shall within 14 days serve on the execution creditor and the sheriff an affidavit specifying any money and describing any goods and chattels claimed and setting out the grounds upon which such claim is based.

(7) Where the applicant is a sheriff a summons under this rule must give notice of the requirement in paragraph (6).".

Oaths and affidavits

24. For Order 32, rule 8, there shall be substituted the following new rule:—

"Officers may administer oaths

8. The following persons shall have authority to administer oaths and take affidavits for the purpose of proceedings in the Supreme Court, namely—

(*a*) the holder of any office which is listed in column 1 of Part II or III of Schedule 2 to the Act and any person appointed to act as a deputy for a person holding any such office or as a temporary additional officer in any such office, and

(*b*) any district registrar, deputy district registrar or assistant district registrar, and

(*c*) any officer in the court service established by section 27 of the Courts Act 1971(**a**) who is for the time being authorised in that behalf by the Lord Chancellor.".

Interest on legacies

25. Order 44, rule 10 shall be amended by substituting, for the figure "£5", the figure "£6".

Enforcement of orders for the payment of money: appeals

26. Order 56, rule 5(2)(*a*) shall be amended by inserting, after the words "Matrimonial Proceedings (Magistrates' Courts) Act 1960", the words ", the Guardianship of Minors Act 1971(**b**)".

27. Order 90, rule 9(1) shall be amended by substituting, for the word "Every", the words "Subject to Order 56, rule 5(2), every".

Court of Appeal

28. Order 59, rule 9 shall be amended as follows:—

(i) In paragraph (1) there shall be substituted, for the words "Not more than 7 days", the words "Not more than 14 days".

(ii) There shall be inserted, at the beginning of item (*e*) of paragraph (1), the words "the originating process by which the proceedings in the court below were begun, any interlocutory or other related process which is the subject of the appeal,".

(iii) There shall be substituted, for item (*f*), the words "the transcript of the official shorthand note or record, if any, of the judge's reasons for giving the judgment or making the order of the court below or, in the absence of such a note or record, the judge's note of his reasons or, if the judge's note is not available, counsel's note of the judge's reasons approved wherever possible by the judge;".

(iv) There shall be substituted, for item (*g*), the words "such parts of the transcript of the official shorthand note or record, if any, of the

(**a**) 1971 c. 23.
(**b**) 1971 c. 3.

evidence given in the court below as are relevant to any question at issue on the appeal or, in the absence of such a note or record, such parts of the judge's note of the evidence as are relevant to any such question;".

(v) There shall be inserted, after paragraph (2), the following new paragraph:—

"(2A) When the transcripts, if any, referred to in items (*f*) and (*g*) of paragraph (1) have been bespoken by the appellant and paid for, the number of such transcripts required in accordance with paragraph (2) shall be sent by the official shorthand writer or transcriber direct to the registrar.".

(vi) There shall be substituted, in paragraph (3), for the words from "After the documents" to "registrar shall", the words "At any time after an appeal has been set down in accordance with rule 5 the registrar may".

29. Order 59, rule 14 shall be amended as follows:—

(i) There shall be substituted, for paragraph (1), the following new paragraph:—

"(1) Unless otherwise directed, every application to the Court of Appeal, a single judge or the registrar which is not made ex parte must be made by summons and such summons must be served on the party or parties affected at least 2 clear days before the day on which it is heard or, in the case of an application which is made after the expiration of the time for appealing, at least 7 days before the day on which the summons is heard.".

(ii) There shall be inserted, at the beginning of paragraph (2), the words "Unless otherwise directed,".

(iii) There shall be substituted, for paragraph (7), the following new paragraph:—

"(7) An application, not being an application for leave to appeal, which may be heard by a single judge shall unless otherwise directed be heard in chambers.".

(iv) There shall be substituted, for paragraph (12), the following new paragraph:—

"(12) An appeal shall lie to the Court of Appeal from any determination by a single judge, not being the determination of an application for leave to appeal, and shall be brought by way of fresh application made within 10 days of the determination appealed against.

Provided that an appeal shall not lie to the Court of Appeal without the leave of that Court in respect of a determination of the registrar which has been reviewed by a single judge.".

30. Order 68 shall be amended by omitting rule 6, and in rule 8, the words from "and, in relation" to the end.

Arbitration proceedings

31. Order 73 shall be amended by omitting rule 1.

32. Order 73 shall be further amended by omitting rule 2(1)(*d*), and the word "or" immediately following it, and by substituting, for rule 3(2), the following new paragraph—

"(2) Any application

(*a*) for leave to appeal under section 1(2) of the Arbitration Act 1979(**a**), or

(*b*) under section 1(5) of that Act (including any application for leave), or

(*c*) under section 5 of that Act,

shall be made to a judge in chambers.".

Applications for leave to adopt a minor who is a ward of court

33. Order 90 shall be amended by inserting, after rule 4, the following new rule:—

"*Applications for leave to adopt a minor who is a ward of court*

4A. An application for leave to commence proceedings to adopt a minor who is a ward of court may be made ex parte to a registrar and if the applicant so requests the registrar may direct that any subsequent proceedings shall be conducted with a view to securing that the proposed adopter is not seen by or made known to any respondent or prospective respondent who is not already aware of his identity except with his consent.".

Appeals from magistrates in custody or access cases

34. Order 90, rule 16(9) shall be amended as follows:—

(1) for the words "or to access, where the extent of access only is in dispute", there shall be substituted the words "or to custody or access";

(2) for sub-paragraph (*b*), there shall be substituted the following:—

"(*b*) the parties may agree in writing or the President may direct that the appeal be heard and determined at a divorce town within the meaning of the matrimonial causes rules.".

Mental Health Act 1983(**b**)

35. Order 94 shall be amended by substituting for rule 11 the following rule:—

"*Case stated by Mental Health Review Tribunal*

11.—(1) In this rule, "the Act" means the Mental Health Act 1983.

(2) The reference in paragraph (3) to a party to proceedings before a Mental Health Review Tribunal, and the references in Order 56, rules 8(1), 9(2) and 10 to a party to proceedings shall be construed as references to—

(*a*) the person who initiated the proceedings; and

(*b*) any person to whom, in accordance with rules made under section 78 of the Act, the Tribunal sent notice of the application or reference or a request instead of notice of reference.

(**a**) 1979 c. 42.
(**b**) 1983 c. 20.

(3) A party to proceedings before a Mental Health Review Tribunal shall not be entitled to apply to the High Court for an order under section 78(8) of the Act directing the Tribunal to state a case for determination by the Court unless—

(*a*) within 21 days after the decision of the Tribunal was communicated to him in accordance with rules made under section 78 of the Act he made a written request to the Tribunal to state a case, and

(*b*) either the Tribunal failed to comply with the last-mentioned request within 21 days after it was made or the Tribunal refused to comply with it.

(4) The period for entry of the originating motion by which an application to the Court for such an order as is mentioned in paragraph (3) is made, and for service of notice thereof, shall be—

(*a*) where the Tribunal refused the applicant's request to state a case, 14 days after receipt by the applicant of notice of the refusal of his request;

(*b*) where the Tribunal failed to comply with that request within the period mentioned in paragraph (3)(*b*), 14 days after the expiration of that period.

(5) A Mental Health Review Tribunal by whom a case is stated shall be entitled to appear and be heard in the proceedings for the determination of the case.

(6) If the Court is of opinion that any decision of such a Tribunal on the question of law raised by the case was erroneous, the Court may give any direction which the Tribunal ought to have given under Part V of the Act.".

36. The rules cited in the first column of the Schedule to these Rules shall be amended by omitting the words in the second column and by substituting the words in the third column.

Forms

37. Appendix A shall be amended as follows:—

(1) In Form 62 there shall be substituted for the words from "register for Irish judgments" to "Inferior Courts Extension Act 1882]" the words "register for Judgments in our High Court of Justice in England and Wales pursuant to Schedule 6 to the Civil Jurisdiction and Judgments Act 1982.".

(2) In Form 63 there shall be inserted after the words "[*or* the Foreign Judgments (Reciprocal Enforcement) Act 1933, Part I]" the words "[*or* the Civil Jurisdiction and Judgments Act 1982]" and after the words "[*or* Part I of the Foreign Judgments (Reciprocal Enforcement) Act 1933]" the words ", [*or* the Civil Jurisdiction and Judgments Act 1982]".

(3) In Form 109 there shall be inserted after the words "European Coal and Steel Community", the words, "*or* for a ruling under Schedule 2 to the Civil Jurisdiction and Judgments Act 1982".

(4) The following new forms shall be added at the end of Appendix A:—

"   No. 110

Certificate under section 12 of the
Civil Jurisdiction and Judgments Act 1982

In the High Court of Justice   19   , No.

      Division

Between   [AB]   Plaintiff

and   [CD]   Defendant

   I, a   of the Supreme Court of England and Wales,
hereby certify:—

1. That the Writ of Summons [*or as the case may be*], a copy of which is annexed, was issued out of the High Court of Justice on the   day of   , 19   , by AB the above-named plaintiff against CD, the above-named defendant, for [payment of the sum of £   ]

   [*or state any other relief claimed*].

2. That the said writ [*or other originating process as the case may be*] was duly served on the   day of   , 19   , upon the said defendant CD by (*state mode of service.*)

3. [That the said CD acknowledged service of the writ on the   day of   , 19   .]

4. That the said plaintiff [*or* defendant] obtained judgment against the said defendant [*or* plaintiff] in the   Division of the High Court of Justice for [payment of the sum of £   ] [*or state any other relief ordered*], together with the sum of £   for costs.

5. That [no] objection has been made to the jurisdiction of the Court [on the grounds that *state grounds of objection*   ].

6. That the judgment carries interest at the rate of .... per cent per annum calculated on the judgment debt and costs from the date of judgment until payment.

7. That the judgment has been served on the defendant in accordance with the provisions of Order 65, rule 5.

8. [That no application to set the judgment aside] [*or* to appeal against the judgment] [has been brought within the time prescribed].

9. [That an application to set the judgment aside] [*or* to appeal against the judgment] [has been finally disposed of].

10. That enforcement of the judgment is not for the time being stayed or suspended and that the time available for its enforcement has not expired.

11. This certificate is issued under section 12 of the Civil Jurisdiction and Judgments Act 1982.

   Dated this   day of   , 19   .

           (*Signed*) a   of the Supreme Court
                                        of England and Wales.

No. 111

Certificate of Money Provisions contained in a Judgment
for Registration under Schedule 6 to the Civil
Jurisdiction and Judgments Act 1982

I, a   of the Supreme Court of England and Wales, hereby
certify:—

1. That AB (*state the name, address and description of plaintiff*) obtained judgment
   against CD (*state the name, address and description of defendant*) on the
   day of   19   in the   Division of the High
   Court of England and Wales for payment of the sum of £   in respect of
   (*state shortly nature of claim*) together with £............ for costs.

2. That the judgment carries interest at the rate of .... per cent per annum
   calculated on the judgment debt and costs from the date of judgment until
   payment.

3. That the conditions specified in paragraph 3(a) and (b) of Schedule 6 to the Civil
   Jurisdiction and Judgments Act 1982 are satisfied in relation to the judgment.

4. That enforcement of the judgment is not for the time being stayed or suspended
   and that the time available for its enforcement has not expired.

5. This certificate is issued under Schedule 6 to the Civil Jurisdiction and Judgments
   Act 1982.

Dated the   day of   19

(Signed) a   of the Supreme Court
                                      of England and Wales.

Produced for registration under Schedule 6 to the Civil Jurisdiction and Judgments Act
1982 by AB/CD.

No.112

Certificate issued under Schedule 7 to the
Civil Jurisdiction and Judgments Act 1982
in respect of Non-Money Provisions

I certify that the annexed copy judgment is a true copy of a judgment obtained in the High Court, that it is issued in accordance with section 18 of the Civil Jurisdiction and Judgments Act 1982 and that the conditions specified in paragraph 3(a) and (b) of Schedule 7 to that Act are satisfied in relation to the judgment.

This certificate is issued under paragraph 4(1)*(b)* of Schedule 7 to the Civil Jurisdiction and Judgments Act 1982.

Dated this   day of   , 19

                    (Signed) a   of the Supreme Court
                                                        of England and Wales.".

Hailsham of St. Marylebone, C.
Lane, C.J.
Donaldson, M.R.
John Arnold, P.
R.E. Megarry, V-C.
Oliver, L.J.
Lloyd, J.
Mark Potter.
John G. Mck. Laws.
P.F. Carter-Ruck.
R.J. Pannone.

Dated 25th July 1983

SCHEDULE

AMENDMENTS TO OBSOLETE REFERENCES

Order and rule	Words to be omitted	Words to be substituted
Order 1, rule 2(2)	"Part VIII of the Mental Health Act 1959"	"Part VII of the Mental Health Act 1983"
	"Mental Health Act 1959, section 112"	"Mental Health Act 1983, section 106"
Order 32, rule 9(1)(b)	"section 141 of the Mental Health Act 1959"	"section 139 of the Mental Health Act 1983"
Order 32, rule 9(3)	"section 141"	"section 139"
Order 52, rule 6(1)(b)	"Mental Health Act 1959"	"Mental Health Act 1983"
Order 62, rule 29(4)(a)	"Mental Health Act 1959"	"Mental Health Act 1983"
	"Part VIII"	"Part VII"
Order 62, rule 29(5)	"Section 118(2) and (3) of the Mental Health Act 1959"	"Section 111, (3) and (4) of the Mental Health Act 1983"
	"Part VIII"	"Part VII"
Order 62, rule 30(1)(a)	"Mental Health Act 1959"	"Mental Health Act 1983"
Order 62, rule 30(3)(b)	"Mental Health Act 1959"	"Mental Health Act 1983"
Order 62, rule 30(7)(a)	"Mental Health Act 1959"	"Mental Health Act 1983"
Order 80, rule 1	"Mental Health Act 1959"	"Mental Health Act 1983"
Order 80, rule 3(3)	"Part VIII"	"Part VII"
Order 80, rule 3(8)(b)	"Part VIII" wherever occuring	"Part VII"
Order 80, rule 16(2)(b)	"Part VIII"	"Part VII"
Order 112, rule 3(b)	"Mental Health Act 1959"	"Mental Health Act 1983"

EXPLANATORY NOTE
(This Note is not part of the Rules.)

These Rules amend the Rules of the Supreme Court so as—

(a) to make provision for proceedings under the Civil Jurisdiction and Judgments Act 1982 and to make new provision for service of process out of the jurisdiction (Rules 3 to 18);

(b) to make provision for the recognition and enforcement of judgments under the Civil Jurisdiction and Judgments Act 1982 (Rules 19 to 21 and Rule 37);

(c) to amend the provision for giving notice of a claim in interpleader proceedings (Rules 22 and 23);

(d) to make new provision for the swearing of affidavits (Rule 24);

(e) to amend the provision for interest on legacies (Rule 25);

(f) to amend the provision for an appeal from the enforcement of an order of a magistrates' court for the payment of money (Rules 26 and 27);

(g) to amend the provisions for appeals to the Court of Appeal (Rules 28 to 30);

(h) to amend the provisions for appeals in arbitration proceedings (Rules 31 and 32);

(i) to make new provision for applications for leave to adopt a minor who is a ward of court (Rule 33);

(j) to amend the provision for appeals from magistrates' courts in custody or access cases (Rule 34);

(k) to provide for appeals from Mental Health Review Tribunals under the Mental Health Act 1983, and to make minor amendments consequential on that Act (Rules 35 and 36).

STATUTORY INSTRUMENTS

1983 No. 1182

PUBLIC HEALTH, ENGLAND AND WALES

PUBLIC HEALTH, SCOTLAND

The Control of Pollution (Exemption of Certain Discharges from Control) Order 1983

Made - - - -	*1st August* 1983
Laid before Parliament	*10th August* 1983
Coming into Operation	*31st August* 1983

Whereas section 32(1) of the Control of Pollution Act 1974 (a) has not yet come into force:

And whereas discharges of the kinds or in the areas mentioned in article 3 of this order are discharges for which consent would not have been required by the Rivers (Prevention of Pollution) Acts 1951 to 1961 or the Rivers (Prevention of Pollution) (Scotland) Acts 1951 to 1965 or section 72 of the Water Resources Act 1963 (b) if the said Act of 1974 had not been passed:

Now therefore the Secretary of State for the Environment as respects England, the Secretary of State for Wales as respects Wales and the Secretary of State for Scotland as respects Scotland, in exercise of their powers under section 32(3)*(a)* of the said Act of 1974 and of all other powers enabling them in that behalf, hereby order as follows:—

Citation and commencement

1. This order may be cited as the Control of Pollution (Exemption of Certain Discharges from Control) Order 1983, and shall come into operation on 31st August 1983.

Interpretation

2. In this order, unless the context otherwise requires—

"the Act" means the Control of Pollution Act 1974;

"aldrin" means the chemical compound 1,2,3,4,10,10 – hexachloro – 1,4,4a,5,8,8a – hexahydro – 1,4 – endo – 5,8 – exo – dimethanonaphthalene;

"dieldrin" means the chemical compound 1,2,3,4,10,10 – hexachloro – 6,7 – epoxy – 1,4,4a,5,6,7,8,8a – octahydro – 1,4 – endo – 5,8 – exo – dimethanonaphthalene;

"endrin" means the chemical compound 1,2,3,4,10,10 – hexachloro – 6,7 – epoxy – 1,4,4a,5,6,7,8,8a – octahydro – 1,4 – endo – 5,8 – endo – dimethanonaphthalene; and

"underground stream" means a stream which is below ground.

(a) 1974 c.40.   **(b)** 1963 c.38.

Certain discharges to be exempt from control

3. Subsection (1) of section 32 of the Act (which provides for the control of discharges of trade and sewage effluent, etc., into rivers and coastal waters, etc.) shall not apply to discharges specified in column (1) of the Schedule to this order except in the case of the discharges specified in column (2) thereof:

Provided that paragraphs 7 and 9 of the Schedule, and paragraph 8 so far as it operates by reference to paragraph 7, shall not extend to Scotland.

4.—(1) Each water authority shall publish a notice stating the general effect of this order, and specifying a place or places in the water authority area where a copy of the order may be inspected by any person free of charge at all reasonable times.

(2) A notice under the last preceding paragraph shall be published either—

(a) at least once in each of two successive weeks in one or more newspapers circulating in the water authority area, or

(b) in any other manner which, in any particular case, may be certified by the Secretary of State to be expedient in that case.

SCHEDULE

(1) Discharges to which section 32(1) does not apply	(2) Discharges excepted from the exemption granted by the order
1. Discharges begun on or before 30th April 1974 of any trade or sewage effluent to controlled waters or to any underground stream.	1. *(a)* Discharges containing mercury from premises used for the purposes of— (i) the manufacture of chemicals, where mercury is used as a catalyst; (ii) the manufacture of catalysts containing mercury; (iii) the manufacture of organic or inorganic mercury compounds (except catalysts); (iv) the manufacture of mercury batteries; (v) the extraction, recovery or refining of mercury or any other non-ferrous metal; (vi) the treatment of industrial waste; (vii) a laboratory, where mercury and its compounds are used; *(b)* discharges containing cadmium from premises used for the purposes of— (i) zinc mining, lead and zinc refining, the manufacture of cadmium metal or the extraction, recovery or refining of cadmium or any other non-ferrous metal;

(1) Discharges to which section 32(1) does not apply	(2) Discharges excepted from the exemption granted by the order
	(ii) the manufacture of cadmium compounds;
	(iii) the manufacture of pigments containing cadmium or cadmium compounds;
	(iv) the manufacture of stabilisers containing cadmium or cadmium compounds;
	(v) the manufacture of primary or secondary batteries;
	(vi) electroplating;
	(vii) the manufacture of phosphoric acid or phosphate fertiliser from phosphate rock;
	(c) discharges from premises in which dieldrin is used for the mothproofing of woollen materials;
	(d) discharges (other than of a kind specified in sub-paragraphs (a) to (c) above) containing free or combined mercury, free or combined cadmium, aldrin, dieldrin, endrin, lead, copper, nickel, chromium, zinc or arsenic in such quantities as are liable to give rise to pollution within the meaning of Article 1.2(e) of Council Directive No. 76/464/EEC on pollution caused by certain dangerous substances discharged into the aquatic environment of the Community;
	(e) discharges (other than of a kind specified in sub-paragraphs (a) to (d) above) which are liable to affect the quality of waters identified for the purposes of Council Directive No. 76/160/EEC concerning the quality of bathing water, or designated for the purposes of Council Directive No. 79/923/EEC on the quality required of shellfish waters, in such a manner as to result in non-compliance with one (or both) of those Directives;
	(f) discharges containing waste produced in the course of the manufacture of titanium dioxide;
	(g) discharges for which consent is required under any byelaw made in pursuance of section 5(1)(c) of the Sea Fisheries Regulation Act 1966 (a) ;
	(h) discharges of trade and sewage effluent to the estuary of the river Mersey east of a line drawn across Liverpool Bay between the points identified by the undermentioned groups of two letters and eight figures

(a)   1966 c.38.

(1) Discharges to which section 32(1) does not apply	(2) Discharges excepted from the exemption granted by the order
	representing the map co-ordinates of those points on the grid of the National Reference System used by the Ordnance Survey on its maps and plans, that is to say, SJ20368867 and SD26950595.
2. Discharges begun on or before 30th April 1974 of any trade or sewage effluent from land in Great Britain through a pipe into the sea outside controlled waters.	2. Discharges of the kinds specified in paragraph 1 of this column.
3. Discharges begun on or before 30th April 1974 of any trade or sewage effluent from a building or from plant on to or into any lake, loch or pond which does not discharge into a stream.	3. *(a)* Discharges of the kinds specified in paragraph 1*(a)* to *(d)* of this column; *(b)* discharges which are liable to affect the quality of waters designated for the purposes of Council Directive No. 78/659/EEC on the quality of fresh waters needing protection or improvement in order to support fish life, or which are subject to the provisions of Council Directive No. 75/440/EEC concerning the quality required of surface water intended for the abstraction of drinking water in the Member States, in such a manner as to result in non-compliance with one (or both) of those Directives.
4. Discharges begun on or before 30th April 1974 of any matter other than trade or sewage effluent into any stream or controlled waters from a sewer or drain as respectively defined by section 343 of the Public Health Act 1936 (a) or, in Scotland, by section 59(1) of the Sewerage (Scotland) Act 1968 (b) .	4. Discharges of the kinds specified in paragraphs 1*(d)* and *(e)* and 3*(b)* of this column.
5. Discharges begun on or before 30th April 1974 of any trade or sewage effluent direct to specified underground water (other than an underground stream).	5. *(a)* Discharges which are liable to result in any substance mentioned in List I of the Annex to Council Directive No. 80/68/EEC (on the protection of groundwater against pollution caused by certain dangerous substances) reaching specified underground water in a quantity or concentration likely to give rise to deterioration in the quality of such water; *(b)* discharges which are liable to result in any substance mentioned in List II of the said Annex reaching specified underground water in such quantities as to give rise to pollution within the

(1) Discharges to which section 32(1) does not apply	(2) Discharges excepted from the exemption granted by the order
	meaning of Article 1.2(d) of the said Council Directive No. 80/68/EEC.
6. Discharges begun on or before 30th April 1974 of any trade or sewage effluent from a building or from plant on to or into any land.	6. Discharges of the kinds specified in paragraph 5 of this column.
7. Discharges (other than discharges which are the subject of an order under the proviso to section 2(4) of the Rivers (Prevention of Pollution) Act 1951 (a)) of water raised or drained from any underground part of a mine into a stream in the same condition in which it is raised or drained from underground, where such discharges were begun on or before 30th April 1974.	7. *(a)* Discharges containing free or combined mercury, free or combined cadmium, lead, copper, nickel, chromium, zinc or arsenic in such quantities as are liable to give rise to pollution within the meaning of Article 1.2(e) of Council Directive No. 76/464/EEC on pollution caused by certain dangerous substances discharged into the aquatic environment of the Community; *(b)* discharges of the kinds specified in paragraph 3*(b)* of this column.
8. Discharges begun after 30th April 1974 but before the day on which section 34 of the Act comes into force which are of a kind exempted under paragraphs 1 to 7 of this column.	8. None.
9. Discharges begun after the day on which section 34 of the Act comes into force which are of a kind exempted under paragraphs 1 to 7 of this column and are made from a pipe or outlet the construction of which was begun before 31st August 1983.	9. None.

28th July 1983.

Signed by authority
of the Secretary of State

29th July 1983.

1st August 1983.

Patrick Jenkin,
Secretary of State for the
Environment.

John Stradling Thomas,
Minister of State for Wales.

George Younger,
Secretary of State for Scotland.

(a) 1951 c.64.

EXPLANATORY NOTE

(This Note is not part of the Order.)

This Order exempts from control certain discharges of trade and sewage effluent, and certain other discharges, which would otherwise be controlled when the appropriate provisions of the Control of Pollution Act 1974 come into force. The Order provides for exceptions from these exemptions where control is necessary in order to implement Council Directives No. 76/464/EEC (dangerous substances discharged into aquatic environment), No. 76/160/EEC (quality of bathing water), No. 78/659/EEC (quality of fresh waters), No. 75/440/EEC (quality of surface water intended for abstraction of drinking water) No. 79/923/EEC (quality of shellfish waters) and No. 80/68/EEC (dangerous substances into groundwater).

Copies of the EEC Directives referred to in this Order may be obtained from Her Majesty's Stationery Office.

Information concerning waters designated or identified for the purposes of the above-mentioned EEC Directives is obtainable from the water authority concerned.

STATUTORY INSTRUMENTS

1983 No. 1183 (C. 34)

OPEN SPACES

The National Heritage Act 1983 (Commencement No. 2) Order 1983

Made -   -   -   -   28th July 1983

The Minister of Agriculture, Fisheries and Food, in exercise of the power conferred on him by section 41(2) of the National Heritage Act 1983(**a**), hereby makes the following order:—

1. This order may be cited as the National Heritage Act 1983 (Commencement No. 2) Order 1983.

2. The following provisions of the National Heritage Act 1983 (relating to the establishment of the Board of Trustees of the Royal Botanic Gardens, Kew) shall come into force on 8th August 1983:—

    (*a*) sections 23 and 29,

    (*b*) Part IV of Schedule 1, and

    (*c*) paragraphs 3 and 4 of Schedule 5 so far as they relate to the Royal Botanic Gardens, Kew.

In Witness whereof the Official Seal of the Minister of Agriculture, Fisheries and Food is hereunto affixed on 28th July 1983.

(L.S.)

Michael Jopling,
Minister of Agriculture, Fisheries and Food.

(**a**) 1983 c. 47.

EXPLANATORY NOTE

(This Note is not part of the Order.)

This order brings into force on 8th August 1983 the provisions of sections 23 and 29 of the National Heritage Act 1983 together with Part IV of Schedule 1. These relate to the establishment of the Board of Trustees of the Royal Botanic Gardens, Kew.

This order also brings into force paragraphs 3 and 4 of Schedule 5 to the Act so far as they relate to the Gardens. Paragraph 3 inserts the Gardens into the list of establishments and organisations whose administrative and departmental records are public records for the purposes of the Public Records Act 1958 (c. 51). Paragraph 4 inserts the Board of Trustees of the Gardens into the list of institutions which so far as they are charities are exempt charities within the meaning of that Act.

NOTE AS TO EARLIER COMMENCEMENT ORDERS

(This Note is not part of the Order.)

The following provisions of the Act have been brought into force by commencement order which was made on 20th July 1983.

Provision	Date of commencement	S.I. No.
s. 40, sch. 5 partially and sch. 6 partially	3.8.1983	1983/1062

and the following provisions of the Act will be brought into force by that commencement order after the date of this order:—

Provision	Date of commencement	S.I. No.
ss.1 & 9, sch. 1 partially and sch. 5 partially	30.9.1983	1983/1062

STATUTORY INSTRUMENTS

1983 No. 1184

EUROPEAN COMMUNITIES

The European Communities (ECSC Treaty Amendment) (Iron and Steel) Regulations 1983

Made - - - -	*2nd August* 1983
Laid before Parliament	*9th August* 1983
Coming into Operation	*1st September* 1983

Whereas the Council of the European Communities has, by Council Decision 83/83/ECSC of 21st February 1983(**a**), added certain products to the list of products set out in Annex 1 to the ECSC Treaty;

Now therefore the Secretary of State, being a Minister designated for the purposes of section 2(2) of the European Communities Act 1972(**b**) in relation to matters relating to the pricing of iron and steel products(**c**) and in relation to measures relating to redundancy among steel workers(**d**), in exercise of the powers conferred by that section, hereby makes the following Regulations:—

Citation and commencement

1. These Regulations may be cited as the European Communities (ECSC Treaty Amendment) (Iron and Steel) Regulations 1983, and shall come into operation on 1st September 1983.

ECSC Treaty amendment

2. The references in paragraph 1 of Schedule 1 to the European Communities (Iron and Steel Employees Re-adaptation Benefits Scheme) Regulations 1979(**e**) (definition of "steel company") and in regulation 2(1) of the Distributors of Iron and Steel Products (ECSC Requirements) Regulations 1982(**f**) (definition of "steel product") to Annex 1 of the ECSC Treaty shall, as from the date of coming into operation of these Regulations, have effect as references to that Annex as extended by Council Decision 83/83/ECSC of 21st February 1983.

(**a**) O.J. No. L56, 3.3.83, p.25.   (**b**) 1972 c. 68.
(**c**) S.I. 1981/1536.   (**d**) S.I. 1972/1811.
(**e**) S.I.1979/954; these Regulations were amended by S.I. 1980/1912, 1981/1102, 1776, 1982/1045.
(**f**) S.I. 1982/1590.

Transitional provision

3. For the avoidance of doubt it is hereby declared that if but for this regulation the relevant date for the purposes of regulation 3 (application) of the Distributors of Iron and Steel Products (ECSC Requirements) Regulations 1982 would by virtue of regulation 2, above, be before 1st September 1983, the relevant date shall be 1st September 1983.

Norman Lamont,
Minister of State,
Department of Industry.

2nd August 1983.

EXPLANATORY NOTE

(This Note is not part of the Regulations.)

These Regulations amend the European Communities (Iron and Steel Employees Re-adaptation Benefits Scheme) Regulations 1979 and the Distributors of Iron and Steel Products (ECSC Requirements) Regulations 1982 by causing references therein to Annex 1 to the ECSC Treaty (which defines the expressions "coal" and "steel" for the purposes of that Treaty) to have effect as references to that Annex as it has been extended by a recent Council Decision (to include cold rolled plate, in coil and in strips, of a thickness of 3 mm or more). In the case of the latter Regulations a transitional provision is included making it clear that the amendment has no retrospective effect.

STATUTORY INSTRUMENTS

1983 No. 1185

EDUCATION, ENGLAND AND WALES

The Education (Students' Dependants Allowances) Regulations 1983

Made - - - - -	*3rd August* 1983
Laid before Parliament	*10th August* 1983
Coming into Operation	*1st September* 1983

The Secretary of State for Education and Science, in exercise of the powers conferred by section 3 of the Education Act 1973**(a)**, hereby makes the following Regulations:—

Citation and commencement

1. These Regulations may be cited as the Education (Students' Dependants Allowances) Regulations 1983 and shall come into operation on 1st September 1983.

Interpretation

2.—(1) In these Regulations, except where the context otherwise requires—

"award" means an award bestowed under the principal Regulations or previous Awards Regulations;

"child", in relation to a student, includes a person adopted in pursuance of adoption proceedings, a step-child and an illegitimate child of whom the student is the mother or in whose case he has admitted paternity or been adjudged the putative father;

"eligible dependant" has the meaning assigned thereto by Regulation 4;

"the principal Regulations" means the Education (Mandatory Awards) Regulations 1983**(b)**;

"spouse" includes a woman who cohabits with a man as his wife and a man who cohabits with a woman as her husband but nothing in this definition shall affect the meaning of "wife" or "husband";

"student" means a person who holds an award;

and other expressions have the same meanings as in the principal Regulations.

(2) In these Regulations, except where the context otherwise requires, a reference to a Regulation is a reference to a Regulation of these Regulations and a reference in a Regulation to a paragraph is a reference to a paragraph of that Regulation.

(a) 1973 c. 16.   **(b)** S.I. 1983/1135.

Revocations and transitional provisions

3.—(1) Subject to paragraph (2), the Education (Students' Dependants Allowances) Regulations 1982**(a)** are hereby revoked.

(2) The Regulations revoked by paragraph (1) shall continue to have effect in relation to an allowance payable thereunder in respect of a period falling before the coming into operation of these Regulations but Regulation 8(2) of these Regulations shall apply for the purpose of correcting any overpayment or underpayment of such an allowance as it applies in the case of an allowance under these Regulations.

Power to pay allowances

4.—(1) Subject to Regulation 5, the Secretary of State may pay an allowance to a student in respect of any eligible dependant within the meaning of paragraph (2) where his requirements in respect of that dependant are not taken into account for the purposes of his award in pursuance of Part 3 of Schedule 2 to the principal Regulations.

(2) The eligible dependants of a student shall be—

(*a*) the student's wife or husband, where they ordinarily live together, if—

(i) the wife or husband does not hold a statutory award and they have a dependent child, or

(ii) it is for the time being certified by a registered medical practitioner that the wife or husband is incapable of being gainfully employed for a period of at least eight weeks, or

(iii) the wife or husband is for the time being registered for employment with the Manpower Services Commission or a local education authority and is available for employment within the meaning of section 17(1)(*a*)(i) of the Social Security Act 1975**(b)** or of regulations made for the purposes thereof (availability for employment for the purposes of unemployment benefit) and is neither entitled to supplementary benefit under the Supplementary Benefits Act 1976**(c)** nor receiving unemployment benefit under the Social Security Act 1975;

(*b*) a child wholly or mainly financially dependent on the student unless—

(i) the parents do not ordinarily live together and the child resides with the other parent, or

(ii) the student's spouse holds a statutory award in the calculation of which account is taken of the child.

(**a**) S.I. 1982/1041.
(**b**) 1975 c. 14, amended by section 22 of the Social Security Pensions Act 1975 (c. 60).
(**c**) 1976 c. 71, amended by section 6 of the Social Security Act 1980 (c. 30).

Exceptions

5. No allowance shall be payable to a student if—

(*a*) no payment in respect of maintenance falls to be made to him under Regulation 17(*b*) of the principal Regulations (whether by reason of Regulation 20 or 23 thereof (sandwich courses; assisted students) or otherwise) and no such payment is made to him under Regulation 26 (discretionary payments), or

(*b*) in pursuance of Regulation 16 or 27 of the principal Regulations (withholding of payments), payments in respect of maintenance falling to be made to him under the said Regulation 17(*b*) are—

   (i) wholly withheld, or

   (ii) except where the payments fall to be determined in accordance with Regulation 24 of the principal Regulations (students provided with free board and lodging), withheld in such part that the partial payment does not exceed the minimum maintenance payment.

Amount of allowance

6.—(1) Subject to paragraphs (5) and (6), an allowance shall be payable to a student with an eligible dependant in any week in a year at the weekly rate determined in accordance with paragraphs (2), (3) and (4)—

(*a*) where he ordinarily lives with his spouse, for any week or part of a week for which—

   (i) the student attends his course at the establishment, or

   (ii) he is pursuing a period of vacation study undertaken as mentioned in paragraph 8(1) of Part 2 of Schedule 2 to the principal Regulations or a period of term-time residential study such as is mentioned in paragraph 9(1) of the said Part 2 (whether or not the establishment is such as is mentioned in the said paragraphs);

(*b*) where he does not so live, irrespective of whether he is attending his course, or pursuing a period of study, as aforesaid.

(2) The weekly amount of the allowance shall, subject to paragraphs (3), (4) and (6), be the amount by which the aggregate of—

(*a*) one fifty-second of the relevant sums mentioned in paragraph 18(4) of Part 3 of Schedule 2 to the principal Regulations so, however, that for the purposes hereof any reference in the said paragraph to the student's spouse or child shall be construed as a reference to an eligible dependant who is his spouse or, as the case may be, child for the purposes of these Regulations and the reference therein to an adult dependant shall be disregarded, and (*b*) where the student maintains a home for himself and an eligible dependant at a place within the United Kingdom, other than that at which he resides while attending the course, the sum specified in paragraph 19 of the said Part 3 divided by the number of weeks in the year for which he attends his course,

exceeds one fifty-second of the annual income of the student's family (within the meaning of Regulation 7) for the year in question.

(3) If the weekly amount of the allowance ascertained in accordance with paragraph (2) would exceed one fifty-second of the amount by which the student's award would be increased if his eligible dependants were all dependants for the purposes of Part 3 of Schedule 2 to the principal Regulations, then the weekly amount of the allowance shall instead equal one fifty-second of the amount of that increase.

(4) If an allowance is payable by virtue of these Regulations to both the student and the student's spouse the weekly amount shall, in both cases, be—

(*a*) unless sub-paragraph (*b*) below applies, a half of the amount ascertained in accordance with paragraphs (2) and (3);

(*b*) if the amounts so ascertained in both cases are not the same, a half of whichever is the higher of those amounts.

(5) No allowance shall be paid for any week in which the capital resources of the student's household exceed £3,000; and, for the purposes hereof, those resources shall be taken to be the capital resources of the student aggregated with those of any person whose resources would fall to be aggregated with his for the purposes of the Supplementary Benefits Act 1976, in each case as for the time being calculated for those purposes.

(6) Where the student in any week has an eligible dependant whom he maintains outside the United Kingdom then, as the Secretary of State considers reasonable in all the circumstances, either no allowance shall be paid for that week or the amount thereof shall be such as he so considers reasonable not exceeding the amount ascertained in accordance with paragraphs (2), (3) and (4).

(7) For the purposes of this Regulation a student shall be treated as having attended at an establishment, or as having pursued a period of study, for a part of a week if and only if he attends at an establishment, or pursues a period of study, on four consecutive days; and, in determining whether he has attended the establishment or pursued a period of study, any period during which he is absent on account of illness shall be ignored.

Income of student's family

7.—(1) For the purposes of these Regulations the income of the student's family in any year shall be taken to be the aggregate of—

(*a*) any sums disregarded under Part 1 of Schedule 3 to the principal Regulations in calculating a student's income for the purposes there mentioned except—

  (i) the first £915 of any such income as is mentioned in paragraph 1(1)(*b*) thereof (awards and payments by employer) so, however, that in relation to a student who holds an Industrial Scholarship this sub-paragraph shall have effect as if for the sum "£915" there were substituted the sum "£1,170";

  (ii) such income as is mentioned in paragraph 1(1)(*f*), (*i*), (*j*), (*k*), (*l*), (*m*), (*n*) or (*o*) thereof (vacation earnings, child benefit, supplementary benefit, attendance or mobility allowance, rent allowance, adoption allowance, guardian's allowance and boarding-out allowance);

  (iii) where the student's course is a sandwich course, such income as is mentioned in paragraph 4(*b*) of Schedule 5 to the principal Regulations (payments in respect of periods of experience);

(*b*) the income, disregarding such income as is mentioned in paragraph (3), of a member of the student's household being his spouse or child, less income tax thereon and any social security contributions paid by the recipient thereof; and

(*c*) in the case of a student to whom the minimum maintenance payment is paid under the principal Regulations, the amount (if any) by which his resources exceed his requirements (ascertained as provided in Regulation 18 of those Regulations).

(2) For the purposes of paragraph (1)(*a*)(i), the reference therein to an Industrial Scholarship is a reference to a scholarship awarded by the Industrial Scholarships Trust.

(3) The income to be disregarded under paragraph (1)(*b*) is—

(*a*) except where the student's spouse attends such a course as is mentioned in sub-paragraph (*c*) below and the provisions thereof apply, a half of any earned income she may have or £375 thereof, whichever is the less;

(*b*) any payment under a statutory award;

(*c*) all income of a person who attends—

  (i) a designated course not being a part-time course, or the part-time part of a course which is partly full-time and partly part-time, prescribed (in either case) under sub-paragraph (*d*)(iii) of Regulation 10(1) of the principal Regulations (certain courses of teacher training); or

  (ii) a full-time course of further education which is not prescribed by or under the said Regulation 10(1) as a designated course;

(*d*) any income by way of child benefit;

(*e*) any income by way of attendance or mobility allowance under section 35 or 37A of the Social Security Act 1975;

(*f*) any income by way of an allowance payable by an adoption agency in pursuance of a scheme approved by the Secretary of State under section 50 of the Adoption Act 1958**(a)**;

(*g*) any income by way of guardian's allowance under section 38 of the Social Security Act 1975;

(*h*) where a child in the care of a local authority is boarded out with the person, any payment made to that person in pursuance of section 21(1) of the Child Care Act 1980**(b)**.

Supplementary

8.—(1) An allowance may be paid in instalments.

(2) An allowance, and an instalment of an allowance, may be paid before the end of the year by reference to which, in accordance with Regulation 6, it falls to be assessed; and—

(*a*) any underpayment, or

(*b*) if the Secretary of State so determines, any overpayment,

in any year shall be corrected by way of an addition to, or deduction from, any allowance payable in the next following year or, if no such allowance is payable, by payment to or repayment by the Secretary of State.

Keith Joseph,
Secretary of State for Education and Science.

3rd August 1983.

(a) 1958 c. 5, amended by section 32 of the Children Act 1975 (c. 72).

(b) 1980 c. 5.

EXPLANATORY NOTE

(This Note is not part of the Regulations.)

These Regulations ("the present Regulations") consolidate the Education (Students' Dependants Allowances) Regulations 1982 with amendments. They empower the Secretary of State to pay allowances in respect of the dependants of students holding local education authority awards, in cases where the dependants' requirements are not taken into account in calculating such awards.

The present Regulations are drafted by reference to the Education (Mandatory Awards) Regulations 1983 ("the principal Regulations"), which come into operation on the same day. The principal Regulations supersede the Education (Mandatory Awards) Regulations 1982 (S.I. 1982/954) and generally alter the amounts payable in respect of students' dependants. An allowance payable under the present Regulations is payable at a rate determined by reference to the principal Regulations (*Regulation 6(2)*) and, accordingly, is payable at a new rate in most cases.

The other changes of substance incorporated in the present Regulations are as follows: the level at which the capital resources of a student's household preclude the payment of an allowance is raised from £2,500 to £3,000 (*Regulation 6(5)*); the sums to be disregarded in determining the income of a student's family, and thereby the amount of any allowance payable, are increased (*Regulation 7(1)(a)(i) and (3)(a)*); provision is also made for the disregard of any guardian's allowance payable to the student or his spouse or child (*Regulation 7(1)(a)(ii) and (3)(g)*).

STATUTORY INSTRUMENTS

1983 No. 1186

SOCIAL SECURITY

The Mobility Allowance Amendment Regulations 1983

Made - - - - - - -	*2nd August* 1983
Laid before Parliament	*8th August* 1983
Coming into Operation	
Except for regulation 2	*29th August* 1983
Regulation 2	*21st November* 1983

The Secretary of State for Social Services, in exercise of the powers conferred upon him by sections 85(1)(*a*) and 114(1) and (2) of the Social Security Act 1975**(a)** and of all other powers enabling him in that behalf, after consultation with the Council on Tribunals in accordance with section 10 of the Tribunals and Inquiries Act 1971**(b)** and after agreement by the Social Security Advisory Committee that proposals to make these regulations should not be referred to it**(c)**, hereby makes the following regulations:—

Citation and commencement

1. These regulations, which may be cited as the Mobility Allowance Amendment Regulations 1983, amend the Mobility Allowance Regulations 1975**(d)** (hereinafter referred to as "the principal regulations") and shall come into operation on 29th August 1983 except for regulation 2 which shall come into operation on 21st November 1983.

Amendment of regulation 8 of the principal regulations

2. In regulation 8(1) of the principal regulations (cases where mobility allowance not to be payable) for sub-paragraph (*b*) there shall be substituted the following sub-paragraph:—

(**a**) 1975 c. 14, as amended by section 21(1) of, and paragraph 28 of Schedule 4 to, the Child Benefit Act 1975 (c. 61).

(**b**) 1971 c. 62.

(**c**) *See* Social Security Act 1980 (c. 30), section 10(2)(*b*).

(**d**) S.I. 1975/1573, as amended by S.I. 1981/1817.

"(*b*) in respect of which that person has received, or is receiving, any payment—

(i) by way of grant under the said section 5(2) and Schedule 2 or section 46 towards the costs of running a private car, or

(ii) of mobility supplement under the Naval, Military and Air Forces etc. (Disablement and Death) Service Pensions Order 1983**(a)** or the Personal Injuries (Civilians) Scheme 1983**(b)**, or under the said Order by virtue of the War Pensions (Naval Auxiliary Personnel) Scheme 1964**(c)**, the Pensions (Polish Forces) Scheme 1964**(d)**, the War Pensions (Mercantile Marine) Scheme 1964**(e)** or an Order of Her Majesty in relation to the Home Guard dated 21st December 1964**(f)** or 22nd December 1964**(g)**, or in relation to the Ulster Defence Regiment dated 4th January 1971**(h)**,

or any payment out of public funds which the Secretary of State is satisfied is analogous thereto."

Amendment of regulation 15 of the principal regulations
3. In regulation 15(2) of the principal regulations (procedure on receipt of medical practitioner's report) after sub-paragraph (*c*) there shall be added the words—

"and for the purposes of sub-paragraph (*b*) above the question specified in regulation 13(1)(*c*) shall be treated as having been determined adversely to the person in respect of whom the allowance is claimed where it is determined by reference to a period ending on some definite date earlier than the date on which that person will attain the age of 75.".

Signed by the authority of the Secretary of State for Social Services.

Rhodes Boyson,
Minister of State,
Department of Health and Social Security.

2nd August 1983.

(**a**) S.I. 1983/883, as amended by S.I. 1983/1116.
(**b**) S.I. 1983/686, as amended by S.I. 1983/1164.
(**c**) S.I. 1964/1985.
(**d**) S.I. 1964/2007, as extended by S.I. 1967/293, 1972/95, 1981/1876.
(**e**) S.I. 1964/2058.
(**f**) Cmnd 2563.
(**g**) Cmnd 2564.
(**h**) Cmnd 4567.

EXPLANATORY NOTE

(This Note is not part of the Regulations.)

These Regulations amend the Mobility Allowance Regulations 1975 ("the principal regulations").

Regulation 8 of the principal regulations is amended so as to provide that from 21st November 1983 a mobility allowance shall not be payable to persons who are in receipt of mobility supplement to pensions payable in respect of disablement due to service in the armed forces of the Crown, the Polish Forces, the Merchant Navy or the fishing service, the Home Guard or the Ulster Defence Regiment, or disablement due to war injuries sustained by civilians or naval auxiliaries.

Regulation 15 of the principal regulations is amended so as to secure that a determination of an insurance officer to the effect that a person may not be expected to continue to be unable, or virtually unable, to walk until he reaches the age of 75 is treated as a decision which is adverse to the claimant, thereby giving the claimant a right of appeal to a medical board.

STATUTORY INSTRUMENTS

1983 No. 1190

TOWN AND COUNTRY PLANNING, ENGLAND AND WALES

The Town and Country Planning (Local Plans for Greater London) Regulations 1983

Made - - - -	*2nd August* 1983
Laid before Parliament	*17th August* 1983
Coming into Operation	*8th September* 1983

ARRANGEMENT OF REGULATIONS

PART I

APPLICATION, CITATION, COMMENCEMENT AND INTERPRETATION

PART II

PUBLICITY IN CONNECTION WITH THE PREPARATION OF LOCAL PLANS: SALE OF DOCUMENTS AND PRESCRIBED PERIOD FOR MAKING REPRESENTATIONS

PART III

FORM AND CONTENT OF LOCAL PLANS

PART IV

PROCEDURE FOR THE ADOPTION, ABANDONMENT, APPROVAL OR REJECTION OF LOCAL PLANS

PART V

AVAILABILITY AND SALE OF DOCUMENTS; REGISTER AND INDEX MAP

PART VI

ALTERATION, REPEAL OR REPLACEMENT OF LOCAL PLANS

PART VII

PREPARATION AND MAKING, ETC., OF LOCAL PLANS BY THE SECRETARY OF STATE

PART VIII

RECONCILIATION OF CONTRADICTIONS

PART IX

REVOCATION

SCHEDULE

FORMS OF NOTICES

The Secretary of State for the Environment in exercise of the powers conferred on him by sections 13(1), 18(1) and (2), 19 and 287 and paragraphs 11(2)*(b)*, (3) and (4)*(b)*, 12(1), and 17(4) of Schedule 4(**a**) to the Town and Country Planning Act 1971(**b**), and of all other powers enabling him in that behalf, hereby makes the following regulations:—

PART I

APPLICATION, CITATION, COMMENCEMENT AND INTERPRETATION

Application

1. These regulations shall apply only to Greater London.

Citation and commencement

2. These regulations may be cited as the Town and Country Planning (Local Plans for Greater London) Regulations 1983 and shall come into operation on 8th September 1983.

Interpretation

3.— (1) In these regulations:—

"the Act" means the Town and Country Planning Act 1971;

"action area" means an area or part of an area treated by virtue of a direction under paragraph 5(3) of Schedule 4 to the Act as an action area within the meaning of section 7(5) of the Act;

"adopt" means adopt within the meaning of section 14(1) of the Act, and "adopted" and "adoption" shall be construed accordingly;

"appropriate form" means the relevant form specified in the Schedule, or a form substantially to the like effect;

"certified copy" means a copy certified by the proper officer of the local planning authority or, in the case of a joint local plan, by the proper officer of any of the local planning authorities concerned, as being a true copy;

"deposited" means made available for inspection in accordance with paragraph 12(2) of Schedule 4 to the Act;

"document" includes a map, diagram, illustration or other descriptive matter in any form, and also includes where appropriate, a copy of a document;

"duly made" in relation to objections, means duly made in accordance with a notice given or served under these regulations;

"Greater London development plan" has the meaning assigned to it in section 290(1) of the Act;

(a) Substituted by the Town and Country Planning (Amendment) Act 1972 (c. 42), s. 4(1) and amended by the Local Government Planning and Land Act 1980 (c. 65), Schedule 14.
(b) 1971 c. 78.

"G.L.C. action area" has the meaning assigned to it by paragraph 8(1) of Schedule 4 to the Act;

"joint local plan" means a local plan prepared by two or more local planning authorities;

"local plan" means a local plan within the meaning of paragraph 11 of Schedule 4 to the Act;

"local planning authority" means the Greater London Council, the council of a London borough or the Common Council of the City of London, as the case may be;

"notice by advertisement" means a notice published in the London Gazette and in each of two successive weeks in at least one local newspaper circulating in the locality in which the land to which the notice relates is situated;

"notice by local advertisement" means a notice published in each of two successive weeks in at least one local newspaper circulating in the locality in which the land to which the notice relates is situated;

"proper officer" means, in relation to the certification of a document as a true copy, the officer appointed for that purpose by the local planning authority or, in the case of a joint local plan, any of the local planning authorities concerned;

"written statement" means the written statement required by paragraph 11(2) of Schedule 4 to the Act.

(2) In relation to a joint local plan reference in these regulations (except in this regulation and in regulations 22 and 23) to a local planning authority shall be read as references to the local planning authorities concerned save that in regulation 6 the reference shall not include a reference to the Greater London Council.

(3) A regulation referred to in these regulations only by number means the regulation so numbered in these regulations, and references to 'the Schedule' are to the Schedule to these regulations.

PART II

PUBLICITY IN CONNECTION WITH THE PREPARATION OF LOCAL PLANS: SALE OF DOCUMENTS AND PRESCRIBED PERIOD FOR MAKING REPRESENTATIONS

Sale of copies of documents made public for the purposes mentioned in paragraph 12(1)(a) of Schedule 4 to the Act

4. The local planning authority shall, in such particular cases as the Secretary of State may direct, provide persons making a request in that behalf with copies of any plan or other document which has been made public for the purposes mentioned in paragraph 12(1)*(a)* of Schedule 4 to the Act, subject to the payment of a reasonable charge therefor.

Prescribed period for making representations

5. The prescribed period for the purpose of paragraph 12(1) of Schedule 4 to the Act shall be six weeks, commencing with such date as the authority shall specify when giving publicity thereunder to the matters proposed to be included in a local plan.

Part III

Form and Content of Local Plans

Title

6. Every local plan shall be given a title which shall include an indication of the area to which the plan relates and any name given to the particular plan by virtue of regulation 7 and there shall be stated separately from the title the name or names of the local planning authority or authorities who prepared the plan; and each document contained in or accompanying a local plan shall bear the title of the plan and, stated separately from the title, the name or names of the relevant authority or authorities.

Names to be given to local plans

7. A local plan shall be given the name "local plan" preceded—

(a) if the local plan is for an action area, by the words "action area";

(b) if the local plan is for a G.L.C. action area by the words "G.L.C. action area";

(c) if the local plan is based on a consideration of a particular description or descriptions of development or other use of land in the area to which it relates, by the name of the subject or subjects to which it relates.

Proposals

8.— (1) The proposals formulated in a local plan written statement shall be set out so as to be readily distinguishable from the other contents thereof.

(2) A local plan written statement shall contain a reasoned justification of the proposals formulated therein.

Maps and diagrams

9.— (1) The map comprised in a local plan in compliance with paragraph 11(2) of Schedule 4 to the Act shall be called the proposals map, and shall be prepared on a map base reproduced from, or based on, the Ordnance Survey map, and show National Grid Lines and numbers.

(2) Insets, prepared as specified for the proposals map, may be contained in or accompany the proposals map to show the proposals for any part of the area to which a local plan relates to a larger scale than that selected for the main body of the proposals map: the boundary of any inset shall be shown on the main body of the proposals map, and proposals relating to land within that boundary shall be shown only on the inset, and not in the main body of the proposals map.

(3) Any map forming part of a local plan shall show the scale to which it has been prepared; and any map or diagram contained in, or accompanying, a local plan shall include such explanation as the local planning authority preparing the plan may think necessary of the notation used thereon.

PART IV

PROCEDURE FOR THE ADOPTION, ABANDONMENT, APPROVAL OR REJECTION OF LOCAL PLANS

Preparation of local plan

10. A local plan shall be prepared in duplicate; the local planning authority who prepared the plan shall, not later than the date on which notice is first given under regulation 11, send to the Secretary of State one duplicate and two certified copies and a statement of the matters specified in paragraph 12(3)(a) and (b) of Schedule 4 to the Act.

Notice of preparation of local plan

11. Subject to the provisions of paragraph 14(4) of Schedule 16 to the Local Government Act 1972(**a**), a local planning authority who have prepared and deposited a local plan shall give notice by advertisement in the appropriate form (Form 1).

Notice of withdrawal of copies of local plan and subsequent action

12.— (1) A local planning authority who are given directions by the Secretary of State under paragraph 14(2) of Schedule 4 to the Act and who, in accordance with paragraph 14(3) of Schedule 4 to the Act, withdraw the copies of a local plan made available for inspection as required by paragraph 12(2) of Schedule 4 to the Act, shall give notice by advertisement in the appropriate form (Form 2) and, for the purpose of complying with paragraph 14(3) of Schedule 4 to the Act, shall serve a notice in the same terms on any person by whom objections to the plan have been made to the authority.

(2) After satisfying the Secretary of State as mentioned in paragraph 14(2) of Schedule 4 to the Act and before taking any further steps for the adoption of the plan, the local planning authority shall again make copies of the plan available for inspection at the places where they were previously available for inspection, and shall give notice by advertisment in the appropriate form (Form 3) and shall serve a notice in the same terms on any person who made objections to the plan to the local planning authority when copies were previously available for inspection.

Local inquiry to be a public local inquiry

13. A local inquiry held for the purposes of considering objections made to a local plan shall be a public local inquiry.

Notice of local inquiry or other hearing

14. Subject to the provisions of paragraph 14(4) of Schedule 16 to the Local Government Act 1972, where a local planning authority cause a local inquiry to be held for the purpose of considering objections made to a local plan, they shall, at least six weeks before the date of the inquiry, give notice by local

---

(**a**) 1972 c. 70.

advertisement in the appropriate form (Form 4) and shall serve a notice in the same terms on any person whose objections have been duly made and are not withdrawn and on such other persons as they think fit; and, where the authority cause a hearing (other than a local inquiry) to be held for the said purpose, they shall, at least six weeks before the date of the hearing, serve a notice in the appropriate form (Form 4) on any person whose objections have been duly made and are not withdrawn and on such other persons as they think fit.

Report of local inquiry or other hearing

15.— (1) Where, for the purpose of considering objections made to a local plan, a local inquiry or other hearing is held, the local planning authority who prepared the plan shall, as part of the consideration of those objections, consider the report of the person appointed to hold the inquiry or other hearing and decide whether or not to take any action as respects the plan in the light of the report and each recommendation, if any, contained therein; and that authority shall prepare a statement of their decisions, giving their reasons therefor.

(2) The local planning authority shall make certified copies of the report, and of the statement prepared under paragraph (1) above, available for inspection when they give notice by local advertisement in compliance with regulation 17 if applicable, and in any event not later than the date on which notice is first given under regulation 18.

Procedure where no local inquiry or other hearing is held

16.— (1) Where by virtue of section 13(3) or, as the case may be, section 15(4) of the Act no local inquiry or other hearing for the purpose of considering objections made to a local plan is held, the local planning authority shall prepare a statement of their decision with respect to each objection made, giving their reasons therefor.

(2) Paragraph (2) of regulation 15 shall apply for the making available of a certified copy of the statement prepared under paragraph (1) above, as it applies for the making available of such a document prepared under paragraph (1) of that regulation.

Proposed modifications

17.— (1) Where the local planning authority who prepared a local plan propose to modify it, they shall, except as respects any proposed modification which they are satisfied will not materially affect the content of the plan—

    (a) prepare a list of the proposed modifications, giving their reasons for proposing them;

    (b) give notice by local advertisement in the appropriate form (Form 5) and serve a notice in the same terms on any person whose objections to the plan have been duly made and are not withdrawn and on such other persons as they think fit;

    (c) consider any objections duly made to the proposed modifications;

    (d) decide whether or not to afford to persons whose objections so made are not withdrawn, or to any of them, an opportunity of appearing before,

and being heard by, a person appointed by the Secretary of State for the purpose; and

(e) if a local inquiry or other hearing is held, also afford the like opportunity to such other persons as they think fit:

Provided that unless the Secretary of State directs them to do so, the local planning authority shall not be obliged to cause a local inquiry or other hearing to be held for the purpose of considering objections made to proposed modifications; but if a local inquiry is held it shall be a public local inquiry.

(2) Regulations 14 and 15 shall apply in relation to proposed modifications as they apply in relation to a local plan.

Action where local planning authority are disposed to adopt local plan

18.— (1) Where a local planning authority are disposed to adopt a local plan they shall, before adopting the plan, give notice by local advertisment in the appropriate form (Form 6) and shall serve a notice in the same terms on any person whose objections to the plan have been duly made and are not withdrawn, and on such other persons as they think fit.

(2) After complying with paragraph (1) above, the local planning authority shall send to the Secretary of State by recorded delivery service a certificate that they have complied therewith; and, subject also to section 14(1A) of the Act, the authority shall not adopt the plan until the expiration of twenty-eight days from the date on which the certificate is sent.

(3) If, before the plan is adopted, the Secretary of State directs the local planning authority not to adopt the plan until he notifies them that he has decided not to give a direction under section 14(3) or, as the case may be, section 14(3A) of the Act, the authority shall not adopt the plan until they receive such notification.

Notice of adoption or abandonment of local plan

19.— (1) Where a local planning authority adopt or abandon a local plan, they shall give notice by advertisement in the appropriate form (Form 7) and shall serve a notice in the same terms on any person who, in accordance with a notice given or served under this part of these regulations, has requested the authority to notify him of the adoption, abandonment, approval or rejection of the plan, and on such other persons as they think fit, and a copy of the notice in the form advertised shall be made available, together with a copy of the plan to which it relates, at every place at which a copy of the operative local plan is made available in accordance with regulation 23 (availability of operative local plans).

(2) The local planning authority shall, not later than the date on which notice is first given under paragraph (1) above, send two certified copies of the plan adopted to the Secretary of State.

Notice of approval, modification or rejection of local plan by the Secretary of State

20.— (1) Where a local planning authority are required by a direction under section 14(3) or (3A) of the Act to submit a local plan to the Secretary of State for his approval and the Secretary of State causes a local inquiry to be held for the purpose of considering objections duly made to the local plan, he shall, at least six weeks before the date of the inquiry, give notice by local advertisement in the appropriate form (Form 4) and shall serve a notice in the same terms on any person whose objections have been duly made and are not withdrawn and on such other persons as he thinks fit; and when the Secretary of State causes a hearing (other than a local inquiry) to be held for the said purpose, he shall, at least six weeks before the date of the hearing, serve a notice in the appropriate form (Form 4) on any person whose objections have been duly made and are not withdrawn and on such other persons as he thinks fit.

(2) A local inquiry held for the purpose of paragraph (1) above shall be a public local inquiry.

(3) Where the Secretary of State proposes to modify a local plan he shall, subject to paragraph (4) below—

(a) notify the local planning authority who prepared the plan of the proposed modifications, and the authority shall give notice by local advertisement in the appropriate form (Form 8) and shall serve a notice in the same terms on such persons as the Secretary of State may direct;

(b) consider any objections duly made to the proposed modifications;

(c) decide whether or not to afford to persons whose objections so made are not withdrawn, or to any of them, an opportunity of appearing before, and being heard by, a person appointed by him for the purpose; and

(d) if a local inquiry or other hearing is held, also afford the like opportunity to the local planning authority who prepared the plan and to such other persons as he thinks fit:

Provided that the Secretary of State shall not be obliged to cause a local inquiry or other hearing to be held for the purpose of considering objections made to proposed modifications; but if a local inquiry is held it shall be a public local inquiry.

(4) Paragraph (3) above shall not apply where the Secretary of State is satisfied that either—

(a) the proposed modification will not materially affect the content of the plan; or

(b) the local planning authority have advertised the proposed modification and considered any objections to it in accordance with regulation 17.

(5) The Secretary of State shall send notification in writing to the local planning authority who prepared the plan of his decision on a local plan and that authority shall forthwith give notice by advertisement in the appropriate form (Form 9) and shall serve a notice in the same terms on any person who, in accordance with a notice given or served under this part of these regulations, has requested to be notified of the decision and on such other persons as the Secretary of State may direct,

Documents to be sent to the Secretary of State

21. In addition to the documents mentioned in regulation 18(2), the local planning authority who prepared the plan shall send to the Secretary of State—

(a) not later than the date on which notice is first given or served under any provision in this part of these regulations, a copy of each document (other than a document mentioned in regulation 10 or 19(2)) referred to in the notice as having been deposited;

(b) on first giving or serving the notice under any provision in this part of these regulations, a certified copy of the notice; and

(c) any other relevant document which the Secretary of State may at any time require.

PART V

AVAILABILITY AND SALE OF DOCUMENTS; REGISTER AND INDEX MAP

Availability of documents referred to in notices

22.— (1) Where a notice given or served under these regulations refers to a deposited document (not being a copy of a local plan or accompanying statement required to be made available for inspection by paragraph 12(2) of Schedule 4 to the Act at the office of the local planning authority who prepared the plan) the local planning authority who prepared the plan, or, in the case of a joint local plan, each of the local planning authorities concerned, shall make that document or a copy thereof available for inspection at their main offices and at such other places as they think appropriate.

(2) Any document made available for inspection under paragraph 12(2) of Schedule 4 or under paragraph (1) above shall, unless it is withdrawn in accordance with paragraph 14(3)(a) of Schedule 4 to the Act, or unless the relevant plan is rejected or abandoned, be available for inspection free of charge, at all reasonable hours from a date not later than the date on which the notice is given or served until the expiration of six weeks from the date of the publication of the first notice of the approval or adoption of the plan required by these regulations.

Availability of operative local plans

23.— (1) The local planning authority who prepared a local plan (not being a joint local plan) shall make copies of the operative local plan available for inspection at their main office and at such other places as they may think appropriate; and in the case of a joint local plan, the local planning authorities who prepared the plan shall make copies of the operative local plan available for inspection at the main office of one of them and at such other places as they may think appropriate.

(2) Any document made available for inspection under paragraph (1) above shall be accompanied by a statement setting out the provisions of section 244(1) and (2) of the Act, and that statement shall remain on deposit until the expiration of the period specified in the said section 244(1).

(3) Any document made available for inspection under this regulation shall be available for inspection free of charge at all reasonable hours.

Printing and sale of documents

24.— (1) The local planning authority who prepared a local plan shall—

(a) provide persons making a request in that behalf with copies of that plan or any other document which has been made available for inspection under paragraph 12(2) of Schedule 4 to the Act, subject to the payment of a reasonable charge therefor; and

(b) as soon as possible after a local plan becomes operative arrange for its printing in the form in which it was approved or, as the case may be, adopted (excluding any material not forming part of the plan as approved or adopted) together with, where applicable, the Secretary of State's notice of approval thereof and thereafter, at such times as the authority may think fit, arrange for the reprinting of these documents; and make available printed copies thereof for sale to the public at a reasonable charge:

Provided that, unless the Secretary of State otherwise directs, it shall suffice, in relation to the application of this paragraph to any operative alteration of a local plan, if the alteration is taken into account when the plan is next reprinted.

Register and index map

25.— (1) The Greater London Council and the London borough council or, as the case may be, the Common Council of the City of London shall each prepare and keep up-to-date at their respective main offices a register containing the following information in respect of their respective areas, namely—

(a) brief particulars of any local plan, copies of which have been made available for inspection under paragraph 12(2) of Schedule 4 to the Act, and of any action taken in connection with any such plan, including, in the case of an operative plan, the date on which the plan became operative and a reference to the boundary of the plan as shown on the index map prepared under paragraph (2) below;

(b) brief particulars of any proposals for the alteration, repeal or replacement of any local plan, copies of which have been made available for inspection under paragraph 12(2) of Schedule 4 to the Act as applied by paragraph 16(1) of Schedule 4 to the Act, and of any action taken in connection with any such proposals, including, in the case of an operative alteration, repeal or replacement, the date on which it became operative.

(2) The council of a London borough and the Common Council of the City of London shall include in the register kept pursuant to paragraph (1) above particulars of the Greater London development plan so far as it relates to or affects their area.

(3) The Greater London Council and the London borough council or, as the case may be, the Common Council of the City of London shall also each prepare and keep up-to-date in their respective main offices an index map for their respective areas showing the boundary of any operative local plan, together with a reference to the appropriate entry in the register prepared under paragraph (1) above.

(4) The Greater London Council and the London borough council or, as the case may be, the Common Council of the City of London shall each make their register and index map available for inspection with any operative local plan made available for inspection at their respective main office under regulation 25 and where, pursuant to that regulation, copies of any plan are also made available for inspection at some other place, they shall include in their register a notice indicating with respect to each operative plan where, apart from their main office, copies are available, and display at each other place where copies are available a notice indicating where the register is available; and documents made available for inspection under this paragraph shall be available for inspection free of charge at all reasonable hours.

PART VI

ALTERATION, REPEAL OR REPLACEMENT OF LOCAL PLANS

Alteration, repeal or replacement of local plans

26. The provisions of these regulation relating to local plans shall apply, with any necessary modifications, in relation to proposals for the alteration, repeal or replacement of a local plan as they apply in relation to a local plan.

PART VII

PREPARATION AND MAKING, ETC., OF LOCAL PLANS BY THE SECRETARY OF STATE

Preparation and making, etc., of local plans by the Secretary of State

27. The provisions of these regulations shall apply, with any necessary modifications, in relation to the preparation and making of a local plan or, as the case may be, the alteration, repeal or replacement of a local plan, by the Secretary of State under section 17 of the Act:

Provided that the local planning authority to whom it fell to prepare the local plan shall, unless the Secretary of State otherwise directs, give and serve such notices as are required by these regulations and comply with Part V hereof.

PART VIII

RECONCILIATION OF CONTRADICTIONS

Reconciliation of contradictions in local plans

28. In the case of any contradiction between the written statement and any other document forming part of a local plan, the provisions of the written statement shall prevail.

Reconciliation of contradictions between local plans

29. In the case of any contradiction between local plans for the same part of any area, the provisions which are more recently adopted, approved or made shall prevail.

PART IX

REVOCATION

Revocation

30. The Town and Country Planning (Local Plans for Greater London) Regulations 1974(a) are hereby revoked.

SCHEDULE

FORMS OF NOTICES

Regulation 11

Form 1: Form of notice of preparation of local plan

NOTICE OF PREPARATION OF LOCAL PLAN

Town and Country Planning Act 1971
(Title of local plan)

(1) have prepared the above-named local plan. [The plan relates to land in the following London borough(s):–(2)](3).

Certified copies of the plan and of the statement mentioned in paragraph 12(3) of Schedule 4 to the Act have been deposited at (4).

The deposited documents are available for inspection free of charge (5).

Objections to the plan should be sent in writing to: (6) before (7). Objections should state the matters to which they relate and the grounds on which they are made*, and may include a request (stating the address to which notice is to be sent) to be notified of the decision on the plan.

19

(Signature)

*Forms for making objections are obtainable at the places where documents have been deposited.

Regulation 12(1)

Form 2: Form of notice of withdrawal of copies of local plan

NOTICE OF WITHDRAWAL OF COPIES OF LOCAL PLAN

Town and Country Planning Act 1971
(Title of local plan)

[To:](8)

The Secretary of State for the Environment has directed (1) not to take any further steps for the adoption of the above-named local plan without taking certain further action as respects publicity in connection with the plan and satisfying him that they have done so.

(a) S.I. 1974/1481.

The copies of the plan made available for inspection have been withdrawn. Before (1) take further steps for the adoption of the plan, copies of the plan will again be made available for inspection at the places where they were previously available for inspection. Objections made to the plan when copies were previously available for inspection will be considered, and there will be a further opportunity to make objections to the plan.

19   .

(Signature)

Regulation 12(2)

Form 3: Form of notice of re-deposit of copies of local plan

NOTICE OF RE-DEPOSIT OF COPIES OF LOCAL PLAN

Town and Country Planning Act 1971
(Title of local plan)

[To:](8)

(1) have decided to take further steps for the adoption of the above-named local plan. [The plan relates to land in the following London borough(s):—(2)](3).

Certified copies of the plan and of the statement mentioned in paragraph 12(3) of Schedule 4 to the Act have been deposited at (4).

The deposited documents are available for inspection free of charge (5).

Objections to the plan should be sent in writing to (6) before (7). Objections should state the matters to which they relate and the grounds on which they are made*, and may include a request (stating the address to which notice is to be sent) to be notified of the decision on the plan. Objections made to the plan when copies were previously available for inspection will be considered.

19   .

(Signature)

*Forms for making objections are obtainable at the places where documents have been deposited.

Regulations 14 and 20

Form 4: Form of notice of local inquiry or other hearing

NOTICE OF [PUBLIC LOCAL INQUIRY] [HEARING] (3)

Town and Country Planning Act 1971
(Title of local plan)

(9) WILL HOLD A [PUBLIC LOCAL INQUIRY] [HEARING] (3) AT (10) INTO OBJECTIONS MADE [TO PROPOSED MODIFICATIONS] (3) TO THE ABOVE-NAMED LOCAL PLAN.

19   .

(Signature)

Regulation 17

Form 5: Form of notice of proposal to modify local plan

NOTICE OF PROPOSAL TO MODIFY LOCAL PLAN

Town and Country Planning Act 1971
(Title of local plan)

[To:](8)

(1) propose to modify the above-named local plan.

Certified copies of the plan, [of the report of the [inquiry into] [hearing of] (3) objections] (3), of the council's statement prepared following the consideration of the [report] [objections] (3)](12) and of the list of proposed modifications (other than modifications which the council are satisfied will not materially affect the content of the plan) have been deposited at (4).

The deposited documents are available for inspection free of charge (5).

Objections to the proposed modifications should be sent in writing to (6) before (7). Objections should state the matters to which they relate and the grounds on which they are made*, and may include a request (stating the address to which notice is to be sent) to be notified of the decision on the plan.

19 .

(Signature)

*Forms for making objections are available at the places where documents have been deposited.

Regulation 18

Form 6: Form of notice of disposition to adopt local plan

NOTICE OF DISPOSITION TO ADOPT LOCAL PLAN

Town and Country Planning Act 1971
(Title of local plan)

[To:](8)

(1) have resolved that they are disposed to adopt the above-named plan [as modified by them] (3) on or after (11), unless, before the plan has been adopted, the Secretary of State for the Environment directs that the plan shall not be adopted until further notice or shall not have effect unless approved by him.

Certified copies of the plan [together with certified copies of the reports of all local inquiries or other hearings held] (12) and of the council's statements prepared following the consideration of [such reports] [objections] (3)(12) have been deposited at (4).

The deposited documents are available for inspection free of charge (5).

19 .

(Signature)

Regulation 19

Form 7: Form of notice of adoption or abandonment of local plan

NOTICE OF [ADOPTION] [ABANDONMENT] (3) OF LOCAL PLAN

Town and Country Planning Act 1971
(Title of local plan)

[To:](8)

On   19   (1) [adopted] [abandoned] (3) the above-named local plan [as modified by the council] (3) [having received the authority of the Secretary of State for the Environment under section 14(1A)(ii) of the Act to do so](12).

Certified copies of the plan and of the resolution [together with certified copies of the reports of all local inquiries or other hearings held and of the council's statements prepared following the consideration of such reports] (12) have been deposited at (4).

The deposited documents are available for inspection free of charge (5).

[The plan became operative on (13), but if any person aggrieved by the plan desires to question its validity on the ground that it is not within the powers conferred by Part II of the Town and Country Planning Act 1971, or that any requirement of the said Part II or of any regulations made thereunder has not been complied with in relation to the adoption of the plan, he may, within six weeks from (14), make an application to the High Court under section 244 of the Town and Country Planning Act 1971] (15).

19   .

(Signature)

Regulation 20

Form 8: Form of notice of proposed modifications to local plan

NOTICE OF PROPOSED MODIFICATIONS TO LOCAL PLAN

Town and Country Planning Act 1971
(Title of local plan)

[To:](8)

The Secretary of State for the Environment proposes to modify the above-named plan.

Certified copies of the plan and of the list of proposed modifications (other than modifications which the Secretary of State is satisfied will not materially affect the content of the plan) have been deposited at (4).

The deposited documents are available for inspection free of charge (5).

Objections to the proposed modifications should be sent in writing to the Secretary, Department of the Environment, 2 Marsham Street, London SW1P 3EB before (7). Objections should state the matters to which they relate and the grounds on which they are made*. A person making objections may send a written request (stating his name and the address to which notice is to be sent) to (6) to be notified of the decision on the plan.

19   .

(Signature)

*Forms for making objections are obtainable at the places where documents have been deposited.

Regulation 20

Form 9: Form of notice of approval or rejection of local plan

NOTICE OF [APPROVAL] [REJECTION] (3) OF LOCAL PLAN

Town and Country Planning Act 1971
(Title of local plan)

[To:](8)

On   19   the Secretary of State for the Environment
[approved] [rejected] (3) the above-named local plan [so far as it relates to (18)] [with modifications] [and] [with reservations] (3).

Certified copies of the plan and of the Secretary of State's letter notifying his decision have been deposited at (4).

The deposited documents are available for inspection free of charge (5).

[The plan became operative on (17), but if any person aggrieved by the plan desires to question its validity on the ground that it is not within the powers conferred by Part II of the Town and Country Planning Act 1971, or that any requirement of the said Part II or of any regulations made thereunder has not been complied with in relation to the approval of the plan, he may, within six weeks from (14) make an application to the High Court under section 244 of the Town and Country Planning Act 1971] (16).

19   .

(Signature)

Footnotes to forms 1 to 9

(1) Insert name of local planning authority.
(2) Insert names of boroughs.
(3) Insert as appropriate.
(4) Insert address of local planning authority's office and addresses of other places at which documents deposited.
(5) Specify days and hours during which deposited documents are available for inspection by public.
(6) State appropriate officer and name and address of local planning authority.
(7) Specify date six weeks after date on which notice first published in local newspaper.
(8) Insert, together with name and address of addressee, in personal notice.
(9) Insert name of person appointed to hold local inquiry or hearing.
(10) State time and date of local inquiry or other hearing and address at which it is to be held.
(11) Specify date, taking account of the period of 28 days specified in regulation 18(2).
(12) Modify as necessary or omit where appropriate.
(13) Insert date appointed in the resolution.
(14) Insert date of first publication of the notice.
(15) Insert paragraph only if plan is adopted.
(16) Insert paragraph only if plan is approved.
(17) Insert date appointed in Secretary of State's letter.
(18) Give indication of area.

Patrick Jenkin,
2nd August 1983.   Secretary of State for the Environment.

EXPLANATORY NOTE
(This Note is not part of the Regulations.)

These Regulations revoke and re-enact the Town and Country Planning (Local Plans for Greater London) Regulations 1974 with amendments which take into account the provisions of the Local Government, Planning and Land Act 1980.

The regulations make provision with respect to the form and content of local plans prepared under Part II of the Town and Country Planning Act 1971 by London authorities and with respect to their preparation, approval or adoption. There is also provision for the procedure to be followed in connection with their alteration, repeal or replacement.

The principal changes made by these regulations are as follows. Local authorities are allowed to advertise certain stages in the local plan process in local newspapers only, (the previous requirement for advertisement in the London Gazette being omitted) (regulations 3, 14, 17, 18 and 20). The period for the making of representations is fixed at 6 weeks, rather than not less than 6 weeks (regulation 5). A procedure is prescribed for use when a local authority dispenses with a local inquiry because objectors to the local plan do not wish to appear. Modifications to local plans which do not materially affect the plans' content need not now be advertised (regulation 17).

STATUTORY INSTRUMENTS

1983 No. 1191

LOCAL GOVERNMENT, ENGLAND AND WALES

The Local Government (Prescribed Expenditure) (Wales) Regulations 1983

Made - - - -	*29th July* 1983
Laid before Parliament	*15th August* 1983
Coming into Operation	*5th September* 1983

The Secretary of State for Wales, in respect of Wales, in exercise of the powers conferred on him by section 84 of, and paragraph 4 of Schedule 12 to, the Local Government, Planning and Land Act 1980(**a**) and of all other powers enabling him in that behalf, hereby makes the following regulations:—

Title and commencement

1. These regulations may be cited as the Local Government (Prescribed Expenditure) (Wales) Regulations 1983 and shall come into effect on 5th September 1983.

Expenditure not to be prescribed expenditure

2. Expenditure of any description mentioned in paragraph 1 of Schedule 12 to the Local Government, Planning and Land Act 1980 so far as it is met by a payment made by the Secretary of State for Wales under section 28B of the National Health Service Act 1977(**b**) to—

(*a*) a local social services authority in Wales towards expenditure incurred or to be incurred by them in connection with any function which, by virtue of section 2(1) or (2) of the Local Authority Social Services Act 1970(**c**), is to be performed through their social services committee, other than functions under section 3 of the Disabled Persons (Employment) Act 1958(**d**);

(*b*) a district council in Wales towards expenditure incurred or to be incurred by them in connection with their functions under section 8 of the Residential Homes Act 1980(**e**) or Part II of Schedule 9 to the

---

(**a**) 1980 c.65.
(**b**) 1977 c.49; section 28B was added by section 1 of the Health and Social Services and Social Security Adjudications Act 1983 (c.41).
(**c**) 1970 c.42.
(**d**) 1958 c.33.
(**e**) 1980 c.7.

Health and Social Services and Social Security Adjudications Act 1983(a) (meals and recreation for old people);

(c) an authority in Wales who are a local education authority for the purposes of the Education Acts 1944 to 1981, towards expenditure incurred or to be incurred by them in connection with their functions under those Acts, in so far as they perform those functions for the benefit of disabled persons; and

(d) an authority in Wales who are a local authority for the purposes of the Housing Act 1957(b), towards expenditure incurred or to be incurred by them in connection with their functions under Part V of that Act (provision of housing accommodation),

shall not be prescribed expenditure.

Signed by authority of the Secretary of State.

John Stradling Thomas,
Minister of State, Welsh Office.

29th July 1983.

EXPLANATORY NOTE
(This Note is not part of the Regulations.)

Paragraph 1 of Schedule 12 to the Local Government, Planning and Land Act 1980 defines "prescribed expenditure" (the expenditure to which Part VIII of the Act relates). Paragraph 4 of that Schedule permits the Secretary of State to make regulations exempting certain types of expenditure from this definition. The Local Government (Prescribed Expenditure) Regulations 1983 (S.I. 1983/296) specified certain items of expenditure which the Secretary of State had decided should not be prescribed expenditure.

Under the provisions of section 28B of the National Health Service Act 1977, as added by section 1 of the Health and Social Services and Social Security Adjudications Act 1983, the Secretary of State for Wales is able to make payments to local authorities in Wales towards expenditure for disabled people in the fields of education, housing and personal social services. Expenditure incurred by the local authorities in Wales will, to the extent of the said payments by the Secretary of State, add a further category, as respects local authorities in Wales, to those items of expenditure already excluded from the definition of "prescribed expenditure" by the 1983 Regulations.

(a) 1983 c.41.
(b) 1957 c.56.

STATUTORY INSTRUMENTS

1983 No. 1192

INSURANCE

INDUSTRIAL ASSURANCE

The Insurance Companies (Accounts and Statements) (Amendment) Regulations 1983

Made - - - -	*3rd August* 1983
Laid before Parliament	*9th August* 1983
Coming into Operation	*5th September* 1983

The Secretary of State, in exercise of his powers under sections 17, 18, 21, 96(1) and 97 of the Insurance Companies Act 1982(**a**) and of all other powers enabling him in that behalf, hereby makes the following Regulations:—

Preliminary

Citation, commencement and transitional provisions

1.—(1) These Regulations may be cited as the Insurance Companies (Accounts and Statements) (Amendment) Regulations 1983 and shall come into operation on 5th September 1983 but, apart from Regulations 3 and 5(3), shall not apply in relation to any financial year of a company ending before 15th March 1984.

(2) A company shall not be required to include in any document submitted to the Secretary of State pursuant to section 22 of the Insurance Companies Act 1982 any information relating to the financial year of the company immediately preceding that financial year of the company to which an amendment made to the Insurance Companies (Accounts and Statements) Regulations 1980(**b**) by any provision of these Regulations shall first apply in accordance with paragraph (1) above.

Interpretation

2. In these Regulations, except where the context otherwise requires, references to numbered Regulations and Schedules are references to Regulations and Schedules respectively so numbered in the Insurance Companies (Accounts and Statements) Regulations 1980.

(**a**) 1982 c. 50.
(**b**) S.I. 1980/6, as amended by S.I. 1981/1656, 1982/305, 1795, 1983/469.

Amendment of the Industrial Assurance Companies (Accounts and Statements) Regulations 1980

3. The Industrial Assurance Companies (Accounts and Statements) Regulations 1980(**a**) are hereby amended—

(a) in regulation 3 by the insertion at the end of the definition of "the Insurance Companies Regulations" of the words "as amended by the Insurance Companies (Accounts and Statements) (Amendment) Regulations 1981(**b**), the Insurance Companies (Accounts and Statements) (Amendment) Regulations 1982(**c**) and the Insurance Companies (Accounts and Statements) (Amendment) Regulations 1983(**d**); and

(b) in Regulation 5*(a)* by the insertion after the words "Forms 55 to 58" of the words ", 60 and 61".

Amendment of the Insurance Companies (Accounts and Statements) Regulations 1980

Amendment of Regulation 2

4. In paragraph (2) of Regulation 2 for the number "17" there shall be substituted the words "17*(a)* and *(b)*".

Amendment of Regulation 3

5.—(1) In paragraph (1) of Regulation 3—

(a) the following definitions shall be inserted in the appropriate places in alphabetical order—

""mathematical reserves" has the same meaning as in Part I of the Insurance Companies Regulations 1981;"

""required margin of solvency" has the same meaning as in Part II of the Insurance Companies Regulations 1981;" and

""required minimum margin" means the greater of the appropriate required margin of solvency and the amount of the appropriate minimum guarantee fund and "required Community minimum margin" and "required United Kingdom minimum margin" shall be construed accordingly;" and

(b) in the definition of "subordinated" for the words "share capital," there shall be substituted the words "share capital and amounts which the company may be liable to pay by virtue of section 59(4) of the Companies Act 1981(**e**),".

(2) For sub-paragraph (b) of Regulation 3(3) there shall be substituted the following sub-paragraph—

"*(b)* any reference to long term business or to general business shall, in

---

(**a**) S.I. 1980/1820.
(**b**) S.I. 1981/1656.
(**c**) S.I. 1982/305.
(**d**) S.I. 1983/1192.
(**e**) 1981 c. 62.

relation to an external company (other than a pure reinsurer), be taken to refer to its entire long term business or to its entire general business and to any long term business or general business carried on by it through an agency or branch in the United Kingdom and, in relation to a United Kingdom deposit company, be taken to refer to its entire long term business or entire general business and to any long term business or general business carried on by it through an agency or branch in any member State; and accordingly any reference to, or requirement imposed in respect of, the accounts and balance sheet (including any notes, statements, reports and certificates annexed thereto) relevant to long term business or to general business shall be taken as referring to, or as the case may be, imposing the requirement in respect of—

(i) accounts prepared in respect of its entire long term business or entire general business, and

(ii) accounts prepared in respect of the long term business or the general business carried on, in the case of an external company, by the agency or branch in question in the United Kingdom, and, in the case of a United Kingdom deposit company, by the agencies or branches in question in any member State taken together.".

(3) After paragraph (3) of Regulation 3 there shall be inserted—

"(4) Regulation 2(2) of the Insurance Companies Regulations 1981 shall have effect for the purposes of these Regulations as it has effect for the purposes of those Regulations and "ECU" shall be construed accordingly.",

and in the Insurance Companies (Accounts and Statements) Regulations 1980 for references to EUA wherever they occur there shall be substituted references to ECU.

Amendment of Regulation 6

6. In Regulation 6—

(a) in paragraph 1 for the words "Forms 10 to 15" there shall be substituted the words "Forms 9 to 15" and for the words "paragraphs (2) to (6) below" there shall be substituted the words "paragraphs (1A) to (6) below";

(b) after paragraph (1) there shall be inserted the following paragraph—

"(1A) Form 9 shall be completed by every United Kingdom company, external company, United Kingdom deposit company and pure reinsurer."; and

(c) for the words "general business" in both places where they occur in paragraph (4)*(e)* and *(f)* there shall be substituted the words "long term or general business".

Amendment of Regulation 17

7. After paragraph *(a)* of Regulation 17 there shall be added the following paragraph—

"*(aa)* except in the case of a Community company (other than a United Kingdom company or a pure reinsurer) and a Community deposit company, the abstract of the actuary's report shall also include Form 60 and, where appropriate, Form 61 in respect of all long term business;".

Amendment of Schedule 1

8. In Schedule 1—

    (a) for the words "Forms 10 to 16" in the heading and in paragraph 1 there shall be substituted the words "Forms 9 to 16";

    (b) for the words "of general business" in paragraphs 3(2)*(a)* and 3(2)*(b)* there shall be substituted the words "of long term or general business";

    (c) for Forms 10, 13 and 14 and Instructions for their completion there shall be substituted Forms 9, 10, 13 and 14 and Instructions for their completion as set out in Schedule 1 hereto;

    (d) for the heading to Form 11 there shall be substituted the heading "General Business: Calculation of required margin of solvency—first method"; and

    (e) in Form 12—

        (i) for the heading there shall be substituted the heading "General Business: Calculation of required margin of solvency—second method, and statement of required minimum margin"; and

        (ii) for the words "Margin of Solvency" in line 43 there shall be substituted the words "Required margin of solvency" and for the words "Required solvency margin" in line 49 there shall be substituted the words "Required minimum margin (the higher of lines 43 and 44)".

Amendment of Schedule 3

9.—(1) In paragraph 2 of Schedule 3, for the first sentence there shall be substituted the words "All amounts shall be shown in sterling. In Forms 40 to 42 amounts shall be shown to the nearer £1,000. In Forms 43 to 51 amounts may be shown to the nearer £1,000.".

(2) At the end of paragraph 4 of Schedule 3 there shall be inserted the following words—

"The box marked "No. of Fund/Summary" in Forms 40, 41 and 42 shall be completed by the inclusion of a discrete number to identify each fund or, if the Form relates to a part of a fund, the fund of which it is part. Where there is only one fund for ordinary long term insurance business or for industrial assurance business, as the case may be, the number "1" is to be shown in the box marked "No. of Fund/Summary". Where there is more than one fund for ordinary long-term insurance business or for industrial assurance business, a summary form shall also be prepared for ordinary long-term insurance business or for industrial assurance business, as the case may require, and the number "99" shall be inserted in the box marked "No. of Fund/Summary". The box marked "No. of part of Fund" should show a discrete number for each part of a fund or the figure "0" if the Form is a statement of the whole fund.".

(3) In each of Forms 40 to 51 for the words "Global business/UK branch business" in the heading there shall be substituted the words "Global business/UK branch business/Community branch business".

(4) In each of Forms 40, 41 and 42 for the word "Fund" in the heading there

shall be substituted the words "Name and number of Fund/Summary" and at the top of each of those forms there shall be inserted the following—

	Company registration number	Global/ UK/CM	Period ended			Units	No. of Fund/ Summary	No. of part of Fund	For official use
			day	month	year				
State whether Form 40, 41 or 42					19	£000			

(5) For Form 45 in Schedule 3 there shall be substituted Form 45 as set out in Schedule 1 below.

Amendment of Schedule 4

10.—(1) For the word "liabilities" in paragraph 7*(d)* of Schedule 4 there shall be substituted the words "mathematical reserves".

(2) For the words "valuation net liability" in paragraph 8*(a)* of Schedule 4 there shall be substituted the words "mathematical reserves".

(3) For the words "net liabilities" in paragraph 8A of Schedule 4 there shall be substituted the words "mathematical reserves".

(4) After paragraph 16 of Schedule 4 there shall be inserted the following paragraph—

"**17.** Separate statements of the required minimum margin for long term business in the form set out in Form 60, and of the required margin of solvency for Supplementary Accident and Sickness Insurance in the form set out in Form 61.

N.B. If the gross annual office premiums for Supplementary Accident and Sickness Insurance in force on the valuation date do not exceed 1 per cent of the gross annual office premiums in force on that date for all long term business, Form 61 need not be completed provided it can be stated that the entry in line 10 of Form 60 exceeds the amount that would be obtained if Form 61 were to be completed. In this circumstance, the method of estimating the entry in line 10 of Form 60, together with a statement of the gross annual office premiums in force at the valuation date in respect of Supplementary Accident and Sickness Insurance, should be given".

(5) For the words "net liability" where they occur in Forms 55, 56 and 58 and in paragraphs 5, 6 and 7 of the Instructions for the completion of Forms 55 and 56 there shall be substituted the words "mathematical reserves".

(6) In the Instructions for completion of Forms 55 and 56—

(*a*) in paragraph 10 for the words "the net liability" to "the total net liability of" there shall be substituted the words "mathematical reserves for business shown under all such headings in any one valuation summary do not exceed 5% of the total mathematical reserves for"; and

(b) in paragraph 17, for the words "net liability at the valuation date is based on that" there shall be substituted the words "mathematical reserves at the valuation date are based on those".

(7) At the end of paragraph 4 of the Instructions for completion of Forms 55 and 56 there shall be added the words "and particulars are also to be shown of any subsidiary provisions within general business class 1 or 2 which, by virtue of section 1(2) and (3) of the Insurance Companies Act 1982 are to be taken to be included in long term business of any class (Supplementary Accident and Sickness Insurance— see Form 61).".

(8) In Form 58—

(a) for the words in line 10 there shall be substituted the words "Surplus including contingency and other reserves held towards the solvency margin (deficiency)(6—9)".

(b) for the words in line 24 there shall be substituted the words "Balance of surplus (including contingency and other reserves held towards the solvency margin) carried forward unappropriated".

(9) After the Instructions for completion of Form 58 in Schedule 4 there shall be inserted Forms 60 and 61 as set out in Schedule 1 hereto.

Amendment of Schedule 5

11. In Form 71, for the words "net liability" there shall be substituted the words "mathematical reserves".

Amendment of Schedule 6

12. For Schedule 6 there shall be substituted that Schedule as set out in Schedule 2 hereto.

Revocation

13. The Regulations mentioned in Schedule 3 below are hereby revoked to the extent therein specified.

3rd August 1983.

Alexander Fletcher,
Parliamentary Under Secretary of State,
Department of Trade and Industry.

(Regulations 8(c), 9(5) and 10(9))

SCHEDULE 1

Forms

Returns under Insurance Companies Legislation

Form 9
(Sheet 1)

Statement of solvency

Name of Company

Global business/UK branch business/Community branch business

Financial year ended

	Company registration number	Global/ UK/CM	Period ended day	month	year	Units	For official use
F9					19	£000	

		As at the end of the financial year 1	As at the end of the previous year 2	Source Form	Line	Column

GENERAL BUSINESS
Available assets

		1	2	Source		
Other than long term business assets allocated towards general business required minimum margin	11			See Instructions (a) and (b) below		

Required minimum margin

Required minimum margin for general business	12			12.49		
Excess of available assets over the required minimum margin (11 − 12)	13					
Implicit items admitted under regulation 10(4) of the Insurance Companies Regulations 1981	14					

LONG TERM BUSINESS
Available assets

Long term business admissible assets	21			10.11		
Other than long term business assets allocated towards long term business required minimum margin	22			See Instructions (a) and (c) below		
Total mathematical reserves (after distribution of surplus)	23			See note 1 below		
Other insurance and non-insurance liabilities	24			See note 2 below		
Available assets for long term business required minimum margin (21 + 22 − 23 − 24)	25					

Implicit items admitted under regulation 10(4) of the
Insurance Companies Regulations 1981

Future profits	31					
Zillmerising	32					
Hidden reserves	33					
Total of available assets and implicit items (25 + 31 + 32 + 33)	34					

Required minimum margin

Required minimum margin for long term business	41			60.13		
Explicit required minimum margin (1/6 x 41, or minimum guarantee fund if greater)	42					
Excess (deficiency) of available assets over explicit required minimum margin (25 − 42)	43					
Excess (deficiency) of available assets and implicit items over the required minimum margin (34 − 41)	44					

V5409
7/83

FORM 9

(Sheet 2)

Returns under Insurance Companies Legislation

Statement of solvency

Name of Company

Global business/UK branch business/Community branch business

Financial year ended

		Company registration number	Period ended Global/ UK/CM day month year Units		For official use

F9   19   £000

		As at the end of the financial year 1	As at the end of the previous year 2	Source Form / Line / Column

ALLOCATION OF OTHER THAN LONG TERM BUSINESS ASSETS

		1	2	Source
Other than long term business assets allocated towards general business required minimum margin	51			
Other than long term business assets allocated towards long term business required minimum margin	52			
Net other than long term business assets (51 + 52)	53			10.29

CONTINGENT LIABILITIES

		1	2	Source
Quantifiable contingent liabilities in respect of other than long term business as shown in a supplementary note to Form 15	60			See note 3 below
Quantifiable contingent liabilities in respect of long term business as shown in a supplementary note to Form 14	61			See note 3 below

Instructions

(a)   For a composite company, the whole Form should be completed, with the entries at lines 11 and 22 being equal to the entries at lines 51 and 52 respectively.

(b)   For a company transacting only general business, only lines 11 to 14 and line 60 should be completed, with the entry at line 11 being equal to the entry at Form 10 line 29.

(c)   For a company transacting only long term business, only lines 21 to 44 and lines 60 and 61 should be completed, with the entry at line 22 being equal to the entry at Form 10 line 29.

Notes   (1)   The entry at line 23 should be equal to the sum of lines 11 and 15 in Form 14 and the amount (if any) stated in a footnote to that Form in accordance with Instruction 3 to that Form.

(2)   The entry at line 24 should be equal to the total of lines 21 to 47 in Form 14 and the amount of any cash bonuses stated in a footnote to that Form in accordance with Instruction 2 to that Form.

(3)   The entries at lines 60 and 61 should not include provision for any liability to tax on capital gains referred to in paragraph 10(2) (b) of Schedule 1.

V 5409
7/83

Form 10

Returns under Insurance Companies Legislation

Statement of net assets

Name of Company

Global business/UK branch business/Community branch business

Financial year ended

	Company registration number	Global/ UK/CM day	Period ended month	year	Units	For official use
F10				19	£000	

		As at the end of the financial year 1	As at the end of the previous year 2	Source Form / Line / Column
Long Term business-admissible assets	11			13.93
Long Term business-liabilities and margins	12			14.59
Other than Long Term business-admissible assets	21			13.93
Other than Long Term business-liabilities	22			15.59
Net admissible assets (21-22)	27			
Unpaid capital — as per line 53	28			
Net assets (27 + 28)	29			
Authorised share capital	41			
Paid up share capital	51			
Share premium account	52			
Unpaid amounts (including share premium) on partly paid shares within the limits allowed by Regulation 10 of the Insurance Companies Regulations 1981	53			
Amounts representing the balance of net assets	54			
Total (51 to 54) and equal to line 29 above	59			

Analysis of admissible assets

Business: Long Term/Other than Long Term

Name of Company

Financial year ended

Category of Assets

Company registration number	Global/UK/CM day month year	Period ended		
F13		19	£000	Category of assets / For official use
			Units	

Admissible assets			Line	As at the end of the financial year 1	As at the end of the previous year 2
Land	Issued by, or guaranteed by, any government or public authority		11		
Fixed interest securities	Issued by, or guaranteed by, any government or public authority	listed	12		
	Other fixed interest securities except those which must be included in lines 31 to 34 and any to be included in lines 61 or 62	unlisted debentures	13		
		other unlisted	14		
Variable interest securities except those included at lines 21 to 34	Issued by, or guaranteed by, any government or public authority, except those included at line 17		15		
	Issued by, or guaranteed by, any government or public authority, where the capital value or interest is determined by an index of prices		16		
	Other		17		
Other variable interest investments	Equity shares except those in dependants which must be included in lines 29, 31 or 33	listed	18		
		unlisted	21		
	Holdings in authorised unit trust schemes		22		
Investments in dependants	Companies authorised to transact insurance business in the United Kingdom	Value of any shares held	23		
		Debts, other than amounts which must be included in lines 41 or 51 to 54	29		
	Other insurance companies	Value of any shares held	30		
		Debts, other than amounts which must be included in lines 41 or 51 to 54	31		
	Non-insurance companies	Value of any shares held	32		
		Debts, other than amounts which must be included in lines 41 or 51 to 54	33		
Share options and debenture options			34		
			35		
Total (11 to 35)			39		

Form 13
(Sheet 2)

Analysis of admissible assets

Name of Company

Financial year ended

Category of Assets

Global business/UK branch business/Community branch business

Business: Long Term/Other than Long Term

	Company registration number	Global/ UK/CM	Period ended day	month	year	£000 Units	As at the end of the financial year 1	As at the end of the previous year 2	Category of assets	For official use
F13				19						

Admissible assets		Line		
Loans secured by policies of insurance issued by the company		41		
Tax recoveries due from taxation authorities		42		
Deposit and current accounts with approved financial institutions, and deposits with local authorities and Building Societies	Current accounts and amounts on deposit for a fixed term of, or on deposit and withdrawable after giving notice of, 12 months or less after the end of the financial year, and certificates of deposit maturing during that period	43		
	Other	44		
Insurance debts including those due from dependants and individuals	Premium income in respect of direct insurance and facultative reinsurance contracts accepted not yet paid to the company less commission payable thereon	51		
	Amounts due from ceding insurers and intermediaries under reinsurance treaties accepted	52		
	Amounts due from reinsurers and intermediaries under reinsurance contracts ceded	53		
	Recoveries due by way of salvage or from other insurers in respect of claims paid other than recoveries under reinsurance contracts ceded	54		
Debts fully secured on land except listed debentures, (which must be included in line 13), debts due from dependants (which must be included in lines 30, 32 or 34), and debts due from individuals (which must be included in lines 64 or 66)	due more than 12 months after the end of the financial year	61		
	due in 12 months or less after the end of the financial year, or which would become due if the company exercised any right to require repayment within that period	62		
	due from companies and unincorporated bodies of persons	63		
	due from individuals	64		
Debts except those which must be included in other lines	due from companies and unincorporated bodies of persons	65		
	due from individuals	66		
Total (41 to 66)		69		

M242
7/83

Returns under Insurance Companies Legislation

Analysis of admissible assets

Name of Company

Financial year ended

Category of Assets

Form 13
(Sheet 3)

Global business/UK branch business/Community branch business

Business: Long Term/Other than Long Term

	Company registration number	Global/ UK/CM	Period ended day month year				
F13				19			

		As at the end of the financial year 1 £000	As at the end of the previous year 2	Units Category of assets	For official use

Admissible assets					
Shares in Building Societies and Industrial and Provident Societies		71			
Cash		72			
Computer equipment		81			
Other office machinery, furniture, motor vehicles and other equipment		82			
Life interests, reversionary interests and similar interests in property		83			
Linked assets	linked assets in internal linked funds (as shown in line 12 on Form 49)	85			
	other linked assets	86			
		87			
Total of Sheet 1 (13.39)		91			
Total of Sheet 2 (13.69)		92			
Gross Total of admissible assets (71 to 92)		93			
Total of assets valued in accordance with valuation regulations which would have been included in one of the headings above but for the admissibility limits applied by which certain assets are required to be taken into account only to a specified extent		94			
Amount included in line 93 attributable to debts due from related companies, other than those under contracts of insurance or reinsurance		95			

INSTRUCTIONS FOR COMPLETION OF FORM 13

1   Long-term business: Form 13 should be completed for the total long-term business assets of the company or branch and for each fund or group of funds for which separate assets are appropriated. The word "Total" or the name of the fund should be shown against the heading "Category of assests". The corresponding code box should contain "10" for the total assets and, in the case of separate funds, code numbers allocated sequentially beginning with code "11".

2   Other than long-term business: Form 13 should be completed in respect of the total assets of the company or branch (other than any long-term business assets) and code "1" entered in the code box "Category of assets". Additionally —

    (a)   In the case of the United Kingdom branch return of an external company (other than a pure reinsurer) Form 13 shall be completed for the following categories of assets —

Category	Code
Assets deposited with the Accountant General	2
Assets maintained in the United Kingdom	3
Assets maintained in the United Kingdom and the other member States	4

    (b)   In the case of a community branch return of a United Kingdom deposit company, Form 13 shall be completed for the following categories of assets —

Category	Code
Assets deposited with the Accountant General	2
Assets maintained in the United Kingdom and the other member States where business is carried on	5
Assets maintained in the United Kingdom and the other member States	4

3   Linked assets should be included in lines 85 and 86 wherever appropriate and not in lines 11 to 83.

4   In line 83 "life interests, reversionary interests and similar interests in property" means those interests of the kind described in Regulation 47 of the Insurance Companies Regulations 1981.

Returns under Insurance Companies Legislation   **Form 14**

Long Term business liabilities and margins

Name of Company

Global business/UK branch business

Financial year ended

	Company registration number	Global/ UK.	Period ended day	month	year	Units	For official use
F14					19	£000	

			As at the end of the financial year 1	As at the end of the previous year 2	Source Form / Line / Column
Ordinary Long Term Business (all funds)	Mathematical reserves as shown in Schedule 4, after distribution of surplus	11			See Instruction 1 below
	Balance of long term business funds	12			See Instruction 2 below
	Ordinary long term business funds (11 + 12)	13			40 . 16
	Valuation deficiencies	14			
Industrial Long Term Business	Mathematical reserves as shown in Schedule 4, after distribution of surplus	15			See Instruction 1 below
	Balance of long term business funds	16			See Instruction 2 below
	Industrial long term business funds (15 + 16)	17			40 . 16
	Valuation deficiencies	18			
Other Insurance Liabilities	Claims admitted but not paid	21			
	Amounts due in respect of direct insurance and facultative reinsurance contracts accepted except amounts which must be included in line 21	31			
	Amounts due to ceding insurers and intermediaries under reinsurance treaties accepted except amounts which must be included in line 21	32			
	Amounts due to reinsurers and intermediaries under reinsurance contracts ceded	33			
Other Liabilities	Loans secured	41			
	Loans unsecured	42			
	Taxation	44			
	Other creditors	47			
Excess of the value of admissible assets representing the long term business funds over the amount of those funds		51			See Instruction 3 below
Total (13 + 14 + 17 to 51)		59			

Amount included in line 59 attributable to liabilities to related companies, other than those under contracts of insurance or reinsurance	61			
Amount included in line 59 attributable to liabilities in respect of property linked benefits	62			

Instructions:

1   The entries at 14.11 and 14.15 should equal the sum of lines 9, 19 and 20 of the appropriate Form 58.

2   The amount of any cash bonuses allocated but not yet paid to policy holders, as shown in 58.18, (which together with 58.24 constitutes the balance of the long-term business funds) should be stated in a footnote.

3   The value of admissible assets representing the long term business funds is determined by deducting from the total value of the admissible assets an amount equal to the liabilities itemised in lines 21 to 47. The amount of any additional mathematical reserves included in line 51 which have been taken into account in the actuary's certificate because the amount of the mathematical reserves determined in Schedule 4 were not calculated in all respects in relation to assets valued in accordance with Part V of the Insurance Companies Regulations 1981, as shown in Form 13, should be stated in a footnote.

V5431

7/83

Returns under Insurance Companies Legislation

Form 45

Long Term business: Expected income from admissible non-linked assets

Name of Company

Global business/UK branch business/Community branch business

Financial year ended

Fund

Type of asset			Value of admissible assets as shown on Form 13 1	Expected income from admissible assets 2	Yield % 3
Land		I			
Fixed interest securities	issued by, or guaranteed by, any government or public authority	2			
	other	3			
Variable interest securities excluding equity shares	issued by, or guaranteed by, any government or public authority except those included at line 5	4			
	issued by, or guaranteed by, any government or public authority where the capital value or interest is determined by an index of prices	5			
	other	6			
Equity shares		7			
Debts fully secured on land	due more than 12 months after the end of the financial year	8			
	due in 12 months or less after the end of the financial year	9			
All other assets	producing income	10			
	not producing income	11			
Total		12			

Instructions

1. Where Form 13 is for the same fund or group of funds:—

   The entry at 45.1.1 should be equal to 13.11.1.
   the entry at 45.2.1 should be equal to 13.12.1.
   the entry at 45.3.1 should be equal to 13.13.1 + 13.14.1 + 13.15.1
   the entry at 45.4.1 should be equal to 13.16.1.
   the entry at 45.5.1 should be equal to 13.17.1.
   the entry at 45.6.1 should be equal to 13.18.1.

   the entry at 45.7.1 should be equal to 13.21.1 + 13.22.1 + 13.23.1.
   the entry at 45.8.1 should be equal to 13.61.1 + part of 13.64.1
   the entry at 45.9.1 should be equal to 13.62.1+ part of 13.66.1 and
   the entry at 45.12.1 should be equal to 13.93.1 — (13.85.1 + 13.86.1).

2. The expected income is to be given as the amounts before deduction of tax which would be received in the next financial year on the assumptions that the assets will be held throughout that year and that the factors which affect income will remain unchanged but account should be taken of any changes in those factors known to have occurred by the valuation date (in particular, changes of the type *(a)*, *(b)*, *(c)* or *(d)* denoted in Regulation 59(5) of the Insurance Companies Regulations 1981). The figures shown in this Form should be those determined before any adjustments considered necessary because of Regulation 59(6).

3. Where a particular asset is required to be taken into account only to a specified extent by the application of the admissibility limits, the expected income from that asset should be included only to the same extent.

4. The treatment of the expected income from any asset where the payment of interest is in default and the amount of interest involved should be stated.

5. The entries at 45.2.3 and 45.3.3 should be the gross redemption yields calculated in accordance with Instruction number 1 to Form 46 weighted by the value of the assets shown in column 1 of that Form; the yields to be inserted in column 3 for other categories of asset should be the running yields. The entry at 45.12.3 should be the weighted average of the yields in column 3, where the weight given to each asset is the value of that asset applicable for entry into column 1; assets not producing income should be included in the calculation.

M273
7/83

REQUIRED MINIMUM MARGIN — LONG TERM BUSINESS

Form 60

CLASS	Classes I and II	Class III business with relevant factor of				Classes IV and VI	Class VII business with relevant factor of				Unallocated additional mathematical reserves with relevant factor of		Total for all classes	
													The financial year	The previous year
Relevant factor (Note 5)	4%	4%	1%	Nil	Total	4%	4%	1%	Nil	Total	4%	1%		
1 Mathematical reserves before deduction for reinsurance:														
(a) Reserves before distribution of surplus														
(b) Reserves for bonus allocated to policyholders														
(c) Reserves after distribution of surplus														
2 Mathematical reserves after deduction for reinsurance:														
(a) Reserves before distribution of surplus														
(b) Reserves for bonus allocated to policyholders														
(c) Reserves after distribution of surplus														
3 Ratio of 2 (c) to 1 (c), or 0.85 if greater (see Note 1)														
4 Required margin of solvency — first result = 1 (c) x 3 x relevant factor														
5 Non-negative capital at risk before reinsurance: (see Note 2)														
(a) Temporary assurances with required margin of solvency of .001														
(b) Temporary assurances with required margin of solvency of .0015														
(c) All other contracts with required margin of solvency of .003														
(d) Total for (a) + (b) + (c)														
6 Non-negative capital at risk after reinsurance (all contracts): (see Note 2)														
7 Ratio of 6 to 5 (d), or 0.50 if greater														
8 Required margin of solvency - second result (see Note 3)														
9 Sum of first and second result = 4 + 8														
10 Required margin of solvency for Supplementary, Accident and Sickness Insurance														
11 Total required margin of solvency for long term business = 9 + 10														
12 Minimum guarantee fund														
13 Required minimum margin (greater of 11 and 12)														

NOTES

1 For a pure reinsurer, the factor of 0.85 should be replaced by 0.50

2 After distribution of surplus

3 Line 8 equals line 7 x [5 (a) x .001 + 5 (b) x .0015 + 5 (c) x .003] for Classes I and II,

4 Any additional mathematical reserves referred to in the footnote to Form 14 shall be included on this Form.

5 The appropriate factor specified in regulations 5 (2) (a) and 6 (3) and (4) of the Insurance Companies Regulations 1981.

7/83   V4AR

INSURANCE

Returns under Insurance Companies Legislation

Global business/UK branch business/Community branch business

Supplementary Accident and Sickness Insurance

Calculation of required margin of solvency

			The financial year 1	The previous year 2
Gross premiums receivable		1		
Premium taxes and levies (included in line 1)		2		
Sub-total A (1—2)		3		
Adjusted sub-total A if financial year is not a 12 month period to produce an annual figure		4		
Division of sub-total A (or adjusted sub-total A if appropriate)	Up to and including sterling equivalent of 10M ECU x 18/100	5		
	Excess (if any) over 10M ECU x 16/100	6		
Sub-total B (5 + 6)		7		
Claims paid		8		
Claims outstanding carried forward at end of financial year		9		
Claims outstanding brought forward at beginning of financial year		10		
Sub-total C (8 + 9 — 10)		11		
Amounts recoverable from reinsurers in respect of claims included in sub-total C		12		
Sub-total D (11—12)		13		
Required margin of solvency for Supplementary Accident and Sickness Insurance:- Sub-total B x sub-total D ———————— (or, if ½ is a greater fraction, x ½) sub-total C		14		

Note

"Supplementary Accident and Sickness Insurance" means the subsidiary provisions in Class 1 (Accident) and Class 2 (Sickness) of general business included in contracts to which section 1(3) of the Insurance Companies Act 1982 applies.

SCHEDULE 2   (Regulation 12)

"SCHEDULE 6   (Regulations 18 and 19)

PART I

Certificate by directors etc.

1. Subject to paragraph 7 below, the certificate required by Regulation 18*(a)* above shall state, in relation to the part of the return comprising Forms 9 to 16, 20 to 29, 31 to 37 and 40 to 51—

(a) that for the purposes of preparing the return—

(i) proper records have been maintained and adequate information has been obtained by the company, and

(ii) an appropriate system of control has been established and maintained by the company over its transactions and records;

(b) that the value shown for each category of asset has been determined in conformity with Regulation 4 above and includes the value of only such assets or such parts thereof as are permitted to be taken into account;

(c) that the amount shown for each category of liability (including contingent and prospective liabilities) has been determined in conformity with Regulation 4 above; and

(d) that in respect of the company's business which is not excluded by Regulation 27 of the Insurance Companies Regulations 1981, the assets held at the end of the financial year enabled the company to comply with Regulations 25 and 26 (matching and localisation) of the said Regulations.

2. Subject to paragraph 7 below, the certificate required by Regulation 18*(a)* above shall state in relation to the part of the return comprising a statement required by Regulation 15A, 15B, or 15BB above that, for the purposes of preparing the statement,—

(a) proper records have been maintained and, as necessary, reasonable enquiries have been made by the company for the purpose of finding whether any person and any body corporate are connected for the purposes of Regulations 15A(1)*(b)* and (2), 15B*(b)* and 15BB(1)*(b)* and (2) above, and

(b) an appropriate system of control has been established and maintained by the company over its transactions and records.

3. The certificate required by Regulation 18(a) above shall, subject to paragraph 7 below, also state separately in respect of long term business and of general business,—

(a) in the case of a United Kingdom company, a pure reinsurer or (in respect of its global business) United Kingdom deposit company or external company, that—

(i) immediately following the end of the financial year the amount of the company's required minimum margin was as shown in Form 9; and

(ii) at the end of the financial year the amount of the company's available assets and quantifiable contingent liabilities (other than those included in Form 14 or Form 15 in accordance with paragraph 10(1) of Schedule 1 above) and the identity and value of items admitted as implicit items in accordance with Regulation 10(4) of the Insurance Companies Regulations 1981 were as shown in Form 9;

(b) in the case of a Community company (other than a United Kingdom company or a pure reinsurer) and of a Community deposit company, that the value of the admissible assets of the long term business or of the general business carried on by the company through an agency or branch in the United Kingdom was maintained at not less than the amount of the liabilities of that business;

(c) in the case of an external company (other than a pure reinsurer),—

(i) in relation to the long term business or to the general business carried on by the company through an agency or branch in the United Kingdom that—

(aa) immediately following the end of the financial year the amount of the company's required United Kingdom minimum margin was as shown in Form 9; and

(bb) at the end of the financial year the amount of the company's available assets and quantifiable contingent liabilities (other than those included in Form 14 or in Form 15 in accordance with paragraph 10(1) of Schedule 1 above) and the identity and value of items admitted as implicit items in accordance with Regulation 10(4) of the Insurance Companies Regulations 1981 were as shown in Form 9;

(ii) that the company has kept admissible assets representing the required United Kingdom minimum margin of an amount at least equal to the appropriate guarantee fund or minimum guarantee fund, whichever was the greater, within the United Kingdom and has kept admissible assets representing the remainder of that minimum margin within the United Kingdom and the other member States; and

(iii) that the deposit made in accordance with section 9(1)*(c)* of the Insurance Companies Act 1982 has been maintained at a level equal to at least the minimum as defined in Regulation 14 of the Insurance Companies Regulations 1981;

(d) in the case of a United Kingdom deposit company,—

(i) in relation to the long term business or to the business carried on by the company through agencies and branches in the member States that—

(aa) immediately following the end of the financial year the amount of the company's required Community minimum margin was as shown in Form 9; and

(bb) at the end of the financial year the amount of the company's available assets and quantifiable contingent liabilities (other than those included in Form 14 or in Form 15 in accordance with paragraph 10(1) of Schedule 1 above) and the identity

and value of items admitted as implicit items in accordance with Regulation 10(4) of the Insurance Companies Regulations 1981 were as shown in Form 9.

(ii) that the company has kept admissible assets representing the required Community minimum margin of an amount at least equal to the appropriate guarantee fund or minimum guarantee fund, whichever was the greater, within the member States concerned and has kept admissible assets representing the remainder of that minimum margin within the member States concerned and the other member States; and

(iii) that the deposit made in accordance with section 9(2) of the Insurance Companies Act 1982 has been maintained at a level equal to at least the minimum as defined in Regulation 14 of the Insurance Companies Regulations 1981.

4. If a company accounts for any of its general business over periods longer than twelve months the certificate required by Regulation 18*(a)* above shall also state subject to paragraph 7 below, that all premiums and considerations receivable in respect of any such business so accounted for (and in relation to which separate provision is not made for unearned premiums and claims outstanding) have been retained in the fund or funds of the account, subject only to—

(i) the discharge of liabilites (including expenses) proper to the execution of that business, and

(ii) the transfer of any profits after the closing of the account at the end of the appropriate accounting period,

and that any shortfall of any such fund below the amount which is estimated to be required to meet outstanding liabilities (net of reinsurance and other recoveries) has been made good by transfers into the fund.

5. If a company carries on long term business the certificate required by Regulation 18*(a)* above shall also state, subject to paragraph 7 below,—

(a) except in the case of a company which has no shareholders and carries on no business whatsoever other than long term insurance business, that the requirements of sections 28 to 31 of the Insurance Companies Act 1982 have been fully complied with and in particular that, subject to the provisions of section 29(2) to (4) and section 30 of the Insurance Companies Act 1982, assets attributable to long term business, the income arising therefrom, the proceeds of any realisation of such assets and any other income or proceeds allocated to the long term business fund or funds have not been applied other than for the purposes of the long term business;

(b) that any amount payable from or receivable by the long term business fund or funds in respect of services rendered by or to any other business carried on by the company or by a person connected with it for the purposes of section 31 of the Insurance Companies Act 1982 has been determined and where appropriate apportioned on terms which are believed to be no less than fair to that fund or those funds, and any exchange of assets representing such fund or funds for other assets of the company has been made at fair market value;

(c) that all guarantees given by the company of the performance by a

related company of a contract binding on the related company which would fall to be met by any long term business fund have been disclosed in the return, and that the fund or funds on which each such guarantee would fall has been identified therein; and

(d) in the case of a United Kingdom company, pure reinsurer, United Kingdom deposit company or external company which has financial, commercial or administrative links with any other company carrying on insurance business, that the returns in respect of long term business are not distorted by agreements between the companies concerned or by any arrangements which could affect the apportionment of expenses and income.

6. Except in the case of a Community company, the certificate required by Regulation 18*(a)* above shall also state, subject to paragraph 7 below, that proper accounts and records have been maintained in the United Kingdom in respect of business carried on through an agency or branch in the United Kingdom.

7.—(1) Where, in the opinion of those signing the certificate, the circumstances are such that any of the statements required by paragraphs 1 to 6 above (other than sub-paragraphs *(a)*, *(c)*(i) and *(d)*(i) of paragraph 3) cannot truthfully be made, the relevant statements shall be omitted.

(2) Where, by virtue of sub-paragraph (1) of this paragraph, any statements have been omitted from the certificate, this fact shall be stated in a note attached to the certificate.

PART II

Certificate by appointed actuary

8. The certificate required by Regulation 18(b) above to be signed by the appointed actuary—

(a) shall state, if such be the case,—

(i) that in his opinion proper records have been kept by the company adequate for the purpose of the valuation of the liabilities of its long term business;

(ii) that the mathematical reserves as shown in Form 14, together, if the case so require, with an amount specified in the certificate (being part of the excess of the value of the admissible assets representing the long term business funds over the amount of those funds shown in Form 14) constitute proper provision at the end of the financial year for the liabilities (other than liabilities which had fallen due before the end of the financial year) arising under or in connection with contracts for long term business including any increase in those liabilities arising from a distribution of surplus as a result of an investigation as at that date into the financial condition of the long term business; and

(iii) that for the purposes of sub-paragraph (ii) above the liabilities have been assessed in accordance with Part VI of the Insurance Companies Regulations 1981 in the context of assets valued in accordance with Part V of those Regulations, as shown in Form 13; and

(b) shall state the amount of the required minimum margin, required Community minimum margin or required United Kingdom minimum margin, as the case may be, applicable to the company's long term business immediately following the end of the financial year (including any amounts resulting from any increase in liabilities arising from a distribution of surplus as a result of the investigation into the financial condition of the long term business).

9. If he considers it necessary, the appointed actuary shall add to the certificate such qualification, amplification or explanation as may be appropriate.

PART III

Auditors' report

10. The report required by Regulation 19 above shall, in addition to any statement required by section 14(4) and (6) of the Companies Act 1967(a) as applied by the said Regulation 19, state,—

(a) in the auditors' opinion, whether the parts of the return required to be audited (that is Forms 9 to 16, 20 to 29, 31 to 37 and 40 to 51 and information furnished pursuant to Regulations 15A and 15BB above) have been properly prepared in accordance with the provisions of these Regulations;

(b) in the auditors' opinion and according to the information and explanations they have received,—

(i) whether the certificate required to be signed in accordance with Regulation 18(a) above has been properly prepared in accordance with these Regulations; and

(ii) whether it was reasonable for the persons giving the certificate to have made the statements therein,

but, in so far as the certificate is given pursuant to paragraph 2 above only to the extent that it applies to information required by Regulation 15A and 15BB above; and

(c) that in giving their opinion the auditors have relied,—

(i) in the case of a company carrying on long term business, on the certificate of the actuary given in accordance with the requirements of Part II of this Schedule with respect to the mathematical reserves and required minimum margin, required Community minimum margin or required United Kingdom minimum margin, as the case may be, of the company; and

(ii) in the case of a company carrying on long term or general business, on the identity and value of any implicit items as they have been admitted in accordance with Regulation 10(4) of the Insurance Companies Regulations 1981."

(a) 1967 c. 81.

(Regulation 13)   SCHEDULE 3

REVOCATIONS

Number	Title	Extent of revocation
S.I. 1981/ 1656	The Insurance Companies (Accounts and Statements) (Amendment) Regulations 1981.	Regulation 5
S.I. 1982/ 305	The Insurance Companies (Accounts and Statements) (Amendment) Regulations 1982.	Regulations 14, 16(4) 19 and 20 and, in the Schedule, Form 10 and the Instructions for its completion
S.I. 1982/ 1795	The Insurance Companies (Accounts and Statements) (Amendment) (No.2) Regulations 1982.	Regulation 3(2)
S.I. 1983/ 469	The Insurance Companies (Accounts and Statements) (Amendment) (General Business Reinsurance) Regulations 1983.	Regulation 8

EXPLANATORY NOTE

(This Note is not part of the Regulations.)

These Regulations further amend the Insurance Companies (Accounts and Statements) Regulations 1980 which prescribe the form and content of the annual returns which insurance companies authorised to carry on business in the United Kingdom are required to make to the Secretary of State. They also amend the Industrial Assurance Companies (Accounts and Statements) Regulations which adapt those Regulations in relation to industrial assurance companies.

The principal amendments are as follows.

The Insurance Companies Regulations 1981 (S.I. 1981/1654), among other things, prescribe the margin of solvency to be maintained by an insurance company which carries on long term insurance business and to which Part II of the Insurance Companies Act 1982 applies. New forms are therefore introduced, by amendment to Schedules 1 and 4 to the Insurance Companies (Accounts and Statements) Regulations 1980, upon which an insurance company is to demonstrate the amount of its required margin of solvency in respect of that business, the amount of its actual margin of solvency and how these amounts have been calculated (Regulations 8 and 10). The directors', actuary's and auditors' certificates described in Schedule 6 to those Regulations are amended to take account of the additional information (Regulation 10).

The Industrial Assurance Companies (Accounts and Statements) Regulations 1980 are amended so as to apply in relation to industrial assurance companies the amendments described above together with amendments previously made to the Insurance Companies (Accounts and Statements) Regulations 1980.

STATUTORY INSTRUMENTS

1983 No. 1199 (C. 35) (S. 105)

MENTAL HEALTH

The Mental Health (Amendment) (Scotland) Act 1983 (Commencement No. 1) Order 1983

Made -   -   -   -   *26th July* 1983

In exercise of the powers conferred upon me by section 41(2) of the Mental Health (Amendment) (Scotland) Act 1983 (**a**) and of all other powers enabling me in that behalf, I hereby make the following order:—

1.—(1) This order may be cited as the Mental Health (Amendment) (Scotland) Act 1983 (Commencement No. 1) Order 1983.

(2) In this order, the expression "the Act" means the Mental Health (Amendment) (Scotland) Act 1983.

2. The provisions of the Act specified in the Schedule to this order shall come into force on 16th August 1983.

George Younger,
One of Her Majesty's Principal
Secretaries of State.

New St Andrew's House,
Edinburgh.
26th July 1983.

(**a**) 1983 c.39.

SCHEDULE

PROVISIONS OF THE ACT COMING INTO FORCE ON 16TH AUGUST 1983.

Provisions of the Act	Subject matter of provisions
Section 7(1) and (2).	Appointment of mental health officers.
Section 38.	Expenses.
Section 39(1) to the extent necessary to bring into operation the provisions of Schedule 1 specified below.	Transitional provisions and savings.
Section 39(2) to the extent necessary to bring into operation the provisions of Schedule 2 specified below.	Minor and consequential amendments.
Section 39(3) to the extent necessary to bring into operation the provisions of Schedule 3 specified in the Appendix hereto.	Repeals.
Section 40.	Interpretation.
In Schedule 1— Paragraph 1.	General transitional provision.
In Schedule 2— Paragraph 6*(a)*.	Amendment of section 7(1A) of the Mental Health (Scotland) Act 1960 (c.61).
So much of Schedule 3 as is specified in the Appendix hereto.	Repeals.

APPENDIX TO THE SCHEDULE

REPEALS COMING INTO FORCE ON 16TH AUGUST 1983.

Chapter	Short title	Extent of repeal
1960 c.61.	Mental Health (Scotland) Act 1960.	In section 7, subsections (1) and (1A)*(b)*, in subsection (2) the words "Notwithstanding anything in subsection (1) of the said section twenty-seven," and subsection (3).

EXPLANATORY NOTE

(This Note is not part of the Order.)

This Order brings into force on 16th August 1983 the provisions of the Mental Health (Amendment) (Scotland) Act 1983 which are set out in the Schedule to the order.

STATUTORY INSTRUMENTS

1983 No. 1200

SOCIAL SECURITY

The Pensioners' Lump Sum Payments Order 1983

Laid before Parliament in draft

Made - - - -	*5th August* 1983
Coming into Operation	*28th November* 1983

Whereas a draft of this order was laid before Parliament in accordance with the provisions of section 4(1)(*a*) of the Pensioners' Payments and Social Security Act 1979(**a**) and approved by resolution of each House of Parliament:

Now, therefore, the Secretary of State for Social Services, in exercise of the powers conferred upon him by section 4(1) and (2) of the Pensioners' Payments and Social Security Act 1979 and of all other powers enabling him in that behalf, hereby makes the following order:—

Citation, commencement and interpretation

1.—(1) This order may be cited as the Pensioners' Lump Sum Payments Order 1983 and shall come into operation on 28th November 1983.

(2) In this order "the Act" means the Pensioners' Payments and Social Security Act 1979.

Substitution in the Act for references to the relevant week and to the passing of the Act

2. Sections 1 to 3 of the Act shall have effect as if—

(*a*) for reference to the relevant week there were substituted references to the week beginning 28th November 1983; and

(*b*) for references to the passing of the Act there were substituted references to the making of this order.

Norman Fowler,
Secretary of State for Social Services.

5th August 1983.

(**a**) 1979 c. 48.

EXPLANATORY NOTE

(This Note is not part of the Order.)

This Order, a draft of which has been laid before and approved by resolution of each House of Parliament, provides for a lump sum payment (Christmas bonus) to be made in respect of a person in whose case the provisions of sections 1 to 3 of the Pensioners' Payments and Social Security Act 1979 are satisfied for a day in the week beginning Monday, 28th November 1983. The power in section 4(3) of the Act to provide for a larger lump sum payment than £10 not having been exercised in this order, such payments will be of £10 as provided for in the Act.

STATUTORY INSTRUMENTS

1983 No. 1201

SOCIAL SECURITY

The Family Income Supplements (Computation) Regulations 1983

Laid before Parliament in draft

Made - - - -	*5th August* 1983
Coming into Operation	*22nd November* 1983

The Secretary of State for Social Services, in exercise of the powers conferred on him by sections 2(1) and 3(1) and (1A) of the Family Income Supplements Act 1970(**a**), and of all other powers enabling him in that behalf, hereby makes the following regulations of which a draft has, in accordance with section 10(5) of that Act, been laid before Parliament and approved by resolution of each House of Parliament.

Citation and commencement

1. These regulations may be cited as the Family Income Supplements (Computation) Regulations 1983 and shall come into operation on 22nd November 1983.

Prescribed amount

2. The prescribed amount for any family for the purposes of section 2 of the Family Income Supplements Act 1970 shall be—

   (*a*) if the family includes only one child, £85.50; and

   (*b*) if the family includes more than one child, £85.50 plus £9.50 for each child additional to the first.

Maximum amount of family income supplement

3. The weekly rate of family income supplement shall not exceed—

   (*a*) if the family includes only one child, £22.00; and

   (*b*) if the family includes more than one child, £22.00 plus £2.00 for each child additional to the first.

(**a**) 1970 c. 55; section 2(1) was amended by paragraph 3 of Schedule 4 to the Child Benefit Act 1975 (c. 61) and section 3 was amended by paragraph 4 of that Schedule.

Revocation

4. The Family Income Supplements (Computation) Regulations 1982(**a**) are hereby revoked.

Norman Fowler,
Secretary of State for Social Services.

5th August 1983.

EXPLANATORY NOTE

(This Note is not part of the Regulations.)

These Regulations specify increased prescribed amounts for the purposes of section 2 of the Family Income Supplements Act 1970 ("the 1970 Act") and increased maximum weekly rates of family income supplement payable under that Act, replacing those set out in the Family Income Supplements (Computation) Regulations 1982 which are revoked. Under sections 2 and 3 of the 1970 Act a family income supplement is calculated by reference to the amount by which the family's resources falls short of the prescribed amount but is not to exceed a maximum specified in regulations. Under these regulations—

(*a*) the amount prescribed for the purposes of section 2 of the 1970 Act for a family is raised from £82.50 plus £9.00 for any child additional to the first to £85.50 plus £9.50 for any such child; and

(*b*) the maximum weekly rate of family income supplement is raised from £21.00 to £22.00. The addition of £2 for any child additional to the first remains unchanged.

(**a**) S.I. 1982/1107.

STATUTORY INSTRUMENTS

1983 No. 1202

SEX DISCRIMINATION
NURSES, MIDWIVES AND HEALTH VISITORS

Sex Discrimination Act 1975 (Amendment of section 20) Order 1983

Laid before Parliament in draft

Made - - - -	*5th August* 1983
Coming into Operation	1*st September* 1983

In exercise of powers conferred on me by section 80(1)(*a*) of the Sex Discrimination Act 1975(**a**), and of all other powers enabling me in that behalf, after consultation with the Equal Opportunities Commission in accordance with section 80(2) of that Act, I hereby make the following order, a draft of which has been laid before Parliament and has been approved by each House of Parliament:—

Citation and commencement

1. This Order may be cited as the Sex Discrimination Act 1975 (Amendment of section 20) Order 1983 and shall come into operation on 1st September 1983.

Amendment of Sex Discrimination Act

2. Subsections (1), (2) and (3) of section 20 of the Sex Discrimination Act 1975 (certain provisions of Act not to apply to midwives) shall be amended by the insertion at the beginning of each of those subsections the words "Until 1st September 1983".

Norman Fowler,
One of Her Majesty's Principal
Secretaries of State.

5th August 1983.

(**a**) 1975 c. 65.

EXPLANATORY NOTE

(This Note is not part of the Order.)

This Order amends section 20 of the Sex Discrimination Act 1975 so that from 1st September 1983 the provisions of that Act concerning employment, promotion, transfer and training will apply to midwives.

STATUTORY INSTRUMENTS

1983 No. 1203

COAST PROTECTION

The Coast Protection (Variation of Excluded Waters) (River Mersey) Regulations 1983

Made - - - - -	*1st August* 1983
Laid before Parliament	*16th August* 1983
Coming into Operation	*7th September* 1983

The Secretary of State for the Environment in exercise of the powers conferred by paragraph 113 of Schedule 4 to the Coast Protection Act 1949**(a)** and now vested in him**(b)** and of all other powers enabling him in that behalf, hereby makes the following regulations:—

1. These regulations may be cited as the Coast Protection (Variation of Excluded Waters) (River Mersey) Regulations 1983 and shall come into operation on 7th September 1983.

2. For paragraph 91 of Schedule 4 to the Coast Protection Act 1949 (which excludes part of the River Mersey for the purposes of the definitions of "sea" and "seashore" in that Act) there shall be substituted the following, namely—

"91. The River Mersey, above a line drawn from the south corner of Royal Seaforth Dock to the point where the north side of the Seacombe Ferry Landing Stage meets the Mersey River Wall.".

Patrick Jenkin,
Secretary of State for the Environment.

1st August 1983.

(a) 1949 c. 74.   **(b)** S.I. 1951/142, 1900, 1970/1681.

EXPLANATORY NOTE

(This Note is not part of the Regulations.)

Schedule 4 to the Coast Protection Act 1949 excludes certain waters for the purposes of definitions of "sea" and "seashore" in the Act but provides that the Schedule may be varied by regulations.

Paragraph 91 of the Schedule excludes part of the River Mersey above a line drawn from the seaward end of the New Brighton Ferry Pier to the point where the southern boundary of the Borough of Crosby crosses the high water mark of ordinary spring tides. These regulations vary the Schedule by substituting a new paragraph 91 which sets new boundaries reducing that part of the River Mersey which is excluded.

STATUTORY INSTRUMENTS

1983 No. 1204

SEA FISHERIES

CONSERVATION OF SEA FISH

The Herring and White Fish (Specified Manx Waters) Licensing Order 1983

Made - - - -	*27th July* 1983
Laid before Parliament	*15th August* 1983
Coming into Operation	*5th September* 1983

The Minister of Agriculture, Fisheries and Food and the Secretaries of State respectively concerned with the sea fish industry in Scotland, Wales and Northern Ireland, acting jointly, in exercise of the powers conferred on them by sections 4, 15(3) and 20(1) of the Sea Fish (Conservation) Act 1967(**a**), and of all other powers enabling them in that behalf, hereby make the following order:—

Title and commencement

1. This order may be cited as the Herring and White Fish (Specified Manx Waters) Licensing Order 1983 and shall come into operation on 5th September 1983.

Interpretation

2. In this order—

"length" means—

(*a*) in relation to boats registered under Part I of the Merchant Shipping Act 1894(**b**), the length entered in the certificate of registry pursuant to the requirements of that Part;

(**a**) 1967 c. 84; section 4 was amended by the Fishery Limits Act 1976 (c. 86), section 3 and by the Fisheries Act 1981 (c. 29), section 20; section 15(3) was amended by the Sea Fisheries Act 1968 (c. 77), Schedule 1, paragraph 38(3) and by the Fishery Limits Act 1976, Schedule 2, paragraph 16(1); section 4 was applied in relation to British fishing boats registered in the Isle of Man and any of the Channel Islands by the Sea Fish (Conservation) (Manx Boats) Order 1978 (S.I. 1978/281) and the Sea Fish (Conservation) (Channel Islands Boats) Order 1978 (S.I. 1978/280); section 22(2)(*a*) which contains a definition of "the Ministers" for the purposes of sections 4 and 15(3) was amended by the Fisheries Act 1981, sections 19(2)(*d*) and 45(*b*).
(**b**) 1894 c. 60.

(*b*) in relation to boats not registered under Part I of that Act, the register length calculated in accordance with the rules specified in Schedule 4 to the Merchant Shipping (Fishing Boats Registry) Order 1981(**a**);

"mile" means an international nautical mile of 1,852 metres;

"specified white fish" means the descriptions of white fish set out in Schedule 1 to this order.

Prohibition of fishing without licence and exception thereto

3.—(1) Subject to paragraph (2) of this article, fishing by British fishing boats in the area of sea described in Schedule 2 to this order for herring (*Clupea harengus*) or any specified white fish is hereby prohibited unless authorised by a licence granted by the Isle of Man Board of Agriculture and Fisheries.

(2) The prohibition in paragraph (1) above shall not apply to fishing for any of the specified white fish by any boat whose length is less than 12.19 metres (40 feet).

Retention on board of fish

4. Notwithstanding the provisions of section 4(9A)(*b*) of the Sea Fish (Conservation) Act 1967 (return to the sea of fish the fishing for which is prohibited), there may be retained on board any fishing boat to which this order applies a quantity of sea fish consisting of one or more of the specified white fish, the fishing for which is for the time being prohibited by or under this order, which—

(*a*) has been taken on board that fishing boat in the area of sea described in Schedule 2 to this order in the course of fishing in that area for other specified white fish or any other description of sea fish the fishing for which is not for the time being prohibited by or under this order or any other enactment; and

(*b*) does not exceed 10 per cent by weight of the total catch of sea fish on board that fishing boat.

Enforcement

5. For the purposes of the enforcement of this order, there are hereby conferred on every British sea-fishery officer all the powers of a British sea-fishery officer under section 8(2) to (4) of the Sea Fisheries Act 1968(**b**).

Revocation

6. The Herring (Isle of Man) Licensing Order 1977(**c**) and the Sea Fishing (Specified Western Waters) (Isle of Man) Licensing Order 1980(**d**) are hereby revoked.

(**a**) S.I. 1981/740.
(**b**) 1968 c. 77; section 8(3) and (4) was amended by the Fisheries Act 1981, section 26(2) and (3).
(**c**) S.I. 1977/1389.   (**d**) S.I. 1980/334.

In Witness whereof the Official Seal of the Minister of Agriculture, Fisheries and Food is hereunto affixed on 25th July 1983.

(L.S.)

Michael Jopling,
Minister of Agriculture, Fisheries and Food.

George Younger,
Secretary of State for Scotland.

26th July 1983.

Nicholas Edwards,
Secretary of State for Wales.

27th July 1983.

James Prior,
Secretary of State for Northern Ireland.

26th July 1983.

Article 2   SCHEDULE 1

SPECIFIED WHITE FISH

Cod	(*Gadus morhua*)
Haddock	(*Melanogrammus aeglefinus*)
Hake	(*Merluccius* spp)
Megrim	(*Lepidorhombus whiffiagonis*)
Monkfish	(*Lophius* spp)
Plaice	(*Pleuronectes platessa*)
Saithe	(*Pollachius virens*)
Sole	(*Solea solea*)
Whiting	(*Merlangius merlangus*)

SCHEDULE 2 Articles 3 and 4

AREA OF SEA IN RESPECT OF WHICH PROHIBITION OF FISHING WITHOUT LICENCE
APPLIES

The area of sea within 12 miles of the baselines from which the breadth of the territorial sea adjacent to the Isle of Man is measured(**a**) but not extending beyond a line every point of which is equidistant from the nearest points of such baselines and the corresponding baselines of the United Kingdom, and excluding the territorial sea around the Isle of Man.

EXPLANATORY NOTE

(*This Note is not part of the Order.*)

This order consolidates with amendments that part of the Herring (Isle of Man) Licensing Order 1977 which prohibited fishing for herring without a licence by British fishing boats within the twelve-mile belt around the Isle of Man but outside territorial waters and the Sea Fishing (Specified Western Waters) (Isle of Man) Licensing Order 1980, which prohibited fishing in that area of sea by British fishing boats for cod, haddock, whiting, plaice and sole without a licence.

The changes of substance are—

(*a*) the addition of hake, megrim, monkfish and saithe to the list of species for which it is prohibited to fish without a licence; and

(*b*) the inclusion of a provision permitting the retention on board of a 10% by-catch of a species (except herring) for which it is prohibited to fish, if taken in the course of fishing for a species for which it is not prohibited to fish.

(**a**) See the Territorial Waters Order in Council 1964 (1965 III, p.6452A, amended by 1979 II, p. 2866).

STATUTORY INSTRUMENTS

1983 No. 1205

SEA FISHERIES

CONSERVATION OF SEA FISH

The Sea Fishing (Specified Western Waters) (Restrictions on Landing) (Variation) Order 1983

Made - - - -	*27th July* 1983
Laid before Parliament	*15th August* 1983
Coming into Operation	*5th September* 1983

The Minister of Agriculture, Fisheries and Food and the Secretaries of State respectively concerned with the sea fishing industry in Scotland, Wales and Northern Ireland, acting jointly, in exercise of the powers conferred on them by section 6(1) and 20(1) of the Sea Fish (Conservation) Act 1967(**a**), and of all other powers enabling them in that behalf, after consultation with the Secretary of State for Trade, hereby make the following order:—

Title and commencement

1. This order may be cited as the Sea Fishing (Specified Western Waters) (Restrictions on Landing) (Variation) Order 1983 and shall come into operation on 5th September 1983.

Variation of the Sea Fishing (Specified Western Waters) (Restrictions on Landing) Order 1980

2. The Sea Fishing (Specified Western Waters) (Restrictions on Landing) Order 1980(**b**) shall be varied—

(*a*) by inserting in article 2 thereof after the definition of "ICES sub-area VII e" the following definition:—

' "ICES area VIII" means that statistical area of the International Council for the Exploration of the Sea described in Part 4 of Schedule 1 to this order;';

(*b*) by inserting in article 3 and article 4 thereof in each case after the words "in ICES area VII" the word "or in ICES area VIII";

(*c*) by adding at the end of Schedule 1 thereto the following Part:—

(**a**) 1967 c. 84; section 6(1) was amended by S.I. 1970/1537, Schedule 2, paragraph 10 and S.I. 1974/692, Schedule 1, Part III; section 22(2)(*a*) which contains a definition of "the Ministers" for the purposes of section 6(1) was amended by the Fisheries Act 1981 (c. 29), sections 19(2)(*d*) and 45(*b*).

(**b**) S.I. 1980/335.

"PART 4
ICES AREA VIII

The waters bounded by a line beginning at a point on the coast of France in 48°00′ north latitude; thence due west to 18°00′ west longitude; thence due south to 43°00′ north latitude; thence due east to the coast of Spain; thence in a northerly direction along the coasts of Spain and France to the point of beginning.".

(*d*) by adding at the end of Schedule 2 thereto the following descriptions of sea fish—

"Hake (*Merluccius* spp)
Megrim (*Lepidorhombus whiffiagonis*)
Monkfish (*Lophius* spp)
Saithe (*Pollachius virens*)".

In Witness whereof the Official Seal of the Minister of Agriculture, Fisheries and Food is hereunto affixed on 25th July 1983.

(L.S.)

Michael Jopling,
Minister of Agriculture, Fisheries
and Food.

George Younger,
Secretary of State for Scotland.

26th July 1983.

Nicholas Edwards,
Secretary of State for Wales.

27th July 1983.

James Prior,
Secretary of State for Northern Ireland.

26th July 1983

EXPLANATORY NOTE

(This Note is not part of the Order.)

This order extends the Sea Fishing (Specified Western Waters) (Restrictions on Landing) Order 1980, which, subject to specified exceptions, prohibits the landing in the United Kingdom of cod, haddock, whiting, plaice or sole caught in ICES area VII (Irish Sea, South Coast of Ireland, Bristol Channel and English Channel) by British fishing boats of 40 feet and over in length. The variation made by this order extends this prohibition so as to apply also—

(*a*) to hake, megrim, monkfish or saithe caught by such boats in ICES area VII; and

(*b*) to cod, haddock, hake, megrim, monkfish, plaice, saithe, sole or whiting caught by such boats in ICES area VIII (Bay of Biscay).

STATUTORY INSTRUMENTS

1983 No. 1206

SEA FISHERIES

CONSERVATION OF SEA FISH

The Sea Fish Licensing Order 1983

Made - - - - -	*27th July* 1983
Laid before Parliament	*15th August* 1983
Coming into Operation	*5th September* 1983

The Minister of Agriculture, Fisheries and Food, and the Secretaries of State respectively concerned with the sea fishing industry in Scotland, Wales and Northern Ireland, acting jointly, in exercise of the powers conferred on them by sections 4, 15(3) and 20(1) of the Sea Fish (Conservation) Act 1967(a), and of all other powers enabling them in that behalf, hereby make the following order:—

Title and commencement

1. This order may be cited as the Sea Fish Licensing Order 1983 and shall come into operation on 5th September 1983.

Interpretation

2. In this order—

"Community waters" means any waters which are under the sovereignty or jurisdiction of a member State;

"ICES" followed by a roman numeral with or without a letter shall be construed as a reference to whichever of the statistical sub-areas and divisions of the International Council for the Exploration of the Sea(b) described in Schedule 1 to this order is identified therein by that roman numeral or that roman numeral and letter as the case may be;

(a) 1967 c. 84; section 4 was amended by the Fishery Limits Act 1976 (c. 86), section 3 and by the Fisheries Act 1981 (c. 29), section 20; section 15(3) was amended by the Sea Fisheries Act 1968 (c. 77), Schedule 1, paragraph 38(3) and by the Fishery Limits Act 1976, Schedule 2, paragraph 16(1); section 4 was applied in relation to British fishing boats registered in the Isle of Man and any of the Channel Islands by the Sea Fish (Conservation) (Manx Boats) Order 1978 (S.I. 1978/281) and the Sea Fish (Conservation) (Channel Islands Boats) Order 1978 (S.I. 1978/280); section 22(2)(*a*) which contains a definition of "the Ministers" for the purposes of sections 4 and 15(3) was amended by the Fisheries Act 1981, sections 19(2)(*d*) and 45(*b*).

(b) Cmnd. 2586.

"length" means—

(*a*) in relation to boats registered under Part I of the Merchant Shipping Act 1894**(a)**, the length entered in the certificate of registry pursuant to the requirements of that Part;

(*b*) in relation to boats not registered under Part I of that Act, the register length calculated in accordance with the rules specified in Schedule 4 to the Merchant Shipping (Fishing Boats Registry) Order 1981**(b)**;

"mile" means an international nautical mile of 1,852 metres;

"NAFO sub-area 1" means the area of sea which is described in paragraph 2(a) of Annex III to the Convention on Future Multilateral Co-operation in the Northwest Atlantic Fisheries**(c)** and is commonly known as *West Greenland*;

"NAFO sub-area 2" means the area of sea which is described in paragraph 3(a) of Annex III to the Convention on Future Multilateral Co-operation in the Northwest Atlantic Fisheries;

"NAFO sub-area 3" means the area of sea which is described in paragraph 4(a) of Annex III to the Convention on Future Multilateral Co-operation in the Northwest Atlantic Fisheries;

"third country waters" means any waters which are not under the sovereignty or jurisdiction of a member State.

Prohibition of fishing without a licence and exceptions thereto

3.—(1) Subject to paragraph (2) of this article, fishing by British fishing boats in an area of sea specified in column 1 of Schedule 2 to this order for a description of sea fish specified in relation to that area in column 2 of that Schedule is hereby prohibited unless authorised by a licence granted, in the case of fishing by British fishing boats registered in the Isle of Man for herring (*Clupea harengus*) in ICES VIIa (*Irish Sea*), by the Isle of Man Board of Agriculture and Fisheries and, in any other case, by one of the Ministers.

(2) The prohibition in paragraph (1) above shall not apply to fishing—

(*a*) by handline for mackerel (*Scomber scombrus*);

(*b*) by any boat whose length is less than 12.19 metres (40 feet), except in the case of a boat fishing for herring—

(i) in ICES VIIa (*Irish Sea*) north of 52°30' north latitude and outside the Mourne fishery, that is to say the area of sea adjacent to the eastern coasts of Ireland and Northern Ireland which lies between latitudes 53°00' north and 55°00' north and within 12 miles from the baselines from which the breadth of the territorial seas of those countries is measured**(d)**;

(a) 1894 c. 60.   **(b)** S.I. 1981/740.
(c) Annexed to Council Regulation (EEC) No. 3179/78 concerning the conclusion by the European Economic Community of the Convention on Future Multilateral Co-operation in the Northwest Atlantic Fisheries (OJ No L 378, 30.12.78, p. 1) as amended by article 1 of, and the Annex to, Council Regulation (EEC) No 654/81 amending Regulation (EEC) No 3179/78 (OJ No L 69, 14.3.81, p. 1).
(d) See the Territorial Waters Order in Council 1964 (1965 III, p. 6452A, amended by 1979 II, p. 2866).

(ii) in ICES VIIg (*South-east of Ireland*);

(iii) in ICES VIIh (*Little Sole Bank*);

(iv) in ICES VIIj (*Great Sole Bank*);

(v) in ICES VIIk (*West of Great Sole Bank*); or

(vi) in the Thames and Blackwater coastal area, that is to say the area of sea adjacent to England which lies between a line drawn due east from Landguard Point, Felixstowe and a line drawn due east from North Foreland lighthouse and within 6 miles from the baselines from which the breadth of the territorial sea is measured.

Retention on board of fish

4. Notwithstanding the provisions of section 4(9A)(*b*) of the Sea Fish (Conservation) Act 1967 (return to the sea of fish the fishing for which is prohibited), there may be retained on board any fishing boat to which this order applies a quantity of sea fish consisting of any descriptions of sea fish (except herring, mackerel or sprat (*Sprattus sprattus*)) the fishing for which is for the time being prohibited by or under this order, which—

(*a*) has been taken on board that fishing boat in any part of ICES VII (*Irish Sea, West of Ireland and Porcupine Bank, South Coast of Ireland, Bristol Channel and English Channel*) or ICES VIII (*Bay of Biscay*) in the course of fishing in that area for any description of sea fish the fishing for which is not for the time being prohibited by or under this order or any other enactment; and

(*b*) does not exceed 10 per cent by weight of the total catch of sea fish on board that fishing boat.

Enforcement

5. For the purposes of the enforcement of this order, there are hereby conferred on every British sea-fishery officer all the powers of a British sea-fishery officer under section 8(2) to (4) of the Sea Fisheries Act 1968**(a)**.

(a) 1968 c. 77; section 8(3) and (4) was amended by the Fisheries Act 1981, section 26(2) and (3).

Revocation

6. The orders mentioned in Schedule 3 to this order are hereby revoked.

In Witness whereof the Official Seal of the Minister of Agriculture, Fisheries and Food is hereunto affixed on 25th July 1983.

(L.S.)

Michael Jopling,
Minister of Agriculture, Fisheries and Food.

George Younger,
Secretary of State for Scotland.

26th July 1983.

Nicholas Edwards,
Secretary of State for Wales.

27th July 1983.

James Prior,
Secretary of State for Northern Ireland.

26th July 1983.

SCHEDULE 1 Article 2

STATISTICAL SUB-AREAS AND DIVISIONS OF THE
INTERNATIONAL COUNCIL FOR THE EXPLORATION OF THE SEA

ICES Statistical Sub-Area I (Barents Sea)

The waters bounded by a line from the geographic North Pole along the meridian of 30°00′ east longitude to 72°00′ north latitude; thence due west to 26°00′ east longitude; thence due south to the coast of Norway; thence in an easterly direction along the coasts of Norway and the Union of Soviet Socialist Republics to Khaborova; thence across the western entry of the Strait of Yugorskiy Shar; thence in a westerly and northerly direction along the coast of Vaygach Island; thence across the western entry of the Strait of the Karskiye Vorota, thence west and north along the coast of the south island of Novaya Zemlya; thence across the western entry of the Strait of Matochkin Shar; thence along the west coast of the north island of Novaya Zemlya to a point in 68°30′ east longitude; thence due north to the geographic North Pole.

ICES Statistical Division IIa (Norwegian Sea)

The waters bounded by a line beginning at a point on the coast of Norway in 62°00′ north latitude; thence due west to 4°00′ west longitude; thence due north to 63°00′ north latitude; thence due west to 11°00′ west longitude; thence due north to 73°30′ north latitude; thence due east to 30°00′ east longitude; thence due south to 72°00′ north latitude; thence due west to 26°00′ east longitude; thence due south to the coast of Norway; thence in a westerly and south-westerly direction along the coast of Norway to the point of beginning.

ICES Statistical Division IIb (Spitzbergen and Bear Island)

The waters bounded by a line drawn from the geographic North Pole along the meridian of 30°00′ east longitude to 73°30′ north latitude; then due west to 11°00′ west longitude; thence due north to the geographic North Pole.

ICES Statistical Division IIIa (Skagerak and Kattegat)

The waters bounded by a line beginning at a point on the coast of Norway in 7°00′ east longitude; thence due south to 57°30′ north latitude; thence due east to 8°00′ east longitude; thence due south to 57°00′ north latitude; thence due east to the coast of Denmark; thence along the north-west and east coasts of Jutland to Hals; thence across the eastern entrance of the Limfjord to Egensekloster Point; thence in a southerly direction along the coast of Jutland to Hasenore Head; thence across the Great Belt to Gniben Point; thence along the north coast of Zealand to Gilbierg Head; thence across the northern approaches of the Oresund to the Kullen, on the coast of Sweden; thence in an easterly and northerly direction along the west coast of Sweden and the south coast of Norway to the point of beginning.

ICES Statistical Division IIIb, c (Sound and Belt Sea or Transition Area)

The waters bounded by a line drawn from Hasenore Head on the east coast of Jutland to Gniben Point on the west coast of Zealand; thence along the north coast of Zealand to Gilbierg Head; thence across the northern approaches of the Oresund to the Kullen, on the coast of Sweden; thence in a southerly direction along the coast of Sweden to Falsterbo Light; thence across the southern entrance of the Oresund to Stevns Light; thence along the south-east coast of Zealand; thence across the eastern entrance of the Storstrom Sound; thence along the east coast of the island of Falster to Gedser; thence to Darsser-Ort on the coast of the German Democratic Republic; thence in a south-westerly direction along the coasts of the German Democratic Republic, the Federal Republic of Germany and the east coast of Jutland to the point of beginning.

ICES Statistical Division IIId (Baltic Sea)

The waters of the Baltic Sea and its dependent gulfs, bights and firths, bounded to the west by a line drawn from Falsterbo Light on the south-west coast of Sweden, across the southern entrance of the Oresund to Stevns Light; thence along the south-east coast of Zealand; thence across the eastern entrance of the Storstrom Sound; thence along the east coast of the island of Falster to Gedser; thence to Darsser-Ort on the coast of the German Democratic Republic.

ICES Statistical Sub-area IV (North Sea)

The waters bounded by a line beginning at a point on the coast of Norway in 62°00′ north latitude; thence due west to 4°00′ west longitude; thence due south to the coast of Scotland; thence in an easterly and southerly direction along the coasts of Scotland and England to a point in 51°00′ north latitude; thence due east to the coast of France; thence in a north-easterly direction along the coasts of France, Belgium, the Netherlands and the Federal Republic of Germany to the western terminus of its boundary with Denmark; thence along the west coast of Jutland to Thyboron; thence in a southerly and easterly direction along the south coast of the Limfjord to Egensekloster Point; thence across the eastern entrance of the Limfjord to Hals; thence in a westerly direction along the north coast of Limfjord to the southernmost point of Agger Tange; thence in a northerly direction along the west coast of Jutland to a point in 57°00′ north latitude; thence due west to 8°00′ east longitude; thence due north to 57°30′ north latitude; thence due west to 7°00′ east longitude; thence due north to the coast of Norway; thence in a north-westerly direction along the coast of Norway to the point of beginning.

ICES Statistical Division Va (Iceland Grounds)

The waters bounded by a line beginning at a point in 68°00′ north latitude, 11°00′ west longitude; thence due west to 27°00′ west longitude; thence due south to 62°00′ north latitude; thence due east to 15°00′ west longitude; thence due north to 63°00′ north latitude; thence due east to 11°00′ west longitude; thence due north to the point of beginning.

ICES Statistical Division Vb (Faroes Grounds)

The waters bounded by a line beginning at a point in 63°00′ north latitude, 4°00′ west longitude; thence due west to 15°00′ west longitude; thence due south to 60°00′ north latitude; thence due east to 5°00′ west longitude; thence due north to 60°30′ north latitude; thence due east to 4°00′ west longitude; thence due north to the point of beginning.

ICES Statistical Sub-Area VI (Rockall and West of Scotland)

The waters bounded by a line beginning at a point on the north coast of Scotland in 4°00′ west longitude; thence due north to 60°30′ north latitude; thence due west to 5°00′ west longitude; thence due south to 60°00′ north latitude; thence due west to 18°00′ west longitude; thence due south to 54°30′ north latitude; thence due east to the coast of the Republic of Ireland; thence in a northerly and easterly direction along the coasts of the Republic of Ireland and of Northern Ireland to a point on the east coast of Northern Ireland in 55°00′ north latitude; thence due east to the coast of Scotland; thence in a northerly direction along the west coast of Scotland to the point of beginning.

ICES Statistical Sub-Area VII (Irish Sea, West of Ireland and Porcupine Bank, South Coast of Ireland, Bristol Channel and English Channel)

The waters bounded by a line beginning at a point on the west coast of the Republic of Ireland in 54°30′ north latitude; thence due west to 18°00′ west longitude; thence due south to 48°00′ north latitude; thence due east to the coast of France; thence in a northerly and north-easterly direction along the coast of France to a point in 51°00′ north latitude; thence due west to the south-east coast of England; thence in a westerly and northerly direction along the coasts of England, Wales and Scotland to a point on the West coast of Scotland in 55°00′ north latitude; thence due west to the coast of Northern Ireland; thence in a northerly and westerly direction along the coasts of Northern Ireland and the Republic of Ireland to the point of beginning.

ICES Statistical Division VIIa (Irish Sea)

The waters bounded by a line beginning at a point on the west coast of Scotland in 55°00′ north latitude; thence due west to the coast of Northern Ireland; thence in a southerly direction along the coasts of Northern Ireland and Ireland to a point on the south-east coast of the Republic of Ireland in 52°00′ north latitude; thence due east to the coast of Wales; thence in a north-easterly and northerly direction along the coasts of Wales, England and Scotland to the point of beginning.

ICES Statistical Division VIIb, c (West of Ireland and Porcupine Bank)

The waters bounded by a line beginning at a point on the west coast of Ireland in 54°30′ north latitude; thence due west to 18°00′ west longitude; thence due south to 52°30′ north latitude; thence due east to the coast of Ireland; thence in a northerly direction along the west coast of Ireland to the point of beginning.

ICES Statistical Division VIId (Eastern English Channel)

The waters bounded by a line beginning at a point on the west coast of France in 51°00′ north latitude; thence due west to the coast of England; thence in a westerly direction along the south coast of England to 2°00′ west longitude; thence south to the coast of France at Cape de la Hague; thence in a north-easterly direction along the coast of France to the point of beginning.

ICES Statistical Division VIIe (Western English Channel)

The waters bounded by a line beginning on the south coast of England in 2°00′ west longitude; thence in a southerly and westerly direction along the coast of England to a point on the south-west coast in 50°00′ north latitude; thence due west to 7°00′ west longitude; thence due south to 49°30′ north latitude; thence due east to 5°00′ west longitude; thence due south to 48°00′ north latitude; thence due east to the coast of France; thence in a northerly and north-easterly direction along the coast of France to Cape de la Hague; thence due north to the point of beginning.

ICES Statistical Division VIIf (Bristol Channel)

The waters bounded by a line beginning at a point on the south coast of Wales in 5°00′ west longitude; thence due south to 51°00′ north latitude; thence due west to 6°00′ west longitude; thence due south to 50°30′ north latitude; thence due west to 7°00′ west longitude; thence due south to 50°00′ north latitude; thence due east to the coast of England; thence along the south-west coast of England and the south coast of Wales to the point of beginning.

ICES Statistical Division VIIg (South-east of Ireland)

The waters bounded by a line beginning at a point in 9°00' west longitude on the south coast of Ireland; thence due south to 50°00' north latitude; thence due east to 7°00' west longitude; thence due north to 50°30' north latitude; thence due east to 6°00' west longitude; thence due north to 51°00' north latitude; thence due east to 5°00' west longitude; thence due north to the south coast of Wales; thence in a north-westerly direction along the coast of Wales to a point in 52°00' north latitude; thence due west to the south-east coast of the Republic of Ireland; thence in a south-westerly direction along the coast of the Republic of Ireland to the point of beginning.

ICES Statistical Division VIIh (Little Sole Bank)

The waters bounded by a line beginning at a point in 50°00' north latitude 7°00' west longitude; thence due west to 9°00' west longitude; thence due south to 48°00' north latitude; thence due east to 5°00' west longitude; thence due north to 49°30' north latitude; thence due west to 7°00' west longitude; thence due north to the point of beginning.

ICES Statistical Division VIIj (Great Sole Bank)

The waters bounded by a line beginning at a point in 52°30' north latitude on the west coast of the Republic of Ireland; thence due west to 12°00' west longitude; thence due south to 48°00' north latitude; thence due east to 9°00' west longitude; thence due north to the south coast of the Republic of Ireland; thence in a westerly and northerly direction along the coast of the Republic of Ireland to the point of beginning.

ICES Statistical Division VIIk (West of Great Sole Bank)

The waters bounded by a line beginning at a point in 52°30' north latitude, 12°00' west longitude; thence due west to 18°00' west longitude; thence due south to 48°00' north latitude; thence due east to 12°00' west longitude; thence due north to the point of beginning.

ICES Statistical Sub-Area VIII (Bay of Biscay)

The waters bounded by a line beginning at a point on the coast of France in 48°00' north latitude; thence due west to 18°00' west longitude; thence due south to 43°00' north latitude; thence due east to the coast of Spain; thence in a northerly direction along the coasts of Spain and France to the point of beginning.

ICES Statistical Sub-Area XII (North of Azores)

The waters bounded by a line beginning at a point in 62°00' north latitude, 15°00' west longitude; thence due west to 27°00' west longitude; thence due south to 59°00' north latitude; thence due west to 42°00' west longitude; thence due south to 48°00' north latitude; thence due east to 18°00' west longitude; thence due north to 60°00' north latitude; thence due east to 15°00' west longitude; thence due north to the point of beginning.

ICES Statistical Sub-Area XIV (East Greenland)

The waters bounded by a line from the geographic North Pole along the meridian of 40°00' west longitude to the north coast of Greenland; thence in an easterly and southerly direction along the coast of Greenland to a point in 44°00' west longitude; thence due south to 59°00' north latitude; thence due east to 27°00' west longitude; thence due north to 68°00' north latitude; thence due east to 11°00' west longitude; thence due north to the geographic North Pole.

SCHEDULE 2   Article 3

AREAS OF SEA AND DESCRIPTIONS OF SEA FISH
IN RESPECT OF WHICH PROHIBITION OF FISHING
WITHOUT LICENCE APPLIES

Column 1	Column 2
Area of sea	Description of sea fish
ICES I	All
ICES IIa excluding third country waters	Cod (*Gadus morhua*), haddock (*Melanogrammus aeglefinus*), hake (*Merluccius* spp), herring (*Clupea harengus*), mackerel (*Scomber scombrus*), plaice (*Pleuronectes platessa*), saithe (*Pollachius virens*), sole (*Solea solea*), whiting (*Merlangius merlangus*)
ICES IIa excluding Community waters	All
ICES IIb	All
ICES IIIa	Mackerel, saithe
ICES IIIb, c excluding third country waters	Mackerel, saithe
ICES IIId excluding third country waters	Mackerel, saithe
ICES IV	Cod, haddock, hake, herring, mackerel, plaice, saithe, sole, whiting
ICES Va	All
ICES Vb excluding third country waters	Cod, Greenland halibut (*Reinhardtius hippoglossoides*), haddock, hake, herring, mackerel, megrim (*Lepidorhombus whiffiagonis*), monkfish (*Lophius* spp), plaice, redfish (*Sebastes spp*), saithe, sole, whiting
ICES Vb excluding Community waters	All
ICES VI	Cod, haddock, hake, herring, mackerel, megrim, monkfish, plaice, saithe, sole, whiting
ICES VIIa*	Cod, haddock, hake, herring, mackerel, megrim, monkfish, plaice, saithe, sole, whiting
ICES VIIb, c	Cod, haddock, hake, mackerel, megrim, monkfish, plaice, saithe, sole, whiting
ICES VIId	Cod, haddock, hake, herring, mackerel, megrim, monkfish, plaice, saithe, sole, sprat (*Sprattus sprattus*), whiting
ICES VIIe*	Cod, haddock, hake, herring, mackerel, megrim, monkfish, plaice, saithe, sole, sprat, whiting
ICES VIIf to k	Cod, haddock, hake, herring, mackerel, megrim, monkfish, plaice, saithe, sole, whiting

SEA FISHERIES

Column 1	Column 2
Area of sea	Description of sea fish
ICES VIII excluding third country waters	Cod, haddock, mackerel, megrim, monkfish, saithe
ICES XII	All
ICES XIV	All
NAFO sub-area 1	All
NAFO sub-area 2	All
NAFO sub-area 3	All

Note: Where an entry in column 1 of this Schedule is marked with an asterisk the following waters are excluded from the area of sea referred to in that entry:—

Waters lying within 12 miles of the baselines from which the breadth of the territorial sea adjacent to the Isle of Man and the Channel Islands respectively is measured, but not extending beyond a line every point of which is equidistant from the nearest points of such baselines and the corresponding baselines adjacent to the United Kingdom and France respectively.

SCHEDULE 3   Article 6

ORDERS WHICH ARE REVOKED BY THIS ORDER

Column 1 Orders revoked	Column 2 References
The Sea Fishing (North-West Atlantic) Licensing Order 1973	S.I. 1973/2084
The Cod (North East Arctic) Licensing Order 1975	S.I. 1975/340
The Herring (Irish Sea) Licensing Order 1977	S.I. 1977/1388
The Mackerel Licensing Order 1977	S.I. 1977/1497
The Haddock (North Sea) Licensing Order 1978	S.I. 1978/1285
The Mackerel Licensing (Manx and Channel Islands Boats) Order 1978	S.I. 1978/1537
The Mackerel Licensing (Variation) Order 1978	S.I. 1978/1538
The Haddock (West of Scotland and Rockall) Licensing Order 1979	S.I. 1979/71
The Cod and Whiting (Licensing) Order 1979	S.I. 1979/268
The Sea Fishing (Specified Western Waters) (Manx and Channel Island Boats) Licensing Order 1980	S.I. 1980/332
The Sea Fishing (Specified Western Waters) Licensing Order 1980	S.I. 1980/333
The West Coast Herring Licensing Order 1981	S.I. 1981/1183
The Herring (North Sea and Specified Western Waters) (Manx and Channel Islands Boats) Licensing Order 1981	S.I. 1981/1293
The Herring (North Sea and Specified Western Waters) Licensing Order 1981	S.I. 1981/1295
The Herring (North Sea and Specified Western Waters) Licensing (Variation) Order 1981	S.I. 1981/1662
The Mackerel Licensing (Variation) Order 1982	S.I. 1982/281
The Mackerel Licensing (Manx and Channel Islands Boats) (Variation) Order 1982	S.I. 1982/282

EXPLANATORY NOTE

(This Note is not part of the Order.)

This order, which consolidates with amendments earlier licensing orders, prohibits fishing by British fishing boats (including boats registered in the Isle of Man and the Channel Islands) in specified areas of sea for the principal species of sea fish, unless authorised by a licence granted—

    (*a*) in the case of fishing by Isle of Man registered boats for herring in ICES VIIa (Irish Sea), by the Isle of Man Board of Agriculture and Fisheries; and

    (*b*) in any other case, by one of the Fisheries Ministers.

There is excepted from this prohibition fishing—

    (i) by boats whose length is under 12.19 metres (40 feet), except in the case of a boat fishing for herring in specified areas;

    (ii) for mackerel by handline.

The amendments made by this order extend licensing requirements in British fishery limits and in the North-West Atlantic and the North-East Arctic. The following table shows, by reference to each area of sea, the species of fish in respect of which licensing requirements under the Sea Fish (Conservation) Act 1967 are introduced for the first time:—

Areas of sea	*Species of fish*
ICES I	All
ICES IIa excluding third country waters	Cod, haddock, hake, herring, plaice, saithe, sole, whiting
ICES IIa excluding Community waters	All
ICES IIb	All
ICES IIIa	Mackerel, saithe
ICES IIIb, c excluding third country waters	Mackerel, saithe
ICES IIId excluding third country waters	Mackerel, saithe
ICES IV	Hake, plaice, saithe, sole
ICES Va	All
ICES Vb excluding third country waters	Cod, Greenland halibut, haddock, hake, herring, megrim, monkfish, plaice, redfish, saithe, sole, whiting

Areas of sea	Species of fish
ICES Vb excluding Community waters	All
ICES VI	Hake, megrim, monkfish, plaice, saithe, sole
ICES VIIa	Hake, megrim, monkfish, saithe
ICES VIIb, c	Hake, megrim, monkfish, saithe
ICES VIId	Hake, megrim, monkfish, saithe, sprat
ICES VIIe	Hake, megrim, monkfish, saithe, sprat
ICES VIIf to h	Hake, megrim, monkfish, saithe
ICES VIIj to k	Hake, herring, megrim, monkfish, saithe
ICES VIII excluding third country waters	Cod, haddock, mackerel, megrim, monkfish, saithe
ICES XII	All
ICES XIV	All
NAFO sub-area 1	All
NAFO sub-area 2	All
NAFO sub-area 3	All

The order permits the retention on board of a 10% by-catch of specified species of fish for which it is prohibited to fish, if taken in the course of fishing in ICES VII or VIII for a species fishing for which is not prohibited.

The order applies the power of British sea-fishery officers for the purposes of enforcement.

STATUTORY INSTRUMENTS

1983 No. 1210 (S. 106)

COURT OF SESSION, SCOTLAND

Act of Sederunt (Rules of Court Amendment No. 6) (Simplified Divorce Procedure) 1983

Made	-	-	-	-	*4th August* 1983
Coming into Operation					*1st September* 1983

The Lords of Council and Session, under and by virtue of the powers conferred upon them by section 16 of the Administration of Justice (Scotland) Act 1933(a) and of all other powers competent to them in that behalf, do hereby enact and declare:—

Citation and commencement

1.—(1) This Act of Sederunt may be cited as the Act of Sederunt (Rules of Court Amendment No. 6) (Simplified Divorce Procedure) 1983 and shall come into operation on 1st September 1983.

(2) This Act of Sederunt shall be inserted in the Books of Sederunt.

Amendment to Rules of Court

2. In the appendix (forms) to the Rules of Court(b) for forms 19A, 19B, 19C, 19D and 19E substitute forms 19A, 19B, 19C, 19D and 19E respectively in the Schedule to this Act of Sederunt.

Emslie,
Lord President,
I.P.D.

Edinburgh
4th August 1983

(a) 1933 c. 41.
(b) S.I. 1965/321; relevant amendment is SI. 1982/1679.

SCHEDULE

FORM 19A

UNDER THE DIVORCE (SCOTLAND) ACT 1976, SECTION 1(2)(d)
SIMPLIFIED PROCEDURE

Court of Session
Divorce Section (SP)
Parliament House
Edinburgh EH1 1RQ
Tel: 031-225 2595 Ext 316

APPLICATION FOR DIVORCE (WITH CONSENT OF OTHER PARTY TO
THE MARRIAGE) HUSBAND AND WIFE HAVING LIVED APART FOR
AT LEAST 2 YEARS

Before completing this form, you should have read the leaflet entitled "Do it
yourself Divorce", which explains the circumstances in which a divorce may
be sought by that method. If the simplified procedure appears to suit your
circumstances, you may use this form to apply for divorce.

Below you will find directions designed to assist you with your application.
Please follow them carefully. In the event of difficulty, you may contact the
Court's Divorce Section at the above address, or any Sheriff Clerk's Office or
Citizens Advice Bureau.

Directions for making Application

WRITE IN INK. USING BLOCK CAPITALS

1. Complete and sign Part 1 of the form (pages 3–7), paying particular attention to the notes opposite each section.

   Application (Part 1)

2. When you have filled in Part 1 of the form, attach the (blue) Instruction Sheet SP3 to it and send both documents to your husband/wife for completion of the consent at Part 2 (page 9).

   Consent of Husband/ Wife (Part 2)

   NOTE: If your husband/wife does NOT complete and sign the form of consent, your application cannot proceed further under the simplified procedure. In that event, if you still wish to obtain a divorce, you should consult a solicitor.

3. When the application has been returned to you with the Consent (Part 2) duly completed and signed, you should then take the form to a Justice of the Peace, Notary Public, Commissioner for Oaths or other duly authorised person so that your affidavit in Part 3 (page 10) can be completed and sworn.

   Affidavit (Part 3)

4. When directions 1–3 above have all been carried out, your application is now ready to be sent to the Court. With it you must enclose:

   Returning completed Application Form to Court

   (i) Your marriage certificate (the document headed "Extract of an entry in a register of Marriages"), which will be returned to you in due course, and

   (ii) Either a cheque or postal order for the sum of £40 in respect of the Court fee, crossed and made payable to "Court of Session",

   or a completed form SP15, claiming exemption from the Court fee.

5. Receipt of your application will be promptly acknowledged. Should you wish to withdraw the application for any reason, please contact the Court immediately.

WRITE IN INK, USING BLOCK CAPITALS

1.
NAME AND ADDRESS OF APPLICANT

Surname.................................   Other name(s) ....
                                              in full
Present ....
Address   Daytime
          ....   Telephone
                                              Number
          ....   (if any)   ....

2.
NAME AND ADDRESS OF HUSBAND/WIFE

Surname.................................   Other name(s) ....
                                              in full
Present ....
Address   Daytime
          ....   Telephone
                                              Number
          ....   (if any)   ....

3.
JURISDICTION

Please indicate with a tick (√) in the appropriate box or boxes which of the following apply:

    (i) I consider myself to be domiciled in Scotland   ☐

    or

    (ii) I have lived in Scotland for a period of at least 12
        months immediately before the date of signing this   ☐
        application

    or

    (iii) My husband/wife considers himself/herself to be   ☐
        domiciled in Scotland

    or

    (iv) My husband/wife has lived in Scotland for a period
        of at least 12 months immediately before the date of   ☐
        signing this application

4.
DETAILS OF PRESENT MARRIAGE

Place of Marriage .... (Registration District)

Date of Marriage: Day .... month .... year ....

5.
PERIOD OF SEPARATION

(i) Please state the date on which you ceased to live with your husband/wife. (If more than 2½ years, just give the month and year)

Day... month ...Year ...

(ii) Have you lived with your husband/wife since that date? *(Tick box which applies)*   ☐ YES NO ☐

(iii) If yes, for how long in total did you live together before finally separating again?

.....................months

6.
RECONCILIATION

Is there any reasonable prospect of reconciliation with your husband/wife? *(Tick box which applies)*   ☐ YES NO ☐

Do you consider that the marriage has broken down irretrievably? *(Tick box which applies)*   ☐ YES NO ☐

7.
CONSENT

Does your husband/wife consent to a divorce being granted? *(Tick box which applies)*   ☐ YES NO ☐

8.
MENTAL DISABILITY

Is your husband/wife incapable of managing his/her affairs because of a mental disorder (whether illness or deficiency?) *(Tick box which applies)*   ☐ YES NO ☐

(If yes, give details)

9.
CHILDREN

Are there any children of the marriage under the age of 16? *(Tick box which applies)*   ☐ YES NO ☐

10.
OTHER COURT ACTIONS

Are you aware of any Court actions currently proceeding in any country (including Scotland) which may affect your marriage? *(Tick box which applies)*   ☐ YES NO ☐

(If yes, give details)

11.
REQUEST FOR DIVORCE AND DISCLAIMER OF FINANCIAL PROVISION

I confirm that the facts stated in Sections 1–10 above apply to my marriage.

I do NOT ask the Court to make any financial awards in connection with this application.

I request the Court to grant decree of divorce from my husband/wife.

....
             (Date)   (Signature)

IMPORTANT—Part 1 MUST be completed, signed and dated before sending the application form to your husband/wife.

PART 2

CONSENT BY APPLICANT'S HUSBAND/WIFE TO DIVORCE

NOTE: Before completing this Part of the form,
please read Part 1 and the notes opposite (page 8).

I, ...

(Full names, in BLOCK letters, of Applicant's husband/wife)

residing at

....

(Address, also in BLOCK letters)

....

....

HEREBY STATE THAT

a. I have read Part 1 of this application;

b. The Applicant has lived apart from me for a continuous period of 2 years
immediately preceding the date of the application (Section 11 of Part 1);

c. I do not ask the Court to make any order for payment to me by the
Applicant of a periodical allowance (ie a regular payment of money
weekly or monthly, etc for maintenance);

d. I do not ask the Court to make any order for payment to me by the
Applicant of a capital sum (ie a lump sum payment);

e. I understand that divorce may result in the loss to me of property rights;

and

f. I CONSENT TO DECREE OF DIVORCE BEING GRANTED IN
RESPECT OF THIS APPLICATION.

....
            (Date)   (Signature)

NOTE: You may withdraw your consent, even after giving it, at any time before
divorce is granted by the Court. Should you wish to do so, you must immediately
advise:

The Court of Session
Divorce Section (SP)
Parliament House
Edinburgh EH1 1RQ

PART 3

APPLICANT'S AFFIDAVIT

To be completed only after Parts 1 and 2 have been signed and dated.

I, (*insert Applicant's full name*) ....

residing at (*insert Applicant's present home address*) ....

....

Town .... Country ....

SWEAR that to the best of my knowledge and belief:

    (1) the facts stated in Part 1 of this Application are true; and

    (2) the signature in Part 2 of this Application is that of my *husband/wife.

Signature of Applicant ....

To be completed
by Justice of Peace,
Notary Public or
Commissioner for
Oaths

SWORN at (Place) ·.

this............... day of .... 19.......

before me (full name) ....

           (full address) ....

....

....

Signature ....

*Justice of Peace/*Notary Public/*Commissioner
   for Oaths

*Delete as appropriate

FORM 19B

UNDER THE DIVORCE (SCOTLAND) ACT 1976, SECTION 1(2)(e)
SIMPLIFIED PROCEDURE

Court of Session
Divorce Section (SP)
Parliament House
Edinburgh EH1 1RQ

Tel: 031-225 2595 Ext 316

APPLICATION FOR DIVORCE
HUSBAND AND WIFE HAVING LIVED APART FOR AT LEAST 5 YEARS

Before completing this form, you should have read the leaflet entitled "Do it yourself Divorce", which explains the circumstances in which a divorce may be sought by that method. If the simplified procedure appears to suit your circumstances, you may use this form to apply for divorce.

Below you will find directions designed to assist with your application. Please follow them carefully. In the event of difficulty, you may contact the Court's Divorce Section at the above address, or any Sheriff Clerk's Office or Citizens Advice Bureau.

Directions for making application

WRITE IN INK. USING BLOCK CAPITALS

1. Complete and sign Part 1 of the form (pages 3–7), paying particular attention to the notes opposite each section.

   Applicatic (Part 1)

2. When you have completed Part 1, you should take the form to a Justice of the Peace, Notary Public, Commissioner for Oaths or other duly authorised person so that your affidavit in Part 2 (page 8) can be completed and sworn.

   Affidavit (Part 2)

4. When directions 1 and 2 above have all been carried out, your application is now ready to be sent to the Court. With it you must enclose:

   Returning completed Applicatio Form to Court

   (i) Your marriage certificate (the document headed "Extract of an entry in a register of Marriages")—check the notes on page 2 to see if you need an up-to-date one (the certificate will be returned to you in due course), and

   (ii) Either   a cheque or postal order for the sum of £40 in respect of the Court fee, crossed and made payable to "Court of Session",

       or   a completed form SP15, claiming exemption from the Court fee.

4. Receipt of your application will be promptly acknowledged. Should you wish to withdraw the application for any reason, please contact the Court immediately.

PART 1 SP5

WRITE IN INK, USING BLOCK CAPITALS

1.
NAME AND ADDRESS OF APPLICANT

Surname... Other name(s) ....
in full
Present ....
Address Daytime
.... Telephone
Number
.... (if any) ....

2.
NAME OF HUSBAND/WIFE

Surname... Other name(s) ....
in full
....

3.
ADDRESS OF HUSBAND/WIFE (if the address of your husband/wife is not
known, please enter "not known" in this
section and proceed to section 4)

Present ....
Address Daytime ....
.... Telephone
Number
.... (if any) ....

4.
Only complete this section if you do not know the present address of your
husband/wife

NEXT-OF-KIN

Name .... Address ....

Relationship ....
to your
husband/wife ....

CHILDREN OF THE MARRIAGE

Names and dates of birth   Addresses

....

                                      ....

....

                                      ....

....

                                      ....

If insufficient space is available here to list all the children of the marriage, please continue on a separate sheet and attach to this form.

5.
JURISDICTION

Please indicate with a tick (√) in the appropriate box or boxes which of the following apply:

(i) I consider myself to be domiciled in Scotland

or

(ii) I have lived in Scotland for a period of at least 12 months immediately before the date of signing this application

or

(iii) My husband/wife considers himself/herself to be domiciled in Scotland

or

(iv) My husband/wife has lived in Scotland for a period of at least 12 months immediately before the date of signing this application

6.
DETAILS OF PRESENT MARRIAGE

Place of Marriage .... (Registration District)

Date of Marriage: (Day) .... (Month) .... (Year) ....

7.
PERIOD OF SEPARATION

(i) Please state the date on which you ceased to live with your husband/wife. (If more than 5½ years, just give the month and year)
                      Day... month ...Year ...

(ii) Have you lived with your husband/wife since that date?   *(Tick box which applies)*   YES NO

(iii) If yes, for how long in total did you live together before finally separating again?

                                                    ....months

8.
RECONCILIATION

Is there any reasonable prospect of reconciliation with your husband/wife?   *(Tick box which applies)*   ☐ YES NO ☐

Do you consider that the marriage has broken down irretrievably?   *(Tick box which applies)*   ☐ YES NO ☐

9.
MENTAL DISABILITY

A far as you are aware is your husband/wife incapable of managing his/her affairs because of a mental disorder (whether illness or deficiency?)   *(Tick box which applies)*   ☐ YES NO ☐

(If yes, give details)

10.
CHILDREN

Are there any children of the marriage under the age of 16?   *(Tick box which applies)*   ☐ YES NO ☐

11.
OTHER COURT ACTIONS

Are you aware of any Court actions currently proceeding in any country (including Scotland) which may affect your marriage?   *(Tick box which applies)*   ☐ YES NO ☐

(If yes, give details)

12.
DECLARATION AND REQUEST FOR DIVORCE

I confirm that the facts stated in sections 1–11 above apply to my marriage.

I do not ask the Court to make any financial awards in connection with this application.

I believe that no grave financial hardship will be caused to my husband/wife as a result of the granting of this application.

I request the Court to grant decree of divorce from my husband/wife.

....
(Date)

....
(Signature of Applicant)

PART 2

APPLICANT'S AFFIDAVIT

To be completed only after Part 1 have been signed and dated.

I, (*insert Applicant's full name*) ....

residing at (*insert Applicant's present home address*) ....

....

Town .... Country ....

Swear that to the best of my knowledge and belief the facts stated in Part 1 of this Application are true.

Signature of Applicant ....

To be completed
by Justice of Peace,
Notary Public or
Commissioner for
Oaths

{

SWORN at (Place) ....

this............... day of .... 19.......

before me (full name) ....

(full address) ....

....

....

....

Signature ....

*Justice of Peace/*Notary Public/*Commissioner
  for Oaths

*Delete as appropriate

FORM 19C

CITATION IN SECTION 1(2)(D) CASES

UNDER THE DIVORCE (SCOTLAND) ACT 1976, SECTION 1(2)(d) SIMPLIFIED PROCE-
DURE

M ....

....

....

Edinburgh 19

APPLICATION FOR DIVORCE (WITH CONSENT OF OTHER PARTY TO THE MARRIAGE) HUSBAND AND WIFE HAVING LIVED APART FOR AT LEAST 2 YEARS

You are hereby served with an aplication by your husband/wife which asks the Court to grant a decree of divorce.

If you wish to oppose the granting of such decree, you should put your reasons in writing and send your letter to the address shown below. Your letter must reach the Court before

Assistant Clerk of Session/
Messenger-at-Arms

IMPORTANT NOTE:
If you wish to exercise your right to claim a financial award you should immediately advise the Court that you oppose the application for that reason, and thereafter consult a solicitor.

Court of Session
Divorce Section (SP)
Parliament House
EDINBURGH EH1 1RQ
Tel: 031-225 2595 Ext 316

FORM 19D

CITATION IN SECTION 1(2)(E) CASES

UNDER THE DIVORCE (SCOTLAND) ACT 1976, SECTION 1(2)(e)
SIMPLIFIED PROCEDURE

M ....

....

....

Edinburgh   19

APPLICATION FOR DIVORCE
HUSBAND AND WIFE HAVING LIVED APART FOR AT LEAST 5
YEARS

Your husband/wife has applied to the Court for divorce on the ground that the marriage has broken down irretrievably *because you and s(he) have lived apart for a period of at least 5 years.*

A copy of the application is hereby served upon you.

1. Please note:

    (a) that the Court may not make financial awards under this procedure and that your husband/wife is making no claim against you for payment of a periodical allowance (i.e. regular payment of money weekly, monthly etc for his/her maintenance) or a capital sum (i.e. lump sum).

    (b) that your husband/wife states that you will not suffer grave financial hardship in the event of decree of divorce being granted.

2. Divorce may result in the loss to you of property rights (eg the right to succeed to the Applicant's estate on his/her death) or the right, where appropriate, to a widow's pension.

3. If you wish to oppose the granting of a divorce, you should put your reasons in writing and send your letter to the address shown below. Your letter must reach the Court before

4. In the event of the divorce being granted, you will be sent a copy of the extract decree. (Should you change your address before receiving the copy extract decree, please notify the Court immediately.)

Assistant Clerk of Session/
Messenger-at-Arms

IMPORTANT NOTE:
If you wish to exercise your right to claim a financial award you should immediately advise the Court that you oppose the application for that reason, and thereafter consult a solicitor.

Court of Session
Divorce Section (SP)
Parliament House
Edinburgh EH1 1RQ
Tel: 031-225 2595 Ext 316

FORM 19E

INTIMATION TO CHILDREN/NEXT OF KIN IN SIMPLIFIED DIVORCE APPLICATION

UNDER THE DIVORCE (SCOTLAND) ACT 1976, SECTION 1(2)(e)
SIMPLIFIED PROCEDURE

M ....

....

....

Edinburgh   19

APPLICATION FOR DIVORCE
HUSBAND AND WIFE HAVING LIVED APART FOR AT LEAST 5 YEARS

.... (Applicant) v. .... (Respondent)

1. In the above application, a copy of which is enclosed, the Applicant has indicated that you are the   of whose present address is unknown to the Applicant.

2. Should you know the present address of your   or how he/she may be contacted, your are requested to give this information at once to:

   Court of Session
   Divorce Section (SP)
   Parliament House
   Edinburgh EH1 1RQ

   Tel: 031-225 2595 Ext 316

This will enable the Court to inform the Respondent that the Application has been made.

3. If you are unable to provide the above information, and/or you desire for your own interest to oppose the application for divorce, you should write to the above address not later than   stating the reason for your opposition.

Assistant Clerk of Session/
Messenger-at-Arms

EXPLANATORY NOTE

(This Note is not part of the Act of Sederunt.)

This Act of Sederunt amends the Rules of Court of the Court of Session by substituting amended forms for Forms 19A–19E in the Appendix (being forms for use in the Simplified Divorce Procedure). The amendments include *(a)* minor textual alterations; *(b)* clarification of notes for completion of forms, with use of 'tick boxes'; *(c)* amendments to take into account the provision in section 2 of the Divorce Jurisdiction, Court Fees and Legal Aid (Scotland) Act 1983 (c.12) for the Court to dispense with corroboration in certain cases.

STATUTORY INSTRUMENTS

1983 No. 1211

FOOD

COMPOSITION AND LABELLING

The Sweeteners in Food Regulations 1983

Made - - - -	*4th August* 1983
Laid before Parliament	*16th August* 1983
Coming into Operation	*6th September* 1983

The Minister of Agriculture, Fisheries and Food, the Secretary of State for Social Services and the Secretary of State for Wales, acting jointly, in exercise of the powers conferred by sections 4, 7 and 123 of the Food and Drugs Act 1955 (**a**) , and now vested in them (**b**) , and of all other powers enabling them in that behalf, hereby make the following regulations, after consultation in accordance with section 123(6) of the said Act with such organisations as appear to them to be representative of interests substantially affected by the regulations and after reference in accordance with section 82(4) of the said Act to the Food Hygiene Advisory Council (in so far as the regulations are made in exercise of the powers conferred by the said section 7):—

Title and commencement

1. These regulations may be cited as the Sweeteners in Food Regulations 1983 and shall come into operation on 6th September 1983.

Interpretation

2.—(1) In these regulations, unless the context otherwise requires—

"the Act" means the Food and Drugs Act 1955;

"the British Pharmacopoeia 1980" means the edition of the British Pharmacopoeia published in 1980 in London by the Department of Health and Social Security, the Scottish Home and Health Department, the Welsh Office and the Department of Health and Social Services for Northern Ireland, ISBN 0 11 320688 7*;

"the British Pharmacopoeia 1980 Addendum 1982" means the Addendum to the British Pharmacopoeia 1980 published in 1982 in London by the Department of Health and Social Security, the Scottish Home and Health Department, the Welsh Office and the Department of Health and Social Services for Northern Ireland, ISBN 0 11 320738 7;

"carbohydrate" means a substance which contains carbon, hydrogen and oxygen only, and in which the hydrogen and oxygen occur in the same proportion as in water;

"catering establishment" has the meaning assigned to it by the Food Labelling Regulations 1980 (**c**) ;

(**a**) 1955 c.16 (4 & 5 Eliz. 2); section 4 was amended by paragraph 3(1) of Schedule 4 to the European Communities Act 1972 (c.68); section 123 was amended by section 4 of the Food and Drugs (Amendment) Act 1982 (c.26).
(**b**) In the case of the Secretary of State for Social Services by virtue of S.I. 1968/1699 and in the case of the Secretary of State for Wales by virtue of S.I. 1978/272.
(**c**) S.I. 1980/1849, to which there are amendments not relevant to these regulations.

"food and drugs authority" has the meaning assigned to it by section 198 of the Local Government Act 1972 (a) ;

"natural food substance" means any substance, suitable for use as food and commonly used as food, which is wholly a natural product, whether or not that substance has been subjected to any process or treatment;

"permitted antioxidant" means any antioxidant in so far as its use is permitted by the Antioxidants in Food Regulations 1978 (b) ;

"permitted bleaching agent" means any bleaching agent in so far as its use is permitted by the Bread and Flour Regulations 1963 (c) ;

"permitted colouring matter" means any colouring matter in so far as its use is permitted by the Colouring Matter in Food Regulations 1973 (d) ;

"permitted emulsifier" means any emulsifier in so far as its use is permitted by the Emulsifiers and Stabilisers in Food Regulations 1980 (e) ;

"permitted improving agent" means any improving agent in so far as its use is permitted by the Bread and Flour Regulations 1963;

"permitted miscellaneous additive" means any miscellaneous additive in so far as its use is permitted by the Miscellaneous Additives in Food Regulations 1980 (f) ;

"permitted preservative" means any preservative in so far as its use is permitted by the Preservatives in Food Regulations 1979 (g) ;

"permitted solvent" means any solvent in so far as its use is permitted by the Solvents in Food Regulations 1967 (h) ;

"permitted stabiliser" means any stabiliser in so far as its use is permitted by the Emulsifiers and Stabilisers in Food Regulations 1980;

"permitted sweetener" means any sweetener specified in Part I of Schedule 1 which satisfies the specific purity criteria for that sweetener specified or referred to in Part II of that Schedule and, so far as is not otherwise provided for by any such specific purity criteria, satisfies the general purity criteria specified in Part III of that Schedule;

"sell" includes offer or expose for sale and includes have in possession for sale, and "sale" shall be construed accordingly;

"sweetener" means any substance, other than a carbohydrate, whose primary organoleptic characteristic is sweetness, but does not include—

(a) any natural food substance,

(b) any permitted antioxidant,

(c) any permitted bleaching agent,

(d) any permitted colouring matter,

(e) any permitted emulsifier,

(f) any permitted improving agent,

(g) any permitted miscellaneous additive,

(h) any permitted preservative,

(a) 1972 c.70.
(b) S.I. 1978/105; the relevant amending instrument is S.I. 1980/1831.
(c) S.I. 1963/1435; the relevant amending instrument is S.I. 1972/1391.
(d) S.I. 1973/1340; relevant amending instruments are S.I. 1975/1488, 1976/2086, 1978/1787.
(e) S.I. 1980/1833; the relevant amending instrument is S.I. 1982/16.
(f) S.I. 1980/1834; the relevant amending instrument is S.I. 1982/14.
(g) S.I. 1979/752; relevant amending instruments are S.I. 1980/931, 1981/1063, 1982/15.
(h) S.I. 1967/1582; relevant amending instruments are S.I. 1967/1939, 1980/1832.

(i) any permitted solvent,

(j) any permitted stabiliser,

(k) any starch, whether modified or not;

"ultimate consumer" has the meaning assigned to it by the Food Labelling Regulations 1980.

(2) For the purposes of these regulations, the supply of food, otherwise than by sale, at, in or from any place where food is supplied in the course of a business shall be deemed to be a sale of that food.

(3) Unless a contrary intention is expressed, all proportions mentioned in these regulations are proportions calculated by weight of the product as sold.

(4) Any reference in these regulations to a numbered regulation or schedule shall, unless the reference is to a regulation of, or schedule to, specified regulations, be construed as a reference to the regulation or schedule so numbered in these regulations.

Exemptions

3. These regulations do not apply to any food (including any sweetener) which is—

(a) not intended for sale for human consumption; or

(b) intended at the time of sale or importation, as the case may be, for exportation to any place outside the United Kingdom.

Sale and importation of food containing added sweeteners

4. No person shall sell or import any food which has in it or on it any added sweetener other than a permitted sweetener.

Sale, importation and advertisement of sweeteners

5.—(1) No person shall sell or import any sweetener (including any sweetener with which any other substance has been mixed) which is intended for use in a catering establishment or for use by the ultimate consumer other than a permitted sweetener.

(2) No person shall sell or advertise for sale any sweetener (including any sweetener with which any other substance has been mixed) for use as an ingredient in the preparation of food unless the sweetener is a permitted sweetener.

Food for babies and young children

6.—(1) No person shall sell any food that is specially prepared for babies or young children if it has in it or on it any added sweetener.

(2) Paragraph (1) of this regulation shall not apply to food specially prepared for babies or young children with special dietary requirements.

Labelling provisions

7.—(1) No person shall sell a permitted sweetener (including a permitted sweetener with which any other substance has been mixed) which is not ready for delivery to the ultimate consumer or a catering establishment unless it is marked or labelled with—

(a) the name of the permitted sweetener;

(b) the serial number, if any, specified for the permitted sweetener in column 2 of Part I of Schedule 1;

(c) the words "for foodstuffs (restricted use)";

(d) the name or business name and an address or registered office of the manufacturer or packer, or of a seller established within the European Economic Community; and

(e) in the case of the permitted sweetener sorbitol syrup (E420) which contains after hydrolysis a level of total sugars exceeding 1%, the words "contains after hydrolysis a level of total sugars of more than 1%" or substantially similar words.

(2) Without prejudice to paragraph (1) of this regulation, no person shall sell a permitted sweetener with which any other substance (including another permitted sweetener) has been mixed and which is not ready for delivery to the ultimate consumer or a catering establishment unless it is marked or labelled with the name of every other substance in the mixture.

(3) A permitted sweetener (including a permitted sweetener with which any other substance has been mixed) shall not be regarded as being marked or labelled in accordance with the foregoing paragraphs of this regulation unless the particulars with which it is required to be marked or labelled by those paragraphs appear—

(a) on the packaging, or

(b) on a label attached to the packaging, or

(c) on a label that is clearly visible through the packaging,

in such a way that they are easy to understand, clearly legible and indelible and are not hidden, obscured or interrupted by any other written or pictorial matter.

Condemnation of food

8. Where any food is certified by a public analyst as being food which it is an offence against regulation 4 to sell or import, that food may be treated for the purposes of section 9 of the Act (under which food may be seized and destroyed on the order of a justice of the peace) as being unfit for human consumption.

Penalties and enforcement

9.—(1) If any person contravenes or fails to comply with any of the foregoing provisions of these regulations he shall be guilty of an offence and shall be liable on summary conviction to a fine not exceeding £1,000.

(2) Subject to paragraph (3) of this regulation, each food and drugs authority shall enforce and execute these regulations in its area.

(3) Each port health authority shall enforce and execute these regulations in its district in so far as they relate to importation.

Application of various provisions of the Act

10.—(1) Subject to paragraph (2) of this regulation, the following provisions of the Act shall apply for the purposes of these regulations as if references therein to proceedings, or a prosecution, under or taken or brought under the Act included references to proceedings, or a prosecution, as the case may be, taken or brought for an offence under these regulations:—

(*a*) section 108(3) and (4) (which relates to prosecutions);

(*b*) section 110(1), (2) and (3) (which relates to evidence of analysis);

(*c*) section 112 (which relates to the power of a court to require analysis by the Government Chemist);

(*d*) section 113 (which relates to a contravention due to some person other than the person charged);

(*e*) section 115(2) (which relates to the conditions under which a warranty may be pleaded as a defence);

(*f*) section 116 (which relates to offences in relation to warranties and certificates of analysis).

(2) Section 112 of the Act shall apply for the purposes of these regulations as if the reference therein to section 108(4) of the Act included a reference to that subsection as applied by paragraph (1) of this regulation.

Amendments

11. The regulations specified in Schedule 2 are hereby amended in accordance with that Schedule.

Revocation

12. The Artificial Sweeteners in Food Regulations 1969 (**a**) are hereby revoked.

Transitional provisions

13.—(1) In any proceedings for an offence against regulation 7 in respect of an act committed after 5th September 1983 and before 1st January 1986 in relation to saccharin, sodium saccharin or calcium saccharin, it shall be a defence for the defendant to prove that the act would not have constituted an offence against regulation 6(1) of the Artificial Sweeteners in Food Regulations 1969 if those regulations had been in operation when the act was committed.

(2) In any proceedings for an offence against regulation 7 in respect of an act committed after 5th September 1983 and before 1st January 1986 in relation to mannitol, sorbitol or sorbitol syrup, it shall be a defence for the defendant to prove that the act would not have constituted an offence against regulation 5(2) of the Miscellaneous Additives in Food Regulations 1980 if those regulations had not been amended by these regulations.

In Witness whereof the Official Seal of the Minister of Agriculture, Fisheries and Food is hereunto affixed on 28th July 1983.

L.S.

Michael Jopling,
Minister of Agriculture, Fisheries
and Food.

(**a**) S.I. 1969/1817; the relevant amending instrument is S.I. 1980/1849.

Norman Fowler,
Secretary of State for Social Services.

3rd August 1983.

Nicholas Edwards,
Secretary of State for Wales.

4th August 1983.

Regulation 2(1)   SCHEDULE 1

PART I

PERMITTED SWEETENERS

Column 1	Column 2
Name of Sweetener	Serial Number
Acesulfame potassium	——
Aspartame	——
Hydrogenated glucose syrup	——
Isomalt	——
Mannitol	E 421
Saccharin	——
Sodium saccharin	——
Calcium saccharin	——
Sorbitol	E 420
Sorbitol syrup	E 420
Thaumatin	——
Xylitol	——

SCHEDULE 1 *continued*

PART II

SPECIFIC PURITY CRITERIA
FOR PERMITTED SWEETENERS

Acesulfame potassium

Synonym	Acesulfame K.
Chemical name	Potassium 3,4-dihydro-6-methyl-2,2,4-trioxo-1,2λ^6,3-oxathiazin-3-ide.
Empirical formula	$C_4H_4KNO_4S$.
Molecular weight	201·2.
Description	White, odourless, crystalline powder or granules with an intensely sweet taste.
Content	Not less than 99·0% of $C_4H_4KNO_4S$ on a volatile matter-free basis.
Volatile matter	Not more than 1·0% (determined by drying at 105°C to constant weight).
pH of a 1% aqueous solution	Not less than 6·5 and not more than 7·5.
Potassium acetate	Not more than 0·5%.
Fluoride	Not more than 30 mg/kg.

Aspartame

Chemical name	(3s)-3-Amino-N[(αs)-α-methoxycarbonyl-phenethyl]succinamic acid.
Synonym	L-Aspartyl-L-phenylalanine methyl ester.
Empirical formula	$C_{14}H_{18}N_2O_5$.
Molecular weight	294·3.
Description	White, odourless, crystalline powder with an intensely sweet taste.
Content	Not less than 98·0% of $C_{14}H_{18}N_2O_5$ on a volatile matter-free basis.
Volatile matter	Not more than 4·5% (determined by drying at 105°C to constant weight).
Specific rotation, $[\alpha]_D^{20°C.}$	Not less than +12·5° and not more than +17·5° (determined using a 4% weight/volume solution on a volatile matter-free basis in 15M formic acid).
pH of a 0·8% aqueous solution	Not less than 4·0 and not more than 6·5.
Sulphated ash	Not more than 0·2% after ignition at 800 ± 25°C.
5-Benzyl-3,6-dioxo-2-piperazineacetic acid	Not more than 1·5%.

Hydrogenated glucose syrup

Synonym	Hydrogenated high maltose glucose syrup.
Description	Clear, colourless, sweet-tasting, aqueous solution of sorbitol, hydrogenated oligosaccharides and hydrogenated polysaccharides prepared by the catalytic hydrogenation of glucose syrup. When dried or crystallised the product is white and crystalline.

SCHEDULE 1 PART II *continued*

Content	D-glucitol: not more than 8%.
	4-O-α-D-glucopyranosyl-D-glucitol: not less than 50% and not more than 90%.
	O-α-D-glucopyranosyl-[1→ 4]-O-α-D-glucopyranosyl-[1→ 4]-D-glucitol: not less than 5% and not more than 20%.
	Hydrogenated tetrasaccharides and hydrogenated higher polysaccharides: not less than 2% and not more than 30%.
	Hydrogenated polysaccharides containing 21 or more D-glucopyranosyl or D-glucitol units: not more than 3%.
	The percentages referred to are calculated on a dry weight basis in each case.
Water	Not more than 26% (Karl Fischer).
Reducing sugars	Not more than 0·3% on a dry weight basis, expressed as dextrose.
pH of a 40% aqueous solution	Not less than 4·0 and not more than 7·0.
Sulphur dioxide	Not more than 10 mg/kg on a dry weight basis.
Sulphated ash	Not more than 0·1% after ignition at $800 \pm 25°C$, calculated on a dry weight basis.
Sulphate	Not more than 0·01% on a dry weight basis, expressed as SO_4.
Chloride	Not more than 50 mg/kg on a dry weight basis, expressed as Cl.
Nickel	Not more than 2 mg/kg on a dry weight basis, expressed as Ni.
Lead	Not more than 1 mg/kg on a dry weight basis, expressed as Pb.

Isomalt

Chemical description	An approximately equimolar mixture of 6-O-α-D-glucopyranosyl-D-glucitol and 1-O-α-D-glucopyranosyl-D-mannitol.
Empirical formula	$C_{12}H_{24}O_{11}$.
Molecular weight	6-O-α-D-glucopyranosyl-D-glucitol ($C_{12}H_{24}O_{11}$): 344·3.
	1-O-α-D-glucopyranosyl-D-mannitol ($C_{12}H_{24}O_{11}$. $2H_2O$): 380·3.
Description	White, odourless, crystalline, slightly hygroscopic solid with a sweet taste.
Content	Not less than 98·0% of 6-O-α-D-glucopyranosyl-D-glucitol and 1-O-α-D-glucopyranosyl-D-mannitol; each shall be present in a proportion of not less than 43% (on a dry weight basis in each case).
Water	Not more than 7·0% (Karl Fischer).
Specific rotation, $[\alpha]_D^{20°C}$.	Not less than $+91·5°$ (using a 4% weight/volume aqueous solution).
Reducing sugars	Not more than 1·5% on a dry weight basis, expressed as dextrose.
D-Mannitol	Not more than 0·5% on a dry weight basis.
D-Sorbitol	Not more than 0·5% on a dry weight basis.
Ash	Not more than 50 mg/kg after ignition at $800 \pm 25°C$, calculated on a dry weight basis.

SCHEDULE 1 PART II *continued*

Nickel	Not more than 2 mg/kg on a dry weight basis, expressed as Ni.
Lead	Not more than 1 mg/kg on a dry weight basis, expressed as Pb.

E421 Mannitol

The criteria for mannitol contained in Council Directive 78/663/EEC (**a**) and in article 6(1)*(a)* of Council Directive 74/329/EEC (**b**) , as amended (**c**) .

Saccharin

The criteria in the monograph for saccharin contained in the British Pharmacopoeia 1980 at page 393.

Sodium saccharin

The criteria in the monograph for saccharin sodium contained in the British Pharmacopoeia 1980 at page 394, as amended by the British Pharmacopoeia 1980 Addendum 1982 at page 99.

Calcium saccharin

Chemical name	1,2-Benzisothiazol-3(2*H*)-one 1,1-dioxide, calcium salt.
Empirical formula	$C_{14}H_8CaN_2O_6S_2$.
Molecular weight	404·4.
Description	White crystals or a white, crystalline powder; odourless or with a faint aromatic odour; with an intensely sweet taste.
Content	Not less than 99·0% of $C_{14}H_8CaN_2O_6S_2$ on a volatile matter-free basis.
Volatile matter	Not less than 11·0% and not more than 15·0% (determined by drying at 105°C to constant weight).
Free acid or alkali	Complies with the test in the monograph for saccharin sodium in the British Pharmacopoeia 1980.
Melting point of isolated saccharin	Complies with the test in the monograph for saccharin sodium in the British Pharmacopoeia 1980.
Related substances	Complies with the test in the monograph for saccharin sodium in the British Pharmacopoeia 1980.
Arsenic	Complies with the test in the monograph for saccharin sodium in the British Pharmacopoeia 1980.
Heavy metals	Complies with the test in the monograph for saccharin sodium in the British Pharmacopoeia 1980.

E420 Sorbitol

The criteria for sorbitol contained in Council Directive 78/663/EEC and in article 6(1)*(a)* of Council Directive 74/329/EEC, as amended.

(**a**) O.J. No. L223, 14.8.78, p.7.
(**b**) O.J. No. L189, 12.7.74, p.1.
(**c**) The relevant amending instrument is Council Directive 78/612/EEC (O.J. No. L197, 22.7.78, p.22).

SCHEDULE 1 PART II *continued*

E420 Sorbitol syrup

The criteria for sorbitol syrup contained in Council Directive 78/663/EEC and in article 6(1)*(a)* of Council Directive 74/329/EEC, as amended.

Thaumatin

Description	Odourless, cream coloured, proteinaceous powder with an intensely sweet taste obtained from aqueous extracts of the arils of the fruit of *Thaumatococcus daniellii* (Benth).
Specific absorption, $E_{1cm}^{1\%}$	Not less than 12·0 and not more than 12·5 (determined at the wavelength of maximum absorbance, about 279 nm, using a 0·1% weight/ volume aqueous solution at pH 2·7).
Nitrogen	Not less than 16·0% on a volatile matter-free basis.
Carbohydrate	Not more than 3·0% on a volatile matter-free basis.
Volatile matter	Not more than 9·0% (determined by drying at 105°C to constant weight).
Sulphated ash	Not more than 2·0% after ignition at 800 ± 25°C, calculated on a volatile matter-free basis.
Aluminium	Not more than 0·01% on a volatile matter-free basis.

Xylitol

Chemical name	*meso*-Xylitol.
Empirical formula	$C_5H_{12}O_5$.
Description	White, odourless, crystalline powder or crystals with a sweet taste.
Content	Not less than 98·0% of *meso*-xylitol, $C_5H_{12}O_5$, on a volatile matter-free basis.
Volatile matter	Not more than 0·5% (determined by drying at 60°C over phosphorus pentoxide in a vacuum for 4 hours).
Reducing sugars	Not more than 0·2% on a volatile matter-free basis, expressed as dextrose.
pH of a 10% aqueous solution	Not less than 5·0 and not more than 7·0.
Other polyols	Not more than 0·5% singly and not more than 1·0% in total on a volatile matter-free basis in each case.
Ash	Not more than 0·1% after ignition at 800 ± 25°C, on a volatile matter-free basis.
Nickel	Not more than 2 mg/kg on a volatile matter-free basis, expressed as Ni.
Lead	Not more than 1 mg/kg on a volatile matter-free basis, expressed as Pb.

PART III

GENERAL PURITY CRITERIA APPLICABLE TO PERMITTED SWEETENERS EXCEPT WHERE OTHERWISE PROVIDED BY SPECIFIC PURITY CRITERIA

No permitted sweetener shall contain more than—

   (a) 3 milligrams per kilogram of arsenic;

   (b) 10 milligrams per kilogram of lead.

SCHEDULE 2   Regulation 11

AMENDMENTS

The Soft Drinks Regulations 1964

1.—(1) In regulation 2(1) of the Soft Drinks Regulations 1964 (a)   (in this paragraph called "the 1964 regulations")—

(a) the definition of "permitted artificial sweetener" shall be deleted;

(b) for the definition of "saccharin" there shall be substituted the following definition:—

' "saccharin" includes sodium saccharin and calcium saccharin;';

(c) in the definition of "sweetened" for the words "polyhydric alcohol or any permitted artificial sweetener" there shall be substituted the word "sweetener"; and

(d) after the definition of "sweetened" there shall be inserted the following definition:—

' "sweetener" has the meaning assigned to it by regulation 2(1) of the Sweeteners in Food Regulations 1983;'.

(2) Regulation 5(1) of the 1964 regulations shall be deleted.

(3) In regulations 5(2), (3), (4) and (5), 7A and 12 of the 1964 regulations and in Schedules 2 and 3 to those regulations for the words "permitted artificial sweetener", wherever they occur, there shall be substituted the word "saccharin".

(4) Schedule 1 to the 1964 regulations shall be deleted.

The Solvents in Food Regulations 1967

2.   In regulation 2(1) of the Solvents in Food Regulations 1967 (b)—

(a) the definition of "permitted artificial sweetener" shall be deleted;

(b) after the definition of "permitted stabiliser" there shall be inserted the following definition:—

' "permitted sweetener" means any sweetener inasmuch as its use is permitted by the Sweeteners in Food Regulations 1983;'; and

(c) in the definition of "solvent" the word "artificial" shall be deleted.

The Ice-Cream Regulations 1967

3.—(1) In regulation 2(1) of the Ice-Cream Regulations 1967 (c)   the definition of "artificial sweetener" shall be deleted.

(2) For regulation 4(8) of the Ice-Cream Regulations 1967 there shall be substituted the following paragraph:—

"(8) No ice-cream of any kind nor any Parev ice shall have in or on it any added acesulfame potassium, aspartame, saccharin, sodium saccharin, calcium saccharin or thaumatin.".

The Antioxidants in Food Regulations 1978

4.   In regulation 2(1) of the Antioxidants in Food Regulations 1978 (d) —

(a) in the definition of "antioxidant" the word "artificial" shall be deleted;

(b) the definition of "permitted artificial sweetener" shall be deleted;

(c) in the definition of "permitted diluent" for the words "miscellaneous additive" there shall be substituted the word "sweetener"; and

(a) S.I. 1964/760; relevant amending instruments are S.I. 1969/1818, 1972/1510 and 1976/295.
(b) S.I. 1967/1582, to which there are amendments not relevant to this Schedule.
(c) S.I. 1967/1866, to which there are amendments not relevant to these regulations.
(d) S.I. 1978/105, to which there are amendments not relevant to this Schedule.

SCHEDULE 2 *continued*

(d) after the definition of "permitted stabiliser" there shall be inserted the following definition:—

' "permitted sweetener" means any sweetener in so far as its use is permitted by the Sweeteners in Food Regulations 1983;'.

The Preservatives in Food Regulations 1979

5.—(1) In regulation 2(1) of the Preservatives in Food Regulations 1979 **(a)** (in this paragraph called "the 1979 regulations")—

(a) the definition of "permitted artificial sweetener" shall be deleted;

(b) after the definition of "permitted stabiliser" there shall be inserted the following definition:—

' "permitted sweetener" means any sweetener in so far as its use is permitted by the Sweeteners in Food Regulations 1983;';

(c) the definition of "polyhydric alcohol" shall be deleted;

(d) in the definition of "preservative" the word "artificial" shall be deleted; and

(e) in the definition of "sweetened" for the words "polyhydric alcohol or any permitted artificial sweetener" there shall be substituted the words "permitted sweetener".

(2) In paragraph *(b)* (iii) of the proviso to regulation 4(1) of the 1979 regulations for the words "permitted artificial sweetener" there shall be substituted the words "saccharin, sodium saccharin or calcium saccharin".

(3) In column 1 of the item in Schedule 2 to the 1979 regulations relating to preparations of permitted artificial sweetener and water only for the words "permitted artificial sweetener" there shall be substituted the words "saccharin, sodium saccharin or calcium saccharin".

The Emulsifiers and Stabilisers in Food Regulations 1980

6. In regulation 2(1) of the Emulsifiers and Stabilisers in Food Regulations 1980 **(b)** —

(a) in the definition of "emulsifier" and "stabiliser" the word "artificial" shall be deleted;

(b) the definition of "permitted artificial sweetener" shall be deleted; and

(c) after the definition of "permitted solvent" there shall be inserted the following definition:—

' "permitted sweetener" means any sweetener in so far as its use is permitted by the Sweeteners in Food Regulations 1983;'.

The Miscellaneous Additives in Food Regulations 1980

7.—(1) In regulation 2(1) of the Miscellaneous Additives in Food Regulations 1980 **(c)** (in this paragraph called "the 1980 regulations")—

(a) in the definition of "miscellaneous additive" the word "artificial" shall be deleted;

(b) the definition of "permitted artificial sweetener" shall be deleted; and

(c) after the definition of "permitted stabiliser" there shall be inserted the following definition:—

' "permitted sweetener" means any sweetener in so far as its use is permitted by the Sweeteners in Food Regulations 1983;'.

(a) S.I. 1979/752, to which there are amendments not relevant to these regulations.
(b) S.I. 1980/1833, to which there are amendments not relevant to this Schedule.
(c) S.I. 1980/1834, to which there are amendments not relevant to this Schedule.

SCHEDULE 2 *continued*

(2) In Parts I and II of Schedule 1 to the 1980 regulations the items relating to mannitol, sorbitol and sorbitol syrup shall be deleted.

(3) Paragraph 1*(d)* of Schedule 3 to the 1980 regulations shall be deleted.

The Food Labelling Regulations 1980

8.   In regulation 2(1) of the Food Labelling Regulations 1980 **(a)** at the end of the definition of "serial number" there shall be inserted the words "or Schedule 1 to the Sweeteners in Food Regulations 1983".

The Jam and Similar Products Regulations 1981

9.—(1) In regulation 2(1) of the Jam and Similar Products Regulations 1981 **(b)** (in this paragraph called "the 1981 regulations") for the definition of "permitted artificial sweetener" there shall be substituted the following definition:—

' "permitted sweetener" means any sweetener in so far as its use is permitted by the Sweeteners in Food Regulations 1983;'.

(2) For regulation 13(2) of the 1981 regulations there shall be substituted the following paragraph:—

"(2) The permitted sweeteners acesulfame potassium, aspartame, saccharin, sodium saccharin, calcium saccharin and thaumatin may be used in the preparation of reduced sugar products.".

(3) In regulation 13(3) of the 1981 regulations for the words "artificial sweeteners and sorbitol" there shall be substituted the word "sweeteners".

(a) S.I. 1980/1849, to which there are amendments not relevant to these regulations.
(b) S.I. 1981/1063, to which there are amendments not relevant to these regulations.

EXPLANATORY NOTE

(This Note is not part of the Regulations.)

These regulations, which apply to England and Wales only, control the use of non-carbohydrate sweeteners in food. The regulations—

(a) specify permitted sweeteners and prescribe purity criteria for those sweeteners (regulation 2(1) and Schedule 1);

(b) prohibit the sale and the importation of food which contains any added sweetener other than a permitted sweetener (regulation 4);

(c) prohibit the sale and the importation of sweeteners for catering purposes or table-top use other than permitted sweeteners (regulation 5(1));

(d) prohibit the sale and the advertisement for sale of sweeteners, other than permitted sweeteners, for use as ingredients in the preparation of food (regulation 5(2));

(e) restrict the sale of food for babies or young children that contains added sweeteners (regulation 6); and

(f) prescribe labelling requirements for permitted sweeteners in circumstances where their labelling is not controlled by the Food Labelling Regulations 1980 (regulation 7).

The regulations supersede the Artificial Sweeteners in Food Regulations 1969. The changes of substance are—

(a) the addition of nine substances to the list of permitted sweeteners (including mannitol, sorbitol and sorbitol syrup, which were previously permitted miscellaneous additives under the Miscellaneous Additives in Food Regulations 1980); and

(b) the removal of the detailed controls on the composition and labelling of saccharin tablets.

Amendments are made to other regulations so as to—

(a) permit the use of acesulfame potassium, aspartame and thaumatin in reduced sugar jam, reduced sugar jelly and reduced sugar marmalade; and

(b) permit the use of all permitted sweeteners in jam and similar products intended for diabetics and in soft drinks.

Certain consequential amendments to other regulations are also made.

STATUTORY INSTRUMENTS

1983 No. 1212

MEDICINES

The Medicines (Products Other Than Veterinary Drugs) (Prescription Only) Order 1983

Made	-	-	-	*3rd August* 1983
Laid before Parliament				*24th August* 1983
Coming into Operation				*14th September* 1983

The Secretary of State concerned with health in England, the Secretaries of State respectively concerned with health and with agriculture in Wales and in Scotland, the Minister of Agriculture, Fisheries and Food, the Department of Health and Social Services for Northern Ireland and the Department of Agriculture for Northern Ireland, acting jointly, in exercise of powers conferred by sections 58(1) and (4), 59 and 129(4) of the Medicines Act 1968(a) and now vested in them (b) and of all other powers enabling them in that behalf, after consulting such organisations as appear to them to be representative of interests likely to be substantially affected by this order pursuant to section 129(6) of that Act, and after consulting and taking into account the advice of the Medicines Commission pursuant to sections 58(6) and 129(7) of that Act, hereby make the following order:—

Citation, commencement and interpretation

1.—(1) This order may be cited as the Medicines (Products Other Than Veterinary Drugs) (Prescription Only) Order 1983 and shall come into operation on 14th September 1983.

(2) In this order, unless the context otherwise requires—

(a) "the Act" means the Medicines Act 1968;

"aerosol" means a product which is dispersed from its container by a propellent gas or liquid;

"controlled drug" has the meaning assigned to it by section 2 of the Misuse of Drugs Act 1971(c);

(a) 1968 c. 67.
(b) In the case of the Secretaries of State concerned with health in England and in Wales by virtue of Article 2(2) of, and Schedule 1 to, the Transfer of Functions (Wales) Order 1969 (S.I. 1969/388), in the case of the Secretary of State concerned with agriculture in Wales by virtue of Article 2(3) of, and Schedule 1 to, the Transfer of Functions (Wales) (No. 1) Order 1978 (S.I. 1978/272) and in the case of the Northern Ireland Departments by virtue of section 40 of, and Schedule 5 to, the Northern Ireland Constitution Act 1973 (c. 36), and section 1(3) of, and paragraph 2(1)*(b)* of Schedule 1 to, the Northern Ireland Act 1974 (c. 28).
(c) 1971 c. 38.

"dosage unit" means—

    (i) where a medicinal product is in the form of a tablet or capsule or is an article in some other similar pharmaceutical form, that tablet, capsule or other article, or

    (ii) where a medicinal product is not in any such form, that quantity of the product which is used as the unit by reference to which the dose is measured;

"external use" means application to the skin, hair, teeth, mucosa of the mouth, throat, nose, ear, eye, vagina or anal canal when a local action only is intended and extensive systemic absorption is unlikely to occur; and references to medicinal products for external use shall be read accordingly except that such references shall not include throat sprays, throat pastilles, throat lozenges, throat tablets, nasal drops, nasal sprays, nasal inhalations or teething preparations;

"health prescription" means a prescription issued by a doctor or dentist under or by virtue of—

    (i) in England and Wales, the National Health Service Act 1977(**a**),

    (ii) in Scotland, the National Health Service (Scotland) Act 1978(**b**), and

    (iii) in Northern Ireland, the Health and Personal Social Services (Northern Ireland) Order 1972(**c**);

"inhaler" does not include an aerosol;

"master" has the same meaning as in the Merchant Shipping Act 1894(**d**);

"maximum daily dose" or "MDD" means the maximum quantity of a substance contained in the amount of a medicinal product for internal use which it is recommended should be taken or administered in a period of 24 hours;

"maximum dose" or "MD" means the maximum quantity of a substance contained in the amount of a medicinal product for internal use which it is recommended should be taken or administered at any one time;

"maximum strength" means such of the following as may be specified—

    (i) the maximum quantity of a substance by weight or volume contained in a dosage unit of a medicinal product, and

    (ii) the maximum percentage of a substance contained in a medicinal product calculated in terms of weight in weight, weight in volume, volume in weight or volume in volume, as appropriate;

"medicinal product" has the same meaning as in the Act except that it does not include a medicinal product which is a veterinary drug as defined in section 132(1) of the Act;

"the Misuse of Drugs Regulations" means, in relation to England, Wales and Scotland, the Misuse of Drugs Regulations 1973(**e**) and, in relation to

---

(**a**) 1977 c. 49.
(**b**) 1978 c. 29.
(**c**) S.I. 1972/1265 (N.I. 14).
(**d**) 1894 c. 60.
(**e**) S.I. 1973/797; relevant amending instruments are S.I. 1975/499, 1623, 1977/1380 and 1979/326.

Northern Ireland, the Misuse of Drugs (Northern Ireland) Regulations 1974(a);

"occupational health scheme" means a scheme in which a person, in the course of a business carried on by him, provides facilities for his employees for the treatment or prevention of disease;

"operator", in relation to an aircraft, means the person for the time being having the management of the aircraft;

"parenteral administration" means administration by breach of the skin or mucous membrane;

"prescription only medicine" means a medicinal product of a description or falling within a class specified in Article 3 of this order;

"registered ophthalmic optician" means a person who is registered in either of the registers of ophthalmic opticians established and maintained under section 2(a) of the Opticians Act 1958(b);

"repeatable prescription" means a prescription which contains a direction that it may be dispensed more than once;

"sell" means sell by retail as defined in section 131 of the Act and "sale" has a corresponding meaning;

"soap" means any compound of a fatty acid with an alkali or amine;

"state registered chiropodist" means a person who is registered in the register established and maintained under section 2(1) of the Professions Supplementary to Medicine Act 1960(c) by the Chiropodists Board;

"supply" means supply in circumstances corresponding to retail sale as defined in section 131 of the Act;

"unit preparation" means a preparation, including a mother tincture, prepared by a process of solution, extraction or trituration with a view to being diluted tenfold or one hundredfold, either once or repeatedly, in an inert diluent, and then used either in this diluted form or, where applicable, by impregnating tablets, granules, powders or other inert substances; and

  (b) a reference—

      (i) to a numbered section is to the section of the Act which bears that number,

      (ii) to a numbered Article or Schedule is to the Article of, or Schedule to, this order which bears that number,

      (iii) in an Article or in a Part of a Schedule to a numbered paragraph is to the paragraph of that Article or that Part of that Schedule which bears that number, and

      (iv) in a paragraph to a lettered sub-paragraph is to the sub-paragraph of that paragraph which bears that letter.

(3) In Schedule 1—

  (a) entries specified in columns 2, 3 and 4 of Parts I and II relate to the substances listed in column 1 against which they appear and where, in relation to a particular substance listed in column 1, an entry in

---

(a) S.R. (N.I.) 1974 No. 272, amended by S.R. (N.I.) 1975 No. 140, 326 and 1977 No. 290.
(b) 1958 c. 32.
(c) 1960 c. 66.

column 2, 3 or 4 bears a number or letter it relates only to such entries in the other of those columns as bear the same number or letter;

(b) the entries in column 4 of Part I shall be read subject to the note at the end of that Part; and

(c) the following abbreviations are used:

"g" for gram,
"mcg" for microgram,
"mg" for milligram,
"ml" for millilitre.

Appropriate Practitioners

2. For the purposes of section 58 (medicinal products on prescription only), doctors, dentists, veterinary surgeons and veterinary practitioners shall be appropriate practitioners in relation to all the descriptions and classes of medicinal products specified for the purposes of that section in Article 3.

Medicinal products on prescription only

3.—(1) There are hereby specified descriptions and classes of medicinal products for the purposes of section 58, namely—

(a) subject to Article 4(1), medicinal products consisting of or containing a substance listed in column 1 of Part I of Schedule 1;

(b) subject to Article 4(2) and Part II of Schedule 1, medicinal products that are controlled drugs;

(c) medicinal products specified in Part III of Schedule 1;

(d) subject to Article 4(3), medicinal products that are for parenteral administration whether or not they fall within sub-paragraph *(a)* or *(b)*;

(e) medicinal products—

(i) which are not of a description and do not fall within a class specified in any of sub-paragraphs *(a), (b), (c)* or *(d)*,

(ii) which are of a description in respect of which the conditions specified in section 59(1) are fulfilled, and

(iii) in respect of which a product licence is granted after the date of coming into operation of this order containing a provision to the effect that the method of sale or supply of the medicinal product is to be only in accordance with a prescription given by an appropriate practitioner.

(2) For the purposes of section 59(2)*(a)* (duration of restrictions for certain new products) the duration shall be a period of five years.

Medicinal products that are not prescription only

4.—(1) Notwithstanding Article 3(1)*(a)*, a medicinal product shall not be a prescription only medicine by reason that it consists of or contains a particular substance listed in column 1 of Part I of Schedule 1 where—

(a) in relation to that substance there is an entry in one or more of columns 2, 3 and 4;

(b) the maximum strength in the product of that substance does not exceed the maximum strength, if any, specified in column 2; and

(c) the medicinal product is sold or supplied—

(i) if a pharmaceutical form or a route of administration is specified in column 3, in such pharmaceutical form, and for administration only by such route, as may be so specified,

(ii) if a use is specified in column 3, in a container or package labelled to show a use so specified to which the medicinal product is to be put but no use not so specified,

(iii) if a maximum dose is specified in column 4, in a container or package labelled to show a maximum dose not exceeding that specified, and

(iv) if a maximum daily dose is specified in column 4, in a container or package labelled to show a maximum daily dose not exceeding that specified.

(2) Notwithstanding Article 3(1)(b), a medicinal product shall not be a prescription only medicine by reason that it is a controlled drug where it—

(a) contains not more than one of the substances listed in column 1 of Part II of Schedule 1 (which substances are amongst the controlled drugs listed in Schedule 2 to the Misuse of Drugs Act 1971) and no other controlled drug;

(b) contains that substance at a strength that does not exceed the maximum strength specified in column 2; and

(c) is sold or supplied—

(i) in such pharmaceutical form as may be specified in column 3, and

(ii) in or from a container or package labelled to show a maximum dose not exceeding that specified in column 4.

(3) Notwithstanding Article 3(1)(d), the following medicinal products for parenteral administration shall not be prescription only medicines—

Biphasic Insulin Injection
Globlin Zinc Insulin Injection
Insulin Injection
Insulin Zinc Suspension
Insulin Zinc Suspension (Amorphous)
Insulin Zinc Suspension (Crystalline)
Isophane Insulin Injection
Neutral Insulin Injection
Protamine Zinc Insulin Injection.

Exemption for parenteral administration to human beings of certain prescription only medicines

5. The restriction imposed by section 58(2)(b) (restriction on administration) shall not apply to the administration to human beings of any of the following medicinal products for parenteral administration—

Adrenaline Injection BP
Atropine Sulphate Injection
Chlorpheniramine Injection
Cobalt Edetate Injection
Dextrose Injection Strong B.P.C.
Diphenhydramine Injection
Hydrocortisone Injection
Mepyramine Injection
Promethazine Hydrochloride Injection
Snake Venom Antiserum
Sodium Nitrite Injection
Sodium Thiosulphate Injection
Sterile Pralidoxime

if and so long as the administration is for the purpose of saving life in an emergency.

Exemptions for emergency sale or supply

6.—(1) The restrictions imposed by section 58(2)*(a)* (restrictions on sale and supply) shall not apply to the sale or supply of a prescription only medicine by a person lawfully conducting a retail pharmacy business if and so long as the conditions specified in paragraph (2) are fulfilled.

(2) The conditions referred to in paragraph (1) are—

(a) that the pharmacist by or under whose supervision the prescription only medicine is to be sold or supplied is satisfied that the sale or supply has been requested by a doctor who by reason of any emergency is unable to furnish a prescription immediately;

(b) that that doctor has undertaken to furnish the person lawfully conducting a retail pharmacy business with a prescription within 72 hours;

(c) that the prescription only medicine is sold or supplied in accordance with the directions of the doctor requesting it;

(d) subject to paragraph (5), that the prescription only medicine is not a controlled drug specified in Schedule 2, 3 or 4 to the Misuse of Drugs Regulations;

(e) that an entry is made in the register kept under regulation 6 of the Medicines (Sale or Supply) (Miscellaneous Provisions) Regulations 1980**(a)** within the time specified in that regulation stating the particulars set out in paragraph 1 of Schedule 2 to those regulations.

(3) The restrictions imposed by section 58(2)*(a)* also shall not apply to the sale or supply of a prescription only medicine by a person lawfully conducting a retail pharmacy business if and so long as the conditions specified in paragraph (4) are fulfilled.

(4) The conditions referred to in paragraph (3) are—

(a) that the pharmacist by or under whose supervision the prescription only medicine is to be sold or supplied has interviewed the person

---

(a) S.I. 1980/1923, to which there are amendments not relevant to this Order.

requesting a prescription only medicine and has satisfied himself—

    (i) that there is an immediate need for the prescription only medicine requested to be sold or supplied and that it is impracticable in the circumstances to obtain a prescription without undue delay,

    (ii) that treatment with the prescription only medicine requested has on a previous occasion been prescribed by a doctor for the person requesting it, and

    (iii) as to the dose which in the circumstances it would be appropriate for that person to take;

(b) that no greater quantity of the prescription only medicine than will provide 5 days' treatment is sold or supplied except that there may be sold or supplied where the prescription only medicine—

    (i) is an aerosol for the relief of asthma, an ointment or a cream, and has been made up for sale in a container elsewhere than at the place of sale or supply, the smallest pack that the pharmacist has available for sale or supply,

    (ii) is an oral contraceptive, sufficient for a full cycle,

    (iii) is an antibiotic for oral administration in liquid form, the smallest quantity that will provide a full course of treatment;

(c) subject to paragraph (5), that the prescription only medicine does not consist of or contain a substance specified in Schedule 2 to this order and is not a controlled drug specified in Schedule 2, 3 or 4 to the Misuse of Drugs Regulations;

(d) that an entry is made in the register kept under regulation 6 of the Medicines (Sale or Supply) (Miscellaneous Provisions) Regulations 1980 within the time specified in that regulation stating the particulars set out in paragraph 3 of Schedule 2 to those regulations;

(e) that the container or package of the prescription only medicine is labelled so as to show—

    (i) the date on which the prescription only medicine is sold or supplied,

    (ii) the name, quantity and, except where it is apparent from the name, the pharmaceutical form and strength of the prescription only medicine,

    (iii) the name of the person requesting the prescription only medicine,

    (iv) the name and address of the registered pharmacy from which the prescription only medicine was sold or supplied, and

    (v) the words "Emergency Supply".

(5) The conditions specified in paragraphs (2)(d) and (4)(c) shall not apply where the prescription only medicine consists of or contains Phenobarbitone or Phenobarbitone Sodium (but no other substance specified in Schedule 2 to this order or Schedule 2, 3 or 4 to the Misuse of Drugs Regulations) and is sold or supplied for use in the treatment of epilepsy.

Exemption for non-parenteral administration to human beings

7. The restriction imposed by section 58(2)(b) (restriction on administration) shall not apply to the administration to human beings of a prescription only medicine which is not for parenteral administration.

Exemption for medicinal products at high dilutions

8. The restrictions imposed by section 58(2) (restrictions on sale, supply and administration) shall not apply to the sale, supply or administration of a medicinal product which is not for parenteral administration and which consists of or contains, of the substances listed in column 1 of Part I or Part II of Schedule 1, only one or more unit preparations of such substances, if—

(a) each such unit preparation has been diluted to at least one part in a million (6x), and the person selling, supplying or administering the medicinal product has been requested by or on behalf of a particular person and in that person's presence to use his own judgment as to the treatment required, or

(b) each such unit preparation has been diluted to at least one part in a million million (6c).

Exemptions for certain persons

9.—(1) The restrictions imposed by section 58(2)(a) (restrictions on sale and supply) shall not apply—

(a) to the sale or supply by a person listed in column 1 of Part I of Schedule 3, or

(b) to the supply by a person listed in column 1 of Part II of Schedule 3

of the prescription only medicines listed in column 2 of Part I or Part II, as the case may be, of Schedule 3 in relation to that person if and so long as the conditions specified in the corresponding paragraphs in column 3 of Part I or Part II, as the case may be, of Schedule 3 are fulfilled.

(2) The restriction imposed by section 58(2)(b) (restriction on administration) shall not apply to the administration by a person listed in column 1 of Part III of Schedule 3 of the prescription only medicines for parenteral administration listed in column 2 of that Part in relation to that person if and so long as the conditions specified in the corresponding paragraphs in column 3 of that Part are fulfilled.

Exemption for sale or supply in hospitals

10. The restrictions imposed by section 58(2)(a) (restrictions on sale and supply) shall not apply to the sale or supply of any prescription only medicine in the course of the business of a hospital where the prescription only medicine is sold or supplied in accordance with the written directions of a doctor or dentist notwithstanding that those directions do not fulfil the conditions specified in Article 12(2).

Exemption in cases involving another's default

11. The restrictions imposed by section 58(2)(a) (restrictions on sale and supply) shall not apply to the sale or supply of a prescription only medicine by a person who, having exercised all due diligence, believes on reasonable grounds that the product sold or supplied is not a prescription only medicine, where it is due to the act or default of another person that the product is a product to which section 58(2)*(a)* applies.

Prescriptions

12.—(1) For the purposes of section 58(2)*(a)* a prescription only medicine shall not be taken to be sold or supplied in accordance with a prescription given by a practitioner unless the conditions specified in paragraph (2) are fulfilled.

(2) The conditions referred to in paragraph (1) are that the prescription—

(a) shall be signed in ink with his own name by the practitioner giving it;

(b) shall, without prejudice to sub-paragraph *(a)*, be written in ink or otherwise so as to be indelible, unless it is a health prescription which is not for a controlled drug specified in Schedule 2, 3 or 4 to the Misuse of Drugs Regulations, in which case it may be written by means of carbon paper or similar material;

(c) shall contain the following particulars—

(i) the address of the practitioner giving it,

(ii) the appropriate date,

(iii) such particulars as indicate whether the practitioner giving it is a doctor, a dentist, a veterinary surgeon or a veterinary practitioner,

(iv) where the practitioner giving it is a doctor or dentist, the name, address and the age, if under 12, of the person for whose treatment it is given, and

(v) where the practitioner giving it is a veterinary surgeon or a veterinary practitioner, the name and address of the person to whom the prescription only medicine is to be delivered and a declaration by the veterinary surgeon or veterinary practitioner giving it that the prescription only medicine is prescribed for an animal or herd under his care;

(d) shall not be dispensed after the end of the period of six months from the appropriate date, unless it is a repeatable prescription in which case it shall not be dispensed for the first time after the end of that period nor otherwise than in accordance with the direction contained in the repeatable prescription;

(e) in the case of a repeatable prescription that does not specify the number of times it may be dispensed, shall not be dispensed on more than two occasions unless it is a prescription for oral contraceptives in which case it may be dispensed six times before the end of the period of six months from the appropriate date.

(3) The restrictions imposed by section 58(2)*(a)* (restrictions on sale and supply) shall not apply to a sale or supply of a prescription only medicine which is not in accordance with a prescription given by an appropriate practitioner by reason only that a condition specified in paragraph (2) is not fulfilled, where the person selling or supplying the prescription only medicine, having exercised all due diligence, believes on reasonable grounds that that condition is fulfilled in relation to that sale or supply.

(4) In paragraph (2) "the appropriate date" means—

    (a) in the case of a health prescription, the date on which it was signed by the practitioner giving it or a date indicated by him as being the date before which it shall not be dispensed, and

    (b) in every other case, the date on which the prescription was signed by the practitioner giving it;

and, for the purposes of sub-paragraphs *(d)* and *(e)* of that paragraph, where a health prescription bears both the date on which it was signed and a date indicated as being that before which it shall not be dispensed, the appropriate date is the later of those dates.

Revocations and transitional provision

13.—(1) The orders specified in Schedule 4 are hereby revoked.

(2) Where immediately before the coming into operation of this order, the restrictions imposed by section 58 applied to the sale, supply or administration of a medicinal product of a particular description either by reason that the product fell within a class specified in Article 3(1)*(e)* (certain new products), or by virtue of Article 14(2) (transitional provision), of the Medicines (Prescription Only) Order 1980(**a**), those restrictions shall continue to apply to products of that description as though Article 3(1)*(e)* and (2), or, as the case may be, Article 14(2) of that order had remained in force.

Signed by authority of the Secretary of State for Social Services.

K. Clarke,
Minister of State,
Department of Health and Social Security.

26th July 1983.

Signed by authority of the Secretary of State for Wales.

John Stradling Thomas,
Minister of State, Welsh Office.

28th July 1983.

George Younger,
Secretary of State for Scotland.

28th July 1983.

(**a**) S.I. 1980/1921; relevant amending instrument is S.I. 1982/29.

In witness whereof the official seal of the Minister of Agriculture, Fisheries and Food is hereunto affixed on 28th July 1983.

Michael Jopling,
Minister of Agriculture, Fisheries and Food.

Sealed with the official seal of the Department of Health and Social Services for Northern Ireland this 3rd day of August 1983.

N. Dugdale,
Permanent Secretary.

Sealed with the official seal of the Department of Agriculture for Northern Ireland this 3rd day of August 1983.

W. H. Jack,
Permanent Secretary.

SCHEDULE 1

DESCRIPTIONS AND CLASSES OF PRESCRIPTION ONLY MEDICINES

Articles 3(1)*(a)*, 4(1) and 8   PART I

Column 1	CIRCUMSTANCES EXCLUDING MEDICINAL PRODUCTS FROM THE CLASS OF PRESCRIPTION ONLY MEDICINES		
	Column 2	Column 3	Column 4
Substance(a)	Maximum strength	Use, pharma-ceutical form or route of admini-stration	Maximum dose and maximum daily dose
Acebutolol Hydrochloride			
Acetarsol			
Acetazolamide			
Acetazolamide Sodium			
Acetohexamide			
Acetylcholine Chloride	0.2 per cent	External	
Acetylcysteine			
Aconite	1.3 per cent	External	
Acrosoxacin			
Actinomycin C			
Actinomycin D			
Acyclovir			
Adrenaline		(1) By inhaler (2) External	
Adrenaline Acid Tartrate		(1) By inhaler (2) External	
Adrenaline Hydrochloride		(1) By inhaler (2) External	
Adrenocortical Extract			
Alclofenac			
Alcuronium Chloride			

(a) Substances added by this order are indicated by the use of bold type.

Sch. 1 (I)

| Column 1 | CIRCUMSTANCES EXCLUDING MEDICINAL PRODUCTS FROM THE CLASS OF PRESCRIPTION ONLY MEDICINES | | |
| | Column 2 | Column 3 | Column 4 |
Substance(a)	Maximum strength	Use, pharmaceutical form or route of administration	Maximum dose and maximum daily dose
Aldosterone			
Alfacalcidol			
Allergen Extracts			
Allopurinol			
Allyloestrenol			
Alphadolone Acetate			
Alphaxalone			
Alprazolam			
Alprenolol			
Alprenolol Hydrochloride			
Alprostadil			
Alseroxylon			
Amantadine Hydrochloride			
Ambenonium Chloride			
Ambutonium Bromide			
Amcinonide			
Ametazole Hydrochloride			
Amethocaine		Any use except local ophthalmic use	
Amethocaine Gentisate		Any use except local ophthalmic use	
Amethocaine Hydrochloride		Any use except local ophthalmic use	

(a) Substances added by this order are indicated by the use of bold type.

Sch. 1 (I)

Column 1	Circumstances Excluding Medicinal Products from the Class of Prescription Only Medicines		
	Column 2	Column 3	Column 4
Substance(a)	Maximum strength	Use, pharmaceutical form or route of administration	Maximum dose and maximum daily dose
Amikacin Sulphate			
Amiloride Hydrochloride			
Aminocaproic Acid			
Aminoglutethimide			
Aminopterin Sodium			
Amiodarone Hydrochloride			
Amiphenazole Hydrochloride			
Amitriptyline			
Amitriptyline Embonate			
Amitriptyline Hydrochloride			
Ammonium Bromide			
Amoxapine			
Amoxycillin			
Amoxycillin Trihydrate			
Amphomycin Calcium			
Amphotericin			
Ampicillin			
Ampicillin Sodium			
Ampicillin Trihydrate			
Amygdalin			
Amylobarbitone			
Amylobarbitone Sodium			

(a) Substances added by this order are indicated by the use of bold type.

Sch. 1 (I)

Column 1	CIRCUMSTANCES EXCLUDING MEDICINAL PRODUCTS FROM THE CLASS OF PRESCRIPTION ONLY MEDICINES		
	Column 2	Column 3	Column 4
Substance(a)	Maximum strength	Use, pharmaceutical form or route of administration	Maximum dose and maximum daily dose
Amylocaine Hydrochloride		Any use except local ophthalmic use	
Ancrod			
Androsterone			
Angiotensin Amide			
Anterior Pituitary Extract			
Antimony Barium Tartrate			
Antimony Dimercaptosuccinate			
Antimony Lithium Thiomalate			
Antimony Pentasulphide			
Antimony Potassium Tartrate			
Antimony Sodium Tartrate			
Antimony Sodium Thioglycollate			
Antimony Sulphate			
Antimony Trichloride			
Antimony Trioxide			
Antimony Trisulphide			
Apiol			
Apomorphine			
Apomorphine Hydrochloride			

(a) Substances added by this order are indicated by the use of bold type.

Sch. 1 (I)

	CIRCUMSTANCES EXCLUDING MEDICINAL PRODUCTS FROM THE CLASS OF PRESCRIPTION ONLY MEDICINES		
Column 1	Column 2	Column 3	Column 4
Substance(a)	Maximum strength	Use, pharmaceutical form or route of administration	Maximum dose and maximum daily dose
Aprotinin			
Arecoline Hydrobromide			
Argipressin			
Arsenic			
Arsenic Triiodide			
Arsenic Trioxide			
Arsphenamine			
Atenolol			
Atropine		(1) Internal: (a) by inhaler (b) otherwise than by inhaler (2) External (except local ophthalmic use)	(b) 300 mcg (MD) 1 mg (MDD)(**b**)
Atropine Methobromide		(1) Internal: (a) by inhaler (b) otherwise than by inhaler (2) External (except local ophthalmic use)	(b) 400 mcg (MD) 1.3 mg (MDD)(**b**)
Atropine Methonitrate		Internal: (a) by inhaler (b) otherwise than by inhaler	(b) 400 mcg (MD) 1.3 mg (MDD)(**b**)
Atropine Oxide Hydrochloride		(1) Internal: (a) by inhaler (b) otherwise than by inhaler (2) External (except local ophthalmic use)	(b) 360 mcg (MD) 1.2 mg (MDD)(**b**)

(**a**) Substances added by this order are indicated by the use of bold type.
(**b**) Subject to the note at the end of Part I of Schedule 1.

Sch. 1 (I)

	CIRCUMSTANCES EXCLUDING MEDICINAL PRODUCTS FROM THE CLASS OF PRESCRIPTION ONLY MEDICINES		
Column 1	Column 2	Column 3	Column 4
Substance(a)	Maximum strength	Use, pharma-ceutical form or route of admini-stration	Maximum dose and maximum daily dose
Atropine Sulphate		(1) Internal: (a) by inhaler (b) otherwise than by inhaler (2) External (except local ophthalmic use)	(b) 360 mcg (MD) 1.2mg (MDD)(b)
Azapropazone			
Azathioprine			
Azathioprine Sodium			
Azidocillin Potassium			
Azlocillin Sodium			
Bacampicillin Hydrochloride			
Bacitracin			
Bacitracin Methylene Disalicylate			
Bacitracin Zinc			
Baclofen			
Barbitone			
Barbitone Sodium			
Barium Carbonate			
Barium Chloride			
Barium Sulphide			
Beclamide			
Beclomethasone			

(a) Substances added by this order are indicated by the use of bold type.
(b) Subject to the note at the end of Part I of Schedule 1.

Sch. 1 (I)

| Column 1 | CIRCUMSTANCES EXCLUDING MEDICINAL PRODUCTS FROM THE CLASS OF PRESCRIPTION ONLY MEDICINES | | |
	Column 2	Column 3	Column 4
Substance(a)	Maximum strength	Use, pharma-ceutical form or route of admini-stration	Maximum dose and maximum daily dose
Beclomethasone Dipropionate			
Belladonna Herb		(1) Internal (2) External	(1) 1 mg of the alkaloids (MDD)
Belladonna Root		(1) Internal (2) External	(1) 1 mg of the alkaloids (MDD)
Bemegride			
Bemegride Sodium			
Benapryzine Hydrochloride			
Bendrofluazide			
Benethamine Penicillin			
Benoxaprofen			
Benperidol			
Benserazide Hydrochloride			
Benzathine Penicillin			
Benzbromarone			
Benzhexol Hydrochloride			
Benzilonium Bromide			
Benzocaine		Any use except local ophthalmic use	
Benzoctamine Hydrochloride			
Benzoyl Peroxide	10.0 per cent	External	

(a) Substances added by this order are indicated by the use of bold type.

Sch. 1 (I)

	CIRCUMSTANCES EXCLUDING MEDICINAL PRODUCTS FROM THE CLASS OF PRESCRIPTION ONLY MEDICINES		
Column 1	Column 2	Column 3	Column 4
Substance(a)	Maximum strength	Use, pharmaceutical form or route of administration	Maximum dose and maximum daily dose
N-Benzoyl Sulphanilamide			
Benzquinamide			
Benzquinamide Hydrochloride			
Benzthiazide			
Benztropine Mesylate			
Benzylpenicillin Calcium			
Benzylpenicillin Potassium			
Benzylpenicillin Sodium			
Betahistine Hydrochloride			
Betamethasone			
Betamethasone Adamantoate			
Betamethasone Benzoate			
Betamethasone Sodium Phosphate			
Betamethasone Valerate			
Bethanechol Chloride			
Bethanidine Sulphate			
Bezafibrate			
Biperiden Hydrochloride			
Biperiden Lactate			
Bismuth Glycollylarsanilate			

(a) Substances added by this order are indicated by the use of bold type.

Sch. 1 (I)

	CIRCUMSTANCES EXCLUDING MEDICINAL PRODUCTS FROM THE CLASS OF PRESCRIPTION ONLY MEDICINES		
Column 1	Column 2	Column 3	Column 4
Substance(a)	Maximum strength	Use, pharma-ceutical form or route of admini-stration	Maximum dose and maximum daily dose
Bleomycin			
Bleomycin Sulphate			
Bretylium Tosylate			
Bromazepam			
Bromhexine Hydrochloride			
Bromocriptine Mesylate			
Bromvaletone			
Brotizolam			
Budesonide			
Bufexamac			
Bumetanide			
Buphenine Hydrochloride			6 mg (MD) 18 mg (MDD)
Bupivacaine		Any use except local ophthalmic use	
Bupivacaine Hydrochloride		Any use except local ophthalmic use	
Buprenorphine			
Buprenorphine Hydrochloride			
Busulphan			
Butacaine Sulphate		Any use except local ophthalmic use	
Butobarbitone			

(a) Substances added by this order are indicated by the use of bold type.

Sch. 1 (I)

| Column 1 | CIRCUMSTANCES EXCLUDING MEDICINAL PRODUCTS FROM THE CLASS OF PRESCRIPTION ONLY MEDICINES | | |
| | Column 2 | Column 3 | Column 4 |
Substance(a)	Maximum strength	Use, pharmaceutical form or route of administration	Maximum dose and maximum daily dose
Butobarbitone Sodium			
Butriptyline Hydrochloride			
Calcitonin			
Calcitriol			
Calcium Amphomycin			
Calcium Benzamidosalicylate			
Calcium Bromide			
Calcium Bromidolactobionate			
Calcium Carbimide			
Calcium Folinate			
Calcium Metrizoate			
Calcium Sulphaloxate			
Candicidin			
Canrenoic Acid			
Cantharidin	0.01 per cent	External	
Capreomycin Sulphate			
Carbachol			
Carbamazepine			
Carbenicillin Sodium			
Carbenoxolone Sodium		(1) Pellet	(1) 5 mg (MD) 25 mg (MDD)
	(2) 2.0 per cent	(2) Gel	

(a) Substances added by this order are indicated by the use of bold type.

Sch. 1 (I)

| Column 1 | Circumstances Excluding Medicinal Products from the Class of Prescription Only Medicines | | |
| | Column 2 | Column 3 | Column 4 |
Substance(a)	Maximum strength	Use, pharma-ceutical form or route of admini-stration	Maximum dose and maximum daily dose
Carbidopa			
Carbimazole			
Carbocisteine			
Carbon Tetrachloride			
Carboprost Trometamol			
Carbuterol Hydrochloride			
Carfecillin Sodium			
Carindacillin Sodium			
Carisoprodol			
Carmustine			
Carperidine			
Cefaclor			
Cefadroxil			
Cefazedone Sodium			
Cefotaxime Sodium			
Cefoxitin Sodium			
Cefsulodin Sodium			
Cefuroxime Sodium			
Cephalexin			
Cephalexin Sodium			
Cephaloridine			
Cephalothin Sodium			

(a) Substances added by this order are indicated by the use of bold type.

Sch. 1 (I)

Column 1	CIRCUMSTANCES EXCLUDING MEDICINAL PRODUCTS FROM THE CLASS OF PRESCRIPTION ONLY MEDICINES		
	Column 2	Column 3	Column 4
Substance(a)	Maximum strength	Use, pharmaceutical form or route of administration	Maximum dose and maximum daily dose
Cephamandole Nafate			
Cephazolin Sodium			
Cephradine			
Cerium Oxalate			
Chenodeoxycholic Acid			
Chloral Hydrate		External	
Chlorambucil			
Chloramphenicol			
Chloramphenicol Cinnamate			
Chloramphenicol Palmitate			
Chloramphenicol Sodium Succinate			
Chlordiazepoxide			
Chlordiazepoxide Hydrochloride			
Chlorhexadol			
Chlormadinone Acetate			
Chlormerodrin			
Chlormethiazole			
Chlormethiazole Edisylate			
Chlormezanone			

(a) Substances added by this order are indicated by the use of bold type.

Sch. 1 (I)

Column 1	CIRCUMSTANCES EXCLUDING MEDICINAL PRODUCTS FROM THE CLASS OF PRESCRIPTION ONLY MEDICINES		
	Column 2	Column 3	Column 4
Substance(a)	Maximum strength	Use, pharmaceutical form or route of administration	Maximum dose and maximum daily dose
Chloroform(b)	(1) 5.0 per cent	(1) Internal (2) External	
Chloroquine Phosphate		Prophylaxis of malaria	
Chloroquine Sulphate		Prophylaxis of malaria	
Chlorothiazide			
Chlorotrianisene			
Chlorphenoxamine Hydrochloride			
Chlorpromazine			
Chlorpromazine Embonate			
Chlorpromazine Hydrochloride			
Chlorpropamide			
Chlorprothixene			
Chlortetracycline			
Chlortetracycline Calcium			
Chlortetracycline Hydrochloride			
Chlorthalidone			
Chlorzoxazone			
Cholestyramine			

(a) Substances added by this order are indicated by the use of bold type.
(b) Additional restrictions on the retail sale or supply of products containing chloroform are imposed by the Medicines (Chloroform Prohibition) Order 1979 (S.I. 1979/382, amended by S.I. 1980/263).

Sch. 1 (I)

Column 1	CIRCUMSTANCES EXCLUDING MEDICINAL PRODUCTS FROM THE CLASS OF PRESCRIPTION ONLY MEDICINES		
	Column 2	Column 3	Column 4
Substance(a)	Maximum strength	Use, pharmaceutical form or route of administration	Maximum dose and maximum daily dose
Chorionic Gonadotrophin			
Ciclacillin			
Ciclobendazole			
Cimetidine			
Cimetidine Hydrochloride			
Cinchocaine	3.0 per cent	Any use except local ophthalmic use	
Cinchocaine Hydrochloride	Equivalent of 3.0 per cent of Cinchocaine	Any use except local ophthalmic use	
Cinchophen			
Cinoxacin			
Cisplatin			
Clenbuterol Hydrochloride			
Clidinium Bromide			
Clindamycin			
Clindamycin Hydrochloride			
Clindamycin Palmitate Hydrochloride			
Clindamycin Phosphate			

(a) Substances added by this order are indicated by the use of bold type.

Sch. 1 (I)

| Column 1 | CIRCUMSTANCES EXCLUDING MEDICINAL PRODUCTS FROM THE CLASS OF PRESCRIPTION ONLY MEDICINES | | |
	Column 2	Column 3	Column 4
Substance(a)	Maximum strength	Use, pharmaceutical form or route of administration	Maximum dose and maximum daily dose
Clioquinol	(1) 35 mg	(1) Treatment of mouth ulcers (2) External (other than treatment of mouth ulcers)	(1) 350 mg (MDD)
Clobazam			
Clobetasol Propionate			
Clobetasone Butyrate			
Clofazimine			
Clofibrate			
Clomiphene Citrate			
Clomipramine			
Clomipramine Hydrochloride			
Clomocycline			
Clomocycline Sodium			
Clonazepam			
Clonidine			
Clonidine Hydrochloride			
Clopamide			
Clopenthixol Decanoate			
Clorexolone			
Clostebol Acetate			
Clotrimazole		External: (1) cream (2) powder (3) solution	

(a) Substances added by this order are indicated by the use of bold type.

Sch. 1 (I)

Column 1	CIRCUMSTANCES EXCLUDING MEDICINAL PRODUCTS FROM THE CLASS OF PRESCRIPTION ONLY MEDICINES		
	Column 2	Column 3	Column 4
Substance(a)	Maximum strength	Use, pharma-ceutical form or route of admini-stration	Maximum dose and maximum daily dose
Cloxacillin Benzathine			
Cloxacillin Sodium			
Cocculus Indicus			
Co-dergocrine Mesylate			
Colaspase			
Colchicine			
Colestipol Hydrochloride			
Colistin Sulphate			
Colistin Sulphomethate			
Colistin Sulphomethate Sodium			
Coniine			
Conium Leaf	7.0 per cent	External	
Corticotrophin			
Cortisone			
Cortisone Acetate			
Co-Trimoxazole			
Cropropamide			
Crotethamide			
Croton Oil			
Croton Seed			
Curare			
Cyclobarbitone			

(a) Substances added by this order are indicated by the use of bold type.

Sch. 1 (I)

| Column 1 | Circumstances Excluding Medicinal Products from the Class of Prescription Only Medicines | | |
	Column 2	Column 3	Column 4
Substance(a)	Maximum strength	Use, pharma-ceutical form or route of admini-stration	Maximum dose and maximum daily dose
Cyclobarbitone Calcium			
Cyclofenil			
Cyclopenthiazide			
Cyclopentolate Hydrochloride			
Cyclophosphamide			
Cycloserine			
Cyclothiazide			
Cyproterone Acetate			
Cytarabine			
Cytarabine Hydrochloride			
Dacarbazine			
Danazol			
Dantrolene Sodium			
Dapsone			
Dapsone Ethane Ortho Sulphonate			
Daunorubicin Hydrochloride			
Deanol Bitartrate			26 mg (MDD)
Debrisoquine Sulphate			
Demecarium Bromide			
Demeclocycline			

(a) Substances added by this order are indicated by the use of bold type.

Sch. 1 (I)

Column 1	CIRCUMSTANCES EXCLUDING MEDICINAL PRODUCTS FROM THE CLASS OF PRESCRIPTION ONLY MEDICINES		
	Column 2	Column 3	Column 4
Substance(a)	Maximum strength	Use, pharmaceutical form or route of administration	Maximum dose and maximum daily dose
Demeclocycline Calcium			
Demeclocycline Hydrochloride			
Deoxycortone Acetate			
Deoxycortone Pivalate			
Deptropine Citrate			
Dequalinium Chloride	(1) 0.25 mg (2) 1.0 per cent	(1) Internal: throat lozenges or throat pastilles (2) External: paint	
Deserpidine			
Desferrioxamine Mesylate			
Desfluorotriamcinolone			
Desipramine Hydrochloride			
Deslanoside			
Desmopressin			
Desonide			
Desoxymethasone			
Dexamethasone			
Dexamethasone Acetate			
Dexamethasone Isonicotinate			
Dexamethasone Phenylpropionate			
Dexamethasone Pivalate			

(a) Substances added by this order are indicated by the use of bold type.

Sch. 1 (I)

| Column 1 | CIRCUMSTANCES EXCLUDING MEDICINAL PRODUCTS FROM THE CLASS OF PRESCRIPTION ONLY MEDICINES | | |
| | Column 2 | Column 3 | Column 4 |
Substance(a)	Maximum strength	Use, pharmaceutical form or route of administration	Maximum dose and maximum daily dose
Dexamethasone Sodium *m*-Sulphobenzoate			
Dexamethasone Sodium Phosphate			
Dexamethasone Troxundate			
Dextromethorphan Hydrobromide		Internal	Equivalent of 15 mg of Dextromethorphan (MD) Equivalent of 75 mg of Dextromethorphan (MDD)
Dextropropoxyphene Hydrochloride			
Dextropropoxyphene Napsylate			
Dextrothyroxine Sodium			
Diazepam			
Diazoxide			
Dibenzepin Hydrochloride			
Dichloralphenazone			
Dichlorphenamide			
Diclofenac Sodium			
Dicyclomine Hydrochloride			10 mg (MD) 60 mg (MDD)
Dienoestrol			
Diethanolamine Fusidate			
Diethylpropion Hydrochloride			

(a) Substances added by this order are indicated by the use of bold type.

Sch. 1 (I)

	CIRCUMSTANCES EXCLUDING MEDICINAL PRODUCTS FROM THE CLASS OF PRESCRIPTION ONLY MEDICINES		
Column 1	Column 2	Column 3	Column 4
Substance(a)	Maximum strength	Use, pharmaceutical form or route of administration	Maximum dose and maximum daily dose
Diflucortolone Valerate			
Diflunisal			
Digitalin			
Digitalis Leaf			
Digitalis Prepared			
Digitoxin			
Digoxin			
Dihydralazine Sulphate			
Dihydroergotamine Mesylate			
Dihydrostreptomycin			
Dihydrostreptomycin Sulphate			
Diloxanide Furoate			
Dimercaprol			
Dimethisoquin Hydrochloride		Any use except local ophthalmic use	
Dimethisterone			
Dimethothiazine Mesylate			
Dimethyl Sulphoxide			
Dimethyltubocurarine Bromide			
Dimethyltubocurarine Chloride			

(a) Substances added by this order are indicated by the use of bold type.

Sch. 1 (I)

| Column 1 | CIRCUMSTANCES EXCLUDING MEDICINAL PRODUCTS FROM THE CLASS OF PRESCRIPTION ONLY MEDICINES | | |
| | Column 2 | Column 3 | Column 4 |
Substance(a)	Maximum strength	Use, pharmaceutical form or route of administration	Maximum dose and maximum daily dose
Dimethyltubocurarine Iodide			
Dinoprost			
Dinoprost Trometamol			
Dinoprostone			
Dipyridamole			
Disopyramide			
Disopyramide Phosphate			
Distigmine Bromide			
Disulfiram			
Dithranol	1.00 per cent		
Dobutamine Hydrochloride			
Domperidone			
Dopamine Hydrochloride			
Dothiepin			
Dothiepin Hydrochloride			
Doxapram Hydrochloride			
Doxepin Hydrochloride			
Doxorubicin			
Doxycycline			
Doxycycline Calcium Chelate			
Doxycycline Hydrochloride			

(a) Substances added by this order are indicated by the use of bold type.

Sch. 1 (I)

| Column 1 | CIRCUMSTANCES EXCLUDING MEDICINAL PRODUCTS FROM THE CLASS OF PRESCRIPTION ONLY MEDICINES | | |
	Column 2	Column 3	Column 4
Substance(a)	Maximum strength	Use, pharmaceutical form or route of administration	Maximum dose and maximum daily dose
Droperidol			
Drostanolone			
Drostanolone Propionate			
Dydrogesterone			
Dyflos			
Econazole		External (except vaginal use)	
Econazole Nitrate		External (except vaginal use)	
Ecothiopate Iodide			
Edrophonium Chloride			
Embutramide			
Emepronium Bromide			
Emetine	1.0 per cent		
Emetine Bismuth Iodide			
Emetine Hydrochloride	Equivalent of 1.0 per cent of Emetine		
Encephalitis Virus, Tick-borne, Cent Eur			
Ephedrine	(2) 2.0 per cent	(1) Internal (other than nasal sprays or nasal drops) (2) Nasal sprays or nasal drops (3) External	(1) 30 mg (MD) 60 mg (MDD)

(a) Substances added by this order are indicated by the use of bold type.

Sch. 1 (I)

Column 1	Circumstances Excluding Medicinal Products from the Class of Prescription Only Medicines		
	Column 2	Column 3	Column 4
Substance(a)	Maximum strength	Use, pharmaceutical form or route of administration	Maximum dose and maximum daily dose
Ephedrine Hydrochloride		(1) Internal (other than nasal sprays or nasal drops)	(1) Equivalent of 30 mg of Ephedrine (MD) Equivalent of 60 mg of Ephedrine (MDD)
	(2) Equivalent of 2.0 per cent of Ephedrine	(2) Nasal sprays or nasal drops	
		(3) External	
Ephedrine Sulphate		(1) Internal (other than nasal sprays or nasal drops)	(1) Equivalent of 30 mg of Ephedrine (MD) Equivalent of 60 mg of Ephedrine (MDD)
	(2) Equivalent of 2.0 per cent of Ephedrine	(2) Nasal sprays or nasal drops	
		(3) External	
Epicillin			
Epithiazide			
Epoprostenol Sodium			
Ergometrine Maleate			
Ergometrine Tartrate			
Ergot, Prepared			
Ergotamine Tartrate			
Erythromycin			
Erythromycin Estolate			
Erythromycin Ethyl Carbonate			

(a) Substances added by this order are indicated by the use of bold type.

Sch. 1 (I)

| Column 1 | CIRCUMSTANCES EXCLUDING MEDICINAL PRODUCTS FROM THE CLASS OF PRESCRIPTION ONLY MEDICINES | | |
	Column 2	Column 3	Column 4
Substance(a)	Maximum strength	Use, pharma-ceutical form or route of admini-stration	Maximum dose and maximum daily dose
Erythromycin Ethyl Succinate			
Erythromycin Lactobionate			
Erythromycin Phosphate			
Erythromycin Stearate			
Erythromycin Thiocyanate			
Estramustine Phosphate			
Etafedrine Hydrochloride			
Ethacrynic Acid			
Ethambutol Hydrochloride			
Ethamivan			
Ethamsylate			
Ethchlorvynol			
Ethiazide			
Ethinyloestradiol			
Ethionamide			
Ethisterone			
Ethoglucid			
Ethoheptazine Citrate			
Ethopropazine Hydrochloride			
Ethosuximide			
Ethotoin			

(a) Substances added by this order are indicated by the use of bold type.

Sch. 1 (I)

| Column 1 | CIRCUMSTANCES EXCLUDING MEDICINAL PRODUCTS FROM THE CLASS OF PRESCRIPTION ONLY MEDICINES | | |
| | Column 2 | Column 3 | Column 4 |
Substance(a)	Maximum strength	Use, pharma-ceutical form or route of admini-stration	Maximum dose and maximum daily dose
Ethyl Biscoumacetate			
Ethyloestrenol			
Ethynodiol Diacetate			
Etidronate Disodium			
Etomidate			
Etoposide			
Fazadinium Bromide			
Felypressin			
Fenbufen			
Fencamfamin Hydrochloride			
Fenclofenac			
Fenfluramine Hydrochloride			
Fenoprofen			
Fenoprofen Calcium			
Fenoterol Hydrobromide			
Feprazone			
Ferrous Arsenate			
Flavoxate Hydrochloride			
Fluanisone			
Flubendazole			
Fluclorolone Acetonide			
Flucloxacillin Sodium			

(a) Substances added by this order are indicated by the use of bold type.

Sch. 1 (I)

| Column 1 | CIRCUMSTANCES EXCLUDING MEDICINAL PRODUCTS FROM THE CLASS OF PRESCRIPTION ONLY MEDICINES | | |
	Column 2	Column 3	Column 4
Substance(a)	Maximum strength	Use, pharmaceutical form or route of administration	Maximum dose and maximum daily dose
Flucytosine			
Fludrocortisone Acetate			
Flufenamic Acid			
Flumethasone			
Flumethasone Pivalate			
Flunisolide			
Flunitrazepam			
Fluocinolone Acetonide			
Fluocinonide			
Fluocortin Butyl			
Fluocortolone			
Fluocortolone Hexanoate			
Fluocortolone Pivalate			
Fluorometholone			
Fluorouracil			
Fluorouracil Trometamol			
Fluoxymesterone			
Flupenthixol Decanoate			
Flupenthixol Hydrochloride			
Fluperolone Acetate			
Fluphenazine Decanoate			
Fluphenazine Enanthate			

(a) Substances added by this order are indicated by the use of bold type.

Sch. 1 (I)

	CIRCUMSTANCES EXCLUDING MEDICINAL PRODUCTS FROM THE CLASS OF PRESCRIPTION ONLY MEDICINES		
Column 1	Column 2	Column 3	Column 4
Substance(a)	Maximum strength	Use, pharma-ceutical form or route of admini-stration	Maximum dose and maximum daily dose
Fluphenazine Hydrochloride			
Fluprednidene Acetate			
Fluprednisolone			
Fluprostenol Sodium			
Flurandrenolone			
Flurazepam Hydrochloride			
Flurazepam Monohydrochloride			
Flurbiprofen			
Fluspirilene			
Folic Acid			200 mcg (MDD)
Formocortal			
Fosfestrol Sodium			
Framycetin Sulphate			
Frusemide			
Furazolidone			
Fusafungine			
Fusidic Acid			
Gallamine Triethiodide			
Gelsemine	0.1 per cent		
Gelsemium			25 mg (MD) 75 mg (MDD)

(a) Substances added by this order are indicated by the use of bold type.

Sch. 1 (I)

| Column 1 | CIRCUMSTANCES EXCLUDING MEDICINAL PRODUCTS FROM THE CLASS OF PRESCRIPTION ONLY MEDICINES | | |
| | Column 2 | Column 3 | Column 4 |
Substance(a)	Maximum strength	Use, pharmaceutical form or route of administration	Maximum dose and maximum daily dose
Gentamicin			
Gentamicin Sulphate			
Gestronol			
Gestronol Hexanoate			
Glibenclamide			
Glibornuride			
Gliclazide			
Glipizide			
Gliquidone			
Glucagon			
Glutethimide			
Glycopyrronium Bromide			1 mg (MD) 2 mg (MDD)
Glymidine			
Gonadorelin			
Gramicidin	0.2 per cent	External	
Griseofulvin			
Growth Hormone			
Guanethidine Monosulphate			
Guanoclor Sulphate			
Guanoxan Sulphate			
Halcinonide			
Haloperidol			

(a) Substances added by this order are indicated by the use of bold type.

Sch. 1 (I)

Column 1	Column 2	Column 3	Column 4
	CIRCUMSTANCES EXCLUDING MEDICINAL PRODUCTS FROM THE CLASS OF PRESCRIPTION ONLY MEDICINES		
Substance(a)	Maximum strength	Use, pharmaceutical form or route of administration	Maximum dose and maximum daily dose
Heparin		External	
Heparin Calcium		External	
Heptabarbitone			
Hexachlorophane	(a) 2.0 per cent (b) 0.1 per cent (c) 0.75 per cent	External: (a) soaps (b) aerosols (c) preparations other than soaps and aerosols	
Hexamine Phenylcinchoninate			
Hexobarbitone			
Hexobarbitone Sodium			
Hexoestrol			
Hexoestrol Dipropionate			
L-Histidine Hydrochloride		Dietary or nutritive use	
Homatropine		(1) Internal (2) External (except local ophthalmic use)	(1) 0.15 mg (MD) 0.45 mg (MDD)
Homatropine Hydrobromide			0.2 mg (MD) 0.6 mg (MDD)
Homatropine Methylbromide			2 mg (MD) 6 mg (MDD)
Hydralazine Hydrochloride			

(a) Substances added by this order are indicated by the use of bold type.

Sch. 1 (I)

| Column 1 | CIRCUMSTANCES EXCLUDING MEDICINAL PRODUCTS FROM THE CLASS OF PRESCRIPTION ONLY MEDICINES | | |
| | Column 2 | Column 3 | Column 4 |
Substance(a)	Maximum strength	Use, pharma-ceutical form or route of admini-stration	Maximum dose and maximum daily dose
Hydrargaphen		Local application to skin	
Hydrobromic Acid			
Hydrochlorothiazide			
Hydrocortisone			
Hydrocortisone Acetate			
Hydrocortisone Butyrate			
Hydrocortisone Caprylate			
Hydrocortisone Hydrogen Succinate			
Hydrocortisone Sodium Phosphate			
Hydrocortisone Sodium Succinate			
Hydroflumethiazide			
Hydroxychloroquine Sulphate		Prophylaxis of malaria	
Hydroxyprogesterone			
Hydroxyprogesterone Enanthate			
Hydroxyprogesterone Hexanoate			
Hydroxyurea			
Hydroxyzine Embonate			
Hydroxyzine Hydrochloride			

(a) Substances added by this order are indicated by the use of bold type.

Sch. 1 (I)

Column 1	CIRCUMSTANCES EXCLUDING MEDICINAL PRODUCTS FROM THE CLASS OF PRESCRIPTION ONLY MEDICINES		
	Column 2	Column 3	Column 4
Substance(a)	Maximum strength	Use, pharmaceutical form or route of administration	Maximum dose and maximum daily dose
Hyoscine	(1) 0.15 per cent	(1) Internal (2) External (except local ophthalmic use)	
Hyoscine Butylbromide		(1) Internal: (a) by inhaler (b) otherwise than by inhaler (2) External	(b) 3 mg (MD) 9 mg (MDD)(b)
Hyoscine Hydrobromide		(1) Internal: (a) by inhaler (b) otherwise than by inhaler (2) External (except local ophthalmic use)	(b) 300 mcg (MD) 900 mcg (MDD)(b)
Hyoscine Methobromide		(1) Internal: (a) by inhaler (b) otherwise than by inhaler (2) External	(b) 2.5 mg (MD) 7.5 mg (MDD)(b)
Hyoscine Methonitrate		(1) Internal: (a) by inhaler (b) otherwise than by inhaler (2) External	(b) 2.5 mg (MD) 7.5 mg (MDD)(b)
Hyoscyamine		(1) Internal: (a) by inhaler (b) otherwise than by inhaler (2) External (3) Preparations for the relief of asthma in the form of cigarettes, smoking mixtures or fumigants which contain Hyoscyamine as an alkaloid of Stramonium	(b) 300 mcg (MD) 1 mg (MDD)(b)

(a) Substances added by this order are indicated by the use of bold type.
(b) Subject to the note at the end of Part I of Schedule 1.

Sch. 1 (I)

Column 1	CIRCUMSTANCES EXCLUDING MEDICINAL PRODUCTS FROM THE CLASS OF PRESCRIPTION ONLY MEDICINES		
	Column 2	Column 3	Column 4
Substance(a)	Maximum strength	Use, pharmaceutical form or route of administration	Maximum dose and maximum daily dose
Hyoscyamine Hydrobromide		(1) Internal: (a) by inhaler (b) otherwise than by inhaler (2) External	(b) Equivalent of 300 mcg of Hyoscyamine (MD) Equivalent of 1 mg of Hyoscyamine (MDD)(b)
Hyoscyamine Sulphate		(1) Internal: (a) by inhaler (b) otherwise than by inhaler (2) External	(b) Equivalent of 300 mcg of Hyoscyamine (MD) Equivalent of 1 mg of Hyoscyamine (MDD)(b)
Ibuprofen		Rheumatic and muscular pain, back-ache, neuralgia, migraine, headache, dental pain, dysmenorrhoea, feverishness, symptoms of colds and influenza	400mg (MD) 1200 mg (MDD)
Idoxuridine			
Ifosfamide			
Ignatius Bean			
Imipramine			
Imipramine Hydrochloride			
Imipramine Ion Exchange Resin Bound Salt or Complex			
Indapamide Hemihydrate			

(a) Substances added by this order are indicated by the use of bold type.
(b) Subject to the note at the end of Part I of Schedule 1.

Sch. 1 (I)

| Column 1 | CIRCUMSTANCES EXCLUDING MEDICINAL PRODUCTS FROM THE CLASS OF PRESCRIPTION ONLY MEDICINES | | |
| | Column 2 | Column 3 | Column 4 |
Substance(a)	Maximum strength	Use, pharmaceutical form or route of administration	Maximum dose and maximum daily dose
Indomethacin			
Indoramin Hydrochloride			
Indoprofen			
Iodamide			
Iodamide Meglumine			
Iodamide Sodium			
Iopamidol			
Ipratropium Bromide			
Iprindole Hydrochloride			
Iproniazid Phosphate			
Isoaminile			
Isoaminile Citrate			
Isocarboxazid			
Isoetharine			
Isoetharine Hydrochloride			
Isoetharine Mesylate			
Isoniazid			
Isoprenaline Hydrochloride			
Isoprenaline Sulphate			
Isopropamide Iodide			Equivalent of 2.5 mg of Isopropamide ion (MD) Equivalent of 5.0 mg of Isopropamide ion (MDD)

(a) Substances added by this order are indicated by the use of bold type.

Sch. 1 (I)

Column 1	Column 2	Column 3	Column 4
	CIRCUMSTANCES EXCLUDING MEDICINAL PRODUCTS FROM THE CLASS OF PRESCRIPTION ONLY MEDICINES		
Substance(a)	Maximum strength	Use, pharmaceutical form or route of administration	Maximum dose and maximum daily dose
Jaborandi		External	
Kanamycin Sulphates			
Ketamine Hydrochloride			
Ketazolam			
Ketoconazole			
Ketoprofen			
Ketotifen Fumarate			
Labetolol Hydrochloride			
Lanatoside C			
Lanatoside Complex A, B and C			
Latamoxef Disodium			
Levallorphan Tartrate			
Levodopa			
Levonorgestrel			
Lidoflazine			
Lignocaine		Any use except local ophthalmic use	
Lignocaine Hydrochloride		Any use except local ophthalmic use	
Lincomycin			
Lincomycin Hydrochloride			
Liothyronine Sodium			

(a) Substances added by this order are indicated by the use of bold type.

Sch. 1 (I)

| Column 1 | CIRCUMSTANCES EXCLUDING MEDICINAL PRODUCTS FROM THE CLASS OF PRESCRIPTION ONLY MEDICINES | | |
| | Column 2 | Column 3 | Column 4 |
Substance(a)	Maximum strength	Use, pharmaceutical form or route of administration	Maximum dose and maximum daily dose
Lithium Carbonate			Equivalent of 5 mg of Lithium (MD) Equivalent of 15 mg of Lithium (MDD)
Lithium Sulphate			Equivalent of 5 mg of Lithium (MD) Equivalent of 15 mg of Lithium (MDD)
Lobeline		(1) Internal (2) External	(1) 3 mg (MD) 9 mg (MDD)
Lobeline Hydrochloride		(1) Internal (2) External	(1) Equivalent of 3 mg of Lobeline (MD) Equivalent of 9 mg of Lobeline (MDD)
Lobeline Sulphate		(1) Internal (2) External	(1) Equivalent of 3 mg of Lobeline (MD) Equivalent of 9 mg of Lobeline (MDD)
Lofepramine			
Lomustine			
Loperamide Hydrochloride		Treatment of acute diarrhoea	
Lorazepam			
Luteinising Hormone			
Lymecycline			
Lynoestrenol			
Lypressin			
Mafenide			

(a) Substances added by this order are indicated by the use of bold type.

Sch. 1 (I)

Column 1	CIRCUMSTANCES EXCLUDING MEDICINAL PRODUCTS FROM THE CLASS OF PRESCRIPTION ONLY MEDICINES		
	Column 2	Column 3	Column 4
Substance(a)	Maximum strength	Use, pharma-ceutical form or route of admini-stration	Maximum dose and maximum daily dose
Mafenide Acetate			
Mafenide Hydrochloride			
Mafenide Propionate	5.0 per cent	Eye drops	
Magnesium Fluoride			
Magnesium Metrizoate			
Mandragora Autumnalis			
Mannomustine Hydrochloride			
Maprotiline Hydrochloride			
Mazindol			
Mebanazine			
Mebendazole			
Mebeverine Hydrochloride			100 mg (MD) 300 mg (MDD)
Mebhydrolin			
Mebhydrolin Napadisylate			
Mecamylamine Hydrochloride			
Mecillinam			
Meclofenoxate Hydrochloride			
Medazepam			
Medigoxin			
Medroxyprogesterone Acetate			

(a) Substances added by this order are indicated by the use of bold type.

Sch. 1 (I)

Column 1	CIRCUMSTANCES EXCLUDING MEDICINAL PRODUCTS FROM THE CLASS OF PRESCRIPTION ONLY MEDICINES		
	Column 2	Column 3	Column 4
Substance(a)	Maximum strength	Use, pharmaceutical form or route of administration	Maximum dose and maximum daily dose
Mefenamic Acid			
Mefruside			
Megestrol			
Megestrol Acetate			
Meglumine Iodoxamate			
Meglumine Iotroxate			
Melphalan			
Melphalan Hydrochloride			
Menotrophin			
Mepenzolate Bromide			25 mg (MD) 75 mg (MDD)
Mephenesin			
Mephenesin Carbamate			
Mepivacaine Hydrochloride		Any use except local ophthalmic use	
Meprobamate			
Meptazinol Hydrochloride			
Mequitazine			
Mercaptopurine			
Mersalyl			
Mersalyl Acid			
Mesterolone			

(a) Substances added by this order are indicated by the use of bold type.

Sch. 1 (I)

	CIRCUMSTANCES EXCLUDING MEDICINAL PRODUCTS FROM THE CLASS OF PRESCRIPTION ONLY MEDICINES		
Column 1	Column 2	Column 3	Column 4
Substance(a)	Maximum strength	Use, pharmaceutical form or route of administration	Maximum dose and maximum daily dose
Mestranol			
Metaraminol Tartrate			
Metformin Hydrochloride			
Methacycline			
Methacycline Calcium			
Methacycline Hydrochloride			
Methallenoestril			
Methandienone			
Methicillin Sodium			
Methixene			
Methixene Hydrochloride			
Methocarbamol			
Methocidin		Throat lozenges and throat pastilles	
Methohexitone Sodium			
Methoin			
Methoserpidine			
Methotrexate			
Methotrexate Sodium			
Methotrimeprazine			
Methotrimeprazine Hydrochloride			
Methotrimeprazine Maleate			

(a) Substances added by this order are indicated by the use of bold type.

Sch. 1 (I)

| Column 1 | CIRCUMSTANCES EXCLUDING MEDICINAL PRODUCTS FROM THE CLASS OF PRESCRIPTION ONLY MEDICINES | | |
	Column 2	Column 3	Column 4
Substance(a)	Maximum strength	Use, pharmaceutical form or route of administration	Maximum dose and maximum daily dose
Methoxamine Hydrochloride	0.25 per cent	Nasal sprays or nasal drops not containing liquid paraffin as a vehicle	
Methsuximide			
Methyclothiazide			
Methyldopa			
Methyldopate Hydrochloride			
Methylephedrine Hydrochloride			30 mg (MD) 60 mg (MDD)
Methylphenobarbitone			
Methylprednisolone			
Methylprednisolone Acetate			
Methylprednisolone Sodium Succinate			
Methyltestosterone			
Methylthiouracil			
Methyprylone			
Methysergide Maleate			
Metirosine			
Metoclopramide Hydrochloride			
Metolazone			
Metoprolol Tartrate			

(a) Substances added by this order are indicated by the use of bold type.

Sch. 1 (I)

| Column 1 | CIRCUMSTANCES EXCLUDING MEDICINAL PRODUCTS FROM THE CLASS OF PRESCRIPTION ONLY MEDICINES | | |
| | Column 2 | Column 3 | Column 4 |
Substance(a)	Maximum strength	Use, pharmaceutical form or route of administration	Maximum dose and maximum daily dose
Metronidazole			
Metyrapone			
Mexiletine Hydrochloride			
Mezlocillin Sodium			
Mianserin Hydrochloride			
Miconazole		External (except vaginal use)	
Miconazole Nitrate		External (except vaginal use)	
Minocycline			
Minocycline Hydrochloride			
Mithramycin			
Mitobronitol			
Mitomycin C			
Molindone Hydrochloride			
Morazone Hydrochloride			
Mustine Hydrochloride			
Nadolol			
Naftidrofuryl Oxalate			
Nalbuphine Hydrochloride			
Nalidixic Acid			
Nalorphine Hydrobromide			

(a) Substances added by this order are indicated by the use of bold type.

Sch. 1 (I)

| Column 1 | CIRCUMSTANCES EXCLUDING MEDICINAL PRODUCTS FROM THE CLASS OF PRESCRIPTION ONLY MEDICINES | | |
	Column 2	Column 3	Column 4
Substance(a)	Maximum strength	Use, pharma-ceutical form or route of admini-stration	Maximum dose and maximum daily dose
Naloxone Hydrochloride			
Nandrolone Decanoate			
Nandrolone Laureate			
Nandrolone Phenylpropionate			
Naphazoline Hydrochloride	(1) 0.05 per cent	(1) Nasal sprays or nasal drops not containing liquid paraffin as a vehicle	
	(2) 0.015 per cent	(2) Eye drops	
Naphazoline Nitrate	0.05 per cent	Nasal sprays or nasal drops not containing liquid paraffin as a vehicle	
Naproxen			
Naproxen Sodium			
Natamycin			
Nefopam Hydrochloride			
Neomycin			
Neomycin Oleate			
Neomycin Palmitate			
Neomycin Sulphate			
Neomycin Undecanoate			
Neostigmine Bromide			
Neostigmine Methylsulphate			

(a) Substances added by this order are indicated by the use of bold type.

Sch. 1 (I)

Column 1	CIRCUMSTANCES EXCLUDING MEDICINAL PRODUCTS FROM THE CLASS OF PRESCRIPTION ONLY MEDICINES		
	Column 2	Column 3	Column 4
Substance(a)	Maximum strength	Use, pharmaceutical form or route of administration	Maximum dose and maximum daily dose
Netilmicin Sulphate			
Nicoumalone			
Nifedipine			
Nifenazone			
Nikethamide			
Niridazole			
Nitrazepam			
Nitrofurantoin			
Nitrofurazone			
Nomifensine Maleate			
Noradrenaline			
Noradrenaline Acid Tartrate			
Norethandrolone			
Norethisterone			
Norethisterone Acetate			
Norethisterone Heptanoate			
Norethynodrel			
Norgestrel			
Nortriptyline Hydrochloride			
Novobiocin Calcium			
Novobiocin Sodium			

(a) Substances added by this order are indicated by the use of bold type.

Sch. 1 (I)

Column 1	Circumstances Excluding Medicinal Products from the Class of Prescription Only Medicines		
	Column 2	Column 3	Column 4
Substance(a)	Maximum strength	Use, pharmaceutical form or route of administration	Maximum dose and maximum daily dose
Nux Vomica Seed			
Nystatin			
Octacosactrin			
Oestradiol			
Oestradiol Benzoate			
Oestradiol Cypionate			
Oestradiol Dipropionate			
Oestradiol Diundecanoate			
Oestradiol Enanthate			
Oestradiol Phenylpropionate			
Oestradiol Undecanoate			
Oestradiol Valerate			
Oestriol			
Oestriol Di-Hemi Succinate			
Oestrogenic Substances Conjugated			
Oestrone			
Orciprenaline Sulphate			
Orphenadrine Citrate			
Orphenadrine Hydrochloride			
Ouabain			
Ovarian Gland Dried			

(a) Substances added by this order are indicated by the use of bold type.

Sch. 1 (I)

| Column 1 | CIRCUMSTANCES EXCLUDING MEDICINAL PRODUCTS FROM THE CLASS OF PRESCRIPTION ONLY MEDICINES | | |
	Column 2	Column 3	Column 4
Substance(a)	Maximum strength	Use, pharmaceutical form or route of administration	Maximum dose and maximum daily dose
Oxamniquine			
Oxandrolone			
Oxantel Pamoate			
Oxatomide			
Oxazepam			
Oxedrine Tartrate			
Oxolinic Acid			
Oxpentifylline			
Oxprenolol Hydrochloride			
Oxybuprocaine Hydrochloride		Any use except local ophthalmic use	
Oxymetholone			
Oxypertine			
Oxypertine Hydrochloride			
Oxyphenbutazone			
Oxyphencyclimine Hydrochloride			
Oxyphenonium Bromide			5 mg (MD) 15 mg (MDD)
Oxytetracycline			
Oxytetracycline Calcium			
Oxytetracycline Dihydrate			
Oxytetracycline Hydrochloride			

(a) Substances added by this order are indicated by the use of bold type.

Sch. 1 (I)

	CIRCUMSTANCES EXCLUDING MEDICINAL PRODUCTS FROM THE CLASS OF PRESCRIPTION ONLY MEDICINES		
Column 1	Column 2	Column 3	Column 4
Substance(a)	Maximum strength	Use, pharmaceutical form or route of administration	Maximum dose and maximum daily dose
Oxytocin, natural			
Oxytocin, synthetic			
Pancuronium Bromide			
Papaverine		(1) By inhaler (2) Otherwise than by inhaler	(2) 50 mg (MD) 150 mg (MDD)
Papaverine Hydrochloride		(1) By inhaler (2) Otherwise than by inhaler	(2) Equivalent of 50 mg of Papaverine (MD) Equivalent of 150 mg of Papaverine (MDD)
Paraldehyde			
Paramethadione			
Paramethasone Acetate			
Parathyroid Gland			
Pargyline Hydrochloride			
Pecilocin			
Pemoline			
Penamecillin			
Penbutolol Sulphate			
Penicillamine			
Penicillamine Hydrochloride			
Pentazocine Hydrochloride			
Pentazocine Lactate			
Penthienate Methobromide			5 mg (MD) 15 mg (MDD)

(a) Substances added by this order are indicated by the use of bold type.

Sch. 1 (I)

| Column 1 | CIRCUMSTANCES EXCLUDING MEDICINAL PRODUCTS FROM THE CLASS OF PRESCRIPTION ONLY MEDICINES | | |
| | Column 2 | Column 3 | Column 4 |
Substance(a)	Maximum strength	Use, pharmaceutical form or route of administration	Maximum dose and maximum daily dose
Pentobarbitone			
Pentobarbitone Sodium			
Pentolinium Tartrate			
Perhexiline Maleate			
Pericyazine			
Perphenazine			
Phenacetin(b)	0.1 per cent		
Phenazone		External	
Phenazone and Caffeine Citrate			
Phenazone Salicylate			
Phenbutrazate Hydrochloride			
Phenelzine Sulphate			
Phenethicillin Potassium			
Phenformin Hydrochloride			
Phenglutarimide Hydrochloride			
Phenindione			
Phenobarbitone			
Phenobarbitone Sodium			
Phenoxybenzamine Hydrochloride			

(a) Substances added by this order are indicated by the use of bold type.
(b) *See also* the Medicines (Phenacetin Prohibition) Order 1979 (S.I. 1979/1181).

Sch. 1 (I)

| Column 1 | Circumstances Excluding Medicinal Products from the Class of Prescription Only Medicines | | |
	Column 2	Column 3	Column 4
Substance(a)	Maximum strength	Use, pharmaceutical form or route of administration	Maximum dose and maximum daily dose
Phenoxymethylpenicillin			
Phenoxymethylpenicillin Calcium			
Phenoxymethylpenicillin Potassium			
Phenprocoumon			
Phensuximide			
Phentermine Hydrochloride			
Phentermine Resin Complex			
Phentolamine Hydrochloride			
Phentolamine Mesylate			
Phenylbutazone			
Phenylbutazone Sodium			
Phenylmethylbarbituric Acid			
Phenylpropanolamine Hydrochloride		Internal: (1) all preparations except controlled release capsules, nasal sprays and nasal drops	(1) 50 mg (MD) 150 mg (MDD)
		(2) controlled release capsules	(2) 75 mg (MD) 150 mg (MDD)
	(3) 2.0 per cent	(3) nasal sprays and nasal drops	
Phenytoin			

(a) Substances added by this order are indicated by the use of bold type.

Sch. 1 (I)

| Column 1 | CIRCUMSTANCES EXCLUDING MEDICINAL PRODUCTS FROM THE CLASS OF PRESCRIPTION ONLY MEDICINES | | |
	Column 2	Column 3	Column 4
Substance(a)	Maximum strength	Use, pharmaceutical form or route of administration	Maximum dose and maximum daily dose
Phenytoin Sodium			
Phthalylsulphathiazole			
Physostigmine			
Physostigmine Aminoxide Salicylate			
Physostigmine Salicylate			
Physostigmine Sulphate			
Picrotoxin			
Pilocarpine			
Pilocarpine Hydrochloride			
Pilocarpine Nitrate			
Pimozide			
Pindolol			
Pipenzolate Bromide			5 mg (MD) 15 mg (MDD)
Piperacillin Sodium			
Piperazine Oestrone Sulphate			
Piperidolate Hydrochloride			50 mg (MD) 150 mg (MDD)
Pipothiazine Palmitate			
Piracetam			
Piroxicam			
Pituitary Gland (Whole Dried)		By inhaler	

(a) Substances added by this order are indicated by the use of bold type.

Sch. 1 (I)

	CIRCUMSTANCES EXCLUDING MEDICINAL PRODUCTS FROM THE CLASS OF PRESCRIPTION ONLY MEDICINES		
Column 1	Column 2	Column 3	Column 4
Substance(a)	Maximum strength	Use, pharmaceutical form or route of administration	Maximum dose and maximum daily dose
Pituitary Powdered (Posterior Lobe)		By inhaler	
Pivampicillin Hydrochloride			
Pivmecillinam			
Pivmecillinam Hydrochloride			
Pizotifen			
Pizotifen Maleate			
Podophyllum			
Podophyllum Indian			
Podophyllum Resin	20.0 per cent	External	
Poldine Methylsulphate			2 mg (MD) 6 mg (MDD)
Polidexide			
Polymyxin B Sulphate			
Polyestradiol Phosphate			
Polythiazide			
Poppy Capsule			
Potassium Arsenite	0.0127 per cent		
Potassium Bromide			
Potassium Canrenoate			
Potassium Clorazepate			
Potassium Perchlorate			

(a) Substances added by this order are indicated by the use of bold type.

Sch. 1 (I)

	CIRCUMSTANCES EXCLUDING MEDICINAL PRODUCTS FROM THE CLASS OF PRESCRIPTION ONLY MEDICINES		
Column 1	Column 2	Column 3	Column 4
Substance(a)	Maximum strength	Use, pharma-ceutical form or route of admini-stration	Maximum dose and maximum daily dose
Practolol			
Pralidoxime Chloride			
Pralidoxime Iodide			
Pralidoxime Mesylate			
Prazepam			
Prazosin Hydrochloride			
Prednisolone			
Prednisolone Acetate			
Prednisolone Butylacetate			
Prednisolone Hexanoate			
Prednisolone Pivalate			
Prednisolone Sodium Phosphate			
Prednisolone Sodium m-Sulphobenzoate			
Prednisolone 21-Steaglate			
Prednisolone m-Sulphobenzoate			
Prednisone			
Prednisone Acetate			
Prenalterol Hydrochloride			
Prenylamine Lactate			

(a) Substances added by this order are indicated by the use of bold type.

MEDICINES

Sch. 1 (I)

| Column 1 | CIRCUMSTANCES EXCLUDING MEDICINAL PRODUCTS FROM THE CLASS OF PRESCRIPTION ONLY MEDICINES | | |
| | Column 2 | Column 3 | Column 4 |
Substance(a)	Maximum strength	Use, pharma-ceutical form or route of admini-stration	Maximum dose and maximum daily dose
Prilocaine Hydrochloride		Any use except local ophthalmic use	
Primidone			
Probenecid			
Probucol			
Procainamide Hydrochloride			
Procaine Hydrochloride		Any use except local ophthalmic use	
Procaine Penicillin			
Procarbazine Hydrochloride			
Prochlorperazine Edisylate			
Prochlorperazine Maleate			
Prochlorperazine Mesylate			
Procyclidine Hydrochloride			
Progesterone			
Prolactin			
Proligestone			
Prolintane Hydrochloride			
Promazine Embonate			
Promazine Hydrochloride			

(a) Substances added by this order are indicated by the use of bold type.

Sch. 1 (I)

	CIRCUMSTANCES EXCLUDING MEDICINAL PRODUCTS FROM THE CLASS OF PRESCRIPTION ONLY MEDICINES		
Column 1	Column 2	Column 3	Column 4
Substance(a)	Maximum strength	Use, pharmaceutical form or route of administration	Maximum dose and maximum daily dose
Propanidid			
Propantheline Bromide			15 mg (MD) 45 mg (MDD)
Propranolol Hydrochloride			
Propylthiouracil			
Proquazone			
Protamine Sulphate			
Prothionamide			
Protirelin			
Protriptyline Hydrochloride			
Proxymetacaine Hydrochloride		Any use except local ophthalmic use	
Pseudoephedrine Hydrochloride			60 mg (MD) 180 mg (MDD)
Pseudoephedrine Sulphate			60 mg (MD) 180 mg (MDD)
Pyrantel Embonate			
Pyrantel Tartrate			
Pyrazinamide			
Pyridostigmine Bromide			
Quinalbarbitone			
Quinalbarbitone Sodium			
Quinestradol			

(a) Substances added by this order are indicated by the use of bold type.

Sch. 1 (I)

Column 1	CIRCUMSTANCES EXCLUDING MEDICINAL PRODUCTS FROM THE CLASS OF PRESCRIPTION ONLY MEDICINES		
	Column 2	Column 3	Column 4
Substance(a)	Maximum strength	Use, pharma- ceutical form or route of admini- stration	Maximum dose and maximum daily dose
Quinestrol			
Quinethazone			
Quinidine			
Quinidine Bisulphate			
Quinidine Phenylethylbarbiturate			
Quinidine Polygalacturonate			
Quinidine Sulphate			
Quinine			100 mg (MD) 300 mg (MDD)
Quinine Bisulphate			Equivalent of 100 mg of Quinine (MD) Equivalent of 300 mg of Quinine (MDD)
Quinine Dihydrochloride			Equivalent of 100 mg of Quinine (MD) Equivalent of 300 mg of Quinine (MDD)
Quinine Ethyl Carbonate			Equivalent of 100 mg of Quinine (MD) Equivalent of 300 mg of Quinine (MDD)
Quinine Glycerophosphate			Equivalent of 100 mg of Quinine (MD) Equivalent of 300 mg of Quinine (MDD)
Quinine Hydrobromide			Equivalent of 100 mg of Quinine (MD) Equivalent of 300 mg of Quinine (MDD)

(a) Substances added by this order are indicated by the use of bold type.

Sch. 1 (I)

| Column 1 | CIRCUMSTANCES EXCLUDING MEDICINAL PRODUCTS FROM THE CLASS OF PRESCRIPTION ONLY MEDICINES | | |
| | Column 2 | Column 3 | Column 4 |
Substance(a)	Maximum strength	Use, pharma-ceutical form or route of admini-stration	Maximum dose and maximum daily dose
Quinine Hydrochloride			Equivalent of 100 mg of Quinine (MD) Equivalent of 300 mg of Quinine (MDD)
Quinine Iodobismuthate			Equivalent of 100 mg of Quinine (MD) Equivalent of 300 mg of Quinine (MDD)
Quinine Phenylcinchoninate			Equivalent of 100 mg of Quinine (MD) Equivalent of 300 mg of Quinine (MDD)
Quinine Phosphate			Equivalent of 100 mg of Quinine (MD) Equivalent of 300 mg of Quinine (MDD)
Quinine Salicylate			Equivalent of 100 mg of Quinine (MD) Equivalent of 300 mg of Quinine (MDD)
Quinine Sulphate			Equivalent of 100 mg of Quinine (MD) Equivalent of 300 mg of Quinine (MDD)
Quinine Tannate			Equivalent of 100 mg of Quinine (MD) Equivalent of 300 mg of Quinine (MDD)
Quinine and Urea Hydrochloride			
Ranitidine Hydrochloride			
Rauwolfia Serpentina			
Rauwolfia Vomitoria			

(a) Substances added by this order are indicated by the use of bold type.

Sch. 1 (I)

| Column 1 | CIRCUMSTANCES EXCLUDING MEDICINAL PRODUCTS FROM THE CLASS OF PRESCRIPTION ONLY MEDICINES | | |
	Column 2	Column 3	Column 4
Substance(a)	Maximum strength	Use, pharmaceutical form or route of administration	Maximum dose and maximum daily dose
Razoxane			
Reproterol Hydrochloride			
Rescinnamine			
Reserpine			
Rifampicin			
Rifamycin			
Rimiterol Hydrobromide			
Ritodrine Hydrochloride			
Rolitetracycline Nitrate			
Sabadilla			
Salbutamol			
Salbutamol Sulphate			
Salcatonin			
Salcatonin Hydrated Polyacetate			
Salmefamol			
Salsalate			
Secbutobarbitone			
Secbutobarbitone Sodium			
Sera and Antisera—			
Botulin Antitoxin			
Diphtheria Antitoxin			

(a) Substances added by this order are indicated by the use of bold type.

Sch. 1 (I)

| Column 1 | CIRCUMSTANCES EXCLUDING MEDICINAL PRODUCTS FROM THE CLASS OF PRESCRIPTION ONLY MEDICINES | | |
	Column 2	Column 3	Column 4
Substance(a)	Maximum strength	Use, pharma-ceutical form or route of admini-stration	Maximum dose and maximum daily dose
Gas-gangrene Antitoxin (Oedematiens)			
Gas-gangrene Antitoxin (Perfringens)			
Gas-gangrene Antitoxin (Septicum)			
Mixed Gas-gangrene Antitoxin			
Leptospira Antiserum			
Rabies Antiserum			
Scorpion Venom Antiserum			
Snake Venom Antiserum			
Tetanus Antitoxin			
Serum Gonadotrophin			
Silver Sulphadiazine			
Sissomicin			
Sissomicin Sulphate			
Snake Venoms			
Sodium Acetrizoate			
Sodium Aminosalicylate			
Sodium Antimonylgluconate			
Sodium Arsanilate			
Sodium Arsenate			
Sodium Arsenite	0.013 per cent		

(a) Substances added by this order are indicated by the use of bold type.

Sch. 1 (I)

Column 1	CIRCUMSTANCES EXCLUDING MEDICINAL PRODUCTS FROM THE CLASS OF PRESCRIPTION ONLY MEDICINES		
	Column 2	Column 3	Column 4
Substance(a)	Maximum strength	Use, pharmaceutical form or route of administration	Maximum dose and maximum daily dose
Sodium Bromide			
Sodium Cromoglycate		Administration through the nose	
Sodium Ethacrynate			
Sodium Fluoride	(1) 0.33 per cent	(1) Dentifrices	
		(2) Other preparations for use in the prevention of dental caries in the form of:	
		(a) tablets or drops	(a) 2.2 mg (MDD)
	(b) 0.2 per cent	(b) mouth rinses other than those for daily use	
	(c) 0.05 per cent	(c) mouth rinses for daily use	
Sodium Fusidate			
Sodium Metrizoate			
Sodium Monofluorophosphate	1.14 per cent	Dentifrice	
Sodium Stibogluconate			
Sodium Valproate			
Sotalol Hydrochloride			
Spectinomycin			
Spectinomycin Hydrochloride			
Spiramycin			

(a) Substances added by this order are indicated by the use of bold type.

Sch. 1 (I)

| Column 1 | CIRCUMSTANCES EXCLUDING MEDICINAL PRODUCTS FROM THE CLASS OF PRESCRIPTION ONLY MEDICINES | | |
| | Column 2 | Column 3 | Column 4 |
Substance(a)	Maximum strength	Use, pharma-ceutical form or route of admini-stration	Maximum dose and maximum daily dose
Spiramycin Adipate			
Spironolactone			
Stannous Fluoride	0.62 per cent	Dentifrice	
Stanolone			
Stanozolol			
Stilboestrol			
Stilboestrol Dipropionate			
Streptodornase		External	
Streptokinase		External	
Streptomycin			
Streptomycin Sulphate			
Strychnine			
Strychnine Arsenate			
Strychnine Hydrochloride			
Styramate			
Succinylsulphathiazole			
Sucralfate			
Sulfacytine			
Sulfadoxine			
Sulfamonomethoxine			
Sulindac			
Sulphacetamide			

(a) Substances added by this order are indicated by the use of bold type.

Sch. 1 (I)

Column 1	CIRCUMSTANCES EXCLUDING MEDICINAL PRODUCTS FROM THE CLASS OF PRESCRIPTION ONLY MEDICINES		
	Column 2	Column 3	Column 4
Substance(a)	Maximum strength	Use, pharmaceutical form or route of administration	Maximum dose and maximum daily dose
Sulphacetamide Sodium			
Sulphadiazine			
Sulphadiazine Sodium			
Sulphadimethoxine			
Sulphadimidine			
Sulphadimidine Sodium			
Sulphafurazole			
Sulphafurazole Diethanolamine			
Sulphaguanidine			
Sulphaloxic Acid			
Sulphamerazine			
Sulphamerazine Sodium			
Sulphamethizole			
Sulphamethoxazole			
Sulphamethoxydiazine			
Sulphamethoxypyridazine			
Sulphamethoxypyridazine Sodium			
Sulphamoxole			
Sulphanilamide			
Sulphaphenazole			
Sulphapyridine			
Sulphapyridine Sodium			

(a) Substances added by this order are indicated by the use of bold type.

Sch. 1 (I)

| Column 1 | CIRCUMSTANCES EXCLUDING MEDICINAL PRODUCTS FROM THE CLASS OF PRESCRIPTION ONLY MEDICINES | | |
| | Column 2 | Column 3 | Column 4 |
Substance(a)	Maximum strength	Use, pharma- ceutical form or route of admini- stration	Maximum dose and maximum daily dose
Sulphasalazine			
Sulphathiazole			
Sulphathiazole Sodium			
Sulphaurea			
Sulphinpyrazone			
Sulpiride			
Sulthiame			
Sutoprofen			
Suxamethonium Bromide			
Suxamethonium Chloride			
Suxethonium Bromide			
Tacrine Hydrochloride			
Talampicillin			
Talampicillin Hydrochloride			
Talampicillin Napsylate			
Tamoxifen			
Tamoxifen Citrate			
Temazepam			
Terbutaline			
Terbutaline Sulphate			
Testosterone			
Testosterone Acetate			

(a) Substances added by this order are indicated by the use of bold type.

Sch. 1 (I)

Column 1	Column 2	Column 3	Column 4
	CIRCUMSTANCES EXCLUDING MEDICINAL PRODUCTS FROM THE CLASS OF PRESCRIPTION ONLY MEDICINES		
Substance(a)	Maximum strength	Use, pharmaceutical form or route of administration	Maximum dose and maximum daily dose
Testosterone 17B Chloral Hemiacetal			
Testosterone Cyclohexylpropionate			
Testosterone Cypionate			
Testosterone Decanoate			
Testosterone Enanthate			
Testosterone Isocaproate			
Testosterone Phenylpropionate			
Testosterone Propionate			
Testosterone Undecanoate			
Tetrabenazine			
Tetracosactrin			
Tetracosactrin Acetate			
Tetracycline			
Tetracycline Hydrochloride			
Tetracycline Phosphate Complex			
Thallium Acetate			
Thallous Chloride			
Thiambutosine			
Thiethylperazine			
Thiethylperazine Malate			
Thiethylperazine Maleate			

(a) Substances added by this order are indicated by the use of bold type.

Sch. 1 (I)

Column 1	CIRCUMSTANCES EXCLUDING MEDICINAL PRODUCTS FROM THE CLASS OF PRESCRIPTION ONLY MEDICINES		
	Column 2	Column 3	Column 4
Substance(a)	Maximum strength	Use, pharmaceutical form or route of administration	Maximum dose and maximum daily dose
Thiocarlide			
Thioguanine			
Thiopentone Sodium			
Thiopropazate Hydrochloride			
Thioproperazine Mesylate			
Thioridazine			
Thioridazine Hydrochloride			
Thiosinamine			
Thiotepa			
Thiothixene			
Thiouracil			
Thymoxamine Hydrochloride			
Thyroid			
Thyrotrophin			
Thyroxine Sodium			
Tiamulin Fumarate			
Ticarcillin Sodium			
Tigloidine Hydrobromide			
Timolol Maleate			
Tinidazole			
Tobramycin Sulphate			
Tocainide Hydrochloride			

(a) Substances added by this order are indicated by the use of bold type.

Sch. 1 (I)

Column 1	CIRCUMSTANCES EXCLUDING MEDICINAL PRODUCTS FROM THE CLASS OF PRESCRIPTION ONLY MEDICINES		
	Column 2	Column 3	Column 4
Substance(a)	Maximum strength	Use, pharmaceutical form or route of administration	Maximum dose and maximum daily dose
Tofenacin Hydrochloride			
Tolazamide			
Tolazoline Hydrochloride		External	
Tolbutamide			
Tolbutamide Sodium			
Tolmetin Sodium			
Tranexamic Acid			
Tranylcypromine Sulphate			
Trazodone Hydrochloride			
Treosulfan			
Tretinoin			
Triamcinolone			
Triamcinolone Acetonide			
Triamcinolone Diacetate			
Triamcinolone Hexacetonide			
Triamterene			
Triazolam			
Triclofos Sodium			
Trifluoperazine			
Trifluoperazine Hydrochloride			
Trifluperidol			
Trifluperidol Hydrochloride			

(a) Substances added by this order are indicated by the use of bold type.

Sch. 1 (I)

| Column 1 | CIRCUMSTANCES EXCLUDING MEDICINAL PRODUCTS FROM THE CLASS OF PRESCRIPTION ONLY MEDICINES | | |
	Column 2	Column 3	Column 4
Substance(a)	Maximum strength	Use, pharmaceutical form or route of administration	Maximum dose and maximum daily dose
Trilostane			
Trimeprazine			
Trimeprazine Tartrate			
Trimetaphan Camsylate			
Trimetazidine			
Trimetazidine Hydrochloride			
Trimethoprim			
Trimipramine Maleate			
Trimipramine Mesylate			
Tropicamide			
Troxidone			
L-Tryptophan		(1) Dietary or nutritive use (2) Any external use	
Tubocurarine Chloride			
Tyrothricin		Throat lozenges or throat pastilles	
Uramustine			
Urea Stibamine			
Urethane			
Uridine-5-Triphosphoric Acid			
Urofollitrophin			
Urokinase			
Ursodeoxycholic Acid			

(a) Substances added by this order are indicated by the use of bold type.

Sch. 1 (I)

	CIRCUMSTANCES EXCLUDING MEDICINAL PRODUCTS FROM THE CLASS OF PRESCRIPTION ONLY MEDICINES		
Column 1	Column 2	Column 3	Column 4
Substance(a)	Maximum strength	Use, pharmaceutical form or route of administration	Maximum dose and maximum daily dose
Vaccines— **Anthrax Vaccine (Bacillus Anthracis)**			
Bacillus Calmette-Guerin Vaccine			
Percutaneous Bacillus Calmette-Guerin Vaccine			
Cholera Vaccine			
Diphtheria Vaccine			
Adsorbed Diphtheria Vaccine			
Diphtheria and Tetanus Vaccine			
Adsorbed Diphtheria and Tetanus Vaccine			
Diphtheria, Tetanus and Pertussis Vaccine			
Adsorbed Diphtheria, Tetanus and Pertussis Vaccine			
Diphtheria, Tetanus and Poliomyelitis Vaccine			
Diphtheria, Tetanus, Pertussis and Poliomyelitis Vaccine			
Eltor Vaccine			
Influenza Vaccine			
Measles Vaccine (Live Attenuated)			
Pertussis Vaccine			
Plague Vaccine			

(a) Substances added by this order are indicated by the use of bold type.

Sch. 1 (I)

| Column 1 | CIRCUMSTANCES EXCLUDING MEDICINAL PRODUCTS FROM THE CLASS OF PRESCRIPTION ONLY MEDICINES | | |
	Column 2	Column 3	Column 4
Substance(a)	Maximum strength	Use, pharmaceutical form or route of administration	Maximum dose and maximum daily dose
Pneumococcal Vaccine (Bacterial Antigen)			
Poliomyelitis Vaccine (Inactivated)			
Poliomyelitis Vaccine (Oral)			
Rabies Vaccine			
Rubella Vaccine (Live Attenuated)			
Smallpox Vaccine			
Dried Smallpox Vaccine			
Schick Control			
Schick Test Toxin			
Tetanus Vaccine			
Adsorbed Tetanus Vaccine			
Tetanus and Pertussis Vaccine			
Tuberculin Purified Protein Derivative			
Old Tuberculin			
Typhoid Vaccine			
Typhoid and Tetanus Vaccine			
Typhoid – paratyphoid A and B Vaccine			
Typhoid – paratyphoid A and B and Cholera Vaccine			
Typhoid – paratyphoid A and B and Tetanus Vaccine			

(a) Substances added by this order are indicated by the use of bold type.

Sch. 1 (I)

| Column 1 | Circumstances Excluding Medicinal Products from the Class of Prescription Only Medicines | | |
	Column 2	Column 3	Column 4
Substance(a)	Maximum strength	Use, pharmaceutical form or route of administration	Maximum dose and maximum daily dose
Typhus Vaccine			
Yellow Fever Vaccine			
Valproic Acid			
Vancomycin Hydrochloride			
Vasopressin Injection			
Vasopressin Tannate			
Verapamil Hydrochloride			
Veratrine			
Veratrum (Green and White)			
Vidarabine			
Viloxazine Hydrochloride			
Vinblastine Sulphate			
Vincristine Sulphate			
Vindesine Sulphate			
Viomycin Pantothenate			
Viomycin Sulphate			
Warfarin			
Warfarin Sodium			
Xipamide			
Yohimbine Hydrochloride			

(a) Substances added by this order are indicated by the use of bold type.

Sch. 1 (I)

	CIRCUMSTANCES EXCLUDING MEDICINAL PRODUCTS FROM THE CLASS OF PRESCRIPTION ONLY MEDICINES		
Column 1	Column 2	Column 3	Column 4
Substance(a)	Maximum strength	Use, pharma-ceutical form or route of admini-stration	Maximum dose and maximum daily dose
Zimeldine Hydrochloride			
Zomepirac Sodium			

Note: In relation to a medicinal product which contains more than one of the substances Atropine, Atropine Methobromide, Atropine Methonitrate, Atropine Oxide Hydrochloride, Atropine Sulphate, Hyoscine, Hyoscine Butylbromide, Hyoscine Hydrobromide, Hyoscine Methobromide, Hyoscine Methonitrate, Hyoscyamine, Hyoscyamine Hydrobromide or Hyoscyamine Sulphate, for the purposes of column 4, the maximum daily dose is 1 mg of the total alkaloids contained in the product which are derived from belladonna, hyoscyamus, stramonium or other solanaceous plant, and there is no maximum dose.

(a) Substances added by this order are indicated by the use of bold type.

Articles 3(1)*(b)* and 4(2)   PART II

	CIRCUMSTANCES EXCLUDING MEDICINAL PRODUCTS FROM THE CLASS OF PRESCRIPTION ONLY MEDICINES		
Column 1	Column 2	Column 3	Column 4
Substance	Maximum strength	Pharmaceutical form	Maximum dose
Codeine; its salts	Equivalent of 1.5 per cent of Codeine		Equivalent of 20 mg of Codeine
Dihydrocodeine; its salts	Equivalent of 1.5 per cent of Dihydro-codeine		Equivalent of 10 mg of Dihydrocodeine
Ethylmorphine; its salts	Equivalent of 0.2 per cent of Ethyl-morphine		Equivalent of 7.5 mg of Ethylmorphine
Morphine; its salts	(1) Equiv-alent of 0.02 per cent of anhydrous morphine	(1) Liquid	(1) Equivalent of 3 mg of anhydrous morphine
	(2) Equiv-alent of 0.04 per cent of anhydrous morphine; equivalent of 300 mcg of anhydr-ous morphine	(2) Solid	(2) Equivalent of 3 mg of anhydrous morphine
Medicinal Opium	(1) Equiv-alent of 0.02 per cent of anhydrous morphine	(1) Liquid	(1) Equivalent of 3 mg of anhydrous morphine
	(2) Equiv-alent of 0.04 per cent of anhydrous morphine	(2) Solid	(2) Equivalent of 3 mg of anhydrous morphine

Sch. 1 (II)

	CIRCUMSTANCES EXCLUDING MEDICINAL PRODUCTS FROM THE CLASS OF PRESCRIPTION ONLY MEDICINES		
Column 1	Column 2	Column 3	Column 4
Substance	Maximum strength	Pharmaceutical form	Maximum dose
Pholcodine; its salts	Equivalent of 1.5 per cent of Pholcodine		Equivalent of 20 mg of Pholcodine

Article 3(1)*(c)* PART III

NAME AND PRODUCT LICENCE NUMBER OF MEDICINAL PRODUCTS

Ancoloxin
0021/5060

Anhydrol Forte
0173/0030

Cedocard 20
0424/0036

Debendox
0027/5001

Debrisan
0009/0021

Mucaine
0011/5014

Nicorette
0458/0020
0458/0021

Perstorp Dextrinomer Iodine
3863/0001

SCHEDULE 2   Article 6(4)(c)

SUBSTANCES NOT TO BE CONTAINED IN A PRESCRIPTION ONLY MEDICINE SOLD
OR SUPPLIED UNDER THE EXEMPTION CONFERRED BY ARTICLE 6(3)

Ammonium Bromide
Amylobarbitone
Amylobarbitone Sodium
Barbitone
Barbitone Sodium
Butobarbitone
Butobarbitone Sodium
Calcium Bromide
Calcium Bromidolactobionate
Cyclobarbitone
Cyclobarbitone Calcium
Embutramide
Fencamfamin Hydrochloride
Fluanisone
Heptabarbitone
Hexobarbitone
Hexobarbitone Sodium
Hydrobromic Acid
Meclofenoxate Hydrochloride
Methohexitone Sodium
Methylphenobarbitone

Pemoline
Pentobarbitone
Pentobarbitone Sodium
Phenobarbitone
Phenobarbitone Sodium
Phentermine Hydrochloride
Phentermine Resin Complex
Phenylmethylbarbituric Acid
Piracetam
Potassium Bromide
Prolintane Hydrochloride
Quinalbarbitone
Quinalbarbitone Sodium
Quinidine Phenylethylbarbiturate
Secbutobarbitone
Secbutobarbitone Sodium
Sodium Bromide
Strychnine Hydrochloride
Tacrine Hydrochloride
Thiopentone Sodium

SCHEDULE 3

EXEMPTION FOR CERTAIN PERSONS FROM SECTION 58(2) OF THE ACT

Article 9(1)*(a)*   PART I

Column 1	Column 2	Column 3
Persons exempted	Prescription only medicines to which the exemption applies	Conditions
1. Persons selling or supplying prescription only medicines to universities, other institutions concerned with higher education or institutions concerned with research.	**1.** All prescription only medicines.	**1.** The sale or supply shall be— *(a)* subject to the presentation of an order signed by the principal of the institution concerned with education or research or the appropriate head of department in charge of a specified course of research stating— (i) the name of the institution for which the prescription only medicine is required, (ii) the purpose for which the prescription only medicine is required, and (iii) the total quantity required, and *(b)* for the purposes of the education or research with which the institution is concerned.
2. Persons selling or supplying prescription only medicines to any of the following— (1) a public analyst appointed under section 89 of the Food and Drugs	**2.** All prescription only medicines.	**2.** The sale or supply shall be subject to the presentation of an order signed by or on behalf of any person listed in sub-paragraphs (1), (2), (3) or (4) of column 1 of this paragraph stating the status

Sch. 3 (I)

Column 1	Column 2	Column 3
Persons exempted	Prescription only medicines to which the exemption applies	Conditions
Act 1955(**a**), section 27 of the Food and Drugs (Scotland) Act 1956(**b**) or section 31 of the Food and Drugs Act (Northern Ireland) 1958(**c**), (2) a sampling officer within the meaning of the Food and Drugs Act 1955, the Food and Drugs (Scotland) Act 1956 or the Food and Drugs Act (Northern Ireland) 1958, (3) a person duly authorised by an enforcement authority under sections 111 and 112, or (4) a sampling officer within the meaning of Schedule 3 to the Act.		of the person signing it and the amount of the prescription only medicine required, and shall be only in connection with the exercise by those persons of their statutory functions.
3. Persons selling or supplying prescription only medicines to any person employed or engaged in connection with a scheme for testing the quality and checking the amount of the drugs and appliances supplied under the National Health Service Act 1977(**d**), the National Health Service (Scotland) Act 1978(**e**) and the Health and Personal Social Services (Northern Ireland) Order 1972(**f**), or under any subordinate legislation made under those Acts or that order.	**3.** All prescription only medicines.	**3.** The sale or supply shall be— *(a)* subject to the presentation of an order signed by or on behalf of the person so employed or engaged stating the status of the person signing it and the amount of prescription only medicine required, and *(b)* for the purposes of a scheme referred to in column 1 in this paragraph.

(**a**) 1955 c. 16.
(**b**) 1956 c. 30.
(**c**) 1958 c. 27 (N.I.).
(**d**) 1977 c. 49.
(**e**) 1978 c. 29.
(**f**) S.I. 1972/1265 (N.I. 14).

Sch. 3 (I)

Column 1	Column 2	Column 3
Persons exempted	Prescription only medicines to which the exemption applies	Conditions
4. Registered midwives.	**4.** Prescription only medicines containing any of the following substances— Chloral hydrate Dichloralphenazone Ergometrine maleate Pentazocine hydrochloride Triclofos sodium.	**4.** The sale or supply shall be only in the course of their professional practice and in the case of Ergometrine maleate only when contained in a medicinal product which is not for parenteral administration.
5. Persons lawfully conducting a retail pharmacy business within the meaning of section 69.	**5.** Prescription only medicines which are not for parenteral administration and which— *(a)* are eye drops or eye ointments and are prescription only medicines by reason only that they contain: (i) Mafenide propionate, (ii) not more than 30.0 per cent Sulphacetamide Sodium, or (iii) Sulphafurazole diethanolamine equivalent to not more than 4.0 per cent Sulphafurazole, or *(b)* are prescription only medicines by reason only that they contain any of the following substances: Atropine sulphate	**5.** The sale or supply shall be subject to the presentation of an order signed by a registered ophthalmic optician.

Sch. 3 (I)

Column 1	Column 2	Column 3
Persons exempted	Prescription only medicines to which the exemption applies	Conditions
	Bethanecol chloride Carbachol Cyclopentolate hydrochloride Homatropine hydrobromide Hyoscine hydrobromide Naphazoline hydrochloride Naphazoline nitrate Neostigmine methylsulphate Physostigmine salicylate Physostigmine sulphate Pilocarpine hydrochloride Pilocarpine nitrate Tropicamide.	
6. Registered ophthalmic opticians.	6. Prescription only medicines listed in column 2 of paragraph 5.	6. The sale or supply shall be only— (a) in the course of their professional practice, and (b) in an emergency.
7. Persons selling or supplying prescription only medicines to the British Standards Institution.	7. All prescription only medicines.	7. The sale or supply shall be— (a) subject to the presentation of an order signed on behalf of the British Standards Institution stating the status of the person signing it and the amount of the prescription only medicine required, and

Sch. 3 (I)

Column 1	Column 2	Column 3
Persons exempted	Prescription only medicines to which the exemption applies	Conditions
		(b) only for the purpose of testing containers of medicinal products or determining the standards for such containers.
8. Holders of product licences and holders of manufacturer's licences.	**8.** Prescription only medicines referred to in the licences.	**8.** The sale or supply shall be only—
		(a) to a pharmacist,
		(b) so as to enable that pharmacist to prepare an entry relating to the prescription only medicine in question in a tablet or capsule identification guide or similar publication, and
		(c) of no greater quantity than is reasonably necessary for that purpose.

PART II

Article 9(1)*(b)*

Column 1	Column 2	Column 3
Persons exempted	Prescription only medicines to which the exemption applies	Conditions
1. Royal National Lifeboat Institution and certificated first aiders of the Institution.	**1.** All prescription only medicines.	**1.** The supply shall be only so far as is necessary for the treatment of sick or injured persons.
2. The owner or the master of a ship which does not carry a doctor on board as part of her complement.	**2.** All prescription only medicines.	**2.** The supply shall be only so far as is necessary for the treatment of persons on the ship.
3. Persons authorised by licences granted under regulation 5 of the Misuse of Drugs Regulations to supply a controlled drug.	**3.** Such prescription only medicines, being controlled drugs, as are specified in the licence.	**3.** The supply shall be subject to such conditions and in such circumstances and to such an extent as may be specified in the licence.
4. Persons requiring prescription only medicines for the purpose of enabling them, in the course of any business carried on by them, to comply with any requirements made by or in pursuance of any enactment with respect to the medical treatment of their employees.	**4.** Such prescription only medicines as may be specified in the relevant enactment.	**4.** The supply shall be— *(a)* for the purpose of enabling them to comply with any requirements made by or in pursuance of any such enactment, and *(b)* subject to such conditions and in such circumstances as may be specified in the relevant enactment.
5. Persons operating an occupational health scheme.	**5.** Prescription only medicines sold or supplied to a person operating an occupational health scheme in response to an order in writing signed by a doctor or a registered nurse.	**5.**—(1) The supply shall be in the course of an occupational health scheme. (2) The individual supplying the prescription only medicine, if not a doctor, shall be a registered nurse acting in accordance with the written instructions of a doctor as to the circumstances in which prescription only medicines of the description in question are to be used in the course of the occupational health scheme.

Sch. 3 (II)

Column 1	Column 2	Column 3
Persons exempted	Prescription only medicines to which the exemption applies	Conditions
6. The operator or commander of an aircraft.	**6.** Prescription only medicines which are not for parenteral administration and which have been sold or supplied to the operator or commander of the aircraft in response to an order in writing signed by a doctor.	**6.** The supply shall be only so far as is necessary for the immediate treatment of sick or injured persons on the aircraft and shall be in accordance with the written instructions of a doctor as to the circumstances in which prescription only medicines of the description in question are to be used on the aircraft.

PART III   Article 9(2)

Column 1	Column 2	Column 3
Persons exempted	Prescription only medicines to which the exemption applies	Conditions
1. State registered chiropodists who hold a certificate of competence in the use of analgesics issued by or with the approval of the Chiropodists Board.	1. Prescription only medicines for parenteral administration that contain, as the sole active ingredient, not more than one of the following substances— Bupivacaine hydrochloride Lignocaine hydrochloride Mepivacaine hydrochloride Prilocaine hydrochloride.	1. The administration shall be only in the course of their professional practice.
2. Registered Midwives.	2. Prescription only medicines for parenteral administration containing any of the following substances but no other substance specified in column 1 of Schedule 1 to this order— Ergometrine maleate Levallorphan tartrate Lignocaine Lignocaine hydrochloride Naloxone hydrochloride Oxytocins, natural and synthetic Pentazocine lactate Pethidine Pethidine hydrochloride Phytomenadione Promazine hydrochloride.	2. The administration shall be only in the course of their professional practice and in the case of Promazine hydrochloride, Lignocaine and Lignocaine hydrochloride shall be only while attending on a woman in childbirth.
3. Persons who are authorised as members of a group by a group authority granted under regulations 8(3) or 9(3) of the Misuse of Drugs Regulations to supply a controlled drug by way of administration only.	3. Prescription only medicines that are specified in the group authority.	3. The administration shall be subject to such conditions and in such circumstances and to such extent as may be specified in the group authority.

Sch. 3 (III)

Column 1	Column 2	Column 3
Persons exempted	Prescription only medicines to which the exemption applies	Conditions
4. The owner or the master of a ship which does not carry a doctor on board as part of her complement.	**4.** All prescription only medicines that are for parenteral administration.	**4.** The administration shall be only so far as is necessary for the treatment of persons on the ship.
5. Persons operating an occupational health scheme.	**5.** Prescription only medicines for parenteral administration sold or supplied to the person operating an occupational health scheme in response to an order in writing signed by a doctor or a registered nurse.	**5.**—(1) The administration shall be in the course of an occupational health scheme. (2) The individual administering the prescription only medicine, if neither a doctor nor acting in accordance with the directions of a doctor, shall be a registered nurse acting in accordance with the written instructions of a doctor as to the circumstances in which prescription only medicines of the description in question are to be used in the course of the occupational health scheme.
6. The operator or commander of an aircraft.	**6.** Prescription only medicines for parenteral administration which have been sold or supplied to the operator or commander of the aircraft in response to an order in writing signed by a doctor.	**6.** The administration shall be only so far as is necessary for the immediate treatment of sick or injured persons on the aircraft and shall be in accordance with the written instructions of a doctor as to the circumstances in which prescription only medicines of the description in question are to be used on the aircraft.
7. Persons who are, and at 11th February 1982 were, persons customarily administering medicinal products to human beings by parenteral administration in the course of a business in the field of osteopathy, naturopathy, acupuncture or other similar field except chiropody.	**7.** Medicinal products that are prescription only medicines by reason only that they fall within the class specified in Article 3(1)*(d)* (products for parenteral administration).	**7.** The person administering the prescription only medicine shall have been requested by or on behalf of the person to whom it is administered and in that person's presence to use his own judgment as to the treatment required.

SCHEDULE 4   Article 13(1)

ORDERS REVOKED

Column 1 Orders Revoked	Column 2 References
The Medicines (Prescription Only) Order 1980	S.I. 1980/1921
The Medicines (Prescription Only) Amendment Order 1981	S.I. 1981/80
The Medicines (Prescription Only) Amendment Order 1982	S.I. 1982/29
The Medicines (Prescription Only) Amendment (No. 2) Order 1982	S.I. 1982/1596
The Medicines (Prescription Only) Amendment (No. 3) Order 1982	S.I. 1982/1801
The Medicines (Prescription Only) Amendment Order 1983	S.I. 1983/341
The Medicines (Prescription Only) Amendment (No. 2) Order 1983	S.I. 1983/957

EXPLANATORY NOTE
(This Note is not part of the Order.)

This Order re-enacts, with amendments, the provisions of the Medicines (Prescription Only) Order 1980 and its amending instruments, which are revoked. The Order specifies descriptions and classes of medicinal products which may be sold or supplied by retail only in accordance with a prescription given by a doctor, dentist, veterinary surgeon or veterinary practitioner and which may be administered only by or in accordance with the directions of such a person. The Order also confers exemptions from those restrictions and prescribes conditions which must be fulfilled if a sale or supply is to be taken as being in accordance with a prescription.

The principal changes made by the Order are—

(a) that the medicinal products, the descriptions and classes of which are specified, no longer include products which are veterinary drugs within the meaning given in section 132(1) of the Medicines Act 1968 (such products are now included in the Medicines (Veterinary Drugs) (Prescription Only) Order 1983 (S.I. 1983/1213)), and

(b) changes (including additions and omissions) in and relating to the list of substances (in column 1 of Part I of Schedule 1) which, if contained in a medicinal product, make that product a prescription only medicine and changes to the list of named products (in Part III of Schedule 1) which are prescription only medicines.

Where a substance or product appears in such a list for the first time it is shown in Schedule 1 in bold type, except where the addition results solely from a change in name. There are also various consequential and minor changes.

STATUTORY INSTRUMENTS

1983 No. 1213

MEDICINES

The Medicines (Veterinary Drugs) (Prescription Only) Order 1983

Made - - - -	*3rd August* 1983
Laid before Parliament	*24th August* 1983
Coming into Operation	14*th September* 1983

The Secretary of State concerned with health in England, the Secretaries of State respectively concerned with health and with agriculture in Scotland and in Wales, the Minister of Agriculture, Fisheries and Food, the Department of Health and Social Services for Northern Ireland, and the Department of Agriculture for Northern Ireland, acting jointly, in exercise of powers conferred by sections 58(1) and (4) and 59 of the Medicines Act 1968(a) and now vested in them (b) and of all other powers enabling them in that behalf, after consulting such organisations as appear to them to be representative of interests likely to be substantially affected by the following order in accordance with section 129(6) of the said Act, and after consulting and taking into account the advice of the Veterinary Products Committee in accordance with sections 58(6) and 129(7) of the said Act, hereby make the following order:—

Title, commencement and interpretation

1.—(1) This order may be cited as the Medicines (Veterinary Drugs) (Prescription Only) Order 1983 and shall come into operation on 14th September 1983.

(2) In this order, unless the context otherwise requires,—

(*a*) "the Act" means the Medicines Act 1968;

"controlled drug" has the meaning assigned to it by section 2 of the Misuse of Drugs Act 1971(**c**);

"dosage unit" means—

(i) where a veterinary drug is in the form of a tablet or capsule or is an article in some other similar pharmaceutical form, that tablet, capsule or other article, or

---

(**a**) 1968 c. 67.
(**b**) In the case of the Secretaries of State concerned with health in England and Wales by virtue of S.I. 1969/388, in the case of the Secretary of State concerned with agriculture in Wales by virtue of S.I. 1978/272 and in the case of the Northern Ireland Departments by virtue of section 40 of, and Schedule 5 to, the Northern Ireland Constitution Act 1973 (c. 36) and section 1(3) of, and paragraph 2(1)*(b)* of Schedule 1 to, the Northern Ireland Act 1974 (c. 28).
(**c**) 1971 c. 38.

(ii) where a veterinary drug is not in any such form, that quantity of the drug which is used as the unit by reference to which the dose is measured;

"external use" means application to the skin, hair, fur, feathers, scales, hoof, horn, ear, eye, mouth or mucosa of the throat or prepuce;

"inhaler" does not include an aerosol;

"maximum daily dose" or "MDD" means the maximum quantity of a substance contained in the amount of a veterinary drug for internal use which it is recommended should be taken or administered in any period of 24 hours;

"maximum dose" or "MD" means the maximum quantity of a substance contained in the amount of a veterinary drug for internal use which it is recommended should be taken or administered at any one time;

"maximum strength" means such of the following as may be specified—

(i) the maximum quantity of a substance by weight or volume contained in a dosage unit of a veterinary drug,

(ii) the maximum percentage of a substance contained in a veterinary drug calculated in terms of weight in weight (w/w), weight in volume (w/v), volume in weight (v/w) or volume in volume (v/v), as appropriate, and

(iii) the maximum amount of a substance contained in a stated weight of a veterinary drug calculated in terms of international units (iu) of biologically determined potency;

"the Misuse of Drugs Regulations" means, in relation to England, Wales and Scotland, the Misuse of Drugs Regulations 1973(a) and, in relation to Northern Ireland, the Misuse of Drugs (Northern Ireland) Regulations 1974(b);

"parenteral administration" means administration to an animal by breach of the skin or mucous membrane;

"prescription only medicine" means a medicinal product of a description or falling within a class specified in Article 3;

"repeatable prescription" means a prescription which contains a direction that it may be dispensed more than once;

"sell" means sell by retail as defined in section 131 and "sale" has a corresponding meaning;

"soap" means any compound of a fatty acid with an alkali or amine;

"supply" means supply in circumstances corresponding to retail sale as defined in section 131;

"unit preparation" means a preparation, including a mother tincture, prepared by a process of solution, extraction or trituration with a view to being diluted tenfold or one hundredfold, either once or repeatedly, in an inert diluent, and then used either in this diluted form or, where

(a) S.I. 1973/797; relevant amending instruments are S.I. 1975/499, 1623, 1977/1380 and 1979/326.
(b) S.R. (N.I.) 1974 No. 272, amended by S.R. (N.I.) 1975 Nos. 140, 326 and 1977 No. 290.

applicable, by impregnating tablets, granules, powders or other insert substances for the purpose of being administered to animals;

"the Veterinary Drugs Exemption Order" means the Medicines (Exemptions from Restrictions on the Retail Sale or Supply of Veterinary Drugs) Order 1979(a); and

(b) a reference—

(i) to a numbered section is to the section of the Act which bears that number,

(ii) to a numbered Article or Schedule is to the Article of, or Schedule to, this order which bears that number,

(iii) in an Article or in a Part of a Schedule to a numbered paragraph is to the paragraph of that Article or that Part of that Schedule which bears that number, and

(iv) in a paragraph to a lettered sub-paragraph is to the sub-paragraph of that paragraph which bears that letter.

(3) In Schedule 1—

(a) entries specified in columns 2, 3 and 4 of Parts I and II relate to the substances listed in column 1 against which they appear and where, in relation to a particular substance listed in column 1, an entry in column 2, 3 or 4 bears a number or letter it relates only to such entries in the other of those columns as bear the same number or letter;

(b) the entries in column 4 of Part I shall be read subject to the note at the end of that Part; and

(c) the following abbreviations are used:

"g" for gram,

"mcg" for microgram,

"mg" for milligram,

"ml" for millilitre.

Appropriate practitioners

2. For the purposes of section 58 (medicinal products on prescription only), veterinary surgeons and veterinary practitioners shall be appropriate practitioners in relation to all the descriptions and classes of medicinal products specified for the purposes of that section in Article 3.

Medicinal products on prescription only

3.—(1) There are hereby specified descriptions and classes of medicinal products for the purposes of section 58, namely—

(a) subject to Article 4(1) and (2), veterinary drugs consisting of or containing a substance listed in column 1 or Part I of Schedule 1;

(b) veterinary drugs that are controlled drugs;

(a) S.I. 1979/45; relevant amending instruments are S.I. 1980/283, 1981/793 and 1983/274.

(c) veterinary drugs specified in Part II of Schedule 1;

(d) subject to Article 4(2), veterinary drugs for parenteral administration whether or not they fall within sub-paragraph *(a)* or *(b)*;

(e) veterinary drugs—

    (i) which are not of a description and do not fall within a class specified in any of sub-paragraphs *(a), (b), (c)* or *(d),*

    (ii) which are of a description in respect of which the conditions specified in Section 59(1) are fulfilled, and

    (iii) in respect of which a product licence is granted after the date of coming into operation of this order containing a provision to the effect that the method of sale or supply of the veterinary drug is to be only in accordance with a prescription given by an appropriate practitioner;

(f) medicinal products which are veterinary drugs by reason of their having been sold or supplied for administration to animals and which, prior to such sale or supply, were prescription only medicines as defined in Article 1(2) of the Medicines (Products Other Than Veterinary Drugs) (Prescription Only) Order 1983**(a)**.

(2) For the purposes of section 59(2)*(a)* (duration of restrictions for certain new products) the duration shall be a period of five years.

Medicinal products that are not prescription only

4.—(1) Notwithstanding Article 3(1)*(a),* a veterinary drug shall not be a prescription only medicine by reason that it consists of or contains a particular substance listed in column 1 of Part I of Schedule 1 where—

(a) in relation to that substance there is an entry in one or more of columns 2, 3 and 4;

(b) the maximum strength in the drug of that substance does not exceed the maximum strength, if any, specified in column 2; and

(c) the veterinary drug is sold or supplied—

    (i) if a pharmaceutical form or a route of administration is specified in column 3, in such pharmaceutical form, and for administration only by such route, as may be so specified,

    (ii) if a use is specified in column 3, in a container package labelled to show a use so specified to which the veterinary drug is to be put but no use not so specified, and

    (iii) if a maximum dose or a maximum daily dose is specified in column 4, in a container or package labelled to show, where a maximum dose is specified, a maximum dose not exceeding that specified, and, where a maximum daily dose is specified, a maximum daily dose not exceeding that specified.

(2) Notwithstanding Article 3(1)*(a)* and *(d),* a veterinary drug for parenteral administration consisting of or containing a substance listed in column 1 of

---

(**a**) S.I. 1983/1212.

Schedule 2 shall not be a prescription only medicine where the maximum strength of that substance does not exceed the maximum strength, if any, specified in column 2 and the veterinary drug in question is sold or supplied only for the purpose or in the circumstances specified in column 3.

Exemption for medicinal products at high dilutions

5. The restrictions imposed by section 58(2) (restrictions on sale, supply and administration) shall not apply to the sale, supply or administration of a veterinary drug which is not for parenteral administration and which consists of or contains, of the substances listed in column 1 of Part I of Schedule 1, only one or more unit preparations of such substances, if—

(a) each such unit preparation has been diluted to at least one part in a million (6x), and the person selling, supplying or administering the veterinary drug has been requested by or on behalf of a particular person and in that person's presence to use his own judgment as to the treatment required, or

(b) each such unit preparation has been diluted to at least one part in a million million (6c).

Exemptions for certain persons

6.—(1) The restrictions imposed by section 58(2)*(a)* (restrictions on sale and supply) shall not apply—

(a) to the sale or supply by a person listed in column 1 of Part I of Schedule 3, or

(b) to the supply by a person listed in column 1 of Part II or Schedule 3,

of the prescription only medicines listed in column 2 of Part I or Part II, as the case may be, of Schedule 3 in relation to that person if and so long as the conditions specified in the corresponding paragraphs in column 3 of Part I or Part II, as the case may be, of Schedule 4 are fulfilled.

(2) The restriction imposed by section 58(2)*(b)* (restriction on administration) shall not apply to the administration by a person listed in column 1 of Part III of Schedule 3 of the prescription only medicines for parenteral administration listed in column 2 of that Part in relation to that person if and so long as the conditions specified in the corresponding paragraphs in column 3 of that Part are fulfilled.

Exemption in cases involving another's default

7. The restrictions imposed by section 58(2)*(a)* (restrictions on sale and supply) shall not apply to the sale or supply of a prescription only medicine by a person who, having exercised all due diligence, believes on reasonable grounds that the product sold or supplied is not a prescription only medicine, where it is due to the act or default of another person that the product is a product to which section 58(2)*(a)* applies.

Prescriptions

8.—(1) For the purposes of sections 58(2)*(a)* a prescription only medicine shall not be taken to be sold or supplied in accordance with a prescription given by an appropriate practitioner unless the conditions specified in paragraph (2) are fulfilled.

(2) The conditions referred to in paragraph (1) are that the prescription—

(a) shall be signed in ink with his own name by the veterinary surgeon or veterinary practitioner giving it;

(b) shall, without prejudice to sub-paragraph *(a)*, be written in ink or otherwise so as to be indelible;

(c) shall contain the following particulars—

(i) the address of the veterinary surgeon or veterinary practitioner giving it,

(ii) the appropriate date,

(iii) such particulars as indicate whether it is given by a veterinary surgeon or veterinary practitioner, and

(iv) the name and address of the person to whom the prescription only medicine is to be delivered and a declaration by the veterinary surgeon or veterinary practitioner giving it that the prescription only medicine is prescribed for an animal or herd under his care;

(d) shall not be dispensed after the end of the period of six months from the appropriate date, unless it is a repeatable prescription in which case it shall not be dispensed for the first time after the end of that period nor otherwise than in accordance with the direction contained in the repeatable prescription;

(e) in the case of a repeatable prescription that does not specify the number of times it may be dispensed, shall not be dispensed on more than two occasions.

(3) The restrictions imposed by section 58(2)*(a)* (restrictions on sale and supply) shall not apply to a sale or supply of a prescription only medicine which is not in accordance with a prescription given by an appropriate practitioner by reason only that a condition specified in paragraph (2) is not fulfilled, where the person selling or supplying the prescription only medicine, having exercised all due diligence, believes on reasonable grounds that that condition is fulfilled in relation to that sale or supply.

(4) In paragraph (2) "the appropriate date" means the date on which the prescription was signed by the veterinary surgeon or practitioner giving it.

Transitional provision

9. Where, immediately before the coming into operation of this order, the restrictions imposed by section 58 applied to the sale, supply or administration of a medicinal product of a particular description by reason that the product fell within the class specified in Article 3(1)*(e)* (certain new products) of the Medicines (Prescription Only) Order 1980(**a**) those restrictions shall continue to apply to products of that description as though Article 3(1)*(e)* and (2) of that order had remained in force.

(**a**) S.I. 1980/1921; relevant amending instrument is S.I. 1982/29.

Signed by authority of the Secretary of State for Social Services.

K. Clarke,
Minister of State,
26th July 1983. Department of Health and Social Security.

George Younger,
28th July 1983. Secretary of State for Scotland.

John Stradling Thomas,
28th July 1983. Minister of State for Wales.

In witness whereof the official seal of the Minister of Agriculture, Fisheries and Food is hereunto affixed on 28th July 1983.

Michael Jopling,
Minister of Agriculture, Fisheries and Food.

Sealed with the official seal of the Department of Health and Social Services for Northern Ireland this 3rd day of August 1983.

N. Dugdale,
Permanent Secretary.

Sealed with the official seal of the Department of Agriculture for Northern Ireland this 3rd day of August 1983.

W. H. Jack,
Permanent Secretary.

SCHEDULE 1

DESCRIPTIONS AND CLASSES OF PRESCRIPTION ONLY MEDICINES

PART I   Articles 3(1)*(a)*, 4(1) and 5

| Column 1 | CIRCUMSTANCES EXCLUDING MEDICINAL PRODUCTS FROM THE CLASS OF PRESCRIPTION ONLY MEDICINES | | |
| | Column 2 | Column 3 | Column 4 |
Substance	Maximum strength	Use, pharmaceutical form or route of administration	Maximum dose and maximum daily dose
Acebutolol Hydrochloride			
Acepromazine			
Acepromazine Maleate			
Acetanilide			
Acetarsol			
Acetazolamide			
Acetazolamide Sodium			
Acetohexamide			
Acetylcarbromal			
Acetylcholine Chloride	0·2 per cent	External	
Acetylcysteine			
Acetyldigitoxin			
Acetylstrophanthidin			
Acetyl Sulphafurazole			
Acetyl Sulphamethoxypyridazine			
Aconitine	0·02 per cent	External	
Aconitine Hydrobromide	Equivalent of 0·02 per cent of Aconitine	External	
Aconitine Hydrochloride	Equivalent of 0·02 per cent of Aconitine	External	

Sch. 1

	CIRCUSTANCES EXCLUDING MEDICINAL PRODUCTS FROM THE CLASS OF PRESCRIPTION ONLY MEDICINES		
Column 1	Column 2	Column 3	Column 4
Substance	Maximum strength	Use, pharmaceutical form or route of administration	Maximum dose and maximum daily dose
Aconitine Nitrate	Equivalent of 0·02 per cent of Aconitine	External	
Aconite Root	1·3 per cent	External	
Actinomycin C			
Actinomycin D			
Adicillin			
Adiphenine Hydrochloride			
Adrenaline		External	
Adrenaline Acid Tartrate		External	
Adrenaline Hydrochloride		External	
Aklomide			
Alclofenac			
Alcuronium Chloride			
Aldosterone			
Alfacalcidol			
Algestone			
Algestone Acetonide			
Algestone Acetophenide			
Allobarbitone			
Allopurinol			
Allyloestrenol			
Alphadolone Acetate			
Alphaxalone			
Alprenolol			

Sch. 1

| Column 1 | CIRCUMSTANCES EXCLUDING MEDICINAL PRODUCTS FROM THE CLASS OF PRESCRIPTION ONLY MEDICINES | | |
	Column 2	Column 3	Column 4
Substance	Maximum strength	Use, pharma-ceutical form or route of admini-stration	Maximum dose and maximum daily dose
Alprenolol Hydrochloride			
Alseroxylon			
Altizide			
Amantadine Hydrochloride			
Ambenonium Chloride			
Ambuside			
Ambutonium Bromide			
Amcinonide			
Ametazole Hydrochloride			
Amidopyrine			
Amikacin Sulphate			
Amiloride Hydrochloride			
Aminocaproic Acid			
Aminopterin Sodium			
Aminosalicylic Acid			
Amiodarone Hydrochloride			
Amiphenazole Hydrochloride			
Amitriptyline			
Amitriptyline Embonate			
Amitriptyline Hydrochloride			
Ammonium Bromide			
Amoxycillin			
Amoxycillin Trihydrate			
Amphomycin			
Amphotericin			

Sch. 1

Column 1	Circumstances Excluding Medicinal Products from the Class of Prescription Only Medicines		
	Column 2	Column 3	Column 4
Substance	Maximum strength	Use, pharmaceutical form or route of administration	Maximum dose and maximum daily dose
Ampicillin			
Ampicillin Sodium			
Ampicillin Trihydrate			
Amylobarbitone			
Amylobarbitone Sodium			
Amylocaine Hydrochloride		Any use except local ophthalmic use	
Ancrod			
Androsterone			
Angiotensin Amide			
Anterior Pituitary Extract			
Antimony Barium Tartrate			
Antimony Dimercaptosuccinate			
Antimony Lithium Thiomalate			
Antimony Pentasulphide			
Antimony Potassium Tartrate			
Antimony Sodium Tartrate			
Antimony Sodium Thioglycollate			
Antimony Sulphate			
Antimony Trichloride			
Antimony Trioxide			
Antimony Trisulphide			
Apiol			
Apomorphine			

Sch. 1

Column 1	Column 2	Column 3	Column 4
	CIRCUMSTANCES EXCLUDING MEDICINAL PRODUCTS FROM THE CLASS OF PRESCRIPTION ONLY MEDICINES		
Substance	Maximum strength	Use, pharmaceutical form or route of administration	Maximum dose and maximum daily dose
Apomorphine Hydrochloride			
Apramycin			
Apramycin Sulphate			
Aprobarbitone			
Aprobarbitone Sodium			
Aprotinin			
Arecoline			
Arecoline-Acetarsol			
Arecoline Hydrobromide			
Arprinocid		Incorporation in Feed for chickens for Fattening at levels not exceeding 60 parts per million	
Arsanilic Acid			
Arsenic			
Arsenic Triiodide			
Arsenic Trioxide			
Arsphenamine			
Atenolol			
Atropine		External (except local ophthalmic use)	
Atropine Methobromide		External (except local ophthalmic use)	
Atropine Methonitrate			

Sch. 1

| Column 1 | Circumstances Excluding Medicinal Products from the Class of Prescription Only Medicines | | |
	Column 2	Column 3	Column 4
Substance	Maximum strength	Use, pharmaceutical form or route of administration	Maximum dose and maximum daily dose
Atropine Oxide Hydrochloride		External (except local ophthalmic use)	
Atropine Sulphate		External (except local ophthalmic use)	
Azacyclonol			
Azacyclonol Hydrochloride			
Azaperone			
Azaproprazone			
Azathioprine			
Azathioprine Sodium			
Azidocillin Potassium			
Bacampicillin Hydrochloride			
Bacitracin			
Bacitracin Methylene Disalicylate			
Bacitracin Zinc	6,300,000 iu/kg	Incorporation in feed as growth promoter	
Baclofen			
Bambermycin	3·0 per cent	Incorporation in feed as growth promoter	
Barbitone			
Barbitone Sodium			
Barium Carbonate			
Barium Chloride			
Barium Sulphide			

Sch. 1

Column 1	Column 2	Column 3	Column 4
	CIRCUMSTANCES EXCLUDING MEDICINAL PRODUCTS FROM THE CLASS OF PRESCRIPTION ONLY MEDICINES		
Substance	Maximum strength	Use, pharmaceutical form or route of administration	Maximum dose and maximum daily dose
Beclamide			
Beclomethasone			
Beclomethasone Diproprionate			
Belladonna Herb		External	
Belladonna Root		External	
Bemegride			
Bemegride Sodium			
Benactyzine Hydrochloride			
Benapryzine Hydrochloride			
Bendrofluazide			
Benethamine Penicillin			
Benoxaprofen			
Benperidol			
Benserazide			
Benzathine Penicillin			
Benzbromarone			
Benzhexol Hydrochloride			
Benzilonium Bromide			
Benzocaine		Any use except local ophthalmic use	
Benzoctamine Hydrochloride			
Benzoestrol			
N-Benzoyl Sulphanilamide			
Benzquinamide			

Sch. 1

Column 1	Circumstances Excluding Medicinal Products from the Class of Prescription Only Medicines		
	Column 2	Column 3	Column 4
Substance	Maximum strength	Use, pharmaceutical form or route of administration	Maximum dose and maximum daily dose
Benzquinamide Hydrochloride			
Benzthiazide			
Benztropine Mesylate			
Benzylpenicillin			
Benzylpenicillin Calcium			
Betahistine Hydrochloride			
Betamethasone			
Betamethasone Adamantoate			
Betamethasone Benzoate			
Betamethasone Sodium Phosphate			
Betamethasone Valerate			
Bethanechol Chloride			
Bethanidine Sulphate			
Biperiden Hydrochloride			
Biperiden Lactate			
Bismuth Glycollylarsanilate			
Bleomycin Sulphate			
Boldenone Undecylenate			
Bretylium Tosylate			
Bromhexine Hydrochloride		Internal for ailments of pet birds and pigeons	
Bromocriptine Mesylate			
Bromvaletone			

Sch. 1

Column 1	Column 2	Column 3	Column 4
	CIRCUMSTANCES EXCLUDING MEDICINAL PRODUCTS FROM THE CLASS OF PRESCRIPTION ONLY MEDICINES		
Substance	Maximum strength	Use, pharmaceutical form or route of administration	Maximum dose and maximum daily dose
Budesonide			
Bufexamac			
Bumetanide			
Buphenine Hydrochloride			
Bupivacaine		Any use except local ophthalmic use	
Bupivacaine Hydrochloride		Any use except local ophthalmic use	
Buprenorphine			
Buprenorphine Hydrochloride			
Busulphan			
Butacaine Sulphate		Any use except local ophthalmic use	
Butalbital			
Butalbital Sodium			
Butanilicaine Phosphate		Any use except local ophthalmic use	
Butobarbitone			
Butobarbitone Sodium			
Butriptyline Hydrochloride			
Butychloral Hydrate			
Calcitonin			
Calcitriol			
Calcium 5-Allyl-5-N-Butylbarbiturate			

Sch. 1

	CIRCUMSTANCES EXCLUDING MEDICINAL PRODUCTS FROM THE CLASS OF PRESCRIPTION ONLY MEDICINES		
Column 1	Column 2	Column 3	Column 4
Substance	Maximum strength	Use, pharmaceutical form or route of administration	Maximum dose and maximum daily dose
Calcium Aminosalicylate			
Calcium Amphomycin			
Calcium Benzamidosalicylate			
Calcium Bromide			
Calcium Bromidolactobionate			
Calcium Carbimide			
Calcium Folinate			
Calcium Sulphaloxate			
Candicidin			
Cantharidin	0·01 per cent	External	
Capreomycin Sulphate			
Caramiphen Hydrochloride	(1) Equivalent of 7·5 mg of Caramiphen (2) Equivalent of 0·1 per cent of Caramiphen	(1) Tablet (2) Liquid	
Carbachol			
Carbadox			
Carbamazepine			
Carbenicillin Sodium			
Carbenoxolone Sodium	2·0 per cent	Gel	
Carbidopa			
Carbidopa Monohydrate			

Sch. 1

Column 1	Column 2	Column 3	Column 4
	CIRCUMSTANCES EXCLUDING MEDICINAL PRODUCTS FROM THE CLASS OF PRESCRIPTION ONLY MEDICINES		
Substance	Maximum strength	Use, pharmaceutical form or route of administration	Maximum dose and maximum daily dose
Carbimazole			
Carbocisteine			
Carbon Tetrachloride		as a liver fluke remedy	
Carbromol			
Carfecillin Sodium			
Carisoprodol			
Carmustine			
Carperidine			
Cefaclor			
Cefadroxil			
Cefoxitin Sodium			
Cephalexin			
Cephalexin Sodium			
Cephaloglycin			
Cephaloram			
Cephaloridine			
Cephalosporin C			
Cephalosporin E			
Cephalosporin N			
Cephalothin Sodium			
Cephazolin Sodium			
Cephradine			
Cerium Oxalate			
Chenodeoxycholic Acid			
Chloral Antipyrine			

Sch. 1

| Column 1 | CIRCUMSTANCES EXCLUDING MEDICINAL PRODUCTS FROM THE CLASS OF PRESCRIPTION ONLY MEDICINES | | |
	Column 2	Column 3	Column 4
Substance	Maximum strength	Use, pharmaceutical form or route of administration	Maximum dose and maximum daily dose
Chloral Betaine			
Chloral Formamide			
Chloral Glycerolate			
Chloral Hydrate			
Chloralose			
Chloralurethane			
Chlorambucil			
Chloramphenicol			
Chloramphenicol Cinnamate			
Chloramphenicol Palmitate			
Chloramphenicol Sodium Succinate			
Chlordiazepoxide			
Chlordiazepoxide Hydrochloride			
Chlohexadol			
Chlorisondamine Chloride			
Chlormadinone Acetate			
Chlormerodrin			
Chlormethiazole			
Chlormethiazole Edisylate			
Chlormezanone			

Sch. 1

	CIRCUMSTANCES EXCLUDING MEDICINAL PRODUCTS FROM THE CLASS OF PRESCRIPTION ONLY MEDICINES		
Column 1	Column 2	Column 3	Column 4
Substance	Maximum strength	Use, pharma-ceutical form or route of admini-stration	Maximum dose and maximum daily dose
Chloroform (a)		Any external use	
Chloroquine Phosphate			
Chloroquine Sulphate			
Chlorothiazide			
Chlorotrianisene			
Chlorphenoxamine Hydrochloride			
Chlorpromazine			
Chlorpromazine Embonate			
Chlorpromazine Hydrochloride			
Chlorpropamide			
Chlorprothixene		For pigs	
Chlortetracycline			
Chlortetracycline Calcium			
Chlortetracycline Hydrochloride			
Chlorthalidone			
Chlorzoxazone			
Cholestyramine			
Chorionic Gonadotrophin			
Ciclacillin			
Cimetidine			

(a) Additional restrictions on the retail sale or supply of products containing chloroform are imposed by the Medicines (Chloroform Prohibition) Order 1979 (S.I. 1979/382), amended by S.I. 1980/263.

Sch. 1

Column 1	CIRCUMSTANCES EXCLUDING MEDICINAL PRODUCTS FROM THE CLASS OF PRESCRIPTION ONLY MEDICINES		
	Column 2	Column 3	Column 4
Substance	Maximum strength	Use, pharmaceutical form or route of administration	Maximum dose and maximum daily dose
Cimetidine Hydrochloride			
Cinchocaine	3·0 per cent	Any use except local ophthalmic use	
Cinchocaine Hydrochloride	Equivalent of 3·0 per cent of Cinchocaine	Any use except local ophthalmic use	
Cinchophen			
Cinoxacin			
Clenbuterol Hydrochloride			
Clidinium Bromide			
Clindamycin			
Clindamycin Hydrochloride Hydrate			
Clindamycin Palmitate Hydrochloride			
Clindamycin Phosphate			
Clobazam			
Clobetasol 17-Propionate			
Clobetasone Butyrate			
Clofazimine			
Clofibrate			
Clomiphene Citrate			
Clomipramine			
Clomipramine Hydrochloride			
Clomocycline			

Sch. 1

Column 1	Column 2	Column 3	Column 4
	CIRCUMSTANCES EXCLUDING MEDICINAL PRODUCTS FROM THE CLASS OF PRESCRIPTION ONLY MEDICINES		
Substance	Maximum strength	Use, pharma-ceutical form or route of admini-stration	Maximum dose and maximum daily dose
Clomocycline Sodium			
Clonazepam			
Clonidine			
Clonidine Hydrochloride			
Clopamide			
Cloprostenol Sodium Salt			
Clorexolone			
Clorprenaline Hydrochloride			
Clostebol Acetate			
Clotrimazole		External: (1) Cream (2) Powder (3) Solution	
Cloxacillin Benzathine			
Cloxacillin Sodium			
Cocculus Indicus			
Co-dergocrine Mesylate			
Colaspase			
Colchicine			
Colestipol Hydrochloride			
Colistin Sulphate			
Colistin Sulphomethate			
Colistin Sulphomethate Sodium			
Coniine			
Conium Leaf	7·0 per cent	External	

Sch. 1

	CIRCUMSTANCES EXCLUDING MEDICINAL PRODUCTS FROM THE CLASS OF PRESCRIPTION ONLY MEDICINES		
Column 1	Column 2	Column 3	Column 4
Substace	Maximum strength	Use, pharma-ceutical form or route of admini-stration	Maximum dose and maximum daily dose
Corticotrophin			
Cortisone			
Cortisone Acetate			
Cortodoxone			
Cotarnine Chloride			
Co-Trimoxazole			
Cropropamide			
Crotethamide			
Croton Oil			
Croton Seed			
Curare			
Cyclobarbitone			
Cyclobarbitone Calcium			
Cyclofenil			
Cyclopenthiazide			
Cyclopentolate Hydrochloride			
Cyclophosphamide			
Cycloserine			
Cyclothiazide			
Cyproterone Acetate			
Cytarabine			
Cytarabine Hydrochloride			
Dacarbazine			
Danazol			

Sch. 1

| Column 1 | CIRCUMSTANCES EXCLUDING MEDICINAL PRODUCTS FROM THE CLASS OF PRESCRIPTION ONLY MEDICINES | | |
	Column 2	Column 3	Column 4
Substance	Maximum strength	Use, pharmaceutical form or route of administration	Maximum dose and maximum daily dose
Dantrolene Sodium			
Dapsone			
Dapsone Ethane Ortho Sulphonate			
Daunorubicin Hydrochloride			
Deanol Bitartrate			
Debrisoquine Sulphate			
Dehydroemetine Hydrochloride			
Dehydroepiandrosterone			
Delmadinone Acetate			
Demecarium Bromide			
Demeclocycline			
Demeclocycline Calcium			
Demeclocycline Hydrochloride			
Deoxycortone Acetate			
Deoxycortone Pivalate			
Deptropine Citrate			
Dequalinium Chloride	1·0 per cent	External: paint	
Deserpidine			
Desferrioxamine Mesylate			
Desfluorotriamcinolone			
Desipramine Hydrochloride			
Deslanoside			

Sch. 1

| Column 1 | Circumstances Excluding Medicinal Products from the Class of Prescription Only Medicines | | |
	Column 2	Column 3	Column 4
Substance	Maximum strength	Use, pharmaceutical form or route of administration	Maximum dose and maximum daily dose
Desmopressin			
Desonide			
Desoxymethasone			
Dexamethasone			
Dexamethasone Acetate			
Dexamethasone 21-Isonicotinate			
Dexamethasone Phenylpropionate			
Dexamethasone Pivalate			
Dexamethasone Sodium m-Sulphobenzoate			
Dexamethasone Sodium Phosphate			
Dexamethasone Trioxaundecanoate			
Dexetimide			
Dextromethorphan Hydrobromide			
Dextropropoxyphene Hydrochloride			
Dextropropoxyphene Napsylate			
Dextrothyroxine Sodium			
Diazepam			
Diazoxide			
Dibenzepin Hydrochloride			
Diclofenac Sodium			
Dichloralphenazone			

Sch. 1

	CIRCUMSTANCES EXCLUDING MEDICINAL PRODUCTS FROM THE CLASS OF PRESCRIPTION ONLY MEDICINES		
Column 1	Column 2	Column 3	Column 4
Substance	Maximum strength	Use, pharmaceutical form or route of administration	Maximum dose and maximum daily dose
Dichlorophenarsine Hydrochloride			
Dichlorphenamide			
Dicyclomine Hydrochloride			
Dienoestrol			
Diethanolamine Fusidate			
Diethylamine Acetarsol			
Diethylpropion Hydrochloride			
Diflucortolone Valerate			
Diflunisal			
Digitalin			
Digitalis Leaf			
Digitalis Prepared			
Digitoxin			
Digoxin			
Dihydralazine Sulphate			
Dihydroergotamine Mesylate			
Dihydrostreptomycin			
Dihydrostreptomycin Sulphate			
Diloxanide Furoate			
Dimepregnen			
Dimercaprol			
Dimethisoquin Hydrochloride		Any use except local ophthalmic use	

Sch. 1

Column 1	CIRCUMSTANCES EXCLUDING MEDICINAL PRODUCTS FROM THE CLASS OF PRESCRIPTION ONLY MEDICINES		
	Column 2	Column 3	Column 4
Substance	Maximum strength	Use, pharmaceutical form or route of administration	Maximum dose and maximum daily dose
Dimethisterone			
Dimethothiazine Mesylate			
Dimethytubocurarine Bromide			
Dimethyltubocurarine Chloride			
Dimethyltubocurarine Iodide			
Dimetridazole		(1) Incorporation in feed for turkeys at levels not exceeding 200 parts per million and in feed for guinea fowl at levels not exceeding 150 parts per million for the prevention of histomoniasis (blackhead) (2) Incorporation in water for the prevention and treatment of histomoniasis (blackhead) in turkeys and game birds, for the prevention and treatment of trichomoniasis in pigeons and for the treatment of histomoniasis in chickens	
Dinitrodiphenylsulphonylethylenediamine			
Dinoprost			
Dinoprostone			
Diphetarsone			
Diprenorphine Hydrochloride			

Column 1	CIRCUMSTANCES EXCLUDING MEDICINAL PRODUCTS FROM THE CLASS OF PRESCRIPTION ONLY MEDICINES		
	Column 2	Column 3	Column 4
Substance	Maximum strength	Use, pharmaceutical form or route of administration	Maximum dose and maximum daily dose
Dipyridamole			
Dipyrone			
Disopyramide			
Disopyramide Phosphate			
Distigmine Bromide			
Disulfiram			
Disulphamide			
Dobutamine Hydrochloride			
Dopamine Hydrochloride			
Dothiepin			
Dothiepin Hydrochloride			
Doxapram Hydrochloride			
Doxepin Hydrochloride			
Doxorubicin			
Doxycycline			
Doxycycline Calcium Chelate			
Doxycycline Hydrochloride			
Droperidol			
Drostanolone			
Drostanolone Propionate			
Dydrogesterone			
Dyflos			
Econazole		External (except vaginal use)	
Econazole Nitrate		External (except vaginal use)	

	CIRCUMSTANCES EXCLUDING MEDICINAL PRODUCTS FROM THE CLASS OF PRESCRIPTION ONLY MEDICINES		
Column 1	Column 2	Column 3	Column 4
Substance	Maximum strength	Use, pharmaceutical form or route of administration	Maximum dose and maximum daily dose
Ecothiopate Iodide			
Edogestrone			
Edrophonium Chloride			
Embutramide			
Emepronium Bromide			
Emetine	1·0 per cent		
Emetine Bismuth Iodide			
Emetine Hydrochloride	Equivalent of 1·0 per cent of Emetine		
Enilconazole			
Ephedrine		External	
Ephedrine Hydrochloride		External	
Ephedrine Sulphate		External	
Epicillin			
Epioestriol			
Epithiazide			
Ergometrine Maleate			
Ergometrine Tartrate			
Ergot, Prepared			
Ergotamine Tartrate			
Ergotoxine Esylate			
Erythromycin			
Erythromycin Estolate			
Erythromycin Ethyl Carbonate			

Sch. 1

Column 1	CIRCUMSTANCES EXCLUDING MEDICINAL PRODUCTS FROM THE CLASS OF PRESCRIPTION ONLY MEDICINES		
	Column 2	Column 3	Column 4
Substance	Maximum strength	Use, pharmaceutical form or route of administration	Maximum dose and maximum daily dose
Erythromycin Ethyl Succinate			
Erythromycin Lactobionate			
Erythromycin Phosphate			
Erythromycin Stearate			
Erythromycin Thiocyanate			
Estramustine Phosphate			
Etafedrine Hydrochloride			
Ethacrynic Acid			
Ethambutol Hydrochloride			
Ethamivan			
Ethamsylate			
Ethchlorvynol			
Ethebenecid			
Ethiazide			
Ethinyloestradiol			
Ethionamide			
Ethisterone			
Ethoglucid			
Ethoheptazine Citrate			
Ethopropazine Hydrochloride			
Ethosuximide			
Ethotoin			
Ethyl Acetanilide			

	CIRCUMSTANCES EXCLUDING MEDICINAL PRODUCTS FROM THE CLASS OF PRESCRIPTION ONLY MEDICINES		
Column 1	Column 2	Column 3	Column 4
Substance	Maximum strength	Use, pharmaceutical form or route of administration	Maximum dose and maximum daily dose
Ethyl Biscoumacetate			
Ethyloestrenol			
Ethylstibamine			
Ethynodiol Diacetate			
Etidronate Disodium			
Etomidate			
Famprofazone			
Fazadinium Bromide			
Fenbufen			
Fencamfamin Hydrochloride			
Fenfluramine Hydrochloride			
Fenoprofen			
Fenoprofen Calcium			
Fenoterol Hydrobromide			
Fenpipramide Hydrochloride			
Fenpiprane Hydrochloride			
Fentin Compounds			
Feprazone			
Ferrous Arsenate			
Flavoxate Hydrochloride			
Fluanisone			
Fluclorolone Acetonide			
Flucloxacillin Sodium			
Flucytosine			

Sch. 1

	CIRCUMSTANCES EXCLUDING MEDICINAL PRODUCTS FROM THE CLASS OF PRESCRIPTION ONLY MEDICINES		
Column 1	Column 2	Column 3	Column 4
Substance	Maximum strength	Use, pharmaceutical form or route of administration	Maximum dose and maximum daily dose
Fludrocortisone Acetate			
Flufenamic Acid			
Flugestone			
Flugestone Acetate			
Flumedroxone Acetate			
Flumethasone			
Flumethasone Pivalate			
Flumethiazide			
Flunisolide			
Flunixin and its salts			
Fluocinolone Acetonide			
Fluocinonide			
Fluocortolone			
Flucortolone Hexanoate			
Fluocortolone Pivalate			
Fluopromazine Hydrochloride			
Fluorometholone			
Fluorouracil			
Fluorouracil Trometamol			
Fluoxymesterone			
Flupenthixol Decanoate			
Flupenthixol Dihydrochloride			
Fluperolone Acetate			
Fluphenazine Decanoate			
Fluphenazine Enanthate			

Column 1	CIRCUMSTANCES EXCLUDING MEDICINAL PRODUCTS FROM THE CLASS OF PRESCRIPTION ONLY MEDICINES		
	Column 2	Column 3	Column 4
Substance	Maximum strength	Use, pharma-ceutical form or route of admini-stration	Maximum dose and maximum daily dose
Fluphenazine Hydrochloride			
Fluprednidene Acetate			
Fluprednisolone			
Fluprostenol Sodium Salt			
Flurandrenolone			
Flurazepam Hydrochloride			
Flurazepam Monohydrochloride			
Flurbiprofen			
Fluspirilene			
Folic Acid			
Formocortal			
Formosulphathiazole			
Fosfestrol Tetrasodium			
Framycetin Sulphate			
Frusemide			
Fumagillin		Treatment of nosema apis infection in bees	
Fumagillin Bicyclohexylamine		Treatment of nosema apis infection in bees	
Furaltadone			
Furazolidone			
Fusafungine			
Fusidic Acid			

Sch. 1

	CIRCUMSTANCES EXCLUDING MEDICINAL PRODUCTS FROM THE CLASS OF PRESCRIPTION ONLY MEDICINES		
Column 1	Column 2	Column 3	Column 4
Substance	Maximum strength	Use, pharma-ceutical form or route of admini-stration	Maximum dose and maximum daily dose
Gallamine Triethiodide			
Gelsemine	0·1 per cent		
Gelsemium			
Gentamicin			
Gentamicin Sulphate			
Gestronol			
Gestronol Hexanoate			
Glibenclamide			
Glibornuride			
Glipizide			
Gliquidone			
Glutethimide			
Glycopyrronium Bromide			
Glymidine			
Gonadorelin			
Gramicidin	0·02 per cent	External	
Griseofulvin			
Growth Hormone			
Guanethidine Monosulphate			
Guanoclor Sulphate			
Guanoxan Sulphate			
Hachimycin			
Halcinonide			

Sch. 1

	CIRCUMSTANCES EXCLUDING MEDICINAL PRODUCTS FROM THE CLASS OF PRESCRIPTION ONLY MEDICINES		
Column 1	Column 2	Column 3	Column 4
Substance	Maximum strength	Use, pharma-ceutical form or route of admini-stration	Maximum dose and maximum daily dose
Halofuginone		Incorporation in feed for chickens for fattening at levels not exceed-ing 3 parts per million	
Haloperidol			
Heparin		External	
Heparin Calcium		External	
Heptabarbitone			
Heptaminol Hydrochloride			
Hexachlorophane	(i) 2·0 per cent (ii) 0·1 per cent (iii) 0·75 per cent	(a) Internal as a liver fluke remedy (b) External: (i) soaps and shampoos (ii) aerosols (iii) preparations other than soaps, shampoos and aerosols	
Hexamine Phenylcinchoninate			
Hexobarbitone			
Hexobarbitone Sodium			
Hexoestrol			
Hexoestrol Dipropionate			
L-Histidine Hydrochloride		Dietary or nutritive use	
Homatropine		External (except local ophthalmic use)	

Sch. 1

Column 1	CIRCUMSTANCES EXCLUDING MEDICINAL PRODUCTS FROM THE CLASS OF PRESCRIPTION ONLY MEDICINES		
	Column 2	Column 3	Column 4
Substance	Maximum strength	Use, pharmaceutical form or route of administration	Maximum dose and maximum daily dose
Homatropine Hydrobromide			
Homatropine Methylbromide			
Hydrallazine Hydrochloride			
Hydrargaphen		Local application to skin	
Hydrobromic Acid			
Hydrochlorothiazide			
Hydrocortamate Hydrochloride			
Hydrocortisone			
Hydrocortisone Acetate			
Hydrocortisone 17-Butyrate			
Hydrocortisone Caprylate			
Hydrocortisone Hydrogen Succinate			
Hydrocortisone Sodium Phosphate			
Hydrocortisone Sodium Succinate			
Hydroflumethiazide			
Hydrogen Cyanide	0·1 per cent		
Hydroxychloroquine Sulphate			
4-Hydroxy-3-Nitrophenylarsonic Acid			
Hydroxymethylgramicidin			
Hydroxyprogesterone			

Sch. 1

Column 1	Circumstances Excluding Medicinal Products from the Class of Prescription Only Medicines		
	Column 2	Column 3	Column 4
Substance	Maximum strength	Use, pharmaceutical form or route of administration	Maximum dose and maximum daily dose
Hydroxyprogesterone Enanthate			
Hydroxyprogesterone Hexanoate			
Hydroxyurea			
Hydroxyzine Embonate			
Hydroxyzine Hydrochloride			
Hyoscine	(1) 0·15 per cent	(1) Internal (2) External (except local ophthalmic use)	
Hyoscine Butylbromide		External	
Hyoscine Hydrobromide		External (except local ophthalmic use)	
Hyoscine Methobromide		External	
Hyoscine Methonitrate		External	
Hyoscyamine		External	
Hyoscyamine Hydrobromide		External	
Hyoscyamine Sulphate		External	
Ibuprofen			
Idoxuridine			
Ifosfamide			
Ignatius Bean			
Imipramine			
Imipramine Hydrochloride			
Imipramine Ion Exchange Resin Bound Salt or Complex			

Sch. 1

	CIRCUMSTANCES EXCLUDING MEDICINAL PRODUCTS FROM THE CLASS OF PRESCRIPTION ONLY MEDICINES		
Column 1	Column 2	Column 3	Column 4
Substance	Maximum strength	Use, pharma-ceutical form or route of admini-stration	Maximum dose and maximum daily dose
Indapamide Hemihydrate			
Indomethacin			
Indoramin Hydrochloride			
Ipratropium Bromide			
Iprindole Hydrochloride			
Iproniazid Phosphate			
Isoaminile			
Isoaminile Citrate			
Isocarboxazid			
Isoetharine			
Isoetharine Hydrochloride			
Isoetharine Mesylate			
Isoniazid			
Isoprenaline Hydrochloride			
Isoprenaline Sulphate			
Isopropamide Iodide			
Isopyrin			
Jaborandi		External	
Kanamycin Sulphates			
Ketamine Hydrochloride			
Ketazolam			
Ketoprofen			
Khellin			
Labetolol Hydrochloride			
Lactogenic Hormone			

Column 1	CIRCUMSTANCES EXCLUDING MEDICINAL PRODUCTS FROM THE CLASS OF PRESCRIPTION ONLY MEDICINES		
	Column 2	Column 3	Column 4
Substance	Maximum strength	Use, pharma-ceutical form or route of admini-stration	Maximum dose and maximum daily dose
Lanatoside C			
Lanatoside Complex A, B and C			
Lead Arsenate			
Levallorphan Tartrate			
Levodopa			
Lidoflazine			
Lignocaine		Any use except local ophthalmic use	
Lignocaine Hydrochloride		Any use except local ophthalmic use	
Lincomycin			
Lincomycin Hydrochloride			
Liothyronine Sodium			
Lithium Carbonate			
Lithium Sulphate			
Lobeline		External	
Lobeline Hydrochloride		External	
Lobeline Sulphate		External	
Lofepramine			
Lomustine			
Loperamide Hydrochloride			
Lorazepam			
Luprostiol			
Luteinising Hormone			
Lymecycline			

Sch. 1

| Column 1 | CIRCUMSTANCES EXCLUDING MEDICINAL PRODUCTS FROM THE CLASS OF PRESCRIPTION ONLY MEDICINES | | |
	Column 2	Column 3	Column 4
Substance	Maximum strength	Use, pharmaceutical form or route of administration	Maximum dose and maximum daily dose
Lynoestrenol			
Lypressin			
Mafenide			
Mafenide Acetate			
Mafenide Hydrochloride			
Mafenide Proprionate	5·0 per cent	Eye drops	
Magnesium Bromide			
Magnesium Fluoride			
Mandragora Autumnalis			
Mannomustine Hydrochloride			
Maprotiline Hydrochloride			
Mazindol			
Mabanazine			
Mebeverine Hydrochloride			
Mebezonium Iodide			
Mecamylamine Hydrochloride			
Meclofenoxate Hydrochloride			
Medazepam			
Medigoxin			
Medroxyprogesterone Acetate			
Mefenamic Acid			
Mefruside			
Megestrol			

Sch. 1

	CIRCUMSTANCES EXCLUDING MEDICINAL PRODUCTS FROM THE CLASS OF PRESCRIPTION ONLY MEDICINES		
Column 1	Column 2	Column 3	Column 4
Substance	Maximum strength	Use, pharmaceutical form or route of administration	Maximum dose and maximum daily dose
Megestrol Acetate			
Melarsonyl Potassium			
Melarsoprol			
Melengestrol			
Melengestrol Acetate			
Melphalan			
Melphalan Hydrochloride			
Menotrophin			
Mepenzolate Bromide			
Mephenesin			
Mephenesin Carbamate			
Mepivacaine Hydrochloride		Any use except local ophthalmic use	
Meprobamate			
Mequitazine			
Mercaptopurine			
Mercuderamide			
Mersalyl			
Mersalyl Acid			
Mesoridazine			
Mestanolone			
Mesterolone			
Mestranol			
Metabutethamine Hydrochloride		Any use except local ophthalmic use	

Sch. 1

Column 1	Column 2	Column 3	Column 4
	CIRCUMSTANCES EXCLUDING MEDICINAL PRODUCTS FROM THE CLASS OF PRESCRIPTION ONLY MEDICINES		
Substance	Maximum strength	Use, pharma- ceutical form or route of admini- stration	Maximum dose and maximum daily dose
Metaraminol Tartrate			
Metformin Hydrochloride			
Methacycline			
Methacycline Calcium			
Methacycline Hydrochloride			
Methallenoestril			
Methandienone			
Methandriol			
Metharbitone			
Methdilazine Hydrochloride			
Methenolone Acetate			
Methenolone Enanthate			
Methicillin Sodium			
Methindizate Hydrochloride			
Methixene			
Methixene Hydrochloride			
Methocarbamol			
Methohexitone Sodium			
Methoin			
Methorserpidine			
Methotrexate			
Methotrexate Sodium			
Methotrimeprazine			
Methotrimeprazine Hydrochloride			

Column 1	Column 2	Column 3	Column 4
	CIRCUMSTANCES EXCLUDING MEDICINAL PRODUCTS FROM THE CLASS OF PRESCRIPTION ONLY MEDICINES		
Substance	Maximum strength	Use, pharmaceutical form or route of administration	Maximum dose and maximum daily dose
Methotrimeprazine Maleate			
Methoxamine Hydrochloride	0·25 per cent	Nasal drops not containing liquid paraffin as a vehicle	
Methoxyflurane			
Methsuximide			
Methyclothiazide			
N-Methyl Acetanilide			
Methyl Benzoquate		Incorporation in feed as a coccidiostat for poultry when combined with Clopidol	
Methyldopa			
Methyldopate Hydrochloride			
Methylephedrine Hydrochloride			
Methylergometrine Maleate			
Methylpentynol			
Methylpentynol Carbamate			
Methylphenobarbitone			
Methylprednisolone			
Methylprednisolone Acetate			
Methylprednisolone Sodium Succinate			
Methylsulphonal			
Methyltestosterone			
Methylthiouracil			

Sch. 1

Column 1	CIRCUMSTANCES EXCLUDING MEDICINAL PRODUCTS FROM THE CLASS OF PRESCRIPTION ONLY MEDICINES		
	Column 2	Column 3	Column 4
Substance	Maximum strength	Use, pharmaceutical form or route of administration	Maximum dose and maximum daily dose
Methyprylone			
Methysergide Maleate			
Metirosine			
Metoclopramide Hydrochloride			
Metolazone			
Metomidate Hydrochloride			
Metoprolol Tartrate			
Metronidazole			
Metyrapone			
Mexiletine Hydrochloride			
Mainserin Hydrochloride			
Miconazole		External (except vaginal use)	
Miconazole Nitrate		External (except vaginal use)	
Minocycline			
Minocycline Hydrochloride			
Mithramycin			
Mitobronitol			
Mitomycin C			
Mitopodozide			
Molindone Hydrochloride			
Monensin Sodium		Incorporation in feed (1) as a coccidiostat for chickens for fattening at levels not exceeding 125 parts per million	

Sch. 1

Column 1	Column 2	CIRCUMSTANCES EXCLUDING MEDICINAL PRODUCTS FROM THE CLASS OF PRESCRIPTION ONLY MEDICINES	
		Column 3	Column 4
Substance	Maximum strength	Use, pharmaceutical form or route of administration	Maximum dose and maximum daily dose
		(2) as a growth promoter for cattle for fattening at levels not exceeding 40 parts per million (3) as a coccidiostat for chickens reared for laying at levels not exceeding 120 parts per million	
Morazone Hydrochloride			
Mustine Hydrochloride			
Nadolol			
Naftidrofuryl Oxalate			
Nalidixic Acid			
Nalorphine Hydrobromide			
Naloxone Hydrochloride			
Nandrolone Decanoate			
Nandrolone Laureate			
Nandrolone Phenylpropionate			
Naphazoline Hydrochloride	0·015 per cent	Eye drops	
Naphazoline Nitrate	0·05 per cent		
Naproxen			
Naproxen Sodium			
Narasin		Incorporation in feed for chickens for fattening at levels not exeeding 80 parts per million	
Natamycin			
Nealbarbitone			

Sch. 1

Column 1	Column 2	Column 3	Column 4
	CIRCUMSTANCES EXCLUDING MEDICINAL PRODUCTS FROM THE CLASS OF PRESCRIPTION ONLY MEDICINES		
Substance	Maximum strength	Use, pharma-ceutical form or route of admini-stration	Maximum dose and maximum daily dose
Neoarsphenamine			
Neomycin			
Neomycin Oleate			
Neomycin Palmitate			
Neomycin Sulphate			
Neomycin Undecanoate			
Neostigmine Bromide			
Neostigmine Methylsulphate			
Nialamide			
Nicotinaldehyde Thio-Semicarbazone			
Nicoumalone			
Nifedipine			
Nifenazone			
Nifuroquine			
Nikethamide			
Niridazole			
Nitrazepam			
Nitrofurantoin			
Nitrofurazone			
Nitroxoline			
Nomifensine Hydrogen Maleate			
Noradrenaline			
Noradrenaline Acid Tartrate			

Sch. 1

	CIRCUMSTANCES EXCLUDING MEDICINAL PRODUCTS FROM THE CLASS OF PRESCRIPTION ONLY MEDICINES		
Column 1	Column 2	Column 3	Column 4
Substance	Maximum strength	Use, pharmaceutical form or route of administration	Maximum dose and maximum daily dose
Norethandrolone			
Norethisterone			
Norethisterone Acetate			
Norethynodrel			
Norgestrel			
d-Norgestrel			
Nortriptyline Hydrochloride			
Novobiocin Calcium			
Novobiocin Sodium			
Nux Vomica Seed			
Nystatin			
Octacosactrin			
Oestradiol			
Oestradiol Benzoate			
Oestradiol Cypionate			
Oestradiol Dipropionate			
Oestradiol Diundecanoate			
Oestradiol Enanthate			
Oestradiol Phenylpropionate			
Oestradiol Undecanoate			
Oestradiol Valerate			
Oestriol			
Oestriol Di-Hemi Succinate			
Oestrogenic Substances Conjugated			

Sch. 1

Column 1	CIRCUMSTANCES EXCLUDING MEDICINAL PRODUCTS FROM THE CLASS OF PRESCRIPTION ONLY MEDICINES		
	Column 2	Column 3	Column 4
Substance	Maximum strength	Use, pharma- ceutical form or route of admini- stration	Maximum dose and maximum daily dose
Oestrone			
Oleandomycin Phosphate			
Opipramol Hydrochloride			
Orciprenaline Sulphate			
Orphenadrine Citrate			
Orphenadrine Hydrochloride			
Orthocaine		Any use except local ophthalmic use	
Ouabain			
Ovarian Gland Dried			
Oxamniquine			
Oxandrolone			
Oxantel Pamoate			
Oxazepam			
Oxedrine Tartrate			
Oxolinic Acid			
Oxophenarsine Hydrochloride			
Oxophenarsine Tartrate			
Oxpentifylline			
Oxprenolol Hydrochloride			
Oxybuprocaine Hydrochloride		Any use except local ophthalmic use	
Oxymsterone			
Oxymetholone			
Oxypertine			

Sch. 1

	CIRCUMSTANCES EXCLUDING MEDICINAL PRODUCTS FROM THE CLASS OF PRESCRIPTION ONLY MEDICINES		
Column 1	Column 2	Column 3	Column 4
Substance	Maximum strength	Use, pharmaceutical form or route of administration	Maximum dose and maximum daily dose
Oxypertine Hydrochloride			
Oxyphenbutazone			
Oxyphencyclimine Hydrochloride			
Oxyphenonium Bromide			
Oxytetracycline			
Oxytetracycline Calcium			
Oxytetracycline Dihydrate			
Oxytetracycline Hydrochloride			
Oxytocin, natural			
Oxytocin, synthetic			
Pancuronium Bromide			
Papaverine			
Papverine Hydrochloride			
Papveroline			
Papaveroline 2-Sulphonic Acid			
Paraldehyde			
Paramethadione			
Paramethasone Acetate			
Parathyroid Gland			
Parglyine Hydrochloride			
Paromomycin Sulphate			
Pecilocin			
Pemoline			
Pempidine Tartrate			

Sch. 1

	CIRCUMSTANCES EXCLUDING MEDICINAL PRODUCTS FROM THE CLASS OF PRESCRIPTION ONLY MEDICINES		
Column 1	Column 2	Column 3	Column 4
Substance	Maximum strength	Use, pharmaceutical form or route of administration	Maximum dose and maximum daily dose
Penamecillin			
Penethamate Hydriodide			
Penicillamine			
Penicillamine Hydrochloride			
Pentacosactride			
Pentazocine Hydrochloride			
Pentazocine Lactate			
Penthienate Methobromide			
Pentobarbitone			
Pentobarbitone Sodium			
Pentolinium Tartrate			
Perhexiline Hydrogen Maleate			
Pericyazine			
Perphenazine			
Phenacaine		Any use except local ophthalmic use	
Phenacemide			
Phenacetin (a)	0·1 per cent		
Phenarsone Sulphoxylate			
Phenazone		External	
Phenazone and Caffeine Citrate			

(a) *See also* the Medicines (Phenacetin Prohibition) Order 1979 (S.I. 1979/1181).

Sch. 1

Column 1	CIRCUMSTANCES EXCLUDING MEDICINAL PRODUCTS FROM THE CLASS OF PRESCRIPTION ONLY MEDICINES		
	Column 2	Column 3	Column 4
Substance	Maximum strength	Use, pharma-ceutical form or route of admini-stration	Maximum dose and maximum daily dose
Phenazone Salicylate Phenbenicillin Potassium			
Phenbutrazate Hydrochloride			
Phenelzine Sulphate			
Phenethicillin Potassium			
Pheneturide			
Phenformin Hydrochloride			
Phenglutarimide Hydrochloride			
Phenindione			
Phenobarbitone			
Phenobarbitone Sodium			
Phenoxybenzamine Hydrochloride			
Phenoxymethylpenicillin			
Phenoxymethylpenicillin Calcium			
Phenoxymethylpenicillin Potassium			
Phenprocoumon			
Phensuximide			
Phentermine Hydrochloride			
Phentermine Resin Complex			
Phentolamine Hydrochloride			
Phentolamine Mesylate			
Phenyl Aminosalicylate			

Sch. 1

	CIRCUMSTANCES EXCLUDING MEDICINAL PRODUCTS FROM THE CLASS OF PRESCRIPTION ONLY MEDICINES		
Column 1	Column 2	Column 3	Column 4
Substance	Maximum strength	Use, pharma-ceutical form or route of admini-stration	Maximum dose and maximum daily dose
Phenylbutazone			
Phenylbutazone Sodium			
Phenylmethylbarbituric Acid			
Phenylpropanolamine Hydrochloride			
Phenytoin			
Phenytoin Sodium			
Phthalylsulphacetamide			
Phthalysulphathiazole			
Physostigmine			
Physostigmine Aminoxide Salicylate			
Physostigmine Salicylate			
Physostigmine Sulphate			
Picrotoxin			
Pilocarpine			
Pilocarpine Hydrochloride			
Pilocarpine Nitrate			
Pimozide			
Pindolol			
Pipenzolate Bromide			
Piperazine Oestrone Sulphate			
Piperidolate Hydrochloride			
Pipothiazine Palmitate			
Piracetam			

| Column 1 | CIRCUMSTANCES EXCLUDING MEDICINAL PRODUCTS FROM THE CLASS OF PRESCRIPTION ONLY MEDICINES | | |
| | Column 2 | Column 3 | Column 4 |
Substance	Maximum strength	Use, pharma-ceutical form or route of admini-stration	Maximum dose and maximum daily dose
Piroxicam			
Pituitary Gland (Whole Dried)			
Pituitary Powdered (Posterior Lobe)			
Pivampicillin Hydrochloride			
Pivmecillinam			
Pivmecillinam Hydrochloride			
Pizotifen			
Pizotifen Hydrogen Maleate			
Podophyllum			
Podophyllum Indian			
Podophyllum Resin	20·0 per cent	External	
Poldine Methylsulphate			
Polidexide			
Polidexide Hydrochloride			
Polidexide Sulphate			
Polymyxin B Sulphate			
Polyoestradiol Phosphate			
Polythiazide			
Poppy Capsule			
Potassium Aminosalicylate			
Potassium Arsenite	0·0127 per cent		

Sch. 1

| Column 1 | CIRCUMSTANCES EXCLUDING MEDICINAL PRODUCTS FROM THE CLASS OF PRESCRIPTION ONLY MEDICINES | | |
| | Column 2 | Column 3 | Column 4 |
Substance	Maximum strength	Use, pharma-ceutical form or route of admini-stration	Maximum dose and maximum daily dose
Potassium Bromide			
Potassium Clorazepate			
Potassium Perchlorate			
Practolol			
Pralidoxime Chloride			
Pralidoxime Iodide			
Pralidoxime Mesylate			
Prazosin Hydrochloride			
Prednisolone			
Prednisolone Acetate			
Prednisolone Butylacetate			
Prednisolone Hexanoate			
Prednisolone Pivalate			
Prednisolone Sodium Phosphate			
Prednisolone Sodium m-Sulphobenzoate			
Prednisolone 21-Steaglate			
Prednisolone m-Sulphobenzoate			
Prednisone			
Prednisone Acetate			
Prenylamine Lactate			
Prilocaine Hydrochloride		Any use except local ophthalmic use	
Primidone			

Sch. 1

Column 1	CIRCUMSTANCES EXCLUDING MEDICINAL PRODUCTS FROM THE CLASS OF PRESCRIPTION ONLY MEDICINES		
	Column 2	Column 3	Column 4
Substance	Maximum strength	Use, pharmaceutical form or route of administration	Maximum dose and maximum daily dose
Probenecid			
Probucol			
Procainamide Hydrochloride			
Procaine Hydrochloride		Any use except local ophthalmic use	
Procaine Penicillin			
Procarbazine Hydrochloride			
Prochlorperazine Edisylate			
Prochlorperazine Maleate			
Prochlorperazine Mesylate			
Procyclidine Hydrochloride			
Progesterone			
Proligestone			
Prolintane Hydrochloride			
Promazine Embonate			
Promazine Hydrochloride			
Propanidid			
Propantheline Bromide			
Propicillin Potassium			
Propiomazine Hydrogen Maleate			
Propranolol Hydrochloride			
Propylhexedrine			

Sch. 1

Column 1	Circumstances Excluding Medicinal Products from the Class of Prescription Only Medicines		
	Column 2	Column 3	Column 4
Substance	Maximum strength	Use, pharmaceutical form or route of administration	Maximum dose and maximum daily dose
Propylhexedrine Hydrochloride			
Propylthiouracil			
Propyphenazone			
Proquamezine Fumarate			
Prostaglandin F2 Alpha Tromethamine			
Protamine Sulphate			
Prothionamide			
Prothipendyl Hydrochloride			
Protoveratrines A and B			
Protriptyline Hydrochloride			
Proxymetacaine Hydrochloride		Any use except local ophthalmic use	
Pseudoephedrine Hydrochloride			
Pyrantel Embonate		as an anthelmintic	
Pyrantel Tartrate		as an anthelmintic	
Pyrazinamide			
Pyridostigmine Bromide			
L-Pyroglutamyl-L-Histidyl-L-Proline Amide			
Quinalbarbitone			
Quinalbarbitone Sodium			
Quinestradol			
Quinestrol			
Quinethazone			

Column 1	CIRCUMSTANCES EXCLUDING MEDICINAL PRODUCTS FROM THE CLASS OF PRESCRIPTION ONLY MEDICINES		
	Column 2	Column 3	Column 4
Substance	Maximum strength	Use, pharmaceutical form or route of administration	Maximum dose and maximum daily dose
Quingestanol			
Quinidine			
Quinidine Bisulphate			
Quinidine Phenylethylbarbiturate			
Quinidine Polygalacturonate			
Quinidine Sulphate			
Quinine		As a fish ectoparasiticide	
Quinine Bisulphate			
Quinine Dihydrochloride			
Quinine Ethyl Carbonate			
Quinine Glycerophosphate			
Quinine Hydrobromide			
Quinine Hydrochloride			
Quinine Iodobismuthate			
Quinine Phenylcinchoninate			
Quinine Phosphate			
Quinine Salicylate			
Quinine Sulphate			
Quinine Tannate			
Quinine and Urea Hydrochloride			
Racephedrine Hydrochloride		External	

Sch. 1

| Column 1 | CIRCUMSTANCES EXCLUDING MEDICINAL PRODUCTS FROM THE CLASS OF PRESCRIPTION ONLY MEDICINES | | |
	Column 2	Column 3	Column 4
Substance	Maximum strength	Use, pharmaceutical form or route of administration	Maximum dose and maximum daily dose
Rauwolfia (Serpentina and Vomitoria)			
Razoxane			
Reproterol Hydrochloride			
Rescinnamine			
Reserpine			
Rifamide			
Rifampicin			
Rifamycin			
Rimiterol Hydrobromide			
Ritodrine Hydrochloride			
Rolitetracycline Nitrate			
Sabadilla			
Salazosulphadimidine			
Salbutamol			
Salbutamol Sulphate			
Salcatonin			
Salcatonin Hydrated Polyacetate			
Salmefamol			
Salsalate			
Secbutobarbitone			
Secbutobarbitone Sodium			

Sch. 1

Column 1	Circumstances Excluding Medicinal Products from the Class of Prescription Only Medicines		
	Column 2	Column 3	Column 4
Substance	Maximum strength	Use, pharma-ceutical form or route of admini-stration	Maximum dose and maximum daily dose
Sera and Antisera— Bovine Gammaglobulin Joint Ill Antiserum Streptococcal, E. Coli Erysipelothrix Rhusiopathiae Antiserum Feline Infectious Enteritis (Panleucopaenia) Antiserum			
Serum Gonadotrophin			
Silver Sulphadiazine			
Sissomicin			
Sodium Aminosalicylate			
Sodium Antimonylgluconate			
Sodium Apolate		External	
Sodium Arsanilate			
Sodium Arsenate			
Sodium Arsenite	0·013 per cent		
Sodium Bromate			
Sodium Bromide			
Sodium Cacodylate			
Sodium Cromoglycate			
Sodium Ethacrynate			
Sodium Fluoride			
Sodium Fusidate			
Sodium Methylarsinate			
Sodium Monofluorophosphate			

Sch. 1

Column 1	CIRCUMSTANCES EXCLUDING MEDICINAL PRODUCTS FROM THE CLASS OF PRESCRIPTION ONLY MEDICINES		
	Column 2	Column 3	Column 4
Substance	Maximum strength	Use, pharma-ceutical form or route of admini-stration	Maximum dose and maximum daily dose
Sodium Stibogluconate			
Sodium Valproate			
Solapsone			
Sotalol Hydrochloride			
Spectinomycin			
Spiramycin		Incorporation in feed as a growth promoter	
Spiramycin Adipate			
Spironolactone			
Stannous Fluoride			
Stanolone			
Stanozolol			
Stibocaptate			
Stibophen			
Stilboestrol			
Stilboestrol Dipropionate			
Streptodornase		External	
Streptokinase		External	
Streptomycin			
Streptomycin Sulphate			
Strontium Bromide			
Strophanthin-K			
Strychnine			
Strychnine Arsenate			

Sch. 1

	CIRCUMSTANCES EXCLUDING MEDICINAL PRODUCTS FROM THE CLASS OF PRESCRIPTION ONLY MEDICINES		
Column 1	Column 2	Column 3	Column 4
Substance	Maximum strength	Use, pharmaceutical form or route of administration	Maximum dose and maximum daily dose
Strychnine Hydrochloride			
Styramate			
Succinylsulphathiazole			
Sulfabenz			
Sulfacytine			
Sulfadicramide			
Sulfadoxine			
Sulfametopyrazine			
Sulfamonomethoxine			
Sulfapyrazole			
Sulindac			
Sulphabromomethazine			
Sulphacetamide			
Sulphacetamide Sodium			
Sulphachlorpyridazine			
Sulphadiazine			
Sulphadiazine Sodium			
Sulphadimethoxine			
Sulphadimidine			
Sulphadimidine Sodium			
Sulphaethidole			
Sulphafurazole			
Sulphafurazole Diethanolamine			
Sulphaguanidine			
Sulphaloxic Acid			

Sch. 1

	CIRCUMSTANCES EXCLUDING MEDICINAL PRODUCTS FROM THE CLASS OF PRESCRIPTION ONLY MEDICINES		
Column 1	Column 2	Column 3	Column 4
Substance	Maximum strength	Use, pharma- ceutical form or route of admini- stration	Maximum dose and maximum daily dose
Sulphamerazine			
Sulphamerazine Sodium			
Sulphamethizole			
Sulphamethoxazole			
Sulphamethoxydiazine			
Sulphamethoxypyridazine			
Sulphamethoxypyridazine Sodium			
Sulphamethylphenazole			
Sulphamoprine			
Sulphamoxole			
Sulphanilamide	5·0 per cent	Powdered surface wound dressings for farm animals	
Sulphanitran			
Sulphaphenazole			
Sulphapyridine			
Sulphapyridine Sodium			
Sulphaquinoxaline		Incorporation in feed as a coccidiostat for poultry when combined with Amprolium Hydrochloride and Ethopabate with or without Pyrimethamine	
Sulphaquinoxaline Sodium			
Sulpharsphenamine			
Sulphasalazine			

| Column 1 | CIRCUMSTANCES EXCLUDING MEDICINAL PRODUCTS FROM THE CLASS OF PRESCRIPTION ONLY MEDICINES | | |
| | Column 2 | Column 3 | Column 4 |
Substance	Maximum strength	Use, pharmaceutical form or route of administration	Maximum dose and maximum daily dose
Sulphasomidine			
Sulphasomidine Sodium			
Sulphathiazole			
Sulphathiazole Sodium			
Sulphathiourea			
Sulphatolamide			
Sulphaurea			
Sulphinpyrazone			
Sulphomyxin Sodium			
Sulphonal			
Sulpiride			
Sulthiame			
Suxamethonium Bromide			
Suxamethonium Chloride			
Suxethonium Bromide			
Tacrine Hydrochloride			
Talampicillin			
Talampicillin Hydrochloride			
Talampicillin Napsylate			
Tamoxifen			
Tamoxifen Citrate			
Teclothiazide Potassium			
Temazepam			
Terbutaline			
Terbutaline Sulphate			

Sch. 1

Column 1	Column 2	Column 3	Column 4
	CIRCUMSTANCES EXCLUDING MEDICINAL PRODUCTS FROM THE CLASS OF PRESCRIPTION ONLY MEDICINES		
Substance	Maximum strength	Use, pharmaceutical form or route of administration	Maximum dose and maximum daily dose
Testosterone			
Testosterone Acetate			
Testosterone 17B Chloral Hemiacetal			
Testosterone Cyclohexylpropionate			
Testosterone Cypionate			
Testosterone Decanoate			
Testosterone Enanthate			
Testosterone Isocaproate			
Testosterone Phenylpropionate			
Testosterone Propionate			
Tetrabenazine			
Tetracosactrin			
Tetracosactrin Acetate			
Tetracycline			
Tetracycline Hydrochloride			
Tetracycline Phosphate Complex			
Thallium Acetate			
Thialbarbitone			
Thialbarbitone Sodium			
Thiambutosine			
Thiethylperazine			
Thiethylperazine Malate			
Thiethylperazine Maleate			

Sch. 1

Column 1	CIRCUMSTANCES EXCLUDING MEDICINAL PRODUCTS FROM THE CLASS OF PRESCRIPTION ONLY MEDICINES		
	Column 2	Column 3	Column 4
Substance	Maximum strength	Use, pharmaceutical form or route of administration	Maximum dose and maximum daily dose
Thiocarlide			
Thioguanine			
Thiopentone Sodium			
Thipropazate Hydrochloride			
Thioproperazine Mesylate			
Thioridazine			
Thioridazine Hydrochloride			
Thiosinamine			
Thiosinamine and Ethyl Iodide			
Thiostrepton			
Thiotepa			
Thiothixene			
Thiouracil			
Thymoxamine Hydrochloride			
Thyroid			
Thyrotrophin			
Thyrotrophin Releasing Hormone			
Thyroxine Sodium			
Tiamulin and its salts			
Tiamulin Hydrogen Fumarate			
Tigliodine Hydrobromide			
Timolol Maleate			

Sch. 1

	Circumstances Excluding Medicinal Products from the Class of Prescription Only Medicines		
Column 1	Column 2	Column 3	Column 4
Substance	Maximum strength	Use, pharma-ceutical form or route of admini-stration	Maximum dose and maximum daily dose
Tinidazole			
Tobramycin Sulphate			
Tofenacin Hydrochloride			
Tolazamide			
Tolazoline Hydrochloride		External	
Tolbutamide			
Tolbutamide Sodium			
Tolmetin Sodium Dihydrate			
Tolperisone			
Totaquine			
Tranexamic Acid			
Tranylcypromine Sulphate			
Trazodone			
Treosulphan			
Tretamine			
Tretinoin			
Triacetyloleandomycin			
Triamcinolone			
Triamcinolone Acetonide			
Triamcinolone Diacetate			
Triamcinolone Hexacetonide			
Triamterene			
Triaziquone			
Triazolam			
Tribromoethyl Alcohol			

Sch. 1

	CIRCUMSTANCES EXCLUDING MEDICINAL PRODUCTS FROM THE CLASS OF PRESCRIPTION ONLY MEDICINES		
Column 1	Column 2	Column 3	Column 4
Substance	Maximum strength	Use, pharmaceutical form or route of administration	Maximum dose and maximum daily dose
Triclofos Sodium			
Tricyclamol Chloride			
Trienbolone Acetate			
Trifluoperazine			
Trifluoperazine Hydrochloride			
Trifluperidol			
Trilostane			
Trimeprazine			
Trimeprazine Tartrate			
Trimetaphan Camsylate			
Trimetazidine			
Trimetazidine Hydrochloride			
Trimethoprim			
Trimipramine Maleate			
Trimipramine Mesylate			
Trimustine Hydrochloride			
Tropicamide			
Troxidone			
L-Tryptophan		(1) Dietary or nutritive use (2) Any external use	
Tubocurarine Chloride			
Tybamate			
Tylosin			
Tylosin Phosphate		Incorporation in feed as a growth promoter for pigs	

Sch. 1

	CIRCUMSTANCES EXCLUDING MEDICINAL PRODUCTS FROM THE CLASS OF PRESCRIPTION ONLY MEDICINES		
Column 1	Column 2	Column 3	Column 4
Substance	Maximum strength	Use, pharmaceutical form or route of administration	Maximum dose and maximum daily dose
Tylosin Tartrate			
Tyrothricin			
Uramustine			
Urea Stibamine			
Uredofus			
Urethane			
Uridine-5-Triphosphoric Acid			
Urokinase			
Vaccines— Anthrax Spore Vaccine, Living			
Bovine lungworm Oral Vaccine, Living			
Bovine Parainfluenza/ Bedsonia/Adenovirus Vaccine			
Brucella Abortus (Strain 45/20) Vaccine			
Corynebacterium Pyogenes Vaccine			
E. Coli Oral Vaccine, Inactivated			
Joint Ill Vaccine			
Salmonella Cholerae Suis Vaccine, Living			
Staphylococcal Vaccine			
For cats:			
Vaccines for Feline Calici Virus Infections			

Sch. 1

	CIRCUMSTANCES EXCLUDING MEDICINAL PRODUCTS FROM THE CLASS OF PRESCRIPTION ONLY MEDICINES		
Column 1	Column 2	Column 3	Column 4
Substance	Maximum strength	Use, pharma-ceutical form or route of admini-stration	Maximum dose and maximum daily dose
Vaccines for Feline Infectious Enteritis (Panleucopaenia)			
Vaccines for Feline Viral Rhinotracheitis			
For dogs:			
Vaccines for Bordetella bronchiseptica			
Vaccines for Canine Distemper (both canine distemper and measles antigens)			
Vaccines for Canine Viral Hepatitis			
Vaccines for Lepto-spirosis (both L. canicola and L. icterohaemorrhagiae antigens)			
Vaccines for Rabies			
For horses:			
Vaccines for Brucellosis			
Vaccines for Equine Influenza			
Vaccines for Tetanus			
For rabbits:			
Vaccines for Myxomatosis			
Valproic Acid			
Vancomycin Hydrochloride			
Vasopressin Injection			

Sch. 1

| Column 1 | CIRCUMSTANCES EXCLUDING MEDICINAL PRODUCTS FROM THE CLASS OF PRESCRIPTION ONLY MEDICINES | | |
	Column 2	Column 3	Column 4
Substance	Maximum strength	Use, pharma-ceutical form or route of admini-stration	Maximum dose and maximum daily dose
Vasopressin Tannate			
Verapamil Hydrochloride			
Veratrine			
Veratrum (Green and White)			
Vidarabine			
Viloxazine Hydrochloride			
Vinbarbitone			
Vinbarbitone Sodium			
Vinblastine Sulphate			
Vincristine Sulphate			
Viomycin Pantothenate			
Viomycin Sulphate			
Virginiamycin	2·0 per cent	Incorporation in feed as growth promoter	
Warfarin			
Warfarin Sodium			
Xipamide			
Xylazine Hydrochloride			
Yohimbine Hydrochloride			
Zeranol		As implant	

Note: In relation to a medicinal product which contains more than one of the substances Atropine, Atropine Methobromide, Atropine Methonitrate, Atropine Oxide Hydrochloride, Atropine Sulphate, Hyoscine, Hyoscine Butylbromide, Hyoscine Hydrobromide, Hyoscine Methobromide, Hyoscine Methonitrate, Hyoscyamine, Hyoscyamine Hydrobromide or Hyoscyamine Sulphate, for the purposes of column 4, the maximum daily dose is 1 mg of the total alkaloids contained in the product which are derived from belladonna, hyoscyamus, stramonium or other solanaceous plant, and there is no maximum dose.

Article 3(1)(c)   PART II

NAME AND PRODUCT LICENCE NUMBER OF VETERINARY DRUGS

Dermisol Cream
0038/4067

Dermisol Multicleanse Solution
0038/4059

Eustidil Tablets for Dogs and Cats
0003/4109

Fortracin 100
1654/4012

Genebile
0015/4014

Lopatol 100
1728/4056

Lopatol 500
1728/4057

Neguvon Paste
0010/4053

Quixalud Feed Additive
0034/4001

Quixalud Premix
0034/4026

Synanthic I.R.
0286/4040

Tracherine
0002/4068

Walpole's Buffer Solution
1732/4057

Whitsyn 10
0038/4037

SCHEDULE 2

Article 4(2)

Column 1	Column 2	Column 3
Substance	Maximum strength	Purpose or circumstances
Azaperone		Only for administration to pigs.
Lignocaine	2·0 per cent	In all circumstances except that where the veterinary drug contains Adrenaline, Adrenaline Acid Tartrate or Noradrenaline, only when the maximum strength of Adrenaline, Adrenaline Acid Tartrate or Noradrenaline does not exceed 0·002 per cent.
Lignocaine Hydrochloride	2·0 per cent	In all circumstances except that where the veterinary drug contains Adrenaline, Adrenaline Acid Tartrate or Noradrenaline, only when the maximum strength of Adrenaline, Adrenaline Acid Tartrate or Noradrenaline does not exceed 0·002 per cent.
Procaine Hydrochloride	2·0 per cent	In all circumstances except that where the veterinary drug contains Adrenaline, Adrenaline Acid Tartrate or Noradrenaline, only when the maximum strength of Adrenaline, Adrenaline Acid Tartrate or Noradrenaline does not exceed 0·002 per cent.

SCHEDULE 3

Article 6(1)(*a*)   PART I

Column 1	Column 2	Column 3
Persons exempted	Prescription only medicines to which the exemption applies	Conditions
1. Persons selling or supplying prescription only medicines to universities, other institutions concerned with higher education or institutions concerned with research.	**1.** All prescription only only medicines.	**1.** The sale or supply shall be— (*a*) subject to the presentation of an order signed by the principal of the institution concerned with education or research or the appropriate head of department in charge of a specified course of research stating— (*i*) the name of the institution for which the prescription only medicine is required, (*ii*) the purpose for which the prescription only medicine is required, and (*iii*) the total quantity required, and (*b*) for the purposes of the education or research with which the institution is concerned.
2. Persons selling or supplying prescription only medicines to any of the following— (1) a public analyst appointed under section 89 of the Food and Drugs Act 1955(**a**), section 27 of the Food and Drugs (Scotland) Act 1956(**b**) or section 31 of the Food and Drugs Act (Northern Ireland) 1958(**c**),	**2.** All prescription only medicines.	**2.** The sale or supply shall be subject to the presentation of an order signed by or on behalf of any person listed in subparagraphs (1), (2), (3), (4) or (5) of column 1 of this paragraph stating the status of the person signing it and the amount of the prescription only medicine required, and shall be only in connection with the exercise by those persons of their statutory functions.

(**a**) 1955 c. 16 (4 & 5 Eliz. 2).   (**b**) 1956 c. 30.   (**c**) 1958 c. 27 (N.I.).

Sch.3(I)

Column 1	Column 2	Column 3
Persons exempted	Prescription only medicines to which the exemption applies	Conditions
(2) a sampling ofice within the meaning of the Food and Drugs Act 1955, the Food and Drugs (Scotland) Act 1956 or the Food and Drugs Act (Northern Ireland) 1958, (3) an agricultural analyst appointed under section 67 of the Agriculture Act 1970(**a**), (4) a person duly authorised by an enforcement authority under sections 111 and 112, or (5) a sampling officer within the meaning of Schedule 3 to the Act.		
3. Persons lawfully conducting a retail pharmacy business within the meaning of section 69.	**3.**—(1) Any veterinary drug such as is described in paragraph (1)*(a)*(i) or (ii) of Article 3 of the Veterinary Drugs Exemption Order, which, if or when for parenteral administration is a prescription only medicine, other than those the entry in relation to which in the fourth column of Part A of Schedule 1 to that order does not permit sale for parenteral use. (2) Prescription only medicines which are not for parenteral administration and which— *(a)* are eye drops or eye ointments and are prescription only medicines by reason only that they contain: (i) Mafenide propionate. (ii) not more than 30·0 per cent Sulphacetamide Sodium, or	**3.**—(1) In the case of the veterinary drugs, the sale or supply shall be subject to the conditions specified in Article 3(2)*(d)* and (4) of the Veterinary Drugs Exemption Order.

(**a**) 1970 c. 40.

Sch.3(I)

Column 1	Column 2	Column 3
Persons exempted	Prescription only medicines to which the exemption applies	Conditions

	(iii) Sulphafurazole diethanolamine equivalent to not more than 4·0 per cent Sulphafurazole or
	(b) are prescription only medicines by reason only that they contain any of the following substances:
	  Atropine sulphate
	  Bethanecol chloride
	  Carbachol
	  Cyclopentolate hydrochloride
	  Homatropine hydrobromide
	  Hyoscine hydrobromide
	  Naphazoline hydrochloride
	  Naphazoline nitrate
	  Neostigmine methylsulphate
	  Physostigmine salicylate
	  Physostigmine sulphate
	  Pilocarpine hydrochloride
	  Pilocarpine nitrate
	  Tropicamide.	

4. Persons the sale or supply by whom is exempted by Article 3 of the Veterinary Drugs Exemption Order from the restrictions imposed by section 52.	**4.** Any veterinary drug such as is described in paragraph (1)*(a)*(i) or (ii) of Article 3 of the Veterinary Drugs Exemption Order which, if or when for parenteral administration, is a prescription only medicine, other than those the entry in relation to which in the fourth column of Part A of Schedule 1 to that order does not permit sale for parenteral use.	**4.** The sale or supply shall be subject to the conditions specified in Article 3(2) to (8) of the Veterinary Drugs Exemption Order.

Sch.3(I)

Column 1	Column 2	Column 3
Persons exempted	Prescription only medicines to which the exemption applies	Conditions
5. Persons the sale supply by whom is exempted by Article 4 of the Veterinary Drugs Exemption Order from the restrictions imposed by section 52.	**5.** Any veterinary drug such as is described in paragraph (1)*(a)*(i) or (ii) of Article 4 of the Veterinary Drugs Exemption Order which is a prescription only medicine.	**5.** The sale or supply shall be subject to— *(a)* the presentation of an order signed by or on behalf of the purchaser stating— (i) the name and address of the purchaser, *(ii)* the name and address of the purchaser's business, and *(iii)* the amount of the veterinary drug required, and *(b)* the conditions specified in Article 4(2) to (6) of the Veterinary Drugs Exemption Order.
6. Persons providing a poultry vaccination service.	**6.** Any veterinary drug such as is described in paragraph (1)*(a)*(i) or (ii) of Article 3 of the Veterinary Drugs Exemption Order which is a poultry vaccine and which, if or when for parenteral administration, is a prescription only medicine.	**6.** The sale or supply shall be only to a person who has charge of animals for the purpose of and in the course of carrying on a business, either as his sole business activity or as a substantial part of his business activities.
7. Persons selling or supplying prescription only medicines to the persons referred to in paragraph 6.	**7.** The veterinary drugs referred to in paragraph 6.	**7.** The sale or supply shall be subject to the presentation of an order signed by the purchaser stating the amount of the prescription only medicine required.
8. Persons selling or supplying prescription only medicines to veterinary surgeons and veterinary practitioners.	**8.** All prescription only medicines.	**8.** No conditions.
9. Persons selling or supplying prescription only medicines to the British Standards Institution.	**9.** All prescription only medicines.	**9.** The sale or supply shall be— *(a)* subject to the presentation of an order signed on behalf of the British Standards Institution stating the status of the person signing it and the amount of the prescription only medicine required, and

Sch.3(I)

Column 1	Column 2	Column 3
Persons exempted	Prescription only medicines to which the exemption applies	Conditions
		(b) only for the purpose of testing containers of medicinal products or determining the standards for such containers.
10. Holders of product licences and holders of manufacturer's licences.	**10.** Prescription only medicines referred to in the licenses.	**10.** The sale or supply shall be only— *(a)* to a pharmacist, *(b)* so as to enable that pharmacist to prepare an entry relating to the prescription only medicine in question in a tablet or capsule identification guide or similar publication, and *(c)* of no greater quantity than is reasonably necesary for that purpose.

Column 1	Column 2	Column 3
Persons exempted	Prescription only medicines to which the exemption applies	Conditions
1. Persons authorised by licenses granted under regulation 5 of the Misuse of Drugs Regulations to supply a controlled drug.	**1.** Such prescription only medicines, being controlled drugs, as are specified in the licence.	**1.** The supply shall be subject to such conditions and in such circumstances and to such an extent as may be specified in the licence.

Column 1	Column 2	Column 3
Persons exempted	Prescription only medicines to which the exemption applies	Conditions
1. Persons providing a poultry vaccination service.	**1.** Any veterinary drug such as is described in paragraph (1)*(a)*(i) or (ii) of Article 3 of the Veterinary Drugs Exemption Order which is a poultry vaccine and which, if or when for parenteral administration, is a prescription only medicine.	**1.** The administration shall be only in the course of providing a poultry vaccination service.
2. Persons who are authorised as members of a group by a group authority granted under regulations 8(3) or 9(3) of the Misuse of Drugs Regulations to supply a controlled drug by way of administration only.	**2.** Prescription only medicines that are specified in the group authority.	**2.** The administration shall be subject to such conditions and in such circumstances and to such extent as may be specified in the group authority.
3. Persons who have in their charge or who maintain animals for the purposes of and in the course of carrying on a business either as their sole business activity or as a part of their business activities.	**3.** Any veterinary drug such as is described in paragraph (1)*(a)*(i) or (ii) of Article 3 of the Veterinary Drugs Exemption Order which, if or when for parenteral administration, is a prescription only medicine, other than those the entry in relation to which in the fourth column of Part A of Schedule 1 to that order does not permit sale for parenteral use.	**3.** The administration shall be only to animals in their charge or under their maintenance for the purposes of and in the course of carrying on a business.

EXPLANATORY NOTE
(This Note is not part of the Order.)

This Order specifies descriptions and classes of medicinal products (being veterinary drugs) for the purposes of section 58 of the Medicines Act 1968 and states that veterinary surgeons and veterinary practitioners are to be appropriate practitioners for the purposes of that section in relation to such products (Articles 2 and 3). By virtue of section 58 such products may be sold or supplied by retail only in accordance with a prescription given by a veterinary surgeon or veterinary practitioner and may be administered only by or in accordance with the directions of such a person. The Order also confers exemptions from those restrictions (Articles 5, 6 and 7) and prescribes conditions which must be fulfilled if a sale or supply is to be taken as being in accordance with a prescription (Article 8).

The provisions of this Order were previously contained in the Medicines (Prescription Only) Order 1980 ("the 1980 Order") as amended except that changes (including additions and omissions) have been made by this Order—

(a) in and relating to the list of substances (in column 1 of Part I of Schedule 1) which, if contained in a veterinary drug, make that drug a prescription only medicine, and

(b) to the list of named veterinary drugs (in Part II of Schedule 1) which are prescription only medicines.

Where a substance or drug appears in such a list for the first time it is shown in Schedule 1 in bold type, except where the addition results solely from a change in name.

The 1980 Order also specified other descriptions and classes of medicinal products for the purposes of section 58 and contained provisions relating to them; such products are now (with certain exceptions) specified in, and such provisions contained in, the Medicines (Products Other than Veterinary Drugs) (Prescription Only) Order 1983 which revoked the 1980 Order and its amending instruments.

STATUTORY INSTRUMENTS

1983 No. 1214

TERMS AND CONDITIONS OF EMPLOYMENT

The Job Release Act 1977 (Continuation) Order 1983

Laid before the House of Commons in draft

Made - - - -	*5th August* 1983
Coming into Operation	*30th September* 1983

The Secretary of State, in exercise of the powers conferred on him by section 1(4)*(b)* of the Job Release Act 1977 (**a**) and of all other powers enabling him in that behalf, hereby makes the following Order, a draft of which was laid before the House of Commons and approved by resolution of that House in accordance with section 1(5) of the Job Release Act 1977:—

Citation and commencement

1. This Order may be cited as the Job Release Act 1977 (Continuation) Order 1983 and shall come into operation on 30th September 1983.

Continuation

2. Section 1 of the Job Release Act 1977 shall continue in force until the expiration of the period ending with 29th September 1984.

Signed by order of the Secretary of State.

Alan Clark,
Joint Parliamentary Under Secretary of State,
Department of Employment.

5th August 1983.

EXPLANATORY NOTE

(This Note is not part of the Order.)

This Order continues in force until 29th September 1984 section 1 of the Job Release Act 1977 which would otherwise have ceased to have effect on 29th September 1983, the section having been continued in force until that date by the Job Release Act 1977 (Continuation) Order 1982 (S.I. 1982/910).

Section 1 of the Job Release Act 1977 provides financial authorisation for any sums required by the Secretary of State or the Department of Manpower Services for Northern Ireland in paying temporary allowances to persons approaching pensionable age, under schemes made and implemented with a view to creating job vacancies and otherwise mitigating the effects of high unemployment.

(**a**) 1977 c.8.

STATUTORY INSTRUMENTS

1983 No. 1215 (S. 107)

EDUCATION, SCOTLAND

The Education (Fees and Awards) (Scotland) Regulations 1983

Made - - - -	*26th July* 1983
Laid before Parliament	*11th August* 1983
Coming into Operation	*15th August* 1983

In exercise of the powers conferred on me by sections 1 and 2 of the Education (Fees and Awards) Act 1983(a), I hereby make the following regulations:—

PART I

GENERAL

Citation and commencement

1. These regulations may be cited as the Education (Fees and Awards) (Scotland) Regulations 1983 and shall come into operation on 15th August 1983.

Interpretation

2.—(1) In these regulations:—

"education" includes post-graduate research otherwise than in the course of employment;

"education authority" means a regional or islands council;

"employment" means full-time employment or part-time employment which, in a normal week, involves a significant number of hours of work and "employed" shall be construed accordingly, and for the purposes hereof the references to employment include references to the holding of any office and to any occupation for gain;

"European Community" means the area comprised by the member states of the European Economic Community (including the United Kingdom) as constituted from time to time;

"fees" includes charges however described;

"the Islands" means the Channel Islands and the Isle of Man;

(a) 1983 c. 40.

"national of a member state of the European Community" means a person who is a national for the purposes of the Community Treaties of any member state of the European Economic Community (including the United Kingdom) as constituted from time to time;

"refugee" means a person who is recognised by Her Majesty's Government as a refugee within the meaning of the United Nations Convention relating to the Status of Refugees done at Geneva on 28th July 1951 as extended by the Protocol thereto which entered into force on 4th October 1967 or a person who enjoys asylum in the United Kingdom in pursuance of a decision of Her Majesty's Government though not so recognised;

(2) In these regulations a reference to a person's son or daughter includes a reference to a person adopted in pursuance of adoption proceedings, a step-child and an illegitimate child of whom the person concerned is the mother or in whose case he has admitted paternity or been adjudged the putative father.

(3) Notwithstanding section 11 of the Interpretation Act 1978(a) section 3(2) of the Education (Fees and Awards) Act 1983 (references to the United Kingdom to include references to the Islands) shall not apply for the purpose of the interpretation of these regulations.

(4) In these regulations, unless the context otherwise requires, a reference to a regulation, Part or Schedule is a reference to a regulation or Part of these regulations or to a Schedule thereto, a reference in a regulation or Schedule to a paragraph is a reference to a paragraph of that regulation or Schedule and a reference in a paragraph to a sub-paragraph is a reference to a sub-paragraph of that paragraph.

Lawful acts

3.—(1) Nothing in Part II shall be construed as rendering unlawful any discrimination arising from the remission in whole or in part of any fee (on grounds of financial hardship or otherwise) if it would have been lawful had these regulations not been made.

(2) Nothing in Part III shall be construed as rendering unlawful any discrimination arising from any rule of eligibility for an award if it would have been lawful had these regulations not been made.

PART II

FEES FOR TUITION ETC.

Scope of Part II

4.—(1) This Part shall have effect as respects the charging of relevant fees in respect of students attending a full-time or sandwich course provided by a central institution or college of education being an institution or, as the case may be, a college which is substantially dependent for its maintenance on public funds within the meaning of section 1(4) of the Education (Fees and Awards)

(a) 1978 c. 30.

Act 1983 or further education establishment; and any reference in this Part to a student shall be construed accordingly.

(2) In this regulation the following expressions have the meaning respectively assigned to them:—

"central institution" means an educational establishment for the provision of further education recognised as a central institution by regulations made by the Secretary of State;

"college of education" means an educational establishment in which further education is provided and the primary purpose of which is the education and training of teachers;

"full-time course" means a course normally involving not less than 15 hours attendance a week in term-time for the organised day-time study of a single subject or related subjects;

"further education establishment" means such an establishment which is provided by an education authority;

"sandwich course" means a course consisting of alternate periods of full-time study in an establishment and periods of experience so organised that, taking the course as a whole, the student attends the periods of full-time study for an average of not less whan 19 weeks in each year (the course being treated for the purpose of calculating attendance as beginning with the first period of full-time study and ending with the last such period) and, for the purposes hereof "periods of experience" means periods of industrial, professional or commercial experience associated with full-time study at the establishment but at a place outside the establishment except that, in the case of a student studying modern languages whose course includes periods of residence in a country whose language is the main language of that course, it means such periods of residence for which he is in gainful employment.

Relevant fees

5.—(1) For the purpose of this Part "relevant fees" means the aggregate of—

    (*a*) any fees for admission, registration or matriculation (including matriculation exemption);

    (*b*) any sessional or tuition fees;

    (*c*) any composition fee; and

    (*d*) any graduation fee,

in each case excluding any element thereof representing or attributable to such fees as are mentioned in paragraph (2).

(2) The fees last referred to in paragraph (1) are:—

    (*a*) any fees charged by an external body in respect of an examination or validation of a course or otherwise charged by such a body whose requirements must (for the purposes of a course) be met; and

    (*b*) charges for board and lodging.

Relevant connection with the United Kingdom and Islands

6. For the purposes of this Part a student has a relevant connection with the United Kingdom and Islands if:—

    (*a*) he has been ordinarily resident therein throughout the 3 year period preceding 1st September, 1st January or 1st April closest to the beginning of the first term of the student's course, and

    (*b*) he has not been resident therein, during any part of that 3 year period, wholly or mainly for the purpose of receiving full-time education.

Charging of higher relevant fees

7.—(1) Subject to Schedule 1, it shall be lawful to charge higher relevant fees in the case of students who have not a relevant connection with the United Kingdom and Islands than in the case of students having such a connection:

Providing that, in the case of a student pursuing a course which he began before 1st September 1980, the annual rate of the relevant fees shall not exceed—

    (*a*) £2,406, where the student's course is a post-graduate or comparable course;

    (*b*) £1,575, where the student's course, not being such as aforesaid, is a course of advanced further education, or

    (*c*) £843, in any other case.

(2) For the purposes of this regulation:—

"post-graduate or comparable course" means a course above first degree level and research training;

"course of advanced further education" means (*a*) a course designated above Scottish Certificate of Education Higher Grade or equivalent standard leading directly to a university degree or equivalent qualification, or (*b*) a course of equivalent standard to that referred to in paragraph (*a*) but not necessarily leading to a university degree or equivalent qualification.

PART III

POST-GRADUATE AGRICULTURAL STUDENTSHIPS

Scope of Part III

8. This Part shall have effect as respects the adoption by the Secretary of State of rules of eligibility for awards (however described) made by him in pursuance of section 4 of the Small Landholders (Scotland) Act 1911(a) and any reference in this Part to an award or a candidate for an award shall be construed accordingly.

(a) 1911 c. 49.

Relevant connection with Scotland

9. For the purposes of this Part a candidate for an award has a relevant connection with Scotland if—

(*a*) he has been ordinarily resident therein throughout the 3 year period preceding the date of his application for an award;

(*b*) he has not been resident therein during any part of that 3 year period wholly or mainly for the purpose of receiving full-time education; and

(*c*) he is a British citizen or otherwise enjoys in the United Kingdom the status of a commonwealth citizen.

Authorised eligibility rules

10. Subject to Schedule 2, it shall be lawful to adopt rules of eligibility for awards which confine the awards to candidates having a relevant connection with Scotland.

SCHEDULE 1

Excepted Students

1. It shall not be lawful in pursuance of regulation 7 to charge higher fees in the case of a student who is an excepted student within the meaning of this Schedule.

2.—(1) A person who—

(*a*) is a national of a member state of the European Community;

(*b*) is the son or daughter of such a national; or

(*c*) began his course before 1st January 1984;

shall be an excepted student if he satisfies the conditions mentioned in sub-paragraph (2).

(2) The conditions referred to in sub-paragraph (1) are that—

(*a*) he has been ordinarily resident in the European Community throughout the 3 year period referred to in regulation 6(*a*); and

(*b*) he has not been resident therein, during any part of that 3 year period, wholly or mainly for the purpose of receiving full-time education.

3. A refugee ordinarily resident in the United Kingdom and Islands who has not ceased to be so ordinarily resident since he was recognised as a refugee or was granted asylum, and the spouse, son or daughter of such a refugee, shall be an excepted student.

4.—(1) A person shall be an excepted student if—

(*a*) at the date referred to in regulation 6(*a*) he is settled in the United Kingdom, and

(*b*) he neither had the right of abode in the United Kingdom nor was settled therein at, or at a time before, the beginning of the 3 year period so referred to.

(2) References in this paragraph to a person having a right of abode in the United Kingdom or being settled therein have the same meanings as in the Immigration Act 1971(**a**).

(**a**) 1971 c. 77, amended by section 39 of the British Nationality Act 1981 (c. 61).

5. A person shall be an excepted student if—

(*a*) he has not been ordinarily resident throughout the 3 year period referred to in regulation 6(*a*) in the United Kingdom and Islands, or

(*b*) being a national of a member state of the European Community or the son or daughter of such a national he has not been so ordinarily resident in the European Community,

only because he, his spouse or his parent was temporarily employed outside the United Kingdom and Islands or, as the case may be, outside the European Community.

6. A person shall be an excepted student if he was admitted to his course in pursuance of arrangements with an institution outside the United Kingdom for the exchange of students on a fully reciprocal basis.

SCHEDULE 2

Awards—Excepted Candidates

1.—(1) It shall not be lawful in pursuance of regulation 10 to adopt rules of eligibility for awards which exclude from eligibility a person who is an excepted candidate within the meaning of this Schedule.

(2) In this Schedule "the relevant date" means, in relation to a candidate for an award, the date of his application therefor.

2. A person shall be an excepted candidate, if he was resident in Scotland on the relevant date and is the child of a national of a member state of the European Community who—

(*a*) where he was employed on the said date, was then in employment in Scotland;

(*b*) where he was not employed on that date (by reason of retirement or otherwise), was previously last employed in such employment, or

(*c*) whether or not he was employed on that date, had, during the period of 3 years ending therewith, been in such employment for an aggregate period of not less than a year,

and where he would have a relevant connection with the European Community for the purposes of Part III, had any reference in regulation 9 to Scotland been a reference to the European Community and had sub-paragraph (*c*) of regulation 9 been omitted.

3.—(1) A national of a member state of the European Community shall be an excepted candidate, if he—

(*a*) was resident in Scotland on the relevant date;

(*b*) entered the United Kingdom wholly or mainly for the purpose of taking up, or of seeking, employment;

(*c*) during the year preceding the relevant date has been in employment in Scotland for an aggregate period of not less than 9 months;

(*d*) seeks an award in respect of a course provided by a vocational training establishment, being a course leading to a qualification which is needed for, or is designed to fit a person for, engagement in a specific profession or trade; and

(*e*) would have a relevant connection with the European Community for the purposes of Part III, had any reference in regulation 9 to Scotland been a reference to the European Community and had sub-paragraph (*c*) of regulation 9 been omitted.

(2) For the purposes of this paragraph—

"qualification" includes authorisation, recognition, registration, enrolment, approval and certification;

"vocational training establishment" means a further education establishment being a vocational school within the meaning of Article 7 of Council Regulation (EEC) No. 1612/68 on freedom of movement of workers within the Community(a).

4. Subject to paragraph 6, a refugee ordinarily resident in the United Kingdom and Islands who has not ceased to be so ordinarily resident since he was recognised as a refugee or was granted asylum, and the spouse, son or daughter of such a refugee, shall be an excepted candidate.

5.—(1) Subject to paragraph 6, a person shall be an excepted candidate for the purposes of Part III, if he has not the relevant connection with Scotland mentioned in regulation 9, by reason only that—

(a) he, his spouse or his parent was temporarily employed outside Scotland; or

(b) he or his spouse was temporarily receiving full-time education outside Scotland.

(2) Subject to paragraph 6, a person shall be an excepted candidate if he would be such in pursuance of paragraph 2 or 3 but for his not having such a relevant connection with the European Community as is mentioned in the paragraph in question for the purposes of Part III where he has not that relevant connection by reason only that—

(i) he, his spouse or his parent was temporarily employed outside the European Community; or

(ii) he or his spouse was temporarily receiving full-time education outside the European Community.

6. Such persons as are mentioned in paragraph 4 or, as the case may be, in paragraph 5 shall only be excepted candidates where the Secretary of State has so determined.

New St. Andrew's House,
Edinburgh.
26th July 1983.

George Younger,
One of Her Majesty's
Principal Secretaries of State.

(a) O.J. No. L257, 19.10.68, p.2 (O.J./S.E. 1968 (II), p.475).

EXPLANATORY NOTE

(This Note is not part of the Regulations.)

These Regulations which come into operation on 15th August 1983 provide (subject to specified exceptions) that in the cases mentioned below it shall be lawful to differentiate between students with, and those without, a specified connection with the United Kingdom (including the Channel Islands and the Isle of Man) or with a particular part of the United Kingdom either as respects fees charged or in rules of eligibility for awards. Nothing in the regulations is to be construed as rendering unlawful anything done in this behalf which would have been lawful had the regulations not been made (regulation 3).

Part II relates to tuition and certain other fees (referred to as "relevant fees") in respect of full-time or sandwich courses provided by a central institution, a college of education or a further education establishment (regulations 4 and 5). Students who have not 3 years' ordinary residence in the United Kingdom and Islands or who, having such ordinary residence, have during the 3 year period been resident wholly or mainly for the purposes of receiving full-time education may be charged higher relevant fees unless they are "excepted students"; excepted students for the purposes of Part II include nationals of member states of the European Community with a corresponding connection with the Community, refugees and recently arrived immigrants (regulations 6 and 7 and Schedule 1).

Part III relates to rules of eligibility for post-graduate agricultural studentships (regulation 8) and makes provision similar to that for Part II save that, first, the required connection is with Scotland instead of the United Kingdom and Islands and, secondly, the rules may require a candidate to be a British or Commonwealth citizen (regulations 9 and 10 and Schedule 2).

"Excepted candidates" for the purposes of Part III include the children of European Community migrant workers, such workers themselves who seek an award in respect of a vocational training course at a vocational training establishment, and refugees. (Schedule 2).

STATUTORY INSTRUMENTS

1983 No. 1217

LICENSING (LIQUOR)

The Airports Licensing (Liquor) Order 1983

Made - - - -	*5th August* 1983
Coming into Operation	*26th August* 1983

Whereas it appears to the Secretary of State that the airports specified in Schedule 1 hereto are airports at which there is a substantial amount of international passenger traffic:

And whereas the Secretary of State is satisfied that arrangements have been made for affording reasonable facilities on licensed premises within the examination station approved for those airports under section 22 of the Customs and Excise Management Act 1979(**a**) for obtaining hot and cold beverages other than intoxicating liquor at all times when intoxicating liquor is obtainable on those premises:

Now therefore the Secretary of State, in exercise of powers conferred by sections 87 and 198 of the Licensing Act 1964(**b**), and now vested in him(**c**), and of all other powers enabling him in that behalf, hereby makes the following Order:

1. This Order may be cited as the Airports Licensing (Liquor) Order 1983 and shall come into operation on 26th August 1983.

2. Section 87 of the Licensing Act 1964 is hereby brought into operation at the airports specified in Schedule 1 hereto.

3. The Orders specified in Schedule 2 hereto are hereby revoked.

Signed by authority of the Secretary of State

David B. Mitchell,
Parliamentary Under Secretary of State,
Department of Transport.

5th August 1983.

(**a**) 1979 c. 2.
(**b**) 1964 c. 26; s. 87 was amended by the Customs and Excise Management Act 1979, Schedule 4, para. 12.
(**c**) S.I. 1966/741, 1970/1537.

SCHEDULE 1

Birmingham	London—Heathrow
Bristol	London—Stansted
Cardiff—Wales	Luton
East Midlands	Manchester International
London—Gatwick	Newcastle

SCHEDULE 2

Orders Revoked

Order	Reference
The Airports Licensing (Liquor) Order 1977	S.I. 1977/1113
The Newcastle Airport Licensing (Liquor) Order 1982	S.I. 1982/204

EXPLANATORY NOTE

(This Note is not part of the Order.)

Section 87 of the Licensing Act 1964 provides that, at an international airport where that section is in operation, section 59 of that Act (which prohibits the sale or supply of intoxicating liquor except during permitted hours) shall not apply to licensed premises which are within the examination station approved for the airport under section 22 of the Customs and Excise Management Act 1979. This Order brings section 87 of the 1964 Act into operation at Bristol and Cardiff-Wales airports and revokes and consolidates the two Orders previously in force bringing section 87 of the 1964 Act into operation at other international airports.

STATUTORY INSTRUMENTS

1983 No. 1219

NURSES, MIDWIVES AND HEALTH VISITORS

The Nurses, Midwives and Health Visitors (Mental Health Committee of the Welsh National Board) Order 1983

Made - - - -	*4th August* 1983
Laid before Parliament	*18th August* 1983
Coming into Operation	*15th September* 1983

The Secretary of State for Wales, in exercise of powers conferred on him by section 7(6) and (7) of the Nurses, Midwives and Health Visitors Act 1979(a) and of all other powers enabling him in that behalf, hereby makes the following order:–

Citation and commencement

1. This order may be cited as the Nurses, Midwives and Health Visitors (Mental Health Committee of the Welsh National Board) Order 1983 and shall come into operation on 15th September 1983.

Interpretation

2. In this order, unless the context otherwise requires—

"the Act" means the Nurses, Midwives and Health Visitors Act 1979;

"the Committee" means the standing committee of the Board constituted by article 3(1) of this order;

"the Welsh National Board" and "the Board" both mean the National Board for Nursing, Midwifery and Health Visiting in Wales established by section 5(1) of the Act.

Constitution of Mental Health Committee

3.—(1) There is hereby constituted for the Welsh National Board a standing committee of the Board which shall be known as the Mental Health Committee of the Board.

(2) The Committee shall consist of not less than nine and not more than fifteen members appointed by the Board of whom a majority shall be persons who work or have worked in either of the professional fields of nursing persons suffering from mental illness or mental handicap.

(a) 1979 c.36.

(3) The Board may appoint as members of the Committee persons who are not members of the Board: Provided that at all times the Committee shall include at least five persons who are also members of the Board.

(4) The members of the Committee shall include at least one registered medical practitioner appointed after consultation with the Royal College of Psychiatrists.

(5) The Board shall, after consultation with the Committee, appoint one of the members of that Committee who is also a member of the Board to be chairman of the Committee.

Duty to consult Mental Health Committee

4. The Board shall consult the Committee on all mental nursing matters.

Nicholas Edwards,
Secretary of State for Wales.

4th August 1983.

EXPLANATORY NOTE

(This Note is not part of the Order.)

This Order constitutes the Mental Health Committee of the Welsh National Board for Nursing, Midwifery and Health Visiting and requires the Board to consult the Mental Health Committee on all mental nursing matters.

STATUTORY INSTRUMENTS

1983 No. 1232

ROAD TRAFFIC

The Heavy Goods Vehicles (Drivers' Licences) (Amendment) Regulations 1983

Made - - - -	*9th August* 1983
Laid before Parliament	*22nd August* 1983
Coming into Operation	*13th September* 1983

The Secretary of State for Transport, in exercise of the powers conferred by sections 114(3), 115(1A), and 119(1) of the Road Traffic Act 1972(**a**), and now vested in him(**b**), after consultation with representative organisations in accordance with section 199(2) of that Act, hereby makes the following Regulations:—

1. These Regulations shall come into operation on 13th September 1983, and may be cited as the Heavy Goods Vehicles (Drivers' Licences) (Amendment) Regulations 1983.

2. The Heavy Goods Vehicles (Drivers' Licences) Regulations 1977(**c**) are further amended in accordance with the following provisions of these Regulations.

3. In Regulation 2 (Interpretation)—

(*a*) after the definition of "ordinary driving licence" insert the following definition:—

" "penalty points" means penalty points endorsed on an ordinary driving licence pursuant to section 19 of, and Schedule 7 to, the Transport Act 1981(**d**) or counted as having been so endorsed pursuant to section 19(7)(*a*) of that Act;"

(*b*) after the definition of "registered" insert the following definition:—

" "relevant endorsement" means an endorsement on a Northern Ireland (ordinary) driving licence of particulars of a conviction in pursuance of that provision for the time being in force in Northern Ireland that corresponds to section 101 of the Act of 1972;".

(**a**) 1972 c. 20; section 115(1A) was inserted by section 15(3) of the Road Traffic Act 1974 (c. 50) and section 119(1) was amended by section 1(2) of, and paragraph 10 of Schedule 1 to, the Road Traffic (Drivers' Ages and Hours of Work) Act 1976 (c. 3).
(**b**) S.I. 1979/571 and 1981/238.
(**c**) S.I. 1977/1309; the relevant amending Instrument is S.I. 1980/1821.
(**d**) 1981 c. 56; Schedule 7 to the said Act of 1981 has been amended by section 58 of the Transport Act 1982 (c. 49).

ROAD TRAFFIC

4. In Regulation 4 (Qualifications of applicants)—

(*a*) for paragraph (*d*) substitute the following paragraph:—

"(*d*) in the case of an applicant for an hgv trainee driver's licence he shall be a registered employee of a registered employer and—

(i) if he is applying for his first hgv driver's licence, the licence referred to in paragraph (*c*) above, if it is an ordinary driving licence, shall have no penalty points endorsed on it, or if it is a Northern Ireland (ordinary) driving licence, shall be free from a relevant endorsement;

(ii) in any other case, the licence referred to in paragraph (*c*) above, if it is an ordinary driving licence shall not have more than three penalty points endorsed on it, or if it is a Northern Ireland (ordinary) driving licence, shall bear not more than one relevant endorsement;"; and

(*b*) delete the paragraph which follows the Table in that Regulation.

5. In Regulation 11 (Suspension or revocation), for paragraph (4), substitute the following paragraph—

"(4) The circumstances prescribed for the purposes of section 115(1A) of the Act of 1972 (obligatory revocation of hgv driver's licence when the holder is under the age of 21) are that the holder's ordinary driving licence has more than three penalty points endorsed on it, or that the holder's Northern Ireland (ordinary) driving licence bears more than one relevant endorsement.".

Signed by authority of the Secretary of State

Lynda Chalker,
Parliamentary Under Secretary of State,
Department of Transport.

9th August 1983.

EXPLANATORY NOTE

(This Note is not part of the Regulations.)

1. These Regulations further amend the Heavy Goods Vehicles (Drivers' Licences) Regulations 1977.

2. They amend Regulation 4 of the 1977 Regulations (as to the qualifications of applicants for hgv trainee drivers' licences) by providing that a holder of an ordinary driving licence must hold a licence which has no penalty points endorsed on it if he is applying for a hgv trainee driving licence for the first time (in place of the previous provisions that the ordinary driving licence should have no endorsement) and that the holder of an ordinary driving licence shall have no more than three penalty points endorsed on it if he is applying for a hgv trainee driver's licence if he has previously held such a licence (in place of the provision that the ordinary driving licence should bear not more than one endorsement). Regulation 4 refers.

3. These Regulations also amend Regulation 11(4) of the 1977 Regulations by providing that the circumstances in which hgv licences shall be revoked by virtue of section 115(1A) of the Road Traffic Act 1972 are that the holder of an ordinary driving licence has more than three penalty points endorsed on his licence (in place of the previous circumstances of the ordinary driving licence bearing more than one endorsement). Regulation 5 refers.

4. "Penalty Points" are defined as the penalty points endorsed on a licence under the provisions of section 19 of, and Schedule 7 to, the Transport Act 1981, and the term "relevant endorsement" is defined. Regulation 2 refers.

5. No amendments are made to the substance of Regulations 4 and 11 as to the holder of a Northern Ireland (ordinary) driving licence.

STATUTORY INSTRUMENTS

1983 No. 1234 (C. 36)

WATER, ENGLAND AND WALES
WATER SUPPLY, SCOTLAND
WATER, NORTHERN IRELAND

The Water Act 1983 (Commencement No. 2) Order 1983

Made -   -   -   -   *9th August* 1983

The Secretary of State for the Environment, as respects England, the Secretary of State for Wales, as respects Wales, the Secretary of State for Scotland, as respects Scotland, and the Secretary of State for Northern Ireland, as respects Northern Ireland, in exercise of their powers under section 11(5) and (6) of the Water Act 1983 (a) and of all other powers enabling them in that behalf, hereby order as follows:—

1.   This order may be cited as the Water Act 1983 (Commencement No. 2) Order 1983.

2.   The provisions of the Water Act 1983 which are specified in column 1 of the Schedule to this order (as respects England, Wales, Scotland and Northern Ireland as specified in Part I, as respects England, Wales and Scotland only as specified in Part II and as respects England and Wales only as specified in Part III of the said Schedule respectively) and which relate to the subject matter specified in column 2 thereof shall come into force on 1st October 1983.

3.—(1) Any person (other than the chairman of a water authority) who, but for the coming into force of section 1 of the Water Act 1983 in accordance with the provisions of paragraph 2 above, would have been holding office as a member of any such authority on 1st October 1983, shall vacate office immediately before that day; but this provision shall not be taken as preventing the reappointment of any such person under the provisions of section 3 of the Water Act 1973 (b), as substituted by the said section 1.

(2) This article extends to England and Wales only.

(a)   1983 c.23.   (b)   1973 c.37.

SCHEDULE

PART I

ENGLAND, WALES, SCOTLAND AND NORTHERN IRELAND

Column 1 Provisions of the Act	Column 2 Subject matter of provisions
Section 1(2)	Amendment of House of Commons Disqualification Act 1975 (a) .
Section 11(3) so far as it applies to the provision of Schedule 5, Part I which is specified below	Repeal or revocation of enactments and instruments.
In Schedule 5 Part I	
House of Commons Disqualification Act 1975 In Part III of Schedule 1, the entry relating to a regional water authority and the Welsh Water Authority	

PART II

ENGLAND, WALES AND SCOTLAND

Column 1 Provisions of the Act	Column 2 Subject matter of provisions
Section 11(2) so far as it applies to the provision of Schedule 4 which is specified below	Minor and consequential amendments.
Section 11(3) so far as it applies to the provision of Schedule 5, Part I which is specified below	Repeal or revocation of enactments and instruments.
In Schedule 4 Paragraph 4(1)	
In Schedule 5, Part 1 the entry relative to the Public Bodies (Admission to Meetings) Act 1960 (b)	

(a) 1975 c.24.   (b) 1960 c.67.

PART III

ENGLAND AND WALES

(1) Provisions of the Act	(2) Subject matter of provisions
Section 1(1) and (3)	Constitution and procedure of water authorities.

Section 11(2)
  so far as it applies to the provisions of
  Schedule 4 which are specified below
	Minor and consequential amendments.

Section 11(3)
  so far as it applies to the provisions of
  Schedule 5 which are specified below
	Repeal or revocation of enactments and instruments.

Schedule 1	
In Schedule 4 paragraphs 4(2), 5, 6 and 7	

In Schedule 5, Part 1
  the entries relative to the Local
  Government Act 1972 (a)	

Water Act 1973	
Section 6	
In section 17(5), the words "under section 6 above" Local Government Planning and Land Act 1980 (b)	
Section 25(4)	
In Schedule 5, Part II all the entries	

Patrick Jenkin,
Secretary of State for the
Environment.

27th July 1983.

Signed by authority of the
Secretary of State
29th July 1983.

John Stradling Thomas,
Minister of State for Wales.

(a) 1972 c.70.   (b) 1980 c.65.

George Younger,
Secretary of State for Scotland.

1st August 1983.

James Prior,
Secretary of State for
Northern Ireland.

9th August 1983.

EXPLANATORY NOTE

(*This Note is not part of the Order.*)

This order brings certain provisions of the Water Act 1983 into force on 1st October 1983. Some apply to the United Kingdom as a whole and others to part only thereof, the Schedule showing these divided up accordingly. The Order also provides, so far as England and Wales are concerned, for the vacation of office by existing members (other than the chairmen) of water authorities before 1st October 1983.

NOTE AS TO EARLIER COMMENCEMENT ORDER

(*This Note is not part of the Order.*)

Provision	Date of Commencement	S.I. No.
ss.7,8,11(3) (partially) Schedule 5 (partially)	10.8.1983	1983/1173 (C. 32)

STATUTORY INSTRUMENTS

1983 No. 1235

WATER, ENGLAND AND WALES
WATER SUPPLY, SCOTLAND
WATER, NORTHERN IRELAND

The Water Act 1983 (National Water Council Appointed Day) Order 1983

Made - - - - - *9th August* 1983

The Secretary of State for the Environment as respects England, the Secretary of State for Wales as respects Wales, the Secretary of State for Scotland as respects Scotland, and the Secretary of State for Northern Ireland as respects Northern Ireland, in exercise of their powers under sections 3(1) and 9(2) of the Water Act 1983**(a)** and of all other powers enabling them in that behalf, hereby make the following order:—

1. This order may be cited as the Water Act 1983 (National Water Council Appointed Day) Order 1983.

2. The day appointed for the purposes of section 3(1) of the Water Act 1983 (which provides for the determination of the functions of the National Water Council) shall be 1st October 1983.

3. The provisions of the Water Act 1983 which are specified in column 1 of the Schedule to this order and which relate to the subject matter specified in column 2 thereof shall come into force on 1st October 1983.

SCHEDULE

Column 1 Provisions of the Act	Column 2 Subject matter of provisions
Section 11(2) so far as it applies to the provisions of Schedule 4 which are specified below	Minor and consequential amendments.
Section 11(3) so far as it applies to the provisions of Schedule 5 which are specified below	Repeal or revocation of enactments and instruments.
In Schedule 4 Paragraphs 1, 2 and 3	
In Schedule 5, Part I the entry relative to the Public Health Act 1961**(b)**	

(a) 1983 c. 23. **(b)** 1961 c. 64.

Column 1 Provisions of the Act	Column 2 Subject matter of provisions
Water Act 1973(a)	
Section 4	
In section 5(3), the words from "but before" to the end.	
In section 26, subsections (2) to (4).	
In section 29(2), the words "and after consultation with the Council".	
In section 30(6), the words "after consultation with the Council".	
In section 38(1), the definitions of "the Council", "regional water board" and "water development board".	
In Schedule 3, paragraphs 22 to 30; in paragraph 31(1), the words from "and including" to the end; in paragraph 31(2), the words "and of any payment to the Council under paragraph 33 below"; in paragraph 32(1), the words "and after consultation with the Council"; paragraph 33; in paragraphs 34, 39F(1), 40(1) and 41, the words "and the Council", wherever they occur; in paragraphs 34(6) and 40(6), the words "or of the Council"; in paragraphs 35(2) and 39E(1), the words "or to the Council"; in paragraphs 36, 38(5) and (6), 39(1), 39E(1)(b) and 39F(1)(a), the words "or the Council", wherever they occur; in paragraph 36(4), the words "or, as the case may be, the Council"; in paragraph 38(1), the words "and of the Council"; paragraph 39F(2); in paragraph 40(3) the words "to the Council and", sub-paragraph (4) and in sub-paragraph (8) the words from "the Council" to "Commission".	
In Schedule 8, paragraph 90 the entries relative to the Health and Safety at Work etc. Act 1974(b)	

(a) 1973 c. 37.   (b) 1974 c. 37.

II/2dd

Column 1 Provisions of the Act	Column 2 Subject matter of provisions
House of Commons Disqualification Act 1975**(a)**. In Part III of Schedule 1, the entry relating to the National Water Council. the entry relative to the Land Drainage Act 1976**(b)** the entry relative to the Water (Scotland) Act 1980**(c)**	

Patrick Jenkin,
Secretary of State for
the Environment.

27th July 1983.

Signed by authority of the Secretary of State

John Stradling Thomas,
Minister of State for
Wales.

29th July 1983.

George Younger,
Secretary of State for
Scotland.

1st August 1983.

James Prior,
Secretary of State for
Northern Ireland.

9th August 1983.

(a) 1975 c. 24.   **(b)** 1976 c. 70.   **(c)** 1980 c. 45.

EXPLANATORY NOTE

(This Note is not part of the Order.)

This Order appoints 1st October 1983 as the day on which the functions of the National Water Council shall determine, and as the day on which certain enactments relating to those functions shall be repealed or modified.

STATUTORY INSTRUMENTS

1983 No. 1239

HOUSING, ENGLAND AND WALES
HOUSING, SCOTLAND
RATING AND VALUATION

The Housing Benefits Amendment (No. 2) Regulations 1983

Made - - - -	*12th August* 1983
Laid before Parliament	*15th August* 1983
Coming into Operation	*1st September* 1983

The Secretary of State for Social Services, in exercise of the powers conferred on him by section 28(1) of the Social Security and Housing Benefits Act 1982(**a**) and of all other powers enabling him in that behalf, with the consent of the Treasury, hereby makes the following regulations:—

Citation and commencement

1. These regulations may be cited as the Housing Benefits Amendment (No. 2) Regulations 1983 and shall come into operation on 1st September 1983.

Amendment of regulations

2. Regulation 16(2)(*e*) of the Housing Benefits Regulations 1982(**b**) (deductions for the purposes of computing eligible rent for certain grant-aided students) is amended as follows:—

    (*a*) in head (i) (students at establishments in the London area) for "£18.65" there is substituted "£19.45"; and

    (*b*) in head (ii) (other cases) for "£14.10" there is substituted "£14.70".

Signed by authority of the Secretary of State for Social Services.

Rhodes Boyson,
Minister of State,
Department of Health and Social Security.

2nd August 1983.

(**a**) 1982 c. 24.
(**b**) S.I. 1982/1124; the relevant amending instrument is S.I. 1982/1519.

We consent,

Nigel Lawson,
D. J. F. Hunt,
Two of the Lords Commissioners
of Her Majesty's Treasury.

12th August 1983.

EXPLANATORY NOTE

(This Note is not part of the Regulations.)

These Regulations amend the Housing Benefits Regulations 1982 ("the 1982 regulations"). Under those regulations, in the assessment of eligible rent for the purposes of calculating rent rebate or rent allowance for a person not receiving supplementary benefit, certain deductions are made from the rent actually payable. One such deduction is made in the case of grant-aided students for certain periods (mainly term-time) set out in Part II of Schedule 1 to the 1982 regulations. For the period for which that deduction is made, an equivalent amount of the student's income is disregarded for the purposes of ascertaining his weekly income for rate rebate, rent rebate or rent allowance. These regulations increase the amount of the deduction from £18.65 to £19.45 in the case of students in the London area and from £14.10 to £14.70 in other cases.

STATUTORY INSTRUMENTS

1983 No. 1240

SOCIAL SECURITY

The Supplementary Benefit (Requirements, Resources and Single Payments) Amendment Regulations 1983

Laid before Parliament in draft

Made - - - - - -	*12th August* 1983

Coming into Operation

Except for regulations 2(2)(*a*), 2(4)(*a*), (*b*) and (*c*), (6), (7), (10), (12)(*a*) and (13)(*b*), 3(2)(*b*), 3(4) *in so far as it adds a sub-paragraph (j)*, 4 *and* 5	*15th August* 1983
Regulations 2(2)(*a*), 2(4)(*a*), (*b*) and (*c*), (6), (7), (10), (12)(*a*) and (13)(*b*), 3(2)(*b*), 3(4) *in so far as it adds a sub-paragraph (j)*, 4 *and* 5	*21st November* 1983

Whereas a draft of the following regulations was laid before Parliament and approved by a resolution of each House of Parliament:

Now therefore the Secretary of State for Social Services, with the consent of the Treasury, in exercise of the powers conferred upon him by section 3(1) and paragraphs 1(2) and 2(1), (3) and (4) of Schedule 1 to the Supplementary Benefits Act 1976(**a**) and of all other powers enabling him in that behalf, after reference to the Social Security Advisory Committee, hereby makes the following regulations:—

Citation and commencement

1. These regulations may be cited as the Supplementary Benefit (Requirements, Resources and Single Payments) Amendment Regulations 1983 and shall come into operation on 15th August 1983 except for regulations 2(2)(*a*), 2(4)(*a*), (*b*) and (*c*), (6), (7), (10), (12)(*a*) and (13)(*b*), 3(2)(*b*), 3(4) in so far as it adds a sub-paragraph (*j*), 4 and 5, which shall come into operation on 21st November 1983.

(**a**) 1976 c.71; Schedule 1 was substituted by section 6(1) of, and paragraph 30 of Schedule 2 to, the Social Security Act 1980 (c.30); the Act is amended by sections 38 and 48(5) of, and Schedule 4 to, the Social Security and Housing Benefits Act 1982 (c.24).

Amendment of the Supplementary Benefit (Requirements) Regulations 1980

2.—(1) Subject to regulation 5 of these regulations the Supplementary Benefit (Requirements) Regulations 1980(a) shall be amended in accordance with the following provisions of this regulation.

(2) In regulation 2(1) (interpretation) there shall be inserted—

(a) after the definition of "prisoner" the following definition:—

""qualifying benefit" means any of the following, namely invalidity benefit or non-contributory invalidity pension under Part II of the Social Security Act, unemployability supplement (increase of industrial injuries disablement pension) under section 58 of that Act or an allowance in respect of unemployability under article 18 of the Naval Military and Air Forces etc. (Disablement and Death) Service Pensions Order 1978(b);" and

(b) after the definition of "single claimant" the following definition:—

""student" means a person under pensionable age who has ceased relevant education and who during a course of full-time education is either attending that course or is on vacation for any period constituting a normal vacation from it;".

(3) In regulation 5(2) (meaning of householder) there shall be substituted for sub-paragraph (c) the following sub-paragraph:—

"(c) is either not absent from the home or if absent is absent only—

(i) otherwise than as a student on normal vacation, and

(ii) for a period which has not yet continued for more than 13 weeks.".

(4) In regulation 7 (conditions for long-term rates of normal requirements)—

(a) in paragraph (1)(a) there shall be inserted after the words "condition of availability" the words "or is eligible for an allowance while the partner of a person aged not less than 60",

(b) in paragraph (1)(b) there shall be substituted for the words "if he is a person aged less than 60" the words "unless he is a person aged not less than 60 or is the partner of such a person",

(c) for sub-paragraph (a) of paragraph (2) there shall be substituted the following sub-paragraph:—

"(a) any period in respect of which he was in receipt of a qualifying benefit;", and

(d) for sub-paragraph (c) of paragraph (2) there shall be substituted the following sub-paragraph:—

"(c) any other period of 8 weeks or less (or of 13 weeks or less in the case of a period ending before 15th August 1983) in respect of which he was not in receipt of an allowance not

---

(a) S.I. 1980/1299; relevant amending instruments are S.I. 1980/1774, 1981/1016, 1197, 1982/1125, 1126, 1127, 1983/505.
(b) S.I. 1978/1525.

subject to the condition of availability and which fell immediately between periods—

(i) in respect of which he was in receipt of an allowance not subject to the condition of availability, or

(ii) to which sub-paragraph (*a*) or (*b*) applies.".

(5) In regulation 8(3) (modification of normal requirements in certain cases of unemployment benefit disqualification) there shall be substituted for sub-paragraph (*b*) the following sub-paragraph:—

"(*b*) any member of the assessment unit is either pregnant or seriously ill,".

(6) In regulation 9(1)(*a*) (boarders) for the words from "except where" to "paragraph (4)" there shall be substituted the words "subject to paragraph (5) shall not exceed the maximum amount in respect of the assessment unit as a whole referred to in paragraph (4)".

(7) For paragraphs (4) and (5) of regulation 9 there shall be substituted the following paragraphs:—

"(4) Subject to paragraph (4A) the maximum amount in respect of the assessment unit as a whole referred to in paragraph (1)(*a*) shall be—

(*a*) in respect of any dependant aged less than 11, $1\frac{1}{2}$ times the amount referred to in paragraph (3)(*c*), and

(*b*) in respect of any member of the assessment unit other than a dependant to whom sub-paragraph (*a*) applies, the amount estimated by a benefit officer as representing the reasonable weekly charge for the relevant area for full board and lodging (inclusive of all meals) which is available in that area or, if the level of charges there is unusually high, in an adjoining area, and which is of a standard suitable for claimants resident in the type of accommodation which is provided either—

(i) in a nursing home or mental nursing home within the meaning of sections 1 and 2 of the Nursing Homes Act 1975(**a**) or in a nursing home as defined in section 10 of the Nursing Homes Registration (Scotland) Act 1938(**b**) or a private hospital within the meaning of Part II of the Mental Health (Scotland) Act 1960(**c**), or

(ii) in a home which satisfies the provisions of the Residential Homes Act 1980, or of section 61 of the Social Work (Scotland) Act 1968(**d**), or

(iii) in any other type of accommodation,

whichever may be appropriate to the accommodation provided in respect of the claimant in that assessment unit save that, in respect of persons referred to in paragraph (4A)(*c*)(vii) or (viii), the amount shall be the amount in respect of accommodation specified under head (iii) hereof.

(**a**) 1975 c.37.
(**b**) 1938 c.73.
(**c**) 1960 c.61.
(**d**) 1968 c.49.

(4A) The maximum amount specified in paragraph (4) shall be increased by any excess of the actual charge over that maximum up to £15.35 or, if the increase is payable under sub-paragraph (*a*) or (*c*) of that paragraph and the claimant is a relevant person, up to £30.70, in the case of—

    (*a*) a claimant who has attained pensionable age or a relevant person or his partner either of whom is aged 65 or over, or

    (*b*) a claimant or any other member of the assessment unit who is infirm by reason of physical or mental disability, or

    (*c*) a claimant in respect of whom or of whose accommodation one or more of the following conditions are satisfied namely that—

        (i) he is a person in respect of whom a local authority has power to make arrangements pursuant to section 26(1)(*a*)(ii) of the National Assistance Act 1948(**a**) (provision of accommodation in premises registered under the Residential Homes Act 1980) but has declined to exercise that power,

        (ii) the accommodation is provided in a nursing home or mental nursing home as defined in sections 1 and 2 of the Nursing Homes Act 1975 where a health authority has power pursuant to section 23(1) of the National Health Service Act 1977(**b**) (voluntary organisations and other bodies) to make contractual arrangements for the provision of accommodation but has declined to exercise that power,

        (iii) the accommodation is provided in a nursing home as defined in section 10 of the Nursing Home Registration (Scotland) Act 1938 or in a private hospital within the meaning of Part III of the Mental Health (Scotland) Act 1960 where the Secretary of State has power pursuant to section 16 of the National Health Service (Scotland) Act 1978(**c**) (assistance to voluntary organisations) to make contractual arrangements for the provision of accommodation but has declined to exercise that power,

        (iv) he is a person in respect of whom a local social services authority has power to provide residential accommodation pursuant to section 21 of, and paragraph 1 of Schedule 8 to, the National Health Service Act 1977 (care of mothers and young children) but has declined to exercise that power,

        (v) he is a person—

           (*aa*) in respect of whom a local social services authority has power to provide residential accommodation pursuant to section 21 of, and paragraph 2 of Schedule 8 to, the National Health Service Act

(**a**) 1948 c.29.
(**b**) 1977 c.49.
(**c**) 1978 c.29.

1977 (prevention, care and after-care) but has declined to exercise that power, and

(*bb*) whose accommodation is in premises registered under the Residential Homes Act 1980 (registration of disabled persons, and old persons, homes),

(vi) he is a person in need within the meaning of section 94(1) of the Social Work (Scotland) Act 1968 who does not come within the provisions of section 12 of that Act,

(vii) he is a person suffering from a mental disorder within the meaning of the Mental Health Act 1959(**a**) or the Mental Health (Scotland) Act 1960 in respect of whom a local social services authority has, pursuant to section 21 of, and paragraph 2 of Schedule 8 to, the National Health Service Act 1977 (prevention care and after-care), made arrangements for the provision of residential accommodation in a private household or in premises which are not required to be registered under the Residential Homes Act 1980,

(viii) he is a person who is resident in premises which are used for the rehabilitation of alcoholics or drug addicts,

so however that only one increase shall be applicable under this paragraph in respect of any member of the assessment unit and the amount payable by virtue of this paragraph in respect of a claimant and his partner shall not exceed £30.70 and, if any member of the assessment unit who is a boarder is receiving attendance allowance under section 35 of the Social Security Act, an increase of disablement pension under section 61 of that Act, constant attendance allowance by virtue of article 14 of the Naval, Military and Air Forces etc. (Disablement and Death) Service Pensions Order 1983(**b**), or constant attendance allowance by virtue of article 14 of the Personal Injuries (Civilians) Scheme 1983(**c**), an increase shall only be payable to the extent that the excess of the actual charge over the maximum amount is more than the amount of whichever of the aforementioned allowances or increase of pension is in payment up to a maximum of the higher rate of attendance allowance specified in Schedule 4 to the Social Security Act.

(4B) The maximum amount applicable in respect of a dependant aged less than 11 calculated in the manner referred to in paragraph 4(a) shall be rounded to the nearest multiple of 5p. by treating an odd amount of 2·5p. or more as 5p. and by disregarding an odd amount of less than 2·5p.

(5) This paragraph shall apply for a period not exceeding 13 weeks to a claimant who has lived in the same accommodation for more than 12 months and who could afford the charges in respect of that accommodation when he took up residence, if, having regard to the availability of and level of charges for board and lodging accommodation and to the circumstances mentioned in regulation 21(5)(*b*), this is

(**a**) 1959 c.72.
(**b**) S.I. 1983/883.
(**c**) S.I. 1983/686.

reasonable to allow him time to find alternative accommodation provided that he is not a person who is being accommodated by a housing authority pursuant to the Housing (Homeless Persons) Act 1977(**a**) or by a local authority pursuant to section 1 of the Child Care Act 1980(**b**) or, in Scotland, section 12 of the Social Work (Scotland) Act 1968(**c**); and in such a case paragraph (4) shall not apply except to the extent that he is able to meet the balance of the actual charge over the maximum amount out of income which is disregarded for the purposes of the Resources Regulations.".

(8) In regulation 9(9) there shall be inserted at the beginning the words "Subject to paragraph (10)," and there shall be deleted the words from and including "but excluding" to the end of the paragraph.

(9) In regulation 9 there shall be added after paragraph (9) the following paragraphs:—

"(10) There shall be excluded from the definition of "boarder" in paragraph (9) any person—

  (*a*) whose accommodation and meals (if any) are provided by a close relative or other than on a commercial basis, or

  (*b*) who is in the opinion of the benefit officer on holiday and during a period which has not yet continued for more than 13 weeks is absent from the home or from a hospital or similar institution in which he is normally a patient, or

  (*c*) who is aged under 19 but not less than 16 and is in the care of a local authority under the provisions of a relevant enactment, except such a person who is personally liable to pay the cost of his accommodation and maintenance direct to someone other than a local authority.

(11) In this regulation "a relevant enactment" means the Social Work (Scotland) Act 1968, the Family Law Reform Act 1969(**d**), the Children and Young Persons Act 1969(**e**), the Matrimonial Causes Act 1973(**f**), the Guardianship Act 1973(**g**), the Children Act 1975(**h**), the Domestic Proceedings and Magistrates Courts Act 1978(**i**) or the Child Care Act 1980(**j**).".

(10) In regulation 10(4) (modification of normal requirements in special cases) the words "other than in premises which are registered under section 1 of the Residential Homes Act 1980(**k**) and which are used for the rehabilitation of alcoholics and drug addicts" shall be inserted both in sub-paragraph (*a*) after the words "(local authority services)" and in sub-paragraph (*c*) after the words "(registration of disabled persons' and old persons' homes)", and in the latter sub-paragraph for the reference to regulation 9(4)(*a*) there shall be substituted a reference to regulation 9(4A)(*c*).

(**a**) 1977 c.48.
(**b**) 1980 c.5.
(**c**) 1968 c.49.
(**d**) 1969 c.46.
(**e**) 1969 c.54.
(**f**) 1973 c.18.
(**g**) 1973 c.29.
(**h**) 1975 c.72.
(**i**) 1978 c.22.
(**j**) 1980 c.5.
(**k**) 1980 c.7.

(11) In regulation 13(6) (additional requirements for items other than heating) there shall be substituted for the words "and 18" the words ", 18 and 18A".

(12) In regulation 14 (housing requirements)—

(a) in paragraph (3)(b) the words from "but" to the end shall be omitted, and

(b) in paragraph (4) the words ", as defined in the Resources Regulations," shall be deleted and before the word "vacation" there shall be inserted the word "normal".

(13) In Schedule 2 (modification of normal requirements in special cases)—

(a) in column (3) of paragraph 2, for the words "the long-term rate for householders" where they first appear there shall be substituted the words "the higher of the two sums for the time being specified in section 6(1)(a) of the Social Security Pensions Act 1975(a) (hereafter in this paragraph referred to as "the relevant sum specified in section 6(1)(a)")" and wherever they otherwise appear there shall be substituted the words "the relevant sum specified in section 6(1)(a)", and

(b) for column (3) of paragraph 4 there shall be substituted the following:—

"4. A weekly amount equal to 7 times the combined total of the rates for the time being specified in regulation 9(2)(b)(i), (ii) and (iii) (daily rates for breakfast and midday and evening meals).".

(14) In Schedule 3, Part II (additional requirements for items other than heating)—

(a) in sub-paragraph (1) of paragraph 14, column (2) the words "provided this does not exceed twice the ordinary rate for non-householders" shall be enclosed in brackets and there shall be inserted in that sub-paragraph at the end the words ", and, where applicable, an amount equal to the amount, calculated on a weekly basis, of any secondary Class 1 contribution payable under the Social Security Act arising from employment consisting of the rendering of that assistance",

(b) in head (iv) of paragraph 16(a), column (2) there shall be substituted for the words "Great Britain" the words "the United Kingdom", and

(a) 1975 c.60; see section 23(1)(a) of that Act and section 1(3) of the Social Security (No. 2) Act 1980 (c.39).

(c) after paragraph 18 there shall be inserted the following paragraph:—

"Special clothing or footwear

18A. Where the cost of an item of necessary clothing or footwear for any person, other than an item available under the National Health Service Act 1977, significantly exceeds the cost of such an item in standard sizes or fittings by reason of his stature or size or of any physical disability of his.

18A. The estimated extra cost, calculated on a weekly basis, of the item above that of such an item in standard sizes or fittings."

Amendment of the Supplementary Benefit (Resources) Regulations 1981

3.—(1) The Supplementary Benefit (Resources) Regulations 1981(**a**) shall be amended in accordance with the following provisions of this regulation.

(2) In regulation 2(1) (interpretation)—

(a) there shall be inserted in the definition of "liable relative" immediately after the words "deceased liable relative" the words "or to a payment resulting from a disposition of property, whether voluntary or by order of the court as the case may be, made in or in connection with an agreement to separate or proceedings for a decree of divorce or judicial separation or for a decree or declarator of nullity"; and

(b) there shall be inserted after the definition of "liable relative" the following definition:—

""life policy" means any instrument by which the payment of money is assured on death (except death by accident only) or the happening of any contingency dependent on human life, or any instrument evidencing a contract which is subject to payment of premiums for a term dependent on human life;".

(3) In regulation 3(2) (calculation of resources)—

(a) in sub-paragraph (b) there shall be substituted for the word "sum" the word "payment", and

(b) after sub-paragraph (f) there shall be added the following sub-paragraph:—

"(g) any payment by way of an annual bounty to a member of any territorial or reserve force mentioned in Part I of Schedule 3 to the Social Security (Contributions) Regulations 1979(**b**) shall be treated as a capital resource.".

(4) In regulation 6(1) (disregarded capital resources) there shall be added after sub-paragraph (h) the following sub-paragraphs:—

"(i) any sum attributable to savings made out of income for the purpose of

(a) S.I. 1981/1527; relevant amending instruments are S.I. 1982/1125, 1126, 1983/505.
(b) S.I. 1979/591; Part I of Schedule 3 substituted by S.I. 1980/1975.

meeting any periodically recurring liability in respect of such personal living expenses and expenses of the home as are reasonable in the opinion of the benefit officer, including in particular charges for:—

 (i) rent

 (ii) rates

 (iii) fuel

 (iv) telephone rental or calls

for such a period and up to such an amount as are reasonable in the opinion of the benefit officer, having regard respectively to the time when the liability falls to be met and its expected amount;

(j) the first £1500 of the surrender value of any life policy or, in any case where there are two or more such policies, of their combined surrender value;

(k) a sum representing the market value of the equitable interest of a member of the assessment unit in trust funds—

 (i) which are derived from a payment, whether in pursuance of a court order or otherwise, in consequence of a personal or criminal injury to him, and

 (ii) to which as sole beneficiary under the trust he is entitled absolutely,

so however that where that member is the claimant or his partner that sum shall only be disregarded for such a period, not normally exceeding 12 months from the date on which the payment would, but for this sub-paragraph, fail to be taken into account for the purposes of a claim for pension or allowance or a review of a determination pursuant to regulation 4 of the Determination of Questions Regulations, as is reasonable in the circumstances in the opinion of the benefit officer.".

(5) In regulation 9(2) (calculation of income resources)—

(a) in sub-paragraph (b) there shall be added after head (ii) the following words:—

"so however that in either case where the payment in question is the last of two or more consecutive payments of any benefit to which regulation 15 of the Social Security (Claims and Payments) Regulations 1979(a) applies (unemployment, sickness and certain other benefits under the Social Security Act) it shall be treated as paid on the date immediately following the last day of the period to which the payment immediately preceding it is attributable in accordance with the provisions of this paragraph;", and

(b) there shall be inserted after sub-paragraph (c) the following sub-paragraph:—

"(cc) where any payment of income from a particular source, whether payable weekly or attributable at a weekly rate in accordance with sub-paragraph (c), is paid regularly, the amount of that income attributable to any one benefit week shall not exceed the amount of or, as the case may be, the weekly rate of one such payment;".

(a) S.I. 1979/628, to which there are amendments not relevant to these regulations.

(6) In regulation 10 (calculation of earnings)—

(a) in paragraph (1) after the words "Subject to" there shall be inserted the words "regulation 3(2)(g) and",

(b) in paragraph (3)—

(i) in head (iv) of sub-paragraph (d) the words "for periods of less than 8 hours a week" shall be deleted, and

(ii) there shall be inserted after sub-paragraph (e) the following sub-paragraph:—

"(f) any payment of bonus or commission which under paragraph (1)(b) of regulation 9 of the Supplementary Benefit (Conditions of Entitlement) Regulations 1981(a) has been taken into account for the purposes of that regulation (claimants treated as engaged in remunerative full time work for the purposes of section 6(1) of the Act) as a claimant's earnings for a period subsequent to the termination of his employment or during which he was a person affected by a trade dispute;", and

(c) in head (ii) of paragraph (4)(b) there shall be substitued for the words "that period", where they first occur, the words "the period to which his earnings from that employment relate".

(7) In regulation 11 (calculation of other income)—

(a) in sub-paragraph (2) there shall be inserted between the words "as" and "the" the words "regulation 3(2)(a) and",

(b) at the end of paragraph (2) there shall be added the following sub-paragraph:—

"(q) any payment of pension or allowance under the Act.", and

(c) in sub-paragraph (l) of paragraph (4) there shall be substituted for the words "or (e)" the words "(e), (g) or (i)".

Amendment of regulation 17(1)(b) of the Supplementary Benefit (Single Payments) Regulations 1981

4. In sub-paragraph (b) of regulation 17(1) of the Supplementary Benefit (Single Payments) Regulations 1981(b) (essential repairs and maintenance of the home) there shall be substituted for the sum of "£225" the sum of "£325".

Transitional provision

5.—(1) Subject to paragraphs (2) and (3) of this regulation,—

(a) in respect of any person to whom the provisions of paragraph (5) of regulation 9 of the Supplementary Benefit (Requirements) Regulations 1980 (hereafter in this regulation referred to as "the Requirements Regulations") applied immediately prior to the date of the coming into operation of this regulation by virtue of sub-paragraph *(a)* of that paragraph those provisions shall continue to apply for 12 months from that date so long as the claimant remains in the same accommodation or is temporarily absent for a period not exceeding 8 weeks;

(a) S.I. 1981/1526.
(b) S.I. 1981/1528, to which there are amendments not relevant to these regulations.

(b) in respect of any person to whom the provisions of paragraph (5) of regulation 9 of the Requirements Regulations applied immediately prior to the coming into operation of this regulation by virtue of sub-paragraph *(b)* of that paragraph, those provisions shall apply for the period for which they would otherwise have applied.

(2) Subject to paragraph 3 of this regulation, a claimant who was entitled to an increase by virtue of regulation 9(4)*(a)* of the Requirements Regulations immediately prior to the date of the coming into operation of these regulations shall continue to be entitled to such an increase up to a maximum of, if he is a relevant person, £12.60, or, in any other case, £6.30, for 12 months from that date so long as he remains in the same accommodation or is temporarily absent for a period not exceeding 8 weeks.

(3) Paragraphs (1) and (2) of this regulation shall not apply in respect of any person who is resident in premises which are used for the rehabilitation of alcoholics or drug addicts and paragraph (2) shall not apply to a claimant who is entitled to an increase by virtue of regulation 9(4A) of the Requirements Regulations.

5th August 1983.

Norman Fowler,
Secretary of State for Social Services.

We consent,

Nigel Lawson,
D. J. F. Hunt,
Two of the Lords Commissioners
of Her Majesty's Treasury.

12th August 1983.

EXPLANATORY NOTE
(This Note is not part of the Regulations.)

These Regulations further amend the Supplementary Benefit (Requirements) Regulations 1980 ("the Requirements Regulations"), the Supplementary Benefit (Resources) Regulations 1981 ("the Resources Regulations") and the Supplementary Benefit (Single Payments) Regulations 1981 ("the Single Payments Regulations").

Various provisions of the Requirements Regulations are amended by regulation 2, as set out in this paragraph. In regulation 2 two new definitions, of "qualifying benefit" and "student", are inserted to clarify amendments made elsewhere in the Regulations. In regulation 5(2) the condition relating to permitted absences from where they normally reside of persons qualifying as householders under the table in Schedule 1 to the Supplementary Benefits Act 1976 is amended so as to exclude absences of students on normal vacations. Certain minor amendments are made to regulation 7 to conform to changes introduced by the Supplementary Benefit (Equal Treatment) Regulations 1983 (S.I. 1983/1004). That regulation is also amended to enable persons in receipt of certain long-term incapacity benefits, and because of the level of those benefits ineligible for the ordinary (lower) rate of supplementary benefit, to count periods in receipt of those incapacity benefits towards the qualifying period for the long-term (higher) rate of supplementary benefit. Regulation 7 is also amended to reduce the length of the gap permitted between periods in receipt of supplementary benefit in reckoning the 52 week qualifying period for benefit at the long-term rate. Regulation 8(3) is amended to restrict the special circumstances in which a smaller reduction is made in benefit payable to persons actually or notionally disqualified from receiving unemployment benefit. Regulation 9 is amended so as to alter the basis on which the rates for board and lodging allowance is calculated and the circumstances in which amounts above the normal maximum limit can be paid and to ensure that the general rates apply to persons in accommodation for the treatment of alcoholism and drug addiction. The exclusion from the definition of "boarder" in paragraph (9) is also expanded to cover certain persons in holiday accommodation or in the care of a local authority. Regulation 14(3)*(b)* is amended so as to make joint householders eligible only for their actual housing requirement, in line with the position under the Housing Benefits scheme, and not, as previously, for a housing requirement equal to the amount of the non-householder contribution in cases where the actual requirement fell below the amount of that contribution. Schedule 2 is amended so as to ensure that the supplementary benefit rate for hospital in-patients remains as the same proportion of the weekly rate of the basic component of a Category A retirement pension by linking it directly to that rate instead of to the long-term supplementary benefit rate for householders which is no longer the same as that retirement pension rate. That Schedule is also amended to give single homeless claimants a different higher rate of benefit to meet the cost of meals. Schedule 3 Part II is amended so as to extend additional requirements to include in the cost of residential domestic assistance payable in special cases of disability etc. the cost of any secondary class 1 contributions payable by the employer under the Social Security Act 1975 (c.14), to include in the cost of travelling expenses for hospital visits the cost of travel to Northern Ireland and to add to the list of additional requirements a new item, the cost of special clothing and footwear for persons unable to wear standard sizes.

Various provisions of the Resources Regulations are amended by regulation 3, as set out in this paragraph. In regulation 2, the definition of "payments made by or derived from a liable relative" (appended to the definition of "liable relative") is amended to exclude payments resulting from certain dispositions of property in the matrimonial field and a definition of "life policy" is added to clarify an amendment elsewhere in the Regulations. Regulation 3(2) is amended so as to include among capital resources certain annual bounties for members of territorial and reserve forces. Regulation 6(1) is amended to add three new items to capital resources disregarded, namely amounts saved to meet certain regularly recurring liabilities, the first £1,500 of the surrender value of life insurance policies and the market value of a sole beneficiary's right to trust funds in certain circumstances where that right is an actual resource. Regulation 9(2) is amended to ensure that certain income resources are not indirectly taken into account twice over. Regulation 10 is amended so as to relax the disregard of earnings from service in the territorial and reserve forces and to prevent certain payments of bonus and commission being taken account of twice over in different ways. Regulation 11 is amended to add supplementary pension or allowance to the categories of income taken into account in full and to provide for the disregard of income from two additional categories of capital disregarded under regulation 6(1).

Regulation 4 amends regulation 17(1)*(b)* of the Single Payments Regulations so as to increase the maximum cost of repairs to and redecoration of the home for which a single payment will be made.

Regulation 5 makes certain transitional provisions in connection with the amendments to regulation 9 of the Requirements Regulations affecting board and lodging rates made by regulation 2 of these regulations.

The report of the Social Security Advisory Committee dated 24th May 1983 on the proposals for these regulations which had been referred to them together with a statement showing that the Regulations give effect to the Committee's recommendations, except that they include the amendment to regulation 8(3) of the Requirements Regulations (made by regulation 2(5)) which the Committee recommended should not be made, is contained in Command Paper No. 8978 published by Her Majesty's Stationery Office.

STATUTORY INSTRUMENTS

1983 No. 1242

HOUSING, ENGLAND AND WALES
HOUSING, SCOTLAND
RATING AND VALUATION

The Housing Benefits (Increase of Needs Allowances) Regulations 1983

Laid before Parliament in draft

Made - - - -	*12th August* 1983
Coming into Operation	*21st November* 1983

The Secretary of State for Social Services, in exercise of the powers conferred on him by sections 28(1) and 29(2) and (3) of the Social Security and Housing Benefits Act 1982 (**a**) and of all other powers enabling him in that behalf, with the consent of the Treasury, and having made the reviews under section 29 of that Act, hereby makes the following regulations of which a draft has been laid before Parliament in accordance with section 29(2) of that Act and approved by resolution of each House of Parliament.

Citation and commencement

1. These regulations may be cited as the Housing Benefits (Increase of Needs Allowances) Regulations 1983 and shall come into operation on 21st November 1983.

Increase of needs allowances

2. Regulation 13 of the Housing Benefits Regulations 1982 (**b**) (needs allowances) is amended as follows:—

(a) in paragraph (1)—

    (i) in sub-paragraph *(a)* (single person, no dependent child) for "£41.40" there is substituted "£43.05", and

    (ii) in sub-paragraphs *(b)* (married or unmarried couple) and *(c)* (single person with dependent child) for "£61.00" there is substituted in each case "£63.50";

(b) in paragraph (2) (handicapped persons)—

    (i) in sub-paragraph *(a)* (single person, no dependent child) for "£46.15" there is substituted "£48.00",

    (ii) in sub-paragraphs *(b)* (married or unmarried couple, one handicapped) and *(c)* (single person with dependent child) for "£65.75" there is substituted in each case "£68.45", and

---

(**a**) 1982 c.24; section 29 was amended by section 2 of the Social Security and Housing Benefits Act 1983 (c.36).

(**b**) S.I. 1982/1124, to which there are amendments not relevant to these regulations.

    (iii) in sub-paragraph *(d)* (married or unmarried couple, both handicapped) for "£68.00" there is substituted "£70.80"; and

  (c) in paragraph (3)*(b)* (increase for dependent child) for "£11.40" there is substituted "£11.90".

Norman Fowler,
Secretary of State for Social Services.

5th August 1983.

We consent,

Nigel Lawson,
D. J. F. Hunt,
Two of the Lords Commissioners
of Her Majesty's Treasury.

12th August 1983.

EXPLANATORY NOTE

(This Note is not part of the Regulations.)

    These Regulations increase the amounts specified as needs allowances in the Housing Benefits Regulations 1982 ("the 1982 regulations"). Needs allowances are amounts used in the calculation of rate rebates, rent rebates or rent allowances for persons other than those in receipt of supplementary benefit. A person's income is compared with the relevant needs allowance as part of this calculation, in accordance with regulation 19 of the 1982 regulations.

STATUTORY INSTRUMENTS

1983 No. 1243

SOCIAL SECURITY

The Child Benefit (Up-Rating) Regulations 1983

Laid before Parliament in draft

Made - - - - -   12*th August* 1983

Coming into Operation   21*st November* 1983

Whereas a draft of the following regulations was, in accordance with the provisions of section 22(3) of the Child Benefit Act 1975(a), laid before Parliament and approved by resolution of each House of Parliament:

Now, therefore, the Secretary of State for Social Services, in conjunction with the Treasury(b), and in exercise of the powers conferred upon him by section 5 of the Child Benefit Act 1975 and of all other powers enabling him in that behalf, hereby makes the following regulations:—

Citation, interpretation and commencement

1. These regulations, which may be cited as the Child Benefit (Up-Rating) Regulations 1983, amend the Child Benefit and Social Security (Fixing and Adjustment of Rates) Regulations 1976(c) (hereinafter referred to as "the principal regulations") and shall come into operation on 21st November 1983.

(a) 1975 c. 61.
(b) *See* section 22(1)(*a*) of the Child Benefit Act 1975.
(c) S.I. 1976/1267; relevant amending instruments are S.I. 1977/1328, 1980/110, 1982/1128.

Amendment of regulation 2 of the principal regulations

2. In regulation 2 of the principal regulations (weekly rates of child benefit)—

  (*a*) in paragraph (1) for "£5.85" there shall be substituted "£6.50";

  (*b*) in paragraph (2) for "£3.65" there shall be substituted "£4.05".

Norman Fowler,
Secretary of State for Social Services.

5th August 1983.

Nigel Lawson,
D. J. F. Hunt,
Two of the Lords Commissioners of
Her Majesty's Treasury.

12th August 1983.

EXPLANATORY NOTE

(This Note is not part of the Regulations.)

These Regulations put up the rates of child benefit applicable under the Child Benefit and Social Security (Fixing and Adjustment of Rates) Regulations 1976 from £5.85 to £6.50 for child benefit and from £3.65 to £4.05 for the increase in child benefit known as "one parent benefit", as from 21st November 1983.

STATUTORY INSTRUMENTS

1983 No. 1244

SOCIAL SECURITY

The Social Security Benefits Up-rating Order 1983

Laid before Parliament in draft

Made - - - -	*12th August* 1983
Coming into Operation	*21st November* 1983

Whereas, the Secretary of State for Social Services having made reviews under sections 125 and 126A of the Social Security Act 1975(a) and having considered under section 37A(4) of that Act whether the rate of mobility allowance should be increased, a draft of the following order was laid before Parliament in accordance with the provisions of sections 125(3) and 126A(2) of that Act and approved by resolution of each House of Parliament:

Now, therefore, the Secretary of State for Social Services, in conjunction with the Treasury(b), in exercise of the powers conferred upon him by sections 124 and 126A of the above-mentioned Act(c), and of all other powers enabling him in that behalf, hereby makes the following order:—

Citation, commencement and interpretation

1.—(1) This order may be cited as the Social Security Benefits Up-rating Order 1983 and shall come into operation on 21st November 1983.

(2) In this order, unless the context otherwise requires—

(a) 1975 c. 14. Section 125 was extended in application by section 23(1) of, and amended by section 65(1) of, and Part I of Schedule 4 to, the Social Security Pensions Act 1975 (c. 60). It was further amended by sections 1(1) and 21(4) of, and Part I of Schedule 5 to, the Social Security Act 1980 (c. 30). It was modified in application by section 1(3) of, and further amended by sections 2(1) and 7(6) of, and the Schedule to, the Social Security (No. 2) Act 1980 (c. 39). It was further amended by section 1(1) of the Social Security Act 1981 (c. 33) and by section 1(1) and (2) of the Social Security and Housing Benefits Act 1983 (c. 36). Section 126A was inserted by section 12 of the Social Security Act 1979 (c. 18); it was amended by section 1(2) of the Social Security Act 1981 and by section 1(4) and (5) of the Social Security and Housing Benefits Act 1983. Section 37A was inserted by section 22(1) of the Social Security Pensions Act 1975.
(b) *See* section 166(5) of the Social Security Act 1975.
(c) Section 124 was modified in application by section 17(4) of the Child Benefit Act 1975 (c. 61) and by section 1(3) of the Social Security (No. 2) Act 1980, and amended by section 5(1) of the Social Security (Miscellaneous Provisions) Act 1977 (c. 5) and by section 7(6) of, and the Schedule to, the Social Security (No. 2) Act 1980. Section 124 was also extended in application by section 23(1) of the Social Security Pensions Act 1975, which was itself amended by section 21(4) of, and Schedule 3 to, the Social Security Act 1979, and by section 21(4) of, and Part I of Schedule 5 to, the Social Security Act 1980.

"the Act" means the Social Security Act 1975, and

"the Pensions Act" means the Social Security Pensions Act 1975.

Alteration in rates or amounts of certain benefits under the Act

2.—(1) In this Article, "Schedule 4" means Schedule 4 to the Act(**a**).

(2) The sums specified in paragraph (3) below shall be altered from and including the respective dates specified in Article 4 below; and Schedule 4 shall accordingly have effect as set out in the Schedule to this order.

(3) The sums mentioned in paragraph (2) above are the sums specified in Parts I, III, IV and V of Schedule 4 (contributory periodical benefits, non-contributory periodical benefits, increases of benefits for dependants and rate or amount of industrial injuries benefits, respectively), except the sum specified in the said Part III for age addition.

Increase of rates or amounts of certain benefits under the Pensions Act

3.—(1) The sums mentioned in paragraphs (2) to (5) below shall be increased from and including the respective dates specified in Article 4 below.

(2) In section 6(1)*(a)* of the Pensions Act (basic component of Category A retirement pension)—

- *(a)* so far as the sum is relevant for the purpose of calculating under section 14(6) of the Act the rate of unemployment benefit, for the sum of £31.45(**b**) there shall be substituted the sum of £34.05;

- *(b)* so far as the sum is relevant for the purpose of calculating under section 14(6) of the Act the rate of sickness benefit and of calculating under section 15(4) of the Act or section 14, 15 or 16 of the Pensions Act the rate of an invalidity pension, for the sum of £31.45(**b**) there shall be substituted the sum of £32.60; and

- *(c)* except so far as mentioned in sub-paragraphs *(a)* and *(b)* above, for the sum of £32.85(**b**) there shall be substituted the sum of £34.05.

(3) It is hereby directed that the sums which are the additional components in the rates of long-term benefits calculated by reference to any final relevant year earlier than the tax year 1983/1984 shall be increased by 3.7 per cent. of their amount apart from this order.

(4) It is hereby directed that the sums payable by way of increases of retirement pensions under Schedule 1 to the Pensions Act (increase of pension where pensioner defers retirement) shall be increased by 3.7 per cent.

(5) It is hereby directed that an amount equal to 3.7 per cent of the aggregate amount of—

(**a**) Schedule 4 was amended by section 21(1) and (2) of, and Schedules 4 and 5 to, the Child Benefit Act 1975, section 22(2) of, and paragraphs 62 and 63 of Schedule 4 to, the Social Security Pensions Act 1975, paragraph 13 of Schedule 1 to the Social Security Act 1979, and the Social Security Benefits Up-rating Order 1982 (S.I. 1982/1130).

(**b**) *See* Social Security (No. 2) Act 1980 (c. 39), section 1(1) and (2), and S.I. 1980/1245, Article 3(2).

(a) the sums payable to a person by virtue of section 35(6) of the Pensions Act (which provides for increases in a person's guaranteed minimum pension if payment of his occupational pension is postponed after he attains pensionable age), including such sums which are payable by virtue of section 36(3) of that Act; and

(b) the amount by which that person's Category A or Category B retirement pension has been increased under section 126A of the Act (up-rating of increments in guaranteed minimum pensions),

shall be payable by way of an increase of his Category A or Category B retirement pension.

Dates on which sums specified for rates or amounts of benefit under the Act or the Pensions Act are altered by this order

4.—(1) Subject to paragraph (8) of the Article, the alterations made by this order in the sums specified for rates or amounts of benefit under the Act or the Pensions Act shall take effect for each case on the date specified in relation to such case in the following provisions of this Article.

(2) In relation to the case of a person over pensionable age who has not retired from regular employment and for whom the rate of unemployment benefit, sickness benefit or invalidity pension falls to be calculated in accordance with section 14(6) or 15(4) of the Act, the increases in the sums mentioned in Articles 2, 3 and 6 for Category A and B retirement pension and graduated retirement benefit (together with, where appropriate, increases for dependants) shall take effect on 24th November 1983 and in relation to all other cases the increases in such sums shall take effect on 21st November 1983.

(3) The increase mentioned in Article 3(5) shall take effect on 21st November 1983.

(4) The alterations in the amounts of maternity allowance, widow's allowance, widowed mother's allowance, widow's pension, Category C and D retirement pension, child's special allowance, attendance allowance, invalid care allowance (except in a case where the Secretary of State has made arrangements for it to be paid on a Wednesday), guardian's allowance and industrial death benefit by way of widow's and widower's pension and allowance in respect of children (together with, where appropriate, increases for dependants) shall in all cases take effect on 21st November 1983.

(5) The sums specified for the rate of mobility allowance, invalid care allowance (in a case where the Secretary of State has made arrangements for it to be paid on a Wednesday), disablement benefit (together with increases of disablement pension), maximum disablement gratuity under section 57(5) of the Act, increase of unemployability supplement under section 59 of the Act and maximum, under section 91(1) of the Act, of aggregate of weekly benefit payable for successive accidents, shall be increased in all cases with effect from 23rd November 1983.

(6) In relation to the case of a person whose weekly rate of Category A or B retirement pension falls to be increased under the provisions of section 28(7) or 29(8) of the Act by reference to the weekly rate of invalidity allowance to which he was previously entitled, the increase in the sum specified for the appropriate rate of invalidity allowance shall take effect on 21st November 1983 and in

relation to all other cases the increase in such sum shall take effect on 24th November 1983.

(7) The alterations in the rates or amounts of unemployment and sickness benefit, invalidity pension and non-contributory invalidity pension (together with, where appropriate, increases for dependants), shall take effect in all cases on 24th November 1983.

Increase in rates of certain benefits under the Industrial Injuries and Diseases (Old Cases) Act 1975

5. In the Industrial Injuries and Diseases (Old Cases) Act 1975(a) the sum of £19.70 referred to in section 2(6)*(c)* (maximum weekly rate of lesser incapacity allowance supplementing workmen's compensation) and section 7(2)*(b)* (industrial diseases benefit schemes: weekly rate of allowance payable where disablement is not total) shall be further increased; and from and including 23rd November 1983 the reference to that sum in section 2(6)*(c)*, and from and including 24th November 1983 the reference to that sum in section 7(2)*(b)*, shall accordingly have effect as references to £20.45.

Increase in rate of graduated retirement benefit and increments thereof

6.—(1) In the National Insurance Act 1965(b) the sum of 4.28 pence referred to in section 36(1) (graduated retirement benefit) shall be increased by 3.7 per cent; and from and including 21st November 1983 the reference in that provision to that sum shall accordingly have effect as a reference to 4.44 pence.

(2) It is hereby directed that the aggregate amount of any increases of graduated retirement benefit payable under Schedule 2 to the Social Security (Graduated Retirement Benefit) (No. 2) Regulations 1978(c) (increases for deferred retirement) shall be increased by 3.7 per cent.

Increase of amount specified in section 30(1) of the Act

7. The amount specified in section 30(1) of the Act, excluding paragraphs *(a)* and *(b)* of that provision (amount of weekly earnings which must be exceeded before a Category A or Category B retirement pension is reduced by reference to earnings), shall be increased to £65.00.

(a) 1975 c. 16; sections 2(6)*(c)* and 7(2)*(b)* were amended by the Social Security Benefits Up-rating Order 1982 (S.I. 1982/1130).
(b) 1965 c.51; section 36 was repealed by the Social Security Act 1973 (c. 38) but subsection (1) is now continued in force by regulation 3 of the Social Security (Graduated Retirement Benefit) (No. 2) Regulations 1978 (S.I. 1978/393) in the modified form set out in the Schedule to those regulations as amended by Article 6 of the Social Security Benefits Up-rating Order 1982.
(c) S.I. 1978/393.

Revocations

8. The Social Security Benefits Up-rating Order 1982(a) is hereby revoked.

Norman Fowler,
Secretary of State for Social Services.

5th August 1983.

Nigel Lawson,
D. J. F. Hunt,
Two of the Lords Commissioners of
Her Majesty's Treasury.

12th August 1983.

(a) S.I. 1982/1130.

Article 2(2)   SCHEDULE

Schedule 4 to the Act as Amended by this Order

SCHEDULE 4

Rates of Benefits, Grants and Increases for Dependants

PART I

Contributory Periodical Benefits (Sections 14–31)

Description of benefit	Weekly rate		
1. Unemployment or sickness benefit (section 14).	(a) unemployment benefit	...	£27.05
	(b) sickness benefit	... ...	£25.95
3. Invalidity allowance (section 16).	(a) higher rate	... ...	£7.15
	(b) middle rate	... ...	£4.60
	(c) lower rate		£2.30
	(the appropriate rate being determined in accordance with section 16(2)(a)).		
4. Maternity allowance (section 22).	£25.95		
5. Widow's allowance (section 24).	£47.65		
9. Category B retirement pension where section 29(7)(a)(i) applies.	£20.45		
10. Child's special allowance (section 31).	£7.60		

PART II

Maternity Grant and Death Grant

Description of Grant	Amount
	£
1. Maternity grant (section 21)	25.00
2. Death grant (section 32), where the deceased was at his death—	
(a) under the age of 3	9.00
(b) between the ages of 3 and 6	15.00
(c) between the ages of 6 and 18	22.50
(d) over the age of 18—	
(i) if on 5th July 1948 that person had attained the age of 55 in the case of a man or 50 in the case of a woman ...	15.00
(ii) in any other case	30.00

(a) Section 16(2) was amended by paragraph 10 of Schedule 1 to the Social Security Act 1979.

PART III

Non-contributory Periodical Benefits (Sections 34–40)

Description of benefit	Weekly rate
1. Attendance allowance (section 35).	*(a)* higher rate ... ... £27.20 *(b)* lower rate ... ... £18.15 (the appropriate rate being determined in accordance with section 35(3)(**a**)).
2. Non-contributory invalidity pension (section 36).	£20.45
3. Invalid care allowance (section 37).	£20.45
3A. Mobility allowance (section 37A).	£19.00
4. Guardian's allowance (section 38).	£7.60
5. Category C or Category D retirement pension (section 39).	*(a)* lower rate ... ... £12.25 *(b)* higher rate ... ... £20.45 (the appropriate rate being determined in accordance with section 39(2)).
6. Age addition (to a pension of any category, and otherwise under section 40).	£ 0.25

(**a**) Section 35(3) was amended by section 2(4) of the Social Security Act 1979.

PART IV

Increases for Dependants (Sections 41–49)

Benefit to which increase applies (1)	Increase for qualifying child (2)	Increase for adult dependant (3)
	£	£
1. Unemployment or sickness benefit—		
(a) unemployment benefit, where the beneficiary is under pensionable age ...	0.15	16.70
(b) unemployment benefit, where the beneficiary is over pensionable age ...	7.60	20.45
(c) sickness benefit, where the beneficiary is under pensionable age	0.15	16.00
(d) sickness benefit, where the beneficiary is over pensionable age	7.60	19.55
2. Invalidity pension	7.60	19.55
3. Maternity allowance	0.15	16.00
4. Widow's allowance	7.60	—
5. Widowed mother's allowance ...	7.60	—
6. Category A or B retirement pension	7.60	20.45
7. Category C retirement pension	7.60	12.25
8. Child's special allowance	7.60	—
9. Non-contributory invalidity pension	7.60	12.25
10. Invalid care allowance	7.60	12.25

PART V

Rate or Amount of Industrial Injuries Benefit

Description of benefit, etc.	Rate or Amount
2. Maximum disablement gratuity under section 57(5).	£3,690
3. Disablement pension under section 57(6) (weekly rates).	For the several degrees of disablement set out in column (1) of the following Table, the respective amounts in that Table, using—

(a) column (2) for any period during which the beneficiary is over the age of 18 or is entitled to an increase of benefit in respect of a child or adult dependant;

(b) column (3) for any period during which the beneficiary is not over the age of 18 and not so entitled;

TABLE

Degree of disablement   Amount

(1) Per cent.	(2) £	(3) £
100	55.60	34.05
90	50.04	30.65
80	44.48	27.24
70	38.92	23.84
60	33.36	20.43
50	27.80	17.03
40	22.24	13.62
30	16.68	10.22
20	11.12	6.81

Description of benefit, etc.	Rate or Amount
4. Unemployability supplement under section 58 (increase of weekly rate of disablement pension).	£32.60
5. Increase under section 59 of weekly rate of unemployability supplement (early onset of incapacity for work).	

(a) if on the qualifying date the beneficiary was under the age of 35, or if that date fell before 5th July 1948 ... ...   £7.15

(aa) if head *(a)* above does not apply and on the qualifying date the beneficiary was under the age of 40 and he had not attained pensionable age before 6th April 1979 ... ...   £7.15

(b) if heads *(a)* and *(aa)* above do not apply and on the qualifying date the beneficiary was under the age of 45 ... ...   £4.60

PART V *(continued)*

Rate or Amount of Industrial Injuries Benefit

Description of benefit, etc.	Rate or Amount
	(bb) if heads *(a)*, *(aa)* and *(b)* above do not apply and on the qualifying date the beneficiary was under the age of 50 and had not attained pensionable age before 6th April 1979 ... £4.60
	(c) in any other case ... £2.30
6. Maximum increase under section 60 of weekly rate of disablement pension in cases of special hardship.	£22.24 or the amount (if any) by which the weekly rate of the pension, apart from any increase under section 61, 63, 64 or 66, falls short of £55.60, whichever is the less.
7. Maximum increase under section 61 of weekly rate of disablement pension where constant attendance needed.	*(a)* except in cases of exceptionally severe disablement £22.30
	(b) in any case... ... ... £44.60
8. Increase under section 63 of weekly rate of disablement pension.(exceptionally severe disablement).	£22.30
10. Increase under section 64 of weekly rate of disablement pension (dependent children).	£7.60
12. Increase under section 66(2) of weekly rate of disablement pension (adult dependant).	£19.55
13. Widow's pension under section 68 (weekly rates)—	
(a) initial rate	£47.65
(b) higher permanent rate	£34.60
(c) lower permanent rate	30 per cent. of the sum specified in section 6(1)*(a)* of the Pensions Act.
14. Widower's pension under section 69 (weekly rate).	£34.60
15. Allowance under section 70 in respect of children—	
(a) weekly rate of allowance at higher rate	in respect of each qualifying child £7.60
(b) weekly rate of allowance at lower rate	in respect of each qualifying child £0.15
16. Maximum under section 91(1) of aggregate of weekly benefit payable for successive accidents.	*(a)* for any period during which the beneficiary is over the age of 18 or is entitled to an increase of benefit in respect of a child or adult dependant ... £55.60
	(b) for any period during which the beneficiary is not over the age of 18 and not so entitled £34.05

EXPLANATORY NOTE

(This Note is not part of the Order.)

This Order, a draft of which has been laid before and approved by resolution of each House of Parliament, is made as a consequence of reviews under sections 125 and 126A of the Social Security Act 1975. It alters with effect from dates in the week beginning 21st November 1983, which are specified in Articles 4 to 6, the rates and amounts of certain benefits and other sums.

Article 2 alters the benefits and increases of benefit (except age addition) specified in Parts I, III, IV and V of Schedule 4 to that Act; Article 3 increases the rates and amounts of certain benefits under Part II of the Social Security Pensions Act 1975 (including increases of Category A or B retirement pension payable by reference to the increases of increments in guaranteed minimum pensions payable by virtue of section 35(6) of that Act); Article 5 increases the rates laid down in the Industrial Injuries and Diseases (Old Cases) Act 1975 for the maximum weekly rate of lesser incapacity allowance supplementing workmen's compensation and the weekly rate of allowance under the Industrial Diseases Benefit Schemes where disablement is not total; Article 6 increases the rate of graduated retirement benefit under the National Insurance Act 1965; and Article 7 increases the amount, specified in section 30(1) of the Social Security Act 1975, of weekly earnings which must be exceeded before retirement pension is reduced by reference to earnings.

In accordance with section 124(3) of the Social Security Act 1975, a copy of a report by the Government Actuary (Cmnd. 8969) giving his opinion on the likely effect on the National Insurance Fund of the making of this Order was laid before Parliament with the draft Order.

STATUTORY INSTRUMENTS

1983 No. 1245

SOCIAL SECURITY

The Supplementary Benefit Up-rating Regulations 1983

Laid before Parliament in draft

Made- - - -	*12th August* 1983
Coming into Operation	*21st November* 1983

The Secretary of State for Social Services, in exercise of the powers conferred upon him by section 3(1) and (2) of, and paragraphs 1(2)*(b)* and (3) and 2(1) and (4) of Schedule 1 to, the Supplementary Benefits Act 1976 (a) and of all other powers enabling him in that behalf, with the consent of the Treasury, and after agreement by the Social Security Advisory Committee that proposals to make these regulations should not be referred to it (b), hereby makes the following regulations of which a draft has, in accordance with section 33(3) of that Act, been laid before Parliament and approved by resolution of each House of Parliament.

Citation and commencement

1. These regulations, which may be cited as the Supplementary Benefit Up-rating Regulations 1983, amend the Supplementary Benefit (Requirements) Regulations 1980 (c), the Supplementary Benefit (Resources) Regulations 1981 (d) and the Supplementary Benefit (Single Payments) Regulations 1981 (e) (hereinafter referred to respectively as the "Requirements Regulations", the "Resources Regulations" and the "Single Payments Regulations") and shall come into operation on 21st November 1983.

Increase of amounts specified in the Requirements Regulations

2.—(1) Amounts specified in the Requirements Regulations (which provide for the calculation of a person's normal, additional and housing requirements for the purposes of supplementary benefit) are increased in accordance with the following paragraphs of this regulation, and the table of normal requirements of relevant persons and householders set out in paragraph 2(3) of Schedule 1 to the Supplementary Benefits Act 1976 shall have effect as modified by the Requirements Regulations as amended by paragraph (2) of this regulation.

(a) 1976 c.71; sections 3 and 33 of, and Schedule 1 to, the Act were amended by paragraphs 3, 28 and 30 of Schedule 2 to the Social Security Act 1980 (c.30).
(b) *See* section 10(2)*(b)* of the Social Security Act 1980.
(c) S.I. 1980/1299; relevant amending instruments are S.I. **1980/1774, 1981/1016, 1982/1125,** 1126, 1127 and 1983/505.
(d) S.I. 1981/1527; the relevant amending instrument is S.I. 1982/1127.
(e) S.I. 1981/1528; the relevant amending instrument is S.I. 1982/1127.

(2) In regulation 5 (normal requirements of relevant persons and householders) for paragraphs (1) to (1C) there are substituted the following paragraphs:—

"(1) Paragraph 1 of the table (long-term rate for couples) shall have effect as if in the second column—

(a) after "aggregate of the" there were inserted "higher of the";

(b) after "Social Security Pensions Act 1975 and" there were inserted "the sum for the time being specified in"; and

(c) at the end there were added "increased by £0.05".

(1A) Paragraph 2 of the table (ordinary rate for couples) shall have effect as if in the second column—

(a) after "specified" there were inserted "in relation to sickness benefit";

(b) for "paragraph 1*(a)*" there were substituted "paragraph 1*(c)*";

(c) the words "unemployment or" were omitted; and

(d) at the end there were added "increased by £1.55".

(1B) Paragraph 3 of the table (long-term rate for householders) shall have effect as if in the second column—

(a) for "The sum" there were substituted "The higher of the sums"; and

(b) at the end there were added "increased by £0.05".

(1C) Paragraph 4 of the table (ordinary rate for householders) shall have effect as if in the second column—

(a) after "specified" there were inserted "in relation to sickness benefit"; and

(b) at the end there were added "increased by £0.85".

(1D) The amounts in the second column of paragraphs 1 to 4 of the table as modified by paragraphs (1) to (1C) above are shown in paragraphs A and B of Schedule 1.".

(3) In regulation 9 (modification of normal requirements for boarders)—

(a) in paragraph (2)*(b)* (increase where charge is not inclusive of all meals)—

(i) in head (i) (breakfast) for "£0.95" there is substituted "£1.00",

(ii) in head (ii) (midday meals) for "£1.35" there is substituted "£1.45", and

(iii) in head (iii) (evening meals) for "£1.35" there is substituted "£1.45"; and

(b) in paragraph (8) (personal expenses)—

(i) in sub-paragraph *(a)* (relevant persons) for "£18.90" (long-term rate) and "£17.00" (ordinary rate) there are substituted "£19.70" and "£17.70" respectively,

(ii) in sub-paragraph *(b)* (other claimants) for "£9.45" (long-term rate) and "£8.50" (ordinary rate) there are substituted "£9.85" and "£8.85" respectively, and

(iii) in sub-paragraph *(c)* (dependants) for "£8.50" (not less than 18), "£5.10" (less than 18, not less than 16), "£4.35" (less than 16, not less than 11) and "£2.85" (less than 11) there are substituted "£8.85", "£5.30", "£4.55" and "£2.95" respectively.

(4) In regulation 18 (interest on loans for repairs and improvements) in paragraph (2) (available capital threshold) for "£300" there is substituted "£500".

(5) In regulation 22(2) (reduction where home is let) in sub-paragraph *(c)* (ii) (available capital threshold) for "£300" there is substituted "£500".

(6) In Schedule 1 (normal requirements)—

(a) in column (1)—

    (i) in paragraph A for "regulation 5(1A)" and "regulation 5(1)" there are substituted "regulation 5(1)" and "regulation 5(1A)" respectively, and

    (ii) in paragraph B for "regulation 5(1)" there is substituted "regulation 5(1C)"; and

(b) in column (2) in each of the provisions of that Schedule 1 indicated in column 1 of Schedule 1 to these regulations, for the amount specified therein set out in column 3 of Schedule 1 to these regulations there is substituted the amount specified in relation to it in column 2 of Schedule 1 to these regulations.

(7) In Schedule 3 (additional requirements)—

(a) in column (1) in paragraph 15*(d)* (available capital threshold relating to hire purchase) for "£300" there is substituted "£500"; and

(b) in column (2) in each of the provisions of that Schedule 3 indicated in column 1 of Schedule 2 to these regulations, for the amount specified therein set out in column 3 of that Schedule 2 there is substituted the amount specified in relation to it in column 2 of that Schedule 2.

Increase of amounts specified in the Resources Regulations

3. Amounts specified in the Resources Regulations (which provide for the calculation of a person's resources for the purposes of supplementary benefit) are increased as follows:—

(a) in regulation 6(2) (capital resources to be disregarded) for "£2,500" there is substituted "£3,000"; and

(b) in regulation 7 (maximum capital resources for entitlement to pension or allowance) for "£2,500" there is substituted "£3,000".

Increase of amounts specified in the Single Payments Regulations

4.—(1) Amounts specified in the Single Payments Regulations (which provide for supplementary benefit to be paid by way of a single payment to meet an exceptional need) are increased in accordance with the following paragraphs of this regulation.

(2) In regulation 5 (disregarded capital threshold) for "£300" there is substituted "£500".

(3) In Schedule 1 (bedclothes) for column 2 (which is set out in column 3 of Schedule 3 to these regulations) there is substituted the column 2 set out in column 2 of Schedule 3 to these regulations, the item to which each amount specified in that column relates being indicated in column 1 of that Schedule 3.

(4) In Schedule 2 (clothing and footwear), in each of Parts I (men's clothing and footwear), II (working clothes and footwear), III (women's clothing and footwear), IV (boys' clothing and footwear) and V (girls' clothing and

footwear), for column 2 (which is set out in column 3 of the corresponding
Part of Schedule 4 to these regulations) there is substituted the column 2 set
out in column 2 of the corresponding Part of Schedule 4 to these regulations,
the item to which each amount specified in that column relates being
indicated in column 1 of that Schedule 4.

Norman Fowler,
Secretary of State for Social Services.

5th August 1983.

We consent,

Nigel Lawson,
D. J. F. Hunt,
Two of the Lords Commissioners of
Her Majesty's Treasury.

12th August 1983.

Regulation 2(6)*(b)* SCHEDULE 1

AMOUNTS SUBSTITUTED IN SCHEDULE 1 TO THE REQUIREMENTS REGULATIONS

Column 1	Column 2	Column 3
Provision of Schedule 1 to the Requirements Regulations	Amount from 21st November 1983	Amount before 21st November 1983
Paragraph A (Couples)—		
sub-paragraph *(a)* (long-term)	£54.55	£52.30
sub-paragraph *(b)* (ordinary)	£43.50	£41.70
Paragraph B (Householders)—		
sub-paragraph *(a)* (long-term)	£34.10	£32.70
sub-paragraph *(b)* (ordinary)	£26.80	£25.70
Paragraph 1 (Non-householders not less than 18, or less than 18 with dependant)—		
sub-paragraph *(a)* (long-term)	£27.25	£26.15
sub-paragraph *(b)* (ordinary)	£21.45	£20.55
Paragraph 2 (Non-householders less than 18 without dependant)—		
sub-paragraph *(a)* (long-term)	£20.90	£20.05
sub-paragraph *(b)* (ordinary)	£16.50	£15.80
Paragraph 3 (Dependants)—		
sub-paragraph *(a)* (not less than 18)	£21.45	£20.55
sub-paragraph *(b)* (less than 18 but not less than 16)	£16.50	£15.80
sub-paragraph *(c)* (less than 16 but not less than 11)	£13.70	£13.15
sub-paragraph *(d)* (less than 11)	£ 9.15	£ 8.75

SCHEDULE 2
Regulation 2(7)(b)

AMOUNTS SUBSTITUTED IN SCHEDULE 3 TO THE REQUIREMENTS REGULATIONS

Column 1	Column 2	Column 3
Provision of Schedule 3 to the Requirements Regulations	Amount from 21st November 1983	Amount before 21st November 1983
Part I — *Heating*		
Paragraph 1 (ill health)—		
sub-paragraph (1)	£ 2.05	£ 1.90
sub-paragraph (2)	£ 5.05	£ 4.65
sub-paragraph (3)	£ 5.05	£ 4.65
Paragraph 2 (householder, home difficult to heat)—		
sub-paragraph *(a)*	£ 2.05	£ 1.90
sub-paragraph *(b)*	£ 5.05	£ 4.65
Paragraph 3 (central heating)—		
sub-paragraph *(a)*	£ 2.05	£ 1.90
sub-paragraph *(b)*	£ 4.10	£ 3.80
Paragraph 5 (estate heating system)	£ 4.10	£ 3.80
	£ 8.20	£ 7.60
Paragraph 6 (persons receiving certain benefits for disability)	£ 5.05	£ 4.65
Paragraph 7 (persons 70 or over or under 5)	£ 2.05	£ 1.90
Part II — *Items other than heating*		
Paragraph 10 (baths)	25p	20p
Paragraph 16 (hospital fares)—		
sub-paragraph *(b)* (i)	£13.65	£13.05
sub-paragraph *(b)* (ii)	£ 9.90	£ 9.45
sub-paragraph *(c)* (i)	£ 6.85	£ 6.50
sub-paragraph *(c)* (ii)	£ 3.10	£ 2.90
sub-paragraph *(d)* (i)	£14.65	£14.00
sub-paragraph *(d)* (ii)	£ 9.70	£ 9.25
sub-paragraph *(d)* (iii)	£ 6.90	£ 6.60
sub-paragraph *(d)* (iv)	£ 2.35	£ 2.20
sub-paragraph *(e)* (i)	£27.30	£26.15
sub-paragraph *(e)* (ii)	£20.00	£19.15
sub-paragraph *(e)* (iii)	£20.45	£19.60
sub-paragraph *(e)* (iv)	£14.65	£14.00

Regulation 4(3) SCHEDULE 3

AMOUNTS SUBSTITUTED IN SCHEDULE 1 TO THE SINGLE PAYMENTS REGULATIONS (BEDCLOTHES)

Column 1	Column 2	Column 3
Item	Amount from 21st November 1983	Amount before 21st November 1983
	£	£
Blanket (cot)	5.70	5.70
Blanket (single)	12.00	9.80
Blanket (double)	16.75	12.50
Pillow	4.70	4.70
Pillow-case	2.10	2.10
Quilt—terylene (single)	14.50	14.50
Quilt—terylene (double)	17.25	16.75
Sheet—cotton (single)	6.80	6.80
Sheet—cotton (double)	8.90	8.90
Sheet—flannelette (cot)	3.00	3.00
Sheet—flannelette (single)	6.50	6.50
Sheet—flannelette (double)	8.50	7.80
Sheet—nylon (single)	5.20	5.20
Sheet—nylon (double)	6.80	6.80

SCHEDULE 4   Regulation 4(4)

AMOUNTS SUBSTITUTED IN SCHEDULE 2 TO THE SINGLE PAYMENTS REGULATIONS
(CLOTHING AND FOOTWEAR)

PART I

Men's Clothing and Footwear

Column 1	Column 2	Column 3
Item	Amount from 21st November 1983	Amount before 21st November 1983
	£	£
Anorak	21.00	21.00
Cap	7.00	5.20
Cardigan	11.00	10.75
Dressing-gown	17.75	17.75
Overcoat	49.50	49.50
Pullover	10.00	9.40
Pyjamas	9.20	9.20
Raincoat	31.00	31.00
Shirt	8.30	8.30
Shoes	17.00	16.75
Slippers	5.50	4.70
Socks	1.50	1.30
Sports-jacket	37.00	36.50
Suit	58.00	58.00
Trousers	16.00	15.50
Underpants—briefs	1.75	1.65
Underpants—woollen (long)	9.50	7.30
Underpants—woollen (short)	5.90	5.20
Vest—singlet	2.05	2.05
Vest—woollen	8.50	6.20

PART II

Working clothes and footwear

Column 1	Column 2	Column 3
Item	Amount from 21st November 1983	Amount before 21st November 1983
	£	£
Boiler suit	12.00	11.50
Boots	16.75	16.75
Donkey-jacket	19.75	19.75
Dungarees	11.50	11.50
Jeans	12.50	12.50
Overalls	10.50	10.50
Suit	58.00	58.00
Wellingtons	12.00	12.00

PART III

Women's clothing and footwear

Column 1	Column 2	Column 3
Item	Amount from 21st November 1983	Amount before 21st November 1983
	£	£
Blouse...	9.00	8.30
Boots (ankle)...................................	18.00	17.75
Brassiere	4.50	4.15
Briefs..	1.40	1.40
Cardigan...	10.00	9.40
Corset..	12.50	12.50
Dress—summerweight.......................	15.00	13.50
Dress—winterweight.........................	18.50	17.75
Dressing-gown................................	15.00	14.50
Hat..	5.50	5.20
Jumper...	9.00	8.30
Knickers...	2.60	2.60
Nightdress (standard length)	7.00	6.80
Nightdress (full length)	8.60	8.60
Overcoat	43.00	43.00
Pantie-girdle...................................	9.00	8.30
Petticoat..	5.20	5.20
Pyjamas..	10.00	9.40
Raincoat...	31.00	31.00
Shoes...	15.00	14.50
Skirt	11.00	9.40
Slippers..	5.20	5.20
Stockings/tights	0.75	0.75
Trousers	12.00	11.50
Vest—cotton	2.50	2.10
Vest—woollen	4.70	4.70

PART IV

Boys' clothing and footwear

Column 1	Column 2		Column 3	
Item	Amount from 21st November 1983 Small to Large		Amount before 21st November 1983 Small to Large	
	£	£	£	£
Dressing-gown	8.60	12.00	8.60	12.00
Dufflecoat	15.50	21.00	15.50	21.00
Jacket/anorak	11.00	16.00	11.00	15.50
Overcoat	18.25	26.00	18.25	26.00
Pyjamas	4.90	8.00	4.90	6.15
Raincoat	13.50	20.75	13.50	20.75
Shirt	4.30	6.50	4.30	6.50
Shoes	8.90	12.50	8.90	12.50
Slippers	3.50	5.00	3.25	4.15
Socks	0.70	1.05	0.70	1.05
Sweater	5.00	7.50	4.90	7.30
Trousers—long	6.80	10.00	6.80	9.90
Trousers—short	4.50	5.50	4.30	5.50
Underpants	—	1.25	—	1.25
Vest	—	1.45	—	1.45
Wellingtons	4.15	6.20	4.15	6.20

PART V

Girls' clothing and footwear

Column 1	Column 2		Column 3	
Item	Amount from 21st November 1983 Small to Large		Amount before 21st November 1983 Small to Large	
	£	£	£	£
Blouse	4.70	8.30	4.70	8.30
Brassiere	—	3.00	—	2.70
Briefs	—	1.10	—	1.10
Cardigan	5.00	8.00	4.60	6.80
Dress—summerweight	5.50	10.00	5.50	9.40
Dress—winterweight	7.50	13.00	7.50	12.50
Dressing-gown	8.60	13.00	8.60	11.75
Dufflecoat	15.50	21.00	15.50	21.00
Jacket/anorak	11.00	16.00	11.00	15.50
Jumper	4.90	7.50	4.90	7.30
Nightdress	4.90	7.30	'4.90	7.30
Overcoat	17.25	25.00	17.25	25.00
Pantie-girdle	—	9.00	—	5.20
Petticoat	2.00	3.05	1.80	3.05
Pyjamas	4.90	8.00	4.90	7.30
Raincoat	13.50	19.75	13.50	19.75
Shoes	8.90	12.50	8.90	12.50
Skirt	5.90	9.40	5.90	9.40
Slippers	3.50	5.00	3.25	4.15
Socks	0.70	1.05	0.70	1.05
Stockings/tights	—	0.75	—	0.75
Trousers	6.50	10.00	6.50	9.70
Vest	—	1.35	—	1.35
Wellingtons	4.15	6.20	4.15	6.20

EXPLANATORY NOTE

(This Note is not part of the Regulations.)

These Regulations increase certain amounts specified in regulations made under the Supplementary Benefits Act 1976 for the purposes of determining supplementary benefit under that Act.

Regulation 2 and Schedules 1 and 2 relate to the increase of amounts specified in the Supplementary Benefit (Requirements) Regulations 1980 in relation to a person's normal, additional and housing requirements. Schedule 1 shows higher amounts applicable as normal requirements, and certain amounts relating to the normal requirements of boarders are increased by regulation 2(3). Regulation 2(4), (5) and (6)*(a)* increases a capital limit affecting the amount applicable as housing requirements for interest on a loan for repairs or improvements to the home, affecting the amount of a reduction from housing requirements when the home is sub-let, and affecting the amount applicable as an additional requirement for certain instalments under hire purchase agreements. Schedule 2 shows higher amounts applicable for certain additional requirements.

Regulation 3 increases the limit of a person's capital resources, specified in the Supplementary Benefit (Resources) Regulations 1981, which are disregarded for the purposes of a supplementary pension or allowance and which, if exceeded, will render him not entitled to such a pension or allowance.

Regulation 4 and Schedules 3 and 4 increase amounts specified in the Supplementary Benefit (Single Payments) Regulations 1981 ("the 1981 Regulations") under which supplementary benefit may be paid by way of a single payment to meet an exceptional need. Schedules 3 and 4 replace the columns of amounts relating to bedclothes, clothing (other than baby clothing amounts for which are not increased) and footwear set out in Schedules 1 and 2 to the 1981 Regulations; not all of those amounts are thereby increased, but the amount relevant before the coming into operation of these regulations, whether different or not, is shown in column 3 of Schedules 3 and 4 to these regulations.

STATUTORY INSTRUMENTS

1983 No. 1246

GAS

The Measuring Instruments (EEC Requirements) (Gas Volume Meters) Regulations 1983

Made - - - -	*2nd August* 1983
Laid before Parliament	16*th August* 1983
Coming into Operation	6*th September* 1983

The Secretary of State, being a Minister designated (**a**) for the purposes of section 2(2) of the European Communities Act 1972(**b**) in relation to the regulation of specifications, construction, placing on the market and use of equipment intended for weighing, measuring or testing or for purposes ancillary thereto, in exercise of the powers conferred by that section and in exercise of his powers under section 30(6)*(a)* and *(e)* of the Gas Act 1972(**c**), and of all other powers enabling him in that behalf, hereby makes the following Regulations:—

1. These Regulations may be cited as the Measuring Instruments (EEC Requirements) (Gas Volume Meters) Regulations 1983 and shall come into operation on 6th September 1983.

2. The Measuring Instruments (EEC Requirements) Regulations 1980(**d**) as originally made shall apply to gas volume meters to which Council Directive No. 71/318/EEC(**e**), as amended by Commission Directive No. 74/331/ EEC(**f**), Commission Directive No. 78/365/EEC(**g**) and Commission Directive No. 82/623/EEC(**h**), applies subject to the modifications specified in Schedule 1 to these Regulations.

3. The Regulations specified in Schedule 2 to these Regulations are hereby revoked.

Alick Buchanan-Smith,
Minister of State,
Department of Energy.

2nd August 1983.

(**a**) S.I. 1975/427.
(**b**) 1972 c. 68.
(**c**) 1972 c. 60.
(**d**) S.I. 1980/1058.
(**e**) O.J. No. L202, 6.9.71, p. 21 (O.J./S.E. 1971 (III), p. 729).
(**f**) O.J. No. L189, 12.7.74, p. 9.
(**g**) O.J. No. L104, 18.4.78, p. 26.
(**h**) O.J. L252, 27.8.82, p. 5.

SCHEDULE 1 Regulation 2

MODIFICATIONS TO THE MEASURING INSTRUMENTS
(EEC REQUIREMENTS) REGULATIONS 1980

1.—(1) In Regulation 2, in paragraph (1)—

(a) the following definition shall be inserted after that of "the Directive on medium accuracy bar weights and cylindrical weights":—

"'the Directive on gas volume meters' means Council Directive No. 71/318/EEC as amended by Commission Directive No. 74/331/EEC, Commission Directive No. 78/365/EEC and Commission Directive No. 82/623/EEC"; and

(b) the following definition shall be inserted after that of "manufacturer":—

"'meter examiner' means a meter examiner appointed or holding office under section 30 of the Gas Act 1972, or in Northern Ireland, under Article 8(1) of the Gas (Northern Ireland) Order 1977(**a**)."

(2) In paragraph (3) of that Regulation, for the words from "means" to the end of the paragraph, there shall be substituted the words "means the Directive on gas volume meters".

(3) In paragraph (4) of that Regulation, the words from the beginning of the paragraph to "hereto" shall have no effect.

2. For Regulation 5 there shall be substituted the following Regulation:—

"**5.** Nothing in section 30 of the Gas Act 1972 (meters not to be used for ascertaining the quantity of gas supplied unless stamped under that section) or, in Northern Ireland, Article 9 of the Gas (Northern Ireland) Order 1977 (meters not to be used for ascertaining the quantity of gas supplied unless stamped) shall restrict the use in Great Britain and Northern Ireland respectively of any instrument which bears the mark of EEC initial verification for ascertaining the quantity of gas supplied provided that the mark remains undefaced otherwise than by reason of fair wear and tear".

3. In Regulation 6(2)—

(a) for the words "Regulation 3(1) above" there shall be substituted the words "Regulation 3 above and the Directive on gas volume meters"; and

(b) the following entry shall be inserted in the Table after the entry relating to the Directive on medium accuracy bar weights and cylindrical weights:—

"The Directive on gas   Yes   Yes"
volume meters.

(**a**) S.I. 1977/596 (N.I.7).

4. Regulations 7(4) and 11(3) shall have no effect.

5. For Regulation 13 there shall be substituted the following Regulation:—

"EEC initial verification

13.—(1) An application for consideration of any instrument of a category to which the Directive on gas volume meters applies for EEC initial verification shall be made to a meter examiner in such manner as the Secretary of State or, as respects an application made in Northern Ireland, the Department of Economic Development may direct.

(2) The meter examiner shall determine whether an EEC pattern approval is in force in respect of the instrument and, if so, whether it conforms to the approved pattern, and where he is satisfied—

> *(a)* that the instrument conforms to the requirements of the Directive on gas volume meters; and

> *(b)* that an EEC pattern approval is in force in respect of the instrument and that the instrument conforms to the approved pattern

he shall affix or authorise to be affixed to the instrument the United Kingdom mark of EEC initial verification, and shall at the same time apply or authorise the application of any seals required by that Directive to be applied in connection with initial verification.

(3) If the meter examiner refuses to affix or authorise to be affixed any EEC mark he shall give to the applicant a statement in writing of his reasons for refusal.

(4) Schedule 3 to these regulations shall apply for regulating the conduct in the United Kingdom of EEC initial verification in relation to instruments of a category to which the Directive on gas volume meters applies.".

6. For Part IV of the Regulations (Supplementary Provisions) there shall be substituted the following Part:—

"PART IV

SUPPLEMENTARY AND CONSEQUENTIAL PROVISIONS

Effect of revocation of EEC pattern approval

14.—(1) Where—

> *(a)* the Secretary of State revokes an EEC pattern approval relating to instruments of a category to which the Directive on gas volume meters applies; or

> *(b)* it appears to the Secretary of State that any such pattern approval has been revoked by any Member State other than the United Kingdom;

the Secretary of State may publish in the London Gazette, the Edinburgh Gazette and the Belfast Gazette a notice requiring all instruments of the pattern in question used for the purpose of ascertaining the quantity of gas supplied to any person in England and Wales, Scotland and Northern

Ireland respectively to be replaced within a period of six months beginning with the date of the notice; and if after the end of that period any person supplies gas through such an instrument he shall be guilty of an offence.

(2) For the purposes of this regulation where a person provides through an instrument of a category to which the Directive on gas volume meters applies, for use in a flat or part of a building let by him, gas supplied to him, he and not the person supplying the gas to him shall be deemed to supply gas through the instrument.

Instruments of defective pattern

15.—(1) Where the Secretary of State is satisfied that instruments of a category to which the Directive on gas volume meters applies constructed according to a pattern in respect of which an EEC pattern approval granted by a Member State other than the United Kingdom is in force reveal in service a defect of a general nature which makes them unsuitable for their intended use, he may publish in the London Gazette, the Edinburgh Gazette and the Belfast Gazette a notice requiring all instruments of the pattern in question used for the purposes of ascertaining the quantity of gas supplied to any person in England and Wales, Scotland and Northern Ireland respectively to be replaced within a period of six months beginning with the date of the notice; and if after the end of that period any person supplies gas through such an instrument he shall be guilty of an offence.

(2) A notice under this regulation shall give particulars of the pattern to which it relates and shall include a statement of the grounds for the publication of the notice.

(3) Paragraph (2) of regulation 14 above shall apply for the purposes of this regulation as it applies for the purposes of that regulation.

(4) The Secretary of State may at any time withdraw a notice under this regulation by publishing a notice of withdrawal in the London, Edinburgh and Belfast Gazettes.

Unauthorised application of EEC signs and marks, etc.

16.—(1) Subject to paragraph (2) below, any person who, in the case of an instrument of a category to which the Directive on gas volume meters applies—

(a) not being a meter examiner or a person acting under the authority of a meter examiner, marks in any manner any plug, seal or plate used or designed for use for the reception of any EEC mark; or

(b) not being a manufacturer authorised or required to do so under any provision of these regulations, or the duly authorised agent of any such manufacturer, marks any such instrument with any EEC sign; or

(c) forges, counterfeits or, except pursuant to a duty imposed on a meter examiner, in any way alters or defaces any EEC sign or mark; or

(d) removes any EEC sign or mark and inserts it into any other measuring instrument; or

(e) makes any alteration in the instrument after any EEC sign or mark has been applied to it in accordance with these regulations, so that it no longer complies with the requirements of the relevant Directive;

shall be guilty of an offence.

(2) A person shall not be guilty of an offence under paragraph (1) above by reason solely of the destruction or obliteration of any sign, mark, plug, seal or plate in the course of the adjustment or repair of any instrument of a category to which the Directive on gas volume meters applies by, or by the duly authorised agent of, a person who is a manufacturer of, or regularly engaged in the business of repairing, such instruments.

(3) Any person who supplies gas through any instrument of a category to which the Directive on gas volume meters applies which to his knowledge—

(a) bears any EEC sign or mark which is a forgery or counterfeit, or which has been transferred from another instrument, or which has been altered or defaced otherwise than pursuant to a duty imposed on a meter examiner or as permitted by virtue of paragraph (2) above; or

(b) does not comply with the requirements of the Directive on gas volume meters by reason of any alteration made in it after any EEC sign or mark was applied to it in accordance with these regulations;

shall be guilty of an offence.

Offences by corporations

17.—(1) Where an offence under any provision of these regulations which has been committed by a body corporate is proved to have been committed with the consent or connivance of, or to be attributable to any neglect on the part of, any director, manager, secretary or other similar officer of the body corporate, or any person who was purporting to act in any such capacity, he as well as the body corporate shall be deemed to be guilty of that offence and shall be liable to be proceeded against and punished accordingly.

(2) Where the affairs of a body corporate are managed by its members, paragraph (1) above shall apply in relation to the acts and defaults of a member in connection with his functions of management as if he were a director of the body corporate.

Prosecutions and punishment of offences under these regulations

18. Proceedings for any offence under regulation 16 above shall not, in England and Wales, be instituted except by or with the consent of the Secretary of State or by the Director of Public Prosecutions.

19. Any person guilty of an offence under regulations 14 and 15 above shall be liable on summary conviction to a fine not exceeding £100 and any person guilty of any offence under regulation 16 above shall be liable on summary conviction to a fine not exceeding £200.

Restriction of application of section 1 of the Trade Descriptions Act 1972

20. Nothing in section 1 of the Trade Descriptions Act 1972(a) shall require a United Kingdom name or mark (as therein defined) applied to any gas volume meter bearing the EEC type approval sign and the mark of EEC initial verification to be accompanied by an indication of the country in which the meter was manufactured if the United Kingdom name or mark is the name or trade mark of the manufacturer.

Consequential provisions

21.—(1) In Schedule 4 to the Gas Act 1972 (gas supply code regulating supply of gas by the British Gas Corporation) references in paragraphs 7 and 10, however expressed, to a meter stamped under section 30 of that Act shall be construed as including references to a meter bearing the mark of EEC initial verification.

(2) In Schedule 1 to the Gas (Northern Ireland) Order 1977 (gas supply code regulating supply of gas by undertakers) references in paragraphs 7 and 10, however expressed, to a meter stamped under Article 9 of that Order shall be construed as including references to a meter bearing the mark of EEC initial verification.

(3) In Regulation 4 of the Gas (Meters) Regulations 1983(b) references, however expressed, to a meter stamped under section 30 of the Gas Act 1972 shall be construed as including references to a meter bearing the mark of EEC initial verification and references to a stamp shall be construed as including references to that mark.

(4) In the Gas (Meter) Regulations (Northern Ireland) 1975(c) references in regulation 4, however expressed, to a meter stamped under section 13 of the Gas Regulation Act 1920 shall be construed as including references to a meter bearing the mark of EEC initial verification and references to a stamp shall be construed as including references to the mark.".

7. In paragraph 5(6) of Schedule 1, after the word "person", there shall be inserted the words "or, where the instrument in question is an instrument to which the Directive on gas volume meters applies, the office of the meter examiner, ".

8. Schedule 3 shall have effect as if the reference in paragraph 3(1) to the inspector dealing with the application were a reference to the Secretary of State or, as respects an application made in Northern Ireland, the Department of Economic Development, and as if the remaining references to an inspector were references to a meter examiner.

9. Schedules 4 and 5 shall have no effect.

(a) 1972 c. 34.
(b) S.I. 1983/684.
(c) S.R. (N.I.) 1975 No. 156.

Regulation 3 SCHEDULE 2

REGULATIONS REVOKED

Regulations revoked	References
The Measuring Instruments (EEC Requirements) (Gas Volume Meters) Regulations 1975.	S.I. 1975/1873.
The Measuring Instruments (EEC Requirements) (Gas Volume Meters) (Amendment) Regulations 1979.	S.I. 1979/1224.

EXPLANATORY NOTE

(This Note is not part of the Regulations.)

The Measuring Instruments (EEC Requirements) (Gas Volume Meters) Regulations 1975, as amended, applied the Measuring Instruments (EEC Requirements) Regulations 1975 (S.I. 1975/1173) subject to modifications to certain gas volume meters to which Council Directive No. 71/318/EEC, as amended, applied, and implemented the obligations of the United Kingdom under that Directive and under Council Directive No. 71/316/EEC, as amended.

The Measuring Instruments (EEC Requirements) Regulations 1975 were revoked by the Measuring Instruments (EEC Requirements) Regulations 1980 (S.I. 1980/1058).

These Regulations therefore revoke the Measuring Instruments (EEC Requirements) (Gas Volume Meters) Regulations 1975 as amended and apply, subject to similar modifications, the Measuring Instruments (EEC Requirements) Regulations 1980 to those gas volume meters.

The principal modifications to the Measuring Instruments (EEC Requirements) Regulations 1980 are as follows:

(a) The substitution for regulation 5 of a regulation providing that the prohibition on the use of meters not stamped under section 30 of the Gas Act 1972 and, as regards Northern Ireland, under Article 9 of the Gas (Northern Ireland) Order 1977 shall not restrict the use of meters bearing the mark of EEC initial verification.

(b) The requirements in regulation 7(4) and 11(3) for publication of EEC pattern approval or revocations of such approvals respectively are to have no effect.

(c) The substitution for regulation 13 of a regulation providing for EEC initial verification of gas volume meters by meter examiners.

(d) The substitution for Part IV of supplementary provisions in respect of gas volume meters relating to—

  (i) the effect of revocation of EEC pattern approval (regulation 14),

  (ii) instruments of a defective pattern (regulation 15),

  (iii) the unauthorised application of EEC signs and marks etc. (regulation 16),

  (iv) offences by corporations and the prosecution and punishment of offences (regulations 17 to 19),

  (v) the restriction of the application of section 1 of the Trade Descriptions Act 1972 in relation to names and trade marks on such meters (regulation 20).

The changes of substance made by these Regulations are—

(a) in regulation 2 and paragraph 1(1)*(a)* of Schedule 1, the inclusion of a reference to Commission Directive No. 82/623/EEC which further amends Council Directive No. 71/318/EEC;

(b) in paragraph 6 of Schedule 1, the insertion of regulation 20 (restriction of application of Section 1 of the Trade Descriptions Act 1972); and

(c) in paragraph 6, the substitution in substituted regulation 21(3) of a reference to the Gas (Meters) Regulations 1983 for the references to the superseded Gas (Meter) Regulations 1974 (S.I. 1974/848) as amended.

STATUTORY INSTRUMENTS

1983 No. 1247

FEES AND CHARGES

The Measuring Instruments (EEC Requirements) (Gas Volume Meters) (Fees) Regulations 1983

Made - - - - -	*12th August* 1983
Laid before Parliament	*16th August* 1983
Coming into Operation	*6th September* 1983

The Secretary of State for Energy, in exercise of the powers conferred on him by section 30(6)(*d*) of the Gas Act 1972(**a**) and, with the consent of the Treasury, in exercise of the powers conferred on him by section 56(1) and (2) of the Finance Act 1973(**b**) and of all other powers enabling him in that behalf, hereby makes the following Regulations:—

1. These Regulations may be cited as the Measuring Instruments (EEC Requirements) (Gas Volume Meters) (Fees) Regulations 1983 and shall come into operation on 6th September 1983.

2. In these Regulations—

"the principal regulations" mean the Measuring Instruments (EEC Requirements) Regulations 1980(**c**) as originally made, as applied to gas volume meters by the Measuring Instruments (EEC Requirements) (Gas Volume Meters) Regulations 1983(**d**);

"the relevant Community obligations" mean the Community obligations of the United Kingdom under Council Directive No. 71/316/EEC(**e**) as amended(**f**) (which relates to measuring instruments in general) and Council Directive 71/318/EEC(**g**) as amended by Commission Directive No. 74/331/EEC(**h**), Commission Directive No. 78/365/EEC(**i**) and Commission Directive No. 82/623/EEC(**j**) (which relates to gas volume meters in particular) relating to gas volume meters.

(**a**) 1972 c. 60.
(**c**) S.I. 1980/1058.
(**b**) 1973 c.51.
(**d**) S.I. 1983/1246.
(**e**) O.J. No. L202, 6.9.71, p. 1 (O.J./S.E. 1971 (II), p. 707).
(**f**) Council Directive No. 72/427/EEC (O.J. No. L291, 28.12.1972, p. 156, O.J./S.E. 1972, 28–30 Dec., p. 71) and Cmnd. 7463, p. 174.
(**g**) O.J. No. L202, 6.9.71, p. 21 (O.J./S.E. 1971 (III), p. 729).
(**h**) O.J. No. L189, 12.7.74, p. 9.
(**i**) O.J. No. L104, 18.4.78, p. 26.
(**j**) O.J. No. L252, 27.8.82, p. 5.

FEES AND CHARGES

3. The fee payable in connection with the services provided by the Department of Energy in pursuance of the relevant Community obligations relating to EEC pattern approval implemented by regulation 7 of, and Schedule 2 to, the principal regulations, shall be, in respect of a category of pattern of instrument and nature of application mentioned in columns 1 and 2 respectively of Schedule 1 to these regulations, the fee specified in column 3 of that Schedule, which fee shall be payable on the making of the application.

4. The fee payable in connection with the services provided by the Department of Energy in pursuance of the relevant Community obligations relating to EEC initial verification implemented by regulation 13 of, and Schedule 3 to, the principal regulations shall be, in respect of a designation of instrument mentioned in column 1 of Schedule 2 to these regulations, the fee specified in column 2 of that Schedule, which fee shall be payable on the making of the application for consideration of the instrument for initial verification.

5. All fees received under Regulations 3 and 4 above shall be paid into the Consolidated Fund.

6. Regulation 4(1) of the Gas (Meters) Regulations 1983**(a)** shall have effect in relation to a meter bearing the mark of EEC initial verification as if the reference to the fee prescribed by any provision of Regulation 5 of those Regulations were, in respect of a designation of instrument mentioned in column 1 of Schedule 2 to these Regulations, the fee specified in column 2 of that Schedule together with an additional fee of £1.

7. The Regulations specified in Schedule 3 hereto are hereby revoked.

Alick Buchanan-Smith,
Minister of State,
Department of Energy.

2nd August 1983.

We consent to the making of these Regulations.

Nigel Lawson,
D. J. F. Hunt,
Two of the Lords Commissioners
of Her Majesty's Treasury.

12th August 1983.

(a) S.I. 1983/684, amended by S.I. 1983/1246.

SCHEDULE 1 Regulation 3

FEES FOR EEC PATTERN APPROVAL

(1) Category of pattern of instrument in respect of which application is made	(2) Nature of application	(3) Fee £
Gas volume meter with deformable walls	Under regulation 7(1) of the principal regulations ... ... Under regulation 7(2) of the principal regulations	340.00 30.00
Rotary piston gas meter	Under regulation 7(1) of the principal regulations ... ... Under regulation 7(2) of the principal regulations	800.00 80.00
Turbine gas meter	Under regulation 7(1) of the principal regulations ... ... Under regulation 7(2) of the principal regulations	900.00 90.00

SCHEDULE 2 Regulations 4 and 6

FEES FOR EEC INITIAL VERIFICATION AND RE-EXAMINATION

(1) Designation (G) (in accordance with item 2 of Chapter II and item 2 of Chapter III of the Annex to Council Directive No. 71/318/EEC, as amended) of instrument in respect of which application is made	(2) Fee £
1.6, 2.5, 4 or 6	0.70
10	1.00
16 or 25	3.00
40, 65 or 100	10.00
160, 250, 400, 650 or 1,000 or any decimal multiple of 160, 250, 400, 650 or 1,000	25.00

FEES AND CHARGES

Regulation 7   SCHEDULE 3

REGULATIONS REVOKED

Regulations revoked	References
The Measuring Instruments (EEC Requirements) (Gas Volume Meters) (Fees) Regulations 1975	S.I. 1975/1874.
The Measuring Instruments (EEC Requirements) (Gas Volume Meters) (Fees) (Amendment) Regulations 1979	S.I. 1979/1257.
The Measuring Instruments (EEC Requirements) (Gas Volume Meters) (Fees) (Amendment) (No. 2) Regulations 1981 ...	S.I. 1981/505.

EXPLANATORY NOTE

(This Note is not part of the Regulations.)

These Regulations prescribe the fees payable in connection with the services provided by the Department of Energy in respect of EEC pattern approval and EEC initial verification of gas volume meters under the Measuring Instruments (EEC Requirements) Regulations 1980 as applied to gas volume meters by the Measuring Instruments (EEC Requirements) (Gas Volume Meters) Regulations 1983. They also prescribe the fees payable where a meter bearing the mark of EEC initial verification is required to be re-examined by a party to a dispute under Regulation 4(1) of the Gas (Meters) Regulations 1983.

They supersede the Measuring Instruments (EEC Requirements) (Gas Volume Meters) (Fees) Regulations 1975 as amended, which referred to the Measuring Instruments (EEC Requirements) Regulations 1975 (S.I. 1975/1173), and the Measuring Instruments (EEC Requirements) (Gas Volume Meters) Regulations 1975 (S.I. 1975/1873), which have been revoked.

The fees for EEC pattern approval and EEC initial verification which are payable on the making of the appropriate application are unaltered.

STATUTORY INSTRUMENTS

1983 No. 1248

ROAD TRAFFIC

The Road Vehicles (Registration and Licensing) (Amendment) Regulations 1983

Made - - - -	*15th August* 1983
Laid before Parliament	*23rd August* 1983
Coming into Operation	*14th September* 1983

The Secretary of State for Transport, in exercise of the powers conferred by section 37(1)(*b*) of the Vehicles (Excise) Act 1971(**a**), now vested in him(**b**), and of all other enabling powers, hereby makes the following Regulations:—

1. These Regulations shall come into operation on 14th September 1983 and may be cited as the Road Vehicles (Registration and Licensing) (Amendment) Regulations 1983.

2. The Road Vehicles (Registration and Licensing) Regulations 1971(**c**) are hereby amended so that in Part I, after Regulation 3, there is inserted the following new Regulation:—

"Exclusion for electrically assisted pedal cycles

3A. The provisions of Parts II and III of these Regulations do not apply to an electrically assisted pedal cycle for the time being prescribed for the purposes of section 103 of the Road Traffic Regulation Act 1967(**d**) and section 193 of the Road Traffic Act 1972(**e**).".

Signed by authority of the Secretary of State.

Lynda Chalker,
Parliamentary Under Secretary of State,
Department of Transport.

15th August 1983.

(**a**) 1971 c. 10.   (**b**) S.I. 1979/371 and 1981/238.

(**c**) S.I. 1971/450, to which there is no relevant amending Instrument.

(**d**) 1967 c. 76; section 103(1) of which Act has been amended by section 24 of the Transport Act 1981 (c. 56).

(**e**) 1972 c. 20; section 193(1) of which Act has been amended by section 24 of the Transport Act 1981.

EXPLANATORY NOTE

(This Note is not part of the Regulations.)

These Regulations amend the Road Vehicles (Registration and Licensing) Regulations 1971 by providing that Parts II and III of those Regulations (which deal, respectively, with licensing and registration of mechanically propelled vehicles and the exhibition of licences and registration marks) do not apply to an electrically assisted pedal cycle for the time being prescribed for the purposes of section 103 of the Road Traffic Regulation Act 1967 and section 193 of the Road Traffic Act 1972. The cycles at present prescribed for those purposes are those to which the Electrically Assisted Pedal Cycles Regulations 1983 (S.I. 1983/1168) apply.

S T A T U T O R Y   I N S T R U M E N T S

1983 No. 1256

OFFSHORE INSTALLATIONS

The Offshore Installations (Safety Zones) (No. 25) Order 1983

Made - - - -	*15th August* 1983
Coming into Operation	*17th August* 1983

The Secretary of State, in exercise of the powers conferred on him by section 21(1), (2) and (3) of the Oil and Gas (Enterprise) Act 1982(a) (hereinafter referred to as "the Act"), and of all other powers enabling him in that behalf, hereby makes the following Order:—

1. This Order may be cited as the Offshore Installations (Safety Zones) (No. 25) Order 1983 and shall come into operation on 17th August 1983.

2.—(1) A safety zone is hereby established around the installation specified in Column 1 of the Schedule hereto (being an installation maintained in waters in an area designated under section 1(7) of the Continental Shelf Act 1964(b)) having a radius of five hundred metres from the point as respects that installation which has the co-ordinates of latitude and longitude according to European Datum (1950) specified in Columns 2 and 3 of the Schedule.

(2) The prohibition under section 21(3) of the Act on a vessel entering or remaining in a safety zone without the consent of the Secretary of State shall not apply to a vessel entering or remaining in the safety zone established under paragraph (1) above:

(*a*) in connection with the laying, inspection, testing, repair, alteration, renewal or removal of any submarine cable or pipe-line in or near that safety zone;

(*b*) to provide services for, to transport persons or goods to or from, or under the authority of a government department to inspect, any installation in that safety zone;

(*c*) if it is a vessel belonging to a general lighthouse authority performing duties relating to the safety of navigation;

(*d*) in connection with the saving or attempted saving of life or property;

(*e*) owing to stress of weather; or

(*f*) when in distress.

(a) 1982 c. 23.　　　(b) 1964 c. 29.

Avon,
Parliamentary Under Secretary of State,
Department of Energy.

15th August 1983.

Article 2(1)   SCHEDULE

SAFETY ZONE

1	2	3
Name or other designation of the offshore installation	Latitude North	Longitude West
DP4	53° 52′ 34.00″	03° 33′ 39.00″

EXPLANATORY NOTE

(This Note is not part of the Order.)

This Order establishes, under section 21 of the Oil and Gas (Enterprise) Act 1982, a safety zone, having a radius of 500 metres from a specified point, around the installation known as DP4 maintained in waters (that is Morecambe Bay) in an area designated under section 1(7) of the Continental Shelf Act 1964.

Vessels (which includes hovercraft, submersible apparatus and installations in transit) are prohibited from entering or remaining in the safety zone except with the consent of the Secretary of State or in the circumstances mentioned in Article 2(2) of the Order.

STATUTORY INSTRUMENTS

1983 No. 1257

OFFSHORE INSTALLATIONS

The Offshore Installations (Safety Zones) (Revocation) (No. 18) Order 1983

Made - - - - -	15*th August* 1983
Coming into Operation	17*th August* 1983

The Secretary of State, in exercise of the power conferred on him by section 21(1) of the Oil and Gas (Enterprise) Act 1982**(a)**, and of all other powers enabling him in that behalf, hereby makes the following Order:—

1. This Order may be cited as the Offshore Installations (Safety Zones) (Revocation) (No. 18) Order 1983 and shall come into operation on 17th August 1983.

2. The Offshore Installations (Safety Zones) (No. 18) Order 1983**(b)** is hereby revoked.

Avon,
Parliamentary Under Secretary of State,
Department of Energy.

15th August 1983.

EXPLANATORY NOTE

(This Note is not part of the Order.)

This Order revokes the Offshore Installations (Safety Zones) (No. 18) Order 1983. The installation known as Pentagone 84 which was protected by the safety zone established by that Order has been removed and accordingly that Order is no longer required.

(a) 1982 c. 23.

(b) S.I. 1983/854.

STATUTORY INSTRUMENTS

1983 No. 1258

OFFSHORE INSTALLATIONS

The Offshore Installations (Life-Saving Appliances and Fire-Fighting Equipment) (Amendment) Regulations 1983

Made - - - -	*15th August*	1983
Laid before Parliament	*17th August*	1983
Coming into Operation	*8th September*	1983

The Secretary of State, in exercise of the powers conferred on him by section 6 of the Mineral Workings (Offshore Installations) Act 1971(**a**) and of all other powers enabling him in that behalf, and after consulting with organisations appearing to him to be representative of those persons who will be affected, hereby makes the following Regulations:—

1. These Regulations may be cited as the Offshore Installations (Life-saving Appliances and Fire-fighting Equipment) (Amendment) Regulations 1983 and shall come into operation on 8th September, 1983.

2. The following table shall be substituted for the table set out in sub-paragraph (*a*) of the Schedule to the Offshore Installations (Life-saving Appliances) Regulations 1977(**b**)and for the table set out in sub-paragraph (*a*) of the Schedule to the Offshore Installations (Fire-fighting Equipment) Regulations 1978(**c**):—

"TABLE

Time spent	Rate per hour or part thereof
On any day except a Saturday, Sunday or public holiday—	
between 8 a.m. and 6 p.m.	£36.95
before 8 a.m. or after 6 p.m.	£55.43
On a Saturday	£55.43
On a Sunday or public holiday	£73.90"

Avon,
Parliamentary Under Secretary of State,
Department of Energy.

15th August 1983.

(**a**) 1971 c. 61; section 6 was extended by section 44(5) of the Petroleum and Submarine Pipelines Act 1975 (c. 74).
  (**b**) S.I. 1977/486, amended by S.I. 1981/364, 1982/360.
  (**c**) S.I. 1978/611, amended by S.I. 1981/364, 1982/360.

EXPLANATORY NOTE

(This Note is not part of the Regulations.)

The Offshore Installations (Life-saving Appliances) Regulations 1977 prohibit the presence of any person on an installation to which the Regulations apply unless the life-saving appliances on that installation have been examined by a person acting at the direction of the Secretary of State. The Offshore Installations (Fire-fighting Equipment) Regulations 1978 contain a similar prohibition in respect of the fire-fighting equipment provided on an offshore installation. Both the 1977 and the 1978 Regulations require the owner of an installation on which an examination is carried out to pay a fee to the Secretary of State, comprising a sum based on the time spent by the examiner in carrying out the examination and in travelling to and from the installation, calculated in accordance with a table set out in the Schedule to the Regulations, and the cost of his travelling and subsistence expenses. These Regulations substitute in the 1977 Regulations and the 1978 Regulations a new table specifying the rates payable in respect of the time spent by an examiner. These new rates replace those having effect by virtue of the Offshore Installations (Life-saving Appliances and Fire-fighting Equipment) (Amendment) Regulations 1982 which were as follows:—

Time spent	Rate per hour or part thereof
Between 6 a.m. and 8 p.m. on any day except a Saturday, Sunday or public holiday—	£33.35
At any time on a Saturday, Sunday or public holiday and before 6 a.m. and after 8 p.m. on any other day	£50.03

STATUTORY INSTRUMENTS

1983 No. 1261

OFFSHORE INSTALLATIONS

The Offshore Installations (Safety Zones) (No. 26) Order 1983

Made - - - - -	16*th August* 1983
Coming into Operation	18*th August* 1983

The Secretary of State, in exercise of the powers conferred on him by section 21(1), (2) and (3) of the Oil and Gas (Enterprise) Act 1982(a) (hereinafter referred to as "the Act"), and of all other powers enabling him in that behalf, hereby makes the following Order:—

1. This Order may be cited as the Offshore Installations (Safety Zones) (No. 26) Order 1983 and shall come into operation on 18th August 1983.

2.—(1) A safety zone is hereby established around the installation specified in Column 1 of the Schedule hereto (being an installation maintained in waters in an area designated under section 1(7) of the Continental Shelf Act 1964(b)) having a radius of five hundred metres from the point as respects that installation which has the co-ordinates of latitude and longitude according to European Datum (1950) specified in Columns 2 and 3 of the Schedule.

(2) The prohibition under section 21(3) of the Act on a vessel entering or remaining in a safety zone without the consent of the Secretary of State shall not apply to a vessel entering or remaining in the safety zone established under paragraph (1) above:

(*a*) in connection with the laying, inspection, testing, repair, alteration, renewal or removal of any submarine cable or pipe-line in or near that safety zone;

(*b*) to provide services for, to transport persons or goods to or from, or under the authority of a government department to inspect, any installation in that safety zone;

(*c*) if it is a vessel belonging to a general lighthouse authority performing duties relating to the safety of navigation;

(*d*) in connection with the saving or attempted saving of life or property;

(*e*) owing to stress of weather; or

(*f*) when in distress.

(a) 1982 c. 23.   (b) 1964 c. 29.

Alick Buchanan-Smith,
Minister of State,
Department of Energy.

16th August, 1983.

SCHEDULE

Article 2(1)

SAFETY ZONE

1	2	3
Name or other designation of the offshore installation	Latitude North	Longitude West
Pentagone 84	58° 07′ 20.59″	00° 05′ 17.72″

EXPLANATORY NOTE

(This Note is not part of the Order.)

This Order establishes, under section 21 of the Oil and Gas (Enterprise) Act 1982, a safety zone, having a radius of 500 metres from a specified point, around the installation known as Pentagone 84 maintained in waters in an area designated under section 1(7) of the Continental Shelf Act 1964.

Vessels (which includes hovercraft, submersible apparatus and installations in transit) are prohibited from entering or remaining in the safety zone except with the consent of the Secretary of State or in the circumstances mentioned in Article 2(2) of the Order.

STATUTORY INSTRUMENTS

1983 No. 1262

OFFSHORE INSTALLATIONS

The Offshore Installations (Safety Zones) (Revocation) (No. 19) Order 1983

Made - - - - -	*16th August* 1983
Coming into Operation	*18th August* 1983

The Secretary of State, in exercise of the power conferred on him by section 21(1) of the Oil and Gas (Enterprise) Act 1982**(a)**, and of all other powers enabling him in that behalf, hereby makes the following Order:—

1. This Order may be cited as the Offshore Installations (Safety Zones) (Revocation) (No. 19) Order 1983 and shall come into operation on 18th August 1983.

2. The Offshore Installations (Safety Zones) (No. 23) Order 1983**(b)** is hereby revoked.

Alick Buchanan-Smith,
Minister of State,
Department of Energy.

16th August 1983.

EXPLANATORY NOTE

(This Note is not part of the Order.)

This Order revokes the Offshore Installations (Safety Zones) (No. 23) Order 1983. The installation known as Dundee Kingsnorth which was protected by the safety zone established by that Order has been removed and accordingly that Order is no longer required.

(a) 1982 c. 23. **(b)** S.I. 1983/1012.

STATUTORY INSTRUMENTS

1983 No. 1264

PENSIONS

The Pensions Increase (Review) Order 1983

Made - - - -	*28th July* 1983
Laid before Parliament	*18th August* 1983
Coming into Operation	*21st November* 1983

Whereas by virtue of section 23 of the Social Security Pensions Act 1975 (**a**) a direction has been given (**b**) under section 124 of the Social Security Act 1975 (**c**) by the Secretary of State for Social Services that the sums mentioned in section 23(1)*(b)* are to be increased:

Now therefore the Treasury, in exercise of the powers conferred by section 59(1), (2) and (5) of the Social Security Pensions Act 1975 (**d**) and now vested in them (**e**), and of all other powers enabling them in that behalf, hereby make the following Order:—

Citation and commencement

1. This Order may be cited as the Pensions Increase (Review) Order 1983 and shall come into operation on 21st November 1983.

Interpretation

2.—(1) In this Order—

"the 1971 Act" means the Pensions (Increase) Act 1971 (**f**) ;

"the 1974 Act" means the Pensions (Increase) Act 1974 (**g**) ;

"the 1975 Act" means the Social Security Pensions Act 1975;

"basic rate" has the meaning given by section 17(1) of the 1971 Act as amended by section 1(3) of the 1974 Act;

"the existing Orders" means the Pensions Increase (Annual Review) Order 1972 (**h**), the Pensions Increase (Annual Review) Order 1973 (**i**), the Pensions Increase (Annual Review) Order 1974 (**j**), the Pensions Increase (Annual Review) Order 1975 (**k**), the Pensions Increase (Annual Review) Order 1976 (**l**), the Pensions Increase (Annual Review) Order 1977 (**m**), the Pensions Increase (Annual Review) Order 1978 (**n**), the Pensions Increase (Review) Order 1979 (**o**), the Pensions Increase (Review) Order 1980 (**p**), the Pensions Increase (Review) Order 1981 (**q**) and the Pensions Increase (Review) Order 1982 (**r**) ;

(**a**) 1975 c.60.
(**b**) The direction is contained in S.I. 1983/1244.
(**c**) 1975 c.14; section 1 of the Social Security and Housing Benefits Act 1983 (c.36) made provision for increases to reflect actual, rather than estimated, rises in the general level of prices.
(**d**) Section 59 was amended and section 59A was added by section 11 of the Social Security Act 1979 (c.18).

	(**e**) S.I. 1981/1670.	(**f**) 1971 c.56.
(**g**) 1974 c.9.	(**h**) S.I. 1972/1298.	(**i**) S.I. 1973/1370.
(**j**) S.I. 1974/1373.	(**k**) S.I. 1975/1384.	(**l**) S.I. 1976/1356.
(**m**) S.I. 1977/1387.	(**n**) S.I. 1978/1211.	(**o**) S.I. 1979/1047.
(**p**) S.I. 1980/1302.	(**q**) S.I. 1981/1217.	(**r**) S.I. 1982/1178.

"official pension" has the meaning given by section 5(1) of the 1971 Act;

"pension authority" has the meaning given by section 7(1) of the 1971 Act;

"qualifying condition" means one of the conditions laid down in section 3 of the 1971 Act as amended by section 3(2) and (3) of the 1974 Act;

"widow's pension" means a pension payable in respect of the services of the pensioner's deceased husband.

(2) For the purposes of this Order the time when a pension "begins" is that stated in section 8(2) of the 1971 Act, and the "beginning date" shall be construed accordingly.

(3) Where, for the purposes of this Order, it is necessary to calculate the number of complete months in any period an incomplete month shall be treated as a complete month if it consists of at least 16 days.

Pension increases

3.   The annual rate of an official pension may, if a qualifying condition is satisfied or the pension is a widow's pension, be increased by the pension authority in respect of any period beginning on or after 21st November 1983 as follows:—

(1) a pension beginning before 22nd November 1982 may be increased by 3.7 per cent of the basic rate as increased by the amount of any increase under section 1 of the 1971 Act or the existing Orders;

(2) a pension beginning on or after 22nd November 1982 and before 21st November 1983 may be increased by 3.7 per cent multiplied by $\frac{A}{B}$ where

(a) A is the number of complete months in the period between the beginning date of the pension and 21st November 1983, and

(b) B is 12.

Increases in certain lump sums

4.   In respect of any lump sum or instalment of a lump sum which became payable before 21st November 1983 but after 21st November 1982 there may be paid an increase of 3.7 per cent of the amount of the lump sum or instalment (as increased by the amount of any increase under section 1 of the 1971 Act or under the existing Orders) multiplied by $\frac{A}{B}$ where

(a) A is the number of complete months in the period between the beginning date for the lump sum or, if later, 22nd November 1982 and the date on which it became payable; and

(b) B is 12.

Reductions in respect of guaranteed minimum pensions

5.   The amount by reference to which any increase in the rate of an official pension provided for by this Order is to be calculated shall, in the case of a person who

(a) is entitled to a guaranteed minimum pension on 21st November 1983, and

(b) where entitlement to that guaranteed minimum pension arises from an employment from which (either directly or by virtue of the payment of a transfer credit under section 38 of the 1975 Act) entitlement to the official pension also arises,

be reduced by an amount equal to the rate of the guaranteed minimum pension unless the Treasury **(a)** shall, in accordance with the provisions of section 59A of the 1975 Act, otherwise direct.

T. Garel-Jones,
Ian B. Lang,
Two of the Lords Commissioners
of Her Majesty's Treasury.

28th July 1983.

EXPLANATORY NOTE

(This Note is not part of the Order.)

Under section 59 of the Social Security Pensions Act 1975 as amended by section 11 of the Social Security Act 1979 and as modified by section 59A of the 1975 Act (introduced by section 11(4) of the 1979 Act) the Treasury (in whom the functions conferred by those provisions are now vested) are required to provide by order for the increase in the rates of public service pensions. The increase is the percentage (or in some circumstances a fraction of the percentage) by which the Secretary of State for Social Services has, by directions given under the provisions of sections 23 of the Social Security Pensions Act 1975, increased the sums referred to in section 23(1)*(b)* of the 1975 Act. These are the sums which are the additional components in the rates of long term benefits namely the additional pension entitlements accruing to employees in respect of their earnings after 5th April 1978.

For pensions which began before 22nd November 1982 the increase is 3.7 per cent. For pensions which began on or after 22nd November 1982, the increases are as follows:

Pensions Beginning	Percentage Increase	Pensions Beginning	Percentage Increase
22nd November 1982 to 5th December 1982	3.7%	6th May 1983 to 5th June 1983	1.9%
6th December 1982 to 5th January 1983	3.4%	6th June 1983 to 5th July 1983	1.5%
6th January 1983 to 5th February 1983	3.1%	6th July 1983 to 5th August 1983	1.2%
6th February 1983 to 5th March 1983	2.8%	6th August 1983 to 5th September 1983	0.9%
6th March 1983 to 5th April 1983	2.5%	6th September 1983 to 5th October 1983	0.6%
6th April 1983 to 5th May 1983	2.2%	6th October 1983 to 5th November 1983	0.3%

(a) *See* S.I. 1981/1670, Arts. 2(1)*(c)* and 3(5).

Deferred lump sums beginning on or before 5th November 1983 and which become payable after 20th November 1983 receive the same percentage increase as pensions which began on the same date. Also Article 4 of the Order provides for increases on certain deferred lump sums which became payable after 21st November 1982 and before 21st November 1983.

The Order also makes provision for the amount by reference to which any increase in the rate of an official pension is to be calculated to be reduced by the amount equal to the rate of the guaranteed minimum pension entitlement deriving from the employment which gives rise to the official pension. This is required by section 59(5) of the Social Security Pensions Act 1975 but by virtue of section 59A of that Act and the Transfer of Functions (Minister for the Civil Service and Treasury) Order 1981 the Treasury is empowered to direct that in respect of specified cases or classes of case either no such reduction be made or the reduction shall be less than the rate of the guaranteed minimum pension.

STATUTORY INSTRUMENTS

1983 No. 1266

CUSTOMS AND EXCISE

The Export of Goods (Control) (Amendment No. 4) Order 1983

Made - - - - -	17*th August* 1983
Coming into Operation	19*th August* 1983

The Secretary of State, in exercise of powers conferred by section 1 of the Import, Export and Customs Powers (Defence) Act 1939(a) and now vested in him(b), and of all other powers enabling him in that behalf, hereby makes the following Order:—

1. This Order may be cited as the Export of Goods (Control) (Amendment No. 4) Order 1983 and shall come into operation on 19th August 1983.

2. The Export of Goods (Control) Order 1981(c) shall be further amended by substituting for Group C of Part I of Schedule 1 thereto the new Group C which appears in the Schedule hereto.

P. M. S. Corley,
An Under Secretary,
17th August 1983.   Department of Trade and Industry.

SCHEDULE

GROUP C

STEEL PRODUCTS PROHIBITED TO BE EXPORTED TO THE UNITED STATES OF AMERICA OR THE COMMONWEALTH OF PUERTO RICO

NOTE: The following goods are specified by reference to headings in the Common Customs Tariff of the European Economic Community. For information, the corresponding Nimexe Codes in the Nomenclature of Goods of the External Trade Statistics of the European Community and Statistics of Trade between Member States (NIMEXE)(d) are also specified.

(a) 1939 c. 69.   (b) *See* S.I. 1970/1537.
(c) S.I. 1981/1641; the only relevant amending instrument is S.I. 1982/1556.
(d) *See* Commission Regulation (EEC) No. 3407/82, OJ No. L366, 27.12.1982, p. 1, amending Council Regulation (EEC) No. 1445/72, OJ No. L161, 17.7.1972, p. 1.

Tariff Heading No.	Nimexe Code	Description of Goods
ex 73.08		Steel coils (ECSC), the following:—
		(1) Less than 1.50 m in width, intended for re-rolling,
	730801	(a) for "electrical" sheets and plates, other than silicon electrical;
		(b) other, of a thickness of—
	730803	(i) more than 4.75 mm;
	730805	(ii) not less than 3 mm but not more than 4.75 mm;
	730807	(iii) less than 3 mm;
		(2) Less than 1.50 m in width, not intended for re-rolling, of a thickness of:
	730821	(a) more than 4.75 mm;
	730825	(b) not less than 3 mm but not more than 4.75 mm;
	730829	(c) less than 3 mm;
		(3) 1.50 m or more in width, of a thickness of:
	730841	(a) more than 4.75 mm;
	730845	(b) not less than 3 mm but not more than 4.75 mm;
	730849	(c) less than 3 mm.
ex 73.09	730900	Steel universal plates (ECSC).
ex 73.10		Steel bars and rods (including wire rod), the following:—
		(1) Not further worked than hot-rolled or extruded, the following:
	731011	(a) wire rod (ECSC), of circular section 0.2 in or more in diameter, or of any other solid section;
	731016	(b) bars and rods (ECSC), other than—
		(i) concrete reinforcing bars with minor indentations, flanges, grooves or other deformations produced during the rolling process, whether or not twisted after rolling, and
		(ii) round blooms and billets;
	731030	(2) Not further worked than cold-formed or cold-finished, of rectangular section more than 1.2 in in thickness and more than 12 in in width;
		(3) Clad or surface-worked, the following:
		(a) not further worked than clad—
	731042	(i) hot-rolled or extruded (ECSC), coated or plated with metal and of rectangular section less than 3/16 in in thickness and more than 12 in in width, or 3/16 in or more in thickness and more than 8 in in width;
	731045	(ii) cold-formed or cold-finished, coated or plated with metal and of rectangular section more than 12 in in width;
	731049	(b) other, of circular section, except with a diameter of 18.8 mm or less and in coils, or of rectangular section, except cold-finished less than 12 in in width, or of any other solid section.

Tariff Heading No.	Nimexe Code	Description of Goods
ex 73.11		Angles, shapes and sections of steel, the following:—
		(1) Not further worked than hot-rolled or extruded (ECSC), the following:
	731111	(a) U, I or H sections of a height of less than 80 mm and having a maximum cross-sectional dimension of 3 in or more;
	731112	(b) H sections (broad-flanged beams) of a height of 80 mm or more;
		(c) U or I sections of a height of 80 mm or more—
	731114	(i) with parallel flange faces;
	731116	(ii) other;
	731119	(d) other angles, shapes and sections having a maximum cross-sectional dimension of 3 in or more;
	731120	(2) Not further worked than forged and having a maximum cross-sectional dimension of 3 in or more;
		(3) Not further worked than cold-formed or cold-finished and having a maximum cross-sectional dimension of 3 in or more, the following:
	731131	(a) from coils for re-rolling, universal plates, hoop, strip, sheets or plates;
	731139	(b) other;
	731150	Steel sheet piling, whether or not drilled, punched or made from assembled elements.
ex 73.12		Steel hoop and strip, the following:—
		(1) Not further worked than hot-rolled (ECSC), the following:
	731211	(a) "electrical", other than silicon electrical;
	731219	(b) other;
		(2) Not further worked than cold-rolled, more than 12 in in width, the following:
	731221	(a) in coils for the manufacture of tin plate, other than black plate, of a thickness of 0.0142 in or more;
	731225	(b) "electrical", other than silicon electrical;
	731229	(c) other, except black plate, of a thickness of 0.0142 in or more;
		(3) Clad, coated or otherwise surface-worked, more than 12 in in width or, in the case of hot-rolled more than 3/16 in in thickness, more than 8 in in width, the following:
	731240	(a) enamelled;
	731251	(b) tinplate (ECSC), not including black plate, (over 12 in in width only);
	731259	(c) other tinned (over 12 in in width only);
	731261	(d) electrolytically zinc-coated (electro-galvanised);
	731263	(e) otherwise zinc-coated (including hot-dipped galvanised);

Tariff Heading No.	Nimexe Code	Description of Goods
	731265	(f) lead-coated;
		(g) not further worked than clad, coated or plated with metal—
	731271	(i) hot-rolled (ECSC);
	731275	(ii) cold-rolled;
	731281	(h) copper-plated;
	731285	(i) nickel-plated or chrome-plated;
	731287	(j) aluminium-coated;
	731288	(k) lacquered, varnished, painted or plastic-coated;
	731289	(l) other, except silvered, gilded or platinum-plated.
ex 73.13		"Electrical" steel sheets and plates (ECSC), except silicon electrical, the following:—
	731311	(1) With a watt-loss, regardless of thickness, of 0.75 watt or less;
	731316	(2) Other.
		Steel sheets and plates, other than "electrical", the following:—
		(1) Not further worked than hot-rolled (ECSC), of a thickness of:
		(a) more than 4.75 mm—
	731317	(i) with raised or indented patterns;
	731319	(ii) other;
		(b) not less than 3 mm but not more than 4.75 mm—
	731321	(i) with raised or indented patterns;
	731323	(ii) other;
	731326	(c) not less than 2 mm but less than 3 mm;
	731332	(d) more than 1 mm but less than 2 mm;
	731334	(e) not less than 0.5 mm but not more than 1 mm;
	731336	(f) less than 0.5 mm;
		(2) Not further worked than cold-rolled, of a thickness of:
	731341	(a) 3 mm or more;
	731343	(b) not less than 2 mm but less than 3 mm (ECSC);
	731345	(c) more than 1 mm but less than 2 mm (ECSC);
	731347	(d) not less than 0.5 mm but not more than 1 mm (ECSC);
	731349	(e) less than 0.5 mm but not less than 0.36 mm [0.0142 in], and not including black plate;
	731350	(3) Not further worked than varnished, polished or glazed (ECSC), of a thickness of not less than 0.36 mm, and not including black plate;
		(4) Clad, coated or otherwise surface-treated (ECSC), the following:
	731362	(a) enamelled more than 12 in in width;
	731364	(b) tinplate, not including black plate;
	731365	(c) other tinned;
	731367	(d) electrolytically zinc-coated (electro-galvanised);
		(e) otherwise zinc-coated (including hot-dipped galvanised)—

Tariff Heading No.	Nimexe Code	Description of Goods
	731368	(i) corrugated;
	731372	(ii) other;
	731374	(f) lead-coated;
	731376	(g) tinned and printed;
		(h) clad, of a thickness of—
	731378	(i) 3 mm or more;
	731379	(ii) less than 3 mm;
	731384	(i) copper-plated;
	731386	(j) nickel-plated or chrome-plated;
	731387	(k) aluminium-plated;
	731388	(l) lacquered, varnished, painted or plastic-coated;
	731389	(m) other coated or plated with metal.
ex 73.15		High carbon steel, the following:—
	736210	(1) Coils for re-rolling (ECSC);
	736230	(2) Universal plates (ECSC);
		(3) Bars and rods (including wire rod); angles, shapes and sections; the following:
	736310	(a) structural shapes, not further worked than forged, having a maximum cross-sectional dimension of 3 in or more;
		(b) not further worked than hot-rolled or extruded (ECSC)—
	736321	(i) wire rod of circular section 0.2 in or more in diameter, or of any other solid section;
	736329	(ii) bars and rods, of circular section, other than round blooms and billets, or of any other solid section; and structural shapes having a maximum cross-sectional dimension of 3 in or more;
	736350	(c) not further worked than cold-formed or cold-finished—
		(i) bars and rods of rectangular section and over 12 in in width;
		(ii) structural shapes having a maximum cross-sectional dimension of 3 in or more;
		(d) clad or surface-worked—
		(i) not further worked than clad—
	736372	(a) hot-rolled or extruded (ECSC), coated or plated with metal and of rectangular section, of a thickness of less than 3/16 in and more than 12 in in width or of a thickness of 3/16 in or more and more than 8 in in width;
	736374	(b) cold-formed or cold-finished, coated or plated with metal, of rectangular section and more than 12 in in width;
	736379	(ii) other, of circular section, except with a diameter of 18.8 mm or less and in coils, or of rectangular section, except cold-finished less than 12 in in width, or of any other solid section;

Tariff Heading No.	Nimexe Code	Description of Goods
		(4) Hoop and strip, the following:
	736420	(a) not further worked than hot-rolled (ECSC);
	736450	(b) not further worked than cold-rolled, more than 12 in in width;
		(c) clad, coated or otherwise surface-treated
	736472	(i) not further worked than clad, hot-rolled (ECSC), more than 8 in in width;
	736475	(ii) not further worked than clad, cold-rolled, coated and plated with metal, more than 12 in in width;
	736479	(iii) other, of a thickness of less than 3/16 in and more than 12 in in width or of a thickness of 3/16 in or more and more than 8 in in width;
		(5) Sheets and plates, the following:
		(a) not further worked than hot-rolled (ECSC), of a thickness of—
	736521	(i) more than 4.75 mm;
	736523	(ii) not less than 3 mm but not more than 4.75 mm;
	736525	(iii) less than 3 mm;
		(b) not further worked than cold-rolled, of a thickness of—
	736553	(i) 3 mm or more;
	736555	(ii) less than 3 mm (ECSC) but not less than 0.36 mm [0.0142 in], and not including black plate;
	736570	(c) polished, clad, and coated, other than with metal, or otherwise surface-treated (ECSC), not less than 0.36 mm in thickness and not including black plate.
		Alloy steel, the following:—
		(1) Coils for re-rolling (ECSC), other than tool steel, high-speed tool steel and chipper knife steel, the following:
	737211	(a) for "electrical" sheets and plates, other than silicon electrical;
	737219	(b) other, except stainless or heat-resisting;
	737239	(2) Universal plates (ECSC), other than stainless or heat-resisting or tool steel, high-speed tool steel or chipper knife steel, more than 8 in in width;
		(3) Bars and rods (including wire rod); angles, shapes and sections; the following:
		(a) structural shapes, not further worked than forged, of—
	737313	(i) stainless or heat-resisting;
	737314	(ii) high-speed steel;
	737319	(iii) other;
		(b) not further worked than hot-rolled or extruded (ECSC)—
		(i) wire rod—
	737325	(a) of S, Pb and P steels (free-cutting and other), of circular section, 0.2 in or more in diameter, or of any other solid section;

Tariff Heading No.	Nimexe Code	Description of Goods
	737326	(b) of mangano-silicon steel;
	737329	(c) other, except tool steel, high-speed tool steel and chipper knife steel, of rectangular section 3/16 in or more in thickness and 8 in or less in width, or of any other solid section;
		(ii) other bars and rods; angles, shapes and sections—
	737333	(a) stainless or heat-resisting (structural shapes only);
	737334	(b) high-speed steel (structural shapes only);
	737335	(c) S, Pb and P steels (free-cutting and other), other than round blooms and billets;
	737336	(d) mangano-silicon structural shapes; and mangano-silicon bars and rods, other than round blooms and billets;
	737339	(e) other, except bars and rods of tool steel, high-speed tool steel or chipper knife steel and round blooms and billets;
		(c) not further worked than cold-formed or cold-finished—
		(i) angles, shapes and sections made from coils for re-rolling, universal plates, hoop, strip, sheets or plates—
	737343	(a) stainless or heat-resisting;
	737349	(b) other;
		(ii) other angles, shapes and sections; bars and rods—
	737353	(a) stainless or heat-resisting (structural shapes only);
	737354	(b) high-speed steel (structural shapes only);
	737355	(c) S, Pb and P steels (free-cutting or other);
	737359	(d) other, except bars and rods of tool steel, high-speed tool steel and chipper knife steel;
		(d) clad or surface-worked—
		(i) not further worked than clad—
	737372	(a) hot-rolled or extruded (ECSC), clad, or coated or plated with metal;
	737374	(b) cold-formed or cold-finished, more than 12 in in width and, if coated or plated with metal, less than 3/16 in in thickness;
	737383	(ii) stainless or heat-resisting, clad, of rectangular section and more than 12 in in width or, in the case of hot-rolled 3/16 in or more in thickness, more than 8 in in width;
	737389	(iii) other, except tool steel, high-speed tool steel or chipper knife steel, of rectangular section and more than 12 in in width or, in the case of hot-rolled 3/16 in or more in thickness, more than 8 in in width, or of circular section except with a diameter of 18.8 mm or less and in coils, or of any other solid section;

Tariff Heading No.	Nimexe Code	Description of Goods
		(4) Hoop and strip, the following:
		(a) not further worked than hot-rolled (ECSC)—
	737421	(i) "electrical", other than silicon electrical;
	737428	(ii) other, except stainless or heat-resisting and tool steel, high-speed tool steel or chipper knife steel;
		(b) not further worked than cold-rolled, less than 3/16 in in thickness and more than 12 in in width—
		(i) "electrical", other than silicon electrical—
	737451	(a) with watt loss, regardless of thickness, of 0.75 watt or less;
	737452	(b) other;
	737459	(ii) other, except tool steel, high-speed tool steel and chipper knife steel;
		(c) clad, coated or otherwise surface-treated—
		(i) not further worked than clad—
	737472	(a) hot-rolled (ECSC), coated or plated with metal;
	737474	(b) cold-rolled, coated or plated with metal, more than 12 in in width;
	737483	(ii) stainless or heat-resisting, clad, and coated or plated with metal;
	737489	(iii) other, except tool steel, high-speed tool steel or chipper knife steel, more than 12 in in width or, in the case of hot-rolled 3/16 in or more in thickness, more than 8 in in width;
		(5) Sheets and plates, the following:
	737511	(a) "electrical" (ECSC), other than silicon electrical—
		(i) with a watt loss, regardless of thickness, of 0.75 watt or less;
		(ii) other;
	737519	(b) not further worked than hot-rolled (ECSC) and other than stainless or heat-resisting, high-speed steel or tool steel, high-speed tool steel and chipper knife steel, of a thickness of—
	737529	(i) more than 4.75 mm;
	737539	(ii) not less than 3 mm but not more than 4.75 mm;
	737549	(iii) less than 3 mm;
		(c) not further worked than cold-rolled and other than stainless or heat-resisting, high-speed steel or tool steel, high-speed tool steel and chipper knife steel, of a thickness of—
	737559	(i) 3 mm or more;
	737569	(ii) less than 3 mm;
		(d) polished, clad, or otherwise surface treated (ECSC)—
	737573	(i) stainless or heat-resisting, clad, or plated or coated with metal;
	737579	(ii) other, except tool steel, high-speed tool steel and chipper knife steel, clad, or coated or plated with metal.

Tariff Heading No.	Nimexe Code	Description of Goods
ex 73.16		Steel railway and tramway track construction material (ECSC), the following:—
		(1) New rails, with weight per metre of:
	731614	(a) not less than 20 kg;
	731616˙	(b) less than 20 kg;
	731617	(2) Used rails;
	731620	(3) Check-rails.

EXPLANATORY NOTE

(This Note is not part of the Order.)

This Order further amends the Export of Goods (Control) Order 1981 by substituting for Group C of Part I of Schedule 1 to that Order (added by S.I. 1982/1556) a revised Group C which is set out in the Schedule to this Order.

The Order implements Commission Decision No. 2192/83/ECSC of 20th April 1983 (OJ No. L215, 5.8.1983, p. 24) and Council Regulation (EEC) No. 2190/83 of 18th April 1983 (OJ No. L215, 5.8.1983, p. 10), amending respectively Commission Decision No. 2872/82/ECSC (OJ No. L307, 1.11.1982, p. 27) and Council Regulation (EEC) No. 2870/82 (OJ No. L307, 1.11.1982, p. 3) which provided for the restriction of exports of certain steel products of Community origin to the United States of America or the Commonwealth of Puerto Rico.

The revised list of products identifies certain of the products more precisely in terms of form or dimensions and extends control to certain products not identified in the earlier list of NIMEXE codes on which the original Group C was based. These include steel coils for "electrical" sheets and plates, "electrical" steel hoop and strip, certain kinds of clad and metal-plated steel products, certain kinds of alloy wire rod and certain stainless steel products.

STATUTORY INSTRUMENTS

1983 No. 1267

WATER, ENGLAND AND WALES

The Water (Compensation) Regulations 1983

Made - - - -	*17th August* 1983
Laid before Parliament	*30th August* 1983
Coming into Operation	*30th September* 1983

The Secretary of State for the Environment, in exercise of the powers conferred upon him by paragraph 8 of Schedule 2 to the Water Act 1983(**a**) and of all other powers enabling him in that behalf, hereby makes the following regulations:—

Title and commencement

1. These regulations may be cited as the Water (Compensation) Regulations 1983 and shall come into operation on 30th September 1983.

Interpretation

2. In these regulations, unless the context otherwise requires—

"the Act" means the Water Act 1983, and "paragraph 8" means paragraph 8 of Schedule 2 to the Act;

"the 1978 Act" means the Employment Protection (Consolidation) Act 1978(**b**);

"the compensation authority" has the meaning assigned to it by regulation 3 below;

"the date of transfer" means 30th September 1983.

Designation of compensation authority

3. For the purposes of paragraph 8, the Severn-Trent Water Authority is hereby designated as the compensation authority.

Transfer of specified liabilities

4. On the date of transfer, the liabilities of the National Water Council relating to—

(*a*) the payment of benefits or compensation in respect of early retirement or for loss of employment, and

(*b*) redundancy payments within the meaning of the 1978 Act

(**a**) 1983 c. 23.   (**b**) 1978 c. 44.

shall be transferred to the compensation authority and shall become liabilities of that authority.

Recovery of cost by compensation authority

5.—(1) Where, in respect of any year or other period to which any determination is expressed to relate, the compensation authority has calculated and notified in writing to any water authority the amount of the total cost, the compensation authority may recover the relevant proportion of that cost from that authority.

(2) In this regulation, "determination" means a determination made and issued by the Secretary of State in pursuance of paragraph 8; "the total cost" means the cost incurred by the compensation authority in consequence of these regulations; and, in relation to any water authority other than the compensation authority, "the relevant proportion" means the proportion of the total cost specified in any determination in respect of that authority.

Signed by authority of the Secretary of State

Ian Gow,
Minister for Housing and Construction,
Department of the Environment.

17th August 1983.

EXPLANATORY NOTE

(This Note is not part of the Regulations.)

Section 3(1) and (3) of the Water Act 1983 provides that the Secretary of State may by order determine the functions of the National Water Council. Paragraph 8 of Schedule 2 to the Act empowers the Secretary of State to transfer to a specified water authority certain named liabilities of the Council.

By the Water Act 1983 (National Water Council Appointed Day) Order 1983 (S.I. 1983/1235) the Secretary of State for the Environment has appointed 1st October 1983 as the day on which the functions of the National Water Council are to determine.

These Regulations provide (regulations 3 and 4) that the liabilities of the National Water Council relating to certain specified payments shall be transferred to the Severn-Trent Water Authority on 30th September 1983 and shall become liabilities of that authority.

The Regulations also provide (regulation 5) that the Severn-Trent Water Authority ("the compensation authority") may recover from each of the other water authorities a proportion of the cost incurred by the compensation authority under the Regulations, as determined by the Secretary of State from time to time.

STATUTORY INSTRUMENTS

1983 No. 1268

PENSIONS

The Local Government Superannuation (Transferred Water Employees) (No. 2) Regulations 1983

Made - - - - -	*17th August* 1983
Laid before Parliament	*30th August* 1983
Coming into Operation	*30th September* 1983

The Secretary of State for the Environment, in exercise of the powers conferred upon him by sections 7 and 12 of the Superannuation Act 1972**(a)**, and of all other powers enabling him in that behalf, after consultation with such associations of local authorities as appeared to him to be concerned, the local authorities with whom consultation appeared to him to be desirable and such representatives of other persons likely to be affected by the regulations as appeared to him to be appropriate, hereby makes the following regulations:—

Citation and commencement

1.—(1) These regulations may be cited as the Local Government Superannuation (Transferred Water Employees) (No. 2) Regulations 1983.

(2) The Local Government Superannuation Regulations 1974 to 1983**(b)** and these regulations may be cited together as the Local Government Superannuation Regulations 1974 to 1983.

(3) These regulations shall come into operation on 30th September 1983.

(a) 1972 c. 11.
(b) S.I. 1974/520, 1977/1121, 1845, 1978/266, 822, 1738, 1739, 1979/2, 592, 1534, 1980/216, 233, 234, 1981/1250, 1509, 1982/908, 1514, 1983/178, 1269, 1270, 1271.

Interpretation

2. In these regulations "the principal regulations" means the Local Government Superannuation Regulations 1974**(a)** and "the 1983 regulations" means the Local Government Superannuation (Transferred Water Employees) Regulations 1983**(b)**.

Elections as to superannuation terms

3. Regulation 4 of the 1983 regulations is amended—

> (*a*) by substituting for the words "the National Water Council" in paragraphs (5) and (7) the words "the Severn–Trent Water Authority"; and

> (*b*) by substituting for the words "the Council" in paragraph (5) the words "that authority".

Preservation of rights on dissolution of National Water Council

4. The 1983 regulations are amended by inserting after regulation 5 the following:

"*Preservation of rights on dissolution of National Water Council*

5A.—(1) This regulation applies where—

> (*a*) an election has been made under regulation 4(2) or (3)(*b*), or by virtue of regulation 5 the principal regulations are deemed to have been modified in accordance with Case A in Part IV of the Schedule, and

> (*b*) the transferred employee has, not earlier than 9th May 1983, ceased to hold an employment under the National Water Council ("the first employment") and has, within 12 months after ceasing to hold the first employment and without having entered any other employment in which he was or was deemed to be a pensionable employee, or which he held for a period of more than 3 months, entered a new employment which is—
>
>> (i) an employment under a water authority in which he becomes a pensionable employee, or
>>
>> (ii) an employment in which he is admitted under an agreement made under regulation B4 of the principal regulations with the Severn–Trent Water Authority to participate in the benefits of a superannuation fund maintained by them.

(2) Subject to paragraph (4), where paragraph (1)(*b*)(i) applies the new employment shall for the purposes of the principal regulations as modified by these regulations be deemed to be a continuation of the first employment.

(**a**) S.I. 1974/520; relevant amending instruments are S.I. 1979/2, 1534, 1980/234, 1981/1250, 1509, 1983/1271.
(**b**) S.I. 1983/178.

(3) Subject to paragraph (4), but notwithstanding anything in regulation B4 of the principal regulations, every agreement made under that regulation with the Severn–Trent Water Authority shall provide that where paragraph (1)(*b*)(ii) applies the transferred employee's rights and liabilities are to be those which he would have had by virtue of regulation 4 or 5 if the new employment had been a continuation of the first employment.

(4) Nothing in this regulation shall be taken—
- (*a*) to make any contributions payable in respect of, or
- (*b*) to make reckonable as reckonable service or as qualifying service,

any period between the cessation of the first employment and the commencement of the new employment.".

Continuation of certain rights and liabilities
5. Regulation 7 of the 1983 regulations is amended—
- (*a*) by inserting after the words "1st April 1974" in paragraph (2) the words ", and the Severn–Trent Water Authority shall be deemed to have had from 30th September 1983"; and

- (*b*) by inserting at the end of paragraph (4)(*b*) the words ", and became on 30th September 1983 references to payment to or receipt from the fund maintained under those regulations by the Severn–Trent Water Authority".

Actuary's certificates
6. Regulation 8 of the 1983 regulations is amended by substituting for the words "the National Water Council" the words "the Severn–Trent Water Authority".

Right to opt out
7. Regulation 9 of the 1983 regulations is amended by substituting for the words "the National Water Council" the words "the Severn–Trent Water Authority".

Modification of principal regulations
8.—(1) Where regulation 5A of the 1983 regulations applies by virtue of an election under regulation 4(3)(*b*) of those regulations, regulation E2 of the principal regulations as modified by paragraph 29 of the Schedule to the 1983 regulations applies as if references to the employee's new employing body included references to the water authority by whom he has become employed or, as the case may be, to the body who made the agreement under regulation B4 of the principal regulations.

(2) Where notice for the purposes of regulation E19 of the principal regulations as modified by paragraph 44 of the Schedule to the 1983 regulations was not given before 30th September 1983, it may be given to, and the time for giving it may be extended by, the Severn–Trent Water Authority.

Signed by authority of the Secretary of State.

Ian Gow,
Minister for Housing and Construction,
Department of the Environment.

17th August 1983.

EXPLANATORY NOTE

(This Note is not part of the Regulations.)

These regulations adapt the provision made by the Local Government Superannuation (Transferred Water Employees) Regulations 1983 ("the 1983 regulations") so as to take account of the determination of the functions of the National Water Council ("the Council").

By virtue of the Local Government Superannuation (National Water Council Dissolution) Regulations 1983 (S.I. 1983/1271) the superannuation fund maintained by the Council is transferred to the Severn–Trent Water Authority, who become the administering authority for the purposes of the Local Government Superannuation Regulations 1974. Regulations 3, 5, 6, 7 and 8(2) substitute for references in the 1983 regulations to the Council references to that authority.

Regulation 4 inserts into the 1983 regulations a new regulation 5A. By virtue of the 1983 regulations certain employees who had been transferred to new employments when the water industry was reorganised under the Water Act 1973 (c.37) retained, or could elect to retain, while they remained in those employments, superannuation rights embodying features of their previous superannuation schemes. New regulation 5A preserves those rights in cases where the employment was with the Council, has ceased after the enactment of the Water Act 1983 (c. 23), and is followed, within 12 months and without any other intervening pensionable or more than temporary employment, by further employment in the water industry. Regulation 8(1) makes a consequential change in the body by whom certain discretionary powers become exercisable in some of these cases.

STATUTORY INSTRUMENTS

1983 No. 1269

PENSIONS

The Local Government Superannuation (Amendment) Regulations 1983

Made - - - -	*17th August* 1983
Laid before Parliament	*30th August* 1983
Coming into Operation	*1st October* 1983

The Secretary of State for the Environment, in exercise of the powers conferred upon him by sections 7 and 12 of the Superannuation Act 1972(a), and of all other powers enabling him in that behalf, after consultation with such associations of local authorities as appeared to him to be concerned, the local authorities with whom consultation appeared to him to be desirable and such representatives of other persons likely to be affected by the regulations as appeared to him to be appropriate, hereby makes the following regulations:—

Citation and commencement

1.—(1) These regulations may be cited as the Local Government Superannuation (Amendment) Regulations 1983.

(2) The Local Government Superannuation Regulations 1974 to 1983(b) and these regulations may be cited together as the Local Government Superannuation Regulations 1974 to 1983.

(3) These regulations shall come into operation on 1st October 1983 and, except as provided in paragraph (4), shall have effect from that date.

(4) Regulations 6 and 11 shall have effect as from 1st April 1980 and regulations 3 and 5 shall have effect as from 1st April 1983.

Interpretation

2. In these regulations "the principal regulations" means the Local Government Superannuation Regulations 1974(c).

Definition in principal regulations

3. Regulation A3(1) of the principal regulations is amended by inserting after the definition of "service" the following definition:

(a) 1972 c. 11.

(b) S.I. 1974/520, 1977/1121, 1845, 1978/266, 822, 1738, 1739, 1979/2, 592, 1534, 1980/216, 233, 234, 1981/1250, 1509, 1982/908, 1514, 1983/178, 1268, 1270, 1271.

(c) S.I. 1974/520; relevant amending instruments are S.I. 1978/1738, 1739, 1979/2, 1980/234, 1981/1509.

" "standard rate" means 1% above the rate which is for the time being the base rate published by members of the Committee of London Clearing Bankers or, where there is for the time being more than one such base rate, the lowest of them;".

Payments by employees to avoid reduction under regulation E3(5) or (6) of retiring allowance and under regulation E11(2)(aa) or (3) of death gratuity

4. Regulation C2A of the principal regulations is amended—

(*a*) by substituting for paragraph (10)(*aa*) the following:

"(*aa*) he ceases to hold his employment and—

(i) one of the conditions prescribed in regulation E2(3)(*a*) and (*b*) applies in his case,

(ii) the last day of his employment is not less than 12 months later than the date of receipt of the notice given under paragraph (3) or, as the case may be, paragraph (4),

(iii) payment by him in accordance with paragraph (3) or, as the case may be, paragraph (4) has not been discontinued by virtue of paragraph (9), and

(iv) he gives notice in writing for the purpose to the appropriate administering authority within the period of 3 months beginning on the day after the last day of his employment,

he may pay to the appropriate superannuation fund within the period specified in paragraph (11) an amount calculated by the fund's actuary to represent the capital value of the payments remaining to be made, and shall in that event be treated as having completed payment in accordance with paragraph (3) or, as the case may be, paragraph (4); or"; and

(*b*) by inserting after paragraph (10) the following:

"(10A) An administering authority may accept a notice given under paragraph (10)(*aa*)(iv) notwithstanding that paragraph (10)(*aa*)(ii) is not satisfied.".

Employer's contributions

5. The principal regulations are amended by substituting for regulation C5 the following:

"**C5.**—(1) An employing authority shall contribute to the appropriate superannuation fund in each year of any period of 5 years for which a certificate is required to be obtained under regulation B8 a sum of an amount equal to the rate per cent specified in the certificate in relation to that year, increased or, as the case may be, reduced by any such amount as is, in respect of the employing authority, specified under regulation B8(1)(ii) as the amount by which the employer's contribution should in that year be increased or, as the case may be, reduced.

(2) An employing authority shall, during each year of every such period as is mentioned in paragraph (1), pay to the appropriate super-

annuation fund at the end of each of the intervals determined under regulation L5, on account of the sum required by paragraph (1) to be paid in that year, a sum equal to the remuneration on which contributions have during the interval been paid to the fund under regulation C1 or C2 by their employees multiplied by the rate per cent specified under regulation B8(1)(i) for that year, increased or, as the case may be, reduced by—

(a) any rate per cent, or

(b) a part, proportionate to the length of the interval, of any amount expressed in money terms,

that has been specified for the year in respect of the authority under regulation B8(1)(ii).

(3) If all or part of any sum due under paragraph (2) remains unpaid at the end of the period of one month after the date on which it becomes due, or one month after 1st October 1983 if later, the administering authority may require the employing authority to pay interest, calculated at the standard rate on a day to day basis from the due date of payment to the date of payment, and compounded with 3-monthly rests, on the amount remaining unpaid.

(4) Interest paid under paragraph (3) shall be carried to the appropriate superannuation fund.".

Employer's additional contributions

6. Regulation C6 of the principal regulations is amended—

(a) by inserting before the words "Where a consent is given" the figure "(1)", and

(b) by adding at the end the following:

"(2) Where on the employee's ceasing to hold his employment the employing authority agree to pay a sum under paragraph 4A(5) of Schedule 5 and the employee pays the required amount for the purposes of that paragraph, the employing authority shall pay the agreed sum to the appropriate superannuation fund before the end of the period of 1 month beginning on the date of the employee's payment.

(3) If all or part of the agreed sum remains unpaid at the end of that period, the administering authority may require the employing authority to pay interest, calculated at the standard rate on a day to day basis from the day after the end of the period to the date of payment, and compounded with 3-monthly rests, on the amount remaining unpaid.

(4) Interest paid under paragraph (3) shall be carried to the appropriate superannuation fund.".

Amount of retirement pension and retiring allowance

7. Regulation E3(6AA) of the principal regulations is amended by substituting for the words "when she gave the notification under regulation E12(b) had no husband" the words "has not given any notification under regulation E12(a)".

Power to compound certain small pensions

8. Regulation E11A of the principal regulations is amended—

(*a*) by substituting for the figure "£39", in paragraph (1), the figure "£78"; and

(*b*) by substituting for the figure "£52", in paragraphs (4) and (6), the figure "£104".

Pensions of widowers, etc.

9. Regulation E12 of the principal regulations is amended—

(*a*) by substituting for paragraphs (*a*) and (*b*) the following:

"(*a*) has a husband who is permanently incapacitated by reason of ill-health or infirmity of mind or body and who is wholly or mainly dependent on her, and notifies the appropriate administering authority in writing that she wishes to have the provisions of this regulation applied to her, or

(*b*) has no husband but has an eligible child or eligible children,";

(*b*) by substituting for the words "after giving a notification under paragraph (*b*)", in the proviso, the words "after this regulation has become applicable to her"; and

(*c*) by inserting at the end of the proviso the words "and she gives a notification, or as the case may be a further notification, under paragraph (*a*)".

Payments by employing authorities to administering authorities

10. Regulation L5 of the principal regulations is amended—

(*a*) by inserting after paragraph (1)(*a*) the following:

"(*aa*) any amount received by the employing authority under regulation C1A, by deduction from remuneration or otherwise, during the interval; and

(*aaa*) any extra charge or additional benefit repayable under regulation C7 the amount of which has been notified by the administering authority to the employing authority during the interval; and ";

(*b*) by substituting for paragraph (2) the following:

"(2) Payments made in pursuance of, and interest paid under paragraph (5) on sums due under, paragraph (1)(*a*) to (*aaa*) shall be carried to the appropriate superannuation fund."; and

(*c*) by substituting for paragraph (5) the following:

"(5) If all or part of any sum due under the provisions of this regulation remains unpaid at the end of the period of one month after the date on which it becomes due, the administering authority may require the employing authority to pay interest, calculated at the standard rate on a day to day basis from the due date of payment to the date of payment, and compounded with 3-monthly rests, on the amount remaining unpaid.".

PENSIONS

Provisions applicable as respects additional contributions while any amount remains outstanding

11. Schedule 5 to the principal regulations is amended—

(a) by substituting for the words "paragraph 5", in paragraph 3, the words "paragraphs 4A and 5"; and

(b) by inserting after paragraph 4 the following:

"4A.—(1) If—

(a) one of the conditions prescribed in regulation E2(3)(a) and (b) applies in the case of an employee falling within paragraph 3(a),

(b) the last day of his employment is not less than 12 months later than the date of notification of the consent given under regulation D10(2) or, as the case may be, the date of the notice given under regulation D13(1), and

(c) he gives notice in writing for the purpose to the appropriate administering authority within the period of 3 months beginning on 1st October 1983 or the day after the last day of his employment if later,

he shall if he pays the required amount to the appropriate superannuation fund within the period specified in sub-paragraph (3) be treated as having completed payment in accordance with regulation D10(4) or, as the case may be, regulation D13(2).

(2) An administering authority may accept a notice given under sub-paragraph (1)(c) notwithstanding that sub-paragraph (1)(b) is not satisfied.

(3) The period mentioned in sub-paragraph (1) is the period of 1 month beginning on the date on which the person is notified by the appropriate administering authority of the required amount.

(4) For the purposes of this paragraph the required amount is, subject to sub-paragraph (5), an amount calculated by the fund's actuary to represent—

(a) where the employee has commenced payment in accordance with regulation D10(4), the capital value of—

(i) the additional contributions remaining to be paid by him under regulation D10, and

(ii) the additional contributions remaining to be paid by the employing authority under regulation C6, or

(b) where the employee has commenced payment in accordance with regulation D13(2), the capital value of the additional contributions remaining to be paid by him under regulation D13.

(5) Where sub-paragraph (4)(a) applies, the employing authority may notify the administering authority (if different) and the employee that they agree to pay to the appropriate superannuation fund a sum not exceeding half of the amount calculated in accordance with sub-

paragraph (4), and in that event the required amount is the balance of the amount so calculated.".

Amount to be paid for additional period

12. Schedule 8 to the principal regulations is amended—

(*a*) by substituting for paragraph 2 the following:

"2. The formula mentioned in paragraph 1 is—

$$\frac{T \times R \times F}{100}$$

where—

T is the length (expressed in terms of complete years and a fraction of a year) of the additional period the employee desires to reckon as reckonable service,

R is the remuneration of the employee at the time he made the election under regulation D12, and

F is the figure specified, opposite to the age of the employee on his birthday next following the date on which he made the election under regulation D12, in the relevant column of Table I or II below appropriate to his pensionable age as defined in paragraph 6.

TABLE I

MALES

Age on birthday next following election	Employee to whom on retirement regulation E3(2) would apply	Others						
	65	60	Over 60 and under 61	61 and under 62	62 and under 63	63 and under 64	64 and under 65	65
26		22·20						
27		21·40						
28		20·80						
29		20·30						
30		19·90						
31		19·60						
32		19·30						
33		19·10						
34		18·90						
35		18·80						
36		18·70	18·50					
37		18·60	18·40	18·00				
38		18·60	18·40	17·90	17·50			
39		18·60	18·40	17·90	17·50	17·10		
40		18·60	18·40	17·90	17·50	17·10	16·70	
41		18·70	18·40	18·00	17·60	17·20	16·70	16·50
42		18·80	18·50	18·00	17·60	17·20	16·80	16·60
43		18·90	18·60	18·10	17·70	17·20	16·80	16·60
44		19·00	18·70	18·20	17·80	17·30	16·90	16·70
45		19·10	18·80	18·30	17·90	17·40	16·90	16·70
46	17·30	19·20	18·90	18·40	18·00	17·50	17·00	16·80
47	17·40	19·30	19·00	18·50	18·10	17·60	17·10	16·90
48	17·50	19·40	19·10	18·60	18·20	17·70	17·20	17·00
49	17·60	19·50	19·20	18·70	18·30	17·80	17·30	17·10
50	17·70	19·70	19·40	18·80	18·40	17·90	17·40	17·20
51	17·80	19·90	19·60	19·00	18·50	18·00	17·50	17·30
52	17·90	20·10	19·80	19·20	18·70	18·10	17·60	17·40
53	18·00	20·30	20·00	19·40	18·90	18·30	17·70	17·50
54	18·10	20·50	20·20	19·60	19·10	18·50	17·80	17·60
55	18·30	20·70	20·40	19·80	19·30	18·70	18·00	17·80
56	18·50	20·90	20·60	20·00	19·50	18·90	18·20	18·00
57	18·70	21·20	20·90	20·20	19·70	19·10	18·40	18·20
58	18·90	21·50	21·20	20·50	19·90	19·30	18·60	18·40
59	19·10	21·80	21·50	20·80	20·10	19·50	18·80	18·60
60	19·40			21·10	20·40	19·70	19·10	18·80
61	19·70				20·70	19·90	19·30	19·00
62	20·00					20·10	19·50	19·30
63	20·30						19·70	19·60
64	20·70							19·90

TABLE II

FEMALES

Age on birthday next following election	Employee to whom on retirement regulation E3(2) would apply	Others						
	65	60	Over 60 and under 61	61 and under 62	62 and under 63	63 and under 64	64 and under 65	65
26		20·40						
27		19·80						
28		19·40						
29		19·00						
30		18·70						
31		18·60						
32		18·60						
33		18·70						
34		18·70						
35		18·80						
36		18·90	18·60					
37		19·00	18·70	18·20				
38		19·10	18·80	18·30	17·80			
39		19·30	19·00	18·40	17·90	17·30		
40		19·40	19·10	18·60	18·00	17·40	16·90	
41		19·60	19·30	18·70	18·10	17·50	17·00	16·70
42		19·70	19·40	18·80	18·20	17·60	17·10	16·80
43		19·80	19·50	18·90	18·30	17·80	17·20	16·90
44		19·90	19·60	19·00	18·40	17·90	17·30	17·00
45		20·10	19·70	19·10	18·50	18·00	17·40	17·10
46	18·80	20·20	19·90	19·20	18·60	18·10	17·50	17·20
47	18·90	20·40	20·00	19·40	18·80	18·20	17·60	17·30
48	19·00	20·50	20·20	19·50	18·90	18·30	17·70	17·40
49	19·10	20·60	20·30	19·60	19·00	18·40	17·80	17·50
50	19·20	20·80	20·40	19·80	19·20	18·60	17·90	17·60
51	19·30	21·00	20·60	19·90	19·30	18·70	18·00	17·70
52	19·40	21·10	20·80	20·10	19·40	18·80	18·20	17·90
53	19·50	21·30	21·00	20·30	19·60	19·00	18·30	18·00
54	19·60	21·50	21·20	20·40	19·80	19·10	18·40	18·10
55	19·80	21·70	21·40	20·60	19·90	19·20	18·60	18·20
56	20·00	21·90	21·60	20·80	20·10	19·40	18·70	18·30
57	20·20	22·10	21·80	21·00	20·30	19·60	18·80	18·50
58	20·40	22·30	22·00	21·20	20·50	19·80	19·00	18·70
59	20·60	22·60	22·20	21·40	20·70	20·00	19·20	18·90
60	20·80			21·70	20·90	20·20	19·40	19·10
61	21·10				21·20	20·40	19·60	19·30
62	21·40					20·50	19·80	19·50
63	21·70						20·00	19·80
64	22·00							20·10

"";

(b) by substituting for the words "paragraph 4(1)"; in paragraph 3, the words "paragraph 4";

(c) by substituting for paragraph 4 the following:

"4. The formula mentioned in paragraph 3 is—

$$\frac{T \times R \times F}{100}$$

where—

T is the length (expressed in terms of complete years and a fraction of a year) of the additional period the employee desires to reckon as reckonable service,

R is the remuneration for the time being of the employee, and

F is the figure specified, opposite to the age of the employee on his birthday next following the date on which he made the election under regulation D13, in the relevant column of Table I or II below appropriate to his pensionable age as defined in paragraph 6.

TABLE I

MALES

Age on birthday next following election	Employee to whom on retirement regulation E3(2) would apply	Figure to be used by reference to the under-mentioned pensionable age — Others						
	65	60	Over 60 and under 61	61 and under 62	62 and under 63	63 and under 64	64 and under 65	65
26		0·58						
27		0·60						
28		0·62						
29		0·64						
30		0·66						
31		0·68						
32		0·71						
33		0·74						
34		0·77						
35		0·80						
36		0·84	0·83					
37		0·88	0·87	0·82				
38		0·93	0·91	0·86	0·81			
39		0·98	0·96	0·90	0·85	0·80		
40		1·03	1·01	0·95	0·90	0·84	0·80	
41		1·09	1·07	1·00	0·95	0·89	0·84	0·81
42		1·16	1·14	1·06	1·00	0·94	0·88	0·85
43		1·23	1·22	1·13	1·06	0·99	0·93	0·89
44		1·31	1·30	1·20	1·12	1·05	0·98	0·93
45		1·40	1·39	1·28	1·19	1·11	1·04	0·98
46	1·08	1·51	1·49	1·37	1·27	1·18	1·10	1·04
47	1·15	1·64	1·61	1·48	1·36	1·26	1·17	1·11
48	1·23	1·79	1·75	1·61	1·47	1·35	1·25	1·18
49	1·31	1·97	1·92	1·76	1·60	1·45	1·34	1·26
50	1·40	2·18	2·13	1·93	1·75	1·57	1·44	1·35
51	1·50	2·42	2·38	2·12	1·92	1·71	1·56	1·45
52	1·62	2·74	2·69	2·36	2·11	1·88	1·70	1·57
53	1·76	3·15	3·09	2·66	2·33	2·08	1·86	1·71
54	1·92	3·68	3·62	3·05	2·63	2·31	2·05	1·87
55	2·12	4·44	4·36	3·57	3·02	2·60	2·28	2·06
56	2·36	5·53	5·45	4·30	3·53	2·98	2·56	2·29
57	2·66	7·40	7·28	5·36	4·23	3·49	2·94	2·58
58	3·04	11·08	10·90	7·17	5·30	4·18	3·43	2·95
59	3·56	22·25	21·88	10·70	7·06	5·21	4·12	3·45
60	4·26			21·50	10·55	6·95	5·12	4·12
61	5·32				21·11	10·37	6·83	5·14
62	7·09					20·41	10·18	6·84
63	10·64						20·14	10·25
64	21·10							20·32

TABLE II

FEMALES

Age on birthday next following election	Employee to whom on retirement regulation E3(2) would apply	Others						
	65	60	Over 60 and under 61	61 and under 62	62 and under 63	63 and under 64	64 and under 65	65
26		0.59						
27		0.61						
28		0.63						
29		0.65						
30		0.68						
31		0.71						
32		0.74						
33		0.77						
34		0.80						
35		0.83						
36		0.87	0.86					
37		0.91	0.90	0.85				
38		0.96	0.94	0.89	0.83			
39		1.01	0.99	0.93	0.87	0.82		
40		1.07	1.05	0.98	0.91	0.86	0.80	
41		1.13	1.11	1.03	0.96	0.90	0.84	0.80
42		1.20	1.18	1.09	1.01	0.95	0.88	0.84
43		1.28	1.26	1.16	1.07	1.00	0.93	0.88
44		1.37	1.34	1.23	1.14	1.06	0.98	0.93
45		1.46	1.43	1.31	1.21	1.12	1.04	0.98
46	1.14	1.57	1.54	1.40	1.29	1.19	1.11	1.04
47	1.21	1.70	1.67	1.51	1.38	1.27	1.18	1.11
48	1.29	1.85	1.82	1.64	1.49	1.36	1.26	1.18
49	1.38	2.03	1.99	1.79	1.62	1.46	1.35	1.26
50	1.48	2.24	2.20	1.96	1.77	1.58	1.45	1.35
51	1.59	2.50	2.46	2.17	1.94	1.72	1.57	1.45
52	1.72	2.83	2.78	2.42	2.14	1.89	1.71	1.57
53	1.87	3.24	3.19	2.73	2.38	2.09	1.87	1.71
54	2.05	3.80	3.73	3.13	2.69	2.33	2.06	1.87
55	2.26	4.58	4.50	3.67	3.08	2.63	2.30	2.06
56	2.52	5.73	5.64	4.40	3.60	3.02	2.59	2.30
57	2.84	7.66	7.53	5.51	4.33	3.54	2.96	2.59
58	3.24	11.47	11.26	7.36	5.40	4.24	3.47	2.96
59	3.79	22.86	22.45	11.05	7.20	5.30	4.15	3.46
60	4.53			22.15	10.79	7.05	5.17	4.14
61	5.65				21.64	10.59	6.89	5.17
62	7.52					20.72	10.24	6.87
63	11.28						20.34	10.29
64	22.44							20.46

".

and

(d) by inserting after paragraph 5 the following:

"6. In paragraphs 2 and 4 "pensionable age" means the earliest age at which, if the employee were to remain a pensionable employee without any break of service, he would become entitled by virtue of regulation E2(1)(a) or (b)(ii), if he then ceased to be employed, to a retirement pension.".

Reduction of benefits under regulation E3(9)

13. Schedule 10 to the principal regulations is amended by substituting for the table the following table:

"TABLE

1. Number of years	Percentage reduction to be made under regulation E3(9)		
	Retirement pension		Retiring allowance
	2. Male	3. Female	4. Both sexes
0	0	0	0
1	8	7	2
2	15	13	5
3	22	18	7
4	28	23	9
5	33	27	11 ".

Method and calculation of payment by employees to avoid reduction under regulation E3(5) or (6) of retiring allowance

14.—(1) Paragraph 2 of Part I of Schedule 20 to the principal regulations is amended—

(a) by substituting for the words from "F is the figure" to "that election" the following:

"F is, in the case of a man, the figure specified in column 2 of the table below opposite to his age on his birthday next following the date on which he made that election; and in the case of a woman, a figure to be specified by the Government Actuary"; and

(b) by substituting for the table the following table:

"TABLE

1. Age on birthday next following election	2. Figure to be used
25	2·76
26	2·61
27	2·51
28	2·44
29	2·39
30	2·35
31	2·31
32	2·28

1. Age on birthday next following election	2. Figure to be used
33	2·25
34	2·23
35	2·21
36	2·20
37	2·18
38	2·17
39	2·16
40	2·15
41	2·14
42	2·13
43	2·12
44	2·11
45	2·10
46	2·09
47	2·08
48	2·08
49	2·09
50	2·10
51	2·12
52	2·14
53	2·16
54	2·18
55	2·20
56	2·22
57	2·24
58	2·26
59	2·28
60	2·30
61	2·31
62	2·32
63	2·33
64	2·34 ”

(2) Paragraph 3 of Part III of Schedule 20 to the principal regulations is amended—

(a) by substituting for the words from "F is the figure" to "specified birthday" the following:

"F is, in the case of a man, the figure specified, opposite to his age on his birthday next following the date on which he made that election, in the relevant column of the table below appropriate to his specified birthday; and in the case of a woman, a figure to be specified by the Government Actuary"; and (*b*) by substituting for Table I and Table II the following table:

"Table

Age on birthday next following election	Figure to be used by reference to the under-mentioned specified birthday					
	60	61	62	63	64	65
25	·07					
26	·07					
27	·07					
28	·07					
29	·08					
30	·08					
31	·08					
32	·08					
33	·09					
34	·09					
35	·09					
36	·10					
37	·10	·10				
38	·11	·10	·10			
39	·12	·11	·10	·09		
40	·12	·11	·11	·10	·09	
41	·13	·12	·11	·10	·10	·09
42	·14	·13	·12	·11	·10	·10
43	·14	·13	·12	·12	·11	·10
44	·15	·14	·13	·12	·11	·11
45	·16	·15	·14	·13	·12	·11
46	·17	·16	·15	·14	·13	·12
47	·19	·17	·16	·15	·14	·13
48	·21	·19	·17	·16	·15	·14
49	·23	·21	·18	·17	·16	·15
50	·25	·23	·20	·18	·17	·16
51	·28	·25	·22	·20	·18	·17
52	·32	·28	·25	·22	·20	·18
53	·37	·32	·28	·24	·22	·20
54	·43	·36	·31	·27	·24	·22
55	·52	·42	·36	·31	·27	·24
56	·65	·51	·42	·35	·30	·27
57	·87	·63	·50	·41	·34	·30
58	1·30	·84	·62	·49	·40	·35
59	2·62	1·26	·83	·61	·48	·41
60		2·53	1·24	·82	·60	·48
61			2·48	1·22	·80	·60
62				2·40	1·20	·80
63					2·37	1·21
64						2·39 "·

Transitional

15.—(1) If all or part of an employer's contribution payable under regulation C5 of the principal regulations for the year ending with 31st March 1983 remains unpaid at the end of the period of one month beginning on 1st October 1983 the administering authority may require the employing authority to pay interest on the amount remaining unpaid as if the contribution were a sum due under regulation C5(2) of the principal regulations.

(2) Where immediately before 1st October 1983 interest was payable under regulation L5(5) of the principal regulations on a sum remaining unpaid on that date, the administering authority may require interest to be paid from that date as if the sum had remained unpaid at the end of one month after that date.

Right to opt out

16. No provision of these regulations shall apply to any person to whom at any time before 1st October 1983 any benefit (including a return of contributions and any pension payable to a widow or any dependant by virtue of a surrender) was or is being paid or became or may become payable if—

   (*a*) he is placed by that provision in a worse position than he would have been if it had not applied in relation to that benefit; and

   (*b*) that provision relates to a benefit paid or payable in respect of a person who—

      (i) ceased before 1st October 1983 to hold an employment in respect of which he was a pensionable employee, or

      (ii) died before that date while still in such an employment; and

   (*c*) the first-mentioned person, by notice in writing given to the appropriate administering authority within 3 months after 1st October 1983, elects that the provision shall not apply to him.

Right of appeal

17. The provisions of Part H of the principal regulations (determination of questions and appeals) shall apply in relation to rights and liabilities under these regulations as they apply in relation to rights and liabilities under the principal regulations.

Signed by authority of the Secretary of State

Bellwin,
Minister of State, Department of the Environment
(Minister for Local Government).

17th August, 1983.

EXPLANATORY NOTE

(This Note is not part of the Regulations.)

These regulations further amend the Local Government Superannuation Regulations 1974 ("the principal regulations") as follows:

(*a*) Regulations 4 and 11 allow an employee who is made redundant after electing to pay additional contributions for certain purposes to be treated as having completed payment if he pays the capitalised value of the outstanding contributions, and of any related contributions payable by the employing authority. The latter element, or part of it, may be met by that authority, and regulation 6 obliges them to give effect to any undertaking to do so.

(*b*) Regulations 5 and 10 require that payments are to be made, at the same determined intervals, on account of the employing authority's annual contribution and in respect of certain other amounts due from them to the administering authority. In each case provision is made (in transitional cases, by regulation 15) for the payment of interest, at the rate specified in regulation 3, on late payments.

(*c*) Regulations 7 and 9 enable the dependent children of a female employee who has no husband to become prospectively entitled to benefits under the principal regulations without the election on her part that was formerly required.

(*d*) Regulation 8 increases the maximum pensions that may be compounded.

(*e*) Regulations 12, 13 and 14 substitute new tables of factors to be used in calculating, respectively, payments to be made for securing additional reckonable service, the reduction of benefits if paid early, and amounts paid to avoid reduction of a retiring allowance in respect of certain early service.

Section 12 of the Superannuation Act 1972 confers express power to make regulations retrospective in effect. These regulations are to a certain extent retrospective. Where rights in relation to ex-employees could be adversely affected, provision is made for opting out and for the determination of related questions (regulations 16 and 17).

STATUTORY INSTRUMENTS

1983 No. 1270

PENSIONS

The Local Government Superannuation (Amendment) (No. 2) Regulations 1983

Made - - - -	*17th August* 1983
Laid before Parliament	*30th August* 1983
Coming into Operation	*1st October* 1983

The Secretary of State for the Environment, in exercise of the powers conferred upon him by section 7 of the Superannuation Act 1972 (a), and of all other powers enabling him in that behalf, after consultation with such associations of local authorities as appeared to him to be concerned, the local authorities with whom consultation appeared to him to be desirable and such representatives of other persons likely to be affected by the regulations as appeared to him to be appropriate, hereby makes the following regulations:—

Citation, commencement and interpretation

1.—(1) These regulations may be cited as the Local Government Superannuation (Amendment) (No. 2) Regulations 1983 and shall come into operation on 1st October 1983.

(2) The Local Government Superannuation Regulations 1974 to 1983 (b) and these regulations may be cited together as the Local Government Superannuation Regulations 1974 to 1983.

(3) In these regulations "the principal regulations" means the Local Government Superannuation Regulations 1974 (c).

Use and investment of superannuation fund's moneys

2. The principal regulations are amended by substituting for regulation B6 the following:

"**B6.**—(1) Subject to paragraphs (3) to (7), an administering authority—

   (a) shall invest any moneys forming part of the superannuation fund maintained by them ("fund moneys") that are not for the time being required to meet payments to be made out of the fund under these regulations, and

   (b) may vary the manner in which any fund moneys are for the time being invested.

(2) For the purposes of this regulation and of regulation B5(c), investment includes use by the administering authority for any purpose for which they have a statutory borrowing power.

(a) 1972 c.11.
(b) S.I. 1974/520, 1977/1121, 1845, 1978/266, 822, 1738, 1739, 1979/2, 592, 1534, 1980/216, 233, 234, 1981/1250, 1509, 1982/908, 1514, 1983/178, 1268, 1269, 1271.
(c) S.I. 1974/520, to which there are amendments not relevant to these regulations.

(3) On the total from day to day of any fund moneys used by them and for the time being not repaid an administering authority shall pay interest to the fund at a rate no lower than the lowest rate at which that amount could have been borrowed by them at arm's length, otherwise than by way of overdraft from a bank, at 7 days' notice.

(4) An administering authority shall not—

(a) make any investment in securities of companies other than listed securities so as to cause the total value of such investments (except investments made in accordance with a scheme under section 11 of the Trustee Investments Act 1961 (a)) to exceed 10% of the value at the time of all investments of fund moneys, or

(b) make any investment, other than—

(i) an investment made in accordance with a scheme under section 11 of the Trustee Investments Act 1961, or

(ii) an investment falling within paragraph 1 of Part I or paragraph 1 or 2 of Part II of the First Schedule to that Act, or

(iii) a deposit with a bank, institution or person falling within section 2 of the Banking Act 1979 (b),

so as to result in more than 5% of the value at the time of all investments of fund moneys being represented by a single holding, or

(c) make any deposit falling within sub-paragraph *(b)*(iii) so as to bring the aggregate of fund moneys deposited with any one bank, institution or person other than the National Savings Bank to an amount which exceeds 10% of the value at the time of all investments of fund moneys, or

(d) lend to any person other than Her Majesty's Government in the United Kingdom or the Government of the Isle of Man, or use as mentioned in paragraph (2), or deposit with a person specified in paragraph 13 or 14 of Schedule 1 to the Banking Act 1979, any further fund moneys so as to bring the aggregate of all fund moneys so lent, used or deposited to an amount which exceeds 10% of the value at the time of all investments of fund moneys.

(5) For the purposes of paragraph (4)*(d)* moneys are not lent if they are—

(a) invested in registered securities to which section 1 of the Stock Transfer Act 1963(c) applies or in listed securities, or

(b) deposited with a bank or institution falling within section (2)(1)*(a)* to *(c)* of the Banking Act 1979, or a person specified in paragraphs 1 to 12 of Schedule 1 to that Act.

(6) In the discharge of their functions under this regulation an administering authority shall have regard—

(a) to the need for diversification of investments of fund moneys,

(b) to the suitability of investments of any description of investment proposed and of any investment proposed as an investment of that description, and

(c) to proper advice, obtained at reasonable intervals.

(a) 1961 c.62.
(b) 1979 c.37.
(c) 1963 c.18; section 1 was amended by virtue of the Interpretation Act 1889 (c.63), section 38(1), and by the Finance Act 1964 (c.49), section 26(7) and Schedule 9, and the Post Office Act 1969 (c.48), section 108(1)*(f)*.

(7) Paragraph (6)*(c)* does not apply where functions under this regulation are lawfully discharged, under arrangements made under section 101 of the Local Government Act or otherwise, by an officer who is competent to give proper advice.

(8) Where any fund moneys are used as mentioned in paragraph (2), sub-paragraphs (2) and (4) of paragraph 19 of Schedule 13 to the Local Government Act (repayment of money used, and deemed exercise of the statutory power to borrow) shall apply as they apply in the case of money so used under that paragraph; but except as aforesaid that paragraph shall not apply to a superannuation fund maintained under these regulations.

(9) An administering authority may pay out of fund moneys any costs, charges and expenses incurred by them in the discharge of their functions under this regulation.

(10) For the purposes of this regulation—

"companies" includes companies established under the law of any territory outside the United Kingdom;

"listed securities" means securities in respect of which a listing has been granted and not withdrawn—

(a) on a stock exchange in the United Kingdom which is a recognised stock exchange within the meaning of the Prevention of Fraud (Investments) Act 1958 **(a)** , or

(b) on a stock exchange outside the United Kingdom of international repute;

"proper advice" means the advice of a person, including an officer of theirs, who is reasonably believed by the administering authority to be qualified by his ability in and practical experience of financial matters;

"securities" includes shares, stock and debentures;

"single holding" means investments—

(a) in securities of, or in units or other shares of the investments subject to the trusts of unit trust schemes managed by, or in loans to or deposits with, any one body, or

(b) in the acquisition, development or management of, or in any advance of money upon the security of, any one piece of land, or

(c) in the acquisition of any one chattel;

and the value at any time of all investments of fund moneys is to be taken to include the amount of any fund moneys used as mentioned in paragraph (2) and for the time being not repaid.".

_____

(a) 1958 c.45.

Modifications to the Trustee Investments Act 1961 in its application to investment of superannuation fund's moneys

3. The principal regulations are amended by deleting Schedule 2.

Signed by authority of the Secretary of State.

Bellwin,
Minister of State, Department of the Environment
(Minister for Local Government).
17th August 1983.

EXPLANATORY NOTE

(This Note is not part of the Regulations.)

These regulations further amend the Local Government Superannuation Regulations 1974 ("the principal regulations") by revising the rules governing the investment of local government superannuation funds.

Regulation B6 of the principal regulations is deleted, as is Schedule 2 (application of Trustee Investments Act 1961). A new regulation B6 is substituted which requires administering authorities to invest any moneys forming part of their superannuation funds that are not for the time being required to meet payments to be made out of the fund under the principal regulations. The use of superannuation fund moneys by the administering authority for purposes for which they have a statutory borrowing power is treated as investment, and interest is to be paid to the fund on any moneys so used.

New regulation B6(4) places limits on certain types of investment:

(a) investment in unlisted securities is not to exceed 10% of the value of all investments;

(b) with certain exceptions, no more than 5% of the value of all investments is to be represented by a single holding;

(c) deposits with a single bank or other authorised deposit-taker are not to exceed 10% of the value of all investments; and

(d) the total of amounts lent, deposited with other local authorities and used by the administering authority is not to exceed 10% of the value of all investments.

New regulation B6(6) requires administering authorities to have regard to the need to diversify their investments, to the suitability of proposed investments, and to proper investment advice.

STATUTORY INSTRUMENTS

1983 No. 1271

PENSIONS

The Local Government Superannuation (National Water Council Dissolution) Regulations 1983

Made - - - -	*17th August* 1983
Laid before Parliament	*30th August* 1983
Coming into Operation	*30th September* 1983

The Secretary of State for the Environment, in exercise of the powers conferred upon him by section 7 of the Superannuation Act 1972(a), and of all other powers enabling him in that behalf, after consultation with such associations of local authorities as appeared to him to be concerned, the local authorities with whom consultation appeared to him to be desirable and such representatives of other persons likely to be affected by the regulations as appeared to him to be appropriate, hereby makes the following regulations:—

Citation, commencement and interpretation

1.—(1) These regulations may be cited as the Local Government Superannuation (National Water Council Dissolution) Regulations 1983, and shall come into operation on 30th September 1983.

(2) The Local Government Superannuation Regulations 1974 to 1983 (b) and these regulations may be cited together as the Local Government Superannuation Regulations 1974 to 1983.

(3) In these regulations "the principal regulations" means the Local Government Superannuation Regulations 1974 (c) and, unless the context otherwise requires, expressions used in these regulations have the same meaning as they have in the principal regulations.

Transfer of superannuation fund maintained by the National Water Council

2.—(1) The superannuation fund maintained under the principal regulations by the National Water Council ("the old fund") is transferred to and vests in the Severn-Trent Water Authority, and shall be carried by them to the fund which they are required to maintain under the principal regulations ("the new fund").

(2) All liabilities attaching to the National Water Council in respect of the old fund shall attach to the Severn-Trent Water Authority in respect of the new fund.

(3) Any liability of any body or person to make payments into the old fund shall become a liability to make payments into the new fund.

(a) 1972 c.11.
(b) S.I. 1974/520, 1977/1121, 1845, 1978/266, 822, 1738, 1739, 1979/2, 592, 1534, 1980/216, 233, 234, 1981/1250, 1509, 1982/908, 1514, 1983/178, 1268, 1269, 1270.
(c) S.I. 1974/520, to which there are amendments not relevant to these Regulations.

(4) All contracts, deeds, bonds, agreements and other instruments subsisting in favour of, or against, and all notices in force which were given by or to the National Water Council or any other body on their behalf for the purposes of the old fund shall be of full force and effect in favour of, or against, the Severn-Trent Water Authority.

(5) Without prejudice to the generality of paragraph (4), any admission agreement in force immediately before 30th September 1983 whereby employees of any body specified in regulation B4(4) of the principal regulations (or deemed to be such a body) are, or can be, admitted to participate in the benefits of the old fund shall have effect as an agreement under regulation B4 of the principal regulations between the body and the Severn-Trent Water Authority.

(6) Any action or proceeding or cause of action or proceeding pending or existing immediately before 30th September 1983 by or against the National Water Council in respect of the old fund shall be of full force and effect in favour of, or against, the Severn-Trent Water Authority.

(7) Where the National Water Council would have become liable, or would have been empowered, on the happening of any event, to make a payment out of the old fund or take any other action as administering authority in respect of any person who has ceased to participate in the benefits of the old fund before 30th September 1983, then on the happening of that event such payment or action shall, or as the case may be may, be made out of the new fund or taken by the Severn-Trent Water Authority.

(8) Where a person has ceased to contribute to the old fund before 30th September 1983 and has not become a contributor to any other superannuation fund maintained under the principal regulations, the new fund shall after 29th September 1983 be deemed to be the fund to which he was last a contributor.

(9) All legal proceedings pending on 30th September 1983 may be amended in such manner as may be necessary or proper in consequence of these regulations.

Division of new superannuation fund

3.—(1) Not later than 31st December 1983 the Severn-Trent Water Authority ("the fund authority") shall establish a second superannuation fund ("the second fund") which they shall maintain in addition to the new fund mentioned in regulation 2 above ("the main fund").

(2) On the establishment of the second fund the fund authority shall cease to hold as part of the main fund assets to a value to be specified by an actuary, which shall then become part of the second fund.

(3) When they obtain from the actuary, in accordance with regulation B7 of the principal regulations, valuations of the main fund and the second fund as at 31st March 1984, the fund authority shall also obtain from him a statement specifying the value to which further assets should in his opinion cease to be held by them as part of the main fund and become part of the second fund.

(4) On a day to be selected by them, which shall be as soon as is reasonably practicable after they obtain the statement mentioned in paragraph (3), the fund authority shall cease to hold as part of the main fund assets to the value specified, which shall then become part of the second fund.

(5) After the establishment of the second fund, references in the principal regulations to the appropriate superannuation fund, to the superannuation fund maintained by the fund authority, and to participation in the benefits of a superannuation fund shall be construed—

(a) in relation to a water authority, and to a person employed by a water authority, as references to, or to participation in the benefits of, the main fund, and

(b) in relation to a body who are a party to an agreement made (or having effect as an agreement made) with the fund authority under regulation B4 of those regulations ("an admitted body"), and to a person employed by such a body, as references to, or to participation in the benefits of, the second fund.

(6) After the establishment of the second fund, references in the principal regulations to the superannuation fund maintained by an administering authority shall in relation to the fund authority be construed as references to both the main fund and the second fund.

(7) As soon as is reasonably practicable after the establishment of the second fund the fund authority shall obtain from the actuary consulted by them for the purposes of paragraph (2) a certificate specifying in respect of the second fund, for the years ending with 31st March 1984, 31st March 1985 and 31st March 1986, the matters referred to in regulation B8(1) of the principal regulations (rate of employer's contribution and any adjustments in respect of particular employers).

(8) For the years mentioned in paragraph (7) regulation C5 of the principal regulations (employer's contributions) shall in relation to an admitted body apply as if for references to a certificate under regulation B8 of those regulations there were substituted references to the certificate required by paragraph (7).

(9) On the establishment of the second fund all rights to payment out of the main fund in respect of service in employment under an admitted body shall become rights to payment out of the second fund.

Continuance of employer's functions

4.—(1) As from the day appointed under section 3(1) of the Water Act 1983(**a**) (determination of functions of National Water Council), every employer's function not already exercised shall become a function of the Severn-Trent Water Authority.

(2) In paragraph (1) "employer's function" means a function under the principal regulations or the former regulations which—

(a) had, or but for the determination of their functions would have, become exercisable in relation to a person by the Council, and

(b) had or would have become so exercisable by virtue only of his having been at some time before the determination of their functions an employee of theirs and in relation to that employment.

(3) The Severn-Trent Water Authority may pay out of the main fund referred to in regulation 3 any costs, charges and expenses incurred by them in the discharge of functions which have become theirs by virtue of this regulation.

(**a**) 1983 c.23.

Superannuation funds

5. Regulation B1 of the principal regulations is amended by substituting for paragraph *(d)* the following:

"*(d)* the Severn-Trent Water Authority".

Appropriate superannuation fund

6. Regulation B3 of the principal regulations is amended by substituting for the words "the National Water Council", in paragraph (3), the words "the Severn-Trent Water Authority".

Power to admit employees of other bodies

7. Regulation B4(4) of the principal regulations is amended—

(a) by inserting after the words "local authorities" wherever they occur in sub-paragraph *(b)* the words "or water authorities";

(b) by inserting at the end of sub-paragraph *(b)* the words "or the functions of water authorities"; and

(c) by inserting after sub-paragraph *(i)* the following:

"*(j)* the company (limited by shares) incorporated on 1st July 1983 under the Companies Acts 1948 to 1981(**a**) under the name of British Water International Limited.".

Certain persons who become subject to certain other superannuation schemes

8. Regulation G9 of the principal regulations is amended by deleting paragraph (4)*(a)*.

Certain persons who were transferred etc, to the employment of the National Water Council or the Thames Water Authority

9. Regulation G10 of the principal regulations is amended by deleting paragraph (2)*(b)* (i).

Bodies whose whole-time employees are to be compulsorily superannuable

10. Part I of Schedule 1 to the principal regulations is amended by deleting the words "the National Water Council".

Modifications to the Trustee Investments Act 1961 in its application to the investment of superannuation fund's moneys

11. Paragraph 3 of Schedule 2 to the principal regulations is amended by substituting for the words "the National Water Council" the words "the Severn-Trent Water Authority".

Transitional

12. Notwithstanding regulation 10 above, any person who—

(a) immediately before the day appointed under section 3(1) of the Water Act 1983 is a pensionable employee in the employment of the National Water Council, and

(b) continues in their employment after the determination of their functions,

---

(**a**) 1948 c.38; 1967 c.81, Parts I and III; 1972 c.67; 1972 c.68, section 9; 1976 c.47, sections 1 to 4; 1976 c.60, section 9; 1976 c.69; 1980 c.22; 1981 c.62 (except sections 28 and 29).

shall, while he remains in their employment, be deemed for the purposes of regulation B2 of the principal regulations (pensionable employees) to be an employee of a scheduled body, and for the purposes of regulation B3 of those regulations (appropriate superannuation fund) to be an employee of an employing authority who are a water authority.

Signed by authority of the Secretary of State.

Ian Gow,
Minister for Housing and Construction,
Department of the Environment.

17th August 1983.

EXPLANATORY NOTE

(This Note is not part of the Regulations.)

These regulations make provision, in connection with the determination of the functions of the National Water Council, for the continued administration of the superannuation fund hitherto administered by the Council under the Local Government Superannuation Regulations 1974 ("the principal regulations").

Regulation 2 transfers the fund and its liabilities to the Severn-Trent Water Authority, with necessary incidental and consequential provisions as to agreements and other matters.

Regulation 3 requires the transferred fund to be divided, the second fund established on the division becoming the fund for bodies whose employees are admitted to the superannuation scheme by agreement, and for those employees.

Regulation 4 provides for the continuance, as functions of the Severn-Trent Water Authority, of superannuation functions which were, or would have become, exercisable by the Council by virtue of employment relationships.

Regulations 5, 6 and 8 to 11 make consequential amendments to the principal regulations.

Regulation 7 amends the principal regulations so as to allow the admission to the superannuation scheme, by agreement, of employees of non-statutory bodies connected with the water industry.

The determination of the Council's functions does not affect the continuance of employment with the Council during the period before it ceases to exist. Regulation 12 makes transitional provision for preserving the pensionable status of persons who continue in employment with the Council during that period.

STATUTORY INSTRUMENTS

1983 No. 1273

OFFSHORE INSTALLATIONS

The Offshore Installations (Safety Zones) (No. 27) Order 1983

Made - - - -	*18th August* 1983
Coming into Operation	*22nd August* 1983

The Secretary of State, in exercise of the powers conferred on him by section 21(1), (2) and (3) of the Oil and Gas (Enterprise) Act 1982(**a**) (hereinafter referred to as "the Act"), and of all other powers enabling him in that behalf, hereby makes the following Order:—

1. This Order may be cited as the Offshore Installations (Safety Zones) (No. 27) Order 1983 and shall come into operation on 22nd August 1983.

2.—(1) A safety zone is hereby established around the installation specified in Column 1 of the Schedule hereto (being an installation maintained in waters in an area designated under section 1(7) of the Continental Shelf Act 1964(**b**)) having a radius of five hundred metres from the point as respects that installation which has the co-ordinates of latitude and longitude according to European Datum (1950) specified in Columns 2 and 3 of the Schedule.

(2) The prohibition under section 21(3) of the Act on a vessel entering or remaining in a safety zone without the consent of the Secretary of State shall not apply to a vessel entering or remaining in the safety zone established under paragraph (1) above:

    (*a*) in connection with the laying, inspection, testing, repair, alteration, renewal or removal of any submarine cable or pipe-line in or near that safety zone;

    (*b*) to provide services for, to transport persons or goods to or from, or under the authority of a government department to inspect, any installation in that safety zone;

    (*c*) if it is a vessel belonging to a general lighthouse authority performing duties relating to the safety of navigation;

    (*d*) in connection with the saving or attempted saving of life or property;

    (*e*) owing to stress of weather; or

    (*f*) when in distress.

(**a**) 1982 c. 23.   (**b**) 1964 c. 29.

Avon,
Parliamentary Under Secretary of State,
Department of Energy.

18th August 1983.

SCHEDULE   Article 2(1)

Safety Zone

1	2	3
Name or other designation of the offshore installation	Latitude North	Longitude East
Dundee Kingsnorth	58° 42′ 02·95′′	01° 24′ 34·62′′

EXPLANATORY NOTE

(*This Note is not part of the Order.*)

This Order establishes, under section 21 of the Oil and Gas (Enterprise) Act 1982, a safety zone, having a radius of 500 metres from a specified point, around the installation known as Dundee Kingsnorth maintained in waters in an area designated under section 1(7) of the Continental Shelf Act 1964.

Vessels (which includes hovercraft, submersible apparatus and installations in transit) are prohibited from entering or remaining in the safety zone except with the consent of the Secretary of State or in the circumstances mentioned in Article 2(2) of the Order.

STATUTORY INSTRUMENTS

1983 No. 1274

EDUCATION, ENGLAND AND WALES

The State Awards (State Bursaries for Adult Education) (Wales) (Amendment) Regulations 1983

Made - - - -	16*th August* 1983
Laid before Parliament	30*th August* 1983
Coming into Operation	20*th September* 1983

The Secretary of State for Wales, in exercise of the powers conferred upon him by sections 3*(c)* and 4(2) of the Education Act 1962(a), hereby makes the following Regulations:—

1. These Regulations may be cited as the State Awards (State Bursaries for Adult Education) (Wales) (Amendment) Regulations 1983 and shall come into operation on 20th September 1983.

2. In these Regulations a reference to the principal Regulations is a reference to the State Awards (State Bursaries for Adult Education) (Wales) Regulations 1979(**b**).

3. In Regulation 2(2) of the principal Regulations (Interpretation) after the word "regulation" in each place where it occurs there shall be added the words "or a Schedule".

4. In Regulation 3 of the principal Regulations (Revocations and transitional provisions) for the words "the Schedule" there shall be substituted the words "Schedule 1".

5. At the beginning of Regulation 5(1) of the principal Regulations (Authority to bestow state bursaries for adult education) there shall be inserted the words "Subject to the provisions of Schedule 2 hereto relating to eligibility for state awards and".

6. After the Schedule to the principal Regulations, which shall stand as Schedule 1, there shall be added the Schedule set out in the Appendix hereto.

(**a**) 1962 c.12; the relevant provisions, as amended, are set out in Schedule 5 to the Education Act 1980 (c.20).
(**b**) S.I. 1979/333.

APPENDIX

SCHEDULE 2   Regulation 5.

ELIGIBILITY FOR STATE AWARDS

1.—(1) In this Schedule—

"employment" means full-time employment or part-time employment which, in a normal week, involves a significant number of hours of work and "employed" shall be construed accordingly, and for the purposes hereof the references to employment include references to the holding of any office and to any occupation for gain;

"European Community" means the area comprised by the member states of the European Economic Community (including the United Kingdom) as constituted from time to time;

"national of a member state of the European Community" means a person who is a national for the purposes of the Community Treaties of any member state of the European Economic Community (including the United Kingdom) as constituted from time to time;

"refugee" means a person who is recognised by Her Majesty's government as a refugee within the meaning of the United Nations Convention relating to the Status of Refugees done at Geneva on 28th July 1951 as extended by the Protocol thereto which entered into force on 4th October 1967 or a person who enjoys asylum in the United Kingdom in pursuance of a decision of Her Majesty's government though not so recognised;

"relevant date", in relation to an applicant for a state award, means the date of his application therefore; and

"United Kingdom and Islands" means the United Kingdom, the Channel Islands and the Isle of Man.

(2) A person shall be treated for the purposes of Regulation 5(2)*(b)* or of paragraph 2(1) or 3*(a)* of this Schedule as ordinarily resident in Wales, in the United Kingdom and Islands or in the European Community ("the relevant area") if the Secretary of State is satisfied that he was only not so resident for the purposes of the said Regulation or not so resident in the relevant area at the date, or throughout the period, mentioned in the paragraphs in question because:—

(a) he, his spouse or his parent was temporarily employed outside the relevant area, or

(b) he or his spouse was temporarily receiving full-time education, or undertaking post-graduate research, outside the relevant area.

2.—(1) The Secretary of State shall not bestow a state award upon a person unless he is ordinarily resident in Wales on the relevant date and he is not then resident therein wholly or mainly for the purpose of receiving full-time education.
Provided that a state award may be bestowed upon a person if:—

(a) he is ordinarily resident in the United Kingdom and Islands on the relevant date and satisfies the Secretary of State that, on 30th June next following the relevant date he will be ordinarily resident in Wales and will not then be resident therein wholly or mainly for the purpose of receiving full-time education; or

(b) he is the child of a national of a member state of the European Community who—

(i) where he is employed on the relevant date, is then in employment in England and Wales; or

(ii) where he is not employed on that date (by reason of retirement or otherwise), was last employed in such employment; or

(iii) whether or not he is employed on that date, he has, during the period of 3 years ending therewith, been in such employment for an aggregate period of not less than a year; or

(c) he is a national of a member state of the European Community who:—

(i) entered the United Kingdom wholly or mainly for the purpose of taking up, or seeking, employment,

(ii) during the year preceding the relevant date has been in employment in England and Wales for an aggregate period of not less than 9 months, and

(iii) seeks an award in respect of a course provided by a vocational training establishment, being a course leading to a qualification which is needed for, or is designed to fit a person for, engagement in a specific profession or trade.

(2) In sub-paragraph (1)*(c)*:—

"qualification" includes authorisation, recognition, registration, enrolment, approval and certification; and

"vocational training establishment" means a further education establishment being a vocational school within the meaning of Article 7 of EEC Regulation 1612/68.

3. Subject to paragraphs 4 and 5, the Secretary of State shall not bestow a state award upon a person who is ordinarily resident in Wales on the relevant date:—

(a) unless he has been ordinarily resident, throughout the period of 3 years preceding the relevant date, in the United Kingdom and Islands or, in the case of such a person as is mentioned in paragraph 2*(b)* or *(c)*, has been so ordinarily resident in the European Community, or

(b) if his residence in the United Kingdom and Islands or, as the case may be, the European Community has during any part of that period been wholly or mainly for the purposes of receiving full-time education or undertaking post-graduate research otherwise than in the course of employment.

4.—(1) Paragraph 3 shall not apply in the case of:-

(a) a refugee who has not been ordinarily resident outside the United Kingdom and Islands since he was recognised as a refugee or was accorded asylum, or

(b) the spouse, son or daughter of such a refugee.

(2) The reference in this paragraph to a refugee's son or daughter includes a reference to a person adopted in pursuance of adoption proceedings, a step-child and an illegitimate child of whom the refugee is the mother or in whose case he has admitted paternity or been adjudged the putative father.

5. Paragraph 3*(b)* shall not apply in the case of a person who, in pursuance of paragraph 1(2), is treated as ordinarily resident in the United Kingdom and Islands or, as the case may be, the European Community throughout the period mentioned in paragraph 3*(a)*.

16th August 1983.

Nicholas Edwards,
Secretary of State for Wales.

EXPLANATORY NOTE
(This Note is not part of the Regulations.)

These Regulations amend the provisions of the State Awards (State Bursaries for Adult Education) (Wales) Regulations 1979 relating to the bestowal of state awards on persons ordinarily resident in Wales other than awards in respect of post-graduate and comparable courses.

The general arrangements made by the Secretary of State for the purposes of his functions under the Regulations of 1979 have provided that a state award should not be bestowed on a person, who, throughout the three years preceding his application for an award has not been ordinarily resident in the British Islands. These arrangements are relaxed or modified in the case of applicants for awards who are refugees or are the children of workers from the European Community.

The present Regulations make express provision in that behalf and further provide that a state award shall not be bestowed on a person if his residence in the British Islands (or the European Community, as appropriate) has, during any part of the three year period preceding his application, been wholly or mainly for purposes of receiving full-time education or undertaking post-graduate research otherwise than in the course of employment.

The Regulations also extend the existing arrangements relating to the eligibility of refugees for awards to their spouses and children. They take account of the provisions of Article 7 of EEC Regulation 1612/68 relating to the access of workers from the European Community to training in vocational schools by providing that such persons and the children of workers from the European Community are not subject to the requirement imposed by the Regulations that a person cannot receive a state award if he is receiving full-time education.

STATUTORY INSTRUMENTS

1983 No. 1275

NATIONAL HEALTH SERVICE, ENGLAND AND WALES

The National Health Service (Appointment of Consultants) (Wales) Regulations 1983

Made - - - -	*16th August* 1983
Laid before Parliament	*2nd September* 1983
Coming into Operation	*23th September* 1983

The Secretary of State for Wales, in exercise of powers conferred on him by paragraph 10 of Schedule 5 to the National Health Service Act 1977(a), and of all other powers enabling him in that behalf, after consultation in accordance with paragraph 11(1) of the said Schedule 5 with bodies recognised by him as representing persons likely to be affected, hereby makes the following regulations:—

Citation and commencement

1. These regulations may be cited as the National Health Service (Appointment of Consultants) (Wales) Regulations 1983 and shall come into operation on 23rd September 1983.

Interpretation

2.—(1) In these regulations, unless the context otherwise requires—

"appropriate body" in relation to a proposed appointment, means such of the following bodies, namely, the Royal College of Physicians of London and its associated Faculty of Occupational Medicine, the Royal College of Surgeons of England and its associated Faculties of Anaesthetists and Dental Surgery, the Royal College of Obstetricians and Gynaecologists, the Royal College of Pathologists, the Royal College of Psychiatrists or the Royal College of Radiologists, as, in the opinion of the Authority concerned, is substantially concerned with the specialty in which the appointment will be made;

"Authority" means a District Health Authority for a district in Wales or two or more such authorities;

"Committee" means an Advisory Appointments Committee constituted pursuant to the provisions of regulation 6;

"consultant" in relation to a relevant specialty, means a consultant specialising or who has recently specialised in the relevant specialty, or

---

(a) 1977 c. 49.

where such specialty has not yet been established, a consultant specialising or who has recently specialised in a specialty which in the opinion of the appropriate body is closely related to the relevant specialty;

"hospital" means premises in which or an institution to or for which an Authority provides facilities or staff for the provision of personal services to a patient for the purpose of the prevention, diagnosis and treatment of illness;

"lay member" means a person who is not a registered medical or dental practitioner or an officer of any Authority;

"member of the clinical staff", in relation to a proposed appointment, means a person of consultant status on the medical or dental staff of a hospital or a group of hospitals in which the duties or the major part of the duties of the appointment will be performed, or where there is no such person, a person of consultant status employed in a hospital;

"professional member", in relation to a proposed appointment, means, if it is a medical appointment, a registered medical practitioner and, if it is a dental appointment, a registered dental practitioner;

"relevant specialty", in relation to a proposed appointment, means the branch of medicine or dentistry in which it is proposed to make the appointment;

"Teaching Authority" for the purpose of regulation 4(1)(e) has the same meaning as in regulation 2(1) of the National Health Service (Appointment of Consultants) Regulations 1982(a) and otherwise for the purpose of these regulations means a District Health Authority the membership of which specified in the Order establishing it includes more than one member nominated by the University so specified as being associated with the provision of the health services in that Authority's district;

"University" means a University providing substantial facilities for undergraduate or postgraduate clinical teaching;

"Welsh Medical Committee" means the Committee recognised by the Secretary of State under section 19 of the National Health Service Act 1977 as being representative of the medical practitioners of Wales;

"Welsh Dental Committee" means the Committee recognised by the Secretary of State under section 19 of the National Health Service Act 1977 as being representative of the dental practitioners of Wales.

(2) For the purposes of these regulations and Schedule 4 a body shall be deemed to have a substantial interest in an appointment where the duties of the appointment include duties on behalf of that body or duties which will be carried out in association with that body, or where that body proposes to invite the person appointed to undertake duties on behalf of that body otherwise than as part of the duties of the appointment.

(3) Unless the context otherwise requires, any reference in these regulations to a numbered regulation or Schedule is a reference to the regulation in, or, as the case may be, the Schedule to these regulations which bears that number, and any reference in a regulation or Schedule to a numbered paragraph is a reference to the paragraph bearing that number in that regulation or Schedule.

(a) S.I. 1982/276.

Regulated appointments

3. These regulations apply to appointments of whatever nature to consultant posts on the staff of an Authority in Wales except appointments which are exempted appointments under regulation 4.

Exempted appointments

4.—(1) Appointments which are exempted appointments are of:—

(a) professors, readers or other members of the academic staff of a University who will receive no remuneration from an Authority in respect of their tenure of their post;

(b) consultants who have reached the age of 65, or in the case of mental health officers as defined in the National Health Service (Superannuation) Regulations 1980(**a**), the age of 60, and who will receive no remuneration from an Authority in respect of their tenure of their post;

(c) persons who are primarily engaged in research which necessitates their appointment to the staff of an Authority and who will receive no remuneration from an Authority in respect of their tenure of their post;

(d) persons whose employment in a post will be limited in duration to carry out the duties of that post—

    (i) until a permanent appointment to it can properly be made provided that such employment shall not be for a period exceeding 12 months; or

    (ii) the duties of or continued existence of which is subject to a review as part of a local reorganisation of the health service: Provided that such employment shall not without the express prior consent of the Secretary of State be for a period exceeding two years;

(e) persons whose last employment by an Authority, a Regional Health Authority or a Teaching Authority in England or two or more such authorities, or a Health Board in Scotland was in a post as consultant, the termination of which employment was certified by the Secretary of State to be by reason of redundancy and who is appointed to a consultant post in Wales within two years of that termination of employment;

(f) persons who are transferred, with the approval of the Secretary of State, from employment as a consultant by an Authority to another such post with that Authority or to employment by another Authority where the employment of the officer would otherwise be terminated by reason of redundancy;

(g) persons whose employment is, with the approval of the Secretary of State, transferred from one Authority to another Authority without any significant alteration in the duties of the post, as part of a local reorganisation of the health service;

(h) persons who are engaged in providing medical or dental services but are employed by bodies referred to in paragraph 1*(b)* or *(c)* of Schedule 4 in posts equivalent to posts in the health service to which consultants are normally appointed, on transfer with the approval of the Secretary of

---

(**a**) S.I. 1980/362; the amending regulations are not relevant to the subject matter of these regulations.

State to the employment of an Authority to fill posts the duties of which are substantially the same as those of the posts in which they were employed immediately before the date of such transfer;

(i) persons employed as consultants by an Authority other than an appointing Authority and whose duties for the appointing Authority will be limited to the equivalent of one day's work in each fortnight;

(2) In this regulation—

(a) "employment" includes part-time employment, whether or not the person is also employed by another Authority, and "employed" shall be construed accordingly;

(b) "remuneration" does not include any distinction award or the defrayment of expenses involved in the carrying out of the duties of a hospital appointment.

Advertisement of proposed appointment

5.—(1) When an Authority proposes to make an appointment to which these regulations apply, it shall arrange for advertisements setting out the general duties of the post and the closing date for receipt of applications to appear in not less than two publications circulating throughout England and Wales which are commonly used for similar advertisements relating to the profession concerned:

Provided that where compliance with the foregoing provisions of this paragraph is not reasonably practicable the Authority shall arrange for such advertisements to appear in such other publications as it thinks appropriate.

(2) Where such an advertisement is in respect of a whole-time post, the advertisement shall include a statement to the effect that applicants for appointment for less time than is required to carry out the full duties of the post will be considered if they are unable to undertake whole-time professional work, unless that advertisement appears in a publication which states the effect of this paragraph in such manner that it applies to the advertisement.

(3) The Secretary of State may if he thinks fit authorise an Authority to dispense with the requirements of paragraph (1) in relation to an appointment to any post or class of post.

Constitution of Committees

6. For the purposes of making any appointment to which these regulations apply a Committee to be called an Advisory Appointments Committee shall, subject to any applicable provisions of Schedule 4 be constituted—

(a) where the appointment is to be made by a single District Health Authority, in accordance with Schedule 1;

(b) where the appointment is to be made by a single Teaching Authority in accordance with Schedule 2;

(c) where two or more Authorities agree to combine in the selection of a person for appointment to employment by one of those authorities, in accordance with Schedule 3.

Selection by Committees

7.—(1) An appointing Authority shall refer to the Committee all applications received by the Authority on or before the advertised closing date and any received after that date but before the Committee has met pursuant to the requirements of paragraph 6(1) of Schedule 4 if the Authority is satisfied that there is a reasonable explanation for their late receipt.

(2) The Committee, acting in accordance with Schedule 4, shall consider all applications so referred to them, shall select from the applicants any persons whom the Committee consider suitable for the appointment and submit their names to the Authority, together with such comments as they consider appropriate.

(3) The Committee shall not submit the name of any person under paragraph (2) without having interviewed him.

(4) Where an Authority proposes to make an appointment to a whole-time post but in the opinion of the Committee one or more of the applicants would be suitable for appointment for less than whole-time they shall submit to the Authority the names of any such applicants and may add such comments as they consider appropriate.

(5) If in the opinion of the Committee none of the applicants is suitable for appointment they shall so inform the Authority.

Appointment by Authority

8.—(1) An Authority shall not make an appointment to which these regulations apply—

(a) except from persons whose names have been submitted to it by a Committee under regulation 7;

(b) of any person who has canvassed, in respect of his application for an appointment to which these regulations apply, any member of the Authority or of the Committee.

(2) In any case where an Authority has been informed as provided for by regulation 7(4), it may appoint for less than whole-time employment one or more of the persons named as suitable for such employment.

(3) Where an Authority decides not to make an appointment from persons named by a Committee or where an Authority is informed pursuant to regulation 7(5) that none of the applicants is suitable, the Committee shall be discharged and these regulations shall apply to any further proposal by the Authority to make an appointment to the relevant post as they applied to the original proposal.

Travelling and subsistence

9. Members of the Committee shall be entitled to receive from the Authority or, where Authorities are acting jointly, from the Authority by which is employed the administrator specified in paragraph 12 of Schedule 4, such payments in respect of travelling and subsistence allowances as are payable to members of the Authority performing an approved duty.

Employment by a single Authority of a consultant appointed jointly

10. Where two or more Authorities agree to appoint the same person to fill posts in hospitals in respect of which they respectively exercise functions, those Authorities shall make arrangements for the person appointed to be employed by such one of those Authorities as may be agreed, or failing agreement as the Secretary of State may direct and for the services of the person appointed to be made available to the other Authority or Authorities so as to enable all the posts to which he was appointed to be filled.

Revocation of Regulations

11. The National Health Service (Appointment of Consultants) (Wales) Regulations 1974(**a**) are hereby revoked.

Transitional provisions

12.—(1) Where before 23rd September 1983 an Advisory Appointments Committee has been constituted under the National Health Service (Appointment of Consultants) (Wales) Regulations 1974 to select a person for appointment after that date to an employment to which these regulations apply, the selection shall be made by that Committee in accordance with those regulations and the appointment shall be made by the appropriate Authority.

(2) Subject to paragraph 1 anything done or begun for the purposes of those regulations in relation to such an appointment shall be treated as having been begun or done under the corresponding provisions of these regulations.

Nicholas Edwards,
Secretary of State for Wales.

16th August 1983.

(**a**) S.I. 1974/477, amended by S.I. 1982/288.

Regulation 6*(a)*   SCHEDULE 1

APPOINTMENTS BY A DISTRICT HEALTH AUTHORITY

1.   The Authority shall constitute a Committee of seven members.

2.   All the members shall be appointed by the Authority and of those members—

(1) one shall be a lay member of the Authority,

(2) one shall be a lay member of another Authority,

(3) one shall be a member of the clinical staff of the Authority,

(4) one shall be a consultant in the relevant specialty not being employed in Wales appointed after consultation with the appropriate body,

(5) one shall be a professional member appointed after consultation with the Welsh National School of Medicine, and

(6) two shall be professional members employed within the district of another Authority nominated by the Welsh Medical Committee in the case of a medical appointment, or by the Welsh Dental Committee in the case of a dental appointment.

Regulation 6*(b)*   SCHEDULE 2

APPOINTMENTS BY A TEACHING AUTHORITY

1.   The Authority shall constitute a Committee of seven members.

2.   All the members shall be appointed by the Authority and of those members—

(1) two shall be lay members one of whom shall be appointed after consultation with the Welsh National School of Medicine,

(2) two shall be consultants in the relevant specialty and of those two—

    (a) one, not being employed in Wales, shall be appointed after consultation with the appropriate body, and

    (b) one, being employed within the district of another Authority, shall be nominated by the Welsh Medical Committee in the case of a medical appointment, or by the Welsh Dental Committee in the case of a dental appointment.

(3) one shall be a member of the clinical staff of the Authority, and

(4) two shall be professional members appointed after consultation with the Welsh National School of Medicine.

Regulation 6*(c)*   SCHEDULE 3

APPOINTMENTS BY AUTHORITIES ACTING TOGETHER

1.   The Authorities acting together shall constitute a Committee.

2.   Where the Authorities acting together are a District Health Authority and a Teaching Authority they shall appoint a Committee of nine members of which—

(1) five members shall be appointed by the Authorities jointly, the five consisting of—

    (a) two lay members, one appointed after consultation with the Welsh National School of Medicine,

    (b) three professional members of whom—

(i) one shall be a consultant in the relevant specialty not being employed in Wales appointed after consultation with the appropriate body;

(ii) two shall be appointed after consultation with the Welsh National School of Medicine, and

(2) two professional members shall be appointed by each Authority one of each pair being a member of the clinical staff of that authority, and the other appointed after consultation with the Welsh Medical Committee in the case of a medical appointment or with the Welsh Dental Committee in the case of a dental appointment.

3. Where the Authorities acting together are—

(a) more than two in number and

(b) one Authority is a Teaching Authority

then they shall comply with paragraph 2 with Authorities of the same description acting jointly as though they were a single Authority.

4. Where the Authorities acting together are two or more District Health Authorities and no Authority is a Teaching Authority they shall comply jointly with Schedule 1 as though their districts were a single district.

SCHEDULE 4   Regulation 7(1) and 7(2)

GENERAL PROVISIONS APPLYING IN ALL CASES

1. Where—

(a) the person to be appointed will be required to carry out duties on behalf of a local authority; or

(b) the person to be appointed may be required or invited to carry out duties on behalf of the Medical Research Council, the Armed Forces, the Public Health Laboratory Service Board, a Government Department or any body provided or constituted under the National Health Service Act 1977(a); or

(c) a University proposes to invite the person appointed to undertake duties on behalf of the University otherwise than as part of the duties of the appointment by the Authority; or

(d) the person to be appointed will be required to carry out duties in more than one place within the district of an Authority and where the Authority feels that the organisation of services in that district is such that the views of all clinical staff with whom the appointee will work for a significant part of his time cannot be represented solely by the member of the clinical staff appointed to the Committee under paragraph 2(3) of Schedule 1, 2(3) of Schedule 2 or 2(2) of Schedule 3;

then the Authority may appoint one or more additional members to the Committee after consultation—

(i) with any of the bodies mentioned in sub-paragraph *(a)* or *(b)* as the case may require, where the Authority feels those bodies have a substantial interest in the appointment; and

(ii) with the University mentioned in sub-paragraph *(c)* in a case to which that sub-paragraph applies:

so however that the Authority may not under the provision of this paragraph, appoint to the Committee more than three additional members.

(a) 1977 c. 49.

2. Where an appointed member is unwilling or unable to perform his functions another person may be appointed in the same manner to be a member in his place.

3.—(1) An Authority entitled to appoint any members of the Committee shall send the name of its appointee to the administrator.

(2) If more than one body appoints the same person the administrator shall forthwith inform each of those bodies of the identity of the other or others.

(3) Where any body is so informed, it shall either confirm its appointment or appoint another person in place of the person originally appointed, and if more than one such body confirms its appointment the membership of the Committee shall be reduced accordingly.

4. The administrator shall provide the Committee with such clerical or other assistance as the Committee may require.

5.—(1) The Chairman of the Committee shall be the lay member or such one of the lay members (not being an additional member appointed under paragraph 1 above) as shall be so designated by the Authority.

(2) The Chairman shall convene, and if present shall preside at any meeting of the Committee.

(3) If the Chairman is not present at any meeting of the Committee, they shall select one of the members present to preside.

6.—(1) For the purposes of regulation 7(2) the Committee shall meet and may adjourn as necessary.

(2) Subject to the provisions of this Schedule the procedure of the Committee shall be such as they think fit.

7. The Committee may invite any applicant to attend before them for the purpose of an interview.

8. In the event of an equality of votes the Chairman shall not have a second or casting vote and no applicant shall be considered suitable for appointment unless a majority of the Committee considers him to be so suitable.

9. The Committee shall not transact any business in the absence of either more than one of the lay members or more than one of the professional members, in each case being members other than additional members appointed under paragraph 1 above.

10. Subject to the provisions of paragraphs 5 and 9 above the proceedings of the Committee shall not be invalidated by any vacancy in, or failure to appoint to, or defect in the appointment or qualification of any member of, the Committee.

11. When in the opinion of the Authority there is more than one appropriate body, the Authority may appoint for each such body after consultation therewith a member to the Committee who shall be a consultant in a relevant specialty, not being a consultant employed within the district of the Authority, and the Committee shall be enlarged accordingly.

12. In this Schedule—

"administrator" means the Chief administrator of the Authority by which the Committee is constituted or where Authorities are acting jointly in constituting the Committee, the Chief administrator of such one of those Authorities as they may agree;

"local authority" means a County Council or a District Council; and

"the Authority" means the Authority or Authorities by which the Committee is constituted.

EXPLANATORY NOTE

(This Note is not part of the Regulations.)

These regulations make provision for the constitution by District Health Authorities in Wales of Advisory Appointment Committees to select candidates for appointments as clinical consultants. They lay down the procedure to be followed and include provision for the making of part-time appointments. These regulations supersede the National Health Service (Appointment of Consultants) (Wales) Regulations 1974.

STATUTORY INSTRUMENTS

1983 No. 1287

TRIBUNALS AND INQUIRIES

The Tribunals and Inquiries (Discretionary Inquiries) (Amendment) Order 1983

Made - - - - -	*9th August* 1983
Laid before Parliament	*26th August* 1983
Coming into Operation	*30th September* 1983

The Lord Chancellor and the Lord Advocate, in exercise of the powers conferred by section 19(2) as read with section 16(2) of the Tribunals and Inquiries Act 1971**(a)**, on the Lord Chancellor and the Lord Advocate**(b)**, hereby make the following Order:—

1. This Order may be cited as the Tribunals and Inquiries (Discretionary Inquiries) (Amendment) Order 1983 and shall come into operation on 30th September 1983.

2. Part I of the Schedule to the Tribunals and Inquiries (Discretionary Inquiries) Order 1975**(c)** shall be amended as follows:—

(*a*) For paragraph 23 there shall be substituted:—

"23. Any inquiry held under section 40 of the British Nationality Act 1981."**(d)**

(*b*) After paragraph 72 there shall be inserted the following paragraphs:—

"72A. Any inquiry held under Part I of the Schedule to the Control of Off-Street Parking (England and Wales) Order 1978."**(e)**

"72B. Any inquiry held under Part I of the Schedule to the Control of Off-Street Parking (Scotland) Order 1979."**(f)**

(a) 1971 c. 62.
(b) See the Transfer of Functions (Secretary of State and Lord Advocate) Order 1972 (S.I. 1972/2002).
(c) S.I. 1975/1379, amended by S.I. 1976/293.
(d) 1981 c. 61.
(e) S.I. 1978/1535.
(f) S.I. 1979/119.

"72C. Any inquiry held under section 4(2) or 5(3) of the Pneumoconiosis etc. (Workers' Compensation) Act 1979."**(a)**

"72D. Any inquiry held under section 90C of the Highways Act 1980."**(b)**

"72E. Any inquiry held under paragraph 6(4) of Schedule 10 to the Transport Act 1981."**(c)**

3. Part II of the Schedule to the Tribunals and Inquiries (Discretionary Inquiries) Order 1975 shall be amended as follows:—

(*a*) For paragraph 79 there shall be substituted:—

"79. Any inquiry held under section 28(6) of and paragraph 8 of Part I of Schedule 3 to the Salmon and Freshwater Fisheries Act 1975."**(d)**

(*b*) After paragraph 105 there shall be inserted the following paragraphs:—

"106. Any hearing held pursuant to regulations made under section 16(1) of the Health Services Act 1976."**(e)**

"107. Any inquiry held under section 11(3) of the Social Security and Housing Benefits Act 1982."**(f)**

Dated the 9th August 1983.

Hailsham of St. Marlebone, C.
Mackay of Clashfern, Lord Advocate.

(**a**) 1979 c. 41.
(**b**) As inserted by section 32 of and paragraph 2 of Part I of Schedule 10 to the Transport Act 1981 (c. 56).
(**c**) 1981 c. 56.
(**d**) 1975 c. 51.
(**e**) 1976 c. 83.
(**f**) 1982 c. 24.

EXPLANATORY NOTE

(This Note is not part of the Order.)

This Order amends the Tribunals and Inquiries (Discretionary Inquiries) Order 1975 ("the 1975 Order") by including in the Schedule to that Order the discretionary inquiries specified, thus applying sections 1 and 11 of the Tribunals and Inquiries Act 1971 to those inquiries. This brings the specified inquiries within the jurisdiction of the Council on Tribunals and gives the Lord Chancellor and, in Scotland, the Lord Advocate, power to make rules regulating their procedures.

Section 12 of the Tribunals and Inquiries Act 1971 applies to the inquiries listed in Part I of the Schedule to the 1975 Order. It will thus be the duty of any Minister who takes a decision after any such inquiry has been held by him or on his behalf to give the reasons for the decision unless he is relieved of the duty by virtue of section 12(2) or (4). There will be no duty to give reasons for the decision in the case of any inquiry listed in Part II of the Schedule to the 1975 Order since section 12 does not apply in relation to such inquiries.

STATUTORY INSTRUMENTS

1983 No. 1288

OFFSHORE INSTALLATIONS

The Offshore Installations (Safety Zones) (No. 28) Order 1983

Made - - - -	*23rd August* 1983	
Coming into Operation	*25th August* 1983	

The Secretary of State, in exercise of the powers conferred on him by section 21(1), (2) and (3) of the Oil and Gas (Enterprise) Act 1982(**a**) (hereinafter referred to as "the Act"), and of all other powers enabling him in that behalf, hereby makes the following Order:—

1. This Order may be cited as the Offshore Installations (Safety Zones) (No. 28) Order 1983 and shall come into operation on 25th August 1983.

2.—(1) A safety zone is hereby established around the installation specified in Column 1 of the Schedule hereto (being an installation maintained in waters in an area designated under section 1(7) of the Continental Shelf Act 1964(**b**)) having a radius of five hundred metres from the point as respects that installation which has the co-ordinates of latitude and longitude according to European Datum (1950) specified in Columns 2 and 3 of the Schedule.

(2) The prohibition under section 21(3) of the Act on a vessel entering or remaining in a safety zone without the consent of the Secretary of State shall not apply to a vessel entering or remaining in the safety zone established under paragraph (1) above:

(*a*) in connection with the laying, inspection, testing, repair, alteration, renewal or removal of any submarine cable or pipe-line in or near that safety zone;

(*b*) to provide services for, to transport persons or goods to or from, or under the authority of a government department to inspect, any installation in that safety zone;

(*c*) if it is a vessel belonging to a general lighthouse authority performing duties relating to the safety of navigation;

(*d*) in connection with the saving or attempted saving of life or property;

(**a**) 1982 c. 23.   (**b**) 1964 c. 29.

(*e*) owing to stress of weather; or

(*f*) when in distress.

Avon,
Parliamentary Under Secretary of State,
Department of Energy.

23rd August 1983.

Article 2(1)   SCHEDULE

SAFETY ZONE

1	2	3
Name or other designation of the offshore installation	Latitude North	Longitude East
47/3 B(BP)	53° 50′ 04·46″	00° 26′ 34·43″

EXPLANATORY NOTE

(*This Note is not part of the Order.*)

This Order establishes, under section 21 of the Oil and Gas (Enterprise) Act 1982, a safety zone, having a radius of 500 metres from a specified point, around the installation known as 47/3 B(BP) maintained in waters in an area designated under section 1(7) of the Continental Shelf Act 1964.

Vessels (which includes hovercraft, submersible apparatus and installations in transit) are prohibited from entering or remaining in the safety zone except with the consent of the Secretary of State or in the circumstances mentioned in Article 2(2) of the Order.

STATUTORY INSTRUMENTS

1983 No. 1289

OFFSHORE INSTALLATIONS

The Offshore Installations (Safety Zones) (No. 29) Order 1983

Made - - - -	*23rd August* 1983
Coming into Operation	*25th August* 1983

The Secretary of State, in exercise of the powers conferred on him by section 21(1), (2) and (3) of the Oil and Gas (Enterprise) Act 1982(a) (hereinafter referred to as "the Act"), and of all other powers enabling him in that behalf, hereby makes the following Order:—

1. This Order may be cited as the Offshore Installations (Safety Zones) (No. 29) Order 1983 and shall come into operation on 25th August 1983.

2.—(1) A safety zone is hereby established around the installation specified in Column 1 of the Schedule hereto (being an installation maintained in waters in an area designated under section 1(7) of the Continental Shelf Act 1964(b)) having a radius of five hundred metres from the point as respects that installation which has the co-ordinates of latitude and longitude according to European Datum (1950) specified in Columns 2 and 3 of the Schedule.

(2) The prohibition under section 21(3) of the Act on a vessel entering or remaining in a safety zone without the consent of the Secretary of State shall not apply to a vessel entering or remaining in the safety zone established under paragraph (1) above:

(*a*) in connection with the laying, inspection, testing, repair, alteration, renewal or removal of any submarine cable or pipe-line in or near that safety zone;

(*b*) to provide services for, to transport persons or goods to or from, or under the authority of a government department to inspect, any installation in that safety zone;

(*c*) if it is a vessel belonging to a general lighthouse authority performing duties relating to the safety of navigation;

(*d*) in connection with the saving or attempted saving of life or property;

(*e*) owing to stress of weather; or

(*f*) when in distress.

Avon,
Parliamentary Under Secretary of State,
Department of Energy.

23rd August 1983.

(**a**) 1982 c. 23. (**b**) 1964 c. 29.

Article 2(1)
SCHEDULE
SAFETY ZONE

1	2	3
Name or other designation of the offshore installation	Latitude North	Longitude East
Apollo II	58° 05′ 05·88″	03° 09′ 05·72″

EXPLANATORY NOTE

(This Note is not part of the Order.)

This Order establishes, under section 21 of the Oil and Gas (Enterprise) Act 1982, a safety zone, having a radius of 500 metres from a specified point, around the installation known as Apollo II maintained in waters in an area designated under section 1(7) of the Continental Shelf Act 1964.

Vessels (which includes hovercraft, submersible apparatus and installations in transit) are prohibited from entering or remaining in the safety zone except with the consent of the Secretary of State or in the circumstances mentioned in Article 2(2) of the Order.

STATUTORY INSTRUMENTS

1983 No. 1290

OFFSHORE INSTALLATIONS

The Offshore Installations (Safety Zones) (No. 30) Order 1983

Made - - - -	*23rd August* 1983
Coming into Operation	*25th August* 1983

The Secretary of State, in exercise of the powers conferred on him by section 21(1), (2) and (3) of the Oil and Gas (Enterprise) Act 1982(**a**) (hereinafter referred to as "the Act"), and of all other powers enabling him in that behalf, hereby makes the following Order:—

1. This Order may be cited as the Offshore Installations (Safety Zones) (No. 30) Order 1983 and shall come into operation on 25th August 1983.

2.—(1) A safety zone is hereby established around the installation specified in Column 1 of the Schedule hereto (being an installation maintained in waters in an area designated under section 1(7) of the Continental Shelf Act 1964(**b**)) having a radius of five hundred metres from the point as respects that installation which has the co-ordinates of latitude and longitude according to European Datum (1950) specified in Columns 2 and 3 of the Schedule.

(2) The prohibition under section 21(3) of the Act on a vessel entering or remaining in a safety zone without the consent of the Secretary of State shall not apply to a vessel entering or remaining in the safety zone established under paragraph (1) above:

(*a*) in connection with the laying, inspection, testing, repair, alteration, renewal or removal of any submarine cable or pipe-line in or near that safety zone;

(*b*) to provide services for, to transport persons or goods to or from, or under the authority of a government department to inspect, any installation in that safety zone;

(*c*) if it is a vessel belonging to a general lighthouse authority performing duties relating to the safety of navigation;

(*d*) in connection with the saving or attempted saving of life or property;

(**a**) 1982 c. 23.   (**b**) 1964 c. 29.

(*e*) owing to stress of weather; or

(*f*) when in distress.

Avon,
Parliamentary Under Secretary of State,
Department of Energy.

23rd August 1983.

Article 2(1)   SCHEDULE

SAFETY ZONE

1	2	3
Name or other designation of the offshore installation	Latitude North	Longitude West
Neddrill 3	50° 24′ 22·75″	01° 35′ 58·61″

EXPLANATORY NOTE

(*This Note is not part of the Order.*)

This Order establishes, under section 21 of the Oil and Gas (Enterprise) Act 1982, a safety zone, having a radius of 500 metres from a specified point, around the installation known as Neddrill 3 maintained in waters in an area designated under section 1(7) of the Continental Shelf Act 1964.

Vessels (which includes hovercraft, submersible apparatus and installations in transit) are prohibited from entering or remaining in the safety zone except with the consent of the Secretary of State or in the circumstances mentioned in Article 2(2) of the Order.

STATUTORY INSTRUMENTS

1983 No. 1297

OVERSEAS DEVELOPMENT AND CO-OPERATION

The International Bank for Reconstruction and Development (1979 General Capital Increase) Order 1983

Laid before the House of Commons in draft

Made - - - -	*12th August* 1983
Coming into Operation	*12th August* 1983

Whereas it is provided in section 4(1) of the Overseas Development and Co-operation Act 1980 ("the Act") (**a**) that if the Government of the United Kingdom becomes bound by any arrangements for the making of any further payment to an international development bank beyond the initial subscription or other initial contribution to its capital stock, the Secretary of State may with the approval of the Treasury by order made by statutory instrument make provision for any of the purposes specified in that subsection;

And whereas a draft of this Order has been laid before the House of Commons in accordance with section 4(3) of the Act and has been approved by a resolution of that House;

Now, therefore, the Secretary of State, in exercise of the powers conferred upon him by section 4 of the Act and with the approval of the Treasury, hereby makes the following Order:—

1.—(1) This Order may be cited as the International Bank for Reconstruction and Development (1979 General Capital Increase) Order 1983 and shall come into operation forthwith.

(2) In this Order—

"the Agreement" means the Articles of Agreement of the International Bank for Reconstruction and Development(**b**);

"the International Bank" means the International Bank for Reconstruction and Development established by the Agreement;

"the Resolution" means Resolution No. 346 adopted by the Board of Governors of the International Bank on 4th January 1980.

2. The Secretary of State may make payment on behalf of the Government of the United Kingdom out of money provided by Parliament of an additional subscription to the capital stock of the International Bank of sums not exceeding in the aggregate the equivalent of 1,467,886,680 United States dollars in accordance with arrangements made between the Government and the International Bank in accordance with the Resolution.

3. The Secretary of State may out of money provided by Parliament make payment of sums required to redeem any non-interest-bearing and non-negotiable notes or other obligations which may be issued or created by him and accepted by the International Bank in accordance with the Agreement or the said arrangements.

(**a**) 1980 c.63.   (**b**) Cmd. 6885.

4. Any sums received by the Government of the United Kingdom in pursuance of the Agreement or the said arrangements shall be paid into the Consolidated Fund.

Geoffrey Howe,
One of Her Majesty's Principal
Secretaries of State.

27th July 1983.

We approve,

Nigel Lawson,
D. J. F. Hunt,
Two of the Lords Commissioners
of Her Majesty's Treasury.

12th August 1983.

EXPLANATORY NOTE

(*This Note is not part of the Order.*)

This Order provides for the payment to the International Bank for Reconstruction and Development, in accordance with arrangements made with it relating to the 1979 General Capital Increase of the resources of the Bank, of an additional subscription equivalent to US $1,467,886,680. The Order also provides for the redemption of non-interest-bearing and non-negotiable notes issued by the Secretary of State in payment of the additional subscription. The Order further provides that certain sums which may be received by the Government of the United Kingdom from the Bank shall be paid into the Consolidated Fund. The provisions of Resolution No. 346 may be obtained by application to the Overseas Development Administration, Eland House, Stag Place, London, SW1E 5DH.

STATUTORY INSTRUMENTS

1983 No. 1298

OVERSEAS DEVELOPMENT AND CO-OPERATION

The International Bank for Reconstruction and Development (1979 Additional Increase in Capital Stock) Order 1983

Laid before the House of Commons in draft

Made - - - - -	*12th August* 1983
Coming into Operation	*12th August* 1983

Whereas it is provided in section 4(1) of the Overseas Development and Co-operation Act 1980 ("the Act")**(a)** that if the Government of the United Kingdom becomes bound by any arrangements for the making of any further payment to an international development bank beyond the initial subscription or other initial contribution to its capital stock, the Secretary of State may with the approval of the Treasury by order made by statutory instrument make provision for any of the purposes specified in that subsection;

And whereas a draft of this Order has been laid before the House of Commons in accordance with section 4(3) of the Act and has been approved by a resolution of that House;

Now, therefore, the Secretary of State, in exercise of the powers conferred upon him by section 4 of the Act and with the approval of the Treasury, hereby makes the following Order:—

1.—(1) This Order may be cited as the International Bank for Reconstruction and Development (1979 Additional Increase in Capital Stock) Order 1983 and shall come into operation forthwith.

(2) In this Order:—

"the Agreement" means the Articles of Agreement of the International Bank for Reconstruction and Development**(b)**;

"the International Bank" means the International Bank for Reconstruction and Development established by the Agreement;

"the Resolution" means Resolution No. 347 adopted by the Board of Governors of the International Bank on 4th January 1980.

(a) 1980 c. 63.   **(b)** Cmd. 6885.

2. The Secretary of State may make payment on behalf of the Government of the United Kingdom out of money provided by Parliament of an additional subscription to the capital stock of the International Bank of sums not exceeding in the aggregate the equivalent of 30,158,750 United States dollars in accordance with arrangements made between the Government and the International Bank in accordance with the Resolution.

3. The Secretary of State may out of money provided by Parliament make payment of sums required to redeem any non-interest-bearing and non-negotiable notes or other obligations which may be issued or created by him and accepted by the International Bank in accordance with the Agreement or the said arrangements.

4. Any sums received by the Government of the United Kingdom in pursuance of the Agreement or the said arrangements shall be paid into the Consolidated Fund.

Geoffrey Howe,
One of Her Majesty's Principal
Secretaries of State.

27th July 1983.

We approve,

Nigel Lawson,
D. J. F. Hunt,
Two of the Lords Commissioners
of Her Majesty's Treasury.

12th August 1983.

EXPLANATORY NOTE

(*This Note is not part of the Order.*)

This Order provides for the payment to the International Bank for Reconstruction and Development, in accordance with arrangements made with it relating to the 1979 Additional Increase in Authorised Capital Stock, of sums not exceeding US$30,158,750. The Order also provides for the redemption of non-interest-bearing and non-negotiable notes issued by the Secretary of State in payment of the additional subscription. The Order further provides that certain sums which may be received by the Government of the United Kingdom from the Bank shall be paid into the Consolidated Fund. The provisions of Resolution No. 347 may be obtained by application to the Overseas Development Administration, Eland House, Stag Place, London, SW1E 5DH.

STATUTORY INSTRUMENTS

1983 No. 1299

OVERSEAS DEVELOPMENT AND CO-OPERATION

The International Development Association (Special Contributions) Order 1983

Laid before the House of Commons in draft

Made - - - -	*12th August* 1983
Coming into Operation	*12th August* 1983

Whereas it is provided in section 6(2) of the Overseas Development and Co-operation Act 1980 ("the Act")(**a**) that if the Government of the United Kingdom becomes bound by arrangements for the making of additional payments to the International Development Association the Secretary of State may with the approval of the Treasury by order made by statutory instrument provide for the payment out of money provided by Parliament of any sums required by him for any of the purposes specified in that subsection;

And whereas a draft of this Order has been laid before the House of Commons in accordance with section 6(3) of the Act and has been approved by a resolution of that House;

Now, therefore, the Secretary of State, in exercise of the powers conferred upon him by section 6 of the Act and with the approval of the Treasury, hereby makes the following Order:—

1.—(1) This Order may be cited as the International Development Association (Special Contributions) Order 1983 and shall come into operation forthwith.

(2) In this Order—

"the Association" means the International Development Association established by the Agreement;

"the Agreement" means the Articles of Agreement of the International Development Association dated 29th January 1960 and accepted on behalf of the Government of the United Kingdom on 14th September 1960(**b**);

"the Resolution" means Resolution No. IDA 82-6 of the Executive Directors of the Association entitled "Arrangements for Special Contributions" adopted on 26th October 1982 the text of which was presented to Parliament by Command of Her Majesty in May 1983(**c**).

(**a**) 1980 c. 63.   (**b**) Cmnd. 1244.   (**c**) Cmnd. 8867.

2. The Secretary of State may make payment on behalf of the Government of the United Kingdom out of money provided by Parliament of additional contributions to the Association of sums not exceeding in the aggregate £105,000,000 in accordance with arrangements made between the Government and the Association in accordance with the terms of the Resolution.

3. The Secretary of State may out of money provided by Parliament make payment of sums required to redeem any non-interest-bearing and non-negotiable notes or other obligations which may be issued or created by him and accepted by the Association in accordance with the said arrangements or any provision of the Agreement as applied by the said arrangements.

4. Any sums received by the Government from the Association in pursuance of the Agreement as applied by the said arrangements shall be paid into the Consolidated Fund.

Geoffrey Howe,
One of Her Majesty's Principal
Secretaries of State.

27th July 1983.

We approve,

Nigel Lawson,
D. J. F. Hunt,
Two of the Lords Commissioners
of Her Majesty's Treasury.

12th August 1983.

EXPLANATORY NOTE

(*This Note is not part of the Order.*)

The Overseas Development and Co-operation Act 1980, section 6(2), provides that if the Government of the United Kingdom becomes bound by arrangements for the making of additional payments to the International Development Association, the Secretary of State may, with the approval of the Treasury, provide by order for the payment out of money provided by Parliament of any sums required by him for any of the purposes specified in that subsection.

This Order provides for the payment to the Association of sums not exceeding £105,000,000 as an additional contribution to the resources of the Association, and for the redemption of non-interest-bearing and non-negotiable notes issued by the Secretary of State in payment of those additional contributions. The Order further provides that certain sums which may be received by the Government of the United Kingdom from the Association shall be paid into the Consolidated Fund.

STATUTORY INSTRUMENTS

1983 No. 1312 (C. 37)

MERCHANT SHIPPING

The Merchant Shipping Act 1979 (Commencement No. 8) Order 1983

Made - - - - 26*th August* 1983

The Secretary of State for Transport, in exercise of powers conferred on him by section 52(2) of the Merchant Shipping Act 1979(a) (hereinafter referred to as "the Act") and of all other powers enabling him in that behalf hereby makes the following Order:—

1. This Order may be cited as the Merchant Shipping Act 1979 (Commencement No. 8) Order 1983.

2. The provision of the Act specified in the first column of the Schedule to this Order (which relates to the matters specified in the second column of that Schedule) shall come into force on 14th September 1983.

Tom King,
Secretary of State for Transport.

26th August 1983.

SCHEDULE

PROVISION COMING INTO FORCE ON 14TH SEPTEMBER 1983

Provision of the Act	Subject matter of the provisions
Section 47(2) so far as it is not already in force	Provisions of the Act which may be extended to certain countries etc.

(a) 1979 c. 39.

EXPLANATORY NOTE

(This Note is not part of the Order.)

This Order brings into force the remainder of section 47(2) of the Merchant Shipping Act 1979 and thus adds to the number of sections of the Act which may be extended to the Isle of Man, the Channel Islands and dependent territories and to ships registered in those countries and their crews.

The sections added are sections 23 to 25 (discipline) (not yet in force), 29 and 30 (deaths on ships), 31 (dues for space occupied by deck cargo), 32(2) and (3) (investigation of incidents), 35(1) in its application to fishing vessels and 35(2) (limitation of liability) (not yet in force), 37(1) (wages in the case of wreck or loss), 37(4) (powers of persons holding inquiries), 37(6) (extension of certain provisions to unregistered British ships) and 40 (foreign action affecting shipping) and Schedule 7 (repeals) to the extent that it is not already in force except so far as it relates to the Pilotage Act 1913 (c.31).

NOTE AS TO EARLIER COMMENCEMENT ORDERS

(This Note is not part of the Order.)

The following provisions of the Merchant Shipping Act 1979 have been brought into force by commencement orders made before the date of this Order:—

Provision	Date of commencement	S.I. No.
ss. 1 to 6, Sch. 1	1.8.79	1979/807
ss. 7, 8(1), (2), (4) and that part of (6) which relates to s. 14 of the Pilotage Act 1913, 9 to 11	4.7.80 and 1.9.80	1980/923
ss. 12, 13(1) in relation to Sch. 2, paras. 1 to 4, 5(2), 6, 7, 10(2), 11, 12, 14 to 19, 20(1), the former part of 20(2), 21 to 27	1.8.79, 1.10.79 and 1.1.80	1979/807
s. 13(1) in relation to Sch. 2, paras. 5(1), 8, 9, 10(1), 13(3) and the latter part of 20(2)	1.1.80 4.7.80 and 1.9.80	1979/807 1980/923
s. 13(2) to (5)	1.8.79	1979/807
s. 15(1) and the latter part of (2)	17.12.79	1979/1578
s. 16	1.8.79	1979/807
s. 19(2), (3)	17.12.79	1979/1578
ss. 20 to 22, 26 to 30, 32(1), 33, 34, 35(1) except in relation to fishing vessels, 36(1)	1.8.79, 1.10.79 and 1.1.80	1979/807
s. 31	3.5.83	1983/440
s. 32(2), (3)	1.7.83	1982/1616
s. 36(2)	1.4.80	1980/354
ss. 36(3), 37(1) to (3), (5),(7), (8)	1.8.79	1979/807
s. 37(4)	1.1.83	1982/1616
s. 38(5)	17.12.79	1979/1578

s. 38(1), (2), (3) and (6)	8.4.81	1981/405
ss. 39 to 45, 46 (partially), Sch. 6	1.8.79 and 1.1.80	1979/807
s. 46 (remainder)	4.7.80	1980/923
s. 47(1), (2) (partially), (3)	1.8.79, 1.10.79 and 1.1.80	1979/807
s. 47(2) (partially)	17.12.79	1979/1578
ss. 48, 49, 50(1), (2)	1.8.79	1979/807
s. 50(3)	4.7.80	1980/923
s. 50(4) and Sch. 7 (partially)	1.8.79, 1.10.79 and 1.1.80 1.4.80 4.7.80 and 1.9.80 8.4.81 3.5.83	1979/807 1980/354 1980/923 1981/405 1983/440
s. 51(1), (3), 52	1.8.79	1979/807
s. 51(2) partially	1.1.83	1982/1616
Sch. 3, Part I has been brought into force for some purposes, with modifications, by the Carriage of Passengers and their Luggage by Sea (Interim Provisions) Order 1980 (S.I. 1980/1092) made under the powers in section 16(1), (2) and (5).	1.1.81	1980/1092.

STATUTORY INSTRUMENTS

1983 No. 1314

PRISONS

The Transfer of Offenders (Designation of Equivalent Sentences) Order 1983

Made - - - - -	*30th August* 1983
Coming into Operation	*26th September* 1983

In exercise of the powers conferred upon me by section 38(6) of the Criminal Justice Act 1961(a), I hereby make the following Order:—

1. This Order may be cited as the Transfer of Offenders (Designation of Equivalent Sentences) Order 1983 and shall come into operation on 26th September 1983.

2. For the purposes of the Criminal Justice Act 1961 and of any enactment referred to in Part III of that Act (which relates to the transfer, supervision and recall of prisoners within the British Islands)—

 (*a*) a description of sentence which a court with jurisdiction in one part of the United Kingdom or in the Channel Islands or the Isle of Man may pass specified in column 1 of the table set out in Schedule 1 to this Order is hereby designated as equivalent to such descriptions of sentence which a court with jurisdiction elsewhere in the United Kingdom or in those Islands may pass as are specified in the entry corresponding thereto in column 2 of the said table; and

 (*b*) a description of sentence which a court with jurisdiction in one part of the United Kingdom or in the Channel Islands or the Isle of Man may pass specified in Part I of Schedule 2 to this Order is hereby designated as equivalent to any other description of sentence which a court with jurisdiction elsewhere in the United Kingdom or those Islands may pass specified in the said Part I; and a description of such sentence specified in Part II of the said Schedule is hereby designated as equivalent to any other description of such sentence specified in the said Part II, for the like term.

Leon Brittan,
One of Her Majesty's Principal
Secretaries of State.

Home Office.
30th August 1983.

(a) 1961 c. 39; subsection (6) of section 38 was inserted by the Criminal Justice Act 1982 (c. 48), Schedule 14, paragraph 15(*b*).

SCHEDULE 1   Article 2(*a*)

EQUIVALENT SENTENCES—GENERAL

PART I

Column 1	Column 2
Description of sentence which may be passed in England and Wales.	Equivalent sentence which may be passed elsewhere in the United Kingdom, the Channel Islands or the Isle of Man.
Imprisonment for life.	Imprisonment for life.
Imprisonment for a determinate period.	Imprisonment for the like term.
Custody for life under section 8 of the Criminal Justice Act 1982.	In Scotland— (*a*) in the case of a person aged less than 18 when sentenced, detention without limit of time under section 205(2) of the Criminal Procedure (Scotland) Act 1975**(a)**; and (*b*) in the case of a person aged 18 or over when sentenced, detention for life under section 205(3) of that Act. In Northern Ireland, the Channel Islands or the Isle of Man, imprisonment for life.
Youth custody sentence under section 6 of the Criminal Justice Act 1982.	In Scotland— (*a*) in the case of a person aged less than 16 when sentenced, detention under section 206(1) of the Criminal Procedure (Scotland) Act 1975**(b)** for the like term; and (*b*) in the case of a person aged 16 or over when sentenced, detention in a young offenders institution under section 208(3) of that Act for the like term. In Northern Ireland— (*a*) in the case of a sentence for a term of 3 years or more, imprisonment for the like term; and (*b*) in the case of a sentence for a term of less than 3 years, detention in a young offenders centre for the like term. In the Channel Islands or the Isle of Man, imprisonment for the like term.

(a) 1975 c. 21; section 205 was substituted by section 43 of the Criminal Justice (Scotland) Act 1980 (c. 62).

(b) Section 206(1) was substituted by section 44 of the Criminal Justice (Scotland) Act 1980.

SCHEDULE 1—PART I—(continued)

Column 1	Column 2
Description of sentence which may be passed in England and Wales.	Equivalent sentence which may be passed elsewhere in the United Kingdom, the Channel Islands or the Isle of Man.
Detention centre order under section 4 of the Criminal Justice Act 1982.	In Scotland— (a) in the case of a person aged less than 16 when sentenced, detention under section 206(1) of the Criminal Procedure (Scotland) Act 1975 for the like term; and (b) in the case of a person aged 16 or over when sentenced— (i) in the case of a sentence for a term exceeding 3 months, detention in a young offenders institution under section 208(3) of that Act for the like term; and (ii) in the case of a sentence for a term not exceeding 3 months, detention in a detention centre for the like term. In Northern Ireland, detention in a young offenders centre for the like term. In Jersey, detention in a young offenders centre for the like term.

PART II

Column 1	Column 2
Description of sentence which may be passed in Scotland.	Equivalent sentence which may be passed elsewhere in the United Kingdom, the Channel Islands or the Isle of Man.
Imprisonment for life.	Imprisonment for life.
Imprisonment for a determinate period.	Imprisonment for the like term.
Detention for life under section 205(3) of the Criminal Procedure (Scotland) Act 1975.	In England and Wales, custody for life under section 8(1) of the Criminal Justice Act 1982. In Northern Ireland, the Channel Islands or the Isle of Man, imprisonment for life.
Detention in a young offenders institution under section 208(3) of the Criminal Procedure (Scotland) Act 1975.	In England and Wales— (a) in the case of a sentence for a life term, custody for life under section 8(2) of the Criminal Justice Act 1982; and (b) in the case of a sentence for a determinate period, a youth custody sentence under section 6 of the Criminal Justice Act 1982 for the like term. In Northern Ireland— (a) in the case of a sentence for a life term, imprisonment for life; (b) in the case of a sentence for a determinate period of 3 years or more, imprisonment for the like term; and (c) in the case of a sentence for a term of less than 3 years, detention in a young offenders centre for the like term. In the Channel Islands or the Isle of Man, imprisonment for the like term.
Borstal training.	In England and Wales, a youth custody sentence under section 6 of the Criminal Justice Act 1982 for a term of 12 months. In Northern Ireland, detention in a young offenders centre for a term of 2 years. In the Channel Islands or the Isle of Man, imprisonment for a term of 12 months.
Detention in a detention centre.	In England and Wales, a detention centre order under section 4 of the Criminal Justice Act 1982 for the like term. In Northern Ireland, detention in a young offenders centre for the like term. In Jersey, detention in a young offenders centre for the like term.

PART III

Column 1 Description of sentence which may be passed in Northern Ireland.	Column 2 Equivalent sentence which may be passed elsewhere in the United Kingdom, the Channel Islands or the Isle of Man.
Imprisonment for life.	In England and Wales— (a) in the case of a person aged 21 or over when sentenced, imprisonment for life; and (b) in the case of a person aged not less than 18 but under 21 when sentenced, custody for life under section 8 of the Criminal Justice Act 1982. In Scotland— (a) in the case of a person aged 21 or over when sentenced, imprisonment for life; and (b) in the case of a person aged not less than 18 but under 21 when sentenced, detention for life under section 205(3) of the Criminal Procedure (Scotland) Act 1975. In the Channel Islands or the Isle of Man, imprisonment for life.
Imprisonment for a determinate period.	In England and Wales— (a) in the case of a person aged 21 or over when sentenced, imprisonment for the like term; and (b) in the case of a person aged not less than 15 but under 21 when sentenced, a youth custody sentence under section 6 of the Criminal Justice Act 1982 for the like term. In Scotland— (a) in the case of a person aged 21 or over when sentenced, imprisonment for the like term; (b) in the case of a person aged not less than 16 but under 21 when sentenced, detention in a young offenders institution under section 208(3) of the Criminal Procedure (Scotland) Act 1975 for the like term; and (c) in the case of a person aged less than 16 when sentenced, detention under section 206(1) of that Act for the like term. In the Channel Islands or the Isle of Man, imprisonment for the like term.

SCHEDULE 1—PART III—(continued)

Column 1 Description of sentence which may be passed in Northern Ireland.	Column 2 Equivalent sentence which may be passed elsewhere in the United Kingdom, the Channel Islands or the Isle of Man.
Detention in a young offenders centre.	In England and Wales— (a) in the case of a sentence for a term of not more than 4 months imposed on a male offender, a detention centre order under section 4 of the Criminal Justice Act 1982 for the like term; and (b) in the case of any sentence imposed on a female offender or a sentence for a term of more than 4 months imposed on a male offender, a youth custody sentence under section 6 of that Act for the like term. In Scotland, detention in a young offenders institution under section 208(3) of the Criminal Procedure (Scotland) Act 1975 for the like term. In the Channel Islands or the Isle of Man, imprisonment for the like term.

PART IV

Column 1	Column 2
Description of sentence which may be passed in the Channel Islands or the Isle of Man.	Equivalent sentence which may be passed in the United Kingdom.
Imprisonment for life.	In England and Wales— (a) in the case of a person aged 21 or over when sentenced, imprisonment for life; and (b) in the case of a person aged not less than 17 but under 21 when sentenced, custody for life under section 8 of the Criminal Justice Act 1982. In Scotland— (a) in the case of a person aged 21 or over when sentenced, imprisonment for life; and (b) in the case of a person aged not less than 18 but under 21 when sentenced, detention for life under section 205(3) of the Criminal Procedure (Scotland) Act 1975. In Northern Ireland, imprisonment for life.
Imprisonment for a determinate period.	In England and Wales— (a) in the case of a person aged 21 or over when sentenced, imprisonment for the like term; and (b) in the case of a person aged under 21 when sentenced, a youth custody sentence under section 6 of the Criminal Justice Act 1982 for the like term. In Scotland— (a) in the case of a person aged 21 or over when sentenced, imprisonment for the like term; and (b) in the case of a person aged under 21 when sentenced, detention in a young offenders institution under section 208(3) of the Criminal Procedure (Scotland) Act 1975 for the like term. In Northern Ireland— (a) in the case of a person aged 21 or over when sentenced, imprisonment for the like term; and (b) in the case of a person aged under 21 when sentenced— (i) if the term specified is less than 3 years, detention in a young offenders centre for the like term; (ii) if the term specified is 3 years or more, imprisonment for the like term.
Borstal training.	In England and Wales, a youth custody sentence under section 6 of the Criminal Justice Act 1982 for a term of 12 months. In Scotland, borstal training. In Northern Ireland, detention in a young offenders centre for a term of 2 years.

SCHEDULE 2   Article 2(*b*)

EQUIVALENT SENTENCES OF DETENTION UNDER
ENACTMENTS RELATING TO CHILDREN AND
YOUNG PERSONS

PART I

1. In England and Wales, detention during Her Majesty's pleasure under section 53(1) of the Children and Young Persons Act 1933**(a)**.

2. In Scotland, detention without limit of time under section 205(2) of the Criminal Procedure (Scotland) Act 1975**(b)**.

3. In Northern Ireland, detention during pleasure under section 73(1) of the Children and Young Persons Act (Northern Ireland) 1968**(c)**.

4. In Jersey, detention under Article 12 of the Children (Jersey) Law 1969.

5. In Guernsey, detention under section 1(2) of the Homicide (Guernsey) Law 1965.

6. In the Isle of Man, detention under section 47(1) of the Children and Young Persons Act 1966 (an Act of Tynwald).

PART II

1. In England and Wales, detention under section 53(2) of the Children and Young Persons Act 1933.

2. In Scotland, detention under section 206(1) of the Criminal Procedure (Scotland) Act 1975**(d)**.

3. In Northern Ireland, detention under section 73(2) of the Children and Young Persons Act (Northern Ireland) 1968.

4. In Jersey, detention under Article 13 of the Children (Jersey) Law 1969.

5. In Guernsey, detention under section 34 of the Loi ayant rapport a la Protection des Enfants et des Jeunes Personnes 1917.

6. In the Isle of Man, detention under section 47(2) of the Children and Young Persons Act 1966 (an Act of Tynwald).

(a) 1933 c. 12.
(b) 1975 c. 21; section 205(2) was substituted by section 43 of the Criminal Justice (Scotland) Act 1980 (c. 62).
(c) 1968 c. 34.
(d) Section 206(1) was substituted by section 44 of the Criminal Justice (Scotland) Act 1980.

EXPLANATORY NOTE

(This Note is not part of the Order.)

This Order designates as equivalent sentences various descriptions of sentence which may be passed in one part of the United Kingdom or in the Channel Islands or the Isle of Man and descriptions of sentence which may be passed elsewhere in the United Kingdom or in those Islands, for the purposes of the provisions of the Criminal Justice Act 1961 (as amended) which relate to the transfer of offenders (to serve their sentences or for temporary purposes) to another area of jurisdiction within the United Kingdom or those Islands. The broad effect of sections 26, 27 and 39 of the 1961 Act is that an offender is upon transfer to be removed to any institution which would be appropriate for the detention of an offender of the same age serving an equivalent sentence, as designated by this Order, in the place to which he is transferred.

STATUTORY INSTRUMENTS

1983 No. 1315

PENSIONS

The Pensions Increase (Local Authorities' etc. Pensions) (Amendment) Regulations 1983

Made - - - - -	*31st August* 1983
Laid before Parliament	*8th September* 1983
Coming into Operation	*30th September* 1983

The Treasury, in exercise of the powers conferred upon the Minister for the Civil Service by section 5(2) of the Pensions (Increase) Act 1971(a), and now vested in them(b), and of all other powers enabling them in that behalf, hereby make the following regulations:—

1.—(1) These regulations may be cited as the Pensions Increase (Local Authorities' etc. Pensions) (Amendment) Regulations 1983, and shall come into operation on 30th September 1983.

(2) In these regulations "the 1974 regulations" means the Pensions Increase (Local Authorities' etc. Pensions) Regulations 1974(c).

2. Regulation 4 of the 1974 regulations is amended—

   (a) by substituting for the words ", 3 or 4", in paragraph (1), the words "or 3";

   (b) by inserting after the words "this paragraph", in paragraph (1), the words "and in paragraph (1A)"; and

   (c) by inserting after paragraph (1) the following:

   "(1A) In the case of a pension specified in paragraph 6 of the Schedule to these Regulations, any increase of pension payable by virtue of these Regulations (including any amount by which the basic rate of the pension has been increased before 30th September 1983 shall be paid by the authority by whom the pension is payable ("the pension authority"), but—

(a) 1971 c. 56.   (b) S.I. 1981/1670.   (c) S.I. 1974/1740.

(*a*) where the functions in connection with which the latest services in respect of which the pension is payable were rendered—

(i) are no longer exercisable by any statutory authority, or

(ii) are superannuation functions or compensation functions,

the pension authority shall be reimbursed 82% of the cost of any such increase by the other water authorities in accordance with the Table below, and

(*b*) where sub-paragraph (*a*) does not apply and the pension authority are not the last employing authority, the pension authority shall be reimbursed the cost of any such increase by the last employing authority.

TABLE

Water authority	Percentage of total Cost
Anglian	11
Northumbrian	4
North West	15
Southern	6
South West	4
Thames	19
Wessex	4
Welsh	9
Yorkshire	10

(1B) In paragraph (1A)—

"superannuation functions" means the functions of an administering authority under the Local Government Superannuation Regulations 1974 to 1983**(a)**, and

"compensation functions" means functions relating to—

(*a*) the payment of benefit or compensation in respect of early retirement or for loss of employment, or

(*b*) redundancy payments within the meaning of the Employment Protection (Consolidation) Act 1978**(b)**,

which were exercisable by the National Water Council, or which are exercisable by the pension authority by virtue of regulations under paragraph 8 of Schedule 2 to the Water Act 1983**(c)**.".

(a) S.I. 1974/520, 1977/1121, 1845, 1978/266, 822, 1738, 1739, 1979/2, 592, 1534, 1980/216, 233, 234, 1981/1250, 1509, 1982/908, 1514, 1983/178.

(b) 1978 c. 44.

(c) 1983 c. 23.

3. The Schedule to the 1974 regulations is amended by deleting paragraphs 4 and 5.

D. J. F. Hunt,
Donald Thompson,
Two of the Lords Commissioners
of Her Majesty's Treasury.

31st August 1983.

EXPLANATORY NOTE

(This Note is not part of the Regulations.)

These regulations amend the Pensions Increase (Local Authorities' etc. Pensions) Regulations 1974 so as to secure that the cost of increasing certain pensions is borne by appropriate authorities. The pensions are those which become payable by the Severn–Trent Water Authority ("the pension authority") instead of by the National Water Council ("the Council"), in consequence of the dissolution of the latter body.

Where the pensioner's last employment was in connection with superannuation on compensation functions of, or transferred to the pension authority from, the Council, or functions which have ceased to be exercisable by any statutory authority, the cost is to be apportioned among all the water authorities. In other cases where the relevant functions are exercisable by the pension authority, that authority are to bear the cost themselves. Where the relevant functions are still exercisable by a statutory authority other than the pension authority, the cost is to be borne by the former authority.

APPENDIX

CERTAIN INSTRUMENTS NOT REGISTERED AS STATUTORY INSTRUMENTS

Orders in Council

Letters Patent

and Royal Instructions

relating to the Constitutions etc. of Overseas Territories or to appeals to the Judicial Committee

Royal Proclamations etc.

BY THE QUEEN

A PROCLAMATION

ALTERING THE PROCLAMATION OF THE 20TH APRIL 1983 DETERMINING
THE DESIGN FOR THE ONE POUND COIN

ELIZABETH R.

Whereas under section 3(1)(*b*) and (*h*) of the Coinage Act 1971 We have power, with the advice of Our Privy Council, by Proclamation to determine the design of any coin to be made at Our Mint and to alter any Proclamation previously made under the said section:

And Whereas by Our Proclamation dated the twentieth day of April 1983 We ordered that a new coin of nickel brass of the denomination of one pound should be made at Our Mint:

And Whereas it appears to Us desirable to determine new designs for the said one pound coin.

We, therefore, in pursuance of the said section 3(1)(*b*) and (*h*) and of all other powers enabling Us in that behalf do hereby, by and with the advice of Our Privy Council, proclaim, direct and ordain as follows:—

1. The following section shall be substituted for section 2 of Our said Proclamation of the twentieth day of April 1983:—
   "2. The design for the said coin shall be as follows:—
For the obverse impression Our effigy with the inscription "ELIZABETH·II D·G·REG·F·D·" and the date of the year, and for the reverse either

   (*a*) the Ensigns Armorial of Our United Kingdom of Great Britain and Northern Ireland,

   (*b*) an Oak Tree enfiling a representation of Our Royal Diadem,

   (*c*) a Thistle eradicated enfiling a representation of Our Royal Diadem,

   (*d*) a Leek eradicated enfiling a representation of Our Royal Diadem, or

   (*e*) a Flax Plant eradicated enfiling a representation of Our Royal Diadem

and beneath the same the words "ONE POUND". The coin shall have a graining upon the edge and in incuse letters the inscription "DECUS ET TUTAMEN" or, in the case of a coin bearing the impression of a Thistle, "NEMO ME IMPUNE LACESSIT" or, in the case of a coin bearing the impression of a Leek, "PLEIDIOL WYF I'M GWLAD"."

2. This Proclamation shall come into force on the twenty-third day of June One thousand nine hundred and eighty-three.

Given at Our Court at Buckingham Palace, this twenty-second day of June in the year of our Lord One thousand nine hundred and eighty-three and in the thirty-second year of Our Reign.

GOD SAVE THE QUEEN

BY THE QUEEN

A PROCLAMATION

APPOINTING TUESDAY, 27TH DECEMBER 1983 AND MONDAY, 28TH MAY 1984 AS BANK HOLIDAYS IN SCOTLAND AND APPOINTING MONDAY, 2ND JANUARY 1984 AND MONDAY, 7TH MAY 1984 AS BANK HOLIDAYS IN ENGLAND, WALES AND NORTHERN IRELAND.

ELIZABETH R.

Whereas We consider it desirable that Tuesday, the twenty-seventh day of December in the year 1983 and Monday, the twenty-eighth day of May in the year 1984 should be bank holidays in Scotland:

And whereas We consider it desirable that Monday, the second day of January and Monday, the seventh day of May in the year 1984 should be bank holidays in England, Wales and Northern Ireland:

We, therefore, in pursuance of section 1(3) of the Banking and Financial Dealings Act 1971, do hereby appoint Tuesday, the twenty-seventh day of December in the year 1983 and Monday, the twenty-eighth day of May in the year 1984 to be bank holidays in Scotland and Monday, the second day of January and Monday, the seventh day of May in the year 1984 to be bank holidays in England, Wales and Northern Ireland.

Given at Our Court at Buckingham Palace this twenty-second day of June in the year of our Lord One thousand nine hundred and eighty-three and in the thirty-second year of Our Reign.

GOD SAVE THE QUEEN

HONG KONG

THE HONG KONG ADDITIONAL INSTRUCTIONS 1983

Dated: 24th August 1983.   *ELIZABETH, R.*

ADDITIONAL INSTRUCTIONS to Our Governor and Commander-in-Chief in and over Our Colony of Hong Kong and its Dependencies or other Officer for the time being Administering the Government of Our said Colony and its Dependencies.

We do hereby direct and enjoin and declare Our will and pleasure as follows:—

Citation, construction and commencement.

1.—(1) These Instructions may be cited as the Hong Kong Additional Instructions 1983 and shall be construed as one with the Hong Kong Royal Instructions of 1917 as amended (hereinafter called "the principal Instructions").

(2) The Hong Kong Royal Instructions 1917 to 1980 and these Instructions may be cited together as the Hong Kong Royal Instructions 1917 to 1983.

(3) These Instructions shall come into effect on the first day of September, 1983.

Amendment of Clause II of principal Instructions.

2. Clause II of the principal Instructions is amended by deleting the words "of Secretary for Home Affairs,".

Amendment of Clause XIII of principal Instructions.

3. Clause XIII of the principal Instructions is amended by—
  (*a*) deleting the words "Secretary for Home Affairs,"; and
  (*b*) substituting for the word "twenty-two" the word "twenty-five" and for the word "twenty-seven" the word "twenty-nine".

Amendment of Clause XIX of principal Instructions.

4. Clause XIX of the principal Instructions is amended by substituting for the word "ten" the word "twenty".

Given at Our Court at St. James's this twenty-fourth day of August 1983 in the thirty-second year of Our Reign.

NOTE
For List of Abbreviations used in this table, see p. ix in part I of this Edition.

Modifications to Legislation

Year and Number (or date)	Act or instrument	How affected
1824	Vagrancy Act (c. 83)	s. 4 **r.**, 1983/201
1854	Lands Valuation (S.) Act (c. 91)	s. 42 **am.**, 1983/120
1867	Lyon King of Arms Act (c. 17)	Sch. B **am.**, 1983/1072
1871	Prevention of Crime Act (c. 112)	ss. 7, 15 **r.**, 1983/201
1875	Explosives Act (c. 17)	ss. 15, 18, 21 **am.**, 1983/219
1877	Colonial Stock Act (c. 59)	s. 20 **am.**, 1983/882
1885	Sea Fisheries (S.) Amdt. Act (c. 70)	s. 4 **am.**, 1983/24
1892	Sheriff Cts. (S.) Extracts Act (c. 17)	s. 9 **am.**, 1983/409
1894	Merchant Shipping Act (c. 60)	ss. 418, 419 **r.** (with savings), 1983/708, 762 (as extended by the latter to certain overseas territories) ss. 420, 424 **r.**, 1983/708, 762 (as extended by the latter to certain overseas territories) s. 427 **am.**, 1983/882 s. 460 **am.**, 1983/808 s. 680 **am.**, 1983/24 s. 692 **am.**, 1983/762, 808
1898	Criminal Evidence Act (c. 36)	s. 1, proviso, para. (*h*)— **r.** (not S.), 1983/182 **r.** (S.), 1983/758
1899	Electric Lighting (Clauses) Act (c. 19)	ss. 2, 52, 54(2) **r.**, Sch. **r.**, 1983/790
1903	Licensing (S.) Act (c. 25)	**r.**, 1983/201
1906	Alkali, &c. Works Regulation Act (c. 14)	ss. 1, 2 **am.**, ss. 6, 7 **r.**, ss. 9, 16, 27 **am.**, Sch. 1 **r.**, 1983/943
	Dogs Act (c. 32)	s. 3 **am.**, 1983/201
1907	Sheriff Cts. (S.) Act (c. 51)	Sch. 1 **replaced**, 1983/747
1909	Electric Lighting Act (c. 34)	s. 23 **r.**, 1983/790
1912 348	Public Trustee Rules	**am.**, 1983/1050
1919	Electricity (Supply) Act (c. 100)	s. 11 **r.**, s. 36 **am.**, 1983/790
1922	Electricity (Supply) Act (c. 46)	s. 23 **r.**, 1983/790
329	Indiarubber Regs.	**am.**, 1983/714
731	Chemical Works Regs.	**am.**, 1983/714

Year and Number (or date)	Act or instrument	How affected
1925	Criminal Justice Act (c. 86).. ..	s. 12 **r.** (not S.), 1983/182
	Imperial Institute Act (c.xvii) ..	s. 8 **am.**, 1983/882
231	Docks Regs.	**am.**, 1983/644
1934		
276	Docks Regs.	**am.**, 1983/644
1321	Public Service Vehicles (Drivers' and Conductors' Licences) Regs.	**am.**, 1983/916
1346	London Cab O.	**am.**, 1983/653
1936	Electricity Supply (Meters) Act (c. 20)	s. 1 **am.**, 1983/790
	Public Health Act (c. 49)	s. 92 **am.**, 1983/943
1297	Fowl Pest O.	**am.**, 1983/941
1938		
661	Trade Marks Rules	**am.**, 1983/181
1944		
119	Prevention of Fraud (Investments) Act Licensing Regs.	**r.**, 1983/587
334	Parliamentary Writs O.	**r.** (with saving), 1983/605
750	Parliamentary Writs (N.I.) O. ..	**r.**, 1983/606
1946	Acquisition of Land (Authorisation Procedure) Act (c. 49)	Sch. 4 **am.**, 1983/790
258	Patent Fuel Manufacture (Health and Welfare) Special Regs.	**am.**, 1983/714
424	Educational Services and Research Grant Regs.	**r.**, 1983/74
1947	Electricity Act (c. 54)	ss. 2, 37 **am.**, Sch. 4 **am.**, 1983/790
1948	Companies Act (c. 38)	6th Sch., Pt. II, form **replaced**, 1983/1023
	Criminal Justice Act (c. 58).. ..	ss. 19, 20, 48(2), 52, 76(2) **r.** (not S.), 1983/182
	Representation of the People Act (c. 65)	Sch. 1 **replaced**, 1983/417, 418, 422
960	Ice Cream (S.) Regs.	**am.**, 1983/270
1949	Merchant Shipping (Safety Convention) Act (c. 43)	s. 2 **am.**, 1983/882 s. 21 **am.**, 1983/708
	Coast Protection Act (c. 74) ..	Sch. 4, para. 91 **replaced**, 1983/1203
316	Enrolment of Deeds (Change of Name) Regs.	**r.**, 1983/680
330	Companies (Winding-up) Rules ..	**am.**, 1983/727
386	Heather and Grass Burning (E. and W.) Regs.	**r.**, 1983/425
495	Heather and Grass Burning (Railways) General Licence	**r.**, 1983/425
789	Gas (Testing) Regs.	**am.**, 1983/363
2224	Dry Cleaning Special Regs... ..	**am.**, 1983/977
1950		
533	Assurance Companies Rules ..	**r.**, 1983/224
1650	Civil Defence (Designation of the Min. of Food) O.	**am.**, 1983/609

Year and Number (or date)	Act or instrument	How affected
1951		
322	H.C. (Redistribution of Seats) (No. 3) O.	**am.,** 1983/417
323	H.C. (Redistribution of Seats) (No. 4) O.	**am.,** 1983/417
324	H.C. (Redistribution of Seats) (No. 5) O.	**am.,** 1983/417
325	H.C. (Redistribution of Seats) (No. 6) O.	**am.,** 1983/417
326	H.C. (Redistribution of Seats) (No. 7) O.	**am.,** 1983/417
327	H.C. (Redistribution of Seats) (No. 8) O.	**am.,** 1983/417
431	H.C. (Redistribution of Seats) (No. 9) O.	**am.,** 1983/417
432	H.C. (Redistribution of Seats) (No. 10) O.	**am.,** 1983/417
1390	H.C. (Redistribution of Seats) (Cardiff, Barry and Monmouth) O.	**am.,** 1983/418
1952	Prison Act (c. 52)..	ss. 44 – 46, 49(2)(*b*) **r.** (not S.), 1983/182
		s. 55 **am.,** 1983/24
	Visiting Forces Act (c. 67)..	s. 1 **am.,** 1983/882
452	H.C. (Redistribution of Seats) (Bristol, North Somerset and Weston Super Mare) O.	**am.,** 1983/417
453	H.C. (Redistribution of Seats) (Sunderland and Houghton-le-Spring) O.	**am.,** 1983/417
1348	H.C. (Redistribution of Seats) (Stockton-on-Tees and Sedgefield) O.	**am.,** 1983/417
1350	H.C. (Redistribution of Seats) (Worcester and South Worcestershire) O.	**am.,** 1983/417
1432	Detention Centre Rules	**r.,** 1983/569
1464	Central Midwives Bd. for Scotland (Reconstitution) O.	**am.,** 1983/134
1689	Factories (Testing of Aircraft Engines and Accessories) Special Regs.	**am.,** 1983/979
1859	Civil Defence (Designation of the Min. of Transport) O.	**r.,** 1983/609
2230	Methylated Spirits Regs.	**r.,** 1983/252
1953		
741	H.C. (Redistribution of Seats) (The Hartlepools, Bishop Auckland and Sedgefield) O.	**am.,** 1983/417
742	H.C. (Redistribution of Seats) (Stockport South and Cheadle) O.	**am.,** 1983/417
744	H.C. (Redistribution of Seats) (Ipswich, Eye and Sudbury and Woodbridge) O.	**am.,** 1983/417
1196	Civil Defence (Designation of the Min. of Fuel and Power) O.	**r.,** 1983/609
1545	Mule Spinning (Health) Special Regs...	**am.,** 1983/714
1954		
796	Mines and Quarries Act (c. 70)	s. 182 **am.,** 1983/710
	Non-Contentious Probate Rules	**am.,** 1983/623
966	Brakes on Pedal Cycles Regs.	**r.,** 1983/1176
1711	Juvenile Cts. (Constitution) Rules	**am.,** 1983/675

Year and Number (or date)	Act or instrument	How affected
1955	Army Act 1955 (c. 18)	s. 71A(2)— **r.** (not S.), 1983/182 **r.** (S.), 1983/758 s. 225 **am.**, 1983/882
	Air Force Act 1955 (c. 19)	s. 71A(2)— **r.** (not S.), 1983/182 **r.** (S.), 1983/758 s. 223 **am.**, 1983/882
1125	Cinematograph (Safety) (S.) Regs. ..	**am.**, 1983/367
1993	Slaughter of Animals (Prevention of Cruelty) (S.) Regs.	**am.**, 1983/874
1956	Admin. of Justice Act (c. 46) ..	s. 8 **am.**, 1983/762 Sch. 1, Pt. I **am.**, 1983/708
	South of Scotland Electricity Order Confirmation Act (c. xciv)	s. 40 **r.**, 1983/790
235	Civil Defence (Designation of the Min. of Fuel and Power) (Amdt.) O.	**r.**, 1983/609
419	Civil Defence (Designation of the Min. of Transport and Civil Aviation) (Amdt.) O.	**r.**, 1983/609
1423	Oil in Navigable Waters (Ships' Equipment) (No. 1) Regs.	**r.**, 1983/1106
1611	Fowl Pest (Infected Areas Restrictions) O.	**am.**, 1983/941
1765	Coal and Other Mines (Safety-Lamps and Lighting) Regs.	**am.**, 1983/710
1778	Misc. Mines O.	**am.**, 1983/994
1779	Misc. Mines (Electricity) O. ..	**am.**, 1983/994, 1130
1780	Quarries O.	**am.**, 1983/1026
1781	Quarries (Electricity) O. ..	**am.**, 1983/1026
1957	Electricity Act (c. 48)	ss. 2, 30 **am.**, Sch. 4 **am.**, 1983/790
	Naval Discipline Act (c. 53).. ..	s. 43A(2)— **r.** (not S.), 1983/182 **r.** (S.), 1983/758 s. 135 **am.**, 1983/882
1157	Landlord and Tenant (Notices) Regs.	**am.**, 1983/133
1424	Oil in Navigable Waters (Ships' Equipment) Regs.	**r.**, 1983/1106
1958	Prevention of Fraud (Investments) Act (c. 45)	s. 3 **am.**, 1983/586
	North of Scotland Electricity Order Confirmation Act (c. ii)	s. 27 **r.**, 1983/790
61	Work in Compressed Air Special Regs.	**am.**, 1983/714
1526	Oil in Navigable Waters (Enforcement of Convention) O.	**r.**, 1983/1106
1971	Slaughter of Pigs (Anaesthesia) Regs.	**am.**, 1983/689
1990	Attendance Centre Rules	**am.**, 1983/621
1991	Magistrates' Cts. (Attendance Centre) Rules	**am.**, 1983/525
2110	Quarries (Ropeways and Vehicles) Regs.	**am.**, 1983/1026
2166	Slaughter of Animals (Prevention of Cruelty) Regs.	**am.**, 1983/688

Year and Number (or date)	Act or instrument	How affected
1959	County Cts. Act (c. 22)	s. 70 **am.**, 1983/708
366	Special Schools and Establishments (Grant) Regs.	**r.**, 1983/74
377	Maintenance Orders (Facilities for Enforcement) O.	**r.** (with saving), 1983/1124
928	Arsenic in Food (S.) Regs... ..	**am.**, 1983/270
1832	Direct Grant Schools Regs... ..	**am.**, 1983/74
1860	Nat. Insurance (Non-participation—Certificates) Regs.	**am.**, 1983/118
2119	Nat. Insurance (Non-participation—Appeals and References) Regs.	**am.**, 1983/118
2182	Fluorine in Food (S.) Regs... ..	**am.**, 1983/270
2258	Misc. Mines (Explosives) Regs. ..	**am.**, 1983/994
2259	Quarries (Explosives) Regs... ..	**am.**, 1983/1026
1960		
449	Parliamentary Constituencies (Barnsley and Wakefield) O.	**am.**, 1983/417
450	Parliamentary Constituencies (Coventry and Mid-Warwickshire) O.	**am.**, 1983/417
451	Parliamentary Constituencies (Gateshead) O.	**am.**, 1983/417
452	Parliamentary Constituencies (Gloucester and Stroud) O.	**am.**, 1983/417
453	Parliamentary Constituencies (Grimsby and Louth) O.	**am.**, 1983/417
454	Parliamentary Constituencies (Ilford and Woodford) O.	**am.**, 1983/417
455	Parliamentary Constituencies (Leeds, York and Barkston Ash) O.	**am.**, 1983/417
456	Parliamentary Constituencies (Lincoln and Grantham) O.	**am.**, 1983/417
457	Parliamentary Constituencies (Middlesbrough) O.	**am.**, 1983/417
458	Parliamentary Constituencies (North Somerset and Wells) O.	**am.**, 1983/417
459	Parliamentary Constituencies (Oxford and Henley) O.	**am.**, 1983/417
460	Parliamentary Constituencies (Portsmouth, Langstone and Petersfield) O.	**am.**, 1983/417
461	Parliamentary Constituencies (Preston South and South Fylde) O.	**am.**, 1983/417
462	Parliamentary Constituencies (Reading Newbury and Wokingham) O.	**am.**, 1983/417
463	Parliamentary Constituencies (South-West Lancashire) O.	**am.**, 1983/417
464	Parliamentary Constituencies (Walsall) O.	**am.**, 1983/417
465	Parliamentary Constituencies (Wandsworth, Kingston-upon-Thames and Richmond) O.	**am.**, 1983/417

Year and Number (or date)	Act or instrument	How affected
1960 *contd*		
468	Parliamentary Constituencies (S.) (Midlothian, Edinburgh East, Edinburgh South, Edinburgh West, Edinburgh, Pentlands) O.	**am.**, 1983/422
469	Parliamentary Constituencies (S.) (West Fife and Dunfermline Burghs) O.	**am.**, 1983/422
470	Parliamentary Constituencies (S.) (West Renfrewshire and Greenock) O.	**am.**, 1983/422
1015	Coal Mines (Firedamp Drainage) Regs.	**am.**, 1983/1130
1139	Mental Health Review Tribunal Rules	**r.**, 1983/942
1216	Licensed Dealers (Conduct of Business) Rules	**r.**, 1983/585
1241	Mental Health (Hospital and Guardianship) Regs.	**r.**, 1983/893
1337	Agricultural Holdings (Specification of Forms) (S.) Instrt.	**r.**, 1983/1073
1932	Shipbuilding and Ship-repairing Regs.	**am.**, 1983/644
1935	Investigation Ctee. Rules	**am.**, 1983/545
2437	Skimmed Milk with Non-Milk Fat (S.) Regs.	**am.**, 1983/270
1961	Factories Act (c. 34)	ss. 2, 3, 18, 19, 26, 27, 29, 30, 39, 68, 175, 176 **am.**, 1st Sch. **replaced**, 1983/978
	Criminal Justice Act (c. 39).. ..	ss. 1, 3 – 7, 10 – 13 **r.** (not S.), 1983/182 s. 32(2)(*a*)(*c*)(*e*)— **r.** (not S.), 1983/182 **r.** (S.), 1983/758 s. 34 **r.** (not S.), 1983/182 ss. 38(5), 39(1)— **am.** (not S.), 1983/182 **am.** (S.), 1983/758 Schs. 1 **r.** (not S.), 4 **am.** (not S.), 6 **r.** (not S.), 1983/182
	Trustee Investments Act (c. 62) ..	1st Sch., Pt. II **am.**, 1983/772
243	Food (Meat Inspection) (S.) Regs. ..	**am.**, 1983/702
431	Shipbuilding (Lifting Appliances etc. Forms) O.	**am.**, 1983/644
1962		
1593	Mental Health (Hospital and Guardianship) Amdt. Regs.	**r.**, 1983/893
2045	Building Societies (Forms and Fees) Regs.	**am.**, 1983/372
2557	Veterinary Surgery (Exemptions) O...	**am.**, 1983/6

Year and Number (or date)	Act or instrument	How affected
1963	Weights and Measures Act (c. 31) ..	Sch. 3, Pt. VI **am.**, 1983/1077
795	Landlord and Tenant (Notices) Regs.	**r.**, 1983/133
1229	Meat Inspection Regs.	**am.**, 1983/174
1461	Bread and Flour (S.) Regs... ..	**am.**, 1983/270
1591	Liquid Egg (Pasteurisation) (S.) Regs.	**am.**, 1983/270
1710	Weights and Measures Regs... ..	**am.**, 1983/914
1830	Betting Levy Appeal Tribunal (S.) Rules	**am.**, 1983/72
1888	Slaughter of Animals (Stunning Pens) (S.) Regs.	**am.**, 1983/874
1964	Agriculture and Horticulture Act (c. 28)	Pt. III, s. 20(1) **replaced**, 1983/1053
44	Meat (Treatment) (S.) Regs. ..	**am.**, 1983/270
388	Prison Rules	**am.**, 1983/568
760	Soft Drinks Regs...	**am.**, 1983/1211
1083	Special Schools and Establishments (Grant) (Amdt.) Regs.	**r.**, 1983/74
1255	Diseases of Animals (Seizure of Carcases, etc.) O.	**am.**, 1983/346
1410	Act of Adj. (Criminal Legal Aid Fees)	**am.**, 1983/972
1736	Docks Certificates (No. 2) O. ..	**am.**, 1983/644
1965	Merchant Shipping Act (c. 47) ..	s. 1 **am.**, Sch. 1 **am.**, 1983/440
	Nat. Insurance Act (c. 51).. ..	s. 36 **am.**, (21.11.83), 1983/1244
	Hire-Purchase Act (c. 66)	s. 2 **am.**, 1983/611
	Hire-Purchase (S.) Act (c. 67) ..	s. 2 **am.**, 1983/611
321	A.S. (Rules of Ct., consolidation and amdt.)	**am.**, 1983/397, 398, 656, 826, 971, 1210
1500	County Ct. Funds Rules	**am.**, 1983/291
1776	Rules of the Supreme Ct.	**am.**, 1983/531, 1181
1995	Industrial and Provident Societies Regs.	**am.**, 1983/350
1966	Housing (S.) Act (c. 49) .. —.	s. 185 **am.**, 1983/24
164	Pneumoconiosis, Byssinosis and Misc. Diseases Benefit Scheme	**r.**, 1983/136
581	Pneumoconiosis, Byssinosis and Misc. Diseases Benefit (Amdt.) Scheme	**r.**, 1983/136
1143	Alkali, &c. Works O.	**r.**, 1983/943
1206	Salad Cream (S.) Regs.	**am.**, 1983/270
1252	Butter (S.) Regs.	**am.**, 1983/270
1263	Mineral Hydrocarbons in Food (S.) Regs.	**am.**, 1983/270
1967	West Indies Act (c. 4)	s. 6 **am.**, 1983/1107
	Parliamentary Commr. Act (c. 13) ..	Sch. 2 **am.**, 1983/879, 1127
	Legal Aid (S.) Act (c. 43) {. ..	ss. 2, 3 **am.**, 1983/532
	Criminal Justice Act (c. 80)..	s. 60(3)(b)(5A)(b)(c) **r.** (not S.), 1983/182 s. 60 **am.** (S.), 1983/758 ss. 63, 66(1), 67(1)(b) **r.** (not S.), 1983/182
	Countryside (S.) Act (c. 86).. ..	s. 56 **r.**, s. 57 **am.**, 1983/201

Year and Number (or date)	Act or instrument	How affected
1967 *contd*		
223	West Indies Associated States Supreme Ct. O.	**am.**, 1983/1108
224	West Indies Associated States (Appeals to Privy Council) O.	**r.** (with saving), 1983/1109
228	Saint Christopher, Nevis and Anguilla Constitution O.	**r.** (19.9.83), 1983/881
230	Montserrat O.	**am.**, 1983/1112
231	Virgin Is. (Cts.) O.	**am.**, 1983/1112
233	Montserrat (Appeals to Privy Council) O.	**am.**, 1983/1108
234	Virgin Is. (Appeals to Privy Council) O.	**am.**, 1983/1108
388	Food (Control of Irradiation) (S.) Regs.	**am.**, 1983/270
879	Carcinogenic Substances Regs. ..	**am.**, 1983/714
1077	Meat Pie and Sausage Roll (S.) Regs.	**am.**, 1983/270
1078	Sausage and Other Meat Product (S.) Regs.	**am.**, 1983/270
1079	Canned Meat Product (S.) Regs. ..	**am.**, 1983/270
1141	Clyde Dockyard Port of Gareloch and Loch Long O.	**am.**, 1983/878
1205	Pneumoconiosis, Byssinosis and Misc. Diseases Benefit (Amdt.) Scheme	**r.**, 1983/136
1233	Pneumoconiosis, Byssinosis and Misc. Diseases Benefit (Amdt.) (No. 2) Scheme	**r.**, 1983/136
1310	Industrial and Provident Societies Regs.	**am.**, 1983/350
1462	Local Review Ctee. Rules	**am.**, 1983/622
1582	Solvents in Food Regs.	**am.**, 1983/1211
1792	Land Registration (Matrimonial Homes) Rules	**r.**, 1983/40
1831	Landlord and Tenant (Notices) Regs.	**am.**, 1983/133
1866	Ice-Cream Regs.	**am.**, 1983/1211
1968	Criminal Appeal Act (c. 19) ..	s. 20 **am.** (not S.), 1983/182
	Theatres Act (c. 54)	s. 2 **am.**, 1983/201
	Clean Air Act (c. 62)	s. 11(2) **r.**, 1983/943
	Gaming Act (c. 65)	s. 48 **am.**, 1983/127, 333
	Medicines Act (c. 67)	ss. 112, 113, 115 **am.**, 1983/62
208	Police Cadets (S.) Regs.	**am.**, 1983/318
263	Solvents in Food (S.) Regs... ..	**am.**, 1983/270
392	Town and Country Planning (Grants) (S.) Regs.	**am.**, 1983/108
780	Ionising Radiations (Unsealed Radio-active Substances) Regs.	**am.**, 1983/714
1014	Detention Centre (Amdt.) Rules ..	**r.**, 1983/569
1163	Pensions Commutation Regs. ..	**am.**, 1983/1052
1314	Wireless Telegraphy (General Licence Charges) Regs.	**am.**, 1983/670
1978	County Cts. (Race Relations Jurisdiction) O.	**r.**, 1983/713

Year and Number (or date)	Act or instrument	How affected
1968 *contd*		
2076	Immature Cod and Haddock (Distant Waters) O.	r., 1983/255
1969	Post Office Act (c. 48)	Sch. 4, para. 11 r., 1983/790
	Trustee Savings Bank Act (c. 50) ..	s. 34 am., 1983/647
	Children and Young Persons Act (c. 54)	ss. 7(1)(3)(4), 31, 34(1)(*d*)(*f*) r. (not S.), Sch. 4, para. 6 r. (not S.), Sch. 5, paras. 5, 23, 44 r. (not S.), 1983/182
269	Public Path Orders and Extinguishment of Public Right of Way Orders Regs.	r., 1983/23
410	Special Schools and Establishments (Grant) (Amdt.) Regs.	r., 1983/74
575	Town and Country Planning (Public Path Orders) Regs.	r., 1983/22
722	Pneumoconiosis, Byssinosis and Misc. Diseases Benefit (Amdt.) Scheme	r., 1983/136
808	Ionising Radiations (Sealed Sources) Regs.	am., 1983/714
833	Civil Aviation (Investigation of Accidents) Regs.	r. (with saving), 1983/551
857	St. Helena Supreme Ct. O.	s. 4 am., 1983/1113
905	Representation of the People (N.I.) Regs.	r. (with saving), 1983/436
1079	Medical Practitioners (Saint Christopher and Nevis) O.	am., 1983/882
1196	Pneumoconiosis, Byssinosis and Misc. Diseases Benefit (Amdt.) (No. 2) Scheme	r., 1983/136
1432	Enrolment of Deeds (Change of Name) (Amdt.) Regs.	r., 1983/680
1771	Landlord and Tenant (Notices) Regs.	r., 1983/133
1817	Artificial Sweeteners in Food Regs. ...	r., 1983/1211
1822	Foreign Sea-Fishery Officers (North-East Atlantic Fisheries Commn. Scheme) O.	r., 1983/254
1848	Artifical Sweeteners in Food (S.) Regs.	am., 1983/270
1970	Income and Corporation Taxes Act (c. 10)	s. 8 am., 1983/404
16	County Ct. Districts O.	r., 1983/713
108	Cheese (S.) Regs.	am., 1983/270
231	Justices' Clerks Rules	am., 1983/527
294	Merchant Shipping (Certificates of Competency as A.B.) Regs.	am., 1983/1167
781	Gaming Clubs (Hours and Charges) (S.) Regs.	am., 1983/80

Year and Number (or date)	Act or instrument	How affected
1970 *contd*		
799	Gaming Clubs (Hours and Charges) Regs.	**am.,** 1983/5
904	County Ct. Districts (Misc.) O. ..	**r.,** 1983/713
1065	Fish and Meat Spreadable Products (S.) Regs.	**am.,** 1983/270
1191	Cream (S.) Regs. ...	**am.,** 1983/270
1285	Ice Cream (S.) Regs.	**am.,** 1983/270
1286	Margarine (S.) Regs.	**am.,** 1983/270
1341	Veterinary Surgery (Exemption) O. ...	**r.,** 1983/6
1440	Trustee Savings Banks (Channel Is.) O.	**r.,** 1983/1126
1674	Parliamentary Constituencies (E.) O.	**am.,** 1983/417
1675	Parliamentary Constituencies (W.) O.	**am.,** 1983/418
1680	Parliamentary Constituencies (S.) O.	**am.,** 1983/422
1792	Magistrates' Cts. (Children and Young Persons) Rules	**am.,** 1983/526
2031	County Ct. Districts (Misc. No. 2) O.	**r.,** 1983/713
1971	Cts. Act (c. 23) ..	Sch. 8, para. 22 **r.** (not S.), 1983/182
	Misuse of Drugs Act (c. 38)..	Sch. 2, Pts. I, III **am.,** 1983/765
	Prevention of Oil Pollution Act (c. 60)	ss. 1(1)(3)(4), 2(1)(*a*)(*b*), 4, 8(1) **r.,** 1983/1106
	Finance Act (c. 68)	s. 32 **am.,** 1983/404
	Immigration Act (c. 77)	s. 6 **am.,** 1983/24
90	A.S. (Alteration of Sheriff Ct. Fees)..	**am.,** 1983/970
124	Students' Allowances (S.) Regs.	**am.,** 1983/798
171	Salmon (Northwest Atlantic) O.	**r.,** 1983/255
249	Residential Establishments (Payments by Local Authies.) (S.) O.	**am.,** 1983/430
253	Iron Casting Industry (Scientific Research Levy) O.	**am.,** 1983/1149
415	Agricultural and Horticultural Co-operation Scheme	**am.,** 1983/1157
450	Road Vehicles (Registration and Licensing) Regs.	**am.,** 1983/1248
454	County Cts. (Race Relations Jurisdiction) (Amdt.) O.	**r.,** 1983/713
560	Mines and Quarries (Valuation) O.	**r.,** 1983/547
656	County Cts. (Bankruptcy and Companies Winding-up Jurisdiction) O.	**r.,** 1983/713
661	Slaughter of Poultry (Humane Conditions) Regs.	**am.,** 1983/943
960	Alkali, &c. Works O.	**r.,** 1983/943
1081	County Ct. Districts (Misc.) O.	**r.,** 1983/713
1103	Foreign Sea-Fishery Officers (International Commn. for the Northwest Atlantic Fisheries Scheme) O.	**r.,** 1983/254
1152	County Cts. (Admiralty Jurisdiction) O.	**r.,** 1983/713
1172	Fishing Nets (Northwest Atlantic) O...	**r.,** 1983/255

Year and Number (or date)	Act or instrument	How affected
1971 *contd*		
1222	Pneumoconiosis, Byssinosis and Misc. Diseases Benefit (Amdt.) Scheme	r., 1983/136
1772	Mental Health Review Tribunal (Welsh Forms) Rules	r., 1983/942
1983	County Cts. (Bankruptcy and Companies Winding-up Jurisdiction) (Amdt.) O.	r., 1983/713
1984	County Cts. (Admiralty Jurisdiction) (Amdt.) O.	r., 1983/713
1985	County Cts. (Race Relations Jurisdiction) (Amdt. No. 2) O.	r., 1983/713
2084	Indictments (Procedure) Rules ..	am., 1983/284
1972	Finance Act (c. 41)	s. 52 am., 1983/140 Sch. 1, paras. 1, 2 am., 1983/401 Sch. 5— Group 7 am., 1983/499 Group 11 **inserted,** 1983/809
	Legal Advice and Assistance Act (c. 50)	s. 1 am., 1983/533 s. 4 am., 1983/384 Sch. 1 am., 1983/384
	Gas Act (c. 60)	s. 30 am., 1983/684
	Local Govt. Act (c. 70)	ss. 154, 156, 159, 160, 162 – 165 am., Sch. 29, para. 7 am., 1983/249
	Criminal Justice Act (c. 71).. ..	s. 42 r. (not S.), Sch. 5 am. (not S.), 1983/182
178	Civil Aviation Authy. Regs. ..	r., 1983/550
188	Salmon and Migratory Trout (Prohibition of Fishing) O.	am., 1983/59
189	Salmon and Migratory Trout (North-East Atlantic) O.	am., 1983/59
207	Salmon and Migratory Trout (Prohibition of Fishing) (No. 2) O.	am., 1983/60
316	Rules of Procedure (Army) ..	am., 1983/719
319	Community Homes Regs.	am., 1983/652
419	Rules of Procedure (Air Force) ..	am., 1983/718
641	Savings Certificates Regs.	am., 1983/495, 1063
758	Foreign Sea-Fishery Officers (North-East Atlantic Fisheries Commn. Scheme) Variation O.	r., 1983/254
868	Foreign Sea-Fishery Officers (International Commn. for the Northwest Atlantic Fisheries Scheme) Variation O.	r., 1983/254
919	Merchant Shipping (Crew Agreements, Lists of Crew and Discharge of Seamen) (Fishing Vessels) Regs.	am., 1983/478

Year and Number (or date)	Act or instrument	How affected
1972 *contd*		
971	Hovercraft (Application of Enactments) O.	**am.**, 1983/769
1012	Detention Centre (Amdt.) Rules ..	**r.**, 1983/569
1096	Judicial Trustee Rules	**r.**, 1983/370
1289	Pneumoconiosis, Byssinosis and Misc. Diseases Benefit (Amdt.) Scheme	**r.**, 1983/136
1330	Alkali, &c., Works (S.) O... ..	**r.**, 1983/943
1345	Car Tax Regs.	**am.**, 1983/140
1758	Immigration (Registration with Police) Regs.	**am.**, 1983/442
1804	Gas Quality Regs...	**am.**, 1983/363
1928	Oil in Navigable Waters (Exceptions) Regs.	**r.**, 1983/1106
1929	Oil in Navigable Waters (Records) Regs.	**r.** (with saving), 1983/1106
1941	County Ct. Districts (Misc.) O. ..	**r.**, 1983/713
1966	Salmon and Migratory Trout (Restrictions on Landing) O.	**am.**, 1983/58
2026	Fishing Boats (EEC) Designation O...	**r.**, 1983/253
1973	Water Act (c. 37)	Sch. 3, para. 39 **am.**, 1983/249
	Social Security Act (c. 38)	s. 86 **am.**, 1983/118
	Powers of Criminal Cts. Act (c. 62)..	s. 14 **am.**, s. 19 **r.**, ss. 21, 23, 29, 32, 45 **am.**, Sch. 5, paras. 1, 13, 33 **r.** (not S.), 1983/182 Sch. 5, para. 13 **r.** (S.), 1983/758
	Local Govt. (S.) Act (c. 65).. ..	s. 111 **am.**, 1983/1074
7	Abstract of Factories Act O. ..	**am.**, 1983/978
22	Grading of Horticultural Produce (Amdt.) Regs.	**am.**, 1983/1053
79	Local Elections (Principal Areas) Rules	**am.**, 1983/1154
127	Foreign Sea-Fishery Officers (North-East Atlantic Fisheries Commn. Scheme) Variation (No. 2) O.	**r.**, 1983/254
428	Police Pensions Regs.	**am.**, 1983/996
430	Police Cadets (Pensions) Regs. ..	**am.**, 1983/990
789	Foreign Sea-Fishery Officers (North-East Atlantic Fisheries Commn. Scheme) Variation (No. 3) O.	**r.**, 1983/254
792	Landlord and Tenant (Notices) Regs.	**r.**, 1983/133
797	Misuse of Drugs Regs.	**am.**, 1983/788
966	Firemen's Pension Scheme.. ..	**am.**, 1983/614
1268	Redundant Mineworkers and Concessionary Coal (Payments Schemes) O.	**am.**, 1983/506

Year and Number (or date)	Act or instrument	How affected
1973 *contd*		
1286	N.H.S. (Regional and Area Health Authies.: Membership and Procedure) Regs.	**r.**, 1983/315
1310	Colouring Matter in Food (S.) Regs.	**am.**, 1983/270
1439	Pneumoconiosis, Byssinosis and Misc. Diseases Benefit (Amdt.) Scheme	**r.**, 1983/136
1701	Foreign Sea-Fishery Officers (North-East Atlantic Fisheries Commn. Scheme) Variation (No. 4) O.	**r.**, 1983/254
1910	Local Elections (Parishes and Communities) Rules	**am.**, 1983/1153
1911	Parish and Community Meetings (Polls) Rules	**am.**, 1983/1151
1929	Civil Aviation Authy. (Amdt.) Regs...	**r.**, 1983/550
1958	Is. of Scilly (Sale of Intoxicating Liquor) O.	**am.**, 1983/1136
2004	Haddock (Restrictions on Landing) O.	**r.**, 1983/255
2045	County Ct. Districts (Misc.) O. ..	**r.**, 1983/713
2084	Sea Fishing (North-West Atlantic) Licensing O.	**r.**, 1983/1206
2185	Sea Fishing (Faroes Region) Licensing and Prohibition of Fishing Method O.	**r.**, 1983/255
1974	Legal Aid Act (c. 4)	ss. 1, 4 **am.**, 1983/618 ss. 6, 9 **am.**, 1983/617
	Control of Pollution Act (c. 40) ..	s. 78(3) **r.**, 1983/943
	Merchant Shipping Act (c. 43) ..	Pt. II, ss. 10−13, Schs. 2, 3 **r.**, 1983/1106
	Housing Act (c. 44)	s. 7 **am.**, 1983/664 ss. 64, 68, 70A, 72 **am.**, 1983/613 s. 78 **am.**, 1983/95 Sch. 6, Pt. I **replaced**, 1983/613
	Housing (S.) Act (c. 45)	Sch. 1, Pt. I **replaced**, 1983/492
	Rehabilitation of Offenders Act (c. 53)	s. 5— **am.** (not S.), 1983/182 **am.** (S.), 1983/758
160	N.H.S. (General Medical and Pharmaceutical Services) Regs.	**am.**, 1983/313
192	Fishing Nets (Northwest Atlantic) (Variation) O.	**r.**, 1983/255
241	N.H.S. Reorganisation (Consequential Amdts.) O.	**r.**, 1983/893
243	Returning Officers (Parliamentary Constituencies) O.	**r.** (with saving), 1983/468
273	Local Authies. (Social Services and Food and Drugs) O.	**am.**, 1983/893

Year and Number (or date)	Act or instrument	How affected
1974 *contd*		
447	Local Govt. (Allowances) Regs.	**am.,** 1983/574
466	N.H.S. (Functions of Health Bds.) (S.) O.	**r.,** 1983/1027
477	N.H.S. (Appointment of Consultants) (W.) Regs.	**r.,** 1983/1275
519	Local Authy. (Stocks and Bonds) Regs.	**am.,** 1983/529
520	Local Govt. Superannuation Regs.	**am.,** 1983/178, 1269, 1270, 1271
556	Reciprocal Enforcement of Maintenance Orders (Designation of Reciprocating Countries) O.	**am.,** 1983/1125
648	Representation of the People Regs.	**r.** (with saving), 1983/435
668	Magistrates' Cts. (Reciprocal Enforcement of Maintenance Orders) Rules	**am.,** 1983/1148
701	Foreign Sea-Fishery Officers (International Commn. for the Northwest Atlantic Fisheries Scheme) Variation O.	**r.,** 1983/254
848	Gas (Meter) Regs.	**r.,** 1983/684
944	Pneumoconiosis, Byssinosis and Misc. Diseases Benefit (Amdt.) Scheme	**r.,** 1983/136
1100	Northwest Atlantic (Demersal Fish) O.	**r.,** 1983/255
1169	Accounts and Audit Regs.	**am.,** 1983/249
1356	Milk and Dairies (Semi-skimmed and Skimmed Milk) (Heat Treatment and Labelling) (S.) Regs.	**am.,** 1983/940
1377	N.H.S. (Remission of Charges) Regs.	**am.,** 1983/309
1389	Civil Aviation Authy. (Second Amdt.) Regs.	**r.,** 1983/550
1440	N.H.S. (Remission of Charges) (S.) Regs.	**am.,** 1983/335
1481	Town and Country Planning (Local Plans for Greater London) Regs.	**r.,** 1983/1190
1555	Molluscan Shellfish (Control of Deposit) O.	**am.,** 1983/159
1740	Pensions Increase (Local Authies.' etc. Pensions) Regs.	**am.,** 1983/1315
1807	Foreign Sea-Fishery Officers (International Commn. for the Northwest Atlantic Fisheries Scheme) Second Variation O.	**r.,** 1983/254
1837	Legal Officers' Fees O.	**am.,** 1983/1048
1937	Enrolment of Deeds (Change of Name) (Amdt.) Regs.	**r.,** 1983/680
2042	Prevention of Fraud (Investments) Act Licensing (Amdt.) Regs.	**r.,** 1983/587
2057	Nat. Insurance (Non-participation—Transitional Provns.) Regs.	**am.,** 1983/118
2058	Nat. Insurance (Non-participation—Transitional Provns.) (No. 2) Regs.	**am.,** 1983/118

Year and Number (or date)	Act or instrument	How affected
1975	Finance Act (c. 7)..	s. 37, Tables **am.**, 1983/403
		Sch. 4, para. 17 **am.**, 1983/879
	Social Security Act (c. 14) ..	s. 30 **am.**,
		Sch. 4 **replaced**, 1983/1244
	Industrial Injuries and Diseases (Old Cases) Act (c. 16)	s. 2 **am.** (23/11/83), s. 7 **am.** (24/11/83), 1983/1244
	Criminal Procedure (S.) Act (c. 21)..	s. 8 **am.**, 1983/24
		ss. 289D, 291 **am.**, 1983/24
		s. 421 **am.**, 1983/24
	H.C. Disqualification Act (c. 24) ..	Sch. 1 **am.**, 1983/608
	Ministerial and other Salaries Act (c. 27)	s. 1 **am.**,
		Sch. 1, Pts. I—IV **replaced**,
		Sch. 2, Pt. I **replaced**, 1983/1128
	Air Travel Reserve Fund Act (c. 36) ..	s. 1 **am.**, 1983/1127
	Social Security Pensions Act (c. 60) ..	s. 6 **am.**, 1983/1244
		ss. 33, 34, 36 – 39 **am.**, 1983/722
	Sex Discrimination Act (c. 65) ..	s. 20 **am.**, 1983/1202
	Community Land Act (c. 77) ..	ss. 1, 2, 7, 26, 40, 43, 44, 51 – 58, Sch. 2 **r.**, 1983/673
112	Heather and Grass Burning (Amdt.) (Northumberland and Durham) Regs.	**r.**, 1983/425
170	Sea Fishing (Waters off Norway) (Prohibition of Trawling) O.	**r.**, 1983/255
171	Foreign Sea-Fishery Officers (Norway) O.	**r.**, 1983/254
205	Friendly Societies Regs.	**am.**, 1983/351
308	Public Health (Infectious Diseases) (S.) Regs.	**am.**, 1983/1008
340	Cod (North-East Artic) Licensing O.	**r.**, 1983/1206
345	Internal Drainage Bds. (Audit) Directions	**am.**, 1983/249
469	Social Security (Industrial Injuries) (Airmen's Benefits) Regs.	**am.**, 1983/186
470	Social Security (Industrial Injuries) (Mariners' Benefits) Regs.	**am.**, 1983/186
499	Misuse of Drugs (Amdt.) Regs. ..	**am.**, 1983/788
514	Pneumoconiosis, Byssinosis and Misc. Diseases Benefit (Amdt.) Scheme	**r.**, 1983/136
532	Civil Aviation Authy. (Third Amdt.) Regs.	**r.**, 1983/550
555	Social Security (Hospital In-Patients) Regs.	**am.**, 1983/186
556	Social Security (Credits) Regs. ..	**am.**, 1983/197, 463

Year and Number (or date)	Act or instrument	How affected
1975 *contd*		
563	Social Security Benefit (Persons Abroad) Regs.	**am.**, 1983/186
564	Social Security (Unemployment, Sickness and Invalidity Benefit) Regs.	**am.**, 1983/463
598	Social Security (Attendance Allowance) (No. 2) Regs.	**am.**, 1983/1015, 1137
628	Social Security (Claims and Payments) Regs.	**am.**, 1983/1015
637	Sheriff Ct. Districts Reorganisation O.	**am.**, 1983/1028
686	Local Authies. (Allowances) (S.) Regs.	**am.**, 1983/579
734	Local Govt. (Compensation) (S.) Regs.	**am.**, 1983/264
850	Representation of the People (S.) Regs.	**r.** (with saving), 1983/548
1036	Merchant Shipping (Oil Pollution) (Parties to Conventions) O.	**r.**, 1983/416
1054	Further Education Regs. ..	**am.**, 1983/74
1071	Gas (Meter) (Amdt.) Regs... ..	**r.**, 1983/684
1139	Pneumoconiosis, Byssinosis and Misc. Diseases Benefit (Amdt.) (No. 2) Scheme	**r.**, 1983/136
1263	Detention Centre (Amdt.) Rules ..	**r.**, 1983/569
1337	Mental Health (Hospital and Guardianship) Amdt. Regs.	**r.**, 1983/893
1379	Tribunals and Inquiries (Discretionary Inquiries) O.	**am.**, 1983/1287
1573	Mobility Allowance Regs.	**am.**, 1983/186, 1186
1623	Misuse of Drugs (Amdt.) (No. 2) Regs.	**r.**, 1983/788
1800	Fire Services (Compensation) (S.) Regs.	**am.**, 1983/263
1803	Supreme Ct. Funds Rules	**am.**, 1983/290
1873	Measuring Instrts. (EEC Requirements) (Gas Volume Meters) Regs.	**r.**, 1983/1246
1874	Measuring Instrts. (EEC Requirements) (Gas Volume Meters) (Fees) Regs.	**r.**, 1983/1247
1929	Further Education (Transitional Exemption Order) Regs.	**r.**, 1983/74
2101	Occupational Pension Schemes (Contracting-out) Regs.	**am.**, 1983/338
2119	County Cts. (Admiralty Jurisdiction) (Amdt.) O.	**r.**, 1983/713
2192	Trial of the Pyx O.	**am.**, 1983/612
2233	Rating (Timetable and Procedures) (S.) (No. 2) Regs.	**am.**, 1983/862
1976	Nat. Coal Bd. (Finance) Act (c. 1) ..	s. 2 **am.**, 1983/459
	Finance Act (c. 40)	s. 64 **am.**, 1983/1102 s. 64A(2), Tables A, B **replaced**, 1983/1101

Year and Number (or date)	Act or instrument	How affected
1976 *contd*		Sch. 7— Pt. I, Tables A – C **replaced,** 1983/1102 Pt. II **am.**, 1983/1102
	Armed Forces Act (c. 52)	s. 13— **am.** (not S.), 1983/182 **am.** (S.), 1983/758
	International Carriage of Perishable Foodstuffs Act (c. 58)	ss. 2, 3, 6, 7, 9 – 11, 19 **am.**, 1983/1123
	Bail Act (c. 63)	Sch. 2, paras. 40, 42 **r.** (not S.), 1983/182
	Sexual Offences (S.) Act (c. 67) ..	s. 13 **am.**, 1983/201
	Energy Act (c. 76)..	s. 14(6)(*b*) **r.**, 1983/790
29	County Ct. Districts (North Shields) O.	**r.**, 1983/713
30	Medicines (Animal Feeding Stuffs) (Enforcement) Regs.	**r.**, 1983/62
143	Contracted-out Employment (Notifications, Premium Payment and Misc. Provns.) Regs.	**am.**, 1983/338
201	County Ct. Districts (Misc.) (Amdt.) O.	**r.**, 1983/713
281	County Ct. Districts (Thanet) O. ..	**r.**, 1983/713
440	Herring (Atlanto-Scandian) (Prohibition of Fishing) O.	**r.**, 1983/255
442	Soft Drinks (S.) Amdt. Regs. ..	**am.**, 1983/270
447	Mental Health Review Tribunal (Amdt.) Rules	**r.**, 1983/942
475	Grant-Aided Secondary Schools (S.) Grant Regs.	**am.**, 1983/908
476	A.S. (Summary Cause Rules, Sheriff Ct.)	**am.**, 1983/747
585	Personal Injuries (Civilians) Scheme..	**r.**, 1983/686
604	County Ct. Distrists (Staines) O. ..	**r.**, 1983/713
605	County Ct. Districts (Medway) O. ..	**r.**, 1983/713
797	County Ct. Districts (Staines) (Amdt.) O.	**r.**, 1983/713
850	County Ct. Districts (Wales and Chester Circuit) O.	**r.**, 1983/713
851	County Cts. (Admiralty Jurisdiction) (Amdt.) O.	**r.**, 1983/713
852	County Cts. (Bankruptcy and Companies Winding-up Jurisdiction) (Amdt.) O.	**r.**, 1983/713
890	County Ct. Districts (Newton Abbot) O.	**r.**, 1983/713
914	Cocoa and Chocolate Products (S.) Regs.	**am.**, 1983/270
946	Specified Sugar Products (S.) Regs...	**am.**, 1983/270
965	Child Benefit (General) Regs. ..	**am.**, 1983/3
1016	Iron Casting Industry (Scientific Research Levy) (Amdt.) O.	**r.**, 1983/1149

Year and Number (or date)	Act or instrument	How affected
1976 *contd*		
1026	Civil Aviation Authy. (Fourth Amdt.) Regs.	**r.**, 1983/550
1073	Police (S.) Regs. ..	**am.**, 1983/317
1167	Personal Injuries (Civilians) (Amdt.) Scheme	**r.**, 1983/686
1191	Further Education (Amdt.) Regs. ..	**r.**, 1983/74
1267	Child Benefit and Social Security (Fixing and Adjustment of Rates) Regs.	**am.**, 1983/1243
1600	Prevention of Fraud (Investments) Act Licensing (Amdt.) Regs.	**r.**, 1983/587
1676	Building Regs.	**am.**, 1983/195
1818	Honey (S.) Regs. ..	**am.**, 1983/270
2012	Nat. Savings Stock Register Regs. ..	**am.**, 1983/1103
2019	Motor Vehicles (Competitions and Trials) (S.) Regs.	**am.**, 1983/354
2095	Herring (Restrictions on Landing) O.	**r.**, 1983/255
2149	Trustee Savings Banks Act (Channel Is.) O.	**r.**, 1983/1126
2162	Petroleum Stocks O.	**am.**, 1983/909
2182	Scottish Development Agency (Compensation) Regs.	**am.**, 1983/265
2216	Fishing Boats (EEC) Designation O...	**r.**, 1983/253
1977	Aircraft and Shipbuilding Industries Act (c. 3)	s. 11 **am.**, 1983/1076
	Criminal Law Act (c. 45)	s. 36(1)(9) **am.** (not S.), s. 37(1) **r.** (not S.), Sch. 12 **am.** (not S.), 1983/182 Schs. 11, 12 **am.** (S.), 1983/758
87	Cts.-Martial and Standing Civilian Cts. (Additional Powers on Trial of Civilians) Regs.	**am.**, 1983/717
88	Standing Civilian Cts. O.	**am.**, 1983/716
96	Representation of the People (N.I.) (Amdt.) Regs. 1976	**r.** (with saving), 1983/436
105	Representation of the People (Amdt.) Regs. 1976	**r.** (with saving), 1983/435
111	Representation of the People (S.) Amdt. Regs. 1976	**r.** (with saving), 1983/548
149	County Ct. Districts (South Eastern Circuit) O.	**r.**, 1983/713
150	County Cts. (Admiralty Jurisdiction) (Amdt.) O.	**r.**, 1983/713
151	County Cts. (Bankruptcy and Companies Winding-up Jurisdiction) (Amdt.) O.	**r.**, 1983/713
176	Gen. Optical Council (Registration and Enrolment Rules) O. of C.	**am.**, 1983/1
278	Non-maintained Special Schools (Fees) Regs.	**r.** (with saving), 1983/74

Year and Number (or date)	Act or instrument	How affected
1977 *contd*		
314	Civil Aviation (Canadian Navigation Services) Regs.	am., 1983/969
343	Social Security Benefit (Dependency) Regs.	am., 1983/186, 1001
348	County Ct. Districts (Western Circuit) O.	r., 1983/713
349	County Cts. (Admiralty Jurisdiction) (Amdt. No. 2) O.	r., 1983/713
350	County Cts. (Bankruptcy and Companies Winding-up Jurisdiction) (Amdt. No. 2) O.	r., 1983/713
380	Pneumoconiosis, Byssinosis and Misc. Diseases Benefit (Amdt.) Scheme	r., 1983/136
404	Personal Injuries (Civilians) Scheme..	r., 1983/686
486	Offshore Installations (Life-saving Appliances) Regs.	am., 1983/1258
887	Further Education (Amdt.) Regs. ..	r., 1983/74
888	Conveyance by Road of Military Explosives Regs.	am., 1983/1140
889	Conveyance by Rail of Military Explosives Regs.	am., 1983/1140
890	Conveyance in Harbours of Military Explosives Regs.	am., 1983/1140
910	Inward Processing Relief Regs. ..	am., 1983/877
918	Explosives (Registration of Premises) Variation of Fees Regs.	r., 1983/219
956	Social Security Benefit (Persons Residing Together) Regs.	am., 1983/186
982	Collision Regulations and Distress Signals O.	r. (with savings), 1983/708, 762, 768, 769
992	Pneumoconiosis, Byssinosis and Misc. Diseases Benefit (Amdt.) (No. 2) Scheme	r., 1983/136
1010	Merchant Shipping (Signals of Distress) Rules	am., 1983/708
1026	Fruit Juices and Fruit Nectars (S.) Regs.	am., 1983/270
1027	Condensed Milk and Dried Milk (S.) Regs.	am., 1983/270
1028	Erucic Acid in Food (S.) Regs. ..	am., 1983/270
1063	Workmen's Compensation Supplementation and Pneumoconiosis, Byssinosis and Misc. Diseases Benefit (Further Amdt.) Scheme	r., 1983/136
1067	Prevention of Fraud (Investments) Act Licensing (Amdt.) Regs.	r., 1983/587
1097	R.A.F. Terms of Service Regs. ..	am., 1983/343, 898
1113	Airports Licensing (Liquor) O. ..	r., 1983/1217
1173	Sheep Scab O.	am., 1983/210
1188	Contracted-out Employment (Misc. Provns.) Regs.	am., 1983/338

Year and Number (or date)	Act or instrument	How affected
1977 *contd*		
1189	County Ct. Districts (Camborne and Redruth) O.	**r.**, 1983/713
1257	Hovercraft (Application of Enactments) (Amdt.) O.	**r.**, 1983/769
1301	Collision Regulations and Distress Signals (Amdt.) O.	**r.** (with savings), 1983/708, 762, 768, 769
1309	Heavy Goods Vehicles (Drivers' Licences) Regs.	**am.**, 1983/1232
1360	Teachers' Superannuation (S.) Regs.	**am.**, 1983/639
1368	Companies (Annual Return) Regs. ..	**r.**, 1983/1023
1388	Herring (Irish Sea) Licensing O. ..	**r.**, 1983/1206
1389	Herring (Is. of Man) Licensing O. ..	**r.**, 1983/1204
1497	Mackerel Licensing O.	**r.**, 1983/1206
1584	Medicines (Animal Feeding Stuffs) (Enforcement) (Amdt.) Regs.	**r.**, 1983/62
1640	Personal Injuries (Civilians) (Amdt.) Scheme	**r.**, 1983/686
1679	Social Security Benefit (Persons Abroad) Amdt. Regs.	**am.**, 1983/186
1753	Alcoholometers and Alcohol Hydrometers (EEC Requirements) Regs.	**am.**, 1983/530
1911	County Ct. Districts (Southwark) O.	**r.**, 1983/713
2112	Agricultural Products Processing and Marketing (Improvement Grant) Regs.	**am.**, 1983/641
2182	Herring (Specified Western Waters) (Prohibition of Fishing) (No. 2) O.	**r.**, 1983/255
1978	Export Guarantees and Overseas Investment Act (c. 18)	s. 5 **am.**, 1983/198 s. 6(1) **am.**, 1983/278 s. 6(2) **am.**, 1983/279 s. 11 **am.**, 1983/281
	N.H.S. (S.) Act (c. 29)	Sch. 9, para. 1 Sch. 10, para. 7 **am.**, 1983/24
	Employment Protection (Consolidation) Act (c. 44)	s. 81 **am.**, ss. 82(7A), 84(7A) **inserted**, s. 94 **am.**, 1983/1160 ss. 141, 146 **am.**, 1983/624 Sch. 4, para. 1 **replaced**, Sch. 6, para. 1 **am.**, 1983/1160
	Community Service by Offenders (S.) Act (c. 49)	s. 6(3) and Sch. 1— **r.** (not S.), 1983/182 **r.** (S.), 1983/758
32	Diseases of Animals (Approved Disinfectants) O.	**am.**, 1983/32, 1071
105	Antioxidants in Food Regs. ..	**am.**, 1983/1211

Year and Number (or date)	Act or instrument	How affected
1978 *contd*		
197	Representation of the People (Amdt.) Regs.	r. (with saving), 1983/435
198	Representation of the People (N.I.) (Amdt.) Regs.	r. (with saving), 1983/436
205	Representation of the People (S.) Amdt. Regs.	r. (with saving), 1983/548
209	Packaging and Labelling of Dangerous Substances Regs.	am., 1983/17
250	Contracted-out Employment (Misc. Provns.) Regs.	am., 1983/338
270	Explosives (Licensing of Stores) Variation of Fees Regs.	r., 1983/219
332	Prescription Pricing Authy. Regs. ..	am., 1983/315
384	Personal Injuries (Civilians) (Amdt.) Scheme	r., 1983/686
393	Social Security (Graduated Retirement Benefit) (No. 2) Regs.	am., 1983/1244
397	County Ct. Districts (Devizes) O. ..	r., 1983/713
415	Redundant Mineworkers and Concessionary Coal (Payments Schemes) O.	am., 1983/506
461	Hire-Purchase (Increase of Limit of Value) (G.B.) O.	r., 1983/611
492	Antioxidants in Food (S.) Regs. ..	am., 1983/270
611	Offshore Installations (Fire-fighting Equipment) Regs.	am., 1983/1258
817	County Ct. Districts (Warminster) O.	r., 1983/713
934	Diseases of Animals (Approved Disinfectants) (Amdt.) O.	r., 1983/1071
950	N.H.S. (Dental and Optical Charges) Regs.	am., 1983/309
998	Education Authy. Bursaries (S.) Regs.	am., 1983/1051
1017	Motor Vehicles (Construction and Use) Regs.	am., 1983/112, 471, 932
1096	State Awards Regs.	am., 1983/188, 920
1285	Haddock (North Sea) Licensing O. ..	r., 1983/1206
1426	Personal Injuries (Civilians) Amdt. (No. 2) Scheme	r., 1983/686
1525	Naval, Military and Air Forces etc. (Disablement and Death) Service Pensions O.	r., 1983/883
1527	Social Security (Jersey and Guernsey) Regs.	am., 1983/604
1537	Mackerel Licensing (Manx and Channel Is. Boats) O.	r., 1983/1206
1538	Mackerel Licensing (Variation) O. ..	r., 1983/1206
1759	Divorce County Cts. O.	r., 1983/713
1884	African Development Bank (Privileges) O.	r., 1983/142
1902	Naval, Military and Air Forces etc. (Disablement and Death) Service Pensions Amdt. O.	r., 1983/883

Year and Number (or date)	Act or instrument	How affected
1979	Customs and Excise Management Act (c. 2)	s. 147 **am.**, 1983/24 Sch. 4 **am.** (not S.), 1983/182
	Electricity (S.) Act (c. 11)	ss. 7, 9, 22, 35 **am.**, 1983/790 s. 41 **am.**, 1983/24
	Capital Gains Tax Act (c. 14) ..	s. 5 **am.**, 1983/402
	Nurses, Midwives and Health Visitors Act (c. 36)	s. 11 **am.**, s. 11A **inserted,** ss. 12, 13 **am.**, ss. 22A, 22B **inserted,** 1983/884
	Merchant Shipping Act (c. 39) ..	s. 43 **am.**, 1983/24
	Pensioners' Payments and Social Security Act (c. 48)	ss. 1 – 3 **am.**, 1983/1200
37	Diseases of Animals (Approved Disinfectants) (Amdt.) O.	**r.**, 1983/1071
45	Medicines (Exemptions from Restrictions on the Retail Sale or Supply of Veterinary Drugs) O.	**am.**, 1983/274, 1156
54	Companies (Annual Return) (Amdt.) Regs.	**r.**, 1983/1023
71	Haddock (West of Scotland and Rockall) Licensing O.	**r.**, 1983/1206
113	Naval, Military and Air Forces etc. (Disablement and Death) Service Pensions Amdt. O.	**r.**, 1983/883
218	Misuse of Drugs (Licence Fees) Regs.	**am.**, 1983/196
221	Agricultural or Forestry Tractors and Tractor Components (Type Approval) Regs.	**am.**, 1983/709
253	Housing (Improvement of Amenities of Residential Areas) (S.) O.	**r.**, 1983/271
268	Cod and Whiting (Licensing) O. ..	**r.**, 1983/1206
270	Personal Injuries (Civilians) Amdt. Scheme	**r.**, 1983/686
333	State Awards (State Bursaries for Adult Education) (W.) Regs.	**am.**, 1983/1274
379	Scottish Land Ct. Rules	**am.**, 1983/1058
383	Coffee and Coffee Products (S.) Regs.	**am.**, 1983/270
429	Returning Officers' Expenses (E. & W.) Regs.	**r.**, 1983/735
430	Returning Officers' Expenses (S.) Regs.	**r.**, 1983/736
431	Returning Officers' Expenses (N.I.) Regs.	**r.**, 1983/737
514	Civil Aviation Authy. (Fifth Amdt.) Regs.	**r.**, 1983/550
591	Social Security (Contributions) Regs.	**am.**, 1983/10, 53, 73, 395, 496
597	Social Security (Overlapping Benefits) Regs.	**am.**, 1983/186
628	Social Security (Claims and Payments) Regs.	**am.**, 1983/186

Year and Number (or date)	Act or instrument	How affected
1979 *contd*		
705	N.H.S. (Dental and Optical Charges) (S.) Regs.	**am.**, 1983/335
743	Nephrops Tails (Restrictions on Landing) O.	**r.**, 1983/255
748	Iron Casting Industry (Scientific Research Levy) (Amdt.) O.	**r.**, 1983/1149
752	Preservatives in Food Regs. ..	**am.**, 1983/1211
757	Domestic Cts. (Constitution) Rules ..	**am.**, 1983/676
758	Domestic Cts. (Constitution) (Inner London) Rules	**am.**, 1983/677
773	Diseases of Animals (Approved Disinfectants) (Amdt.) (No. 2) O.	**r.**, 1983/1071
781	Social Security (Claims and Payments) Amdt. Regs.	**am.**, 1983/186
800	Agricultural Holdings (Specification of Forms) (S.) Amdt. Instrt.	**r.**, 1983/1073
937	Industrial and Provident Societies (Credit Unions) Regs.	**am.**, 1983/352
954	European Communities (Iron and Steel Employees Re-adaptation Benefits Scheme) Regs.	**am.**, 1983/1184
996	Pneumoconiosis, Byssinosis and Misc. Diseases Benefit (Amdt.) Scheme	**r.**, 1983/136
1073	Preservatives in Food (S.) Regs. ..	**am.**, 1983/270
1092	Motor Vehicles (Type Approval) (G.B.) Regs.	**am.**, 1983/328
1176	Irish Sea Herring (Prohibition of Fishing) O.	**r.**, 1983/255
1183	Trustee Savings Banks (Fund for the Banks for Savings) (No. 2) O.	**am.**, 1983/636
1203	Coal and Other Mines (Electric Lighting for Filming) Regs.	**am.**, 1983/710
1204	Banking Act 1979 (Exempt Transactions) Regs.	**am.**, 1983/510
1224	Measuring Instrts. (EEC Requirements) (Gas Volume Meters) (Amdt.) Regs.	**r.**, 1983/1246
1232	Personal Injuries (Civilians) Amdt. (No. 2) Scheme	**r.**, 1983/686
1257	Measuring Instrts. (EEC Requirements) (Gas Volume Meters) (Fees) (Amdt.) Regs.	**r.**, 1983/1247
1312	Naval, Military and Air Forces etc. (Disablement and Death) Service Pensions Amdt. (No. 2) O.	**r.**, 1983/883
1317	Reciprocal Enforcement of Maintenance Orders (Hague Convention Countries) O.	**am.**, 1983/885
1450	Merchant Shipping (Oil Pollution) (Parties to Conventions) (Amdt.) O.	**r.**, 1983/416
1470	Police Regs.	**am.**, 1983/160
1547	Companies (Forms) Regs.	**am.**, 1983/1021

Year and Number (or date)	Act or instrument	How affected
1979 *contd*		
1604	Nursing Qualifications (EEC Recognition) O.	**r.**, 1983/884
1605	Measuring Instrts. (Liquid Fuel and Lubricants) Regs.	**r.**, 1983/592
1641	Lead in Food (S.) Regs.	**am.**, 1983/270
1657	Representation of the People (N.I.) (Amdt.) Regs.	**r.** (with saving), 1983/436
1659	Safety (Collision Regulations and Distress Signals) Regs.	**r.** (with saving in application to seaplanes and hovercraft), 1983/708 **r.** (in application to hovercraft), 1983/769
1679	Representation of the People (Amdt.) Regs.	**r.** (with saving), 1983/435
1727	Police Cadets Regs.	**am.**, 1983/161
1770	Representation of the People (S.) Amdt. Regs.	**r.** (with saving), 1983/548
1980	Child Care Act (c. 5)	s. 21A **am.**, 1983/652
	Nat. Heritage Act (c. 17)	ss. 2, 4, 5, 7 – 10, 12, 14, 16, 18 **am.**, 1983/879
	Magistrates' Cts. Act (c. 43) ..	ss. 76, 81, 131 **am.** (not S.), Sch. 7—para. 38 – 42, 79, 84 **r.** (not S.), para. 120 **am.** (not S.), 1983/182
	Water (S.) Act (c. 45)	Sch. 4, para. 10 **am.**, 1983/24
	Housing Act (c. 51)	ss. 111, 155 **am.**, 1983/1122

	Criminal Justice (S.) Act (c. 62) ..	s. 7 **am.**,
		s. 8 **r.**,
		ss. 46, 55 **am.**,
		Sch. 7—
		  paras. 7, 12 **r.**, 1983/758
		  para. 50 **am.**, 1983/24

	Local Govt., Planning and Land Act (c. 65)	ss. 7, 9 **am.**, 1983/685
6	Insurance Companies (Accounts and Statements) Regs.	**am.**, 1983/1192
25	Diseases of Animals (Approved Disinfectants) (Amdt.) O.	**r.**, 1983/1071
30	N.H.S. (Vocational Training) (S.) Regs.	**am.**, 1983/948
54	Consumer Credit (Advertisements) Regs.	**am.**, 1983/110
55	Consumer Credit (Quotations) Regs.	**am.**, 1983/110

Year and Number (or date)	Act or instrument	How affected
1980 *contd*		
182	Car Tax (Is. of Man) O.	**r.** (with saving), 1983/140
222	Motor Vehicles (Type Approval) (G.B.) (Fees) Regs.	**am.**, 1983/536
223	Motor Vehicles (Type Approval and Approval Marks) (Fees) Regs.	**am.**, 1983/537
289	Chloroform in Food (S.) Regs. ..	**am.**, 1983/270
330	Seeds (Nat. Lists of Varieties) (Fees) Regs.	**am.**, 1983/293
332	Sea Fishing (Specified Western Waters) (Manx and Channel Is. Boats) Licensing O.	**r.**, 1983/1206
333	Sea Fishing (Specified Western Waters) Licensing O.	**r.**, 1983/1206
334	Sea Fishing (Specified Western Waters) (Is. of Man) Licensing O.	**r.**, 1983/1204
335	Sea Fishing (Specified Western Waters) (Restrictions on Landing) O.	**am.**, 1983/1205
350	Prevention of Fraud (Investments) Act Licensing (Amdt.) Regs.	**r.**, 1983/587
351	Plant Breeders' Rights (Fees) Regs. ...	**am.**, 1983/292
356	Civil Aviation (Route Charges for Navigation Services) Regs.	**am.**, 1983/332
370	Public Trustee (Fees) O.	**r.**, 1983/443
377	Social Security (Industrial Injuries) (Prescribed Diseases) Regs.	**am.**, 1983/185, 1094
449	Import and Export of Trees, Wood and Bark (Health) (G.B.) O.	**am.**, 1983/807
457	New Street Byelaws (Ext. of Operation) O.	**am.**, 1983/483
495	Motor Vehicles (Competitions and Trials) (S.) Amdt. Regs.	**r.**, 1983/354
694	County Ct. Districts (Frome) O. ..	**r.**, 1983/713
725	Upholstered Furniture (Safety) Regs.	**am.**, 1983/519
790	Divorce County Cts. (Amdt.) O. ..	**r.**, 1983/713
797	Health Service Supply Council Regs.	**am.**, 1983/315
867	International Oil Pollution Compensation Fund (Parties to Convention) O.	**r.**, 1983/415
895	Nurses, Midwives and Health Visitors Act 1979 (Membership of Nat. Bds.) O.	**am.**, 1983/725
901	Seeds (Fees) Regs.	**am.**, 1983/928
917	Education (Areas to which Pupils belong) Regs.	**am.**, 1983/260
952	Legal Officers' Fees O.	**am.**, 1983/1048
955	Diseases of Animals (Approved Disinfectants) (Amdt.) (No. 2) O.	**r.**, 1983/1071
1031	Representation of the People (Amdt.) Regs.	**r.** (with saving), 1983/435
1033	Representation of the People (N.I.) (Amdt.) Regs.	**r.** (with saving), 1983/436

Year and Number (or date)	Act or instrument	How affected
1980 *contd*		
1050	Police (S.) Amdt. Regs.	am., 1983/317
1058	Measuring Instrts. (EEC Requirements) Regs.	am., 1983/530, 1246
1072	Agriculture and Horticulture Grant Scheme	am., 1983/273, 923
1080	Naval, Military and Air Forces etc. (Disablement and Death) Service Pensions Amdt. O.	r., 1983/883
1081	Naval, Military and Air Forces etc. (Disablement and Death) Service Pensions Amdt. (No. 2) O.	r., 1983/883
1088	Criminal Justice and Armed Forces (N.I.) Consequential Amdts. O.	am. (not S.), 1983/182 am. (S.), 1983/758
1102	Personal Injuries (Civilians) Amdt. Scheme	
1103	Personal Injuries (Civilians) Amdt. (No. 2) Scheme	r., 1983/686
1133	Representation of the People (S.) Amdt. Regs.	r. (with saving), 1983/548
1177	N.H.S. (Superannuation) (S.) Regs...	am., 1983/272
1215	County Ct. Districts (Romford) O. ..	r., 1983/713
1216	District Registries O.	r., 1983/713
1217	Divorce County Cts. (Amdt. No. 2) O.	r., 1983/713
1233	Mines and Quarries (Fees for Approvals) Regs.	am., 1983/484
1298	Agriculture and Horticulture Development Regs.	am., 1983/508, 924
1299	Supplementary Benefit (Requirements) Regs.	am., 1983/505, 700, 1240, 1245
1319	Scottish Land Ct. (Fees) Amdt. Rules	r., 1983/1058
1437	Family Income Supplements (General) Regs.	am., 1983/1003
1438	Family Income Supplements (Claims and Payments) Regs.	am., 1983/1003
1459	Road Transport (International Passenger Services) Regs.	am., 1983/1025
1503	N.H.S. (Charges for Drugs and Appliances) Regs.	am., 1983/306, 1165
1536	V.A.T. (General) Regs.	am., 1983/295
1578	Sheep Variable Premium (Recovery Powers) Regs.	r., 1983/1010
1580	Supplementary Benefit (Duplication and Overpayment) Regs.	am., 1983/1000
1630	Legal Aid (Assessment of Resources) Regs.	am., 1983/423
1641	Supplementary Benefit (Trade Disputes and Recovery from Earnings) Regs.	am., 1983/1000
1643	Supplementary Benefit (Determination of Questions) Regs.	am., 1983/337, 1000
1648	Welfare Food O.	am., 1983/379
1657	Herring (Restrictions on Landing) O.	r., 1983/255

Year and Number (or date)	Act or instrument	How affected
1980 *contd*		
1674	N.H.S. (Charges for Drugs and Appliances) (S.) Regs.	am., 1983/334, 1172
1721	Medical, Nursing and Dental Qualifications (EEC Recognition) (Greek Qualifications) O.	am., 1983/884
1743	Education (Assisted Places) Regs. ..	am., 1983/189
1811	Sheep Variable Premium (Protection of Payments) (No. 2) O.	am., 1983/1009
1820	Industrial Assurance Companies (Accounts and Statements) Regs.	am., 1983/1192
1826	Companies (Forms) Regs.	am., 1983/1021
1833	Emulsifiers and Stabilisers in Food Regs.	am., 1983/1211
1834	Misc. Additives in Food Regs. ..	am., 1983/1211
1836	Welfare Food (Amdt.) O.	r., 1983/379
1849	Food Labelling Regs.	am., 1983/1211
1851	Gas (Metrication) Regs.	am., 1983/684
1866	Milk (Special Designations) (S.) O. ..	am., 1983/939
1878	Measuring Instrts. (Liquid Fuel and Lubricants) (Amdt.) Regs.	r., 1983/592
1888	Emulsifiers and Stabilisers in Food (S.) Regs.	am., 1983/270
1889	Misc. Additives in Food (S.) Regs. ..	am., 1983/270
1894	Legal Aid (General) Regs.	am., 1983/424
1898	Legal Advice and Assistance Regs. (No. 2)	am., 1983/392, 470, 1142
1918	County Ct. Districts (Ellesmere Port and Birkenhead) O.	r., 1983/713
1921	Medicines (Prescription Only) O. ..	am., 1983/341, 957 r. (with saving), 1983/1212
1950	Personal Injuries (Civilians) Amdt. (No. 3) Scheme	r., 1983/686
1955	Naval, Military and Air Forces etc. (Disablement and Death) Service Pensions Amdt. (No. 3) O.	r., 1983/883
1990	Butter Subsidy (Protection of Community Arrangements) Regs.	am., 1983/1098
2007	Bankruptcy Fees O.	am., 1983/775
2008	Companies (Dept. of Trade) Fees O.	am., 1983/774
1981	Finance Act (c. 35)	Sch. 9 am., 1983/1127
	Contempt of Ct. Act (c. 49) ..	ss. 12(3), 14(3) r. (not S.), 1983/182
	British Nationality Act (c. 61) ..	Schs. 3, 6 am., 1983/882
	Transport Act (c. 62)	s. 10 am., 1983/559
	Trustee Savings Banks Act (c. 65)— as extending to the Bailiwick of Guernsey	ss. 7(6), 11(5) r., s. 24 am., s. 31, para. (*b*) **replaced,** ss. 35, 36 am.,

Year and Number (or date)	Act or instrument	How affected
1981 *contd*		s. 40(1) **replaced,** ss. 40(3), 41, 45, 50, 52, 54 **am.,** s. 56(2) **inserted,** Sch. 2 **am.,** Sch. 4, Pt. II, para. 23 **inserted,** 1983/1126
	as extending to the Bailiwick of Jersey	ss. 7(6), 11(5) **r.,** ss. 24, 31, 35 **am.,** s. 36(3) **replaced,** s. 36(4) **r.,** s. 38(4)(5) **replaced,** s. 38(6) **r.,** s. 40(1) **replaced,** ss. 40(3), 41, 45, 52, 54(1) **am.,** s. 54(2) **r.,** s. 56 **am.,** Sch. 2 **am.,** Sch. 4, Pt. II, para. 23 **inserted,** 1983/1126
	Acquisition of Land Act (c. 67)　..	Sch. 4, para. 1 **am.,** 1983/790
	Wildlife and Countryside Act (c. 69)	Pts. II, III **am.,** 1983/512
7	Diseases of Animals (Approved Disinfectants) (Amdt.) O.	**r.,** 1983/1071
30	Air Navigation (Restriction of Flying) (Atomic Energy Establishments) Regs.	**r.,** 1983/640
61	Civil Aviation Authy. (Sixth Amdt.) Regs.	**r.,** 1983/550
80	Medicines (Prescription Only) Amdt. O.	**r.,** 1983/1212
106	N.H.S. (Functions of Health Bds.) (S.) O.	**r.,** 1983/1027
137	Food Labelling (S.) Regs. ..　　..	**am.,** 1983/270
174	Education (Assisted Places) (Incidental Expenses) Regs.	**am.,** 1983/205
199	Agricultural Levies (Export Control) Regs.	**r.,** 1983/61
248	Trade Marks (Amdt.) Rules　　..	**r.,** 1983/181
251	Lotteries (Gaming Bd. Fees) O.　..	**r.,** 1983/126
324	Public Trustee (Fees) (Amdt.) O.　..	**r.,** 1983/443
327	Rate Product Rules　　..　　..	**am.,** 1983/268
334	Health and Safety (Fees for Medical Examinations) Regs.	**r.,** 1983/714
348	Local Govt. (Prescribed Expenditure) Regs.	**r.,** 1983/296
354	Merchant Shipping (Light Dues) Regs.	**am.,** 1983/573, 1080
362	Civil Aviation (Navigation Services Charges) Regs.	**am.,** 1983/349

Year and Number (or date)	Act or instrument	How affected
1981 *contd*		
396	Hovercraft (Fees) Regs.	r., 1983/1166
404	Army Terms of Service Regs. ..	am., 1983/899
454	Fresh Meat Export (Hygiene and Inspection) Regs.	am., 1983/173
504	Gas (Meter) (Amdt.) (No. 2) Regs. ...	r., 1983/684
505	Measuring Instrts. (EEC Requirements) (Gas Volume Meters) (Fees) (Amdt.) (No. 2) Regs.	r., 1983/1247
535	Immature Bass O...	am., 1983/552
552	Magistrates' Cts. Rules	am., 1983/523
553	Magistrates' Cts. (Forms) Rules ..	am., 1983/524
573	Merchant Shipping (Cargo Ship Safety Equipment Survey) Regs.	am., 1983/708
630	Education (School Information) Regs.	am., 1983/41
637	Housing (Standard Amenities Approved Expense) (S.) O.	r., 1983/492
638	Housing (Improvement and Repair Grants) (Approved Expenses Maxima) (S.) Regs.	r., 1983/493
728	Rampton Hospital Review Bd. (Functions and Membership) Regs.	am., 1983/315
786	Education (Grants) (Music and Ballet Schools) Regs.	am., 1983/169, 1017
859	Traffic Signs General Directions ..	am., 1983/1086
	Traffic Signs Regs.	am., 1983/1088
861	Non-Contentious Probate Fees O. ..	am., 1983/1180
880	Capital Transfer Tax (Delivery of Accounts) Regs.	am., 1983/1039
881	Capital Transfer Tax (Delivery of Accounts) (S.) Regs.	am., 1983/1040
932	Nursing Homes and Mental Nursing Homes Regs.	am., 1983/901
933	N.H.S. (Health Authies.: Membership) Regs.	r., 1983/315
1034	Fresh Meat Export (Hygiene and Inspection) (S.) Regs.	am., 1983/703
1045	Rating (Repayment Procedures etc.) (S.) Regs.	am., 1983/1095
1050	Diseases of Animals (Approved Disinfectants) (Amdt.) (No. 2) O.	r., 1983/1071
1061	Home Purchase Assistance (Pricelimits) O.	r., 1983/82
1063	Jam and Similar Products Regs. ..	am., 1983/1211
1086	Education (Schools and Further Education) Regs.	am., 1983/262
1110	Naval, Military and Air Forces etc. (Disablement and Death) Service Pensions Amdt. O.	r., 1983/883
1126	Home Purchase Assistance (Pricelimits) (Hertfordshire and Lincolnshire) O.	r., 1983/82
1143	Personal Injuries (Civilians) Amdt. Scheme	r., 1983/686

Year and Number (or date)	Act or instrument	How affected
1981 *contd*		
1183	West Coast Herring Licensing O. ..	r., 1983/1206
1240	Merchant Shipping (Sterling Equivalents) (Various Enactments) O.	r., 1983/36
1252	Carriage by Air (Sterling Equivalents) O.	superseded, 1983/43
1261	Milk Prices (S.) O.	r., 1983/491
1293	Herring (North Sea and Specified Western Waters) (Manx and Channel Is. Boats) Licensing O.	r., 1983/1206
1294	Herring (Specified Western Waters) (Prohibition of Fishing) (No. 2) (Variation) O.	r., 1983/255
1295	Herring (North Sea and Specified Western Waters) Licensing O.	r., 1983/1206
1296	Irish Sea Herring (Prohibition of Fishing) (Variation) O.	r., 1983/255
1297	Herring (Specified North Sea Waters) (Prohibition of Fishing) O.	r., 1983/255
1306	Measuring Instrts. (Liquid Fuel and Lubricants) (Amdt.) Regs.	r., 1983/592
1320	Jam and Similar Products (S.) Regs.	am., 1983/270
1524	Supplementary Benefit (Aggregation) Regs.	am., 1983/1000, 1004
1525	Supplementary Benefit (Claims and Payments) Regs.	am., 1983/337, 1000, 1004
1526	Supplementary Benefit (Conditions of Entitlement) Regs.	am., 1983/463, 1000
1527	Supplementary Benefit (Resources) Regs.	am., 1983/503, 505, 1240, 1245
1528	Supplementary Benefit (Single Payments) Regs.	am., 1983/1000, 1240, 1245
1529	Supplementary Benefit (Urgent Cases) Regs.	am., 1983/1000
1568	Smoke Control Areas (Exempted Fireplaces) O.	r., 1983/277
1624	County Cts. (Bankruptcy and Companies Winding-up Jurisdiction) (Amdt.) O.	r., 1983/713
1625	District Registries (Amdt.) O. ..	r., 1983/713
1641	Export of Goods (Control) O. ..	am., 1983/1006, 1266
1653	Marine Fish Farming (Financial Assistance) Scheme	am., 1983/626
1654	Insurance Companies Regs. ..	am., 1983/48, 224, 396
1655	Lloyd's (Financial Resources) Regs...	r., 1983/224
1656	Insurance Companies (Accounts and Statements) (Amdt.) Regs.	am., 1983/1192
1662	Herring (North Sea and Specified Western Waters) Licensing (Variation) O.	r., 1983/1206
1672	Naval, Military and Air Forces etc. (Disablement and Death) Service Pensions Amdt. (No. 2) O.	r., 1983/883

Year and Number (or date)	Act or instrument	How affected
1981 *contd*		
1678	Personal Injuries (Civilians) Amdt. (No. 2) Scheme	r., 1983/686
1694	Motor Vehicles (Tests) Regs. ..	am., 1983/1147
1707	Farm and Horticulture Development Regs.	am., 1983/507, 925
1729	Merchant Shipping (Means of Access) Regs.	am., 1983/117
1752	Lyon Ct. and Office Fees (Variation) O.	r., 1983/1072
1753	Building Societies (Fees) Regs. ..	r., 1983/372
1754	Industrial Assurance (Fees) Regs. ..	r., 1983/373
1769	Customs Duties (ECSC) O... ..	am., 1983/342
1792	Children Act 1975 (Commencement No. 5) O.	am., 1983/86
1800	British Telecommunications (Pensions) O.	r., 1983/326
1825	Measuring Instrts. (EEC Pattern Approval Requirements) (Fees) (No. 2) Regs.	am., 1983/280
1831	Friendly Societies (Fees) Regs. ..	r., 1983/351
1832	Industrial and Provident Societies (Credit Unions) (Amdt. of Fees) Regs.	r., 1983/352
1833	Industrial and Provident Societies (Amdt. of Fees) Regs.	r., 1983/350
1837	N.H.S. (Determination of Districts) O.	am., 1983/30, 336
1838	N.H.S. (Constitution of District Health Authies.) O.	am., 1983/31, 1090
1852	Milk Prices (S.) Amdt. O... ..	am., 1983/491
1869	Fishing Nets O.	r., 1983/255
1870	Immature Sea Fish O.	r., 1983/255
1873	Specified Sea Fish (Prohibition of Fishing and of Fishing Methods) O.	r., 1983/255
1982	Social Security and Housing Benefits Act (c. 24)	s. 7 am., 1983/123
	Finance Act (c. 39)	s. 26 am., 1983/368 s. 154 am., 1983/958 Sch. 7 am., 1983/368
10	Rampton Hospital Review Bd. (Functions and Membership) Amdt. Regs. 1981	r., 1983/315
29	Medicines (Prescription Only) Amdt. O.	r., 1983/1212
33	Children Act 1975 (S.) (Commencement No. 3) O.	am., 1983/107
35	Diseases of Animals (Approved Disinfectants) (Amdt.) O.	r., 1983/1071
80	Receiving of Trans-shipped Sea Fish (Licensing) O.	am., 1983/1139
84	Gaming Clubs (Hours and Charges) (Amdt.) Regs.	r., 1983/5
115	Local Authies. (Allowances) (S.) Amdt. Regs.	r., 1983/579

Year and Number (or date)	Act or instrument	How affected
1982 *contd*		
125	Local Govt. (Allowances) (Amdt.) Regs.	am., 1983/574
130	Gaming Clubs (Hours and Charges) (S.) Amdt. Regs.	r., 1983/80
136	Lloyd's (Audit Certificate) Regs. ..	r., 1983/224
169	Specified Sea Fish (Prohibition of Fishing and of Fishing Methods) (Variation) O.	r., 1983/255
192	Registration of Births, Deaths and Marriages (Fees) (S.) Regs.	am., 1983/221
216	Legal Advice and Assistance (S.) (Financial Conditions) (No. 2) Regs.	r., 1983/384
220	Aviation Security Fund Regs. ..	am., 1983/81
235	Trustee Savings Banks (Interest-bearing Receipts) O.	r., 1983/647
241	Housing Support Grant (S.) O. ..	am., 1983/105
247	Mines and Quarries (Fees for Approvals) (Amdt.) Regs.	r., 1983/484
248	Ironstone Restoration Fund (Standard Rate) O.	r. (with saving), 1983/225
267	Block Grant (Education Adjustments) (E.) Regs.	am., 1983/261
281	Mackerel Licensing (Variation) O. ..	r., 1983/1206
282	Mackerel Licensing (Manx and Channel Is. Boats) (Variation) O.	r., 1983/1206
288	Health Services Act 1980 (Consequential Amdts.) O.	am., 1983/893
302	Local Govt. (Prescribed Expenditure) (Amdt.) Regs.	r., 1983/296
304	Block Grant (Education Adjustments) (W.) Regs.	am., 1983/238, 310
305	Insurance Companies (Accounts and Statements) (Amdt.) Regs.	am., 1983/1192
315	Authies. for London Post-Graduate Teaching Hospitals Regs.	am., 1983/315
316	Public Trustee (Fees) (Amdt.) O. ..	r., 1983/443
328	County Ct. Districts (Western Circuit) O.	r., 1983/713
334	Anguilla Constitution O.	am., 1983/1108
342	Prevention of Fraud (Investments) Act Licensing (Amdt.) Regs.	r., 1983/587
345	N.H.S. (Constitution of District Health Authies.) Amdt. O.	am., 1983/31
355	Merchant Shipping (Fees) Regs. ..	r., 1983/1167
361	Hovercraft (Fees) (Amdt.) Regs. ..	r., 1983/1166
453	Fishing Nets (Variation) O... ..	r., 1983/255
454	Immature Sea Fish (Variation) O. ..	r., 1983/255
455	Specified Sea Fish (Prohibition of Fishing and of Fishing Methods) (Variation) (No. 2) O.	r., 1983/255
456	Milk Prices (S.) Amdt. O... ..	r., 1983/491
507	Legal Advice and Assistance (S.) (Financial Conditions) Regs.	r., 1983/533

Year and Number (or date)	Act or instrument	How affected
1982 *contd*		
508	Legal Aid (S.) (Financial Conditions) Regs.	r., 1983/532
565	Gas (Meter) (Amdt.) Regs... ..	r., 1983/684
573	Fishing Nets (Variation) (No. 2) O...	r., 1983/255
578	C.A.P. (Wine) Regs. ..	am., 1983/1042
608	Aujesky's Disease of Swine O. ..	r., 1983/344
681	Police (S.) Amdt. Regs. ..	am., 1983/317
698	Seed Potatoes (Fees) Regs... ..	r., 1983/707
717	Patents Rules	am., 1983/180
718	Trade Marks (Amdt.) Rules ..	am., 1983/181
719	Public Lending Right Scheme ..	am., 1983/480
721	Seed Potatoes (Fees) (S.) Regs. ..	r., 1983/544
810	Personal Injuries (Civilians) Amdt. Scheme	r., 1983/686
824	Falkland Is. and Dependencies (Interim Admin.) O.	am., 1983/1110
828	Registered Housing Assocns. (Accounting Requirements) O.	am., 1983/207
829	Betting Levy Appeal Tribunal (S.) Amdt. Rules	am., 1983/72
834	Royal Navy Terms of Service (Ratings) Regs.	am., 1983/897
845	Naval, Military and Air Forces etc. (Disablement and Death) Service Pensions Amdt. O.	r., 1983/883
848	Ministerial and other Salaries O. ..	r., 1983/1128
863	N.H.S. (Charges to Overseas Visitors) (No. 2) Regs.	am., 1983/302
864	Merchant Shipping (Fees) (Amdt.) Regs.	r., 1983/1167
873	Immature Sea Fish (Variation) (No. 2) O.	r., 1983/255
874	Fishing Nets (Variation) (No. 3) O...	r., 1983/255
875	Specified Sea Fish (Prohibition of Fishing and of Fishing Methods) (Variation) (No. 3) O.	r., 1983/255
894	Statutory Sick Pay (General) Regs. ...	am., 1983/376
898	N.H.S. (Charges to Overseas Visitors) (S.) Regs.	am., 1983/362
914	Supplementary Benefit (Housing Benefits) (Misc. Consequential Amdts.) Regs.	am., 1983/337
939	Legal Officers' Fees O.	am., 1983/1048
947	Diseases of Animals (Approved Disinfectants) (Amdt.) (No. 2) O.	r., 1983/1071
949	Education (Assisted Places) (S.) Regs.	am., 1983/1030
954	Education (Mandatory Awards) Regs.	r., 1983/1135
969	Excise Duties (Deferred Payment) Regs.	r., 1983/947
1018	Meat (Sterilisation and Staining) Regs.	am., 1983/704
1032	Occupational Pension Schemes (Connected Employers) Regs.	am., 1983/338

Year and Number (or date)	Act or instrument	How affected
1982 *contd*		
1036	Local Govt. (Direct Labour Organisations) (Competition) Regs.	r., 1983/685
1041	Education (Students' Dependants Allowances) Regs.	r. (with saving), 1983/1185
1047	Personal Injuries (Civilians) Amdt. (No. 2) Scheme	r., 1983/686
1076	Medical, Nursing, Dental and Veterinary Qualifications (EEC Recognition) O.	am., 1983/884
1077	Naval, Military and Air Forces etc. (Disablement and Death) Service Pensions Amdt. (No. 2) O.	r., 1983/883
1107	Family Income Supplements (Computation) Regs.	r., 1983/1201
1124	Housing Benefits Regs.	am., 1983/57, 1014, 1239, 1242
1126	Supplementary Benefit (Housing Benefits) (Requirements and Resources) Consequential Amdts. Regs.	am., 1983/505
1130	Social Security Benefits Up-rating O.	r., 1983/1244
1163	Motorways Traffic (E. and W.) Regs.	am., 1983/374
1171	Gaming Act (Variation of Fees) O. ..	r., 1983/127
1172	Lotteries (Gaming Bd. Fees) (Amdt.) O.	r., 1983/126
1197	Legal Aid in Criminal Proceedings (Costs) Regs.	am., 1983/235, 1049
1227	Savings Certificates (Amdt.) (No. 3) Regs.	r., 1983/1063
1236	Income Tax (Interest Relief) Regs. ..	am., 1983/311, 368
1253	Gaming Act (Variation of Fees) (S.) O.	r., 1983/333
1295	Education (Mandatory Awards) (Amdt.) Regs.	r., 1983/1135
1367	District Registries (Amdt.) O. ..	r., 1983/713
1372	Fishing Nets (Variation) (No. 4) O...	r., 1983/255
1373	Immature Sea Fish (Variation) (No. 3) O.	r., 1983/255
1374	Specified Sea Fish (Prohibition of Fishing and of Fishing Methods) (Variation) (No. 4) O.	r., 1983/255
1408	Social Security (General Benefit) Regs.	am., 1983/186, 981
1478	Goods Vehicles (Plating and Testing) Regs.	am., 1983/239
1487	Police Cadets (Amdt.) (No. 2) Regs.	am., 1983/161
1516	Central Blood Laboratories Authy. Regs.	am., 1983/315
1520	Housing Benefits (Transitional) Regs.	am., 1983/57, 438, 912
1541	Acquisition of Land (Rate of Interest after Entry) (No. 4) Regs.	r., 1983/33
1542	Acquisition of Land (Rate of Interest after Entry) (S.) (No. 4) Regs.	r., 1983/34

Year and Number (or date)	Act or instrument	How affected
1982 *contd*		
1590	Distributors of Iron and Steel Products (ECSC Requirements) Regs.	**am.**, 1983/1184
1596	Medicines (Prescription Only) Amdt. (No. 2) O.	**r.**, 1983/1212
1606	Offshore Installations (Safety Zones) O.	**am.**, 1983/222
1684	Offshore Installations (Safety Zones) (No. 4) O.	**r.**, 1983/39
1685	Offshore Installations (Safety Zones) (No. 5) O.	**r.**, 1983/69
1760	Customs Duties (Quota Relief) (Paper, Paperboard and Printed Products) O.	**am.**, 1983/1038
1766	Offshore Installations (Safety Zones) (No. 6) O.	**r.**, 1983/38
1769	Divorce County Cts. (Amdt.) O. ..	**r.**, 1983/713
1782	Customs Duties (ECSC) (Quota and Other Reliefs) O.	**am.**, 1983/501
1794	County Ct. Rules 1981 (Amdt. No. 3) Rules	**am.**, 1983/275
1795	Insurance Companies (Accounts and Statements) (Amdt.) (No. 2) Regs.	**am.**, 1983/469, 1192
1801	Medicines (Prescription Only) Amdt. (No. 3) O.	**r.**, 1983/1212
1844	Fishing Nets (Variation) (No. 5) O...	**r.**, 1983/255
1845	Specified Sea Fish (Prohibition of Fishing and of Fishing Methods) (Variation) (No. 5) O.	**r.**, 1983/255
1846	Immature Sea Fish (Variation) (No. 4) O.	**r.**, 1983/255
1847	Western Mackerel (Danish Fishing Boats) (Prohibition of Fishing) O.	**r.**, 1983/15
1848	Sea Fish (Specified Waters of Member States) (Prohibition of Fishing) O.	**r.**, 1983/255
1849	Sea Fish (Specified U.K. Waters) (Prohibition of Fishing) O.	**r.**, 1983/255
1850	Demersal Fish (Specified Northern Waters) Licensing O.	**r.**, 1983/255
1852	Offshore Installations (Safety Zones) (No. 8) O.	**r.**, 1983/575
1983	Mobile Homes Act (c. 34)	s. 1 **am.**, 1983/749 Sch. 1, Pt. I **am.**, 1983/748
14	Specified Sea Fish (U.K. Fishing Boats) (Prohibition of Fishing) O.	**r.**, 1983/255
15	Specified Sea Fish (U.K. Waters) (Prohibition of Fishing) O.	**r.**, 1983/255
32	Diseases of Animals (Approved Disinfectants) (Amdt.) O.	**r.**, 1983/1071
33	Acquisition of Land (Rate of Interest after Entry) Regs.	**r.**, 1983/863

Year and Number (or date)	Act or instrument	How affected
1983 *contd*		
34	Acquisition of Land (Rate of Interest after Entry) (S.) Regs.	r., 1983/864
36	Merchant Shipping (Sterling Equivalents) (Various Enactments) O.	r., 1983/582
37	Offshore Installations (Safety Zones) O.	r., 1983/777
43	Carriage by Air (Sterling Equivalents) O.	superseded, 1983/593
48	Insurance Companies (Advertisements) (Amdt.) Regs.	r., 1983/396
68	Offshore Installations (Safety Zones) (No. 3) O.	r., 1983/347
79	Offshore Installations (Safety Zones) (No. 4) O.	r., 1983/502
114	Education (Mandatory Awards) (Amdt.) Regs.	r., 1983/1135
131	Offshore Installations (Safety Zones) (No. 5) O.	r., 1983/646
136	Pneumoconiosis, Byssinosis and Misc. Diseases Benefit Scheme	am., 1983/504
171	Offshore Installations (Safety Zones) (No. 6) O.	r., 1983/620
178	Local Govt. Superannuation (Transferred Water Employees) Regs.	am., 1983/1268
182	Criminal Justice Act 1982 (Commencement No. 2) O.	am., 1983/627
295	V.A.T. (General) (Amdt.) Regs.	am., 1983/475
330	Offshore Installations (Safety Zones) (No. 7) O.	r., 1983/1134
341	Medicines (Prescription Only) Amdt. O.	r., 1983/1212
348	Offshore Installations (Safety Zones) (No. 8) O.	r., 1983/812
413	Offshore Installations (Safety Zones) (No. 9) O.	r., 1983/776
469	Insurance Companies (Accounts and Statements) (Amdt.) (General Business Reinsurance) Regs.	am., 1983/1192
477	Education (Mandatory Awards) (Amdt.) (No. 2) Regs.	r., 1983/1135
495	Savings Certificates (Amdt.) Regs.	r., 1983/1063
543	Offshore Installations (Safety Zones) (No. 10) O.	r., 1983/852
595	Offshore Installations (Safety Zones) (No. 11) O.	r., 1983/811
648	Offshore Installations (Safety Zones) (No. 12) O.	r., 1983/835
659	Divorce County Cts. (Amdt.) O.	r., 1983/713
686	Personal Injuries (Civilians) Scheme	am., 1983/1164
708	Merchant Shipping (Distress Signals and Prevention of Collisions) Regs.	am., 1983/768

Year and Number (or date)	Act or instrument	How affected
1983 *contd*		
813	Offshore Installations (Safety Zones) (No. 14) O.	**r.**, 1983/1316
853	Offshore Installations (Safety Zones) (No. 17) O.	**r.**, 1983/933
854	Offshore Installations (Safety Zones) (No. 18) O.	**r.**, 1983/1257
855	Offshore Installations (Safety Zones) (No. 19) O.	**r.**, 1983/1011
883	Naval, Military and Air Forces etc. (Disablement and Death) Service Pensions O.	**am.**, 1983/1116
957	Medicines (Prescription Only) Amdt. (No. 2) O.	**r.**, 1983/1212
1012	Offshore Installations (Safety Zones) (No. 23) O.	**r.**, 1983/1262

Index to Parts I and II

HMSO
£10
2 vols